U S

THE ROU

THE ROUGH GUIDES

OTHER AVAILABLE ROUGH GUIDES
**AMSTERDAM • BARCELONA • BERLIN • BRAZIL
BRITTANY & NORMANDY • BULGARIA • CALIFORNIA & WEST COAST USA
CANADA • CRETE • CZECH & SLOVAK REPUBLICS • CYPRUS • EGYPT
EUROPE • FLORIDA • FRANCE • GERMANY • GREECE • GUATEMALA & BELIZE
HOLLAND, BELGIUM & LUXEMBOURG • HONG KONG • HUNGARY • IRELAND
ISRAEL • ITALY • KENYA • MEDITERRANEAN WILDLIFE • MEXICO • MOROCCO
NEPAL • NEW YORK • NOTHING VENTURED • PARIS • PERU • POLAND
PORTUGAL • PRAGUE • PROVENCE • PYRENEES • SAN FRANCISCO
SCANDINAVIA • SICILY • SPAIN • THAILAND • TUNISIA • TURKEY
TUSCANY & UMBRIA • VENICE • WEST AFRICA • WOMEN TRAVEL
ZIMBABWE & BOTSWANA**

FORTHCOMING
AUSTRALIA • ST PETERSBURG

USA: THE ROUGH GUIDE CREDITS

Text Editor: Greg Ward
Typesetting, Layout and Design: Greg Ward
Production: Susanne Hillen, Kate Berens, Andy Hilliard, Gail Jammy
Series Editor: Mark Ellingham

ACKNOWLEDGEMENTS

This book could never have been written without the assistance of the many people in the United States who gave us their unstinting help. A partial list appears on page vi.

Greg: Thanks to everybody at Rough Guides, especially Mark and Susanne for having the confidence to leave me to my own devices and encouraging me when I needed it, Martin Dunford for starting me off, Martin and Jules for preparing drafts of New York and Florida, Gail and Andy for sitting in the same room for 18 months, always being ready to help, and putting up with all that Al Green, Richard for his continued interest, Celia for her good sense, Deborah for being so reasonable, and Kate Berens and Margaret Doyle for imaginative proofreading. Thanks also to Jon Dear, and above all to all the authors and contributors for their unfailing hard work and enthusiasm over such a protracted period.
 I'd also like to thank Robert, Jamie and cousin Barbara for fun in America; Sandra, Deborah, Alex, Jules, Marion, Mark, Jennie and especially Sam for friendship and support; and my parents and family for all their help.

Sam: In the USA, special mention should go to Evelyn Hall, Diane Wolfe, Suzann Stewart, Nancy Miller, Anne-Marie Quagliaroli, Beryl Fishbone, Errin Cecil, Charles and Virginia Grenier, and, for hospitality and friendship, Jane DeBlieux, Sandra and Chris Curphey, Shelby Redden, Vivian Stanley, Jerry Olson, Tamara Ferguson, E J Farhood, Chris Szalay, Shirley Condiff, Jim and Doris Begnaud, Pam Renfro, and my English friends Ed Buscombe, Sarah Boston and Josephine Newell. Back home, big thanks to Jim Cook, Nat "I've been to Little Rock" Payne, Nick Thomas and Ally Scott, and to Leslie Faizi, whose patience and support lasted from day one (see you in P-Town). Thanks also to all the team, especially Greg for inspired editing and invaluable friendship, but above all this is for Pam Cook, who I hope will enjoy using it.

Tim: Thanks to all in Manchester, especially Chris Wren for the Rocky Mountain adventure, and Cath Wade & Myc Kay (reading and writing). Also Rick Stern, Jacquie, Nathan, Tony and Karl for putting up with all the carry on. Eternal gratitude to John Breslin for loads of help and to the other Londoners: Kev, Danny, Col and Ali. Hi again to: Jill Abrahamson (Omaha), the Martins (Toronto), Tracey Swope (Traverse City CVB) and Jimmy Williams (Sugarhill Int. House, NY). Finally, the red pen of the ever-patient Greg Ward, Rachel Kennedy for a good idea and Bill & Madge in Ireland.

Jamie: For putting me up, and putting up with me, a round of drinks and affectionate gratitude to Hilary Delamere, Jules Brown, Greg Ward, Ian and Jane (and Sam and Mully) in the UK, and Danny, Maayan (and Leore) Klein in New York, Mom in DC, Randy Terry and James T Gibson in Chicago, Greg, Syvilla and Kyle Rachal in LA, and, more than ever, to Catherine, Brando and Judah. I'd also like to dedicate the best parts to the memory of "Ice Box" Julian Hancock, who never made it across.

The publishers and authors have done their best to ensure the accuracy and currency of all the information in
USA: The Rough Guide; however, they can accept no responsibility for any loss, injury or inconvenience sustained
by any traveller as a result of information or advice contained in the guide.

First edition published in March 1992 by Harrap Columbus Ltd and reprinted April 1992.
Reprinted 1992 and 1993 by Rough Guides Ltd, 1 Mercer Street, London WC2H 9QJ.
Distributed by Penguin Books, 27 Wrights Lane, London W8 5TZ.

Typeset in Linotron Univers and Century Old Style to an original design by Andrew Oliver.

Printed in the UK by Cox & Wyman, Reading, Berks.

Incidental illustrations in Parts One and Three by Ed Briant.

992pp. includes index
British Library Cataloguing in Publication Data
A catalogue record for this book is available from the British Library.

ISBN 1-85828-028-1 (previously published by Harrap Columbus Ltd, under ISBN 0-7471-0274-0).

USA
THE ROUGH GUIDE

Written and researched by

SAMANTHA COOK, TIM PERRY,

JAMIE JENSEN and GREG WARD

with additional contributions by
Mick Sinclair, Deborah Bosley, Wendy Ferguson,
Donald Hutera, Martin Dunford, Andrew Gilchrist,
Andrew Neather and Jack Holland

THE ROUGH GUIDES

CONTENTS

Introduction x

PART THREE CONTEXTS   923

HELP US UPDATE

A lot of hard work has gone into making this first edition of the *Rough Guide: USA* as comprehensive and accurate as possible. However, from the moment of publication things will, of course, begin to change. Prices will rise, opening hours will alter, restaurants and hotels will close, and new ones will appear.

A crucial element in the monumental task of keeping this book up to date is the response we get from readers. Please write and let us know if you spot anything that is no longer true, or if you feel we have omitted anything that deserves inclusion. We will send a copy of any *Rough Guide* to the writers of the best letters. We would also welcome correspondence from the owners of any establishments reviewed in this book, with news of updated prices or facilities, and will send researchers to those who are not mentioned and feel that they should be.

Please write to Greg Ward, Rough Guides (USA), 1 Mercer Street, London WC2H 9QJ.

THANKS TO EVERYONE

Such is the legendary American hospitality that the list below can only represent a small fraction of the many people who helped in the preparation of this book. Behind each name there's a fondly remembered story; thanks for the good times.

Carol Ann Anderson, Carla Andrews, Ira Babin, Bonnie Barness, Brenda Bear, J Ray Bennison, Darla Bigler, Emma Blocher, Bill Blumensaadt, Becky Bovell, Barb Bowman, Lindy Boyes, Jeannine Breshears, Dana Brockway, Colin Brodie, Dan Brown, Barbara Campbell, Linda Carlson, Fay Carpenter, Mark Cestari, Anita Clark, Mary Kay Cline, Marcia Cobun, Cynthia Collyer, Dorothy Coyle, Tom Crain, Karen Culp, Tim Culver, Karen Cummings, Mary Denis, Cindy DePierri, Judy Draucker, Andrea Ernst, Preston Friedley, Beverly Gianna, Robert Gibbons, Wadine Gibbons, Jane Gillespie, Lucinda Hampton, Tyler Hardeman, Shelly Helmerick, Chuck Hillestad, Pamela Hoedel, Nancy Milton Holtzscher, Karen Howard, Dana Johnson, Donna Jung, Jim Karras, Connie Kenney, Kurt Kosmowski, Rosetta Stone Land, Shelly Lau, Blair Learn, David Lee, Joyce Lee, Cheryl Lewis, Karl Lion, Jim Lovejoy, Sharon Maloof, John McIlhenny, Ellen McMahon, Stephen Martin, Sharon McKeague, Margaret MeGee, Deborah Milo, Tania Moore, Kevin Morrissey, Gordon Morse, Kathleen Myers, Timothy Olsen, Joe O'Mealy, Jim Pape, Ann Parthé, Carol Pasternak, Lynn Pearce, Tracy Potter, Rob Powers, Shelly Pritikin, Becky Purdy, Susan Ricciardi, Mike Robertson, Wendy Roe, Judy Salisbury, Cindy Sanders, Susanne Satagaj, Fred Sater, Linda Sauer, Jennifer Schmits, Mary Schmitz, Ray Shepard, Ami Simpson, Nancy Smith, Sandy Spayo, Jackie Stewart, Tom Stilz, Kelly Strenge, Betty Szerencse, Sandy Torres, Candee Treadway, Ro Trent, Mark Waldo, Floyd Williams Jr, Christy Walker, Ellen Wein, Don Wick, Kim Williamson, Doreen Willis-Bailey, Maggie Wilson, Connie Wright.

One last hello to Bob Sylvia and Susan Middleton, day one in Boston; Robert Stevens at the Grand Canyon; Kay and Peter Shumway at *Moose Mountain Lodge*; Nancy Gray in Freeport; Kelly in St Louis; Rich Grant, John Hickenlooper, and Gully Stanford in Denver; and John Erickson and Bob Levine in Hawaii.

LIST OF MAPS

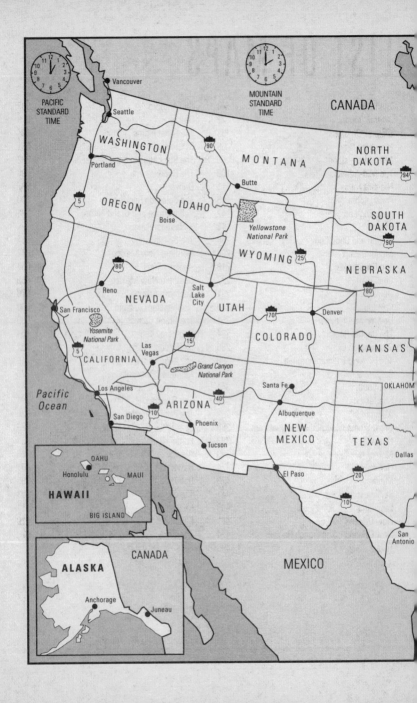

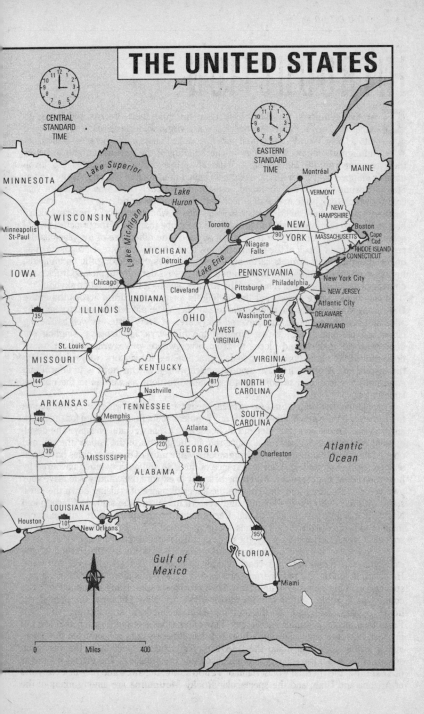

INTRODUCTION

For five centuries, travellers have been bringing their dreams and hopes to America. For the earliest pioneers, it was a virgin wilderness ready to be shaped into a "New World", a potential paradise wasted on its native peoples. Millions of immigrants followed, to share in the building of the new nation and to better their lives, far from the hidebound societies of Europe and Asia; the slaves, too, involuntarily shipped over from Africa, eventually joined them as free citizens. As the United States expanded to fill the continent, something genuinely new was created: a vast country which took pride in defining itself in the eyes of the world.

Every visitor to the United States has some idea of what to expect. American culture has become so thoroughly shared throughout the globe that one of the principal joys of seeing the country for the first time is not so much the difference of the place as the repeated delicious shock of the familiar. Yellow taxis on busy city streets; roadside mailboxes straight out of *Peanuts* cartoons; wooden porches overlooking the cottonfields; tumbleweed rolling across the desert; endless highways dotted with pick-up trucks and chrome-plated diners; the first sight of the Grand Canyon, or the Manhattan skyline.

In this book, we've picked out the highlights for travellers from across the entire USA, from Maine to Hawaii, and Alaska to Florida. We've divided the country state by state and region by region, and covered every area of every state. As well as the big cities and national parks, we've explored the highways and byways, singling out detours worth making and places to avoid. Everywhere we've written about, we've done more than simply provide up-to-date practicalities for visitors: we've delved into the history and people who have made America what it is. Our hope is to inform and entertain travellers, and to point in unexpected directions as well as to the obvious landmarks.

Travelling in the United States is extremely easy; in a country where everyone seems to be forever on the move, there's rarely any problem about finding a room for the night, and you can almost invariably depend on being able to eat well and cheaply. The development of transport has played a major role in the growth of the nation; the railroad opened the way for transcontinental migrations, while most of the great cities have been shaped by the automobile. Your experience of the USA will be very much flavoured by how you choose to get around. Much the best way to explore the country is to drive your own vehicle: it takes a long time before the sheer pleasure of cruising down the interstate, with the radio playing country and western music and the signs to Chicago and Nashville flashing past, begins to pall. Car rental is far cheaper than in Europe, every main road is lined with budget motels charging around $25 per night for a good room, and, whatever Americans may say, the price of petrol remains absurdly low.

We have also detailed public transport options everywhere; with the aid of the excellent-value nationwide rail, coach and air passes, you can get wherever you want. However, if you do use public transport, there's a real temptation to see America as a succession of big **cities**. Dynamic **New York** provides a stimulating introduction to the country as a whole, and among its worthy rivals are **New Orleans**, the flamboyant home of jazz; **Chicago**, at the cutting edge of modern architecture; and **San Francisco**, on its beautiful Pacific bay. Few other cities can quite match this level of interest, however, and following a heavily urban itinerary cuts you off from the astonishing **landscapes** that make the USA truly distinctive. Especially in the vast open spaces of the west, the scenery is often absolutely breathtaking. The glacial splendour of **Yosemite**, the thermal wonderland of **Yellowstone**, the awesome red-rock **canyons** of Arizona and Utah, and the spectacular **Rocky Mountains** are among many of the treasures preserved and protected in the splendid national park system. Once you reach such places, the potential for **hiking** and **camping** is magnificent – the United States possesses wildernesses in a sense you simply don't get in Europe – but all too often it's essential to have a car to get near them.

Above all, most visitors come for the sheer thrill of experiencing American culture on its own ground. Place names from rock'n'roll songs and western novels suddenly spring into life; landscapes straight out of Hollywood movies spread across the horizon. For **music** fans, the chance to hear country music in Nashville or rhythm and blues in New Orleans, or to visit Elvis in Memphis, verges on a religious experience; readers brought up on the **books** of Mark Twain can ride a paddle-wheeler on the Mississippi; **moviegoers** can live out their *Thelma and Louise* fantasies in the Utah desert.

Europeans are often all too ready to dismiss the United States as a land almost devoid of **history**. Though mainstream America tends to trace its roots back to the Pilgrims and Puritans of New England – an area which to European sensibilities can seem somewhat twee – the rest of the continent has an even longer past, stretching back way beyond the French culture of Lousiana and the Spanish presence in California to the majestic cliff palaces built by the Anasazi in the Southwest a thousand years ago. There are also any number of fascinating strands to America's post-revolutionary history – relics of the Gold Rush in California, of the civil rights years in the South, or of the Civil War anywhere east of the Mississippi.

Though we've had to structure this book regionally, much the best idea on any trip to the USA is to get to know more than one area. You do not, however, have to cross the entire continent from shore to shore in order to appreciate its amazing diversity. It would take forever to see the whole place, and the more time you spend on the road the less time you'll have to savour the small-town pleasures and backroads oddities that may well provide your strongest memories. It doesn't take long to realise that there is no such thing as a typical American person, any more than there is a typical American landscape, but there can be few places where strangers can feel so confident of a warm reception.

AVERAGE MAXIMUM DAILY TEMPERATURES (°F)												
	Jan	Feb	March	April	May	June	July	Aug	Sept	Oct	Nov	Dec
Anchorage	19	27	33	44	54	62	65	64	57	43	30	20
Atlanta	51	54	62	71	79	86	87	86	82	72	61	52
Boston	36	37	43	54	66	75	80	78	71	62	49	40
Chicago	32	34	43	55	65	75	81	79	73	61	47	36
Honolulu	76	76	77	78	80	81	82	83	83	82	80	78
Las Vegas	60	67	72	81	89	99	103	102	95	84	71	61
Los Angeles	65	66	67	70	72	76	81	82	81	76	73	67
Miami	74	75	78	80	84	86	88	88	87	83	78	76
Nashville	47	50	59	69	78	86	89	88	82	72	58	49
New Orleans	62	65	71	77	83	88	90	90	86	79	70	64
New York City	37	38	45	57	68	77	82	80	79	69	51	41
San Francisco	55	59	61	62	63	66	65	65	69	68	63	57
Seattle	45	48	52	58	64	69	72	73	67	59	51	47
Washington DC	42	44	53	64	75	83	87	84	78	67	55	45

PART ONE

THE
BASICS

GETTING THERE

Over twenty US cities are accessible by non-stop flights from the UK (see box). At these "gateway cities", airport hubs for US air carriers, you can connect with extensive networks of domestic flights on into the rest of the country. Direct services (which may land once or twice on the way, but are called direct if they keep the same flight number throughout their journey) fly from Britain to nearly every other major US city.

You can fly to the US from Heathrow, Gatwick, Glasgow, Manchester and Stansted. Flight routes and prices vary widely. Although fares change extremely fast, competition between airlines is intense, which gives rise to occasional dramatic fare-cuts and special promotional deals – albeit with a whole pile of restrictions attached. On top of this, travel operators can offer **inclusive holidays** and **fly-drive deals** at only a little above the regular air fare. **Charter flights** from all over the UK to holiday resorts in the States throw up even more low-cost options. Britain is one of the best places in Europe to obtain cut-price air fares; we have listed some of the most reliable discount operators below. It is also worthwhile to call the airlines (see below) themselves as they sometimes offer bargain deals that undercut even the cheapest Apex fares available from the agents. The comments below can only act as a general guide, so be sure to shop around carefully for the best offers by checking the travel ads in the Sunday papers, and, in London, scouring *Time Out*, *City Limits* and the *Evening Standard*. Giveaway magazines aimed at young travellers, like *TNT*, are also useful resources.

SAMPLE AIR FARES FROM BRITAIN

The prices given below (in £ sterling) are a general indication of the (minimum) transatlantic air fares obtainable from specialist companies in 1992. Each airline decides the exact dates of its seasons.

	LOW Nov 1–Dec 11, Dec 25–Mar 14		SHOULDER Mar 15–Jun 14, Sep 16–Oct 31		HIGH Jun 15–Sep 15, Dec 12–Dec 24	
From **London** to	one-way	return	one-way	return	one-way	return
New York	119	229	166	331	175	349
Boston	130	229	171	345	175	349
Washington	140	280	166	331	213	426
Miami	137	273	187	374	213	426
Denver	154	307	154	307	213	426
Chicago	157	314	173	345	234	468
Houston	123	245	123	245	189	377
Seattle	164	328	223	446	259	517
Los Angeles	157	314	223	446	259	517
San Francisco	164	328	223	446	266	531
From **Manchester** to						
New York	174	249	214	398	228	357
Chicago	180	348	180	348	234	468
Los Angeles	234	468	274	518	282	564

NON-STOP FLIGHTS TO THE US FROM BRITAIN

FROM LONDON
(Heathrow or Gatwick)
Anchorage British Airways
Atlanta British Airways, Delta
Baltimore TWA
Boston American Airlines,
British Airways, Northwest,
Virgin Atlantic
Charlotte US Air
Chicago American Airlines,
British Airways
Cincinnati Delta
Dallas/Fort Worth American
Airlines, British Airways
Denver Continental
Detroit Delta
Houston British Airways,
Continental

Los Angeles Air New Zealand,
American Airlines, British
Airways, United, Virgin Atlantic
Miami American Airlines,
British Airways, Delta, Virgin
Atlantic
Minneapolis Northwest
New York Air India, American
Air, British Airways, Continental,
Kuwait Air, United, Virgin
Atlantic
Orlando British Airways, Virgin
Atlantic
Philadelphia British Airways,
TWA
St Louis TWA
San Francisco British Airways,
United

Seattle British Airways, United
Tampa British Airways
Washington DC British
Airways, United

FROM MANCHESTER
Atlanta Delta
Chicago American Airlines
New York American Airlines,
British Airways
Orlando Virgin Atlantic

FROM GLASGOW
Boston Northwest
Chicago American Airlines
New York British Airways,
Northwest

AIRLINE ADDRESSES

Air India 17–18 New Bond St, London W1 (☎071/
493 4050).

Air New Zealand Elsenore House, Fulham Palace
Rd, London W6 (☎081/741 2299).

American Airlines 15 Berkeley St, London W1
(☎081/572 5555 or ☎0800/010151).

British Airways 156 Regent St, London W1R 5TA
(☎081/897 4000).

Continental Airlines 52 Conduit St, London W1
(no phone; booking office). Head Office: Beulah
Court, Albert Rd, Horley, Surrey RH6 7HZ (☎0293/
776464).

Delta Victoria Plaza, Victoria Station, London SW1
(☎0800/414767).

Kuwait Air 16–20 Baker St, London W1 (☎071/
486 6666).

Northwest Airlines 8–9 Berkeley St, London W1
(no phone; booking office). Head office: Northwest
House, Tinsley Lane, Crawley, W Sussex RH10 2TP
(☎0345/747800).

TWA 200 Piccadilly, London W1N OHA (☎071/439
0707).

United Airlines 193 Piccadilly, London W1
(☎081/990 9900 or ☎0800/888555)

US Air Piccadilly House, Regent St, London SW1
(☎0800/777333).

Virgin Atlantic Sussex House, High St, Crawley,
West Sussex RH10 1PH (☎0293/562000)

Toll-free phone numbers for airlines **in the United States** are listed on p.23.

Generally, the most expensive time to fly is **high season**, roughly between June and August and around Christmas. May and September are slightly less pricey, and the rest of the year is considered low season and cheaper still. Remember, however, that high season in the UK can sometimes be the least costly and crowded season at your destination. For example, South Florida and New Orleans are both unbearably hot – almost swampy – in the summer, so the extra you might spend on a summer flight might be more than compensated for by low prices once

you're on the ground. Keep an eye out for slack season bargains, and, additionally, make sure to check the exact dates of the seasons with your operator or airline; you might be able to make major savings by shifting your departure date by a week – or even a day. Midweek flights tend to cost less than weekend ones.

Once in the US, a **Visiting US Airpass** (VUSA) can be a good idea if you want to see a lot of the country. These are only available to non-US residents, and must be bought before reaching the States (see p.23).

FARES

Standby deals (under which you buy an open-dated ticket and decide later when to fly) are uncommon, and are often no more economical than the more standard **Apex** returns. Apex fares, which are offered by agents (see below), must be booked at least three weeks in advance, and you must stay for a minimum of seven nights. Tickets are then valid for six months. **Instant Savers**, which can result in considerable savings, are booked one day in advance and are completely inflexible. Some airlines do a **Super-Apex** ticket, cheaper than an ordinary Apex fare, which often has to be booked thirty days in advance and is only valid for up to three weeks; usually it isn't refundable or even changeable. With an **open-jaw** ticket you can fly into one city and out of another; fares are calculated by halving the return fares to each destination and adding the two figures together. This is a convenient option for those who want a fly-drive holiday (see below).

AGENTS

For a precise picture of all the available options at any given time, contact an agent specialising in low-cost flights (see below), who may – especially if you're under 26 or a student – be able to knock down the regular Apex fares when there are no special airline deals. You'll need to be pretty flexible about your destination and travel date, however. These agents also offer cut-price seats on charter flights, which are good value if you're travelling from somewhere other than London, but tend to be limited in the summer. They're restricted to so-called "holiday destinations" and have fixed departure and return times. Look out, too, for fly-drive packages and all-inclusive flight-plus-accommodation deals. Brochures are available at high-street travel agents, or contact the agents direct at the addresses below.

COURIER FLIGHTS

It is possible for those on a very tight budget to travel as **couriers**. Most of the major courier firms offer opportunities to travel for up to fifty percent off the cheapest fare (as low as £150–200 return to New York, or £200 return to the West Coast) in return for delivering a package. There'll be someone to check you in and to meet you at your destination, which minimises any red-tape

LOW-COST FLIGHT AGENTS IN BRITAIN

Campus Travel 52 Grosvenor Gardens, London W1 (☎071/836 3343), and nationwide branches.

Council Travel 28a Poland St, London W1V 3DB (☎071/437 7767).

CTS Travel 44 Goodge St, London W1P 2AD (☎071/323 5130).

Destinations 200–208 Tottenham Court Rd, London W1 (☎071/436 6676).

Flightfile 49 Tottenham Court Rd, London W1P 9RE (☎071/323 4340).

STA Travel. All US enquiries on ☎071/937 9971. Offices at 74 Old Brompton Rd, London SW7 3LH; 117 Euston Rd, London NW1; 2SX; 25 Queen's Rd, Bristol BS8 1QE; 38 Sidney St, Cambridge CB2 3HX; 36 George St, Oxford OX1 2BJ; 88 Vicar Lane, Leeds LS1 7JH; 75 Deansgate, Manchester M3 2BW.

Touropa 52 Grosvenor Gardens, London SW1W ONP (☎071/730 2101).

Trailfinders 42–50 Earl's Court Rd, London W8 6EJ (☎071/937 5400).

Travel Cuts 295 Regent St, London W1 (☎071/637 3161).

SPECIALIST US FLIGHT AGENTS IN BRITAIN

Airborn 48 Crawford St, London W1H 1HA (☎071/706 2288).

Falcon 33 Notting Hill Gate, London W11 (☎071/221 6298); Birmingham, ☎021/666 7000; Manchester, ☎061/831 7000; Glasgow, ☎041/248 7911.

Globespan 236 Atlantic House, Gatwick Airport, W Sussex RH6 ONP (☎0293/541541). Also PO Box 149, Glasgow G2 3EJ (☎041/332 6600).

Jetsave Sussex House, London Rd, East Grinstead, W Sussex RH19 1LD (☎0342/327711).

North American Travel Club 38 High St, Hurstpierpoint, W Sussex BN6 9RG (☎0273/835095).

Unijet "Sandrocks", Rocky Lane, Haywards Heath, W Sussex (☎0444/458181).

COURIER FIRMS IN BRITAIN

Courier Travel Service (CTS) Ltd ☎071/351 0300.

DHL ☎081/890 9393.

IML ☎081/847 5621.

Nomad ☎081/570 9277.

Polo Express ☎081/759 5383.

TNT Skypack is operated by CTS (above).

hassle. However, you'll have to travel light, with only a cabin-bag, and accept tight restrictions on travel dates – stays of more than a fortnight are rare. For phone numbers, see above or check the Yellow Pages.

FROM LONDON

Non-stop flights to **Los Angeles** from London take ten or eleven hours and cost around £500–600, although many carriers have occasional offers as low as £300; the London–**Miami** flight, which varies a lot in price, takes eight hours, while flying time to **New York** is seven or so hours, and the fare will range from £300 to £600. Due to the time-change (the East Coast is five hours behind GMT, the West Coast is eight hours behind), return flights are always an hour or two shorter than outward journeys. One-stop direct flights to destinations beyond the East Coast obviously add time to the journey, but can work out cheaper than non-stop flights.

FROM ELSEWHERE IN BRITAIN

Outside London, there are fewer choices as regards non-stop flights to the US (see box). Travel to the West Coast is particularly tricky. As yet, there are no non-stop flights to LA or San Francisco from Manchester or Glasgow, although *American Airlines* does have a service from Manchester, via Chicago, to the West Coast. From Glasgow, *Northwest* flies via New York or Boston to the West Coast, and also via Boston to Florida. Cheap **charters** from the larger regional airports (especially Stansted or Manchester) are run by specialist operators, and some of these fares include accommodation.

FROM EIRE

The cheapest flights **from Eire** – if you're under 26 or a student – are available from *USIT* (see

below). Student-only fares to **New York** or **Boston** go for around IR£369 return, the fare to **Chicago** is about IR£429. You can get to **Florida** and the East Coast via London on *Northwest* for around £420 return. *Aer Lingus* has occasional special offers to gateway cities, with services from Dublin and Shannon to Florida via New York from IR£500. *Delta* flies to Florida, via Atlanta, for the same fare. Flights from Shannon may be IR£15 or so cheaper than those from Dublin.

AIRLINE ADDRESSES IN IRELAND

Aer Lingus 41 Upper O'Connell St, Dublin 1 (☎010 3531/377777)

Delta 24 Merrion Square, Dublin 2 (☎010 3531/768080)

Northwest Air 47 Dawson St, Dublin (☎010 3531/717766)

USIT Aston Quay, O'Connell Bridge, Dublin 2 (☎010 3531/778117); 13b College St, Belfast BT1 6ET (☎0232/324073).

FROM EUROPE

It is generally far cheaper to fly non-stop to the States – especially the West Coast – from London than any other European city. However, for the best deals to New York from Brussels and Paris, contact **Nouvelles Frontières**, 66 boulevard St-Michel, Paris (☎4634-5530) and 21 rue de La Violette (Grand Place), Brussels (☎02511/8013). Their London branch is at 1–2 Hanover St, W1 (☎071/629 7772). Other options are the cut-price charter flights occasionally offered from major European cities; ask at your nearest travel agent for details. The cheapest deals from all continental Europe are with *Icelandair*, who have offices in London (☎071/388 5599) and who fly from Luxembourg to Baltimore, Chicago, Detroit, New York and Orlando.

FROM AUSTRALIA AND NEW ZEALAND

Travelling from **Australia** and **New Zealand** to the States, there are very few cheap alternatives to Apex fares. *Qantas, Air New Zealand, Northwest, Continental, United, Delta, American, Garuda, JAL* and *Thai* all fly from **Sydney** to **LA**; all except *Delta* operate from **Melbourne** too, and *Continental* and *Qantas* use **Brisbane** as well. A peak-season return will cost around

Aus$1400, dropping to Aus$1300 off-season. Most of these services are routed via New Zealand; *Air New Zealand*, *Northwest*, *Continental*, *United*, *Delta* and *American* fly from **Auckland** to LA for about NZ$1800 return.

With any of the American carriers from Australasia, you can continue on to **New York** for something in the region of US$170 extra. If you want to get to **Florida**, *American Airlines* leaves Auckland and stops at Dallas/Fort Worth on the way to Miami; an Apex return costs Aus$1520–1720 or NZ$2600–2800, depending on the season. Most flights stop off in Honolulu, Hawaii; you can usually stay over for as long as you like for no extra charge.

In Australia, **STA** have offices at 1a Lee St, Railway Square, Sydney 2000 (☎2/519-9866), and 222–224 Faraday St, Carlton 3053 (☎03/347-4711. In New Zealand, they're at 64 High St, Auckland (☎09/309-0458).

INCLUSIVE HOLIDAYS AND CHARTERS

Packages – fly-drive, flight/accommodation deals and guided tours (or a combination of all three) – can work out cheaper than arranging the same trip yourself, especially for a short-term stay. To take a typical example, a return flight plus middle-range midtown hotel accommodation for three nights in New York City costs around £350 per person. Drawbacks include the loss of flexibility and the fact that you'll probably be made to stay in hotels in the mid-range to expensive bracket, even though cheaper accommodation is almost always readily available.

High street travel agents have plenty of brochures and information about the various combinations available. Most charter deals from agents include accommodation along with the flight. Prices are based on two or more people travelling together; and this can be such a bargain that even if you do end up paying for a hotel room, which, of course, you don't have to use, it may still be cheaper than the standard fare. Flight-only deals do turn up at the last minute to fill unused seats; scan high street travel agents for the latest offers.

FLY-DRIVE

Fly-drive deals, which give cut-rate (sometimes free) car rental when buying a transatlantic ticket from an airline or tour operator, are always cheaper than hiring on the spot and give great value if you intend to do a lot of driving. On the other hand, you'll have to pay more for the flight than if you booked it through a discount agent. Competition between airlines (especially *Northwest* and *TWA*) and tour operators means that it's well worth phoning to check on current special promotions. *Northwest Flydrive*, PO Box 45, Bexhill-on-Sea, East Sussex TN40 1PY (☎0424/224400) offer excellent deals for not much more than an ordinary Apex fare. For example, a return flight to Boston and a week's car rental might cost as little as £333 per person; a mere £14 more than the cheapest air fare. *Poundstretcher*, *Renown Holidays* and *Destination USA* (see below) offer similar packages. However, there will often be little to choose between them; prices begin at £55 per week for a small family saloon, working up to £130 per week for an estate, usually including 750 to 1000 free miles. Watch out for hidden extras, though, like the car "drop-off" charge, which can be as much as a week's rental, and Collision Damage Waiver insurance which is about £8 per day. Remember, too, that while you can drive in the States with a British licence, there can be problems renting vehicles if you're under 25. For complete car-rental and driveaway details, see "Getting Around" (p.24)

FLIGHT AND ACCOMMODATION DEALS

There are no end of **flight and accommodation** packages to all the major American cities, and although you can do things cheaper independently, you won't be able to do the same things cheaper. *STA Travel* (see above) offer "City Packages" using hostel accommodation (not available in every US city) for around $15 per night plus airfare. Among the many tour operators which offer more costly deals, *Virgin Holidays* are about the cheapest: for example, seven nights in San Francisco plus return flight will cost around £600–700 per person, and the same deal in a Florida destination, with car rental included, can be as low as £400–500. See also "Accommodation", p.27, for details of pre-booked accommodation schemes.

TOURING AND ADVENTURE PACKAGES

A simple and exciting way to see a chunk of America's Great Outdoors, without being hassled by too many practical considerations, is to take a specialist **touring and adventure package**, which includes transport, accommodation, food

SPECIALIST HOLIDAY OPERATORS IN BRITAIN

GENERAL

Destination USA 1a Martindale Rd, Hounslow West, Middlesex TW4 7EW (☎081/891 3131).

Poundstretcher Atlantic House, Hazelwick Ave, Three Bridges, Crawley, W Sussex RH10 1NP (☎0293/518022).

Renown Holidays 19 Connaught St, London W2 2AY (☎071/723 6689).

Thomson Greater London House, Hampstead Rd, London NW1 7SD (☎071/387 6534).

Travelscene 94 Baker St, London W1M 2HD (☎071/935 1025).

Virgin Holidays Sussex House, High St, Crawley, W Sussex RH10 1BZ (☎0293/617181).

ADVENTURE TOURS

Adventure Travel Centre/Top Deck 131–135 Earl's Court Rd, London SW5 (☎071/370 4555).

Airtours Helmshore Rossendale, Lancs BB4 4NB (☎0706/260000).

AmeriCan Adventures, 45 High St, Tunbridge Wells, Kent TN1 1XL (☎0892/511894).

American Pioneers PO Box 229, Westlea, Swindon SN5 7HJ (☎0793/881882).

Contiki Travel 7 Rathbone Place, London W1 (☎071/637 2121).

Enterprise Groundstar House, London Rd, Crawley, W Sussex RH10 2HB (☎0293/560777).

Exodus Expeditions 9 Weir Rd, London SW12 OLT (☎081/675 5550).

Explore Worldwide I Frederick St, Aldershot, Hampshire GU11 1LQ (☎0252/319448).

Greyhound Sussex House, London Rd, East Grinstead, W Sussex RH19 (☎0342/317317).

Poundstretcher Atlantic House, Hazelwick Avenue, Three Bridges, Crawley, W Sussex RH10 1NP (☎0293/615538).

Premier Westbrook, Milton Rd, Cambridge CB4 1YQ (☎0223/355977).

TransAmerica 3a Gatwick Metro Centre, Balcombe Rd, Horley, Surrey RH6 9GA (☎0293/774099).

TrekAmerica Trek House, The Bullring, Deddington, Oxford OX15 OTT (☎0869/38777).

Unijet "Sandrocks", Rocky Lane, Haywards Heath, W Sussex RH16 4RH (☎0444/459191 or ☎0345/600800).

Virgin Holidays Sussex House, High St, Crawley, W Sussex RH10 1BZ (☎0293/617181).

and a guide. Some of the more adventurous carry small groups around on minibuses and use a combination of budget hotels and camping (equipment, except sleeping bag, is provided). Most also have a food kitty of maybe £25 per week, with many meals cooked and eaten communally, although there's plenty of time to leave the group and do your own thing.

TrekAmerica is one UK-based company to offer such deals; a typical package would be ten days in California and the "Wild West" for £400 or so excluding flights. Other operators are listed below. *Green Tortoise*, PO Box 24459, San Francisco CA 94214 (☎415/821-0803) (see p.21) is a more unorthodox, US-based company whose tours include an annual summer trip to Alaska. Also in California, the *Sierra Club*, c/o Outings Dept, 730 Polk St, San Francisco CA 94110 (☎415/776-2211), offers a range of backcountry hikes into otherwise barely accessible parts of the High Sierra wilderness, with food and guide provided. The tours are summer-only, cost around $300 for a fortnight and are heavily subscribed, making it essential to book at least three months in advance. You'll also have to pay about $40 to join the club.

VISAS AND RED TAPE

British citizens who wish to enter the US for less than ninety days (three months) will need a full UK passport (not a one-year British Visitors Passport) and a visa waiver form. You can get this form either from your travel agent, the airline when you check in, or on the plane. Fill it in and present it to the immigration officials when you arrive in the States. The visa waiver scheme also allows you to re-enter the US if you cross the border into Canada or Mexico.

Anyone who is not a British citizen (for example British overseas citizens or British subjects – including citizens of Eire, Australia, Portugal and Greece), or British citizens who wish to stay in the States for longer than ninety days, must have a non-immigrant visitor's visa before arriving. To obtain one, fill in the form available at most travel agents, and send or take it, with a full passport and photograph, to the visa department of your nearest US Embassy or Consulate (for addresses, see below). You'll need to give precise dates of your trip, and declare that you're not intending to live or work in the US (if, however, you do intend to do either of those two things, see p.49). Personal interviews can be arranged, at a week's notice, for those who need a visa in a hurry. Visas aren't issued to convicted criminals and anyone who admits to ever having been a fascist, communist or drug dealer. You may also have problems if you admit to being HIV positive or having AIDS. The American Embassy in London makes an unwarranted heavy charge for calls to its "Visa Information Line" on ☎0898/200 290 (36p per min cheap rate, 48p per min all other times).

IMMIGRATION

During the flight you'll be handed an **immigration form** (and a customs declaration; see below). Fill this out and hand it, with your passport, to the immigration officials on landing. Part of the form will be attached to your passport where it must stay until you fly back. On the form you'll have to give details of where you intend to stay during your trip. If you don't know, write "touring", but be prepared to give an idea of your schedule and destinations. You'll probably be asked by the officials where you intend to stay your first night. Sounding confident and saying "a hotel" or "a hostel" should suffice. If you're staying with friends, give their address and phone number, which the officer might check. You must also give the date that you intend to leave the US.

In addition, the officer will want to know how you intend to support yourself during your visit. If you're going to be in the country for more than a fortnight, you may be asked to show your return ticket and ample means of support: about $250 per week is considered enough, so flash as many credit cards and travellers' cheques as you can muster.

There are, of course, ways to bend the rules a bit; you could, for example, borrow enough money to get into the country, and return it afterwards using an international money order (see p.13). Overall, it will help if you look reasonably respectable. It's unfortunately true that entry will be more straightforward if you're white, conventional looking, and are well-spoken and polite. And, whatever you do, if you are thinking of working in the States, never let on; this, of course, is exactly what the officials are trying to find out.

CUSTOMS

Customs officers will relieve you of your customs declaration and ask if you have any fresh foods. If you do, you'll have to hand them over, and won't get them back; say "no" and your baggage might be searched anyway. You'll also be asked if you visited a farm in the last month; if yes, don't be surprised if they take away your shoes. The duty-free allowance if you're over seventeen is two hundred cigarettes and one hundred cigars, and if you're over 21, a litre of spirits or wine.

US EMBASSIES AND CONSULATES OVERSEAS

Great Britain
5 Upper Grosvenor
 Street
London W1
☎071/499 7010

3 Regent Terrace
Edinburgh EH7 5BW
☎031/556 8315

Queens House
14 Queen Street
Belfast BT1 6EQ
☎0232/228239

Australia
Moonhah Place
Canberra
☎62/733 711

Canada
100 Wellington St, K1P 5Tl
Ottawa, Ontario
☎238-0430

Denmark
Dag Hammerskjöld Alle 24
2100 Copenhagen
☎01/423144

Eire
42 Elgin Road
Ballsbridge, Dublin 4
☎01/688777

France
2 avenue Gabriel
75382 Paris Cedex 08
☎42.96.12.02

Netherlands
Museumplein 19
Amsterdam
☎020/790 321

Norway
Drammensveien 18
Oslo
☎02/448 550

Sweden
Strandvagen 101
Stockholm
☎08/783 53000

New Zealand
29 Fitzherbert Terrace
Thorndon, Wellington
☎4/722 068

FOREIGN EMBASSIES AND CONSULATES IN THE US

Great Britain
Embassy:
3100 Massachusetts
 Ave NW
Washington DC 20008
☎202/462-1340

Consulates:
33 N Dearborn St
Chicago IL 60602
☎312/346 1810

3701 Wilshire Blvd,
 Suite 312
Los Angeles CA90010
☎213/385-7381

Suite 2110, 1001 S
 Bayshore Drive
Miami FL 33101
☎305/374-1522

845 Third Ave
New York NY 10022
☎212/745-0202

Australia
1601 Massachusetts
 Ave NW
Washington DC 20036-
 2273
☎202/797-3000

Canada
501 Pennsylvania Ave
 NW
Washington DC 20001
☎202/682-1740

Denmark
3200 White Haven St
 NW
Washington DC 20008
☎202/234-4300

Eire
2234 Massachusetts
 Ave NW
Washington DC 20008
☎202/462-3939

France
4101 Reservoir Rd NW
Washington DC 20007
☎202/944-6000

Germany
4645 Reservoir Rd NW
Washington DC 20007
☎202/298-4000

Japan
2520 Massachusetts
 Avenue NW
Washington DC 20008
☎202/234-2266

Mexico
2829 16th St NW
Washington DC 20009
☎202/234-6000

Netherlands
4200 Linnean Ave
Washington DC 20008
☎202/244-5304

New Zealand
37 Observatory Circle
 NW
Washington DC 20008-
 3686
☎202/328-4800

Norway
2820 34th St NW
Washington DC 20008-
 2799
☎202/33-6000

Spain
270 15th St NW
Washington DC 20009
☎202/265-0190

Sweden
600 New Hampshire
 Ave NW, #1200
Washington DC 20037-
 2462
☎202/944-5600

As well as food and anything agricultural, it's also prohibited to carry into the country any articles from Vietnam, North Korea, Kampuchea or Cuba (including cigars), obscene publications, lottery tickets, Pre-Columbian artefacts and chocolate liqueurs. Anyone caught smuggling drugs of any kind will not only face prosecution but be entered in the records as an Undesirable and probably denied re-entry for life.

EXTENSIONS AND LEAVING

The date stamped on your passport is the latest you're legally allowed to stay. Leaving a few days later may not matter, especially if you're heading home, but more than a week or so can result in a protracted, rather unpleasant, interrogation from officials which may cause you to miss your flight. Overstaying may also cause you to be turned away next time you try to enter the US.

To get an extension before your time is up, apply at the nearest **US Immigration and Naturalization Service** (INS) office (their address will be under the Federal Government Offices listings at the front of the phone book). They will assume that you're working illegally and it's up to you to convince them otherwise. Do this by providing evidence of ample finances, and, if you can, bring along an upstanding American citizen to vouch for your worthiness. Obviously you'll also have to explain why you didn't plan for the extra time initially – saying your money lasted longer than you expected, or that a close relative is coming over, are well-worked excuses.

HEALTH AND INSURANCE

If you're coming from Europe, you don't require any inoculations to enter the US. But insurance, while not compulsory, is essential. The US has no national health system, and you can lose an arm and a leg (so to speak) having even minor medical treatment.

Insurance policies can be bought through any high street travel agent or insurance broker. In Britain, the cheapest is through *Touropa* (see above under "Low-Cost Flight Agents"), who charge around £40 for six weeks to cover life, limb and luggage, with the needs of young travellers and students in mind. The forms are availa-ble from *Touropa* itself, or call ☎0800/262299. On all policies, read the small print to ensure that the cover includes a sensible amount for medical expenses – at least $100,000 – and that they'll fly you home in the event of serious injury. Also, if you'll be doing a lot of travelling around the States by bus or train, make sure your baggage is well insured against loss or theft. If you do have anything stolen (including cash), register the loss immediately at the nearest police station (if in doubt call ☎911). They will give you a reference number to pass on to your insurance company – an accepted alternative to the full statement insurers usually require.

If you need a doctor, lists can be found in the Yellow Pages under "Clinics" or "Physicians and Surgeons". British Consulates in individual cities can also provide selected names. A basic consultancy fee is from $50 to $75, payable in advance; medicines aren't cheap either – keep receipts for all you spend and claim it back on your insurance.

Most minor ailments can be remedied by a simple trip to the drugstore, but bear in mind that many painkillers available over the counter in Britain need a prescription in the US. Brand names can be confusing; if in doubt, ask at the nearest pharmacy (there's one in every drug store). More seriously, if you're involved in an accident, medical services will come to your aid and charge you later.

COSTS, MONEY AND BANKS

Assuming that exchange rates remain as favourable for visitors as they have been in recent years – when the English pound has fluctuated between $1.50 and $2 – the US is a pretty cheap place to visit. Items such as petrol, booze and cigarettes (as well as electronic equipment, cameras and, of course, Levi jeans) cost a whole lot less than they do at home. That said, you will still need to watch your wallet carefully if you're on any kind of budget; and be prepared for regional variances. Most New York prices, for example, are well above those in rural America.

Your biggest single expense is likely to be **accommodation**. You're unlikely to find a hotel or motel room in a city for under $25 – $40 would be more usual – and rates in rural areas are not all that much cheaper. Although hostels offering dorm beds for $8 to $15 per night are reasonably common, they're by no means everywhere. Camping, of course, is cheap, ranging from free to perhaps $15 per night, but rarely practical in or around the big cities. Bear in mind that immigration officers may well want you to prove when you arrive that you have sufficient funds to finance your stay, and their criteria are more likely to be based on motel prices.

Food is no problem at all. Ten dollars a day is enough to get you a fairly basic life-support diet, while for a daily total of around $20 you can dine pretty well. Portions tend to be bigger and better in the US than virtually anywhere. Beyond this, everything hinges on how much sightseeing, taxi-taking, drinking, clubbing and socialising you're intending to do. Much of any of these – especially in a major city – and you're likely to be getting through upwards of $50 a day.

If you're planning to **travel** around the country to any significant extent, rates for buses and trains, even planes, may look cheap on paper, but the distances involved are so great that the costs will soon mount up. For a group of two or more, renting a **car** can be a very good investment, not least because it will enable you to stay in the ubiquitous cheap motels along the interstates instead of expensive city-centre hotels.

All the specific **prices** given in this book were applicable at the start of 1992; as time goes by, you can expect inflation to send them creeping up. For **museums** and similar attractions, the admission fees we quote are for adults; you can assume that children get in half-price. Prices for **accommodation**, unless otherwise stated, are for high-season double rooms, and do not include local taxes.

MONEY

US currency comes in **bills** worth $1, $5, $10, $20, $50 and $100, plus various rarely seen larger denominations. Confusingly, all are the same size and same green colour, making it necessary to check each bill carefully before handing it over. The dollar is made up of 100 cents in **coins** of 1 cent (known as a **penny**), 5 cents (a **nickel**), 10 cents (a **dime**) and 25 cents (a **quarter**). Very occasionally you might come across **JFK half-dollars** (50¢), **Susan B. Anthony dollar coins**, or a **two-dollar bill**. Change (quarters are the most useful) is needed for buses, vending machines and telephones, so always carry plenty.

TRAVELLERS' CHEQUES

The bulk of your money should be carried as **US dollar travellers' cheques** (US *travelers' checks*); cheques in other currencies, including sterling, might just as well be from the moon. Dollar cheques can be changed in banks, but are accepted as cash virtually everywhere – $10 and $20 cheques are the most useful, as shops may be unhappy to give you $49.50 in change just because you buy a candy bar.

Travellers' cheques can be bought in Britain over the counter at any bank and many building societies, irrespective of whether you have an account or not. There's usually a charge of 1 to 2 percent of the amount ordered. The most widely recognised cheques are *American Express*, available from Lloyds, Natwest, the Royal Bank of Scotland and the TSB; *Visa* travellers' cheques from the Co-op, Yorkshire and Barclays banks; and *Thomas Cook* travellers' cheques, sold by their major agents and the Midland Bank.

When changing travellers' cheques, you'll be asked for **identification**; a passport is best. Though you often see signs in the States saying "no checks", this refers to personal cheques — there should be no problem using travellers' cheques. For **emergency phone numbers** to call if your cheques (and/or credit cards) should be stolen, see p.46.

CREDIT CARDS AND CASH MACHINES

If you don't already have a **credit card**, you should think seriously about getting one before you go. In the United States, it'll prove invaluable. For many services, it's simply taken for granted that you'll be paying with plastic. When renting a car (or even a bike) or checking into a hotel you may well be asked to show a credit card to establish your creditworthiness — even if you intend to settle the bill in cash. *Visa, Access* (known in the US as *Mastercard*) and *American Express* are the most widely used. Bear in mind that fluctuating exchange rates may result in spending more (or less) than you expect when the item shows up on your statement.

Provided you know your PIN (personal identification number), most major credit cards, and some bank and building society cash cards (such as Abbey National's *Abbeylink*) can be used to draw up to $500 a day from the **cash machines** (US *Automated Teller Machines* or *ATMs; Cirrus* and *Plus* are the biggest networks). It's essential, though, that you check the latest details with your credit card company before departing — otherwise the machine may simply gobble up your plastic friend. *American Express* card holders can use the travellers' cheque and cash dispensers found at airports and in larger cities.

BANKS

Banking hours are generally from 10am until 4pm Monday to Thursday, and 10am to 6pm on Friday, although the trend is towards longer opening hours. Until recently, banks in the US were organised along state lines, which meant that even the largest US banks only had branches in a single state. This is rapidly changing, but it can still be an awkward task to keep track of who's who. Most major banks will change travellers' cheques for their face value (not that there's much point doing this — and some charge for the privilege, so ask before you do); banks can also **change foreign travellers' cheques and currency** — usually a frustratingly tedious task. Depending on the amount and number of cheques, you may well end up paying a lower commission at an exchange bureau; *Thomas Cook* or *American Express* are the most widely found names, but there are always exchange offices at airports. Rarely, if ever, do hotels change foreign currency.

EMERGENCIES

If you're flat broke and at a loss for what to do, don't give up hope: there are several alternatives before breaking down in tears.

The easiest way to get money is to have someone in the UK send you some through **Western Union**. All they need do is hand over the loot to any UK Western Union agent (call Freefone 100 and ask for the nearest one). You can then collect it (less a hefty ten percent commission) from any Western Union office in the US (for the nearest one phone: ☎1-800/326 6000). The transfer is instantaneous.

Alternatively, arrange someone to transfer cash from any branch of **Thomas Cook** in Britain via telex to one of their US branches; they're all in local phone books. The actual transfer of funds is, again, instantaneous; the cost is £25.

If there's time, get someone to buy an **international money order** and post it to you. The cost of this is minimal (around £5), but you have to rely on air mail and should allow seven days for arrival. The money order can be cashed at any post office, and is a quicker way to acquire funds than being sent an ordinary cheque, which takes two or three weeks to clear. If you know someone with a US bank account, you can have money sent by wire through your UK bank to their US account, but this is more expensive.

Other possibilities include **working illegally** (see p.49) or throwing yourself on the mercy of your nearest national consulate. **British consulates** will — in worst cases only — repatriate

British citizens (on arrival in the UK, you'll have to surrender your passport until you've repaid the cost of the flight) but will never, under any circumstances, lend money. As a last resort, you might try **selling blood**, for perhaps $15 for a pint – check the Yellow Pages for agencies and hospitals. Teaching hospitals in California will also pay for donations to their sperm banks.

TELEPHONES, POST AND TIME ZONES

Because of the strong emphasis placed on business efficiency, and the fact that Americans in general are avid complainers, all forms of communication (apart from the US Mail, which is incredibly slow and careless) in the US are very good. In rural areas you may find it slightly frustrating just getting to the nearest public phone – which may be many miles away – but in general keeping in touch is easy.

TELEPHONES

US **telephones** are run by a huge variety of local companies, many of which were hived off from the previous *Bell System* monopoly – the successor to which is the nationwide *AT&T* network. No matter which system is providing the local service, most things are identical across the country: the **dialling tone** is a continuous lowish hum; the **ringing tone** is a long nasal squawk with short gaps; the **engaged** (US *busy*) tone a series of rapid blips; **number unobtainable** (rare) is a single high-pitched squeak. Dial-phones are scarce: the vast majority are the push-button kind, emitting a different audio tone for each button pressed. Some numbers, particularly those of consumer services, employ letters as part of their "number", for example ☎1-800/822-TAXI to call a cab company in Los Angeles,

or ☎1-800/USA-RAIL for *Amtrak* train information; the letters are on the buttons. For help, call the **operator** (☎0).

Public telephones invariably work, and in cities at any rate can be found everywhere – on street corners, in railway and bus stations, hotel lobbies, bars and restaurants. They take 25¢, 10¢ and 5¢ coins. The cost of a **local call** from a public phone (ie within the same area code) varies, from a minimum of 20¢, according to the actual distance being called.

Some numbers covered by the same area code are considered so far apart that calls between them count as **non-local** (*zone calls*). These cost much more and sometimes require you to dial 1 before the seven-digit number. Pricier still are **long-distance calls** (ie to a different area code), for which you'll need plenty of change. An assertive female voice tells you how much money to insert whenever your time is running out. If you still owe money at the end of the call, the phone will ring immediately and you'll be asked for the outstanding amount (if you don't cough up, the person you've been calling will get the bill). Non-local calls and long-distance calls are far cheaper if made between 6pm and 8am, and calls from **private phones** are always much cheaper than those from public phones. Detailed rates are listed at the front of the **telephone directory** (the "White Pages", a copious source of information on many matters).

Phone calls from a hotel room are usually more expensive than from a public phone (and there are usually public phones in hotel lobbies). On the other hand, some hotels offer free local calls from rooms – ask when you check in. An increasing number of phones accept **credit cards** – simply swipe the card through the slot and dial. Another way to avoid the necessity of carrying copious quantities of change everywhere is to obtain an **AT&T charge card** (information on ☎412/553-7458 or ☎1-800/874-4000 ext 359), for which you have to have an *AMEX* or credit card issued by an American bank.

INTERNATIONAL TELEPHONE CODES

The telephone code to dial **TO the US** from the outside world is 1.
To make international calls **FROM the US**, dial 011 followed by the country code:

Australia 61	**Germany** 49	**Netherlands** 31	**Sweden** 46
Denmark 45	**Ireland** 353	**New Zealand** 64	**United Kingdom** 44

TELEPHONE AREA CODES WITHIN THE US

Alabama (AL) 205
Alaska (AK) 907
Arizona (AZ) 602
Arkansas (AR) 501

California (CA)
 Los Angeles 213
 West Los Angeles 310
 Orange County 714
 San Francisco 415
 East Bay 510
 Monterey 408
 Santa Barbara 805
 San Diego & eastern California 619
 Wine Country & North Coast 707
 Sacramento & northern California 916
Colorado (CO)
 Denver & northern Colorado 303
 Colorado Springs 719
Connecticut (CT) 203

Delaware (DE) 302

Florida (FL)
 Miami 305
 Orlando 407
 Tampa 813
 Fort Lauderdale 305
 Jacksonville & Tallahassee 904

Georgia (GA)
 Atlanta 404
 Savannah 912

Hawaii (HI) 808

Idaho (ID) 208
Illinois (IL)
 Chicago 312
 Peoria 309
 Springfield 217
 Centralia 618
Indiana (IN)
 Indianapolis 317
 South Bend 219
Iowa (IA)
 Des Moines 515
 Dubuque 319
 Council Bluffs 712

Kansas (KS)
 Kansas City & east Kansas 913
 Dodge City & Wichita 316
Kentucky (KY)
 Louisville 502
 Covington 606

Louisiana (LA)
 New Orleans 504
 The rest 318

Maine (ME) 207
Maryland (MD)
 Frederick 301
 Baltimore 410
Massachusetts (MA)
 Boston 617
 Eastern Massachusetts 508
 Western Massachusetts 413
Michigan (MI)
 Detroit 313
 Lansing 517
 Grand Rapids 616
Minnesota (MN)
 Minneapolis 612
 Rochester 507
 Duluth 218
Mississippi (MS) 601
Missouri (MO)
 Kansas City 816
 St Louis 314
 Springfield 417
Montana (MT) 406

Nebraska (NE)
 Omaha and the east 402
 Western Nebraska 308
Nevada (NV) 702
New Hampshire (NH) 603
New Jersey (NJ)
 Princeton & the coast 609
 Newark 201
New Mexico (NM) 505
New York (NY)
 Manhattan & the Bronx 212
 Brooklyn & Queens 718
 Long Island 516
 Hudson Valley 914
 Buffalo & Rochester 716
 Syracuse 315
 Albany 518
 Binghampton 607

North Carolina (NC)
 Charlotte 704
 Raleigh 919
North Dakota (ND) 701

Ohio (OH)
 Southern & Central Ohio 614
 Cleveland 216
 Cincinnati 513
 Toledo & Lake Erie Islands 419
Oklahoma (OK)
 Oklahoma City & west 405
 Eastern Oklahoma 918
Oregon (OR) 503

Pennsylvania (PA)
 Philadelphia 215
 Harrisburg & central Pennsylvania 717
 Pittsburgh & southwest 412
 Altoona & the north 814

Rhode Island (RI) 401

South Carolina (SC) 803
South Dakota (SD) 605

Tennessee (TN)
 Memphis 901
 Nashville 615
Texas (TX)
 Central Texas & Corpus Christi 512
 Dallas 214
 West Texas 915
 Houston 713
 Fort Worth 817
 The Panhandle 806
 Paris 903
 Galveston 409

Utah (UT) 801

Vermont (VT) 802
Virginia (VA)
 Richmond 804
 Lexington 703

Washington (WA)
 Seattle 206
 Eastern Washington 509
Washington DC (DC) 202
West Virginia (WV) 304
Wisconsin (WI) 414
Wyoming (WY) 307

Many government agencies, car rental firms, hotels and so on have **toll-free numbers**, which always have the prefix ☎1-800. From within the US, you can dial any number which starts with those digits free of charge. Phone numbers with the prefix ☎1-900 are pay-per-call lines, generally quite expensive and almost always involving either sports or phone sex.

The US has around 100 **area codes** – three-digit numbers which must precede the seven-figure number if you're calling from abroad or from a region with a different code. In this book, we've highlighted the local area codes at appropriate moments in the text, and they're also listed in the box on p.15. On any specific number we give, we've only included the area code if it's not clear from the text which one you should use, or if a given phone number lies outside the region currently being described.

International calls from the US can be dialled direct from private or public phones, though obviously you'll need to load the (public) phone with money first. If after a few attempts you haven't succeeded in getting through, you can get assistance from the **international operator** (☎1-800/874-4000), who may also interrupt every three minutes asking for more money, and again call you back for any money still owed immediately after you hang up. One alternative is to **reverse the charges** (US *call collect*) by dialling ☎1-800/445-5667, which will connect you free with a British operator. The **cheapest rates** for international calls to Europe are between 11pm and 7am on weekdays and all day on weekends, when a direct-dialled call costs roughly $1 a minute.

POST

Post offices are usually open Monday to Friday from 9am until 5pm, and Saturday from 9am to noon. They're the best places to buy **stamps** and send mail you want to arrive quickly. Stamps are also available from vending machines on the walls outside, and there are blue **mail boxes** on many street corners (in the US, one *mails* a letter, one doesn't *post* it). **Air mail** between the US and Europe generally takes about a week. Postcards are the cheapest things to send home (40¢); aerogrammes are slightly dearer (45¢); letters weighing up to half an ounce (a single thin sheet) will set you back 50¢, and the cost mounts steadily with every sheet you add.

Sending ordinary **mail within the US** is fairly slow but generally reliable, taking around a week to get across the country (or across town) and costing 29¢ for a letter weighing up to an ounce. The last line of the address is made up of an abbreviation denoting the state (California is "CA", Texas is "TX", for example, though you can spell it in full if you're unsure; see the list in the phone codes box) and a five-figure number – the **zip code** – denoting the local post office. Letters which don't carry the zip code are liable to get lost or at least delayed; if you don't know it, phone books carry a list for their service area, and post offices – even in Britain – have directories.

In the US, **poste restante** is called "**General Delivery**". Letters can be sent *c/o General Delivery* to any post office in the country but *must* include the zip code (we've given them for each major city). Such letters are held for thirty days before being returned to sender – so make sure there's a **return address** on the envelope. If you're receiving mail at someone else's address, it should include "c/o" and the regular occupants' name; otherwise it too is likely to be returned.

The rules on sending **parcels** from the US are very rigid. Packages must be in special containers bought from post offices, and sealed according to their instructions. Parcels are sent by land, which takes up to six weeks, unless air mail is specified. To send anything out of the country, you'll need to fill out a **green customs declaration label**, available from a post office.

To send a **telegram** (sometimes called a *wire*), don't go to a post office but to a *Western Union* office (listed in the Yellow Pages). Credit card holders can dictate messages over the phone. **International telegrams** are slightly cheaper than the cheapest international phone call: one sent in the morning from the US should arrive at a British address the following day. For domestic telegrams ask for a **mailgram**, which will be delivered to any address in the country the next morning. Public fax machines, in photocopying shops, both send and receive **faxes** very cheaply.

TIME ZONES

The continental USA is so big that it spreads over four different time zones, plus another one for Alaska and Hawaii; these are shown on the map at the start of this book. The **Eastern** zone, which covers the area inland to the Great Lakes and the Appalachian mountains, is five hours behind

Greenwich Mean Time; so 10am London time is 5am in New York City. The **Central** zone, starting at Chicago and spreading west to Texas and the Great Plains, is an hour behind the east; the **Mountain** zone covers the Rocky Mountains and the Southwest states and is two behind the East Coast, seven behind Britain; and the **Pacific** zone includes the three coastal states and Nevada and is three hours behind New York, eight behind London. **Alaska** is another two hours behind the **Pacific** zone, as is Hawaii. Daylight Savings Time corresponds pretty closely to UK dates.

INFORMATION AND MAPS

The most useful source of information on the United States is the wide range of free maps, leaflets and brochures produced by each of the various State Tourist Offices. The box on the next two pages contains a full list; if you write well in advance of your departure, and are as specific as possible about your interests, they should be able to tell you all you want to know. The United States Travel and Tourism Administration (USTTA) has offices in capital cities throughout the world, also listed below, which serve mainly as clearing houses; they can send you vast quantities of printed information, but tend not to be able to help very much with specific queries.

In the US, state-run **Welcome Centers** dispense all sorts of glossy but usually fairly practical information along the main highways, especially at state borders, and most large towns have a **visitor centre** (typically open Mon–Fri 9am–5pm, Sat 9am–1pm), with detailed information on their area. These often go under the name of "Convention and Visitors Bureau", abbreviated to CVB. In addition, there are **Chambers of Commerce** almost everywhere – designed to promote local business interests but also holding local maps and information. In most communities, a number of **free newspapers** are also available, which carry local news and entertainment listings.

MAPS

The **free maps** issued by each state are usually fine for general driving and route planning. To get hold of one, either write to the office directly or call at any visitor centre. The best of the commercially available maps are those published by *Rand McNally*, bound together in their *Rand McNally Road Atlas* (£9.95), which also covers Mexico and Canada, or printed separately for £1.99 per state. For something more detailed, say for **hiking** purposes, camping shops generally have a good selection, and park ranger stations in national parks, state parks and wilderness areas all sell good quality local hiking maps for $1 to $3.

Most good UK bookshops carry a fair selection of maps of the US, though rarely much on hiking. If you can't find what you want, try a specialist map stockist such as *Stanfords*, 12–14 Long Acre, London WC2 (☎071/836 1321), who also run a mail-order service. Bear in mind, too, that if you're an *AA* or *RAC* member, a reciprocal agreement entitles you to free maps (and help) from the *American Automobile Association* (*AAA*) (toll-free ☎1-800/336-4357), based at 1000 AAA Drive, Heathrow, Florida 32746, but with offices in every US city.

USTTA OFFICES ABROAD

Almost always, USTTA offices share the buildings of US embassies or consulates (see p.10).
BRITAIN 22 Sackville St, London W1X 2EA (Mon–Fri 10am–4pm; ☎071/439 7433).
NORTHERN IRELAND & EIRE US Consulate, Queen's House, 14 Queen St, Belfast BT1 6EQ (☎0232/228239).
AUSTRALIA 4 Cliff St, Milsons Point, NSW 2061 Sydney (☎612-957 3144).

STATE TOURIST OFFICES IN THE US

Alabama
Alabama Bureau of Tourism &
  Travel,
401 Adams Ave, PO Box 4309
Montgomery AL 36103
☎205/242-4169
☎1-800/ALABAMA

Alaska
Alaska Division of Tourism
PO Box E
Juneau AK 99811 0800
☎907/465-2015

Arizona
Arizona Office of Tourism
1100 W Washington St
Phoenix AZ 85007
☎602/542-TOUR

Arkansas
Arkansas Department of Parks &
  Tourism
One Capitol Mall
Little Rock AR 72201
☎501/682-7777
☎1-800/828-8974

California
California Office of Tourism
1121 L St, Suite 103
Sacramento CA 95814
☎916/322-1396

Colorado
Colorado Tourism Board
Box 38700, Department CVB
Denver CO 80238
☎303/ 592 5510
☎1-800/433-2656

Connecticut
Connecticut State Information
  Bureau
165 Capital Ave
Hartford CT 06106
☎203/842-2200

Delaware
Delaware State Tourism Office
99 Kings Hwy, Box 1401
Dover DE 19903
☎302/736-4271

Florida
Florida Division of Tourism
126 Van Buren St
Tallahassee FL 32301
☎904/487-1462

Georgia
Georgia Department of Industry,
  Trade & Tourism
285 Peachtree Center Ave NE
Suite 1000
Marquis Two Tower
Atlanta GA 30303-1232
☎404/651-9038

Hawaii
Hawaii Visitors Bureau
Waikiki Business Plaza
2270 Kalakaua Ave
Honolulu HI 96815
☎808/923-1811

Idaho
Idaho Travel Council
700 W State St
Rm 108, State Capitol Building
Boise ID 83720
☎208/334-2470
☎1-800/635-7820

Illinois
Illinois Office of Tourism
620 E Adams St
Springfield IL 62701
☎217/782-7500

Indiana
Indiana Division of Tourism
1 N Capitol Ave #700
Indianapolis IN 46204
☎317/232-8860

Iowa
Iowa Division of Tourism
200 E Grand Ave
Des Moines IA 50309
☎515/242-4705

Kansas
Kansas Department of Economic
  Development
Travel & Tourism Division
400 SW 8th St
Topeka KS 66603-3450
☎913/296-2009

Kentucky
Kentucky Department of Travel
  Development
2200 Capital Plaza Tower
500 Mero St
Frankfort KY 40601
☎502/564-4930
☎1-800/225-8747

Louisiana
Louisiana Office of Tourism
Box 94291
Baton Rouge LA 70804-9291
☎504/342-8100

Maine
Maine Publicity Bureau
97 Winthrop St
Hallowell ME 04347
☎207/289-2423

Maryland
Maryland Office of Tourism
  Development
217 E Redwood St
Baltimore MD 21202
☎301/333-6611

Massachusetts
Massachusetts Division of Tourism
100 Cambridge St
Boston MA 02202
☎617/727-3201
☎1-800/632-8038

Michigan
Michigan Travel Bureau
333 S Capitol Avenue
Lansing MI 48909
☎517/373-1220
☎1-800/543-2937

Minnesota
Minnesota Office of Tourism
250 Skyway Level, 375 Jackson St
St Paul MN 55101
☎1-800/657-3700

Mississippi
Mississippi Department of
  Economic Development –
  Tourism Division,
PO Box 22825
Jackson MS 39205
☎601/359-3297
☎1-800/647-2290

Missouri
Missouri Division of Tourism
PO Box 1055, Jefferson City
Missouri MO 65102
☎341/751-4133

Montana
Montana Department of Commerce
1424 Ninth Ave
Helena MT 59620-0401
☎406/444-2564

Remember that **toll-free** (☎1-800) numbers can only be used within the United States.

STATE TOURIST OFFICES IN THE US

Nebraska
Nebraska Division of Tourism & Travel
PO Box 94666
Lincoln NE 68509
☎402/471-3796
☎1-800/228-4307

Nevada
Nevada Commission on Tourism
5151 S Carson St
Carson City NV 89710
☎702/687-4322

New Hampshire
New Hampshire Office of Vacation Travel
105 Loudon Rd, PO Box 856
Concord NH 03301
☎603/271-2666

New Jersey
New Jersey Division of Travel & Tourism
20 West State St
Trenton NJ 08625-0826
☎609/292-2470

New Mexico
New Mexico State Tourism
1100 St Francis Drive
Santa Fe NM 87503
☎505/827-0318

New York City
New York City CVB
Two Columbus Circle
New York NY 10019
☎212/397-8222

New York State
New York Division of Tourism
1 Commerce Plaza
Albany NY 12445
☎518/474-4116
☎1-800/225-5697

North Carolina
North Carolina Travel & Tourism Division
430 N Salisbury St
Raleigh NC 27611
☎919/733-4171
☎1-800/VISIT-NC

North Dakota
North Dakota Tourism Division
Liberty Memorial Building
Bismarck ND 58505
☎1-800/437-2077
☎1-800/472-2100 in state

Ohio
Ohio Office of Travel & Tourism
Box 1001
Columbus OH 43216
☎614/466-8844

Oklahoma
Oklahoma Tourism & Recreation
500 Will Rogers Building
Oklahoma City OK 73105
☎405/521-3981

Oregon
Oregon Tourism Division
775 Summer Street NE
Salem OR 97310
☎503/378-3451

Pennsylvania
Pennsylvania Bureau of Travel Development
416 Forum Building
Harrisburg PA 17120
☎717/787-5453

Rhode Island
Rhode Island Department of Economic Development
7 Jackson Walkway
Providence RI 02903
☎401/277-2601

South Carolina
South Carolina Department of Parks, Recreation & Tourism
1205 Pendleton St #522
Columbia SC 29201
☎803/734-0129

South Dakota
South Dakota Department of Tourism
711 Wells Ave
Pierre SD 57501
☎605/773-3301
☎1-800/843-1930
☎1-800/952-2217 in state

Tennessee
Tennessee Department of Tourism Development
PO Box 23170
Nashville TN 37202
☎615/741-2158

Texas
Texas Department of Commerce, Tourism Division
Box 12008
Austin TX 78711
☎512/463-8585

Utah
Utah Travel Council
Council Hall
Capitol Hill
Salt Lake City UT 84114
☎801/538-1030

Vermont
Vermont Travel Division
134 State St
Montpelier VT 05602
☎802/828-3236

Virginia
Virginia Division of Tourism
1021 E Cary St, 14th Floor
Richmond VA 23219
☎804/786-4484

Washington
Washington State Tourism Development Division
Department of Trade & Economic Development
101 General Administration Building
Olympia WA 98504-0613
☎206/586-3024

Washington DC
Washington Convention & Visitors Association
1575 I St NW
Washington DC 20005
☎202/ 789-7000

West Virginia
Travel West Virginia
State Capitol Complex
2101 Washington St
E Charleston WV 25305
☎1-800/CALL-WVA

Wisconsin
Wisconsin Tourism Development
123 West Washington Ave
PO Box 7970
Madison WI 53707
☎608/266-7621
☎1-800/432-TRIP national
☎1-800/372-2737 in-state

Wyoming
Wyoming Division of Tourism
I-25 at College Drive
Cheyenne WY 82002
☎307/777-7777
☎1-800/225-5996

GETTING AROUND

Distances in the US are so great that it's essential to think carefully in advance about how you plan to get from place to place. How you choose to travel will have a crucial impact on your experience of the country.

Between the major cities there are usually good **bus** links – though ***Greyhound***, the mainstay of the US bus services, is in deep financial trouble and services are subject to sudden changes. ***Amtrak*** provides a skeletal but often scenic **rail** service across the US. Things only get difficult in the isolated rural areas, though even here, by adroit forward planning, you'll usually be able to reach the main points of interest without too much trouble by using local buses and charter services, as detailed in this book.

It has to be said, however, that things are always easier if you have a **car**. Many of the most worthwhile and memorable destinations in the United States are far removed from the cities. Even if a bus or train can take you to the general vicinity of one of the great National Parks, for example, it can be quite impossible to explore the area without your own vehicle. For that matter, the cities themselves can be so vast, and so heavily car-oriented, that the lack of a car can seriously impair your enjoyment.

BY BUS

If you're travelling on your own, **buses** are by far the cheapest way to get around. The main long-distance service is *Greyhound*, who link all major cities and many smaller towns. Out in the country, buses are fairly scarce, sometimes only appearing once or twice a week, and here you'll need to plot your route with care. But between the big cities, buses run around the clock to a fairly full timetable, stopping only for meal breaks (almost always fast-food dives) and driver change-overs. *Greyhound* buses are slightly less uncomfortable

than you might expect, too, and it's feasible to save on a night's accommodation by travelling overnight and sleeping on the bus – though you may not feel up to much the next day, and this is not recommended for lone female travellers. (If you want to avoid trouble, incidentally, it's not a good idea to sit at the back of a *Greyhound* bus.) Any sizeable community will have a *Greyhound* station; in smaller places the post office or petrol station doubles as the bus stop and ticket office. All seats are on a first-come, first-served basis; there are no reservations.

Fares – for example $49 from Los Angeles to San Francisco one-way – are expensive but not staggeringly so, and can be sometimes be reduced by travelling on weekdays (except Friday). Foreign travellers exploring the US by bus can save a packet by buying a *Greyhound* **Ameripass** before leaving home. In the UK, they're available from *London Student Travel*, 52 Grosvenor Gardens, London SW1W 0AG (☎071/730 3402); through any branch of *Thomas Cook;* or from *Greyhound*'s office at Sussex House, London Road, East Grinstead, West Sussex RH19 1LD (☎0342/317317). The passes give unlimited travel within a set time limit: four days (£49), seven days (£75), fifteen days (£120) or thirty days (£150). Extensions can be bought in the US for the dollar equivalent of £10 per day. The first time you use your pass, present it to the ticket clerk saying where you want to go. The pass will

---

THE TROUBLES OF *GREYHOUND*

A few years ago, *Greyhound* absorbed its major rival, *Trailways*, and incorporated all their routes into its own schedules. You may still, however, occasionally spot a *Trailways* depot that hasn't been closed down or a bus that hasn't been renamed. During 1990, many *Greyhound* drivers went on strike protesting against "unfair management practices", only to be sacked by the company, who then recruited new staff. There were fraught scenes as buses arrived at picketed *Greyhound* stations. Timetables were totally disrupted, and the dismissed drivers vowed to set up a rival bus company. *Greyhound* services are for the moment running fairly normally, though there's every indication that many of their routes may be sold off to local companies in the near future.

be dated (which becomes the commencement date of the ticket) and your destination is written on a page which the driver will tear out and keep as you board the bus. Repeat this procedure for every subsequent journey.

Greyhound does produce a condensed **timetable** of major country-wide routes, but for some reason they're now unwilling to distribute it to travellers. In any case, for most needs it isn't particularly useful; you'd do better to plan your route with the fuller regional timetables available free from *Greyhound* stations in the US. *Greyhound*'s only toll-free information service is in Spanish (☎1-800/531-5332). Double-check routes and times by phoning the local terminal (we've included *Greyhound* numbers for most towns; others will be in the phone book).

One West Coast **alternative**, in every sense, is *Green Tortoise*, whose buses, furnished with foam cushions, bunks, fridges and rock music, ply the major cities, running between Los Angeles, San Francisco and Seattle; they also run low-priced tours of the US, taking in the national parks (in 17 days for $399) or travelling to New Orleans for Mardi Gras. Reservations are recommended and can be made by calling their head office in San Francisco (☎415/821-0803 or toll-free on ☎1-800/227-4766).

BY TRAIN

Travelling by **rail** is not all that viable a way of getting about, though if you have the time it can be a pleasant and relaxing experience. As you will see from our map, the *Amtrak* system isn't at all comprehensive — some surprisingly large cities are bypassed, and certain states are missed out altogether. What's more, the cross-country routes tend to be served by one or at most two trains per day, so there are large areas of the nation where the only train of the day passes through at 3 or 4 in the morning. For any one specific journey, it's also much more expensive than taking a *Greyhound* or even a plane — New York to Los Angeles, for example, costs $300 one-way. That said, it certainly has its fans: all the major cities are connected and the carriages clean, comfortable and tidy, and rarely crowded.

Visitors from overseas can, however, cut **fares** greatly by buying a discount **rail pass**. Several are available, each giving pretty much unlimited travel for 45 days (children up to age 12 travel for half the adult rate, under-2s ride free).

For all information on ***Amtrak* fares and schedules** in the US, ring the toll-free number
☎1-800/USA-RAIL
Do not ring individual stations.

The best value of the lot, the **National Rail Pass** ($299), covers the entire US rail network. The **Eastern Region Rail Pass** ($179) reaches from New York to Chicago; the **Western Region Rail Pass** ($229) covers everywhere west of Chicago and New Orleans; and the **Far Western Rail Pass** ($179) is good for all the Pacific coastal routes and extends as far east as Salt Lake City and Flagstaff (for the Grand Canyon). The handy **Florida Region Rail Pass** costs just $59. All can be bought from *Amtrak* stations in the US on production of your passport, or from *Amtrak*'s UK agent: **Destination Marketing Limited**, 2 Cinnamon Row, Plantation Wharf, York Place, London SW11 3TW (☎071/978 5222).

Once you have a pass, you still have to make reservations for travel, as far in advance as possible, as some trains — especially those between major East Coast cities — are booked solid and all passengers must have a seat. There are also a number of supplements payable, for sleeping cars and the plush *Metroliner* carriages, for example.

HISTORIC RAILROADS

While *Amtrak* has a monopoly on long-distance rail travel, a number of **historic** or **scenic railways**, some of them steam-powered or running along narrow-gauge mining tracks, do much to bring back the glory days of train travel. Many are purely tourist attractions, doing a full circuit through beautiful countryside in two or three hours, though a couple — like the Mount Hood Railroad in Oregon, or the Durango–Silverton line in Colorado, can drop you off in otherwise hard-to-reach wilderness areas.

Popular lines include the **Cass Scenic Railroad** in West Virginia (☎304/456-4300); the **Cumbres and Toltec** line in Chama, New Mexico (☎505/756-2151); **Durango & Silverton Narrow Gauge Railroad** in southern Colorado (☎303/247-2733); the **Big Trees and Roaring Camp Railroad** in Santa Cruz (☎408/335-4484) and the **Fort Bragg–Willitts** line (☎707/964-6371), both in California; and the **Mount Hood Railroad** (☎503/386-3556) outside Portland, Oregon.

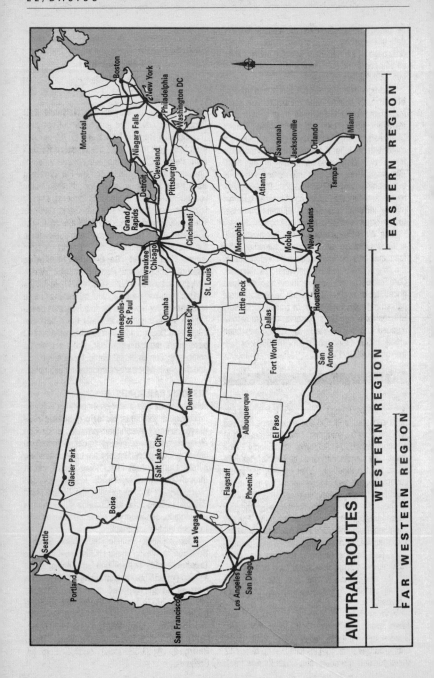

AMTRAK ROUTES

FAR WESTERN REGION

WESTERN REGION

WESTERN REGION

EASTERN REGION

BY PLANE

Don't be too misled by the scenes from Hollywood movies in which characters stroll into large airports and casually buy cross-country air tickets; that kind of plane travel is just as expensive in the US as it is anywhere else.

However, if you plan ahead, **air** travel can work out reasonably cheap, as well as obviously being the quickest way to get around. Indeed, it can cost less than the train – especially if you take into account how much you save not having to pay for food and drink while on the move – and only a little more than the bus.

If you buy your tickets outside the United States, a **VUSA** (Visiting US Airpass) ticket can provide for unlimited internal air travel at special rates. It's useful if you just want to make a couple of hops to cover long distances quickly, but can be extended to range as far afield as Alaska, Hawaii, Mexico, Canada and the Caribbean. The passes are available in the UK from most of the main American airlines (and by *British Airways* in conjunction with *US Air*), usually with the proviso that you cross the Atlantic with that carrier, and that you fly to that carrier's hub airport before making any journey. All the air-pass deals are broadly similar, involving the purchase of at least three **coupons** (for around £150; £45–55 for each additional coupon), each valid for a flight of any duration within the US. The best deal really depends on which airline has the strongest connections in the region you intend to visit: study the possibilities carefully before committing yourself. Both *Delta* and *Northwest* do thirty-day **standby passes**, covering over 200 cities, with no limit on mileage or

number of flights, for the sterling equivalent of $449 (or $749 for sixty days on *Delta*). Standby passes are obviously subject to the same restrictions as any standby tickets.

Flying can also make sense for relatively short local hops, turning a full day's cross-desert $25 bus journey in the Southwest, for example, into a quick and scenic $50 hour's flight. We've mentioned such options wherever appropriate.

In the US, the computerised **Fare Assurance Program** processes all the ticket options offered by participant travel agents and automatically searches for the cheapest fare, taking into account any special requirements of individual travellers. One agent using the service is *Travel Avenue* (☎1-800/333-3335).

BY CAR

For many people, the concept of cruising down an American highway, preferably in an open-top convertible with the radio blaring, is one of the major reasons to plan a visit to the US in the first place. The romantic images of countless road movies, from *Bonnie and Clyde* to *Thelma and Louise*, are not far from the truth, though you don't have to embark on a wild spree of drink, drugs, crime and murder to enjoy driving in America. Apart from anything else, a car makes it possible to choose your own itinerary, and to explore the wide-open landscapes that may well provide your most enduring memories of the continent.

Driving in the cities, on the other hand, is not exactly fun, but American metropolises tend be so large that a car can be by far the most conven- ient way of negotiating your way around cities have grown up and assumed th

TOLL-FREE AIRLINE NUMBERS IN THE

Aer Lingus ☎1-800/223-6537
Air France ☎1-800/237-2747
Alitalia ☎1-800/223-5730
American Airlines ☎1-800/433-7300
America West ☎1-800/247-5692
British Airways ☎1-800/247-9297
Continental Airlines ☎1-800/231-0856
Delta ☎1-800/221-1212
Iberia ☎1-800/772-4642
Icelandair ☎1-800/223-5500
KLM ☎1-800/777-5553

L'Express ☎1-800/3
Lufthansa ☎1-8 ☎1-800/225-2525
Midway 1-800/531-5601
Nort ☎1-800/221-7370
...ans World Airlines ☎1-800/892-4141
United Airlines ☎1-800/241-6522
US Air ☎1-800/622-1015
Virgin Atlantic Airways ☎1-800/862-8621

<table>
<tr><th colspan="3">MAJOR CAR RENTAL COMPANIES</th></tr>
</table>

IN THE UK

Alamo ☎0800/272200	**Budget** ☎0800/181181	**Hertz** ☎081/679 1799
Avis ☎081/848 8733	**Europcar** ☎081/950 5050	**Holiday Autos** ☎071/491 9000

IN THE US

Alamo ☎1-800/327-9633	**National** ☎1-800/227-7368
American International ☎1-800/527-0202	**Rent-a-Wreck** ☎1-800/535-1391
Avis ☎1-800/331-1212	**Snappy** ☎1-800/669-4800
Budget ☎1-800/527-0700	**Thrifty** ☎1-800/367-2277
Dollar ☎1-800/421-6868	**USA Rent-a-Car System** ☎1-800/872-2277
Hertz ☎1-800/654-3131	**Value** ☎1-800/327-2501

shape since cars were invented, sprawling for so many miles in all directions — Los Angeles and Houston are the classic examples — that your hotel may be fifteen or twenty miles from the sights you came to see. Not all cities even have a "centre" in the European sense, where the main attractions and facilities are concentrated within walking distance of each other. In smaller towns, the motels may be six miles or more out along the interstate, and the restaurants in a brand-new shopping mall on the far side of town — or perhaps simply on the other side of a freeway which there's literally no way of crossing on foot.

Any UK national over the age of 21 who holds a full UK driving licence is allowed to drive in the US — and to **rent a car** (Americans say *rent* where the English say *hire*; we've followed US usage throughout this book). Drivers wishing to rent cars are supposed to have held their licences for at least one year (though this is rarely checked); 25s may encounter problems, and will prob-also umbered with a higher than normal have one mium. Car rental companies will (at least $200) ave a credit card; if you don't

Often the cheap ou leave a hefty **deposit** to take a fly-drive det on it.

advance with a major agent a car is either *Budget, Hertz, Holiday Autos* or or book **in** which have offices in Britain. *Holiday Avis,* to be the cheapest by a whisker, charging of £70 a week for a four-door saloon, with sub compacts going for as low as £58 a week with **free unlimited mileage** — an important consideration if you're planning to cover long distances.

Alternatively, a number of local companies **in the US** (*Rent-a-Heap, Rent-a-Wreck, Dollar* and many others) rent out new — and not so new — vehicles. They are certainly cheaper than the big chains if you just want to spin around a city for a day, but free mileage is not included, so they work out far more costly for long-distance travel. Most firms have offices at airports, and addresses and phone numbers are comprehensively documented in the Yellow Pages. Leaving the car in a different city to the one in which you rented it will incur a **drop-off charge** that can be as much as a week's rental.

When you rent a car, read the small print carefully for details on **Collision Damage Waiver (CDW)**, a form of insurance which often isn't included in the initial rental charge but which you should think about taking out. This specifically covers the car you are driving yourself — you are in any case insured for damage to other vehicles. At $10 to $12 a day, it can add substantially to the total cost, but without it you're liable for every scratch to the car — even if it wasn't your fault. Some credit card companies (*AMEX* for example) offer automatic CDW coverage to anyone using their card; read the fine print beforehand in any case.

DRIVEAWAYS

One variation on renting is a **driveaway**, whereby you drive a car from one place to nother on behalf of the owner. The same rules any renting apply, but you should look the car cle's a bous taking it as you'll be lumbered with and a large fuel bill if the vehi-

Most driveaway companies

will want you to give a personal reference from someone either in the town you're leaving or in the car's eventual destination, and it makes obvious sense to get in touch in advance, to spare yourself waiting around for a week for a car to turn up. The most common routes are between the coasts, although there's a fair chance you'll find something that needs shifting more or less to where you want to go. You needn't drive flat out, although four hundred miles a day is expected. Look under "Automobile Driveaways" in the local Yellow Pages and phone around for the latest offers; or try one of the ninety branches of *Auto Driveaway*, whose national headquarters are at 310 SA Michigan Avenue in Chicago (☎312/341-1900).

RENTING AN RV

Besides cars, **campervans** (US *Recreational Vehicles* or *RVs*) can be rented for around £170 per week, although outlets are not as common as you might expect. – Americans tend to own RVs rather than rent them. Most travel agents who specialise in the US can arrange RV rental, and usually do it cheaper if you book a flight through them as well. You can rent a huge variety of RVs, from campervans to giant mobile homes – some with two bedrooms, showers and entire fully fitted kitchen. These are good for groups or families travelling together, but they can be quite unwieldy on the road. A price of around £400 for a five-berth van for two weeks is fairly typical, and on top of that you have to take into account mileage charges, the cost of petrol (some RVs do fifteen miles to the gallon or less) and any drop-off charges, in case you plan to do a one-way trip across the country. It is rarely legal simply to pull up and spend the night at the roadside in an RV;

you are expected to stay in designated parks, which cost up to $20 per night.

DRIVING

Once you have a vehicle, you'll find **petrol** (US *gasoline* or just *gas*) is relatively cheap at around $1.25 a gallon (that's a US gallon, roughly twenty percent smaller than the imperial gallon) for **unleaded** petrol, used by most cars. Most rental cars have **automatic transmission**, and power-assisted brakes and steering. If you're unfamiliar with these features, take a steady chug around the block to get used to them.

There are certain differences between driving in the US and elsewhere, not least the fact that some rules and regulations are specific to individual states, though the most basic ones are fairly uniform across the country. One rule which is national, of course, is **driving on the right**; this is surprisingly easy to forget.

ROADS

There are several **types of road**. The best for covering long distances quickly are the wide, straight and fast **Interstate Highways**, usually at least six-lane motorways and always prefixed by "I" (eg I-5 or I-80) – marked on maps by a red, white and blue shield bearing the number. Even-numbered Interstates usually run east–west and those with odd numbers north–south.

A grade down, and broadly similar to British dual carriageways and main roads, are the **US Highways** (eg US-395) and the **State Highways** (eg Hwy-1). Some major roads in cities are technically state highways but are better known by their local name: Hwy-2 in Los Angeles, for instance, is far more commonly called Santa Monica Boulevard. In rural areas, you'll also find much

AMERICAN DRIVING/CAR TERMS

Antennae	Aerial	Parking Brake	Hand brake
Denver Boot	Wheel clamp	Speed zone	Area where speed limit decreases
Divided Highway	Dual carriageway	Stickshift	Gear stick/manual transmission
Fender	Bumper/Car wing	Trailer	Caravan
Freeway	Limited access multi-lane motorway, often raised above street level	Trunk	Boot
		Turn-out	Lay-by
Gas(oline)	Petrol	RV	Recreational vehicle, often a massive mobile home with multiple bedrooms, kitchen and bathroom
Gridlock	Traffic jammed in every direction		
Hood	Bonnet	Windshield	Windscreen
No standing	No parking or stopping		

smaller **County Roads**; their number is some-times preceded by a letter denoting their county, but in this book we've used the "Hwy" convention for these as well as for state highways. Ranch Roads (RR) and Farm Roads (FR) may well be little more than dirt tracks.

The few **toll roads** in the US – the New Jersey Turnpike, for example – cost very little, at around $3 for a 200-mile journey. **Bridges** however can be quite expensive: the Golden Gate Bridge costs $3, and the Verrazano Narrows Bridge in New York around twice that.

RULES OF THE ROAD

In **urban areas** streets are arranged on a grid system and labelled at each junction, often with octagonal red "**Stop**" **signs** at all four corners: priority is given to the first car to arrive, and to the car on the right if two or more cars arrive at the same time. One rule that is very different from the UK is that, in most states, you can turn right on a red light if there is no traffic approach-ing from the left. **Traffic signals** are much the same as in the UK, with the exception that there is no amber between a red (stop) signal and a green (go) signal.

Driving on American **highways** is easier than it looks, but you need to adapt quickly to the national habit of **changing lanes**: US drivers do this frequently, and overtake on both sides. Big overhead signs warn you if the road is about to split towards two different destinations, or if an exit is coming up. Sometimes a lane *must* exit, and if you lose concentration you're liable to leave the Interstate accidentally – no great calamity as it's easy enough to get back on again. **Missing an exit** is more annoying; U-turns are strictly ille-gal, and you have to continue on to the next exit, which may be miles away.

Although the law says that drivers must keep up with the flow of traffic, which is often hurtling along at 70mph, the official **maximum speed limit** in the US is 55mph (65mph on most stretches of Interstate), with lower signposted limits – usually around 30 to 35mph – in built-up areas. There's also a legal **minimum speed** on Interstates of 45mph, though this will rarely be an issue. There are no **spot fines**; if you're given a ticket for **speeding**, your case will come to court and the size of the fine will be at the discretion of the judge; $75 is a rough minimum, and you may well be forced to return to the US to plead your case. If the police do **pull you over**, don't get out of the car and don't reach into the glove compart-ment – the cops may think you have a gun and will respond quite aggressively. Simply sit still with your hands on the wheel; when questioned, be polite and don't attempt to make jokes.

When driving, you must carry your licence with you at all times. The police will not take ignorance of this law as an excuse, and you might even find yourself detained in custody until they find the time to sort the matter out. As for other possible violations, US law requires that any **alcohol** be carried unopened in the boot of the car, and it can't be stressed enough that **driv-ing under the influence (DUI)** is a very serious offence. If a police officer smells alcohol on your breath, he/she is entitled to administer a breath, saliva or urine test. If you fail, they'll lock you up with other inebriates in the "drunk tank" of the nearest jail until you sober up – at least over-night, and sometimes for a minimum of 24 hours. Your case will later be heard by a judge, who can fine you $200 or, in extreme (or repeat) cases, imprison you for thirty days. Less serious offences include making a **U-turn** on an Interstate or anywhere where a pair of unbroken parallel lines (known as a "double yellow" line) runs along the centre of the road; **parking on a highway**; or allowing front-seat passengers to ride without fastened **seatbelts**.

Once at your destination, you'll find in cities at least that **parking meters** are commonplace, charging from 25¢ to $1 per hour. **Car parks** (US *parking lots*) charge up to $10 a day. If you park in the wrong place (such as within ten feet of a fire hydrant) your car is very likely to be towed away or **wheel-clamped**; a sticker on the windscreen will tell you where to pay the fine, which can range from $5 up to $35 or more.

If you **break down** in a rented car, there'll be an emergency number pinned to the dashboard. Otherwise you should sit tight and wait for the Highway Patrol or State Police, who cruise by regularly. Raising your car bonnet is recognised as a call for assistance, although women travel-ling alone should, obviously, be wary of doing this. Another tip, for women especially, is to rent a **mobile telephone** from the car rental agency – you often only have to pay a nominal amount until you actually use it, but having a phone can be reassuring at least, and a potential life-saver should something go terribly wrong. (See "Police and Trouble" below for more on the potential downsides of travelling in the US.)

HITCHHIKING

Where it's legal – and on any freeway or Interstate, it isn't – **hitchhiking** may be the cheapest way to get around but it is also unpredictable and potentially dangerous. Small country roads are your best bet: in rural areas it's quite common for the locals to get around by thumb, and it's an unbeatable way of getting to meet people. Big cities, and the routes in and out of them, are definite places *not* to hitch; if you do, you'll be lucky to live to regret it. Anywhere else, use your common sense: sit next to an unlocked door, keep your luggage within reach, refuse the ride if you feel unsure of the driver, and ask to be let out if you become in any way suspicious of his/her intentions.

Besides the standard method of standing by the road, or at freeway on-ramps, with your thumb out and maybe holding a sign with your destination written on it, another technique is to strike up a conversation with likely-looking drivers in roadside diners or gas stations. Safer still is to scrutinise the "**ride boards**" on university campuses, although this can entail a couple of days' wait, and drivers found this way will usually expect a contribution towards fuel costs.

In order to minimise hassle from police, always carry ID, and try to have at least $20 in your pockets – in quite a few places, being broke and homeless is grounds for being arrested as a vagrant, and you may be obliged to spend time in jail before being deposited at the county or state line.

CYCLING

In general, **cycling** is a cheap and healthy method of getting around all the big **cities**, some of which have cycle lanes and local buses equipped to carry bikes – strapped to the outside. *Greyhound* will take bikes for free (so long as they're in a box) but *Amtrak* charges $5 every time you board with one. In **country areas**, roads are usually well maintained and with wide shoulders. A number of companies organise multi-day cycle tours, either camping out or staying in country inns; we've mentioned local firms where appropriate. The biggest of the nationwide organisations is the non-profit *Bikecentennial* (PO Box 8308, Missoula MT 59807; ☎406/721-1776), founded in 1976, as part of the national bicentennial celebrations, to promote transcontinental cycle trips. It publishes maps ($6.95 each) of several 400-mile routes, detailing campgrounds, motels, restaurants, bike shops and sites of interest. *Backroads Bicycle Tours*, 1516 Fifth Street, Berkeley CA 94704 (☎510/527-1888), and the *AYH* hostelling group (see below) also arrange group tours. Many individual states issue their own cycling guides; contact the offices listed on p.18–19.

For more casual riding, bikes can be **rented** for $8 to $25 per day, or at discounted weekly rates, from outlets which are usually found close to beaches, university campuses, or simply in areas that are good for cycling, although rates in heavily touristed areas can be much higher. Local visitor centres should have details. For **long-distance cycling** you'll need a good quality, multi-speed bike, panniers, maps, padded shorts, a helmet (not a legal obligation but a very good idea), and a route avoiding Interstates (on which cycling is unpleasant and usually illegal). Of **problems** you'll encounter, the main one is traffic – mobile homes driven by buffoons who can't judge their width, and huge lorries which scream past and create intense back-draughts capable of pulling you out into the middle of the road.

ACCOMMODATION

Your major expense while travelling in the US is probably going to be accommodation; in part, at least, because Americans insist on, and get, an exceptionally high standard of comfort and service. To some extent it's possible to trim costs by sleeping in dormitory-style hostels, which can cost from nothing to around $10. However, such hostels are in short supply, and you're likely to have to make regular use of hotels and motels, costing anything upwards of $25. **Many hotels will set up a third single bed for around $10 on top of the regular price, reducing costs for three people sharing. On the other hand, the lone traveller will have a hard time of it: "singles" are usually double rooms at an only slightly reduced rate.**

Wherever you stay, you'll be expected to **pay in advance**, at least for the first night and perhaps for further nights too, particularly if it's high season and the hotel's expecting to be busy. Payment can be in cash or in dollar travellers' cheques, though it's more common to give your credit card number and sign for everything when you leave. **Reservations** are only held until 5pm or 6pm unless you've told the hotel you'll be arriving late. Most of the larger chains have an advance booking form in their brochures and will make reservations at another of their premises for you; alternately you can take advantage of the toll-free phone numbers of the national chain motels and hotels (listed opposite), which handle bookings for properties across the country.

Since cheap beds tend to be taken up quickly, always **book ahead** if possible in the cities. In major cities **campgrounds** tend to be on the outskirts if they exist at all, but there are excellent opportunities for camping in the many parks and natural areas all over the US – see the "Outdoors" section below for an overview.

Ys AND YOUTH HOSTELS

Aside from the odd private hostel in the larger cities, there are two kinds of cheap hostel-type accommodation in the US: YMCA/YWCA hostels (known as "*Y's*"), which offer mixed-sex or, in a few cases, women-only accommodation, and official *AYH* youth hostels.

Prices in the less plentiful **YMCAs** range from around $8 for a dormitory bed to $18–30 for a single or double room. Ys offering accommodation (and not all do, many being basically health clubs) are often in older buildings and in less than ideal neighbourhoods, but facilities can include a gymnasium and swimming pool, and sometimes a cheap cafeteria.

There are about sixty regular *AYH* **youth hostels** in the US, most in popular hiking areas, a few in the bigger cities and tourist centres. At $6–10 (a few dollars more for non-members) per night per person they are clearly the cheapest option under a roof. The *International Youth Hostel Handbook – Volume 2* (£5.99) has a full list, and is

available from the British *Youth Hostel Association* headquarters/shop, at 14 Southampton Street, London WC2 (☎071/836 8541), where you can also buy a year's *IYHF* **membership** for £8.30 (£4.40 if you're under 21). The informative *American Youth Hostel (AYH) Handbook* ($5) is only available from hostels in the US or direct from the *AYH* national office: PO Box 37613, Washington, DC 20013 (☎202/783-6161).

Particularly if you're travelling in high season, it's advisable to **book ahead** by writing to the relevant hostel and enclosing a deposit, or by sending an *IYHF Advance Booking Voucher*, which costs £4 – a sum then knocked off the bill at the hostel – available from any *IYHF* office or specialist travel agent (though first check that the hostel you're after accepts them – a few don't). Beds reserved in this way will be held until 9pm. Some hostels will allow you to use a **sleeping bag**, but officially they should (and many do) insist on a **sheet sleeping bag**. You can buy these for around £10 from any *YHA* shop in Britain, or they can be rented at the hostel. The maximum stay at each hostel is technically three days, though this is again a rule which is almost always ignored if there's space. Few hostels provide meals but most have **cooking** facilities, and there's usually a curfew some time between 10pm and midnight; alcohol, drugs and smoking are banned.

Certain larger cities also have hostels which are not affiliated to the *AYH*. Their independent status may be due to a failure to come up to the *AYH*'s (fairly undemanding) criteria, but often it's simply because the owners prefer not to be tied down by *AYH* regulations. Standards range from the abysmal and unsafe to very good; naturally, we've included the latter in this book.

HOTELS AND MOTELS

It is consistently easy to find a basic hotel room in the United States. Motorists approaching any significant town are confronted by endless lines of motels along the highway, with prominent neon signs flashing their rates. Along the major cross-country routes the choice is phenomenal; Tucumcari in New Mexico, for example, is not a place that anyone would set out to visit, but its location on I-40 means that it's not far off having the *200 Motels* Frank Zappa made a movie about. In every town mentioned in this book we have recommended particular establishments, but you can also assume that there are a whole lot more we haven't got the space to list. Only where

NATIONAL MOTEL AND HOTEL CHAINS

Rooms in the budget **chains** such as *Motel 6* cost around $25 to $35, while *Days Inn, Howard Johnson's, Travelodge*, and *Quality Inns* all provide reasonable accommodation for $40 to $60. All the chains listed below publish handy free directories (with maps and illustrations) of their properties.

Best Western, PO Box 10203, Phoenix AZ 85064. ☎1-800/528-1234.

Comfort Inns, 10750 Columbia Pike, Silver Spring MD 20901. ☎1-800/228-5150.

Days Inn, 2751 Buford Highway NE, Atlanta GA 30324. ☎1-800/325-2525.

Econolodge, 6135 Park Road, Suite 2000, Charlotte NC 28210. ☎1-800/446-6900.

Hilton Hotels, PO Box 5567, Beverly Hills CA 90209. ☎1-800/445-8667.

Holiday Inns, 1100 Ashwood Parkway, Atlanta GA 30338. ☎1-800/465-4329.

Howard Johnson, PO Box 29004, 3838 E Van Buren, Phoenix AZ 85038. ☎1-800/654-2000.

La Quinta Inns, PO Box 790064, San Antonio, TX 78279. ☎1-800/531-5900.

Motel 6, 51 Hitchcock Way, Santa Barbara CA 93105. ☎505/891-6161.

Red Roof Inns, 4355 Davidson Rd, Hilliard OH 43026. ☎1-800/848-7878.

Super 8 Motels, PO Box 4090, Aberdeen, SD 57402. ☎1-800/848-8888.

Susse Chalet, Chalet Drive, Wilton NH 03086. ☎1-800/628-7727.

Travelodge, 5700 Broadmoor, Mission KS 66202. ☎1-800/225-3050.

---

there is a genuine shortage of accommodation have we explicitly said so.

Hotels and **motels** are essentially the same thing, although motels tend to be located beside the main roads away from city centres – and thus are much more accessible to drivers. The cheaper ones are pretty basic affairs, but in general there's a uniform standard of comfort everywhere – double rooms with bathroom, TV and phone – and you won't get a much better deal by paying, say, $50 instead of $30. Over $50, the room and its fittings simply get bigger and more luxurious, and there'll probably be a swimming pool which guests can use for free. Paying over $100 brings you into the decadent realms of the en suite jacuzzi.

Very few hotels or motels bother to compete with the ubiquitous diners and offer **breakfast**, although there's a trend towards providing free self-service coffee and sticky buns.

Many of the higher-rung chains offer **pre-paid discount vouchers**, which in theory save you money if you're prepared to pay in advance – British travellers must purchase them in the UK. These usually cost between £30 and £60 per night for a minimum of two people sharing, and it's hard to think of a good reason to buy them. True, you may save a nominal amount on the fixed rates, but better-value accommodation is not exactly difficult to find in the US, and you may well regret the lack of flexibility such schemes will give your travels.

When it's worth blowing a whole lot of cash on somewhere really atmospheric we've said as much. The most upscale establishments have all manner of services which may appear to be free, but for which you will be expected to **tip** in a style commensurate with the hotel's status – ie *big*. If you don't want to pay to have your bags carried, then don't let anyone get hold of them.

BED AND BREAKFAST

Forget English seaside resorts and greasy bacon and eggs: **bed and breakfast** in the US is often luxurious. Typically, the bed and breakfast inns, as they're usually known, are restored buildings in the smaller cities and more rural areas – although these days you also find plenty in big cities. Sometimes a B&B may just be a couple of furnished rooms in someone's home, and even the larger establishments tend to have no more than ten rooms, without TV and phone but often with plentiful flowers, stuffed cushions and an almost over-contrived homely atmosphere. Extended conversations with the hosts and other guests are all but compulsory, and can be a great way of meeting people. Occasionally, though, a B&B will consist of an entire apartment where you won't even see your host.

For advice on **camping**, see the "Outdoors" section on p.36.

The price you pay for a B&B always includes a huge and wholesome breakfast (sometimes a buffet on a sideboard, but more often a full-blown cooked meal with unlimited fruit juice and coffee) and prices vary greatly: anything from $30 to $200 depending on location and season. Most fall between $45 and $75 per night for a double,

a little more for a whole apartment – and tend to be booked well in advance.

In many areas, individual bed and breakfast inns have grouped together to form central **booking agencies**, thereby making it much easier for the traveller to find a room at short notice; we've given addresses for these where appropriate.

EATING

The term "junk food" may be American in origin, but most visitors find the sheer variety – and, for the most part, quality – of the food available in the United States quite staggering. It's not too much of an exaggeration to say that you can eat whatever you want, whenever you want. Whether it's for basic sustenance or for a special social occasion, Americans love to dine out. On every main street, a mass of restaurants, fast-food places and coffeeshops try to outdo one another with their bargains and special offers.

BREAKFAST

The daily round of eating gets going pretty early. **Breakfast** is taken very seriously, and with prices averaging between $3 and $5 it can be the best value and most filling meal of the day. For a real American experience, go to a **diner**, which should serve breakfast until at least 11am. At earlier times, say between 6am and 8am, the price may be even cheaper. The breakfasts themselves are pretty much the same all over the

country. **Eggs** are the staple ingredient, in a variety of styles: "sunny side up" is fried on one side, leaving a runny yolk, "over" is slipped over in the pan to stiffen the yolk, and "over easy" is flipped for a few seconds to give a hint of solidity. **Scrambled** and **poached eggs** and **omelettes** are popular too. The usual **meat** is ham or bacon, streaky and fried to a crisp, or sausages, skinless and spicier than the British version. **Hash browns** and **home fries** are different forms of fried potatoes. Other breakfast options include white, dense and tangy **sourdough bread**, an **English muffin** (actually a crispy crumpet), or, in trendier places, a **bran muffin** – a fruitcake made with bran and sugar. There's no hesitation when it comes to mixing sweet and savoury on the same plate; if you wish, you can add **waffles** or **pancakes** to the combination, swamped in butter with lashings of maple syrup.

COPING AS A VEGETARIAN

For **vegetarians**, in the big cities of the United States, at least, eating shouldn't present too much of a problem. Cholesterol-fearing Americans are turning to healthfoods in a big way, and most towns of any size boast a wholefood or vegetarian cafe, while the ubiquitous Mexican restaurants tend to include at least one vegetarian item on their menus. However, don't be too surprised in rural areas if you find yourself restricted to a diet of eggs, cheese sandwiches (you might have to ask them to leave the ham out), salads and pizza. In the southeast, most soulfood cafes offer great-value vegetable plates (four different vegetables, including potatoes) for $2 to $4, but these are often cooked with pork fat. Similarly, baked beans, and the nutritious-sounding red beans and rice, usually contain bits of diced pork. None of the major fast-food chains includes a vegetarian burger on its menu, but the Mexicanesque *Taco Bell* sells meatless tostadas and burritos.

GLOSSARY OF AMERICAN FOOD TERMS

A la mode	With ice cream	Jello	Jelly
Au jus	Meat served with a gravy made from its own juices	Jelly	Jam
Biscuit	Scone	Kalua pork	Hawaiian pig, roasted whole in an underground oven – *imu* – at a traditional *luau* or feast
BLT	Bacon, lettuce and tomato toasted sandwich		
Broiled	Grilled	Muffuletta	Italian French-bread sandwich, served in Louisiana
Brownie	A fudgy, filling chocolate cake		
Burrito	Folded *tortilla* stuffed with refried beans or beef, and grated cheese	Muffin	Small cake made with bran and/ or fruit and other sweeteners
		Nachos	Tortilla chips with melted cheese
Caesars Salad	Cos lettuce in egg dressing with anchovy paste, olives and lemon served with garlic croutons and parmesan cheese	Pecan pie	Pastry shell filled with pecan nuts and syrupy goo
		Po'Boy	Southern equivalent of a sub sandwich, often filled with deep-fried seafood
Calf fries	Deep-fried calfs' testicles, served in Texas		
		Poi	Tasteless Hawaiian paste made from *taro* root
Check	Bill		
Chips	Potato crisps	Popsicle	Ice lolly
Chitterlings	Pigs' intestines	Pretzels	Savoury circles of glazed pastry
Cilantro	Coriander	Quahog	Large clam, served in New England
Clam chowder	A thick soup made with clams and other seafood.		
		Salsa	Chilis, tomato, onion and cilantro, served in varying degrees of spiciness
Club sandwich	Large, overstuffed sandwich		
Cookie	Biscuit		
Crawfish (also crayfish)	Crustacean, resembling a baby lobster	Sashimi	Thinly sliced raw fish eaten with soy sauce or *wasabi*
Eggplant	Aubergine	Seltzer	Fizzy/soda water
Enchiladas	Soft *tortillas* filled with meat and cheese or chili and baked	Sherbet	Sorbet
		Shrimp	Prawns
English muffin	Toasted bread roll, like a crumpet	Soda	Generic term for any soft drink
Fajitas	Soft *taco*-like flour *tortilla* stuffed with shrimp, chicken or beef	Squash	Marrow
		Steamers	Steamed clams, served with butter
Frank	Frankfurter (hot dog)		
(French) fries	Chips	Sub	French-bread sandwich
Frijoles	Refried beans, ie mashed fried beans.	Sushi	Japanese speciality; raw fish wrapped with rice in seaweed.
		Tab	Bill
Gravy	White lard-like sauce poured over biscuits for breakfast	Tacos	Folded, fried *tortillas*, stuffed with chicken, beef or (occasion-ally) cow's brains
Grits	Southern breakfast of ground white corn, served hot with butter		
		Tamales	Corn meal dough with meat and chili, wrapped in a corn husk and baked
Gumbo	Thick Cajun soup of seafood, chicken and vegetables, named for the Bantu word for okra		
		Tempura	Seafood and vegetables deep-fried in batter
Half-and-half	Half cream, half milk		
Hash browns	Fried chopped or grated potato	Teriyaki	Chicken or beef, marinated in soy sauce and grilled
Hero	French-bread sandwich		
Hoagie	Another French-bread sandwich	To go	Take away
Hot cakes	Pancakes	Tortillas	Maize dough pancakes used in most Mexican dishes
Home fries	Thick-cut fried potatoes		
Jambalaya	A sort of Cajun paella, containing seafood, chicken, sausage and vegetables	Waldorf salad	Celery, chopped apple and walnuts served on lettuce leaves with mayonnaise
		Zucchini	Courgettes

Wherever you eat, it'll be washed down by as much **coffee** as you can stomach, virtually always fresh and served as "regular"or "decaff". Refills are usually free; waiters and waitresses keep supplying mug-fulls until you ask them to stop. English-style **tea** is much less commonly drunk; you will normally be able to find it, but if you do, it's likely to be a poor-quality brew made with lukewarm water and stale tea bags. A cup of tea will cost 45¢ to $1, and be served straight, or with lemon; if you want milk, you'll have to ask for it. A wide range of **herbal teas** is also available. In many parts of the country, especially the southern states, **iced tea** is the most common refreshing day-time drink, served in tall glasses with lots of ice, a slice of lemon, and (usually) large quantities of sugar.

LUNCH, SNACKS AND FAST FOOD

During the standard lunch-break hours, between 11.30am and 2.30pm, most eating places offer special low-cost **set menus** – generally excellent value. In **Chinese** restaurants, for example, you'll normally find rice and noodles, or dim sum feasts, for $4 to $6, and many Japanese restaurants give you a chance to eat sushi much more cheaply ($7 to $10) than usual. **Mexican** restaurants tend to be well-priced at all times, and you can get a good-sized lunch in one for $4 to $5. **Pizza** is also widely available, from both familiar chains like *Pizza Hut* and *Domino's*, and unfamiliar ones like *Shakey's*, all dependable and with broadly the same range. Count on paying $5 to $8 for a basic two-person pizza. If it's a warm day and you can't face hot food, look for a deli with a **salad bar**, where you can help yourself for around $2. There's even healthy fast food: ice cream-like **frozen yoghurt** is sold in most places by the tub for $1.50, and sometimes blended with fresh fruit to make a "**smoothie**".

For **quick snacks**, many **delis** do ready-cooked meals for $2 to $3, as well as a range of **sandwiches** and filled **bagels**. **Street stands** sell hot dogs, burgers, tacos or slices of pizza for around $1, and most shopping malls have ethnic fast-food stalls, often pricier than their equivalent outside. Be a little wary of the grungier **Mexican fast-food** stands if you're buying meat, although they're generally filling and cheap. Franchises such as *El Pollo Loco* and *Taco Bell* sell swift tacos and burritos for around $3. And the inevitable **burger chains** are all over the US: *Wendy's*, *Burger King* and *McDonalds* are the familiar names; others have yet to cross the Atlantic, such as *Jack-in-the-Box* – a drive-through takeaway where you place your order by talking to a plastic clown (and with a recently updated menu including croissants and shrimp salads).

Some seafood restaurants sell **fish and chips**: the fish is usually breaded and then fried, and the chips are actually chipped potatoes rather than the American french-fry matchsticks you'll normally find; a plateful will be about $4. In New England, or in the Pacific Northwest, look out for **clam chowder**, a thick, creamy shellfish and potato soup served for $2 to $3 a bowl.

HAPPY HOURS AND BRUNCH

Some **bars** in the US are used as much by diners as drinkers, who turn up in droves to gorge themselves on the free **hors d'oeuvres** laid out by a lot of city bars between 5pm and 7pm Monday to Friday – an attempt to nab the commuting classes before they head off to the suburbs. For the price of a drink you can stuff yourself silly on chili, seafood or pasta, though bear in mind it will help to look like an office worker; look like a tramp and you won't get in.

Brunch is another deal worth looking out for: a cross between breakfast and lunch that's indulged in at weekends (especially on Sunday) between 11am and 2pm. For a set price ($8 and up) you get a light meal and a variety of complimentary cocktails or champagne. Perfect for serious day-time boozing.

RESTAURANTS

Even if it often seems swamped by the more fashionable regional and ethnic cuisines, traditional **American cooking** is found all over the country. Portions are big and you start with **salad**, eaten before the main course arrives. Of the usual salad dressings, **Italian** is like the oil-and-vinegar French dressing familiar in Europe, whereas what Americans call **French** is much creamier, with more lemon.

Main dishes are dominated by **meat** – enormous steaks, burgers, piles of ribs or half a chicken (roast turkey is only eaten hot on Thanksgiving Day, otherwise it's served cold in sandwiches). **Vegetables** include french fries or baked potatoes, the latter commonly topped with sour cream and chives. There's also a good choice of **fish and seafood**, especially in Florida, Louisiana, around the Chesapeake Bay, and in the

Pacific Northwest. **Shellfish**, such as the highly rated dungeness crab – smoother and creamier than the average crab – and the unique soft-shell crab, highly spiced and eaten whole, is popular too. Maine lobsters and *steamers* (clams) provide a reason to visit New England in themselves.

Cajun food, which originated in the bayous of Louisiana as a way of using up left-overs, is centred on red beans and rice, enlivened with unusual seafood like crawfish and catfish and always highly spiced. The often-misunderstood distinction between Cajun and **creole** cooking is explained in our "Louisiana" chapter, on p.479. It's rarely inexpensive, outside New Orleans and the Mississippi Delta; its current cachet has pushed prices up tremendously.

Traditional **southern American cooking** – also known as "soul food" – is not always easy to find away from the South, but is well worth seeking out for an authentic taste of America. You may not fancy the bland **grits** for breakfast (ground white corn served hot, mixed with butter) but full meals can be delicious, and incredibly filling. Vegetables such as **collard greens**, **black-eyed peas**, fried **eggplant** (aubergines) and **okra** (a staple ingredient of the Cajun gumbo) are added to staples such as fried chicken, roast beef, and **hogjaw** – meat from the mouth of a pig. **Chitterlings** (or chitlins) are a delicacy prepared from the entrails of a pig. Meat dishes are usually accompanied by **cornbread** to soak up the thick gravy poured over everything; with fried fish, you'll get **hush puppies** – fried corn balls with tiny bits of chopped onion.

By contrast, another American innovation, **California cuisine**, is geared towards health and aesthetics. Raved about by foodies, it's basically a development of French *nouvelle cuisine*, utilising the wide mix of fresh, locally available ingredients. The theory is to eat only what you need, and what your body can process. Vegetables are harvested before maturity and steamed to preserve both vitamins and flavour. Seafood comes from oyster farms and the catches of small-time fishermen, and what little meat there is tends to be from animals reared on organic farms. The result is small but beautifully presented portions, and high, high prices: not unusually $50 a head for a full dinner with wine; the minimum you'll need for a sample is $15, which will buy an entree.

A spin-off from California Cuisine is the so-called New New Mexican or **Santa Fe-style** food, again emphasising ultra-fresh and unusual ingredients, and spiced to reflect the Spanish and Mexican heritage of the Southwest desert region.

Although technically ethnic, **Mexican** food is so common it often seems like (and, historically, often is) an indigenous cuisine, especially in Southern California. In Texas, **Tex-Mex** food is a less spicy local version, responsible for developing *chili con carne*. Day or night, it's the cheapest type of food to eat: even a full dinner with a few drinks will rarely be over $10 anywhere except in the most upmarket establishment. Mexican food in the States is different from that found in Mexico, making more use of fresh vegetables and fruit, but the essentials are the same. Lots of rice and kidney beans, often served refried (ie boiled, mashed and fried), with variations on the **tortilla**, a thin maize dough pancake that can be wrapped around the food and eaten by hand (a **burrito**); folded, fried and filled (a **taco**); rolled, filled and baked (an **enchilada**); or fried flat and topped with a stack of food (a **tostada**). Meals are usually served with complimentary **nachos** (chips) and a hot **salsa** dip. The **chile relleno** is a good vegetarian option – a green pepper stuffed with cheese, dipped in egg batter and fried.

Other ethnic cuisines are plentiful too. **Chinese** food is everywhere, and can often be as cheap as Mexican; **Japanese** is more expensive and fashionable, especially on the coasts (sushi is worshipped by some Californians), but it does at least cost less than in Britain. **Italian** food is popular, but can be expensive once you leave the simple pastas and explore the exotic pizza toppings or the specialist Italian regional cooking that's fast catching on in the major cities; **French** food, too, is available, though always pricey, the cuisine of social climbers and power-lunchers and rarely found outside the larger cities. **Thai**, **Korean** and **Indonesian** food is similarly city-based, though usually cheaper; **Indian** restaurants, on the other hand, are thin on the ground just about everywhere except New York – although as Indian cuisine catches on the situation is gradually changing for the better, with a sprinkling of moderately priced Southern Indian food outlets. Local variations are endless. Many farming and ranching regions have a surprising number of **Basque** restaurants; the **Amish** communities of Pennsylvania have their own traditions; and **Portuguese** restaurants, dating originally from whaling days, abound in New England.

TIPPING

Whatever you eat and wherever you eat, **service** will always be enthusiastic – thanks in large part to the American institution of **tipping**. Waiting staff depend on tips for the bulk (and sometimes all) of their earnings. You should always top up the bill by fifteen to twenty percent; not to tip at all will result in short pay-packets for your servers, and consequently is severely frowned upon. Many (not all) restaurants accept **payment** in the form of credit/charge cards: if you use one, a space will be left to fill in the appropriate tip.

DRINKING

American bars and cocktail lounges are pretty true to their popular image: long dimly lit counters with a few punters perched on stools before a bartender-cum-guru, and tables and booths for those who don't want to join in the drunken bar-side debates. Of the main US centres, New York, Chicago, New Orleans and San Francisco are the consummate boozing towns, but almost anywhere, men, at any rate, shouldn't have to search very hard for a comfortable place to drink. Don't forget to leave a tip – a dollar or so – on the bar when you leave.

To **buy and consume alcohol** in the US, you need to be 21, and could well be asked for ID even if you look much older. Each state makes its own licensing laws – Mormon Utah has the most byzantine restrictions, while many others have prohibitions about selling alcohol on Sunday, during elections, or – in the case of various counties in the Midwest – at all, ever. In more liberal areas, alcohol can be bought and drunk any time between 6am and 2am, seven days a week (New Orleans is a law unto itself, with certain bars open 24 hours and a far from rigid policy on ID). You can get a drink almost anywhere; bars, nightclubs, cafes and restaurants are nearly always fully licensed. More cheaply, you can buy beer, wine or spirits easily in supermarkets, many delis, and, of course, liquor stores – no matter where you buy it, prices are certainly much lower than in the UK, even for UK products.

BEER

For the most part, American **beer** is as unremarkable as its European reputation suggests: freezing cold, fizzy and tasteless lager, designed to quench your thirst rather than to satisfy your palate. Major national brands such as *Budweiser*, *Miller* and *Coors* – all of them lager-style

concoctions – are found everywhere, as is *Michelob*, the only nationally sold variety likely to find many fans among British beer drinkers. Happily, there are alternatives: on the East Coast look out for Boston-based *Samuel Adams* or *New Amsterdam Bitter*, not to mention the budget beer turned UK style accessory *Rolling Rock*. Around the Great Lakes, traditional brewing capital of the US, some of the better brews include *Schlitz*, and the Texan brand *Lone Star* has its dedicated followers; out in California, the full-bodied, San Francisco-brewed *Anchor Steam* beer is available all over, while the rarer *Red Tail Ale* is among the finest brews in the country.

Microbreweries and **brewpubs** are springing up everywhere, in which you can drink excellent beers, brewed on the premises and often not available anywhere else. Otherwise, do what most locals do and stick to **imported** beers, such as the Mexican brands *Bohemia*, *Corona*, *Dos Equis*, *Superior* and *Tecate* (for the really unadventurous, British brands are easily found in the big cities). Expect to fork out $1.50 for a glass (just over half a British pint) of good draught beer, slightly more for a bottle or an imported beer. In all but the more pretentious bars, several people can save money by buying a "**pitcher**" of beer, getting about three pints for $5. If bar prices are a problem, you can stock up with **six-packs** from a supermarket ($2–4 for domestic, $4–7 for imported brews).

WINE

Most of the American **wine** exported to the rest of the world comes from California, although there are lesser-known vineyards in the Texan Panhandle, Ohio, and even Hawaii. If you're partial to the likes of *Gallo* and *Paul Masson*, you may be surprised to learn that they are held in low regard in America, and produced in plants resembling oil refineries. Most people prefer to drink the produce of California's innumerable smaller wineries – invariably good, with the best of the lot in the Napa and Sonoma Valleys, made from French-strain grapes and predominantly dry.

In the relevant areas, it's possible to take a **winery tour**, most of which include free tastings (although some charge $4–5 for a full glass or two). The best lesson of all, of course, is simply to buy the stuff. It's fairly inexpensive: a glass of the house wine in a bar or restaurant costs about $2, a bottle $5 to $8. Buying from a supermarket is cheaper still – just $3 to $6 a bottle.

SPIRITS

As for **spirits** ("hard liquor"), this is where the US really excels: the range, even in a run-of-the-mill bar is enough to put the best-stocked British pub to shame. Whatever you order you'll get it in a glass full of ice – "on the rocks". The American taste for putting copious amounts of ice in all drinks should not, incidentally, be seen as a device to charge you more and give you less; they genuinely don't seem to understand that you might prefer your drink "straight up".

You need to be careful when ordering whiskey. Unless you ask for Scotch or Irish you'll be served the heavier-tasting bourbon, the more common brands of which are *Jim Beam*, *Old Grandad* and *Wild Turkey*. Some of the most famous **distilleries** in Tennessee and Kentucky, including *Jack Daniels*, can be visited; though maddeningly, several are in "dry" counties so they don't offer samples. There are startling arrays of different gins and vodkas (*Stolychnaya* or "stoly" is the most popular), and always a good selection of rums from white to dark and every shade in between, including the explosive *Bacardi 151* – 75 percent pure alcohol. Remember that, in America, a Martini is a cocktail made with gin and a dash of white vermouth; if you want the British kind use the generic term, pronouced "vermooth". Spirits generally cost $1 "a shot" – a slightly larger measure than the UK "single".

Cocktails are extremely popular, especially during **happy hours** (usually any time between 5pm and 7pm) when drinks are half-price and there's often a buffet thrown in. Varieties are innumerable, sometimes specific to a single bar or cocktail lounge, though there are a few standards, any of which will cost $2 to $5.

FESTIVALS AND HOLIDAYS

Someone, somewhere is always celebrating something in the USA, although apart from national holidays, few festivities are shared throughout the country. Instead, there is a disparate multitude of local events: art and craft shows, county fairs, ethnic celebrations, music festivals, rodeos, sandcastle building competitions, and many others of every hue and shade.

Tourist offices for each state (see p.18–19) can provide full lists, or you can just phone the visitor centre in a particular region ahead of your arrival and ask what's coming up. Certain festivities, such as **Mardi Gras** in New Orleans (p.482), are well worth planning your holiday around; obviously other people will have the same idea, and visiting during these times requires an extra amount of advance effort.

The biggest and most all-American of the US **national festivals and holidays** is **Independence Day** (the "Fourth of July"), when the entire country grinds to a standstill as Americans get drunk, salute the flag and partake of firework displays, marches, beauty pageants and more, all in commemoration of the signing of the Declaration of Independence in 1776. **Halloween** (October 31) lacks any such patriotic overtones, and is not a public holiday despite being one of the most popular yearly flings. Traditionally, kids run around the streets banging on doors demanding "trick or treat", and being given pieces of candy. These days that sort of activity is mostly confined to rural areas, while in bigger cities Halloween has grown into a massive gay celebration: in West Hollywood in LA, in New York's Greenwich Village and San Francisco's Castro district, the night is marked by mass cross-dressing, huge block parties and general licentiousness. More sedate is **Thanksgiving Day** (last Thursday in November), the third big event of the year and essentially a domestic affair with relatives returning to the familial nest to stuff themselves with roast turkey, and (supposedly) fondly recall the first harvest of the Pilgrim Fathers in Massachusetts – though in fact Thanksgiving was already a national holiday before anyone thought to make that connection.

On the national **public holidays** listed below, shops, banks and offices are liable to be closed all day. Many states also have their own additional holidays, and in some places Good Friday is a half-day holiday. The traditional summer season for tourism runs from Memorial Day to Labor Day; some tourist attractions are only open during that period.

January 1 **New Year's Day**
January 15 **Martin Luther King's Birthday**
Third Monday in February **President's Day**
Easter Monday
Last Monday in May **Memorial Day**
July 4 **Independence Day**
First Monday in September **Labor Day**
Second Monday in October **Columbus Day**
November 11 **Veterans' Day**
Last Thursday in November **Thanksgiving Day**
December 25 **Christmas Day**

OUTDOORS

The US has some fabulous backcountry and wilderness areas, coated by dense forests, cut by deep canyons and capped by great mountains. Even the heavily populated East Coast has its share of open space, most notably along the Appalachian Trail, which starts on top of Mount Katahdin in Maine and winds south through the Green Mountains of Vermont, into Virginia, and on to the Blue Ridge Mountains of Tennessee –

some two thousand miles of surprisingly untramelled forest. In order to experience the full breathtaking sweep of America's wide-open stretches, however, head west to the Rockies, to the red-rock deserts of the Southwest, or across the continent to the amazing variety of wild spaces that fill the three West Coast states. The shoreline itself, however, particularly in the East but also in the West, is often disappointingly hard to access, with a high proportion firmly under private ownership.

The US's protected backcountry areas fall into a number of potentially confusing categories, especially so since the various federal, state and local jurisdictions do not necessarily reflect any real hierarchy of beauty. **National Parks** are federally controlled (and usually very popular and heavily if sensitively developed) areas of great natural beauty or historical significance: places like **Yellowstone**, with its teeming geysers and wildlife, **Yosemite**, with its towering granite walls, or the **Grand Canyon**. Don't blithely expect to tour such parks on foot; it can be done, of course, but they are huge places, and you can't just turn up and stroll around. (Yellowstone is, for example, bigger than the states of Delaware and

Rhode Island combined.) **National Monuments** tend to be outstanding geological features (such as Devil's Tower, Wyoming), covering smaller areas than national parks and not having quite the same facilities or broad tourist appeal; National Seashores, Lakeshores and so on are self-explanatory. Around national parks you'll find areas of **National Forest**: also federally-administered but with much less protection, often allowing some limited logging and other land-based industry – ski resorts more often than strip mines, fortunately. If you plan to visit more than a couple of such sites, all of which charge an admission fee per carload (between $3 and $10 per car), you'll save money buying a *Golden Eagle* pass, which gives unlimited access to any national park, monument or whatever, for $25 for a calendar year.

State Parks, operated by the individual states, tend to focus on sites of geological or historical importance. Various government departments administer a whole range of wildlife refuges, national scenic rivers, recreation areas and the like – such administration consisting basically of leaving the natural landscape alone. The **Bureau of Land Management (BLM)**, a sub-department of the US Government, has the largest holdings of all, most of it open rangeland, such as in Nevada and Utah, but also including some enticingly out-of-the-way reaches.

Any of the above areas will have at least basic facilities for **camping**, but, in general, the more well-known a place is, the more likely it will be to have some semblance of the comforts of home, with shops and petrol stations and lodges – all of which are handy, but tend to detract from the natural splendour. Whenever possible, set off on trails and camp out overnight.

CAMPING AND BACKPACKING

If your time and money are limited, but you really want to get a feel for America's vast wild spaces, one of the best options is to tour around by car, camping out at night and cooking your own meals (either on a camp stove or an open fire). If you don't fancy roughing it all the way, there is also a wide selection of public and commercially run **campgrounds** (in the US, camping is done at a camp*ground*; a camp*site* is the spot where one pitches one's tent – we've used the word in its American sense throughout this book) in or very near areas of great beauty. Every state produces comprehensive lists of the campgrounds in its state parks; there are so many that it would be impossible to list them in this book. The spectrum of campgrounds ranges from the primitive (a flat piece of ground that may or may not have a water tap) to some which are more like open-air hotels, with shops, restaurants and washing facilities. Naturally enough, prices vary accord to facilities, ranging from nothing at all for the most basic plots up to $15 a night for something comparatively luxurious. There are plenty of campgrounds but often plenty of people intending to use them: take special care over plotting your route if you're camping during public holidays or the high season, when many sites will be either full or very crowded. By contrast, some of the more basic campgrounds in isolated areas may well be completely empty whatever time of year you're there, and if there's any charge at all you'll need to pay by leaving the money in the bin provided.

Half of the land in the US is in the public domain, and, if you're backpacking, you can **camp** in the gaping **wilderness areas** and **deserts** pretty much anywhere you want. In certain areas, including the backcountry reaches of most national parks, you'll need to get a **Wilderness Permit** (either free or $1) from the nearest park rangers' office. Before you set off on anything more than a half-day hike, and anytime you're headed for anywhere at all isolated, be sure to inform the park ranger of your travel plans, and ask for weather conditions and general information about the hike you're undertaking. You should also take the proper precautions: carry sufficient food and drink to cover emergencies, as well as all the necessary equipment and maps.

When **camping rough**, check that fires are permitted before you start one; even if they are, try to use a campstove in preference to local materials – in some places firewood is scarce, although you may be allowed to use deadwood. In wilderness areas, try to camp on previously used sites. Where there are no toilets, **bury human waste** at least four inches into the ground and a hundred feet from the nearest water supply and campground. **Burn rubbish**, and what you can't burn, carry away. One very serious problem is *Giardia*, a water-borne bacteria causing an intestinal disease, of which the symptoms are chronic diarrhoea, abdominal cramps, fatigue and loss of weight. Treatment at that stage is essential; much better to avoid catching it in the first place. **Never drink** from rivers and streams, however clear and inviting they may look (you never know what unspeakable acts people – or animals – further upstream have performed in them); **water** that isn't from taps should be boiled for at least five minutes, or cleansed with an iodine-based purifier (such as *Potable Aqua*) or a *Giardia*-rated filter, available from any camping or sports shop, before you drink it.

Hiking at **lower elevations** should present few problems but a number of pesky blood-sucking insects are known to carry diseases and, in the case of the thick swarms of **mosquitos** you're likely to encounter near any body of water, can drive you crazy or at least ruin a trip; *DEET* and *Avon Skin-so-soft* handcream, are two fairly reliable repellents. **Ticks** – tiny beetles that plunge their heads into your skin and swell up – are another hazard. They sometimes leave their heads inside to cause blood clots or infections, so get advice from a park ranger if you've been bitten. Beware, too, of **Poison Oak**, a allergenic shrub that grows all over the western states, usually among oak trees, with leaves in groups of three with prominent veins and shiny surfaces. If you come into contact with this, wash your skin (with soap and cold water) and clothes as soon as possible – and don't scratch: the only way to ease the itching is to smother yourself in cala-mine lotion or to take regular dips in the sea. In serious cases, hospital emergency rooms can give antihistimine or adrenaline jabs.

MOUNTAIN HIKES

Hiking at **higher elevations**, as in the fourteen-thousand-foot peaks of the Rockies or California's Sierra Nevada, and certainly in Alaska, you need to take especial care: late snows are common, even into July, and in spring there's a real danger of avalanches, not to mention meltwaters making otherwise simple stream crossings hazardous. Altitude sickness, brought on by the depletion of oxygen in the atmosphere, can affect even the fittest of athletes. Take it easy for the first few days you go above seven thousand feet; drink lots of water, avoid alcohol, eat plenty of carbohy-drates, and protect yourself from the increased power of the sun.

DESERT HIKES

If you plan to hike in the **desert**, the crucial thing is to *think*. Tell somebody where you are going, and write down all the pertinent information, including your expected time of return. Carry an extra two days' food and water and never go anywhere without a map. Try and cover most of your ground early morning: the midday heat is too debilitating, and you shouldn't even think about it when the mercury goes over 90°F (temperatures in California's Death Valley, for example, can reach 136°F). If you get lost, find some shade and wait. So long as you've registered, the rangers will eventually come and fetch you.

Not only are you doing battle with incredible heat, but at high elevations at night you should be prepared for below-freezing temperatures too. At any time of year, you'll stay cooler during the day if you wear full-length sleeves and trousers: shorts and a vest will expose you to far too much sun – something you won't be aware of until it's too late. A wide-brimmed hat and a pair of good sunglasses will spare you the blinding headaches that can result from the desert light. You may also have to contend with **flash floods**, which can appear from nowhere: an innocent-looking dark cloud can turn a dry wash into a raging river. Never camp in a dry wash and don't attempt to cross flooded areas until the water has receded.

You can never drink enough **liquid** in the desert: the body loses up to a gallon every day and even when you're not thirsty you should keep drinking. Before setting off on any expedition, whether on foot or in a car, *two* gallons of water per person should be prepared. Waiting for thirst, dizziness, nausea or other signs of dehydration before doing anything can be dangerous. If you notice any of these symptoms, or feel weak and have stopped sweating, it's time to get to the doctor. Watch your alcohol intake, too: if you must booze during the day, compensate heavily with pints of water between each drink.

Driving in the desert, you should always take along an emergency pack with flares, a first aid and snakebite kit, matches and a compass. A shovel, tyre pump and extra petrol are always a good idea. If the car's engine overheats, don't turn it off; instead, turn the front end towards the wind and pour some water on the front of the radiator, turn the air-conditioning off and heating up full blast to cool the engine quickly. In an emergency, never panic and leave the car: you'll be harder to find wandering around alone.

ADVENTURE TRAVEL

The opportunities for active travelling in the US are all but endless, from whitewater rafting down the Colorado River, to mountain biking in the volcanic Cascades, canoeing down the headwaters of the Mississippi River, horse riding in the Big Bend on the Rio Grande in Texas, and Big Wall rock-climbing on the sheer granite monoliths of Yosemite Valley. While an exhaustive listing of the possibilities could fill another volume of this book, certain places have an especially high concentration of adventure opportunities, such as Moab, Utah; Hood River or Bend, Oregon; or Bishop, California. Throughout this book, we've recommended guides and outfitters.

WILDLIFE

It's crucial in the backcountry to watch out for bears, deer, moose, mountain lions and rattlesnakes, and the effect your presence can have on their environment.

Other than in a national park, you're highly unlikely to encounter a **bear**. Even there, it's rare to stumble across one in the wilderness. If you do, don't try to run, just back away slowly. As friendly as they appear, they are *wild* animals.

Most fundamentally, they will be after your food, which should be stored in airtight containers when camping. Ideally, you should hang both food and garbage from a high branch (too weak to support the weight of a bear) some distance from your camp. Never attempt to feed bears (frequently they'll beg, but once fed will become aggressive in their demands for more), and never get between a mother and her young. Young animals are cute, irate mothers are not.

Particularly in the deserts, there's a danger of being bitten or stung by various **poisonous creatures**. You'll soon know if this happens. Current medical thinking rejects the concept of cutting yourself open and attempting to suck out venom; whether snake, scorpion or spider is responsible, you should apply a cold compress to the wound, constrict the area with a tourniquet to prevent the spread of venom, drink lots of water and bring your temperature down by resting in a shady area. Stay as calm as possible and seek medical help **immediately**.

ENTERTAINMENT AND MEDIA

Even if you've never been to the United States before, to travel through the country is to find yourself in a landscape that is already intensely familiar, where the place names come from classic rock 'n' roll songs and the wide-open spaces seem straight out of Hollywood westerns. Exploring the reality behind the glamorous media images of America – and experiencing at first hand the mighty entertainment industry responsible for all your preconceived ideas of the country – are two of the greatest pleasures of coming here.

Whether you want to follow in the footsteps of Bob Dylan in north-country Minnesota or Robert Johnson in Mississippi, see Woody Allen's Manhattan or JR's Dallas, there's nowhere like the USA for living out musical and movie fantasies. Mickey Mouse and Dolly Parton have their own theme parks, the buffalo still roam the Great Plains, Route 66 still winds from Chicago to LA, and Elvis still lives in Graceland.

MUSIC

Music fans make pilgrimages from all over the world to the cities that spawned jazz, blues, country, soul and rap. No country devotee could fail to enjoy the rhinestone glitter, halls of fame, honky-tonks and stars' homes of **Nashville**. **Memphis**, the home of Sun, Stax and the Reverend Al Green, and **Chicago** are the prime destinations for live blues. The party town of **New Orleans**, with its legendary Bourbon Street, boasts an unrivalled jazz and R&B scene, while hard-core rock fans head for **Los Angeles**, where heavy metal is starting to supplant Hollywood, **Boston**, or Prince's **Minneapolis**. Not everywhere lives up to the myth, however; Motown fans may well, for example, be disappointed by Detroit.

The musical excitement is by no means confined to the big cities. Travel through rural Appalachia and you'll soon find ensembles of hillbilly **fiddlers**; the otherwise sleepy bayous of southern Louisiana are enlivened by the footstomping **Cajun** and **zydeco** sounds; and the little jook-joints of Mississippi Delta hamlets enrapture **blues** purists. The influence of **country** music extends well beyond Tennessee; the south, particularly Texas, is awash with unpretentious honky-tonk bars and the cowboy bars of southern Wyoming play nothing but good old C&W. Towns as far flung as **Bakersfield**, California, with its gutsy honky-tonk style, and tiny but more mainstream **Branson**, Missouri, boasts almost as many live country venues as Nashville.

Today's rock and soul superstars may play virtually all their gigs in huge 30,000-seater stadia, but there are innumerable smaller venues where you can see the latest up-and-coming groups. College towns in particular play a major role in introducing new artists to wider audiences, and you shouldn't pass through **Ann Arbor**, Michigan, **Austin**, Texas (also the home of progressive country music) or Athens, Georgia (where REM and the B-52's come from) without checking on what's going on.

The **clubs** of Chicago, Detroit, Miami and New York have given innovative dance sounds like house, techno and rap their first exposure over the last decade. In cities like these, the scene changes and evolves non-stop; the hipness quotient of a club or style of music can change at the drop of a hat, and although we've tried to list the best in this book there's no substitute for checking things out for yourself.

Getting to see **classical music** concerts is easier than in Britain. Even towns of 200,000 or so manage to support an orchestra of reasonable standard and tickets are not too prohibitive. Some of the nation's top orchestras are to be found in Chicago, Los Angeles, Philadelphia and Boston.

CINEMA AND THEATRE

If you want to be ahead of the crowds back home then take in a film or two while in the States; **movies** are generally on show three to six months before they arrive elsewhere. Most cities have good cinemas downtown, though in smaller places you often have to make your way out to the multiscreen venues in the malls on the edge of town. Sadly, you don't come across many drive-ins these days.

Theatre is very hit and miss in the big cities. The international reputation of New York's Broadway theatres is generally well-deserved but it costs a small fortune to get a seat even for most of the "Off-Broadway" productions. The larger college towns tend to feature well-funded performances of Shakespeare and the usual canon, while throughout the country – in Minneapolis, for example – local companies provide their own stimulating alternatives.

Every major town and city has at least one **comedy club**. Standards vary enormously; you may come across sexist xenophobes pandering to the basest of prejudices, in other places the material is fresh, incisive and above all funny. We've listed the best venues, though as ever you should consult the local entertainment weeklies.

NEWSPAPERS

Due mainly to its vast size, the US had no national **newspaper** (aside from the staid financial *Wall Street Journal* and the tacky sex-and-scandal weekly, the *National Enquirer*) until the arrival of the colour *USA Today* a few years back. Most Americans still prefer their newspapers grainy, inky and local. Every large town has at least one morning and/or evening paper, generally excellent at covering its own area but relying on agencies for foreign – and even national – reports.

One good thing most US newspapers share is their low cost – normally 25¢ to 40¢, with the enormous Sunday editions selling for $1 to $1.25. You buy newspapers from vending machines on street corners; newsagents are very rare.

Every community of any size has at least a few **free newspapers**, found in street distribution bins or in shops and cafes. These can be handy sources for bar, restaurant and nightlife information, and we've mentioned the most useful titles in the relevant cities.

TELEVISION

For travellers operating on a low budget, watching cable **television** in an anonymous motel room may well be the predominant form of entertainment.

American TV can be quite insanely addictive; it certainly comes in quantity, and the quality of the best of it can keep you watching indefinitely. With perhaps thirty-odd channels to choose from, there's always something to grab your attention. The schedules are packed with sycophantic chat-shows, outrageous quizzes and banal sit-coms, persistently interrupted by commercials. As for **news** coverage, local reports are comprehensive: a couple of hours each night, usually from 5pm until 6pm and 10pm until 11pm. The hour of national and international news which normally follows tends to be much less thorough, and world events which don't directly affect the US barely get a look-in.

The major networks (*ABC*, *CBS* and *NBC*), which have affiliated local stations in each area, have long dominated US broadcasting, although Rupert Murdoch's *Fox* network has recently made a big impact (largely through shows like *The Simpsons* and *America's Most Wanted*). Every major city also has a number of independent stations.

You won't find adverts – or any sort of news – on the non-profit **PBS** channels. Programmes are paid for by viewer subscriptions, individuals or special interest groups – a policy which gives rise to anything from entire evenings of British comedy to hours of high-class costume drama. Similarly with the public access channels, which give airtime to anyone – New Age astrologists, right-wing fanatics – organised enough to put a half-hour programme together.

Cable TV is widely found in motels and hotels, although sometimes you have to pay a couple of dollars to watch it. Most cable stations are no better than their network rivals, though some of the more specialised channels are consistently interesting. The *ARTS* channel broadcasts enjoyable, if po-faced, arts features, imported TV plays and the like. *CNN* (*Cable Network News*), already well known in Europe, offers round-the-clock news; *HBO* (*Home Box Office*) shows recent big-bucks movies, *AMC* (*American Movie Company*) old black-and-white films, and *ESPN* exclusively covers sport. Finally, there's *MTV* (Music Television), which, with the exception of its slots on rap, heavy metal and the like, is wearingly mainstream.

Other cable channels – each major city has at least a dozen – are even more narrowcast. You'll frequently find Japanese soaps and earnest half-hour interviews with people claiming to have come back from the dead. Soccer fans should scan the Spanish-language channels, which often show matches from Europe and South America.

There's an increasing trend toward major sporting occasions being transmitted on a pay-per-view basis. To watch events like world heavyweight boxing bouts you may have to pay as much as $40, either to your motel or to a bar that's putting on a live screening.

RADIO

Radio stations are even more abundant than TV channels, and the majority, again, stick to a bland commercial format. Except for news and chat, stations on the **AM** band are best avoided in favour of **FM**, in particular the nationally funded public and college stations, found between 88 and 92 FM. These provide diverse and listenable programming, be it bizarre underground rock or obscure theatre, and they're also good sources for local nightlife news.

Though the large cities boast good specialist **music** stations, for most of the time you'll probably have to resort to skipping up and down the frequencies, between re-run Eagles tracks, country and western tunes, fire-and-brimstone Bible thumpers and crazed phone-ins. Driving through rural areas can be frustrating; for hundreds of miles you might only be able to receive one or two (very dull) stations. It's not usual for car rental firms to equip their vehicles with cassette players.

WORLD SERVICE

You can keep in touch with British and world events by listening to the World Service of the BBC, broadcast to the US for eight hours daily. Programmes are on the short wave band but frequencies and timings vary. For the latest details write for the free *Programme Guide* from BBC External Services Publicity, Bush House, PO Box 76, Strand, London WC2. Many public FM radio stations in the US rebroadcast World Service news programmes as part of the daily schedules.

SPORT

Americans are sports-mad, and athletic activity and competition have a high profile. All the big cities have at least one team in each of the major professional sports – baseball, football and basketball – sometimes as well as supporting sides in the more unusual spectator sports of indoor soccer, volleyball, ice hockey, wrestling, even roller derby. Chicago, home of Michael "Air" Jordan and the basketball world-champion *Bulls*, as well as the baseball *Cubs* and *White Sox*, and football *Bears*, is probably the best US city for sports-watching; New York, Boston, LA and San Francisco are also good.

Just as exciting as the professional games, and usually much less expensive, are the **inter-collegiate sports**. College and university teams compete against one another with an enthusiasm fuelled by passionate local rivalries, and the fans are as vociferous as any European soccer crowd.

Throughout this book, we've detailed the major stadia, as well as sporting outlets and facilities which can be enjoyed by the humble travelling amateur.

BASEBALL

Baseball, much like cricket in its relaxed, summertime pace and (to the uninitiated) byzantine rules, is often called "America's pastime". Games are played all over the US just about every day during the summer, from April to September, with the league championships and the (somewhat misnamed) **World Series**, the final seven-game playoff, extending the season into October.

Watching a game, even if you don't understand what's going on, can be at the least a pleasant day out, drinking beer and eating hot dogs in the sun: tickets are cheap and the crowds usually friendly and sociable. Two of the teams most worth catching – if only for the experience of spending some time at their evocatively antique grounds – are the Boston *Red Sox*, based at Fenway Park, and the Chicago *Cubs*, who play at ivy-clad Wrigley Field.

There are also numerous **minor league** clubs, known as **farm teams** because they supply the top clubs with talent, in small towns across the fifty states

THE RULES OF BASEBALL

The setup for baseball looks like the English game of rounders, with four **bases** set at the corners of a 90-foot-square **diamond**. The base at the bottom corner is called **home plate**, and serves much the same purpose as do the stumps in cricket. Play begins when the **pitcher**, standing on a low **pitcher's mound** in the middle of the diamond, throws a ball at upwards of a hundred miles an hour, making it curve and bend as it travels towards the **catcher**, who crouches behind home plate; seven other defensive players take up **positions**, one at each base and the others spread out around the field of play.

A **batter** from the opposing team stands beside home plate and tries to hit the ball. If the batter swings and misses, or if the pitched ball crosses the plate above the batter's knees and below his chest, it counts as a **strike**; if he doesn't swing and the ball passes outside of this **strike zone**, it counts as a **ball**. If the batter gets **three strikes** against him he is **out**; **four balls** and he gets a free **walk**, and takes his place as a **runner** on first base.

If he succeeds in hitting the pitched ball into **fair territory**, the wedge between the first and third bases, the batter runs towards first base; if the opposing players catch the ball before it hits the ground, the batter is **out**. Otherwise they field the ball and attempt to relay it to first base before the batter gets there; if they do he is **out**, if they don't the batter is **safe** – and stays there, being moved along by subsequent batters until he makes a complete circuit of the bases and scores a **run**. The most exciting moment in baseball is the **home run**, when a batter hits the ball over the outfield fences, a boundary 400 feet away from home plate; he and any runners on base when he hits the ball each score a run. If there are runners on all three bases it's called a **grand slam**, and earns four runs.

The nine players per side bat in rotation; each side gets **three outs** per **inning**, and there are **nine innings** per **game**. Games normally last two to three hours, and are never tied; if the scores are level after nine innings, extra innings are played until one side pulls ahead and wins.

THE RULES OF AMERICAN FOOTBALL

The **rules of American football** are fairly simple: the **field** is 100 yards long by 40 yards wide, plus two **endzones** at each end; there are two teams of eleven men. The game begins with a **kickoff**, after which the team in possession of the ball tries to move downfield to score a **touchdown**, while the opposing team tries to stop them. The attacking team has four chances to move the ball forward 10 yards and gain a **first down**; otherwise they forfeit possession to the opposition. After the kickoff the **quarterback**, the leader of the attack, either passes the ball to a **running back**, or throws the ball through the air downfield to a **receiver**. Play ends when the man with the ball is tackled to the ground, or if the pass attempt falls incomplete.

A **touchdown**, worth six points, is made when a player crosses into the defending team's endzone carrying the ball; a **field goal**, worth three points, is scored when the **placekicker** – always the smallest man on the team and usually the lone foreigner – kicks the ball, as in rugby, through the **goalposts** that stand in the endzone. If the attacking team has failed to move the ball within scoring range, and seems unlikely to gain the required ten yards for another first down, they can elect to **punt** the ball, kicking it to the other team.

A change of possession can also occur if the opposition players manage to **intercept** an attempted pass.

AMERICAN FOOTBALL

Football in America attracts the most obsessive and devoted fans of any sport, perhaps because fewer games are played – only sixteen in the season, which lasts throughout the autumn. With its many quick skirmishes, and the quasi-military movement up and down the field, it makes an ideal sport for television.

The game lasts for four fifteen-minute quarters, with a fifteen-minute break at half-time. However, time is only counted when a play is in progress, and so a match can take up to three hours to complete, mainly due to interruptions for TV advertising. Whether or not you flounder in the accompanying deluge of statistics, American football is an enjoyable spectacle. The players tend to be huge, averaging about six feet five inches and weighing upwards of seventeen stone; they look even bigger when they're suited up for battle in shoulder pads and helmets. The best of them rake in millions of dollars for product endorsements on top of astronomical salaries.

Watching football isn't anything like the aesthetic experience of a baseball game, however. For a start, the weather is different: football games go on in rain, sleet, heat and snow, from the frigid cold of Chicago's Soldier Field to the sweltering heat of Miami. With tickets expensive ($25–60) and hard to come by, in many ways it's best to watch the games in a bar on TV.

The football weekend gets rolling on Friday night, when **High School** games can attract 20,000-strong crowds. Saturday is the preserve of **college** football. Tickets for popular teams usually sell out well in advance; the Michigan Wolverines regularly fill their 102,000-seater stadium in Ann Arbor, while grudge matches such as Tennessee versus Alabama draw 98,000 to Knoxville. The 24 professional teams of the **National Football League** (NFL) play their matches on Sunday, with the exception of one televised encounter each Monday.

BASKETBALL

Basketball is, with baseball, one of the few sports that ordinary Americans actually play; all you need is a ball and a hoop. It's particularly popular in inner-city areas, where school playgrounds are packed with young hopefuls.

The professional game is played by athletes of phenomenal agility, seven-foot giants who float through the air over a wall of equally tall defenders, seeming to change direction in mid-flight before slam-dunking the ball (smashing it through the hoop with such force that the backboard sometimes shatters) to score two points. Games last for an exhausting 48 minutes of playing time, around two hours total. The most exciting clubs are the **Chicago Bulls**, led by megastar Michael Jordan, the **Los Angeles Lakers**, who play their games in front of a crowd of celebrities (actor Jack Nicholson, for example, has a season-long front court seat), the **Detroit Pistons** and the "Rip City" **Portland Trailblazers**. The **Boston Celtics** are the grand old men of basketball, and play their games in the venerable Boston Garden; most other venues are modern municipal stadia, and not especially atmospheric.

SURFING

Surfing is probably the best-known American pastime, invented in ancient **Hawaii** (where rock-carvings show primeval surfers) long before the white men arrived. The north-coast beaches of the various Hawaiian islands – particularly the Banzai Pipeline on Oahu – remain the finest places to catch a wave. Since the Sixties, however, surfing has become inextricably identified with **California** by the songs of the Beach Boys and Frankie Avalon; southern California is dotted with excellent surfing beaches, such as Tourmaline Beach near San Diego, and Huntington Beach and Malibu in Los Angeles. **Windsurfing**, too, is extremely popular.

CYCLING

The sport of **cycling** has been given a boost by the phenomenal success of triple Tour de France winner Greg Lemond. The Rockies, and Colorado in particular, play host to highly competitive, world-class road races; many of the country's top professionals live and train in Boulder Colorado. An innovation developed in the US in the late Seventies, and since adopted around the globe, is the heavy-duty, all-terrain **mountain bike**, originally designed to tackle the slopes of Mount Tamalpais near San Francisco. Bikes are available for rent in most towns and cities. See "Getting Around", p.20, for more on general cycling.

SKIING

Skiing is the biggest mass-market participant sport, and downhill resorts can be found all over the US. The eastern resorts of Vermont and New York State, however, pale by comparison with those of the Rockies, such as Vail and Aspen in Colorado, and the Californian Sierra Nevada. You can usually rent equipment for about $30 per weekend, and expect to pay another $20 to $40 a day for lift tickets.

A cheaper option is **cross-country skiing**, or ski-touring. Backcountry ski lodges dot mountainous areas along both coasts and in the Rockies, offering a range of rustic accommodation, equipment rental and lessons, from as little as $10 a day for skis, boots and poles, up to about $100 for an all-inclusive weekend tour.

HORSE RACING

The **Kentucky Derby**, held in Louisville on the first Saturday in May (see p.382), is the biggest event in the **horse racing** calendar, but many other towns across the nation have good racecourses. Races are held on tracks of dirt, not grass; one popular variation is harness racing, where a couple of horses pull a buggy and driver around an oval circuit. As off-course betting is illegal in the US, the only place you can bet is at the trackside, and meetings are usually well attended.

THE 1994 WORLD CUP

The decision of the governing body of world soccer, FIFA, to hold the **1994 World Cup** in the US shocked fans throughout the world. This is a country where "football" very definitely means the gridiron variety, and soccer has been reported as ranking below tractor racing in national popularity. The abortive experiment of the early Eighties, when teams such as the New York Cosmos hired over-the-hill megastars such as Pele, Beckenbauer and Cruyff, has long since foundered, and professional participation is confined to a barely watched indoor six-a-side league. Since the USA beat England 1-0 in the 1950 tournament, its only appearance in the World Cup finals has been the unremarkable performance in Italy in 1990. Bookmakers will certainly be offering long odds against the hosts lifting the trophy in 1994.

That said, over eleven million Americans, the vast majority of them under eighteen, now play soccer regularly. The low cost of equipping players, in contrast to the paraphernalia of American football, means that much to the chagrin of the NFL the sport is starting to take off in schools, and in Hispanic areas above all soccer seems to be acquiring ever-greater significance.

All indications are that the 52-game tournament, to be held from June 17 to July 17 1994, will be a glitzy affair, run on the same private-sector lines, and by many of the same people, as the successful and money-spinning LA Olympics. Former Secretary of State Henry Kissinger is chair of the organising committee. Although the venues have yet to be finalised, matches are certain to take place in LA, Miami, and somewhere close to, but not in, New York City.

For more details, contact World Cup USA 1994 Inc, Suite 300, 4300 Fair Lakes Court, Fairfax VA 22033 (☎703/631-1994).

POLICE AND TROUBLE

No one could pretend that America is trouble-free, although away from the major urban centres violent crime is a lower-key issue than you might think. Even the lawless reputation of New York, Detroit or Los Angeles is far in excess of the truth, and most parts of these cities, by day at least, are fairly safe; at night, though, quite a few areas are completely off-limits.

Members of the notorious **gangs** are a rare sight outside their own territories (which are usually well away from where you're likely to be), and they tend to kill each other rather than tourists – despite the horror stories in 1991 of British visitors being shot in Miami. Similarly, deaths in the so-called murder cities, such as Washington DC and Houston, are mainly confined to domestic attacks. By being careful, planning ahead, and taking care of your possessions, you should, generally speaking, have few real problems. If you do, the police are usually helpful and obliging to foreign visitors, although they'll be less sympathetic if they think you brought the trouble on yourself.

POLICE

It helps to be familiar with the hierarchy of the various **police** forces – there are innumerable levels of city, county, state and federal authorities. Confusingly, most of the jurisdictions overlap and you may well find yourself having to deal with more than one. The caricatured figure of the overweight, usually bumbling but always southern-drawling **County Sheriff** represents the

lowest rung of authority; larger cities and sizeable towns within a county will usually have their own **Police Department**. On a statewide level you'll most likely see **Highway Patrol** officers or **State Troopers**, generally responsible for writing speeding tickets; the elite of the law enforcement bunch are the **FBI** agents – à la Dale Cooper in *Twin Peaks* – who are rarely seen but deal with the most important cases of kidnappings, bank robberies and organised crime. Outnumbering all the official law enforcement officers are the ranks of private **security guards** – untrained, poorly paid and heavily armed misfits standing guard at *7-Elevens*, company headquarters and late-night liquor stores.

THIEVES

The biggest problem for most travellers is the threat of **mugging**. It's impossible to give hard and fast rules about what to do if you're confronted by a mugger. Whether to run, scream or fight depends on the situation – but most locals would just hand over their money. Of course, the best thing is simply to avoid being mugged, and a few basic rules are worth remembering: *don't* flash money around; *don't* peer at your map (or this book) at every street corner, thereby announcing that you're a lost stranger; even if you're terrified or drunk (or both), *don't* appear so; avoid dark streets, especially ones you can't see the end of; and in the early hours stick to the roadside edge of the pavement so it's easier to run into the road to attract attention. If you have to ask for directions, choose your target carefully. Another idea is to carry a wad of cash, perhaps $50 or so, separate from the bulk of your holdings so that if you do get confronted you can hand over something of value without it costing you everything.

If the worst happens and your assailant is toting a gun or (more likely) a knife, try to stay calm: remember that he (for this is generally a male pursuit) is probably scared too. Keep still, don't make any sudden movements – and hand over your money. When he's gone, you should, despite your shock, try to find a phone and dial ☎911 (the nationwide emergency number), or hail a cab and ask the driver to take you to the nearest police station. Here, report the theft and get a

reference number on the report to claim
insurance (see p.11) and travellers' cheque
refunds. For advice specifically for women in case
of mugging or attack, see below.

Needless to say, having bags snatched which
contain travel documents can be a big headache,
none more so than **losing your passport**. If you
do lose your passport, go to the nearest consulate and get them to issue you a **temporary
passport**, basically a sheet of paper saying
you've reported the loss, which will get you out
of America and back to the UK. If you plan to
travel on from America – say into Mexico or
further afield, you'll need to get a new passport –
an extremely tough and time-consuming, not to
mention expensive, process.

Another common problem is **lost travellers'
cheques**. You should keep the receipt, or at least
a record of the numbers of your cheques, separately from the actual cheques, and if you lose
them ring the issuing company on their toll-free
number. They'll ask you for the cheque numbers,
the place you bought them and when and how you
lost them and whether it's been reported to the
police. All being well, the missing cheques should
be reissued within a couple of days – and you may
get an emergency advance to tide you over.

GAY AND LESBIAN USA

**The gay scene in America is huge, albeit
heavily concentrated in the major cities.
San Francisco, where between a quarter
and a third of the voting population is reckoned to be gay or lesbian, is probably the
premier gay city of the world; New York
runs a close second, and up and down both
coasts gay men and women enjoy the kind
of visibility and influence those in other
places can only dream about. Gay politicians, and even policemen, are more than a
novelty, and representation at every level is
for real. Resources, facilities and organisations are endless. However, head into the
heartland and life more than looks like the
Fifties – away from large cities homosexu-
als are still oppressed and commonly
reviled, and gay travellers would regrettably
be well advised to watch their step to avoid
hassles and possible aggression.**

Ghettoisation is no longer the self-defensive
manoeuvre it used to be, but almost all the major
cities have sizeable, predominantly gay areas –
Christopher Street in New York City, Los
Angeles' **West Hollywood**, San Francisco's
Castro district, Houston's **Montrose**, Seattle's
Capitol Hill, and so on. But while gay life
exploded into the public eye in the Seventies, in
the face of the AIDS pandemic the energies of
gay men and women have been directed to the
protection of existing rights, and to increasing
support and help for victims of the disease.
Activist groups like *ACT-UP* (the AIDS Coalition
To Unleash Power) and *Queer Nation* hold sit-ins
(and kiss-ins) as part of continuing efforts to
maintain a high profile in the face of increasing
intolerance and isolation.

Things change as quickly in the gay and
lesbian (and emerging bisexual) scene as they do
everywhere else, but we've tried to give a overview of local **resources**, **bars** and **clubs** in each
of the major cities. Of national **publications** to
look out for, most of which are available from any
good bookshop, by far the best is *Bob Damron's
Address Book* (PO Box 11270, San Francisco CA
94101; $12), a pocket-sized yearbook full of list-
ings of hotels, bars, clubs and resources. *Gay
Yellow Pages* (PO Box 292, Village Station, New
York NY 10011; $8.95) is also useful. *The
Advocate* (Liberation Publications, 6922
Hollywood Blvd, Los Angeles CA 90028; $2.95) is
a bi-monthly national gay news magazine, with
features, general info and classified ads (not to
be confused with *Advocate Men*, which is a soft-
porn magazine). Specifically lesbian publications
are harder to find: the most useful is *Gaia's Guide*
(132 W 24th St, New York NY 10011; $6.95), a
yearly international directory with a lot of US
info. There's also a national, toll-free gay and
lesbian **crisis line** (☎1-800/767-4297).

WOMEN

Women in the US have made great advances since the housewifely Fifties, and although the women's movement has lost some impetus in recent years its achievements persist: women's bars, bookstores and support centres are testimony to continuing, and widespread, commitment to female self-determination. The US is also remarkable in that it has a central and voluble group protesting women's issues; lobbying by the National Organisation for Women (featuring Gloria Steinem and Betty Friedan) has done much to affect positive legislation.

At the same time, women are beginning to achieve positions of real power – there's a woman on the US Supreme Court, for instance, and a number of state governors are female. However, the recent and very discouraging failure to pass the **Equal Rights Amendment**, which would have assured all people equal treatment under the law regardless of gender, and the simultaneous rise to power of fundamentalist Christian **anti-abortion activism** (the US government no longer provides funding or medical help to women seeking to terminate a pregnancy) have together had a demoralising effect on women's solidarity.

Practically speaking, a woman **travelling alone** in America is not usually made to feel conspicuous, or liable to attract unwelcome attention. US **cities** can feel a whole lot safer than you might expect from the images of demented urban jungles that are so prevalent abroad, simply because there are so many people about. But as with anywhere, particular care has to be taken at night: walking through unlit, empty streets is never a good idea, and if there's no bus service (and you can afford it), take cabs. It's true that women who look confident are less likely to encounter trouble – those who stand around looking lost and a bit scared are prime targets.

In the major urban centres, provided you listen to advice and stick to the better parts of town, going into **bars** and **clubs** alone should pose few problems: there's generally a pretty healthy attitude towards women who do so and your privacy will be respected – although the existence of unevolved specimens who'll assume you're available is undeniable. Gay and lesbian bars are usually a trouble-free and welcoming alternative.

However, **small towns** tend not to be blessed with the same liberal or indifferent attitudes toward lone women travellers. People seem to jump immediately to the conclusion that your car has broken down, or that you've suffered some terrible tragedy; in fact, you may get fed up with well-meant offers of help. If your **vehicle breaks down** in a country area, walk to the nearest house or town for help; on Interstate highways or heavily travelled roads, wait in the car for a police or highway patrol car to arrive. One increasingly available option is to rent a portable telephone with your car, for a small additional charge – a potential lifesaver.

You shouldn't expect life in the US to be free from the sort of daily harassment familiar from home; if anything, it's liable to be less subtle (as with other things here). That said, many Americans are genuinely friendly and interested in travellers; it is sometimes difficult to distinguish harassment from eagerness to talk to someone with a foreign (and especially British or Irish) accent. If in doubt, be aloof and firm.

Rape statistics in the US are outrageously high, and it goes without saying that you should *never* **hitch** alone – this is widely interpreted as an invitation for trouble, and there's no shortage of weirdos to give it. Similarly, if you have a car, be careful who you pick up: just because you're in the driving seat doesn't mean you're safe. Avoid travelling at night by public transport – deserted bus stations, if not actually threatening, will do little to make you feel secure – and where possible you should team up with a fellow traveller. There really is security in numbers. On *Greyhound* buses, follow the example of other lone women and make a point of sitting as near to the front – and the driver – as possible. Should disaster strike, all major towns have some kind of rape counselling service; if not, the local sheriff's office will make adequate arrangements for you to get help, counselling, and, if necessary, get you home.

Specific **women's contacts** are listed in the city sections of this book; for good back-up material, get hold of *Places of Interest to Women* ($7; Ferrari Publications, PO Box 35575, Phoenix AZ; ☎602/863-2408), a yearly guide for women travelling in the US, Canada, the Caribbean and Mexico. The National Organisation for Women has branches in most cities – check the phone book.

DISABLED TRAVELLERS

Travellers with mobility problems or other physical disabilities will probably find the US more accommodating than Britain or much of Europe. All public buildings have to be wheelchair accessible and provide suitable toilet facilities, street corners almost all have dropped kerbs, and most public transport systems have facilities for "physically challenged" individuals – subways have lifts, many buses are able to "kneel" down to let people board, and staff are generally understanding.

Most **airlines**, either transatlantic or within the US, will do whatever they can to ease your journey, and will usually let attendants of more seriously disabled people accompany them at no extra charge. The Americans with Disabilities Act 1990 obliges all air carriers to make the majority of their services accessible to travellers with disabilities within five to nine years. It always helps to give at least a day's notice if you have special needs, and it's generally a good idea to allow plenty of time so you don't have to feel rushed around. The larger **car rental** companies, *Hertz* and *Avis* for example, can provide cars with hand-controls at no extra charge, though these are only available on their full-size (ie most expensive) models; book one as far in advance as you can. Many *Amtrak* **trains** are equipped with specially adapted sleeping quarters for handicapped travellers. Taking *Greyhound*, however, is really not to be recommended, except perhaps for shorter journeys (though if you do somehow manage to get a wheelchair-user on board, the helper travels free).

Larger **hotels** – including most *Holiday Inns* – have at least one or two suites designed specifically for their disabled guests, and the entire *Red Roof* chain of motels (☎1-800/848-7878) is accessible to travellers with disabilities.

The **Sierra Club** (730 Polk St, San Francisco, CA 94110; ☎415/776-2211) have recently published *Easy Access to National Parks*, by Wendy Roth and Michael Tompane ($15), a detailed guide to all fifty US national parks for people with disabilities, senior citizens and families with young children.

Most individual states in the US can provide information specifically geared at disabled travellers. Among **national organisations** worth contacting are **SATH**, the **Society for the Advancement of Travel for the Handicapped** (26 Court Street, Brooklyn, NY 11242; ☎718/858-5483), a non-profit travel-industry grouping which includes travel agents, tour operators, hotel and airline management, and people with disabilities. They will refer any enquiry about the States to the appropriate member, but they are hard up and busy, so send an International Reply Coupon and allow plenty of time for a response. **Mobility International USA** (PO Box 3551, Eugene, OR 97403; ☎503/343-1248) answer transport queries and operate an exchange programme for disabled people and their friends. They also have an office in Britain, at 62 Union Street, London SE11 TD (☎071/403 5688).

TRAVELLING WITH CHILDREN

Children are far more accepted – and welcomed – in public places in the US than in Britain. Travelling with kids is relatively problem-free: hotels and especially restaurants are well-used to them, most state and national parks organise children's activities, every town or city will have a large number of good clean and safe playgrounds – and of course Disneyland in Los Angeles, and Disney World in Florida, are the ultimate in kids' entertainment.

In addition, almost any large city will have a natural history museum or a good aquarium, and quite a few have children's museums specialising in hands-on, interactive education and recreation. State tourist bureaux can provide specific information, and various guidebooks have been written for parents travelling with children.

On a more practical level, children under two years old fly for free – though that doesn't mean they get a seat, which is a pretty major consideration on transatlantic flights – and when aged from two to twelve they are usually entitled to half-price tickets. The same goes for air, train or bus travel within the States.

Don't set yourself unrealistic targets if you're hoping to drive in the US with your kids. Distances are colossal, and those long, boring journeys on the Interstate can be disastrous. When renting a car, note that the companies are obliged to provide free car seats for kids if requested.

One of the real joys of bringing kids to the US is the good deal you get in its **restaurants**. Almost every one offers bolster chairs and a special kids menu, packed with huge, excellent value (though not necessarily healthy) meals – cheeseburger and chips for 99¢, and so on. Children's **toys** are also exceptionally good value – a much better selection, at around half the cost of what you'd find in Britain.

WORK AND STUDY

While the United States may be a great place to live, it's becoming increasingly difficult for foreigners to obtain work there. For an extended legal stay, you should apply for a special working visa at any American Embassy *before* you set off for the States. (For other ways of extending your stay, see "Visas and Red Tape", p.9). Different types of visas are issued, depending on your skills and length of stay, but unless you've got relatives (parents or children over 21) or a prospective employer to sponsor you, your chances are at best slim. Finding long-term accommodation is a lot simpler, although by no means cheap.

WORKING AND STAYING ON

Illegal work is nothing like as easy to find as it once was, now that the Government has introduced fines of up to $10,000 for companies caught employing anyone without the legal right to work in the US. Understandably, most are now reluc-

tant to hire travellers. Even in the traditionally more casual establishments like restaurants and bars, things have really tightened up, and if you do find work it's likely to be of the less visible, poorly paid kind – washer-up instead of waiter. Temporary **agency work** without papers is a long shot too; opt for short-term manual labour jobs and your chances are better. **Agricultural work** is often available on farms during harvest, but can entail working miles from major centres, and back-breaking labour. If you stick it out, the pay can be good, often including board and accommodation. Another idea is to take a summer job in one of Alaska's fish **canneries**, well paid but messy work; the best time to enquire is April or May. Finally, **housecleaning** and **babysitting** are feasible, if not very well-paid options. Check the notices in supermarkets, drugstores, local papers and universities. As with anything, it's who you know that counts; the more contacts you make, the better the chance that somebody will put some work your way. Don't be afraid to ask around: Americans respond to an enterprising spirit.

There is, of course, the option of making up a social security number (the national ID number that shows you have the right to work) or borrowing somebody else's, but this means borrowing their identity, too – it's too tricky to bother with really, as well as highly illegal. In an effort to get around the recent stringency, more and more people are opting into **marriages of convenience**, usually on the basis of some kind of payment (in the region of $5000 is a usual amount) to the person willing to marry you, though if you encounter someone similarly desirous of access to Britain, no money need change hands. While such marriages are common enough, they're no guarantee of a **Green Card** (the cherished document that declares you legally entitled to work and reside in the US). Indeed, the authorities treat all marriages involving foreigners with suspicion, and will interview you rigorously; should they suspect that your marriage is not legitimate, you qualify for immediate deportation.

STUDYING

Students have the best chance of prolonging their stay in the US. One way is to get on to an Exchange Visitor Programme, for which participants are given a J-1 visa that entitles them to accept paid summer employment and apply for a social security number. However, you should note that most of these visas are issued for jobs in American **summer camps**, which aren't everybody's idea of a good time; they fly you over, and after a summer's work you end up with around $500 and a month to blow it in. If you live in Britain and are interested, contact *BUNAC* (232 Vauxhall Bridge Road, London SW1; ☎071/630 0344), or *Camp America* (37 Queens's Gate, London SW7; ☎071/589 3223). If you want to **study** at an American university, apply to that institution directly; if they accept you, you're more or less entitled to unlimited visas so long as you remain enrolled in full-time education.

DIRECTORY

ADDRESSES Though initially confusing, American addresses are masterpieces of logic. Generally speaking, roads in built-up areas are laid out to a grid system, creating "blocks" of buildings. The first one or two digits of a specific address refer to the block, which will be numbered in sequence from a central point, usually downtown; for example, 620 S Cedar Avenue will be six blocks south of downtown. It is crucial, therefore, to take note of components such as "NW" or "SE" in addresses; 3620 SW Washington Boulevard will be a very long way indeed from 3620 NE Washington Boulevard.

AIRPORT TAX Around $35 – this pays for security checks, as well as customs and immigration – but always included in the price of your ticket.

CIGARETTES AND SMOKING The country which first gave tobacco to the world – and which continues assiduously to push it all over the globe – is now probably the most concerned about its detrimental effects on health. Smoking is now severely frowned upon in the US, although no government measures have been taken against tobacco advertising. It's possible to spend a month here without ever smelling tobacco; most cinemas are non-smoking, restaurants are usually divided into non-smoking and smoking sections, and smoking is universally forbidden on public transport – including almost all domestic airline flights. Work places, too, tend to be smoke-free zones, so employees are reduced to smoking on the street outside. Cigarettes are, however, widely sold. A packet of twenty costs a mere $1.50, though most smokers buy cigarettes by the carton for around $10.

DATES In the American style, the date 4.9.92 means not September 4 but April 9.

DONATIONS Many museums request donations rather than an admission fee; usually you'll be expected to put $2 or so into the collection box as you enter. If you don't, you won't be turned away but will suffer the indignity of being considered a complete cheapskate.

DRUGS The precise legal position of someone found to be possessing under an ounce of marijuana varies from state to state – it's legal in Alaska, but the norm elsewhere would be for it to be an offence punishable by a $200 fine. Being caught with more than an ounce, however, means facing a criminal charge for dealing, and a possible prison sentence. Other drugs are, of course, completely illegal and it's a much more serious offence if you're caught with any.

ELECTRICITY 110V AC. All plugs are two-pronged and rather insubstantial. Some travel plug adapters don't fit American sockets.

FLOORS The *first* floor in the US is what would be the ground floor in Britain; the *second* floor would be the first floor, and so on.

ID Should be carried at all times. Two pieces should suffice, one of which should have a photo: a passport and credit card(s) are your best bets.

LAUNDERETTES All but the most basic hotels do laundry, but a wash and tumble dry in a launderette (US *laundromat*) works out a lot cheaper, at about $1.50. Take plenty of quarters.

MEASUREMENTS AND SIZES The US has yet to go metric, so measurements are in inches, feet, yards and miles; weight in ounces, pounds and tons. Liquid measurements differ too: American pints and gallons are about four-fifths of British ones. Clothing sizes are always two figures less what they would be at home. For example, a British women's size 12 is a US size 10. To work out shoe sizes, simply add 1 ½ to your British size.

PUBLIC TOILETS Don't exist as such in cities. Bars, restaurants and fast-food outlets are your best bets, though really you should be a customer.

TAX Be warned that **sales tax** (like VAT only different) is added to virtually everything you buy in a shop, but it isn't part of the marked price.

The actual rate varies from place to place: in New York and parts of California it's over 8 percent, while other states – Alaska, Delaware, Montana and Oregon – have no sales tax at all. **Hotel tax** will add 5 to 10 percent to most bills.

TEMPERATURES Always given in Fahrenheit.

TICKETS For music, theatre, sports and camping reservations, use *Ticketron*, whose offices are everywhere and listed in the phone book, and through whom you can buy tickets over the phone using your credit card number.

TIME See p.16.

TIPPING Many first-time visitors to the US think of tipping as a potential source of huge embarrassment. It's nothing of the sort; tipping is universally expected, and you quickly learn to tip without a second thought. You really shouldn't depart a bar or restaurant without leaving a tip of *at least* 15 percent (unless the service is utterly disgusting): the whole American system of service is predicated on tipping, and not to do so causes a great deal of resentment, and a short paypacket for the waiter or waitress at the end of the week. About the same amount should be added to taxi fares – and round them up to the nearest 50¢ or dollar. A hotel porter who has lugged your suitcases up several flights of stairs should get $3 to $5. When paying by credit or charge card, you're expected to add the tip to the total bill before filling in the amount and signing.

VIDEOS The standard format used for video cassettes in the US is different from that used in Britain. You cannot buy videos in the US compatible with a video camera bought in Britain.

PART TWO

THE

GUIDE

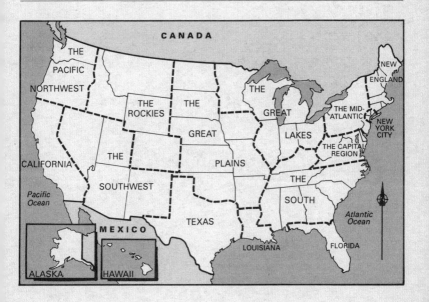

CHAPTER ONE

NEW YORK CITY

New York City is the most beguiling city in the United States. You may not think so at first – for the place is nothing short of mad, epitomising all that is wrong (and really drastically wrong) in modern America. But spend even a few days here and the adrenalin takes hold. Walking through the city streets *is* an experience, the buildings like icons to the modern age. And despite all the hype, the movie-image sentimentalism, Manhattan – the central island and the city's real core – has massive romance. Whether it's the flickering lights of the midtown skyscrapers, the 4am half-life in Greenwich Village, or just wasting the morning on the Staten Island Ferry, you really would have to be made of stone not to be moved by it all.

New York is not a conventionally pleasing city – or for that matter conventional in any respect. The divisions between rich and poor in Manhattan could hardly be more extreme, and the city's problems – racism, the drug trade, homelessness – are increasing. New York is a city on the brink, one of the world's most spectacular cases of urban blight, and whether you seek it or not it's hard not to become aware of this; indeed, in a perverse way, it's these tangible and potent contrasts that give New York much of its excitement.

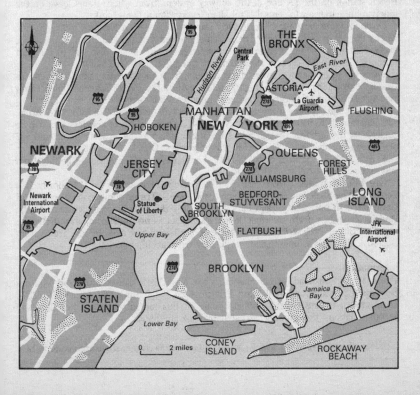

The city does have more straightforward pleasures, such as its different **ethnic neighbourhoods** in Lower Manhattan, from Chinatown to the Jewish Lower East Side, the arty concentrations of SoHo and TriBeCa, Greenwich and East Village; its **architecture** (the whole city reads like an illustrated history of modern design); and its **art**, to which you could devote weeks of wandering in the Metropolitan and Modern Art museums and countless smaller collections. And there is, of course, the opportunity to consume. You can **eat** anything, cooked in any style; **drink** in any kind of company; sit through any amount of **movies**. The established arts – **dance, theatre, music** – are superbly catered for, and New York's **clubs** are varied and exciting. As for **shops**, the choice in this heartland of the great capitalist dream is almost numbingly exhaustive.

Arriving and Information

New York City is served by two **international airports**: most flights use **John F Kennedy (JFK)** (☎718/656-4520) in Queens, but some *Virgin* and *Continental* flights touch down at **Newark** (☎201/961-2000) in New Jersey. In addition, some **domestic** arrivals come in at **La Guardia** (☎718/476-5000), also in Queens. From all the airports, the cheapest and most straightforward way into Manhattan is by **bus**.

From **JFK**, *Carey* buses run to the Port Authority Bus Terminal and Grand Central Station in Manhattan; journey time is between forty minutes and one hour ($11; every 30min, 5am–12.30am; ☎718/632-0500). The alternative bus/subway link (☎718/330-1234) costs just $1.15; take the shuttle bus (labelled "Long-term parking") to Howard Beach station on the #A line of the subway system, from where trains leave on the ninety-minute journey to central Manhattan (every 20min, 6am–1am).

Olympia Trails buses take up to forty minutes to get from **Newark** to Manhattan, where they stop at the World Trade Center, Grand Central and Penn stations ($7; every 30min, 5am–1am; ☎964-6233). *New Jersey Transit* buses also run to the Port Authority Terminal ($7; every 15–30min, day and night; ☎201/762-5100).

Carey buses (see above) every thirty minutes from **La Guardia** take 45 minutes to Grand Central ($8.50; 6am–midnight) and Port Authority ($8.50; 7.30am–10pm). *Carey* also link **JFK and La Guardia**, taking 45 minutes ($9.50; every 30min, 6am–11pm).

Taxis are fairly pricey from all the airports; reckon on paying $20 from La Guardia, $30-plus from JFK, $40 or more from Newark. **Car and minibus services** can also be costly *from* the airports, though prices from Manhattan *to* the airports are around $12 per person to La Guardia, $15 to JFK, $18 to Newark. Check with the company first or call *Gray Line Air Shuttles* on ☎757-6840. For **general information** on getting from and to the airports, call ☎1-800/AIR RIDE.

Greyhound buses (☎635-0800) pull in to New York at the Port Authority Bus Terminal, 41st Street and Eighth Avenue (☎564-8484). **Trains** come in at either **Grand Central Terminal**, 42nd St and Park Ave (☎532-4900), which takes arrivals from the Hudson Valley, the north and west US and Canada, or **Penn Station**, at Seventh Avenue and 33rd Street (☎868-8970), which serves Long Island and New Jersey. Trains from Boston, Chicago, Washington and Florida may arrive at either station.

Information

The best place to head for information is the **New York Convention and Visitors Bureau** at 2 Columbus Circle (Mon–Fri 9am–6pm, Sat & Sun 10am–6pm; ☎397-8222). They have up-to-date leaflets on what's going on, bus and subway maps, and details of accommodation – though they can't actually book anything.

Unless otherwise specified, all telephone numbers in this chapter share **area code** ☎212.

Getting Around

Few American cities equal New York for sheer street-level stimulation, and **walking** is much the most exciting method of exploring. However, it's also exhausting, and at some point you'll need to use some other form of **transport**. The fastest way to get from A to B in Manhattan and the boroughs is the dirty, noisy, and intimidating – but reasonably efficient – **subway**. Each train and route is identified by a number or letter; the majority of routes run uptown or downtown, following the great avenues, rather than crosstown. The subway is open 24 hours a day, but most routes operate at certain times only. Every journey, whether on the **express** lines, which stop only at major stations, or the **locals**, which stop at them all, costs $1.15, bought in the form of a **token** from station booths. There's no discount for buying several, but stocking up means less queueing, and they can be used for buses too. Subway and bus maps can be obtained from token booths, or from the concourse office at Grand Central. At night always try to use the crowded centre cars, and while you're waiting, keep to the area marked in yellow where you can be seen by the booth attendants. By day the whole train is safe, at least in theory.

New York's **bus system** is a lot simpler than the subway, and fairly frequent. Its one disadvantage is that it can be extremely slow – in peak hours almost down to walking pace. Buses stop every two or three blocks, at five- to ten-minute intervals. Anywhere in Manhattan the fare is $1.15, payable on entry with either a subway token or with the correct change – but not pennies or dollar bills. Ask for a transfer if you need to change buses anywhere along your journey, valid for an hour from boarding.

Taxis are reasonably priced, and much the best way of getting around in the evening, although New York taxi drivers don't always know their way around terribly well and often speak little English. Basic fares are $1.50 for the first eighth of a mile, 25¢ for each fifth of a mile thereafter, rising by 50¢ after 8pm and all day Sunday.

Guided Tours

Grayline are the biggest operators of guided **bus** tours, with three terminals in midtown Manhattan: on Eighth Avenue between 53rd and 54th streets (☎397-2600); on West 49th Street between Sixth and Seventh avenues (☎869-5005); and at 166 West 46th Street (☎354-5122). Half-day tours, taking in the main sights of Manhattan, go for around $23, and a full day costs $32.50, bookable through any travel agent.

The **Circle Line Ferry** takes three hours to sail right round Manhattan from Pier 83 at the far west end of 42nd Street, taking in everything from soaring views of Lower Manhattan to the bleaker stretches of Harlem, with a commentary and on-board bar ($16; March–Dec with varying regularity; ☎563-3200). The **Staten Island Ferry** (see p.83), lays on a staggering panorama of the downtown skyline for just 50¢.

Island Helicopter, at the far eastern end of East 34th Street (☎683-4575), and *Liberty Helicopter Tours*, at the western end of 30th Street, near the Jacob Javits Convention Center (☎465-8905), offer **helicopter** flights from around $40 upwards.

WALKING TOURS

Municipal Arts Society, 457 Madison Ave (☎935-3960). Architectural or cultural tours. Regular trips around Harlem, and other neighbourhoods. Prices from $14.

The 92nd Street Y, 1395 Lexington Ave (☎996-1105). A mixed bag of walking tours, from art tours to political New York and pre-dawn visits to the wholesale meat and fish markets. $8–12 per person.

The Penny Sightseeing Company, 1565 Park Ave (☎410-0080). Black-run company specialising in tours of Harlem. Trips run on Tuesdays and Saturdays at 11am; $15. Their Gospel Tours take in the rousing singing of a Baptist service: Thursdays at 10am, Sundays at 10.30am; $17. Reservations for all *Penny Sightseeing* tours have to be made two days in advance.

The City

New York City comprises the central island of Manhattan along with four outer boroughs – Brooklyn, Queens, The Bronx and Staten Island. **Manhattan**, to many, is New York; certainly, this where you're likely to spend most time, and to stay. The island is broadly divided into three districts: **Downtown** (below 14th St); **Midtown** (from 14th St up as far as Central Park); and **Upper Manhattan** (north of Central Park). The southern (downtown) part of Manhattan was first to be settled, which means that its streets have names and are somewhat randomly arranged. Uptown, above Houston Street on the east side, 14th Street on the west, the streets are numbered and follow a grid pattern, the numbers increasing as you move north.

Fifth Avenue, the greatest of the main avenues, cuts along the east side of Central Park and serves as a dividing line between east streets (the "East Side") and west streets ("the West Side"). House numbers increase as you walk away to either side; numbers on avenues increase as you move north. It's useful also to know that traffic on **odd**-numbered streets runs from east to west, and on **even**-numbered streets from west to east, though major crosstown streets run in both directions. Apart from Park, Broadway, and Eleventh Avenue, which are two-way, avenues run in alternate directions.

Manhattan is a hard act to follow, and the four **outer boroughs** – Brooklyn, Queens, The Bronx and Staten Island – inevitably pale in comparison, with fewer specific sights and a life, essentially residential, which is less obviously dynamic. There are, however, good reasons for stepping off the island: Brooklyn Heights is one of the city's most beautiful neighbourhoods, and the faded resort of Coney Island, also in Brooklyn, along with nearby Brighton Beach, are well worth the trip out on the subway; the Staten Island Ferry is worth a trip in its own right. The outer boroughs also harbour some thriving ethnic quarters, and so make good places to go to eat, while Queens and the Bronx are where to head for if you want to watch a baseball game.

Lower Manhattan

LOWER MANHATTAN harbours its extremes in close proximity. For some it's the most spectacular, most glamorous skyline in the world, for others a rundown and seedy home. But whatever your perspective, it is undeniably archetypal New York, encompassing Greenwich Village and the East Village, Chinatown and Little Italy, and, at the skyscraper heart of things, the corporate monoliths of the Financial District.

As a prelude to neighbourhood wanderings, the **Statue of Liberty** provides an obvious focus – not so much for the vaunted symbol (though this is hard to ignore) as for the views of southern Manhattan. This lower part of the island begins with the shoreline **Financial District** – Wall Street at its centre – and then drifts, within half a mile, into the first of the city's ethnic districts: **Chinatown**, a bustling, insular area that's expanding fast into adjacent **Little Italy**. Over to the west, the one-time industrial areas of **SoHo** and **TriBeCa** are now up-and-coming residential blocks, home to Manhattan's (alternative) art scene. Further north, a less radical shift are traditionally politicised/literary **Greenwich Village** (touristy now but fun) and the **East Village**, which has taken on much of Greenwich's alternative mantle. All of which makes for enjoyable walking and cafe browsing. Walk beyond, though, into the **Lower East Side**, and the riches fade fast – New York's very real poverty quite unhidden and not a little threatening.

The Statue of Liberty and Ellis Island

The tip of Manhattan island, and the enclosing shores of New Jersey, Staten Island and Brooklyn, form the broad expanse of **New York Harbor**, one of the finest natural harbours in the world, stretching as far as the Verrazano Narrows – the narrow neck of land between Staten Island and Long Island. It's possible to appreciate it by simply

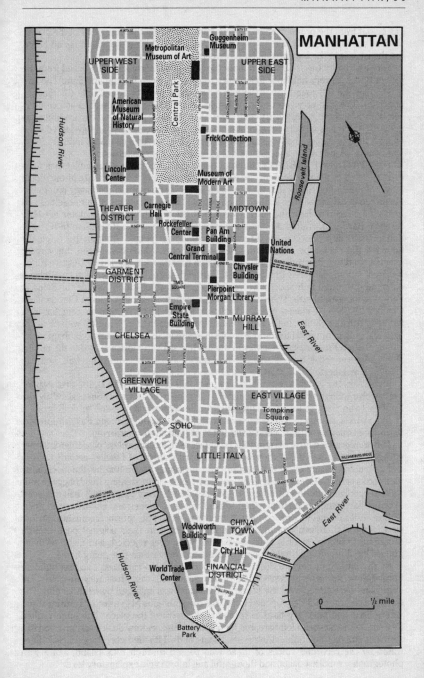

MANHATTAN

UPPER WEST SIDE

Metropolitan Museum of Art

Guggenheim Museum

UPPER EAST SIDE

Central Park

American Museum of Natural History

Frick Collection

Hudson River

Lincoln Center

Museum of Modern Art

Roosevelt Island

THEATER DISTRICT

Carnegie Hall

MIDTOWN

Rockefeller Center

Pan Am Building

Grand Central Terminal

United Nations

GARMENT DISTRICT

Chrysler Building

TIMES SQUARE

Pierpoint Morgan Library

Empire State Building

MURRAY HILL

CHELSEA

GREENWICH VILLAGE

EAST VILLAGE

Tompkins Square

SOHO

East River

LITTLE ITALY

WILLIAMSBURG BRIDGE

HOLLAND TUNNEL

GRAND STREET

CHINA TOWN

Woolworth Building

East River

City Hall

BROOKLYN BRIDGE

World Trade Center

FINANCIAL DISTRICT

Hudson River

WALL STREET

0   ½ mile

Battery Park

gazing out from the promenade on Battery Park. But to get the best views of the classic skyline, you should really take to the water. You can do this on the Staten Island Ferry, but the islands in the bay provide far more compelling targets.

Ferries, run by *Circle Line*, go to both the Statue of Liberty and Ellis Island from the pier in Battery, every half-hour in summer roughly between 9.15am and 5pm. The fare is $6.50 for the full round trip, half-price for children (tickets from Castle Clinton, see opposite). The last ferry you can feasibly take is at 3.30pm, and even then you couldn't see both islands. It's best to try and leave as early as possible, thereby avoiding the queues (which can be very long in high season, and at weekends) and giving yourself enough time to explore both islands properly: each deserves a couple of hours at least, and Liberty Island can be a pleasant place to spend an entire afternoon.

The **STATUE OF LIBERTY**, torch in hand and clutching a stone tablet, has for a century acted as a figurehead for the American Dream, and it's a measure of the global power of the United States that there is today probably no more immediately recognisable profile in existence. The statue, which depicts Liberty throwing off her shackles and holding a beacon to light the world, was the creation of the French sculptor Frédéric Auguste Bartholdi, crafted a hundred years after the American Revolution in recognition of fraternity between the French and American people (though he originally intended the statue for Alexandria in Egypt). Liberty, which consists of thin copper sheets bolted together and supported by an iron framework designed by Gustave Eiffel, was built in Paris between 1874 and 1884. Bartholdi started with a terracotta model and enlarged it through four successive versions – one of which stands beside the Seine in Paris – to its present size. The statue was formally dedicated by President Cleveland on October 28 1886. It closed a few years back for extensive renovation paid for by a fervently patriotic public, but is now accessible again, opened in July 1986 with plenty of back-slapping ceremonial to commemorate its centennial. You can today climb up to the crown, though the cramped stairway to the torch is sadly to remain closed to the public. Don't be surprised if there's an hour-long queue to ascend; while you wait, you can always enjoy Liberty Park's views of the Lower Manhattan skyline.

Just across the water, a few minutes by ferry, sits **ELLIS ISLAND**, the first stop for over twelve million prospective immigrants. Originally known as Gibbet Island by the English (who used it for punishing unfortunate pirates), it became an immigration station in 1894, mainly to handle the massive influx from southern and Eastern Europe. It remained open until 1954, when it was left to fall into atmospheric ruin.

The immigrants who arrived at Ellis Island were all steerage class passengers; richer voyagers were processed at their leisure on board ship. Most families arrived hungry and penniless, rarely speaking English and invariably overawed by the beckoning metropolis across the water. Con men preyed from all sides, stealing their baggage as it was checked and offering rip-off exchange rates for whatever money they had managed to bring. Each family was split up, men sent to one area, women and children to another, while a series of checks weeded out the undesirables and the infirm. Steamship carriers were obliged to return any immigrants not accepted to their original port, though according to official records only two percent were ever rejected, and many of those jumped into the sea and tried to swim to Manhattan rather than face going home.

By the time of its closure, Ellis Island was a formidable complex. The first building burned down in 1897; its replacement dates from 1903, though sundry hospitals and outhouses were added over the years, as the island was enlarged by fresh landfill. The turretted central building reopened in 1990 as the ambitious **Museum of Immigration**, where films and tapes try hard to recapture the spirit of the place. The huge vaulted Registry Room has been left bare, but for a couple of inspectors' desks, and gives on to a series of suitably institutional interview rooms and white-tiled corridors. Each is illustrated by the recorded voices of those who passed through Ellis Island, along with photographs, small artefacts, and thoughtful and informative explanatory text.

The Financial District

The skyline of Manhattan's **FINANCIAL DISTRICT** is the one you see in all the movies – dramatic skyscrapers crammed into the southern tip of the island and framed by the monumental elegance of the Brooklyn Bridge. At the heart of the nation's wheeler-dealing, this is the place where Manhattan (and indeed America) began, though precious few leftovers of those days remain, shunted out by big corporations eager to boost their images with headquarters at the right addresses.

The Dutch arrived here first, building a wooden wall at the edge of their small settlement as protection from pro-British settlers to the north, and giving the narrow canyon of today's **Wall Street** its name. It's here, behind the thin neoclassical mask of the **New York Stock Exchange**, that the purse strings of the capitalist world are pulled – a process you can view from the **visitors' gallery** (Mon–Fri 9.15am–4pm; free), and have explained by way of a glib introductory film and a small exhibition. The **Federal Hall National Memorial**, at Wall Street's head, looks a little foolish surrounded by skyscrapers. The building was once the Customs House, but the exhibition inside (Mon–Fri 9am–5pm; free) relates the headier days of 1789 when George Washington was sworn in as America's first president from a balcony on this site. Washington's statue stands, very properly, on the steps outside the daintily rotunded hall. At Wall Street's other end, **Trinity Church** (guided tours daily at 2pm) is an ironic onlooker to the street's dealings, a knobbly neo-Gothic structure that went up in 1846 and for fifty years was the city's tallest building. It's got much of the air of an English church, especially in the sheltered graveyard, the resting place of such early luminaries as the first Secretary to the Treasury, Alexander Hamilton.

Broadway comes to a gentle end at the **Bowling Green**, an oval of turf used for the game by eighteenth-century colonial Brits on a lease of "one peppercorn per year". Earlier still the green was the site of one of Manhattan's more memorable business deals, when Peter Minuit, first director general of the Dutch colony of New Amsterdam, bought the whole island from the Indians for a handful of baubles worth 60 guilders (about $25). Today the green is a spot for office people picnicking in the shadow of Cass Gilbert's **US Customs House**, an heroic monument to New York the port. Four statues at the front represent the four continents (sculpted by Daniel Chester French, who also created the Lincoln Memorial in Washington DC) and the twelve near the top personify the world's commercial centres, all fixed in homage to the maritime market. Beyond the Customs House, Lower Manhattan lets out its breath in **Battery Park**, where the nineteenth-century **Castle Clinton** (daily 9am–5pm) formerly protected Manhattan's southern tip and is now the place to buy ferry tickets to the Statue of Liberty and Ellis Island. Turning north up Water Street, on the corner of Pearl and Broad streets, the **Fraunces Tavern** (Mon–Fri 10am–4pm; $2.50) is a partially reconstructed Georgian house where on December 4 1783, with the British conclusively beaten, a weeping George Washington took leave of his assembled officers, intent on returning to rural life in Virginia. "I am not only retiring from all public employments," he wrote, "but am retiring within myself" – with hindsight a hasty statement as six years later he was to return as the new nation's president. The second floor re-creates the simple colonial dining room where this took place – all probably as genuine as the relics of Washington's teeth and hair in the adjacent museum.

Further up Water Street, at the eastern end of Fulton Street, the renovated **South Street Seaport** was formerly New York's sailship port, from where Robert Fulton started a ferry service to Brooklyn. Trade eventually moved elsewhere, and the blocks of warehouses and ship's chandlers were left to rot. Property speculators were gradually and secretively buying them up when they were rescued in the nick of time by an historical monument order. Regular guided tours of the Seaport run from the visitor centre at 207 Water Street, but the best place to start looking around is the so-called **Museum Block**, an assembly of upmarket shops hidden behind Water Street's hotchpotch of Greek Revival and Italianate facades. You might also look in on the **Fulton Fish Market**, a tatty building that wears its eighty years as the city's wholesale outlet with no pretensions. If you can manage it, the time to be here is around 5am (organised tours, $10, reservations required; ☎669-9416) when buyers' lorries park up beneath the highway to collect the catches – invigorating stuff, and a twilight world that probably won't be around that much longer. The adjacent **Pier 17 Pavilion**, a complex of restaurants and shops, could be one nail in its coffin. Next door, around piers 15 and 16, is the **South Street Museum** (daily 10am–5pm; $6), a collection of nimble sailships and chubby ferries slowly being refitted to former glories.

From just about anywhere in the seaport you can see one of New York's most celebrated delights, the much-loved **Brooklyn Bridge**. Now just one of several spans across the East River, it was in its day a technological quantum leap. It towered over the low brick structures around and for twenty years was the world's largest suspension bridge, the first to use steel cables and for many more the longest single span. It didn't go up without difficulties. John Augustus Roebling, its architect and engineer, crushed his foot taking measurements for the piers and died of gangrene three weeks later; his son Washington took over only to be crippled by the bends from working in an insecure underwater caisson, and subsequently directed the work from his sick bed overlooking the site. Twenty workers died during the construction, and, a week after the opening day in 1883, twelve people were crushed to death in a panicked rush on the bridge's footway.

Wherever you are in Lower Manhattan, the twin towers of the **World Trade Center** dominate the landscape. Spirited down to a tenth of their size they wouldn't get a second glance. But the fact is they're *big*, undeniably and frighteningly so, and a walk across the plaza below in summer months (closed in winter as icicles falling from the towers can kill) makes your head reel. The towers were in fact quickly surpassed as the world's tallest building by the Sears Tower in Chicago, and were half empty for several years. Now, however, they're part of a successful five-building development, as the bustling concourses and ritzy *Windows on the World* restaurant and, more affordably, the *City Lights* bar can vouch. With courage, a trip to the 107th floor **observation deck** of Two World Trade Center (daily 9.30am–9.30pm; $3.75) gives a mind-blowing view from a height of 1350 feet; and from the open-air rooftop promenade the silent panorama is more dramatic still – even Jersey City looks exciting. As you timidly edge your way around, ponder the fact that one Philippe Petit once walked a tightrope between the two towers.

Across from the World Trade Center on Vesey Street and Broadway, **St Paul's Chapel** comes from a very different order of things. It's the oldest church in Manhattan, dating from 1766 – eighty years earlier than Trinity Church and almost prehistoric by New York standards. The church's architect was from London – St Martin-in-the-Fields was his model – though his building seems quite American in feel.

City Hall Park and the Civic Center

Immediately north of St Paul's Chapel, Broadway and Park Row form the apex of **City Hall Park**, a noisy, pigeon-splattered triangle of green with Cass Gilbert's 1913 **Woolworth Building** as a venerable onlooker. Some think this is New York's definitive skyscraper, and it's hard to disagree, its soaring lines fringed with Gothic decoration. The famous lobby is one of the city's musts. Frank Woolworth made his fortune from his "five and dime" stores – everything cost either 5¢ or 10¢, strictly no credit. True to his philosophy he paid cash for his skyscraper, and the whimsical reliefs at each corner of the lobby show him doing just that, counting out the money in nickels and dimes. Facing him in caricature are the architect (medievally clutching a model of his building), renting agent and builder. Within, vaulted ceilings ooze honey-gold mosaics, and even the mailboxes are magnificent.

At the top of the park, marking the beginning of the **CIVIC CENTER** and its incoherent jumble of municipal offices and courts, stands **City Hall** (Mon–Fri 10am–4pm), finished in 1812 to a good-looking design that's a marriage of French Chateau and American Georgian. After the city's 1927 feting of the returned aviator Charles Lindbergh, it became the traditional finishing point for Broadway tickertape parades given for triumphant baseball stars, astronauts, and, more recently, returned Iranian hostages. Inside it's an elegant meeting of arrogance and authority, with the sweeping spiral staircase delivering you to the precise geometry of the **Governor's Room** and the self-important rooms that formerly contained the **Board of Estimates Chamber**.

If City Hall is the acceptable face of municipal bureaucracy, the **Tweed Courthouse** behind is a reminder of a seamier underbelly of corruption. William Marcy "Boss" Tweed worked his way from nowhere to become chairman of the Democratic Central Committee at Tammany Hall in 1856, and by a series of adroit and illegal moves manipulated the city's revenues through his own and his supporters' pockets. For a while Tweed's grip strangled all dissent until a political cartoonist, Thomas Nast, and the editor of the *New York Times* (who'd refused a half-million-dollar bribe to keep quiet) turned public opinion against him. With suitable irony Tweed died in 1878 in Ludlow Street jail – a prison he'd had built when Commissioner of Public Works.

Chinatown and Little Italy

A short stroll north from Civic Center, **CHINATOWN** is Manhattan's most thriving ethnic neighbourhood, over recent years pushing its boundaries north across Canal Street into Little Italy, and east as far as the fringes of the Lower East Side. It has close on 100,000 residents (about half of New York's Chinese population), seven Chinese newspapers, around 150 restaurants and over 300 garment factories.

The Chinese began to arrive in the mid-nineteenth century. Most had previously worked out west, building railways and digging gold mines, and few intended to stay: their idea was simply to make a nest-egg and retire to a life of leisure with their families (99 percent were men) back in China. Some did go back, but on the whole the big money took rather longer to accumulate than expected, and so Chinatown took shape as a permanent settlement. It later thrived on the back of the declining midtown garment business, with extensive garment factories that paid below minimum wages in return for enforced long hours. Cheap restaurants boomed, thanks in part to the numbers of working women who had no time to cook, and bought food to take home. Recently the community has swollen once again, with immigrants from Hong Kong anticipating the colony's uncertain future. Today, beneath the blithely prosperous facade, sharp practices continue to flourish, with traditional extortion, protection rackets and non-union sweatshops – not that the casual visitor sees much sign of it. **Mott Street** is the main thoroughfare and the streets around – Canal, Pell, Bayard, Doyers and Bowery – host a positive glut of restaurants, tea and rice shops and grocers.

On the other side of Canal Street, **LITTLE ITALY** is light years away from the solid ethnic enclave of old. Originally settled by New York's huge nineteenth-century influx of Italian immigrants, it is encroached upon a little more each year by Chinatown; few Italians still live here and the restaurants (of which there are plenty) tend to have valet-parking and high prices. However, some of the original delis and bakeries do survive, and there are still plenty of places to indulge yourself with a cappuccino and pastry. If you're here in September the **Festa di San Gennaro** is a wild splurge to celebrate the saint's day, when Italians from all over the city turn up and **Mulberry Street**, Little Italy's main strip, is transformed by street stalls and numerous Italian fast-snack outlets. Of the **restaurants**, *Umberto's Clam House* on Mulberry Street remains most famed, not for the food but as the scene of a vicious gangland murder in 1972, when Joe "Crazy Joey" Gallo was shot dead while celebrating his birthday with his wife and daughter. The bullet holes from the slaying are still visible in the windows.

SoHo and TriBeCa

Since the mid-1960s, **SOHO**, the grid of streets that runs *So*uth of *Ho*uston Street, has meant **art**. Squashed between the Financial District and Greenwich Village to the north, it had long been a no-man's-land of manufacturers and wholesalers, but as the Village declined in hipness, SoHo was suddenly "in". Its loft spaces were ideal for cheap-rental studios, and galleries quickly attracted the city's art crowd, boutiques and restaurants following close behind. Like the Village, gentrification quickly followed, and what remains is a mix of chi-chi antique, art and clothes shops and high living, although no amount of gloss can cover up SoHo's quintessential appearance of dark alleys and shabby factories, fronted by some of the best cast-iron facades in America.

The technique of **cast-iron architecture** originated as a way of assembling buildings quickly and cheaply, with iron beams rather than heavy walls carrying the weight of the floors. The result was the removal of load-bearing walls, greater space for windows, and, most noticeably, decorative facades. Almost any style or whim could be cast in iron and pinned to a building, and architects indulged themselves in Baroque balustrades, forests of Renaissance columns and all the effusion of the French Second Empire to glorify SoHo's sweatshops. Have a look at **72–76 Greene Street**, a neat extravagance whose Corinthian portico stretches the whole five storeys, all in painted metal, and at the strongly composed elaborations of its sister building at nos. **28–30**. At the northeast corner of Broome Street and Broadway the magnificent **Haughwout Building** is perhaps the ultimate in the genre, with rhythmically repeated motifs of colonnaded arches framed behind taller columns in a thin sliver of a Venetian palace.

TRIBECA, the *Tri*angle *Be*low *Ca*nal Street, retains a lived-in, worked-in feel. Less a triangle than a crumpled rectangle – the area bounded by Canal and Chambers streets, Broadway and the Hudson – its spacious industrial buildings house the apartments of TriBeCa's new gentry. Like "SoHo" the name TriBeCa was a 1960s invention to label the suddenly popular residential scramble of warehouses; they're now approaching SoHo in status and price, and it's only a matter of time before TriBeCa becomes just another piece of juicy real estate.

Greenwich Village

If you're a New Yorker, it's fashionable to dismiss **GREENWICH VILLAGE** (or "the Village" as it's most widely known). And it's true that while the bohemian image of Greenwich Village endures well enough if you don't actually live in New York, it's a tag that has long since ceased to hold genuine currency. However, the Village is still exciting, and to a great extent still sports the attractions that brought people here in the first place. Though quiet and residential, it has a busy street life that lasts later than any other part of the city; there are more restaurants per head than anywhere else, and bars, while never cheap, clutter every corner. Indeed there are few better initiations into the city's life, especially at night.

Greenwich Village grew up as a rural retreat from the early and frenetic nucleus of New York City, given impetus during the yellow fever epidemic of 1822, when it served as a refuge from the infected streets downtown. Refined Federal and Greek Revival terraces sprouted throughout the neighbourhood, and lured some of the city's highest society names. Later these large houses were to prove a fertile hunting ground for struggling artists and intellectuals on the lookout for cheap rents, and by the turn of the century Greenwich Village was well on its way to becoming New York's Left Bank.

The best place to start exploring the Village is its natural centre, **Washington Square**. It is not exactly elegant, but it does retain its northern edging of red-brick rowhouses – the "solid, honourable dwellings" of Henry James' eponymous novel – and Stanford White's imposing **Triumphal Arch**, built in 1892 to commemorate the centenary of George Washington's inauguration. It's also the heart of New York University, whose truly urban campus is spread out around the west Village. As soon as the weather gets warm, the park becomes sports field, dance floor, drug den and social club, boiling over with life as frisbees fly, skateboards flip and boom boxes crash through the urgent cries of dope peddlers and the studied patrols of police cars.

Follow **Macdougal Street** south and you hit **Bleecker Street** – Greenwich Village's Main Street, packed with shops, bars, people and restaurants. This junction is also the area's best-known meeting place, a vibrant corner with mock-European sidewalk cafés that have been literary hangouts since the start of this century. Turning right takes you right through the hubbub of Greenwich Village life, which stretches up **Sixth Avenue** to the unmistakable nineteenth-century bulk of the **Jefferson Market Courthouse**, voted fifth most beautiful building in America in 1885 and now serving as the local public library. Cut through from here to **Seventh Avenue**, off which **Bedford Street**, with Barrow and Commerce streets nearby, represents one of the Village's quietest and most desirable corners. Nearby, **Christopher Street** joins Seventh at **Sheridan Square**, site of the **Stonewall** gay bar which in 1969 was raided by police, precipitating a siege which lasted the best part of an hour and ended with several arrests and a number of injured policemen. Though hardly a victory for their rights, it was the first time that gay men had stood up *en masse* to the persecutions of the police, and as such represents a turning point in their struggle, formally instigating the Gay Rights movement and remembered by the annual **Gay Pride march** held on the last Sunday in June.

The East Village

The **EAST VILLAGE** is quite different in look and feel to its western counterpart, Greenwich Village. Once, like the Lower East Side proper which it abuts, a refuge of immigrants, and always solidly working-class, it became home to New York's non-conformist fringe in the earlier part of this century. W H Auden lived at 77 St Mark's Place, the neighbourhood's main street, and from the same building the Communist Journal *Novy Mir* was run, numbering among its more historic contributors Leon Trotsky. Much later the East Village became the New York haunt of the Beats – Kerouac, Burroughs, Ginsberg *et al* – who would get together at Alan Ginsberg's house on East Seventh Street for declamatory poetry readings. Later, Andy Warhol debuted the Velvet Underground; the Fillmore East played host to just about every band you've ever heard of; and Richard Hell proclaimed himself the inventor of punk rock. Perhaps inevitably, a lot has changed over the last decade. Escalating rents have forced many people out and the East Village isn't the hotbed of creativity it once was. But St Mark's Place is still one of Lower Manhattan's more vibrant strips, even if the thrift shops and panhandlers and political hustlers have given way to a range of ritzy boutiques, and this remains one of the city's most happening enclaves.

Though it's hard to believe now, **Astor Place**, at the western end of St Mark's Place, was in the 1830s one of the city's most desirable neighbourhoods. Lafayette Street in particular was home to the city's wealthiest names, not least John Jacob Astor himself, one of New York's most hideously greedy tycoons. The Astor Place **subway station**, bang in the middle of the junction, discreetly remembers the man on the platforms, its coloured reliefs of beavers recalling Astor's first big killings – in the fur trade. **Lafayette Street** is an undistinguished thoroughfare, and all that's left to hint that this might once have been more than a down-at-heel gathering of industrial buildings is **Colonnade Row**, a terrace of four monumental houses, now home to the Colonnade Theater. At the opposite end of St Mark's Place, **Tompkins Square Park** has long acted as focus for the Lower East Side/East Village community, and has a reputation as a centre of political demonstrations. It was here in 1874 that the police massacred a crowd of workers protesting against unemployment, and here too in the 1960s that protests were organised and made themselves heard. The late Yippie leader Abbie Hoffman lived nearby, and residents like him have helped give the East Village its maverick name. Today Tompkins Square Park is a focus of dissent against the gentrification of the East Village and Lower East Side. Between 1988 and 1991 it became more or less a shantytown for the homeless, known locally as "Tent City". In the winter, only the really hardy or really desperate lived here, but in warmer weather the numbers were swollen by activists, anarchists and all manner of statement-makers, hoping to rekindle the spirit of 1988, the year of the massive demonstrations known as the Tompkins Square **riots**. When mayor David Dinkins was reduced to clearing away the homeless by force in June 1991 – having castigated previous administrations during his election campaign for their indifference – it was widely seen as a telling and humiliating failure.

East of Tompkins Square, the island bulges out beyond the city's grid structure, the extra avenues being named A to D, and the area, by its devotees, **Alphabet City**. Until a very few years ago, this was a notoriously unsafe corner of town, run by drug pushers and the hoodlums that controlled them. This was brought to a halt in 1983 with a massive police campaign to clean up the area, although appearances remain much the same: the people who live here are poor Puerto Ricans, and their houses, what's left of them, are bombed-out shells amid fields of flattened rubble, next to which gangs of tramps have erected makeshift shelters.

The Lower East Side

South of Tompkins Square, the **LOWER EAST SIDE** began life towards the end of the last century as an insular slum for over half a million Jewish immigrants. Since then it has become considerably depopulated, and the slum-dwellers are now largely Puerto Rican rather than Jewish; but otherwise little has visibly changed. The area retains a Jewish feel, and if outsiders come here at all it's either to **eat** or for the bargain **shopping**. You can get just about anything cut-price in the stores, especially on Sunday mornings when Orchard Street is filled with stalls and stores selling off hats, clothes and designer labels for hefty discounts. And when you've finished shopping, the **Lower East Side Tenement Museum**, 97 Orchard St (Tues–Fri 11am–4pm, Sun 10am–3pm; free), housed in a former tenement building, is the best place to get the lowdown on the neighbourhood's immigrant past and present.

To the west, the **Bowery** spears up as far as Cooper Square on the edge of the East Village. This wide thoroughfare has gone through many changes over the years: it took its name from "Bouwerie", the Dutch word for farm, when it was the city's main agricultural supplier; later, in the closing decades of the last century, it was flanked by music halls, theatres, hotels and middle-market restaurants, drawing people from all parts of Manhattan. Currently it's a skid row for the homeless, flanked by a demoralising line of boarded-up shops and long-stay hotels near which few New Yorkers venture of their own accord, although it's rarely all that dangerous. The one – bizarre – focus is the **Bowery Savings Bank** on the corner of Grand Street. Designed by Stanford White in 1894, it rises out of the neighbourhood's debris like a god, much as does its sister bank on 42nd Street, a shrine to the virtue of thrift. Inside, the original carved cheque-writing stands are still in place, and the coffered ceiling, together with White's great gilded fake marble columns, couldn't create a more potent feel of security. An inscription above the door as you exit leaves you in no doubt: "Your financial welfare is the business of this bank." Quite so, but back on the Bowery, stepping over the drunks and avoiding the panhandlers, you can't help pondering what went wrong.

Midtown Manhattan

You're likely to spend a fair amount of time in **MIDTOWN MANHATTAN**, which is in many ways the centre of the city. Most of the city's hotels are here, and this is also where you'll most likely arrive – at Penn or Grand Central Station, or the Port Authority. New York's most glamorous (and most expensive) street, **Fifth Avenue**, cuts through its heart, with the theatre strip of **Broadway**, an increasingly disreputable neighbour, just to the west for much of the way. The character of Midtown undergoes a radical transformation depending on which side of Fifth you find yourself. Along Fifth and **east** are the corporate businesses and big prestige skyscrapers – the Chrysler, the Empire State, the Seagram. **West** of Fifth Avenue, and in particular west of Broadway, the area takes a dive. The **Theater District** is a natural entertainment focus, though these days more than a little sleazy, notwithstanding the fact that **Times Square**, the traditional centre of sex shows and petty crime, has recently undergone a multimillion-dollar clean-up. **The Garment District** has a certain throwback interest as a nineteenth-century foil to the corporate skyscrapers across the way, but the residential districts are frankly dull: **Chelsea** is long established but downbeat; **Clinton**, further up the west side, is gentrifying slowly but is still rough down by the West Side Highway.

Fifth Avenue and East: Union Square to 42nd Street

Downtown Manhattan ends with 14th Street, which slices across the island from the housing projects of the east side to the cut-price shops and eventually the meat-packing warehouses on the banks of the Hudson. In the middle, **Union Square**, once known as a gathering point for political demonstrations, was up until the mid-1980s a seedy haunt of dope pushing and street violence, but it's much more inviting now, the spill of shallow steps enticing you in to stroll the paths, feed the squirrels, and gaze at its array of statuary. The stretch of **Broadway** north of here was known once as "Ladies' Mile" for its fancy stores and boutiques, but notwithstanding a few sculpted facades and curvy lintels, it's now hard to imagine as an upmarket shopping mall. Turn right on East 20th Street for **Theodore Roosevelt's Birthplace** at no. 28 (Wed–Sun 9am–5pm; $1) – or

---

THE SKYSCRAPERS OF NEW YORK

Along with Chicago and Hong Kong, Manhattan is one of the best places in the world in which to see **skyscrapers**. In fact there are only two main clusters of skyscrapers, but they set the tone for the city – the **Financial District**, where the combination of narrow streets and tall buildings forms slender, lightless canyons, and **Midtown Manhattan**, where the big skyscrapers, flanking the wide central avenues between the Thirties and the Sixties, have long competed for height and prestige.

The first generally recognised skyscraper in New York was the **Flatiron Building** on Madison Square, designed in 1902, which made the most of the new iron-frame technique of construction. A few years later, in 1913, New York clinched the title of the world's tallest building with the sixty-storey **Woolworth Building** on Broadway, later going on to produce such landmarks as the **Chrysler** and **Empire State** buildings, and, more recently, the **World Trade Center** – though the latter has since been dwarfed by Chicago's Sears Tower. Styles over the years have been influenced by the city's stringent zoning laws. At first skyscrapers were sheer vertical monsters, maximising the floor space possible with no regard to how this affected the neighbouring buildings, which more often than not were thrown into shade by the new arrival. The authorities came up with the concept of "air rights", putting a restriction on how high a building could be before it had to be set back from its base. This forced skyscrapers to be designed in a series of steps – a law most elegantly adhered to by the Empire State Building, which has no less than ten steps. It's a pattern you will see repeated all over the city.

Due to the pressure on space in Manhattan's narrow confines, and the price of real estate, which makes the speculatory building of office blocks so potentially lucrative, the skyscrapers continue to rise, and some steel frame is always slowly rising somewhere in the city. There seems to be almost no limit to the heights envisaged in the future, the most notable plan being Donald Trump's bid to reclaim the tallest-building title for New York with a new structure on the Upper West Side well over a hundred storeys high. Whether or not this comes off, it's certain that even in times of recession skyscrapers remain the "machines for making money" that Le Corbusier originally proclaimed them to be.

at least a reconstruction of it: a grim brownstone mansion that boasts a few rooms with their original furnishings, some of Teddy's hunting trophies and a small gallery documenting the president's life. Past here Manhattan's clutter breaks into the ordered open space of **Gramercy Park**, a former swamp reclaimed in 1831 that is one of the city's best squares, its centre tidily planted and, most noticeably, completely empty for much of the day – principally because the only people who can gain access are those rich enough to live here.

Broadway and Fifth Avenue meet at **Madison Square**, by day a maelstrom of dodging cars and cabs, but possessing a monumentality and neat seclusion that Union Square has long since lost. Most notable among the grand structures that surround it is the **Flatiron Building**, set cheekily on a triangular plot of land on the square's southern side, the city's first true skyscraper, hung on a steel frame in 1902 with its full twenty storeys dwarfing all the other structures around. Its tapered structure creates unusual wind currents at ground level, and years ago police officers were posted to prevent men gathering to watch the wind raise the skirts of women passing on 23rd Street. The cry they gave to warn off voyeurs – "23 Skidoo!" – has passed into the language.

Further up Fifth Avenue is New York's prime **shopping territory**, home to the heavyweight department stores. Overshadowing them all is the **Empire State Building**, on what has always been a prime site. A potent symbol of New York since its completion in 1931, after just two years in the making, its 102 storeys and 1472 feet – toe to TV mast – make it the world's third tallest building; but the height is deceptive, rising in stately tiers with steady panache. Inside, its basement is an underground marbled shopping precinct, finished everywhere with delicate Deco touches. The first lift towards the top takes you to the 86th floor, summit of the building before the radio and TV mast was added. The views from the outside walkways here are as stunning as you'd expect – better than the World Trade Center because Manhattan spreads on all sides. If you're feeling brave, and can stand the queues for the small single lift, go up to the Empire State's last reachable zenith, a small cylinder at the foot of the TV mast which was added as part of a hare-brained scheme to erect a mooring post for airships – a plan subsequently abandoned after some local VIPs almost got swept away by the wind. You can't go outside and the extra sixteen storeys don't really add a great deal to the view, but you will at least have been to the top (daily 9.30am–midnight; $3.75).

East of the Empire State lies **MURRAY HILL**, a residential district formerly dominated by the crusty old financier J P Morgan and his offspring. The **Pierpoint Morgan Library**, 29 E 36th St (Tues–Sat 10.30am–5pm, Sun 1–5pm, closed Sun in July & Aug; suggested donation $3), a gracious Italian-style nest built by McKim, Mead and White in 1917, feathered with the fruits of the Morgan's magpie-ish trips to Europe, is one of New York's best small museums. Its focal points are two main rooms, access to which is along a corridor usually lined with Rembrandt prints. The first, the **West Room**, was Morgan's study, and has been left much as it was when he worked here, with a carved sixteenth-century Italian ceiling, a couple of paintings by Memling and Perugino, and, among the few items contemporary with the building, a custom-carved desk. A portrait of J P's father hangs over the fifteenth-century Florentine fireplace, and there's a portrait of J P Junior on the far wall, swathed in the academic finery of an honorary Cambridge degree conferred in 1919. Through a domed and pillared hallway lies the **East Room** or library, a sumptuous three-tiered cocoon of rare books, autograph musical manucripts and various trinkets culled from European households and churches. A changing exhibit holds original manuscripts by Mahler (the museum has the world's largest collection of his work); a Gutenburg Bible from 1455 (one of eleven surviving); and literary relics ranging from the letters of Vasari and George Washington to works by Keats and Dickens.

North up Fifth Avenue, on the corner of **42nd Street**, the Beaux Arts **New York Public Library** can be viewed on free guided tours (Mon–Sat at 11am & 2pm). Trotsky worked in the large coffered Reading Room at the back of the building on and off during his brief sojourn in New York, just prior to the 1917 Revolution, having been introduced to the place by his friend Bukharin, who was bowled over by a library you could use so late in the evening. The opening times are less impressive now, but the library still boasts one of the five largest collections of books in the world. East down 42nd Street looms the huge bulk of **Grand Central Station**, constructed around a basic iron frame but clothed with a Beaux Arts skin. You can either explore on your own or take one of the excellent free **tours** which leave from under the Kodak hoarding every Wednesday at 12.30pm. The most spectacular aspect of the building is its size, now cowed by the soaring airplane wing of the Pan Am building behind but still no less impressive in the main station **concourse** – one of the world's most imposing open spaces, 470ft long and 150ft high, the barrel-vaulted ceiling speckled like a Baroque church with a painted representation of the winter night sky, its 2500 stars shown back to front: "As God would have seen them", the painter is reputed to have remarked. It's a pity about the broad advertising hoardings, which can't help but obscure the enormous windows, but stand in the middle and you realise that Grand Central represents a time when stations were seen as appropriate dwarfing preludes to great cities.

For the best view of the concourse climb up to the catwalks which span the sixty-feet-high windows on the Vanderbilt Avenue side; then explore the terminal's more esoteric reaches. The **Oyster Bar** in the vaulted bowels of the station – one of the city's most highly regarded seafood restaurants – is cram-packed every lunchtime with the midtown office crowd. You can stand on opposite sides of any of the vaulted spaces here and hold a conversation just by whispering, an acoustic fluke that makes this the loudest place in town.

Across the street, the **Bowery Savings Bank** echoes Grand Central's grandeur, extravagantly lauding the twin shibboleths of sound investment and savings. A Roman-style basilica, the floor is paved with mosaics, each column is fashioned from a different kind of marble, and bronze bas-reliefs on the elevator doors show bank employees hard at various tasks. The more famous **Chrysler Building**, across Lexington Avenue, has equal style. This was for a short while the world's tallest building, and since the rediscovery of Art Deco a decade or so ago has become Manhattan's best loved, its car-motif friezes, jutting gargoyles and arched stainless-steel pinnacle giving the solemn midtown skyline a welcome touch of fun. Chrysler moved out some time ago, and for a while the building was left to degenerate by a company that didn't wholly appreciate its spirited silliness, but now a new owner has pledged to keep it lovingly intact. The lobby, once a car showroom, is for the moment all you can see, its opulently inlaid elevators, walls covered in African marble and murals showing aeroplanes, machines and brawny builders who worked on the tower.

East of here, beyond the deceptively modern headquarters of the **New York Daily News** – whose foyer holds blown-up prints of the paper's more memorable front pages – 42nd Street grows more tranquil. On the left, between Second and First Avenue, is the peaceful 1967 **Ford Foundation Building**, first of the city's long line of atriums and probably the best: a giant greenhouse gracefully supported by soaring granite columns and edged with two walls of offices from which workers can look down onto a subtropical garden which changes naturally with the seasons. At the far end of 42nd Street, steps lead up to **Tudor City**, which with its coats of arms, leaded glass and neat neighbourhood shops is the very picture of dowager respectability, before descending to the **United Nations** complex, which you can view by way of guided tours from the monumental General Assembly lobby (every 15min, 9.15am–4.45pm; $5.50). These take in the main conference chambers of the UN and its constituent parts, foremost of which is the General Assembly Chamber itself, expanded a few years back to accommodate up to 179 delegations; there are for the moment only 159 but the figure seems destined to grow over coming years.

The West Side: Chelsea, the Garment District and Times Square

Few visitors bother with Chelsea and the Garment District, the two areas that fill the West Side between 14th and 42nd streets. **CHELSEA** took shape in 1830 when its owner, Charles Clarke Moore, laid out his land for sale in broad lots. Enough remains to indicate Chelsea's middle-class suburban origins, though in fact the area never quite achieved the desirability it sought. Instead, Manhattan's chic residential focus leap-frogged dreary Chelsea, stuck between the ritziness of Fifth Avenue and the poverty of Hell's Kitchen, straight to the East 40s and 50s.

During the nineteenth century the area was a centre of New York's theatre district. Nothing remains of that now, but the hotel which put up all the actors, writers and bohemian hangers-on – the **Chelsea Hotel** – remains a New York landmark. Mark Twain and Tennessee Williams lived here, Brendan Behan and Dylan Thomas staggered in and out during their New York visits, and in 1951 Jack Kerouac, armed with a customised typewriter (and a lot of Benzedrine) typed the first draft of *On the Road* non-stop onto a 120ft roll of paper. In the 1960s Andy Warhol and his doomed protégé Edie Sedgwick holed up here and made the film *Chelsea Girls* in (sort of) homage; and most recently Sid Vicious stabbed Nancy Spungen to death in their suite, a few months before his own pathetic life ended with an overdose of heroin. With a pedigree like this it's easy to forget the hotel itself, which has a down-at-heel Edwardian grandeur all of its own. A few streets north, Sixth Avenue collides with Broadway at **Greeley Square**, an overblown name for what is a trashy triangle celebrating Horace Greeley, founder of the *Tribune* newspaper, known for his rallying call to the youth of the nineteenth century to explore the continent ("Go West, young man!") and support for women's and trade union rights. His paper no longer exists and the square named after him is one of those bits of Manhattan that looks ready to disintegrate at any moment. Across the way is **Macy's**, the all-American superstore and self-proclaimed largest department store in the world, with some two million square feet of floor space and around $5 million turnover a day.

In a way this part of Broadway is the shopfront to the **GARMENT DISTRICT**, a loosely defined patch between 34th and 42nd streets and Sixth and Eighth avenues that produces around three-quarters of all the women's and children's clothes in America, though you'd never believe it: outlets are strictly wholesale with no need to woo customers, and the only clues to the industry inside are the racks of clothes shunted around on the street and occasional skips of offcuts. The dominant landmark is the **Pennsylvania Station** and **Madison Square Garden** complex, a combined box and drum structure that swallows up millions of commuters in its train station below and accommodates the *Knicks* basketball and *Rangers* hockey teams up top. The original Penn Station, demolished to make way for this, is now hailed as a lost masterpiece. One of McKim, Mead and White's greatest designs, it reworked the ideas of the Roman Baths of Caracalla to awesome effect: "Through it one entered the city like a god . . . . One scuttles in now like a rat" mourned an observer. Immediately behind Penn Station the **General Post Office** is a McKim, Mead and White structure that survived, a relic from an era when municipal pride was all about making statements. The old joke is that it had to be this big to fit in the sonorous inscription above the columns – "Neither snow nor rain nor heat nor gloom of night stays these couriers from the swift completion of their appointed rounds" – a claim about as believable as the official one that the Manhattan postal district handles more mail than Britain, France and Belgium combined.

Further up, the **Port Authority Terminal Building** at 40th Street and Eighth Avenue is another sink for the area, a Dantesque version of a British concrete-and-glass bus station that is an appropriate signal for the squalid stretch of **42nd Street** beyond, a strip of prostitution and petty vice you'll do better to skip altogether – something which also goes for much of Eighth Avenue north of 42nd. **Times Square**, beyond, was in its excess and brashness for years a distillation of the city itself, an increasingly sleazy, sometimes dangerous area that has recently undergone a massive clean-up. Almost all of the peep shows and sex shops have gone, replaced by new office blocks and safely sanitised cinemas and electrical shops. Much of the danger and a lot of the feel have gone too, but you should still be careful in the streets off the square, at least at night.

Further north, the **Equitable Center** at 757 Seventh Avenue is home to a branch of the **Whitney Museum of American Art**, displaying Roy Lichtenstein's 68ft *Mural with Blue Brush Stroke* and Thomas Hart Benton's *America Today* murals, which magnificently portray ordinary American life in the days before the Depression. Otherwise **Carnegie Hall**, an overblown and fussy warehouse-like venue for opera and concert at 154 West 57th Street, is the thing to see. Tchaikovsky conducted the programme on opening night and Mahler, Rachmaninov, Toscanini, Frank Sinatra and Judy Garland played here; and although it's dropped down a league since the Lincoln Center opened, the superb acoustics still ensure full houses most of the year. Tours are held on Tuesdays and Thursdays at 11.30am, 2pm and 3pm ($6).

A block east, **Sixth Avenue** is properly named "Avenue of the Americas", though no New Yorker ever calls it this and the only manifestation of the tag are lamppost flags of Central and South American countries. If nothing else Sixth's distinction is its width, a result of the Elevated Railway that once ran along here, now replaced by the Sixth Avenue subway. In its day the Sixth Avenue "El" marked the borderline between respectability to the east and dodgier areas to the west, and it still separates the glamorous strips of Fifth, Madison and Park avenues and the less salubrious western districts. One odd quirky corner is **Diamond Row** on West 47th Street, between Fifth and Sixth avenues, a short strip of shops chockful of expensive stones and jewellery, managed by ultra-Orthodox Hasidic Jews who seem only to exist in the confines of the street. Further up, Sixth Avenue is solidly corporate, especially between 47th and 50th streets, where the towers of **Rockefeller Center Extension** don't have the romance of their predecessor (see below) but do possess some of its monumentality – although across the avenue at 49th Street, the **Radio City Music Hall** has greater rewards, the last word in 1930s luxury. The staircase is regally resplendent with the world's largest chandeliers, the murals from the men's toilets are now in the Museum of Modern Art and the huge auditorium looks like an extravagant scalloped shell or a vast sunset; "Art Deco's true shrine" as the architecture critic Paul Goldberger called it. To explore, take a tour from the lobby (Mon–Sat 10.15am–4.45pm, Sun 11.15am–4.45pm; $7).

Fifth Avenue and East: 42nd Street to Central Park

Fifth Avenue bowls ahead from 42nd Street with all the confidence of the material world. It's been a great strip for as long as New York has been a great city, and its name is an automatic image of wealth and opulence. Here that image is very real: all that considers itself suave and cosmopolitan ends up on Fifth Avenue, and the shops showcase New York's most opulent and conspicuous consumerism. That the shopping is beyond the means of most people needn't put you off, for Fifth Avenue has some of the city's best architecture; the boutiques and stores are just the icing on the cake.

At the heart of Fifth Avenue's glamour, the **Rockefeller Center**, built between 1932 and 1940 by John D Rockefeller, son of the oil magnate, is one of the finest pieces of urban planning anywhere: office space with cafes, a theatre, underground concourses and rooftop gardens work together with an intelligence and grace rare in any building then or now. It's a combination that shows every other city-centre shopping mall the way, leaving you thinking that Cyril Connolly's snide description – "that sinister Stonehenge of Economic Man" – was way off the mark. The **GE Building** here rises 850 feet, its monumental lines matching the scale of Manhattan itself, though softened by symmetrical setbacks to prevent an overpowering expanse of wall. Down below, the **Lower Plaza** holds a sunken restaurant in the summer months, linked visually to the downward flow of the building by Paul Manship's sparkling *Prometheus*; in winter it becomes an ice rink, giving skaters a chance to show off their skills to passing shoppers. Inside is no less impressive, with José Maria Sert's murals, *American Progress* and *Time*, a little faded but eagerly in tune with the Thirties' Deco ambience – presumably more so than the original paintings by Diego Rivera, which were removed by John D's son Nelson when the artist refused to scrap a panel glorifying Lenin. A leaflet available from the lobby desk details a **self-guided tour** of the center, and while you can't reach the building's summit, a cocktail in the *Rainbow Room* restaurant on the 65th floor gives you Manhattan's best skyscraper view, especially at night. Among the many offices in the GE Building are the **NBC Studios** (one-hour tours leave regularly, Mon–Sat 9.30am–4.30pm, reservations in the foyer; $7.25). If you're a TV freak, pick up a (free) ticket for a **show recording** from the mezzanine lobby, Room 48 or out on the street. The most popular tickets evaporate before 9am.

Almost opposite the Rockefeller Center, **St Patrick's Cathedral**, designed by James Renwick and completed in 1888, seems the result of a painstaking academic tour of the Gothic cathedrals of Europe – perfect in detail, but lifeless in spirit, with a sterility made all the more striking by the glass-black **Olympic Tower** next door, whose exclusive apartments house Jackie Onassis when she's in town. Further up, the **Trump Tower** at 57th Street is the last word in Fifth Avenue opulence, with an outrageously over-the-top atrium that is just short of repellent – perhaps in tune with those who frequent its glamorous designer shops. Perfumed air, polished marble panelling and a five-storey waterfall are calculated to knock you senseless with expensive good taste. But the building is clever, a neat little outdoor garden is squeezed high in a corner, and each of the 230 apartments above the atrium gets views in three directions.

Just off Fifth Avenue, at 1 East 53rd Street, the **Museum of Television and Radio** (Tues, Wed & Fri–Sun noon–6pm, Thurs noon–8pm; suggested $5) is an archive of American TV and radio broadcasts, whose excellent card reference system allows you to trace 1950s comedies, old newsreels and other oddities. Beyond, **Madison Avenue** shadows Fifth Avenue with some of its sweep but less of the excitement. The **AT&T Building**, between 55th and 56th streets, is a Johnson-Burgee collaboration that follows the Post-Modernist theory of eclectic borrowing from historical styles with its Chippendale top and Renaissance base. Inside, the **Infoquest Center** (Wed–Sun 10am–6pm, Tues 10am–9pm; free) is an AT&T-sponsored hands-on museum of modern science, covering computers, holograms and videos, as well as the future.

The next big avenue east, **Park Avenue**, was described in 1929 as the place "where wealth is so swollen that it almost bursts". Things haven't changed much: corporate headquarters jostle for prominence in a triumphal procession to capitalism, pushed apart by Park's broad avenue. It's one of the city's most awesome sights, everything progressing to the high altar of the delicate, energetic **New York Central Building** (now the Helmsley Building), with its lewdly excessive Rococo lobby. In its day it formed a skilled punctuation mark to the avenue, but its thunder was stolen in 1963 by the **Pan Am Building** that looms behind. Headquarters of the (now defunct) airline, the profile is meant to suggest an aircraft wing, and the blue-grey mass certainly adds drama to the cityscape, but it unquestionably robs Park Avenue of the views south it deserves, sealing 44th Street and drawing much of the vigour from the buildings all about. Another black mark was the rooftop helipad, closed in the 1970s after a helicopter undercarriage collapsed shortly after landing, causing a rotor to sheer off and kill four people who had just got off, as well as injuring several people on the ground.

Wherever you placed it, the solid mass of the **Waldorf Astoria Hotel** (between 49th and 50th) would hold its own, a resplendent statement of Art Deco elegance. Crouching behind, the contrasting **St Bartholomew's Church** is a low-slung Byzantine hybrid that adds immeasurably to the street, giving the lumbering skyscrapers a much-needed sense of scale. The spikey-topped **General Electric Building** behind seems like a wild extension of the church, its slender shaft rising to a meshed crown of abstract sparks and lightning strokes that symbolises the radio waves used by its original occupier, RCA. The lobby (entrance at 570 Lexington) is yet another Deco delight. Amongst all this it's difficult at first to see the originality of the **Seagram Building** between 52nd and 53rd streets. Designed by Mies Van der Rohe with Philip Johnson and built in 1958, this was the seminal curtain-wall skyscraper, the floors supported internally, allowing a skin of smoky glass and whisky-bronze metal (Seagram are distillers), now weathered to a dull black. Every interior detail down to the fixtures and lettering on the mailboxes was specially designed. It was the supreme example of Modernist reason, deceptively simple and cleverly detailed, and its opening caused a wave of approval. The plaza, an open forecourt designed to set the building apart from its neighbours and display it to advantage, was such a success as a public space that the city revised the zoning laws to encourage other high-rise builders to supply plazas – the result being the windswept anti-people places now found all over Manhattan. A block east, the chisel-topped **Citicorp Center** on **Lexington Avenue** (between 53rd and 54th streets) was finished in 1979 and is now one of Manhattan's most conspicuous landmarks. The slanted roof was designed to house solar panels and provide power, but the idea was ahead of the technology and Citicorp had to content themselves with adopting the distinctive top as a corporate logo.

The Museum of Modern Art

11 W 53rd St. Subway #E or #F to Fifth Ave–53rd St. Fri–Tues 11am–6pm, Thurs 11am–9pm. $7, students $4,Thurs 5–9pm pay what you wish.

Instigated in 1929, moved to its present permanent home ten years later, and in the mid-1980s extensively updated in a steel pipe and glass renovation that doubled its gallery space, **The Museum of Modern Art** (MoMA) offers probably the finest and most complete account of late nineteenth- and twentieth-century art you're likely to find. It covers every medium – illustration and design, architecture and photography – but focuses primarily on painting and sculpture, divided between pre-war work on the first floor, and post-war stuff on the second.

The first-floor galleries kick off with the Impressionists. Cézanne's 1885 *Bather* leads on to Gauguin, Seurat, and, most famously, Van Gogh, represented by *Starry Night*. In the third room are paintings by the Belgian James Ensor, Redon and Bonnard. Then come galleries of works by the major Cubist painters, including Picasso and Braque. The most notable is Picasso's *Demoiselles d'Avignon of 1907*, a revolutionary clash of tones and planes said to be the heralder (and initial arbiter) of Cubist principles. A room off to the left holds Monet's *Water Lilies,* stirring attempts to abstract colour and form. Later rooms encapsulate entire periods and movements: there are paintings by Chagall; Kirchner's *Dresden* and *Berlin* street scenes dominate a gallery devoted to the glaring realities of the German Expressionists; the whirring abstractions of Boccioni are the mainstay of another, devoted to the Futurists' paeans to the industrial age; and a further room takes in the work of De Stijl, principally Mondrian, following the artist's development from early limp Cubist pieces to later works like *Broadway Boogie Woogie*. Beyond here Matisse has a large room to himself, centring on the *Dancers* of 1909, and then come paintings by Klee, swirling canvases by Kandinsky, and late works by Braque and Picasso. In contrast, a room on, are the brooding skies of de Chirico, a room containing works by Miro, and a handful of dreamlike paintings by Dali, Magritte and Delvaux.

The second Painting and Sculpture gallery continues chronologically, perhaps inevitably with a more American slant, taking in the gloomy canvases of Edward Hopper, and work by the artists of the New York School – Pollock and de Kooning – along with the more ordered efforts of Rothko and Barnett Newman and the later works of Matisse – mainly paper cutouts, most striking the bold blue shapes of his *Swimming Pool* which the ageing artist made to decorate the walls of his apartment in Nice. Pop Art pieces include Jasper Johns' *Flag*, and works by Robert Rauschenberg and Claes Oldenburg.

Upper Manhattan

UPPER MANHATTAN begins above 57th Street, where the prosperity of Midtown gives way abruptly to the smug domesticity of the Upper East and West sides. People come to **Central Park** in between, the city's back garden, to play, jog, and, in summer, to escape midtown's crowds in a particularly intelligent piece of urban landscaping.

The **Upper East Side** is at its most opulent in the mansions of **Fifth** and **Madison avenues**, today taken over by the Metropolitan and other great museums of "Museum Mile". **The Upper West Side** is less refined, though the Lincoln Center here hosts New York's most prestigious arts performances. It is again predominantly residential, well heeled on its southern fringe, especially along stretches of Columbus Avenue, but less so as you move north to its top end, marked at the edge by the monolithic Cathedral of St John the Divine and the precincts of Columbia University – the last gasp of Manhattan's wealth which is creeping ever further into the streets of **Harlem**. Further north is the city's least expected museum, the medieval arts collection of **The Cloisters**.

Central Park

"All radiant in the magic atmosphere of art and taste." So enthused *Harper's* magazine on the opening of **Central Park** in 1876, and though it's hard to be quite so jubilant about the place today, few New Yorkers could imagine life without it. Whether you're into jogging, baseball, boating, botany or just plain walking, or even if you rarely go near the place, there's no question that Central Park is what makes New York a just-about-bearable place to live.

The poet and newspaper editor William Cullen Bryant had the idea for an open public space back in 1844, and spent seven years trying to persuade City Hall to carry it out, while developers leaned heavily on the authorities not to give up any valuable land. Eventually 840 desolate and swampy acres north of the city limits, then occupied by a shantytown of squatters, were set aside. The two architects commissioned to design the landscape, Frederick Olmsted and Calvert Vaux, planned to create a rural paradise, a complete illusion of the countryside bang in the heart of Manhattan, which even then was growing at a fantastic rate. Today, in spite of the advent of motorised traffic, the sense of disorderly nature Olmsted and Vaux intended largely survives, although the skyline has changed greatly and much of the open space has been turned into asphalted playground. Lately, too, the success of Central Park has been its downfall, for as the crowds have become thicker, so the park has become more difficult to keep up to scratch; its lawns have become muddied, the gardens weary-looking and patchy, and the quieter reaches, which the architects imagined a haven of peace and solitude, sites of muggings and attacks. To their credit, the authorities have since 1980 mounted a determined assault on all these evils, renovating large portions, upping the park's policing, and greenifying it at the expense of softball pitches and basketball nets. But it will be some time before Central Park is looking anything like its best.

Much the best way to explore is to rent a **bicycle** (roughly $3 an hour) from either the *Loeb Boathouse* or *Metro Bicycles* (Lexington at 88th Street). **On foot**, there's little chance of getting lost, but to know exactly where you are, find the nearest lamppost: the first two figures signify the number of the nearest street. After dark it's illegal to enter on foot. If you want to see the buildings of Central Park West lit up, à la Woody Allen's *Manhattan*, fork out for a **carriage ride**, as hawked along Central Park South, between Fifth and Sixth avenues – though they cost around $25 per half-hour.

Most things of interest lie in the southern reaches of the park. Near Grand Army Plaza is Central Park **Zoo**, which tries to keep caging to a minimum and the animals as close to the viewer as possible (April–Oct Mon–Fri 10am–5pm, Sat & Sun 10am–5.30pm; Nov–March Mon–Sun 10am–4.30pm; $1). Beyond here, the first point to head for is the **Dairy**, a ranch building originally intended to provide milk for nursing mothers and now the park's **visitor centre** (Tues–Sun 11am–4pm), giving out free leaflets and maps, selling books and putting on sporadic exhibitions. Nearby, the **Wollman Rink** is a lovely place to skate (Mon 9am–5pm, Tues–Thurs 10am–9.30pm, Fri–Sun 10am–11pm; $5 plus $2.50 for skates) in winter. The most obvious route onwards is north up the formal **Mall** to the **Bandshell**, and the terrace and sculpted birds and animals of the **Bethesda Fountain**. To your left, **Cherry Hill Fountain** once provided a turnaround point for carriages, and has deliberately excellent views of the **Lake**, which sprawls across the heart of Central Park. You rent **boats** from the **Loeb Boathouse** on the eastern bank (April–Oct daily 9am–6pm; $20 deposit, $6 per hour); or cross the water by the elegant cast-iron **Bow Bridge** and delve into the wild woods of **The Ramble**, on the far side of which **Belvedere Castle** is a mock citadel giving views over the northern half of the park and mounting small exhibitions.

The Metropolitan Museum of Art

Fifth Ave at 82nd St (Tues–Thurs & Sun 9.30am–5.15pm, Fri & Sat 9.30am–8.45pm; suggested donation $6, $3 for students, includes admission to the Cloisters on same day).

Jutting into the park from the east, the "Met" takes in over three-and-a-half-million works of art, spanning not just America and Europe but also China, Africa, the Far East, and the Classical and Islamic worlds. You could spend days in here and still not see everything, but if you're just making one visit, head first for the **European Painting** galleries. Of the **early Flemish and Netherlandish paintings**, the best are by Jan van Eyck, who is generally attributed with beginning the tradition of North European realism, and Rogier van der Weyden, whose *Christ Appearing to His Mother* is one of his most beautiful works. Later canvases include Brueghel's *Harvesters*, one of the Met's most reproduced pictures, and part of the series of twelve paintings that included his familiar Christmas-card *Hunters in the Snow*. Cutting left at this point brings you to the Spanish paintings and the very different landscape of El Greco's extraordinary *View of Toledo*, and Velazquez's *Portrait of Juan de Parej* – "All the rest are art, this alone is truth," remarked a critic of this sombre portrait when it was first exhibited. The **Italian Renaissance** is less spectacularly represented but a worthy selection includes an early *Madonna and Child Enthroned with Saints* by Raphael, a late Botticelli and Fra Filippo Lippi's *Madonna and Child Enthroned with Two Angels*. The culmination of the European Galleries is the **Dutch paintings** section, dominated by the major works of Rembrandt, Vermeer and Hals. Vermeer, genius of the domestic interior, is represented by five works, most haunting of which is the great *Portrait of a Young Woman*, and there are some fine portraits by Rembrandt – a beautiful painting of his common-law wife, *Hendrike Stoffels*, painted three years before her early death, and a superb *Self-Portrait* from 1660, the year he was declared bankrupt.

The **André Meyer galleries** house a startling array of **Impressionist and Post-Impressionist** art, beginning with Edouard Manet, the movement's most influential precursor, and his striking *Woman with a Parrot*. The prolific Monet is represented by his *Rouen Cathedral*, the *Houses of Parliament from the Thames* and *Poplars* – in which you can detect the beginnings of his final phase of near-Abstract Impressionism. Courbet and Degas are also well represented – Courbet especially, including *Young Ladies from the Village*, a virtual manifesto of his idea of realism, and his own superbly erotic *Woman with a Parrot*. Also here is a vaguely macabre casting of Degas' *Little Dancer*, complete with real tutu, bodice and shoes.

Tacked on to the rear of the Met in 1975 to house the collection of banker Robert Lehman, the **Lehman Pavilion** fills the gaps in the Met's **Italian Renaissance** paintings, most notably with a small Botticelli *Annunciation* and a sculptural *Madonna and Child* by Giovanni Bellini. There are also works from the **Northern Renaissance**, notably Hans Holbein the Younger's *Portrait of Erasmus of Rotterdam* and Rembrandt's *Portrait of Gerard de Lairesse*. By all accounts de Lairesse was disliked for his luxurious tastes and unpleasant character, but mainly for his face, which had been ravaged by congenital syphilis. The nineteenth-century painter Suzanne Valadon is largely ignored today, and is best known as a model for Toulouse-Lautrec, Renoir and Degas. The boldly coloured canvasses here, such as *Reclining Nude*, show her originality and influence on her son, Utrillo, whom she taught to paint as an attempt to wean him off drink and drugs. Utrillo's *Rue Ravignon* stands besides his mother's painting.

Housed over two floors in the **Lila Acheson Wallace Wing**, the Met's compact **twentieth-century collection** features paintings such as Picasso's *Portrait of Gertrude Stein* alongside works by Klee, Matisse, Braque and Klimt, and post-war pieces such as Pollock's masterly *Autumn Rhythm (Number 30)*, Thomas Hart Benton's rural idyll of *July Hay*, RB Kitaj's *John Ford on His Deathbed*, and Andy Warhol's final *Self-Portrait*, along with works by Max Beckmann, Roy Lichtenstein and Gilbert and George.

The **American Wing**, in the northwest corner of the Met, is virtually a museum in its own right, with furnished historical rooms, starting with the Early Colonial period and the Hart room of around 1674, and ending with Frank Lloyd Wright's *Room from the Little House, Minneapolis*, originally windowed on all four sides, in key with Wright's concept of minimising interior–exterior division. **American paintings** include the nine-teenth-century canvases of William Sidney Mount, who depicted genre scenes on his native Long Island, and the landscape artists of the Hudson Valley School – Thomas Cole and his pupil Frederick Church. Winslow Homer is allowed a gallery to himself – fittingly for a painter who was a great influence on the late nineteenth-century artistic scene in America – while later rooms bring the Met's American art into the twentieth century with work by Thomas Eakin, William Merritt Chase, and John Singer Sargent, whose *Portrait of Madam X* was one of the most famous pictures of its day, exhibited at the 1884 Paris salon, and considered so improper that Sargent had to leave the city.

The Met's **Medieval Galleries** are no less exhaustive, with displays of sumptuous Byzantine metalwork and jewellery donated by J P Morgan and a main sculpture hall piled high with religious statuary and carvings, as well as later period rooms – panelled Tudor bedrooms, florid Rococo boudoirs and salons from France, an entire Renaissance patio from Velez Blanco in Spain. The **Egyptian rooms** also have as much to see – huge statuary, smaller sculptural pieces and jewellery – although the most prominent exhibit is the **Temple of Dendur**, housed in its own huge gallery, designed to give hints and symbols of its original site on the banks of the Nile. Built by the Emperor Augustus in 15 BC as an attempt to placate a local chieftain, the temple was moved here as a gift of the Egyptian people during the construction of the Aswan High Dam – it would otherwise have been drowned.

The Upper East Side

A two-square-mile grid, scored with the great avenues of Madison, Park and Lexington, the **Upper East Side**'s defining characteristic is wealth, as you'll appreciate if you've seen any of the many Woody Allen movies set here. **Fifth Avenue** up here has been the patrician face of Manhattan since the opening of Central Park attracted the Carnegies, Astors and Whitneys to migrate north and build fashionable residences alongside. **Grand Army Plaza**, at the junction of Central Park South and Fifth Avenue, serves as the introduction, flanked by the extended chateau of the swanky **Plaza Hotel**. Fifth Avenue's wall continues with Henry Clay Frick's house at 70th Street, marginally less ostentatious than its neighbours and now the tranquil home of the **Frick Collection** (Tues–Sat 10am–6pm, Sun 1–6pm; $3), the first of many prestigious museums in the area. The Frick is perhaps the most enjoyable of the big New York galleries, made up of the art treasures hoarded by Frick during his years as probably the most ruthless of New York's robber barons. The legacy of his self-aggrandisement – he spent millions on the best Europe had to offer – is as good a glimpse of the sump-tuous life enjoyed by New York's big industrialists as you'll find. The collection includes paintings by Reynolds, Hogarth, Gainsborough's *St James's Park* – "Watteau far outdone", wrote a critic at the time – and Bellini's *St Francis*, which suggests his vision of Christ by means of pervading light, a bent tree and an enraptured stare. El Greco's *St Jerome*, above the fireplace, reproachfully surveys the riches all around, and looks out to the South Hall, where hangs one of Boucher's very intimate depictions of his wife and an early Vermeer, *Officer and Laughing Girl*. In the opposite direction are the Library's British works, most notably one of Constable's Salisbury Cathedral series, and in the North hall hangs an engaging and sensitive portrait of the Comtesse de Haussonville by Ingres. But the West Gallery holds Frick's greatest prizes: two Turners, views of Cologne and Dieppe; Van Dyck's informal portraits of Frans Snyders and his wife – two paintings only reunited when Frick purchased them; and a set of piercing self-portraits by Rembrandt, along with the enigmatic *Polish Rider* (although serious doubt has recently thrown on its authenticity). A tiny room on the other side of the West Gallery houses an exquisite set of Limoges enamels, and a collection of small-scale paintings that includes a *Virgin and Child* by Jan van Eyck.

The **Guggenheim Museum**, further up Fifth Avenue past the Met at 89th Street, is probably better known for the building than its collection. This purpose-built structure, designed by Frank Lloyd Wright, caused a storm of controversy when it was unveiled in 1959. Even now, although the years have given it a certain respectability, no one seems to have quite made up their mind, as the recent furore over the extension, built behind the original building to allow a greater proportion of the collection to be shown, has demonstrated. Much of the building is still given over to temporary exhibitions, but the permanent collection includes work by Chagall, Leger, the major Cubists, and, most completely, Kandinsky. There are also a number of late nineteenth-century paintings, not least the exquisite Degas *Dancers* and other Post-Impressionists, Van Gogh's *Mountains at St Remy* and some sensitive early Picassos.

East of here, the **Whitney Museum of American Art**, 945 Madison Avenue (Tues 1–8pm, Wed–Sat 11am–5pm, Sun noon–6pm; $5, students free; free for all Tues 6–8pm), brings things up-to-date, one of the pre-eminent collections of twentieth-century American art and a superb exhibition locale that every other year mounts the Whitney biennial show of contemporary American art. When that's not on, you can view the somewhat arbitrary Highlights of the Permanent Collection, arranged by both chronology and theme. It's particularly strong on Edward Hopper: *Early Sun Morning* is typical, a bleak urban landscape. The Abstract Expressionists feature strongly too, with great works by high priests Pollock and De Kooning, leading on to Rothko and the Colour Field painters, and the later Pop Art works of Warhol, Johns and Oldenburg.

The Upper West Side

North of 59th Street, midtown Manhattan's tawdry west side becomes less commercial, fading after Lincoln Center into a residential area of mixed charms. This is the **Upper West Side**, these days one of the city's most desirable addresses, though unlike its counterpart to the east of the park a neighbourhood whose typical resident would be hard to pin down. There's no shortage of money, but it has to co-exist alongside slum areas that have been little affected by any shifts in status.

Broadway sheers north from Columbus Circle to **Lincoln Center for the Performing Arts**, a marble assembly of buildings put up in the early 1960s on the site of some of the city's worst slums. Home to the Metropolitan Opera and the New York Philharmonic, as well as a host of other smaller companies – see p.93 – this is worth seeing even if you don't catch a performance (organised **tours** leave daily on the hour 10am–5pm; $5.75). At the centre of the complex, the **Metropolitan Opera House** is a rather overdone building, but an impressive one nonetheless, with murals by Marc Chagall behind each of its high front windows. On the left, *Le Triomphe de la Musique* is cast with a variety of well-known performers, landmarks snipped from the New York skyline and a portrait of Sir Rudolph Bing, the man who ran the Met for more than three decades, garbed as a gypsy. The other mural, *Les Sources de la Musique*, is remi-niscent of Chagall's renowned Met production of *The Magic Flute*: the god of music strums a lyre while a Tree of Life, Verdi and Wagner all float down the Hudson River.

A block east from Columbus Avenue, the monumental apartment blocks of **Central Park West** have long been wealthy territory, the most famous being the **Dakota Building**, a grandiose Renaissance-style mansion built in the late nineteenth century to persuade wealthy New Yorkers that life in an apartment could be just as luxurious as in a private house. Over the years few residents have not been publicly known in some way: big-time tenants included Lauren Bacall and Leonard Bernstein, and not so long ago the building was used as the setting for Polanski's film *Rosemary's Baby*. Most people now know the building as the former home of **John Lennon** – and (still) of his wife Yoko Ono, who owns a number of the apartments. It was outside the Dakota, on the night of December 8 1980, that Lennon was murdered – shot by a man who professed to be one of his greatest admirers. Fans may want to light a stick of incense for Lennon across the road in **Strawberry Fields**, a section of Central Park which has been restored and maintained in his memory through an endowment by Yoko Ono; trees and shrubs were donated by a number of countries as a gesture towards world peace.

North up Central Park West, the often-overlooked **New York Historical Society** at 77th Street (Tues–Sun 10am–5pm; $3, Tues pay what you wish) is more a museum of American than of New York history, with a collection that includes the paintings of James Audubon, the Harlem artist and naturalist who specialised in lovingly detailed watercolours of birds, a broad sweep of nineteenth-century American portraiture (including the picture of Alexander Hamilton that found its way onto the $10 bill) and Hudson River School landscapes (among them Thomas Cole's fantastically pompous Course of Empire series), and a glittering display of Tiffany glass, providing an excellent all-round view of Louis Tiffany's attempts "to provide good art for American homes".

Two blocks away, the **American Museum of Natural History** (Mon, Tues, Thurs, Sun 10am–5.45pm, Wed, Fri, Sat 10am–9pm; suggested donation $4, Planetarium $5; free Fri & Sat) claims to be the largest museum of any kind in the world, filling four blocks with its bulk, a strange architectural mélange of heavy neoclassical and rustic Romanesque styles. It houses intelligently mounted artefacts from Asia and Africa, sandwiched between dusty dioramas of the two continents' mammals. There's a wilting array of dinosaurs, a static display of fish, and – rather better – a Hall of Meteorites with some strikingly beautiful crystals, not least the *Star of India*, the largest blue sapphire ever found. The museum's astronomy department, in the adjacent **Hayden Planetarium**, has a variety of astronomical displays and gadgetry, assorted celebrities relating an impassioned tale of space endeavour, and stages a soporifically dull history of the universe (narrator Vincent Price) in the theatre.

The Upper West Side's second best address after Central Park West is **Riverside Drive**, which weaves its way up the western fringe of Manhattan island, flanked by palatial townhouses put up in the early part of this century by those not quite rich enough to compete with the folks down on Fifth Avenue, and by **Riverside Park**, land-scaped in 1873 by Frederick Olmsted of Central Park fame. It makes the most pleasant route up to the prestigious **Columbia University**, whose campus fills seven blocks between Amsterdam and Broadway, and boasts a set of precincts laid out by McKim, Mead and White in grand Beaux Arts style. Regular guided **tours** start from the infor-mation office on the corner of 116th Street and Broadway.

On the eastern side of the Columbia precincts, the **Cathedral Church of St John the Divine** rises out of the burned-out tenements, dumped cars and hustlers of the southern fringes of Harlem with a sure, solid kind of majesty – far from finished but already one of New York's main tourist hotspots, and on the itinerary of a steady stream of coach parties throughout the season. A curious mixture of Romanesque and Gothic styles, the church was begun in 1892, but stopped with the outbreak of war in 1939 and has only resumed recently, fraught with funding difficulties and hard questioning by people who consider that the money might be better spent on something of more obvious benefit to the local community. That said, St John's is very much a community church, housing a soup kitchen and shelter for the homeless, studios for graphics and sculpture, a gymnasium, and (still to be built under the choir) an amphitheatre for the production of drama and concerts. And the building itself is being undertaken by local blacks trained by English stonemasons. Only two-thirds of the cathedral is finished, and completion isn't due until around 2050, when it will be the largest cathedral structure in the world, its floor space – at 600ft long and at the transepts 320ft wide – big enough to swallow both the cathedrals of Notre Dame and Chartres whole, or, as guides take pains to point out, two full-sized American football pitches.

Harlem, El Barrio and the North

HARLEM is the side of Manhattan that few visitors bother to see. Home of a culturally and historically – if not economically – rich **black** community, Harlem is still a focus of black activism. It has its share of racial tension – recently there have been conflicts with Korean shop-owners – and its flavour is inexorably changing with seeping gentrification from the Upper West Side. But, thanks in part to a near-total lack of federal and municipal support, it is an extremely self-reliant community, worth seeing if you can.

Harlem's **sights** are too spread out to amble between. You'll do best to make several trips, preferably getting acquainted with the area via a **guided tour** (see p.57). **125th Street** between Broadway and Fifth Avenue is its working centre, a flattened expanse spiked with the occasional skyscraper. No. 253 is the famous **Apollo Theater** – not much from the outside, but for many years the centre of black entertainment in New York and northeastern America. Almost all the great figures of jazz and blues played here; **James Brown** recorded his seminal *Live At The Apollo* album in 1962.

Close by, **Adam Clayton Powell Jr Boulevard** pushes north, a broad and busy thoroughfare named after the 1930s minister who helped to force the white-owned stores of Harlem to employ the blacks on whom their economic survival depended. Powell later became the first black on the city council, then New York's first black representative at Congress, a career which came to an embittered end in 1967, when amid strong rumours of the misuse of public funds he was excluded from Congress by majority vote. This failed to diminish his standing in Harlem, where voters twice re-elected him before his death in 1972. A block east, the **Schomburg Center for Research in Black Culture** at 515 Lenox Avenue at 135th Street (Mon–Wed 10am–8pm, Fri 10am–6pm) has thought-provoking displays on the history of black culture in the US. Just north at 132 West 138th Street, the **Abyssinian Baptist Church** was where Powell preached, and a small **museum** inside records his life (minus the scandal). The church is also famed for its revival-style Sunday morning services and a gospel choir of gut-busting vivacity. Cross over to 138th Street between Powell and Eighth Avenue, and you're in what many consider the finest, most articulate block of row houses in Manhattan – **Strivers' Row** – commissioned during the 1890s housing boom and taking in designs by three sets of architects – the best McKim, Mead and White's north side of 139th, a dignified Renaissance-derived strip that's an amalgam of simplicity and elegance. Within the burgeoning black community of the turn of the century this came to be *the* desirable place for ambitious professionals to reside; hence its nickname.

From Park Avenue to the East River is Spanish Harlem or **EL BARRIO**, dipping down as far as East 96th Street to collide head on with the affluence of the Upper East Side. The centre of a large Puerto Rican community, it is quite different from Harlem – the streets are dirtier, the atmosphere more intimidating. In the early 1950s the American government offered Puerto Ricans incentives to emigrate to the US under a policy known as "Operation Bootstrap". But the occupants have had little opportunity to evolve Latino culture in any meaningful way, and the only space where cultural roots are in evidence is **La Marqueta** on Park Avenue between 111th and 116th streets, a five-block street market of tropical produce, sinister-looking meats and much shouting, and the **Museo del Barrio** at Fifth Avenue and 104th Street (Wed–Sun 11am–5pm; suggested donation $2), a showcase of Latin American art and culture. Close by, the **Museum of the City of New York**, on the corner of 103rd St (Tues–Sat 10am–5pm, Sun 1–5pm; suggested donation $4), might also grab your interest, with a competent rundown on the history of the city from Dutch times to the present day; it also runs Sunday walking tours of various New York neighbourhoods.

North of Harlem, but easily reached from the #1 train to 157th and Broadway or the #A to 155th or 163rd, **Audubon Terrace** at 155th and Broadway is a weird, clumsy nineteenth-century complex of museums dolled up as Beaux Arts temples, the best of which is the **Museum of the American Indian** (Tues–Sat 10am–5pm, Sun 1–5pm. $3, students $2), a fascinating assembly of artefacts from almost every tribe native to the Americas. Highlights include assorted scalps, the personal knick-knacks of Sitting Bull and Geronimo, shrunken human figures from Ecuador and some amazing Inuit scrimshaw. A very reasonable museum shop sells various authentic items.

The **Morris–Jumel Mansion**, within walking distance on 160th Street between Amsterdam and Edgecombe avenues (Tues–Sun 10am–4pm; $2), is another uptown surprise, its proud Georgian outlines faced with a later Federal portico. Built as a rural retreat in 1765 by Colonel Roger Morris, it was briefly Washington's headquarters before falling into the hands of the British. Later, wealthy wine merchant Stephen Jumel bought the mansion and refurbished it for his wife Eliza, formerly a prostitute and his mistress. New York society didn't take to such a past, but when Jumel died in 1832, Eliza married ex-Vice President Aaron Burr – she for his connections, he for her money. Burr was 78 when they married, 20 years older than Eliza: the marriage lasted for six months before old Burr upped and left, to die on the day of their divorce. Eliza battled on to the age of 91, and on the top floor of the house you'll find her obituary, a magnificently fictionalised account of a "scandalous" life.

From most western stretches of Washington Heights you get a glimpse of the **George Washington Bridge** that links Manhattan to New Jersey, a dazzling concoction of metalwork and graceful lines. "Here, finally, steel architecture seems to laugh," said Le Corbusier of the 1931 construction. **The Cloisters** in Fort Tryon Park (March–Oct Tues–Sun 9.30am–5.15pm, Nov–Feb Tues–Sun 9.30am–4.45pm; suggested donation $6; $3 students, includes Metropolitan Museum on same day) – also reachable by hourly direct shuttle coach from the Met (June, July & Aug, Fri & Sat; $5) – is the handiwork of collectors George Barnard and John D Rockefeller, who spent the early years of this century shipping over all they could buy of medieval Europe. It now houses the pick of the Metropolitan Museum's medieval collection. Among its larger artefacts are a monumental Romanesque Hall made up of French remnants and a frescoed Spanish Fuentiduena Chapel, both thirteenth-century and cornering on the prettiest of the four sets of cloisters here, from St Guilhelm from thirteenth-century France. At the centre of the museum is the Cuxa cloister from a twelfth-century Benedictine monastery in the French Pyrenees, whose capitals are brilliant peasant art, carved with weird, self-devouring grotesque creatures. Among smaller sculpture, the Early Gothic Hall houses a memorably tender *Virgin and Child*, carved in England in the fourteenth century. The collection of tapestries is special, too, including the spectacular *Unicorn Tapestries*. Campin's *Merode Altarpiece*, housed in its own antechamber, depicts the Annunciation in a typical Flemish interior of the day, beyond which life goes on in a fifteenth-century market square, perhaps Campin's native Tournai. The amazing downstairs Treasury houses the *Belles Heures de Jean, Duc de Berry* – perhaps the greatest of all medieval Books of Hours, executed by the Limburg Brothers with dazzling genre miniatures of seasonal life – and the twelfth-century altar cross from Bury St Edmunds in England, a mass of tiny expressive characters from Biblical stories.

The Outer Boroughs

Most visitors to New York don't stray off Manhattan. But if you're staying a while, you might choose to investigate the so-called **Outer Boroughs**. **Brooklyn** is certainly worth a trip out, primarily for the salubrious neighbourhood of Brooklyn Heights just across the East River, the bucolic environment of Prospect Park and the Brooklyn Botanical Garden, and the Brooklyn Museum, whose collection can compete with anything on Manhattan. For inveterate nostalgics, Coney Island and its Russian neighbour, Brighton Beach, lie at the far end of the subway line. Few indeed make it to **Queens**, but it has, among other attractions the bustling Greek community of Astoria and the new Museum of the Moving Image. As for for **Staten Island,** the ferry is its own justification. Even the **Bronx**, renowned for the desolate and bleak environs of its southern reaches, has the city's largest **zoo** and another glorious **botanical garden**.

Brooklyn

If it were still a separate city, **BROOKLYN** would be the fourth largest in the US, but until as recently as the early 1800s it was no more than a group of autonomous towns and villages distinct from the already thriving Manhattan. Robert Fulton's steamship service across the water first changed the shape of Brooklyn, starting with the establishment of a leafy retreat at Brooklyn Heights. What really transformed things, though, was the opening of the Brooklyn Bridge. Thereafter development began to spread deeper inland, as housing was needed to service a more commercialised Manhattan. By the turn of the century, Brooklyn was fully established as part of New York City, and its fate as Manhattan's perennial kid brother was sealed.

Brooklyn Heights is now one of New York Kity's most beautiful and wealthy neighbourhoods, and as such it has little in common with the rest of the borough, a peaceful, tree-lined enclave originally settled by financiers from Wall Street across the water and today still very exclusive. There isn't much to see as you wander its perfectly preserved terraces and breathe in the air of civilised calm, though students of urban architecture could have a field day. The most obvious place to begin a tour is the so-called **Esplanade**, with its fine views of Lower Manhattan across the water, east of which **Pierrepoint and Montague** streets are the Heights' main arteries, studded with delightful – and fantastic – brownstones.

Further into Brooklyn, Flatbush Avenue leads up to **Grand Army Plaza**, a grandiose junction laid out by Calvert and Vaux late in the nineteenth century as a dramatic approach to their new Prospect Park just behind. The triumphal **Soldiers and Sailors' Memorial Arch** was added thirty years later, topped with a fiery sculpture of Victory in tribute to the triumph of the North in the Civil War. **Prospect Park** itself was landscaped in the early 1890s, and remains for the most part remarkably bucolic – far more so than Central Park – as does the adjacent **Brooklyn Botanic Garden** (April–Sept Tues–Fri 8am–6pm, Sat & Sun 10am–4pm; Oct–March Tues–Fri 8am–4.30pm, Sat & Sun 10am–4.30pm) – one of the most enticing park spaces in the city, smaller and more immediately likeable than its more celebrated rival in the Bronx. Behind, the **Brooklyn Museum**, 220 Eastern Parkway (daily 10am–5pm, closed Mon & Tues; $4, students $2), though doomed to stand perpetually in the shadow of the Met, is a major museum, and a good reason in itself for forsaking Manhattan for an afternoon, although its five floors of miscellaneous artefacts demand considerable selectivity. Highlights, depending on your personal interests, include the ethnographic department on the ground floor, with arts and applied arts from Oceania and the Americas, the Classical and Egyptian antiquities on the second floor, and the evocative American Period Rooms on the fourth floor. Be sure, too, to look in on the American and European Picture Galleries on the top storey, which have lots of eighteenth-century portraits, including one of George Washington by Gilbert Stuart; bucolic canvases by William Sidney Mount, alongside the heavily romantic paintings of the Hudson River School; and paintings by Eastman Johnson and John Singer Sargent, especially Johnson's curious *Not at Home*, leading up to twentieth-century work by Charles Sheeler and Georgia O'Keeffe. European artists featured include Degas, Cézanne, Toulouse-Lautrec, Monet, and Dufy. The gift shop sells genuine ethnic items from around the world at reasonable prices.

One of Brooklyn's furthest points, **Coney Island**, reachable direct from Manhattan on the B, D, F or N subway lines, was for years where generations of working-class New Yorkers came to relax, at its height visited by 100,000 people a day. Now, however, it's one of the city's poorest districts: the amusement park is peeling and rundown, and until recently the boardwalk was cracked and broken – although if you like rundown seaside resorts there's no better place on earth. The beach at least is beautiful, a broad swathe of golden sand, and it's not difficult to see what once made people come here. The **New York Aquarium** on the boardwalk (daily 10am–4.45pm; summer weekends 10am–5.45pm; $4.75) first opened in 1896 and is still going strong, displaying fish and invertebrates from the world over in its darkened halls, along with frequent open-air shows of marine mammals.

Further along, **Brighton Beach**, or "Little Odessa", is home to the country's largest community of Russian emigrés, around 20,000 in all, who arrived in the 1970s following a relaxation of immigration restrictions on Soviet citizens. There's also a long-established and now largely elderly Jewish population. It's livelier than Coney Island, and more prosperous, especially along its main drag, **Brighton Beach Avenue**, which runs underneath the El in a hotchpotch of food shops and appetising restaurants.

The Bronx

Everyone's got a horror story to tell about the **BRONX**. In reality, though, as long as you avoid its seriously decayed southern reaches, it's not much different to any other New York borough, and has proved less vulnerable to the racial tensions that have surfaced in other parts of the city during the Eighties. The borough developed – and has since declined – more quickly than any other part of the city. First settled in the seventeenth century by the Swedish Jonas Bronk, like Brooklyn it only became part of the city proper at the turn of the last century. From 1900 onwards things moved fast, and the Bronx became one of the most sought-after parts of the city in which to live, its main thoroughfare, **Grand Concourse**, becoming edged with increasingly luxurious Art Deco apartment blocks – many of which, though greatly rundown, still stand.

The **Bronx Zoo** (Mon–Sat 10am–5pm, Sun 10am–5.30pm; Fri–Mon $4.75, otherwise a donation) is accessible either by its main gate on Fordham Road or by a second entrance on Bronx Park South. This last is the entrance to use if you come directly here by subway (to East Tremont Avenue). Even if you don't like zoos, the largest urban zoo in the US is better than most, and one of the first to realise that animals both looked and felt better out in the open. Its Wild Asia exhibit is an almost forty-acre wilderness through which tigers, elephants and deer roam relatively freely, viewable from a monorail train (May–Oct; $1.25). Look in also on the World of Darkness, which holds nocturnal species, and the simulation of a Himalayan mountain area, with endangered species like the giant panda and snow leopard. Across the road from the zoo's main entrance is the back turnstile of the **New York Botanical Gardens** (Tues–Sun 10am–5pm, last admission 4pm) which in parts is as wild as anything you're likely to see upstate. Leave the gardens by their main entrance and walk west to Grand Concourse and the **Poe Cottage** (Wed–Fri 9am–5pm, Sat 10am–4pm, Sun 1pm–5pm; $1), a tiny white clapboard shack that was Edgar Allan Poe's home for the last three, unhappy years of his life, which saw his wife's death and very little writing beyond the short, touching poem, *Annabel Lee*. Poe left the cottage for the last time in 1849 to secure backing for his long-running dream – his own literary magazine – but got entangled in the election furore in Baltimore, disappeared, and was eventually found delirious in the street, dying in hospital a few days later. What actually happened no one knows, and the house, with its few meagre furnishings spread thinly through half a dozen rooms, tells you little more about the man.

Queens

Of New York City's four outer boroughs, **QUEENS**, named after the wife of Charles II, is the most consistently ignored. Though considerably more accessible than Staten Island, a great deal larger than Brooklyn, and immeasurably safer than the Bronx, it is simply not seen as a desirable place to live. People who live in Queens, the thinking seems to run, are either excruciatingly dull or just can't afford to live anywhere else.

Which belittles its role as one of the rare places where post-war immigrants could buy their own homes and establish their own communities. **Astoria**, for example, holds the largest concentration of Greeks outside Greece itself (Melbourne included). It has a long **film-making** tradition: *Paramount* had their studios here until they were lured away by Hollywood's reliable weather. Astoria was left empty and disused by all except the US Army, until Hollywood's stranglehold on the industry finally weakened. The new studios here – not open to the public – now rank as the country's fourth largest and are set for a major expansion. The **Museum of the Moving Image** in the old Paramount complex at 34–31 35th Street (Tues–Fri noon–4pm, Sat & Sun noon–6pm; $5) is devoted to the history of film, video and TV. Along with posters and kitsch movie souvenirs from the Thirties and Forties, you can listen in on directors explaining sequences from famous movies; watch fun short films made up of well-known clips; add your own sound effects to movies; and view original sets and costumes. A wonderful, mock-Egyptian pastiche of a 1920s movie theatre is used for showings kids' movies and TV classics.

If you're really keen on exploring Queens, the **Queens Museum**, at Flushing Meadows-Corona Park (Tues–Sat 10am–5pm, Sun noon–5.30pm; $2), is another possible target. Its one permanent item is an 18,000-square-foot model of the five boroughs of New York City, spectacularly lit, constantly updated and originally conceived for the 1964 World's Fair by Robert Moses. Great fun if you know the city well, and useful orientation if you don't. Take the subway #7 to Willets Point–Shea Stadium.

Staten Island

Until about 25 years ago **STATEN ISLAND** (officially Richmond County) was isolated – getting to it meant a ferry trip or long ride through New Jersey, and commuting into town was almost an eccentricity. In 1964 the opening of the Verrazano Narrows Bridge changed things; upwardly mobile Brooklynites found cheap property on the island and swarmed over the bridge to buy their parcel of suburbia. Today Staten Island has swollen to accommodate tightly packed residential neighbourhoods amid the rambling greenery, endless backwaters of neat look-don't-touch homes.

The **Staten Island Ferry** sails around the clock with half-hourly departures between 9.30am and 4pm, and is famed as New York's best bargain, giving great wide-angled views of the city for just 50¢ return. The ferry terminal quickly dispels any romance, but it's easy enough to escape to the adjoining bus station and catch the #74 bus to the **Jacques Marchais Center of Tibetan Art** at 338 Lighthouse Avenue (May–Sept Wed–Sun 1pm–5pm; April, Oct, Nov, Fri–Sun 1pm–5pm; $2.50). Jacques Marchais was the alias of Jacqueline Kleber, a New York art dealer who reckoned she'd get on better with a French name. She did, and used her wealth to indulge a passion for Tibetan art, assembling the largest collection in the Western world and reproducing a Buddhist temple on the hillside to house it. Even if you know nothing about such things the exhibition is small enough to be accessible, with magnificent bronze Bodhisattvas, fearsome deities in union with each other, musical instruments, costumes and decorations from Tibet. During the first or second week of October it hosts a **harvest festival**: Tibetan monks in saffron robes perform the traditional ceremonies, and Tibetan food and crafts are sold.

Accommodation

Prices for **accommodation** in New York are well above the norm for the US as a whole; a decent $50 hotel room should be regarded as extraordinarily good value, and **budget** hotels and motels barely exist. If you're just here for a few days, you may well be away from your lodgings for all your waking hours, anyway, so spending $100 on a bed doesn't make all that much sense. On the other hand, there is of course a lot of high-standard accommodation available, and if you pay that bit more you can stay in a much more central location. Getting yourself a room with a **TV** is also a definite plus; New York's cable stations have to be seen to be believed.

Hostels and YMCAs

Chelsea Center Hostel, 511 W 20th St (☎243-4922). Small, clean and safe downtown hostel, with prices from $16. Reservations essential in high season.

International Youth Hostel, 891 Amsterdam Ave, at 103rd St (☎932-2300). Opened in October 1989, this place has dorm beds for $19 per night, and facilities including a restaurant, travel shop and theatre. It's large (480 beds), but you should book well in advance.

Sugar Hill International House, 722 St Nicholas Ave (☎926-7030). A well-run and very friendly place with adequate if noisy dorm accommodation for just $10 a night. Way up in Harlem, opposite the 145th St subway station.

Vanderbilt YMCA, 224 E 47th St (☎755-2410). Smaller and quieter than its handy midtown Manhattan location, five minutes' from Grand Central, might suggest. Inexpensive restaurant, swimming pool, gym and laundromat. Singles $34, doubles $44.

West Side YMCA, 5 W 63rd St (☎787-4400). Well-placed for the Upper West Side, Lincoln Center and Central Park – and with a similarly impressive range of facilities. Singles $39, doubles $44.

Bed & Breakfast

Bed and breakfast – staying in a New Yorker's spare room or subletting an apartment – is an increasingly popular (and inexpensive) option. Normally arranged through an agency, such as those listed below, rates run at about $75 for a double, or $100 a night for a studio apartment. It is essential to book well in advance.

British travellers who wish to reserve their accommodation before leaving the UK can obtain excellent-value B&B double rooms from $65 per night, or studios from $90, through *Colby International*, 139 Round Hey, Liverpool L28 1RG (☎051/220-5848; or ☎1-800/927-7821 in the US).

Bed and Breakfast Network of New York, Suite 602, 134 W 32nd St, NY 10001 (☎645-8134). New and growing network with hosted singles for around $60, doubles $80–90, apartments $130.

Urban Ventures, PO Box 426, NY 10024 (☎594-5650). The first and largest B&B registry in the city. Some budget doubles from $45 upwards, but most start from about $65, apartments from $95. Minimum stay two nights.

Womyn's Bed & Breakfast (☎794-8645). Women-only rooms in central Manhattan.

Hotels

Most of New York's **hotels** are in midtown Manhattan, which is as good a location as any to stay, although you may well travel downtown for food and nightlife. **Booking ahead** is once again very strongly advised; at certain times of the year – Christmas and early summer particularly – you're likely to find everything full. Phone the hotels direct or contact a **booking services** to reserve rooms at no extra charge, such as *Meegan's* (☎718/995-9292 or ☎1-800/221-1235), or *Central Reservations* (☎1-800/356-1123).

Aberdeen, 17 W 32nd St (☎736-1600). Rather spartan rooms, in a good location just off Fifth Avenue. Doubles from $85, quads from $115.

Algonquin, 59 W 44th St (☎840-6800). New York's classic literary hangout. The decor remains little changed; the prices – at $180 for the cheapest double – are, relatively speaking, very good.

Ameritania, 230 W 54th St (☎247-5000). Just opened, and superb value at $110 per night for beautifully furnished double-bedded rooms with private bath (singles $95). Mention *Rough Guides* and this goes down to $90 per night (singles $69).

Carlton Arms, 160 E 25th St (☎679-0680). The latest bohemian dosshouse, with a characterful location, eclectic interior decor, and a clientele made up of Europeans, down-at-heel artists, etc. Doubles around $50 make it one of the city's best bargains.

Chelsea, 222 W 23rd St (☎243-3700). One of New York's most noted landmarks, both for its ageing neo-Gothic building and its bohemian past (see p.70). Still something of a haunt of musicians and arty types, though its days of notoriety are pretty much over. Indifferent doubles from $85.

Chelsea Inn, 46 W 17th St (☎645-8989). Nicely situated in the heart of Chelsea, not too far from the Village, and with double rooms for around $95.

Chelsea Pines Inn, 317 West 14th St (☎929-1023). Well-priced gay-oriented hotel housed in an old brownstone. Clean, comfortable, attractively furnished rooms for $65 a double.

Esplanade, 305 West End Ave (☎874-5000). A good choice if you want to stay in a quieter area within reach of Midtown's attractions. Doubles around $100, multibedded suites for not a lot more.

Excelsior, 45 W 81st St (☎362-9200). Upper West Side hotel in the heart of the liveliest stretch of the Columbus Avenue scene. Decently sized doubles cost around $90.

Gorham, 136th W 55th St (☎245 1800). Excellent-value Midtown hotel, handy for Central Park and with jacuzzis, cable TV and a kitchen in every room. At around $120 a double, the best bargain in the area.

Gramercy Park, 2 Lexington Ave (☎475-4320). Excellent downtown alternative, popular with Europeans. Doubles normally around $140.

Longacre House, 317 W 45th St (☎246-8580). Gay-oriented hotel in the Theatre District. Singles start at $30.

Malibu Studios, 2688 Broadway (☎633-0275). Probably the best-value budget accommodation in the city. A fair step from the heart of things up at the Morningside Heights end of the Upper West Side, but adjacent to the 103rd St stop on the #1 subway line. Prices are $35 for a single room ($50 with bath), $50 for a double ($60 with bath), and $19–24 per person for a triple.

Mansfield, 12 W 44th St (☎944-6050). The real value alternative to both the nearby *Algonquin* and the *Royalton* (see below), with doubles hovering around $85, three-person suites at $100 or so.

Milburn, 242 W 76th St (☎362-1006). Welcoming and well-situated hotel in the heart of the Upper West Side that's in the course of being renovated. A few double rooms for $80–100, one-bedroom suites (complete with kitchen) for a little over $100. Excellent value.

Morgan's, 237 Madison Ave (☎686-0300). Self-consciously – and quite successfully – one of the chicest hotels in town. Good value at around $230 for the cheapest double room.

New York Bed and Breakfast, 134 W 119th St (☎666-0559). Lovely old brownstone with nice double rooms going for just $40. The only drawback is the location, way uptown in El Barrio.

Paramount, 235 W 46th St (☎764-5500). Former budget hotel, renovated by the *Morgan's/Royalton* crew as one of the hippest places in town. Doubles cost $140–190, and all have VCR.

Pickwick Arms, 230 E 51th St (☎355-0300). For the price, one of the best deals you'll get in this part of town. Clean, reasonable doubles go for about $90.

President, 234 W 48th St (☎246-8800). Standard midtown hotel whose doubles, weighing in at $100–120 including breakfast, are excellent value.

Remington, 129 W 46th St (☎221-2600). Good-value Times Square area hotel, with nice doubles from $75.

Royalton, 44 W 44th St (☎869-4400). Owned by the same management as *Morgan's*, the *Royalton* attempts to capture the market for the discerning style person. Doubles from about $240.

Salisbury, 123 W 57th St (☎246-1300). For the location – at the very hub of the 57th Street shopping scene – not an overpriced hotel, and quite cosy too. Doubles around $120.

Southgate Tower, 371 Seventh Ave (☎563-1800). Large and atmospheric old place, specialising in suites. Double rooms start at $135, suites at $165.

Wales, 1295 Madison Ave (☎876-6000). Almost in Spanish Harlem, though very definitely Upper East Side in feel. Fairly recently refurbished elegant doubles range from about $125.

Washington Square, 103 Waverley Place (☎777-9515). One of very few truly downtown hotels, bang in the heart of Greenwich Village, and with double rooms at $90 up. Don't be deceived by the posh-looking refurbished lobby – the rooms don't quite live up to it.

Eating

There isn't anything you can't **eat** in New York. The city has more restaurants per head than anywhere else in the States, and New Yorkers not only eat out often but take their food incredibly seriously, devoting long hours of discussion to the study of different cuisines, new dishes and new restaurants – which can be welcomed with all the fervour of the Second Coming.

Certain areas are pockets of ethnic cuisine: **Chinatown** (including Vietnamese) below Canal Street; **Little Italy** just to the north; **Little India**, Sixth Street east of Bowery; **Little Brazil**, 46th Street between Fifth and Sixth Avenues. On the **Upper West Side**, quite a few places offer the unusual combination of Cuban and Chinese. In the **Outer Boroughs**, **Brooklyn** has some great West Indian and Italian cooking, not to mention its Russian restaurants; **Queens** holds large Greek and Latin American communities; while Belmont in the **Bronx** is renowned for its Italian cuisine.

Lower

Anjelica, 300 E 12th St (☎228-2909). Good-quality vegetarian with various daily specials. Cheap, too. Patronised by an artistic and fashion crowd.

Brother's Bar-B-Q, 228 W Houston St (☎727-2775). Downbeat SoHo diner serving some of the best barbecue food east of the Mississippi. Cheap too.

Café Le Figaro, 184 Bleecker St (☎677-1100). Former Beat hangout during the Fifties; the ersatz Left Bank at its finest. Good views of Bleecker Street, and excellent snacks and meals.

Caribe, 117 Perry St (☎255-9191). Loud and usually crowded Caribbean restaurant filled with a leafy jungle decor serving spicy food and wild tropical cocktails. A fun night out.

Cent' Anni, 50 Carmine St (☎989-9494). Small Village restaurant, serving delicious and well- priced Florentine food.

Cinco de Mayo, 349 W Broadway (☎226-5255). Mexican in SoHo. Authentic food, wild ambience.

Corner Bistro, 331 W Fourth St (☎242-9502). Dingy pub with cavernous cubicles and healthy servings of burgers, etc, for reasonable prices. Long-standing West Village literary haunt.

The Cupping Room Café, 359 W Broadway (☎925-2898). Quaint place, serving good wholesome food with occasional jazz and the odd tarot or palm reader. The brunches are best. Recommended.

Ed Debevic's, 661 Broadway (☎982-6000). A wacky retro diner where the staff are dressed like greasers, cheerleaders and the like, and the food is basic American fare.

El Faro, 823 Greenwich St (☎929-8210). Dark, lively Spanish restaurant. You can't go wrong with the paella or the seafood in green sauce. Moderate prices too, and you can share most main dishes.

Florent, 69 Gansevoort St (☎989-5779). Ultra-fashionable bistro on the edge of the meat-packing district that serves good French food, either à la carte or from a *prix fixe* menu ($16.95). Coffee-shop decor; excellent food and decent service; always busy. They also serve weekend brunch.

Hee Sung Feung ("HSF"), 46 Bowery (☎374-1319). Renowned dim sum restaurant.

Japonica, 90 University Place (☎243-7752). Some of the freshest sushi in the city, at very reasonable prices. Sat and Sun brunch deals are excellent at around $12 a head.

Jeremy's Alehouse, 254 Front St (☎964-3537). South Street Seaport area bar serving well-priced pint mugs of beer and excellent fish, as well as burgers.

Jerry's, 101 Prince St (☎966-9464). American-French restaurant with an upscale diner atmosphere that's one of SoHo's trendier spots. Casual and good for people-watching. Moderate prices.

John's Pizzeria, 278 Bleecker St (☎243-1680). No slices, no takeaways, but one of the city's best (thin crust) pizzas. Be prepared to queue. Another uptown branch at 408 E 64th St (☎935-2895).

Katz's, 205 E Houston St (☎254-2246). Long-established, wisecracking Lower East Side deli that serves archetypal NYC pastrami and corned beef, though it's better known these days as the scene of the faked orgasm in *When Harry Met Sally*.

Life Café, 343 E 10th St (☎477-8791). Peaceful East Village haunt right on Tompkins Square that hosts sporadic concerts. Food is sandwiches, Tex-Mex or vegetarian – around $6–8.

Little Mushroom Café, 183 W 10th (☎242-1058). Fish, pasta and omelettes at $5–12. One of the cheaper places along this stretch of the Village. Bring your own booze from the deli opposite.

Lupe's East LA Diner, 110 Sixth Ave (☎966-1326). Very laid-back, hole-in-the-wall restaurant serving great beer and burritos. Good fun, and cheap.

Nice Restaurant, 35 E Broadway (☎406-9776). Vast, packed restaurant, great for dim sum.

Royal Canadian Pancake Restaurant, 145 Hudson St (☎219 3038). Numerous kinds of vast – and delicious – pancakes, with fillings ranging from lager to white chocolate and almond to berries and bananas. A perfect, if busy venue for Sunday brunch.

Second Avenue Deli, 156 Second Ave (☎677-0606). East Village deli serving up marvellous burgers, pastrami and other goodies in ebullient, snap-happy style.

Whole Wheat'n'Wild Berries, 57 W Tenth St (☎677-3410). Gourmet health food and vegetarian specials, including fresh fish, pasta dishes, salads and homemade soups.

Yonah Schimmel's, 137 E Houston St (☎477-2858). Home-baked knishes and wonderful bagels.

Midtown

The Ballroom, 253 W 28th St (☎244-3005). Long-established Chelsea tapas bar, good both for snacks and for a full feed. Also one of the city's classiest comedy spots.

Carnegie Deli, 854 Seventh Ave (☎757-2245). The most generously stuffed sandwiches in the city.

Genroku Sushi, 365 Fifth Ave (☎947-7940). Sushi and other Japanese-Chinese food. You pick what you fancy off a moving conveyor belt.

Grigori's Gourmet à la Russe, 315 W 54th St (☎246-6341). Russian deli that's half takeout, half small cafe, open for lunch or an early dinner. Closed by 7pm.

Hourglass Tavern, 373 W 46th St (☎265-2060). Tiny Midtown French restaurant. Excellent-value two-course menu for just $11.50. When the hourglass above your table is empty, you're supposed to leave; in fact it seems to last more than an hour, and they only enforce the rule if there's a queue.

Landmark Tavern, 626 Eleventh Ave (☎757-8595). Long-established Irish bar/restaurant popular with the midtown yuppie crowd. Good food, and huge portions.

Lox Around the Clock, 676 Sixth Ave (☎691-3535). Blintzes, bagels and, of course, lox, in a trendy, noisy environment. Good for brunch. Open 24 hours.

Trattoria del'Arte, 900 Seventh Ave (☎245-9800). Airy Italian restaurant, with excellent service. Great crispy pizzas and imaginative pasta for around $15, and mouthwatering antipasto bar. Book.

Oyster Bar, Grand Central Terminal (☎490-6650). Wonderfully atmospheric old place, down in the vaulted dungeons of Grand Central, where midtown office workers break for lunch (see p.69). Clam chowder with bread is around $3 – great bowls of pan-roast oysters or clams more like $10.

Upper

All State Café, 250 W 72nd St (☎874-7883). Interesting mixture of American and French food in a popular Upper West Side hangout. Get here early to be sure of a place.

Asmara, 951 Amsterdam Ave (☎749-9614). African restaurant serving a variety of curried meat dishes, along with a few vegetarian alternatives, eaten with chapati-like *injera* bread. Very cheap.

Brother Jimmy's BBQ, 1461 First Ave (☎545-RIBS). Casual, fun barbecue restaurant whose motto is "Pig Out!" Quite a happening bar scene too.

La Caridad, 2199 Broadway (☎874-2780). Upper West Side institution, doling out plentiful and cheap Cuban-Chinese food to hungry punters. Bring your own beer, and don't expect polite service.

Carmine's, 2450 Broadway (☎362-2200). Large and loud Upper West Side restaurant that has in recent years made a name for decent home-style Southern Italian food, in mountainous portions. Groups of six or more can book; otherwise be prepared to queue for at least thirty minutes.

Dock's Oyster Bar, 2427 Broadway (☎724-5588) and 633 Third Ave (☎986-8080). Uptown restaurants with ultra-freshest seafood. The Upper West Side one is a bit homelier – both can be noisy.

Ecco-la, 1660 Third Ave (☎860-5609). Unique pasta combinations at very moderate prices make this place one of the Upper East Side's most popular Italians. If you don't mind waiting, a real find.

Flor de Mayo, 2651 Broadway (☎595-2525). Very cheap, very popular Cuban-Chinese restaurant with coffeeshop decor, though not much for vegetarians. You can eat well for around $10.

Genoa, 271 Amsterdam Ave (☎787-1094). Small and very authentic Italian restaurant. Cheap, dark and always crowded. Expect to queue for a table.

Malaga, 406 E 73rd St (☎737-7659). Intimate Spanish restaurant frequented by locals. Good, wholesome food at decent prices.

Mme Romaine de Lyon, 29 E 61st St (☎758-2422). The place for omelettes: they've got 550 on the lunch menu and dinner features an expanded non-omelette menu.

New Wave Coffee Shop, 937 Madison Ave (☎734-2467). Standard coffeeshop known as a venue for celebrities. A nice cheap option if you've just blitzed in the nearby designer clothing emporia.

Ollie's, 2315 Broadway (☎362-3712); 2957 Broadway (☎932-3300). Downscale Upper West Side Chinese cafe that serves marvellous noodles. Not, however, a place to hang about.

Pig Heaven, 1540 Second Ave (☎744-4333). Good-value Chinese restaurant decorated with images of pigs. Not surprisingly, the accent is on pork.

Poiret, 474 Columbus Ave (☎724-6880). A trendy – and reasonably inexpensive – French bistro with excellent food and outside seating in summer. A nice place for brunch too.

Rathbones, 1702 Second Ave (☎369-7361). Opposite the more famous *Elaine's*, and an excellent alternative for ordinary humans. Take a window seat, watch the stars arrive, and eat for a fraction of the price. Burgers, steak, fish for under $10.

Vince & Eddie's, 70 W 68th St (☎721-0068). Slightly pseudo-country-style restaurant serving grub like the classic American granny used to make – hearty, wholesome, and delicious.

West Side Storey, 700 Columbus Ave (☎749-1900). A wide range of American-style food, and ultra-friendly management. $8–12 for a main course.

The Outer Boroughs

Carolina, 1409 Mermaid Ave, Coney Island (☎718/714-1294). Inexpensive family-run Italian restaurant that's been around forever. Great food, great prices.

Gage & Tollner, 372 Fulton St, Brooklyn (☎718/875-5181). Old-fashioned downtown Brooklyn seafood restaurant. Not as expensive as it looks; great crab cakes.

Just Omelettes, 150 Bay St, Staten Island (☎718/273-7237). 101 varieties of omelette. Within walking distance of the ferry terminal.

Omonia Café, 32-20 Broadway, Queens (☎718/274-6650). Good Greek food at affordable prices.

Primorski, 282 Brighton Beach Ave, Brighton Beach (☎718/891-3111). Perhaps the best of the area's Russian hangouts. Huge menu of authentic Russian dishes at absurdly cheap prices.

Promenade, 101 Montague St, Brooklyn (☎237-9796). Greek diner in the heart of Brooklyn Heights with a massive menu and good lunch specials for $5–7.

Teresa's, 80 Montague St, Brooklyn (☎718/797-3996). Large portions of Polish homecooking – blintzes, pirogi and the like. Good lunchtime stopoff for those on tours of Brooklyn Heights.

Tierras Columbianas, 82-18 Roosevelt Ave, Queens (☎718/426-8868). One of the most popular of the Jackson Heights Columbians – great food (wonderful soups, and spicy meat dishes), decently priced and in large portions.

Victor's, 6909 Roosevelt Blvd, Queens (☎718/651-9474). Filipino restaurant serving up huge portions of rice, beans, chicken and beef for upwards of $6 a main course.

Drinking

New York's best **bars** are in **lower Manhattan** – Greenwich Village, the East Village and SoHo. The **midtown** places tend to be geared to an after-hours office crowd and (with a few exceptions) are pricey and rather dull; **uptown**, the Upper West Side at least, between 60th and 85th Streets along Amsterdam and Columbus avenues, has several good places to drink. Most of the bars listed below serve food of some kind.

Lower

Broome Street Bar, 363 West Broadway (☎925-2086). A popular and long-established local haunt, now more restaurant than bar, serving reasonably priced burgers and salads in a dimly lit setting. A nice place just to nurse a beer too, especially when footsore from SoHo's shops and galleries.

Cedar Tavern, 82 University Place (☎929-9089). Legendary Fifties Beat meeting point. Cosy place, with well-priced drinks and cheap food; served in summer in their covered roof garden.

Chumley's, 86 Bedford St (☎675-4449). Atmospheric former speakeasy with a good choice of beers and food from around $8. Arrive before 9pm to be sure of one of the battered tables.

Downtown Beirut, 158 First Ave (☎777-9011). Mega-sleaze East Village punk bar with music, live and recorded. Jukebox vintage 1977–79.

Fanelli, 94 Prince St (☎226-9412). SoHo's oldest bar, cosy and informal. Food from $5.

Grassroots Tavern, 20 St Mark's Place (☎475-9443). Basement bar at the centre of the East Village hum: not expensive, and with a good oldies jukebox and two dartboards.

La Jumelle, 55 Grand St (☎941-9551). Trendy, youthful, and normally very crowded SoHo bar.

McSorley's, 15 E Seventh St (☎473-9148). New York City's longest-established bar – male-only until just over a decade ago. Looks like a saloon, and serves nothing but cheap strong ale.

Sugar Reef, 93 Second Ave (☎477-8754). High-spirited East Village bar with 40 different varieties of rum and Caribbean food.

Vazac's, 108 Ave B (☎473-8840). Known as "Seven and B", on the corner of Tompkins Square. East Village hangout used as a sleazy set in films and commercials – most famously in *Crocodile Dundee*.

White Horse Tavern, 567 Hudson St (☎243-9260). Convivial, cheap Village bar where Dylan Thomas supped his last. Excellent jukebox.

Midtown

The Coffee Shop, 29 Union Square West (☎243-7969). Former coffeeshop turned trendy bar and restaurant. Vaguely Caribbean-style food in the noisy adjacent restaurant, and cheaper bar grub too.

Live Bait, 14 E 23rd St (☎353-2400). Cajun bar/restaurant run by the same people as the *Coffee Shop* (above), and popular with the after-office crowd. Not the place for a quiet drink.

Mumbles, 603 Second Ave (☎889-0750). Casual, friendly and cosy bar in which people gather to watch the seasonal sport. Mixed, neighbourhood crowd.

Murphy's, 977 Second Ave (☎751-5400). Irish bar which attracts the midtown singles set. Drinks are costly but food less so – a rare and useful standby in this part of town.

Old Town Bar and Restaurant, 45 E 18th St (☎473-8874). Atmospheric bar popular with publishing types, models and photographers from the surrounding Flatiron district.

PJ Clarke's, 915 Third Ave (☎759-1650). Legendary spit-and-sawdust alehouse with a not-so-cheap restaurant out the back. You may recognise it as the location of the film *The Lost Weekend*.

Upper

Border Café, 244 E 79th St (☎535-4347). Friendly neighbourhood hangout good for satisfying cravings for frozen margaritas. Down to earth despite its upscale location.

Buckaroo's Bar & Rotisserie, First Ave and 74th St (☎861-8844). *The* place to mingle with thirty-somethingish Upper East Siders. Fruity drinks, including jello-shots, and well-priced food.

Ruby's River Road Cafe & Bar, 1754 Second Ave (☎348-2328). Home of the famous jello-shots (shots of liquor made with different coloured jellies), and a fun bar with a Cajun cafe in the back.

Rusty's, 1271 Third Ave (☎861-4518). Small bar, good for burgers and brew, that's run by an ex Mets baseball player and is packed with sporting paraphernalia.

The Saloon, 1920 Broadway (☎874-1500). Large bar/restaurant with a vast menu. Bonuses include outside seating, and waiters serving on roller skates. Good for brunch.

Gay Men's Bars

Badlands, 388 West St (☎741-9236). One of the most popular and most enjoyable Village bars.

Marie's Crisis, 59 Grove St (☎243-9323). Well-known cabaret/piano bar popular with gay men, and featuring old-time singing sessions on Friday and Saturday nights. Often packed, always fun.

The Monster, 80 Grove St (☎924-3558). Large, campy bar with a drag cabaret, piano and video.

South Dakota, 405 Third Ave (☎684-8376). Extremely friendly, excellent food. Recommended.

The Tunnel Bar, 116 First Ave (☎777-9232). Caters to a younger, more activist gay male crowd.

Ty's, 114 Christopher St (☎741-9641). Relaxed but convivial.

Gay Women's Bars

Crazy Nanny's, 21 Seventh Avenue (☎366-6312). Yuppie-orientated, rather stylish lesbian bar.

Pandora's, 70 Grove St (☎242-1408). Formerly known as the *Grove Club*, this is a legendary lesbian dive – small, tacky and overpriced but with a devoted following.

Nightlife and Entertainment

Considering New York's everyday energy and diversity, its **music scene** can be disappointing. There is excellent **jazz**, traditional and contemporary and still concentrated in Greenwich Village, and you'll find a scattering of blues, Latin American and hip hop. But straight **rock music** is something of a write-off – at least as far as originality goes. Admission **prices** vary, but most jazz clubs have a hefty **cover** ($10–12.50) and a **minimum** charge for food and drinks; at rock venues expect to pay anything from nothing to around $15.

With **nightclubs**, New York is more in its element, although the city's clublife is an amorphous creature; the name DJs remain the same, but venues shift around and open and close according to the whims of fashion. Musically **house** holds sway at the moment – with the emphasis on the deep, vocal style that's always been popular in the city – but Latin Freestyle, dance hall reggae and rap all retain interest. The hippest time to club is during the week; only out-of-towners would dream of clubbing at weekends, when prices are in any case much more expensive. Nothing gets going much before midnight; there's no point turning up earlier. Remember, also, to take **ID** with you wherever you go: venues have latterly been obliged to be more observant of laws on entry and under-age drinking (ie under 21). If you look anything around the magic age, you may well not get in at all.

What's on listings can be found in a number of places. Perhaps the most useful general source, clear and comprehensive, is *New York Magazine*, though the *Village Voice* is better for things downtown and anything vaguely "alternative". The Sunday *New York Times Weekly Guide* is also good, especially for mainstream events: on Friday, the paper's *Weekend* section lists "ticket availability" of the major shows. Specific Broadway listings can be found in the widely available free *Official Broadway Theater Guide*.

The Big Performance Venues

Madison Square Garden, between Seventh and Eighth aves, W 31st–33rd St (☎465-6000). New York's principal large stage hosts most of the big rock acts that visit the city. Seating 20,000 people, it's not the most soulful place to see a band.

Radio City Music Hall, Sixth Ave and 50th St (☎247-4777). Not as prestigious a venue as it used to be, although the building itself still has the same sense of a great occasion.

Rock and Pop Venues

The Bottom Line, 15 W Fourth St (☎228-7880). Regular venue for established name bands. Cabaret setup, with tables crowding out any suggestion of a dance floor. $10–15.

Cat Club, 76 E 13th St (☎505-0090). Long-established club and venue with a sumptuous Art Deco interior and live bands most nights of the week. $10–15.

CBGB, 315 Bowery (☎982-4052). Deliberately sleazy, and despite a relative demise in influence still a great place to see (if not actually listen to) a band. $5–10.

Dan Lynch's, 221 Second Ave (☎677-0911). Blues and R&B bands nightly from 10pm.

Delta 88, 332 Eighth Ave (☎924-3499). Live music venue which hosts everything from Cajun to gospel to R&B. No cover Mon, Tues–Sun $5.

King Tut's Wah Wah Hut, 112 Ave A (☎254-7772). Tiny bar that's an East Village institution. Punky crowd; cover varies, though it's usually under $5.

Lone Star Cafe Roadhouse, 240 W 52nd St (☎245-2950). One of the city's better live venues, with all sorts of nightly acts, cheap drinks and good food. Entrance around $10.

Manny's Car Wash, 1558 Third Ave (☎369-2583). Smoky, Chicago-style blues bar with a small dance floor and reasonable prices. Shows from 9.15pm. Covers range from $3 to $10.

Marquee, 547 W 21 St (☎929-3257). Supposedly a sister club to its London namesake, the *Marquee* presents a mixture of blues, rock and, especially, new British bands. Admission $10–20.

Nightingale Bar, Second Ave at 13th St (☎473-9398). Blues and new wave bands nightly.

North River Bar, 145 Hudson St (☎226-9411). Down-to-earth TriBeCa bar that books regular live – mostly rock – bands. Try the shots served in test tubes.

SOB's ("Sounds of Brazil"), 204 Varick St (☎243-4940). Lively club/restaurant, with regular jazz, salsa-tinged and World Music acts. Two performances a night. $15–20.

Tramps, 54 W 21st St (☎727-7788). Blues and new wave bands almost nightly, from 9pm (weekends additional show at midnight). $10–15.

Wetlands, 161 Hudson St (☎966-4225). A self-proclaimed "ecosaloon" that books regular live bands – particularly reggae – and circulates petitions among the punters. Very Sixties. $4–10.

Jazz Venues

Angry Squire, 216 Seventh Ave (☎242-9066). Nightly jazz and solid and affordable food and drink. $5–8 cover, though no cover at all if you sit at the bar. Highly recommended.

The Blue Note, 131 W Third St (☎475-8592). Big names mainly and with high prices – but good music and atmosphere. $5 drinks minimum plus $15–45 cover per table, $10 if you sit at the bar.

Bradley's, 70 University Place (☎228-6440). Neighbourhood bar, good for catching big names jamming in unexpected combinations. $8 minimum at the tables; $5–10 cover, free Mon & Tues.

Condon's, 117 E 15th St (☎254-0960). Big-name venue. Cover $12.50, and a two-drink minimum. Although the sound is good the view is very restricted.

Fat Tuesday's, 190 Third Ave (☎533-7902). Small and atmospheric jazz venue. Prices vary according to who's on, but generally hover around the $12.50 cover, $7.50 minimum mark.

The Knitting Factory, 47 E Houston St (☎219-3055). Small, vibrant club hosting regular live jazz and avant-garde rock. Entrance $5–10.

Sweet Basil, 88 Seventh Ave (☎242-1785). Major jazz spot. $15 cover and a $6 minimum at the tables ($12 at the bar including a drink).

Village Gate, Bleecker St at Thompson (☎475-5120). One of New York's oldest jazz clubs and still one of the best. Monday salsa nights are the current highlight, well worth the $10 entrance.

Village Vanguard, 178 Seventh Ave (☎255-4037). Jazz landmark that still lays on a regular diet of big names. Admission around $10; $5 drink minimum at weekends.

Clubs and Discos

The Building, 51 W 26th St (☎576-1890). Old Con Edison powerstation with its original fittings, save for the introduction of a dance floor overlooked by two mezzanines. Wed–Sun 10pm–4am; $7–15.

Island Club, 285 W Broadway (☎226-4598). Wed, Thurs and Sun hard-core reggae music, Fri and Sat salsa and Latin-edged sounds. Admission $5–10.

Kilimanjaro, W 18th St and Tenth Ave. Great club whose mixture of African jive, soul, soca and reggae, not to mention the resident band "Ethiopia", attracts a mixed crowd. Entrance $18.

Limelight, 660 Sixth Ave (☎807-7850). Long-established club now enjoying something of a renaissance after a lean period, particularly for its UK-influenced Thurs night sessions. Admission $18.

Mars, 28–30 Tenth Ave (☎691-6262). Fashionable club in which each floor sports a different atmosphere and music. $15–20.

Mission, 531 E Fifth St, between aves A and B (☎473-9096). East Village club specialising in goth, punk and new wave music. Thurs–Sat, from 10pm; admission is $6 and drinks are cheap.

Octagon, 555 W 33rd St (☎947-0400). Run-of-the-mill club, except on Sat nights, when Roger Sanchez' *Ego Trip* plays deep house and reggae. Admission $5 on Thurs, $15 Fri & Sat.

Palladium, 126 E 14th St (☎473-7171). Biggest of the New York clubs, housed in an enormous old theatre. The dance floor, light and sound system take some beating. For no-nonsense dancing without the posing, still one of the best. Admission $20.

Red Zone, 440 W 54th St (☎582-2222). Popular place for heavy-duty dance music, catering to a young, mainly Latin crowd. David Morales plays on Sat.

Shelter, 157 Hudson St (☎677 2582). A lethal mixture of deep house and disco classics for a mainly black crowd. Great atmosphere, with the emphasis on serious dancing. Sat is gay night.

Sound Factory, 27th St between 10th and 11th aves. Two of NYC's most renowned DJs play here: Tony Humphries on Fri, Frankie Knuckles on Sat.

Comedy Clubs

Caroline's Comedy Club, 89 South St, Pier 17 (☎620-5971). Glitzy room that books some of the best acts in town. $7.50–10 cover during the week, $12.50–17.50 at weekends.

Catch a Rising Star, 1487 First Ave (☎794-1906). New talent showcase twice nightly, three times on Saturday. Cover around $10.

Comic Strip, 1568 Second Ave (☎861-9386). Famed showcase for stand-up comics and young singers going for the big time. Nightly shows from 9pm, two shows at weekends. Cover $5–12.

Dangerfield's, 1118 First Ave (☎593-1650). New talent showcase run by the established comedian Rodney Dangerfield. Cover $10–15.

Don't Tell Mama, 343 W 46th St (☎757-0788). Lively, convivial piano bar and cabaret featuring rising stars. Shows at 8pm and 10pm. Cover $6–15, two drink minimum.

Duplex, 61 Christopher St (☎255-5438). Village cabaret popular with gays. Cover $7–11. The rowdy piano bar downstairs is also worth catching.

Improvisation, 358 W 44th St (☎765-8268). New comic and singing talent, mostly improvised. Cover $7–8. Shows at 9pm during the week; two shows on Fri, three on Sat.

Stand Up New York, 236 W 78th St (☎595-0850). Upper West Side club that's a forum for established acts. Nightly shows, two, sometimes three, at weekends. Cover about $10.

Theatre

New York is one of the great **theatre** centres of the world. You can find just about any kind of production here, from lavish, over-the-top musicals to experimental productions in converted garages: the variety is endless. Venues are referred to as **Broadway, Off Broadway**, or **Off-Off Broadway**, groupings which represent a descending order of ticket price, production polish, elegance and comfort – but don't necessarily have much to do with the address.

Broadway offerings consist primarily of large-scale musicals, comedies and dramas with big-name actors, with the occasional classic and one-person show. **Off Broadway** theatres also tend to provide polished production qualities, but combine them with a greater willingness to experiment. Off-Broadway is social and political drama, satire, ethnic plays and repertory: in short, anything that Broadway wouldn't consider a sure-fire money-spinner. **Off-Off Broadway** is the fringe – drama on a shoestring, sometimes on subjects other theatres find too sensitive or not profitable enough to mount. Most Broadway theatres are located in the blocks just east or west of Broadway between 40th and 52nd streets; Off and Off-Off Broadway theatres are sprinkled throughout Manhattan, with a concentration in the East and West Villages, Chelsea, and several in the 40s and 50s west of the Broadway Theatre District.

Nowhere are regular **tickets** cheap on Broadway; Off Broadway prices have risen recently too, to as much as $35 in some cases: in general, expect to pay upwards of $15 Off Broadway and $6 Off-Off. If you know where and how to look, even these prices can be cut considerably. You can queue up on the day of the performance at the **TKTS** booth in Times Square (Mon–Sat 3–8pm, noon–2pm for Wed & Sat matinees), where at least one pair of tickets for every performance of every Broadway and Off Broadway show is available at half price (plus a $1.25 ticket service charge). There's another *TKTS* booth in the lobby of 2 World Trade Center. Both take cash or travellers' cheques only.

Twofer discount coupons are available in either of the New York CVBs, as well as many shops, banks, restaurants and hotel lobbies. The days are long gone when they really did offer two-for-the-price-of-one, but they still entitle two people to a hefty discount. Unlike *TKTS*, twofers make it possible to book ahead, though don't expect to find coupons for the latest shows.

If you're prepared to pay **full price** you can, of course, either go directly to the theatre, or *Tickets Central*, 406 West 42nd Street, open 1–8pm daily. Also *Ticketron* (☎399-4444) book seats for those with credit cards for a $2.50 charge.

LINCOLN CENTER

Lincoln Center, on Broadway at 64th Street, is New York's powerhouse of highbrow art. Each of its major auditoria is in active use through the year.

The New York State Theater (☎870-5770). Home for six months of the year to the *New York City Ballet* – considered by many to be the greatest dance company in existence – this more accessible venue is also where the *New York City Opera* plays David to the Met's Goliath. Seats go for less than half the Met's prices, and standing room tickets are available if a performance sells out.

The Avery Fisher Hall (☎874-2424). The permanent base of the *New York Philharmonic* under Zubin Mehta, and a temporary one to visiting orchestras and soloists. Ticket prices range from $10 to $45.

The Metropolitan Opera House (☎362-6000). Hosts the *Metropolitan Opera Company* from September until late April, and the *American Ballet Theater* between early May and July. Tickets are outrageously expensive and difficult to get hold of. Last-minute cancellations and standing-room tickets can in theory be picked up from the box office, but lines are already forming the night before any significant occasion.

The Alice Tully Hall (☎362-1911). Smaller venue used by chamber orchestras, string quartets and instrumentalists. Prices similar to those in the Avery Fisher Hall.

Classical Music, Opera and Dance

New Yorkers take serious music seriously. Long queues form for anything popular, a good many concerts sell out, and summer evenings can see a quarter of a million people turning up in Central Park for free performances by the New York Philharmonic. Half-price **tickets**, on a day-to-day basis only, are available from the **Music & Dance Booth** in Bryant Park on 42nd Street (Tues–Fri noon–2pm & 3–7pm, Wed & Sat 11am–2pm & 3–7pm; Sun noon–6pm; ☎382-2323).

Besides Lincoln Center, (see box), the most important venue is **Carnegie Hall**, 154 W 57th Street (☎247-7800), where the greatest names from all schools of music have performed. The acoustics remain superb, and a patching-up operation is under way to amend years of structural neglect and restore the place to its former glory.

As for **dance**, for which Lincoln Center once again serves as showcase, a number of other venues regularly host events. The **Brooklyn Academy of Music**, 30 Lafayette Street, Brooklyn (☎718/636-4100), universally known as BAM, is America's oldest performing arts academy and one of the most daring producers in New York – definitely worth crossing the river for. The **City Center**, 131 W 55th Street (☎246-8989), has five resident dance troupes including America's two undisputed choreographic giants, the *Merce Cunningham Dance Company* and the *Paul Taylor Dance Company*, as well as the *Ioffrey* and *Dance Theatre of Harlem*. Probably the most important middle-sized dance space in Manhattan is the **Joyce Theater**, 175 Eighth Avenue (☎242-0800), which has the *Eliot Feld Ballet* in residence.

Film

Revival cinemas are increasingly giving way to multi-screen "plexes", but some alternatives still exist.

Anthology Film Archives, 32–34 Second Ave (☎505-5181). Shows many films you thought you'd never have the chance to see again.

Biograph, 225 W 57th St (☎582-4582). Revival house featuring all your favourite movie classics.

The New Cinema 12, 22 E 12th St (☎924-3363). Modern films (1950 onwards) are the standard bill here, plus the occasional festival.

Museum of the Moving Image, 35th Ave and 36th St, Queens (☎718/784-0077). Foreign and avant-garde films.

Theatre 80 St Marks, 80 St Mark's Place (☎254-7400). Classic movies. Don't miss the mini-*Grauman's Chinese Theater* (see p.747) collection of star footprints and autographs in the pavement.

Gay and Lesbian New York

Gay refugees from all over America and the world come to New York, and as many as twenty percent of New Yorkers (or at least Manhattanites) are said to be **lesbian** or **gay**. **Greenwich Village** is the traditional and most established gay neighbourhood, but the **East Village**, too, has a growing scene, especially for younger, more politically active gays and lesbians. Other promising locales include the **East 20s and 30s**, **Chelsea**, and the **Upper West Side**. Two popular **gay hotels**, the *Chelsea Pines* and the *Longacre*, are listed on p.85. Gay and lesbian **bars** can be found on p.89.

For more information get hold of the **Gayellow Pages** ($3.95), available from either of the bookshops below. Up-to-the-minute news can be found in *Outweek*, a provocative weekly magazine for gay men, or *Womanews*, a monthly lesbian/feminist news sheet.

Resources

Community Health Project, 208 W 13th St (☎675-3559). Low-priced gay clinic .

A Different Light, 548 Hudson St (☎989-4850). Excellent selections of gay and lesbian publications. Open late throughout the week, and often hosts book-signing parties and readings.

Gay Switchboard (daily 10.30am–midnight; ☎777-1800). Help and what's on information.

Lesbian and Gay Community Center, 208 W 13th St (☎620-7310). Umbrella group and meeting space for over eighty gay organisations. Regular social events; call to see what's happening.

Lesbian Switchboard (Mon–Fri 6pm–10pm; ☎741-2610). *The* place to phone for information on events, happenings and contacts in the New York community.

The Oscar Wilde Memorial Bookshop, 15 Christopher St (☎255-8097). The first gay bookshop in the US. Unbeatable.

Shops

New York is the consumer capital of the world. Its **shops** cater for every possible taste, creed or perversity, in any combination and at any time of day or night. To enjoy them to the full, it's a good idea to devote a few years before you visit to the single-minded pursuit of colossal riches; but shopping in New York, in the markets of Greenwich Village for example, can be extraordinarily cheap as well as phenomenally expensive, and even if you can't afford to buy the top of the line, browsing is, of course, free.

Midtown Manhattan is mainstream territory, with its department stores, big-name clothes designers and branches of the larger chains; **downtown** plays host to a wide variety of more offbeat stores. **Uptown**, the Upper East Side is uncompromisingly upmarket, while the funkier **Upper West Side** has an array of off-the-wall stores to compare with anything SoHo or the Village can offer.

Department Stores

Bloomingdale's, 1000 Third Ave (☎355-5900). Perhaps Manhattan's most famous department store, packed with designer clothiers, perfume concessions and the like.

Macy's, Broadway at 34th St (☎695-4400). The largest department store in the world; two buildings, two million square feet of floor space, ten floors, and around $5m gross turnover every day.

Saks Fifth Avenue, 611 Fifth Ave (☎753-4000). Although *Saks* remains virtually synonymous with style, it has also updated itself to carry the merchandise of all the big designers.

Books

Brentano's, 597 Fifth Ave (☎826-2450). Housed in the fine old *Scribner's* bookstore, and continuing that shop's tradition of good service and stock in elegant surroundings.

Compleat Traveller, 199 Madison Ave (☎679-4339). Manhattan's premier travel bookshop, excellently stocked, secondhand and new.

Endicott Booksellers, 450 Columbus Ave (☎787-6300). Long-standing store providing helpful service and a wonderful range of titles.

Gotham Book Mart, 41 W 47th St (☎719-4448). Literary bookstore, good on drama and theatre publications, excellent on more obscure stuff.

Rizzoli, 31 W 57th St (☎759 2424); 454a W Broadway (☎674-1616). Manhattan branches of Italian store, specialising in European publications. Good selection of foreign newspapers and magazines.

Strand Bookstore, 828 Broadway (☎473-1452). Gigantic place, one of the few surviving secondhand stores in an area that used to be full of them. Also offers half-price review copies.

Records

Dayton's, 799 Broadway (☎254-5084). Rare records, old review copies, deleted soundtracks.

Footlight Records, 113 E 12th St (☎533-1572). *The* place for show music – everything from Broadway to Big Band, Sinatra to Mermand. A must for record collectors.

The Golden Disc, 239 Bleecker St (☎255-7899). Jazz, rock oldies, blues and gospel.

House of Oldies, 35 Carmine St (☎243-0500). What the name says – oldies but goldies of all kinds.

Second Coming, 235 Sullivan St (☎228-1313). The place for heavy metal and hard-core punk.

Sounds, 20 St Mark's Place (☎677-3444). New and used records.

Vinyl Mania, 60 Carmine St (☎691-1720). This, and two other branches in Carmine St, is where DJs come for the newest, rarest releases, especially of dance music.

Listings

Consulates *Australia*, 630 Fifth Ave (☎245-4000); *Canada*, 1251 Sixth Ave (☎768-2400); *Ireland*, 515 Madison Ave (☎319-2555); *United Kingdom*, 845 Third Ave (☎745-0202).

Dental Treatment In an emergency, ring ☎679-3966 (after 8pm ☎679-4712).

Hospitals For minor accidents, there are 24hr casualty departments at the following Manhattan hospitals: *Bellevue Hospital* at First Avenue and East 29th Street (☎561-4141); *St Vincent's Hospital*, Seventh Ave at 11th St (☎790-7997); *New York Hospital*, E 70th St at York Ave (☎472-5050); *Mount Sinai Hospital*, Madison Ave at 100th St (☎241-7171).

Left Luggage Two of the most likely places to dump your stuff are Grand Central Station at 42nd St and Park Ave (Mon–Fri 7am-8pm, Sat & Sun 10am–6pm), and Port Authority Bus Terminal at 41st St and Eighth Ave (daily 7am–12pm). At both you'll pay around $1 an item.

Lost Property Things lost on buses or on the subway: *MTA Lost Property Division*, 370 Jay St, Brooklyn (☎718/625-6200). Things lost in a cab: *Taxi & Limousine Commission Lost Property Information Dept*, 211 W 41st St (☎869-4513).

Pharmacy *Kaufman*, 557 Lexington Ave (☎755-2266), is open 24hr.

Post Office The main Manhattan office is at 421 Eighth Ave, between W 31st and 33rd sts (Mon–Sat 24hr for important services). Its zip code is the easily memorable 10001.

Out from the City: Long Island

The state of New York – of which New York City is not even the capital – extends five hundred miles west of Manhattan, to Niagara Falls on the Canadian border. That vast area is covered in Chapter Two of this book. However, it makes most sense to see **Long Island**, which unfurls east of the city for 125 miles of lush farmland and broad sandy beaches, as an excursion of perhaps a few days from the metropolis. Its western end includes the urban boroughs of Brooklyn and Queens, but further east, the settlements begin to thin out and the countryside can get surprisingly remote. The **north** and **south shores** differ greatly – the former more immediately beautiful, its cliffs topped with luxurious mansions and estates, while the South Shore is fringed by almost continuous sand, interspersed with holiday resorts such as **Jones Beach** and gay-oriented **Fire Island**. At its far end Long Island splits in two, the **North Fork** retaining a marked rural aspect while the **South Fork**, much of which is known as **The Hamptons**, has long been an enclave of New York's richest and finest.

The quickest way to reach Long Island is via the reliable if rather grubby **Long Island Railroad** from Penn Station (☎718/454-LIRR or ☎718/990-7498), though numerous **bus services** (operated by major companies and the **Hampton Jitney**, ☎212/895-9336 or ☎516/283-4600) cover most destinations. If you **drive**, bear in mind that parking permits for Long Island's **beaches** are issued only to local residents; without one, there's a stiff daily rate (or even steeper fine) to leave a car in any of the car parks. On the whole it works out cheaper to head down to the beach on foot.

The South Shore and Fire Island

Long Island's **SOUTH SHORE** merges gently with the wild Atlantic, shallow and open and slicked with slithers of creamy sand and a succession of luscious duney beaches such as **Long Beach** and **Jones Beach**. Not surprisingly, these get less crowded the further east you go; by the time you get as far as **Gilgo** or **Oak Beach**, or cross the water to **Robert Moses State Park** on the western tip of Fire Island, you should be able to find whatever solitude you want. **Ocean Parkway** leads along the narrow offshore strand from Jones Beach to **Captree**, a good base for early-morning fishing trips or whale-watching expeditions (☎785-1600), before crossing back to Long Island proper over the Robert Moses Causeway to **Bay Shore**, a dull town which serves as a **ferry** terminal for Fire Island ($4). This way you bypass the sprawling mess of **Amityville**, famous for its "horror" of a decade or so ago. The house on the hill, from which a family were driven in terror by some mysterious supernatural force, still stands.

Fire Island
FIRE ISLAND, a slim spit of land parallel to the South Shore, is in many ways a microcosm of New York City. People don't come here to experience something different; they go because they know what to expect, and on summer weekends half of Manhattan seems to be holed up in its tiny settlements. It's primarily a **gay** resort: young gays make for **Cherry Grove**; older and wealthier ones for **Fire Island Pines**; **Kismet** is the hangout of older Jews, **Ocean Bay Park** yuppie and jappie; while **Point O Woods** is probably the most exclusive of the lot. The **season** is as rigidly defined as the people. Memorial Day onwards Fire Island hums with activity and is swamped with crowds – though it's always possible to escape for gorgeous wild walks along the sand – whereas after Labor Day, though the weather may still be very warm, the throngs diminish dramatically.

> The telephone **area code** for Long Island is ☎516.

Most ferries dock at trendy **Ocean Beach**, where trippers pile up groceries on trolleys (cars are forbidden) and set off for their vacation pads. All **accommodation** should be booked in advance: *Jerry's*, 620 Bay Walk, Ocean Beach (☎583-8870), has rooms for roughly $50 per person, or double that at weekends; *Flynn's*, in nearby Ocean Bay Park (☎583-8000), has doubles from $60. *Giovanni's*, opposite the ferry terminal, is the best and most convivial place to **eat** for under $5; on weekends, *Flynn's*, and *Leo's* on Bay Walk, are good for riotous boozing and eating.

The North Shore and North Fork

The **NORTH SHORE** is Long Island at its most rugged, dropping into the sea in a series of bluffs, coves and wooded headlands. The Long Island Expressway beyond Queens leads straight onto the **Gold Coast**, a Twenties and Thirties stomping ground of the rich and elegant. **Great Neck** here became F Scott Fitzgerald's *West Egg* in *The Great Gatsby*, home of the narrator Nick and Gatsby himself. Some of this prime real estate is so expensive that no one can afford to live here, and large houses such as **Sands Point**, on the sharp tip of the next peninsula, stand empty. This motley collection of European-style buildings, once owned by the Guggenheim family, is now a park and museum (May–Oct Sat–Wed 10am–5pm; $1). Its 209 acres of unkempt parkland offer great views over what Fitzgerald called "the most domesticated body of salt water in the Western hemisphere, the great barnyard of Long Island Sound".

Sagamore Hill, on the coast road six miles beyond Glen Cove, is the heavily touristed former country retreat where **Teddy Roosevelt** lived for thirty-odd years (May–Oct daily 9.30am–5pm, Nov–April 9.30am–4.30pm; $1). Its 23 rooms are adorned everywhere by the great man's trophies, sprouting horns from walls or grinning toothily up from the firesides. The **Old Orchard Museum** near the car park recounts Teddy's political and personal life, but the real reason to come is to stroll in the gorgeous grounds, where springy lawns drop to Oyster Bay and the sea.

Nearby **Cold Spring Harbour** grew up as a whaling port, and still retains some of its looks despite commercialisation. Its **Whaling Museum** (Tues–Sun 11am–5pm) recaptures that era better than the town ever could now, featuring a fully equipped whaleboat and a four-hundred-piece assembly of scrimshaw work. The **Vanderbilt Mansion** just outside Centreport (April–Oct Tues–Sat 10am–4pm, Sun noon–5pm; Nov–March Tues–Sun noon–4pm; $1) displays the dubious taste typical of Vanderbilt residences. In the style of a Baroque Spanish palace, it's heavily ornate both outside and in, with marble-encased galleries, swirling staircases and gaudily carved fireplaces.

On the **North Fork**, which sees far fewer tourists, the scenery is at its wildest. Once an independent colony, this region has something of the feel of New England. **Greenport** is its most picturesque town, a clutter of narrow streets and alleys leading down to a harbour pierced by the masts of visiting yachts. **Accommodation** such as *Bartlett House*, 503 Front Street (☎477-0371), where double rooms range from $62 to $88, is plentiful. Regular 15-minute **ferries** connect with Shelter Island and hence the South Fork. **Orient Point**, a few miles east, offers access to the gloriously untouched **Orient Point State Park**, and frequent ferries make the one-and-a-half-hour trip to New London, Connecticut, which is described on p.179 (summer, 6 daily, last leaves 2pm; foot passengers $8 one-way, $12 day-return).

The South Fork

The US has few more wealthy – or status-ridden – quarters than the small towns of Long Island's **SOUTH FORK**. Huge palaces lurk in the trees or stand boldly on the flats behind the dunes, and nowhere, but nowhere, is consumption as deliberately conspicuous as in **The Hamptons**. Though among the oldest communities in the state, settled by restless New Englanders in the mid-1650s, they remained relatively isolated until the rich began to turn up in their motor cars. Now celebrities such as Betty Frieda, Gloria Vanderbilt, and Woody Allen are either residents or frequent visitors, and the area has a gossip column cachet that you'll either love or hate.

Southampton

SOUTHAMPTON hasn't been totally overwhelmed by money, but long association with the smart set has left it unashamedly twee, its streets lined with clothes shops, galleries and jewellery shops. The nearby beaches are superb, though a car can help to escape the summer crowds. The **visitor centre** at 76 Main Street (daily 9am–5pm) has lists of B&B rooms; the *Hill Guest House*, 535 Hill Street (May–Oct only; ☎283-9889), ranges from $60 to $75. For **food**, *Joe's*, 23 Hill Street, does pizzas and pasta at rock-bottom prices, while *Barrister's* on Main Street has marvellous soft-shell crabs.

Sag Harbor

SAG HARBOR, the most historic of the South Fork towns, was once a harbour second only to that of New York, which was designated first Port of Entry to the New Country by George Washington. The **Whaling Museum** on Main Street (mid-May–Sept, Mon–Sat 10am–5pm, Sun 1–5pm) commemorates the town's brief whaling days with a collection of guns and scrimshaw. Nearby the **Whaler's Presbyterian Church** is crenellated with jutting rows of whale blubber spades. Young whalers, most of whom died in their twenties, lie in **Oakland Cemetery**, where beautifully reliefed memorials tell of horrific encounters with "the monsters of the deep".

The harbour lies at the foot of the town's elegantly curving main street. John Steinbeck, who lived here for many years, is remembered by a plaque on the windmill which in summer serves as a **visitor centre**. Only the *Baron's Cove Inn* (☎725-2100) has **rooms**, from $50 in winter but more like $100 in summer, but if you're after **something to eat** Main Street is lined with reasonably priced restaurants.

Montauk

Blustery, wind-battered **MONTAUK**, up beyond Amagansett on the furthest tip of Long Island, would but for a hurricane and the Wall Street Crash of 1929 have been a sizeable resort. As it is, the entrepreneur who hoped to develop the place lost his money and, a weird Florentine tower in its centre apart, Montauk stayed as it was – a not particularly attractive town with access to some enticingly undisturbed country.

Montauk's oldest buildings date from the eighteenth century, when this was a summer pasture for grazing cattle. Later it became better known as a quarantined campground for diseased veterans of the Spanish-American War – Teddy Roosevelt's Rough Riders – who were forced to bivouac on the rocky wilds of **Montauk Point** after being refused entry by a hygiene-conscious New York City.

Today the rare beauty of the cape figures in all the tourist brochures, its **lighthouse** (which you should be able to visit) forming an almost symbolic finale to this stretch of the American coast. Back in the town centre a number of **motels** offer fairly priced rooms: doubles at the *Oceanside Beach Resort* (☎668-9825), on the junction of the Old Montauk Highway and Main Street, flicker between $30 and $70 depending on the season. *The Lobster Roll* on the Montauk Highway serves excellent fresh fish and seafood for between $5 and $15.

CHAPTER TWO

THE MID-ATLANTIC

T he three Mid-Atlantic states – **NEW YORK, PENNSYLVANIA** and **NEW JERSEY** – form a corridor between New England and the Capital region in the most populated, industrialised corner of the States. Although dominated in the popular imagination by the grey smokestacks of New Jersey, and the coalfields and steel factories of western Pennsylvania, as they stretch far from the coast to the north and west they also encompass lakes, forests and rolling green countryside, and, in places, expanses of virtual wilderness.

White settlement was characterised by considerable shifts and turns; the **Dutch**, who arrived in the 1620s under the auspices of the Dutch West Indies Company, were methodically squeezed out by the **English**, who in turn fought off the **French** challenge to secure total control of the colonies by the late eighteenth century. By then, the Native American population, including the **Iroquois** and **Lenni Lenape**, had been confined to reservations or pushed into Canada. At first the economy depended on trade with the West Indies, and the importation of slaves, though Presbyterian Irish landowners had by the 1730s become a significant political force, their holdings extending to the western limits of Pennsylvania and New York.

All three states were important during the **Revolution**; the Declaration of Independence and the Constitution were both written in Philadelphia, and Washington won major victories at Trenton and Princeton in New Jersey. Upstate New York was geographically crucial, as the British forces knew that control of the Hudson River would effectively divide New England from the other colonies.

Even while still under British rule the region began to produce huge amounts of **iron**, much to the distaste of its colonial masters, and in the 1850s large **coalfields** were discovered in northeast Pennsylvania. Though still significant, industry has now dwindled, as other areas – particularly the Great Lakes – have come to prominence.

Although many travellers to the East Coast may not consider venturing much further than New York City itself – covered in *Chapter One* of this book, together with Long Island – the region is much more than just an overspill of the Big Apple, whatever chauvinistic city-dwellers might say. Each state has its own personality. **Upstate New York** is for outdoor-lovers; the wooded **Catskill Mountains** line the Hudson River (which Henry James claimed was "in the geography of the ideal"), the imposing **Adirondack Mountains** spread over a quarter of the state, and the **Finger Lakes** region offers a pastoral interlude en route to the awesome **Niagara Falls** on the Canadian border. **Pennsylvania** is best known for the fertile **Amish** country, and the two great cities of **Philadelphia** and **Pittsburgh**. **New Jersey**, often pictured as one great industrial carbuncle, offers shameless tourist pleasures along the shore; day-trippers in their millions flock to the Boardwalk and casinos of **Atlantic City**.

The entire region is well covered by **public transport**, with New York's JFK and New Jersey's Newark **airports** acting as important international gateways, and New York's La Guardia airport serving domestic flights. *Amtrak* **trains** run Northeast Corridor routes east–west through New York and Pennsylvania, and north–south through New York and New Jersey, while the *New Jersey Transit* rail and bus network serves all of New Jersey, extending west to Philadelphia and north to Manhattan. *Greyhound* **buses** follow the major Interstates, with subsidiary lines running to more out-of-the-way places.

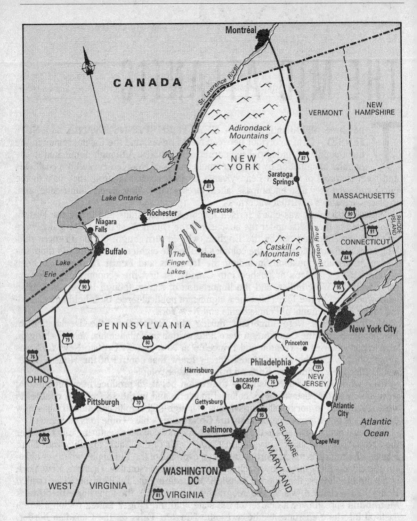

NEW YORK STATE

However much the tourist authorities try to encourage visitors, the large and rambling state of **NEW YORK** remains inevitably in the shadow of America's most celebrated city. The words "New York" bring to mind soaring skyscrapers and traffic-filled streets, rather than rolling dairy farmland, old colonial villages, workaday towns and severe mountains, and the five hundred miles which separate New York City from mighty **Niagara Falls** in the northwest corner of the state are still barely explored by travellers. Their strongest appeal is to the outdoor fanatic – upstate New York offers mountains, lakes, and waterfalls, and forests for the asking. Few of the conurbations hold very much of interest, and the small towns, though they can be quite charming, lack sufficient diversity to make an extensive tour fruitful.

No great distance from downtown New York, the valley of the **Hudson River**, with the moody **Catskill Mountains** rising stealthily from the west bank, is easily accessible to those seeking a brief respite from the intensity of the city. Much wilder and more rugged are the peaks in the vast **Adirondack National Park** further north. They're far beyond the scope of a casual excursion, though getting to the chic spa town of **Saratoga Springs** in the foothills is a comfortable day's drive, and it makes an excellent stop if you're on the way to Canada. As you head for Niagara, the central portion of the state is occupied by the pretty **Finger Lakes**.

In the seventeenth and eighteenth centuries, as nation-moulding political and military battles were taking place around Manhattan, semi-feudal **Dutch landowning dynasties** such as the Van Rensselaers held sway upstate. Their control over tens of thousands of tenant farmers was barely affected by the transference of colonial power from Holland to Britain, or even by American independence. Only with the completion of the **Erie Canal** in 1825, linking New York City with the Great Lakes, did the interior of the state start to open up, with canal-side towns like **Rochester** and **Syracuse** undergoing massive expansion thanks to the improved opportunities for trade. On the other hand, the industrial and agricultural growth in its hinterland served, of course, to increase the financial standing of New York City, and the story of the past century and a half has been one of consistent political and economic domination of city over state.

Getting Around New York State

Greyhound and *Trailways* **buses** run to all the major towns; *Shortline* (☎212/736-4700) serves the Hudson Valley. *Amtrak* operate a relatively good **train** service along a beautiful route through the Hudson Valley to Albany; from there less frequent trains continue to Montreal via the Adirondacks, and to Toronto via Niagara Falls. Many bus and train stations are several miles out from the town centres; the necessary walking can be unpleasant in the muggy heat of summer.

Car rental in New York City is expensive, and restricted to drivers over 25 years of age. If either of these factors causes a problem, try taking public transport over the state line to New Jersey or Connecticut, where the minimum age is 21 and rates can be considerably cheaper. **Flying** too is expensive; by the time you get out to JFK or La Guardia you might just as well be on your way upstate. **Cycling** is best enjoyed as a means of exploring small areas such as the Finger Lakes or Catskills.

The Hudson Valley and the Catskills

To the average commuter, the **Hudson River** is just an inconvenient barrier en route to New Jersey. However, you only need to travel a few miles north of Manhattan before the valley takes on a Rhine-like charm, with prodigious historic homes, such as those of the Roosevelt, Vanderbilt and van Cortland families, rising from its steep and thickly wooded banks. A little further on come the forests of the **Catskill Mountains**, whose brilliant fall colours rival anything to be seen in New England. Few of the valley towns, including the largely lacklustre state capital of **Albany**, hold much to impress the visitor, though it's worth calling in – if just for old times' sake – at the New Age (-ish) village of **Woodstock**, nestled among the Catskills.

The Lower Hudson Valley

A mere 25 miles north of central New York City, leafy **TARRYTOWN** was the original setting for Washington Irving's tales of *Rip Van Winkle* and *The Legend of Sleepy Hollow*. In 1835 the author rebuilt a farm cottage just south of town on West Sunnyside Lane (off US-9) which he named **Sunnyside**: "a little old-fashioned stone mansion, all made up of

The telephone **area code** for the lower Hudson Valley is ☎914.

gable ends, and as full of angles and corners as an old cocked hat." Tours squeeze around its cosy rooms, enjoyable even if you've never read a word of Irving (April–Dec, Wed–Sun 10am–5pm; March, Sat & Sun 10am–5pm; $5). It's also worth looking around the neighbouring village of **LYNDHURST**, where the spikily crenellated **Lyndhurst Castle** is as dapper a piece of nineteenth-century Gothic revivalism as you'll find (May–Oct, Tues–Sun 10am–5pm; Nov, Jan & March, Sat & Sun 10am–5pm; $5).

Congress set up the **United States Military Academy** at **WEST POINT** in 1802 after it realised that the ragged troops who had won the Revolutionary War had been knocked into shape almost exclusively by European officers. Homegrown skills had to be cultivated in case foreign help wasn't so readily forthcoming again. Since then, West Point has provided the military training for generals Grant, Lee, MacArthur, Eisenhower, Patton and Schwartzkopf, to name but a famous few. Today, 4000-odd candidates on a tough four-year course fill the smart showpiece campus, which protectively overlooks the Hudson from a wide, strategic bluff. The free **West Point Museum** (daily 10.30am–4.15pm) shows trophies of war including a pistol that belonged to Hitler and, disturbingly, the pin from the Nagasaki bomb. There may be little mention of Vietnam, but no doubt a full Desert Storm exhibit will be unveiled shortly, which should delight the crowds drawn by the stirring patriotism embodied in the Parade Ground drilling. The **visitor centre** (daily; 8.30am–4.15pm; ☎938-2638) can provide a schedule of parades, at their most frequent in spring and fall.

The Catskill Mountains and the West Bank

The magnificent crests of the **Catskills**, cloaked with maple and beech which turn orange, ochre and gold each fall, have a rich and absorbing beauty. This dislocated branch of the Appalachians is inspiring country, filled with amenities – campgrounds, hiking, floating, fishing and, especially, skiing. To enjoy it to the full, venture onto the trails; the mountains are so tightly packed that good roadside overlooks are rare.

Kingston

Of the various towns on the fringes of the mountains, **KINGSTON**, with its decidedly English air, is the most pleasant and convenient place to stop. It may not quite live up to its billing as "the Williamsburg of the north", but downtown Kingston is an agreeable mix of well-preserved old houses and neat little business premises.

The *Holiday Inn*, 503 Washington Avenue (☎338-0400), complete with sauna, pool and games area, is a fine place to **stay** if you can afford $59 to $79 (increasing to $99 at the weekend); the *Super 8 Motel*, 487 Washington Avenue (☎333-3078), costs $45. The *Market Basket Deli*, 308 Wall Street (☎338-2755), serves fresh breads and bagels, and *Dallas Hot Weiners*, 51 North Street, has cheap burgers.

Woodstock

Beyond Kingston, Hwy-28 meanders into the Catskills, looping past the lovely **Ashokan Reservoir** where Hwy-212 branches off to **WOODSTOCK**. The village, carved out of the lush deciduous woodlands and cut by fast-rushing creeks, was not actually the venue of the famed **psychedelic picnic** of August 1969 – that was some sixty miles southwest in **Bethel**, where a monument at Herd and West Shore roads marks the site on Max Yasgur's farm. However, Woodstock has enjoyed a bohemian reputation since the foundation in 1902 of the Byrdcliffe arts colony. During the Sixties, it was a favourite stomping ground for the likes of Dylan, Hendrix and Van Morrison. It still bears signs of its hippy past – shops sell tie-dyed T-shirts and crystals, and there's even the occasional commune – but for the most part you'll have to search hard to find a truly alternative edge. In the twee cafes, you're more likely to bump into a successful Manhattanite who owns a second home here than a long-haired beatnik (not that those two categories are necessarily mutually exclusive).

Woodstock's best **accommodation** is the *Twin Gables Guest House* (☎679-9479) at 77 Tinker Street, in the centre of the village, where doubles cost $40 (singles $30). If this is full, as is often the case, $60 gets a cabin and breakfast at *Pinecrest Lodge* on Country Club Lane (☎679-2814). *Duey's*, 50 Mill Hill Road (☎679-9593), and the *Woodstock Pizza* on the village green can provide filling, inexpensive **meals**. To savour a little nostalgia, sample the New Age atmosphere at the *Tinker Street Cafe*, 59 Tinker Street, or the *Joyous Lake* on Mill Hill Road (☎679-9300); both feature live bands at the weekend. Several **buses** each day take two-and-a-half hours to reach Woodstock from New York City's Port Authority Bus Terminal (*Adirondack Trailways*; ☎212/947-5300).

For more information tune into the local radio station, WDST (100.1 FM), pick up the *Woodstock Times* or phone the Chamber of Commerce (☎679-6234).

On through Catskill Park

As you continue along Hwy-28, the picturesque hamlet of **PHOENICIA**, in a hollow to the right of the road, is an ideal place to rent floating gear, mountain bikes and rafts. You can also catch the circular **Catskill Mountain Railroad** (summer & fall; ☎688-7400) through scenic Esopus Creek. A few miles further west, Hwy-49A affords a good vista of the rambling Catskills from the car park of the Belleayre ski resort. The *AYH Hostel*, Bonnieview Avenue, Pine Hill (☎254-4200), provides a bed for $10 ($12 in winter).

The return route to I-90 along Hwy-23A includes a breathtaking view of the dramatic gorge between the villages of Hunter and Catskill, along with the area's premier ski runs on **Hunter Mountain**. This is not a cheap place to be during the main November to Easter sports season; daily ski passes cost over $30 and the least expensive rooms start at $75. The resort's chairlifts also run during the summer ($5; ☎518/263-4223).

The East Bank

HYDE PARK, approximately twenty miles south of Kingston, is a peaceful plateau with magnificent views of the Hudson and, signposted off the Albany Post Road, the homes of Franklin Delano and Eleanor **Roosevelt**. In the house where the "New Deal" president was born and spent much of his adult life, a good **museum** displays extensive photos and artefacts, including the specially adapted car he drove after being struck down by polio in 1921, and the letter from Einstein that led to the development of the atomic bomb (daily 9am–5pm; $3).

FDR lies buried in the rose garden, beside his wife (and distant cousin) Eleanor, a gifted and influential Democratic politician without whose help his career might well not have survived his long bouts of illness. She broke away from the tradition that the president's wife should merely serve as a hostess at society functions, by playing a prominent role in the New Deal programme, touring the country and reporting to FDR on the living conditions of the poor. After FDR's death in 1945 she moved to the nearby cottage, **Val-Kill**, from where she carried on her work as chair of the United Nations Human Rights Commission, receiving dignitaries such as Tito, Nehru, Khrushchev and John F Kennedy until her death in 1962. Shuttle buses leave the FDR house every half-hour for free tours (April–Oct daily 9am–5pm).

Admission to the Roosevelt homes also gets you into the Beaux Arts **Vanderbilt Mansion**. This virtual palace – believe it or not, the smallest of the family's residences – was built for Frederick, a grandson of railroad baron Cornelius. The at-times garish furnishings show that money is no guarantee of good taste (April–Oct, daily 9am–5pm; Nov–March, Thurs–Mon 9am–5pm).

Albany

ALBANY made its money by controlling east–west trade along the Erie Canal, and its reputation by being capital of the state. It's not an unpleasant town, just rather boring, with its character almost exclusively shaped by political and bureaucratic affairs.

Piercing like an arrowhead into the otherwise bland-looking downtown Albany, Nelson A Rockefeller's **Empire State Plaza** went up in the Sixties and Seventies, replacing 98 acres of nineteenth-century buildings with a complex which includes a subterranean retail arcade, lined with impressive modern art. The view from the Corning Tower **observation deck** (daily 9am–4pm; free) seems designed to make you feel like the conqueror of an invaded territory, looking out beyond the twisting Hudson to the Adirondack foothills, the Catskills and the Massachusetts Berkshires. It also peers down on the neighbouring **Performing Arts Center** – known locally as "The Egg" – which adds the only curves to the rigid angularity of the Plaza, and is worth a peek inside even if you don't get to a show.

The **New York State Museum** reclines one level down at the end of the Plaza, revealing, free of charge, the whole state in imaginative if static natural history tableaux (most hands-on displays have been discontinued due to state cuts). The excellent section on New York City is better than anything in Manhattan itself, with histories of immigration and skyscraper construction, storefronts and trolley cars along with the original set of *Sesame Street* (daily 10am–5pm; free; ☎474-5877).

Practicalities

Arrive by *Greyhound* (☎434-0121) or *Trailways* (☎436-9651) and it's a short hilly walk to the heart of downtown; come in by *Amtrak* (☎465-9971) and you face a two-mile bus ride (☎482-8822). If you intend to **stay** the night, bear in mind that downtown lodging is not cheap. The *Econolodge*, 300 Broadway (☎434-4111), charges $60 to $90 for a room in summer. A small **youth hostel** offers budget rates at 46 Elm Street (☎434-4963), and the cheapest suburban chain motels start at $40.

The *Victory Cafe*, Sheridan and Chapel streets (☎463-9113), is a lively lunch spot serving quality burgers and tasty, healthy specials at good prices. For cheap gyros, sandwiches and pizza, call in at *Pizzeria 54*, 54 Pearl Street (☎432-5454).

The telephone **area code** for Albany and northern New York state is ☎518.

North through the Adirondacks

Mountaineers, skiiers and dedicated hikers form the majority of visitors to the vast northern region between Albany and the Canadian border. Outdoor pursuits are certainly the main attractions in the rugged wilderness of **Adirondack National Park**, though a few small resorts, especially the former Winter Olympic venue of **Lake Placid**, have a bit of life to offer, and the elegant spa town of **Saratoga Springs** nestles invitingly in the delicate countryside of the southern foothills.

Saratoga Springs

For well over a century, **SARATOGA SPRINGS**, just 42 miles north of Albany on I-87, was very much *the* place to be seen for the northeast's richest and most glittering names. At first, the town's curative **waters** were the main attraction; then John Morrisey, an Irish boxer, transformed things by opening a **racecourse** and **casino** during the 1860s. The Morgans, Vanderbilts and Whitneys all had houses in the town at one time, and Diamond Jim Brady was one of the most ostentatious visitors.

Saratoga Springs retains the feel of an exclusive vintage resort during the August racing season, but for the rest of the summer it is accessible, affordable and fun. **Broadway**, the main axis, takes in just about every aspect of the modern town from the ugly motel signs to the Gothic and Renaissance residential palaces on the northern tip of downtown. The carefully cultivated **Congress Park**, off South Broadway, laid out for the *curistes*, remains a shady retreat from the bustle of the town centre.

The **racetrack** still functions in the same old ultra-formal manner, enforcing strict dress codes for all meetings, but there's no such pretension at the **harness track** on nearby Crescent Avenue (evening meetings several times a week, May–Nov; $2). If you can't get to either, the array of paintings, trophies and brilliant audio-visual displays at the **National Museum of Racing** and **Thoroughbred Hall of Fame** on Union Avenue is well worth seeing (Mon–Sat 10am–4.30pm, Sun noon–4.30pm; $3).

On the southern edge of town, the green **Saratoga State Park** presents opportunities to swim in great old Victorian pools, picnic, hike or even bathe in one of two bathhouses (around $12; ☎584-2011). The **Saratoga Performing Arts Center** here was built during the Sixties in a successful attempt to revive the town's fortunes after a few lean decades. *SPAC* (☎587-3330) is home to the New York City Opera in June, the New York City Ballet in July and the Philadelphia Orchestra in August. It also hosts the "Newport Jazz Festival – Saratoga" in late June, and promotes rock concerts.

Practicalities

Central Saratoga Springs is fairly compact, but to get to most of the attractions you'll need to drive or use the local **bus** service (☎482-8822). **Accommodation** is no real problem, except during the race meeting in August when prices can more than double. The **Chamber of Commerce**, 494 Broadway (☎584-3255), has full lists, with prices; budget motels such as the *Spa Motel*, 73 Ballston Avenue (☎587-5280), ask around $40 per room. **Eating out** is also easy. One real favourite is the soul food at *Hattie's Chicken Shack*, 45 Phila Street (☎584-4790), where lunches cost under $5 and huge dinners are $10; the salads and sandwiches at *Bruegger's Bagels*, 453 Broadway (☎584-4372), are even cheaper. There's usually good Irish music at the *Parting Glass Pub*, 40 Lake Avenue (☎583-1916). *Nine Maple Avenue*, logically enough at 9 Maple Avenue (☎583-CLUB), offers live jazz until 4am, and the folksy *Cafe Lena*, 47 Phila Street – which was where Don McLean first inflicted *American Pie* on the world – still pulls in the crowds.

The Adirondacks

Covering a greater area than Connecticut and Rhode Island combined, **Adirondack National Park** has until recent decades been the almost exclusive preserve of loggers, fur-trappers and a few New York millionaires who really knew how to get away from it all (E L Doctorow's novels *Loon Lake* and *Billy Bathgate* both describe the bucolic retreats of Manhattan mobsters). For sheer grandeur, the region is hard to beat. Forty-three peaks stretch beyond 4000 feet; in summer the purple-green mountains span far into the distance in shaggy tiers, in fall the trees form a woozy russet-red kaleidoscope.

Though *Trailways* **buses** serve the area, you'll find it hard going without a car. The **Adirondack National Park** (☎327-3000) can provide general information, while the *Adirondack Mountain Club* (*ADK*), PO Box 3055, Lake George 12845 (☎668-4447), is best for details on hiking and camping.

Adirondack Towns

Though the undulating scenery around **LAKE GEORGE**, 25 miles up I-87 from Saratoga Springs, is pleasant, the village itself is overrun with cheap souvenir shops, and the eastern fringes of the Adirondacks in general hold little to compete with the splendours of the interior. Seventy miles west, at the junction of highways 28 and 30, stands tiny **Blue Mountain Lake**, where the twenty-building **Adirondack Museum** gives the lowdown on every aspect of regional life including art, sport, mining and wildlife (mid-June to mid-Oct, daily, 9.30am–5.30pm; $6; ☎352-7311).

The winter sports centre of **LAKE PLACID**, conspicuously proud of having twice hosted the Winter Olympics, lies sixty miles north on US-30. Throughout the year, the self-guided **Olympic Tour** takes in various former Olympic sites, including the bobsleigh run, ski jump (via chairlift) and a white-knuckle eight-mile drive up the sharply rising Whiteface Mountain toll road ($15 all-in; ☎1-800/44-PLACID). **John Brown's Farm and Grave**, on Hwy-73 outside the village, was where the famous abolitionist brought his family in 1849 to aid a small colony of black farmers and conceived his kamikaze battle to end slavery. The house is less interesting than his story (see p.318), but at least it's free (late May to late Oct, Wed–Sat 10am–5pm, Sun 1–5pm). In summer, there are **boat trips** on Lake Placid ($6; ☎523-9704).

A good scatter of economical **motels** can be found on Wilmington Road – try the *Cobble Mountain Lodge* (☎523-2040) or *Hi-Ridge Motel* (☎523-3938), both for around $35. The cheapest place to stay is the $10-a-night summer **youth hostel** at Main and Park streets (☎668-2634). The cosy *Artist's Cafe*, 1 Main Street (☎523-9493), provides filling lunches and reasonably priced seafood dinners.

The Thousand Islands

Beyond the Adirondacks, on the broad St Lawrence River that forms the border with Canada, are 1800 barely populated hunks of earth known as the **Thousand Islands**. They share their name with a salad dressing because one turn-of-the-century visitor – George Boldt, president of New York's *Waldorf-Astoria Hotel* – is said to have asked the steward on his yacht to concoct something different for a special luncheon. The resultant sickly pink goo is now famous the world over.

From both **Alexandria Bay** and the smaller fishing port of **Clayton**, boat excursions set out to explore the waterway; the tiny craft are all but swamped by the passing huge cargo ships, larger than many of the islands. For departure times, contact *Empire* (☎315/482-9511) or *Uncle Sam's Tours* (☎315/686-3511).

Central Leatherstocking and the Finger Lakes

Stretching all the way from Albany at the head of the Hudson to Rochester on Lake Erie is a belt of fertile farming country which comprises the agricultural heartland of New York State. **Central Leatherstocking** – named after the protective leggings worn by the area's first settlers – is well off the conventional tourist trails and, unless you want to check out one of its specialist sports museums, is best skipped over. Shortly beyond the manufacturing centre of **Syracuse**, you come to the eleven Finger Lakes, a series of narrow channels gouged out by glaciers which have left tell-tale signs in the form of drumlins, steep gorges and any number of waterfalls. With the exception of well-to-do **Ithaca** and tiny **Skaneatles**, few towns compete with the lakeshore scenery.

Cooperstown

Seventy miles west of Albany, sitting gracefully on the wooded banks of tranquil Otsego Lake, is the almost aggressively pretty village of **COOPERSTOWN**, christened "Glimmerglass" by novelist James Fenimore Cooper, son of the town's founder. The fact that **baseball** is said to have originated here on Doubleday Field is commemorated by the inspired and spacious **National Baseball Hall of Fame**, on Main Street. Everything is displayed in such an attention-grabbing manner that even if you know nothing about the game it's difficult to remain uninterested. Babe Ruth gets a whole

> The telephone **area code** for Central Leatherstocking and the Finger Lakes is ☎607; for Syracuse it's ☎315

display to himself while more of the greats are shown in action in photographs and videos (daily; May–Oct 9am–9pm; Nov–April 9am–5pm; $6; ☎547-9988).

Cooperstown is a pleasant community; it's worth taking a stroll around, or swimming from the beach at Glimmerglass State Park. Except for the **youth hostel** ($5 for AYH members; ☎293-7324), **accommodation** is expensive; the *Lake View* on Hwy-80 (☎547-9740) is one of the cheapest motels at $75 a night. *Obie's Brot und Bier*, 46 Pioneer Alley (☎547-5601), sells cheap sandwiches with a Germanic influence.

Canastota

Just before Syracuse, at exit 34 from I-90, nondescript **CANASTOTA** is the home of the **International Boxing Hall of Fame**. Canastota's links with boxing go back to early in the last century, and this ten-thousand strong village has produced two post-war world champions; Carmen Basilio, who took away the middleweight crown of Sugar Ray Robinson in an epic 1958 encounter, and Billy Backus, a welterweight title-holder during the early Seventies. All the greats are represented in the two-room museum, whether by picture, dressing-gown, mouthpiece, handwraps, gloves or bronze fist impressions, and there's a selection of big fight videos (daily 9am–5pm; $3; ☎697-7095).

Syracuse

SYRACUSE marks the transition between Central Leatherstocking and the Finger Lakes. A lively modern city, it made its name first for the production of salt and, more importantly, for its central position on the Erie Canal. Despite a population nudging half a million, there's little to see, though the presence of the university gives downtown an active and youthful feel. The redevelopment of **Armory Square** as an area of speciality shops, galleries and cafes has added further character to the city centre.

The small **Erie Canal Museum** (Tues–Sun 10am–5pm; $1), housed in an 1850s weighing station at 318 Erie Boulevard, tells the story of the long battle between politicians and taxpayers before work was started on the canal in 1810. The waterway was designed to link the Great Lakes with New York City via the Hudson, so cutting hefty transport costs. At first not everyone was in favour, critics speaking of a "big ditch" in which "would be buried the treasure of the state". The project eventually took fifteen years and one thousand lives, and went three million dollars above budget, but it spawned America's first generation of engineers, and the prosperity of New York City and the towns alongside the canal rose almost overnight. Erie Boulevard, on which the museum stands, was created by filling in the old canal bed.

Downtown's *Comfort Inn*, 454 James Street (☎425-0015), offers rooms for $40 to $50, while dorm beds at the fairly central *Downing International AYH Hostel*, 535 Oak Street (☎472-5788), cost $8. *Niko's*, 135 Water Street (☎475-7000), serves standard cheap food, while the nearby, slightly more healthy, *Pastabilities*, 311 S Franklin Street (☎474-1153), is also reasonable. Student numbers ensure a lively music scene; consult the resourceful *Syracuse New Times* freesheet for details.

Northern Finger Lake Towns

SKANEATLES, crouching at the neck of Skaneatles Lake, is the best place to go bathing in the Finger Lake region. The appealing bay sports a beach and a marina where you can take boat trips and rent water sport equipment. **Accommodation** is sparse but sometimes *Budget Host*, 797 W Genessee Street (☎685-6720), has rooms for $35. The

Sherwood Inn (☎685-3405), overlooking the lake, is not as expensive as you might think; doubles start at $66 including breakfast. For cholesterol-packed but scrumptious cheap **meals**, join the queue at the ever-popular *Doug's Fish Fry*, 8 Jordan Street (☎685-3288).

At **SENECA FALLS**, just west of the northern tip of Cayuga Lake, **Elizabeth Cady Stanton** and a few colleagues planned and held the first **Women's Rights Convention** in 1848 – 72 years before the Nineteenth Amendment gave all US women the vote. The site of the first campaign meeting, the **Wesleyan Chapel**, 126 Fall Street, is due to re-open as a museum in 1993, but the **National Women's Hall of Fame**, 76 Fall Street, where Cady Stanton is among the women honoured in fields such as humanitarianism, sport and the arts, makes an interesting stop (May–Oct, daily 10am–4pm; Nov–April Wed–Sat 10am–4pm, Sun noon–4pm; $3; ☎568-8060). Run by the National Park Service, the **Women's Rights Visitors Center**, 116 Fall Street (daily, 9am–5pm; ☎568-2991), has details of a walking tour that takes in the small museum at the Cady Stanton house and passes the (privately owned) former home of **Amelia Bloomer**, whose crusade to urge women out of their cumbrous undergarments won her a place in the dictionary.

The town itself is an interesting blend of old mills and different-styled homes, tucked away among the mature trees. If you want to stop over, try the *Gould Hotel* on busy Fall Street (☎568-5801), where the slightly tarnished pomp and luxury costs $55 to $75.

Hwy-89 out of Seneca Falls has been dubbed the **Cayuga Wine Trail**, as dozens of small wineries operate from along the west shore of the largest of the Finger Lakes. One of the best is the Lucas Vineyard (☎532-4825).

Ithaca

Cayuga Lake comes to a halt at hilly **ITHACA**, perhaps the most picturesque town in the region, piled like a diminutive San Francisco high above the lakeshore and culminating in the towers, sweeping lawns and shaded parks of the Ivy League **Cornell University**. On campus, the boxy I M Pei-designed **Herbert F Johnson Museum of Art** merits a visit more for its fifth-floor view of the town and lake than for an unspectacular collection of Asian and contemporary art (Tues–Sat 10am–5pm; free). The pick of the countless waterfalls within a few miles of town is the slender 210ft **Taughannock Falls** on Hwy-89, which has a swimming beach close at hand.

Greyhound and local **buses** operate out of the terminal at W State and N Fulton streets (☎272-1313). Cheap places to **stay** are few and far between; the cramped *Hillside Inn*, 518 Stewart Avenue (☎273-6864), and the *Elmshade Guest House*, 402 S Albany Street (☎273-1707), both cost around $40. Ithaca boasts two top-rated **vegetarian restaurants** – *Cabbagetown Cafe*, 404 Eddy Street (☎273-2847), and the inventive *Moosewood*, of cookbook fame, in DeWitt Mall in the central vehicle-free **Commons**, 108 E Green Street (☎273-9610). Numerous cheaper student-oriented places to eat include *Oliver's Deli*, 415 College Avenue. For news of the lively **music scene** – and gigs at the **Haunt**, 114 W Green Street (☎273-3355) – check out the free *Ithaca Times*.

Other Southern Finger Lake Towns

Forty miles southwest of Ithaca, world-famous **Steuben Glass** has been manufactured in the otherwise undistinguished town of **CORNING** since Frederick Carder started making his characteristic Art-Nouveau pieces in 1903. The excellent **Museum of Glass** in the **Corning Glass Center** traces its history from ancient heads and amulets to modern sculptures and paperweights. Also in the complex, where glass is omnipresent in mirrors and motifs, are the **Hall of Science and Technology**, full of push-button exhibits, and the **Steuben Glass Factory** itself, where every stage of the production process can be viewed from behind (glass) screens (daily 9am–5pm; $5; ☎974-8271).

The **Rockwell Museum**, ten minutes' stroll away at Cedar Street and Denison Parkway, has more glass, plus antique toys and a strong collection of western art (summer Mon–Fri 9am–7pm, Sat 9am–5pm, Sun noon–5pm; otherwise less; $4).

The Niagara Frontier

With the captivating exception of **Niagara Falls**, one of the continent's biggest crowd-pullers, there's little to see in the northwest reaches of New York State. The industrial giants of **Rochester** and **Buffalo** each possess one or two worthy museums, but nothing to go out of your way for.

Rochester

In contrast to its sprawling suburbs, downtown **ROCHESTER** is a salubrious place. Loosely corralled by an inner ring road, the central office-block area is bordered by well-heeled mansions on spacious boulevards. Various high-tech companies, such as Bausch & Lomb and Xerox, have brought capital to the city, but by far the most conspicuous names on view are those of **Kodak**, and its founder, **George Eastman**. Legacies throughout the metropolitan area include **Kodak Park**, the **Eastman Theater**, and above all the **International Museum of Photography** at George Eastman House, two miles from downtown at 900 East Avenue. A first-rate exhibition of photographic history ranges from unbelievably clear Civil War prints to modern experimental works, and the twentieth-century gallery forms an A to Z of modern greats – Ansel Adams, Cartier-Bresson, Steiglitz, Weston and lots more. Upstairs is the fun, hands-on Discovery Room, plus cabinets of unusual cameras. Nonetheless, with Kodak cash behind it, you would expect the museum to be much bigger. Good as it is, a visit will leave most people thirsting for more, and frustrated that a large part of the new wing completed in 1990 is given over to research and storage rather than exhibition space (Tues–Sat 10am–5pm, Sun 1–5pm; $4; ☎271-3361).

The **Strong Museum** on Manhattan Square is another gift from a wealthy former resident. Margaret Woodbury Strong (1897–1969), an inveterate collector of domestic artefacts, left everything from stuffed toys to porcelain plates and Shaker furniture. Many see it as an over-the-top souvenir hypermarket, but afficionados of Victoriana should have a field day. Of more general interest are the well-presented temporary exhibits looking at American consumer society; recent topics have included radio, sport and advertising (Mon–Sat 10am–5pm; Sun 1–5pm; $3; ☎263-2700).

Practicalities

To get to the museums from the *Amtrak* and *Greyhound* drop-off at 320 Central Avenue near downtown, you'll have to use *RTS* buses (☎654-0200). The company also runs a free city centre service (Mon–Fri, 11am–2pm). What there is of interest can be seen in a day, which is just as well as **accommodation** is nowhere cheap. Downtown the *Holiday Inn*, 120 E Main Street (☎546-6400), costs $90, as does the excellent *428 Mt Vernon B&B* (☎271-0792) at the entrance to lush **Highland Park**, one mile north. Budget options in the south of the city include the *Red Roof Inn*, 4820 W Henrietta Road, off I-90 Exit 46 (☎359-1100), for around $32. Popular places to **eat** in the fairly lively downtown include *Aladdin's*, 141 State Street (☎546-4320), serving inexpensive Middle Eastern food, the pub-style *Old Toad*, 277 Alexander Street (☎232-2626), where beer and cheap meals are served by mostly British staff, and *Cafe Creme de la Creme*, 295 Alexander Street (☎263-3580), whose magnificent pasties and creative entrees don't cost the earth.

Out from Rochester

The **Lake Ontario State Parkway** is a quiet, scenic way of driving to Niagara Falls from Rochester, taking about an hour longer than the standard route along I-90 via

The telephone **area code** for the Niagara area is ☎716.

Buffalo. The parkway starts eight miles from downtown at the end of Lake Avenue, near the popular **Ontario Beach Park**. This short golden strand, overlooked by exclusive holiday homes, is a real poseur's paradise; you may well feel self-conscious if your shades don't match up to the ubiquitous (locally manufactured) *Ray-Bans*.

If big crowds and the churning noise of speedboats are not your thing, head twenty miles along the parkway to the more secluded **Hamlin Beach State Park** ($3 per car). The parkway passes through few towns, and the best place to stop for refreshments is the small and attractive **Point Breeze** harbour, ten miles on from Hamlin.

Buffalo

As I-90 sweeps down into Buffalo, downtown looms up in a cluster of Art Deco spires and glass box skyscrapers – Manhattan in miniature on the Erie. The city centre smacks of money but the derelict buildings in the immediate environs tell of an uncomfortable ride during past recessions. Today Buffalo has set aside those memories, and stands ready to exploit the recently signed free trade agreement with Canada.

The **Albright-Knox Art Gallery**, 1285 Elmwood Avenue, two miles north of downtown, would hold its own even in New York City. It's especially strong on American and European art of the past thirty years: the Colourfield painters, Abstract Expressionism, Pop, Op and Kinetic Art are on show, Pollock, Rothko and Rauschenberg among the names. There's also a fine selection of pieces by earlier artists including Matisse, Picasso and Monet (Tues–Sat 11am–5pm; Sun noon–5pm; donation).

Apart from its professional **sports** teams – football's Bills (☎649-0015), ice hockey's Sabres (☎856-7300) and baseball's Bisons (☎846-2003), who as the top farm team for the Pittsburgh Pirates attract over a million fans per season to downtown's Pilot Field stadium – Buffalo has surprisingly little to offer the visitor. A clipper boat trip from the redeveloped **lakeshore** is one possibility (daily; $7; ☎856-6696).

Practicalities

Greyhound (☎855-7511), *Metro Bus* and *Metro Rail*, the city's new tramway (both ☎855-7211), all operate from the downtown depot at Ellicott and Church streets. *Amtrak* stops at nearby 75 Exchange Street, and in the eastern suburb of Depew, close to the **airport** (☎632-3115). The one moderately priced place to **sleep** downtown – except for the *YWCA*, 245 North Street (☎884-4761), where women can stay for $7 a night – is the *Hotel Lenox*, 140 North Street (☎884-1700), at $50 ($40 for students). The city's speciality of **buffalo** (spicy chicken) **wings** with blue cheese dressing is said to have been invented at the Anchor Bar, 1047 Main Street (☎886-8920), where lunch costs around $6. *Preservation Hall*, 752 Elmwood Avenue (☎884-4242), serves tasty, keenly priced vegetarian dishes, and during the day the cheap food stalls and tiny Polish cafes of Broadway Market, 999 Broadway, are well worth perusing.

Niagara Falls

Every second, over half a million gallons of water explode over the knife-edge **NIAGARA FALLS**, right on the border with Canada some twenty miles north of Buffalo on I-190. This awesome spectacle is made even more so by the variety of methods laid on to help you get closer: boats, catwalks, observation towers and helicopters all push as near to the curtain of gushing water as they dare. At night the falls are lit up, and the coloured waters tumble dramatically into blackness, while in winter the whole scene changes as the falls freeze to form gigantic razor-tipped icicles.

Many visitors will, however, find the whole experience a bit too gimmicky; no commercial opening has been left unexploited in the attempt to extract cash from tourists (Oscar Wilde quipped that he would have been more impressed if the falls ran

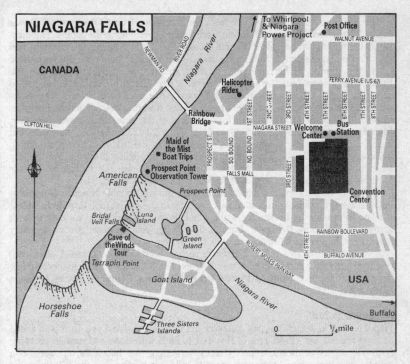

upwards; at least no one's tried that yet). Don't expect too much; neither the small city of **Niagara Falls**, still a shabby industrial eyesore despite recent efforts to spruce it up, nor the more developed tinsel town of **Niagara**, Canada, is a place to savour in any way. Once you've seen the falls, from as many different angles as you can manage, there's no real point in sticking around.

Arrival and Information

Amtrak **trains**, en route between New York and Toronto, stop two miles from downtown at 55 Dick Road. If you arrive at the **bus** station (☎285-9391), on Fourth and Niagara streets, you're next door to the official **Welcome Center** (☎285-2400), who are helpful for accommodation advice. Countless other places in town claim to be tourist centres but in fact are just fronts for tour companies hoping to entice you on one of their trips. *Niagara Frontier Metro Transit System* buses run to all areas of the city and Buffalo ($2). To send the obligatory postcards, you'll need the **post office** at 615 Main Street (Mon–Fri 8.30am–5pm, Sat 9am–noon; ☎285-7561).

The Falls

Niagara Falls is in reality comprised of three distinct cataracts. Though the tallest are the **American** and **Bridal Veil** falls on the American side, plunging straight down in a 180ft drop, the broad **Horseshoe Falls** which curve their way over to Canada are probably the most impressive. All three were formed some twelve thousand years ago, when the retreat of melting glaciers allowed water trapped in Lake Erie to gush north to Lake Ontario. Back then the falls were seven miles downriver, but constant erosion has cut them back to their present site.

The best conventional views are from the **Prospect Point Observation Tower** (daily; 25¢) or from Terrapin Point on **Goat Island** overlooking the rapids. The nineteenth-century tightrope-walker Blondin crossed the Niagara repeatedly near here, and even carried passengers across on his back; other suicidal fools over the years have taken the plunge in barrels. One survivor among the many fatalities was the Englishman Bobby Leach, who went over in a steel barrel in July 1911 and had to spend the rest of the year in hospital. That practice has since been banned, for reasons which become self-evident when you approach the towering cascade on the not-to-be-missed *Maid of the Mist* **boat trip** from the foot of the observation tower (summer, Mon–Fri 10am–5pm; Sat & Sun 10am–6pm; $7; ☎284-4233). A more expensive but equally compelling way to appreciate the grandeur of the falls is to take a six-minute **helicopter ride** from 454 Main Street (daily 9am–dusk; $25; ☎284-2800). For the less adventurous, the *Cave of the Winds* tour leads down to the base of the falls by elevator to within almost touching distance of the water (mid-May–late Oct; $4).

With your own transport it's possible to trace the inhospitable **Niagara Gorge** two miles along the dramatic Robert Moses Parkway to the **Whirlpool Rapids**, a violent maelstrom swollen by broken trees and other flotsam. Alternatively it's easy to walk across the **Rainbow Bridge** to Canada (50¢; bring your passport) for an arguably better view, bigger crowds and even more tawdry commercialism.

As you look on in awe, reflect that you're seeing about half the volume of water – the rest is diverted to hydro-electric power stations. The full story of this engineering feat is related at the free **Niagara Power Project Visitors Center** in nearby Lewiston (daily; ☎285-3211).

Accommodation

Places to **stay** in central Niagara can work out quite expensive if you don't plan ahead or shop around, but US-62, east of Hwy-190, is lined with dozens of **motels** charging from $30. Many of these are pretty tacky, targetting the thousands of honeymoon couples who come here every year (despite Wilde's assertion that the falls "must be one of the earliest if not keenest disappointments of American married life").

The closest place to **camp** is seven miles from downtown at the *Niagara Falls Campground & Lodging*, 2405 Niagara Falls Boulevard in Wheatfield (☎731-3434), for $15 a night.

All Tucked Inn B&B, 574 3rd St (☎282-0919). Cosy, unpretentious B&B for just $54.

Budget Inns, 492 Main St (☎285-8366). No-frills downtown motel; $49–69.

Coachman Motel, 523 3rd St (☎285-2295). Central, fairly basic accommodation for $44.

Days Inn Fallsview, 201 Rainbow Blvd (☎285-9321). Impressive landmark hotel with grand lobby and tastefully decorated rooms. The average double costs nearly $100 but if you book early you should get one of the cheaper $59 rooms.

Frontier AYH Hostel, 1011 Ferry Ave (☎282-3700). Friendly, well-run hostel with around forty beds. Facilities include showers, kitchen and TV lounge. Preference is given to AYH members and it's advisable to book ahead in summer. $10 ($14 non-members).

YMCA, 1317 Portage Rd (☎282-0919). Basic and unremarkable men-only accommodation. $10.

Eating

Though most of the eating options in Niagara Falls are fast-food joints of indifferent quality, there are a few decent local bars and restaurants.

Arterial Restaurant, 314 Niagara St. Tasty burgers for under $2 and generous portions of spicy chicken wings at $3 make this an excellent downtown alternative to the fast-food emporia.

The Bakery and Ports of Call Restaurant, 3004 Niagara St (☎282-9498). A bit out of the way but a wide variety of European dishes for $10–20. The bar is good for a quiet drink.

Cataract House Restaurant, 225 Rainbow Mall (☎282-5635). Posh-looking Greek restaurant. Kebab, pizza and sandwich lunches for around $5, and a slightly more expensive dinner menu.

PENNSYLVANIA

PENNSYLVANIA, which but for a small stretch on Lake Erie is the only landlocked state in the northeast, was explored by the Dutch, in the early 1600s, settled by the Swedes forty years later, and claimed by the British in 1664. Charles II of England, who owed a debt to the Penn family, rid himself of the potentially troublesome young **William Penn**, an enthusiastic advocate of religious freedom, by granting him land in the Colony in 1682. Penn Jr immediately established a "holy experiment" of brotherly love and tolerance, naming the state for his father and setting a good example by signing a peaceful cohabitation treaty with the Native Americans. Most of the early agricultural settlers were religious refugees: Quakers like Penn himself, Mennonites from Germany and Switzerland, and Irish Catholics.

"The keystone state" was crucial in the development of the US. Politicians and thinkers like **Benjamin Franklin** and **Thomas Jefferson** in Philadelphia – home of both the Declaration of Independence and the Constitution – were prominent in articulating the ideas behind the Revolution. Later, the battle in **Gettysburg**, south Pennsylvania – best remembered for Abraham Lincoln's immortal Gettysburg Address – marked a turning point in the Civil War. Pennsylvania was also vital industrially; Pittsburgh, in the west, was the world's leading steel producer in the nineteenth century, and nearly all the nation's anthracite coal is still mined here.

The two great urban centres of **Philadelphia** and **Pittsburgh**, both lively and vibrant tourist destinations, are at opposite ends of the state. The three hundred miles between them, though predominantly agricultural, are topographically diverse. There are over one hundred state parks, with green rolling countryside in the east, brooding forests in the west, and in the northeast, the rivers, lakes and valleys of the Poconos, honeymooners' paradise. **Lancaster County**, home to traditional **Amish** farmers, and the Gettysburg battlefield both heave with busloads of day-trippers, and even the unexciting chocolate-factory town of **Hershey**, minutes away from Harrisburg, the capital, draws thousands of cocoa-loving visitors.

Getting Around Pennsylvania

Although to appreciate the less-populated stretches of Pennsylvania you really need a car, **public transport** is adequate if you organise yourself carefully. Both I-76 (the **Pennsylvania Turnpike**) and I-80 sweep right the way across to Ohio, nearly five hundred miles east to west. US-30 (the **Lincoln Highway**) also runs east–west between Philadelphia and Pittsburgh, past Lancaster City, York and Gettysburg, while the prettiest north–south route is US-15, from Maryland to New York State, which follows the Susquehanna River for about fifty miles.

Amtrak crosses daily from Philadelphia to Pittsburgh, stopping at Lancaster City, Harrisburg and other smaller towns. *Greyhound* covers all the major cities and some small towns not served by rail, but its routes can be circuitous – check arrival times when buying your ticket, especially if you need to make a connection.

Philadelphia

The original capital of the nation, **PHILADELPHIA** was laid out by William Penn, Jr in 1682, on a grid system that was to provide the pattern for most American cities. It was envisaged as a "greene countrie towne", and today, for all its historical and cultural significance, it still manages to retain a certain quaintness. Just a few blocks away from the noise, crowds, heat and dust of downtown, shady cobbled alleys stand lined with red-brick Colonial houses, while the peace and quiet of huge Fairmount Park make it easy to forget you're in a major metropolis.

Settled by **Quakers**, Philadelphia prospered swiftly on the back of trade and commerce, and by the 1750s had become the second largest city in the British Empire. Economic power fuelled strong Revolutionary feeling, and the city was the capital during the **War of Independence** (but for nine months under British occupation in 1777–78). It also served as the US capital until 1800, while Washington DC was being built. The **Declaration of Independence** was written, signed and first publicly read here in 1776, as was the **US Constitution** ten years later. Philadelphia was also a hotbed of new ideas in the arts and sciences, as epitomised by the scientist, philosopher, statesman, inventor and printer **Benjamin Franklin**. Numerous libraries and debating societies, as well as the nation's first hospital, women's medical college, university and zoo all sprang up in this stimulating environment.

A strong mix of **ethnic groups** make up forty percent of the population. Many of the city's **black** community are descendants of the mass black migration after the Civil War when, like Chicago, Philadelphia was seen as a mecca of tolerance and liberalism. More recently, it voted in the nation's first black mayor, and has the country's first museum dedicated to African-Americans. Though the word *Philadelphia* is Greek for "city of brotherly love", brotherly love isn't always evident; a history of racial tension culminated a few years ago when the black mayor – supposedly at the behest of the police chief – ordered the bombing of a building in which the separatist black group MOVE were squatting. Entire blocks were razed, and children were numbered among the dead.

Once known as *Filthydelphia*, and the butt of endless derision from W C Fields in the Thirties (witness, for example, his famous epitaph: "On the whole, I'd rather be in Philadelphia"), the city underwent a remarkable resurgence for the nation's bicentennial in the 1970s. Its strength today is in its great energy – regenerated by history, strong cultural institutions, a buzzing yuppie downtown and the rough edge of its traditional ethnic neighbourhoods, especially Italian South Philadelphia.

Arrival and Information

Philadelphia's **International Airport** (☎492-3181) is eight miles southwest of the city off I-95. Taxis into town cost around $20 (try *United Cabs*, ☎625-2811), and the *South East Pennsylvania Transit Authority* (*SEPTA*), run **trains** every thirty minutes (6am–midnight; $4) to three downtown destinations: 30th Street near the university, Suburban Station near City Hall, and Market East, adjacent to the **Greyhound** terminal at 1001 Filbert Street (☎931-4000). The **Amtrak** station, the second busiest in the States, is in the university area, opposite the city's main (24-hour) **post office** at 30th and Market streets (zip code 19104).

The excellent **visitor centre**, 1525 JFK Boulevard (☎636-1666) at the Penn Center subway station in the heart of downtown, supplies a wealth of interesting information, including the *Afro-American Historical and Cultural Guide* to the city (daily 9am–5pm, 9am–6pm in the summer); another visitor centre can be found at Third and Chestnut streets in Independence National Historic Park (INHP), the main tourist district east of the Delaware River (daily 9am–5pm; ☎597-8974).

Getting Around

SEPTA (☎574-7800) run an extensive **bus** system (6.30am–1am) and a **subway**. The most useful lines cross the city east–west (Market–Frankford line) and north–south (Broad Street line). Both bus and subway require exact fares of $1.50, but unlimited bus day passes and five-token books go for $5.25. **Trolleys** run to Fairmount Park every thirty minutes from the visitor centre (see above).

The telephone **area code** for Philadelphia is ☎215.

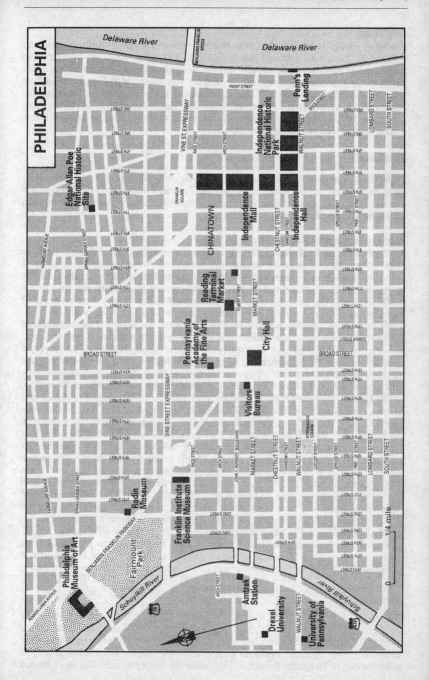

City Tours

American Trolley Tours leave from the visitor centre at 9.40am, 10.10am, 2.10pm, and 2.40pm, on three-hour narrated jaunts ($14). All the major sights are covered, and more detailed stops are made at INHP and the Betsy Ross House. At the end, the guide hands out free postcards, which will be sent for you (from the B Free Franklin Post Office) for no charge. *Candlelight Tours* through the hidden gardens and courtyards of Society Hill leave from the *City Tavern* (May–Oct, Thurs–Sat, 6.30pm; $5; ☎735-3123). *Gray Line* (☎569-3666) have a variety of coach tours from $13.50, including a three-hour historical tour and an all-day bash.

The City

Philadelphia stretches for about two miles from the Schuylkill (pronounced *Schoolkill*) River on the west to the Delaware on the east. The city's districts are compact, walkable and readily accessible from each other; Penn's beautifully planned grid system makes for easy sightseeing.

Independence Hall National Park

Any tour of Philadelphia should start with **Independence National Historic Park**, or **INHP**, "America's most historic square mile", which covers a mere four blocks just west of the Delaware River between Walnut and Arch streets, but can take more than one day to explore in full. The solid red-brick buildings here, not all of which are open to the public, epitomise the Georgian obsession with balance and symmetry. Free tours set off from the rear of the east wing of Independence Hall, the single most important site.

It's best to reach **Independence Hall** early, to avoid the hordes of tourists. Built in 1732 as the Pennsylvania State House, this was where the Declaration of Independence was prepared and signed, and, after the pealing of the Liberty Bell, given its firt public reading on July 8 1776. Today, in the room in which Jefferson *et al.* drafted and signed the United States Constitution, you can see George Washington's high-backed chair with the half-sun on the back – Franklin, in optimistic spirit, called it "the rising sun".

The **Liberty Bell** itself hung in Independence Hall from 1753, ringing to herald vital announcements such as victories and defeats in the Revolutionary War. In the nineteenth century, the bell's inscription from Leviticus, advocating liberty "throughout all the land unto all the inhabitants", made it an anti-slavery symbol for the New England Friends of Freedom – the first to call it the Liberty Bell. Stories as to how it received its famous crack vary; one tells that it occurred while tolling the funeral of Chief Justice Marshall in 1835. Whatever the truth, it rang publicly for the very last time on George Washington's birthday in 1846. After the Civil War the silent bell was adopted as a symbol of reconciliation, and embarked on a national rail tour. The well-travelled and somewhat lumpen icon now rests at eye level in a purpose-built pavilion on Market Street between Fifth and Sixth streets; reverent groups are herded through, given a speedy talk, and invited to take photos from a respectful, cordoned-off distance.

Next door to Independence Hall, **Congress Hall**, built in 1787 as the Philadelphia county courthouse, on Sixth and Chestnut streets, is where the new **United States Congress** first took their places, and where all the patterns for today's government were established. The US Supreme Court sat from 1791 until 1800 in **Old City Hall**, on the other side of Independence Hall on Fifth and Chestnut streets (daily 9am–5pm; free).

In 1774, delegates of the first **Continental Congress** – predecessor of the US Congress – chose defiantly to meet at **Carpenter's Hall**, 320 Chestnut Street, to air their grievances against the English king, rather than the more commodious State House. Today the building exhibits early tools and furniture (Tues–Sun 10am–4pm; ☎925-0167). Directly north, **Franklin Court**, 313 Market Street, is a tribute, on the site of his home, to Benjamin Franklin. The house no longer stands, but steel frames outline the original structure. An underground **museum** has dial-a-quote recordings of his pithy sayings and musings of his contemporaries, and there's a working printshop. The **B Free Franklin Post Office**, 316 Market Street, sells stamps and includes a small postal museum (daily 9am–5pm; free). Other buildings in the park include the **Philosophical Hall**, 104 S Fifth Street, still used today by the nation's first philosophical debating society (founded by Franklin). The building is closed to the public, but features a statue of Ben in intellectual mode, garbed in a fetching toga. The original **Free Quaker Meeting House**, Fifth and Arch streets, was built in 1783 by the small group of Quakers who actually fought in the Revolutionary War.

On the outskirts of the park, the **Norman Rockwell Museum**, Sixth and Sansom streets, has all of Rockwell's *Saturday Evening Post* covers and a slide show (daily 10am–4pm; $1.50). The museum also offers a self-guided audio-cassette tour of INHP, with music and anecdotes and a free map ($8 for one person, $12 for two; pick-up 10am–1pm, return by 4pm). The **Graff House**, Seventh and Market streets, was where Thomas Jefferson stayed while he drafted the Declaration of Independence. His two rooms have been re-created with period furnishings, and there is a short film (daily 9am–5pm; free). Philadelphia has two excellent ethnic museums; the **National Museum of American-Jewish History**, 55 N Fifth Street, which is dedicated to the experiences of Jews in the States and includes a synagogue (Mon–Thurs 10am–5pm, Fri 10am–3pm, Sun noon–5; $1.75), and the emotive and politically informed **Afro-American Historical and Cultural Museum**, Seventh and Arch streets. The latter tells the stories of the thousands of blacks who migrated north to Philadelphia after Reconstruction and in the early twentieth century. As well as lectures, films and concerts, there are photos, personal memorabilia, poems by black poet Langston Hughes and a Billie Holiday soundtrack (Tues–Sat 10am–5pm, Sun noon–6pm; $3.50). The **Edgar Allan Poe House**, ten blocks away from the park, 523 N Seventh Street, is where *The Telltale Heart* and *The Black Cat* were written (daily 9am–5pm; free).

Olde City

INHP runs north into **Olde City**, Philadelphia's earliest commercial area above Market Street near the riverfront. Washington, Franklin and Betsy Ross all worshipped at **Christ Church**, on Second Street just north of Market Street. Dating from 1727, it is surrounded by the gravestones of signatories to the Declaration of Independence (Mon–Sat 9am–5pm, Sun 1–5pm; free). The church's official burial ground, back towards INHP at Fifth and Arch streets, includes **Franklin's grave** (April–Oct). At 239 Arch Street, the **Betsy Ross House**, by means of unimpressive wax dummies, salutes the woman credited with making the first American flag. There's a gift shop and shady garden, an oasis away from the dusty streets outside (Tues–Sun 10am–5pm; free).

The claim of **Elfreth's Alley** – a pretty little cobbled way in the shadow of Philadelphia's downtown skyscrapers on Second Street between Arch and Race streets – to be the "oldest street in the United States" is somewhat nebulous, but it has been in continuous residential use since 1727, and its thirty houses, notable for their wrought-iron gates, water pumps, wooden shutters and attic rooms, date from early Colonial to Federal times. Number 126 is a small **museum** with household goods, and a quaint overgrown back garden (daily 10am–4pm; free).

Penn's Landing

Just to the east of Olde City along the **Delaware River** is one of the largest freshwater ports in the world, where William Penn stepped off in 1682. The **Penn's Landing** development, along Delaware Avenue from Market to Spruce streets, includes a **Port of History Museum** on Delaware Avenue and Walnut Street, which exhibits international arts and crafts (Wed–Sun 10am–4.30pm; $2) and a variety of historical ships including the flagship USS *Olympia* and World War II submarine *Becuna* (both daily

10am–5pm; $3), and the three-masted Portuguese Tall Ship *Gazela*, built in 1883 (while in port Sat & Sun 12.30–5.30pm; donation). The **Maritime Museum** (☎925-5439), based in INHP, runs a wooden-boatmaking workshop from a barge on the water (Wed–Sun 10am–5pm; $1.50; ☎925-7589). There are also plenty of food stalls, landscaped pools and fountains, and regular outdoor concerts and festivals.

Society Hill

Society Hill, an elegant residential area west of the Delaware and directly south of INHP, spreads itself between Walnut and Lombard streets. Though it is indeed Philadelphia's high society who live here now, the hill was named for its first inhabitants, the Free Society of Traders – a rather more fun-loving bunch than the strict Quakers who lived to the north. In one of the city's most picturesque districts, cobbled gaslit streets are lined with immaculately kept Colonial, Federal and Georgian homes. There are markers everywhere for self-guided tours, and the **Hill Keith Physick House**, 321 S Fourth Street, home to an early American surgeon, exhibits eighteenth- and nineteenth-century decorative arts (Tues–Sat 10am–4pm, Sun 1–4pm; $3).

Center City

Center City, Philadelphia's main business and commercial area, stretches from Eighth Street west to the Schuylkill River, dominated by the endearing baroque wedding cake of **City Hall** and its 37ft bronze statue of Penn. Before ascending thirty storeys to the observation deck at Penn's feet, check out the quirky sculptures and carvings around the building, including the cats and mice in the south entry. A couple of blocks north, the **Pennsylvania Academy of the Fine Arts**, Broad and Cherry streets, exhibits three hundred years of American art including works by Mary Cassatt and Thomas Eakins, in a gracious 1805 building with arches, columns, skylights and latticed windows (Tues–Sat 10am–5pm, Sun 11am–5pm; $5, free Sat 10am–1pm).

Beginning at Eighth Street, **Chinatown**, marked by a forty-foot oriental gate around the corner from the bus station, has some of the best budget food in the city. The lively, century-old **Reading Terminal Market**, between City Hall and INHP on Twelfth Street, caters to locals and businesspeople rather than tourists, and is a great place to browse or try out some of Philadelphia's superlative ethnic food. The market is closed at night, when the surrounding area should be avoided.

The Museums

The mile-long Benjamin Franklin Parkway, known as **Museum Row** – or, less convincingly, as "America's Champs-Elysees" – sweeps from City Hall to the colossal Museum of Art in Fairmount Park, an area of countryside annexed by the city in the nineteenth century. Spanning nine hundred scenic acres on both sides of the Schuylkill River, this is the world's largest landscaped city park, with jogging, biking and hiking trails, endless streams and trees, early American homes, an all-wars memorial to the state's black soldiers, and a **zoo**, 3400 Girard Avenue (Mon–Fri 9.30am–5pm, Sat–Sun until 6pm; $5.75, free on Mon Dec–Feb). In the late 1960s, local residents **Muhammad Ali** and **Joe Frazier** all but brought the city to a standstill with the announcement one afternoon that they were heading for Fairmount for an informal slug-out.

Sylvester Stallone later immortalised the steps of the **Philadelphia Museum of Art**, 26th Street and Franklin Parkway, by running up them in the film *Rocky*, but he missed out on a real treat inside; twenty superb galleries, with a twelfth-century French cloister, Renaissance art, Pennsylvania Dutch crafts and Shaker furniture, a strong Impressionist collection and a massive gathering of the works of Duchamp (Tues–Sun 10am–5pm; $5, Sun 10am–1pm free; ☎763-8100). A statue of Stallone as *Rocky* stood for a while on the steps, but the museum authorities shunted it away as soon as discreetly possible, considering it to be out of keeping with the general theme of their decor.

Statuary addicts may find some consolation for that loss in the exquisite **Rodin Museum**, Franklin Parkway and 22nd Street. Marble-walled, and set in a shady garden with a green pool, it holds the largest collection of Rodin's Impressionistic sculptures and casts outside Paris, including *The Thinker*, the *Burghers of Calais* and the *Gates of Hell* (Tues–Sun 10am–5pm; $1). Among rare books at the **Free Library of Philadelphia**, 19th and Vine streets, are cuneiform tablets from 3000 BC, medieval manuscripts, first editions of Dickens and Poe, and intriguing titles like the 1807 *Inquiry into the Conduct of the Princess of Wales* (Mon–Fri 9am–5pm, tours at 11am; free).

Over the road in the vast **Franklin Institute Science Museum** are a **Planetarium** (daily 9.30am–5pm; $5), the four-storey **OMNIVERSE** movie theatre (daily 9.30am–5pm; $6), and the new **Futures Center** – a mind-boggling state-of-the-art facility filled with such entertaining high-tech gadgets as a de-stressing game, and a hugely popular machine on which you can see (disappointingly hazy) images of your face aged by 25 years (Mon–Tues 9.30am–5pm, Wed–Sun 9.30am–9pm; $8.50). A $12.50 combination ticket covers admission to all three. Continuing the educational theme, the nearby **Academy of Natural Sciences** exhibits dinosaurs, mummies and gems (Mon–Fri 10am–4.30pm, Sat & Sun 10am–5pm; $5.50).

West Philadelphia
Across the Schuylkill River, **West Philadelphia** is home to Drexel and Penn universities, and is where Franklin established the country's first medical school. Today this lively student area has two good museums: the small **Institute of Contemporary Art**, 36th and Sansom streets, with cutting-edge travelling exhibitions in an airy white space (Tues–Sun 10am–5pm, Wed 10am–7pm; $2, free on Wed), and the **University Museum of Archaeology and Anthropology**, 33rd and Spruce streets (Sept–June Tues–Sat 10am–4.30pm, Sun 1–5pm; $3).

Rittenhouse Square
Grassy **Rittenhouse Square**, one of Penn's original city squares, is in one of the most fashionable areas in town. On one side it borders chic Walnut Street, on the other, a residential area of solid brownstones with beautifully carved doors and windows. The red-brick 1860 **Rosenbach Museum**, 2010 Delancey Place, holds over thirty thousand rare books and **James Joyce**'s original hand-scrawled manuscripts of *Ulysses* (Tues–Sun 11am–4pm, last tour 2.45pm; $1.50). To the north, the free **Mutter Museum**, 19 S 22nd Street in the College of Physicians (between Chestnut and Market streets), is filled with weird pathological and medical oddities including tumours, skeletons and the death cast of a pair of Siamese twins (Tues–Fri 10am–4pm). On summer evenings there are free outdoor jazz and R&B concerts in the square itself.

South Philadelphia
South Philadelphia, centre of Philadelphia's black community since the Civil War, is also home to the **Italian** district, where, among others, opera singer **Mario Lanza** (who has his own museum at 416 Queen Street) and pop stars Fabian and Chubby Checker grew up. This is where to go to get an authentic – and very messy – cheesesteak, and to rummage through the wonderful **Italian Market**, which begins at Ninth and Christian streets, for junk, flowers, oversized Levis, live seafood, and exquisitely fragrant olive oils in the fading wooden delis that have stood here for generations.

Six blocks away down Washington Avenue, the Art Deco **Mummers Museum** on Second Street and Washington Avenue displays costumes, musical instruments and photographs, illustrating the history of the colourful brass bands who march along Broad Street on New Year's Day (Tues–Sat 9.30am–5pm, Sun noon–5pm; $2).

South Street, the original boundary of the city, sells itself as Philadelphia's answer to New York's Greenwich Village – and is becoming every bit as commercial. There are more college kids and yuppies than starving artists, but it's undeniably lively at night, especially between Front and Tenth streets. At weekends it can be impossible to move, it's so crowded.

Accommodation

Philadelphia's luxury downtown **hotels** are prohibitively expensive; many of them do cheap weekend packages, however, so it's well worth checking with the visitor centre. **B&Bs** are a good option, but often need to be arranged in advance. *B&B Center City*, 1804 Pine Street (☎735-1137), has over fifty rooms throughout the city from $40 to $85. *University City Guest Homes*, 2933 Morris Road, Ardmore (☎387-3731), offers rooms in the homes of academics, predominantly in the west of town, from $25 to $75.

Apollo Hotel, 1918 Arch St (☎567-8925). Decent rooms for under $40.

Chamounix Mansion International AYH Hostel, West Fairmount Park (☎878-3676). Quaker country estate in a gorgeous park setting. A bit of a trek, but on the trolley route from the visitor centre. 11pm curfew, check-in 4.30–8pm, beds $12.50 for non-members.

Comfort Inn, 100 N Delaware Ave (☎627-7900). High-rise hotel, great location near Penn's Landing, with rooms for $75–89 including continental breakfast.

International House, 3701 Chestnut St (☎387-5125). Adjacent to Penn University, giving preference to students and college graduates (proof required), with doubles from $50. More space during the summer, when the international students have returned home.

Quality Inn, 501 N 22nd St (☎568-8300). North of the Franklin Parkway, near the museums. $70–82.

Thomas Bond House, 129 S Second St (☎923-8523). 1769 townhouse near INHP with twelve rooms from $80 including breakfast.

The Village Guest House, 808 S Second St (☎755-9770). Three blocks below South Street, with rooms $55–75 including breakfast.

Eating

Eating out cheaply in Philadelphia is a real treat; try Chinatown, Reading Terminal Market and the Italian Market for ethnic food, South Street for trendy and reasonably priced restaurants, and the ubiquitous street stands for the famous Philly soft pretzels with mustard (around 50¢). The **South Philadelphia cheesesteak** varies from joint to joint around town, though logically enough the best (as in the biggest, freshest and juiciest) are to be found in the Italian cafes of South Philadelphia.

City Tavern, Second and Walnut streets (☎923-6059). Reconstructed 1773 tavern in INHP, familiar to the city's founders, and called by John Adams "the most genteel tavern in America". Costumed staff serve "olde style" food (pasties, turkey rarebit) to a harpsichord accompaniment, but the prices, sadly, are historically inaccurate – from about $16 for dinner. Lunch is cheaper.

Delilah's, Reading Terminal Market, 12th and Spruce streets (☎574-0929). Superb soul food, scatty service. Nigerian stew with cornbread $4.75, beans and rice $3.50.

Diner on the Square, 1839 Spruce St (☎735-5787). 24hr diner off Rittenhouse Square serving staple foods (including a good cheesesteak) from $4 and with a circular soda- and ice-cream bar.

Geno's, Ninth and Passyunk streets (no phone). Beautifully cooked cheesesteak hoagies (bulging French bread sandwiches) in the Italian Market. From $5.

Joe's Peking Duck House, 925 Race St (☎922-3277). Shabby setting, but some of the best food in Chinatown. Dinner from $6.

Lee's Hoagies, 44 S 17th St (☎564-1264). Downtown lunch place; a thousand variations on a single theme. The regular hoagies (from $3.75) are giant; the giants (from $7.50), truly gargantuan.

South Street Diner, 140 South St (☎627-5258). Huge menu with Greek and Italian specialities from $5.25. Seven days, 24hr.

Tuly's, 603 S Fourth St (☎922-3533). Small Middle Eastern restaurant off South St. Dinner from $7. Bring your own bottle.

White Dog Cafe, 3420 Sansom St (☎386-9224). Trendy, creative food in an antique-filled room near the universities. Arty, student crowd. Dinner (Lithuanian salmon on spinach, for example) $12–25.

Nightlife and Entertainment

Few reminders are left of the **Philly Sound**, famous in the Seventies; stars like Patti LaBelle and Harold Melvin and the Blue Notes have waned, and nightlife has shifted more upmarket, with a world-famous orchestra and superb theatres. The **Philadelphia Orchestra** performs at the grand **Academy of Music** on Broad Street (☎893-1930), modelled after Milan's La Scala Opera House, and also holds free summer concerts at the **Mann Music Center** in Fairmount Park (☎567-0707). The **Freedom Theater**, 1346 N Broad Street (☎765-2793), is an excellent black theatre company with performances in the oldest black cultural centre in the US. *TIXSTOP*, in the visitor centre, offers half-price standby tickets (Tues–Thurs 11.30am–3.30pm, Fri & Sat 11.30am–5pm).

A trail of **theme bars** has sprung up along **Penn's Landing** and the Delaware River, but by far the most popular stretch is on **South Street**. Check the listings in the *Friday City Paper* or call the 24-hour **event hotline**, ☎574-1200. In July, there's a week-long **Freedom Fest** around the Fourth, and the superb **Riverblues** weekend festival on the Delaware River at the end of the month features top-name blues artists.

Bars and Live Music Venues

Borgia Cafe, 406 S Second St (☎574-0414). Live jazz, plus food.

Irish Pub, 1123 Walnut St (☎568-5603). Good music and atmosphere near Rittenhouse Square.

Katmandu, Pier 25 N Delaware Ave (☎629-7400). World music in "exotic" surroundings just north of the decidedly unexotic Franklin Bridge. Bar and nightly outdoor barbecue.

The Khyber Pass, 56 S Second St (☎440-9683). Small rock venue with a gargoyle-lined wooden bar, bluesy jukebox and casual young clientele.

Painted Bride Art Center, 230 Vine St (☎925-9914). Art gallery with live folk, jazz, poetry and performance art by night.

Trocadero, Tenth and Arch streets (☎923-ROCK). Trendy downtown dance club with occasional live bands. Cover varies, ID essential. Closed Mon.

Who's on Third, 700 S Third St (☎625-2835). Irish pub a block below South Street. Happy Hour 7–9pm, *Campbells Soup* served at $3 a can. Disco Fri & Sat.

Central Pennsylvania

Central Pennsylvania, cut north to south by the broad **Susquehanna River**, has no major cities, although it holds the state capital, **Harrisburg**, and the important Civil War site of **Gettysburg** at its southern border. Its assorted landscapes are sparsely populated, from the rolling Amish farmlands of **Lancaster County** in the southeast to the mighty northern forests around **Williamsport**, which reveals the legacy of its great nineteenth-century lumber wealth in mansion-lined streets. **Johnstown**, beyond the dramatic Allegheny mountains in the west, is a tough survivor, subject of many folk songs for its tragic history of floods (the most destructive in 1889 when the South Fork Dam, ten miles east, collapsed and killed over two thousand in ten minutes, and the most recent in 1977). The town has developed a tourist industry of sorts by such means as the **Johnstown Flood Museum** on Washington Street (☎539-1889).

Lancaster County – Pennsylvania Dutch Country

Lancaster County, fifty miles west of Pennsylvania, stretches for about thirty miles from Churchtown in the east to the Susquehanna River in the west. Although **Lancaster City**, ten miles east of the river, was US capital for a day in September 1777,

The telephone **area code** for central Pennsylvania is ☎717.

the region is famed more for its preponderance of agricultural religious communities, known collectively as the **Pennsylvania Dutch** (a derivation of *Deutsch*, or German). They originated as **Anabaptists**, founded in sixteenth-century Switzerland by Menno Simons, whose unorthodox advocacy of adult baptism and literal interpretation of the Bible led to the order's persecution. Invited by Penn to settle in Lancaster County in the 1720s, today the 1700 or so Pennsylvania Dutch include the "plain" Old Order **Amish** (a strict order who originally broke away from Simmons in 1693) and freer-living **Mennonites**, as well as the "fancy" **Lutheran** groups (distinguished by the colourful circular "hex" signs on their barns). The Amish are the best known, the men with their wide-brimmed straw hats and beards (but no "military" moustaches), the women in bonnets, plain dresses (with no fripperies like buttons), and aprons. Shunning electricity and any exposure to the corrupting influence of the outside world, the Amish power their farms with generators, and travel (at roughly ten miles per hour) in handmade horse-drawn buggies. For all their insularity, the Amish are very friendly and helpful; resist the temptation to photograph them, however, as the making of "graven images" offends their beliefs.

An extremely touristy place, even before it was brought to international fame by the movie *Witness*, Lancaster County has maintained its natural beauty in the face of encroaching commercialisation. It is a region of gentle countryside and fertile farmlands, mule-drawn ploughs, tiny roadside bake shops crammed with jams and pies, Amish children wending on old-fashioned scooters to and from their one-room schoolhouses, and flower-filled, immaculate farmhouses. However, attempting to live a simple life away from the pressures of the outside world has proved too much for many Pennsylvania Dutch. A few (mainly Mennonites) have succumbed to commercial need by offering rides in their buggies and meals in their homes. Members of the stricter orders in particular have moved away from ceaseless intrusions of privacy – as well as soaring land prices – to less touristed Ohio and Iowa.

Arrival and Information

The Pennsylvania Turnpike sweeps across the north of the region, but most activity is concentrated further south near the east–west US-30. *Greyhound* arrives in Lancaster City at 22 W Clay Street (daily 7am–5.15pm; ☎387-4861), *Amtrak* at 53 McGovern Avenue. The bustling **Pennsylvania Dutch Visitors Bureau**, northeast of town at 501 Greenfield Road, provides orientation and advice on accommodation (Mon–Thurs 8.30am–7pm, Fri & Sat 8.30am–9pm, Sun 8.30am–6pm; ☎299-8901). In Lancaster City itself, the small **visitor centre** at 100 S Queen Street downtown in the Southern Farmers' Market has maps for self-guided walking tours (April–Oct Mon–Fri 8.30am–5pm, Sat 10am–3pm, Sun 9am–3pm; ☎392-1776). They organise guided tours on weekdays at 10am and 1.30pm, and on Sundays at 1.30pm, costing $3.

Visitors keen to learn about Pennsylvania Dutch culture should head to the excellent **People's Place**, Main Street, Intercourse, eleven miles east of Lancaster City, which has a well-stocked bookshop, an informative if sentimental slide show, an Amish world museum, and the feature film *Hazel's People*, plus quilts and artwork (April–Oct Mon–Sat 9.30am–9.30pm, Nov–March 9.30am–4pm). The **Mennonite Information Center**, 2209 Millstream Road off US-30, organises lodging with Mennonite families, and has a wide range of information. Call at least two hours ahead for a guide to come with you for a two-hour, $16.50, tour in your car (April–Oct Mon–Sat 9.30am–9.30pm, Nov–March 9.30am–4.30pm; ☎299-0954).

Getting Around

Winding country lanes weave through Pennsylvania Dutch country, passing small villages with eccentric-sounding names such as **Intercourse** (source of many droll postcards, but simply named for its location on the junction of two main roads).

Although a car will get you to the quieter back roads the tour buses miss, it's more fun to **rent a bike**. Only then can you feel the benefits of all that pure fresh air – and it shows more consideration for the horse-drawn buggies with which you share the road. *New Horizons*, 3495 Horizon Drive, rent bikes by the day or hour, and will meet travellers from the bus or train station if called in advance (☎285-7607).

For those without transport, *Red Rose Transit* (☎397-4246) in Lancaster City run an extensive **bus** and **trolley** system. Flat-fare buses ($1.15) run to Paradise, Bird-in-Hand, Intercourse, Ephrata and Lilitz, but service stops around 5pm. In summer, the trolley follows a useful route along US-30 to Strasburg, with the last trip back at 8pm ($1.50, day pass $2.50). Collect schedules from 47 N Queen Street .

Of the various **tour companies**, *Amish Country Tours*, on US-340 between Bird-in-Hand and Intercourse, do four-hour tours of the farmlands ($19) and special limited-number "VIP" tours which stop at Amish properties – a rare opportunity to talk to the people rather than merely gawp at them ($28; ☎768-7063). *Ed's Buggy Rides*, US-896, north of Strasburg, are lolloping three-mile countryside excursions for $6 (☎687-0360).

Touring Pennsylvania Dutch Country

Though useful for a general overview and historical insights, the "authentic" Amish attractions of Lancaster County – farms, homes, villages and so on – are all much of a muchness. It's far more satisfying just to explore the countryside for yourself. The Pennsylvania Dutch population having doubled in less than twenty years, the scarcity of farmland has led to diversification (look out for wonderful crafts and furniture stores) and some Amish now live on the outskirts of the small towns; however, the majority remain successful and wealthy farmers. Here, among the streams with their wooden covered bridges and fields striped with corn, alfalfa and tobacco, the reality hits you – these aren't just actors re-creating an ancient lifestyle, but a living, working community. There's no guarantee as to what you'll see; on Sunday, for example, there are no quilt sales or bake shops, and the men don't work the fields, but there may well be a large gathering of buggies outside one of the farms, indicating an Amish church service (in High German), or a "visiting day".

Among the widely spread formal "attractions", the **Ephrata Cloister**, 632 W Main Street, Ephrata (on US-272 and 322) re-creates the eighteenth-century settlement of German Protestant celibates that acted, amongst other things, as an early publishing and printing centre (Mon–Sat 9am–5pm, Sun noon–5pm; $3). Further south, about three miles northeast of Lancaster City, the **Landis Valley Museum**, 2451 Kissell Hill Road, is a living history museum of rural life (Tues–Sat 9am–5pm, Sun noon–5pm; $3).

In **Lancaster City** itself, a stolid red-brick town with treelined avenues, the **Heritage Center Museum**, 13 W King Street on the main Penn Square, exhibits Lancaster folk art, including wagons and rifles, ancient *fraktur* calligraphy, wooden toys, weathervanes and quilts (May–Nov Mon–Sat 10am–4pm; free). Along US-30, the most interesting stop is the **Amish Homestead**, 2034 Lincoln Highway E; informative tours of this eighteenth-century working farm include details on Amish clothing and lifestyle, and Amish-led buggy rides in the grounds give an opportunity to talk to the Pennsylvania Dutch first-hand for 75¢. At **Strasburg**, a mixture of tourist tweeness and historical authenticity southeast of Lancaster City on US-896, the **Strasburg Railroad** gives 45-minute round-trip rides in original steam trains through patchwork farmland to **Paradise** (daily; $5.50; ☎687-7522). Disappointingly, Paradise itself holds no heavenly delights, but there are some good views on the way (if little that couldn't be seen by bike or car), and the train makes regular picnic stops. The oldest building in the county, the **Hans Herr House**, 1849 Hans Herr Drive, Willow Street, five miles south of downtown Lancaster City off US-222, is a 1719 Mennonite church with a pretty garden and orchard, a medieval German facade and exhibits of early farm life (April–Dec Mon–Sat 9am–4pm; $2.50).

Lancaster County Accommodation

Accommodation options for those who want to spend more than a day in Pennsylvania Dutch country range from reasonably priced **hotels** in and around Lancaster City, through **farm vacations** (ask at the Pennsylvania Dutch CVB) to **campgrounds**. *White Oak Campgrounds*, 372 White Oak Road, Quarryville, four miles north of Strasburg, overlook the heart of the Dutch farmlands and host a county auction on Saturdays (reservations recommended; $12; ☎687-6207).

Brunswick Hotel, Chestnut and Queen streets (☎397-4801). Seventies-style luxury hotel in the centre of downtown Lancaster City, with spacious comfortable rooms for $62–75.

Countryside Motel, 134 Hartman Bridge Rd (☎687-8431). Six miles east of Lancaster City on Hwy-896, costing from $40.

Dingledein House, 1105 E King St (☎293-1723). Friendly B&B close to Lancaster City. Rooms from $55 – but only four of them, so call ahead. Includes a huge country breakfast.**Lancaster Travelodge**, 2101 Columbia Ave, US-462 (☎397-4201). Standard lodging two miles south of downtown Lancaster. Prices from $66 at weekends, cheaper during the week.

Patchwork Inn, 2319 Old Philadelphia Pike (☎293-9018). Rooms in this nineteenth-century farm between Lancaster City and Smoketown go for $55–75.

Red Caboose Motel, Paradise Lane, Strasburg (☎687-6646). Quirky accommodation in converted train cabooses, from $50.

Lancaster County Eating and Nightlife

Lancaster County **food** is delicious: German-influenced, organic, and served in vast quantities. There are no Amish-owned restaurants, but Amish roadside stalls sell fresh homemade root beer, jams, pickles, breads and pies; if, as occasionally happens in more remote areas, there's no one there, leave the money on the counter. To arrange a meal in a **Mennonite home** (for around $10), ask at the Pennsylvania Dutch CVB.

The huge "all-you-can-eat" **tourist restaurants** on US-30 and US-340 look off-putting, all pseudo-rusticism with costumed waitresses. However, most serve excellent meals (costing around $13.50), "family-style" – which means sharing long tables and limitless mountains of fried chicken, sauerkraut, noodles, pickles, cottage cheese and apple butter, corn, hickory-smoked ham, *schnitz, knepp*, apple dumplings and shoo-fly pie with crowds of other tourists. None stays open later than 8pm.

Rural Lancaster County, where people get up at the crack of dawn, is not known for its wild **nightlife** – or any nightlife for that matter; even the streets of Lancaster City are strangely quiet after dark. Options are not totally limited to early nights or cable TV, however; a couple of good – and very friendly – bars are worth exploring downtown. The *Fulton Opera House*, 12 N Prince Street (☎397-7425), is a plush red and gold restored Victorian theatre, hosting dance, plays and special events (Tues–Sun; $10–25).

Central Market, Penn Square, Lancaster City. Fresh farm produce and sandwiches. Tues & Fri 6am–4.30pm, Sat 6am–2pm.

Family Style Restaurant, 2323 E Lincoln Hwy (☎393-2323). The only "family-style" restaurant open on Sunday, and one of the few to serve alcohol. Also does breakfast.

Good'n'Plenty, East Brook Road, US-896, Smoketown (☎394-7111). Not Amish-owned, but Amish women cook and serve food in the best of the family-style restaurants. Open Mon–Sat until 8pm.

Habibi's, 9 W King St, Lancaster City (☎397-0152). Delicious and very cheap Middle Eastern alternative to wholesome farm food; feta cheese sandwiches, bean salads, felafel and rosewater lemonade in a tiny deli opposite the Central Market.

Lancaster Dispensing Co, 33–35 N Market St, Lancaster City (☎299-4602). Downtown Lancaster's trendiest and friendliest bar. Live jazz and blues at the weekend, plus chili, burgers and sandwiches.

Molly's Pub, 53 E Chestnut St, Lancaster City (☎396-0225). Neighbourhood bar with lively atmosphere and good burgers. Closed Sun.

Tom Paine's Grog House and Restaurant, 317 N Queen St, Lancaster City (☎393-2671). Expensive restaurant (ranging from $13), but also serves drink in ancient candlelit wooden bar where Revolutionary War tactics were whispered and plotted. Closed Sun.

Harrisburg

HARRISBURG, Pennsylvania's capital, lies on the Susquehanna River thirty or so miles northwest of Lancaster City, across the interstate. As you approach, the tower blocks of the skyline appear to lurk miserably on the horizon, but once you arrive it's a surprisingly attractive city, lined with many shuttered colonial buildings and well complemented by its unintentionally kitsch Chocolatetown neighbour **Hershey**.

Harrisburg's ornate **capitol**, Third and State streets, is undeniably beautiful; at its dedication in 1906, Theodore Roosevelt called it "the handsomest building I ever saw". Italian Renaissance in style, it has a dome modelled after St Peter's in Rome (Mon–Sat 9am–4pm; free). The complex includes the archaeological and military artefacts, decorative arts, tools and machinery exhibited in the free **State Museum of Pennsylvania**, a cylindrical building at Third and North streets (Tues–Sat 9am–5pm, Sun noon–5pm) .

One of the nicer ways to spend a Harrisburg afternoon is to cross the Susquehanna along the Walnut Street footbridge and stroll through **City Island**, a waterfront development that, as well as offering vast sports facilities (including a family-filled concrete beach, a baseball stadium and a football ground), gives good views across to downtown, shady picnic areas and riverboat rides, and hosts regular festivals and concerts.

Hershey, ten miles east, is by no means the "sweetest place on earth" – whatever the brochures may say. This sober small town, built in 1903 by candy magnate Milton S Hershey for his chocolate factory, does, however, have streetlamps in the shape of Hershey's chocolate kisses, streets named Chocolate and Cocoa Avenue, and air rich with the smell of cocoa. The excessive **Chocolate World Visitors Center** offers a free mini-train ride through a simulated chocolate factory (accompanied by sugary piped warblings of *It's a chocolate, chocolate world*). Those not content with the free sample given out at the end can guzzle in the vast gift and souvenir shops and cafes (daily 9am–6.45pm).

Hersheypark, which began in 1907 as a picnic ground for Hershey factory workers, is now a routine amusement park (mid-May–Sept daily, hours vary; $20.95; ☎534-3005). The adjacent **Hershey Museum of American Life** has exhibits on the Pennsylvania Dutch and tells the story of Hershey himself, the man who started it all (daily 10am–5pm; $1.25). **Founders Hall**, the centre of the Hershey school which provides free education for over a thousand kids, includes a bronze statue of him, as well as a reverent film on his "vision" (Mon–Fri 10am–4pm, Sat–Sun 10am–3pm; free).

Practicalities

The local **airport** (☎948-3913) is fifteen minutes from downtown; *Amtrak* share the central new station at Fourth and Chestnut streets with *Greyhound* (☎232-4251). *Greyhound* stop additionally in Hershey at 337 W Chocolate Street (☎397-4861). Harrisburg's **visitor centre** at 114 Walnut Street (☎232-1377) provides maps and an excellent historic downtown walking tour.

The **bus** system is negligible; don't try looking for budget accommodation without a car. Even the hotels on the outskirts of town, aimed towards business clientele, are pricey (but considerably cheaper at weekends). Five miles southwest of downtown, the *Quality Inn*, Limekiln Road and Leo Boulevard off I-83, has rooms from $50–70. In Hershey, they go for $55 to $90 at the Fairway, 1034 E Chocolate Avenue (☎533-5179), or, a mile further down the road at 1806 Chocolate Avenue, the *Chocolatetown Motel* (☎533-2330) has rooms from $60–75 (March–Oct only).

Cheap **restaurants** line Second Street in downtown Harrisburg, the very best being *Zephyr Express*, 400 N Second Street, which serves superb gourmet pasta from $5 in a lively chrome Art-Deco setting (☎257-1328). The popular *Roberto's Pizza*, 340 N Second Street, does juicy slices and subs from $1.50 (☎234-6633), and *Kick'n Chicken Cafe*, 900 N Third Street, has good spicy chicken from around $3 (☎236-1930).

Gettysburg

The attractive small town of **GETTYSBURG**, thirty miles south of Harrisburg near the Maryland border, gained tragic notoriety in 1863 for the cataclysmic **Civil War battle**, in which fifty thousand men died. There were more casualties during these three days than in any American battle before or since – a full third of those who fought – and entire regiments were wiped out when the tide finally turned against the South, on July 3.

Four months later, on November 19, **Abraham Lincoln** delivered his **Gettysburg Address** at the dedication of the National Cemetery. His two-minute speech, in memory of all the soldiers who died, is acknowledged as one of the most powerful orations in American history. Lincoln himself was convinced that it was a "flat failure", and prefaced his remarks with the words "the world will little note nor long remember what we say here ...."; you'll be muttering it in your sleep by the time you leave.

Gettysburg is almost overwhelmingly geared towards **tourism**, relentlessly replaying the minutest details of the battle, but fortunately it is perfectly feasible to avoid the commercial overkill and explore for yourself the rolling hills of the battlefield (now a national park) and the tidy town streets with their shuttered historic houses.

Arrival, Information and Getting Around

Greyhound (☎334-7064) makes two stops daily to and from Philadelphia outside the Gettysburg College on Carlisle Street. From here it's a short walk to the **Gettysburg Travel Council**, 35 Carlisle Street, housed in the tiny historic train depot where Lincoln disembarked in November 1863 (☎334-6274). Extremely helpful staff give out free maps and brochures and can help find accommodation.

Though the town is small, and easy to walk around, a car helps when touring the huge battlefield. There are no taxis, but **bikes** can be rented in the battleground at 610 Taneytown Road (April–Oct; from $2 per hour to $16 per day; ☎334-1258). Two-hour *Battlefield Bus Tours*, running through the town and making two stops in the battle- field, depart from 778 Baltimore Street (daily, every thirty minutes; $9.75; ☎334-6296).

The Battleground

It takes most of a day to see the 3500-acre **Gettysburg National Military Park**, which surrounds the town (daily 6am–10pm; free). The excellent **visitor centre** on Taneytown Road (daily 8am–6pm; ☎334-1124) doubles as the best **museum** with guns, uniforms, surgical and musical instruments, tents and flags, as well as touching photos of the 1938 Joint Soldiers Reunion. A thirty-minute – and painstakingly thorough – **electric map** show ($2) plots the intricacies of the battle; you can pick up details of a self-guided driv- ing route or a guide will join you in your car for a personalised two-hour tour ($17.50).

A short walk away, the **Cyclorama Center** holds a 356ft circular painting of **Pickett's Charge**, the suicidal last Confederate thrust across open wheat fields in broad daylight, and is accompanied by a recitation of the Gettysburg address (daily 9am–5pm; $2). The earliest existing draft of the Address (not, as commonly believed, scrawled on the back of an envelope), sits in a hallowed cabinet in a dark room on the lower storey. If you're dissatisfied with mere representations of the battlefield, the **National Tower** opposite the visitor centre gives views of the real thing from 300-foot observation decks (summer daily 9am–7.30pm, winter 9am–6pm; $3.75). The grounds themselves, golden fields reminiscent of an English country landscape, are peaceful now except for the names – **Valley of Death, Bloody Run, Cemetery Hill**. Uncanny statues of key figures stand at appropriate points and heavy stone monuments honour different regiments.

The Town

Pick just a couple of the numerous **museums** in town and follow the Travel Council's fourteen-block **downtown walking tour** for a real sense of the history of the place.

The **National Civil War Wax Museum**, 297 Steinwehr Avenue, shows, using dreadful dummies, the lead-up to the Civil War, the Underground Railroad for escapee slaves, abolitionist John Brown, and the famous Southern belle spies Rose Greenhow and Belle Boyd (daily 9am–9pm; $3.95). Across the National Cemetery in the battlefield, there are yet more dummies in the **Hall of Presidents and their First Ladies**, 504 Baltimore Street, complete with presidential pearls of wisdom and stirring patriotic music (daily, summer 9am–9pm, off-season 9am–5pm; $4). The only civilian to die in the battle, twenty-year-old Jennie Wade, was killed by a stray bullet as she made bread for the Union troops in her sister's kitchen. The **Jennie Wade House**, next to the Gettysburg Tour Center on Baltimore Street, looks exactly as it did on July 3 1863, with bullet holes in the front door and on the bedpost, an artillery shell hole ripped through the wall adjoining the neighbour's house, and a macabre model of Jennie's corpse lying under a sheet in the cellar (daily 9am–10pm, 9am–5pm off-season; $2.95).

President Eisenhower, who retired to Gettysburg, is commemorated to the west of the park at the **Eisenhower National Historic Site**, where his Georgian-style mansion holds an array of memorabilia. The site is only accessible on shuttle bus tours from the National Park visitor centre (daily 8.30am–4.15pm; $2.25).

Accommodation

There are plenty of budget lodgings in Gettysburg itself; choose from B&Bs, luxury motels and a very good hostel.

AYH Gettysburg International Hostel, 27 Chambersburg St (☎334-1020). Historic Civil War building in the centre of downtown. Excellent value at $10 for non-members.

Farnsworth House Inn, 401 Baltimore St (☎334-8838). An 1810 townhouse, used as Union HQ in the war and still riddled with bullet holes. Four rooms go for $65–80, with breakfast, afternoon tea and ghost stories in the cellar.

Heritage Motor Lodge, 64 Steinwehr Ave (☎334-9281). Between downtown and the battlefield, with rooms for $40–50.

Howard Johnson Lodge, 301 Steinwehr Ave (☎334-1181). Directly opposite the entrance to the battleground. Rooms from $69.

Eating and Nightlife

Evenings in Gettysburg tend to be quiet; the tour buses have gone home and many people choose to drink in their hotel bars. However, there are some very good **restaurants**, many in historically important buildings, and for those still hungry for battle trivia, James Getty, an Abe Lincoln lookalike, gives summer evening performances, answering questions and recounting "memories" of his life, at the *Conflict Theater*, 213 Steinwehr Avenue (Mon–Thurs 8pm; $5; ☎334-8003).

Dobbin House Tavern, 89 Steinwehr Ave (☎334-2100). The oldest house in the city, dating from 1776 and once an underground slave hideout. Lunch from $6, candlelit dinners more expensive. Food veers between Pennsylvania Dutch and early American.

Dutch Cupboard, 523 Baltimore St (☎334-6227). Sturdy Pennsylvania Dutch cooking (meatloaf, *snitz und knepp*, chicken and noodles, shoo-fly pie) in simple setting, from $3 for lunch, $8 dinner.

Tavern in the Village, 619 Baltimore St (☎334-5648). Gourmet sandwiches, happy hour 6–8pm.

Western Pennsylvania

Western Pennsylvania, a key point for frontier trade and an important thoroughfare to the west, was the focus of the fighting between English and French in the seven-year French and Indian War for colonial and maritime power (1756–63). It grew to industrial prominence in the nineteenth century, with the exploitation of its **coal** resources gathering pace after the Civil War, and the opening of the world's first **oil well** at Titusville (now Drake Well Memorial Park) in northwestern Pennsylvania in 1859.

Today, tourism in Western Pennsylvania, like the now-depleted coal and steel industries, is concentrated around the surprisingly appealing city of **Pittsburgh**. If you're looking for a more rural experience, however, the lush **Allegheny National Forest** in the north, twenty miles from I-80, is a great place to camp. The summer-only Kinzua Point Information Center on Hwy-59 (☎726-1291) can provide details on campgrounds and trails.

Pittsburgh

The vibrant ten-block district, known as the "**Golden Triangle**", at the heart of downtown **PITTSBURGH** stands at the confluence of the Monongahela, Allegheny and Ohio rivers, once bitterly fought over as the gateway to the west. The French built **Fort Duquesne** on the site in 1754, only for it to be destroyed four years later by the British, who replaced it with **Fort Pitt**. Industrial renown began with the development of **iron** foundries in the early 1800s. During the Civil War, Pittsburgh produced half of the iron and one third of the glass in the country, and soon after it became the world's leading producer of steel, thanks to the vigorous modernisation programmes of Andrew Carnegie – by 1870, the richest man in the world.

Although it has been transformed by two so-called "renaissances" since the Fifties, Pittsburgh still can't quite shake off its grimy Victorian reputation as dirty and polluted. The first face-lift involved large-scale demolition, but incipient yuppification has thus far been kept in check by the student population and the small-town feel of some of the older ethnic neighbourhoods on the north and south sides. Pittsburgh today, with one of the lowest crime rates in the country, has resilience and enthusiasm in the air rather than coal fumes, sleek architecture and green parks rather than smokestacks and slums.

Arrival and Information

Greyhound (☎391-2300) pulls in at Eleventh Street and Liberty Avenue, on the outskirts of downtown, across from *Amtrak* at Liberty and Grant avenues. From the **airport**, fifteen miles west of downtown, the *Airline Transport Company* (☎665-8115) runs **shuttles** downtown (daily 5am–10pm; $9) and to Oakland (daily 7am–8pm).

Pittsburgh has two main **visitor centres**: downtown on Liberty Avenue, adjacent to the Gateway Center (Mon–Fri 9.30am–5pm, Sat & Sun 9.30am–3pm; ☎281-9222), and in Oakland at Forbes Avenue on the University of Pittsburgh campus (Tues–Sun 10am–4pm; ☎624-4660). Additionally, there's a visitor information **hotline** on ☎391-6840. The principal **post office** is at Seventh and Grant streets (Mon–Fri 7am–6pm, Sat 7am–2.30pm; ☎642-4472; zip code 15230).

Getting Around

Though Pittsburgh is a city of distinct districts, transport between them is simple. **Buses** through town ($1.15), the Monongahela **trolley** incline to Mount Washington (daily until late; $1) and a small **subway** system (free downtown, 75¢ to cross the river to the South Side) are all run by *PAT* (☎231-5707). For **taxis**, call *Yellow Cabs* (☎665-8100). *Gray Line* (☎741-2720) runs daily city and area **tours**.

The City

Each of Pittsburgh's close-knit neighbourhoods – the **South Side** and **Mount Washington**, across the Monongahela River from the Golden Triangle, the **North Side** across the Allegheny River, and **Oakland**, the university area in the east – attests in its own way to the city's history and its resurgence. Easily accessible from each other, they retain individual identities while remaining part of a proud whole.

The telephone **area code** for Pittsburgh and southwestern Pennsylvania is ☎412.

The *New York Times* once described Pittsburgh as "the only city with an entrance", and the view of the **Golden Triangle** skyline on emerging from the tunnel on the Fort Pitt Bridge is undeniably breathtaking. Surrounded by water and fronted with a huge fountain, Pittsburgh's downtown pays tribute both to its coal-grimed past and sunny future. In the core of the original city, the Triangle's imaginative contemporary architecture stands comfortably next to Gothic churches and red-brick warehouses and includes, on Fort Pitt Boulevard and Stanwix Street, the **National Steel Center**, a six-sided concrete building covered in marble. Four blocks away, between Third and Fourth avenues, Philip Johnson's magnificent five acres of Post-Modernism, the startling black-glass **PPG Place** complex looms incongruously over the old **Market Square**, lined with historic restaurants and shops. More recent history is apparent on the faded buildings along **Liberty Avenue**, with Forties and Fifties fronts left in peace during successive face-lifts.

Point State Park, at the peak of the Triangle, is where it all began, the site of five different forts during the French and Indian War. This popular gathering area has a 150ft fountain with a pool in which to dip weary feet, as well as great views of port activity on the rivers and across to the colourful old buildings on verdant Mount Washington. The **Fort Pitt Museum**, 101 Commonwealth Place in the park, was once England's largest fort in the States; now its exhibits include dioramas, scale models and reconstructions of three forts (Wed–Sat 9am–5pm, Sun noon–5pm; $1.50). Opposite, the 1764 **Fort Pitt Blockhouse** is the oldest structure in the city, a look-out of sandstone and rough brick.

Northeast of downtown, the **Strip District** is a colourful early-morning **market** with wholesale outlets and fresh produce stalls, popular with bargain hunters and good for cheap breakfasts. Along **Penn Avenue**, its main street, the imminent opening of an entertainment and hotel complex will surely bring gentrification to the old fruit and vegetable warehouses and stores. Guided **walking tours** detail the history and development of the area (☎276-0908).

In the nineteenth century, the four-hundred-foot **Mount Washington**, across the Monongahela River, was the site of most of the city's coal mines. No longer dominated by belching steel mills and industry, the **South Side**, banked by the green "mountain", is an area of many churches, colourful houses nestling in steep hills, and old neighbourhoods. These days only two survive out of the twelve cable cars which, at the height of steel production, used to carry coal up the trolley inclines. The 1877 **Duquesne Incline**, from 1197 W Carson Street to 1220 Grandview Avenue, is the most interesting for its small museum of Pittsburgh history in the waiting room at the top; old photos of the city show workers struggling blindly through the streets in pitch-black midday smog (daily until 1am; $1.50). The outdoor observation platform is a prime spot for views over the Golden Triangle to the hills on the horizon; the prospect is absolutely awesome after dark.

South Side's new gentility begins with red-brick **Station Square**, a complex of renovated railroad warehouses filled with restaurants and shops. The showpiece of the restoration is the beautiful stained glass and marble of the (expensive) **Grand Concourse** restaurant. The **Transportation Museum** in Bessemer Court exhibits old cars and steam train memorabilia, with an emphasis on the history of the Western Pennsylvania train line (summer daily noon–8pm, winter noon–6pm; $1). Further into the residential area at the foot of Mount Washington, shabby East Carson Street, the main drag, is more offbeat and less commercial, with abandoned stores and offices now housing thrift stores, galleries and bookshops.

Revitalisation on the **North Side**, only annexed by Pittsburgh in 1907, centres around the intriguingly named **Mexican War Streets** on the northern edge of Allegheny Commons. In this unevenly restored tree-lined area of nineteenth-century grey brick and limestone terraces, old families, descendants of early German and Scandinavian immigrants, live in an uneasy truce alongside young professionals. The **Pittsburgh Aviary**, Allegheny Commons West, is a huge indoor bird sanctuary where you can see over two hundred species, including foul-mouthed parrots, in free flight (daily 9am–4.30pm; $2).

The **USS Requin**, a 1945 submarine, bobs on the shores of the Allegheny River (daily 10am–6pm; $2), outside the magnificent **Carnegie Science Center**. This huge state-of-the-art interactive museum had not yet opened when this book went to press, but promised to include the world's largest cockroach (from Florida) and a mind-blowing planetarium in which the audience will be able to conduct self-driven tours through the solar system. Pittsburgh's past will be explored by means of a working foundry, and visitors will be invited to abseil and ride bobsleighs. Also on the shore, **Three Rivers Stadium**, 400 Stadium Circle, home to the Pittsburgh Pirates baseball and Steelers football teams, is open for hour-long "behind the scenes" tours when no games are scheduled, and additional tours of the **Hall of Fame Museum** (daily 8am–5pm, reservations required; $1.50, $3 including Hall of Fame; ☎321-0650).

Oakland, Pittsburgh's university area, originally an area where wealthy industrialists built their mansions, is today marked by a strong mixture of Italian and Greek families as well as students. Sights are concentrated around the **University of Pittsburgh** campus and Forbes Street. The 42-storey Gothic-revival **Cathedral of Learning**, (called by architect Frank Lloyd Wright "the world's largest keep off the grass sign"), Fifth Avenue at Bigelow Boulevard, is a university building with a difference; over twenty classrooms are furnished with antiques and specially crafted items donated by the different ethnic groups, from Lithuanian through Chinese to Irish, who have settled in the city. These beautiful rooms, far more interesting than they may sound, have been used by students since the Thirties; all are open to the public except the exotic **Syria-Lebanon** room, and the **Early American** room, complete with trap door and secret passage, which are shown on guided tours only. Tape-recorded tours are available for those with less time (Mon–Sat 9am–4.30pm, Sun 11am–4.30pm; $2). The French Gothic **Heinz Memorial Non-denominational Chapel**, on the campus at Fifth Avenue and Bellefield Street, is notable for its long, skinny, stained glass windows.

Across from the cathedral, the **Carnegie**, 4400 Forbes Avenue, provides the city's two greatest museums, the **Museum of Natural History**, famed for its extensive dinosaur relics and with a sparkling gem collection, and the **Museum of Art**, with Impressionist, Post-Impressionist and American regional art, as well as an excellent modern collection. The building was recently given a well-deserved scrub; spot the sooty square on the wall, left as a memory of grubbier days (Tues–Thurs & Sat 10am–5pm, Fri 10am–9pm, Sun 1–5pm; $5, Fri 3–9pm half-price). Nearby **Schenley Park**, a green space of over four hundred acres, includes the colourful Victorian flower **gardens** of Phipps Conservatory (June–Aug Mon–Fri 9am–5pm, Sept–May Mon–Fri 9am–5pm & 7–9pm; $1).

Shady Side, on the eastern fringes of Oakland, is an upmarket student district with a villagey feel. In Mellon Park the **Pittsburgh Center for the Arts**, 6300 Fifth Avenue, showcases innovative Pittsburgh art in various media (Tues & Thurs–Sat 10am–5pm, Wed 10am–8pm, Sun noon–4pm; free). Further east, the **Frick Art Museum**, 7227 Reynolds Street, has on show Italian, Flemish and French art from the fifteenth to the nineteenth centuries; its stunning decorative art includes two of Marie Antoinette's chairs (Tues–Sat 10am–5.30pm, Sun noon–6pm; free). On the same grounds, Clayton is a mansion furnished exactly as it was when Henry Clay Frick himself, an associate of Carnegie, lived there (Wed–Sat 10am–5.30pm, Sun noon–6pm; tours $4.50).

Accommodation

Pittsburgh's **hotels** are expensive, although weekend packages at luxury downtown hotels can bring rooms down to $75. Oakland has a couple of reasonably priced business hotels and some **student accommodation,** and the *Pittsburgh B&B Registry,* 2190 Ben Franklin Drive (☎367-8080), has details of rooms from $45.

Carnegie-Mellon University, 1060 Morewood St (☎268-2939). College dorm rooms in Oakland, available during the summer for $25, with a $5 reduction for students. Office hours 8am–5pm.

Howard Johnson, 3401 Blvd of the Allies (☎683-6100). One of the best deals in Oakland, with rooms from $70.

Point Park College Youth Hostel (AYH), 201 Wood St (☎392-3824). The best deal in town, with clean dorms and good views for $7.50, but only open Sept–May. Eight blocks from the bus station.

Red Roof Inn, 6404 Stubenville Pike, route 60 (☎787-7870). Standard doubles near the airport from just over $40, reachable from the bus station on bus #26F.

University Inn, Forbes Ave at McKee Place (☎683-6000). Rooms in this luxury Oakland hotel start at $85 for a double.

Eating

Eating downtown can prove expensive, but there are good Italian restaurants around the Convention Center. For cheaper neighbourhood Italian and Eastern European places, try along and around Carson Street on the South Side. Station Square and on Mount Washington cater to a more upmarket crowd, while Oakland is, unsurprisingly, home to an array of cheap student hangouts. Breakfasting on coffee and pastries in the Strip District is fast becoming a Pittsburgh tradition.

1902 Landmark Tavern, 24 Market Square (☎471-1902). Pricey for dinner, but oysters at the city's oldest oyster bar in the centre of downtown go for $7–10.

Grandview Saloon, 1212 Grandview Ave (☎431-1400). The cheapest and most relaxed of Mount Washington's restaurants, usually packed with a young crowd. Huge plates of pasta, salads and meat or fish dinners for $5–12. Get there early to snap up a table with a view.

Great Scot, 413 Craig St (☎683-1450). Dark pub-like restaurant around the corner from the Carnegie, with creative burgers from $7. Dinner might be pasta with shrimp and squash, or grilled tuna with strawberry sauce, from $12.

Richest, 140 Sixth St (☎471-7799). Kosher deli and restaurant, dinner from $4.

South Shore Diner, 1728 E Carson St (☎431-9292). Unpretentious old diner on hip South Side street, full dinners from $5.

Star of India, 412 Craig St (☎681-5700). Functional Indian restaurant in Oakland with cheap lunch specials from $7.

Suzie's Greek Specialities, 1704 Shady Ave (☎422-8066). Homemade Greek dishes including fish and seafood. Good lunchtime sandwiches from $4, with dinner from $9.

Nightlife and Entertainment

With its recent cultural resurgence, Pittsburgh's **nightlife** has soared upmarket, dominated by the performing arts. The *Fulton Theater,* 101 Sixth Street (☎471-9700), puts on small productions such as poetry recitals. *TIX* booth, 209 Ninth Street downtown (☎391-8353), offers half-price theatre and concert tickets on the day. **Jazz** fans should check out the Shady Side district. For other options, *In Pittsburgh,* the free newsweekly, has extensive listings, and there's a 24-hour **Activities Line** (☎391-6840). If all you feel like doing is **drinking,** Pittsburgh's own *Iron City* beer is suitably powerful.

Balcony, 5520 Walnut St (☎687-0110). Shady Side jazz club with no cover charge.

Peter's Pub, 116 Oakland Ave (☎681-7465). Rowdy student bar in Oakland. Cheap beer, but surprisingly, this area can be dodgy at night.

James Street Tavern, 422 Foreland Ave (☎323-2222). An expensive place to eat, well out on the North Side, but they put on good live jazz in the downstairs bar at weekends.

Pittsburgh Sports Garden Bar, 1 Station Square Drive East (☎281-1511). Massive sports bar on the South Side.

NEW JERSEY

The long skinny state of **NEW JERSEY**, squashed between Philadelphia and New York on the Atlantic coast, suffers a severe image problem. Most travellers only see "the Garden State" from the stupendously ugly New Jersey Turnpike toll road, which, heavy with truck traffic, cuts through a landscape of grey smokestacks and industrial estates. Even the songs of **Bruce Springsteen**, Asbury Park's golden boy, paint his home state as a gritty urban wasteland of empty lots, grey highways, lost dreams and blue-collar tragedy. In reality, the majority of the refineries and factories hug a mere fifteen-mile stretch of the turnpike, but bleak cities like **Newark**, home to the major airport, and **Trenton**, the capital, do little to improve the look of the place – even if they do produce some of the best contemporary black music around.

The Dutch, who had snatched New Jersey from the peaceful Lenni Lenape Indians, turned the land over to the English in the 1660s. During the **Revolution** a battle was fought at **Princeton**, and George Washington spent two bleak winters at **Morristown**, west of Newark. When the **Civil War** came, the fact that the state's future obviously lay with industry meant that despite its location (severed by the Mason-Dixon line), and the slave-driven agrarian economy in south New Jersey, it fought with the Union.

There's more to New Jersey than factories and pollution. Both Thomas Paine and Walt Whitman wrote of their years here with fond nostalgia; the **northwest** corner is traced with picturesque lakes, streams and woodlands, while the **Atlantic shore** offers many attractive resorts.

Getting Around New Jersey

With a car, New Jersey is easily accessible from New York City, via I-95, while the notorious **New Jersey Turnpike** sweeps from the northeast down into Delaware. The **Garden State Parkway** runs parallel to the Atlantic from New York to Cape May (with a 35¢ toll every twenty miles), and gives easy access to the shoreline resorts. One nice route in the north of the state is US-29, from Trenton along the Delaware River.

Newark International Airport (☎201/961-2000) is the fastest-growing gateway to the US, used by plenty of visitors who have no intention of staying in New Jersey but who prefer Newark to New York's JFK. The airport is served by all the major international carriers, and is a mere thirty-minute bus ride away from Manhattan.

Numerous *Amtrak* **trains** pass through Newark, Princeton and Trenton, en route between Philadelphia, New York and Washington DC, and *Greyhound* cover most of the state. *New Jersey Transit* (☎201/460-8444 or ☎1-800/772-2222) also offer a good train and bus service, extending to Philadelphia and New York as well as out to the coast. New Jersey's south coast is connected to Delaware by the Cape May–Lewes **ferry** (in Cape May, ☎609/886-7218; in Lewes, ☎302/645-6313).

Inland New Jersey

Travelling west on the interstates from the shore or from New York State, visitors see the New Jersey of popular imagination: heavily industrialised, a cultural and visual desert. **Newark**, the state's largest city, is perhaps the nation's drabbest, redeemed only by its efficient airport and views over the Hudson to the Statue of Liberty (which is, incidentally, in New Jersey waters). Northwest of Newark, on I-287, **Morristown**, the site of two of Washington's harshest winters in the Revolutionary War, is now a National Historic Park. **Trenton**, the state capital, sits on the Delaware River at the border with Pennsylvania, something of a national joke for its motto, "Trenton makes, the world takes". Nearby **Princeton**, an Ivy League town that makes a pretty stop-off, is one place worth visiting.

> The telephone **area code** for Newark is ☎201; for Princeton and the coast it's ☎609.

Princeton

Staid and self-satisfied **PRINCETON**, on US-1 eleven miles north of Trenton, is home to the Ivy League **Princeton University** – the nation's fourth oldest, which broke away from the overly religious Yale in 1756 – and the prestigious **Institute of Advanced Study**. It began its days inauspiciously as Stony Brook, and then in 1724 as Princes Town, a coach stop between New York and Philadelphia. In January 1777, a week after Washington's triumph against the British at Trenton, the **Battle of Princeton** occurred southwest of town. This victory, a turning point in the Revolutionary effort, bolstered the morale of Washngton's troops before their long winter encampment at Morristown to the north. After the war, in 1783, the **Continental Congress**, fearful of potential attack from incensed unpaid veterans in Philadelphia, met here for four months; the leafy, well-kept town was then left in peace to follow its academic pursuits. Graduates of the university include actor James Stewart, jazz-age writer F Scott Fitzgerald, and presidents Wilson and Madison. Today, other than tour the university, there is little to do in this sleepy place but enjoy a stroll through pleasant Colonial streets.

Arrival, Information and Getting Around

A shuttle bus, the *Princeton Airporter*, makes the run from Newark (1hr 30min) and JFK (2hr 40min) **airports** to town (daily 7am–10pm; ☎587-6600). The in-town **train terminal**, on campus at University Place, a block north of Alexander Road, is connected by *New Jersey Transit* "dinky" trains (☎201/378-6300) and *SEPTA* shuttles (☎215/574-7800) to **Princeton Junction**, three miles south, where both *Amtrak* and *New Jersey Transit* stop on their New York–Philadelphia runs. *Suburban Transit* **buses** (☎201/249-1100) from New York stop every thirty minutes at Nassau Street.

Information, including maps and lists of events, is available from Stanhope Hall at the university (Mon–Fri 8.30am–4.30pm; ☎258-3600) or the **CVB**, 20 Nassau Street (☎683-1760). The **Historical Society**, 158 Nassau Street (☎921-6748), leads walking tours through town (Sun 2pm; $3), and provides maps so you can do it yourself.

The Town and the University

Mercer Street, the long road that sweeps southwest past the university campus to Nassau Street, is lined with elegant Colonial houses, graced with shutters, columns and wrought-iron fences. The **Princeton Battlefield State Park**, a mile out, includes the **Thomas Clarke House**, 500 Mercer Street, a Quaker farmhouse that served as a hospital during the battle (Wed–Fri 9am–5pm, Sat 10am–noon, Sun 1–5pm).

In a simple raised house at 112 Mercer Street, back towards town, **Albert Einstein** lived while teaching at the Institute of Advanced Study. North of here, and running into Nassau Street, Stockton Street's pre-Revolutionary clapboard homes include the **Aquinas House**, Stockton Street and Library Place, home of **Thomas Mann**, Einstein's novelist compatriot who also fled Nazi Germany, and the Greek Revival **Drumthwacket**, 354 Stockton Street, the governor's mansion restored to its original 1835 style (tours Wed noon–2pm). Princeton has once again found itself acting as a sanctuary since the **Tiananmen** massacre of 1989, having become a gathering place for exiled members of China's democracy movement.

A substantial number of the tour groups who visit **Princeton University** are disarmingly conservative prospective students and their proud parents, soaking up the tales of old-boy pranks and superstitions (for example, that no student should pass through the main gates for fear of being tarnished by the ugly outside world) that prop up the Ivy League tradition. The tours may be complacent, but the tranquil and shaded campus is beautiful. Just inside the main gates on Nassau Street, **Nassau Hall** was, when constructed in 1756, the largest stone building in the nation; its 26-inch-thick walls (now patterned with plaques and patches of ivy placed by graduating classes) withstood American and British fire during the Revolution. It was also the seat of government during Princeton's brief spell as national capital (Mon–Fri 2–5pm, Sat 9am–5pm, Sun 1–5pm; free). The 1925 **chapel**, based on Kings College Cambridge, has stained glass windows showing scenes from works by Dante, Shakespeare and Milton as well as the Bible, and the **Prospect Gardens**, a flowerbed in the shape of the university emblem, are a blaze of orange in summer. In the middle of the campus, fronted by the Picasso sculpture *Head of a Woman*, the **University Art Museum**, not included on the standard tours, is well worth a look for its collection from the Renaissance to the present, including Modigliani, Van Gogh and Warhol, and Chinese and pre-Columbian art (Tues–Sat 10am–5pm, Sun 1–5pm; tours Sat 2pm, museum talks Fri 12.30pm & Sun 3pm; free).

Free student-led university **tours** leave from the rear of the yellow **Maclean House** at 73 Nassau Street (Mon–Sat 10am, 11am, 1.30pm, & 3.30pm; Sun 1.30pm& 3.30pm).

Accommodation, Eating and Drinking

The only **hotel** in Princeton itself, the luxurious 1756 *Nassau Inn*, Palmer Square (☎921-7500), charges $120 and above for the privilege of staying in its lovely rooms. Budget **motels**, accessible by *Suburban Transit* bus, can be found along US-1 and in the suburb of **Lawrenceville** a few miles south of town. The *Sleep-e-Hollow*, 3000 US-1 (☎896-0900), has functional rooms from $30, and the *McIntosh Inn* (☎896-3700), by the Quaker Bridge Mall on US-1, has doubles from $47.

For cheap diner-type **lunches** try along Witherspoon Street; for a more upmarket feast, the popular *Annex*, 128 Nassau Street, serves quality Italian food in a candlelit setting from $7. **Vegetarians** should try the *Tempting Tiger*, 14 Witherspoon Street (☎924-0644), which serves healthy salads, soups and sandwiches, accompanied by classical music, from around $4 (open until 8.30pm, 5.30pm on Sat). **Nightlife** is limited, especially out of term-time, but the ancient wooden *Tap Room* bar downstairs at the *Nassau Inn* is usually full of revellers drinking and enjoying live **jazz**.

New Jersey Shore

New Jersey's **Atlantic coast**, a 130-mile stretch of almost uninterrupted resorts – some rowdy, many pitifully rundown and faded, a few undeveloped and peaceful – has long been reliant on farming and tourism. No profitable ports were established, nor did short-lived attempts at whaling come to anything. In 1988 the whole coastline suffered severe and well-publicised pollution from ocean dumping, but today the **beaches**, if occasionally somewhat crowded, are now safe and clean, sandy and broad with their characteristic wooden **boardwalks**. Many of them, in an attempt to maintain their condition, charge admission during the summer. The casinos of the tackily surreal **Atlantic City** are the most brazenly obvious attractions, with the restorative peace of **Spring Lake** and the historic importance of Victorian **Cape May** offering quieter charms.

Spring Lake

SPRING LAKE, about twenty miles down the Jersey coast, is one of the smallest, most uncommercial communities on the shore, a gentle respite on the road south to Atlantic City. Tourism in this elegant Victorian resort evolved slowly, without the booms, crises, resurgences and depressions of other seaside towns – partly due to the strict zoning laws prohibiting new building; and stressed-out city dwellers come here to get away from it all. You can walk the totally undeveloped two-mile **boardwalk** and watch the crashing ocean from battered gazebos, swim and bask on the white beaches (in summer, compulsory beach tags cost $2 per day, but most guest houses provide them free) or sit in the shade by the town's namesake, Spring Lake itself. Wooden foot-bridges, swans and geese, and the grand St Catherine's Catholic Church on the banks of the lake give it the feel of a country village. A historical museum is planned for the Municipal Building on Fifth and Warren streets, but for the moment the little activity there is centres on the upmarket shops of Third Avenue.

Bruce Springsteen fans can use the town as a base for visiting nearby **Asbury Park**, a poignantly faded old seaside town where The Boss played his first gigs.

Practicalities

Spring Lake is accessible by US-34 from the New Jersey Turnpike, and served by *New Jersey Transit* from New York. The *Spring Lake Hotel and Guest House Association* (☎449-1332) can help in finding somewhere to stay, especially during summer week-ends. There are no cheap motels, and **B&Bs** can be expensive. One of the nicest is the easy-going *Sea Crest by the Sea*, 19 Tuttle Avenue (☎449-9031), an 1885 inn with rooms furnished individually on quirky themes. Summer rates begin at $85, which includes an excellent all-you-can-eat home-cooked breakfast. *Ashling Cottage*, 106 Sussex Avenue ☎449-3553, overlooks the lake and has rooms from $60 (April–Dec only).

Most of Spring Lake's **restaurants** are in the elegant Victorian hotels along the seafront, and can be pricey. The **North Pavilion** on the boardwalk sells cheap break-fasts and snacks, but there are no fast-food stands along the walk itself. *Jeffrey's*, 1321 Third Avenue (☎449-1661), is a no-nonsense cafe serving breakfast from $2, lunch from $4. *The Beach House*, 901 Ocean Avenue (☎449-9646), is more upmarket, with screened-in verandah seating and healthy lunches from $5, dinner from $16. For a blowout, the *Sandpiper*, 7 Atlantic Avenue (☎449-6060), serves superb fresh fish and seafood in elegant candlelit surroundings. Dinner costs around $20; bring your own bottle.

Nightlife is unsurprisingly quiet, although the lovely old *Community House Theater*, Third and Madison avenues, holds regular musicals and plays (☎449-4530). In July and August, free evening **concerts** are held in the gazebo in Potter Park, Fifth and Warren avenues. The **bars** at neighbouring Belmar to the north attract students and singles.

Atlantic City

What they wanted was Monte Carlo. They didn't want Las Vegas.
What they got was Las Vegas. We always knew that they would get Las Vegas.
                                    Stuart Mendelson, *Philadelphia Journal*, 1978.

ATLANTIC CITY, on Absecon Island just off the midpoint of the Jersey shoreline, has been a seedy tourist mecca since 1854, when Philadelphia speculators created it as a rail terminal resort. In 1909, at the peak of the seaside town's popularity, *Baedeker* wrote "there is something colossal about its vulgarity" – a quality which it sustains today, even while beset by bankruptcy and decay. The real-life model for the board-game **Monopoly**, it has an impressive popular cultural history, boasting the nation's first **Boardwalk** (1870), the first **colour postcards** (1893), the world's first **Big Wheel** (1869) and the first **Miss America Beauty Pageant** (cunningly devised to extend the tourist season in 1921, and still held here yearly).

During Prohibition and the Depression, Atlantic City was a centre for rum-running, packed with speakeasies and illegal gambling dens. Thereafter, in the face of increas-ing competition from Florida, it slipped into apparently terminal decline, until desper-ate city officials decided in 1976 to open up the decrepit resort to legal **gambling**.

The monster **casinos** that replaced the grand old hotels dominate not just the Boardwalk and the skyline, but the whole culture of the city. Their tackiness puts the lie to the would-be glamorous image; *pace* Stuart Mendelson, Atlantic City didn't even quite "get" Las Vegas. The place is not so much limousines and roulette as hamburgers and slot machines; as eighty percent of Atlantic City's millions of visitors are day-trippers, there's definitely more glitz than glamour. Indeed, the gamble on gambling is not paying off. The casinos are in debt, and over-enthusiastic developers have empty lots on their hands. To the glee of the popular press, **Donald Trump**'s multimillion-dollar empire was severely damaged by losses made on his gargantuan **Taj Mahal Casino**, and a mere block or two behind the fairground attractions of the Boardwalk, those locals who don't have the resources to escape (since 1976 the population has dropped by twenty percent) inhabit shanty-town slums. For all its shabbiness, though, the place has an uneasy charm, with determinedly cheerful holiday-makers, more than adequate **beaches**, and, of course, the never-ending allure of the jackpot.

Arrival, Information and Getting Around

Travelling to Atlantic City by **bus** can be a real money-spinner; casino-sponsored buses from New York, Philadelphia and other points along the coast give away vouchers exchangeable for cash and free meals to a value well above the day return fare. It's hoped that you will spend all this money and more in the casinos, but you can easily cash it and leave. The **bus terminal** (☎347-5413) at Arctic and Arkansas avenues is served by *Greyhound* (☎345-6617) and *New Jersey Transit* (☎1-800/582-5946).

Amtrak has express **trains** from New York, Philadelphia, Washington and Baltimore, and *New Jersey Transit* (☎1-800/772-3606) trains run between Atlantic City and south Jersey, with connections to Philadelphia, from 1 Atlantic City Expressway (☎344-9013). **Atlantic City International Airport** is thirteen miles from downtown in Pleasantville (☎645-8882); the smaller **Bader Field Airport** (☎345-6402), in the centre of town, has connections to Boston, Baltimore, Philadelphia and Pittsburgh.

For maps and **information**, head for the **CVB**, 2310 Pacific Avenue (Mon–Fri 9am–5pm; ☎348-7100), or the **visitor centre** next door (Mon–Fri 9am–4.30pm; ☎348-7044).

City Transport

Atlantic City is easy to walk around, although it is unwise to stray farther from the five-mile Boardwalk along the ocean than the parallel Pacific, Atlantic and Arctic avenues. **Ventnor** and **Margate** to the south on Absecon Island are served by **buses** along Atlantic Avenue. *Jitneys* (☎344-8642) offer 24-hour **minibus** service the length of Pacific Avenue, the #1 route travelling as far as Ventnor ($1).

Various **bike rental** stands along the Boardwalk charge about $3 per hour, although cycling is only permitted from 6am until 10am in the summer.

The Town

The hopeful hordes in Atlantic City head straight for the casinos, with an ample over-spill flooding the Boardwalk and beach. Beyond the Boardwalk there is little to see, although a quick walk around the eerily quiet slums of the South Inlet district makes a chilling contrast to the manic jollity a mere block away. This is not an area in which to linger for any length of time, or indeed at all at night – the danger of attack is very real.

Each of Atlantic City's thirteen **casinos**, which also act as luxury hotels, conference centres and concert halls, has a slightly different personality, despite the apparent uniformity of vast, richly ornamented halls, slot machines, relentless flashing lights and incessant noise, chandeliers, mirrors, and a disorienting absence of clocks or windows. Apart from a quick flutter, the real pleasure here is in people-watching; from the frisky pensioners cashing in their chips to the shady-looking compulsive types lurking at the roulette wheel. All casinos are open from 10am until 4am during the week, and until 6am at the weekend, although the restaurants keep their own hours. Costumed wait-resses serve drinks at the baccarat and craps tables, and will supply newcomers with rule books. Although officially jeans and T-shirts are frowned upon, in practice most of the punters are extremely casual, even after 6pm. One rule that is never waived is the age requirement; you must be 21 to gamble and will be asked to show ID.

As time goes on, these overblown amusement arcades have become more and more outrageous in order to compete with each other. By far the most ostentatious is the new kid on the block, Donald Trump's Disneyesque **Taj Mahal**. Occupying nearly twenty acres and over forty storeys high, with glittery minarets and onion domes, this gigantic piece of Far Eastern kitsch stands opposite the steel pier at the north end of the Boardwalk. It is the largest gambling casino on earth, precariously tottering on the edge of bankruptcy (☎449-1000). At the other end of the scale, the **Claridge**, Indiana Avenue and the Boardwalk, dubs itself "the friendly casino" and is smaller, darker and more downmarket than the others (☎340-3400). **Sands**, next door at South Indiana Avenue, is a noisy and popular venue on a pink flamingo theme (☎441-4000). Both these properties are slightly off the Boardwalk, accessible by a glass-covered slow-moving sidewalk with accompanying taped music from the various stars who have played Atlantic City. **Caesars**, Arkansas Avenue and the Boardwalk, has an uninspired Roman theme, with statues of Greek gods, marble columns and laurel wreaths at every turn (☎348-4411).

Atlantic City's wooden **Boardwalk**, the dividing line between the ocean and the slums, was originally built as a temporary walkway, raised above the beach so that holiday-makers could take a seaside stroll without treading sand into the grand hotels. Alongside the brash 99¢ shops and exotically named palm-readers, a few beautiful Victorian buildings invoke a more elegant past, though dwarfed by the casinos and incongruously housing fast-food joints. Early in the morning when the breezes from the ocean are at their most pleasant, the Boardwalk is peaceful, peopled only by keen cyclists and a few lost souls down on their luck.

The **Central Pier** offers all the fun of the fair, with rides, games and old-fashioned "guess your weight" challenges. A few blocks south, another pier has been remodelled into an ocean-liner-shaped shopping centre. The small and faded **Arts Centre and Historic Museum**, at the quiet northern end of the Boardwalk, on the **Garden Pier**, has a free collection of seaside memorabilia, postcards, photos and a special exhibit on Miss America, as well as travelling art shows. A block off the Boardwalk, where Pacific Avenue meets Rhode Island Avenue, and in the heart of some of the city's worst deprivation, the **Absecon Lighthouse** was active until 1933, but is now a small free marine museum, with separate entrance to the 167ft tower (June–Oct Thurs–Tues 10am–5pm, Nov–May Fri–Mon 10am–5pm; 50¢).

Atlantic City's **beach** is free, family filled and surprisingly clean considering its proximity to the Boardwalk. Beaches at neighbouring **Ventnor**, a jitney-ride away, are quieter, but charge users $3.50 per week. For the same fee, New Jersey's beautiful people pose on the beaches of **Margate**, three miles south of Atlantic City; all watched over by **Lucy**, the **Margate Elephant**, 9200 Atlantic Avenue. A 65ft wood and tin Victorian oddity, Lucy was built as a seaside attraction in 1881 and used variously as a tavern and a hotel. Today her huge belly is filled with a museum of Atlantic City memorabilia, and photos and artefacts from her own history (July–Aug daily 10am–8.30pm, April–June and Sept–Oct Sat–Sun 10am–4.30pm; $1.50).

Accommodation

Atlantic City's high **accommodation** rates get even higher at weekends and in summer. Room prices at the casinos are, not surprisingly, astronomical, but motels line Pacific and Atlantic avenues behind the Boardwalk, and things are cheaper in quiet **Ocean City**, a family resort on the mainland to the south.

The Casino Hotel, 28 S Georgia Ave (☎344-0747). Small rooms from $50. Open May–Oct.

The Dunes Motel, 2819 Pacific Ave (☎344-5271). Reasonable rooms from $50 near the Boardwalk.

The Irish Pub, 164 St James Place (☎344-9063). $40 rooms above one of the best bars in town.

Shamrock Hotel, 133 St James Place (☎348-9832). Rooms from $180 per week.

Eating

One side-effect of Atlantic City's rabid commercialisation is an abundance of cheap **fast food**. The Boardwalk is lined with pizza, burger and sandwich joints, and the casino cafes too dole out economical meals. Diners on Atlantic and Pacific Avenues serve soul food and cheap breakfasts.

Hunan Chinese Restaurant, 2323 Atlantic Ave (☎348-5946). Reasonably priced Chinese food two blocks from the Boardwalk. Combination plates from $6.

Los Amigos, 1926 Atlantic Ave (☎344-2293). Mexican restaurant and bar, with good tortillas and enchilada meals from $7. Open until 6am.

Tony's Little Italy, S Carolina Ave and the Boardwalk. One of the better cheap and cheerful Boardwalk joints, with pizza and breakfast from $2.

White House Sub Shop, Mississippi and Arctic avenues (☎345-8599). This bright and super-efficient sandwich bar is where Bill Cosby gets his subs when in town. Prices range from $3 for half a French loaf crammed with omelette, to $7 for a full steak sandwich.

Entertainment and Nightlife

Atlantic City sells itself as the fun nighttime city; but the **nightlife** centres on the casinos and Boardwalk amusements. Once you get bored with slot machines there is little else to do. Big-name entertainers like Frank Sinatra, Bill Cosby and Joan Rivers play regularly at the casinos, with tickets in the $20 range. Both the *Claridge* (☎340-3700) and the *Trop World Casino* (☎340-4000) have comedy clubs with shows from $10. For cheaper informal fun, good neighbourhood **bars** include the friendly, dark-panelled *Irish Pub*, 164 St James Place (☎345-9613), which serves cheap food and often has live Irish music, and *McGuires Pittsburg Cafe*, 142 S Tennessee Avenue (☎345-9607).

Cape May

CAPE MAY was founded in 1620 by the Dutch Captain Mey, on the small hook at the very southern tip of the Jersey coast, jutting out into the Atlantic and washed by the Delaware Bay on the west. After being briefly settled by New England whalers in the late 1600s, it turned in the eighteenth century to more profitable farming and **tourism**. In 1745 the first advert for its restorative air and fine accommodations appeared in the Philadelphia press, heralding a period of great prosperity, when Southern plantation owners, desiring cool sea breezes without having to venture into Yankee land, flocked to the fashionable boarding houses of this genteel "resort of Presidents".

The Victorian era was Cape May's finest; nearly all its gingerbread architecture dates from a mass rebuilding after a severe fire in 1878. However, the increase in car travel after World War I meant that vacationers could go further, more quickly and cheaply, and the little town found itself something of an anachronism, while the gaudier charms of Atlantic City became the brightest stars on the Jersey coast. During the 1950s, Cape May began to dust off its most valuable commodity: its **history**. Today the whole town is a National Historic Landmark, with over six hundred Victorian buildings, tree-lined streets and beautifully kept gardens, and a lucrative B&B industry. Avoid the few inevitable twee olde shoppes and high prices, and concentrate instead on the appealing combination of historical authenticity and good beaches.

Arrival and Information

New Jersey Transit (☎884-6139) runs an express **bus** from Philadelphia and the south Jersey coast, and services from New York and Atlantic City. **Flights** from Philadelphia and Atlantic City touch down at the Cape May County airport (☎886-1500), five miles north on US-47, and **ferries** connect the town to Lewes, Delaware (15 per day in the summer, 4 or 5 off-season; $4; schedules on ☎886-2718). The ferry dock, in west Cape May, is, however, a bit of a trek at the end of US-9.

Maps and information are available from the friendly **Mid-Atlantic Center for the Arts**, 1048 Washington Street, the non-profit organisation that masterminded Cape May's preservation move (Mon–Fri 9am–5pm; ☎884-5404). They also organise guided **walking tours** of the town's central mansions and ninety-minute historical **trolley** tours of the area, and issue details of self-guided cycling tours. The **Welcome Center** at 405 Lafayette Street can help with finding accommodation (April–Oct Mon–Sat 9am–4pm, Sun 1–3pm; ☎884-9562); other sources of information include a small booth on the southern end of Washington Street in the paved mall, and the tiny **Chamber of Commerce**, in the bus depot, 609 Lafayette Street (Mon–Fri 9am–5pm; ☎884-5508).

Though Cape May itself is best enjoyed on foot, to venture out a bit further **bikes** can be rented from the *Village Bike Shop*, Washington and Ocean streets (daily 6.30am–7pm; $9 per day; ☎884-8500). The *Cape May Whale Watch and Research Center*, 1286 Wilson Drive, offers three trips around Cape May Point daily, **dolphin-watching** breakfast and sunset cruises and a four-hour **whale-watching** voyage. Boats leave Cape May harbour at the north end of Lafayette Street (April–Nov daily; ☎898-0055).

The Town

Cape May's brightly coloured **houses** were built by nouveaux riche Victorians with a healthy disrespect for subtlety. Cluttered with cupolas, gazebos, balconies, and "widows walks", the houses follow no architectural rules except excess. They were known as "**thumbprint homes**", with designs and features chosen from catalogues and thrown together in accordance with the owner's taste. The Victorian obsession with the Orient is everywhere; Moorish arches and onion domes sit comfortably next to gingerbread and Queen Anne-style turrets.

The only old home open as a museum, the eighteen-room **Emlen Physick House**, 1048 Washington Street, was built by the popular Philadelphia architect Frank Furness. It has been restored to its 1879 glory, with whimsical "upside down" chimneys, a mock Tudor half-timbered facade, and much original furniture (Mon–Thurs, Sat & Sun 10.30am–3pm; $5). Various B&Bs and hotels, given enough notice, also conduct informal tours of their premises; the **Mainstay Inn**, 635 Columbia Avenue, was an elaborate Italianate 1872 gambling club (guided tour and tea daily 4pm; $5; ☎884-8690), and the **Abbey**, Columbia Avenue and Gurney Street, is a Gothic mansion with a sixty-foot tower and blood-red etched windows (tours Thurs–Sun; $3; ☎884-4506).

West of town, where the Delaware Bay and the ocean meet, the 1859 **Cape May Lighthouse**, visible from 25 miles at sea, offers great views from a gallery below the lantern (199 steps up) and a small exhibit on its history at ground level (Sat–Sun 10am–4pm; $3.50). A mile north of town on US-9, **Historic Cold Spring Village**, 735 Seashore Road, depicts a typical nineteenth-century South Jersey farming community. Restored buildings from the region house a jail, school, an inn and shops, and there are various craft shows and special events (June–Oct 10am–4pm; $2).

Cape May's excellent **beaches** literally sparkle with small quartz pebbles. Beach tags ($2 per day) must be worn from 10am until 6pm in the summer, and are available from B&Bs, official vendors, or at **City Hall**, 643 Washington Street (☎884-9525).

Accommodation

Most of Cape May's pastel Victorian homes seem to be (pricey) **B&Bs** or **guest houses**, but the resort is so popular that choice plummets on summer weekends. Standard **hotels** front the ocean on Beach Drive, and you can **camp** at *Seashore Campsites*, 720 Seashore Road (reservations recommended July–Aug; ☎884-4010).

Abigail Adams Bed and Breakfast, 12 Jackson St (☎884-1371). High-quality lodging, April–Nov only, half a block from the sea. $60–95, including home-cooked breakfast and afternoon tea.

Inn at Cape May, Beach Drive and Ocean Ave (☎884-3500). Once a fashionable Victorian shorefront hotel. Rooms (May–Sept) from $50, or less in the small adjoining motel wing (April–Nov).

The Montreal Inn, Beach Drive and Madison Ave (☎884-7011). Modern motel with standard rooms from $55. Cheaper off-season.

Summer Cottage Inn, 613 Columbia Ave (☎884-4948). 1867 inn, verandahs and cupola. From $60.

Queen Victoria, 102 Ocean St (☎884-8702). Over twenty rooms in four buildings including a cottage and a carriage house. Rooms for $55–120, with use of the library and flower gardens, as well as breakfast (in bed if desired) and afternoon tea.

Eating

Cape May lacks the usual Boardwalk snack bars, but it has plenty of cheap **lunch** places. **Dinner**, however, is far more expensive. If you're staying at a B&B, you can always fill up there with homemade goodies, and make do with bar snacks at night.

Cafe Gazebo, 414 Washington St mall (☎884-4832). Cool, dark cafe with indoor gazebo and wrought-iron benches. Gourmet coffees, speciality ice creams and light lunches from $4.

The Lemon Tree, Washington St mall (☎884-2704). Cheap cheerful deli. Breakfasts, sandwiches, soups and salads. Nothing over $5.

Louie's Pizza, 7 Gurney St (☎884-0305). Fresh pizza opposite the beach from $8, or $2 per slice.

Mad Batter, 19 Jackson St (☎884-5970). Worth splashing out on, with international meals (baked clams in a tomato pesto sauce), served by candlelight in the garden, from $16. Lunch from $7.

Nightlife and Entertainment

Cape May is a friendly and laid-back place to be **after dark**; the day-trippers have gone home and the bars and music venues are enjoyed by locals and tourists alike.

Carney's, 401 Beach Ave (☎884-4424). Spacious and relaxed Irish bar, with raucous live music.

The Shire, 315 Washington St mall (☎884-4700). Hip setting for excellent live blues and jazz, Latin, reggae and world music. Outside seating and reasonably priced food. A real gem.

Ugly Mug, Washington St mall and Decatur St (☎884-3459). Local favourite, with friendly bar, and chowder, sandwiches and seafood from $3.

travel details

TRAINS

Routes (all *Amtrak*)

• Around forty trains pass through **Philadelphia** every day en route between **New York** and **Washington DC**, with onward connections up and down the eastern seaboard and into the South.

• Five trains daily connect **Philadelphia** with **Atlantic City** on the New Jersey coast.

• Four daily trains between **Philadelphia** and **Chicago** call at **Harrisburg** and **Pittsburgh**.

Journey Times

From Philadelphia to New York 1hr 30min; Washington DC 1hr 40min; Atlantic City 1hr 20min; Harrisburg 1hr 30min; Pittsburgh 7hr 30min; Chicago 16hr.

BUSES

All *Greyhound* unless otherwise indicated

From Albany to Lake George (6 daily; 1hr); Lake Placid (6; 3hr 45min); New York City (9; 3hr); Tupper Lake (1; 4hr).

From Buffalo to Boston (5 daily; 12hr); Chicago (6; 12hr); New York City (8; 8hr); Niagara Falls (*Niagara Frontier Metro Transit System*; 17; 1hr).

From Philadelphia to Gettysburg (1 daily; 4hr 40min); Harrisburg (11; 2hr 30min); Hershey (1; 2hr 10min); Lancaster City (1; 1hr 40min); New York City (16; 2hr 30min); Pittsburgh (15; 7hr 30min).

From Pittsburgh to Chicago (4 daily; 10hr); Cleveland (9; 4hr); Harrisburg (7; 4hr); New York City (9; 10hr).

From Princeton to New York City (*Suburban Transit*, 24; 2hr); Trenton (*New Jersey Transit*; 32; 20min).

From Spring Lake to New York City (*Asbury Park Transit Line Inc*; 10 daily; 1hr 50min).

From Atlantic City to Cape May (*New Jersey Transit*, 14 daily; 1hr 45 min); New York City (*New Jersey Transit*, 30; 2hr 30min); Philadelphia (12; 1hr 15min; *New Jersey Transit*; 37; 1hr 30min).

From Cape May to New York City (*New Jersey Transit*, 4; 5hr).

CHAPTER THREE

NEW ENGLAND

E uropeans cannot but see New England differently from Americans. For Americans, the small communities of **MASSACHUSETTS, RHODE ISLAND, CONNECTICUT, NEW HAMPSHIRE, VERMONT** and **MAINE** simply exude history; for visitors used to European cities, which have gradually evolved over the centuries from their original dense cores, they can seem soulless. The European image of an old stone fishing village, huddled around a compact little harbour and battered by the elements, finds few echoes in the genteel seaside towns of Cape Cod and Rhode Island. Much of the coast has only ever been viewed as prime real estate, to be lined with grand patrician homes – such as the presidential compounds of the Bush and Kennedy families.

The six New England states like to view themselves as the repository of all that is intrinsically American. In this version of history, the tangled streets of old Boston, the farms of Connecticut and the village greens of Vermont are the cradle of the nation, and in a sense the nostalgic lure of lost youth is at the basis of the region's tourist trade. Innumerable small towns have been dolled up to recapture a past that is at best wishful, and at times purely fictional, while the real business of making a living goes on in cities for the most part well off the tourist trail.

Although you do now come across picturesque villages, where white-spired churches stand beside immaculate rolling greens, the early settlers did not really congregate in this sort of idealised community. Instead, with so much land to choose from, they spread themselves across existing Indian fields, or straggled their farmhouses in endless strips along the newly built highways (establishing in the process a more genuinely American style of development). In any case, it can be all but impossible to tell whether what you're seeing is authentic or not: there's not much to distinguish a clapboard house built last year from another, two hundred years old, which has just had its annual fresh coat of white paint.

The magnificently colourful displays of **fall foliage** which attract so many people to New England during late September and October give a misleading impression as to quite how fertile this land really is. In fact the great trees of the inland forests are adapted to survive in just a few feet of topsoil, and the pioneers were disappointed as they moved inland to find that an agricultural way of life was hard to sustain.

New England is an **expensive** place to visit, especially in the fall. Its tourist facilities – from the resort hotels to the numerous B&Bs – are aimed at weekenders from the big cities as much as outsiders; places like **Cape Cod** might make convenient short breaks for locals, but they're really *not* the bucolic retreats you might be expecting. **Connecticut** and **Rhode Island** in particular clearly form part of the great East Coast megalopolis which stretches from Washington to Boston – you rarely escape the feeling that you're travelling through some vast suburb of New York. **Boston** itself however is a vibrant and stimulating city, one that can provide an excellent introduction to the US for first-time visitors, while further north up the coast the towns finally thin out and the scenery gets interesting (as indeed does the **seafood**). Inland, too, the lakes and mountains of **Maine** and **New Hampshire** offer rural wildernesses to rival any in the nation, providing opportunities for hiking, skiing and outdoor activities in general.

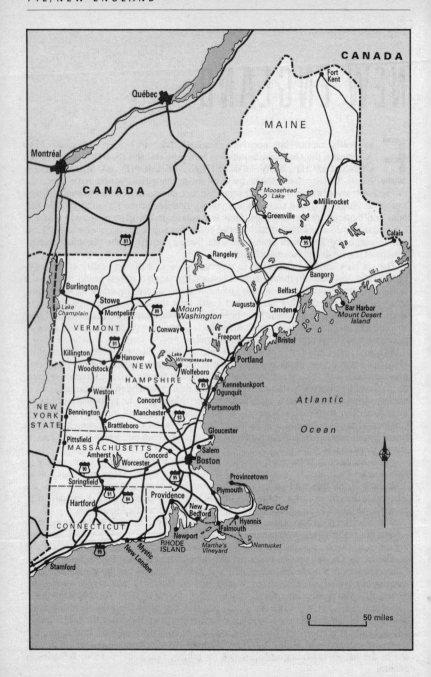

History

The **Native Americans** who first peopled the northeast shoreline lived by farming and fishing along the coast in summer, and retreating with their animals to the relative warmth of the inland valleys in winter. Though the Algonquin did not always live in harmony with each other, they did manage to repel the first European invaders, earning themselves five hundred years' grace, some time around 1000 AD, by forcing the Viking Leif Ericsson to abandon the settlement of **Vinland the Good** – which may have been anywhere between Newfoundland and Massachusetts.

Within five years of Columbus' first voyage, John Cabot nosed by in 1497, in search of the Northwest Passage. Over the next century, European fishermen began to return each year, but it was not until the early 1600s that the French and English attempted to found permanent colonies, in what is now Maine. The name "New England" was given by John Smith in 1614, who particularly appreciated the plentiful lobsters.

This was not particularly promising land: as a character in Robert Lowell's *Endecott and the Cross* put it, "I'm not a birdwatcher or an Indian . . . I don't see the point of this outpost of England". There were no precious metals to be mined, there was no potential to grow lucrative crops; instead the first major impetus for emigration turned out to be **religion**. Refugees from religious intolerance – notably the Puritans, beginning with the **Pilgrim Fathers** in 1620 – made the long and arduous voyage in order to find freedom to build their own communities. The Pilgrims only survived at first thanks to the Indians; they were even aided by a certain Squanto, who had been kidnapped, sold as a slave in Spain and returned home via England. In return, the Pilgrims forced the Indians from the terraces they had farmed for generations, and dismissed as inappropriate a centuries-old solution to the problems of survival in such terrain: as one commented, "their land is spacious and void, and there are few and do but run over the grass . . . They are not industrious, neither have art, science, skill or faculty to use either the land or the commodities of it".

The possibility of a serious Indian threat was removed by victory in **King Philip's War** of 1675–76, when a leader of the Narragansett persuaded feuding groups to bury their differences in one last despairing throw. By then, white colonisation was beyond the stage where it could be controlled by a few high-minded zealots. The **Salem witch trials** of 1692 provided a salutary lesson of the potential dangers of fanaticism, and as immigration became less English-based, with influxes of Huguenots after 1680 and Irish in 1708, Puritan domination decreased and a definite class structure began to emerge.

While the strand of history which began with the Pilgrim Fathers is just one among many – even forgetting the Indians, the Spanish were in Santa Fe before the Pilgrims ever left England – it is true to say that the metropolis of **Boston** deserves to be celebrated as the place where the great project of American **independence** first captured the popular imagination. The leading port of colonial America was always the likeliest focus of resentment against the latest impositions of the British government, and was ready to take up the challenge thrown down by British Prime Minister Townshend in 1766: "I dare tax America". So many of the seminal moments of the **Revolutionary War** took place here: the Boston Massacre of 1770, the Boston Tea Party of 1773, Paul Revere's ride and the first shots at Lexington and Concord in 1775.

Nationhood secured, however, New England's prosperity was ironically hit hard by the loss of trade with England, and Boston was fast eclipsed by Philadelphia, New York, and the new capital, Washington. The **Triangular Trade** in slaves and rum provided one substitute source of income, the brief heyday of **whaling** another, and New England was also briefly at the forefront of the **Industrial Revolution**, when water-powered mills created a booming textile industry. The attempt to farm the north, however, foundered: careless techniques served to exhaust the land, and as the vast spaces of the west opened to settlement many of the inland towns fell silent.

MASSACHUSETTS

To the first colonists of the **Massachusetts Bay Company**, their arrival near the site of modern Salem in 1630 marked a crucial moment in history. **Puritans** who had decided to leave England before it was engulfed by the clearly imminent chaos of civil war, they saw their purpose, in the words of Governor John Winthrop, as the establishment of a Utopian "**City upon a hill**". Their new colony of **MASSACHUSETTS** was to be a beacon to the rest of humanity, an exemplar of sober government along sound spiritual principles. Not all those who followed, however, shared the same motivation; the story is often told of the preacher who told his congregation that they had come to New England to build a new kingdom of God, only to be challenged by a vociferous element who said that they personally had come to fish.

In their own terms, the Puritans were not successful: as waves of immigration carried all kinds of dissenters and free-thinkers from Europe, society in New England inevitably became secular. However, their **influence** remained. A clarity of thought and forcefulness of purpose can be traced from the foundation of Harvard College in 1636, through the intellectual impetus behind the Revolution and the crusade against slavery, to the nineteenth-century achievements of **writers** such as Melville, Poe, Hawthorne and Thoreau.

Other traditions too have helped shape the state – poor migrants from **Ireland** and **Italy**, freed and escaped **slaves** from the southern states, **Portuguese** seamen – even if they have not always been welcome. The anti-immigrant "Know-Nothings" of the 1850s acquired considerable public support; in 1927, the Italian anarchists **Sacco and Vanzetti** came up against conservative old Massachusetts, and were framed and executed on murder charges. As recently as the 1970s, Boston experienced racial conflicts to compare with any in the nation. There is, however, a cosmopolitan side to Massachusetts – witness the extraordinary blend of nationalities involved in the trans-global **whaling** industry of nineteenth-century Nantucket – and a strong liberal undercurrent. The high-tech promise of Governor Michael Dukakis' "Massachusetts Miracle" may not quite have delivered lasting prosperity any more than did John Kennedy, but optimism and resilience still shine through.

Spending a few days in **Boston** is strongly recommended; the city is Massachusetts at its best. It's a place that feels no need to rest on its laurels – the history is there and visible, but there's a great deal of modern life and energy besides. Several further historic towns are within easy reach – **Salem** to the north, **Concord** and **Lexington** just inland, and **Plymouth** to the south. **Provincetown**, a three-hour ferry ride across the bay at the tip of Cape Cod, is a lot of fun to visit, but the rest of the Cape is a little disappointing, at least to a European sensibility. **Inland Massachusetts** is much quieter; its settlements are naturally concentrated where the land gets fertile, such as along the Connecticut River valley and in the Berkshires in the west, and high real estate prices tend to ensure a rich population and a placid atmosphere.

Getting Around Massachusetts

With the single proviso that all roads in Massachusetts seem to lead to Boston, this is an easy state to tour on **public transport**. Planes, trains and buses all radiate out from the one great city; the connections to **Cape Cod** in particular (see p.161) are absolutely legion. The *Amtrak* line which connects Boston with New York, Philadelphia and Washington is the best **train** service in the nation, and the east–west line via Worcester and Springfield gives access to Montréal, Toronto and Chicago. With the exception of the local commuter lines, trains do not, however, continue north of Boston: the only service along the coast is the summer-only service to Hyannis on Cape Cod. **Buses** from Boston are also plentiful, but the only major north–south route inland is that which runs up the Connecticut River valley.

Boston

Although the metropolitan area of **BOSTON** has long since expanded to fill the shoreline of **Massachusetts Bay**, and stretches for miles inland as well, the seventeenth-century port at its heart is still discernible. Forget the neat grids of modern urban America; the twisting streets clustered around **Boston Common** are a reminder of how the nation started out, and the city is enjoyably human in scale.

Boston was until 1755 the biggest city in America; as the one most directly affected by the latest whims of the British Crown, it was the natural focus for the opposition which culminated in the **Revolutionary War**. Numerous evocative sites from that era are preserved along the **Freedom Trail** through downtown. Since then, however, Boston has in effect turned its back on the sea. As the third busiest port in the British empire (after London and Bristol), it stood on a narrow peninsula. What is now Washington Street provided the only access by land, and when the British set off to Lexington in 1775 they embarked in ships from the Common itself. During the nineteenth century, much of the bay was filled in, to create the Back Bay residential area. Central Boston is now slightly but significantly set back from the water, separated by the psychological barrier of the hideous John Fitzgerald Expressway which carries I-93 across downtown.

There is a certain truth in the charge levelled by other Americans that Boston likes to live in the past; echoes of the "Brahmins" of a century ago can be heard in the upper-class drawl of the posher districts. But this is by no means just a city of WASPs: the Irish who began to arrive in quantity after the Great Famine produced their first mayor as early as 1885, and the president of the whole country within a hundred years. The liberal tradition which spawned the Kennedys remains alive, fed in part by the presence in the city of more than one hundred universities and colleges.

The slump of the Depression seemed to linger in Boston for years – even in the 1950s, the population was actually dwindling – but these days the place definitely has a rejuvenated feel to it. **Quincy Market** has served as a blueprint for urban development worldwide, and with its busy street life, imaginative museums and galleries, fine red-brick architecture and palpable history, Boston is the one destination in New England there's no excuse for missing.

> The telephone **area code** for Boston is ☎617.

Arrival and Information

Boston may not be the "hub of the universe", as Oliver Wendell Holmes liked to think, but it is at any rate the centre of all New England's transport networks. Direct flights from Europe mean that for many travellers it provides their first taste of America, while efficient rail and bus services from New York, Montréal and further afield make this the obvious goal, wherever you're heading in New England.

Air

Logan Airport (☎1-800/235-6426 or ☎561-1800), one of the busiest in the US for both international and domestic services, is a mere three miles from downtown Boston. It stands on an artificial peninsula jutting into Boston Harbor, created by levelling three islands and destroying Revolution Wharf. As driving within the city is not to be recommended (see below), it makes little sense to rent a car at the airport. A **taxi** into town costs between $10 and $15; the trip should take twenty minutes, but all traffic has to pass through the Sumner or Callahan tunnels, which can get very congested. Between 5.30am and 1am, free buses run every few minutes from all terminals to the Airport

subway station on the *MBTA Blue* line (also see below), from where it's an easy ten-minute ride to the city centre. Just as quick, and a whole lot more fun, is the **water shuttle** which connects the *Eastern Airlines* terminal with Rowes Wharf across the Harbor (Mon–Fri every 15min, 6am–8pm, Sat & Sun every 30min, noon–8pm; adults $7, kids $3; ☎1-800-23-LOGAN).

Far too many flights use Logan Airport to list here, but it is worth mentioning that two regular **shuttles to New York** leave throughout the day for a flat single fare of around $125. Off-peak and student discounts can make them the same price as the train.

Several **bus** companies offer direct links between Logan Airport and northern New England. *Vermont Transit* (☎1-800/451-3292) cover New Hampshire's White Mountains and continue to Vermont and Montréal, while *Concord Trailways* (☎1-800/258-3722) simply run to New Hampshire.

Trains

Amtrak trains along the Northeast Corridor from Providence, Washington DC and New York, and from Chicago and Canada via Springfield, as well as the summer-only Cape Cod specials, arrive in downtown Boston near the waterfront at **South Station** (☎482-3715), Summer Street and Atlantic Avenue. The station is currently being expanded to coordinate all Boston's buses and trains. Some *Amtrak* services also make an extra stop at **Back Bay Station** (☎348-0601), 145 Dartmouth Street, on the *Orange* subway line near Copley Square. **North Station** is used only by *MBTA* commuter trains.

Buses

Boston's long-distance *Greyhound* terminal at 10 St James Avenue (☎423-5810), two blocks from the Arlington (*Green* line) subway station, is shared with *Bonanza Bus Lines* (also ☎423-5810), who connect the city with Woods Hole, Newport and Providence, and the *Plymouth and Brockton Bus Co* (☎508/746-0378), serving Hyannis. *Peter Pan Bus Lines* – to New York and western Massachusetts – and *Concord Trailways* – north to New Hampshire – are based at 555 Atlantic Avenue (☎426-7838), across from South Station. Some long-distance buses operate out of Logan Airport (see above).

Information

The most convenient place to get advice and maps is the **Visitor Information Center** (daily 8.30am–5pm; ☎267-6466) at Park Street subway on the Tremont Street side of Boston Common. There's also an information booth at the **John Hancock Tower**, at Copley Square in the Back Bay area (Mon–Sat 9am–11pm, Sun noon–11pm).

The city's main **post office** is at McCormack Station, Post Office Square, Boston MA 02109 (Mon–Fri 8am–5pm; ☎654-5686).

Getting Around

Much of the pleasure of visiting Boston comes from being in a city that was built long before cars were invented. Walking around it can be a joy; conversely, driving is an absolute nightmare. The freeways won't take you where you want to be, the one-way traffic systems can have you circling for hours without getting any nearer your destination; and if you ever do arrive there's nowhere to park. There's really no point renting a car in Boston until the day you leave.

The *Massachusetts Bay Transport Authority* (*MBTA*, universally known as the "**T**") is responsible for Boston's **subway** system and **trolley buses**. The subway, which opened in 1897, is the oldest in the US; its first station, Park Street, remains its centre (any train marked "inbound" is headed here), and is the place to pick up all schedules and information. Four lines – *Red*, *Green*, *Blue* and *Orange* – operate daily from 5am until 1am, although certain routes begin to shut down earlier. Away from downtown, the trains emerge from tunnels to run along the city's major arteries, though not all their overground stops are shown on the widely available *Rapid Transit* maps. Trains are fast and safe; only the *Orange* line might be said to be unsafe after dark.

The standard fare is 75¢, paid with tokens inserted into turnstiles, but on some incoming overground routes you have to pay extra, up to $1.75. You can buy eleven tokens for the price of ten, and a **tourist pass** covers all subway and local bus journeys at a cost of $8 for 3 days, or $16 for a week. (All *MBTA* information is on ☎722-3200 Mon–Fri 7am–6pm; ☎722-5000 nights and weekends; ☎1-800/392-6100.)

The normal fare on *MBTA*'s **local buses** is 50¢, but longer distances, such as out to Salem or Marblehead, cost $2.50 single. Red double-decker *Shopper's Shuttle* buses loop regularly between Back Bay, Downtown Crossing and Faneuil, from 10am until 6pm; adults 50¢, kids 25¢. *MBTA* also run **commuter rail lines**, extending as far as Salem, Ipswich, and Concord, New Hampshire; these are based at the venerable **North Station** (☎227-5070) on Causeway Street, under the Boston Garden.

Bicycles can be rented from the *Community Bike Shop* at 490 Tremont Street (☎542-8623) and *Ferris Wheels*, 64 South Street, Jamaica Plain (☎522-7082), among others.

City Tours

It's easy enough to get to know Boston by following the Freedom Trail on foot (see below). If you prefer to be guided, narrated trips run throughout the day aboard the *Beantown Trolley* (☎287-1900), and *Boston By Foot* (77 N Washington St; ☎367-2345) conduct ninety-minute walking tours for $5. More useful are the coach excursions further afield with *Brush Hill Tours* (☎287-1900 or ☎1-800/647-4776), which start from the *Sheraton* at the Prudential Center; their shuttle buses connect with all large hotels.

The City

Boston has grown up around **Boston Common**, which was set aside as common land in 1634, and was for the next two hundred years grazed by cattle and lapped by the sea. As well as being the obvious first stop on a tour of the city, it is also a pleasant place to return to rest your legs at the odd moment throughout the day. You might even choose to take a short ride in one of the two-ton **swan boats** which paddle across the main pond.

The visitor centre, which is the official starting point of the **Freedom Trail**, is near the tapering north end of the Common. As you stand here, facing up Tremont Street with the **State House** away to your left, the main **shopping** district, **Quincy Market**, and the **waterfront** are slightly ahead of you but down to the right. The modern concrete wasteland of **Government Center** is straight up Tremont Street, and beyond that is the **North End**, which was first Irish, then Jewish, and is now very definitely Italian. A short way behind you on the left rises **Beacon Hill**, every bit as elegant as it was when Henry James referred to Mount Vernon Street as "the most prestigious address in America" (and far removed from its eighteenth-century nickname of "Mount Whoredom"). Heading away from the centre down Tremont Street brings you to **Chinatown** and the **Theater District**, while grand boulevards such as Commonwealth Avenue at the Common's inland end lead into **Back Bay**.

The Freedom Trail

Much the best way to orientate yourself to downtown Boston – and to appreciate the city's role in American history – is to walk some or all of the **Freedom Trail**. You can pick up or leave this easy self-guided route anywhere – for most of the way a line of red bricks is embedded in the pavement, elsewhere there's a painted red line – but technically it begins on Boston Common at the **Visitor Information Center**.

BOSTON

To the Airport

To Bunker Hill

US-1

Charles River Dam

Museum of Science

Charles

USS Constitution

CHARLESTOWN BRIDGE

NORTH END

Boston Garden & North Station

BEACON HILL

CAMBRIDGE STREET

State House

Old Granary Burying Ground

Old Court House

Government Center

Old State House

Quincy Market (Faneuil Hall)

Park Columbus

Long Wharf

New England Aquarium

Rowes Wharf

Old South Meeting House

TREMONT STREET

Computer Museum

Children's Museum

Boston Tea Party Ship & Museum

South Station

TUNNEL

SOUTH BOSTON

From here, head for the golden dome of the **State House**, which was completed in 1798 to a design by Charles Bulfinch. It remains the seat of Massachusetts' government; its most famous feature, the wooden Sacred Cod symbolising the wealth Boston accrued from its fisheries, hangs in front of the Speaker, and faces in different directions according to which party is in office (free tours Mon–Fri 10am–4pm).

Henry James described **Park Street Church** as the "most interesting mass of brick and mortar in America"; this was where the orator William Lloyd Garrison launched his campaign to free the slaves on July 4 1829 (July & Aug Tues–Sat 9.30am–3.30pm, otherwise by appointment; free). The 1600 graves of the **Old Granary Burying Ground** just around the corner (daily 8am–5pm; free) include those of Paul Revere, Samuel Adams and John Hancock, as well as the original Mother Goose, while **King's Chapel Burying Ground** (Tues–Sun 10am–4pm; free) contains Boston's earliest colonists and the first governor, John Winthrop. A statue of Benjamin Franklin marks the site of Boston's **First Public School**, attended by Franklin and Samuel Adams. Guests at the nearby **Omni Parker House Hotel** (not officially on the Trail) have included Charles Dickens and John Kennedy; employees, Malcolm X, Red Foxx and Ho Chi Minh. The **Old Corner Bookstore** at the corner of School and Washington streets was a literary salon frequented by Longfellow, Thoreau and Hawthorne; under the auspices of the *Boston Globe*, it's now the atmospheric *Globe Corner Bookstore*, specialising in travel (Mon–Fri 9am–6pm, Sat 9.30am–6pm, Sun noon–5pm).

Next come the Trail's two most striking and significant buildings. At the **Old South Meeting House**, Samuel Adams addressed the patriots about to carry out the Boston Tea Party on December 16, 1773 (April–Oct daily 9.30am–5pm; Nov–March Mon–Fri 10am–4pm, Sat & Sun 10am–5pm; $1.25). According to contemporary accounts this was no raucous and unruly mob: they were solemn men, well aware of the likely impact of their actions. The elegant **Old State House**, built in 1712 and still proud although dwarfed by surrounding skyscrapers, was the seat of Colonial government. From its balcony the Declaration of Independence was read on July 18 1776; exactly two hundred years later Queen Elizabeth II appeared on that same balcony. Inside is a museum of Boston history (daily 9.30am–5pm; $1.25). Outside, a ring of cobblestones marks the site of the **Boston Massacre** on March 5 1770, when British soldiers fired on a crowd which was pelting them with stone-filled snowballs, and killed five, including the black Crispus Attucks.

Modern visitors gravitate to **Quincy Market** and **Faneuil Hall** (it rhymes with *Daniel*; daily 9am–9pm; free) for the lively shops, restaurants and takeaways which made this a pioneer example of successful urban renewal (by the architect who went on to transform London's Covent Garden). Faneuil Hall was, however, once known as the "Cradle of Liberty", a meeting place for Revolutionaries and, later, abolitionists.

Moving into the North End, **Paul Revere House** is the only seventeenth-century house still standing in Boston. It was built after the Great Fire of 1676, and Paul Revere – patriot, silversmith, Freemason, and father of sixteen children – lived here from 1770 until 1800 (mid-April to Oct daily 9.30am–5.15pm; Nov to mid-April daily 9.30am–4.15pm; closed Mon Jan–March; $1.50). Revere's famous **ride** of April 18 1775, to warn Lexington of imminent British attack, was spurred by two signal lanterns ("one if by land, two if by sea") hung from the steeple of **Old North Church** at 193 Salem Street (daily, 9am–5pm; free). A little further up, from **Copp's Hill Burial Ground** (daily 8am–5pm; free) you can see across the harbour to Charlestown; as indeed could the British who planted their artillery here for the Battle of Bunker Hill.

In theory, the Freedom Trail now crosses the Charlestown bridge, but that's a long walk over. Its final two sites are better reached by the frequent **ferries** from Long Wharf to Charlestown Navy Yard (every 15–30min, Mon–Fri 6.30am–8pm, every half-hour at weekends 10am–6pm; $1 each way). First is the **USS Constitution**, also known as "Old Ironsides", the oldest commissioned warship afloat in the world.

Launched in Boston in 1797, it was prominent in the War of 1812. Every July 4 it is ceremonially turned around – sailed out into the bay and its cannon fired – mainly in order to equalise the weathering on its two sides. Free tours of the ship are conducted in period costume (daily 9.30am–3.50pm). Up above, the **Bunker Hill Monument** is in fact on Breed's Hill; but this was the actual site of the battle on June 17 1775, which, although won by the British, did much to convince them that they could not hope to triumph in the end. A spiral staircase of almost three hundred steps leads to the top; nearby, a museum offers a multi-media presentation of the battle (summer daily 9.30am–6pm, winter 9.30am–4pm; monument free, museum $1.50).

The Black Heritage Trail

Massachusetts was the first state to declare slavery illegal, in 1783 – partly as a result of black participation in the Revolutionary War – and a large community of free blacks and escaped slaves swiftly grew up in the North End, and on Beacon Hill. Although ironically very few blacks now live on Beacon Hill, the **Black Heritage Trail** through the area celebrates many important sites in the history of Boston's black community (maps are available from the various visitor centres).

Pick up the Trail either at 46 Joy Street, where the **Abiel Smith School** contains a **Museum of Afro-American History** (Tues–Fri 10am–4pm), illustrating the national civil rights campaign as well as local history, or at the **African Meeting House** at 8 Smith Court (off Joy Street), for displays and talks from well-informed rangers. Built in 1806 as the first African–American church in the United States, this became known as "Black Faneuil Hall" during the abolitionist campaign; Frederick Douglass issued his call here for all blacks to take up arms in the Civil War. Among those who responded were the volunteers of the **Massachusetts 54th Regiment**, commemorated by a monument at the edge of Boston Common, opposite the State House, which depicts their farewell march down Beacon Street. Robert Lowell won a Pulitzer Prize for his poem, *For the Union Dead*, about this monument; and the regiment's tragic end at Fort Wagner was depicted in the movie *Glory*. The Trail then winds around Beacon Hill, passing schools, other institutions, and residences ranging from the small cream clapboard houses of Smith Court to the imposing **Lewis and Harriet Hayden House** at 66 Phillips Street, which was a stop on the famous "Underground Railroad", sheltering runaway slaves from pursuing bounty-hunters.

The waterfront

It comes as a disappointment to realise that you can't walk along Boston's **waterfront** for any distance: most of the wharfs are closed to visitors, and you can see little of the harbour from the roads and footpaths which provide access to them.

If you head straight for the sea from Quincy Market, however, **Columbus Park**, next to the ugly *Marriott Hotel*, is a nice place to sit for a while. Originally, Faneuil Hall stood at the head of **Long Wharf**, which stuck 2000ft out into the harbour, and was the site of the final British evacuation on March 17 1776. Then a thousand feet of water was filled in, and the **Custom House Tower** was erected to mark the end of the wharf. That remained Boston's tallest building until as recently as 1962; it too now finds itself inland, as a further thousand feet of new land has been added.

The **Boston Harbor Cruises** ($8; ☎227-4231) from Long Wharf are not in fact all that exciting. The port is nothing like as busy as it was when fishing boats lined the quays three or four deep on all sides. Instead you pass vast rows of freshly imported Japanese cars on the quayside, and get a close-up view of the airport. It's possible to get off one cruise in Charlestown in order to see the *USS Constitution* (see opposite), and then catch the next one back for no extra charge.

Close at hand on Central Wharf, the **New England Aquarium** (July–Sept Mon, Tues & Thurs 9am–6pm, Wed & Fri 9am–8pm, Sat & Sun 9am–7pm; Oct–June Mon–

Thurs 9am–5pm, Fri 9am–8pm, Sat & Sun 9am–6pm; adults $7, kids $4; ☎873-5200) is marked by an outdoor pool of basking harbour seals. Inside the highlight is the colossal Giant Ocean Tank, a four-storey glass cylinder containing all sorts of sharks, giant turtles and tropical marine life (with an unsettling emphasis on how "delicious" certain specimens are). Scuba divers hand-feed the fish five times a day, and frequent dolphin shows are held in a floating amphitheatre alongside.

If you follow the shoreline past **Rowe's Wharf** (the base for the water shuttles to the airport), a short distance before South Station the **Congress Street Bridge** leads off to the left across the Fort Point Channel. The **Boston Tea Party Ship and Museum** (daily 9am–dusk; adults $4, kids $3) is moored to the bridge itself. This is not the original *Beaver*, one of the three ships stormed by patriots in 1773, but a replica, *Beaver II*, sailed here from Denmark in 1973. Neither is it the original mooring, which was on the now-demolished Griffin's Wharf; instead it's the site of the house where the conspirators prepared their assault. The ship is small and not desperately interesting, for adults at any rate. Displays include a relief model of Boston as it then was – virtually an island – and costumed attendants serve China tea of the self-same type that was thrown in the sea, provoking the British to close the port and place Boston under martial law. From time to time throughout the day there are re-enactments of the Tea Party itself.

On the far side of the bridge, a forty-foot **milk bottle**, which serves as an ice cream store and sandwich bar, marks **Museum Wharf**. Here the two most enjoyable museums in the city share the same modern building (though each has a separate entrance). The **Children's Museum** (Tues–Thurs, and Sat & Sun 10am–5pm, Fri 10am–9pm, closed Mon except during school holidays; adults $5, kids $4) is an absolute kids' paradise – all its galleries invite maximum participation. The central shaft is taken up with a climbing maze-cum-sculpture, stretching three storeys, that no one over fourteen could possibly get into. At one end, a reconstructed Thirties house looks as though the family has just nipped out – the radio is on, and you can browse through the magazines and books on the table, while downstairs in "Grandfather's Cellar" the woodworking tools are laid out for anyone to use, with or without supervision. At the other, a genuine Japanese dwelling offers impromptu art classes. In a soundproof booth upstairs demented kids jam on synthesized guitars; nearby a psychedelic disco raves all day. An impressive display, designed to raise awareness of racism, enables you to explore Boston's ethnic neighbourhoods via inter-active video; another, on disabilities, to tackle an obstacle course in a wheelchair.

The world's first and only **Computer Museum** is right alongside (same hours and prices – you have to pay again – as the Children's Museum). Reached by glass-sided elevator, the collection opens with four history-making computers: the first, *Univac*, is seen predicting the result of the 1952 Presidential election. You progress to hands-on exhibits on artificial intelligence, graphic design, and of course games. The whole thing – heavily corporate-sponsored – stresses that computers "serve mankind and improve the scope of our lives"; there's no reference to defence industries or unemployment. But it's undeniably entertaining, with its showpiece a giant "**Walk-through Computer**", a model personal computer that you can literally walk through, dissected mouse and all. You need to be computer-literate already, or at least confident, to get the best of it, and it's more fun when the place is empty, so come during the week or out of holidays.

Children might also want to visit the **Museum of Science**, in the Science Park on the Charles River Dam at the northern end of the waterfront, not far from North Station (daily 9am–5pm except Fri 9am–9pm, closed Mon except during holidays; adults $6, kids $4). The Sun Room, which takes advantage of the beautiful setting to catch light for its solar panels, and the egg hatchery, in which at least one new chicken always seems to be pecking its way out of the shell to the bewilderment of its older siblings, are its most popular features. An *OMNIMAX* cinema takes up the full height of one end of the building, and the Hayden Planetarium as ever pays its way with Pink Floyd laser shows.

Back Bay and beyond

As each portion of the tidal flats of the Charles River was filled in, from 1857 onwards, more of the spacious boulevards and grand houses of **Back Bay** were built. Thus to walk through the area from east to west gives you an object lesson in the history of Victorian architecture. Much the most distinguished of its buildings is the Romanesque **Trinity Church** on Clarendon Street, which is supported on four thousand wooden pilings which have to be kept permanently moist. The church these days can always be seen reflected in the gleaming windows of the adjacent **John Hancock Tower**, whose rooftop observatory provides a glorious overall view of Boston (Mon–Sat 9am–11pm, Sun noon–11pm; $3). Structural flaws are said to have caused Hancock Tower to shed three thousand panes of glass during its first year; the cost of insuring Trinity Church against damage was so prohibitive that it was cheaper to buy it outright. **Copley Square** nearby is an upmarket shopping mall with several good snack-bars and restaurants.

The **Christian Science Center** at Huntington and Massachusetts Avenue is the "Mother Church" of the Church of Christ Scientist, and the home of the *Christian Science Monitor* newspaper; Nelson Mandela made a point of paying a personal visit here in 1990 to thank the paper for its support. The **Mapparium** (Mon–Fri 8am–4pm, Sat 10am–3.45pm, Sun 11.15am–3.45pm; free) is an impressive, if not utterly logical, glass globe of the world, which you can walk inside on a footbridge. Part of the interest is that it was built in 1932, and thus shows national boundaries as they were then.

Further south, beyond the boundaries of Back Bay and a long enough walk to warrant taking the *Green* subway line instead (get on a car marked "E"), is the **Museum of Fine Arts** at 465 Huntingdon Avenue (Tues & Thurs–Sun 10am–5pm, Wed 10am–10pm; West Wing only is also open Thurs & Fri 5–10pm; adults $6, kids free). From its magnificent collections of Asian and ancient Egyptian art onwards, this holds sufficient marvels to detain you all day. High points include the Babylonian *Lion* (604 BC) and the Sumerian *Head of Gudea* (2200 BC); John Frederick Peto's charming, *trompe l'oeil, Poor Man's Store* (in the American Masters room); Edward Hopper's tranquil, hopeful, *Room In Brooklyn* (American Modern); Andrew Wyeth's *Corner of the Woods* (William Coolidge); Degas' *The Little Dancer*; and Gauguin's *Where do we come from, What are we, Where are we going ?* (Impressionists). A personal favourite is Millet's *The Sower*, in the English and French room – an elemental vision of the catalytic role of humans in the natural cycle. Don't miss the **American Decorative Arts** either: a gloriously nostalgic jamboree of coffee urns, speak-your-weight machines and reconstructed living rooms.

A smaller-scale and rather more idiosyncratic collection of fine arts can be found at the **Isabella Stewart Gardner Museum**, just down the road at 280 The Fenway (Tues noon–6.30pm, Wed–Sun noon–5pm; $5). This reconstructed Italian Renaissance villa, complete with indoor fountain, is crammed with the eclectic harvest of a lifetime spent in pursuit of the sublime – an unclassifiable but breathtaking hotchpotch covering anything from modern American to fifteenth-century Italian. Some of the most interesting works are "unlisted", such as the tapestry above the door of the Italian room, which depicts a lion, a sealion and an elephant, or the sculpted pigeon on the nearby windowsill. Among Gardner's various eccentricities was the injunction declaring the place a pen-free zone; if you're tempted to make any notes, use a pencil.

Cambridge

It's well worth devoting at least half a day to a trip across the Charles River to **Cambridge**. The *Red* "T" line takes fifteen minutes from Park Street to **Harvard Square**, which is not so much a square as a number of interlocking streets, filled with shopping malls and bookstores, at the point where Massachusetts Avenue runs into JFK and Brattle streets. This is an exceptionally lively area, filled with students from nearby Harvard University and MIT; its cafe terraces, such as *Au Bon Pain*, make for enjoyable people-watching. The **Cambridge Discovery Booth** (June to mid-Oct Mon–Sat 9am–

6pm, otherwise Mon–Sat 9am–5pm, Sun all year 1–5pm, ☎497-1630) here organises walking tours in summer, and sells local maps and guides including the *Unofficial Guide to Life at Harvard*, produced by the students responsible for the *Let's Go* travel series.

Feel free to wander into **Harvard Yard** and around the core of the university, founded in 1636; its enormous Widener Library (named to commemorate a victim of the *Titanic*) boasts a Gutenberg Bible and a First Folio of Shakespeare. Five minutes' walk west along Brattle Street is the imposing yellow-fronted mansion known as **Longfellow House** (daily 10.30am–4.30pm; $1), after the author of *Hiawatha* who lived here until 1882; a century earlier it was briefly the headquarters of General George Washington. Dexter Pratt, immortalised in Longfellow's "Under the spreading chestnut tree, the village blacksmith stands", lived at 56 Brattle Street, now a popular bakery and cafe.

Many of Cambridge's wonderful array of **bookstores** stay open until midnight; both *Barillari* (1 Mifflin Place) and *Words Worth* (30 Brattle Street) offer big discounts on their large stock, and there are any number of smaller specialist and secondhand stores. You'll also find a wide range of cheap clothing stores and shops catering for student interests. Things in general get a bit funkier heading down Massachusetts Avenue towards the river. *Cheapo Records* at no. 645, by Central Square (Mon–Wed & Sat 10am–6pm, Thurs & Fri 10am–9pm) has a phenomenal selection of old **records** on two floors – R&B, gospel, blues, jazz, country, cajun, reggae, the works.

Lexington and Concord

On the night of April 18 1775, **Paul Revere** rode down what is now Massachusetts Avenue from Boston, racing through Cambridge and Arlington on his way to warn the American patriots gathered at **Lexington** of an impending British attack. Close behind him was a force of over four hundred British soldiers, intent on seizing the supplies which they knew the "rebels" had hoarded at **Concord**.

Although today Revere's route has been turned into major freeways, and you are barely out of the Boston suburbs before you arrive in Lexington, the various scenes of the first military confrontation of the Revolutionary War – "the shot heard round the world" – remain much as they were that night. The triangular **Town Common** at Lexington was where the British encountered the opposition. Captain John Parker ordered his 77 American **"Minutemen"** to "stand your ground. Don't fire unless fired upon, but if they mean to have a war let it begin here." No-one knows who fired the first shot – it may have come from one of the venerable houses around the green – but the Minuteman Statue commemorates the eight Americans who died. Guides in period costume lead tours of the **Buckman Tavern**, where the Minutemen waited for the British to arrive; the **Hancock-Clarke House** a quarter of a mile north, where Samuel Adams and John Hancock were awakened by Paul Revere, is now a museum.

There were no British casualties in Lexington, but by the time they marched on Concord the next morning the surrounding countryside was up in arms. In running battles in the town itself, and along Battle Road leading back towards Boston, almost three hundred British soldiers were killed over the next two days. The relevant sites are preserved as the **Minuteman National Historic Park**, which has visitor centres at the scenic North Bridge (174 Liberty Street) in Concord and Battle Road in Lexington.

Walden Pond near Concord was where Henry David Thoreau conducted the experiment in solitude and self-sufficiency described in his 1854 book *Walden*. "I did not feel crowded or confined in the least", he wrote of life in his simple log cabin; the site where it stood is now marked with stones, and at dawn you can still watch the pond "throwing off its nightly clothing of mist". However, it's now a busy and crowded state park.

Paul Revere's ride is re-enacted annually on the state holiday of Patriot's Day, the third Monday in April, along with the Battle of Lexington. As well as guided **coach tours** from Boston (see p.147), **buses** run to Lexington from Alewife Station, and commuter **trains** to Concord from North Station.

Accommodation

Good-quality budget **accommodation** is hard to find in Boston. The price you can pay for a hostel here would get you an upmarket motel elsewhere, while any hotel accommodation in walking distance of downtown for under $100 unfortunately has to be considered a bargain. The **Boston Welcome Center** at 140 Tremont Street (☎451-2277) can make hotel bookings in the $60 to $100 price bracket.

While a tremendous number of homes in the Boston area now offer **bed and breakfast** accommodation, it is very unusual for any of the downtown options to advertise themselves directly. Most are simply not equipped to deal with casual enquirers walking in off the street, and deal instead through **agencies**. Any of *Host Homes of Boston* (PO Box 117, Waban Branch, Boston MA 02168; ☎244-1308); *Boston B&B* (16 Ballard St, Newton; ☎332-4199); or *New England B&B* (1045 Centre St, Newton Centre, MA 02159; ☎244-2112) can provide rooms starting at around $60 for a double.

Hostels

Boston International AYH Hostel, 12 Hemenway St, Boston (☎536-9455). A little way out in the Fenway (Hynes Convention subway). Dorms $12 for members, $15 non-members. 10am–5pm lockout; check-in 5–11pm, midnight curfew. Book ahead in summer.

Cambridge YMCA, 820 Massachusetts Ave (☎661-9622) and **Cambridge YWCA**, 7 Temple St, (☎491-6050). Single rooms in single-sex hostels, both near Central subway in Cambridge, for $30 members, $39 non-members. Book in advance.

Greater Boston YMCA, 316 Huntington Ave, Boston (☎536-7800). Near the junction with Massachusetts Ave. Mixed-sex accommodation from $29 single, $42 double with breakfast.

YWCA, 40 Berkeley St, Boston (☎482-8850). Women-only rooms in convenient South End location. $34 single or $44 double for basic rooms, $2 extra for non-members, weekly rates.

Hotels, Motels and B&Bs

Anthony's Town House, 1085 Beacon St, Brookline (☎566-3972). Brownstone house a 15-min ride from downtown, $40–60 double with shared bath.

A Cambridge House, 2218 Massachusetts Ave at Porter Square, Cambridge (☎491-6300). Classy restored house a 15-min walk from Harvard Square. B&B rates start at $60.

Copley Square, 47 Huntington Ave (☎536-9000). Very near Copley Plaza. Double rooms (without bath) start at $95.

Inn at Children's, 342 Longwood Ave, Boston (☎731-1700). A *Best Western* hotel, 10min on subway from downtown (stop Longwood/Hospitals), with a high standard for around $100 double. Good facilities, but this hospital district is not very exciting.

Longwood Inn, 123 Longwood Ave, Boston (☎566-8615). Simple rooms in large Victorian house. Singles and doubles from $48.

Quality Inn, 1651 Massachusetts Ave, Cambridge (☎491-1000). Standard but very comfortable accommodation near Harvard Square, from $76 double.

Susse Chalet Motor Lodge and **Susse Chalet Inn**, 800 and 900 Morrissey Blvd, Dorchester (☎287-9100 or ☎287-9200). Six miles southeast of downtown, just off the Southeast Expressway. High-quality double rooms from $50. There are several *Susse Chalets* in the Boston area.

The Tremont House, 275 Tremont St, Boston (☎426-1400). Doubles for $100 in this well-restored art-deco hotel, now run by *Quality Inns*, an easy walk from the Common.

Eating

There is far more to eating in Boston than its image as "Beantown" might suggest. Above all, there's the **seafood**, especially lobsters, *scrod* (a generic term for young white-fleshed fish), and clams (served as *steamers*, dipped in butter, or as creamy chowder). You could base a day's tour of the different neighbourhoods around the foods on offer: breakfast in the cafes of **Beacon Hill** or **Cambridge**; lunch in the food plazas of

Quincy Market or **The Garage** on JFK Street in Cambridge, or dim sum in **Chinatown**; for dinner, a cheap **Indian** in Cambridge, an **Italian** around Hanover Street in the North End, or expensive seafood overlooking the Harbor.

For cheap eating, and to sample what's available, much the best place to start is the central aisle of **Quincy Market**, which is superb for all kinds of takeaways, including fresh clams and lobster, as well as ethnic dishes, fruit cocktails and cookies. (Here and all over the city, you'll find marvellous chocolate and ice cream.) Groups can buy from different vendors and eat together in the central seating area. There are also restaurants and brasseries on all sides.

Many restaurants in Chinatown stay open until 2 or 3am; otherwise there is very little late-night eating available.

Boston

Addis Red Sea, 544 Tremont St (☎426-7827). Authentic Ethiopian food, which you scoop up, using chunks of doughy flatbread, from communal dishes. Spicy and cheap.

The Blue Diner, 215 South St (☎338-4639). Classic restored diner with lively jukebox, slowly inching its way upmarket but with excellent traditional and unpretentious American food.

Buteco II, 57 W Dedham St, South End (☎247-9249). Wide range of tasty Brazilian dishes served until 11pm, including feijouada stew at weekends, and Brazilian drinks. Moderately priced.

Daily Catch, 323 Hanover St (☎523-8567) and 261 Northern Ave (☎338-3093). Italian-style seafood, with a wonderful way with squid. Expect to pay up to $20.

Durgin-Park, 340 N Market St, Faneuil Hall (☎227-3078). Crowded, hurried and priding itself on surly service, but a Boston institution for its chunky prime ribs and seafood specialities – not to mention the baked beans. Shared tables, no reservations. Anything from $7 upwards.

The European, 218 Hanover St, North End (☎523-5694). Welcoming and high-quality Italian, open at least until midnight. Crowded and a bit raucous, with a menu to suit all budgets.

Golden Palace, 14–20 Tyler St (☎423-4565). Chinese restaurant open until 11.30pm, with cheap and excellent dim sum daily until 3pm. $7 and upwards.

HooDoo Barbeque, 835 Beacon St (☎267-7427). Substantial barbecues, where *Green* "T" line C emerges at Audubon Circle. Good jukebox and a lively atmosphere, but not particularly cheap.

Legal Seafoods at the *Park Plaza Hotel*, 50 Park Plaza (☎426-4444). Fast-growing chain deservedly renowned for top-quality seafood. Around $20.

Rebecca's, 21 Charles Street (☎742-9747). High-quality Continental cuisine on Beacon Hill, open until midnight except 10pm Sun. $15 and upwards. Also good for breakfast.

Ristorante Lucia, 415 Hanover St, North End (☎367-2353). Wonderful Italian with seafood specialities and an intimate atmosphere. $10 and upwards.

Sakura-bana, 57 Broad St (☎542-4311). Smart, highly aesthetic but relaxed and far from exorbitant Japanese restaurant and sushi bar.

Sol Azteca, 914A Beacon St (☎262-0909). Unpretentious Mexican in basement of brownstone a fair way out. Enchiladas, tacos, imported beer and a whole lot more. Dinner only, $10–20.

Thai House Restaurant, 1033 Commonwealth Ave (☎787-4242). Excellent Thai restaurant; steamed seafood and great duck from $15.

Cambridge

Boston Sail Loft, 1 Memorial Drive, Kendall Square (☎225-3888). A fine assortment of cheap seafood, including lobsters.

The Cajun Yankee, 1193 Cambridge St, Inman Square (☎576-1971). Gumbo, crawfish, and other Cajun specialities, with a short menu that changes daily. Reserve. $10–18.

Daily Catch, 1 Kendall Square (☎523-8567). Seafood; see entry under Boston, above.

El Rancho, 1126 Cambridge St, Inman Square (☎868-2309). Tues–Sat until 9pm. Very cheap Salvadorean restaurant; tasty Latin American food, fruit drinks but no alcohol. $4–10.

Kebab'n'Kurry, 30 Massachusetts Ave (☎536-9835). Deservedly the most popular of Cambridge's many Indian restaurants, open to 11pm daily, and reasonably priced.

Lai Lai, 700 Massachusetts Ave, Central Square (☎876-7000). Good, friendly, cheap Chinese.

Nightlife and Entertainment

Mainstream Boston's pride and joy, the **Boston Symphony Orchestra**, is based at the Symphony Hall, 301 Huntington Avenue (☎266-1492) – which Stravinsky called the best auditorium in the world – with a winter season followed by the **Boston Pops** concerts in May and June. The city's **theatre** scene divides into the safe productions of the Theater District (often Broadway try-outs) and more experimental companies in Cambridge. The **Bostix** kiosk (☎723-5181) at Faneuil Hall sells tickets for all major events – as well as tours, "T" passes, and so on – with some half-price day of sale tickets.

Jonathan Richman and his Modern Lovers have long since moved on, but Boston still has an active **rock** scene, while the students of Cambridge support a wide range of alternative live music venues. Note that the city's **bars** are unusually officious about demanding ID. They are not permitted to offer cut-price happy hours, but some provide free early-evening snacks instead.

Bars and Clubs

The Black Rose, 160 State St (☎742-2286). Large Irish pub right beside Faneuil Hall, with traditional music every night and Guinness galore.

Bull and Finch Pub, 84 Beacon St, Beacon Hill (☎227-9605). Its status as the original setting of TV's *Cheers* gives this place an unpleasant streak of smugness, but at least it's central and lively.

Catch A Rising Star, 30 JFK St, Cambridge (☎661-9987). The hottest of Boston's comedy clubs; at least one show every night. Admission $6 and upwards.

Chaps, 27 Huntington Ave (☎266-7778). The biggest, glitziest gay club in town.

Commonwealth Brewery Company, 138 Portland St (☎523-8383). Brew pub right by Boston Garden near North Station, serving good pub food and their own real ale.

Grendel's Den, 89 Winthrop St, Harvard Square (☎491-1050). The liveliest of Cambridge's many student-oriented bars.

Hub Club, 533 Washington St (☎451-6999). Frenzied nightly dance club, up to $12 at weekends.

Indigo, 823 Main St, Cambridge (☎497-7200). Gay women's club, Wed–Sat only. Cover $7 and up.

Paradise, 967 Commonwealth Ave (☎254-2052). Enjoyable rock venue for name touring bands.

Passim, 47 Palmer St, Harvard Square (☎492-7679). Long-standing "coffee-house" folk/blues venue.

The Rat, 528 Commonwealth Ave (☎267-4156). Heavy drinking and heavy music.

Western Front, 343 Western Ave, Cambridge (☎492-7772). Live music every night, usually reggae at weekends. Cover $10.

Sport

The legendary Red Sox play **baseball** at Fenway Park (Kenmore or Fenway subway on the *Green* "T" line). The whole stadium, squeezed in 1912 into the odd-shaped plot that was all its builders could buy, is painted green, including the 37-foot, 6-inch wall in the left field known as the "Green Monster". (Schedules ☎267-8661; tickets, $6–16, ☎267-1700.) **Basketball**'s Celtics (☎523-6050) and **hockey**'s Bruins both play at the Boston Garden, 150 Causeway near North Station (box office ☎227-3200).

The first **Boston Marathon** was run in 1897, and is now held each year on Patriot's Day, finishing beside Trinity Church on Boylston Street (details ☎338-5709).

Listings

Disabled Information The *Center for Individuals with Disabilities* is on ☎727-5540; ☎1-800/462-8015 in Massachusetts only.

Gay and Lesbian Helpline Mon–Thurs 6–11pm, Fri & Sun 6–8.30pm, ☎267-9001.

Pharmacy 24-hour *Phillips Drug*, 155 Charles St (☎523-4372).

Rape Crisis 46 Pleasant St, Central Square, Cambridge. 24-hr hotline ☎492-7273.

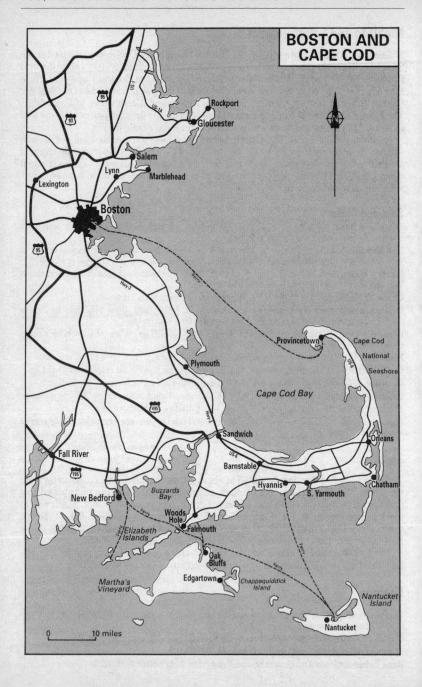

**BOSTON AND
CAPE COD**

Rockport
Gloucester
Salem
Lynn
Marblehead
Lexington
Boston
Provincetown
Cape Cod
National
Seashore
Plymouth
Cape Cod Bay
Sandwich
Orleans
Fall River
Barnstable
Hyannis
Chatham
New Bedford
Buzzards
Bay
S. Yarmouth
Woods
Hole
Falmouth
Elizabeth
Islands
Oak
Bluffs
Edgartown
Chappaquiddick
Island
Martha's
Vineyard
Nantucket
Island
Nantucket

0   10 miles

The North Shore

As you head northwards out of Boston, you pass through a succession of rich little ports which have been all but swallowed up by the suburbs. There are some nice bathing beaches at **Lynn**, which claims to have given the world the game of *Monopoly* and the brown paper bag. Nearby **Marblehead**, on the other hand, gave us the **US Navy**: George Washington's first five vessels were built there. The pineapples you'll notice hanging on the front porches of the grand local homes are a traditional sign of hospitality, originally displayed by sea captains returned from long voyages. If you have the time, **Gloucester** on **Cape Ann** is a more authentic fishing port than any on Cape Cod, (T S Eliot used to come here for his family vacations, and the *Dry Salvages* which gave the title to the third of his *Four Quartets* are a group of offshore rocks), but the obvious day-trip from Boston is the half-hour ride out to **Salem**.

Salem

Ironically, **SALEM** is remembered less as the site where the colony of Massachusetts was first established, with the most elevated of intentions, than as the place where just sixty years later Puritan self-righteousness reached its apogee in the horrific **witch trials** of 1692. While the town itself was to prosper as one of New England's most successful ports – as evidenced by its fine old buildings – the witch scare did much to discredit the idea that the New World conducted its affairs on a different moral plane than the Old. Twenty Salem women were put to death as witches, thanks to a group of impressionable teenage girls who reported as truth a garbled mixture of fireside tales told by a West Indian slave, Tituba, and half-digested scare stories published by Cotton Mather, a pillar of the Puritan community. Encouraged by the judiciary, the girls denounced a widening circle of townspeople; the whole thing stopped not because of its intrinsic lack of plausibility, but because the girls went too far and denounced the wife of the governor. Twenty years on, all the victims received a posthumous official pardon.

That this unpleasant history should now be the basis of a child-oriented tourist industry – all pointed black hats and broom-sticks – makes Salem an unsettling place. The **Salem Witch Museum** in Washington Square (July & Aug daily 10am–7pm, otherwise 10am–5pm; $4) attempts to draw parallels with modern racism and political persecution, but is at heart a rather tacky show of illuminated dioramas and prerecorded commentary, without authentic relics. Innumerable other witch-related attractions in town are best ignored. Salem's later seafaring years are remembered in the **Peabody Museum** in East India Square (Mon–Wed & Fri–Sat 10am–5pm, Thurs 10am–9pm, Sun noon–5pm; $6), which since 1799 has assembled a remarkable collection of objects brought home by voyaging New Englanders. As well as its extensive Japanese and Asian displays, it has one of only three existing breadfruit-wood idols of the Hawaiian god Ku, and details about the town's ships themselves.

The **House of Seven Gables** at 54 Turner Street (summer daily 9.30am–5.30pm; otherwise 10am–4.30pm, $6) is a magnificent rambling old mansion in a perfect waterfront setting, the star of Nathaniel Hawthorne's eponymous novel. Hour-long guided tours of the complex of several ancient wooden houses take in the author's birthplace, which was moved here from its original site in Union Street.

Little of Salem's original waterfront remains, though the long **Derby Wharf** is still standing, together with the imposing **Custom House** at its head, where Hawthorne once worked. **Pickering Wharf** a short way south is very obviously brand new, an ugly little mall of souvenir shops which at least has a lively selection of fast-food stands. The Indian restaurant, *Oh Calcutta*, at 6 Hawthorne Boulevard, with vegetarian specialities.

Regular **buses** (#455) run to Salem from Haymarket Square in Boston, and there are hourly **trains** (every two hours at weekends) from North Station. If you want to **stay**, rooms at *Hotel Lafayette*, 116 Lafayette Street (☎745-5503), start at $40.

The South Shore

It can take a while to get clear of Boston heading south – especially at summer weekends, when the traffic down to Cape Cod can be horrendous. Two historic towns, one north and one south of the Cape, are worth exploring – **Plymouth** and **New Bedford**.

Plymouth

"America's Hometown", **PLYMOUTH**, is on the south shore of Massachusetts Bay, 35 miles south of Boston and halfway to Hyannis. (For details of buses from Boston, see p.146.) It's a small town, given over to commemorating, in various degrees of taste and tack, the landing here of the 102 **Pilgrim Fathers** in December 1620.

A solemn pseudo-Greek Temple by the sea encloses the nondescript **Plymouth Rock** where the Pilgrims are said to have touched land; as they had already spent two months on Cape Cod, and there are no contemporary references to the rock, it is of symbolic importance only. Two worthier memorials make no claim to authenticity, but meticulously reproduce the experience of the Pilgrims. Both the replica of the **Mayflower** in town, and **Plimoth Plantation** three miles south, are staffed by costumed "interpreters", each of whom acts out the part of a specific Pilgrim, Indian, or sailor. The charade visitors are obliged to perform of pretending to have stepped back into the seventeenth century can be a little tiresome, but ultimately the sheer depth of detail in both endeavours makes them fascinating. At the Plantation, everything you see in the Pilgrim Village of 1627, and the Wampanoag Indian Settlement, has been created using traditional techniques (both April–Nov, daily 9am–5pm; *Mayflower* in July & Aug 9am–7pm; Plantation $15, *Mayflower* $6; joint ticket $20; ☎746-1622).

Plymouth's **visitor centre** is in the park on North Park Avenue (☎746-4779). **Motels** in town, such as the *Blue Anchor*, 7 Lincoln Street (☎746-9551), and the *Cold Spring*, 188 Court Street (☎746-2222) start at around $60. Good **seafood** places along the front include the *Lobster Hut* (☎746-2270).

New Bedford

The famous old whaling port of **NEW BEDFORD**, 45 miles due south of Boston, is still home to the nation's most prosperous fishing fleet. New development along the waterfront has obscured some of its past, but on County Street the fine old houses still stand of which Melville commented

> *New Bedford is a queer place. Had it not been for us whalemen, that tract of land would this day perhaps have been in as howling condition as the coast of Labrador . . . all these brave houses and flowery gardens came up from the Atlantic, Pacific and Indian oceans. One and all, they were harpooned and dragged hither from the bottom of the sea.*

The roster of the whaling ship *Acushnet*, in the **New Bedford Whaling Museum** at 18 Johnny Cake Hill (Mon–Sat 9am–5pm, Sun 11am–5pm; $3.50), shows Melville as one of the crew. Other evocative displays include a half-size replica of a whaling vessel. Immediately opposite stands the **Seamen's Bethel**; it really *does* have the ship-shaped pulpit described in *Moby Dick*, but this one was re-built after a later fire.

Much the most atmospheric place to **stay** in town is the *Durant Sail Loft Inn*, in the port at 1 Merrill Wharf (☎999-2700), just across busy MacArthur Drive, where rooms cost from $70. At the same address, the *Pena Branca* (☎999-4495) is a superb and cheap Portuguese-owned **fish restaurant**. The **visitor centre** is at 47 N Second Street (☎991-6200); **ferries** to Martha's Vineyard are detailed on p.165. New Bedford achieved an unwelcome notoriety several years ago, after a brutal bar-room rape was said to have been encouraged by witnesses; the film *The Accused* was loosely based on the incident.

The telephone **area code** for all eastern Massachusetts outside Boston is ☎508.

Cape Cod and the Islands

Here a man may stand, and put all America behind him.

Henry David Thoreau

The trouble with standing on **Cape Cod** these days is that "all America" tends to be a lot closer behind you than you might prefer. The place is packed in summer, its roads circled by a grim procession of crawling vehicles, vaguely searching for some "unspoiled" bit of beach or "undiscovered" old town. If you don't have your own, preferably very secluded, place to stay, it's barely worth turning up between June and August and putting yourself through the hassle of trying to find what little accommodation may be available, invariably at premium prices.

Thinking of the Cape, as everyone does, as an arm, these strictures apply most forcefully to its **upper** section, the thirty-mile eastward stretch from mainland Massachusetts. Much the worst of the beachfront development lies along the southern shore, and it's **Hwy-28**, running from Falmouth via Hyannis to Chatham, that gets especially clogged. The northern coast is boggy and has fewer facilities. **Hwy-6A** here, which began life as the trail to Boston, could be called the oldest road in the country. Only once you get beyond the "elbow" and head north through the spectacular dunes of **Cape Cod National Seashore** do you get a feeling for why the Cape still has a reputation as a seaside wilderness. **Provincetown**, right at the end, is the one town on the Cape that can be unreservedly recommended.

Sadly, the islands of **Martha's Vineyard** and **Nantucket**, off the Cape to the south, are now also dependent on tourism for their livelihood. However, a trip out to Nantucket in particular does still evoke haunting memories of its proud seafaring days.

Cape Cod was named by Bartholomew Gosnold in 1602, on account of the prodigious quantities of cod caught by his crew off Provincetown. Less than twenty years later the Pilgrim Fathers landed nearby; in the few months before moving on to Plymouth they began the process, continued by generations of Europeans, of stripping the interior of the Cape bare of its original covering of thick woods.

Getting to the Cape

It was the Pilgrims who first suggested the construction of a canal between Cape Cod Bay and Buzzards Bay, to enable coastal shipping to avoid the dangers of the open ocean; when that was finally completed at the start of this century, it left the peninsula as an island. Now all traffic to the Cape bottlenecks at one or other of the two enormous bridges across the canal; if you try in summer to **drive** in on a Friday afternoon (3–10pm) or out on a Sunday (noon–9pm) you may well regret it. There is an **information office** for the Cape (daily 9am–7pm) on the mainland side of each bridge.

One way to dodge the traffic is to **fly**. *Business Express* (☎1-800/345-3400) serve Hyannis and Nantucket from Boston and New York; *Continental Express* (☎1-800/525-0280) leave several times daily from Boston to Hyannis, Provincetown and the islands, with single fares starting at around $50. *Continental* also fly direct from New Bedford to the islands. In summer there are usually weekend *Amtrak* **trains** to Hyannis from both New York and Boston. These are dependent on a state subsidy that may not always be forthcoming, so check in advance. *Bonanza* **buses** run regularly from New York (☎564-8484), and the *Plymouth and Brockton Bus Co* (☎1-800/328-9997) runs to Hyannis and Provincetown from Rhode Island, Boston and New York daily (for other Boston services see p.146). **Ferries** take three hours to cross from Boston to Provincetown (see p.163); for boats to the various islands see p.165.

You can also **cycle** from Boston on the 135-mile Boston–Cape Cod Bikeway, which extends all the way up to Provincetown.

The Upper and Mid-Cape

The **Upper Cape**, just across the bridges, was the first part of the peninsula to attract tourists in any numbers – and it shows. To see the various communities of the south coast as "pretty little villages" – the image they hope to project – you'd have to be wearing exceptionally rose-tinted spectacles, or blinkers. In theory, each is coyly arranged around a prim central green; but you have to fight your way through thickets of malls and motels to reach their artificial hearts.

It only makes sense to stay in one of these places if you're catching a **ferry** to the islands (in which case, see p.165). Thus one obvious base is **FALMOUTH**, where the *Falmouth Marina Trade Winds* on Robbins Road (☎548-4300) is the cheapest of the central motels, and the $80 rooms at the luxurious clapboard *Village Green Inn*, 40 West Main Street (☎548-5621) are in Cape terms a bargain. The *Sippewissett Campground* a couple of miles out at 836 Palmer Avenue (☎548-2542) offers a free shuttle service to the ferries and beaches. There are plenty of restaurants around, but the best food in the area is to be found in the assorted moderately priced seafood places along the waterfront at **WOODS HOLE**, four miles southwest; the *Fishmonger's Cafe* at 56 Water Street (☎548-9148) is recommended. Though the **Woods Hole Oceanographic Institute** here won sensational headlines for its discovery of the wreckage of the *Titanic* in 1986, it is actually part of a complex of serious marine science research facilities. The institute itself is not open to the public, but an exhibition near Little Harbor has displays on the *Titanic* and their other activities.

The largest port on the Cape, and its main commercial hub, **HYANNIS**, clings a little desperately to the glamour it earned when the **Kennedy compound** at Hyannisport placed it at the centre of world affairs. The Kennedys are still here, though their property can only be glimpsed, from a considerable distance, from the sea. Coincidentally enough, the town itself has become a rather anonymous playground for the over-privileged young. As well as its many motels, Hyannis has some reasonable **B&Bs**. The *Snow's Creek Inn* (☎778-4758), at 361 Ocean Street near the harbour, and *Sea Gate House*, 94 Seagate Lane (☎778-5783), both offer rooms from $50. There's also a **youth hostel**, the *HyLand (AYH)*, at 465 Falmouth Road (☎775-2970). Dorm beds cost $10 ($14 for non-members), and you have to check in between 5pm and 10.30pm.

Sightseeing trips on the **Cape Cod Railroad** (☎771-3788) run from Center Street in Hyannis along a meandering route to Sandwich, Buzzards Bay and Falmouth. Along the northern side of the peninsula, the **Cape Cod Rail Trail** follows a paved-over railway track from Dennis to Eastham, through cranberry bogs and forests. It makes a good **cycling** trip; bikes can be rented in all the main towns.

Cape Cod National Seashore

After the preceding bustle, the **Cape Cod National Seashore** really does come as the proverbial "breath of fresh air". These protected lands take up virtually the entire "forearm" of the Cape, with the exception of towns such as Provincetown, and by the act of President Kennedy have been spared the rampant development further south. Most of the way along you can park by the road and strike off across the dunes to windswept beaches. A programme of grass-planting is helping to hold the whole place together; three feet of the lower Cape is washed away each year, and much of it is carried here by the sea to extend the endless beaches.

It was on these shifting sands, not then as denuded as today, that the **Pilgrim Fathers** made their first home. They obtained their water from Pilgrim Spring near Truro; at Corn Hill Beach they uncovered the freshly buried cache of Indian corn that kept them alive. After a couple of months, which they survived with the help of the Wampanoag, they moved on to Plymouth (where the reconstructed Indian village at Plimoth Plantation, p.160, is based on one found at Eastham).

Provincetown

The compact and beautiful fishing village of **PROVINCETOWN** ("P-Town") is right on
the knuckle of Cape Cod's clenched fist. Silvery clapboard houses, with glorious unruly
gardens, line its tiny winding streets. Provincetown is far from secluded: its population
of five thousand rises tenfold in summer. Self-professed **bohemians** and **artists** have
always flocked here for the dazzling light and vast beaches, and in 1914 Eugene O'Neill
established the *Provincetown Playhouse* in a small hut. It has also become renowned,
since the beatnik Fifties, as a **gay** and **lesbian** centre. Commercialism, though rampant,
is countercultural. Gay, environmentalist and feminist gift shops join arty (not craftsy)
galleries, restaurants and bars on the aptly named **Commercial Street**, where the
atmosphere is spirited rather than tacky, committed rather than cynical.

Provincetown retains a firm grip on its past. Strict zoning ensures that there are few
new buildings in town, and there is barely a sign of ugly condo development. Albeit
crowded and raucous from July onwards, P-Town remains a place where history, natural beauty, and, above all, difference, are respected and celebrated.

Arrival, Information and Getting Around
Provincetown lies 120 miles from Boston by land, but less than fifty by sea, nestled in
the second largest natural harbour in the world (after Le Havre in France). By far the
nicest way to arrive is on the **ferry**. *Bay State Cruises* leave 20 Long Wharf, Boston, at
9.30am arriving at MacMillan Wharf three hours later, and return at 3.30pm (daily from
mid-June to mid-Sept, weekends only in early June and late Sept; $15 one-way, $25
round trip; ☎723-7800 in Boston). The tiny **information centre** in the Chamber of
Commerce, at the end of the wharf at 307 Commercial Street, sells ferry tickets
(summer daily 9am–5pm, off-season Mon–Sat 10am–4pm; ☎487-3424).

It couldn't be easier to **walk** around tiny P-town, but most visitors prefer to **cycle** the
narrow streets and hills. The ever-packed *Arnold's*, 329 Commercial Street, rents mountain bikes and ten-speeds for $7 to $15 per day (daily 8.30am–5.30pm; ☎487-0844). In
summer, the daytime *Provincetown Shuttle* **bus** runs to Herring Cove Beach. For those
without transport, **tours** to the more isolated dunes and moors include the
Provincetown Trolley Inc from the town hall on Commercial Street (daily 10am–7pm;
$6; ☎487-9483); *Art's Dune Tours* are based at Commercial and Standish Streets (April–
Oct 10am–sunset; $7; ☎487-1950). **Whale-watching** cruises leave from MacMillan
Wharf during May and September. All cost about $15 and sell tickets in the harbour.

The Town and the Beaches
Many visitors head straight for the beaches, but it's a shame to miss Provincetown's tiny
core, centred on the three narrow miles of **Commercial Street**. **MacMillan Wharf**,
always busy with charters, yachts and fishing boats (which unload their catch each afternoon), splits the town in half. Not far away in the quieter **East End**, the **Heritage
Museum**, 356 Commercial Street (summer daily 10am–10pm; otherwise 10am–5pm;
$2), stands in an 1860 Methodist church. This well-loved collection of Provincetown
memorabilia includes a 68-inch striped bass, a Portuguese altar, a model fishing schooner, assorted old photos, and a reconstruction of the beach hut of Harry Kemp, beach-
bum poet and crony of Eugene O'Neill. They also provide leaflets detailing walking
tours. Some distance further out, the delightful **Provincetown Art Association**, 460
Commercial Street (summer daily noon–4pm & 7–10pm; Nov–March Fri–Sun noon–
5pm; $2), displays selections from its many paintings by local artists.

The 250-foot granite tower of the **Pilgrim Monument and Museum** on Town Hill,
in the breathtakingly pretty **West End** of P-Town, has an observation deck (only accessible by stairs and ramps) which looks out over the whole of the Cape (summer daily
9am–9pm; off-season 9am–5pm; $3). At the bottom of the hill on Bradford Street, a bas-

relief marks the few weeks in which the Pilgrims wrote their **Mayflower Compact**. Further from the wharf, the weathered clapboard houses have coloured blinds, white picket fences, and wildflowers spilling out of every possible crevice. The 1746 **Seth Nickerson House**, 72 Commercial Street, is the oldest house in town, built by a ship's carpenter. Tours lead through cabin-like rooms with slanting doors and crazed floorboards (June–Oct daily 10am–5pm; $2). A modest bronze plaque on a boulder at the western end of Commercial Street commemorates the Pilgrims' actual landing-place.

A little way beyond the town's narrow strip of sand, undeveloped **beaches** are marked only by dunes and a few shabby beach huts. You can swim in the clear water from the uneven rocks of the two-mile breakwater, where the seabed crunches with softshell clams, or head onwards through scented wild roses and beach plums to find blissful isolation. West of town, **Herring Cove Beach**, easily reached by bike or through the dunes, is more crowded but never unbearably so. In the wild **Province Lands**, at the Cape's northern tip, vast sweeping moors and bushy dunes are buffeted by a deadly sea, site of three thousand known shipwrecks. The **visitor centre** (summer daily 9am–6pm; off-season 9am–4.30pm; ☎487-1256) in the middle of the dunes on Race Point Road has an observation deck from which you might spot a whale.

Accommodation

As well as the few motels on the outskirts, every second picturesque little cottage in town seems to be a guest house. Prices are reasonable, even until mid-June, and off-season it's possible to find real bargains. Summer weekends can get a bit tight, but the Chamber of Commerce usually manages to rustle up something.

Gull Walk Inn, 300a Commercial St (☎487-9027). All-women guest house in a quiet lane off the town centre, with sun deck and sea views. Doubles from $50.

Hurst House, 384 Commercial St (☎487-0990). Quiet, clean rooms in artistic house. Large doubles with shared bathroom from $45.

Joshua Paine's Guest House, 15 Tremont St (☎487-1551). Four rooms on quiet street, from $40.

Eating

Food in Provincetown can be expensive: the snack bars around MacMillan Wharf are generally extortionate, and the – undeniably good – nouvelle cuisine in the trendy gay restaurants can hit $10 for a salad and a coffee. Portuguese bakeries, relics of early settlement, and bland family restaurants abound on Commercial Street.

Cafe Blase, 328 Commercial St (☎487-9465). Touristy pastel cafe, one of the few places with outdoor seating for people-watching. Pricey for dinner, but delicious $5.50 fresh fruit and waffle breakfasts.

Cafe Heaven, 199 Commercial St (☎487-9639). Light and airy upmarket-looking cafe serving all-day breakfasts, cappuccino and creative salads from $5. Closed 3–6pm, then reopens until 9pm.

Fat Jack's, 335 Commercial St (☎487-4822). Cheap no-nonsense breakfasts and daily specials.

Post Office Cafe, 303 Commercial St (☎487-6400). Small gay restaurant serving lunch from $5. Gay/feminist cabaret nightly.

Nightlife and Entertainment

Boatloads of revellers disembark each weekend to seek out P-Town's notoriously wild nightlife. From house music raves to drag cabarets, from torch singing to R&B, the variety is huge.

The Atlantic House, 6 Masonic Place (☎487-3821). Once the dark drinking hole of Tennessee Williams and Eugene O'Neill, the "A-House" is now one of the trendier gay music clubs and bars.

Colonial Tap Room, Commercial St. Ancient, dimly lit fishermen's bar. Crooked wooden floors and heavy graffiti-carved benches. Clientele includes gruff sea salts and exuberant revellers.

Crown and Anchor, 247 Commercial St (☎487-1430). Noisy pub with regular drag cabaret.

Governor Bradford, 312 Commercial St (☎487-9618). Popular bar with live jazz, reggae and R&B.

Martha's Vineyard

The island of **MARTHA'S VINEYARD**, just seven miles south of Cape Cod, and twenty-four miles long by ten wide, may or may not have been named for Bartholomew Gosnold's daughter Martha (some ancient maps call it *Martin's* Vineyard). The "Vineyard" part, however, was for its "incredible store of vines"; considerably more fertile than bleak little Nantucket, it has never been quite so dependent on the sea to make a living. Now more than ever tourism is at the root of the island's economy. The many second-home owners who spend the summer here get a better deal than mere day-trippers, though – some of the best beaches are off-limits to non-residents.

Ferries to the island arrive at either **Oak Bluffs**, where genteel terraced houses look down on the harbour and there's a colourful century-old fairground carousel near the jetty, or at the more upmarket **Vineyard Haven**. **Edgartown**, over to the east, is the oldest settlement on the island, and has been extravagantly dolled up for visitors (you may recognise it as the location for the *Jaws* films). A little ferry shuttles back and forth from Edgartown to adjacent **Chappaquiddick Island** (the bridge which Senator Edward Kennedy made infamous is on the far side).

The three principal island communities are connected by a regular bus service and offer full facilities and shops of every kind. They're quite mellow places to pass a summer's day, but much the best idea on a visit to Martha's Vineyard is to explore the island for yourself. Bringing a car over is expensive and rather pointless, but as soon as you get off the ferry you encounter rows of **bike** rental places. The best ride is along the State Beach Park between Oak Bluffs and Edgartown, with the dunes to one side and marshy Sengekontacket Pond to the other; purpose-built cycle routes continue to the youth hostel at West Tisbury (see below).

Trips around the west side of the island ("up-island") can be disappointing, with not a peep at the ocean beyond the private estates; however, you do eventually come to the **lighthouse** at **Gay Head Cliffs**, where the multi-coloured clay was once the main source of paint for the island's houses. The cliffs are not vast, and they're crumbling away so fast that it's not safe to approach them too closely. From Philbin Beach below, however, you can get near enough to wallow in some lovely mud holes. Gay Head was once famous for its Wampanoag harpooneers, such as Tashtego in *Moby Dick*.

FERRIES TO MARTHA'S VINEYARD AND NANTUCKET

Unless otherwise specified, all the ferries below run several times daily in midsummer (mid-June to mid-Sept). Most have fewer services from May to mid-June, and between mid-September and October. There is at least a skeleton service to each island, though not on all routes, all year round. Single passenger fares from the Cape to Martha's Vineyard are around $6, to Nantucket $12. Bikes are $5 extra, cars around $40.

To Martha's Vineyard

From **Falmouth** to Oak Bluffs. Passenger only. *The Island Queen* (☎548-4800).

From **Woods Hole** to both Vineyard Haven and Oak Bluffs. Car ferry. *Steamship Authority* (☎540-2022; on Martha's Vineyard ☎693-0367).

From **Hyannis** to Oak Bluffs. Passenger only. *Hy-Line* (☎778-2600 in Hyannis; ☎693-0112 on Martha's Vineyard).

From **New Bedford** to Vineyard Haven. Passenger only, $10. *Cape Island Express*

Lines (☎997-1688 in New Bedford; ☎693-2088 on Martha's Vineyard).

From **Montauk**, Long Island to Oak Bluff. Passenger only, summer Thursdays only, $40. *Viking Ferry* (☎668-5709).

To Nantucket

From **Hyannis**. Cars on *Steamship Authority* (☎228-3274 on Nantucket). Also *Hy-Line* (☎228-3949 on Nantucket).

The *Steamship Authority* in summer also runs one daily connecting service between Martha's Vineyard and Nantucket.

Accommodation

If accommodation is booked up, as is very likely, the main **Chamber of Commerce** office at Beach Road in Vineyard Haven (☎693-0085) may be able to help. There are **campgrounds** near Vineyard Haven (☎693-3772) and Oak Bluffs (☎693-0233).

Attleboro House, 11 Lake Ave, Oak Bluffs (☎693-4346). Old-fashioned B&B in a distinguished harbour-view terrace. Singles from $45, doubles $60, no private bathrooms.

Colonial Inn, North Water St, Edgartown (☎627-4711). Extremely central white clapboard inn, part of a largish mall. Very smallest room is $45 in off-season, but midsummer room rates are $100–195.

Manter Memorial Youth Hostel (AYH), Edgartown Rd, West Tisbury (☎693-2665). A very nice setting, but not that easy to get to. April–Nov, curfew 10pm, $10 members, $13 non-members.

Nashua House, Kennebec Ave, Oak Bluffs (☎693-0043). Small doubles, shared baths, from $35.

Wesley Hotel, 1 Lake Ave, Oak Bluffs (☎693-6611). Huge but characterful hotel near the ferries. Rooms are mostly upwards of $125, but a few with shared bathrooms start at $60.

Eating

It's not at all hard to find something to eat on Martha's Vineyard. The ports in particular have rows of places to tempt tourists catching the ferries back. Only in Edgartown and Oaks Bluff can you order alcohol with meals, but you can bring your own elsewhere.

AJ's Seafood & Steak, Main St, Vineyard Haven (☎693-4480). Good budget food in a nice setting.

Linden Tree, Main St, Vineyard Haven (☎693-4480). Very cheap cafe with seafood and pasta.

Giordano's, Circuit Ave, Oak Bluffs (☎693-0184). Crowded and cheap Italian.

Lawry's, Main St, Edgartown (☎627-8857). Very good back-to-basics fish-market-cum-restaurant.

Louis', 102 State Rd, Vineyard Haven (☎693-3255). Lively Italian place, well priced. Salad bar.

Nantucket

The thirty-mile, two-hour sea crossing to **NANTUCKET** may not be an ocean-going odyssey, but it does set the "Little Grey Lady" apart from her shore-hugging sister, Martha. Halfway here from Hyannis, neither mainland nor island is in sight, and once you've landed you can avert your eyes from the smart-money double-deck cruisers with names like *Pier Pressure* and *Loan Star* and let the place remind you that it hasn't always been a rich folk's playground. Indeed, despite the formidable prowess of its seamen (see box), survival for early settlers on the island's barren soil was always a struggle.

The tiny cobbled alleyways of **Nantucket Town** itself, once one of the largest cities in Massachusetts, were frozen in time when the economic decline hit, 150 years ago. This area of delightful old houses is very much the centre of activity. From the moment you get off the ferry you are besieged by bike rental places and tour companies. **Straight Wharf** leads directly onto **Main Street** with its shops and restaurants; the island's **information office** – which does *not* make accommodation reservations – is nearby at 25 Federal Street (☎228-0925). The main sights in town are the excellent **Whaling Museum** (daily, 9am–6pm, summer only; $3) on Broad Street at the head of Steamboat Wharf, where you should look out especially for such scrimshaw artefacts as a set of 21 whale types carved from whales' teeth, and the astonishing corkscrewed harpoon twisted in the "flurry" or last struggle of a dying whale, and the **Peter Foulger Museum** ($2) of island history next door.

After a stroll around Nantucket Town, the usual procedure is to cycle the seven flat miles east to the village of **Siasconset** (always abbreviated to *Sconset*), where the ancient cottages stand literally encrusted with salt, and then to meander back at will across the heaths and moorland. Buses also link Nantucket Town and Siasconset.

Accommodation

But for the **youth hostel**, accommodation on Nantucket is invariably expensive; the going rate in B&Bs and guest houses starts at $70. There are no **campgrounds**.

THE WHALERS OF NANTUCKET

Scores of anonymous Captains have sailed out of Nantucket, that were as great, and greater than your Cook . . . For in their succorless empty-handedness, they, in the heathenish sharked waters, and by the beaches of unrecorded, javelin islands, battled with virgin wonders and terrors that Cook with all his marines and muskets would not have willingly dared.

Herman Melville, *Moby Dick*

In 1659, a sober group of twenty-seven Quaker and Presbyterian families arrived on Nantucket, and set about imposing order on the haphazard business of **whaling**. Whales had always beached themselves on the treacherous sandy shoals all around – up to a dozen might be washed ashore in a major storm – and the local **Indians** had become skilled in hunting them in nearby waters. At first, the white settlers treated the island itself as their vessel, erecting tall masts from which a permanent watch was kept for passing whales. As the years went by, they stopped waiting at home, and sent large ships out into the ocean to pursue their prey. The Wampanoag played an integral part in the process: the actual kill was effected by two rowboats working in tandem, and at least five of each thirteen-man crew, usually including the crucial **harpooneer**, would be Indian. (The common occurrence when an injured whale would speed away, dragging a boat helter-skelter behind it for endless terrifying hours, was known as a "**Nantucket Sleighride**".)

The early chronicler Crèvecoeur provides an extensive account of Nantucket as it was in 1782 in his *Letters from an American Farmer*. Although perturbed by the islanders' universal habit of taking a dose of opium every morning, he held them up as a model of diligence and good self-government. Whaling was a disciplined profession, unmarred by the stereotyped debauchery of sailors elsewhere, and to feed themselves and equip their ships the islanders kept up a shrewd and extensive trade with the mainland. At that time there were already more than a hundred ships; the whalemen were not paid; instead each had a share (a *lay*) of the final proceeds of the voyage. Crèvecoeur was impressed by the Nantucketers' ambition: "Would you believe that they have already gone to the Falkland Islands and I have heard several of them talk of going to the South Sea".

They did indeed reach the Pacific – see Chapter Sixteen, Hawaii, for an account of their experiences there. The great days of Nantucket were immortalised by Herman Melville:

And thus have these naked Nantucketers, these sea hermits, issuing from their ant-hill in the sea, overrun and conquered the watery world like so many Alexanders . . . Two thirds of this terraqueous globe are the Nantucketer's. For the sea is his; he owns it, as Emperors own empires.

In fact *Moby Dick* is a valediction; by the time it was published in 1851, Nantucket's fortunes had gone into an abrupt decline. Soon after a devastating fire in 1846, reports of the Californian Gold Rush lured young men westwards; the discovery of underground oil in Pennsylvania came as the final blow. A magazine article of 1873 reported "Let no traveler visit Nantucket with the expectation of witnessing the marks of a flourishing trade . . . of the great fleet of ships which dotted every sea, scarcely a vestige remains."

Cliff Lodge, 9 Cliff Rd (☎228-9480). B&B with singles from $60 and doubles from $100.

Hawthorn House, 2 Chestnut St (☎228-1468). Cheap, central and well-appointed guest house. $65.

Hungry Whale, 8 Derrymore Rd (☎228-0793). Good value and friendly, from $73.

Star of the Sea Youth Hostel (AYH), Surfside (☎228-0433). Dorm beds at Surfside Beach, two miles south of town. $10 members, $13 non-members. April–Oct only. Opens 5pm, curfew 10.30pm.

Eating

Crèvecoeur (see box) reported that on Nantucket "music, singing and dancing are holden in equal detestation". **Seafood**, fortunately is not; the only trouble is that Nantucket's restaurants, good as they may be, tend to be exceptionally expensive.

Espresso Cafe, 40 Main St (☎228-6930). Cheap, healthy lunch place. Some vegetarian dishes.

Obadiah's Native Seafood, 2 India St (☎228-4430). Good value for the island.

Rose and Crown, 23 S Water St (☎228-2595). Seafood saloon with music and comedy.

Inland Massachusetts

The 150 miles of Massachusetts which stretch inland to the west of Boston have always been obliged to play second fiddle to the state capital. Just ten years after the Revolution, the farmers who struggled to make a living from this indifferent soil so resented the imposition of taxes by the prosperous merchants of the east that they rose in **Shay's Rebellion**; their pitchforks were no match for the guns of the new nation.

These days the citizens of the west are eager to promote themselves as cultural rivals to the big city. The **Berkshires** host the celebrated **Tanglewood** music festival in summer, while **Amherst**, the home of Emily Dickinson, is a stimulating little college community. Few of the modern towns offer much insight into the region's history, though the reconstructed **Old Sturbridge Village**, halfway between Worcester and Springfield on US-20, is an idealised but entertaining portrait of a small New England town of the 1830s, with all its crafts and diversions (charging a hefty $15 admission). **Hancock Shaker Village** near Pittsfield is somewhat more authentic.

Regular trains and buses run west from Boston through Worcester and Springfield.

Worcester

Forty miles west of Boston on I-90, **WORCESTER** is Massachusetts' second largest city, and the only industrial city in the US beside neither sea, lake nor river. Abbie Hoffman's hometown is not a place to spend any great deal of time, but if you're passing nearby the **Higgins Armory Museum**, at 100 Barber Avenue (Mon–Fri 9am–4pm, Sat & Sun noon–4pm; closed Mon Sept–June; $5) is a remarkable blend of old and new. An enthusiasm for metalworking led the founder of the Worcester Pressed Steel Company to tour Europe after World War I, buying vast quantities of ancient armour. He then built this bizarre steel and glass office-cum-museum (note the conspicuous riveting). Weapons and armour from all over the world have since been added to his collection. You might also drop in at the **American Antiquarian Society**, 185 Salisbury Street (Mon–Fri 9am–5pm, tours Wed 2pm), which holds copies of two-thirds of all the material published in America before 1821, more even than the Library of Congress.

Of local **accommodation**, the *Howard Johnson* at 181 W Boylston Street (☎835-4456) starts at $65; the *Yankee Budget Motor Lodge* at 561 Lincoln Street (☎852-5800) is cheaper. *Legal Seafoods*, 1 Exchange Place (☎792-1600), is a reliable fish restaurant.

Springfield

SPRINGFIELD, at the point where I-90 crosses I-91, ninety miles from Boston at the southern end of the Pioneer Valley, has an odd assortment of claims to fame, including being the home of the Springfield Rifle and the late children's author Dr Seuss. Visitors are drawn to this unwieldy and unattractive city, split by the wide Connecticut River, by the 1890s invention of Dr James Naismith – the sport of **basketball**. Naismith designed the game as a way of providing exercise for athletes at the YMCA, and its popularity spread with amazing rapidity. After a trip to the Berlin Olympics in 1936 Naismith came up with another bright idea, and established the **Basketball Hall of Fame** at 1150 West Columbus Avenue, next to the river just south of Memorial Bridge (July to mid-Sept daily 9am–6pm; otherwise 9am–5pm; $5). This enjoyably traces the history of the game with movies, videos and plenty of memorabilia, and also lets you test your own skills.

Springfield's *Amtrak* station is very central, on Lyman Street. Plenty of **motels** start at around $40; the *Susse Chalet* at exit 6 of I-90 (☎592-5141) is the cheapest. *Chi-Chi's Restaurante*, 955 Riverdale Road in West Springfield (☎781-0442), is a local institution, a massive pseudo-adobe Mexican restaurant on Hwy-5 just south of the I-91 bridge.

The telephone **area code** for Springfield and western Massachusetts is ☎413.

The Berkshires

The **Berkshire Hills**, where Massachusetts borders New York, are a cross between the English Lake District and the grand seafront resort of Newport Connecticut. Especially in the area nearest the Massachusetts Turnpike (I-90), the green hillsides are dotted with ostentatious Victorian mansions, while the towns are chic – if not snooty – summer tourist-traps. Further north, it's easier to escape civilisation and get deep into the woods. The best of the many hiking options is the **Mohawk Trail** in the northwest corner, which passes through North Adams and Williamstown along the route the Indians used to travel between the valleys of the Connecticut and Hudson rivers.

STOCKBRIDGE, just south of I-90 fifty miles west of Springfield, started out as "Indian Town". The Reverend John Sergeant built the simple wooden **Mission House** on Main Street in 1739 in an attempt to live in close proximity with the local Indians, and convert them to Christianity by sheer force of example. His success barely lasted beyond his own death; later settlers were far less keen on having the Indians around.

That Stockbridge today conforms to everyone's idea of the archetypal New England small town – above all when there's snow on the ground – is due largely to the artist **Norman Rockwell**, who lived here for 25 years until his death in 1978. Many of his *Saturday Evening Post* covers, whose sentimentality was made palatable by his sharp wit, featured the town; a collection can be seen at the **museum** on Main Street (May– Oct daily 10am–5pm; otherwise Mon–Fri 11am–4pm, Sat & Sun 10am–5pm; $6). Some of the tour guides modelled for Rockwell as children, and recall that for every few minutes they managed to hold still he'd slip them one more from his large pile of nickels.

Magnificent houses in the hills around include **Naumkeag**, which belonged to Joseph Choate, US ambassador to Queen Victoria (summer daily 10am–4.15pm; winter Sat & Sun only 10am–4.15pm), and **Chesterwood**, the luxurious home and studio of Daniel Chester French, sculptor of the Lincoln Memorial (May–Oct daily 10am–5pm). Stockbridge was also the setting for Arlo Guthrie's song, and movie, *Alice's Restaurant*.

Well-heeled tourists flock to nearby **LENOX** each year for the summer season of the Boston Symphony Orchestra at **Tanglewood**. Open-air concerts are held every Friday, Saturday and Sunday in July and August; the few covered seats are expensive and hard to get, but you can sit and picnic on the lush lawns for an admission fee of around $10. Some midweek rehearsals are also open to the public (☎637-1940 for details), and there's a **jazz** festival on the weekend of Labor Day.

Further north on US-7, **Arrowhead** near Pittsfield was Herman Melville's home while he wrote *Moby Dick*; declining popularity eventually obliged him to sell up and move to New York. The **Hancock Shaker Village** west of Pittsfield survived from 1790 to 1960 (May–Oct daily 9.30am–5pm; April, Oct & Nov daily 10am–3pm; $7). The story of their experiment in communal living begins in the large dwelling place, in which two hundred people slept and ate, and continues through the Round Stone barn for their cattle, to the garage where the last Shakers kept their cars.

Practicalities

Most of the **accommodation** in the Berkshires is concentrated in Lenox and neigh-bouring Lee; when the Tanglewood concerts are on, prices of course go through the roof. The only rooms in Lee for under $50 are in the *Super 8 Motel* at 128 Housatonic Street (☎1-800/843-1991); the *Underledge Inn* at 76 Cliffwood Street in Lenox (☎637-0236) is a welcoming B&B inn, which starts at around $60 out of season. The *Red Lion Inn* is one of the grander edifices on Main Street Stockbridge (☎298-5545); rooms are expensive, but the *Lion's Den* bar and restaurant downstairs is fun. For **food**, the Church Street Cafe, 59 Church Street, Lenox (☎637-2745), is good value. Good **bars** include the *Shaker Mill Tavern*, Albany Road, West Stockbridge (☎232-8565) and *Sullivan Station*, a converted railway station in Lee (☎243-2082).

RHODE ISLAND

RHODE ISLAND is the smallest state of the Union, at a mere 48 miles long by 37 miles wide, and tends to be overlooked as a destination, even if it is home to more than twenty percent of the nation's historical landmarks. It was established by Roger Williams in 1635 as a "lively experiment" in religious freedom. He had been expelled from Puritan Salem for his radical ideas (including the notion that Indians should be paid for their land and that there should be a complete separation of church from state), and the Massachusetts Puritans liked to call the state "**Rogues Island**".

Despite its size, Rhode Island has over four hundred miles of coastline, hacked out of the Narragansett Bay; it is in fact made up of over thirty tiny islands, including Hope and Despair. The "**Ocean State**" therefore developed through sea trade, whaling and smuggling. Partly due to this commercial power, Rhode Islanders were in the front rank of Revolutionary feeling, resenting the increasingly stringent economic pressures placed on them from England. However, no Revolutionary battles were fought on Rhode Island soil, and as it turned out this was the last state to ratify the Constitution, unwilling at first to abandon its new-found freedom. Between the Revolution and the Civil War, Rhode Island shifted from a maritime economy; it led the **Industrial Revolution** with the creation by Samuel Slater of the nation's first water-powered **textile mill** at Pawtucket outside Providence. Today, although still heavily industrialised, the state's main destinations of interest are its two original ports: well-heeled **Newport**, yachting capital of the world with good beaches and outrageously extravagant mansions, and the Colonial college town of **Providence**. **Block Island**, about thirty miles south of Newport, has a popular state beach, while the rest of Rhode Island is largely made up of sleepy small towns and fishing ports.

Getting Around Rhode Island

Rhode Island is tiny enough for getting around it to be ridiculously easy. I-95, the major interstate, runs through **Providence** on its way from Massachusetts to Connecticut. A more scenic route out of Providence is along US-1, which follows the coast of Narragansett Bay into Connecticut. **Newport** is accessible from Hwy-138, which connects the many small islands in Narragansett Bay to the mainland. **Public transport** is good; local buses connect Providence and Newport, and *Amtrak* stops regularly in Providence. Block Island is joined to Newport by **ferries**.

Providence

Splayed across seven hills on the Providence and Seekonk rivers, **PROVIDENCE** was Rhode Island's first settlement, founded "in commemoration of God's providence" on land given to Roger Williams by the Narragansett Indians (his insistence that Indians should be paid for their land being waived in his own case). Now New England's fourth largest city, it has been the **state capital** since 1901, and flourished as one of the most important ports of call in the notorious "triangle trade", where New England rum was exchanged for African slaves to be sold for West Indian molasses. Since Slater's invention of the water-powered textile mill, port trade and industry have been the mainstays of the economy. Today Ivy League **Brown University** and the **Rhode Island School of Design** (RISD or "Rizdee") give the place a certain cultural verve (although admittedly that doesn't stray far from the immediate environs of College Hill on the east bank of the river), and the many original Colonial homes on **Benefit Street** emphasise a historical importance almost absent from the somewhat drab downtown across the river. Ethnic diversity is provided by **Little Italy** on Federal Hill west of the river, and fairly voluble Greek and Portuguese – and especially Cape Verdean – communities.

Arrival and Getting Around

Rhode Island's **T F Green Airport** is in Warwick, nine miles south of Providence. In town, there's a brand-new *Amtrak* station at 100 Gaspee Street, in a domed building a short walk southwest of the Capitol. *Plymouth and Brockton, Greyhound,* and *Bonanza* **bus** lines stop considerably further out at 1 Bonanza Way (exit 25 off I-95) (☎751-8800). Bus transport within the city, and to the rest of the state, is provided by *RIPTA* (Mon–Sat 8.30am–6pm; ☎781-9400), with most local and all longer-distance buses leaving from Kennedy Plaza, where schedules are available from a rarely staffed information booth (Mon–Fri 8am–4.30pm). However, sightseeing is best done on foot.

Information
The **CVB**, 30 Exchange Terrace (Mon–Fri 9am–5pm; ☎274-1636), provides maps and brochures, as does the useful **Providence Preservation Society**, 24 Meeting Street in the 1772 *Shakespeare's Head*, which has self-guided walking and audio-cassette tours of the city's historic areas (Mon–Fri 9am–5pm; ☎831-7440). There's another **information centre** in the Roger Williams National Memorial Park, 282 N Main Street (daily, summer 9am–5pm; winter 9am–4.30pm; ☎528-5385).

The Town

Most of the main attractions in Providence are concentrated around three of its seven hills. Downtown, which centres on **Kennedy Plaza**, is sited just below **Constitution Hill**. **City Hall**, on the western end of the Plaza, is mainly notable for a star-spangled midnight blue ceiling in the Alderman's Chamber. Though no longer used as a train terminal, the nearby 1898 Beaux Arts **Union Station** on Exchange Terrace is a fine example of the historic restoration at which the city excels. Southeast of the Plaza, the 1828 **Westminster Arcade**, the oldest enclosed shopping mall in the nation, features expensive clothes shops and a food court in a small, bright, skylit hall. **Roger Williams National Memorial Park**, at N Main and Smith streets at the foot of Constitution Hill, includes an original well said to be used by Williams and his followers (Nov–April Mon–Fri; ☎528-5385), while at the top of the hill, the white marble **State Capitol** boasts a huge unsupported dome, second only in size to Saint Peters in Rome, topped with a statue of "independent man". There is a handsome full-length portrait of Washington in the Reception Room (free tours Mon–Sat 9am–3.30pm; ☎277-2357).

Laid-back **College Hill**, separated from downtown by the river, is a pretty district of Colonial buildings and museums. Part of Williams' holy experiment was the establishment of the Baptist Church in 1638. The white clapboard **First Baptist Meeting House** at the foot of the hill dates from 1775, and is remarkable for its very tall steeple (free tours by appointment Nov–March Mon–Fri 10am–3pm, Sat 10am–noon, Sun noon; ☎751-2266). This street leads into **South Main Street**, once bustling with waterfront activity, now a small stretch of potpourri and pottery shops. **Benefit Street**, a block up the hill, is Providence's **"mile of history"**, lined with ice-cream coloured eighteenth- and nineteenth-century clapboard houses, originally the homes of merchants and sea captains. Now beautifully restored, the street was just a dirt path leading to graveyards until it was improved in the nineteenth century for the "benefit of the people of Providence" – hence its name. To find out more about the area, take a tour of the elegant **John Brown House**, 52 Power Street at Benefit Street, which was the home of the Donald Trump of the eighteenth century, who made his wealth from trading in slaves and with China. The first house built on the hill (nicely conspicuous from the river), it

The telephone **area code** for the entire state of Rhode Island is ☎401.

retains its original furnishings; there are film-shows on the formidable Brown family, as well as exhibits on the city itself (Tues–Sat 11am–4pm, Sun 1–4pm; $5).

The small but excellent collection of the **RISD Museum of Art**, 224 Benefit Street, is worthy of its status as one of the best art schools in the country, and includes ancient and Oriental works, Impressionists and Post-Impressionists, American art and Rodin's statue of Balzac (mid-June to Aug Wed–Sat noon–5pm; Sept to mid-June Tues, Wed, Fri & Sat 10.30am–5pm, Thurs noon–8pm, Sun 2–5pm; $2, free on Sat). Across the road, the Greek Revival **Providence Athenaeum**, 251 Benefit Street, is where Edgar Allan Poe unsuccessfully wooed fellow-poet Sarah Whitman. Today the library holds original Audubon prints and rare books, and the piano and hand-painted chairs in the cosy reading rooms give it the feel of someone's living room (June–Sept Mon–Fri 8.30am–4.30pm; Oct–May Mon–Fri 8.30am–5.30pm, Sat 9.30am–5.30pm; free).

Ivy League **Brown University** sets the tone for this three-centuries-old district with its relaxed, intellectual feel. Free self-guided walking tours and guided tours of the campus are available at the admissions office, 45 Prospect Street (Mon–Fri 8am–4pm; tours 10am, 11am, 1pm, 3pm & 4pm). Another university building, the **Woods-Gerry Gallery**, 62 Prospect Street, is a solid red-brick mansion set in a tree-shaded garden with heavy stone benches, exhibiting innovative student art (Mon–Fri 11am–4pm; off-season Mon–Sat 11am–4pm, Sun 2–5pm; closed August; free). At the eastern edge of College Hill, **Wickenden Street** buzzes with a creative assortment of bookshops, cafes, and antique and thrift stores.

Federal Hill, west of downtown, is Providence's **Little Italy**, entered through a large arch at Atwells Avenue topped by a bronze pine cone. Long a powerful Mafia stronghold, this area is one of the friendliest and safest in the city; alive with cafes, delis, bakeries and bars, and a large Italianate fountain in the Piazza de Pasquale.

Pawtucket

It was in 1793 that Samuel Slater shoved Rhode Island into the industrial age. His **Old Slater Mill**, an important historical landmark, is still in operation, in suburban Pawtucket. A ten-minute drive north to exit 28 on I-95, the **Slater Mill Historical Site**, on Roosevelt Avenue, also includes in its living museum of the Industrial Revolution the 1810 Wilkinson Mill and the 1758 Sylvanus Brown House (June–Sept Tues–Sat 10am–5pm, Sun 1–5pm; March–May & Sept–Dec Sat & Sun 1–5pm; $3).

Accommodation

There are few cheap **rooms** in downtown Providence, although B&B is a viable option. *B&B of Rhode Island*, Box 3291, Newport (☎401-849-1928) offers accommodation on College Hill from $55. Motorists can take advantage of the cheap hotels along I-95, or north in Pawtucket, and south near the airport at Warwick.

Church House Inn, 122 Fountain St (☎751-7209). B&B above good music venue (see opposite). Rooms $50–70, special deals on extended stays.

Holiday Inn, 21 Atwells Ave (☎831-3900). Next to the Civic Center near Little Italy. From $80.

Howard Johnson Motor Lodge, 2 George St, Pawtucket (☎723-6700). Reasonable hotel close to I-95 and Slater's Mill, with rooms from $60.

The Old Court, 144 Benefit St (☎751-2002). Luxury B&B in old rectory. Ten rooms from $110.

Eating

Studenty **Thayer Street** is lined with cheap lunch places, a few of which remain open after dark. **Wickenden Street** is more alternative, and more expensive. The family-run Italian restaurants on Federal Hill serve good food at reasonable prices, and the Westminster Arcade downtown is your best bet for a quick breakfast or lunch.

Angelo's Civita Farnese, 141 Atwells Ave (☎621-8171). Casual family restaurant. Huge plates of good-value pasta.

The Cafe at Brookes, 244 Wickenden St (☎521-6445). Upbeat restaurant with small garden, serving hefty portions of Californian food from $5.

Cinema Cafe, 204 S Main St (☎272-3315). Joined to Providence's hippest Arts Cinema, this simple cafe has outdoor seating, and is open late for vegetarian and international dishes from $3.

Coffee Exchange, 214 Wickenden St (☎273-1198). Trendy coffee bar. A popular meeting place for arty intellectuals. On the pavement, deckchairs and barrels act as seating and tables.

Le Grecque, 24 Arcade Mall (☎351-3454). The cheapest and most interesting food in the mall. Greek specialities include marinated chick peas and rice or spinach pies.

Nightlife and Entertainment

Because much of Providence's **nightlife** is student-generated, things get pretty quiet during the vacations. Thayer Street, however, is always lively, and on summer Friday and Saturday nights a special **party trolley** complete with balloons and noisy music rumbles through downtown. The $6 fee includes entrance to six nightclubs on its route, and a half-price drink (8.30pm–2am; ☎861-1385). The *Cable Car Cinema* at 204 S Main Street, and the *Avon Rep Cinema*, at 250 Thayer Street (☎421-3315) show good independent and art **films**. The *Providence Performing Arts Center*, downtown at 220 Weybosset Street, is in a grand old art-deco movie house, and hosts various shows and theatre (☎421-2787). The free weekly *Nice Paper* has complete entertainment listings.

Church House Inn Red Brick Tavern, 122 Fountain St (☎351-5505). Two clubs, with live jazz, blues, reggae and Cajun music, and DJ dance one-nighters. Cover varies.

Club Babyhead, 73 Richmond St (☎421-1698). Indie bands and assorted dance nights. No cover before 10pm except for national acts.

The Last Call, 15 Elbow St (☎421-7170). Live R&B and jam sessions. Cover varies.

L'Elizabeths, 285 S Main St (☎621-9113). Upmarket, relaxed bar.

Newport

Thirty miles south of Providence, **NEWPORT** stands at the southern tip of the baggy boot of the largest island in Narragansett Bay, **Aquidneck** (or **Rhode**) **Island**. It was established as a colony by William Coddington of Providence in 1639. Due to its excellent harbour, it grew rapidly as a port for the triangle trade, a privateering centre, and a hotbed of Revolutionary feeling. **Religious tolerance** led to an influx of Jews, Quakers and Baptists who formed lucrative international trade links, but this great prosperity was severely knocked back by the **British occupation** of 1776–79, when half the population fled and much of the town was burnt down. Fortunately, enough buildings survived for Newport now to rival Boston for its number of original eighteenth-century homes.

After a period of readjustment, in the 1850s the town became fashionable again, this time as a coastal resort for wealthy Southern merchants, and very soon nouveau-riche New England industrialists such as the Astors, Belmonts and Vanderbilts were building **"summer cottages"** – better described as palaces – along the rocky coastline. This is now known as Newport's **gilded age**, an era of obscene ostentation that shocked Massachusetts old wealth to the core.

Depression killed off the decadence, but Newport kept going as a naval town until the 1970s. Today the town feeds off tourism; much of it caters to the tennis and yachting set, but there are as many people looking at – and envying – the wealth as enjoying it. Despite being sanitised by the construction of the ugly **America's Cup Avenue**, which replaced the seasalt rawness of the waterfront with bars and boutiques, the rough old port still rears its boozy head, with beer and R&B clubs every bit as evident as cocktails and cruises.

Arrival, Information, and Getting Around

There are actually three towns on Aquidneck Island; **Portsmouth** is at the northern edge, and then comes the appropriately named **Middletown**, with **Newport**, the southernmost, just below it. The mainland is connected to the island from I-95 on US-138 by the **Jamestown Bridge** to Conanincut Island, and from there by the **Newport Bridge**.

Newport itself, spanning only ten miles, is easy to walk around. **Thames** (pronounced *Thaymz*) Street, is the main road, with Bellevue Avenue, or Mansion Row, parallel to the east. Information, auto-tape tours ($10.50), maps and advice are available from the **visitor centre** at 23 America's Cup Avenue (daily 8am–8pm, off-season 9am–5pm; ☎849-8048), and the **Newport Harbour Center**, 365 Thames Street.

The **Gateway Center**, at 23 America's Cup Avenue, is used as a terminal by *Bonanza* (☎846-1820) and *RIPTA* **buses**. The latter provide a regular service to the beaches and onwards to Providence (fares 75¢–$2.25; ☎847-0209). Also based at the Center are the free summer **shuttle bus** which connects all the main sights and shopping areas (daily 10am–7pm); the hourly **Newport Trolley** which stops at sixteen tourist attractions including the mansions (June–Sept daily 10am–3pm; unlimited rides $7.50; ☎849-8005); and *Viking Tours*, whose bus excursions take in admission to one or more mansions (☎847-6921). A rented **bike** is a good way of getting to the quieter beaches; they cost $10 per day from *Ten Speed Spokes*, 18 Elm Street, off America's Cup Avenue (Mon–Sat 9.30am–5.30pm, summer Sun noon–5pm; ☎847-5609).

The Town

Newport's main attractions are obviously its **mansions**, but there is nothing to be gained by attempting to tour them all, and although it is pleasant enough to stroll around the predominantly Colonial **downtown**, the ever-growing profusion of souvenir shops is somewhat off-putting. Otherwise, if you don't fancy beautiful-people-spotting on the harbour, you'll do better following the crowds to one of the **beaches**.

The Mansions

The phrase "**conspicuous consumption**" was first coined by a sociologist who visited Newport at the turn of the century and witnessed the desperate need felt by new entrepreneurial **millionaires** to escape the class conflicts and tensions of urban life, and, in this idyll, define their fragile identities by flaunting their wealth. More than just a summer resort, Newport became an arena in which families competed with increasing mania to outdo each other. The "**season**" lasted only a few weeks and many of the ten-million-dollar mansions lay empty for years at a time, but stories of the wild and decadent parties of society's in-crowd make the "gilded age" (a disparaging term coined by Mark Twain, mindful of Shakespeare's assertion that to gild refined gold is ridiculous and excessive) one of the most fascinating in Newport's chequered past.

It's difficult to grasp the sheer wealth involved by merely gawping at the mansions' facades, but after being herded in and rushed through more than a couple the opulence rapidly begins to pall. Choose one to see, or two at the most. The most important stand on **Bellevue Avenue**, **Ocean Drive** and **Harrison Avenue**. The Astors' **Beechwood**, 580 Bellevue Avenue, is an entertaining antidote to the drier historical drills given on other tours. Costumed actors welcome visitors as house guests who have arrived for a party held by Mrs Astor, the self-proclaimed queen of American society (she devised the notion of the **Four Hundred**, an elite of individuals whose lineage had to go back at least three generations). Anecdotes, bitchy asides and a constant stream of activity – as well as strawberry tea in the servants' kitchen – make it all great fun (mid-May–Oct daily 10am–5pm; Nov–Dec daily 10am–4pm; Feb–May Sat & Sun 10am–4pm; $7).

Also on Bellevue Avenue, the **Marble House**, owned by suffragist Mrs Belmont, which has a golden ballroom and a Chinese teahouse on the grounds, and **Rosecliff**, with its colourful rose garden and heart-shaped staircase, were both used as sets during the filming of *The Great Gatsby*. The most ornate of the lot, Cornelius Vanderbilt's **The Breakers**, on Ochre Point Avenue, is a palace built in the style of the Italian Renaissance, overlooking the ocean. All except Beechwood are run by the **Newport Preservation Society**, 118 Mill Street, who offer combination tickets which slightly help to beat the hefty individual admission prices of at least $6 (April–Sept daily 10am–5pm, otherwise schedules vary; any two houses $11, three $16, four $19; ☎847-1000).

One way to see the Bellevue Avenue mansions on the cheap is to peer in the back gardens from the **Cliff Walk**, which begins on Memorial Avenue where it meets First Beach. This three-and-a-half mile oceanside path alternates from jasmine and wild roses to unappealing concrete subways through perilous rocks. For those with a car, Ocean Drive continues from Bellevue Avenue where the Cliff Walk ends, following the coast eastwards and passing **Hammersmith Farm**, John and Jackie Kennedy's 28-room shingled summer home, originally owned by Jackie's mother (April–Oct daily 10am–7pm; March & Nov Sat & Sun 10am–5pm).

Downtown

Newport's Colonial political and business centre, **Washington Square**, lies just south of the Gateway Centre, beginning where Thames Street meets the Brick Market. The 1762 market, off **Long Wharf** (the most important of Newport's Colonial wharves), has been refurbished to include fairly ordinary galleries and pricey gift shops. The **Old Colony House**, one of Rhode Island's few pre-Revolutionary brick buildings, and seat of government from 1739 to 1900, stands on the other side of the square (July–Sept Mon–Fri 9.30am–noon & 1–4pm, Sat & Sun 9.30am–noon; free). To the north, the **Easton's Point** district, between Washington Street and the water and Spring Street to the east, is lined with the eighteenth-century homes of ship captains; only the 1748 **Hunter House**, 54 Washington Street, is open to the public (May–Oct daily 10am–5pm; ☎847-1000).

The oldest religious building in town is the shabby 1699 **Quaker House**, Marlborough and Farewell streets, restored to its nineteenth-century appearance and completely free of adornment (mid-June to Aug Mon–Sat 10am–5pm; otherwise tours by appointment; $2). In 1790, Newport's Jewish community wrote to George Washington expressing their hopes for his new government. His enthusiastic reply advocating religious liberty is exhibited at the Georgian **Touro Synagogue**, 85 Touro Street, built in 1763 and the oldest in the nation (June–Sept Mon–Fri 10am–5pm, Sun 10am–6pm; Oct–May Sun 2–4pm; free). Just next door, the tiny **Newport Historical Society and Museum**, 83 Touro Street, has changing exhibits on Newport's past, and on Friday and Saturday mornings in summer organises walking tours through Colonial Newport (Tues–Fri 9.30am–4.30pm, Sat 9.30am–noon). Washington himself worshipped at the 1726 **Trinity Church** on Queen Anne Park, a Colonial structure based on the Old North Church in Boston and the designs of Sir Christopher Wren (June–Sept Mon–Sat 10am–4pm; Oct–May Sat & Sun 1–4pm; free). A few blocks south, the Catholic **St Marys Church**, Spring Street and Memorial Boulevard, is the oldest Catholic Church in Rhode Island, where Jackie Bouvier married John Kennedy (Mon–Fri 7–11am; free).

Bellevue Avenue, the street lined with most of Newport's famous mansions, also has two museums of note. The **Newport Art Museum**, at no. 76, is housed in the 1864 mock-medieval Griswold House, and exhibits New England art from the last two centuries (Tues–Sat 10am–5pm, Sun 1–5pm; $2.50). At no. 194, the grand **Newport Casino** was an early country club which held the first national tennis championship in 1881. It is now the **International Tennis Hall of Fame**, and still keeps its grass courts open to the public. The museum includes exhibits on tennis fashion and trophies (May–Sept daily 10am–5pm; Oct–April 11am–4pm; $4).

Beaches

The indubitable attraction of Newport's shoreline, with its many coves and gently sloping beaches, is slightly marred by the fact that many are strictly private. **Gooseberry Beach**, on the southern edge of the island, is surrounded by grand houses and charges $1 admission. The town beach, **First** (or Newport, or Easton's) **Beach**, is at the east end of Memorial Boulevard. **Second** and **Third** beaches are further along the same route towards Middletown. The visitor centre provides a guide to them all.

Accommodation

There are plenty of reasonably priced **guest houses** in Newport, but it's a good idea to book ahead, especially on summer weekends (when prices rocket). The visitor centre (see p.174) has free phone links to inns and motels in varying price ranges. By far the most prevalent form of accommodation is **B&B**. *Bed and Breakfast of Rhode Island* (☎849-1298) can find rooms from around $65, and *Anna's Victorian Connection*, 5 Fowler Avenue, offers a 24-hour reservation service with rooms from $35 (☎849-2489).

Commodore Perry Inn, 348 Thames St (☎848-8000). Clean and comfortable rooms in prime position from $45.

Marion's House, 378 Spring St (☎848-0115). 1861 house, with rooms during the week for $50–70, and $70–95 at weekends.

The Melville House, 39 Clarke St (☎847-0460). Colonial house two blocks from the harbour. Rooms from $75 including homemade breakfast.

Pembroke House, 21 Bedlow Ave (☎849-8786). B&B from $65.

The William Fudder House, 30 Bellevue Ave (☎849-4220). 1875 home near the mansions. Rooms from $55.

Eating

Many of Newport's restaurants are smug and overpriced, with the result that visitors on a budget have to make do with snacks. However, there are some gems, even along touristy Thames Street, and the seafood here is well worth the blow-out if you have the extra cash.

Corner Store Deli, (☎847-1978). Gourmet bagels and breakfast specials from $1.25. Patio garden opens at 4pm, with fresh pizza from $6. Bring your own bottle.

Wave Cafe, 22 Washington Sq (☎846-6060). Hip, upbeat cafe serving aspiring artists and poets rather than the yacht club. Crepes from $4, lunch specials with an international flavour from $5.50, flavoured coffees and teas. Occasional poetry readings and exhibitions.

Muriel's, 58 Spring St (☎849-7780). French restaurant serving chowder, pasta and French dishes from $10.

Salas, 345 Thames St (☎846-8772). Buzzing, friendly Italian family restaurant serving great home-cooked feasts including stuffed quahog (clams) from $2, spaghetti from $3.

Live Music

Newport is historically famed for its duo of music festivals: the **Folk Festival** in August, followed by the **Newport Jazz Festival**. Both are held in Fort Adams State Park (☎847-3700). A lesser-known **Classical Music Festival** takes place in the mansions during July (☎846-1133).

Otherwise, there is plenty of shamelessly unrefined **nightlife**; noisy bars and clubs abound near the waterfront, and among the **live music venues** in town, two of the best are the *Blue Pelican*, 40 W Broadway (☎847-5675), which has jazz, blues, folk, Irish, reggae and world music nightly, and *Thax*, 212 Thames Street (☎849-1112), which puts on R&B and jazz above an upmarket restaurant.

CONNECTICUT

CONNECTICUT was named *Quinnehtukqut* by the Native Americans, for the "great tidal river" which splits it in two before spilling out into the Long Island Sound and washing the old whaling ports of the coast. This small and densely populated state is a sort of conservative suburb of New York City, enabling commuters to earn Big-Apple salaries while avoiding New York state and city taxes. Its first white settlers arrived in the 1630s; refugees from Massachusetts seeking liberty, good farmland and trading opportunities (not necessarily in that order). Connecticut soon became a centre for "**Yankee ingenuity**", prospering through the invention and marketing (often by the notorious and not always honourable Yankee peddlers) of many a useful little household object. Although hit very badly by English raids in the Revolutionary War, its role in providing the war effort with crucial supplies made it known as "the **provisions state**". After the war, the original charter of Connecticut's first colonists was used as a model for the American Constitution, and gave rise to another nickname: "the **Constitution state**". It continued to prosper during the eighteenth and nineteenth centuries, with steady industrialisation, and lucrative whaling along the southeastern coast. Today, much of the old industry, especially in the north, has withered away, leaving areas of green countryside, untroubled by noisy interstates, many verdant forests and the idyllic rural villages that typify New England's PR image – but also unemployment, poverty, and a degree of displacement. **New Haven** in particular, home to Yale University, faces distinctly un-New England problems like drug wars, homelessness and violent crime.

The linchpins of Connecticut's economy – insurance companies, medical research and military bases – hardly make for pleasing aesthetics, as demonstrated by the interminably dull capital city, **Hartford**, and even the historic and otherwise attractive coastline is marred by some unlovely stretches of sprawling grey concrete.

Getting around Connecticut
Except for a few isolated areas in the north, Connecticut is well provided with major **roads**. I-95 is the main interstate, running from New York to Rhode Island along the shore of the Long Island Sound. I-91 travels north from I-95 at New Haven, weaving its way along the Connecticut River to Vermont. However, in Connecticut, as with the other New England states, it's a shame to miss out on the quiet countryside scenery along the side roads. Although it's easy to get lost on poorly signposted backroads, distances are so small that this is unlikely to be a major problem.

All the major east coast air carriers **fly** to Bradley International Airport near Hartford, and *Greyhound* **buses** run to most of the main towns (though not Mystic). *Connecticut Transit* buses (☎525-9181) serve the inland area around Hartford. *Amtrak* **trains** call regularly at New Haven, Hartford, Mystic and New London, and make numerous commuter stops.

Southeastern Connecticut

The **southeastern coast** of Connecticut, spanning fifteen miles from Stonington in the east to Niantic in the west, and bisected by the Thames (pronounced *Thaymz*) River, is one of the state's most touristed areas. Each of the handful of tiny, picturesque Colonial communities and old whaling villages along the Long Island Sound is a mere stone's throw from the next. No longer perhaps are they the iniquitous and rumbustuous ports that so inspired Melville, but they're still keen to preserve a sense of their history. The biggest attraction, the restored nineteenth-century **Mystic Seaport**, justifies at least a day's visit; nearby are the less lovely US Naval submarine base at **Groton** and the pretty fishing harbour of **Stonington Borough**.

Mystic

The old whaling port and shipbuilding centre of **MYSTIC**, the purists will tell you, does not in fact exist (they may also claim that Mystic is a state of mind); it is an area governed partly by Groton and partly by Stonington. Nonetheless, it does have a small, well-kept, and somewhat touristy **downtown**, lined with typically New England-quaint clapboard galleries and antique shops. The old bridge across the bustling **Mystic River** which divides it down the middle still opens hourly, and various self-guided walking tours take in the many old houses built by well-off sea captains. The **Olde Mistick Village**, at the intersection of I-95 and US-27, is a pleasant enough outdoor mall with over sixty upmarket shops in Colonial-style buildings. For a scenic walk or bike ride away from tourists, the four-mile river road is protected from cars and development, and passes by Downes Marsh, a sanctuary for osprey.

What brings the tourists to Mystic is the impeccably reconstructed seventeen-acre waterfront village of **Mystic Seaport**, at the mouth of the river, where more than sixty authentically weathered buildings house old-style workshops, stores and a printing press. Its **Stillman Museum** exhibits exquisitely carved scrimshaw and a vast amount of products made from whales' wax-like spermaceti, as well as film of a bloody whale capture. Demonstrations of shanty-singing, fish-splitting and sail-setting, amongst other sea-salty pastimes, vie with storytelling and theatre, while in the **shipyard** you can watch the building, restoration and maintenance of wooden ships. The piece-de-resistance is the restored *Charles W Morgan*, a three-masted wooden Yankee **whaling ship** built in 1841. The last of its kind, the *Morgan* is an elegy to an age of exploration and arrogant expansion remembered now with an uneasy mixture of nostalgia and shame. Done up ready to embark on a two-year voyage, the ship is filled with whaling memorabilia; below deck, accessible by perilously narrow stairs, the blubber room is crowded with huge iron try-pots in which the stinking blubber was melted down (daily 9am–5pm; $14, late-afternoon arrivals are granted free entrance on the next day; ☎572-0211).

Over six thousand weird and wonderful sea creatures glug about the **Marinelife Aquarium**, at exit 90 off I-95. The hourly *Marine Theater* is more educational than the usual performing seal show, with porpoises and a beluga whale, and there are various gooey-eyed baby seals and cute penguins to coo at (July & Aug daily 9am–7pm, last admission 5.30pm; Sept–June daily until 6pm, last admission 4.30pm; $7.50; ☎536-2563).

Practicalities

Mystic has **information offices** in the Olde Mistick Village shopping mall (Mon–Fri 9.30am–5.30pm, Sat until 6pm, Sun 10am–5pm; ☎536-1641), and in the train station (☎572-9578), from where a special bus transports you straight to the Seaport. Though the town itself is manageable on foot, it also has a tourist trolley service which stops at the major hotels.

Accommodation in town is at a premium in July and August. The small *Comfort Inn*, 132 Greenmanville Avenue (☎572-8531), is handy for the Seaport, and has B&B rooms from $36. *Applewood Farms Inn* is a rural Colonial farmhouse, five minutes north of town at 528 Colonel Ledyard Highway, Ledyard (☎536-2022), with six B&B rooms from $65; the hosts will collect you from the train station if given notice. The *Seaport* **campground** is on US-184 in Old Mystic, three miles from the Seaport (☎536-4044).

Much the best-known **restaurant** is *Mystic Pizza*, at 56 W Main Street (☎536-3700), a small family-run pizza place which remains surprisingly unruffled by the fame it

---

The telephone **area code** for the entire state of Connecticut is ☎203.

achieved by inspiring the 1988 movie *Mystic Pizza*, starring Julia Roberts. The pizzas are still huge, cheap and fresh, and the menus and paper napkins are collectors' items amongst its college-age clientele. A good alternative is ten minutes' drive south of Mystic, in the small fishing port of **Noank**. *Abbott's Lobster in the Rough*, at 117 Pearl Street (☎536-7719), is a casual summer-only venue serving truly superb fresh steamed lobster and seafood, at outdoor picnic tables. A giant New England dinner for four costs $25, a lobster plate around $18; bring your own alcohol.

Stonington Borough

STONINGTON BOROUGH, five miles east of Mystic, is an overwhelmingly pretty old fishing village, originally Portuguese but now very New England, characterised by desirable whitewashed cottages (which were once factory houses), white picket fences and colourful flower gardens. Its main street, **Water Street**, is chock-a-block with antique shops and upmarket thrift stores, crowded with well-heeled bargain hunters at the weekend. The **Old Lighthouse Museum**, at no. 7, dates from 1823 and is full of local memorabilia, maps and drawings; fresh flowers everywhere add a nice touch. You can climb the stone steps and iron staircase to the top for views over the water and Connecticut's neighbouring states (May–Oct Tues–Sun 11am–4.30pm; $2). The waterside itself is a great place to pass a few sunny hours, peaceful and quiet with a few bobbing fishing boats and clean water for swimming.

If you want to **stay**, the *Farnan House*, 10 McGrath Court (☎535-0634), is a simple Colonial guest house with rooms from $65, including breakfast. Authentic New England clam chowder, and full meals, can be had at *Noah's*, 115 Water Street (☎535-3925), an old Portuguese **restaurant** with a friendly, pine-table-trendy atmosphere, and delicious home-baked cakes.

Groton

Seven miles west of Mystic Seaport, **GROTON** is a suitably unpleasant name for the home town of the hideous **US Naval Submarine Base**, headquarters for the North Atlantic fleet. The **USS Nautilus**, America's first nuclear-powered submarine, was built in Groton. In 1958, four years after it was launched, it became the first vessel to sail under the polar icecap. It's now moored on the Thames, and self-guided tours allow access to its terrifyingly claustrophobic corridors, one-person-wide in many places. The sub looks pretty much as it did in the Fifties, complete with pin-ups of Marilyn Monroe. The **Submarine Force Museum** next door has exhibits on the history of submersibles from the minuscule *American Turtle*, built in 1775, to the frighteningly powerful *Trident* (April–Oct Wed–Mon 9am–5pm; Nov–March 9am–3.30pm; free; ☎449-3558).

New London

NEW LONDON, which stands opposite Groton on the west side of the Thames, is the closest thing the region has to a city, although it spreads over only six square miles. Originally settled in 1646, it was a wealthy whaling port in the nineteenth century, and is today home to the **US Coastguard Academy**, Mohegan Avenue off I-95, where visitors can wander around a museum of coastguard history and visit the tall ship *USS Eagle* when it's in port (May–Oct daily 9am–5pm). A self-guided walking tour of downtown passes along the prosperous-looking Huntington Street, where four adjacent Greek Revival mansions known as **Whale Oil Row** stand as testimony to the riches brought by whaling. For swimming and sunbathing, the **Ocean Beach Park**, Ocean Avenue, has a sand beach and huge saltwater pool, as well as a wooden boardwalk (summer daily 9am–10pm; $1).

New London was the birthplace of boozy playwright **Eugene O'Neill**. His childhood home, the **Monte Cristo Cottage**, 325 Pequot Avenue, is open for tours, complete with juicy details of his trauma-ridden early life – though they may already be familiar to you from his *Long Day's Journey Into Night* (Mon–Fri 1–4pm; $3). The writer's influence is felt further at the *O'Neill Memorial Theater Center*, 305 Great Neck Road in nearby **Waterford**, an acclaimed testing ground for playwrights and actors, at which audiences can take potluck and watch new, often experimental shows in rehearsal (performances every other night in July; ☎443-5378).

Practicalities

Groton–New London Airport (☎445-8549) has a limited service to the rest of New England (and several car-rental outlets), and you can also arrive in New London by **ferry** from Orient Point on Long Island (*Cross Sound Ferry*; ☎443-5281). *Greyhound* (☎447-3841) and *Bonanza* both serve the town, which is the centre of *SEAT*'s far from comprehensive local **buses** (☎886-2631).

The **Southeastern Connecticut Chamber of Commerce** is at 1 Whale Oil Row (☎443-8332). New London is generally a less expensive place to stay than Mystic, with plenty of reasonably priced **motels** along I-95. Regional **bed and breakfast** inns can be booked via *Seacoast Landings B&B Registry*, 133 Neptune Drive, Groton 06340 (☎442-1940), and the *Holiday Inn*, I-95 and Frontage Road (☎442-0631), offers standard rooms from $65. Nearby **campgrounds** include the nastily named *Camp Niantic by the Atlantic*, six miles west on Hwy-156.

Central Connecticut

Though **central Connecticut** is dominated by Hartford, the state's largest city is possibly one of the nation's dullest destinations. There's not a great deal of point in straying away from the coast, where **New Haven** is a whole lot more interesting.

Hartford

The capital of Connecticut, **HARTFORD**, is also the insurance centre of the United States, an unattractive modern city on the Connecticut River. The **State Capitol** sits on a hill in Bushnell Park, in the centre of town at the corner of Capitol Avenue. The gold-domed building houses a small museum of Connecticut history; free tours are available during the week from 9.15am until 2.15pm. Marginally more thrilling is the antique merry-go-round in the park, which gives jangling rides for a mere 25¢. The **State Museum** across the road includes in its collection Colt rifles and revolvers, and the desk at which Abraham Lincoln signed the paper that emancipated all slaves during the Civil War.

The small **Hartford Atheneum** at 600 Main Street, the nation's oldest public art museum, is filled with American fine and decorative arts (Tues–Sun 11am–5pm; $3, free Thurs & Sat 11am–1pm; ☎278-2670). Nearby on Main Street, the wide-ranging **Avery Art Memorial** holds works by Picasso, Goya, Rembrandt and Cezanne.

Practicalities

Hartford, which lies at the junction of I-91 (north–south) and I-84 (east–west), is easily accessible by car. *Greyhound* (☎547-1500) and *Bonanza* **buses**, and *Amtrak* **trains**, all pull into the terminal at Union Place. If you have to stay the night, there are cheap **hotels** along the interstates; the *Susse Chalet Inn*, 185 Brainard Road off exit 27 on I-91 (☎525-9306), has doubles from $45. Hotels in Hartford itself cater mainly to business visitors and are correspondingly pricey. A popular **restaurant** downtown is *Brown,*

Thompson & Co (☎525-1600), 924 Main Street, where dinner costs around $6 and there's live comedy at the weekend (for a $10 admission charge). For further information, try the **Hartford Convention and Visitors Bureau**, in the centre of downtown on Civic Center Plaza (Mon–Fri 9am–4.30pm; ☎728-6789).

Farmington

Hartford does have a number of appealing Colonial suburbs, such as Wethersfield and **Farmington**, about seven miles west on Hwy-4. This was home in the 1880s to next-door neighbours **Mark Twain** and **Harriet Beecher Stowe**, when Twain was writing *Huckleberry Finn*. Today their Victorian homes, at 351 Farmington Avenue and adjacent Nook Farm, are furnished much as they were when the authors lived there, and are open for tours (daily in summer, closed Mon in winter; $6.50 for both; ☎525-9317).

New Haven

NEW HAVEN, founded in 1638 by a group of wealthy Puritans from London on a large natural harbour at the mouth of the Quinnipiac River, developed as a solid town, its economy based on shipping and, later, industry. In 1716 it became the seat of **Yale University**, now the third oldest college in the States, but it was manufacturing that really brought the city into its own, late in the nineteenth century. New Haven churned out Winchester rifles, musical instruments, tools, carriages and corsets, and **Eli Whitney**, inventor of the revolutionary cotton gin, discovered in his workshop here a method of mass production that did away with expensive skilled labour. Today, however, there is little manufacturing activity left in New Haven, as it faces a damaging and profound depression.

In the summer of 1991, Yale alumnus George Bush, giving a speech at the university on the horrors of the Tiananmen Square massacre, met with boos and derision from students eager to hear him address more immediate domestic problems, not least those of New Haven itself. It's an uneasy place, half tension-ridden urban wasteland and half Ivy League idyll. Town-versus-gown conflicts are so marked as to give the city a crackling energy, and New Haven is certainly less WASPish and smug than many other Ivy League towns. Drug pushing, gang wars and homelessness notwithstanding, blacks and whites – and Italians, Irish and Asians – coexist, ambivalently, in New Haven in a way unseen in the rest of New England. Even the students themselves seem a different, slightly less self-satisfied, breed from those at Princeton, say, or Harvard. The city's ethnic diversity, and the undeniable vitality provided by the much-maligned Yalies, make it a stimulating place to spend some time.

Arrival, Information and Getting Around

New Haven lies where the interstates I-91 and I-95 fork apart, and is on the main **train** line between Washington and Boston; services also run to Canada and New York. The *Amtrak* terminal is in the colossal and newly renovated **Union Station**, on Union Avenue six blocks southeast of the Yale campus downtown. To or from New York, the *Metro-North Commuter Railroad* (☎497-2089) is a better deal than *Amtrak*. *Greyhound* and *Peter Pan* (to Boston) **buses** arrive at 45 George Street (☎772-2470). Upon arrival, it's advisable to catch a cab to your hotel, as the bus and train terminals are in potentially dodgy areas. One reputable firm is *Metro Taxi* (☎777-7777).

Public transport to areas outside central downtown is provided by *Connecticut Transit* (☎624-0151), 470 James Street, but service is poor after 6pm. An **information booth** two blocks east of the Green at 200 Orange Street gives details of routes and schedules (Mon–Fri 9am–5pm). There is a **visitor centre** nearby at 900 Chapel Street (☎787-8367), and another, smaller, one at Long Wharf on the river.

The Town

A succession of remarkably ugly buildings put up during the 1950s rather blighted New Haven, but its **downtown**, centring on the **Green**, remains both attractive and walkable, thanks in part to some sensitive restoration. This area, laid out in 1638, was the site of the city's original settlement; around the Green are three churches, a grand library and a number of stately government buildings. The park itself is now home to a handful of harmless itinerants, and borders the student-filled College and Chapel Street district. The surrounding five blocks are a genuinely lively place in which to hang out, filled with bookshops, cafes, clubs and hip clothes shops; the **Neon Garage**, an art exhibit in a real parking lot on Crown Street, is especially notable. It's quite safe to wander around, even at night, especially during term-time.

Yale University stands proudly right in the centre of things, revoking the Gothic architecture of Oxford University. You can wander at will through New Haven's prime attraction, though free hour-long student-led **tours** set off daily from the Information Office at 344 College Street opposite the Green (Mon–Fri 10am–4pm; tours Mon–Fri 10.30am–2pm, Sat & Sun 1.30pm; ☎432-2300). The tours, which entail quite a bit of trooping to and fro, begin with the beautiful old spires and ivy-strewn cobbled court-yards of the old campus (mostly built in the Thirties, but painstakingly distressed to look suitably ancient) and finish up at the remarkable **Beinecke Rare Books Library**, 121 Wall Street, where venerable manuscripts and hand-printed books can be seen with the aid of natural light seeping through the translucent marble walls (Mon–Fri 8.30am–5pm, Sat 10am–5pm; closed Sat in Aug; free). Other university buildings of interest include the three-storey **Center for British Art**, 1080 Chapel Street, which exhibits English paintings from Old Masters to works by Peter Blake and Francis Bacon (Tues–Sat 10am–5pm, Sun 2–5pm; free). The **Yale Art Gallery**, just across the road at 1111 Chapel Street, is the nation's oldest university art museum, with an impressive collection of American decorative arts, regional design and furniture, and African and pre-Columbian works. Among its major European paintings is Van Gogh's famous *Night Café*, said by the artist to be "one of the ugliest pictures I have done" (Tues–Sat 10am–5pm, Sun 2–5pm; closed Aug; free). A quirky **Collection of Musical Instruments** is at 15 Hillhouse Avenue (Tues–Thurs 1–4pm, Sun 2–5pm), and the **Peabody Museum of Natural History**, 170 Whitney Avenue, is a solid nineteenth-century collection of fossils, skeletons, gems and dioramas (Mon–Sat 10am–5pm, Sun noon–5pm; closed July; $2, free Mon–Fri 3–5pm).

New Haven's close-knit **Italian District** has been based since 1900 among the well-kept brownstones and colourful window boxes of **Wooster Street**, just beyond Crown Street southeast of the Green. This was where the city's original Italian immigrants set-tled when they came to work on the railroad. There's little to see here except the incredibly popular restaurants, but it's well worth stopping by when there's a festival on.

Accommodation

New Haven has surprisingly few **hotels** for a city of its size; not even expensive ones for visiting Yalie parents. **B&B** from around $45 can be arranged in advance through *Nutmeg Bed and Breakfast*, 222 Girard Avenue, Hartford 06105 (☎236-6698). The down-town hotels, although slightly overpriced, are worth it for their convenient location and safety. Because of the shortage of rooms, be sure to book ahead if you're going to be visiting during graduation.

Colony Inn, 1157 Chapel St (☎776-1234). Luxury hotel in the centre of things, where the plainest rooms go for $100.

Holiday Inn, 30 Whalley Ave (☎777-6221). Generic rooms in good central location from $90.

Hotel Duncan, 1151 Chapel St (☎787-1273). Comfortable rooms in old-fashioned hotel, a few steps away from Yale, from $50.

Eating

You can't leave New Haven without trying the local **pizza** (known by the cognoscenti as tomato pies). The *New York Times* discovered New Haven's pizzas a few years ago, and since then there have been queues down the street at all the family restaurants in Wooster Square. There are also plenty of reasonably priced and innovative restaurants around the Green, on College and Chapel streets.

Atticus Bookstore Cafe, 1082 Chapel St (☎776-4040). Mediocre salads and brioches, good coffee, in a relaxed bookshop open until midnight. Prices range from $2.

Bruxelles Brasserie, 220 College St (☎782-1551). Fashionable restaurant near the theatres with excellent cordon bleu food and smart crowd. Entrees, which include Louisiana stuffed trout and chicken with lemon yoghurt, start at $13.

Claire's Corner Copia, 1000 Chapel St (☎562-3888). Worthy vegetarian food, including many international dishes. Cheap, but a rather dilettante attitude to the microwave.

Daily Caffe, 316 Elm St (☎766-5063). Relaxed and arty cafe, open until 1am, catering to the cappuccino and Sunday papers set. Sandwiches and cakes from $2.

Louis' Lunch, 263 Crown St (☎562-5507). Small and dark ancient burger house that claims to have invented the hamburger. Highly popular, but closed, oddly enough, at the weekend.

Pepe's Pizzeria, 157 Wooster St (☎865-5762). Most popular of the Wooster Street eateries; plain, functional and friendly, with huge "combination pies" starting at $5. The secret is apparently in the coal-fired ovens and the Italian tomatoes.

Spanky's, 238 Crown St (☎562-3530). This brand new "Fifties" diner may look awful; but it can offer great music on the individual jukeboxes, juicy burgers from $5, and no-nonsense blue-plate specials like meatloaf from $8.

Willoughby's, 1006 Chapel St (☎789-8400). Self-consciously trendy gourmet coffee bar frequented by hip intellectuals and fashionable townies. Superb coffee from $1.75, and sticky cakes for slightly more.

Yankee Doodle, 258 Elm St (☎865-1074). Yalies' favourite cheap caff, with original Fifties fittings and shop sign.

Nightlife and entertainment

New Haven has an undeniably rich **cultural scene**, and is especially strong on **theatre**. The *Yale Rep Company*, 1120 Chapel Street (☎432-1234), which boasts amongst its eminent past members Jodie Foster and Meryl Streep, turns out consistently good shows during the school year. The *Long Wharf Theater* (☎787-4282), 222 Sargent Drive just off I-95, has a nationwide reputation for quality performances, as does the refurbished *Schubert Performing Arts Center*, 247 College Street (☎562-5666). During the summer, the *Summer Cabaret* (☎432-1567), 217 Park Street, puts on two comedy shows nightly.

Additionally, there are several good **bars** and **clubs**, concentrated on Chapel and College streets. The free bi-weekly paper *Hip*, available from the clothes shops along Chapel Street, has details of all the happening happenings in and around New Haven, while the *New Haven Advocate*, a free news and arts weekly paper, has more comprehensive listings.

Anchor Bar, 272 College St (☎865-1512). Authentic Fifties bar, one of the best spots in town, complete with snug plastic booths, dim orange lighting, frosted windows and a formidable matronly hostess.

Bopper's, 239 Crown St (☎562-1469). Pseudo-Fifties club with various one-nighters.

Club Heat, 216 Crown St (☎782-1238). Wild club which really wishes it were in New York, and does its best to pretend that it is.

Foundry Cafe, 104 Audubon St (☎776-5144). Laid-back bar with live music and a small, pretty garden.

Toad's, 300 York St (☎777-7431). Big live music venue, where the likes of Dylan and the Stones "pop in" occasionally to play impromptu gigs.

NEW HAMPSHIRE

Long after sailors, fishermen and agricultural colonists had domesticated the entire coastline of New England, the harsh glacier-scarred interior of **NEW HAMPSHIRE**, with its dense forests and forbidding mountains, remained the exclusive preserve of the Algonquin Indians. Only the few miles of seashore held sizeable seventeenth-century communities of European settlers, such as Strawbery Banke at **Portsmouth**.

Even when the Indians were finally driven back, following the defeat of their French allies in Canada, the settlers could make little agricultural impact on the rocky terrain of this "granite state". Towns such as Nashua, Manchester and Concord grew up in the fertile Merrimack Valley, but not until the Industrial Revolution made possible the development of water-powered **textile** mills did the economy take off. For a while, ruthless **timber** companies looked set to strip all northern New Hampshire bare – very few of the trees you see now are original growth – but they were brought under control when it was appreciated that the pristine landscape of the **White Mountains** might turn out to be the state's greatest asset. Large-scale **tourism** began towards the end of last century; at one stage fifty trains daily brought travellers up to Mount Washington.

Ever since becoming the first American state to declare independence, in January 1776, New Hampshire has been proud to go its own idiosyncratic way. The absence of a sales tax, or even a personal income tax, is seen as a fulfilment of the state motto, "Live Free or Die". Alternative sources of revenue include state-owned **liquor stores** – set up after the failure of Prohibition, and so enthusiastically promoted as to seem almost completely opposite in their intention. There are no "bars"; any establishment serving alcohol also has to serve food. The state has long gained inordinate political clout as the venue of the first **primary election** of each US presidential campaign. Its villages are well used to playing host to would-be world leaders; the hopes of Democrat front-runner Ed Muskie were shattered here in 1972, while four years later Jimmy Carter emerged from obscurity to race to the Democratic nomination. State Governor John Sununu's successful efforts to clinch victory for George Bush in 1988 led to his becoming White House Chief of Staff.

One less ideological aspect of New Hampshire's individualism is the emphasis on a healthy outdoor lifestyle. Hiking, climbing, cycling, and **skiing** are enjoyed both by energetic locals and by the many visitors who drive up from Boston and New York. The major destinations are **Lake Winnipesaukee**, and **Conway, Lincoln** and **Franconia** in the mountains further north. Some have grown rather too large and commercial for their own good, but if you steer clear of the paying "attractions", the lakes, islands and snow-capped peaks themselves remain spectacular. To see the bucolic rural scenery more usually associated with New England, take a detour off the main roads up the Merrimack Valley – to **Canterbury Shaker Village** near Concord, for example.

Getting Around New Hampshire

Though Manchester does have a small airport, travellers coming to New Hampshire from far afield usually do so via Boston's Logan Airport. *Concord Trailways* (☎1-800/258-3722, or ☎1-800/852-3317 in NH) run **buses** from there to Manchester, Concord, Conway and Franconia. *Vermont Transit* (☎1-800/451-3292) run from the *Peter Pan* terminal in Boston to Conway and Franconia, and at weekends (Fri, Sat & Sun) also connect Conway with Burlington and Montréal. The closest *Amtrak* service is to White River Junction in Vermont, just across the state line from Hanover. As ever, a **car** makes all the difference for exploring once you've arrived, but a surprising number of **cyclists** set out to tour the mountains.

The telephone **area code** for the entire state of New Hampshire is ☎603.

The Coast

Of all the US states with ocean access, New Hampshire has the shortest coastline – just eighteen miles. Driving north from Boston along either I-95 or the quieter US-1, you enter New Hampshire after roughly forty miles, to be confronted almost immediately by the nuclear power plant at **Seabrook Station**, which finally opened in 1990 after years of determined opposition, not least from the irate state of Massachusetts close by.

Hampton Beach, a little further on, is a traditional family-oriented seaside resort (its free information line has the optimistic number ☎1-800/GET-A-TAN). The usual assortment of motels and fast-food places line the approaches to the crowded beaches (one of New England's main **surfing** spots), but this close to Boston summer **accommodation** rates are high. The *Pine Haven* at 183 Lafayette Road (☎964-8187), on US-1 four miles north of town, is one of the cheaper options, with rooms around $60. Large **campgrounds** in the area include *Tuxbury Pond* in South Hampton (☎394-7660).

Portsmouth

New Hampshire's oldest community, **PORTSMOUTH**, might look like a major city on the map, but once you're there it has much more of the feel of a country town. Its position at the mouth of the Piscataqua River has always made it an important port – it was the state capital until 1808 – but it has barely grown, and the spire of **North Church** in the central **Market Square** remains the highest building you'll see in town.

An official walking trail guides visitors past a striking selection of grand timber mansions, of which the 1758 gambrel-roofed, cream-and-white clapboard **John Paul Jones House** at 43 Middle Street, on the corner of State Street, is the most distinctive (May–Sept only, Mon–Sat 10am–4.15pm; $3). However, with so many old houses to see you might just as contentedly walk at random, and a visit to **Strawbery Banke** (see below) provides a better overview of local history. Antiquarian book dealers, such as the *Book Guild* at 58 State Street, and curio shops like *Garakuta* in Bow Street, add to the pleasures of a stroll. In **Prescott Park** along the waterfront, the **Sheafe Warehouse Museum** has a fascinating free collection of mostly nautical ephemera.

Portsmouth's fortunes have long rested with its **Naval Shipyard**, visible across the bay (in Kittery, Maine; see p.201). Founded in 1800 by John Paul Jones as the first-ever US government shipyard, it has remained active ever since – it launched 31 submarines in 1944 alone, and built the first Polaris in 1962. In 1905 President Teddy Roosevelt hosted the conference here which ended the war between Russia and Japan – and thereby earned himself a Nobel Peace Prize. A few years later, **Humphrey Bogart**, as a junior naval rating, received injuries while attempting to prevent the escape of a prisoner which left him with his trademark permanent sneer and a slight lisp.

Strawbery Banke

Hancock and Marcy streets. May–Oct daily 10am–5pm. $8 adults, $4 kids, $22 families. ☎433-1100.

The lack of any great pressure on space has made it possible to preserve ten acres of Portsmouth's original site as **STRAWBERY BANKE**. This area began life as home to wealthy shipbuilders, and was successively the lair of privateers and a red-light district before turning into respectable – and, in the Fifties, ultimately decaying – suburbia. It was then decided to re-create its former appearance, mainly by clearing away the newer buildings (only two of the houses on display had to be moved here). The old street pattern has once more been marked out, and the Puddle Dock where ships used to come in, now well back from the shore, has been outlined but not re-dug. One or two people still live here, tucked away on the upper floors, but the whole complex serves as a living museum, which you can explore either on a guided tour or at your own whim; in either case, several of the houses have well-informed attendants.

What makes Strawbery Banke particularly intriguing is that the restoration is deliberately piecemeal. Each building is shown in its most interesting former incarnation, whether that be 1695 or 1955; indeed in the **Drisco House**, the very first you come to, each individual *room* dates from a different era. The 1766 **Pitt Tavern** holds the most historic significance, having acted as a meeting place during the Revolution for patriots and loyalists (it still functions as a masonic lodge, one of the four oldest in the US – which explains why you can't go upstairs). Its clientele was segregated by sex, but not by social standing; the tiny glasses remind you that they drank gin rather than beer.

Although during term-time you may have to struggle to keep ahead of school parties, Strawbery Banke continues to undertake serious excavation and academic research, holding symposia on local history, including women's and industrial history. Traditional **crafts** are both studied and practised, for example in the **Dinsmore Shop** where an infinitely patient cooper manufactures barrels with the tools and methods of 1800. The *Mills Zoldak* **pottery** shop produces attractive and low-priced ceramics; they're open year-round, and you can visit them without paying admission.

Practicalities

C&J Trailways **buses** drop passengers off in Portsmouth at 5 Congress Street, on Market Square, en route between Boston and Portland. You can pick up information from the **visitor centre** at 500 Market Street (Mon–Fri 9.30am–5pm; ☎436-1118), and the outside tables of the *Cafe Brioche* in Market Square make an obvious point from which to get your bearings.

Accommodation in the town centre is restricted to B&Bs. The rambling seven-room *Inn at Strawbery Banke* at 314 Court Street (☎436-7242) is very quiet at night, and has rooms from $70; the similarly priced *Martin Hill Inn* at 404 Islington Street (☎436-2287) is a bit more formal. Of the **restaurants**, the *Stockpot*, overlooking the river at 53 Bow Street (☎431-1851), specialises in paella and stir-fries, while the *Szechuan Taste* at 54 Daniels Street (☎431-2226) serves good Thai and Chinese food. The lively *Washington Street Eatery* is part of Strawbery Banke, but accessible without entering the museum.

Hotels and motels along US-1, rarely cheap, include the *Comfort Inn at Yoken's* (☎433-3338), with pool, where rooms start at $60. The adjacent *Yoken's* (☎436-8224) is a popular and inexpensive restaurant for ribs and the like, housed in New England's largest **gift shop**, a veritable goldmine of trivia.

Odiorne Point State Park

The one brief patch of semi-wilderness along the New Hampshire coast was, ironically, where the first white settlers landed in 1623. Some of the scattered ruins in marshy **Odiorne Point State Park** date from those early days; others, far more modern, were World War II defences. The two park entrances are on Hwy-1A near **Rye**, four miles southeast of Portsmouth, and a summer-only visitor centre is open daily from 10am until 4pm. The offshore **Isles of Shoals**, a supposed haunt of Blackbeard the pirate, can be seen close-up on boat trips from Portsmouth Harbor (☎431-5500).

The Merrimack Valley

The financial and political heartland of New Hampshire is the **Merrimack Valley**, which first by water and now by road has always been the main thoroughfare north to the White Mountains and Québec. None is of any great interest to tourists, though all are pleasant enough, and equipped with relatively cheap motels.

The southernmost town on the river, **Nashua**, was even named by *Money* magazine in 1987 as the "number one place to live in America". Plenty of its citizens still choose to work in Boston, although the state of Massachusetts no longer allows employees to escape state taxes by living across the border in New Hampshire. **Manchester**, like its namesake in England, was a major cotton producer in the nineteenth century. Although its massive Amoskeag Mills were forced to close in the Thirties, it remains the largest city in the state, and is now notable mainly for the collection of glassware, furniture and paintings in the recently expanded **Currier Gallery of Art** at 192 Orange Street (Tues–Sun 10am–5pm; free). The focal point of **Concord** is the gold dome of the State House, the seat of New Hampshire's state legislature; despite its small size it has 424 members, making it the fourth largest such body in the world after the parliaments of the United States, Britain and India). Local schoolteacher Christa McAuliffe, a victim of the *Challenger* tragedy, is commemorated by a new planetarium.

Fifteen miles north of Concord on Hwy-106, **Canterbury Shaker Village** (May–Oct Mon–Sat 10am–5pm; $8; ☎783-9511) was the sixth Shaker community (see pp.169, 379 and 384) to be founded by Ann Lee in the 1780s and grew to three-hundred-strong by 1860. On ninety-minute tours, visitors can see traditional Shaker crafts and techniques – such as box-making – and sample their food in the attached *Creamery* restaurant.

America's Stonehenge

Daily June–Aug 9am–5pm; May & Sept 10am–4pm; April & Nov Sat & Sun 10am–3.30pm; $5.

If you enter New Hampshire from Boston along I-93 rather than via Nashua, a ten-mile detour east of **Salem** (not to be confused with witch-trial Salem, fifty miles southeast) will bring you to the archaeological site once known as Mystery Hill, now re-vamped as **America's Stonehenge**. This bewildering thirty-acre jumble of rocks, on an exposed granite hilltop, has been shown to date back four thousand years, but whether it really was an astronomical observatory to rival Stonehenge – let alone whether its builders were Phoenician sailors, as some would have it – is far from proven. The walls, chambers and monoliths are no less impressive for being unexplained.

The nearest budget **accommodation** is the *Susse Chalet* at 6 Keewaydin Drive in Salem, near exit 2 off I-93 (☎893-4722), where doubles cost $50.

The Lakes Region

Of the literally hundreds of lakes created by the snow-melt flowing south from the White Mountains, much the biggest is **Lake Winnipesaukee**, which forms the centre of the vacation-oriented Lakes Region. Long segments of its three-hundred-mile shoreline, especially in the east, consist of thick forests sweeping down to waters which are only disturbed by pleasure craft and dotted with little islands. The most sophisticated of the towns is **Wolfeboro**; the most fun to visit has to be **Weirs Beach**.

Ideally, you would bring your own small boat, and get thoroughly lost in the maze of small channels and islets. Failing that, the **cruise ship** *Mount Washington* does daily three-hour tours in summer of the more open stretches, leaving Weirs Beach at 9am and 12.15pm, and Wolfeboro at 11am. The tours cost $12, and also call at either Center Harbor (Mon, Wed & Fri) or Alton Bay (Tues, Thurs, Sat & Sun). It's certainly a pretty ride, though it can seem a little long in the heat of the day and you might prefer to take an evening dinner cruise (July & Aug Tues–Sat). A smaller mail-boat does more local round-trips from Weirs Beach for $7.50. For all queries, ring ☎366-BOAT.

Wolfeboro

Because Governor Wentworth of New Hampshire built his summer home nearby in 1768, tiny **WOLFEBORO** claims to be "the oldest summer resort in America". Sandwiched between Lakes Winnipesaukee and Wentworth, it has little to show for that history, but it's a relaxing place to spend a few hours, along the short but bustling main street, next to the quay where the *Mount Washington* comes in.

The 1812 *Wolfeboro Inn* (☎1-800/451-2389 or ☎569-3016) stands in a dignified waterfront position at 44 N Main Street, just a few yards from the town proper; **rooms** cost upwards of $100. Also beside the lake, four miles north in Alton Bay, the *Bay Side* motel (☎875-5005) has rooms from $70. *Wolfeboro Campground* is on Haines Hill Road (☎569-9881). Two branches of *Bailey's* (☎569-3662), one on the quayside and one on Main Street, serve basic good-value **food**; *West Lake Asian Cuisine* (☎569-6700) in the Wolfeboro Center on Hwy-109 is an excellent, reasonably priced, **Chinese** restaurant.

The eastern shore of Lake Winnipesaukee is considerably less developed than the area around Weirs Beach, and makes for much better walking. One fascinating stop-off, a few miles north of Wolfeboro on Hwy-109, is the **Libby Museum** (summer only, Tues–Sun 10am–4pm; ☎569-1035). It houses a bizarre collection founded at the start of the century by a local dentist, Henry Forest Libby, who had become fascinated with the theory of evolution. Various rather ineptly stuffed animals (one can only hope that he was a better dentist than he was a taxidermist) are displayed alongside the skeletons of bears, orang-utans, and humans. There's also a mastodon's tooth, a "Niddy Noddy" spinning device, and a fingernail supposedly pulled out by its Chinese owner to demonstrate his new Christian faith. The enthusiastic curator will be more than happy to tell you about the time he met Marlene Dietrich, and to lie about his stuffed alligator. The front steps command a superb view over the lake itself.

Weirs Beach and Laconia

The short boardwalk at **WEIRS BEACH**, the very essence of seaside tackiness even if it is fifty miles inland, is the social centre in summer of the Lakes Region. Its little wooden jetty throngs with holiday-makers, the amusement arcades jingle with cash, and there's even a neat little crescent of sandy beach, suitable for family swimming. The main competing attractions are two **water parks**; *Surf Coaster* (summer daily 10am–8pm; $15 adults, $12 kids) on Hwy-11B just south of town offers dramatic rides and a powerful wave machine, while the *Weirs Beach Water Slide* on US-3 is cheaper but not quite so well equipped.

Nearby **LACONIA** actually controls the purse-strings for Weirs Beach. **Belknap Mill** here claims to be "the oldest unaltered brick textile mill building in the United States". You might think the fact that it is now an arts centre would count as some sort of alteration, but the mill machinery is still in working order in amongst the gallery space, which is the venue for evening concerts and lecture programmes.

One particularly demented time to be in the area is on Father's Day weekend (the third in June), when a gigantic motorcycle race and rally is held at **Loudon**, and at least twenty thousand **bikers** cruise up here looking for action – and **accommodation**. Even at the best of times, rooms do not come cheap, costing $70 or more at the beachfront *Birch Knoll Motel* (April–Oct; ☎366-4958) for example. *Hickory Stick Farm* (☎524-3333) on Bean Hill Road, out in the woods four miles south, is a top-notch restaurant and B&B, where rooms also start at $70. The nearest **campground** is the *Gunstock* (☎293-4341) near Gilford six miles south (a ski resort in winter).

Meredith

MEREDITH, four miles north of Weirs Beach, is the last of Lake Winnipesaukee's resorts. In the modern new waterfront mall, the *Millworks Restaurant* (☎279-4116) is a nice place to eat, while the *Inn at Mill Falls* (☎279-7006) is exceptionally comfortable, if expensive at $85 and up.

The **Winnipesaukee Railroad** (☎279-3196) operates two-hour ($7) and one-hour ($3) scenic trips along the lakeshore between Meredith and Weirs Beach, on weekends from Memorial Day and then daily from mid-June to mid-October, including special fall foliage excursions (and even a Santa Claus special).

The only thing to admire at **Annalee's Doll Museum** (daily 9am–5pm in summer, slightly shorter hours in winter), just outside Meredith, is its effrontery in calling itself a museum. In fact it's a hard-sell toy shop, specialising in painted-felt dolls of quite stunning ugliness. Those items onto which they've managed to stitch the heads back to front are offered at a twenty-five percent reduction.

Northwards to the mountains

Hwy-25 northeast from Meredith leads to Conway in the White Mountains; US-3 northwest on the other hand keeps you in the Lakes Region a little longer, and leads past **Squam Lake**, where the movie *On Golden Pond* was filmed. The **Science Center of New Hampshire** at **Holderness** (July & Aug daily 9.30am–4.30pm, May, June, Sept & Oct Mon–Fri 9.30am–4.30 pm, Sat & Sun 1–4pm; $1; ☎968-7194) is a gentle non-profit institution dedicated to educating children to appreciate and understand the local flora and fauna. Tours lead through a largely natural landscape, in which animals such as deer, bobcat, bears and foxes are kept (mostly short-term) in enclosures.

Five miles on from Holderness at **Plymouth**, you can either rejoin I-93 as it heads into the mountains, or you can continue another five miles west to the **Polar Caves** (mid-May to Oct daily 9am–5pm; $8). Frankly, that would not be a good idea; whatever else the Polar Caves may be, they are not caves. They are no more than a cascade of clammy granite boulders tumbled against a hillside, between which visitors are for no discernible reason expected to find pleasure in squeezing themselves – while paying handsomely for the privilege. A large giftshop sells supremely irrelevant "souvenirs".

The White Mountains

Thanks to their accessibility from both Montréal to the north and Boston to the south, the **White Mountains** have become a year-round tourist destination, popular with summer hikers and winter skiers alike. Commercialised they may be, in built-up strips along the main highways, but the great granite massifs retain much of their majesty and power. **Mount Washington** can claim the severest weather in the world, and conditions are harsh enough for the timberline to be at four thousand feet, as compared to the norm in the Rockies of ten thousand.

Just a few high passes – here called "**notches**", only discovered with infinite pains by the early pioneers – pierce the range, and the roads through these gaps, such as the **Kancamagus Highway** between Lincoln and Conway, make for an enjoyable driving tour. However, you won't really have made the most of the White Mountains unless you also set off, on foot or on skis, across the long expanses of thick evergreen forest which separate them, with snowcapped peaks poking out in all directions.

Hiking in the mountains is co-ordinated by the **Appalachian Mountain Club** (AMC), whose chain of hostels, huts and information centres along the Appalachian Trail, traversing the region from northeast to southwest, is detailed under "White Mountains Accommodation and Eating", below; ring ☎466-2727 for further information, and pick up a copy of the *AMC White Mountain Guide* ($16) before you attempt any serious expedition. Downhill and cross-country **skiers** can choose from several resorts, such as *Loon Mountain* (☎1-800/227-4191 or ☎745-8111) and *Ski Bretton Woods* (☎1-800/258-0330 or ☎278-5000). General information on the skiing centres along I-93 is available from *Ski 93* (PO Box 517, Lincoln, NH 03251; ☎745-8101); those further east are covered by the very helpful Mount Washington Valley Chamber of Commerce (PO Box 2300, North Conway NH03860; ☎356-3171). Once you're in the area, North Conway is the best place for equipment rentals and other supplies. **Bikes** can be rented from the *Loon Mountain Bike Center* on the Kancamagus Highway in Lincoln (☎745-8111) or *Joe Jones* on Main Street in North Conway (☎356-9411).

Franconia Notch and the Old Man of the Mountains

I-93, speeding up towards Canada, and the more leisurely US-3 merge briefly about ten miles beyond **Lincoln**, to pass through **Franconia Notch State Park**. From a roadside pullout, you can look back and upwards to the **Old Man of the Mountains**. This natural rock formation, resembling an old man's profile, will no doubt already be familiar from powerfully magnified photographs – and New Hampshire's licence plates. Seen from a thousand feet below, it's absolutely tiny. It all has to be held together with wires, and one particular family has the annual responsibility of climbing up to plug the cracks made by the winter's ice.

Franconia Notch itself is a slender valley crammed between two great walls of stone. From the park **visitor centre** (May–Oct daily 9am–4.30pm), you can for $6 walk along a two-mile boardwalk-cum-nature-trail to the **Flume**, to look down on the Pemigawasset River as it rages through a narrow rock-filled gorge, or take an $8 **cable-car** ride up the sheer granite face of **Cannon Mountain** (all year; ☎823-5563).

One mile south of **FRANCONIA** further on, the **Frost Place** on Ridge Road (July & Aug daily except Tues 1–5pm; May, June, Sept & Oct Sat & Sun 1–5pm; $3) is the former home of poet Robert Frost, memorable largely for an inspiring panorama of mountains which can look almost undisturbed by human interference.

Bretton Woods

The ease with which US-302 now crosses the middle of the mountains belies the effort that went into cutting a road through **Crawford Notch**, halfway between Franconia and Conway. Just to the north, the magnificent **Mount Washington Hotel** (☎278-1000) stands in splendid isolation in the wide mountain valley of **BRETTON WOODS**. Its imposing red-brick facade, framed by the western slopes of Mount Washington rising behind, is unchanged since the day it was opened in 1902. In its heyday, a stream of horsedrawn carriages brought families and their servants up from the station, deliberately located at a distance in order to increase the sense of grandeur. Displays commemorate the 1944 Bretton Woods Conference, which laid the groundwork for the post-war financial structure of the capitalist world, setting the gold standard at $35 an ounce – it's now $350 – and creating the International Monetary Fund and the World Bank.

Now of course struggling due to its sheer size to remain an economic proposition – rooms start at almost $200 – the hotel remains marvellously evocative, with its quarter-mile terrace and white wicker furniture. It's not the one featured in the movie *The Shining* (see p.855), but it has something of the same feel; you're welcome to pad at will down its endless corridors, past chipmunks scampering across the carpets.

A few miles to the north, the coal-fired steam train of the **Mount Washington Cog Railway** climbs the exposed flank of the mountain, ascending gradients of up to 38 percent on a track which was completed in 1869. The three-hour round-trip costs $35 for adults, $18 for kids over eight (May–Nov ☎1-800/922-8825 or ☎846-5404).

Mount Washington

The 6288-foot **Mount Washington** was named for George Washington before he became President, but over the years other mountains in this "Presidential Range" have taken the names of Madison, Jefferson, and even Eisenhower. (Mount Nancy was called that long before the Reagans; and Mount Deception just happens to be close by.)

You can see all the way to the Atlantic – and right into Canada – from the top of Mount Washington on a clear day, but the real interest in making the ascent lies in the extraordinary severity of the weather up there. The wind exceeds hurricane strength on over one hundred days of each year, and in 1934 it reached the highest speed ever recorded anywhere in the world – 231mph. On the very summit, you'll see the remarkable spectacle of buildings actually held down with great chains; many have over the years been blown away, including the old observatory, said to be the strongest wooden building ever constructed. There's now a viewing platform, with a weatherproof museum and cafe just below. A roll call of the 103 victims to die on the mountain includes two who attempted to slide down the Cog Railway on "improvised boards".

On the way to the top, you pass through four separate climatic zones, with century-old fir and ash trees so stunted as to be below waist-height, before coming out finally amid Arctic tundra. The drive up the **Mount Washington Auto Road** (mid-May to Oct only, 7.30am–6pm in peak season) is not quite as hair-raising as you may be led to expect, though the hairpin bends certainly keep you alert. There is, however, a $12 **toll** for private cars (plus $5 for each additional adult and $3 for kids). Specially adapted minibuses, still known as "stages" in honour of the twelve-person horse-drawn carriages which first used the road, take **narrated tours** ($16 adults, $10 kids). Driving takes thirty or forty minutes under sane conditions, though rally-drivers have done it in under ten. The record for the annual **running** race each June – heading *up* the mountain, naturally – now stands at an incredible 59min 12sec.

North Conway

A few miles south of Mount Washington, heading past **Glen**, US-302 and Hwy-16 as they approach **NORTH CONWAY** become a veritable turmoil of shopping malls, fast-food places and theme parks such as Heritage USA and Storyland. The strip between North Conway and **Conway** proper offers all sorts of "factory outlets" (including a branch of Maine's *L L Bean's* – see p.204) for discount shopping. The towns are not at all interesting, but there are plenty of secluded lodging options in the foothills to either side, and bars and restaurants in the malls (detailed below).

Kancamagus Highway

The **Kancamagus Highway** (Hwy-112) connecting Conway and Lincoln is the least busy road through the mountains, and makes for a very pleasant drive. Several campgrounds are situated in the woods to either side, and various walking trails are signposted. The half-mile hike to **Sabbaday Falls**, off to the south roughly halfway along, leads up a narrow rocky cleft in the forest to a succession of idyllic waterfalls.

White Mountains Accommodation and Eating

So many youthful hikers and skiers come to the White Mountains that for once there is a great deal of **low-budget accommodation**. What the area lacks, however, are cheap motels; there's quite a chasm between the hostels, costing under $20, and the inns and B&Bs which tend to start at over $60. **Campers** can pitch their tents anywhere in the White Mountains National Forest that is below the tree-line and away from the roads, so long as they show consideration for the environment; there are also more than twenty official campgrounds (information ☎528-8727, reservations ☎1-800/283-2267). You can't help but spot any number of cheap **eating places** along the main highways.

Hostels and Mountain Huts

As well as the hostels at Crawford Notch and Pinkham Notch, listed below, which are accessible to motorists, the Appalachian Mountain Club administers eight other huts along the Appalachian Trail, which can be reached only on foot and which in summer provide meals and bedding for up to one hundred people per night. Prices in all the AMC places range from $13 up to $40 according to the amount of privacy (and food) you desire. It's extremely advisable to book ahead, on ☎466-2727.

Berkshire Manor, 133 Main St, Gorham (☎466-9418). Hostel-style accommodation – shared kitchens and so on – but private rooms, from $30 double.

Bowman's Base Camp AYH Hostel, Randolph (☎466-5130). Very basic summer-only hostel, roughly ten miles by road north of Pinkham Notch. $12 AYH members, $13 others.

Crawford Notch Depot, US-302, Carroll (☎846-7773). AMC hostel; two dorms and three cabins in the heart of the mountains. See above for rates. Daily information in summer 8.30am–4.30pm.

Pinkham Notch Camp, Hwy-16 (☎466-2727). AMC hostel – see above for rates – near the base of the Mount Washington Auto Road. Daily information in summer 7am–10pm.

Motels, Hotels and B&Bs

The Bungay Jar, Hwy-116, Franconia (☎823-7775). B&B in superb natural setting. $50.

Eagle Mountain House, 2 Carter Notch Rd, Jackson (☎1-800/777-1700 or ☎383-9111). Highly atmospheric inn, recently re-built, far above the bustle of North Conway. Doubles from $75.

The Forest – A Country Inn, Hwy-16A, Intervale (☎356-9772). Very welcoming B&B between North Conway and Jackson, around $70 per night.

Kancamagus Motor Lodge, two miles east of Lincoln (☎745-3365). Rooms from $65 in summer.

Raynor's Motor Lodge, south of Franconia on Hwy-18 (☎1-800/634-8187 or ☎823-9586). Old-style hotel rooms from $40, plus a dearer fully modernised motel next door. Bicycles for rent.

Saco River Motor Lodge, US-302, Center Conway (☎447-3720). Motel rooms from $48.

Stonybrook Motor Lodge, one mile south of Franconia on Hwy-18 (☎1-800/722-3552 or ☎823-8192). Another motel near the interstate, charging $60 in summer.

Sunny Side Inn, Seavey St, North Conway (☎356-6239). Pleasant B&B, doubles from $52.

Restaurants and Bars

The Cinnamon Tree, Pleasant St Plaza, Conway (☎447-5019). Appetising breakfasts and snacks.

Houlighans, Kearsarge St, North Conway. Just off the main strip, and by far the liveliest bar and restaurant in North Conway, though damnably smoky.

Red Parka Pub, US-302, Glen (☎383-4344). Evening-only barbecue restaurant with bar until 1am, live rock music at weekends.

Truants Taverne, Main St, North Woodstock (☎745-2239). Homely and very reasonable restaurant, with a menu ranging from fancy specials down to sandwiches.

West to Vermont

Much of the western side of New Hampshire, as you approach the Connecticut River which forms the entire border with Vermont, amounts to a less developed – and therefore less touristed – version of the Lakes Region. There's very little cheap accommodation, but for a tranquil day or two the area around **Lake Sunapee** can be very appealing. The *Mountain Lake Inn* (☎938-2136) on Hwy-14, just south of Bradford on tiny Lake Massasecum, is a nice B&B with rooms from $75, and there's a toll-free booking number for all the local inns (☎1-800/662-6005).

Hanover

HANOVER, near Lebanon just across from Vermont, is home to the venerable and elegant **Dartmouth College**, founded in this remote spot in the eighteenth century "for the instruction of the Youth of Indian tribes . . . and others". The main attraction here is the small **Hood Museum of Art** on the college green (Sun & Tues–Fri 11am–5pm, Sat 11am–8pm; free), which contains works by Picasso and Monet alongside genuine Assyrian bas-reliefs. Hanover is a nice place to wander around, and the student population means that it has a few cheap motels, as well as lively eating places such as the panelled cellar of *Peter Christian's Tavern* at 39 S Main Street (☎643-2345).

One unforgettable place to stay nearby is *Moose Mountain Lodge* (☎643-3529), a steep climb up in the hills above **Etna**, looking out over Vermont. All year it feels marvellously remote from the commercial world below, but it really comes into its own for **cross-country skiing** in winter. The friendly owners expect their guests to share their enthusiasm for the country life, and charge $60 per day per person, with a good evening meal.

VERMONT

VERMONT comes closer than any other state in New England to fulfilling the quintessential image of small-town America, with its white churches and red barns, covered bridges and clapboard houses, snowy woods and maple syrup. No city can manage a population of fifty thousand – only **Burlington** has more than twenty thousand – and the chief tourist attraction is *Ben and Jerry's* ice-cream factory. Though the landscape is rural, it's not all that agricultural, and much is still covered by mountainous forests (the state's name is universally said to come from the French *verd mont*, or green mountain – though that is not in fact French at all). The people who choose to live here hold a lot in common; hippies and die-hard conservatives find themselves working together to preserve their environment, and lamenting the advent of yet more ski resorts.

This was the last area of New England to be settled, early in the eighteenth century. As French explorers worked their way down from Canada, American colonists began to spread north; but even as that rivalry died down, a further antipathy developed between settlers from New Hampshire and those from New York. The wealthy New York merchants who built fine homes along the Connecticut River Valley thought of themselves as the "River Gods", but the hardy settlers of the lakes and mountains to the west had little time for their patrician ways. Their leader was the now-legendary **Ethan Allen**, who formed his **Green Mountain Boys** in 1770, proclaiming that "the gods of the hills are not the gods of the valley". When the Revolutionary War superseded such conflicts, this all-but-autonomous force captured Fort Ticonderoga from the British, and helped to win the decisive Battle of Bennington. For fourteen years from 1777, Vermont was an independent republic, with the first constitution in the world explicitly to forbid slavery and grant universal (male) suffrage, but once its boundaries with New York were finally agreed, it joined the Union in 1791. Curiously, the two seminal figures of the **Mormon** religion were both born in Vermont shortly thereafter – Joseph Smith in 1805, and his lieutenant and successor Brigham Young in 1801.

With the occasional exception, such as the extraordinary assortment of Americana at the **Shelburne Museum** near Burlington, there are few specific goals for tourists. Visitors come in great numbers during two well-defined seasons: to see the display of **fall foliage** in the first two weeks of October, and to **ski** in the depths of winter, when the resorts of **Killington**, and **Stowe** further north (home of the *Sound of Music's* Von Trapp family), spring into life. For the rest of the year, you might just as well explore any of the state's minor roads which take your fancy, confident that some picturesque village will be around the next corner. There are far too many to list; we've had to leave out such prime examples as **Peru**, **Grafton** and **Middlebury**. Further information can be picked up from the official Welcome Center on each interstate as it enters Vermont.

Getting Around Vermont

Vermont Transit Lines (☎864-6811) **buses** connect Montréal with both Boston and New York, passing through Burlington, Montpelier, Rutland, White River Junction and Brattleboro. Other services link Stowe with Burlington, run from Newport in the north across to Portland in Maine, and cross the Green Mountains. *Amtrak* **trains** between Washington DC and Montréal stop at Brattleboro, White River Junction, Montpelier and Burlington – though not at convenient hours. The main **airport** is in Burlington.

Lake Champlain Ferries (☎864-9804) carry cars to New York at three points, including Burlington, and a six-minute ferry links Larrabee's Point with Ticonderoga further south. *Vermont Mountain Bike Tours* (PO Box 541, Pittsfield VT 05762; ☎746-8580) and *Vermont Bicycle Touring* (PO Box 711, Bristol VT 05433) both organise **cycle tours**.

The telephone **area code** for the entire state of Vermont is ☎802.

Southern Vermont

Of the two low-key towns at either end of Vermont's southern corridor – a mere forty miles from east to west and linked by Hwy-9 – **Brattleboro** has the atmosphere of a college town, but not the college, while **Bennington** has the college but not the atmosphere. The birthplace of Mormon prophet Brigham Young is marked by a monument at **Whitingham**, halfway between the two.

Brattleboro

If **BRATTLEBORO**, in the very southeast corner of the state, is your first taste of Vermont, it may come as a surprise. It's not the Fifties throwback you might expect, but owes its style more to the Sixties, with numerous little stores catering to the youthful and vaguely "alternative" population which has moved into the surrounding hills over the last two decades. The town's one unlikely claim to fame is that this was where **Rudyard Kipling** wrote his two *Jungle Books*.

Trains follow the river into town and stop behind the Old Railroad Station, which as the **Brattleboro Museum** (May–Oct Tues–Sun noon–6pm; $2) now displays locally made Estey organs and works of art. Buses, on the other hand, merely pick up and set down next to exit 3 off the interstate, a couple of miles north. Much the best place to **stay** is the art-deco *Latchis Hotel* at 50 Main Street (☎254-6300), where very nice rooms overlooking the river cost from $50. It has recently been restored, along with the **movie theater** next door, to which guests receive a free pass. The nearby *Common Ground Community Restaurant* at 25 Elliot Street (☎257-0855) is a long-established **wholefood restaurant**, run by a co-operative, serving international vegetarian specialities in a very pleasant glassed-in conservatory.

Bennington

Little has happened in **BENNINGTON** in the past two hundred years to match the excitement of the days when Ethan Allen's Green Mountain Boys were based here, known as the "Bennington Mob". A 306ft hilltop obelisk (April–Oct daily 9am–5pm; $1) commemorates the **Battle of Bennington** in August 1777, in which they were a crucial factor in defeating the British under General Burgoyne (though the battle itself was probably fought just across the border in New York).

About a mile north of the sleepy intersection at the town centre, three **covered bridges** cross the Walloomsac River. Walkers set out from the southern end of the Long Trail (see below) roughly five miles east. Students from the exclusive arts-oriented Bennington College crowd into the *Blue Benn* **diner** at 102 Hunt Street (☎442-8977), which has vegetarian dishes as well as traditional American diner-food. The *Fife'n'Drum* **motel** (☎442-4074), just south of town on US-7, has rooms from $46.

The Green Mountains

The **Green Mountains** which form the backbone of Vermont are not as harsh as New Hampshire's White Mountains, though the forests for which they are named are invariably buried in snow for most of the winter, and the higher roads are liable to be blocked for long periods. Here and there, denuded patches mark where trees have been shaved away to create ski-runs, but for the most part the usually peaceful Hwy-100 running up from the south offers unspoiled mountain views to either side.

In summer, hikers take up the challenge of the **Long Trail** along the central ridge, 264 miles from north to south. This pre-dates the Appalachian Trail, which now joins its southern portion, and was constructed by the **Green Mountain Club** (PO Box 889, Montpelier VT 05601; ☎223-3463). Their *Guide Book of the Long Trail* is invaluable.

Weston

One of the prettiest villages along Hwy-100 is **WESTON**, spreading beside a little river and centring on a perfect village green. A sombre stone slab on the green commemorates the seventeen soldiers from Weston who were killed on the same day during the Civil War, at Alexandria in Virginia – Vermont suffered the highest proportionate losses of any state in the Union. Nearby, the **Farrar-Mansur House** (July & Aug Wed–Sun 1.30–4.30pm; May, June, Sept & Oct Wed–Fri 1.30–4.30pm; $2) is an early tavern which has been restored to show the lives of early settlers, while the **Weston Playhouse** is typical of many little Vermont theatres, with summer performances of light comedies and musicals (Tues–Sun; ☎824-5288).

An assortment of stores selling antiques, toys and fudge is scattered up and down the main street. The spell is slightly broken when you enter the **Vermont Country Store** a few yards south of the green and realise just how vast – on the scale of Dr Who's *Tardis* – it is, artfully concealed behind its modest facade. It calls itself "the first revived country store in the US", and carries a wide range of vaguely rural and domestic articles; in fact the original *Weston Village Store* opposite is more authentic, if not quite as comprehensive. The **Weston Bowl Mill** on the north side of town has all sorts of finished and unfinished wooden items, including beautifully turned bowls.

Weston's nicest **accommodation** has to be the *1830 Inn on the Green* (☎824-6789), a lovely old house with just four guest rooms, costing from $60 to $80 for B&B. The *Colonial House* (☎824-6286), less than two miles south on Hwy-100, is a motel charging $60, and B&B at the three-room *Hillside* (☎875-3844) in Andover three miles northeast starts at $50. The *Bryant House* **restaurant** (closed Sun; ☎824-6287), two doors down from the *Vermont Country Store* and run by the same management, is a real delight. A magnificent old soda fountain dominates its 1887 mahogany bar, while the menu includes all sorts of country goodies – old-fashioned cream soda with real cream, "johnny cakes" of cornbread with molasses, you name it.

Killington

The ski resort area of **KILLINGTON**, in the centre of the Green Mountains halfway between Woodstock to the east and Rutland to the west, has grown out of nothing since 1957. Despite a permanent population of perhaps fifty, it's estimated that in season there are enough beds within twenty miles to accommodate over ten thousand people each night. The two main slopes are **Killington Peak** itself (for skiing information, ring ☎422-3333) and **Pico Peak** (☎775-4345).

During the winter, the Killington Access Road which climbs up from US-4 is jammed with lively bars and restaurants; most are closed in summer, though you can still take the **cable-car** (☎422-3333) up to the bleak summit, where there's an observation deck and a cafeteria. Several hiking routes meet here, including the Long and Appalachian Trails. The *Cortina Inn* (☎1-800/451-6108 or ☎773-3331) is one of several luxury **motels** on US-4 to offer reduced summer rates; in this instance, around $65.

The spartan clapboard hamlet of **PLYMOUTH**, ten miles south, was the birthplace of **Calvin Coolidge**, who was sworn in as President of the United States (by his father, the local JP) at 2.47am one August morning in 1923, upon receipt of the news of the death of the incumbent President Harding. When she heard of the famously taciturn Coolidge's own death, years later, Dorothy Parker remarked, "How could they tell?"

Woodstock

Since the 1790s, **WOODSTOCK**, a few miles west from the Connecticut River up US-4, has been a refined centre for Vermont's professional life. Hence the distinguished houses around its oval green, now largely taken over by antiques shops and tearooms. It should most certainly not be confused with Woodstock NY, of festival fame; the closest it came to radical action in the Sixties was to build a new covered bridge.

Both of Woodstock's two main paying attractions are geared towards seeing animals close up. Part of **Billings Farm and Museum** (May–Oct daily 10am–5pm; $6) is maintained as it was on the death of its former owner in 1890, while the rest is run as a modern dairy farm; the **Vermont Raptor Center** on Church Hill Road (summer Wed–Mon 10am–4pm; winter Mon & Wed–Sat 10am–4pm; $4) treats injured birds of prey.

An information booth on the Green in summer (☎457-1042) will help to find **accommodation**. The *Village Inn of Woodstock* at 41 Pleasant Street (☎457-1255) has B&B rooms from $55, and also serves dinner; rooms with shared bathroom in the small and very homely *Applebutter Inn* (☎457-4158), just east on US-4 in Taftsville, are $60. You don't have to be a $100-a-night guest at the riverside *Lincoln Inn* (☎457-3312), three miles west, to eat in its very reasonable dining room (Wed–Sun only); in Woodstock itself, the *Rumble Seat Rathskeller* (☎457-3609) is a bar and restaurant with an outside patio, serving snacks and full meals.

Quechee

In recent years, the grand houses on the hills around **QUECHEE**, eight miles west of Woodstock, have been joined by a proliferation of newly developed condos and second homes. It's all reasonably well landscaped, but a shame nonetheless, and adds nothing to the environs of **Quechee State Park**, which was fortunately created in time to spare the splendours of the **Quechee Gorge**. A delicate bridge spans the 165ft chasm of the Ottauquechee River, and hiking trails lead down through the fir trees, where you'll find one of Vermont's many state-run **campgrounds** (☎295-2990).

A waterfall on the river turns the turbines of **Simon Pearce Glass** (daily 9am–9pm; ☎295-1470), on Main Street in Quechee itself. Housed in a former woollen mill, this is an unusual combination of glass-blowing centre and restaurant, where you can watch bowls and pots being made, and then eat off them. Adventurous meals start at $12.

White River Junction

Probably the most exciting thing ever to happen in **WHITE RIVER JUNCTION** was the first use of laughing gas as an anaesthetic, in 1844. But it's an invaluable transport hub; weary *Amtrak* passengers stumble off trains at unearthly hours, straight onto N Main Street, and buses run east into New Hampshire – **Hanover** (see p.192) is just across the river – and west through Vermont.

A good old-fashioned railroad hotel still survives in the town centre, with good old-fashioned prices; clean rooms at the *Hotel Coolidge* at 17 S Main Street (☎295-3118) start at only $30, and its *Cashie's* restaurant is a bargain too. Call in at the *Catamount Brewery* down the road at 28 S Main Street (☎296-2248) to try their fresh-brewed real ale.

Montpelier and Barre

Another fifty miles north up I-89, **MONTPELIER** is the smallest state capital in the nation, with less than ten thousand inhabitants. The golden dome of the **Capitol** is appealing in its leafy gardens, but there's nothing very much to see. Copious information on accommodation possibilities, here and throughout the state, is available from the Vermont Travel Division at 134 State Street (Mon–Fri 7.45am–4.30pm, Sat 9am–3pm, Sun 11am–3pm; ☎828-3236); rooms at the *Vermonter Hotel* (☎479-9014), southeast on US-302, start at $35.

Students from the local New England Culinary Institute run both the *Elm Street Cafe* at 38 Elm Street (☎223-3188) and the more upmarket *Tubbs Restaurant* (☎229-9202) at 24 Elm Street, serving excellent and cheap – if somewhat experimental – dishes from all over the world. The *Horn of the Moon Cafe* at 8 Langdon Street (☎223-2895) is a wholefood bakery, while the menu at *Julio's* at 44 Main Street (☎229-9348) features all kinds of delicious Mexican specialities.

The immigrant stoneworkers of the adjacent town of **BARRE** (pronounced *BA-rie*) were at the turn of this century famed for their militancy. Their most enduring memorials are the gravestones they carved themselves, in **Mount Hope Cemetery** on Hwy-14, though the Scots among them did also erect a rather incongruous statue downtown of Robert Burns. Southeast of town, you can take a free look at the world's biggest granite quarry, the **Rock of Ages**, or pay for a twenty-minute ride on a little train (June–Oct). *Arnholm's* at 891 N Main Street (☎476-5921) is a $30 summer-only motel.

Waterbury

Guidebooks never paid much attention to **WATERBURY** before 1978; even then, the opening of a homemade ice cream stand on the forecourt of a gas station would not have excited much interest. However, **Ben & Jerry's Ice Cream Factory**, one mile north of I-89 in Waterbury Center, on the way up to Stowe, has grown so huge, so fast, that it is now the number-one tourist destination in Vermont. Half-hour tours (Mon–Sat 9am–4pm; $1) feature an audio-visual presentation, a chance to look down on the workforce from an observation platform, and a free scoop of the deliciously rich ice cream that made it all possible. You're then let loose in a massive gift shop.

Waterbury is the closest *Amtrak* stop to Stowe – the station is just south of the interstate – and *Vermont Transit* buses also pass through.

Stowe

There is still a beautiful nineteenth-century village at the heart of **STOWE**, with a white-spired meeting house and a green to stroll around, though a century's experience of catering to large crowds of skiers means that it has become rather swamped by malls full of fast-food outlets and equipment stores, and sprawling complexes of condos and resort facilities. Nonetheless, the setting remains spectacular, at the foot of Vermont's highest mountain, the 4393ft **Mount Mansfield**.

Hwy-108, known as **Mountain Road**, leads close to the mountain through the dramatic **Smugglers' Notch**, which is closed by snow through the winter. Weather permitting, you can get to the very top either by driving up the **Toll Road** which starts seven miles up (May to mid-Oct daily 9.30am–5pm; $8 per car), or by taking the **Gondola** (June–Oct 9am–5pm; $10; ☎253-7311) up to Cliff House, and hiking for another half-hour from there. Vermont's **State Ski Dorm** is on Mountain Road just past the foot of the Toll Road (☎253-4010). In summer, when it doubles up as an AYH **youth hostel**, dorm beds are just $12; in winter the $40 charge includes dinner and breakfast.

What really made Stowe's name as a **cross-country ski** resort was its connection with the **von Trapp family**, of *Sound of Music* fame. After fleeing Austria during the war, they established the *Trapp Family Lodge* on Luce Hill Road (☎253-8511). The original lodge, where Maria von Trapp held her singing camps, has burned down, and she herself died in 1987, but a new and equally luxurious building has taken its place – rooms in winter start at around $200. If you don't want to pay that sort of money, drop in at their *Austrian Tea Room* for some incredibly heavy Germanic cakes and pastries.

Stowe's plentiful **accommodation** options, mostly on Mountain Road, include the *Stoweflake Inn* (☎1-800/782-9009 or ☎253-7355), where rooms start at $75; the *Golden Kitz* (☎253-4217), $60 in winter dropping to $30 in summer; and the small *Charbonneau Guest House* (☎253-7701), $35 and up. Summer rates at the historic 1833 *Green Mountain Inn* (☎1-800/445-6629 or ☎253-7301) in the town centre start at $80, rising to $100 during the foliage and skiing seasons. The *Gold Brook* **campground** is two miles south of town on Hwy-100 (☎253-7683). The sunken lounge of *Hapeltons* (☎253-4653) on Hwy-100 is a nice place for a snack and a drink, and very snug in winter.

For **skiing information**, contact Mount Mansfield (☎253-7311) or Smuggler's Notch (☎1-800/451-8752 or ☎664-8851). **Bikes** can be rented from the *Mountain Bike Shop* on Mountain Road (☎253-7919).

Lake Champlain

The 150-mile long **LAKE CHAMPLAIN**, which forms the boundary between the states of New York and Vermont, and just nudges its way into Canada in the north, never exceeds twelve miles in width. Across the water from the flatlands of the Champlain Valley, the impassive Adirondacks are always visible, looming up in the west. The first white man to see the lake, Samuel de Champlain in 1609, who named it in his own honour, was also the first to claim that it held a sinuous Loch-Ness-style monster. "Champ" is now familiar as an informal symbol of the region.

The life and soul of the valley is the French-influenced city of **Burlington**, whose long-standing trade connections with Montréal have filled it with elegant nineteenth-century architecture. Within just a few miles of the centre, US-2 leads north onto the supremely rural **Champlain Isles**, covered in meadows and orchards.

Lake Champlain Ferries (☎864-9804) cross the lake from Vermont to New York from **Burlington** (to Port Kent; hourly; $12); **Charlotte** (to Essex; hourly; $7); and **Grand Isle** (to Plattsburgh; year-round, every 20min; $7). All these rates are for cars plus driver; foot passengers are much cheaper.

Burlington

Lakeside **BURLINGTON**, Vermont's largest "city", is one of the most purely enjoyable towns in New England, a relaxed and open-minded fusion of Montréal, eighty miles away to the north, and Boston, over two hundred miles southeast. In fact, from its earliest days Burlington looked as much to Canada as to the south. Shipping connections with the St Lawrence River were far easier than the land routes across the mountains, and the harbour became a major supply centre. The city's founding fathers included Ethan Allen and family – far from being some impoverished Robin Hood figure, Ethan was a wealthy landowner, and his brother Ira set up the University of Vermont.

Burlington today is the definitive youthful, outward-looking university town. From the bandstands to the brew pubs, this is simply a nice place to be. It's one of the few American cities to offer something approaching a cafe society, with a downtown you can stroll around on foot, and plenty of open-air terraces. Politically too it's unusual; Bernard Saunders, the former socialist mayor of Burlington, was in 1990 elected to the House of Representatives from Vermont – the first political independent to go to Congress in forty years.

Arrival and information

Vermont Transit **buses** come right into downtown Burlington at the corner of St Paul and Main streets, beside City Hall Park, but the *Amtrak* station is an inconvenient five miles north, in the small community of Essex Junction (connecting buses every half-hour; 1$). The airport is two miles out along US-2, in the same general direction.

Practical **information** is available from the **visitor centre** at 209 Battery Street (July–Sept Mon–Fri 8.30am–5pm, Sat & Sun 10am–2pm; Oct–June Mon–Fri 8.30am–5pm; ☎863-3489). You can rent **bikes** from *Ski Rack* at 85 Main Street (☎658-3313).

Lake Champlain Ferries (see above) leave from the jetty at the end of King Street; daytime and sunset sightseeing cruises on the Spirit of Ethan Allen (☎862-9685; $8) set out from nearby Perkins Pier at the end of Maple Street.

The Town

Your natural inclination on setting out to explore Burlington might be to head for the **waterfront**. In fact, that's surprisingly undeveloped, though Battery Park at its northern end makes a good place to watch the sun go down over the Adirondacks – especially when there's a band playing, as there often is at weekends.

A better target is the pedestrianised **Church Street Marketplace**, a few blocks back, which is where Burlington's finest old buildings, and all its modern cafes and boutiques, are to be found. The free **Robert Hull Fleming Museum** on Colchester Avenue (Tues–Fri 9am–4pm, Sun 1–5pm) has an interesting collection of art and artefacts from all over the world, including pre-Columbian pieces, while back at Essex Junction, the stimulating **Discovery Museum** near the river at 51 Park Street (July & Aug Tues–Sat 10am–4.30pm, Sun 1–4.30pm; otherwise Tues–Fri & Sun 1–4.30pm, Sat 10am–4.30pm; $2.50) aims to excite children's interests in science and nature.

The Shelburne Museum

Hwy-7 in Shelburne, three miles south of Burlington. Mid-May to mid-Oct daily 9am–5pm. ☎985-3344. Adults $15, kids $5. Tickets are valid for two successive days.

The remarkable **SHELBURNE MUSEUM** just south of Burlington should not be missed. In fact you'll need to allow a whole day, if not more, fully to appreciate this fifty-acre collection of pure unalloyed **Americana**, created in 1947 by heiress Electra Webb. At its centre, her parents' collection of French Impressionist paintings, including works by Degas and Monet, is displayed in a meticulous reconstruction of their New York apartment. However, Electra's own interests ranged far wider, and she put together what is probably the nation's finest celebration of its inventive past.

After a brief film show, you're free to wander around more than thirty buildings, some original and some newly constructed, focusing on aspects of American everyday life over the past two centuries and mostly staffed by well-informed attendants happy to share their expertise. The village includes a General Store, complete with painted "**cigar store Indians**", an apothecary, an early print shop, a doctor's, a dentist's and a blacksmith's. There's a **Shaker barn**, a schoolhouse, a meeting house, a covered bridge, a railroad station, and even an enormous **steam paddle-wheeler** from Lake Champlain, the *SS Ticonderoga*, with its own rock-surrounded lighthouse. All are furnished as appropriate, and filled with relevant exhibits; the purpose-built **circus museum** for example has a colourful array of carousel animals.

Accommodation

Burlington has no shortage of affordable accommodation, and for **camping** the lake-side *Northbeach Campsites* (☎862-0942) is less than two miles north on Institute Road.

Ho-Hum Motel, 1660 Williston Rd (☎863-4551). Three miles east of downtown on US-2, with $50 rooms. Also at 1200 Shelburne Rd (☎658-1314), three miles south on US-7, rooms $55.

Mrs Farrell's Home Hostel (AYH), 27 Arlington Court (☎865-3730). A few dorm beds. $10 members, $12 others. Three miles out from the centre.

North Shore B&B, 251 Staniford Rd (☎862-2781). Small lakeside B&B three miles north of downtown on North Avenue bus route. $40 rooms.

Queen City Inn & Motel, 428 Shelburne Rd, South Burlington (☎864-4220). Inn rooms from $50, motel rooms from $40.

YWCA, 278 Main St (☎862-7520). Women-only budget accommodation. Dorms $8, doubles $18.

Eating, Drinking and Entertainment

The presence of ten thousand students during term-time means that Burlington offers any number of cheap and good restaurants, as well as some pretty raucous nightspots.

Bourbon Street Grill, 213 College St (☎865-2800). Crowded and dimly lit. Cajun specials from $8.

Five Spice Café, 175 Church St (☎864-4045). Excellent Asian food. Dim sum and vegetarian.

The Front, 89 Main St (☎658-5631). Student-oriented venue for comedy, jazz, and "indie" bands.

Lazy Dog Deli & Café, 55 Main St (865-0551). Trendy, laid-back snack bar, with great smoothies.

Oasis Diner, 189 Bank St (☎864-5308). Friendly, authentic chrome and leatherette steel-tube diner.

Vermont Pub and Brewery, 144 College St (☎865-0500). Roomy and convivial brew pub. Free little tasters of their various beers – *Dogbite Bitter* is the best – plus a good menu and live music.

MAINE

As big as the other five New England states combined, **MAINE** has barely the population of Rhode Island. In principle, therefore, there's plenty of room for its massive summer influx of visitors; in practice, the majority of these make for the southern stretches of the extravagantly corrugated **coast**. You only really begin to appreciate the size and space of the state further north, or **inland**, where vast tracts of mountainous forests are dotted with lakes, and barely pierced by roads – ideal territory for hiking and canoeing (and spotting the occasional moose).

Although Maine is in many ways inhospitable – the **Algonquin** called it "Land of the Frozen Ground" – it has been in contact with Europe ever since the **Vikings**, around 1000 AD. For the navigator Verrazzano, in 1524, the "crudity and evil manners" of the Indians made this the "Land of Bad People", but before long European fishermen were setting up camps each summer to dry their catch. Francis Bacon in turn said the English were "worse than the very Savages, impudently lying with their Women, teaching their men to drink drunke, and . . . to fall together by the eares".

North America's first agricultural **colonies** were in Maine: de Champlain's **French** Protestants near Mount Desert Island in 1604, and an **English** group which survived one winter at the mouth of the Kennebec three years later. In the face of the unwillingness of subsequent English settlers to let them farm in peace, the local Indians formed a long-term alliance with the French, and until as late as 1700 regularly drove out streams of impoverished English refugees. By 1764, however, the official census could claim that even Maine's black population was more numerous than its Native Americans.

At first considered part of Massachusetts, Maine only became a separate entity in 1820, when the Missouri Compromise made Maine a Free and Missouri a Slave state. In the nineteenth century, its people had a reputation for conservativism and resistance to immigration, manifested in anti-Irish riots. Today, the **economy** remains heavily based on the sea, although many of those who fish also farm, and long expeditions are rare. Recently they have even been selling their catch direct to Russian factory ships anchored just offshore. Lobster fishing in particular has defied gloomy predictions and has boomed again since 1988, as evidenced by the many thriving **lobster pounds**.

In winter, most of Maine is under ice; summer is short and usually heralded in early June by an infestation of tiny black flies. Autumn colours begin to spread from the north in late September – when, unlike elsewhere in New England, off-season prices apply.

Getting Around Maine

The vast majority of visitors to Maine **drive**. Much the most enjoyable route to follow is US-1, which runs within a few miles of the coast all the way to Canada, with innumerable side turnings leading to hidden seaside villages. If you're in a hurry, I-95, initially the (tolled) Maine Turnpike, offers speedy access to Portland and on to Augusta and Bangor. In the **interior**, the roads are quiet and the views spectacular, nowhere more so than as you approach Mount Katahdin in the north. Many of the roads belong to the lumber companies, who keep careful track of who you are and where you're going (and charge you for the privilege). At any time of year bad weather can render these roads suddenly impassable; be sure to check before setting off.

Public transport on the other hand falls a long way short of meeting travellers' needs. The six-times-daily *Greyhound* service from Boston to Portland, three of which continue to Bangor, at least links the main towns of the southern coast, but that's about all there is. Except in high summer, you can't even get a bus any nearer to Acadia National Park or Bar Harbor than Bangor, and nothing at all runs north. Sadly, in a state which once built its industry and tourism on its railroads, there is no longer any *Amtrak* service. A Canadian train runs across the middle of the state to reach New Brunswick, but doesn't connect anywhere useful within Maine itself.

The telephone **area code** for the entire state of Maine is ☎207.

The Maine Coast

Considering that the state has a coastline of three thousand miles, finding access to the sea in Maine can be a frustrating business. The oceanfront is monopolised by an endless succession of private homes and vacation residences – most famously that of President Bush at Kennebunkport. In fact, only two percent of the shore is publicly owned – and not all of that is beach. Rather than long walks on coastal footpaths, travellers should expect attractive if rather commercial harbour villages, linked by roads which are mostly set well back from the water and packed with diners, motels, and factory outlets.

Europeans tend to find the landscape pretty, but not strikingly different to the Atlantic coast back home, and occasionally a bit too well manicured. The liveliest destinations are **Portland** and **Bar Harbor** (at the edge of **Acadia National Park**); there's a wide choice of smaller seaside towns, such as **Belfast** and **Wiscasset**, if you're looking for a more peaceful base. **Beaches** are more common (and the sea is warmer) further south, for example at **Ogunquit**.

The best way to see the coast itself must be by **boat**; ferries and excursions operate from even the smallest harbours, with major routes including the ferries to **Canada** from Portland and Bar Harbor, and the shorter trips to **Monhegan** and **Vinalhaven** Islands from Boothbay Harbor and Rockland respectively.

South of Portland

I-95 crosses from Portsmouth, New Hampshire (see p.185) into an area of Maine so dense with little communities that Mark Twain alleged one couldn't "throw a brick without danger of disabling a postmaster". Three miles over the border, an **information centre** at **Kittery** provides copious details for the whole state (daily summer 8am–9pm; winter 9am–5pm; ☎439-1319).

If you avoid the tolls on the interstate and follow US-1 instead, you'll soon find yourself in **YORK**, which was in 1639 the first English city to be chartered in North America. Its seventeenth-century **Old Gaol** now serves as a museum, commemorating its own past and also that of the local Native Americans.

Ogunquit

The three-mile spit of sand which shields **OGUNQUIT** from the open ocean is Maine's finest **beach**, but the town remains small enough to be a pleasant resort, popular with Boston's **gay** community. The summer season at the *Ogunquit Playhouse* (☎646-5511) usually attracts a few big-name performers. Among dozens of **motels** is the summer-only *Holiday House* (☎646-5020), where rooms cost $40 to $70. The Marginal Way, a not very rural clifftop path, leads from central Ogunquit to **Perkins Cove** a mile south, where the well-priced **seafront restaurants** include *Barnacle Billy's* (☎646-5575).

Kennebunkport

KENNEBUNKPORT was perfectly happy as a self-contained and exclusive residential district, before its worldwide exposure as the home of **George Bush**'s "summer White House". If anything, locals seem to feel that George has lowered the tone of the place by becoming president. There have been complaints at having to bear the extra cost of policing (the far smaller and poorer Plains, Georgia, home of Jimmy Carter, paid up with pride), and talk of a "lower class" of gawking visitor clogging the streets and driving the old money away. Things do get pretty crowded when the president's around; the press corps push accommodation prices right up, and souvenir sellers descend in force. However, Kennebunkport is not actually all that different from anywhere else along the coast – which is presumably what's bothering the locals. The best place to hang out (and eat seafood) is *Alisson's* at 5 Dock Square (☎967-4841), where dinner is served until 10pm, and the bar stays open until 1am. There's no great point paying in-town hotel rates when there are so many motels along the highways.

For those shameless souls who can't resist a quick peep, the **presidential compound** is reached by following Ocean Avenue – a nice drive in its own right – out to Walker's Point. The house itself is surprisingly accessible, at least when there's no one home, but of course secret service agents stop anyone who approaches too close. **Cruise boats** from Kennebunkport (☎967-5955) now combine whale-watching trips with a leisurely look at the compound from the sea.

Five miles south of Portland is the **Cape Elizabeth lighthouse**, commissioned by George Washington in 1791 and familiar from postcards and posters. The *Lobster Shack* (☎799-1677) just below the light (and above the horn) serves cheap fresh seafood.

Portland

The largest city in Maine, **PORTLAND** was founded in 1632 in a superb position on the Casco Bay Peninsula, and quickly prospered, building ships and exporting the great inland pines for use as masts. A long line of wooden **wharves** stretched along the seafront, with the merchants' houses on the hillside above. From the earliest days it was a cosmopolitan city, with a large free black population who traditionally worked as longshoremen; there was great bitterness when Irish immigrants began to displace them in the 1830s. When the **railroads** came, the Canada Trunk Line had its terminus right on Portland's quayside, bringing the produce of Canada and the Great Plains one hundred miles closer to Europe than it would be at any other major US port. Some of the wharves are now taken up by new condo developments, though **Custom House Wharf** remains much as it must have looked when Anthony Trollope passed through in 1861 and said "I doubt whether I ever saw a town with more evident signs of prosperity". Most of the town he saw was destroyed by an accidental **fire** in 1866 (Indians in 1675, and the British in 1775, had previously burned Portland deliberately).

Grand Trunk Station was torn down in 1966, and downtown Portland appeared to be in terminal decline until a group of committed residents undertook the energetic redevelopment of the area now known as **Old Port Exchange**. Their success has revitalised the city, keeping it at the heart of Maine life – but you shouldn't expect a hive of energy. Portland is simply a pleasant, sophisticated, and in places very attractive town, not a major urban centre.

Arrival and Information

Both I-95 and US-1 skirt the promontory of Portland, within a very few miles of the city centre; **Portland International Jetport** (☎779-7301) is next to I-95, and connected with downtown by regular city buses. Driving into the city, Congress Street is the main central thoroughfare, while Fore Street runs along the harbour just to the south. *Greyhound*'s coastal services (around six daily to Boston, three northwards to Bangor and, in summer, Bar Harbor) arrive at 950 Congress Street (☎772-6587), at the eastern edge of downtown; there is no *Amtrak* service.

Between mid-May and October, the Prince of Fundy Company's *Scotia Prince* **ferry** leaves Portland for **Yarmouth** in Nova Scotia at 9pm each evening, returning the next day. The standard high-season fare is $93 car, $68 adult, $34 children, extra for a cabin, though there are various discount and excursion fares (details on ☎775-5616, ☎1-800/482-0955 in Maine, ☎1-800/341-7540 elsewhere).

Downtown Portland is compact enough to stroll around, though there are also buses and trolleys if you need them, and you can rent a **bicycle** from *Portland Bicycle Exchange*, 396 Fore Street (☎772-4137). The **Convention and Visitors Bureau** is near the Art Museum at 142 Free Street (Mon–Fri 9am–5pm; ☎772-4994).

The City

Thanks to the various fires, not all that much of old Portland survives, though various grand mansions can be seen along Congress and Danforth streets. The **Wadsworth-Longfellow House** at 485 Congress Street was Portland's first brick house when built in 1785 by Peleg Wadsworth, but owes its fame primarily to Peleg's grandson, the poet Henry Longfellow, who spent his boyhood here. Tours start every hour on the hour and last around 45 minutes (June to mid-Sept Tues–Sat 10am–4pm; $3).

The **Portland Museum of Art** at 7 Congress Square is a much more modern affair, built in 1988 by the I. M. Pei partnership (Tues, Weds, Fri & Sat 10am–5pm, Thurs 10am–9pm, Sun noon–5pm; $3.50, free Thurs 5–9pm). There are superb views out over the bay from all parts of the museum, including some through porthole windows; indeed on occasions the collection seems subordinate to the design, which does not allow much room for extensive displays. Normally the lower storeys are occupied by temporary exhibitions – though there's a lovely open-air garden cafe as well – while the works upstairs include a lively and flirtatious set of 1880s Winslow Homer engravings, some Andrew Wyeths, and an array of early nineteenth-century European ceramics commemorating heroes of the American Revolution.

For relaxed wandering, the restored **Old Port Exchange** near the quayside is quite entertaining, with all sorts of antiquarian shops, specialist book and music stores (particularly on Exchange Street), and other esoterica. Several companies operate **boat trips** from the nearby wharves, including *Bay View Cruises* of the harbour and bay from Fisherman's Wharf (daily in summer, 90min trips for $8; ☎761-0496), and **whale-watching** on the *Odyssey* from Long Wharf (weekends late May–early Oct, daily in high summer; ☎642-3270). *Casco Bay Lines* offer a twice-daily mailboat all year, and additional cruises in summer, to six of the innumerable **Calendar Islands** in Casco Bay, from their terminal at Commercial and Franklin streets ($8 adult, $4 child; ☎774-7871). **Long**, **Peaks** and **Cliff islands** all have accommodation or camping.

If you follow Portland's waterfront to the end of the peninsula, the **Eastern Promenade**, which became almost exclusively residential after the last fire, is remarkably peaceful so close to downtown. There's a big beach below the headland, while at the top of Munjoy Hill above is the eight-sided shingled 1807 **Portland Observatory** (June Fri–Sun 1–5pm, July–Labor Day Wed–Sun noon–5pm). If you're heading east along the coast, leave Portland over Tukey's Bridge at the end of the Promenade.

Accommodation

Finding a room in Portland is no great problem, though you can expect to pay more to stay in town than in the **budget motels** around exit 8 off I-95. The closest (summer-only) **campground** is *Wassamki Springs* (☎839-4276) off Hwy-114 towards Westbrook.

Hotel Everett, 51A Oak St (☎773-7882). Two blocks from the Wadsworth-Longfellow House, and popular with young long-term residents, with daily summer rates of $38–50.

Sonesta, 157 High St (☎775-5411). Upwards of $100 for luxury central accommodation.

Susse Chalet, 340 Park Ave (☎871-0611). Good-value doubles $48–50 on the western edge of the peninsula near the Maine Medical Center.

Susse Chalet, 1200 Brighton Ave (☎774-6101). At Exit 8 from I-95, and slightly cheaper at $43.

YMCA, 70 Forest Ave (☎874-1105). Men-only hostel accommodation north of Congress St near Deering Oaks Park. $20 per night, $65 per week, cash only and unfortunately often full.

YWCA, 87 Spring St (☎874-1130). Very near the Museum of Art, women-only, charging $25 single, or $20 per bed in a double room.

Eating

Not only is Portland rich in affordable **restaurants**, but most of its entertainment venues and bars, listed under a separate heading below, serve food as well.

Amigos, 9 Dana St (☎772-0772). Good Mexican dinners for around $10, in a distinctive large clapboard property very near the port.

Baker's Table, 434 Fore St (☎775-0303). A wooden-table cafe at lunchtime, costing $4–7, with open-air tables at the rear on Wharf St, which becomes a formal tablecloth restaurant in the evening, entrees $10–16. The clams steamed in *Bass Ale* are recommended.

Boone's, 6 Custom House Wharf (☎774-5725). Traditional waterfront restaurant in old wharf buildings, overlooking the fishing docks. Good lobster and broiled seafood in general. $12–20.

Fresh Market, 58 Market St (☎773-7146). All kinds of fresh pasta and noodles, including ginger and squid's ink, at reasonable prices ($7–10).

Hu-Shang, 29 Exchange St (☎733-0300) and 7–13 Brown St (☎774-0800). Deservedly popular Chinese restaurants. A good lunch at either can easily cost under $8.

Raffles Cafe Bookstore, 555 Congress St (☎761-3930). Wholefood cafe and bookshop.

Raphael's, 36 Market St (☎773-4500). Good but slightly pricey ($15 or more) northern Italian food, in the same premises as *Little Willie's Lounge*, a no-cover comedy and jazz bar.

Nightlife and Entertainment

In addition to the pubs and clubs below, more formal entertainment possibilities range from the tiny and adventurous *Mad Horse Theatre Company* at 955 Forest Avenue (☎797-3338) up to the large productions at the Portland Performing Arts Center, 25A Forest Avenue (☎774-0465). The free *Casco Bay Weekly* has listings of all local events; Maine's biggest gigs each summer take place roughly ten miles south of Portland at **Old Orchard Beach**.

Cafe No, 20 Danforth St (☎772-8114). Part wholefood cafe and part secondhand bookshop, which puts on live jazz and folk at weekends, in a building mostly taken up by artists' studios. Closed Mon.

Gritty McDuff's, 396 Fore St (☎772-2739). Portland's first brew pub, making *Portland Head Pale Ale* and *Black Fly Stout*. Food, folk music, long wooden benches, and a friendly (if a little self-consciously British) atmosphere, which gets rowdy on a Saturday night.

Raoul's Roadside Attraction, 865 Forest Ave(☎773-6886). Music venue – R&B, punk, reggae, etc – which is also a restaurant with vegetarian specials, one mile from downtown.

Three Dollar Dewey's, 135 Fore St. Raucous beer hall, with a wide selection of draft beers.

Zootz, 31 Forest Ave (☎773-8187). "Progressive" dance club hosting world-beat discos and concerts.

North Along the Coast from Portland

The coastal towns immediately north of Portland are no less commercialised than those to the south; **Freeport** for example is one long shopping mall, albeit a good one. However, soon after **Brunswick** I-95 veers away inland towards Augusta (see p.212), and US-1 is left to run on alone parallel to the ocean. Things become much less frenetic, and prices a whole lot cheaper; even on the main road you find pleasant communities like **Bath** and **Belfast**, while the many headlands can be even more peaceful. There's really no need to race the full 160 miles to Acadia National Park in one go.

Freeport

The current prosperity of **FREEPORT**, fifteen miles north of Portland, rests on the invention by Leon L Bean, in 1912, of a particularly ugly rubber-soled fishing boot. That original boot is still selling, and **LL Bean's** has grown into an enormous clothing store on Main Street which literally never closes. In theory, that's so pre-dawn hunting expeditions can stock up; all the relevant equipment is available for rent or sale, and the store runs regular workshops to teach hunting, fishing and backcountry lore. However, with the outdoor look in vogue (President Bush's "preppy" style may have something to do with it), *LL Bean's* is now more of a fashion emporium. Freeport has expanded to welcome its 2.5 million annual customers a year with a mile-long strip of top-name **factory outlets** along US-1, most of which do offer genuine reductions against usual shop prices (though at coastal North Hampton, New Hampshire, you'll find much the same selection without Maine's hefty sales tax).

Freeport is not an ideal place to stay – everything falls quiet once the shoppers have gone home. However, the *Harraseeket Inn* at 162 Main Street (☎1-800/342-6423 or ☎865-9377) is a wonderful clapboard B&B inn, even if rooms do cost upwards of $100.

For a complete change of pace, head a mile south of Freeport to the sea, where the *Harraseeket Lunch & Lobster Co* (☎865-4888), extending on its wooden jetty into the peaceful bay, makes a great outdoor lunch spot. The very green promontory visible just across the water is **Wolfe's Neck Woods State Park**. In summer, for $1, you can follow hiking and nature trails along the unspoiled fringes of the headland.

Brunswick

Only a few miles further on from Freeport is **BRUNSWICK**, home since 1802 of the private Bowdoin College. Free tours of the college itself take in the intriguing **Peary-Macmillan Arctic Museum** (Tues–Fri 10am–4pm, Sat 10am–5pm, Sun 2–5pm). After decades of controversy, experts are now generally agreed that former student Admiral Robert Peary really was the first man to reach the North Pole in 1909; whatever the truth, his assembled equipment and notebooks have a powerful fascination.

It was while her husband Calvin was teaching here in the early 1850s that Harriet Beecher Stowe wrote *Uncle Tom's Cabin*, a book whose portrait of slavery had such an impact that Lincoln is said to have greeted her with the words "so this is the little lady that made this big war". The rambling old **Harriet Beecher Stowe House** at 63 Federal Street (☎725-5543) is now a B&B; guests can use the lounge of the original house, but stay in modern motel rooms around the back, for around $70 per night.

Rooms at the *Mainline Motel*, 133 Pleasant Street (☎725-8761), start in summer at $60, and the *Great Impasta* at 42 Maine Street(☎729-5858) serves excellent Italian **food** at reasonable prices. The ideal moment to visit Brunswick would be on Labor Day Weekend, when the town hosts a **Bluegrass Festival** (☎725-6009) a little way on at Thomas Point Beach, reached by following Hwy-24 from Cook's Corner. On the same road, there's a well-equipped oceanfront **campground** (☎833-5595) at **Orrs Island**.

Bath

The small town of **BATH** has an exceptionally long history of **shipbuilding**; the first vessel to be constructed and launched here was the *Virginia* in 1607, by Sir George Popham's short-lived colony. **Bath Iron Works**, founded in 1833, attracted job-seeking Irishmen in such numbers as to provoke a mob of anti-immigrant "Know-Nothings" to burn down the local Catholic church in July 1854. The works continue to produce ships – during World War II, more destroyers were built here than in all Japan – and only admit visitors for special occasions such as ceremonial launchings. However, at the **Maine Maritime Museum** two miles south of town on US-1, you can tour a function-ing shipyard where apprentices still learn to build wooden schooners using traditional techniques (May–Oct daily 10am–5pm; $6 adults, $3 kids; ☎443-1316).

As you head up the coast, **accommodation** starts to be better value. *Glad II* at 60 Pearl Street (☎442-1191) is a small (and non-smoking) B&B very near the museum, charging from $38 for a double room. West of town on Bath Road, the *New Meadows Inn* (☎443-3921) is similarly priced, as well as serving good basic meals, and has four-person cottages from $58. The *Bakke B&B*, on Foster Point Road in West Bath (☎442-7185), is tiny and very friendly, offering just one suite of two bedrooms for around $60.

The *Soup to Nuts Cafe* at 191 Water Street (☎442-7234) is a cheap vegetarian lunch place, while the *Harbor Lights Cafe*, 166 Front Street (☎443-9883), is a Mexican restaurant putting on live music at weekends. *Montsweag Restaurant* (☎443-6563), on US-1 in **Woolwich** just to the east, is a very cheap and lively seafood place, open for both lunch and dinner but closing very early in the evenings.

Wiscasset and Boothbay Harbor

WISCASSET, ten miles on from Bath, is dominated by the bridge which carries US-1 over the Sheepscot River. In the shallow waters of its narrow and picturesque bay lie two forlorn **shipwrecks**, the *Luther Little* and the *Hesper*, all that remains of the last four-masted schooners in the world. As good a view of them as any is to be had from the seafood restaurant *Le Garage*, on Water Street (☎882-5409). One can only hope that the large nuclear power station south of town on Hwy-144 – the scene in 1991 of what was said to be a very minor accident – proves more robust.

Cheap accommodation possibilities in the area include the down-to-earth summer-only *Whitfield Motel*, three miles south on US-1 (☎882-7137), where rooms cost from $35, or the private lakeside **campground** *Downeast Family Camping* (☎882-5431), at Gardiner Pond, four miles north on Hwy-27, with its cathedral stand of Norway pines.

For no very obvious reason, **BOOTHBAY HARBOR** at the southern tip of Hwy-27 has become one of Maine's most crowded resorts. Don't plan to stay here, but if you're passing by, the *Lobstermen's Coop* at 99 Atlantic Avenue (☎633-4900) dishes up ultra-fresh lobsters at minimal prices.

Moody's Diner (☎236-3391) in **Waldoboro**, back on the main road east, is a long-standing haunt of police and truckers, open 24 hours and oozing nostalgia.

Rockland and Vinalhaven

ROCKLAND, where US-1 reaches Penobscot Bay roughly halfway between Portland and Bar Harbor, is the world's largest distributor of **lobsters**, and holds the Maine Lobster Festival over the first weekend of August. One of the best of its traditional lobster pounds is *Miller's* (☎594-7406), on the shore of Wheeler's Bay in an isolated cove at Spruce Head on Hwy-73, which is open from 10am until 7pm in season, for succulent lobsters and steamers.

Between two and four **ferries** run daily throughout the year from Rockland to the island of **Vinalhaven**, which has one or two inns (but no campgrounds), a few shops, a museum and an impressive lighthouse; slightly fewer serve neighbouring **North Haven**. The boats do carry cars, though the chance to hike is what attracts most visitors. The *Maine State Ferry Service* at 517A Main Street (☎596-2202) has full schedules; they also operate several daily services from **Lincolnville**, north of Rockport, across to **Islesboro** and the **campground** (☎289-3824) on tiny Warren Island.

Camden and Rockport

The adjacent communities of **CAMDEN** and **ROCKPORT** only split into two separate towns in 1891, over a dispute as to who should pay for a new bridge over the Goose River between them. Rockport was at that time a major lime-producer, but a fire at the kilns in 1907 not only put an end to that business but also destroyed the ice-houses which were the town's other main source of income. Now it's a slightly dowdy place, outdone by the much prettier Camden in the competition for tourists.

Camden's speciality is organising sailing expeditions of up to six days in the large schooners known as **windjammers**. Vessels include the *Stephen Taber* (70 Elm Street; ☎236-3520 or ☎1-800/999-7352) and the *Roseway* (PO Box 696X; ☎236-4449). Among busy eating and drinking spots in town are *Cappy's Chowder House* at 1 Main Street (☎236-2254) and *Gilbert's Publick House* on Sharps Wharf (☎236-4320), which has pool tables. The *Maine Stay*, 22 High Street (☎236-9636) is an 1813 white clapboard inn where single rooms start at $55 and doubles at $65, and there's a cinema (☎236-8722) on Bay View Street.

Belfast

Homely **BELFAST** feels like the most lived-in and liveable of the towns along the Maine coast. Here the shipbuilding boom is long since over, but the inhabitants have had the waterfront declared an historic district, sparing it from over-commercialisation and condominium development. As a result, Belfast – early inhabitants tossed a coin to decide between that name and "Londonderry" – is a relaxing place to spend a bit of time, and one with a marked community spirit.

As you stroll around Belfast and its assortment of antique and curio shops, look out for the old-fashioned *Greyhound* and *Western Union* office on the high street (complete with juke-box and wooden seating), and the *Cranberry Tiger* **ice cream shop** (☎338-3531) at 60 Main Street. If love for your product is anything to go by, the claims of Woody, its owner, to make the best ice cream in the world are entirely credible. He'll be happy to demonstrate the entire process – and perhaps show you the bright red fire engine he's done up as a mobile ice cream factory.

The **information office** (☎338-2896) at the foot of Main Street by the sea is next to the old **railroad station** used by the *Belfast and Moosehead Lake Railroad* (☎338-2931). Hour-long excursions in reconditioned Pullman cars run from here up the lush banks of the Passagassawakeag River, along track laid in 1870 to connect logging operations with the sea – though whatever impression you might get from their advertisements, the trains are pulled by diesel not steam. En route to the villages of Brooks and Burnham Junction, you pass through thick forests, at their most colourful in autumn. The fall foliage can also be admired from the daily **sea cruises** out of Belfast – a $12 trip on the *Sea Spirit* (☎338-5191) gives a three-hour stopover in the photogenic village of **CASTINE** across the bay – or even an **air tour** with *Ace Aviation* ($8 per person for 15min, $16 for 30min, $32 for 1hr; ☎338-2970).

Also right beside the rail terminal, *Weathervane's* seafood **restaurant** (☎338-1774) has some tables on the wooden jetty outside. *Rollie's Cafe* back up the hill at 37 Main Street (☎338-9872) is a rough-and-ready bar and burger joint open until 1am every day of the year. For **accommodation**, the *Hiram Alden Inn* at 19 Church Street (☎338-2151) is a beautiful 1840 Greek Revival house run as a B&B by the genial Jim Lovejoy; rooms with shared bathrooms start at $35 for a single and $50 for a double. The *Horatio Johnson House*, 36 Church Street (☎338-5153), is similarly priced, while the three rooms in the *Kingsbury House*, 35 Northport Avenue (☎338-2419), go for $50 including a macrobiotic breakfast.

While you're in the area, it's worth tuning into the mildly offbeat local **radio station** *WERU*, which broadcasts on 89.9FM from the rather snooty resort of **Blue Hill**.

Mount Desert Island

Considering that five million visitors come to **Mount Desert Island** each year, that it contains most of New England's only National Park, and that it boasts not only a genuine fjord but also the highest headland on the entire Atlantic coast north of Rio de Janeiro, it is quite an astonishingly small place, measuring just sixteen miles by thirteen. It is of course simply one among innumerable rugged granite islands along the Maine coast; the reason to come here is that it is the most accessible, linked to the mainland by bridge since 1836, and has the best facilities. The social centre, **Bar Harbor**, has accommodation and restaurants to suit all pockets, there are lower-key communities all over the island, and **Acadia National Park** can offer less sedate travellers camping, cycling, canoeing, kayaking, and birdwatching.

The island was named *Monts Deserts* (bare mountains) by Samuel de Champlain in 1604. and fought over by the French and English for the rest of the century. Although all existing settlements date from long after the final defeat of the French, the name remains, still pronounced in French (more like *dessert*, actually).

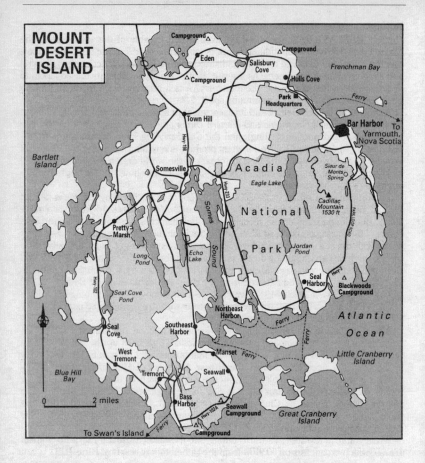

Getting There

If you're **driving**, Mount Desert is easy enough to get to, along Hwy-3 off US-1, though in high summer roads on the island itself get congested (and the horse-drawn tours don't help). **Public transport**, however, is minimal. *Greyhound* buses (☎667-8596) run to Bar Harbor from Bangor for perhaps a couple of months in summer, starting in mid-June, though even that can't be guaranteed. *St Croix Bus Co* (☎454-7526) connects Ellsworth and Bar Harbor, as does *Downeast Transportation* (Mon, Wed & Fri only; ☎667-5796), who also run buses across the island from Bar Harbor to Southwest Harbor (Thurs) and Northeast Harbor (Tues).

Nearby Trenton Airport (☎667-7432) has a limited service on *Continental Airlines* and *Bar Harbor Airlines* (☎1-800/327-8376), while the *Blue Nose* **ferry** takes six hours to link Bar Harbor with Yarmouth, Nova Scotia (cars $70, adults $38, kids $18; late June to late Sept, daily from Bar Harbor at 8am; otherwise Mon, Wed, & Fri only, 8.30am. Reservations are compulsory, from *Marine Atlantic Reservations Bureau*, PO Box 250, North Sydney, NS B2A 3M3, Canada; ☎288-3395; in Maine ☎1-800/432-7344; in US ☎1-800/432-7981).

The Town of Bar Harbor

BAR HARBOR began life as a wealthy and exclusive resort, summer home to the Vanderbilts and the Astors; the great fire of October 1947 which destroyed their opulent "cottages" ended all that. It's now firmly geared towards mass tourism, though it's by no means downmarket. There's not all that much to do in town, even in high summer. However, hordes of young visitors provide enough ambience for it to take a while to realise that once you've strolled around the village green, and walked past the headland of the *Bar Harbor Inn* for views of the ocean and Frenchman Bay, you've seen most of what Bar Harbor has to offer.

In high season up to 21 different **sea trips** set off each day, for purposes ranging from deep sea fishing to cocktail cruises. Among the most popular are the *Acadian* **whale-watcher** expeditions, departing from the *Golden Anchor Inn* (July & Aug 8am & 1.30pm; Sept & Oct 11.30am only; ☎288-9794), and the two-hour cruises on the **three-masted schooner** *Natalie Todd* from the *Bar Harbor Inn* (daily 10am, 2pm & 6pm; $16; summer ☎288-4585, winter ☎546-2927).

One of the town sights in its heyday was the "Indian village", a summer encampment where Native Americans came to sell to tourists; it was cleared away in the 1930s to make room for a new ball park. Now the only signs of the island's first inhabitants are the artefacts at the **Robert Abbe Museum**, found at Fernald Point near Southwest Harbor, overlooking Somes Sound, and attributed to a nomadic people who made birch-bark canoes. What became of them is encapsulated by a classic understatement on a map which contrasts the tribal areas of 1600 with the modern reservations: "the native population did not view territorial boundaries as we do today". The museum is a couple of miles south of Bar Harbor – not a particularly pleasant walk – at Sieur de Monts Spring, just off the Park Loop Road (daily, July & Aug 9am–5pm, mid-May to June, Sept & Oct 10am–4pm; $1.25).

Bar Harbor's main **tourist information** office is at the ferry terminal (☎288-3393); in summer there's another on Kennebec Street beside the village green.

Acadia National Park

Not all of **Acadia National Park** is on Mount Desert Island – there are sections on the Isle au Haut to the west, reached by ferry from Stonington, and on the Schoodic peninsula to the east – but there's all you could want here in terms of mountains and lakes for secluded rambling, and **wildlife** such as seals, beavers, puffins and bald eagles. The two main geographical features are the narrow fjord of **Somes Sound** which almost splits the island in two, and **Mount Cadillac**, only 1530ft high but offering tremendous ocean views. The summit, the first place in the United States to see the sun rise each morning, can be reached either by a moderately strenuous climb – more than you'd want to do before breakfast – or by a very leisurely drive, winding up a low-gradient road.

There's not all that much point setting out to drive around the island, however. The traffic can be terrible, and in any case you can only rarely see the sea from the main road. Much the most enjoyable way to explore is to ride a rented **bicycle** around the fifty-mile system of gravel-surfaced "**carriage roads**", built by John D Rockefeller as a protest against the 1917 vote which first allowed "infernal combustion engines" onto the island. Two companies in Bar Harbor rent mountai.. bikes between 8am and 6pm, at around $9 half-day, $16 all day: *Bar Harbor Bicycle Shop*, at 141 Cottage Street on the edge of town (☎288-3886), and *Acadia Bike & Canoe Co*, across from the post office at 48 Cottage Street (☎288-9605). *Southwest Cycle* do the same in Main Street, Southwest Harbor (☎244-5856). All provide excellent maps. Carry water, as there are very few refreshment stops inside the park.

Canoes are for rent, mid-May to mid-October, from *National Park Canoe Rentals* on Pretty Marsh Road (Rt 102), two miles from Somesville at the northern end of Long Pond (☎244-5854), at daily rates from $25.

The park is open all year, with a summer-only **visitor centre** at the entrance to the Loop Road north of Bar Harbor (daily mid-June to Aug 8am–8pm, May to mid-June & Sept–Nov 8am–6pm; ☎288-3338), and the headquarters at Eagle Lake (daily 8am–4.30pm). There are two official **campgrounds**: *Blackwoods*, five miles south of Bar Harbor off rte 3, and *Seawall*, on rte 102A, four miles south of Southwest Harbor. Both are in woods, near the ocean, and have full facilities in summer; only *Blackwoods* is open in winter, with minimal facilities. Space can be reserved in midsummer from Acadia National Park, PO Box 117, Bar Harbor, ME 04609 (☎288-3338) or *Ticketron* outlets.

Accommodation on Mount Desert Island

Hwy-3 into and out of Bar Harbor (which is Main Street on the way south) is lined with cheap **motels**, which do little to improve the look of the place but satisfy an enormous demand for accommodation. Rates increase drastically in July and August, and anywhere offering sea views will cost a whole lot more. The quieter places elsewhere on the island tend to be booked up early.

Bass Cottage in the Field, Main St, Bar Harbor (☎288-3705). Ten-room old-fashioned white clapboard inn, very near the centre. Doubles $50–90, singles $32.

Cove Farm Inn, RFD #1 Box 420, Bar Harbor (☎288-5355). Peaceful B&B, two miles northwest of Bar Harbor near Lake Wood on the very rural Crooked Road. May–Feb, $35–65.

Maine Street Motel, 315 Main St, Bar Harbor (☎288-3188). April to mid-Nov only. Doubles $74 in summer, otherwise $44–52. Has its own restaurant next door.

McKay Cottages, 243 Main St, Bar Harbor (☎288-3581). B&B in two nice old houses. Doubles from $55.

Moorings Motor Sail, Shore Road, Manset (☎244-5523). Lovely 200-year-old inn, two miles east of Southwest Harbor, May–Oct. $50–80 in high summer. Private beach, boats for rent next door.

Mt Desert Island Youth Hostel, Kennebec St, Bar Harbor (☎288-5587). Mid-June–Aug only, beds in large dormitories for $8 AYH members, $11 non-members. Reservations essential.

Penury Hall, Main St, Southwest Harbor (☎244-7102). Small B&B. $40–55 double.

YWCA, 23 Mt Desert St, Bar Harbor (☎288-5008). Year-round, very central women-only accommodation. Beds in shared rooms start at $18.

Eating, Drinking and Nightlife on Mount Desert Island

Mount Desert's most memorable **eating** experiences are to be found in the many **lobster pounds** all over the island, but for nightlife as such, Bar Harbor is where the people are. Cottage Street is a much more promising area to look for food and evening atmosphere than the surprisingly subdued waterfront. The art-deco *Criterion* cinema at 35 Cottage Street (☎288-3441) puts on 2pm matinees on rainy days.

Beal's Lobster Pier, Clark Point Rd, Southwest Harbor (☎244-7178). Fresh seafood for under $10, on a rickety wooden pier crammed full of lobsters.

Bulger's Dockside Restaurant, across from Manset Town Dock, Shore Rd, Manset (☎244-5221). Ocean views from every table, seafood from $7.

Christopher's, 227 Main St, Bar Harbor (☎288-9089). Seafood restaurant which tries to cut down on deep-fried and cholesterol-heavy dishes. $10 and upwards, live music most nights.

Lompoc Cafe, 34 Rodick St, Bar Harbor (☎288-9392). A healthy Middle-Eastern menu for $10–15, with local *Thunder Hole Ale* on draft and live music every night. Open 3pm–midnight.

The Opera House, 27 Cottage St, Bar Harbor (☎288-3509). Upmarket restaurant serving dinner only at around $20 per head, with framed portraits and recordings of opera legends.

Thirsty Whale, 44 Cottage St, Bar Harbor (☎288-9335). Bar Harbor's busiest late-night bar.

Triangle Seafood Restaurant, Rte 102A, Bass Harbor (244-9608). Excellent-value seafood daily 11am–9pm; "try it all" full meal with lobster, crab and mussels for $9.95.

The Unusual Cabaret, 14A Mount Desert St, Bar Harbor (☎288-3306). Small "innovative Italian" restaurant, where the waiters, all professional actors and singers, take it in turns to perform on the small stage. The evening culminates in a full-scale musical revue. All-inclusive cost around $20.

Downeast Maine: The Coast to Canada

Looking at a typical map of the United States, you'd never dream that Canada stretched for five hundred miles beyond Maine to the east. In fact few travellers venture far beyond Acadia National Park, which is one reason why what's known as **Downeast Maine** remains so little touched by change. Another reason is that this is bleak and windswept country, where high cliffs are battered by harsh seas. In summer, though, the weather is no worse than in the rest of Maine, and the coastal drive can be exhilarating. At those points where the road runs next to the sea, you get a real sense of the overwhelming power of the ocean, sweeping in to create the highest tides in the nation.

A short way northeast of Acadia, a loop road leads from US-1 to the rocky outcrop of **Schoodic Point**, which offers good birdwatching, great views, and a splendid sense of solitude. Tourism is not big business in these parts, but all the villages seem to have one or two B&Bs and cheap restaurants. The fishing harbour at **JONESPORT** on Hwy-187 is well worth a detour, and *Tootsies Bed and Breakfast* (☎497-5414) has a couple of rooms for around $40. A glorious high-arched iron bridge leads to the nature reserve of **Beal's Island**. **MACHIAS** back on US-1 is even more picturesque, with a little waterfall right in the middle, and was the unlikely scene of the first naval battle of the Revolutionary War, in 1775. The townsfolk commandeered the British schooner *Margaretta* and proceeded to terrorise all passing British shipping. That attack was planned in the still-standing gambrel-roofed **Burnham Tavern**. Meals are good value at *Helen's Restaurant*, 32 Main Street (☎255-6506), while the *Clark Perry House* (☎255-8458) at 59 Court Street provides B&B accommodation from $45.

Continuing east, and abandoning US-1 for Hwy-189, you come to the prominently striped **lighthouse** at **West Quoddy Head**, the easternmost point of the US, where an international bridge crosses to Campobello Island in Canada. The nearby settlement of **Bailey's Mistake** is named for a sea captain who beached his lumber vessel in thick fog in 1830, and chose to settle here with his crew, building homes with their erstwhile cargo, rather than face the wrath of the ship's owners back in Boston.

The border between the United States and Canada weaves through the centre of **Passamaquoddy Bay**; the towns to either side get on so well that they refused to fight in the US–UK war of 1812, and promote themselves jointly to tourists on the **Quoddy Loop** (information on ☎454-2597). It's perfectly feasible to take a "two-nation vacation", but each passage through customs and immigration between **CALAIS** (pronounced *callous*) in the States and **St Stephen** in Canada does take a little while – and watch out for confusion stemming from the fact that they're in different time zones. No trace now remains of Samuel de Champlain's 1604 attempt to found a colony on the diminutive St Croix Island, which you can see from an overlook on the main road. The *St Croix Bus Line* (☎454-7526) runs a once-daily van from Calais to Ellsworth and Bar Harbor.

Inland Maine

The vast expanses of the **Maine interior**, stretching up into the cold far north, consist mostly of evergreen forests of pine, spruce and fir, interspersed by the white birches and maples responsible for the spectacular colours of autumn. Only in the remote north is at all much of it genuine wilderness, however; elsewhere, what you see is more likely to be either abandoned farming land, over-exploited by the pioneers, or woodlands cultivated by the timber companies.

Distances are large. Once you get away from the two largest cities nearer the sea – **Augusta**, the capital, and **Bangor** – it's roughly two hundred miles by road to the northern border at **Fort Kent**, while to drive between the two most likely inland bases, **Greenville** and **Rangeley**, takes three hours or more. Driving (there's no public transport) through this mountainous scenery can be a great pleasure, but you do need to know where you're going. There are few places to stay, and many roads are tolled access routes belonging to the lumber companies: gravel-surfaced, vulnerable to bad weather, and in any case often not heading anywhere in particular. This landscape has evolved in a very un-European way. Many waterfront communities grew up without any roads to serve them, in the days when the timber harvest was floated downriver to the sea; other more recent settlements have only ever been accessible by seaplane. Now that mighty trucks carry the tree-trunks instead, roads are finally being pushed through, amid complaints that they are ruining the whole feel of the place.

If you have the time, this is great territory in which to **hike** – the **Appalachian Trail** starts its 2000-mile course down to Georgia at the top of Mount Katahdin – or **rafting** on the **Allagash Wilderness Waterway**. Especially around **Baxter State Park**, the forests are home to deer, beaver, a few bears, some recently introduced caribou . . . and **moose**. These endearingly gawky creatures (they look like badly drawn horses, and are virtually blind), tend to be seen at early morning or dusk; in spring they come to lick the winter's salt off the roads, while in summer you may spot them feeding in shallow water.

Augusta

The capital of Maine since 1832, **AUGUSTA** is a much quieter and less-visited place now than it was a hundred years ago. The lumber industry here really took off after the technique of making paper from wood was rediscovered in 1844, and Augusta also had a lucrative sideline – each winter hundreds of thousands of tons of **ice**, cut from the Kennebec River, were shipped out, as far south as the Caribbean, in a trade now all but forgotten by history. There are informative displays on Maine's landscape and industrial past at the lively **Maine State Museum**, a short way south of the Capitol on State Street (Mon–Fri 9am–5pm, Sat 10am–4pm, Sun 1–4pm).

If you plan to stay in Augusta, as usual the best value **accommodation** is the *Susse Chalet Motor Lodge* (☎622-3776), on Whitten Road at the Maine Turnpike's Augusta-Winthrop exit, where doubles start around $42. For **food**, the lobster rolls and sandwiches at *Burnsie's Homestyle Sandwiches* (☎622-6425) on State Street next to the Capitol are favourites with the politicians, while *Hazel Green's* at 349 Water Street (☎622-9903) is an atmospheric but pricey (up to $30) riverside restaurant.

Bangor

In its prime, **BANGOR**, 120 miles northeast of Portland, was the undisputed "Lumber Capital of the World". Every winter its raucous population of "River Tigers" went upstream to brand the felled logs, which they then manoeuvred down the Penobscot as the thaw came in April, reaching Bangor in time to carouse the summer away in the grog shops of Peppermint Row. (Bangor too exported ice to the West Indies – and got rum in return.) Those days were coming to an end when in October 1882 Oscar Wilde addressed a large crowd at the new Opera House and spoke diplomatically of "such advancement . . . in so small a city".

Bangor today is not a place to spend much time, although with its plentiful motels and the big new Bangor Mall on Hogan Road north of town it makes a good last stop before the interior. Its twin claims to fame are that it's the unlikely home of Stephen King, the horror fiction writer, and that it possesses what, at 31ft, may well be the largest statue of **Paul Bunyan** in the world, excepting perhaps one or two in Minnesota (see p.281) – though it looks more like a brightly painted *Airfix* kit than a statue.

From mid-May until the end of July there's **harness racing** at the *Bangor Raceway* (☎947-3313), just behind the statue; admission is $1 but the potential to lose money is unlimited. The same venue hosts the **Bangor State Fair**, in the last week of July and the first in August. The *Opera House*, 131 Main Street (☎947-0200), was destroyed by fire in 1914, but has now been restored and puts on film, opera, dance and theatre, while a few miles north of Bangor, the *Maine Center for the Arts* (☎581-1755), at the University of Maine in **Orono**, runs a series of big-name concerts each summer. Orono is named after the eighteenth-century Chief Joseph Orono; a small island nearby is now a rather sad reservation running summer Bingo sessions.

Practicalities

Bangor is the last sizeable town along I-95, before it finally veers away from the coast and heads up the Penobscot towards Canada. It's also the end of the line as far as *Greyhound* is concerned, the thrice-daily service from Boston and Portland terminating at 158 Main Street.

Accommodation possibilities include the *Susse Chalet*, near the interstate at 1100 Hammond Street (☎947-6921), and the *Red Carpet Inn*, opposite Paul Bunyan at 480 Main Street (☎942-5282), both charging around $45 per room. The *Holiday Inn* at 500 Main Street (☎947-8651) has rooms for $70, and houses Bangor's liveliest dance venue, the *Bounty Taverne*. The best **restaurant** in town is the massive Mexican *Pepino's* 105 Main Street (☎947-1233), costing $13 and upwards.

Baxter State Park and the Far North

Driving through northern Maine can feel as though you're trespassing on the private fiefdoms of the logging companies; only Baxter State Park is public land. However, you're pretty much free to hike, camp and explore anywhere you like, so long as you let people know what you're doing (only a sensible precaution, after all). The scenery is pretty much the same everywhere, although of course to get the best of it – to experience what Thoreau described in his *Maine Woods* – you need to leave your car at some point and set off into the back woods.

Five miles north of Brownsville Junction on Hwy-11, an inconspicuous left turn leads to the **Katahdin Iron Works** at Silver Lake (daily in summer, 9am–5pm), built in 1843. It's remarkable quite how little remains of what one hundred years ago was a thriving industrial community; one solitary brick oven and the tower of the blast furnace, stark and forlorn at the end of a few miles of gravel track. In good summer weather it's possible to continue along the track across the hills to Greenville.

Further north, **Millinocket** is a genuine company town, built on a wilderness site by the Great Northern Paper Company in 1899–1900 as the "magic city of the North". Public curiosity was so great that three hundred people came on a special train from Bangor to see what was happening. Since then it has produced massive quantities of newsprint, but in 1990 the company was taken over by the Georgia Pacific Corporation, and although the townspeople made a killing from cashing in their stock, their homes are almost unsaleable, and their jobs may well not last.

Next to **Millinocket Lake**, ten miles northwest, the splendidly ramshackle old *Big Moose Inn* (Box 98, Millinocket, ME 04462; ☎723-8391) and adjacent campground makes a great place to stay. Inn rooms cost $22 per person, while 4-person cabins are $48. *Unicorn Expeditions* (☎725-2255) use the inn as a base for day **rafting** and **kayaking** expeditions, and there are **dog-sled races** in February and March, as well as seaplane tours.

By now you're approaching the southern end of **Baxter State Park** itself, with on a clear day the 5268ft peak of **Mount Katahdin** visible from afar. The park was the single-handed creation of former Maine Governor Percival P Baxter, who having failed to persuade the state to buy Katahdin and the land around it, bought it himself between the 1930s and 1960s, and deeded it bit by bit to the state on condition that it remain "forever wild".

Northwards to Canada

The northernmost tip of Maine is taken up by Aroostook County, which covers an area larger than several individual states. Although its main activity is the large-scale cultivation of potatoes, it is also the location of the **Allagash Wilderness Waterway**; this is where most of the **whitewater rafting** companies mentioned in this section actually carry out their expeditions.

Britain and the United States all but went to war over Aroostook in 1839; at **Fort Kent**, the northern terminus of US-1 (which runs all the way from Key West, Florida), the main sight is the solid cedar **Fort Kent Blockhouse** built to defend American integrity, and looking like a throwback to early pioneer days. *Doris' Cafe* (☎834-6262) at Fort Kent Mills on Hwy-11 towards Eagle Lake can provide big cheap breakfasts.

Greenville

GREENVILLE, at the southern end of Moosehead Lake, is another nineteenth-century lumber town which now makes its living primarily from tourism. It's not exceptionally pretty and it's certainly not very large, but it is well positioned for explorations throughout the Maine woods. In town, the main attraction is the restored **steamboat** *Katahdin*, which tours the lake and also serves as the (non-profit) Moosehead Marine Museum (cruises at 10am & 2pm, daily July–Sept, Sat & Sun only in May & June; ☎695-2716).

The **Chamber of Commerce** on Main Street near the T-junction at the lake has details of **accommodation** (daily in summer, Mon–Fri only in winter; ☎695-2702). The *Gray Swan Motor Lodge* (☎695-4470), overlooking the lake from deep in the woods on the hill above town, costs around $60; the *Greenville Inn* on Norris Street (☎695-2206) varies from $40 to $75. Among local **rafting** companies are *Eastern River Expeditions*, PO Box 1173, Moosehead Lake, Greenville ME 04441 (☎695-2411; outside Maine ☎1-800/634-RAFT); *Wilderness Expeditions*, The Birches, PO Box 41, N Rockwood ME 04478 (☎534-2242); and *Allagash Canoe Trips*, Box 713G, Greenville ME 04441 (☎695-3668). A typical price for one day in the water is $50 to $90. Greenville is also the largest **seaplane** base in New England; contact *Currier's Flying Service* (☎695-2778).

Rangeley

RANGELEY is only just in Maine, a short way east of New Hampshire and even less distance south of the border with Québec. Furthermore, as the cheap cafe-bar *Doc Grant's* (☎864-3449) on Main Street makes a great show of telling you, it's equidistant (at 3107.5 miles) from the North Pole and the Equator. That doesn't mean it's on the main road to anywhere, although if you're avoiding the coast altogether you can get here direct from the northern side of the White Mountains (see p.189). It has always been a resort, served in 1900 by two train lines and several steamships, with the main attraction then being the fishing in the spectacularly named Mooselookmeguntic Lake.

This small and very homely place, nestling amidst a complex system of lakes and waterways, serves as base for summer explorations, and in winter as the nearest town (and airport) to the **ski** area at **Saddleback Mountain**. Rangeley Lakes **Chamber of Commerce** at PO Box 317 (☎864-5364) has details of various activities, including snowmobiling, and dawn moose-watching **canoeing** expeditions (☎864-5136). One really fun thing to do is to take a **seaplane** trip with the *Mountain Air Service* (☎864-5307). A fifteen-minute tour, flying low over endless forests and tiny lakes, costs $30 for two; you can also arrange on the spot on the waterfront to go on the regular two-hour fire-watching tours, for $25 each person. Among other outlets, **bicycles** and **canoes** can be rented from the *Rangeley Region Sport Shop* on Main Street (☎864-5615).

Rangeley also has one unlikely and not exactly orthodox tourist attraction. About halfway along the north side of Rangeley Lake, a mile up a side track off route 16, is the

Wilhelm Reich museum at **Orgonon** (PO Box 687, Rangeley ME 04970; July & Aug Tues–Sun 1–5pm, Sept Sun only 1–5pm; $3; ☎864-3443). This remote spot is where Wilhelm Reich eventually made his American home after fleeing Germany in 1933. Although he was an associate of Freud in Vienna, and wrote the acclaimed *Mass Psychology of Fascism*, Reich is best remembered for developing the orgone energy accumulator. He claimed it could create rain and dissipate nuclear radiation; sceptical authorities focused on the not very specific way in which it was said to collect and harness human sexual energy. In a tragic end to his career, Reich was imprisoned after a wayward student broke an injunction forbidding the transportation of his accumulators across state lines, and he died in the Federal Penitentiary in Lewisberg PA in November 1957. He is buried here, amid the neat lawns and darting hummingbirds, and his house remains a centre for the study of his work.

Accommodation in the Rangeley area

The *Rangeley Inn* on Main Street (☎864-3341) stands between Rangeley Lake and the smaller bird sanctuary Haley Pond, so you can stay right in town and have a room that backs onto a scene of utter tranquillity; there's also a gorgeous old wooden dining room. Rooms range from $59 to $100. Otherwise, the Chamber of Commerce can provide lists of "remote campsites" around the lake – which really are remote, several of them inaccessible by road.

Twenty miles north of Rangeley, the peaceful *Grants Camps* beside Kennebago Lake (mid-May–Sept, PO Box 786, Rangeley ME 04970; ☎864-3608) arrange fishing, canoeing and windsurfing, with accommodation in comfortable cabins, with all meals, costing around $70 per person per day, and lower weekly rates. A more accessible campground is *Cathedral Pines* (☎246-3491) just north of **Stratton** on Eustis Road. At its entrance stands a memorial to Benedict Arnold's expedition to Québec in 1775, which passed this way, and to Colonel Timothy Bigelow who climbed the mountain in a "vain endeavour to see the city of Québec".

To the east, the great white *Herbert Inn* in **Kingfield** (PO Box 67, Kingfield, ME 04947; ☎265-2000) is something special, a classic country hotel with rooms at $50 to $75 and good meals for under $15; the *Sherbert* next door is a luxurious sweet-shop and bakery.

travel details

TRAINS
Routes

• Up to eight *Amtrak* trains per day connect **Boston** with **Washington DC**, via **Providence**, **New London**, **New Haven**, **New York**, **Philadelphia** and **Baltimore**. Two also stop at **Mystic**. Another two take an inland route through Massachusetts, calling at **Worcester** and **Springfield** instead of Providence and New London.

• A frequent – hourly on weekdays – rail service between **New Haven** and Grand Central Terminal in **New York** is run by *Metro North* (☎212/532-4900).

• From the end of June until the beginning of September, there is an *Amtrak* weekend service between **Providence** and Hyannis on **Cape Cod**.

• One *Amtrak* train daily between Washington DC and Montréal stops at **New Haven**, **New London**, **Brattleboro**, **White River Junction**, **Montpelier**, Waterbury (for **Stowe**) and Essex Junction (for **Burlington**). However, the New England portion of this journey is in the middle of the night in both directions.

• One *Amtrak* train daily links **Springfield** with **Chicago**; connect at Springfield for other New England destinations.

• The only trains which head north from Boston are the regular *MBTA* commuter lines to places such as **Salem**, **Ipswich** and **Concord**, New Hampshire (see p.146).

Journey Times

From Boston: Providence 45min; Mystic 1hr 30min; New London 1hr 40min; New Haven 2hr 50min; New York 4hr 50min; Philadelphia 6hr 20min; Baltimore 7hr 45min; Washington DC 8hr 30min; Worcester 1hr 10min; Springfield 2hr 45min; Salem 30min; Ipswich 1hr; Rockport 1hr 10min.

From Providence: Hyannis 2hr 30min.

From New Haven: New London 1hr; Brattleboro 5hr; White River Junction 6hr 45min; Montpelier 8hr; Waterbury 8hr 15min; Essex Junction 8hr 45min; New York (on *Metro North*) 1hr 40min.

From Springfield: Chicago 18hr.

BUSES

From Boston: to New York (6 daily; 5hr); Providence (17 daily; 1hr 10min) via Pawtucket; Newport (7; 1hr 40min); Burlington (6 daily, 7hr); Montréal (1 daily, 9hr); Portland (6; 3hr) via Portsmouth; Bangor (3; 5hr).

From Logan Airport, Boston: to Providence (15 daily; 1hr 10min) via Pawtucket; Woods Hole (8; 2hr 10min) via Boston and Falmouth; Franconia (3 daily; 3hr 30min) via Manchester, Concord, and Conway.

See p.146 for more details on buses from Boston. Transportation to Cape Cod is detailed on p.161.

From Providence: to Hyannis (10 daily, 1hr 50min); New Bedford (4; 50min); New York (5; 5hr); Hartford (6; 2hr 10min); Springfield (2; 1hr 40min); Lee (2; 2hr 30min);

From Bennington: to New York (2 daily; 5hr 30min) via Lee and Lenox.

From Burlington: to New York (3 daily, 9–12hr) via Springfield and Hartford, connecting to Montréal (1, 11–14hr).

From Bangor: to Bar Harbor (summer only; 3 daily, 1hr 15min)

FERRIES

From Boston: to **Provincetown**. Details on p.163.

To Martha's Vineyard and **Nantucket**: details on p.165.

From Burlington: to upstate New York. Details on p.198.

From Portland: to **Yarmouth** in Nova Scotia. Daily, summer-only; details on p.202.

From Bar Harbor: to **Yarmouth** in Nova Scotia. Details on p.208.

CHAPTER FOUR

THE GREAT LAKES

S wept by tumultuous storms and traversed by fleets of oceangoing tankers, the
interconnected **Great Lakes** form the largest body of fresh water in the world;
Lake Superior alone is over three hundred miles from east to west. Left
untouched, the shores of these inland seas can rival any coastline: Superior and
the northern reaches of Lake Michigan offer stunning rocky peninsulas, craggy cliffs,
tree-covered islands, mammoth dunes and deserted beaches. For endless stretches
along Lake Erie, and the bottom lips of lakes Michigan and Huron, however, sluggish
waters lap against grimy cities, and the unused wharves of decaying ports.

To varying degrees, all the states which line the American side of the lakes – **OHIO**,
MICHIGAN, **INDIANA**, **ILLINOIS**, **WISCONSIN** and **MINNESOTA** – share this
mixture of natural beauty and industrial blight. Cities such as Chicago and Detroit,
with all their good and bad points – and **Chicago**, with its magnificent architecture,
museums, music and restaurants, is an unmissable destination – should not be seen as
characterising the entire region. Within the first hundred miles or so of the lakeshores,
especially in Wisconsin and Minnesota, tens of thousands of smaller lakes and
tumbling streams are scattered through a spectacular rural wilderness; beyond that,
you are soon in the heart of the corn belt, where you can drive for hours and encounter
nothing more than a succession of crossroads communities, grain silos and giant
barns. Garrison Keillor's wry stories about the fictional backwater town of Lake
Wobegon (where "all the women are strong and all the men are beautiful"), set in
Minnesota, carry more than a ring of truth.

The first foreigner to reach the Great Lakes, the French explorer Champlain in 1603,
found the region inhabited mostly by Huron, Iroquois and Algonquin. France soon
established a network of military forts, Jesuit missions and fur-trading posts – which
entailed treating the Indians as allies rather than subjects. Territorial disputes with their
colonial rivals, however, culminated in the **French and Indian War** with Britain from
1754 to 1761. The victorious British felt under no constraints to deal equitably with the
Indians, and things grew worse with large-scale American settlement after independence. The **Black Hawk War** of 1832 put a bloody end to traditional life.

Settlers from the east were followed to Wisconsin and Minnesota by waves of
Scandinavians and **Germans**, while the lower halves of Illinois and Indiana attracted
southerners, who attempted to maintain slavery and resisted Union conscription
during the Civil War. These areas often still share more in common with neighbouring
Kentucky and Tennessee than with the industrial cities of their own states.

The impetus given to **industry** by the Civil War was encouraged by abundant
supplies of ores and fuel, and efficient transport connections by water and rail. As lakeshore cities like Chicago, Detroit and Cleveland grew, their populations were swollen by
hundreds of thousands of poor **blacks** brought in from the Deep South as cheap labour,
particularly to work in munitions during the two world wars. But a complete lack of planning, inadequate housing provision and mass lay-offs at times of low demand bred conditions which led to the riots of the late Sixties and current inner-city deprivation.
Depression in the Seventies ravaged the economy – especially the **automobile** industry
on which so much else depended – and brought the unwanted title of **"Rust Belt"**. Since
then, urban centres have battled back with varying degrees of success.

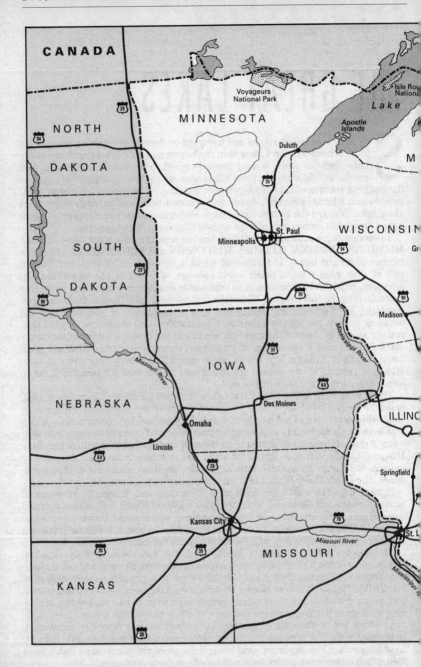

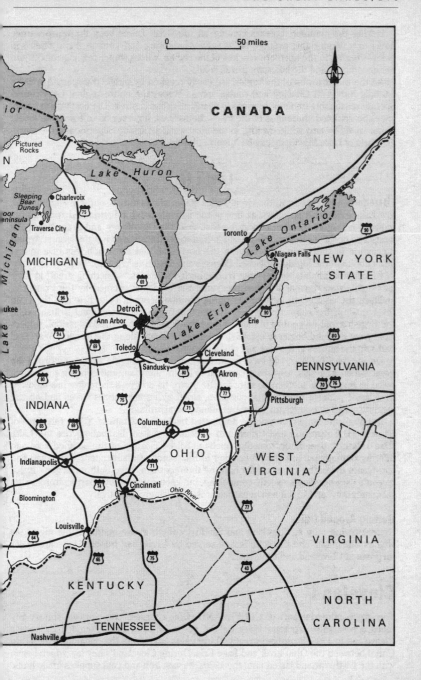

During the summer, breezes coming off the Great Lakes keep the **temperature** down to a comfortable average of 70°f. Even in spring and autumn it can often slip below freezing in the northern reaches of the region, where winter readings of -50° are not uncommon and the lakes are frozen solid.

All the major towns of the region are easily reached by public transport. **Amtrak**'s national hub is in Chicago and routes spread across the entire region; **Greyhound** operate reasonably frequent services to nearly all urban centres. The best way to appreciate the sculpted shorelines of the lakes themselves, however, is to travel the lonely minor roads by **car**, while **cycling** in the northwest, alongside Superior and the northern parts of Lake Michigan, can be hugely enjoyable.

OHIO

OHIO, the furthest east of the Great Lakes states, clings to the southern edge of shallow Lake Erie. This is known as one of the nation's most industrialised regions, but industry is largely concentrated in the east, near the Ohio River, and to the south the landscape becomes less populated and more forested. Ohio also has the largest **Amish** population in the world, who farm in the northeast, and are much less of a tourist attraction than the highly publicised Pennsylvania Dutch (see p.122).

Ohio's first inhabitants were the **Iroquois**, (Ohio means "something great" in their language), who remained undisturbed until the area was claimed by the French in 1669. In the eighteenth century, its prime position between Lake Erie and the Ohio River made it the subject of fierce contention between the French and British; when the British acquired control of most of the French land east of the Mississippi, settlers from New England began to establish communities both along the Iroquois War Trail paths on the shores of the lake and along the Ohio River.

During the Civil War, Ohio was in the forefront of the struggle, producing two of the great Union generals, Ulysses Grant and William Sherman, and sending more than twice its quota of volunteers to fight for the north. Its progress thereafter has followed the classic pattern: rapid industrialisation, aided by its natural resources and crucial location, which has since the Seventies foundered alarmingly.

Although the state is physically dominated by its triumvirate of "C"s – the cities of **Cleveland**, **Columbus** and **Cincinnati** – its most visited destinations are the **Lake Erie Islands**, benefiting from the much-publicised cleanup of the polluted lake and offering outdoor pursuits and relaxation to thousands of mainlanders. Cincinnati and Cleveland, the latter hit especially hard by the recession, have both undergone major face-lifts. Neither city is exactly compelling, but each can proudly boast a strong cultural community, and Cincinnati in particular is surprisingly attractive.

Getting Around Ohio
Amtrak **trains** stop at Cleveland and Sandusky (both in the middle of the night), as well as Cincinnati, and the state is well served by *Greyhound* **buses**. There are major **airports** at Cleveland and Cincinnati.

Cleveland

The great industrial port of **CLEVELAND**, Ohio's largest city, sprawls almost fifty miles across the Cuyahoga River on the shore of Lake Erie. Founded by Moses Cleaveland in 1796, it profited greatly, thirty years later, from the opening of the **Ohio Canal** between the Ohio River and Lake Erie. During Cleveland's heyday, which began with the Civil War and lasted until the 1920s, its vast iron and coal supplies made it one of the most important **steel** and **shipbuilding** cities in the world. **John D Rockefeller** made his billions here, as did the many others whose now-decrepit old mansions line "Millionaires Row". That has become a no-go area, along with many other bleak and faceless danger spots; the scars of deprivation and neglect since the Thirties are often all too visible. However, Cleveland has lately undergone a quite remarkable resurgence, with a superb constellation of **museums** in University Circle, and a sensitive, fond restoration of the **waterfront.**

Arrival, Getting Around and Information
Cleveland's busy **Hopkins International Airport**, 5300 Riverside Drive (✆265-6030), served by 25 airlines, is twelve miles out in the western suburb of Brookpark. The twenty-minute **cab** ride to town costs around $20, but a cheaper shuttle is provided by the *Regional Transit Authority* (*RTA*; ✆566-5074). *Greyhound* (✆781-1400) arrives at 1465 Chester Avenue, which is in a dodgy area, and the *Amtrak* station (✆696-5115) is on the lakefront at 200 Cleveland Memorial Shoreway.

Cleveland is concentrated in different pockets, and as the potentially dangerous areas are scattered pretty wide (it is not safe, for example, to wander into the streets around the three-block-deep *Cleveland Clinic*, very close to the much-frequented University Circle), it's a good idea to have a **car**. *RTA* run an efficient **bus** service (85¢) and a small *Rapid* train line ($1), until about 12.30am. They're based across from Terminal Tower in the centre of town at 2019 Ontario Avenue (schedules Mon–Sat 6am–6pm; ✆621-9500). **City tours** are provided by *Trolley Tours of Cleveland*, W Ninth Street at St Clair Avenue (reservations required, ✆771-4484).

Maps and **information** can be had from the Cleveland **CVB**, 3100 Tower City Center (✆621-4110), in the centre of Public Square, and there's an information booth in the nearby Terminal Tower.

The Town
All the main streets in Cleveland lead to the stately nineteenth-century Beaux Arts **Public Square**, at the very centre of downtown. **Ontario Street**, which runs north–south through the Square, divides the city into east and west. Cleveland's most interesting areas are at two opposite ends of the spectrum: the industrial romance of the **Flats** in the northwest, and the cultural institutions of **University Circle**, east of the river.

Downtown Cleveland has recently been regaining energy; among its glamorous new shopping malls are the **Tower City Center** in the Terminal Tower, which also has an **observation deck** on the 42nd floor (Sat & Sun only) and the **Avenue**, a skylit hall of gleaming white and black marble. **Playhouse Square**, twelve blocks away at 1501 Euclid Avenue, is an impressive complex of three renovated old theatres. Take a look at the gorgeous lobby of the small *Ohio Theatre*, with its starlit-sky ceiling.

Five miles east of downtown, the **University Circle** is a cluster of over seventy cultural institutions. The eclectic and well-contextualised **Museum of Art**, fronted by a lagoon at 11150 East Boulevard, ranges from fifteenth-century Dutch tapestries to African art (Tues, Thurs & Fri 10am–6pm, Wed 10am–10pm, Sat 9am–5pm, Sun 1–6pm; free). Also notable is the **Museum of Natural History**, Wade Oval, with its exhibits on dinosaurs and Native American culture (Mon–Sat 10am–5pm, Sun 1–5.30pm; $4, free Tues & Thurs 3–5pm). The free **Dittrick Museum of Medical History**, 11000 Euclid Avenue, covers all matters surgical, from a re-creation of a nineteenth-century doctor's office to nursing and pharmaceutical memorabilia. Dotted along East and Martin Luther King boulevards, twenty-four small landscaped cultural gardens are dedicated to and tended by Cleveland's diverse ethnic groups, including

The telephone **area code** for Cleveland is ✆216.

Croatians, Estonians and Finns. **Murray Hill**, Cleveland's Little Italy, is adjacent to University Circle: an attractive area of brick streets, small delis and galleries.

In the Seventies the busy **Cuyahoga River** was so polluted that it actually caught fire, a memory that still makes Clevelanders hang their heads in shame. Today, however, it has been cleared up, and the **waterfront** is one of the liveliest areas of the city. The river itself bustles with cargo ships and pleasure boats, its distinctive steel bridges opening at regular intervals. The surrounding **Warehouse District** is still being restored, a stretch of nineteenth-century industrial buildings given over to restaurants and shops. The **Cleveland Flats**, long known for its excellent nightlife, relishes its industrial setting; the old bridges, warehouses and slag heaps appear powerful and romantic rather than depressing, a proud testimony to Cleveland's hard-working history.

To the west of the river, **Ohio City** is one of Cleveland's hipper neighbourhoods, with junk shops, Victorian clapboard houses, and a **farmers' market** on W 25th Street selling all manner of ethnic foods (Mon & Wed 7am–4pm, Fri & Sat 7am–7pm).

Accommodation

Travellers without cars are at a severe disadvantage when it comes to finding somewhere to sleep in Cleveland. The downtown **hotels** are prohibitively expensive, and cheap **motels** are concentrated in the sprawling suburbs or along I-90. **B&B** in town can be arranged through *Private Lodgings*, Box 18590, Cleveland 44118 (☎321-3213).

Gateway Motel, 29865 Euclid Ave (☎943-6777). Ten miles from downtown, but reachable by bus. Rooms from $40.

Glidden House, 1901 Ford Drive (☎231-8900). B&B in a Gothic mansion. From $79.

Holiday Inn – Lakeside, 1111 Lakeside Ave (☎241-5100). Luxury hotel in town. From $75.

Lakewood Manor Motel, 12019 Lake Ave (☎226-4800). In the western suburb of Lakewood, but accessible by public transport. Plain but adequate rooms from $40.

Red Roof Inn, 29595 Clemens Rd, exit 156 off I-90 (☎892-7920). Eleven miles out; rooms from $50.

Eating

The **farmers' market** in Ohio City is one of the best places for cheap and unusual picnic food, but Cleveland is also sprouting some excellent (if slightly pricey) upmarket restaurants downtown. The Italian places on Murray Hill are good value and popular.

Burgess Grand Cafe, 1406 W Sixth St (☎574-2232). Glamorous, stylish downtown cafe in old warehouse. Superb food, reasonably priced. Fruit and waffle breakfasts from $5. Dinner begins at $16.

Isabella's, 2025 Abington Ave (☎229-1177). Popular Italian restaurant in University Circle/Little Italy with lunch from $5, dinner from $9, and live jazz.

New York Spaghetti House, 2173 E Ninth St (☎696-6624). Cheap, family-owned Italian restaurant.

Whole Grain, 55 Public Square (☎861-0999). Healthy weekday breakfast and lunch from $1.

Nightlife and Entertainment

For drinking, live music and dancing, several districts are worth checking out. The crowded and lively bars in the **Flats** – such as *Shooters*, 1148 Main Avenue (☎861-6900) – have great views over the river, while the *Powerhouse* in the **Warehouse District** is packed with places like *Howl at the Moon*, 2000 Sycamore Avenue (☎861-HOWL), a raucous piano bar and Karaoke club. In **Ohio City**, the huge mahogany bar in the *Great Lakes Brewing Co*, 2516 Market Street (☎771-4404), still bears bullet-holes left over from a Twenties shoot-out involving Elliot Ness.

As for more refined entertainments, the *Cleveland Opera* (☎575-0900) and *Ballet* (☎621-2260) perform in **Playhouse Square** (☎241-6000), which also hosts drama, and the *Cleveland Orchestra* (☎231-1111) is based in University Circle at Severance Hall, 11001 Euclid Avenue. The *Great Lakes Theatre Festival* (☎241-5490), 1501 Euclid Avenue, is the state's only classical rep company. Current events listings can be found in the *Cleveland Magazine* and *Northern Ohio Live* available at newsstands.

The Lake Erie Islands

The **LAKE ERIE ISLANDS** – Kelleys Island, and the three **Bass Islands** further north – were early stepping stones for the **Iroquois** on the route to what is now Ontario. French attempts to claim the islands in the 1640s met with considerable hostility, and they were left more or less in peace until 1813, when in the **Battle of Lake Erie**, fought off South Bass Island, the Americans established their control over the Great Lakes by destroying the entire English fleet (for the first time in history).

The islands first tasted prosperity in the 1860s, when a boom in wine production meant that nearly every available acre was planted with grapes. Tourism arrived almost simultaneously, with steamboats bringing wealthy visitors to spend their summers in the grand hotels. However, the economy was hit hard by Prohibition and the emergence of the California wineries, as well as the advent of car travel. In the Seventies, Lake Erie's appalling pollution was the final straw for many inhabitants, who undertook a huge cleanup, both literally, of the lake, and figuratively, of the islands' image. Their plan has worked; today the islands are heavily touristed, especially in summer, with fishing and swimming the two main attractions. Those mainland towns, like **Sandusky**, that act as jump-off points for the islands, are destinations in themselves. One pleasant way to see the shore is to follow the lovely **Lake Erie Circle Tour**, marked by green signs about every ten miles along the two hundred miles of coast road.

The Mainland

The large coal-shipping port of **SANDUSKY**, fifty miles west of Cleveland on US-2, is probably the most visited of the lakeshore towns, thanks to **Cedar Point Amusement Park**, five miles southeast of town (May–Sept daily 9am–10pm; $20, $11 after 5pm). The largest ride park in the nation, now nearly a century old, it claims to have the tallest and fastest **roller coaster** in the US, and also has a mile-long beach.

Sandusky, in its pleasant farmland setting, is a nice enough town, but there's not much to it apart from the billboards and fast-food spots lining US-2. **VERMILION**, further east, just beyond the suburbs of Cleveland, is also known as Harbour Town for its attractive lakeside area, which has thrived since 1837. Today it is a quaint old hamlet lined with clapboard houses, cedar trees and tidy gardens. Olde-style galleries and shops hug the small downtown, a stone's throw from the boat rides, seafood restaurants and fishing boats on the dockside. The maritime collection of the **Great Lakes Historical Society Museum**, 480 Main Street, includes models, photos, paintings and Great Lakes shipping memorabilia (daily; free).

Practicalities

Two *Amtrak* **trains** pass through Sandusky daily to and from Boston; the station, at N Depot and Hayes avenues, is in a distinctly dangerous area, and unstaffed. *Greyhound* **buses** are more convenient; they call at 6513 Milan Road (☎625-6907), with a shuttle to Cedar Point and downtown ($4). Sandusky's **visitor centre** is at 5510 Milan Road (daily in summer, 8am–6pm; ☎625-5721); Vermilion's, 5495 Liberty Avenue (☎216/967-4477).

Motels along Cleveland Road in **Sandusky** include the *Mecca* (☎626-1284), 2227 Cleveland Road, and the *Greentree* (☎626-6761), at the entrance to Cedar Point, which both cost around $55. **Camping** is available at the *Bayshore Campsite*, 2311 Cleveland Road (☎625-7906). In **Vermilion**, the *Motel Plaza*, 4645 Liberty Avenue (☎216/967-3191), offers rooms in summer only from $40. In **Lakeside**, a quiet Methodist retreat across Sandusky Bay, the *Lakeside Hotel* (☎798-4461) offers simple rooms from $35.

The telephone **area code** for Sandusky and the Lake Erie Islands is ☎419.

Kelleys Island

KELLEYS ISLAND is about nine miles north of Sandusky, in the western basin of Lake Erie. Seven miles across at its widest, it's the largest American island on the lake, but it's also one of the most peaceful and picturesque, home to just a hundred or so permanent residents. The whole island, green, dozy and with few buildings less than a century old, is a National Historic District. Its seventy-plus archaeological sites include **Inscription Rock**, a four-hundred-year-old limestone slab carved with Native-American pictographs, east of the dock on the southern shore. The **Glacial Grooves State Memorial**, on the west shore, is a four-hundred-foot trough of solid limestone, scoured with deep ridges by the glacier that carved the Great Lakes.

Settled by two brothers from Cleveland in the 1830s, Kelleys developed as a working island rather than a holiday resort, its economy based first on lumber, then wine, and later limestone quarrying. All three eventually collapsed, but a steady tourist industry also developed. Today, careworn city dwellers from the mainland come here to get away from it all, to walk, swim (there's a sandy public beach on the north shore), and cycle and hike through the dramatic disused quarries, which now sprout cedars.

Practicalities

Kelleys Island's **visitor centre** (☎746-2360) is on the dockside. Getting around is easy; cars are heavily discouraged, and most people, when not strolling, use bikes ($6 per day) or golf carts ($25), available from *1st Place Rentals*, at the top of the ferry dock (☎746-2314). A tram runs downtown from the dock, giving a short narrated tour of the island on its way. There are a few B&Bs and inns, but the island caters more for long-term stays with cottages and apartments. You can **camp** at the State Park on the north bay near the beach (no reservations; $8; ☎746-2546).

South Bass Island

SOUTH BASS ISLAND is the largest and southernmost of the Bass Island chain, three miles from the mainland northwest of Kelleys Island, and named for the excellent bass fishing in the surrounding waters. Also known as Put-in-Bay (either for the sailors who used to "put in" to the safe harbour here, or for its soft "puddingy" seabed), this is the most visited of the American Lake Erie Islands, with its permanent population of 450 swelling to ten times that in summer.

Just a year after its first white settlers turned up and planted their wheat, British troops invaded the island as part of the 1812 war for control of the lakes. The **Battle of Lake Erie**, which took place on its southeastern edge, is commemorated by the Perry's Victory and International Peace Memorial in a 25-acre park where the island dramatically nips in at the waist. You can see the ten miles to the battle site from an observation deck near the top of the 352-foot stone Doric column (May–Oct daily 10am–7pm; $1).

After the war, with the lake safe from Canadian invasion, South Bass Island grew both as a port, transporting cedar to the mainland for the construction of steamboats, and as a tourist destination: in the 1890s its *Victory Hotel* was one of the largest hotels in the world. Today it's pretty much a family resort, where outdoor-lovers come to fish, camp, hike, parasail, or swim at the stone beach in the State Park west of the island (daily 8am–5pm). Wine was also big business, though only one of its twenty-six vineyards survived Prohibition (by producing grape juice). The **Heineman Winery** on Catawba Avenue, the east–west road on the main body of the island, and adjacent **Crystal Cave** (a giant spangly geode of lilac celestite crystals) give combination tours which include a free glass of wine or grape juice (daily May–June & Sept 11am–5pm; July & Aug 10.30am–5.30pm; $3).

Ferries to **Kelleys Island** are operated by *Neuman Boats* from **Sandusky** (☎626-5557) and **Marblehead** (☎798-5800) every hour from dawn until dusk, more frequently at weekends and during peak times (April–Nov; $4 one way, $8 return).

Ferries to **South Bass Island** are operated by *Put-in-Bay* (☎285-3491) from **Port Clinton**, ten miles away on the mainland, at regular intervals during the day; and by *Miller Boats* (☎285-2421) from **Catawba Point** at the end of US-53 N to Lime Kiln Dock on the southern tip of the island (March–Sept daily, hourly 7am–7.30pm; $4).

The **Jet Express** takes a mere fifteen minutes to reach **South Bass Island** from Port Clinton. It runs until 11.30pm in the summer (April–Nov; $7.50 one way; ☎1-800/2451-JET).

The **cruise boat** *Goodtime* (☎625-9692) leaves Sandusky's Jackson Street Pier daily at 9.30am, and calls at both Kelleys Island and South Bass Island, for a roundtrip fare of $19.95.

Flights to both Kelleys Island and South Bass Island leave at least once a day from Sandusky. Contact *Griffing Airlines* (☎626-5161).

Practicalities

Put-in-Bay's **visitor centre** (☎285-2832) is in Harbour Square, downtown, just next to the northern dock. To get around, as on Kelleys Island, most people either rent **golf carts**, for a pricey $10 to $20 per hour, from *Baycarts Rental* on Harbour Square (☎285-5785), or **bikes**, from *Island Bike Rental* at both docks (☎285-2016). A **shuttle bus** runs between the northern dock, the winery and the State Park ($1), and a narrated **tram tour** sets off from the dock every thirty minutes. Call ☎285-6161 for a taxi service which will take you anywhere on the island between 7am and 3am for $2 per person, or $1 if you're staying here.

Hotel rooms, which range from $50 to $95, are heavily booked at the weekends and during the summer, and B&Bs often require a two-night minimum stay at the weekend. There's **camping** for $7 in the State Park (☎797-4530), and at the *Foxes Campground* (☎285-5001) on the southern shore.

Put-in-Bay's wild **nightlife** pulls in revellers not only from the other islands but from the mainland. *Tippers Seafood and Steakhouse* serves fantastic seafood dinners from $14, while numerous **live music** venues include the *Beer Barrel Saloon* – said to have the longest uninterrupted bar in the world, and the *Roundhouse* (☎285-4595), 234 Lorain Avenue.

Cincinnati

CINCINNATI, just across from Kentucky on the southern border of Ohio, and roughly three hundred miles from both Detroit and Chicago, is a city with a definite European flavour. Its tidy centre, rich in architecture and culture, lies within a few minutes' easy walk of the arty **Mount Adams** district and the beautiful **Ohio riverfront**.

This metropolis of 1.7 million people, now one of the most dynamic **industrial** centres in the country, was founded in 1788 at the point where an Indian trading route crossed the Ohio River. Its name comes from a group of Revolutionary War veterans who admired the Roman general Cincinnatus, who, after saving his city in 458 BC, returned to his small farm and refused to accept any reward or glory. Cincinnati quickly became an important supply point for pioneers heading west on flatboats and rafts, and its population rocketed with the establishment of a major steamboat **riverport** in 1811. Tens of thousands of **German** immigrants poured in during the 1830s.

Loyalties were split by the **Civil War**. At first merchants were perturbed by the loss of important markets; then they began to pick up lucrative government contracts, and the city decided its future lay with the Union. In the prosperous post-war decade, Cincinnati acquired Fountain Square, the prodigious Music and Exhibition Hall, a zoo, art museum, public library and the country's first professional baseball team. **Sport** remains a great source of pride; you can't be in the city for long without becoming familiar with the distinctive orange and black colours of the Bengals football side and the epic saga of the Reds' victory in the 1990 World Series.

Charles Dickens, Winston Churchill and Longfellow have all admired Cincinnati; Mark Twain on the other hand, struck by its conservatism, said that when the world ended he hoped to be in Cincinnati, as it's always twenty years behind everywhere else.

Arrival and Information

Greater Cincinnati International Airport (☎283-3151) is twelve miles from downtown, in Covington, Kentucky. Taxis to the city centre cost around $20, though shuttle vans are more like $8. The **Greyhound** station is just off Broadway on the eastern fringe of the centre at 1005 Gilbert Avenue (☎352-6000). *Amtrak* **trains** (☎579-8506) arrive almost two miles out at 1901 River Road, on the regular day-time citywide bus network.

Cincinnati's main **visitor centre** is at 300 W Sixth Street (Mon–Fri 8.45am–5pm; ☎621-2142), though there's also an information booth in Fountain Square.

Downtown

Downtown Cincinnati rolls back from the Ohio River to fill the flat Basin area, ringed by a disarray of rugged hills. During the city's emergent industrial years, the filth, disease, crime and general commotion of the so-called Sausage and Rat rows led the middle classes to abandon downtown en masse, in one of the first instances of what became a common American phenomenon. Nowadays, however, it has been taken over by a continental-style abundance of attractive shops, stores, street vendors, restaurants, cafes, open spaces and gardens. Over, among and even right through the hotel plazas, office lobbies and retail areas, the **Skywalk** network of air-conditioned passages and flyovers spans sixteen city blocks. No one building or sector stands out, but the area's charm, atmosphere and cleanliness, together with the friendliness of the people, simply make it a very enjoyable place to wander round and explore.

At the geographic centre of downtown, the **Genius of the Waters** in **Fountain Square** sprays a cascade of hundreds of jets to symbolise the city's trading links. Once the site of a noisy, fetid nineteenth-century market, the square is now surrounded by a tree-dotted plaza, all but enclosed by soaring facades of glass and steel, and provides an extremely popular lunch spot and venue for day-time concerts. Looming over the square at Fifth and Vine streets, the 48-storey Art Deco **Carew Tower** has a viewing gallery on its top floor giving a wonderful panorama of the tight bends of the Ohio and the surrounding hillsides (Mon–Fri 9am–5pm; $1).

Just east of Fountain Square are the Art Deco headquarters of **Procter and Gamble**, manufacturers of *Ariel*, *Tide*, *Fairy Liquid* and *Old Spice*. The company was formed in 1837, when William Procter, a candlemaker, and James Gamble, a soapmaker, joined forces to take advantage of the supply of animal fat from the slaughterhouses that had earned Cincinnati the nickname of **"Porkopolis"**. The company's less than open style of management has spawned tales of dubious religious and political links; it even had to change its corporate logo in the face of accusations that it was a satanic symbol. The company made social history in 1932 by introducing radio listeners to the "Puddle Family"; because of its sponsor, the programme became known as the first **soap opera**.

The telephone **area code** for Cincinnati is ☎513; for Covington across the river it's ☎606.

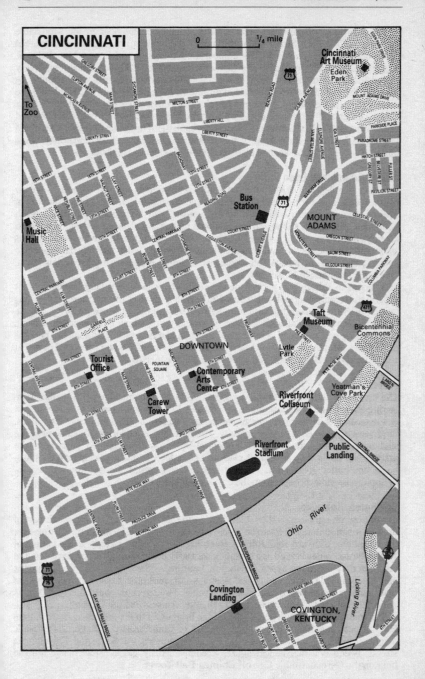

CINCINNATI

0 — ¼ mile

To Zoo

GREGORY STREET
CLIFTON AVENUE
MCMICKEN AVENUE
MAIN STREET
SYCAMORE STREET
15TH AVENUE
MILTON STREET
LIBERTY HILL
READING ROAD

Cincinnati Art Museum
Eden Park
MOUNT ADAMS DRIVE
PARKSIDE PLACE
PARADROME STREET
HATCH STREET
GREGORY ST
ELSINORE AVENUE
VAN METER STREET
BELVEDERE ST
FULLER ST
PAVILION STREET

LIBERTY STREET
LIBERTY STREET
BROADWAY
13TH STREET
14TH STREET
CLAY STREET
WALNUT STREET
13TH STREET
READING ROAD
12TH STREET
REPUBLIC STREET
VINE STREET
11TH STREET

Music Hall

Bus Station
US 71

CENTRAL PARKWAY
SYCAMORE STREET
EGGLESTON AVENUE
COURT STREET
GILBERT AVENUE

MOUNT ADAMS
CELESTIAL STREET
OREGON STREET
MONASTERY STREET
BAUM STREET
KILGOUR STREET
COLUMBIA PARKWAY

CENTRAL PARKWAY
PLUM STREET
ELM STREET
9TH STREET
COURT STREET
BOWEN STREET
MAIN STREET
8TH STREET
9TH STREET
7TH STREET
8TH STREET

GARFIELD PLACE
7TH STREET
DOWNTOWN

Tourist Office
FOUNTAIN SQUARE
VINE STREET
RACE STREET
WALNUT STREET
6TH STREET
8TH STREET

Contemporary Arts Center
6TH STREET

Taft Museum
PIKE STREET
Lytle Park
Bicentennial Commons
PETE ROSE WAY

CENTRAL AVENUE
6TH STREET
Carew Tower
5TH STREET
4TH STREET
3RD STREET

Riverfront Coliseum
POPLAR
Yeatman's Cove Park
L AND N BRIDGE

Riverfront Stadium

Public Landing
CENTRAL BRIDGE

PETE ROSE WAY
CENTRAL AVENUE
PLUM STREET
STADIUM DRIVE
PADDOCK DRIVE
MEHRING WAY

Ohio River

US 71
US 75
CLAY WADE BAILEY BRIDGE

Covington Landing
RIVERSIDE DRIVE
ROEBLING SUSPENSION BRIDGE

COVINGTON, KENTUCKY
2ND STREET
GREENUP STREET
COURT AVENUE
SCOTT BLVD
7TH STREET
GARRARD ST

Licking River

The nearby **Contemporary Arts Center**, on the second floor of the Mercantile Center at 115 E Fifth Street, puts on multi-media modern art exhibitions (Mon–Sat 10am–6pm; $2, free on Mon). The homoerotic photography of Robert Mapplethorpe rocked this sexually restrictive city to such an extent in 1990 that police temporarily closed the museum and its director was taken to court on charges of obscenity. By contrast, the **Taft Museum**, just east of downtown in an immaculate 1820 Federal-style mansion at 316 Pike Street, contains a priceless collection of works by Rembrandt, Hals, Goya, Turner and Gainsborough, plus a staggering collection of Ming porcelain and French enamels (Mon–Sat 10am–5pm, Sun 2–5pm; $2). The statue of a weary Abraham Lincoln in **Lytle Park**, in front of the museum, was criticised as unpatriotic when unveiled in 1917; it's now seen as a great example of sculptural realism.

Mount Adams and Eden Park

Just over a mile from downtown, the land rises suddenly and the streets – narrow courses with tight corners and abrupt dead ends – start to conform to the contours of **Mount Adams**. Century-old town houses coexist with avant-garde galleries, stylish boutiques, trendy gift shops and international restaurants. During the late nineteenth century, the elegant dining rooms of Mount Adams entertained the rich and famous who wanted to escape the squalor and noise of the Basin. Today its lively bars appeal to yuppies, students, hedonists and iconoclasts from all over the city. From downtown, take a taxi (around $3) or #49 bus.

Adjacent to this tightly packed neighbourhood recline the rolling lawns, verdant copses and scenic overlooks of **Eden Park**. A loop road at the northern end of this former vineyard leads to the **Cincinnati Art Museum** on Art Museum Drive. Its one hundred labyrinthine galleries span five thousand years, taking in an excellent Islamic collection as well as a solid selection of European and American paintings by the likes of Matisse, Monet, Picasso, Edward Hopper and Grant Wood (Tues & Thurs–Sat 10am–5pm, Wed 10am–9pm, Sun noon–5pm; $3, free on Sat).

Riverside

The Cincinnati side of the Ohio River seems at first to be dominated by the pallid, uninspiring **Riverfront Stadium**, home of football's Bengals and baseball's Reds. But just to the east, despite its proximity to car parks, concrete edifices and busy interstates, the riverside takes on a greater serenity. The mile-long riverside walk begins near the stadium at **Public Landing** at the bottom of Broadway. The cobbled wharf here, the original site of the city, is a great place to take a look at immaculately painted showboats and other river craft. Further west, **Bicentennial Commons** was a two-hundredth birthday present from the city to itself in 1988.

Covington, Kentucky

Covington, directly across the Ohio River on the Kentucky side, is very much part of the Cincinnati hinterland. It can be reached from downtown Cincinnati by walking over the bright-blue 355-yard 1867 **John A Roebling Suspension Bridge**, at the bottom of Walnut Street, which served as a prototype for the Brooklyn Bridge. Once across, you're confronted by the much-hyped **Covington Landing** – "the largest waterfront complex on inland waters" – a collection of cafes, shops and clubs on permanently moored boats that's little more than an upmarket mall on water. Two riverboat companies, *BB* (☎606/261-8500) and *Barleycorns* (☎606/581-0300), offer cruises from the Landing.

Ten minutes' walk southwest of the bridge brings you to the attractive, narrow, tree-lined streets and nineteenth-century houses of **MainStrasse Village**, a Germanic neighbourhood of antique shops, bars and restaurants. At Sixth and Philadelphia streets, twenty-one mechanical figures accompanied by glockenspiel music toll the hour on the German Gothic **Carroll Chimes Bell Tower**.

Accommodation
Budget travellers may have problems finding affordable downtown rooms; things don't get much cheaper until as far out as the airport. *Ohio Valley B&B*, 6876 Taylor Mill Road, Independence KY 41051 (☎606/356-7865), runs a reservation service for over-night stays in central Cincinnati and beyond. Places to camp are also a long way out; the nearest is the *Florence Overnite RV Park* (☎606/371-8352), 10485 Dixie Highway (US-25), fifteen miles south in Florence, Kentucky.

Budget Inn, 3356 Central Parkway (☎559-1600). The cheapest place in uptown Cincinnati, but doubles are still anywhere from $41 to $70. Just over three miles from downtown.

Cincinnati Home Hostel (AYH), 2200 Maplewood Ave (☎651-2329). Dorm beds in large converted house for only $6. Two miles from downtown.

Holiday Inn Downtown, 800 W Eighth St (☎241-8660). Usually downtown's cheapest rooms. $73.

Motel 6, I-75 Exit 180, Florence, KY (☎606/283-0909). Only $24, but almost twenty miles south.

Eating
Cincinnati has some excellent gourmet and continental restaurants, but it's best known for the chains of local fast-food restaurants that serve up **Cincinnati chili**. Pig out on a *five-way chili* (chili and beans over spaghetti, topped with cheese and chopped onions) with a side order of a *Coney Island* (hot dog with chili and cheese) and oyster crackers, all for under $3. *Skyline Chili*, open from breakfast to midnight, pops up at over forty places, including Vine & Seventh streets downtown.

Celestial Restaurant, 1071 Celestial St, Mt Adams (☎241-4455). Popular French restaurant. Dinner can be very expensive, but it's worth enquiring about the early evening $9.95 specials, Mon–Thurs.

Dee Felice, 529 Main St, Covington KY (☎606/261-2365). Small and atmospheric restaurant/jazz venue, specialising in Cajun cuisine, with lots of fresh seafood dishes. Main courses $12–20.

La Normandie Grill, 118 E Sixth St (☎721-2761). Solid, mid-range downtown choice, well known for great steaks, chops and seafood. Lunches $10, dinner entrees cost $12–20.

Longworth's, 1108 St Gregory St, Mt Adams (☎579-0900). Good quality meals for under $10 in a delightful garden setting. Food served all day until midnight, and the music goes on until 2.30am.

Mike Fink, at the foot of Greenup St, Covington KY (☎606/261-4212). Quality seafood restaurant in a fine old riverboat. Great night views of the Cincinnati skyline. Most main courses around $12.

Riverview Revolving Restaurant, in the *Quality Hotel*, 666 Fifth St, Covington KY (☎606/491-5300). Brilliant views of the river, with a full revolution each hour. The unusual cordon bleu menu, including alligator ravioli, is very expensive, but the excellent Sunday brunch is just $10.95.

Nightlife
The bars, restaurants and cafes of Mount Adams offer a great choice of music, food and atmosphere, especially good on warm summer nights when the narrow streets are full of revellers. What's on listings for the whole city are in the free *Everybody's News*.

Arnold's, 201 E 8th St (☎421-6234). Fun and funky downtown spot. A favourite with jazz fans, though it also puts on folk and acoustic acts. Good restaurant upstairs.

Blind Lemon, 936 Hatch St, Mt Adams (☎241-3885). Extremely popular cocktail bar in a dark, cavernous setting. Acoustic music most nights.

Cory's Old Cincinnati Saloon, 1 E McMillan St, Mt Auburn (☎721-6339). Bar near the University of Cincinnati campus. R&B bands most nights. Open until 2.15am, happy hour from 4pm to 8pm.

The Pavilion, 949 Pavilion St, Mt Adams (☎721-7272). Bar with great view of the city and the Ohio River from its terraced outdoor deck.

Classical Music, Opera, Theatre
Music Hall, at 1241 Elm Street (☎621-1919), an 1870s conglomeration of spires, arched windows and cornices, is said to have near-perfect acoustics. Home to Cincinnati's *Opera* and *Symphony Orchestra*, it also hosts the May Festival of choral music. The *Cincinnati Playhouse in the Park* (☎421-3888), in Eden Park, puts on drama, musicals and comedies with daily performances throughout the year (except Mon).

MICHIGAN

Mention **MICHIGAN** and most people think of cars, heavy industry and the blighted neighbourhoods of Detroit. To midwesterners, this vast state is almost as well known for magnificent scenery: along the 3200 miles of shoreline of its two vividly contrasting **peninsulas** – bordering four of the five Great Lakes – lie beaches, dunes and cliffs to rival many an oceanfront state.

The mitten-shaped **Lower Peninsula** is dominated from its southeastern corner by the industrial giant of **Detroit**, surrounded by satellite cities almost exclusively devoted to the automotive industry. Two hundred miles away, through unremarkable farmland, its balmy northwest corner, centred on **Traverse City**, contains a scattering of pretty little towns, and the stunning **Sleeping Bear Dunes**. The desolate, dramatic and thinly populated **Upper Peninsula**, reaching out from Wisconsin like a claw to separate lakes Superior and Michigan, is a far cry indeed from the cosmopolitan south.

The first whites in Michigan were **French** explorers, who in the mid-seventeenth century forged a successful trading relationship with the Chippewa, Ontario and other tribes. The **British**, who acquired control after 1763, were far more brutal: Governor Henry Hamilton was known as the "Hair Buyer of Detroit" for his advocacy of taking scalps rather than prisoners. Michigan's economy has developed in waves, starting with the fur, timber and copper booms of the early and mid-eighteenth century. By 1870, the majority of the workforce was involved in industry and commerce. The state's abundance of raw materials and good transport links – aided by the genius of innovators such as **Henry Ford** – placed it at the forefront of the nation's manufacturing capacity. It was the automobile that created many of its eastern cities in the Twenties – only to destroy many of them during the slumps of the Sixties and Seventies. Car production remains the major source of income, though tourism is now a four-season money-spinner.

Getting Around Michigan

It's easy to be caught out by Michigan's sheer size; from Ironwood, on the Wisconsin border, to Detroit is over seven hundred miles. *Greyhound* **buses** run regularly throughout its southern end, but journeys elsewhere are less frequent, and those few buses that serve the remote Upper Peninsula travel through at night, en route for Wisconsin. *Amtrak* **trains**, en route between New York and Chicago stop at **Detroit** and **Ann Arbor**, but the only trains to Canada pass through glum, industrial Port Huron. Michigan's principal **airport** is just outside Detroit. **Cycling** is both feasible and rewarding, particularly in the Traverse City area; the *League of Michigan Bicyclists* (☎616/452-BIKE) can help with routes.

Detroit

DETROIT, the birthplace of the mass production **car** industry and the **Motown** sound, is a city with an image problem. It boasts a billion-dollar downtown development, two ultra-modern motor-manufacturing plants, some excellent museums and one of the nation's biggest art galleries. But media attention focuses instead on its huge tracts of inner-city urban wasteland, and the gun-blasted neighbourhoods where the only signs of commerce are heavily fortified loan shops and food stores. If you are to believe all you read, Detroit is the American Beirut.

Such views incur the wrath of **Coleman Young**, the city's mayor, who claims that these are the kind of problems experienced by every US city, magnified by the press for the simple reason that blacks run Detroit and account for 75 percent of its population. That assertion certainly carries some weight, but Detroit – which has lost nearly half its citizens, almost a million people, in less than forty years – has by any standards suffered.

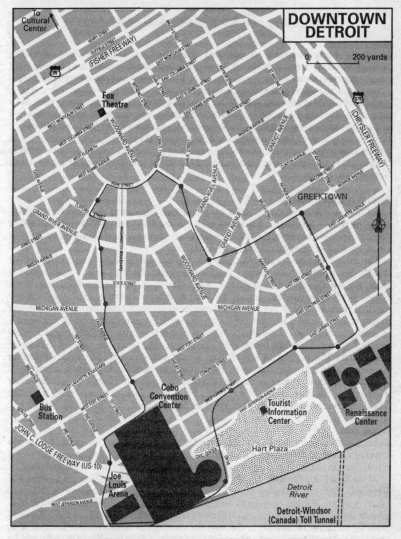

DOWNTOWN DETROIT

0   200 yards

To Cultural Center
(FISHER FREEWAY)
I-75
Fox Theatre
GREEKTOWN
(CHRYSLER FREEWAY) I-375
GRAND RIVER AVENUE
WOODWARD AVENUE
GRATIOT AVENUE
MICHIGAN AVENUE
MICHIGAN AVENUE
Bus Station
Cobo Convention Center
Tourist Information Center
Renaissance Center
JOHN C. LODGE FREEWAY (US-10)
Joe Louis Arena
Hart Plaza
CIVIC CENTER
Detroit River
Detroit-Windsor (Canada) Toll Tunnel
WEST JEFFERSON AVENUE

Founded in 1701 by Antoine de Mothe **Cadillac**, as a trading post for the French to do business with the Chippewa, Detroit was no more than a medium-sized port two hundred years later. Then **Ford**, **Olds**, the **Chevrolets** and the **Dodge** brothers began to build their automobile empires. Thanks to the introduction of the mass assembly line, Detroit sped into full gear in the Twenties, expanding into the countryside and booming like a mining town – fast, compulsive and indifferent to the needs of its population. The auto barons sponsored the construction of segregated neighbourhoods and unceremoniously dispensed with workers during times of low demand. Such policies created huge ghettos, and the city came to the boil in July 1967 in the bloodiest **riot** in the USA for

The telephone **area code** for Detroit and Ann Arbor is ☎313.

fifty years. More than forty people died and over 1300 buildings were destroyed. Nothing was solved, and little even improved; the inner city was left to fend for itself, and the all-important motor industry was rocked by the oil crises and Japanese competition.

No visitor to Detroit could fail to be disturbed by the divisions between rich and poor (and above all between white and black). The fact that other industrial towns have been hit equally hard by the recession is little consolation, and the latest round of closures and lay-offs by General Motors in December 1991 augurs badly for the future. However, whilst heavily scarred and bruised, Detroit is not quite the apocalyptic mess some would have it. Downtown has attracted new businesses and suburban residents have started to return to its clubs and restaurants, especially in the rejuvenated **Theater District** and **Greektown**.

Arrival and Information
Most **flights** still come into **Detroit Metropolitan Airport** in Romulus (☎942-3550), thirty minutes' drive from downtown and a hefty $30 taxi ride, though *Southwest Airlines* and several regional companies now use the expanding **Detroit City Airport** (☎267-6400), five miles out and only $10 in cab fare.

The main *Greyhound* – 1000 W Lafayette Avenue (☎961-2535) – and *Amtrak* – 2601 Rose Street at 17th Street – terminals are not in areas where it's safe to walk around at night. *Amtrak* also stop ten miles out at 16121 Michigan Avenue, Dearborn, next to the Henry Ford Museum and several mid-range motels. The high-tech *People Mover* elevated railway stops at thirteen downtown locations until 11pm during the week and midnight on Friday and Saturday (50¢). Otherwise, public transport is inadequate. Heavily guarded *DOT* buses (☎833-7692) run a patchy service in the inner city, while the slightly better *SMART* buses (☎962-5515) serve the outer communities. Transport in the Motor City is geared firmly toward the car; out-of-towners are often horrified by the vast array of criss-crossing roads, and the local penchant for high-speed driving.

Detroit's **visitor centre** is on Hart Plaza at 2 E Jefferson Street (daily 9am–5pm; ☎567-1170). The main **post office** (Mon–Fri 8.30am–5pm, Sat 8am–noon; zip code 48200) can be found at 1401 W Fort Street, at Eighth Street.

Downtown
Futuristic glass-box office blocks and a tastefully revamped park overlook the deodorant-green **Detroit River**, but for the most part downtown is a rather sad and empty place. Even in the middle of the day its streets are remarkably quiet and uncrowded.

At the heart of downtown, the six gleaming towers of the **Renaissance Center** (the **RenCen**) zoom up 73 storeys from the riverbank. This business, convention and retail centre was one of many complexes developed by **Detroit Renaissance** (a joint public/private sector project) to rejuvenate the city centre in the aftermath of the 1967 riots. Seen by some as the saviour of the city, the consortium is viewed less favourably by those whose small businesses and homes were compulsorily purchased to make way for its multimillion-dollar projects. Outside another massive chunk of steel and concrete, the Rubik-Cube-style **Cobo Convention Center**, stands a powerful-looking bronze statue of home-grown boxer **Joe Louis**. The Brown Bomber's wins, especially over Italian fascist Primo Carnera for the World Heavyweight Championship in 1935, were greeted by a carnival atmosphere in the black neighbourhood of Paradise Valley.

Rare green space comes among the fountains and sculptures of **Hart Plaza**, which rolls down to the river in the shade of the RenCen. It hosts free lunchtime concerts, as well as a succession of well-attended festivals on summer weekends. The USA leg of the **Montreux–Detroit Jazz Festival** takes place here in late May.

THE MOTOWN SOUND

Mo.town (*mo'toun'*) adj [< a trademark for phonograph records, etc. <Mo(tor) Town, nickname for Detroit, Mich] designating or of style of rhythm and blues characterised by a strong, even beat.
Webster's New World Dictionary of the American Language

The legend that is Tamla Motown started in 1959 when Ford worker and part-time songwriter **Berry Gordy Jnr** borrowed $800 to set up a studio. From his first hit onwards – the prophetic *Money (That's What I Want)* – he set out to create a crossover style, targeting his records at white and black consumers alike.

Early Motown hits were pure **formula**. Gordy softened the bluenotes prominent in most black music of the time, in favour of a more danceable, poppy beat, with **gospel**-influenced singing and clapping. Prime examples of the early approach featured all-female groups like the **Marvelettes** (*Needle in a Haystack*), the **Supremes** (*Baby Love*) and **Martha Reeves and the Vandellas** (*Nowhere to Run*), as well as the all-male **Miracles** (*Tracks Of My Tears*) featuring the sophisticated love lyrics of lead singer **Smokey Robinson**. The Motown organisation was an intense, close-knit community: **Marvin Gaye** married Gordy's sister, "Little" **Stevie Wonder** was the child of the family.

In the quest for chart domination Gordy instituted what he called the "Quality Control Department", a backroom team who scrutinised every beat, playing all recordings through speakers modelled on those of cheap transistor radios before the final mix. Motown also moved with the times, utilising such innovations as the wah-wah pedal and synthesiser. By the late Sixties its output had acquired a harder sound, crowned by the acid soul productions of Norman Whitfield working with the versatile **Temptations**.

In 1968 the organisation outgrew its premises on Grand Avenue; four years later it abandoned Detroit altogether for Los Angeles, to be closer to Hollywood's television and film companies. Befitting the MOR tastes of the Seventies, the top sellers now were the high-society soul of **Diana Ross** and the ballads of the **Commodores**. White artists began to appear on the label: Tom Jones is said to have turned down a contract, though R. Dean Taylor (*Indiana Wants Me*) and the less successful Kiki Dee did accept.

The Seventies saw many top artists, dissatisfied with Gordy's constant intervention, leave the label. The crack songwriting team of Holland-Dozier-Holland, responsible for most of the **Four Tops'** hits, stayed in Detroit to produce the seminal **Chairmen of the Board** (*Gimme Just A Little More Time*), along with Aretha Franklin and Jackie Wilson.

Now wholly owned by MCA, Motown still rakes in the royalties, more on the strength of its back catalogue than its current roster of artists like Rockwell and Bruce Willis. More conservative in its output than many black-music divisions of the major record corporations, the Motown of the Nineties is the antithesis of its innovative early years, and a far cry from the "rats, roaches and soul" of the ghetto which Gordy claimed his music represented in the early days.

Three miles further east (take *DOT* bus #25 and transfer to #4 at MacArthur Bridge), the two-mile-long **Belle Isle** public park is a quiet inner-city island retreat with twenty miles of walkways, various sports facilities and free attractions including an aquarium, a Great Lakes Museum and elaborate gardens.

The Cultural Center

Three miles northwest of downtown, next to Wayne State University, the top-class museums of the **Detroit Cultural Center** all lie within easy walking distance of each other. Due to budgetary restrictions imposed by Michigan's monetarist Republican governor, it's best to phone for current opening times.

One hundred galleries in the colossal **Detroit Institute of Art**, 5200 Woodward Avenue, trace a history of civilisation, most notably Chinese, Persian, Egyptian, Greek, Roman, Italian, Dutch and American (Wed–Sun 9.30am–5.30pm; mandatory donation).

No less than 93 Rembrandts, 77 Matisses and 67 Picassos are on display, as are master-pieces like Van Gogh's self-portrait and Joos Van Cleeve's *Adoration of the Magi*; but for many Diego Rivera's enormous 1932 mural *Detroit Industry* steals the show. The main display in the well laid-out **Museum of African-American History**, 301 Frederick Douglass Street, looks at Michigan's role in the Underground Railway, smuggling slaves from the south to Canada (Wed–Sat 9.30am–5pm, Sun 1–5pm; free). Whilst recognising the achievements of the city's African-Americans, the museum doesn't ignore the social and employment problems faced by young people in Detroit today.

Also in the Cultural Center, the **Detroit Historical Museum**, 5401 Woodward Avenue, interprets the city's past through the *Streets of Old Detroit* display (Wed–Sun 9.30am–5pm; donation), and the **Detroit Science Center**, 5020 John R Street, holds assorted hands-on displays (Tues–Fri 9am–4pm, Sat 10am–6pm, Sun noon–6pm; $5).

The Motown Museum

2648 W Grand Blvd. Tues–Sat 10am–5pm, Sun 2–5pm. $3. ☎875-2264.

Unlike cities such as Memphis, Nashville and New Orleans, Detroit is devoid of the bars, clubs and homes of the stars associated with the music that made it famous. The golden age of Motown was very much confined to a time and a place, and, disappoint-ingly, only at the **Motown Museum** can Tamla fans now pay homage to the world's most celebrated record label. The museum is housed in the small white and blue clap-board house that served as Motown's recording studio from 1959 to 1972. On the ground floor, Studio A remains just as it was left: battered instruments stand piled up against the nicotine-stained acoustic wall-tiles, and a well-scuffed Steinway piano all but fills the room. Upstairs, record sleeves, gold and platinum discs, sheet music and photos are diplayed almost at random on the walls and tables. Michael Jackson gets a small room to himself as a thank you for his $125,000 donation. The absence of sophisticated display is more than made up for by the enthusiastic and knowledgeable staff, who will quite happily give one person the full tour.

Henry Ford Museum and Greenfield Village

20900 Oakwood Blvd, Dearborn. 10 miles from downtown, on *SMART* bus routes #200 and #250. Daily 9am–5pm; the interiors of Greenfield Village buildings are closed Jan to mid-March. $10.50 for each attraction or $18 for a two-day combination ticket. ☎271-1620.

The enormous **Henry Ford Museum** pays fulsome tribute to its founder as a brilliant industrialist and do-gooder. The former is certainly true. The hero of the "second indus-trial revolution", he invented the assembly line and guided the company he founded in 1903 with such vision that within two decades it was producing over two million cars per year. However, Ford didn't achieve all this by being a philanthropist. The formation of the Service Department – 3500 private policemen, who terrorised, and on occasion killed, suspected troublemakers – prompted the *New York Times* in 1928 to call him "an industrialist fascist – the Mussolini of Detroit". To Ford, unions were "the worst things that ever struck the earth". He became obsessed by "red agitators" and even argued for the right to arm non-strikers during disputes. But after a ballot in which only 34 out of 78,000 workers voted against joining a union, he was eventually forced to let the UAW into his factories in 1943. Ford also had to bow to the economic necessity of employing blacks, though he banned them from living in the model communities he built for his white workers. Instead,the company constructed a separate town, which he sardonically named Inkster.

Besides the massive **"Automobile in American Life"** exhibit, the twelve-acre museum amounts to a giant curiosity shop, holding several planes and trains, rows and rows of domestic inventions, and cabinets full of schoolboy collectables like dime novels, comics and baseball cards. Real oddities include the chair Lincoln was sitting in, and the car Kennedy was riding in, when each was shot, and even a test tube holding

Edison's last breath. One pertinent item not on view, however, is the Iron Cross which Hitler presented to Ford (a notorious anti-Semite) in 1938.

Ford uprooted the houses of famous Americans from all over the country to relocate them in **Greenfield Village**. Among the 240 buildings, you'll find Ford's own birthplace, the Wright Brothers' cycle shop, Edison's laboratory, and Firestone's farm. Costumed staff give displays of everything from weaving to puncture repairing.

Accommodation

Downtown Detroit caters well for expense-account travellers. The problem for others is to find somewhere to stay that's both safe and cheap. Be sure to bear in mind the cost of reaching your destination at night by taxi if you intend to sample the nightlife.

Country Grandma's AYH Home Hostel, 22330 Bell Rd (☎753-4901). On the outskirts of Dearborn. $8 members; $11 non-members.

Days Inn – Downtown, 231 Michigan Ave (☎965-4646). Just about the cheapest central downtown hotel during the week (some others offer weekend specials). $80.

Fairfield Inn, 31119 Flynn Drive (☎728-2322). The best budget motel near the airport. $40.

Mercy College of Detroit, 8200 W Outer Drive (☎592-6170). Eleven miles from downtown. Singles $20, doubles $32; students get a twenty percent discount.

Motor City AYH Home Hostel, 16901 Burgess Ave (☎533-9597). Twelve miles from downtown. Cyclists well catered for. $8.

Red Roof Inn, 24130 Michigan Ave, Dearborn (44278-9732). Handy for *Amtrak* in Dearborn. $40.

Shorecrest Motor Inn, 1316 E Jefferson Ave (☎568-3000). A friendly family-run business. Clean rooms at a good price, behind an unimpressive exterior. In lively Rivertown, just off downtown. $45.

Eating

The ethnic **restaurants** in Detroit dish up the best (and some of the least expensive) food in the city. **Greektown**, just one block of Monroe Avenue between Beaubien and St Antoine streets, is crammed with authentic Greek places, while nearby **Trappers Alley** is a small mall crammed with good stalls and shops. Less commercial, but offering just as high a standard of food, are the bakeries, bars and cantinas of **Mexican Town**, five minutes from downtown. Suburban **Royal Oak**, ten miles out, has a wide range of vaguely alternative wholefood places, along with its bars, record and book shops.

Elwood Grill, 2100 Woodward Ave (☎961-7485). Wonderful Art-Deco building near to the Fox Theater. Gourmet burgers, sandwiches and entrees from $8 to $15.

El Zocala, 3400 Bagley Ave at 23rd St, Mexican Town (☎841-3700). Aztec-style Mexican restaurant, revered for its margaritas and *botanas* (chips smothered in refried beans). Most entrees $5–7.

New Parthenon, 579 Monroe Ave, Greektown (☎961-5111). Expensive-looking place, with its pillars and Hellenic murals, but entrees are a reasonable $6–8. Great salads, seafood and vegetarian fare.

Niki's Tavern, 735 Beaubien St (☎961-4303). Cheap cafe on the edge of Greektown with tasty deep-dish pizzas and succulent gyros for under $5.

Woodbridge Tavern, 289 St Aubin St, Rivertown (☎259-0578). Excellent burgers and sandwiches, with Twenties decor and a great outdoor terrace. Also live rock music Thurs–Sun.

Xochimilco, 3409 Bagley Ave, Mexican Town (☎843-0179). Basic decor, lots of people, lots of choice and celebrated *tacos al carbon*. Open until 4am; main courses $5–7.

Nightlife

There's lots to do late at night in Detroit – the city where the **techno-house** beat originated and is still going strong – though if you're unfamiliar with the layout it's best to travel by taxi. In the past few years young whites from the suburbs have started to come back downtown for nights out, particularly to the bars and clubs of the **Theater District**. The area centres around the glorious **Fox Theater**, 2111 Woodward Avenue (☎567-6000), a huge old movie palace that's now the city's top concert and drama venue. **Rivertown**, a mile from the RenCen, is renowned for its chic bistros and funky jazz and blues bars, tucked in amongst rambling warehouses.

Windsor, Ontario, just across the Canadian border, also has some good nightlife, as well as a great view of the Detroit skyline. You can get there on the *Tunnel Bus* ($1.50); be sure to take your passport.

The City Club, 400 Bagley Ave, downtown (☎962-2300). Dark, dingy, strobe-lit and oozing atmosphere. The best dance sounds in Detroit for the past few years. Almost anti-trendy in attitude.

Elan, 1314 Broadway (☎965-2196). One of the city's top house joints.

Rhinoceros, 265 Riopelle St, Rivertown (☎259-2208). Poppy jazz hangout. A tight squeeze but fun.

Saint Andrew's Hall, 431 E Congress St, downtown (☎961-8137). Cramped, cavernous club promoting unknown bands and top new acts. Only holds 800, so get a ticket in time.

Soup Kitchen Saloon, 1585 Franklin St, Rivertown (☎259-2643). Detroit's premier venue for gutsy low-down blues. A great old bar but the capacity of just 130 makes it sweaty, smoky and squashed.

Out From Detroit: Ann Arbor

Although its population just tops 100,000, **ANN ARBOR,** 45 minutes' drive west of Detroit along I-94, offers a greater choice of restaurants, live music venues and cultural activities than most conurbations ten times its size. The **University of Michigan** has shaped the growth, economy and character of the town ever since it was moved here from Detroit in 1837, providing the city with a very conspicuous radical edge.

Much the best thing to do in Ann Arbor is to stroll round downtown and the campus which meet at S State and Liberty streets. **Downtown's** twelve blocks of brightly painted shops and sidewalk cafes offer all you would expect from a college town. The huge **campus** doesn't look particularly appealing, but it emanates a buzz that makes it an exciting place to linger. Worth a look are the **Ruthven Exhibit Museum,** 1109 Geddes Avenue, packed with unusual natural history displays including huge dinosaur skeletons, rare Indian artefacts and a planetarium (Tues–Sat 9am–5pm, Sun 1–5pm), and the small but eclectic **Museum of Art,** 525 S State Street (Tues–Fri 10am–4pm, Sat & Sun 1–5pm).

Practicalities

Greyhound operate frequent services to both Detroit ($8) and Chicago, stopping at 116 W Huron Street (☎662-5511), while the *Amtrak* station is on the north edge of downtown at 325 Depot Street. The **visitor centre** is at 211 E Huron Street (☎995-7281).

Although most Ann Arbor **motels** target their prices at conventioneers and academics, the *Red Roof Inn,* 3621 Plymouth Road (☎996-5800), is a reasonable $40. The modern downtown *YMCA,* 350 S Fifth Avenue (☎663-0536), is open to both sexes, charging $23 for a single room with shared bath ($85 per week). You can also get nice en-suite rooms right on campus at the *U of M Cambridge House (West Quad),* 541 Thompson Street (☎764-0185). Singles range from $39 to $49, doubles $49 to $59.

Restaurants worth trying out include the good-value Indian *Raja Rani,* 400 S Division Street (☎995-1545), and the wholefood *Seva,* 314 E Liberty Avenue (☎662-1111). *Jerusalem Garden,* 307 S Fifth Street (☎995-5060), serves the best falafel in town, while *Zingerman's,* 422 Detroit Street (☎663-DELI), is an excellent if expensive deli.

Ann Arbor's **live music** scene has enjoyed a nationwide reputation ever since the Stooges, MC5 and Bob Seger made their names here; and, unlike many college towns, the whole place doesn't go to sleep during the summer. For news of gigs, grab a copy of *Current,* a free monthly, or tune into the excellently eclectic student/community (ie ex-student) station WCBN 88.3FM. Likely venues include the jazz-oriented *Bird of Paradise,* 207 S Ashley Avenue (☎662-8310), *Club Heidelberg,* 215 N Main Street (☎994-3562), which specialises in acoustic and leftish "anti-folk" acts, and *Rick's American Cafe,* 611 Church Street (☎996-2747), where you can see rock, blues and indie bands. *Del Rio,* 122 W Washington Avenue (☎761-2530), is a crowded **bar** which serves great Mexican food and hosts free jazz sessions every Sunday.

The Lower Peninsula

The northern reaches of Michigan's lower peninsula, particularly the area around **Traverse City**, attract sportspeople and tourists from all over the Midwest. Within striking distance of Traverse are the beautiful **Sleeping Bear Dunes** on the Leelanu Peninsula to the west and the charming towns of **Charlevoix** and **Petoskey** to the northeast. Marking the northern tip, messy **Mackinaw City** is the departure point for the state's major tour bus attraction, old-world **Mackinac Island**.

Traverse City

Smooth beaches and striking bay views help make lively **TRAVERSE CITY**, 242 miles northwest of Detroit, the favourite in-state resort for Michiganers. A town of just 17,000 year-round residents, it was saved from the stagnation that overtook many north Michigan communities when their lumber mills closed down, as the stripped fields proved to be ideal for fruit-growing. Today, the area's claim to be "**Cherry Capital of the World**" is no idle boast: thousands of acres of cherry orchards envelop the town, their wispy, pink blossom bringing a delicate beauty each May. The annual **Cherry Festival** is held during the first full week in July. As well as parades, fireworks and concerts, there's a chance to sample every imaginable cherry product; Coca-Cola chose the event to launch its cherry flavour a few years ago.

The neat **downtown** rests along the bottom of the west arm of **Grand Traverse Bay**, below the Old Mission Peninsula. This slender seventeen-mile strip of land, which divides the bay into two inlets, makes for a pleasant short driving tour; narrow roads slice through miles of cherry orchards and vineyards, with tremendous simultaneous views of the bay on either side. Five sandy public **beaches** and a small **harbour** can be found around the town itself. Various companies offer boat, windsurfer, jet ski and mountain bike rental (the surrounding countryside is excellent for cycling).

Practicalities

Greyhound stops near downtown at 3233 Cass Road (☎946-5180). The **visitor centre**, at 415 Munson Avenue (☎947-1120), can help with finding **accommodation**, though Traverse City has a dearth of cheap places to stay. Rooms at the small and attractive *Bay Shore Motel*, 833 E Front Street (☎946-4798), near downtown with its own private beach, cost around $70; the well-maintained *Days Inn*, 420 Munson Avenue (☎941-0208), is similarly priced. The *Sierra Motel*, 230 Munson Avenue (☎946-7720), is a bit shabby but starts at $45. In summer, you can get a single room for as little as $18 at *North Michigan Community College East Hall*, 1701 E Front Street (☎922-1406); doubles are $30. You can **camp** at Traverse City State Park, just outside town at 1132 US-31E (☎947-7193).

Traverse City brochures might tout its exclusive country clubs, but more affordable places to **eat** are easy to find. *Mode's Bum Steer*, 125 E State Street (☎947-9832), is the town's premier rib joint, and *Don's Drive-In*, 2030 US-31N (☎938-1860), is a porky-pink-coloured Fifties-style diner with magnificent burgers and shakes, a couple of miles south of downtown. The best **bar** in town has to be the *U & I Lounge*, 214 E Front Street (☎946-8932), which besides the drink serves up great gyros, burgers and salads for under $5. *Union Street Station*, 117 South Union Street (☎941-1930), has **live music** of all sorts most nights of the week. *Larry's Place* at the *Bay Winds*, 1265 US-31N (☎929-1044), is a hectic beach bar. It's popular with students and great fun – even if there's a limit to the number of Jimmy Buffet songs you can stomach in one night.

> The telephone **area code** for Traverse City and around is ☎616.

The Leelanu Peninsula

The ideal day trip out from Traverse City is to drive or cycle round the ninety-mile loop of heavily wooded **Leelanu Peninsula**, just to the west. The giant sand dunes along its southwestern edge are utterly spectacular, though several easy-going little villages and ports, such as Leland, are also worth calling in on.

The **Sleeping Bear Dunes National Lakeshore**, a constantly re-sculpted area of towering dunes and precipitous 400-foot drops, starts about twenty miles west of town. Only as you approach close enough to realise that the brightly coloured specks on what appear to be insignificant, undulating mounds are in fact people, do you begin to appreciate their true size. They were named by the Chippewa, who saw the mist-shrouded North and South Manitou Islands as the grave-sites of two drowned bear-cubs and the massive mainland dune, covered with dark trees, as their grieving mother. Fierce winds off Lake Michigan cause the dunes to edge inland, burying trees that reappear years later stripped of foliage and life. The continual attack of high water, on the other hand, undercuts the massive sand banks, occasionally sending massive chunks of them into the water.

To see the dunes, take the **Pierce Stocking Scenic Drive**, off Hwy-109, a hilly nine-mile loop affording a number of stunning overlooks and trail routes, or clamber up the strenuous but enjoyable **Dune Climb**, four miles further north on Hwy-109 (take sunscreen and water, and try to do it barefoot, as shoes soon fill with sand). The **visitor centre** (☎326-5134), at the junction of Hwys-22 and 109, can direct you to the trail-heads, the **beach** near the hamlet of Empire, and various **campgrounds**.

LELAND, fifteen miles north, is the best village to stop at on the peninsula. Its harbour, crammed with expensive launches, also shelters a quaint collection of well-weathered sheds, known as **Fishtown**, where the day's catch used to be hauled in for gutting and smoking; most are now touristy knick-knack shops. *The Cove* at 111 River Street here (☎256-9834) serves up tasty Great Lakes fish and is run by the same people as the weirside burger restaurant, *Rick's Place*, downstairs. **Ferries** from Leland (☎256-9061; $15) go to the uninhabited South Manitou Island.

North of Traverse City

Scenic Hwy-31 skims along between Lake Michigan and a number of smaller, more placid lakes before passing through delightful **Charlevoix** and other pretty lakeside towns. The northern tip of the peninsula is sullied by the presence of **Mackinaw City**, a giant parking lot for the tour buses that bring excursionists to much-hyped **Mackinac Island** – roadside hoardings advertise its attractions for a good fifty miles before you arrive.

Charlevoix

CHARLEVOIX boasts a positively idyllic setting, fronting onto three separate lakes: Michigan, Charlevoix and the beautiful, bowl-shaped Round Lake. Petunia-lined **Bridge Street**, the two-block downtown, looks over a picturesque, almost landlocked harbour on Round Lake, hemmed in on other sides by terraced ridges. Various comp-anies offer boat trips; walk down to the harbour for schedules and prices or call in at the **visitor centre**, 408 Bridge Street (☎547-2101). Two fine sandy beaches on the Michigan shoreline lie within easy walking distance of the harbour.

Lakeside condos and hotels charge up to $500 a night; even the best value "budget" **motel**, the *Archway*, 1440 S Bridge Street (☎547-2096), charges $60 to $80. There is, however, a small **home hostel** at 541 N Mercer Street (☎547-2937), understandably very popular, with rates under $5 a night. *Parkside Dining*, 404 Bridge Street (☎547-9111), is a reasonably priced family-style **diner** with a good view of the harbour.

Petoskey and Harbor Springs

Bigger and busier than Charlevoix is **PETOSKEY**, sixteen miles north along US-31, high on a hill above the stony-blue waters of Lake Michigan. Grand old Victorian houses encircle the Gaslight District downtown, which is nicely restored and kitted out with tasteful shops. **Motels** in Petoskey are much cheaper: the *Inland House Motel* (☎347-8127) on US-31N on Crooked Lake has weekday rooms for $38. The cheapest lodgings of all are the clean dorms available year-round at *North Central Michigan College*, 1505 Howard Street (☎347-3973), for only $7 per person. For inexpensive **meals**, choose between the gorgeous deli sandwiches at *Symon's General Store*, 401 E Lake Street (☎347-2438), or *Jesperson's*, 312 Howard Street (☎347-3601), which specialises in pies and pasties.

Twelve miles out from Petoskey along Hwy-119, **HARBOR SPRINGS** is a favourite haunt of the midwestern elite. Its charming main street and small shaded beach with adjacent park are certainly captivating, but the sheer ostentation puts many off this "Cornbelt Riviera" resort. The *Harbor Springs Motor Inn* at Bay and Zoll streets (☎526-5431) is the only place where rooms come as cheap as $65.

Mackinac Island

Viewed from an approaching boat, the tree-blanketed rocky limestone outcrop of **MACKINAC ISLAND** (pronounced *Mackinaw*), suddenly thrusting out from the swirling waters, is an unforgettable sight. As you near the harbour, large Victorian houses come into view, dappling the hillsides with white and pastel shades. The most conspicuous is the imposing facade of the $250-a-night *Grand Hotel*, where even to enter the foyer costs $5. On disembarking, your attention is grabbed by rows of horses and buggies (all motor vehicles are supposedly banned from the island, though some motorised horse trailers are tucked away out the back) and the omnipresent smell of fresh **manure**. Also ubiquitous on the island is **fudge**, a Mackinac "delicacy" which tourists purchase by the boxload from Victorian-style shops.

Mackinac's crowded main street and the contrived nostalgic aura can get irritating, but the island is still worth visiting, not least for the ferry ride over and the opportunity to cycle along the hilly backroads. Underneath all the tourist trimmings is a rich history. The first whites to reach here were French priests who established a mission to the Huron Indians during the winter of 1670–71. The French army built a fort in 1715 but lost control of the island to the British within fifty years. Since independence, Mackinac has been used as a base for John Jacob Astor's American Fur Company, a fishing port, and a jail for Confederate officers during the Civil War. The government acknowledged its beauty by designating it as the country's second national park, two years after Yellowstone in 1875, though management was handed over to the state of Michigan twenty years later. To get a feel for the history, hike or cycle up to the whitewashed stone **Fort Mackinac**, a US Army outpost until 1890. Its ramparts afford a great view of the village and lake below, though admission is a steep $6.

Regular **ferries** run from **MACKINAW CITY**, a parasitic colony of motels, fudge, souvenir and T-shirt emporia, forty miles north of Petoskey. *Shepler's* (☎616/436-5023) operate a smooth, reliable service for $10.50 return and $4 for bikes. If you want to stay, be prepared to part with a lot of money: the average room in the island's many lodging places costs in excess of $120 a night. The cheapest **hotel** is *Murray's* (☎847-3361), where most rooms are around $70, though some go for $50. Unpretentious **B&Bs** are more affordable; the *Bogan Lane Inn* (☎847-3439) costs $45, and the secluded *Small Point* (☎847-3758), $52. The **information** kiosk on Main Street (☎847-3783) provides full prices and details of accommodation, horse rides and bike rental.

The telephone **area code** for Mackinac Island and the Upper Peninsula is ☎906.

The Upper Peninsula

From the map, it would seem more logical for Michigan's **Upper Peninsula**, separated from the rest of the state by the **Mackinac Straits**, to be part of Wisconsin. However, when Michigan entered the Union in 1837 (eleven years before Wisconsin), its legislators, keen to tap its huge mineral wealth, incorporated it into their new state.

Before then the U.P., as it's commonly known, figured prominently in French plans to create an empire in North America. Missionaries such as Father Jacques Marquette made peace with the Indians and established settlements like the port of **Sault Ste Marie** in 1688. The French hoped to press further south, but before they could get much past Detroit, the British inflicted a severe military defeat in 1763.

Vast, lonesome and wild, the Upper Peninsula has lots of stunning landmarks, exemplified by the **Pictured Rocks National Lakeshore**, but few towns of interest. The northwest corner is the most desolate, especially the rough and broken **Keewanaw Peninsula**, and **Isle Royale** fifty miles offshore. Until 1957 you could only get to the U.P. from lower Michigan by ferry. Today, the five-mile **Mackinaw Bridge** ($1.50 toll) stretches elegantly across the bottleneck Straits of Mackinac, with Lakes Superior and Huron to either side. At night its glistening multicoloured lights sparkle in the dark northern sky and are reflected in the black waters of the straits.

Eastern U.P.

Most of the eastern portion of the Upper Peninsula, enveloped by Lakes Superior, Huron and Michigan, is marked by low-lying, sometimes swampy land in between softly undulating limestone hills. The best scenery is on the southern shores of Lake Superior, on the northern side of the peninsula, west of Sault Ste Marie.

Sault Ste Marie

Perched at the northeast corner of the U.P., 340 miles from Detroit, **SAULT STE MARIE** (known locally as "The Soo") lies across St Mary's Rapids from the Canadian town bearing the same name. It's one of the oldest settlements in the US, not that you'd guess that from its bedraggled Fifties-looking downtown and the industrial sprawl of the waterfront. The Soo owes most of its trade and industry to the **St Mary's Locks**, the only water connection between Superior and the other Great Lakes, built in 1855 and later expanded to take oceangoing vessels. Four giant reservoirs raise upbound boats twenty-one feet to the level of Lake Superior. To see this impressive operation, which accounts for more tonnage than the Suez and Panama canals combined, take one of the *Soo Locks Boat Tours* ($10; ☎632-3311) from Dock #1 or Dock #2 on East Portage Avenue, or watch for free from the Soo Locks Visitors Center (daily 7am–11pm).

Despite efforts to increase its tourist trade, the Soo is not a place you'd want to spend much time in, though the *Crestview Thrifty Inn*, 1200 Ashmun Street (☎635-5213), has good, clean, comfortable rooms for $40.

Paradise

Native Americans who lived in the area around **PARADISE**, sixty miles west and north of the Soo, called it *Tahquamenon* (Marsh of the Blueberries). If you get here on a good summer day, the current name of this elongated lakeside village, cut out of thick dark green forests and surrounded by small, reed-cluttered ultramarine lakes, doesn't seem too far amiss. Life is slow and easy here, but the choppy waters of Superior deny absolute calm to the beach. In winter temperatures drop to -40°F and snowmobiles are the usual mode of transport. Ten miles west on Hwy-123, a popular spot for hiking, boating and camping is the **Tahquamenon Falls State Park** (daily; $3 per car), where waters, coloured a translucent brown by tannic acid, spill over two sets of cataracts.

Basic but clean **accommodation** costs $30 at the *Vagabond Motel* (☎492-3477). *Curley's Motel* (☎492-3445), at the road junction, is a definite step up with a nice beach, sports facilities and the *Yukon Bar*, full of stuffed trophies, right across the road. Doubles cost $42 and cabins for six people are only $75. You can pitch a tent at the *Superior Campground* (☎492-3249), one mile south of the town near the *Birch Hill Cafe*, popular for its succulent fried whitefish.

Whitefish Point

Whitefish Road winds its way nine miles north of Paradise to where the shingle shores of **WHITEFISH POINT** nudge into the harsh waters of Lake Superior. Raging northwesterly winds that build up over two hundred miles of open lake have helped to cause over 500 shipwrecks along the eighty-mile stretch of lakeshore to Munising. As you drive the coast road beside this "Graveyard of the Great Lakes", you can spot the skeletons of schooners and steamboats. The **Great Lakes Shipwreck Historical Museum**, gloomily lit with doom-laden background music, tells the stories of the big wrecks. It's not all ancient history; the cargo ship *Edmund Fitzgerald* foundered in 96mph gusts on November 10 1975, with the loss of its 29 crew (June to mid-Oct daily 10am–6pm; $3).

Pictured Rocks National Lakeshore and Munising

The 42 mile between the attractive fishing villages of **Grand Marais** and **Munising** form the **Pictured Rocks National Lakeshore**, a splendid array of multicoloured cliffs, rolling dunes and secluded sandy beaches. Rain, wind, ice and sun have carved and gouged arches, columns and caves into the face of the lakeshore, all stained with different hues. An unpaved road and hiking trails run beside the water, but the best way to see the cliffs is by boat. Three-hour narrated **cruises** leave from the left of the City Pier in Munising (daily; July & Aug 5 trips per day; June, Sept & early Oct, 2 trips; $12.50; ☎387-2379). *Scotty's Motel*, 415 Cedar Street in Munising (☎387-2449), is a comfortable place to stay for $35.

Western U.P.

From the Pictured Rocks onward, the bleak western half of the U.P. contrasts sharply with the low-lying eastern portion, both topographically and economically. Rough-hewn to the extreme, its dramatic shores are potted with crags and precipices. To see it at its most uncouth, travel along the **Keewanaw Peninsula** with its rocky spine and small harbour towns, or take a ferry out to the wilderness of Isle Royale.

The Keewanaw Peninsula and Isle Royale

Very much off the beaten track, the **Keewanaw Peninsula** juts like a dorsal fin eighty miles out into Lake Superior. Halfway up the peninsula in **Houghton**, a small college town overlooking Portage Lake, the *Gateway Motel* on US-41 near the ferry dock (☎482-3511) is good value at $30–40. The *Suomi Home Bakery and Restaurant* (☎482-3220), under the covered street downtown, serves cheap pasties and Finnish food. Right at the northern tip of Keewanaw, the handsome small village of **Copper Harbor** also has budget accommodation in the *Brockway Inn* on Hwy-26 (☎289-4588).

In summer, **ferries** to the 45-mile sliver of **Isle Royale National Park**, fifty miles out in Lake Superior, leave from both Copper Harbor ($30; ☎289-4437) and Houghton ($37; ☎482-0984). In a double sense this is as far as you can get in Michigan from Detroit: all cars are banned, and, instead of freeways, 166 miles of hiking trails lead past Native American copper mines and swampy lakes where moose graze. Canoeing and scuba-diving among shipwrecks are the principal leisure activities. The **park headquarters** at 87 N Ripley Street (☎482-0984) in Houghton can advise on camping, mosquitoes, and how to cope with temperatures that drop well below freezing even in summer.

INDIANA

Thanks to a heavy influx of immigrants from the south at the start of the nineteenth century, once the Miami, Potawatomi and Shawnee had been displaced, northerly **INDIANA** displays vestiges of the easy-going South. Among these early settlers was the family of Abraham Lincoln, who set up home near the present village of Santa Claus, close to the Kentucky border, in 1816, and stayed for fourteen years before moving to Illinois. Unlike the abolitionist Lincolns, many brought slaves to this new territory; slavery was technically banned in all northern states, but Indiana allowed a system of "voluntary servitude" to operate right up to 1843. At the outbreak of the Civil War, thousands of ex-southerners rioted against the draft. Behind such slogans as "We won't fight to free the nigger" lay a real concern that Indiana was every bit as subservient to the northeast as the Deep South. However, since the 1870s, industrialisation has integrated Indiana into the regional economy.

Despite some beautiful dunes and beaches, the most lasting memories provided by Indiana's fifty-mile **lakeshore** (by far the shortest of the Great Lake states) are the grimy steel mills and poverty-stricken neighbourhoods of towns like **Gary** and **East Chicago**. Elsewhere in the state there is little of real interest to travellers. The central plains are characterised by small agricultural settlements, except for the sprawling state capital, **Indianapolis**, which, despite a population close to a million, and a number of attractions lacks the dynamism of nearby cities of similar size such as Louisville and Cincinnati. Hilly southern Indiana, at its most appealing in autumn, is a welcome contrast to the central cornbelt.

Dozens of explanations have been offered as to why Indianans are called "Hoosiers"; the most believable is that its use spread from the days of the Ohio Falls Canal construction in the 1820s, when a contractor, Samuel Hoosier, gave employment preference to those living on the Indiana side of the Ohio River. His workers became known as the Hoosier men and later simply as Hoosiers.

Getting Around Indiana

Nine different interstates – seven of them slicing through Indianapolis – provide boring but fast ways of traversing Indiana. *Greyhound* runs frequent services, particularly on I-65 between Chicago and Louisville and I-70 between the east and St Louis. **Indianapolis**, **Michigan City** and **South Bend** are the major stops on the three different *Amtrak* routes which cut through the state. Flights from most midwestern and eastern cities come in at **Indianapolis International Airport**

Northern Indiana

Lying just off I-80/90, halfway along the northern fringe of Indiana, the industrial centre of **SOUTH BEND** briefly threatened to rival Detroit as the country's leading car manufacturing centre during the early Twenties, when the now-defunct Studebaker marque was going strong. These days it's better known for the **University of Notre Dame**, the most famous Roman Catholic college in the US and home of the widely supported Fighting Irish **football** team. Free tours of the campus (☎219/239-5110) take in the gold-domed Administration Building and sights such as a replica of the grotto at Lourdes. The *Hickory Inn Motel*, 50520 US-33N (☎219/272-7555), three miles from the university, has **rooms** for under $30.

Forty miles west, smaller **MICHIGAN CITY** marks the start of the twenty-mile **Indiana Dunes National Lakeshore**, dedicated in 1972 to prevent further encroachment on the state's shoreline by manufacturing or tourist industries. There's not much to the "city" itself but it is the handiest place to stay near the lake; the *Knights Inn*, 201 W Keiffer Road (☎219/874-9500), presents the best value at under $40. Just to the west of town, the impressive **Mount Baldy** is, in fact, a giant sand dune. Good swimming beaches, and hiking trails through woods and marshes, can be found at **Indiana Dunes State Park**, twelve miles further along.

From here it's another fifteen miles west to the industrial mess of **GARY**, the largest US city founded this century and mildly famous as the birthplace of Michael Jackson. Until the US Steel Corporation built a giant foundry here in 1906, this was uninhabited bogland. By 1920 the population was 55,000 and it has tripled since then. These days it's basically a depressed suburb of Chicago.

Indianapolis

INDIANAPOLIS began life in 1821 when a tract of barely inhabited marshes was designated state capital. Its location in the middle of Indiana's rich farmland bore terrific commercial advantages, but the absence of a navigable river prohibited the transportation of bulky materials like coal and iron to sustain heavy industry. Though home to over sixty car manufacturers by 1910, the city never seriously threatened Detroit's supremacy. Nevertheless, its central Midwest location has attracted food, paper and pharmaceutical industries, including the giant Eli Lilly Corporation, and Indianapolis is one of the biggest cities in the world that can't be reached by water.

Today the city is trying to shake off unflattering nicknames such as *Naptown, Indiano-place* and *Brickhouse in the Cornfield* in favour of its chosen designation as the country's unofficial amateur sports capital. This might seem a rather modest aspiration but, in modern US sport, amateur events like the Pan-American Games and national Olympic trials are worth big money. In recent years, Indianapolis has acquired several world-class sports stadia, along with new hotels, two museums and a zoo, and old landmarks have been turned into downtown shopping and dining complexes. No longer is it (quite) true that nothing happens here except for the glamorous **Indianapolis 500 car race** – "the most televised annual event in the world" – each May.

Arrival and Information

The fast-growing **Indianapolis International Airport** is seven miles west of downtown, on the #9 bus route ($1). A **taxi** into the centre costs around $22, the *Shuttle Express* **van** service $12 (☎247-7301). *Greyhound* (☎635-4501) arrives at 101 W Ohio Street, just off Monument Circle, while *Amtrak*, 350 S Illinois Street, is next to the fairly central Union Station complex. *Metro Bus*, 14 E Washington (☎635-3344), run an inadequate service given that taxis can be prohibitively expensive. The **visitor centre** is at 201 S Capitol Street (☎237-5206 or ☎1-800/323-INDY), beside the Hoosier Dome.

Downtown

Though spacious and unhurried, downtown Indianapolis conspicuously lacks a nerve centre and fails to gel into a coherent entity. Streets radiate from **Monument Circle**, once the focal point of downtown, but now filled with venerable yet collectively dull buildings. The challenge of climbing 32 flights of steep stairs up the 284-foot **Soldiers and Sailors Monument** (there are often queues for the tiny elevator) is rewarded by an unspectacular view of the sprawling city (daily 10am–7pm; free). One reason why the centre seems so dreary and deserted is that, just to the north, five entire blocks are given over to anonymous war memorial buildings and uninspiring fountains; the benches, steps and green spaces now provide a place for the homeless to wait for the nearby food kitchens to open.

The telephone **area code** for Indianapolis is ☎317.

The shops, cafes and lively bars of the tastefully renovated Romanesque red brick and pink granite **Union Station** complex at Capitol and Louisiana streets, southwest of Monument Circle, inject some much-needed energy into downtown, while the serene tree-shaded **Lockerbie Square Historic District**, on the eastern fringe at New York and East streets, provides a small enclave of picturesque charm. Small wood-frame cottages, once home to nineteenth century artisans, line the cobblestone streets, many of them painted in bright pinks, blues and yellows, with ornately carved porches.

Indianapolis seems a strange setting for the **Eiteljorg Museum of American Indian and Western Art** (Tues–Fri 10am–5pm, Sun noon–5pm, $2), located on the western edge of downtown at 500 W Washington Street, in a stone, wood and adobe building among the rolling greenery of White River State Park. Harrison Eiteljorg, an Indianapolis industrialist who went West in the Forties to speculate in minerals, fell so much in love with the art of the region that he decided to bring as much of it back with him as possible. High points are the Southwestern gallery featuring work of many artists from Taos and New Mexico artists, and the American Western gallery which ranges from Frederic Remington to Andy Warhol. Artefacts from all over North America are on display in the Native American gallery.

Out from Downtown

Although the bodies of former US President Benjamin Harrison and Hoosier poet James Whitcomb Riley lie in the enormous **Crown Hill Cemetery**, at 38th Street and Michigan Road, the most frequently visited grave belongs to Thirties bankrobber **John Dillinger**, whose remains are supposedly buried at Section 44 Lot 94. Designated as public enemy number one, he gained a reputation as a daring, sharp-dressed, cavalier gunman who in a brief one-year career completed thirteen bank raids, killing four policemen, three FBI agents, one sheriff and an undetermined number of innocent bystanders. He escaped from jail twice inside a few months, but was eventually ambushed by the FBI outside a Chicago theatre in 1934 (see p.257). However, some researchers believe that another man, not Dillinger, was killed, leaving the bankrobber free to disappear. He became a somewhat macabre folk hero, commemorated by nine movies.

Opposite the cemetery at 1200 W 38th Street, over 150 lush wooded acres accommodate the capacious **Indianapolis Museum of Art**. The main building, surrounded by a lake, botanical garden, sculpture courtyard and concert terrace, is fronted by the original of Robert Indiana's *LOVE* pop-art sculpture. Inside, in the tasteful galleries, the exceptional displays include neo-impressionist works, Chinese art, the Eiteljorg Collection of African Art and the largest collection of Turner paintings outside Britain (Tues–Sat 10am–5pm, Thurs to 8.30pm, Sun noon–5pm; free).

The Indianapolis 500

Seven miles north of downtown, the **Indianapolis Speedway** race track only stages one race per year, but that does happen to be the legendary **Indianapolis 500**. Held on the Sunday before Memorial Day, it's preceded by a month of practice to whittle the hopeful entrants down to a final field of 33 drivers, one of whom will scoop the million-dollar first prize. The two-and-a-half-mile rectangular circuit was originally built as a test track for the city's motor manufacturers, but the first 500-mile race held in 1911 was a huge success, vindicating the organisers' belief that the distance was the optimum length for spectators' enjoyment. An average speed of 74.6mph was enough for Ray Harroun to win the 1911 race in a time of six hours and forty-two minutes; the winner's speed these days is likely to be over one hundred miles an hour faster, with the maximum touching 225mph.

The big race has become the crowning event of one of the nation's largest festivals, watched by 450,000 with up to 100,000 locked outside, hoping to savour at least some of the fume-laden air. At first, the city's conservative hierarchy saw it as a hedonistic infringement on the traditional observance of Memorial Day weekend. However, it brings so much money into the city, with thousands of "Indy Racing" fanatics staying for the month of practice and parties, that it is now exploited to the full with civic events such as the crowning of the Speedway Queen, a Mayor's Ball and street parade. Seats for the race usually sell out well in advance, but you can sometimes gain admittance to the infield, where the atmosphere makes up for the poor view, on the day.

Adjoining the track, the **Indianapolis Motor Speedway Hall of Fame Museum**, 4790 W 16th Street, houses an impressive display of race car history and provides a good background to what all the hysteria is about (daily 9am–5pm; $1). For an extra dollar, a rickety old bus provides an informative saunter round the super-smooth asphalt track ringed by huge banked grandstands.

Accommodation

Indianapolis has plenty of places to **stay**, but few of the cheaper options are convenient for downtown. The huge convention trade means there are usually a lot of empty (and therefore cheap) rooms at weekends. For **camping**, the nearest place to downtown is *Kamper Korner*, one mile south at 1951 W Edgewood Avenue (☎788-1488).

Holiday Inn Union Station, 123 W Louisiana St (☎631-2221). One of downtown's least expensive places, handy for bars and restaurants. Regular rooms cost $80; suites in converted railway carriages are $30 extra.

Motel 6, 2851 N Shadeland Ave (☎546-5864). Ten minutes' drive from downtown, just north of I-70. Functional motel with a pool for only $25.

North Meridian Inn, 1530 N Meridian St (☎634-6100). Medium-range motel with pool and lounge, sixteen blocks north of downtown. $55.

Renaissance Tower Historic Inn, 230 E Ninth St (☎631-2328). Just off central downtown. Rooms come complete with four-poster bed, toaster, coffeemaker and popcorn popper. $50.

YMCA, 860 W 10th St (☎634-2478). For both men and women. Singles $16–20.

Eating

Union Station, at Capitol and Louisiana streets, houses fast-food interpretations of many ethnic cuisines as well as a number of mid-price cafes and lively bars. At lunchtime, **City Market**, 222 Market Street, is a maze of lunch counters and tables where you can feast cheaply on all sorts of international food amidst a cacophonous din.

Bazbeaux, 334 Massachusetts Ave, downtown (☎636-7662), and 832 E Wheatfield Blvd, Broad Ripple Village (☎255-5711). The best pizzas in town, with a great range of toppings.

El Matador, 921 Broad Ripple Ave, Broad Ripple Village (☎251-9722). Unassuming Mexican diner at value-for-money prices.

Mugwumps, 608 Massachusetts Ave (☎635-7115). Halfway between a pub and cafe. International menu featuring vegetarian dishes for under $10. Gourmet coffees and teas. Live jazz Thurs–Sun.

Original Pancake House, 121 W Louisiana St (☎266-0304). Scrumptious German oven-baked pancakes made this one of *Gourmet* magazine's top ten breakfast restaurants in the USA.

St Elmo Steak House, 127 S Illinois St (☎635-0636). One of the top steak restaurants in the meat-mad Midwest. Wonderful food, if rather pompous and expensive. Expect to pay $25–30 for a meal.

Nightlife

Downtown, the area around **Union Station** buzzes in the evening as crowds go in and out of the numerous lively bars and discos. In summer, head for chic **Broad Ripple Village** (#17 bus) at College Avenue and 62nd Street, packed with bars, cafes, galleries and shops. See the *NUVO* or *New Times* free papers for full details of gigs and events.

Two elaborate former movie palaces worth checking out for live performances are the 1927 Spanish baroque *Indiana Repertory Theatre*, 140 W Washington Street (Thurs–Sun; ☎635-5252), which puts on dramatic productions between October and May, and the 1916 *Circle Theatre*, 45 Monument Circle (☎639-4300), where the Indianapolis Symphony Orchestra has weekly concerts.

Chatterbox, 435 Massachusetts Ave (☎636-0584). Bar that's a bit of a dive, but the atmosphere's great, attracting a real social cross-section of punters. Jazz every night except Sun.

Madame Walker Urban Life Center and Theatre, 617 Indiana Ave (☎236-2099). Black cultural and heritage centre. *Jazz on the Avenue* every Fri plus regular dance events, plays and concerts.

Slippery Noodle, 372 S Meridian St (☎631-6968). Indiana's oldest bar, established in 1850. Next to Union Station. Cheap beer Mon and Tues, live blues Wed–Sat.

The Works, 4120 Keystone Ave (☎547-9210). Gay men's social club and resource centre with dancing until dawn every night. Other services include private rooms, sauna and gym.

Out from Indianapolis: Bloomington

BLOOMINGTON, by far the liveliest small city in Indiana, lies 45 miles southwest of Indianapolis on Hwy-39. It owes its vibrancy to the 33,000-student Indiana University, east of downtown, whose best known former pupil is **J Danforth Quayle**. The most closely guarded secret in the administration building is said to be his final examination grading; the university's refusal to release it only adds fuel to the rumours of the US vice president's academic shortcomings. Probably of greater interest anyway, and certainly easier to see, is the fine international collection of paintings and sculptures in the I M Pei-designed **University Art Museum** on E Seventh Street (☎812/855-4826). The Indiana Hoosiers, the best-loved team in a basketball-mad state, play to a sell-out crowd every home game; "Hoosier Hysteria" easily eclipses any passion for Indiana's only professional football team, the floundering Indianapolis Colts.

Practicalities

Greyhound, 535 N Walnut Street (☎812/332-1522), operates a fairly reliable service to Indianapolis. Bloomington's **visitor centre** can be found at 2855 N Walnut Street (☎812/334-8900 or ☎1-800/678-9828). Inexpensive places to **stay** include the *Downtown Motel*, 509 N College Avenue (☎812/336-6881), and *Motel 6*, further out at 1265 Franklin Road (☎812/332-0337); both charge $25 to $30 for a room. The *Indiana Memorial Union* on Seventh and Park streets (☎812/856-6381), a good source of campus information, also offers a range of cheap places to **eat**. Other student bars and cafes are strung out along Kirkwood Avenue; more formal restaurants include *Grisanti's*, 850 Auto Mall Road (behind College Mall), which serves good-value pasta dishes, especially lasagnes, and the *Snow Lion*, 113 S Grant Street, where the Tibetan entrees cost around $10.

ILLINOIS

Nearly everything in **ILLINOIS** revolves around **Chicago**, the largest and most exciting of all the Great Lakes cities. Set at the state's northeastern corner, on the shores of **Lake Michigan**, Chicago has a skyline to rival New York City plus a gamut of top-rated museums, restaurants and cafes, and innumerable bars and nightclubs paying homage to the city's strong jazz and blues heritage. Seventy-five percent of the state's twelve million population live within commuting distance of Chicago's energetic centre, which controls the bulk of the state economy – Illinois is the third largest agricultural producer in the US. The sole exception to the endless flat prairies elsewhere is far to the south, where the forested **Shawnee Hills** rise between the Mississippi and Ohio rivers.

The contrast between the invariably quiet rural hinterlands and the buzzing urban centre could hardly be greater. That said, if you're travelling through Illinois there are a few places to look out for, though most are of historic rather than current interest. First explored and settled by the French, in 1763 the territory that's now Illinois was sold to the English, for whom it was the western extent of their vast Virginia colony. Granted statehood in 1818, Illinois remained a distant frontier until the mid-1830s when, after a series of uprisings, the native **Sauk** and **Black Hawk** tribes were subjugated and settlers began to arrive in sizeable numbers. Among these were the first followers of Joseph Smith, founder of the Mormon Church, who established a large colony along the Mississippi River at Nauvoo. The Mormons met with suspicion and persecution, and, after Smith was murdered by a lynch mob in 1844, fled west to Utah.

Other early immigrants included the young **Abraham Lincoln**, who practiced law from 1837 onwards in the east-central Illinois village of Charleston. A reconstructed two-room log cabin there serves as a reminder of his humble beginnings. One of Illinois' most popular nicknames – as repeated on the state's car licence plates – is "Land of Lincoln", and many other Illinois towns try to claim an important role in the making of the sixteenth US President. **Springfield**, the state capital, holds the best range of Lincolniana, including his restored home, his law offices and various other period buildings and artefacts, as well as his monumental tomb.

Getting Around Illinois

Since Chicago is the site of **O'Hare Airport**, the world's busiest, with more take-offs and landings each year than any other (though both Atlanta and Heathrow handle more passengers), as well as the hub of the national *Amtrak* **train** network, you're likely at least to pass through it. If you plan to spend time in the rest of Illinois, *Amtrak*, numerous commuter railroads, and, to a lesser extent, *Greyhound*, make getting around on public transport feasible, and **cycling** is generally easy on these endless flat plains.

If you're **driving**, half a dozen interstates ray out across the country from Chicago; the famous Chicago-to-LA Route 66 has been defunct since the 1960s, though I-55 southwest to St Louis, followed by I-44 and I-40, follow its general route.

Chicago

CHICAGO is in many ways the last great American city. Though long eclipsed by Los Angeles as America's second-largest centre after New York, Chicago really does have it all, with little of the hassle and infrastructural problems of its coastal rivals. Founded in the early 1800s, Chicago grew up with the country, serving as the main connection between the established East Coast cities and the wide open Wild West frontier. This position on the sharp edge between civilisation and wilderness made Chicago into a crucible of innovation, and many aspects of modern life, from skyscrapers to suburbia, had their start, and their finest expression, here on the shores of Lake Michigan.

Despite burning to the ground in 1871, Chicago boomed thereafter, doubling in population every decade and reaching two million around 1900, swollen by **Irish** and **Eastern European** immigrants (Chicago still ranks as the second largest Polish city in the world, after Warsaw). In the early years of this century, it cemented a reputation as a place of apparently limitless opportunity, with jobs aplenty for those willing to work. The attraction was strongest among Deep South **blacks** suffering from economic deprivation and racist terror: from 1900 to 1920 African-Americans poured in, with over 75,000 arriving during the war years of 1916–19 alone. Not all met with immediate riches, but for the great majority conditions were vastly better, with employment in the huge **Stockyards** – the slaughterhouses of Upton Sinclair's novel *The Jungle* – or on the very railroads that had brought them here. Chicago remains an important centre of black America – both the Reverend Jesse Jackson's **Operation PUSH** (*People United to Save Humanity*) and the more militant **Nation of Islam** (or Black muslims), founded by Elijah Mohammed in the 1940s, have their national headquarters on the South Side.

During the Roaring Twenties, Chicago's self-image as a no-holds-barred free market was pushed to the limit by a new breed of entrepreneur: criminal syndicates, ruthlessly run by the brazen likes of **gangsters** John Dillinger and Al Capone, took advantage of Prohibition to sell bootleg booze. Shoot-outs in the street between sharp-suited, Tommy-gun wielding mobsters were not as common as local legend would have it, but the back-room dealing and iron-handed control they pioneered was later perfected by politicians such former mayor Richard Daley – father of the present incumbent – who ran Chicago single-handedly from the 1950s until his death in 1976. His brutal handling of student anti-war demonstrators at the 1968 Democratic convention remains notorious.

Today, Chicago's towering **skyline** – the city has perhaps the world's best collection of **modern architecture**, from Frank Lloyd Wright houses to the 110-storey **Sears Tower** – still dominates the pancake-flat prairies for hundreds of miles around, and its status as cultural, and financial, heart of middle America is beyond question. **The Loop** downtown houses the offices of many major US companies, and holds some of the nation's most important **markets**, which together handle the buying and selling of one-third of the world's agricultural and industrial products.

For visitors, Chicago offers a wide range of excellent **museums** (especially the **Art Institute of Chicago**), restaurants and high-brow cultural activities, but its strongest suit is **live music**, with a phenomenal array of **jazz** and **blues clubs** packed into the backrooms of its amiable bars and cafes. And almost everything is noticeably **cheaper** than in other US cities – **eating out**, for example, costs much less than in New York or California, but is every bit as good. Though locals might deny it, the city has a surprisingly low-key and generally welcoming population – Chicagoans on the whole are proud of their city and usually keen to point out its best features. Two great ways to get a real feel for the city are to head out to ivy-covered **Wrigley Field** on a sunny summer afternoon to catch baseball's Cubs in action, or to cruise in style at sunset in one of the horse-drawn carriages that amble around Michigan Avenue.

Arrival, Information and Getting Around

Chicago's **O'Hare Airport**, the national HQ for *United, American* and many other US airlines, is well connected to downtown by *CTA* trains, which take around forty minutes and cost just $1.25 (see below). **Taxis** into town cost around $30, and can take 25–45 minutes. If you've got a lot of luggage, another option is the **van** service offered by *Continental Air Transport* ($12.50; ☎454-7800) between the terminals and downtown hotels; because the highway is often clogged, allow at least an hour for the trip. They also connect the city with **Midway Airport**, smaller than O'Hare and used mostly by domestic flights but not much easier to reach; from here the vans take around half an hour to downtown and cost $10.

Coming overland, Chicago is the base of the nationwide **Amtrak rail** system, and almost every cross-country route passes through **Union Station** (☎558-1075) at Canal and Adams streets, which has left luggage lockers (for passengers only) and is open 24 hours. **Greyhound** (☎781-2900) and a number of regional bus companies pull in to a large 24-hour station at Harrison and Jefferson streets, three blocks southwest; this too has left luggage lockers. Arriving in Chicago by **road** can be memorable, racing past the gleaming glass towers of the Loop; however, traffic on the downtown expressways is pretty horrendous, and parking is expensive. Perhaps the best place to leave a car is the garage under Grant Park, between Lake Michigan and the Loop.

Information
Once in Chicago, pick up **information and maps** from the **Chicago Tourism Council**, across Michigan Avenue from the landmark **Historic Water Tower** at 163 E Pearson Street (daily 9.30am–5pm; ☎280-5740 or ☎1-800/487-2446) on the Magnificent Mile shopping strip. The Chicago Architectural Foundation's **Archicenter**, in the Monadnock Building at 330 S Dearborn Street (☎922-3431), has the best range of local guidebooks and walking-tour maps, and runs good guided tourson foot, bus and bike; it also provides the guides for the excellent **Chicago by Boat** tours (see p.252).

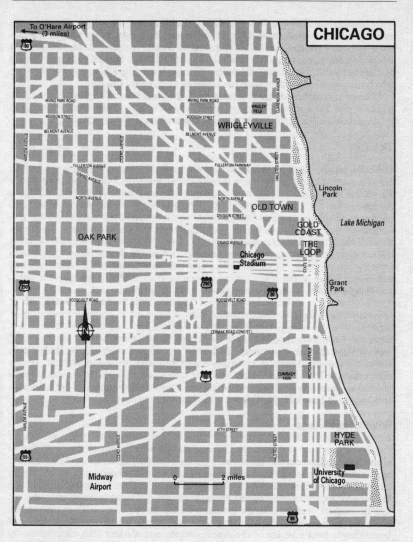

CHICAGO

To O'Hare Airport
(3 miles)

IRVING PARK ROAD
ADDISON STREET
BELMONT AVENUE

HARLEM AVENUE
CICERO AVENUE
FULLERTON AVENUE
GRAND AVENUE
NORTH AVENUE

OAK PARK

ROOSEVELT ROAD

HARLEM AVENUE

Midway
Airport

IRVING PARK ROAD
ADDISON STREET
BELMONT AVENUE

WRIGLEY FIELD
CLARENDON AVENUE

WRIGLEYVILLE

HALSTED STREET
FULLERTON PARKWAY

Lincoln
Park

NORTH AVENUE

OLD TOWN

DIVISION STREET

GOLD COAST

Lake Michigan

GRAND AVENUE

Chicago
Stadium

THE LOOP

STATE ST.

Grant
Park

ROOSEVELT ROAD

CERMAK ROAD (22ND ST.)

N

COMISKEY PARK

MICHIGAN AVENUE

47TH STREET

CICERO AVENUE

HALSTED STREET

HYDE PARK

0   2 miles

University
of Chicago

Getting Around

Getting around Chicago is simple and quick, thanks to the **trains** and **buses** operated 24 hours a day by the *Chicago Transit Authority* (*CTA*; ☎836-7000). Elevated trains circle the Loop before heading out to the North Side and suburbs, and link up with other subway routes criss-crossing the city. A complete network of buses fills out the system. Fares are $1.25 (good for two hours' unlimited riding; be sure to get a transfer when you board) and there's a special all-day fare of $1.75 on Sundays and holidays.

The telephone **area code** for Chicago is ☎312.

In summer, the **Culture Bus** ($2.50) is a double-decker sightseeing bus that runs every twenty minutes on three different routes, making a circuit from the Art Institute south to Hyde Park, the Science Museum and the Prairie Avenue district; west through the city's many ethnic neighbourhoods; and north to Lincoln Park. A *Culture Bus* ticket also saves you $2.50 off the $5 fares of the *Chicago Motor Coach Company* (☎226-2870), which runs open-topped double-decker buses all over central Chicago.

Chicago is compact enough that **taxis** rarely cost more than $5; rates are around $1 per mile plus 25¢ a minute. Cabs are readily available in the Loop (during the day at least) and on the North Side; otherwise you can book one on ☎829-4222.

The City

Lake Michigan, which provides Chicago with some of its most attractive open space (twenty miles of lakeshore lie within the city limits), serves as a clear point of reference for getting your bearings – the lake is always to the east of the urban grid. **Michigan Avenue** is the city's main thoroughfare, running between the lakeside museums and parklands, the densely packed skyscrapers of downtown and the diverse low-rise neighbourhoods that spread to the north, south and west. The **Chicago River**, which cuts through the heart of downtown Chicago out of Lake Michigan, separates the business district from the shopping and entertainment areas of the **North Side**, which range from the upscale **Near North** and **Gold Coast** neighbourhoods, to the artist's lofts and galleries of **River North**, and the more blue-collar areas of **Old Town**, **Lincoln Park**, and **Wrigleyville** – Chicago's hottest spots for nights out on a budget.

In contrast to the wealth and prosperity of the North Side, the deprived **South Side** of Chicago is more like New York's South Bronx, a huge and in places desperately poor expanse with a dangerous reputation. But while large areas are definitely unsafe after dark, and dodgy even at midday, a few corners of the South Side are well worth visiting, especially the spacious **University of Chicago** campus and neighbouring **Hyde Park**, site of the massive **Museum of Science and Industry** – the second most popular museum in the US. Apart from **Oak Park** to the west, which holds the childhood home of **Ernest Hemingway** and over a dozen well maintained examples of the influential architecture of **Frank Lloyd Wright**, **suburban** Chicago has little to offer.

Downtown Chicago

It may not have anything like the sheer mass of Manhattan, or the dense warrens of the City of London, but **downtown Chicago** puts on what is perhaps the finest display of **modern architecture** in the world, from the prototype skyscrapers of the 1890s to Mies van der Rohe's modernist masterpieces and the tallest building in the world, the quarter-mile-high **Sears Tower**. Just about all these edifices are workplaces of one kind or another; the whole place is bustling in the day and virtually empty later on.

The compact heart of Chicago is known as **the Loop**, because it's circled by the elevated tracks of the *CTA* "El" trains; for a first impression of downtown, you can't beat riding a train into any of the dozen stations, and starting your explorations by seeing all the city's energy, drive and unmasked greed exposed in the trading pits of its various **marketplaces**. Half the world's wheat and corn (and pork belly futures) are bought and sold amid the cacophonic roar of the **Chicago Board of Trade**, housed in a gorgeous Art Deco tower, appropriately topped by a 30-foot stainless steel statue of Ceres, Roman goddess of grain. From the entrance at 141 W Jackson Street, at the south end of La Salle Street, take the lift to the fifth-floor visitors' gallery (Mon–Fri 9am–2pm; free), where displays and videos trace the evolution of the various frantic shouts and signals by which trade is actually carried out. A similarly energetic ballet goes on from the early hours on Chicago's stock options exchange, the largest in the US. At the **Chicago Mercantile Exchange**, three blocks away at 30 S Wacker Drive

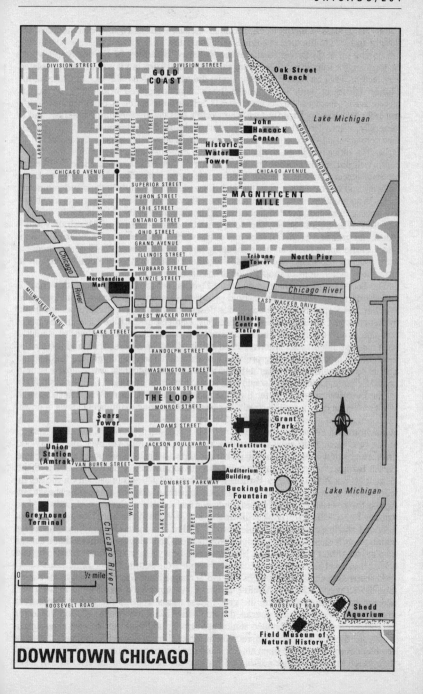

DOWNTOWN CHICAGO

GOLD COAST

DIVISION STREET

DIVISION STREET

Oak Street Beach

Lake Michigan

John Hancock Center

Historic Water Tower

MAGNIFICENT MILE

CHICAGO AVENUE

CHICAGO AVENUE

SUPERIOR STREET

HURON STREET

ERIE STREET

ONTARIO STREET

OHIO STREET

GRAND AVENUE

ILLINOIS STREET

HUBBARD STREET

Tribune Tower

North Pier

KINZIE STREET

Merchandise Mart

Chicago River

MILWAUKEE AVENUE

WEST WACKER DRIVE

EAST WACKER DRIVE

Illinois Central Station

LAKE STREET

RANDOLPH STREET

WASHINGTON STREET

MADISON STREET

THE LOOP

MONROE STREET

Sears Tower

ADAMS STREET

JACKSON BOULEVARD

Grant Park

Art Institute

Union Station (Amtrak)

VAN BUREN STREET

Auditorium Building

CONGRESS PARKWAY

Buckingham Fountain

Lake Michigan

Greyhound Terminal

Chicago River

0   ½ mile

ROOSEVELT ROAD

ROOSEVELT ROAD

Shedd Aquarium

Field Museum of Natural History

LARRABEE STREET

FRANKLIN STREET

ORLEANS STREET

WELLS STREET

LASALLE STREET

CLARK STREET

DEARBORN STREET

STATE STREET

RUSH STREET

NORTH MICHIGAN AVENUE

NORTH LAKE SHORE DRIVE

NORTH MICHIGAN AVENUE

WELLS STREET

CLARK STREET

STATE STREET

WABASH AVENUE

SOUTH MICHIGAN AVENUE

COLUMBUS DRIVE

SOUTH LAKE SHORE DRIVE

(Mon–Fri 7.30am–3.30pm; free), precious metals, currencies and commodities are bought and sold to the tune of some $50 billion a day.

Looking up at the proud facade of the **Reliance Building**, 32 N State Street, you'd be forgiven for thinking it dated from the Art Deco 1930s, but it was in fact completed way back in 1895 by Daniel Burnham, who did much to shape the face of Chicago; his **Fisher Building**, with its tongue-in-cheek, aquatic-inspired ornamental terracotta, stands across from the Archicenter at 343 S Dearborn Street. A block further south, the 1890 **Manhattan Building** was the world's first tall all-steel-frame building, and is generally acknowledged as the progenitor of the modern curtain-walled skyscraper; now converted into luxury flats, it preserves some noteworthy exterior ornament.

Besides office buildings, the Loop also holds some of Chicago's grandest turn-of-the-century **department stores**. The best-looking of these, the **Carson Pirie Scott** store on State Street between Madison and Monroe streets, was designed in 1899 by Louis Sullivan, and boasts a magnificent ironwork facade which blends botanic and geometric forms in an intuitive version of Art Moderne; Sullivan also designed the gorgeous spherical bronze clocks suspended from the building's corners. Two blocks north, on State Street at Washington Street, the comparatively bland exterior of **Marshall Field's** oldest and grandest branch masks one of the world's great stores. Theodore Dreiser's Sister Carrie spent many an hour shopping here, and the seven floors of merchandise were recently revamped and expanded around a multistorey escalator-filled atrium to attract new generations of shop-till-you-drop consumers.

The Loop is usually said to end at the El tracks, but the blocks beyond this core, to either side of the Chicago River, hold plenty more of interest. Broad, double-decked **Wacker Drive**, parallel to the water, was designed as a sophisticated promenade, lined by benches and obelisk-shaped lanterns, by Daniel Burnham in 1909. It was never completed, but, despite the almost constant intrusion of construction works, it makes for a nice extended walk. The river itself had its direction reversed, around the turn of the century, in an engineering project more extensive than the digging of the Panama Canal. As a result, rather than letting its sewage and industrial waste flow east into Lake Michigan, Chicago now sends it all south, toward St Louis and the Mississippi.

The best way to get a feel for the riverfront is on a **boat tour** ($15). These leave at 10am and noon daily from the North Pier (see p.255), giving magnificent views of downtown and a good insight into the city's history. However, half an hour's walk, especially at lunchtime when the office workers are out in force, will do the trick. Burnham's promenade runs along both sides of the river, crossing back and forth over the twenty-odd drawbridges that open and close to let barges and an occasional sailboat pass. The **State Street bridge** is a superb vantage point. On the south bank, at 35 E Wacker Drive, the elegant Beaux Arts **Jewelers Building** was built in 1926 and is capped on the seventeenth floor by a domed rotunda that once housed Al Capone's favourite speakeasy. Across the river stands what's commonly considered the masterpiece of Ludwig Mies van der Rohe – the 1971 **IBM Building** at 330 N Wabash Avenue. The gentle play of light and shadow across the detailed bronze and smoked glass facade was a model for countless other less considered copies worldwide. The building is so huge that it acts as a funnel for winter winds off Lake Michigan, and heavy ropes sometimes have to be tied across the broad plaza at its base to protect people from getting blown away.

Perhaps Chicago's most successful and acclaimed building of recent years stands four blocks west at 333 **W Wacker Drive**. Towering over a broad bend in the river, and bowed to follow its curve, the green glass facade reflects the almost fluorescent green of the river (recently upgraded from "toxic" to merely "polluted"); on the lower floors, a more classically detailed stone base actively addresses its stalwart elder neighbours. Further on, a newly resurrected stretch of the riverfront walk follows the western bank of the river, with open-air cafes and gardens to tempt office workers to extend their lunch breaks. Further south, and back on the Loop side of the river at S Wacker

Drive and Adams Street, is the 1450-foot tall **Sears Tower**, so huge that it has over 100 different lifts. Two of them ascend, in little over a minute, all the way from the ground level shopping mall to the 103rd-floor **Skydeck Observatory** (9am–11.30pm; $5), from where on a clear day you can discern the curvature of the earth.

South Michigan Avenue and the Art Institute of Chicago

Many of Chicago's major cultural attractions are collected together on the eastern edge of the Loop, along Michigan Avenue between the city's commercial core and the shores of Lake Michigan. On the lake side of South Michigan Avenue, at the east end of Adams Street, the top-quality **Art Institute of Chicago** (Mon & Wed–Fri 10.30am–4.30pm, Tues 10.30am–8pm, Sat 10am–5pm, Sun noon–5pm; $6 suggested donation, free last half-hour and all day Tues) has an excellent collection of Impressionist and Post-Impressionist paintings, Asian art (particularly Japanese prints), photography and architectural drawings. The neoclassical facade of the main entrance does its best to pull off a dignified air but, once inside, the numerous added-on wings can make finding your way around a difficult task, especially since the artworks are arranged as much by benefactor as by style or era. A long-term plan to integrate all the artworks into one basically chronological display is due to be completed by the end of 1992.

Most visitors head immediately upstairs to the Impressionist paintings, which include a wall full of Monet's *Haystacks* captured in various lights, next to Seurat's immediately familiar pointillist *Sunday Afternoon*; a handful of Post-Impressionist masterpieces by Van Gogh, Gauguin and Matisse are arrayed nearby. Beyond here, a tortured, tuxedoed self-portrait by Max Beckmann – his last Berlin painting before fleeing the Nazis – welcomes you into a crowded gallery of early twentieth-century American and European works, in which moody portraits by Balthus and Picasso, and Surrealist landscapes by Max Ernst and Yves Tanguy, hang side by side with Edward Hopper's lonely *Nighthawks* and Georgia O'Keeffe's doom-laden *Black Cross, New Mexico*.

Elsewhere in the museum, keep an eye out for the pitchfork-holding farmer of Grant Woods's oft-reproduced *American Gothic* – a picture he painted as a student at the Art Institute school, and sold to the museum for $300 in 1930 – and for the delightful seventh-century Indonesian sculpted stone monkeys, in the Southeast Asian collections displayed around the McKinlock Court Garden, which in summer serves as an open-air cafe. Also here, in the far east end of the complex, is the immaculately reconstructed Art Moderne trading room of the **Chicago Stock Exchange**, designed by Louis Sullivan in 1893 and moved here in the 1970s.

While the hotels and theatres that once lined up around the Art Institute on South Michigan Avenue have since migrated north of the river, around the turn of the century this lakefront strip was the city's prime entertainment district. Many of that era's grand structures preserve a sense of its unabashed artistic aspirations. The world-renowned **Chicago Symphony Orchestra**, now run by Daniel Barenboim after many successful years under the baton of Sir Georg Solti, still performs to sell-out crowds at the (Daniel Burnham-designed) **Orchestra Hall** at 220 S Michigan Avenue. Down the street, the **Fine Arts Building**, at 410 S Michigan Avenue, once held the offices of *Wizard of Oz* author L Frank Baum – who named Oz for a real-life Chicago park – and the draughting studio of the young Frank Lloyd Wright.

Further along stand two of Chicago's most famous old **hotels**, including the recently renovated *Hilton* – the world's largest hotel when it opened in 1927 – and the more affordable and atmospheric *Blackstone*. South of here, the neighbourhood income levels drop off sharply, and, apart from the Prairie Avenue Historic District described on p.259, there isn't much of interest before you hit the Hyde Park district three miles south – though R&B fans may like to know that the southwest corner of Michigan Avenue and 21st Street held the studios and offices of **Chess Records**, immortalised in the early Rolling Stones song *2120 S Michigan Avenue*.

Grant Park

East of the Art Institute towards Lake Michigan, **Grant Park** provides a welcome but not entirely complete break from the downtown urban grid – wide strips of high-speed road and railway slice through it, so casual rambling can be frustrating. The northern half of the park, especially around the immense **Buckingham Fountain**, is its least degraded part, and the whole 200-acre swath is liberally sprinkled with sculptures and monuments, from a moping Columbus to a proud Plains Indian on horseback. Throughout the summer, jazz, blues and classical concerts are held in the Petrillo Music Shell, just behind the Art Institute. The **taste of Chicago** at the end of June, attracts over a million people to a week-long feeding frenzy.

The railway tracks of the Illinois Central make it annoyingly difficult to walk the mile or so from the southern end of the Loop to the southern half of Grant Park, where all the major attractions are gathered; the best route is to walk through the northern half of the park and head south along the lakeshore promenade.

The extensive and engaging **Field Museum of Natural History**, 1200 S Lake Shore Drive at Roosevelt Road (daily 9am–5pm; $3, free Thurs), is ten minutes' walk south of the Art Institute, in a huge, marble-clad, Daniel Burnham-designed Greek temple. "Natural history" here seems to includes anything that's non-white and non-European; the collection ranges from Egyptian tombs – the entire burial chamber of the son of Fifth Dynasty Pharaoh Unis was brought here in 1908 – to a simulated South Pacific Island, complete with mock lava flows. The Native American section features an earthen lodge where folklorists in garb tell myths and legends – intended for young kids but not overly sentimental or simple-minded. As you might expect, acres of embalmed and stuffed specimens highlight the flora and fauna of North America, starring a 75-foot-long skeleton of an Aptosaurus (what used to be called a Brontosaurus), dug up on the Great Plains.

Just across busy Lake Shore Drive, on the shores of Lake Michigan, the **Shedd Aquarium** (daily 9am–5pm; $3, free Thurs) proclaims itself, in true Chicago style, the largest indoor aquarium in the world. The uninspired 1930s structure is rather old-fashioned in its layout, but the lighthearted and often tongue-in-cheek displays – some of which use *Far Side* cartoons, while others describe a Joycean *Portrait of an Otter* – are at once informative and entertaining. The central exhibit, a 90,000-gallon re-creation of a coral reef complete with sharks (who get fed at 11am and 2pm daily), turtles and thousands of tropical fish, is surrounded by over a hundred tanks featuring *Animals of the Cold Oceans* and *Great Lakes Sturgeons*. Highlights include the sluggish and comical South American freckled sideneck turtles, housed across from a four-foot-long, 250lb alligator snapping turtle, who trundles to the surface to breathe every half-hour.

The recently added **Oceanarium** (same hours; $7, includes Aquarium admission) provides an enormous contrast, with its modern Lake Michigan-view home for marine mammals such as Pacific dolphins and beluga whales. Designed to replicate a rocky Alaskan coastline, it's a carefully disguised amphitheatre for demonstrations of the animals' "natural behaviour" such as jumping out of the water and fetching plastic rings. Performances are every ninety minutes and you need a ticket; at other times you can watch the animals cruise around the tank, from underwater galleries where you can listen to the clicks, beeps and whistles they use to communicate with each other. As well as a cramped tank of unhappy-looking penguins, there's an interactive exhibit on sea otters and a detailed look at the repercussions of the devastating Exxon Valdez oil spill.

In summer, tour boats run by *Shoreline Marine Sightseeing* ($5; ☎673-3399) take hour-long **cruises** along the lakeshore from a jetty just north of the Aquarium. The predictable **Adler Planetarium** nearby (9.30am–4.30pm; free) is the smallest, oldest and least interesting of the Grant Park museums, but it does give one of the best views of the towering Chicago skyline; the small Meigs Field airport is just to the south, so don't be surprised if low-flying planes seem about to crash into the lake.

The North Side

Chicago's North Side, where you're likely to spend most of your time, has few big-name attractions, but it's great for simply wandering around, chancing upon odd shops, neighbourhood bars and historic sites, in a generally low-rise tangle containing some of the city's most characteristic corners.

When the Michigan Avenue bridge was built over the Chicago River in 1920, the warehouse district along its north bank quickly changed into one of the city's most upmarket quarters, now known as the **Magnificent Mile** and famed for its fashionable shops and department stores. Throughout the Roaring Twenties one glitzy tower after another was thrown up along Michigan Avenue, starting in the north with the opulent **Drake Hotel** off Lincoln Park, and in the south with the equally ornate **Wrigley Building**, just over the river at 400 N Michigan Avenue. The Wrigley Building, built by the Chicago-based chewing-gum magnates, was eclipsed almost as soon as it was finished by the "Mag Mile's" most famous structure, the **Tribune Tower**. Still housing the editorial offices of Chicago's morning newspaper, as well as, on the ground floor, the studios of its main AM radio station, *WGN* (you can peer in from the street and watch the DJs at work), the tower was completed in 1925, its flying buttresses and Gothic detailing turning its back on the then-prevalent Modern style. Look closely at its lower floors and you'll see various bits of historic buildings – like the Parthenon and the Great Pyramid – purloined from around the world by *Tribune* staffers and embedded here.

While the Tribune Tower anchors its southern end, the Mag Mile's northern reaches are dominated by the quarter-mile-high, cross-braced steel **John Hancock Center** at 875 N Michigan Avenue. Though it's 125 feet shorter than the Empire State Building, and has since been pushed out of the top three by New York's World Trade Center and Chicago's own Sears Tower, the 360° panorama you get on a clear day from its 94th-floor **Skydeck Observatory** (daily 9am–midnight; $4) is unforgettable.

Back at ground level, you're right at the heart of Chicago's prime **shopping district**, where *Bloomingdale's*, *Neiman-Marcus* and *Tiffany & Co* rub shoulders with *Benetton* and *The Gap*. Some front straight onto Michigan Avenue, but many of the shops are enclosed within multistorey, fabulously decorated shopping malls, all of which stay open daily from 9am till midnight, so you can window-shop after the stores have closed. In the newest and most outlandish of these emporia, **Chicago Place** at 700 N Michigan Avenue, an eight-storey shopping mall is topped by a barrel-vaulted glass conservatory where you can sample fast foods from dozens of admittedly anodyne stands. Two blocks north, at 900 N Michigan Ave, *Gucci* and *Aquascutum* fill up the lower floors of the deluxe **Four Seasons Hotel**; this flashy complex is also home to the lavish *Henri Bendel*, Chicago's most exclusive department store.

Across from Water Tower Place, at the very centre of this consumer paradise, stands one of Chicago's best-loved buildings, the **Historic Water Tower**. An exuberant but naive example of frontier Gothic, the stone castle, topped by a 100-foot tower, was built in 1869 and is one of the very few structures to have survived the Chicago Fire of 1871. Chicago's main **visitor centre** is housed across the street in the equally historic Pumping Station, which also holds the multimedia extravaganza *Here's Chicago* (hourly 10am–4pm; $5), a 45-minute guided tour through Chicago's past and present.

Away from the Magnificent Mile, the area along the river, between Michigan Avenue and the Lake, is being redeveloped in a major way, with giant hotel and office block complexes already under construction. The one part so far completed, **City Point**, is quite shamelessly and successfully modelled upon New York's Rockefeller Center; Daniel Burnham's riverfront promenade is also being incorporated into the plans, and, near where the river flows out of Lake Michigan, a large fountain, each hour on the hour, spurts a powerful stream of water arching across to the south bank. A block from the fountain, at 455 E Illinois Street, **North Pier**, one of the few surviving riverfront warehouses, was recently restored into a carnival-like collection of restaurants and gift shops, complete with an indoor crazy golf course that features models of Chicago's many skyscrapers. It's nowhere near as tacky as it might sound, and is certainly worth the walk, if only to board a guided boat tour (detailed above).

The more heavily industrial area west of Michigan Avenue is also experiencing a revival of sorts, though on a smaller scale and with a different character. Re-christened **River North**, the many old brick warehouses and factory premises here have been converted to house avant-garde art galleries, restaurants and nightclubs. **Huron** and **Superior** streets, around their intersection with Wells Street, hold the most concentrated collection; if you're interested in doing any degree of serious gallery-hopping, pick up a copy of the free *Chicago Gallery News*.

As its name suggests, the **Gold Coast** is one of Chicago's wealthiest and most desirable neighbourhoods, stretching north from the Magnificent Mile along the lakeshore. This residential district is primarily notable for holding Chicago's most central (and style-conscious) **beach**, the broad strand of **Oak Street Beach**, reached via a walkway under Lake Shore Drive, across from the *Drake Hotel*. After dark, the summertime crowds are apt to be found in the myriad bars of Rush and Division streets. The more northerly reaches of the Gold Coast, approaching Lincoln Park, are also its most exclusive, nowhere more so than the stretch of Astor Street running south from the park. However, only one of the many fine houses, the Frank Lloyd Wright 1892 **Charnley House** at 1365 N Astor Street, is open to the public.

Old Town, west of LaSalle Street to either side of North Avenue, has a much more lived-in look than does the dandified Gold Coast. Originally a German immigrant community based around the 1888 **St Michaels Church** – whose carrillon is to Old Towners' what Bow Bells are to Cockneys – today the neighbourhood boasts one of the city's broadest ethnic and cultural mixes. While its many century-old row houses and workers' cottages are now prime real estate, as recently as thirty years ago its then-shabby housing stock and derelict factories attracted a variety of creative types. **Wells Street**, the main drag, emerged in the late 1960s as a mini-Haight Ashbury, and while almost all signs of that era have vanished (or, as in the case of the folk club *Earl of Old Town*, moved uptown), at least one survivor, the *Second City* comedy club (see p.264), is still going strong. The rest of the neighbourhood is packed with some of the city's best bars, galleries and barbecue joints, and makes for a diverting afternoon's wander.

The westernmost quarter of this area, stretching from Chicago Avenue north to **Division Street** (locale of Studs Terkel's eponymous social documentary), is a district tourists would do well to avoid: the immense 1960s **Cabrini Green** public housing project has since eroded into one of the city's most poverty-stricken corners. While it's certainly not a place you'd want to wander round aimlessly, especially after dark, it's not as dangerous as some locals like to make out – certainly it's nowhere near as desperate and run-down as the South Bronx, or even parts of South London.

In summer, Chicago's largest green space, **Lincoln Park**, gives a much-needed respite from the gridded pavements of the rest of the city. Unlike Grant Park to the south, Lincoln Park is packed with leafy nooks and crannies, monuments and sculptures, and has a couple of friendly, family-oriented **beaches**, at the eastern ends of North Avenue and Fullerton Avenue. Near the small zoo (daily 9am–5pm; free), at the heart of the park, you can rent paddleboats or bikes. If the weather's bad, head inside the **Chicago Historical Society museum** (Mon–Sat 9.30am–4.30pm, Sun noon–5pm; $3, free Mon), at the south end of the park off Clark Street, and bone up on Chicago's captivating past; it also has a nice skylit cafe.

The neighbourhood called Lincoln Park, inland from Lake Michigan between North Avenue and Diversey Parkway, is centred along **Lincoln Avenue** and **Clark Street**, which run diagonally from near the Historical Society; **Halsted Street**, which holds many of Chicago's better blues bars and nightclubs, runs north–south through the heart of the district. Any of these main roads is worth an extended stroll, popping in to the many book and record shops, while smaller side streets show off why Lincoln Park is one of the city's most popular places to live. Look out for the **Biograph Theatre**, 2433 N Lincoln Avenue, where John Dillinger was ambushed and killed by the FBI in 1934, thanks to a tip-off from his companion, the legendary Lady in Red; and **Oz Park**, at Lincoln and Webster avenues, which was the namesake, if not the inspiration, for Chicago author L Frank Baum's stories, set somewhere over the rainbow.

Chicago spreads north from Lincoln Park for block after low-rise block of houses and shops, many of which date from the late 1800s, when thousands of German immigrants settled in what was then the separate enclave of Lake View. It's now dubbed **Wrigleyville**, in honour of **Wrigley Field**, the ivy-covered 75-year-old stadium of Chicago's much-loved baseball-playing Cubs. The Lord's of baseball, Wrigley Field is the keeper of tradition – it was the last major league stadium to add floodlights for night baseball – and, along with Boston's Fenway Park (see p.157), it remains the best place to get a real feel for the game. Even if you know nothing about the rules, there are few more pleasant and relaxing ways to spend an afternoon than drinking beer, eating hot dogs and watching the Cubs come close to winning a ball game (they haven't won anything important since World War II). See also "Sports" on p.265.

Graceland Cemetery, three blocks north at Clark Street and Irving Park Road, is the city's biggest and best graveyard. Dozens of tombs and monuments mark the final resting place of the men and women who made Chicago. Almost all the big names in Chicago architecture are buried here – including Daniel Burnham, Ludwig Mies van der Rohe, and Louis Sullivan, who also designed some of the more noteworthy memorials – as are Marshall Field, who started the city's most famous department store, and George Pullman, who broke the back of America's railway unions in a bitter 1894 strike and is buried under ten tons of protective concrete and steel.

The West Side

Chicago's West Side, west of the Chicago River, was where the **Great Fire of 1871** started, supposedly when Mrs O'Leary's cow kicked over a lantern. The flames spread quickly east to engulf the entire central city, which was built of wood and fed the fire for three full days. Appropriately enough, the O'Leary cottage is now the site of the Chicago Fire Department training academy. The West Side also saw 1886's **Haymarket Riots**, when striking workers assembled at the old city market at Desplaines and Randolph streets; after a peaceful demonstration, as police began to break up the crowd, a bomb exploded, killing an officer. Another six policemen and four of the workers died in the resulting panic; four labour leaders were later found guilty of murder and hanged, despite the fact that none of them had been present at the event.

Though the West Side has little to see compared to the rest of the city, it does provide a good look at its day-to-day realities. The area served as the port of entry for Chicago's myriad ethnic groups, now congregated in its distinct neighbourhoods. **Milwaukee Avenue**, which stretches under the El tracks diagonally from the Loop out towards O'Hare Airport, has long been home to a sizeable Eastern European community, mainly Poles – over a million altogether, including some 60,000 who came to Chicago during the martial law era of the 1980s. For an introduction, stop by the **Polish Museum of America** (daily noon–5pm; free) at 984 N Milwaukee Avenue, or the **Ukrainian National Museum** (Mon–Fri 11am–4pm, Sun noon–4pm; $1), half a mile west at 2453 W Chicago Avenue. **Greektown**, the few blocks of Halsted Street north of the I-290 freeway, and **Little Italy**, along Taylor Street west of Halsted Street, are both just a short walk from the University of Illinois subway station, on the CTA Congress line. On a Sunday morning, the liveliest spot on the West Side is **Maxwell Street market**, four blocks southeast of Little Italy. It's the closest thing in the US to London's East End street markets, with live blues bands busking on street corners and *kielbasas* replacing bagels among the stallholders.

Ten miles west of the Loop, the affluent and attractive turn-of-the-century suburb of **Oak Park** has been preserved as a national historic district, thanks in part to its early influence on two very different but very American figures, **Ernest Hemingway** and **Frank Lloyd Wright**. Oak Park is easily accessible by public transport: take the Lake–Dan Ryan CTA El train west to the Harlem Avenue stop. The **visitor centre** (daily 9am–5pm; ☎848-1500), a block north of the station at 158 N Forest Avenue, has an excellent walking tour map ($1) as well as guidebooks and free brochures.

Hemingway was born and grew up in Oak Park, editing his high school newspaper and living a normal middle-class life; neither his birthplace (at 339 N Oak Park Ave) nor his boyhood home (600 N Kenilworth Ave) is open to visitors, though an engaging collection of memorabilia can be seen at the **Oak Park Historical Society** (Fri 10am–2pm, Sat & Sun 1–4pm; $3) at 217 Home Avenue, a block south of the station.

In 1889, a decade before Hemingway's birth, an ambitious young architect named Frank Lloyd Wright arrived in Oak Park, which he used for the next twenty years as a testing ground for his innovative design theories. Most of the twenty-five buildings he put up here are in keeping with conventional Victorian design, and few are open to the public; fortunately, however, his most interesting and groundbreaking edifices are maintained as monuments. **Unity Temple**, a boldly geometric, reinforced concrete structure at 875 Lake Street, is the best introduction to his ideal of an "organic architecture", in which all aspects of the design derive from a single unifying concept – quite at odds with the fussy "gingerbread" popular at the time. Built for the Unitarian Universalist congregation of which Wright was a member, Unity Temple's simple, angular form was dictated by economics more than anything else (it cost under $60,000 to build in 1906). However, its unembellished surfaces contribute to a masterful manipulation of space, especially in the skylit interior, where the subtle interplay of overlapping planes and volumes creates a dynamic spatial flow. Though little noticed in the US, Unity Temple was very influential in Europe as a precursor of Modern architecture.

Frank Lloyd Wright's **home and studio** is a short walk away at 951 Chicago Avenue, on the corner of Forest Avenue. He built this small brown-shingled house in 1889 at the age of 22, and remodelled it repeatedly thereafter. It shows all the hallmarks of Wright's domestic ideal: large fireplaces to symbolise the heart of the home and family; free-flowing, open-plan rooms; and the visual linking of interior and exterior spaces. In 1895 he expanded the kitchen and dining rooms , filling them for the first time with furniture of his own design. Three years later Wright added a two-storey studio, featuring a mezzanine draughting area suspended by chains from the roof beams, which is where he worked for the next decade. In 1909 Wright abandoned Oak Park and his family for pastures new (see also pp. 273 and 677); he was eventually to design such landmarks as New York's Guggenheim Museum. You can see the house itself on a 45-minute guided tour (Mon–Fri 11am, 1pm & 3pm, Sat & Sun 11am–4pm; $5), while lengthier walking tours take in the dozen other Wright-designed houses within a two-block radius.

The South Side

The **South Side** of Chicago has always had a rough deal, cursed with the presence of bad-neighbour heavy industries like the sprawling **Chicago Stockyards**, the slaughterhouses and meatpackers which Upton Sinclair exposed in his 1906 novel *The Jungle*, and whose stink covered most of the South Side up through the 1950s. The overriding impression is one of misery and downtrodden poverty, with block after block of deprived and dangerous neighbourhoods. That said, there are exceptions: not just the **Prairie Avenue** and **Hyde Park** districts described below, but also the buzzing **Chinatown** around Wentworth Avenue and 22nd Street; the artsy, predominantly Mexican **Pilsen** district, a few blocks north and west; and the predominantly Irish, blue-collar **Bridgeport**, around Halsted and 37th streets – Mayor Daley's old fiefdom, the home of Comiskey Park and baseball's White Sox (see p.265). To reach the South Side, double-decker *Illinois Central* commuter **trains** run beside the lake to Prairie Avenue (a block from the 18th Street station) and Hyde Park (near the 59th Street station); *CTA* bus #1 follows Michigan Avenue to the same places, while bus #8 bus runs every fifteen minutes, 24 hours a day, south through Pilsen to Bridgeport.

Two blocks east of Michigan Avenue, a mile from the Loop and only a quarter of a mile from the lake, **Prairie Avenue** started life as an exclusive suburb. Though just a ten-minute walk south from Grant Park and the Field Museum, it's best reached by taking a cab, bus or train; the route is confusing and the streets are just not safe. The area had a brief moment of glory as the one part of Chicago to remain unscathed in the Great Fire of 1871. For a few short but vital years this was Chicago's finest address, home to such eminent figures as railway magnate George Pullman, catalogue king Joseph Sears and meatpacker George Armour. However, by the turn of the century the railroads had cut it off from Lake Michigan, and the expansion of the stockyards had encouraged the wealthy to flee back to their traditional North Side haunts.

One of the few structures to have survived the intervening years is the 1886 **Glessner House**, an H H Richardson-designed Romanesque manor, standing sentry on the southwest corner of Prairie Avenue and 18th Street. Behind the forbidding stone facade, the house opens onto a internal garden court, its interior filled with Arts and Crafts furniture and swathed in William Morris fabrics and wall coverings. The place is maintained by the *Chicago Architectural Foundation*, who give hour-long guided tours (Wed–Fri noon–2pm, Sat & Sun 11am–2pm; $6; ☎326-1393). Tickets to the Glessner House also get you inside Chicago's oldest building, the **Clarke House**, a block away at 1855 S Indiana Avenue, a plain white 1836 Greek Revival pioneer home that spent many years as a community centre before being prissied up as a minor museum of interior decor. Much more interesting, and proof of the wealth once concentrated here, is the lavish gothic **Presbyterian Church**, a block away at 1936 S Michigan Avenue, which features Burne-Jones and Tiffany stained-glass windows.

An island of middle-class prosperity surrounded by urban poverty, **Hyde Park** is the most attractive and sophisticated South Side Chicago neighbourhood. It's also one of the more racially integrated areas of the city, and among its more erudite: the **University of Chicago**, endowed by Rockefeller in 1892 and now among the top institutions in the US, has encouraged a college-town atmosphere, with bookshops and numerous cafes around its compact campus, especially along E 57th Street. On the campus itself, two buildings are well worth searching out: the massive gothic pile of the **Rockefeller Memorial Chapel**, at 59th Street and Woodlawn Avenue, and the Frank Lloyd Wright-designed Robie House, two blocks north at 5757 S Woodlawn Avenue.

Woodlawn Avenue runs north from the University of Chicago campus, passing by one of the South Side's most popular taverns, *Jimmy's Woodlawn Tap* at 55th Street, before turning a whole lot grander. Besides its enormous mansions, Woodlawn Avenue illustrates the social and racial mix for which Hyde Park is renowned: within two blocks of each other are the Midwest's largest Jewish temple, the ornate **Isaiah Israel** at 1100 E Hyde Park Boulevard, and the home of Minister Louis Farrakhan, leader of the **Nation of Islam**, which was started here on the South Side in the 1940s by the late Elijah Muhammad. In between, at 4944 S Woodlawn Avenue, stands the huge brick manor where boxer Muhammad Ali lived for many years.

Just west of the university, on the edge of lush Washington Park, the **Du Sable Museum of African-American History** takes a look at the experience of Americans of African descent, from slavery through to contemporary times (Mon–Fri 9am–5pm, Sat & Sun noon–5pm; $2). Named after Jean Du Sable, the Haitian-born Francophone who was Chicago's first permanent settler, it focuses on the works of WPA-sponsored artists of the 1930s, and on the more assertive Black Power-era of the 1960s.

Washington Park wraps around the south of the University of Chicago campus, to join the long green strip of the **Midway** – one of the few reminders that a hundred years ago this was the site of the Chicago **World's Columbian Exposition**. Attracting some thirty million spectators in the summer of 1893 alone, the Midway was then filled with full-size model villages from around the globe, including an Irish market town and a mock-up of Cairo complete with belly dancers; these days it's used mainly by joggers and students tossing Frisbees. The cavernous **Museum of Science and Industry** at the east end of the park (Mon–Fri 9.30am–4pm, Sat & Sun 9.30am–5.30pm; $5) is Chicago's single most popular tourist destination (and ranks second in the US), drawing over four million visitors each year; it will be interesting to see how much attendance drops off since it began charging admission in 1991. Besides interactive computer displays, the best of which explores the inner workings of the brain, exhibits include a captured German U-boat, a trip down a replica coal mine, and a simulated space-shuttle journey; it's fun for kids, but adults may not feel like staying very long.

Promontory Point juts into Lake Michigan just east of the museum, giving great views of the Chicago skyline, including a close-up look at Mies van der Rohe's first high-rise, the Promontory Apartments at 5530 S Lake Shore Drive.

Accommodation

Most of Chicago's central **accommodation** is oriented toward businesspeople rather than tourists, but there are still plenty of moderately priced rooms. A good selection of clean if unexciting pre-war **hotels** in and around the Loop offer reasonable rates, especially at weekends, and motorists can pick from scores of motels along the surrounding Interstates (parking downtown can add $10 a day to your stay). Even the top-class downtown hotels are, comparatively, not that expensive. While they're not as prominent as elsewhere, **bed and breakfast** rooms are available through *Chicago B&B*, PO Box 14088 (☎951-0085), for around $55 a night. Under the *Chicago's Got It* programme, hotels in all price ranges offer discounts of between fifteen and thirty percent on Thursday to Sunday nights, when the business types have gone home. Ten percent room tax is added everywhere to all bills.

Allerton Hotel, 701 N Michigan Ave (☎440-1500 or ☎1-800/621-8311). Nicely renovated grand hotel at the heart of the Gold Coast/Miracle Mile. Weekend rates from $69 per double.

Ascot House, 1100 S Michigan Ave (☎922-2900 or ☎1-800/621-4196). Large central motel – handy for Grant Park and other lakeside attractions. It has a swimming pool, and doubles start at $55.

The Bismarck Hotel, 171 W Randolph St (☎236-0123 or ☎1-800/643-1500). Safe and clean if somewhat faded Loop hotel, offering double rooms for a bargain $58 a night.

Blackstone Hotel, 636 S Michigan Ave (☎427-4300 or ☎1-800/622-6330). Resurgent, once elegant turn-of-the-century hotel overlooking the lake, near Grant Park. Doubles from $58.

Chicago International Hostel, 6318 N Winthrop St (☎262-1011). Clean rooms in a safe if somewhat distant Northside neighbourhood, easily accessible on the subway – take the A or B train north to Loyola Station, then walk two blocks south. Dorm beds $10 *AYH* members, $13 for others.

Comfort Inn of Chicago, 601 W Diversey Parkway (☎348-2810 or ☎1-800/228-5150). Newly renovated medium-sized motel, with free parking near Lincoln Park; doubles from $45.

The Drake Hotel, 140 E Walton Place (☎787-2200). Grand old hotel, modernised without sacrificing its sedate charms. Off the Magnificent Mile; rooms from $150, but you can just pop in for a drink.

The Fairmont Hotel, 200 N Columbus Drive (☎565-8000 or ☎1-800/527-4757). Plush and comfortable modern hotel. Spacious, luxuriously appointed lakeview rooms start at $99 a night.

International House, 1414 E 59th St (☎753-2270). Plain but pleasant rooms on the University of Chicago campus, in summer only. *AYH* members $14, others $23. Reservations essential.

LaSalle Motor Lodge, 720 N LaSalle St (☎664-8100). At the heart of the River North art gallery and nightclub district, with standard doubles from under $50 a night.

The Midland Hotel, 172 W Adams St (☎332-1220 or ☎1-800/621-2360). Long established Loop hotel, popular with brokers and businesspeople. Good-value weekend specials. Doubles from $89.

YMCA/YWCA, 33 W Chicago Ave (☎944-6211). Very plain, safe, and very central private rooms; singles $24, doubles $32. Weekly rates from $70.

Eating

Chicago, famous across America for **"Deep Dish" pizzas** and **barbecued ribs**, is one of the most satisfying US cities for good inexpensive food. Besides its all-American steak-and-potato places, a legacy of Chicago's days as the nation's meatpacker, all sorts of **ethnic** restaurants – Italian, Chinese, South American and Eastern European – energise a very dynamic, and very changeable, eating scene. **Gold Coast** and **Lincoln Park** are the best areas to start looking. Steer clear, though, of the numerous "theme" restaurants, such as replica Fifties diners and places run by retired sports stars – wherein the food is firmly secondary to the surroundings. Many of the establishments listed under "Bars" and "Cafes" in the "Drinking" section also serve snacks and light meals.

Budget Eating: Breakfasts, Burgers and Sandwiches

Little Al's Italian Beef Barbeque, 1079 W Taylor St (☎226-4017). Fight your way to the counter for hearty sandwiches and a groaning pile of fresh french fries – all for under $4. Open until 1am.

Billy Goat Tavern, 430 N Michigan Ave (☎222-1525). Well-worn, fluorescent formica haunt of shift-working *Chicago Tribune* journalists. Cheap breakfasts, burgers and beers 7am–3am daily.

Ceres Cafe, 141 W Jackson Blvd (☎427-3443). Lively, Art Deco coffeeshop, on the ground floor of the Board of Trade building, packed with TV screens quoting the latest pork-belly futures prices.

Lou Mitchell's, 563 W Jackson Blvd (☎939-3111). Excellent coffee, fresh-squeezed fruit juices and delicious fresh pastries, plus carbo-loading breakfasts. Just west of the Loop.

Morrie's Old-Fashioned Deli, 345 S Dearborn St (☎922-2932). Succesful imitation of a Jewish New York deli, with pickles and matzo-ball soups along with delicious pastrami sandwiches.

Oak Tree, 25 E Oak St (☎751-1988). Bustling, all-American diner amongst the high-style haunts of the Gold Coast, open 24 hours for omelettes, waffles and endless cups of coffee.

West Egg Cafe, 620 N Fairbanks St (☎280-8366). Very popular – especially for Sunday brunch – artsy cafe, with sidewalk dining two blocks east of the Magnificent Mile.

American

Army and Lou's, 420 E 75th St (☎483-6550). Top-quality "soul food" in comfortable, friendly South Side setting. Excellent value, down-home cooking – smoked ham hocks with mustard greens, shrimp and chicken gumbos, or mouthwatering fried chicken – plus excellent desserts.

Bay Street, 1024 N Rush St (☎226-7707). Large and lively restaurant serving up some of Chicago's best fresh fish, steamed clams, chowders and gumbos.

Canoe Club, 2843 N Halsted St (☎348-3800). Great stacks of crispy onion rings are the highlight on the huge all-American menu – steaks, meatloaf in creamy gravy, burgers – plus all-you-can-eat fried fish on Friday night. Even with the requisite couple of beers it shouldn't come to more than $15.

Eli's the Place for Steaks, 215 E Chicago Ave (☎642-1393). A favourite of old-time Chicagoans, including Frank Sinatra, who come for the thick steaks and 1940s ambience.

Rooney's Original Lobster House, 431 N Dearborn St (☎467-1100). Juicy steaks and flown-in fresh seafood in a retro-Twenties Chicago tavern.

Twin Anchors, 1655 N Sedgewick St (☎266-1616). Zesty, melt-in-the-mouth barbecued ribs, great onion rings in friendly Old Town landmark. Unless you arrive at 5pm, you'll have to wait at the bar.

Asian

Hatsuhana, 160 E Ontario St (☎280-8287). Sit at the blond wood bar and watch the chefs prepare sea-fresh sushi or sashimi. Expensive, but not outrageous for the prime Magnificent Mile location.

Jun Japanese Restaurant, 434 W Diversey Parkway (☎477-5511). Excellent sushi at amazingly low prices – $7.95 for four pieces plus a pile of tempura shrimp – along with a full menu of traditional Japanese foods in pleasant setting near Lincoln Park.

Pattaya, 114 W Chicago Ave (☎944-3753). Classy and comfortable Thai restaurant. A wide selection of meat and vegetable dishes. Excellent creamy desserts and not that pricey – $20 goes a long way.

Thai Classic, 3332 N Clark St (☎404-2000). Inexpensive, low-key Wrigleyville Thai place with very good seafood specialities.

Three Happiness, 2130 S Wentworth Ave (☎791-1228). Chicago's best dim sum, in a cacophonous Chinatown haunt.

Eastern European

Galan's, 2212 W Chicago Ave (☎292-1000). For groaning plates of Ukrainian food at low prices, this is the place – set meals of cabbage rolls, potato dumplings, sausages, sauerkraut and hunks of beef, pork or chicken paprika, plus a half-bottle of wine for around $15.

Mareva's, 1200 N Milwaukee Ave (☎227-4000). A surprise in the as yet ungentrified Near West Side, this family-run Polish restaurant offers multi-course Slavic meals – *pirogis* and borscht to start, then a range of rich meat-in-cream dishes – for around $20–25, plus vodka.

Zofia's, 6873 N Milwaukee Ave (☎647-7949). Popular if plain Polish diner serving up family-sized portions of *pirogis*, *kielbasas* and plum soup, plus a range of daily specials for under $10. Well out from downtown, near O'Hare Airport.

French, Italian and Pizza

Ambria, 2300 N Lincoln Park West (☎472-5959). One of Chicago's finest nouvelle cuisine restaurants. The Art Nouveau ambience is classy without being stuffy, and the food – tender slices of duck liver in calvados just for starters – is nothing short of exquisite.

Avanzare, 161 E Huron Ave (☎337-8056). Spacious Near North restaurant serving top-quality northern Italian dishes for less than you'd think. Main dishes are $12–15, and the desserts are excellent.

Bacino's, 2204 N Lincoln Ave (☎472-7400). Just off Oz Park, this popular pizza place has great calzones, plus good beers and wines. There's a downtown branch at 75 E Wacker Drive.

Cafe Spiaggia, 980 N Michigan Ave (☎280-2764). Casual but top-rate Italian cafe, in the posey One Magnificent Mile building. Ultra-fresh salads, and great pizzas and pasta dishes.

California Pizza Kitchen, 414 N Orleans St (☎222-9030). Designer pizza par excellence, topped with barbecued chicken and Peking duck and served in a stagey black tiled setting. Very pricey.

Edwardo's Natural Pizza Restaurant, 1212 N Dearborn St (☎337-4490). Exceptional pizza even by Chicago standards. Also at 2120 N Halsted St (☎871-3400) and 521 S Dearborn St (☎939-3366).

Gino's East, 160 E Superior St (☎943-1124). Rough and ready, dark wood and vinyl booth pizza parlour serving up some of the best (and cheapest) pies in the city.

Pizzeria Uno, 29 E Ohio St (☎321-1000). The place that put Chicago Deep Dish pizza on the map, since franchised nationwide.

Middle Eastern and African

Helmand, 3201 N Halsted St (☎935-2447). An unusual Lincoln Park treat: Chicago's only Afghanistani food, with dishes like baked lamb with split peas, onions and a dash of coriander.

Middle East Restaurant, 2701 W Lawrence St (☎878-6533). Low on ambience, with its formica tables, fluorescent lights, video games and screaming jukebox – but the Lebanese food is excellent and cheap. $7 buys a bowl of soup and a huge plate of hummus, lemon chicken and fried eggplant.

Moulibet, 3521 N Clark St (☎929-9383). Low-key but top-quality storefront restaurant, right near Wrigley Field, serving traditional Ethiopian meals. Rich garlicky meat stews, delicately spiced vegetables and tangy *injera* flatbread. Full meals cost around $15.

Spanish, Mexican and South American

Cafe Ba-ba-reeba!, 2024 N Halsted St (☎935-5000). Pricey but fun tapas bar and restaurant. Great garlic shrimp and plentiful paella, cooked in an open kitchen and washed down with Spanish wine.

Frontera Grill, 445 N Clark St (☎661-1434). Excellent, $10-a-plate Mexican-flavoured restaurant using ingredients – Hawaiian seafood or smoked venison – you'd rarely find south of the border.

Marco's Paradise, 3358 N Sheffield St (☎281-4848). Heaped portions of Mexican food, just down the street from Wrigley Field and jam-packed after a game. Fill up for under $5.

Mestizo, 311 W Superior St (☎787-4160). Fairly posey Mexican place, in the River North gallery district, worth a look at least for its ersatz Mayan decor; live salsa music most nights.

Rio's Casa Iberia, 4611 N Kedzie Ave (☎588-7800). Why fly to Rio de Janeiro when you can taste the best of Brasil (and Portugal and Spain) at the end of the Ravenswood CTA line? Not cheap at around $25 for a full meal, but great, especially the shellfish dishes.

Drinking

Though it's not quite as wild as it was in the bootlegging days of speakeasies and Prohibition, Chicago is still a consummate **boozer's town**. From sleekly chic piano bars to spit-on-the-sawdust-floor saloons, the city has somewhere for everybody. As well as the standouts listed below, there are hundreds of equally comfortable haunts all over town, as often as not within stumbling distance of each other, and all are open until 3 or 4am. One thing Chicago has more of than anywhere else on earth is "**sports bars**", where banks of TV screens broadcast Cubs, Sox, Bears and Bulls games – great places for beer drinking and male bonding, but not for thoughtful conversation. **Division Street**, in the two blocks west of State Street, is unreconstructed breeder-bar territory, with a handful of more subtle joints tucked away on side streets off the main drag.

Cafes

Albert's Patisserie, 52 W Elm St (☎751-0666). Tiny cafe, tucked away off Division Street and Michigan Avenue, with great cakes and coffees.

Cafe Voltaire, 3231 N Clark St (☎528-3136). Comfy couches and a nice back garden attract a varied crowd during the day; live music and performances pack the downstairs cabaret most nights.

Caffe Trevi, 2275 N Lincoln Ave (☎871-4310). Cosy neighbourhood cafe that makes an eye-opening antidote to Lincoln Avenue's wall-to-wall saloons, nightclubs and pool halls.

No Exit Cafe, 6970 N Glenwood Ave (☎743-3355). As you might guess from the name, this nearly suburban North Side cafe strives to preserve late 1950s Bohemianism intact for future generations.

Scenes Coffeehouse, 3168 N Clark St (☎525-1007). Clubby cafe just a block from N Halsted Street's alternative theatres and nightclubs, sharing space with the city's best drama bookshop.

Third Coast Coffeehouse, 1260 N Dearborn St (☎649-0730). *The* place to people-watch at 5am after a night in clubland. Trendy cafe open 24hr Tues–Sun; also at 888 N Wabash Ave (☎664-7225).

Bars and Pubs

John Barleycorn Memorial Pub, 658 W Belden St (☎348-8899). Highbrow hangout near Lincoln Park. Lots of room, and a good range of British and Irish beers.

The Berghoff, 17 W Adams St (☎427-3170). Classic and stylish Chicago saloon – sharp-suited gentlemen behind the brass-railed bar have been pouring drinks for almost a century.

Harry Caray's, 33 W Kinzie (☎465-9269). Chicago's biggest and best sports bar, in an old River North brick warehouse. The walls are covered floor to ceiling with Cubs memorabilia – Harry Caray is a radio announcer – and the huge bar is packed with beer drinkers until the early hours.

Coq D'Or, in the *Drake Hotel*, 140 E Walton Place (☎787-2200). Plush, warmly lit hideaway off the Magnificent Mile that's perfect for an intimate evening cocktail or two.

Old Town Ale House, 219 W North Ave (☎944-7020). Bass IPA on draught and the jazziest juke-box in town. Unpretentious well-worn haunt attracting a friendly, varied crowd. Nightly until 4am.

O'Rourke's Pub, 1625 N Halsted St (☎335-1806). Spacious and comfortable Irish bar with a good-jukebox and portraits of notable Irishmen on the walls. Best Guinness in the Midwest.

Slugger's World Class Sports Bar, 3540 N Clark St (☎248-0055). Probably the only bar in the world with its own indoor batting cage, this raucous beer bar fairly rattles and hums during Cubs, Bears and Bulls games. During happy hour beers cost just 25¢.

Tap Root Pub, 636 W Willow St (☎642-5235). Ripe with Old Chicago legend – Al Capone kept his bootleg whisky next door, for example. A great place to soak up some history over a beer or two.

Zebra Lounge, 1220 N State St (☎642-5140). Ironic and erudite contrast to nearby Division Street's meatmarkets. Everything in this basement bar is covered in black-and-white stripes, and the late-night singalongs have to be seen and heard to be believed.

Nightlife and Entertainment

Chicago, from its earliest frontier days, has had some of the best **nightlife** in the US. Sweet Home Chicago, birthplace of Muddy Waters' urban blues as well as R&B label Chess Records, is still going strong, inspiring the energetic dancebeat of 1980s house music and the hardcore punk of bands like Big Black, as well as the groundbreaking jazz of the Art Ensemble of Chicago. There are **nightclubs** aplenty all over town, especially along Halsted Street, Lincoln Avenue and Clark Street on the North Side.

More highbrow pursuits are also well provided for: the Chicago Symphony plays in winter at the **Orchestra Hall**, 220 S Michigan Avenue (☎435-6666), and in summer at the Ravinia Festival, held in the northern suburbs. **Theatre** is not as big as in London or New York, but is certainly of a high standard – David Mamet, John Malkovich and many others got their first break here. The **Comedy** is particularly vibrant and the improvisational troupe at *Second City*, 1616 N Wells Street (☎337-3992), is especially renowned.

The listings below should give a sense of the variety on offer; for a rundown of **what's on** when you're here, check out the free *Chicago Reader*, which comes out every Thursday and has extensive entertainment listings and articles on contemporary local issues and concerns; the colourful *New City* is less comprehensive but still well worth a look. Local **radio stations** are also good sources of information about what to see and do; one of the best is WHPK (88.5FM), which plays great jazz, blues and R&B without commercial interruption. The Friday editions of the daily *Tribune* and the *Sun-Times* also carry up-to-date arts and music information.

Rock Clubs

Avalon Niteclub, 959 W Belmont Ave (☎472-3020). Lots of bands, plus a range of dance floors, all for $5 or less.

Batteries Not Included, 2201 N Clybourn Ave (☎472-9920). Tiny back room, behind an uneventful bar. Sometimes big-name indie artists, but most nights it's young punks or art-rock bands.

Cabaret Metro, 3730 N Clark St (☎549-3604). Multi-level dance club, converted from an old cinema. Regular concerts, often young English bands trying to break in Stateside, and DJ mixes. The best dancing is in the downstairs *Smart Bar*. The whole complex is open late – until 5am Fri and Sat.

Cubby Bear Lounge, 1059 W Addison St (☎327-1662). A sports bar during the day – right next to Wrigley Field – after dark this place transforms itself into one of the city's better live venues, popular with ageing dinosaurs more than up-and-coming bands, but still fun.

Lounge Ax, 2438 N Lincoln Ave (☎525-6620). Small and always crowded old barroom that's emerged as one of Chicago's most happening new clubs.

Blues Clubs

B.L.U.E.S., 2519 N Halsted St (☎528-1012). Small and sweaty club, pulling in some of best blues singers and players on the planet. Cover $5–15. Its more dance-oriented sister club, *B.L.U.E.S. etc*, 1124 W Belmont Ave (☎549-9436), is considerably larger and has a broader range of music.

Kingston Mines, 2548 N Halsted St (☎477-4646). Big names play the main room, local bands a smaller side room, and a huge dance floor grooves until 4am every night; cover $4–9.

New Checkerboard Lounge, 423 E 43rd St/Muddy Waters Drive (☎624-3240). Chicago's oldest blues club, in a slightly dodgy South Side neighbourhood near the *CTA* 43rd Street station.

Rosa's Blues Lounge, 3420 W Armitage Ave (☎342-0452). One of Chicago's most welcoming blues bars, with great bands and an even better sound. Well worth the $6 taxi ride from downtown.

Wise Fool's Pub, 2270 N Lincoln Ave (☎929-1510). Friendly, no-frills beer bar, two blocks from Lincoln Park, with portraits of Chicago's blues musicians covering the walls, and a blues band in the back room most nights.

Folk and World Music Clubs

At the Tracks, 325 N Jefferson St (☎332-1124). Artsy, post-industrial space, across the Chicago and North Western Railroad tracks from the towering skyline of the Loop, with a surprisingly unpretentious range of folksy, usually acoustic live music.

Clearwater Saloon, 3937 N Lincoln Ave (☎549-5599). Cosy, pub-like haunt with good, free (or very cheap) live folk and country most nights.

Earl's Pub, 2470 N Lincoln Ave (☎929-0660). This rough-at-the-edges Sixties holdout has good beers and live acoustic music most nights.

Wild Hare and Singing Armadillo Frog Sanctuary, 3350 N Clark St (☎327-0800). Fun if fairly anodyne reggae dance club that attracts an interesting mix of local rastas and Lincoln Park yuppies; *Exodus II*, up the street at 3477 N Clark Street (☎348-3998), is closer to the real thing.

Jazz Clubs

Andy's, 11 E Hubbard St (☎642-6805). Fairly slick, very central and thus often jam-packed during the lunch hour and early evening – when there are low-priced performances and office workers drop by to unwind; a second wave comes through for the nightly live shows.

The Bulls, 1916 N Lincoln Park West (☎337-3000). Chicago's best late-night hangout, with live jazz three times nightly – last shows kick off at 1am.

Green Mill, 4802 N Broadway (☎878-5552). Atmospheric, 1930s Art Deco tavern with big band swing and other traditional jazz.

Joe Segal's Jazz Showcase, in the *Blackstone Hotel* at 636 S Michigan Ave (☎427-4300). Premier contemporary jazz in top-class setting. Dress to impress, and expect to pay $20 for a big-name star.

Dance Clubs

Cairo, 720 N Wells St (☎266-6620). Very fashionable, high-style River North hangout for civilised decadence, divided into posey jazz bar (upstairs) and cavernous rock club (downstairs).

Carol's Speakeasy, 1355 N Wells St (☎944-4226). Huge, very cruisy gay dance club. Among the hottest and sweatiest nights out in town.

Medusa's, 3257 Sheffield Ave (☎935-3635). Housed in an old school, this offbeat and enthusiastic young people's club – there's no alcohol, and just about everyone's under 18 – is a energised counterpoint to Chicago's more studiously jaded haunts.

Neo, 2350 N Clark St (☎528-2622). Longstanding alternative club. Largest and lively dance floors; good mix in both the music and the crowd. Cover $2–5; open until 4am every night but Mon.

Shelter, 564 W Fulton St (☎648-5500). Chicago's hottest and most expensive nightspot, with a assorted bars and dance floors inside and queues snaking around the block; cover around $10.

Sports

Staunchly blue-collar Chicago must be among the best US cities for watching **sports**. Though the city's two **baseball** teams haven't won anything for years, Chicagoans follow their fortunes with masochistic glee. The perennially mediocre Chicago Cubs baseball team play all summer at historic **Wrigley Field** on the North Side, described on p.257 (☎404-2827); the usually better Chicago White Sox are based at the ultramodern New Comiskey Park, on the South Side (☎924-1000).

In recent years the city's most successful outfit has been the Chicago Bulls **basketball** team, lead by superstar Michael Jordan; they play in winter and spring at Chicago Stadium, 1800 W Madison Street (☎943-5800), as do **hockey's** Chicago Blackhawks (☎733-5300). The fearsome Chicago Bears **football** team can be seen at Soldier Field in Grant Park (☎663-5408).

Listings

Chemists *Walgreen's*, 757 N Michigan Ave (☎664-8686), is open 24 hours.

Dial-a-Poem ☎346-3478.

Hospital Northwestern Memorial Hospital, 233 E Superior Blvd (☎944-2358), has an all-night casualty ward.

Oprah Winfrey TV show Tickets ☎633-1000.

Post Office Chicago has the world's largest post office, at 433 W Van Buren St (☎765-3200). General delivery zip code is 60607.

Record Stores *Jazz Record Mart*, 11 W Grand Ave at N State St (☎222-1467), has one of the world's foremost catalogues of jazz, blues and other American music; *Wax Trax*, 2449 N Lincoln Ave (☎929-0221), sells an unbeatable range of punk and industrial sounds.

WISCONSIN

WISCONSIN is said to be home to as many cows as humans. About four million of each live comfortable lives off this rich, rolling farmland; in fact, there are more overweight people here than in any other state. However, America's self-proclaimed "Dairyland" is more than just one giant pasture. Beyond the massive red barns and silvery silos lie endless pine forests, some 15,000 sky-blue lakes, postcard-pretty valleys and dramatic bluffs. The state, whose name is an Ojibway word meaning "gathering of the waters", is bordered by Lake Michigan to the east, Lake Superior in the north and, westward, the Mississippi and St Croix Rivers; only the southern, Illinois, demarcation is dry.

The **history** of Wisconsin exemplifies the standard formula for westward expansion. French and British explorers came along in the seventeenth century, began trading with the Native Americans and soon ousted them from their land, which was then settled by European immigrants, particularly Germans, Scandinavians and Poles. With some exceptions, their politics tend towards the liberal and progressive. Major national social programmes, such as labour laws for women and children, assistance for the elderly and the disabled, and unemployment compensation, were rooted in Wisconsin. On the down side, Senator Joseph McCarthy, the infamous witch-hunter of the 1950s, was born in Grand Chute, current headquarters of the right-wing John Birch Society.

Wisconsin today is best known for its liquids. The **milk** from all those cattle yields cheeses of all kinds, while the **beer**, as the song says, is what made **Milwaukee** famous. Wisconsin's biggest city encapsulates the state's ethnic mix, although its happy melting pot image was severely bruised in 1991 by the grisly discoveries in the apartment of Jeffrey Dahmer, heir to the horrific throne of Ed Gein, the rural Wisconsinite whose serial killings in the 1950s inspired the novel and film *Psycho*. Sparkling **Madison** apart, its other cities – LaCrosse, Green Bay, Oshkosh – are on the dull side, but they're also clean, safe and amiable, while its smaller towns can be distinctive and charming.

Getting Around Wisconsin

You'll be hard put to explore Wisconsin's remote north, or key locales like Door County peninsula, without a vehicle. Public transport is better in the south. Milwaukee and, to a lesser extent, Madison are hub cities for *Greyhound* and *Amtrak*. Six **trains** daily connect Milwaukee and Chicago, a ninety-minute journey, while one crosses the state in the south en route for Seattle, via Columbus (near Madison) and LaCrosse. Milwaukee-based *Midwest Express* (☎1-800/452-2022, or ☎747-4646 in the city) has **flights** to California, Florida and the East Coast.

Milwaukee

MILWAUKEE, the "Deutsch Athens" of southeastern Wisconsin, is an engaging combination of the down-home and the sophisticated. Spruce and unpretentious, the city is known for its succession of festivals, many held on the lakefront. The secret of its renowned, Old World *gemutlichkeit*, or hospitality, may be that it is really a collection of neighbourhoods in which Germans, Irish, Poles, Hispanics, African-Americans, Hmongs and other groups rub shoulders more or less easily.

Milwaukee was a meeting place for Indian tribes long before white settlers moved in, thanks to its prime position on the shores of huge Lake Michigan, at the confluence of three rivers. The opulent nineteenth-century mansions lining the lake commemorate the industrialists who helped make the city Wisconsin's economic and manufacturing capital. By 1850, less than two decades old and with a population of twenty thousand, Milwaukee already had a dozen breweries and 225 saloons. The contemporary estimate of 6000 bars – one for every hundred residents – is not necessarily apocryphal.

Arrival, Getting Around and Information

As Wisconsin's largest, most visited city, Milwaukee is well-served by air, rail and coach. **Mitchell International Airport**, eight miles south of downtown at 5300 S Howell Avenue, is connected with downtown by **bus #80** to Sixth Street and Wisconsin Avenue ($1), and by a limousine service ($6.50 single). *Amtrak* is at 433 W St Paul Avenue, while *Greyhound* and *Wisconsin Coach*, serving outlying Wisconsin, operate out of the same terminal at 606 N Seventh Street (☎272-8900). *Badger Bus*, 635 N Seventh Street (☎276-7490), runs a daily express service to Madison ($14 return).

Getting around Milwaukee is easy and inexpensive via the county's extensive **transit system** (24-hour info ☎344-6711). Rides, including transfers valid for one hour, cost $1, or less if you buy several tickets at once. They also arrange trolley and coach tours.

Milwaukee's **CVB**, 510 W Kilbourn Avenue (Mon–Fri 8am–6pm; ☎273-3950 or ☎1-800/231-0903), can provide details on such festivals as the Great Circus Parade (mid-July) and the Wisconsin State Fair (early August). The main **post office** is at 345 W St Paul Avenue (Mon–Fri 7.30am–6pm; ☎287-2530; zip code 53201).

The Town

Downtown Milwaukee, split north to south by the **Milwaukee River**, is only a mile long and a few blocks wide. Handsome old buildings and gleaming, modern steel and glass structures are comfortably corralled together on three sides by spaghetti-like strands of freeway. **Lake Michigan** forms the fourth boundary, with its parkland, marina and **Summerfest** grounds (the scene in late June and early July of huge outdoor music gigs). The **Milwaukee Art Museum**, 750 N Lincoln Memorial Drive (Tues, Wed, Fri & Sat 10am–5pm, Thurs noon–9pm, Sun noon–5pm; $4), contains works by European masters and twentieth-century Americans. One wing – with stunning views of the lake – is devoted to the late Peg Bradley's dazzlingly comprehensive collection of Post-Impressionist paintings. At the **Milwaukee Public Museum**, also downtown at 800 W Wells Street (daily 9am–5pm; $4.50), the intertwined histories and mysteries of the earth, nature and humankind are presented with vibrant imagination, through dioramas and reconstructions such as *The Streets of Old Milwaukee*, a Guatemalan public market, a battle of dinosaurs, and a Native American bison hunt.

The **Annunciation Greek Orthodox Church**, 9400 W Congress Street (☎461-9400; nominal admission; bus #57), completed in 1961, was the last major work by native Wisconsin architect Frank Lloyd Wright. It's an imposing blue-domed, neo-Byzantine edifice, resembling a mushroom crossed with a spaceship, with an interior that is a jaw-dropping blend of the streamlined and the ornate. Visiting hours are 9am until 4pm, but call first. The 37-room **Pabst Mansion**, 2000 W Wisconsin Avenue (mid-March to Dec Mon–Sat 10am–3.30pm, Sun noon–3.30pm; otherwise weekends only; $5) is a castle-like reminder of Milwaukee's wealthier past, built in 1893 for a local beer baron. You can see how he made his fortune at **Pabst Brewery**, 915 W Juneau Avenue (Mon–Fri 10am–3pm, June–Aug also Sat 9–11am, bus #71). It and **Miller Brewing Company**, 4251 W State Street (Mon–Sat 10am–3.30pm, bus #71), offer free behind-the-scenes tours, leading you through the brewing and packaging process before pouring generous promotional samples for over-21s. The micro-brewery **Sprecher**, 730 W Oregon Street (Sat 1, 2 & 3pm, $2), is more primitive and more personal, serving samples straight out of the barrel.

Accommodation

Possibilities in Milwaukee run the gamut from low-budget to upmarket chains. *B&B of Milwaukee Inc*, 1916 W Donges Bay Road in nearby Mequon (☎242-9680), is a free

The telephone **area code** for Milwaukee and eastern Wisconsin is ☎414.

reservation service for close on thirty B&Bs in or near the city. The University of Wisconsin (☎229-4065) lets inexpensive rooms June to mid-August.

Edge O'Town Motel, 5105 S 27th St (☎282-8500). Twenty rooms, some with kitchenettes. $26–36.

Marie's, 346 E Wilson St (☎483-1512). B&B in self-contained suburb-that's-not-a suburb Bay View. Excellent morning feeds, rooms $45–65.

Ramada Inn, 633 W Michigan St (☎272-8410). Downtown rooms $56–76.

Red Barn Hostel, 6750 W Loomis Rd (☎529-3299). Thirteen miles southwest of downtown via Hwy-894 or buses #10 and #35. Hiking and biking trails. May–Oct only; $6–9.

Robert Stevens Inn, 1457 N Franklin Place (☎224-1059). Towered Victorian restoration. All eight rooms have private baths; outdoor pool, grand piano, sitting room with fireplace. $75–85.

The Wisconsin, 720 N Third St (☎271-4900). Older downtown hotel half a block from the glassy, classy and sprawling Grand Avenue Mall, with free parking and a lounge. Rooms $40–46.

Eating

The Germans who first settled in Milwaukee determined the city's eating style, heavy on bratwurst, rye bread and beer. Subsequent immigrants threw the collective kitchen wide open, making Milwaukee a culinary cornucopia. With Lake Michigan lapping the city's feet, freshwater fish can hardly be overlooked. Wherever you go, portions tend to be big and prices not exorbitant.

Jack Pandl's Whitefish Bay Inn, 1319 E Henry Clay St (☎964-3800). Suburban landmark famous for broiled whitefish ($7.75), colossal oven-baked pancakes ($7.25), and stein collection.

John Ernst's, 600 E Ogden Ave (☎273-1878). With the similarly pricey *Mader's* and *Karl Ratzsch's*, one of the city's top three German institutions. Assiduous service and excellent Wiener schnitzel.

The Old Town, 522 W Lincoln Ave (☎672-0206). Tasty Serbian food on the Pole-dominated south side. Try a *burek*, a meat or spinach-filled pie the size of a Frisbee ($11). Live music Thurs–Sun.

Shakers, 422 S Second St (☎272-4222). Trendified Victorian wine bar serving an eclectic, fruity-spicy cuisine, for adventurous palates only, late into the night.

Sheila's at the Plaza, 1007 N Cass St (☎272-4661). Gorgeous little Deco-style day-time cafe in a venerable downtown apartment-hotel. Meals $2–6.

Yen Ching, 7630 W Good Hope Rd (☎353-6677). Great Mandarin meals for under $9.

Nightlife

The concept of neighbourhoods is vital to Milwaukee's nightlife. **Brady Street** in the near northeast, where the counterculture flourished in the 1960s, is now a haven of **Italian** restaurants and bars. The **Polish** have their locals on the south side, while nearby **Walker's Point** has all sorts of gay and straight watering holes.

The thriving bar scene somewhat overshadows Milwaukee high culture, the major-ity of which takes place in a two-block area downtown, much of it at the **Performing Arts Center** (PAC), 929 N Water Street (☎273-7206 or ☎1-800/472-4458), or the plush, historic *Pabst Theater*, 414 E Wells Street (☎278-3665; guided tour Sat 11am, call to verify). The nearby *Milwaukee Repertory Theater*, 108 E Wells Street (☎224-9490), has a reputation for risk-taking productions. The repertoire at *Skylight Opera Theatre*, 813 N Jefferson Street (☎271-8815), moves from Mozart to musical comedy.

John Hawk's Pub, 100 E Wisconsin Ave (☎272-3199). Riverside Brit-style establishment down-town. Food all day, jazz on Sat.

Louie's American-Chinese Tavern, 120 W National Ave (☎347-0524). Weird but popular bar where kimonos, a rickshaw and teahouse upstage a patio-cum-volleyball court.

Partners, 813 S First St (☎647-0130). Casual gay chic.

The Safe House, 779 N Front St (☎271-2007). A nightclub straight out of a spy film. This is a camp paean to the lighter side of espionage – with phony entrance, secret password, two-way mirrors, escape route and a phone booth with 92 sound effects. Open from 11am; light meals.

Tamarack, 322 W State St (☎225-2552). One of the city's oldest saloons, with R&B – ribs and blues – served side by side on weekends.

Von Trier's, 2235 N Farwell Ave (☎272-1775). Black Forest decor, lots of imported beers.

Cedarburg

Settled by Irish and German millers in the nineteenth century, **CEDARBURG** is a tranquil, *Currier and Ives*-type village twenty miles north of Milwaukee. Among its beautiful limestone dwellings, **Cedar Creek Settlement** (Mon–Sat 10am–5pm, Sun noon–5pm), a three-storey former woollen mill, has a winery in its bowels (45min tour daily 11.30am, 1.30 & 3.30pm; $2). *Barth's at the Bridge* (☎377-0660) is a classy **restaurant**; *Morton's* on Center Street (☎377-4779) serves lower-cost food in an idiosyncratic bar setting. **Staying** here makes an attractive alternative to Milwaukee. The atmosphere at the *Washington House Inn*, W62 N573 Washington Avenue (☎375-3550 or ☎1-800/369-4088), is countrified de luxe, with rooms costing $59 to $139. The *Stagecoach Inn*, no.W61 N520 (☎375-0208), more modestly rusticated, charges $65 ($10 less in winter). The town's **visitor centre** is at no.W63 N645 (April–Dec daily ; ☎377-9620).

Eastern Shores

North of Milwaukee, **eastern Wisconsin** is a melange of the industrial and the maritime, with a nod to agriculture, its character determined by its proximity to **Lake Michigan** and the smaller **Lake Winnebago**. Of its towns, **Appleton** was the birthplace of escapologist Harry Houdini, **Green Bay** is home to pro football's legendary Packers, and **Oshkosh** is a household word for its overalls and baby clothes, but it's all best seen as a prelude to the most romanticised part of the state, **Door County**.

Door County

DOOR COUNTY, forty-two miles long, sticks out into Lake Michigan like a gradually tapering candle from **Sturgeon Bay**, 140 miles north of Milwaukee. It smacks more of New England than the Midwest, with thirteen lighthouses and a string of fishing villages along its 250-mile coastline. The name derives from "Porte des Morts" or "**Door of Death**", the French name for the treacherous eight-mile strait, scene of countless shipwrecks, which separates the peninsula from Washington Island at its tip. Despite drawing a million-plus warm-weather tourists, this somewhat pricey peninsula (actually an island split off from Wisconsin by a canal) is not yet an extended amusement park; its main attractions are fishing and sightseeing cruises. Highlights of a half-day tour include **Peninsula State Park**, adjacent to **Fish Creek** on the bay side, which has forested biking and hiking trails galore, an observation tower and a lighthouse along its extensive shoreline. **Whitefish Dunes State Park**, off Hwy-57 south of **Jacksonport**, holds a wildlife preserve, trails and dunes. The most remote state park, **Rock Island**, off Washington Island, has no stores, no vehicles, and no way to leave after 4pm when the last cruiser ($6 return) departs for Washington Island.

Accommodation in Door County

Accommodation in Door County ranges from overpriced resorts to modest motels, as well as B&B inns and homes. **Camping** in the state parks costs up to $10 (plus $6 daily admission, annual $28). Recommended private campgrounds include *Patch of Pines* (☎868-3332), County Road F off Hwy-42, near Fish Creek ($15, May–Oct).

Edge of the Park, 200 feet from the entrance to Peninsula State Park (☎868-3344). Cabins from $45 per day. Bicycles, of varying speeds, for rent at hourly, daily and weekly rates.

Hillside Hotel, 9980 Hwy-42 (☎854-2417 or ☎1-800/423-7023). Beautifully restored country inn on Ephraim harbour. Rooms with shared bath $70. Gourmet meals (residents only) on selected nights.

Twin Oaks Lodge, County Rd A and Hwy-42 (☎854-2633). Spotless, cordial motor hotel at edge of Fish Creek. Free bikes, cable TV, heated outdoor pool. Rooms $40–59, depending on season.

The White Gull Inn, 4225 Main St, Fish Creek (☎868-3517). Doubles $58–70, breakfast extra.

Eating in Door County

One reward of a midsummer visit to Door County is the chance to sample the **cherry** in all its guises. Another traditional treat is the **fishboil**, a delicious outdoor ritual involving whitefish steaks, potatoes and onions cooked in a cauldron over a wood fire. Rounded off with coleslaw and cherry pie, it's widely available for less than $10.

Al Johnson's Swedish Restaurant, Hwy-42 (☎854-2626). Pancakes, meatballs and other fine Scandinavian dishes; and there are goats tethered atop the sod roof.

Digger's Grill and Pizza, Hwy-42, Fish Creek (☎868-3095). Big portions, low prices.

Greenwood Supper Club, County Rds A & F, near Fish Creek (☎839-2451). Excellent service, full meals up to $15, and lounge.

Wilson's, Hwy-42, Ephraim (☎854-2041). Burgers, sandwiches and the peninsula's best ice cream.

Upstate Wisconsin

Sparsely settled **northern Wisconsin** has no large cities (and few small ones) and no interstates. Bordered at the top by Lake Superior and the western end of Michigan's upper peninsula (see p.240), it is largely a lake-studded wilderness covered by enormous tracts of forest. You can canoe its rivers, fish for record-breaking whoppers, or ski or snowmobile cross-country trails without having to fight for space. **Bayfield** and the **Apostle Islands** in the northwest are the most obvious destinations, though Hayward, 76 miles southeast of Superior, is home to the amazing **National Fresh Water Fishing Hall of Fame** (mid-April to Nov, 10am–5pm), dominated by a four-storey 500-ton fibreglass fish: "Walk through the biggest fish in the world!"

The Apostle Islands

All but one of the twenty-two **Apostle Islands**, scattered off **Bayfield Peninsula** about eighty miles east of Duluth, Minnesota (see p.279), are designated National Lakeshore Reserve. Most visitors only make it to **Madeline Island**, the largest and easiest to reach, but even that still has its secluded spots to recharge depleted spiritual batteries. **Campers** require free permits from the National Park **Visitor Center**, in the old Bayfield courthouse, Washington Avenue and Fourth Street (daily May–Oct; ☎779-3397). *Apostle Island Cruise Service* (☎779-3925) offers sightseeing **tours**, for $17.

The erstwhile lumbering and fishing village of **BAYFIELD**, now a pleasantly soft-sell tourist trap, serves as jumping-off point to the Apostles. **Rooms** at the *Old Rittenhouse Inn*, 301 Rittenhouse Avenue (☎779-5111), start at $69; gourmet meals cost $30. Clean, simple doubles at *Frostman's*, 24 N Third Street (☎779-3239), cost from $20. The *Village Inn Restaurant* (☎742-3941) in **Cornucopia**, a lakeside hamlet twenty miles west, serves Scandinavian **fishboils** every Friday ($7.95) and keeps four rooms at $49 each. *Rocky Run Resort* (☎373-2551), on the outskirts of Washburn eleven miles south, has thirty private lakeside acres. This may be the most idyllic place to stay on the peninsula; assorted rooms and cottages go for $35–80, summer only.

Madeline Island

The thousands of Ojibway Indians who occupied Madeline Island as early as the fifteenth century knew it as *Mon-a waun-a-kauning* – home of the golden-breasted woodpecker. Frenchman Michel Cadotte founded a fur trading post there for the British in 1793, and subsequently married Equaysayway, daughter of a tribal leader, who took the Christian name the island bears today. Cadotte is buried in an overgrown cemetery in the island's sole town, **La Pointe**, not far from a golf course and marina.

The telephone **area code** for upstate Wisconsin is ☎715.

In summer the *Madeline Island Ferry Line* shuttles between Bayfield and La Pointe (every 30min; passengers $2.25, vehicles $1.50–5.25; ☎747-2051). Madeline Island's 14,000 acres remain relatively undeveloped. La Pointe is a tiny community with an interesting little historical **museum** (May–Oct daily 10am–5pm; $3). Its cheapest indoor **accommodation** is at *Madeline Island Motel* (☎747-3000), $45, and *La Pointe Lodgings* (☎747-5205), $35 to $55, both near the ferry dock. **Eating** options are limited: the *Clubhouse* (☎747-2612) serves fairly pricey but tasty food in season (Wed–Sun only); low-cost *Grandpa Tony's* (☎747-3911) is open daily in summer from 8am.

The island's big sandy beaches, wide bays, scenic points and forests can be explored via forty-five miles of sometimes rough road. As you get off the ferry, you can hire **bicycles** from the Chamber of Commerce (☎747-2801), or **mopeds** from *Motion to Go*. **Camping** sites at *Big Bay State Park* (☎779-3346) cost $12.75 including park admission; reservations required. A wooden footbridge across the lagoon leads to *Big Bay Town Park* (☎747-6913; $6.50, no reservations); the campgrounds share a splendid mile-long beach. At **Big Bay Point**, sandstone cliffs and caves stand at the water's edge.

Southern Wisconsin

The highways and backroads lacing up **southern Wisconsin** pass over the rolling hills and deep dales so typical of the state. The main conurbation of Wisconsin's most populated region, still mainly farmland, is the immensely likeable lakeside college town of **Madison**, which doubles as the state capital. Stretches of the **Mississippi River**, as it undulates down Wisconsin's western border, have been designated **The Great River Road**, a scenic highway that runs from near Canada to the Gulf of Mexico.

Madison

The history books say that **MADISON** was little more than a wooded, mosquito-infested swamp when it was selected to be the political nucleus of Wisconsin Territory in 1836. Today it is one of the country's finest capital cities, more pocket-sized than Milwaukee, just over an hour to the east. Though it has a number of diverting art and heritage museums, plus a small public zoo, Madison's main appeal is as a stimulating, youthful metropolis with few of the problems found in bigger American cities.

Downtown is neatly laid out on an isthmus between lakes **Mendota** and **Monona**, with the sumptuous white granite **State Capitol** (free tours) sitting benignly on a hill at its the centre, surrounded by shady trees, lawns and park benches. Capitol Square itself is the site of a fun **farmers market** (May–Oct, Sat 6am–2pm); browse late for bargains. Numerous streets radiate out from here, and residential areas begin within two blocks.

If the Capitol is the city's governmental heart, the **University of Wisconsin-Madison** (average enrolment 46,000) is its spirited, liberal-thinking head, now mellowed since its hippie/protest heyday in the Sixties and Seventies. **Memorial Union**, 800 Langdon Street (☎262-1583), is the campus "living room", holding a cheap cafeteria and pub, the *Rathskeller*, with tables strewn beneath huge vaulted ceilings and live music most evenings. Out back, the spacious **UW Terrace** faces beautiful Lake Mendota. Capitol and campus are arterially connected by **State Street**, eight tree-lined, pedestrianised blocks of restaurants, cafes and bars, and fun and funky shops.

Practicalities

Greyhound, 931 E Main Street (☎257-9511), has regular runs to Milwaukee, Green Bay and out of state. *Badger Coaches*, 601 W Washington Avenue, make two trips daily to

The telephone **area code** for southern Wisconsin is ☎608.

Milwaukee ($14 return; ☎255-1511). *Alco Bus Company* depart from Memorial Union to Chicago's O'Hare Airport (12 daily; $18; ☎257-5593). The **visitor centre** is at 615 E Washington Avenue (Mon–Fri 8am–5pm; ☎25-LAKES).

There's **accommodation** to be had all over the city, though the cheap chains are near I-90/94 to the east. *Collins House*, 704 E Gorham Street (☎255-4230), is a beautiful B&B just a few blocks from the Capitol, with rooms from $65 to $99. Doubles at the *Colonial Motel*, 3001 W Beltline Hwy (☎836-1131), in the western suburbs, cost from $21 to $37, while in summer *The Towers*, 502 N Frances Street (☎257-0701), offers hundreds of clean central rooms, normally used for conferences, for as little as $25. **State Street** is a veritable smorgasbord of **eating** and **drinking** opportunities; the tiny Nepalese *Himal Chuli* at no. 318 (☎251-9225) serves meals for under $8, while *Ella's Deli*, no. 425 (☎257-8611), has kosher food, daily specials and rich ice creams. Top-quality dining is to be found in *The Fess*, a converted hotel at 123 E Doty Street (☎256-0263); entrees start at a bargain $9. The *Essen Haus*, 514 E Wilson Street (☎255-4674), is a raucous "biergarten" restaurant with a phenomenal selection of beers.

In addition to the (often free) **entertainment** on the university campus, it's worth checking out the converted railroad hotel at 636 W Washington Street, which incorporates a live music bar, a mixed dance club, and a heavy-duty gay leather bar. State Street is packed with bars like *The Pub* and *Mondays*. *Crystal Corner*, 1302 Williamson Street (☎256-2953), is a soulful neighbourhood joint which puts on **blues** acts; the music at *O'Cayz Corral*, 504 E Wilson Street (☎256-1348), ranges through heavy metal, folk and acoustic. *Phaze 2*, 117 W Main Street (☎255-5029), is a friendly, decorative downtown gay bar serving light meals. Full **listings** are carried by the free weekly *Isthmus*.

Baraboo

Between 1884 and 1912, the **Ringling Brothers' Circus** kept winter quarters in **BARABOO**, thirty miles northwest of Madison. The **Circus World Museum**, 426 Water Street, successfully recaptures the pre-TV glory days of big-top history, via an enormous collection of memorabilia and daily performances including an old-time circus show that is both tawdry (elephants with bows on their tails doing leg kicks to *New York, New York*) and irresistible (daily late July & Aug 9am–10pm; May, June, and the first halves of July & Sept 9am–6pm; $9). Every summer, in the second week of July, seventy-five meticulously restored circus wagons set out on a two-day rail journey through small-town Wisconsin and Illinois, culminating in a horse-drawn parade through downtown Milwaukee; an unbeatable extravaganza of Americana.

Baraboo itself is calmer, quieter and more affordable than nearby Wisconsin Dells. The colonial *Barrister's House*, 226 Ninth Avenue (☎356-3344), is a B&B on a high bluff with rooms for $50 to $60. Rooms at the *Spinning Wheel*, 809 Eighth Street (☎356-3977), cost $30 to $50; the friendly all-night store opposite serves as the local *Greyhound* stop. *Kristina's Family Cafe*, 113 Third Street (☎356-3430), and *Susie's*, 146 Fourth Avenue (☎356-9911), on the square around the town hall, serve low-cost **meals**. Baraboo's **visitor centre** is at 124 Second Street (Mon–Fri 10am–4pm; ☎356-8333).

Overlord Master Control

En route to Baraboo from Madison, seven miles beyond **Sauk City**, Hwy-12 passes a junk shop called **Delany's Surplus**, facing the munitions factory Badger Ordinance Power Plant. Out back, Tom Every, formerly in the demolition business, has fashioned his own nascent **sculpture park**. The centrepiece is **Overlord Master Control**, a buoyantly ridiculous conglomeration of thousands of pounds of scrap metal by which Every's fictional nineteenth-century ancestor, the physicist Dr Evermore, hoped to be transported to the heavens. Be sure to sit in the **Ear of the Universe**, a colossal cinema speaker above a filigreed two-person swivel seat attached to a sighting scope.

Wisconsin Dells

The **WISCONSIN DELLS** are fourteen miles of unusual rock formations, gorgeous gorges, and hundred-foot cliffs which rise above the Wisconsin River in weird, pancake-like layers near the eponymous town of Wisconsin Dells. Daily summer tours of the Upper and Lower sections – separated by a hydro-electric dam – take four hours, costing $9.95 and $6.85 respectively (or $13.28 for the two). The more interesting **Upper Dells** tour (board downtown on Broadway Street) includes landings at Witches Gulch, Coldwater Canyon and towering Stand Rock. The remainder of the Dells, spilling over into the community of Lake Delton, is a Midwestern Disneyland gone haywire; if you're in the right mood, the gaudy mini-golf games, giant water parks, foam homes, spook-houses, waxworks and endless hoardings can make for a fun, if tiring, day.

Finding **accommodation** in the Dells can be tricky, especially in summer when prices soar. The *Historic Bennett House*, 825 Oak Street (☎254-2500), is now a B&B with comfy doubles for $50 to $60. Motels along **Wisconsin Dells Parkway** towards Lake Delton – prices start at $35 and head on up – include the *New Concord Inn*, no. 411 (☎254-4338), and *Inn of the Dells*, no. 611 (☎253-1511); you can **camp** at *Dells KOA* (☎254-4177), nine blocks from town at S235 Stand Rock Road. The *Fire Station* (☎254-7127) serves all-you-can-eat pizza and pasta for $5 at two locations here; *Jimmy's Italian* at no. 126 (☎254-8186) is also good value. There's a **visitor centre** at 701 Superior Street (☎254-8088 or ☎1-800/22-DELLS). *Amtrak* makes one stop daily in each direction.

Necedah

The fundamentalist "theme park" of the **Queen of the Holy Rosary Mediatrix of Peace Shrine**, just outside **NECEDAH**, forty miles northwest of the Dells, is Wisconsin's secret answer to Fatima and Lourdes. It was inspired by visitations from the Virgin Mary and various saints received by the late **Mary Ann Van Hoof** from 1949 onwards, as documented in the **information centre** (daily 9.30am–9pm), well stocked with anti-abortion and anti-rock'n'roll pamphlets. The **Shrine** itself consists of fourteen tableaux, including a Crucifixion with a Christ whose skin is so gruesomely full of multi-coloured gashes as to resemble an abstract painting, and a triumvirate of the Lord flanked by George Washington and Abraham Lincoln. Because it is a "place of apparitions", no one, least of all women, is allowed in wearing shorts, low-cut dresses or see-through blouses. A massive House of Prayer is under construction, funded by donation, but no attempt is made to convert or extract cash from guests. Nearby are homes for Unfortunate Men and unwanted children (free pregnancy testing available).

Spring Green

During his seventy-year career, Wisconsin-born architect and social philosopher **Frank Lloyd Wright** designed such structures as the spiralling **Guggenheim Museum** in New York City, and Tokyo's earthquake-proof **Imperial Hotel**. Wright's **Taliesin and Hillside Home School** stands in **SPRING GREEN**, forty miles west of Madison on Hwy-14. Taliesin itself, Wright's home overlooking the river three miles south of town, is not open to the public. Tours of the architectural school he began in 1932, however, with its magnificent studio and jewel-like theatre space, tell a good deal about his life and beliefs (see also pp. 258 and 677). Its streamlined geometry and functional grandeur exemplify the break Wright's work made from the boxy, fustian Victorian style (May to mid-Oct daily 9am–4pm; $6). Among Wright-influenced buildings in Spring Green are the bank, pharmacy and the lounge of a mid-priced restaurant called the *Post House* (☎588-2595). The classy *Spring Green Restaurant* (☎588-2571), a stone's throw from Taliesin on Hwy-23, is the only eating establishment Wright himself designed.

The **House on the Rock**, six miles beyond Taliesin on Hwy-23, was built by Alex Jordan from 1944 onwards for no discernible reason – he certainly never lived in it, nor did he intend it to become Wisconsin's number one tourist attraction (April–Oct daily 8am–5.30pm; $13). Only the first section of the House bears any resemblance to a house of any kind. It's a multi-levelled series of furnished nooks and chambers, built in, on and out of a natural sixty-foot, chimney-like rock, which with its low ceilings, indirect lighting, indoor pools, waterfalls and trees and pervasive shag carpeting, comes across as an eccentric bachelor's digs, sort of Frank Lloyd Wright meets *The Flintstones*. Much of it was wrought by hand, Jordan himself hauling the materials in baskets up rope ladders. The rest of the House is a logic-free labyrinth, containing Jordan's astounding collection of collections (antiques, nickelodeons, miniature circuses, dolls and dolls' houses, maritime memorabilia, armour and firearms, ad infinitum), with little to indicate what is genuine or imitation, and no clue as to what it all means. The net effect is overwhelming and disorienting, alternately great fun and ghastly. Highlights include the **Infinity Room**, composed of three thousand small glass panels tapering to a point and cantilevered several hundred feet above the Wyoming Valley; the utterly dazzling **World's Largest Carousel**, with 269 fabulous figures and some 20,000 lights; and any of several partly pneumatic, partly computerised automated orchestras.

Practicalities

Spring Green is a pretty place to **stay**. The *Round Barn Lodge*, Hwy-14 (☎588-2568), has rooms for $55 to $75, less off-season, and family-style dining in a 1914 round barn. The secluded *Wildwood Lodge* (☎588-2514), between Taliesin and the House on Hwy-3, about two miles off Hwy-23, is a little run-down and hard to find, has rooms from $30 upwards. Locals and thespians hang out at *The Shed* (☎588-9049), an easy-going diner and bar on downtown Lexington Street serving acceptable, low-budget food.

MINNESOTA

Though **MINNESOTA** is about a thousand miles from either coast, it's virtually a seaboard state, thanks to **Lake Superior**, connected to the Atlantic via the St Lawrence Seaway. The glaciers that, millions of years ago, flattened all but its southeast corner gouged out more than 15,000 **lakes**, and major **rivers** run along the eastern and western borders. Ninety-five percent of the population lives within ten minutes of a body of water, and the very name *Minnesota* is a Sioux word meaning "land of sky-tinted water".

French explorers in the sixteenth century encountered prairies to the south and, in the north, dense forests whose abundant waterways were an ideal breeding ground for beavers and muskrats. **Fur trading, fishing** and **lumbering** flourished, and the Ojibway and Sioux tribes were eased out by waves of French, British and American immigrants. Place names throughout the state attest to its Indian and French heritage. Admitted to the Union in 1858, the new state of Minnesota was at first settled by Germans and Scandinavians, who farmed in the west and south. Other ethnic groups followed, many drawn by the discovery of massive **iron ore** deposits in north-central Minnesota, which are expected to hold out for another two hundred years.

Minnesota still thrives on its natural resources, and on a progressive social outlook typified by such liberal political heavyweights as Hubert Humphrey, Eugene McCarthy and Walter Mondale. More than half of its hardy inhabitants, who endure some of the fiercest winters in the nation, live in the southeast, around the so-called Twin Cities of **Minneapolis** and **St Paul**, attractive and basically friendly rivals who together rank as the Midwest's great civic double act for their combined cultural, recreational and business opportunities. Smaller cities include the northern shipping port of **Duluth**, close to pristine wilderness, and **Rochester**, near pretty river towns like Red Wing and Winona.

Getting Around Minnesota

Minneapolis/St Paul **airport**, home base for *Northwest Airlines*, handles overseas traffic, including routes to Great Britain, as well as domestic flights. *Amtrak* **trains** cross the state once a day east and west, with stops in Winona, Red Wing, St Paul, Staples and Detroit Lakes. *Greyhound*, founded upstate in Hibbing although no longer based there, is the largest of the several **bus** companies plying Minnesota's roads.

Minneapolis and St Paul

Commonly known as the **Twin Cities**, **MINNEAPOLIS** (a combined Sioux and Greek word meaning "water city") and **ST PAUL** are competitive yet complementary in the manner of gritty Glasgow and straitlaced Edinburgh. Fraternally rather than identically twinned, they may be even better places to live than they are to visit, thanks to their good looks, cleanliness, cultural activity, social awareness and relatively low crime rates. About thirty of *Fortune Magazine*'s 500 top-ranking corporations are based here; many extend substantial financial support to local arts, community projects and sports. Life for a majority of Twin Citians seems so vibrantly wholesome that the most significant threat would appear to be their own creeping complacency.

St Paul has been called "the last city of the east", making Minneapolis across the curving Mississippi "the first city of the west". Only a twenty-minute expressway ride separates them, but each has its own character, style and strengths. **St Paul**, the state capital, was originally called Pig's Eye, after a scurrilous French-Canadian fur trader who sold whiskey at a landing on the banks of the Mississippi River in the 1840s. Of the twins, it is the staid, slightly older sibling, careful to preserve its buildings and traditions. The residents are mainly German, Irish and Catholic. The compact but stately downtown is built, like Rome, on seven hills; the **Capitol** and the **Cathedral** occupy one each, august monuments that keep the city mindful of its responsibilities. Garrison Keillor, Minnesota's would-be Mark Twain, got his start in St Paul.

Minneapolis, founded on money generated by the Mississippi's hundreds of flour and saw mills, is livelier, artier and more modern, with skyscraping, up-to-date architecture and an upbeat and even brash attitude that never quite jeopardises its essential affability. The mostly Slavonic, Nordic and Lutheran residents are spread over wider ground than in St Paul, with dozens of lakes and parks to underscore the city's appeal. Home-grown superstar **Prince** has cast a global spotlight on the local music scene.

Arrival, Information and Getting Around

Twin Cities International Airport lies about ten miles from either city in suburban Bloomington. **Limousine** service between the airport and major hotels is around $10 return, although some lodgings lay on transport. **Taxis** to Minneapolis will set you back about $20, to St Paul $15. **Bus** #7 goes to Minneapolis; transfer to #9 for St Paul (6am–midnight: $1.60). *Amtrak* is midway between the cities at 730 Transfer Road, off University Avenue. The *Greyhound* terminals, each in a convenient downtown location, are at 29 Ninth Street in Minneapolis (☎371-3311), and, less used, Seventh and St Peter streets in St Paul (☎222-0509). *Metropolitan Transit Commission* **buses** cover both cities; multiple-ride tickets can be had from 719 Marquette Avenue in Minneapolis.

In Minneapolis, the **visitor centre** is at 1219 Marquette Avenue (☎348-4313 or ☎1-800/445-7412), in St Paul at 600 NCL Tower, 445 Minnesota Street (☎297-6985 or ☎1-800/627-6101). The main Minneapolis **post office** is at First Street and Marquette Avenue (zip code 55401); in St Paul it's at 180 E Kellogg Boulevard (zip code 55101).

The telephone **area code** for Minneapolis/St Paul is ☎612.

Exploring Minneapolis

Laid out on a simple grid, **downtown Minneapolis** is bounded by the Mississippi River
on the north side and by lovely Loring Park to the south. The riverfront, dubbed the
"Mississippi Mile", continues to be developed as a place for strolling, dining and entertainment. Each city has its own landing site for narrated **paddleboat** cruises (☎227-
1100; $7.50, seasonal). The vast Third Avenue bridge makes an ideal vantage point for
viewing **St Anthony Falls**, a controlled torrent in a wide stretch of the river. The
missionary Father Hennepin discovered the Falls in 1680; the first permanent settlement of present-day Minneapolis began nearby in the early nineteenth century.

Most of downtown's major stores are stacked along **Nicollet Mall**, a pedestrian thoroughfare. **Hennepin Avenue**, the other main drag, is a block west. The **IDS Center**,
on the Mall, is the tallest building in either city; its indoor glass atrium, the Crystal
Court, is essentially modern Minneapolis' town square. Pedestrians escape the city's
weather extremes via a "skyway" system of elevated, climate-controlled glassed walkways connecting over forty buildings. Culturally, Minneapolis would be poorer without
the **Walker Art Center**, Vineland Place (Tues–Sat 10am–8pm, Sun 11am–5pm; $3, free
Thurs), on the edge of downtown. This multipurpose contemporary arts space balances
its permanent collection of sculpture and paintings (such as German expressionist
Franz Marc's *Blue Horses*) with exciting temporary exhibitions and a programme of
films and performing arts. The seven-acre outdoor **Sculpture Garden** is a work of
genius, its most popular piece the whimsical gigantic *Spoonbridge and Cherry* (not
exactly a bridge, more like a fountain) by Claes Oldenburg and Coosje van Bruggen.

Arctic winters apart, hordes of Minneapolitans flock to the shores of the "big three",
Lakes **Calhoun** and **Harriet** and **Lake of the Isles**, all in residential areas within two
miles south of downtown. Each July the **Minneapolis Aquatennial** celebrates the lifestyle fostered by the lakes with two huge downtown parades and water-based events
such as milk-carton boat races. **Minnehaha Falls**, south of downtown on bus #7, was
featured in Longfellow's 1855 poem *Song of Hiawatha* without his ever having laid eyes
on it. The adjacent park is a favourite haunt for hikes and picnics.

Exploring St Paul

St Paul, reached along Interstate 94 (and served by buses #16A, #21A or express route
#94B) has more wealthy old homes and civic monuments than Minneapolis. Call in at
the jazzy Art Deco lobby of the **City Hall and Courthouse**, Fourth and Wabasha
streets, to see Swedish sculptor Carl Milles' remarkable revolving *Indian God of Peace*,
36ft high and carved in the 1930s from white Mexican onyx. The castle-like **Landmark
Center**, a couple of blocks away at Fifth and Market streets, overlooks **Rice Park**, probably the prettiest little square in either city. As in Minneapolis, downtown buildings are
linked via "skyways"; but here at evenings and weekends things get very quiet. The
beautifully restored **Cafesjian's Carousel** ($1 per ride) is tucked inside **Town Square
Park**, a lush, multilevel indoor garden in a shopping complex. An immense steel iguana
is the doorkeeper at the exciting hands-on **Science Museum of Minnesota**, 30 E
Tenth Street (April–Sept Mon–Sat 9.30am–9pm, Sun 11am–9pm, otherwise closed Mon;
$6), which has a two-storey **Omnitheater** cinema.

As you move away from downtown, five-mile **Summit Avenue** is a well preserved
Victorian boulevard. **F Scott Fitzgerald**, born nearby, finished his first success, *This
Side of Paradise*, in 1918 while living in a modest row house at no. 599; he disparaged the
avenue as a "museum of American architectural failures". Look for the coffin atop no.
465, once the home of an undertaker. Pioneer politico **Alexander Ramsey's** house
(April–Dec Tues–Fri 10am–4pm, Sat & Sun 1–4.30pm; $3), nearby at 265 S Exchange
Street in the fashionable Irvine Park district, remains a showcase of Victorian high style.

Costumed staff do a fine job of interpreting Minnesota's early nineteenth-century past at **Fort Snelling** (May–Oct daily 10am–5pm; Nov–April Mon–Fri 9am–430pm; $3), near the airport off highways 5 and 55. Built between 1819 and 1825 on a strategic bluff at the confluence of the Mississippi and Minnesota rivers, this was Minnesota's first permanent structure – a successful attempt by the US government to establish an official presence in the wilderness that had recently been won from Great Britain.

Annual celebrations in St Paul include a beanfeast called **Taste of Minnesota** (tons of food, live entertainment, rides and fireworks) on Independence Day in early July, the nation's largest State Fair (end of Aug to early Sept), and the **Winter Carnival** (late Jan to early Feb), a frosty gala designed to make the most of the seasonal freeze via ice and snow sculpting, hot air ballooning, team sports, parades and more.

Accommodation

You're likely to pay more for lodgings downtown than in the suburbs, where dozens of cheap **motels** line I-494 near the airport, though some of the pricier central hotels offer reduced rates and special package deals on weekends.

Minneapolis

Brasie House, 2321 Colfax Ave S (☎377-5946). Attractive guest house in lively neighbourhood near downtown. Three rooms with shared bath, continental breakfast. $60.

Caecilian Hall, 2004 Randolph Ave (☎690-6604). Doubles for *AYH* members $20, others $25.

Christopher Inn, 201 Mill St, Excelsior (☎474-6816). Year-round suburban B&B on Lake Minnetonka. Cheaper rooms $65–85, good discounts off-season and midweek.

Evelo's B&B, 2301 Bryant Ave S (☎374-9656). Three comfortable rooms in well-preserved Victorian home near bus lines, lakes and downtown. $35–55. Non-smokers preferred.

Fair Oaks, 2335 Third Ave S (☎871-2000). Friendly, unpretentious motor hotel near downtown, across from the Art Institute. Doubles $43–50.

St Paul

Chatsworth B&B, 984 Ashland Ave (☎227-4288). Beautiful turn-of-the-century home. $58–95.

Como Villa, 1371 W Nebraska Ave (☎647-0471). Gay-owned Victorian B&B by Como Park. $55–70.

Miller B&B, 887 James Ave (☎227-1292). 1920s duplex with shared bath. $35.

Sunwood Inn, 1010 Bandana Blvd W (☎647-1637). Unique lodgings in former railroad car repair shop now attached to Bandana Square mall. $65–70 includes indoor pool, sauna.

Eating

Minneapolis and St Paul belie preconceptions of Midwestern blandness with an almost bewildering number of **restaurants**. In Minneapolis, head for the downtown **warehouse district** or the university's **Dinkytown**; in St Paul try **Galtier Plaza** or the **St Paul Center** downtown. *The Lotus* is a local chain serving Vietnamese meals for under $5. Be sure to sample **wild rice**, a Minnesota speciality.

Minneapolis

Broder's Cucina Italiana, 2308 W 50th St (☎925-3113). Terrific deli for eat-in or takeaway.

Cafe Brenda, 300 First Ave N (☎342-9230). Excellent, moderately priced nouvelle vegetarian cuisine in arty downtown warehouse district.

Chez Bananas, 129 N Fourth St (☎340-0032). Spicy, Caribbean-influenced food and toys on tables.

Emily's Lebanese Deli, 641 University Ave NE (☎379-4069). Warm, low-cost local place.

Korea House, 414½ Cedar Ave S (☎339-9385). Family-owned, authentic, inexpensive.

Odaa, 408 Cedar Ave S (☎338-4959). Fine all-you-can-eat Ethiopian finger food for $10 and less.

Sawatdee, 607 Washington Ave S (☎338-6451). Flavoursome Thai food, always well prepared.

St Paul

Caravan Serai, 2175 Ford Parkway (☎690-1935). Afghani food, tent-like space, pillow seats.
The Deco, 305 St Peter St (☎228-0520). Fabulous buffets ($9 and up) atop riverside art museum.
Mickey's Diner, 36 W Seventh St (☎222-5633). Landmark 24-hr greasy spoon in 1930s dining car.
St Paul Grill, 350 Market St (☎292-9292). Trad but inventive dishes in classic downtown hotel.
WA Frost, Selby and Western Ave (☎224-5715). Former pharmacy and F Scott Fitzgerald hangout converted into plush restaurant with garden patio.

Nightlife and Entertainment

The Greater Twin Cities have been dubbed a "cultural Eden on the prairie", where 2.2 million people support ninety **theatre** companies, ten **dance** troupes, twenty **classical music** ensembles and over a hundred art galleries. Sir Tyrone Guthrie began the theatrical boom back in 1963, enrolling large-scale local assistance to establish the classical repertory company (☎377-2224 or ☎1-800/848-4912) named after him. The cities now have more theatre per capita than anywhere in the US apart from New York City.

Unlike many American cities, **nightlife** in Minneapolis (and, to a lesser extent, St Paul) hasn't been siphoned off by suburbia. The presence of around a hundred thousand students ensures a vibrant **club** scene. **Prince Rogers Nelson**, the *wunderkind* responsible for the so-called "Minneapolis sound", keeps his multimedia **Paisley Park** studio in the suburb of Chanhassen. Another hot Twin Cities recording company, **Flyte Time**, produces Janet Jackson. For complete entertainment information and listings, check out the ubiquitous free weeklies *Twin Cities Reader* and *City Pages*. *Equal Time*, *Gaze* and *GLC Voice* provide a similar service from a gay and lesbian perspective.

Minneapolis and St Paul Theatres

Chanhassen Dinner Theater, 521 W 78th St, Minneapolis (☎934-1525). Mainstream musicals, popular comedies and drama on three stages. Adequate meals. Thirty minutes from downtown.
Dudley Riggs' Brave New Workshop, 2605 Hennepin Ave S, Minneapolis (☎332-6620). The granddad of local satirical comedy troupes.
Great North American History Theater, 30 E Tenth St, St Paul (☎292-3423). Original plays dealing with events and personalities from Minnesota's past.
Jungle Theater, 709 W Lake St, Minneapolis (☎822-7063). Hole-in-the-wall theatre/cabaret.
Park Square, St Peter St and Kellogg Blvd, St Paul (☎291-7005). Classic plays well served.
Penumbra, 270 N Kent St, St Paul (☎224-4601). Professional African-American company.
Red Eye Collaboration, 15 W 14th St, Minneapolis (☎870-0309). Challenging experimental theatre.
Theater de la Jeune Lune, First St and First Ave, Minneapolis (☎333-6200). Unique ensemble of Parisians and Minneapolitans offer dynamic, highly physical productions from a commedia base.

Minneapolis Clubs and Pubs

Fine Line, 318 First Ave (☎338-8100). Sleek, small and musically eclectic downtown club.
First Avenue and 7th St Entry, 701 First Ave (☎338-8388 or ☎332-1775). Landmark rock venue where Prince's *Purple Rain* was shot still packs 'em in with live and canned music.
Gay 90s, 408 Hennepin Ave S (☎333-7755). Sprawling gay club that's a downtown institution with two dance floors, piano lounge, men's and women's bars, dining and weekend drag shows.
Glam Slam, 110 N Fifth St (☎338-3383). State of the art dance club owned by Prince associate, featuring local and national acts. Dress flash and possibly glimpse royalty.
Loon Cafe, 500 First Ave N (☎332-8342). Noisy, likeable sports bar with great grub (try the chilis).
Loring Bohemian Bar and Cafe, 1624 Harmon Place (☎338-6258 or ☎332-1617). Beautiful people with attitude drink, dine or drift upstairs to the dance/theatre Playhouse.
New Riverside Cafe, 329 Cedar Ave S (☎333-4814). Alcohol-free venue; jazz, bluegrass, folk nightly.
Nye's Polonaise Room, 112 E Hennepin Ave (☎379-2021). Plenty of old-time atmosphere with both piano and polka bars, plus Polish-American restaurant.

St Paul Clubs and Pubs

The Dakota Bar and Grill, 1021 Bandana Blvd (☎642-1442). Gourmet Midwestern food and great local and national jazz in converted shopping mall locale.

Gallivan's, 354 Wabasha St (☎227-6688). Downtown white-collar pub with neighbourhood feel.

Heartthrob Cafe and Philadelphia Bandstand, 30 E Eighth St (☎224-2783). Bright, noisy and nostalgic downtown burger joint with rollerskating staff and dancing.

O'Gara's Bar and Grill, 164 N Snelling Ave (644-3333). Mixed clientele drawn by grub, grog and live bands in the adjoining Garage.

Rumors, 490 N Robert St (☎646-2288). Downtown gay/lesbian club; exudes camaraderie.

Town House, 1415 University Ave (☎646-7087). Gay country & western bar where they'll gladly teach you the two-step.

Stillwater

The bluffs, hills and historic small towns strung along the **St Croix River Valley** to the east of the Twin Cities bear some resemblance to Rhineland. The riverside community of **STILLWATER**, twenty-five miles out via I-35 north and Hwy-36 east, is known as the "Birthplace of Minnesota", as it petitioned Congress for the formation of the Minnesota Territory in 1849. It was the state's lumber capital until the forests were depleted and the industry moved north. Now a commuters' retreat, contemporary Stillwater shows off pretty church spires, a courthouse complete with cupola, and some grand old homes, as well as antique shops, boutiques, restaurants and bars. In summer you can ride the **Rivertown Trolley** (☎430-0352; $5.50) or a segment of the old **Stillwater/St Paul Railroad** (☎228-0263; $6). The 1940s railroad dining cars of the *Minnesota Zephyr*, 601 N Main Street (☎430-3000), travel up the valley along the river at five miles per hour, while passengers dine on a four-course meal (3hr; $47.50).

The colonial-style *Lowell Inn*, 102 N Second Street (☎439-1100), serves sumptuous and suitably pricey **meals** amid a riot of Swiss woodcarving; romantic and kitschy **rooms** start at $79 low-season. The gracious *Rivertown Inn*, 306 W Olive Street (☎430-2955 or ☎1-800/562-3632), keeps three rooms at $69, one for $49. The *Best Western Stillwater Inn*, two miles out at 1750 W Frontage Rd (☎430-1300), is a motel refreshingly run like a B&B; rooms cost $44 to $52. **Eat** and **drink** at *The Freight House*, 305 Water Street (☎439-5718), or *Brine's*, 219 S Main Street (☎439-1862); both are moderately priced, informal and friendly. The **visitor centre** is at 423 S Main Street (☎439-7700).

Northern Minnesota

Minnesota's substantial northern half, overrun with forested lakes, remains much as it was when the first Europeans began trading with the Indians. The contemporary tourist can expect secluded outdoor vacations centred around fishing, canoeing and sundry watery pursuits. There's no dearth of campgrounds or "Ma and Pa" lakeside resorts, havens of homely simplicity dedicated to soothing urban-ravaged souls.

Duluth

The port city of **DULUTH**, at the western extremity of Lake Superior 150 miles north of Minneapolis/St Paul, forms a long crescent at the base of a triangular region, abutting Canadian Ontario and nicknamed the **Arrowhead**, It cascades down from granite bluffs surrounding Skyline Drive (an exhilarating thirty-mile route) to a great natural harbour, shared with inferior Superior, Wisconsin. Together these "twin ports" constitute the largest inland shipping centre in the United States, linked to the Atlantic via the St Lawrence Seaway. In the whole nation, only New York City handles greater tonnage.

> The telephone **area code** for Duluth is ☎218.

Named after Daniel Greysolon, Sieur du Lhut, a French officer who first journeyed here in 1678, the port's main cargo in its early days was fur, not the taconite of today. Over the next three centuries, its fortunes fluctuated along with markets for grain, lumber and ore. In the 1980s it had a face-lift and began to encourage tourism.

Duluth is **cold**. The seaway is frozen through the winter, and even spring and autumn evenings can be chilly; the temperature is significantly cooler near the lake at all times. A **harbour cruise** ($7; ☎722-6218) is a surprisingly pleasant way to spend a couple of hours in summer, gawping at huge rusty ships and mounds of ore; boats depart from behind the convention centre on Harbor Drive. **Rail excursions** run along the Superior shoreline (☎722-1273; $12) and the St Louis River (☎624-7549 or ☎727-8025; $5).

Practicalities

Greyhound, 2212 W Superior Street (☎722-5591), has connections with most of the Upper Midwest. *Triangle Transportation* hooks up Duluth with Grand Forks and other North Dakotan destinations via International Falls. The **visitor centre** is in Endion Station, 100 Lake Place Drive (☎722-4011 or ☎1-800/4-DULUTH).

The lavish *Mansion*, 3600 London Road (☎724-0739), leads the pack of **B&Bs**, with a few rooms at $75; prices at the *Best Western Edgewater*, 2400 London Road (☎728-3601 or ☎1-800/777-7925), start at $49. Non-members pay $25 at the **AYH youth hostel** in the YWCA, 202 W Second Street (☎722-7425). *Indian Point* **campground**, 75th and Grand avenues, west off Hwy-23 (☎624-5637), has summer bayside sites. The Italian-American food at *Grandma's Saloon And Deli*, 522 S Lake Avenue (☎727-4192) in view of the aerial-lift bridge, is not for dieters. *Grandma's Sports Garden* (☎722-4722), just across a parking lot at no. 425, has a similarly convivial old-time atmosphere, dishing up tasty food when it isn't functioning as either dance floor or basketball court.

Out from Duluth

Highway 61, popularly known as North Shore Drive, follows Lake Superior 150 miles from Duluth to the tip of the Arrowhead (Minnesota native Robert Zimmerman, himself more popularly known as **Bob Dylan**, memorialised it on his album *Highway 61 Revisited*). Precipitous cliffs and dramatic waterfalls are interspersed with pretty little ports like Two Harbors and Grand Marais. In the Arrowhead's top half, the huge wilderness of the **Boundary Waters Canoe Area** (BWCA) is a canoe, backpack and fishing enthusiast's paradise, where over a thousand lakes are linked by overland trails or "portages"; in winter you can ski cross-country and dogsled. There are no roads, electricity, telephones or trash cans, and most lakes are motor-free. Stringent rules limit entry to the BWCA; in summer you have to have a permit (☎720-5440). Outfitters in the gateway towns of **Ely** and **Grand Marais** can supply everything you'll need (except appropriate clothing) for a daily fee of $20 to $45. The Gunflint Trail, a sixty-mile road into Canada from Grand Marais, is strewn with lodges for those who'd rather not rough it. Minneapolis-based *Wilderness Inquiry*, 1313 Fifth Street SE, arranges five- and seven-day guided holidays ($315–415; ☎379-3858 or ☎1-800/728-0719).

The vagaries of fur trading, logging, mining, fishing and shipping determined northern Minnesota's development. Many mines in the fabulously rich Mesabi and Vermilion Ranges still function over a century after their inception. **Ironworld USA**, in **Chisholm**, puts both the industry and the geology in perspective. Open-pit mining is visible all along Hwy-169 from Chisholm to **Hibbing**, Bob Dylan's birthplace and site of the awesome **Hull-Rust Mahoning Mine**; nearly five miles across and up to 535 feet deep, it's one of the largest man-made holes in the world. You can tour the oldest, deepest and richest of the mines at **Tower-Soudan State Park**, twenty-five miles west of **Ely**.

Towns throughout the Upper Midwest boast huge crude statues of **Paul Bunyan**, the titanic lumberjack, and his sidekick Babe, the equally gargantuan Blue Ox. They can be found standing in **Bemidji**, about thirty miles from Lake Itasca State Park, where the Mississippi River begins its great thirty-one state roll down to the Gulf of Mexico. A seated Paul moves his arms and speaks in **Brainerd**, twenty or so miles from Mille Lacs Lake. In tiny **Akeley**, near large Leech Lake, Paul (minus Babe) kneels so you can sit in his palm. The mid-sized town of **Grand Rapids**, 81 miles northwest of Duluth, contents itself with being the birthplace of **Judy Garland**; the old county schoolhouse contains a small museum dedicated to her, the path leading to it is a Yellow Brick Road.

Southern Minnesota

Southern Minnesota is split between high plains, timbered ravines and slow-flowing Mississippi tributaries in the east, and the drier, flatter prairie and checkerboard farm-land of the west. **Southeast Minnesota**, spared a filing down by the last glacial advance, is the most varied and physically dramatic part of the state. Several attractive small towns sit along the Mississippi, or on bluffs above it, in the ninety-mile **Hiawatha Valley** between Hastings and Winona. The shipping trade on the Mississippi helped sustain resourceful communities like **Winona**, **Red Wing**, **Lake City** (where waterski-ing was invented circa 1922) and **Wabasha**. All share some modest pleasures: well-preserved old homes, comfy historic hotels and inns, and an easy-going pace.

Northfield, only thirty miles south of the Twin Cities on I-35, is an agricultural and college centre that annually commemorates the Jesse James gang's foiled attempt to rob the town bank in September 1876. **Harmony**, almost in Iowa and near Minnesota's largest Amish colony, **Lanesboro**, with a storybook setting on the hillsides of the Root River, and **Mantorville** are the sort of places where time seems to have kept at least one foot in the nineteenth century. Further west, the names of **New Prague** and **New Ulm** betray their European heritage; these settlements were prime targets for the grossly mistreated Sioux during a six-week war with the US government in 1862.

Rochester

The metropolis of **ROCHESTER**, about eighty miles southeast of Minneapolis/St Paul, was settled in the 1850s by immigrants from Rochester, New York, as a humble crossroads campground for wagon trains. After a tornado devastated the town in 1883, the drive to improve its medical facilities resulted in the establishment by Dr William Worral Mayo of the **Mayo Clinic**, 200 First Street SW (☎284-2653). This huge complex of buildings, connected by subways and skyways, now sees an average of four thou-sand patients daily. Free **tours** (Mon–Fri 10am & 2pm) serve as ninety-minute pedes-trianised adverts for "the first and largest private group medical practice in the world".

Rochester is crawling with **accommodation**. The central *Kahler Hotel*, 20 SW Second Avenue (☎282-2581), has standard doubles for $49 to $64, and several dining options. Both the *Civic Inn*, 31 NW 13½ Street (☎289-3343), and *Heritage House*, 103 SW Third Avenue (☎282-2248), cost $26 to $42. The *Broadstreet Cafe and Bar*, 300 NW First Avenue (☎289-1280), a bistro in a renovated warehouse, serves excellent meals at reasonable prices; there's live music in the cosy *Redwood Room* downstairs.

Jefferson Union Bus Depot, 405 SW First Avenue (☎289-4037), is the hub for coach services. *Rochester Express Limousine Service* (☎288-4490) makes around six runs daily to the Twin Cities' airport, and the **visitor centre** is at 150 S Broadway Avenue (☎288-4331 or ☎1-800/426-6025).

The telephone **area code** for southern Minnesota is ☎507.

Pipestone

PIPESTONE, eight miles east of the South Dakota border, is named for a soft red rock found within the local quartzite. The stone was used for centuries by Great Plains Indians – who believed that it was formed from their ancestors' blood – to make ceremonial *calumets*, or peace pipes. The quarry site, a kind of neutral, inter-tribal United Nations, is now a National Monument (daily; $1). A self-guided trail winds from the visitor centre through stands of trees, past rock formations and exposed quarry pits, and over a creek, complete with picturesque falls. It's an exceptionally tranquil spot.

Pipestone township's small historic district includes a sleepy county museum, a century-old hotel and a building with several amusing sandstone gargoyles; pick up a walking tour brochure from the **Chamber of Commerce** (☎825-3316), on the edge of town near the junction of highways 75 and 23. You can sleep and eat at the *Calumet Inn*, Main Street (☎825-5871 or ☎1-800/535-7610), where rooms are about $60, though the generic *Travel Host* (☎825-4217 or ☎1-800/346-4974) and *Kings Kourt* (☎825-3314) motels are both cheaper. For nine days each July the town presents a massive **Indian pageant** in an outdoor amphitheatre.

The **Blue Mounds State Park**, a few miles north of the junction of I-90 and US-75 at Luverne, has seasonal **campgrounds** (☎1-800/765-CAMP) and a permanent small herd of buffalo. The mounds themselves are hard red rocks which slope into a long cliff up to a hundred feet high; from a distance the great hump they create appeared blue to pioneers approaching at sunset. The most curious part of the park is a 1250-foot row of rocks aligned on an east–west axis. Twice a year, at the equinox, the sun lines up with these stones.

travel details

TRAINS
Routes

• All *Amtrak* **train** routes in the Great Lakes region pass through **Chicago**, so that city has direct train links all over the continent, to New York, Boston, Washington DC, New Orleans, Los Angeles, San Francisco and Seattle.

• One service daily (two on Tues, Thurs & Sat) runs between **Chicago** and **Indianapolis**. One train each day travels on to the East Coast via Cincinnati.

• Two trains each way every day connect **Chicago** with **Toledo** via **South Bend**. Services continue either to Sandusky, Buffalo and New York City or Boston, or to Pittsburgh and Washington DC.

• Two trains daily in each direction run between **Chicago** and **Detroit**, stopping at **Battle Creek** and **Ann Arbor**; one continues to Toledo in Ohio, also calling at Ann Arbor and Dearborn. You can transfer to the daily Canada-bound train at Battle Creek; waiting time is 2hr 40min (1hr on Sun).

• One train each way daily from **Chicago** to **Toronto** stops at Battle Creek, Flint and Port Huron.

• Six trains daily connect **Chicago** and **Milwaukee**; one continues across Wisconsin towards Seattle, stopping at Columbus (near Madison), Portage, Wisconsin Dells, Tomah and LaCrosse.

Journey Times

From **Indianapolis**: Cincinnati 3hr; New York 23hr.

From **Detroit**: to Dearborn 15min; Ann Arbor 50min; Toledo 1hr 40min; Michigan City 5hr.

From **Chicago**: to Detroit 4hr 30min; Indianapolis 4hr 20min; Michigan City 1hr; South Bend 1hr 30min; Toledo 5hr; Toronto 12hr; Milwaukee 1hr 30min; New Orleans 19hr; Los Angeles 51hr; Oakland 52hr.

BUSES

All *Greyhound* unless otherwise stated.

From **Indianapolis**: to Bloomington (2 daily; 1hr); Chicago (10; 3hr 30min); Cincinnati (6; 2hr); Louisville (6; 2hr).

From **Cleveland**: to Pittsburgh (8 daily; 2hr); Sandusky (6, 1hr 30min); Cincinnati (4, 4hr 30min).

From **Detroit**: to Ann Arbor (6 daily, 1hr); Traverse City (1, 5hr); Mackinaw City (1, 6hr 30min); Toronto (6, 5hr); Cleveland (8, 4hr); Cincinnati (4, 3hr).

From **Chicago**: to Detroit (10 daily, 3hr); Milwaukee (6, 2hr 30min); Madison (6, 3hr); Minneapolis (6, 9hr); Cincinnati (7, 5hr 30min); Mackinaw City (1, 10hr).

From **Minneapolis/St Paul**: to Duluth (4 daily, 2hr).

From **Duluth**: to Mackinaw City (1 daily, 9hr).

From **Milwaukee**: *Badger Buses* to Madison (6 daily, 1hr).

CHAPTER FIVE

THE CAPITAL REGION

The city of **WASHINGTON DC**, and the four states of **VIRGINIA, WEST VIRGINIA, MARYLAND** and **DELAWARE**, constitute a cross-section of the nation. Since the days of the first American colonies, US history has been shaped here, from agitation towards independence to the battles of the Revolutionary and Civil wars. Now, the sharp contrasts and bizarre incongruities of contemporary America are shown in high relief; the corridors of power in Washington are literally a stone's throw away from dire inner-city poverty, while nearby dozens of time-worn farming and fishing towns seem straight out of some Norman Rockwell idyll.

Early in the seventeenth century, the first British settlements began to take root along the rich estuary of the **Chesapeake Bay**; though the colonists hoped for gold, they found their fortunes growing tobacco. Though even **Maryland** was bigger and more prosperous than Massachusetts, **Virginia**, the first of all, was the largest and most populous. It originally included most of what are now Kentucky, Tennessee and Ohio, and as late as the 1790s had double the residents of any other state. What often goes unsaid, however, is that fully half the people living here were **slaves**, brought from Africa to do the back-breaking work of harvesting the tobacco. Despite its central position on the East Coast, the whole region lies below the Mason-Dixon Line – the symbolic border between North and South, drawn up in 1763 as the boundary between slave and free states – and until the Civil War, one of the country's busiest slave-markets was just two blocks from the White House.

Besides generating the bulk of colonial **wealth** – tobacco from Virginia and Maryland accounted for over half the exports of the original thirteen US states – the region also produced many of early America's great leaders, from firebrand politicians like **Patrick Henry** ("Give me Liberty or Give me Death") to patrician intellectuals like **Thomas Jefferson**. Another Virginian, **George Washington**, lead the Continental Army against the British in the Revolutionary War and served as the first US president, while **James Madison** was the primary author of the country's Constitution.

For all its colonial importance, by the mid-nineteenth century the region had lost power and status to the burgeoning industrial and mercantile centres of Philadelphia and New York. Tensions between North and South finally erupted into the **Civil War**, of which traces are still visible everywhere. The hundred miles between the capital of the Union – Washington DC – and that of the Confederacy – Richmond, Virginia – were a constant and bloody battleground for four long years. This sense of a nation divided against itself is especially acute at the grand manor of **Robert E Lee**, the Confederacy's military leader: high on a hill overlooking the heart of Washington DC, its grounds are now filled with the war dead of the Arlington National Cemetery.

Washington DC itself, with its magnificent national showcases, is an essential stop on any tour of the region. **Virginia**, to the south, holds literally hundreds of historic sites, from the homes of early politicians to the colonial capital of **Williamsburg**, as well as the narrow forested heights of **Shenandoah National Park**, along the crest of the Blue Ridge Mountains. Much greater expanses of wilderness, crashing whitewater rivers, and innumerable backwoods villages await you in less-visited **West Virginia**.

Most tourists come to **Maryland** for the maritime traditions of **Chesapeake Bay** – though many of its quaint old villages have been gentrified by an influx of weekend pleasure-boaters. **Baltimore** is a characterful and enjoyably unpretentious city (with a

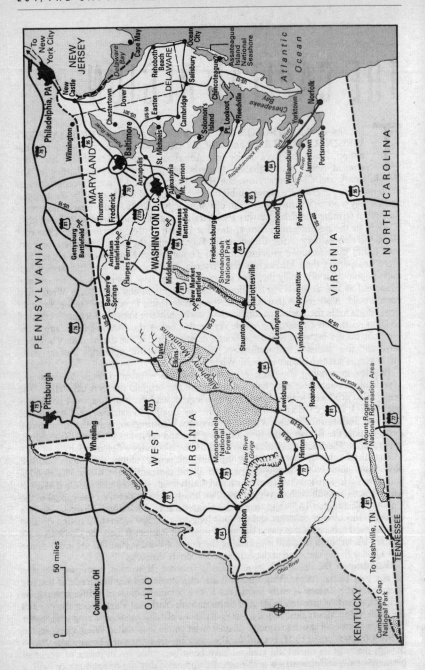

phenomenal concentration of bars), while **Annapolis**, the unassuming but pleasant state capital, is linked by bridge and ferry to the **eastern shore**. This quiet backwater, ideal for cycling, has dozens of two-hundred-year-old hamlets, as well as the untouched Atlantic paradise of **Assateague Island**. **New Castle**, across the border in **Delaware**, is perhaps the most perfectly preserved colonial-era town in the US; the rest of the state is unremarkable, but holds some of the East Coast's best and least crowded beaches.

WASHINGTON DC

That the marshy swamp where **WASHINGTON DC** now stands was chosen to be the **capital** of the newly independent United States of America says a lot about then-prevalent attitudes towards government. Washington, District of Columbia – also known as "DC" and "The District" – can be unbearably hot and humid in summer, and bitterly cold in winter. Such an unpleasant climate, it was hoped, would discourage elected leaders from making government a full-time job. This disdain for politics is still apparent: DC is run as a virtual colony of Congress, where residents have just one, non-voting representative and could not vote in presidential elections until the 1970s.

Another factor in the decision to establish the national capital here was that DC is midway between the northern cities of Boston, New York, and Philadelphia – the latter, the previous capital, was thought too exciting for a seat of government – and the rural south. It was also accessible from the sea, via the Potomac River – a bit too easily so, as demonstrated by the burning and ransacking of the city by the British during the War of 1812. Best of all, the land was cheap – the state of Maryland ceded sovereignty to the federal government, which only had to pay for the individual sites it chose for its buildings. Though the baroque plan of the city was laid out in 1800 – by a Frenchman, **Pierre L'Enfant**, and the black **Benjamin Banneker** – few buildings were put up, apart from the actual houses of government, until near the end of the century. Charles Dickens, visiting in 1842, found "spacious avenues that begin in nothing and lead nowhere".

After the Civil War, thousands of southern **blacks** arrived in search of a sanctuary from racist oppression; to some extent, they found one. Racial segregation was banned in public places, and **Howard University**, the only US institution of higher learning that enrolled black people, was set up in 1867. By the 1870s African-Americans made up over a third of the 150,000 population, but, compounded by government indifference, economic resources were soon stretched to breaking point. As poverty and squalor worsened, official segregation was re-introduced in 1920, banning blacks from government buildings – including, in an ironic twist, the Lincoln Memorial – and the jobs they had come to find. The situation can't be claimed to have improved since: DC currently has the country's highest murder rate, and appalling levels of drug abuse, unemployment and illiteracy. The depth of its troubles was recently highlighted by the conviction of its longtime mayor, **Marion Barry**, for possession of a small amount of crack cocaine – in a massive, federally sponsored sting operation which many saw as racially motivated – and by the riots which rocked the District in the summer of 1991.

Arrival and Information

Washington DC has three major **airports**, two on the outskirts and one right in the city centre. **Dulles International Airport**, thirty miles west in the depths of northern Virginia, and **Baltimore-Washington International** (BWI), halfway between DC and Baltimore, get the majority of the international traffic; **National Airport**, along the Potomac River just west of the Mall, is mostly used by domestic flights. **Shuttle vans** from Dulles (*Washington Flyer*, ☎703/685-1400) or BWI (*Airport Connection*, ☎301/ 261-1091) to downtown Washington will cost around $12 one-way, $20 return. National is a whole lot more convenient, being on the DC Metro subway system.

By **train**, you arrive amid the gleaming malls of bustling **Union Station**, just two blocks north of the US Capitol; *Greyhound* **buses** stop at a modern station at First and L streets NE (☎565-2662) in a fairly dodgy part of town, ten blocks from downtown – take a cab (around $4), especially at night. **Driving** into DC is a sure way to experience some of the worst traffic on the East Coast – the main I-95 freeway circuits Washington on what's known as the **Beltway**, jammed eighteen hours a day.

The helpful **visitor centre**, 1445 Pennsylvania Avenue NW (Mon–Sat 9am–5pm; ☎789-7000), has free handy guides to all the museums and cultural attractions.

Getting Around

Getting around DC is a cinch. Most places downtown, including all the Mall museums, the major monuments and the White House, are easily walkable from one another, and an excellent **public transport** system – including an extensive modern subway and a network of buses – reaches outlying sites and neighbourhoods. **Buses** cost $1, the **Metro subway** $1 to $2 (route information can be had at 12th and F streets NW; ☎637-7000). **Taxis** are also a good option, and not that expensive; few rides will cost over $5. During the day, narrated open-air **Tourmobiles** ($10) do a circuit of the major museums and sites; you can get on and off at any of a dozen different locations, and buy tickets from kiosks on the Mall or on the tram itself.

The City

Because the city was built from scratch, Washington's very regular **town plan** is easy to grasp. Centred on Capitol Hill and its assortment of governmental monoliths, the District is divided into four **quadrants** – northeast, northwest, southeast, southwest. Until you get your bearings, it's wise to stick to the established tourist trail; almost the most famous sights are in the comparatively affluent northwest quarter. To the west of the Capitol, the broad, green **Mall** holds monuments to presidents **Washington**, **Jefferson** and **Lincoln**, as well as the **White House**, official home of the current incumbent. Also here are the bulk of the city's many marvellous museums, including the national collections of the **Smithsonian Institution**.

However, there is more to Washington than an endless succession of museums and monuments, and it's well worth searching out its many attractive **neighbourhoods**. Despite its violent reputation, most of the city is in surprisingly good shape, with row after row of nineteenth-century brick-fronted houses set along leafy boulevards. Dozens of broad **avenues**, all named for states, run diagonally across a standard grid of **streets**, meeting up at monumental roundabouts like du Pont Circle. North–south streets are numbered, east–west ones are lettered in alphabetical order (there's no J Street, an intentional slight to early Supreme Court justice John Jay, and I Street is often written Eye Street). Be very sure to note the relevant two-letter code in any **address** (NW, NE, SW, SE) which shows its quadrant; 1600 Pennsylvania Avenue NW is a long way from 1600 Pennsylvania Avenue SE.

The oldest area, **Georgetown**, where popular bars and restaurants now line M Street and Wisconsin Avenue above the **Potomac River**, actually precedes the establishment of the District: a longish walk from the *Foggy Bottom* Metro. Other neighbourhoods to check out are **du Pont Circle** at the intersection of Massachusetts, Connecticut and New Hampshire avenues, which pulls a dynamic mix of yuppies, guppies and buppies; and the lower-rent, Latin American immigrant community of **Adams Morgan**, a short walk from du Pont Circle up 18th Street.

The telephone **area code** for Washington DC is ☎202.

Capitol Hill

Though there's more than one hill in Washington DC, when people talk about what's going on on "The Hill" they mean Capitol Hill – a shallow knoll topped by the giant white dome of the US Capitol building. Rising at the very centre of the city, when Washington DC was first laid out Capitol Hill was intended to be both the symbolic and real seat of the federal government. Home of both the legislature – Congress – and the judiciary – the Supreme Court – this is still the place where the law of the land is made and refined; it also holds the newly refurbished Library of Congress.

US Capitol

Between Constitution and Independence avenues at the end of E Capitol Street; closest Metro *Capitol South*. Daily 9am–8pm.

Visible from all over the city, and housing the nation's law-makers and tax-takers, the Senate and the House of Representatives, the US Capitol is one of the few places in the District where you can get a sense of the immense power wielded by the nation's elected officials – and watch them at work. The grand halls and public spaces are packed with monuments and statues of ex-politicians, while the current crop of legislators can be seen arguing over the finer points of law and policy in committee rooms and the ornate main chambers. When the lantern above the dome is lit, Congress is in session.

Begun in 1793 – George Washington, in Masonic garb, laid the cornerstone – the Capitol was repeatedly expanded over the ensuing years, and is now a confusing hybrid, hard to find your way around (the almost-constant construction and restoration work doesn't help). It faces the mall on the west, but you have to enter from the east. The free tours (every 15min until 3.45pm) are basically just a walk around the building; US citizens who want to see inside the legislative chambers have to arrange "VIP tours" through their representatives; foreigners, however, can simply show their passports at the visitors gallery entrances. Nine presidents, most recently JFK, have lain in state before burial in the impressive Rotunda, which, capped by a 180ft-tall dome, links the two halves of the Capitol – the Senate is in the north wing, the House in the south.

Library of Congress

10 First Street SE; closest Metro *Capitol South*. Mon–Fri 8.30am– 9.30pm, Sat & Sun 8.30am–6pm.

In the Library of Congress, the largest in the world, over 95 million books and manuscripts, and countless thousands of microfilm rolls and computer discs, are arrayed on 600 miles of shelves. Set up in 1800, the entire library was burned by the British in 1814; to replace the loss, Thomas Jefferson sold the country his six-thousand-volume personal collection. In 1870, when the Library of Congress was declared the national copyright library, the need was felt to build a suitable home; the result, the exuberantly eclectic Thomas Jefferson Building, opened in 1897 across from the Capitol. Though the multitiered, domed octagon of the Reading Room and the hundreds of mosaics, murals and sculptures are well worth a look, much of the building will be closed for renovation until early 1993. Various old books – including a Gutenberg Bible and a first folio of Shakespeare – are on display in the adjacent James Madison Building.

Supreme Court

First Street and Maryland Avenue NE; closest Metro *Union Station*. Mon–Fri 9am–4.30pm.

The Supreme Court, across from the US Capitol, is the final arbiter of what is and isn't legal in the country. The interior spaces of this pseudo-Greek temple, especially the courtroom itself – where guides give lectures when the court is not in session – make it worth climbing the steps and going inside. Each day, the cases to be heard are listed in the *Washington Post* newspaper (or phone ☎479-3499). Sessions begin at 10am, and last one hour per case; arrive early to be assured of getting one of the 150 seats.

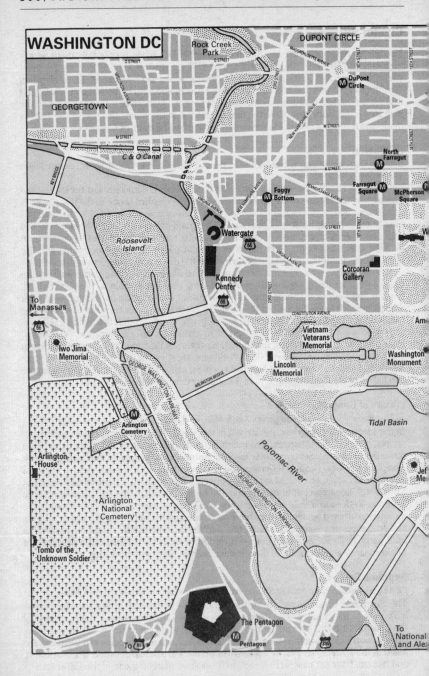

WASHINGTON DC

Rock Creek Park

DUPONT CIRCLE

O STREET

O STREET

Ⓜ DuPont Circle

GEORGETOWN

M STREET

M STREET

C & O Canal

North Farragut Ⓜ

K STREET

Farragut Square Ⓜ

McPherson Square

VIRGINIA AVENUE

Foggy Bottom Ⓜ

G STREET

Ⓦ W

Roosevelt Island

Watergate

65

Corcoran Gallery

Kennedy Center

65

To Manassas

CONSTITUTION AVENUE

Am

66

Vietnam Veterans Memorial

Iwo Jima Memorial

Washington Monument

GEORGE WASHINGTON PARKWAY

Lincoln Memorial

ARLINGTON BRIDGE

Tidal Basin

Ⓜ Arlington Cemetery

Potomac River

† Arlington † House

GEORGE WASHINGTON PARKWAY

Jef Me

Arlington National Cemetery

Tomb of the Unknown Soldier

The Pentagon

To 95

Ⓜ Pentagon

395

To National and Ale

The Mall

One of the main features of L'Enfant's grand plan for Washington was the provision of a large central parkland, a Grand Avenue lined by the mansions of the political elite. Today the mile-long **Mall** stretches west from the Capitol to the Potomac River. It wasn't always such a carefully manicured park, however: when the Capitol was first built, it looked out across a muddy, bug-infested swamp, and by the 1870s, the south side was lined by meat-markets and warehouses and criss-crossed by railroad tracks. A stark reminder of L'Enfant's unfulfilled dream, for over twenty years the Washington Monument was left unfinished, an ugly butt of stone cut off halfway.

DC's most popular green space, used for summer softball games and Fourth of July Beach Boys concerts, is lined by numerous museums, the White House, the understated but powerful Vietnam Memorial and the trio of presidential monuments.

Washington Monument

In the centre of the Mall at 14th Street; closest Metro *Smithsonian*. Daily; summer 8am–midnight, otherwise 9am–5pm.

The Mall's tallest and most prominent feature, the **Washington Monument** is an unadorned marble obelisk built in memory of George Washington, the first US president. At 555 feet it's the tallest all-masonry structure in the world. Volunteers started work on it in 1848, but various internal arguments, and later the Civil War, so disrupted construction that it wasn't completed until 1884. When the US Government took over the project in 1876, they used marble from a slightly different source; the transition line at the 150ft level where work resumed is readily apparent.

You may have to queue at the base for an hour or more to ride the lift to the top. You can't walk up (not that you'd want to), but twice a day (10am & 3pm) guided walks back down point out 200-odd stones donated by various states and national organisations.

The White House

1600 Pennsylvania Avenue NW; closest Metro *McPherson Square*. Continuous tours Tues–Sat, 10am–noon; ticket kiosk opens at 8am.

For nearly two hundred years, the **White House** has been the residence and office of the President of the United States. Standing at the edge of the Mall, due north from the Washington Monument, this grand, neoclassical edifice was completed in 1800 by Irish immigrant James Hoban, who modelled it on the Georgian manors of Dublin. Each of its presidential occupants has made his mark: Thomas Jefferson added the first toilets, just before the British burned it down during the War of 1812. It was quickly rebuilt and expanded, often in such a hurry that the whole building was on the verge of collapse. Harry Truman had to move out for four years from 1948 while the structure was stabilised; all the rooms were dismantled and a modern steel frame inserted. Truman also added the balcony to the familiar south side portico.

Not surprisingly, the White House is one of Washington's most high-security places, and visits (unless you manage to get invited to an official function) are limited to a brief tour of the ground floor reception rooms, all filled with portraits of ex-presidents. In summer, the gardens are sometimes opened for afternoon tours, and during the Christmas holidays there are special evening tours of the festively decorated interior.

Lincoln Memorial

23rd Street between Constitution and Independence avenues; closest Metro *Foggy Bottom*.

Standing at the far west end of the Mall, the **Lincoln Memorial** is modelled upon a Doric temple, enclosed by a colonnade and fronted by a long reflecting pool that provides memorable vistas. During the Civil Rights march on Washington in 1963, Dr Martin Luther King, Jr delivered his epic "I Have a Dream" speech, not from the steps of the White House or the US Capitol, but here. Ironically, when this monument to the Great Emancipator was dedicated in 1922, the crowds were segregated by colour – even black leader Booker T Washington, who gave an address, was forced to watch from a roped-off area to the side.

The Lincoln Memorial is a fitting tribute to the man who held the country together during the Civil War and thereby put an end to slavery in the US. A craggy likeness of Abraham Lincoln sits firmly grasping the arms of his throne-like chair, deep in thought.

Vietnam Memorial

Constitution Avenue at 21st Street; closest Metro *Foggy Bottom*. Daily 8am–midnight.

Cutting sharply into the green lawn of the Mall, the small and simple **Vietnam Veterans Memorial** serves as a sombre and powerful reminder of the nearly 60,000 US soldiers who died in Vietnam. The pathway that slopes down from the grass forms a gash in the earth, its increasing depth symbolising the increasing involvement of US forces in the war. Alongside, a black marble wall is carved with the names of every soldier who died, in chronological order from 1959 to 1975. People often take rubbings from the wall, and it's not uncommon to see friends and family members break into tears at sight of the name of a loved one.

The memorial was designed by Maya Lin, a 21-year-old architecture student. When it was first erected in 1982, there was some outcry by veterans groups about its anti-war connotations. By way of appeasement, in 1984 a more traditional statue of three heroic soldiers was placed nearby, under a floodlit American flag.

Jefferson Memorial

West of 14th Street near Ohio Drive; closest Metro *Smithsonian*. Daily 8am–midnight.

The most recently constructed of the major Mall monuments – it wasn't finished until 1943 – the **Jefferson Memorial** is the best-looking but hardest to reach of the three presidential memorials. Modelled on his country home, Monticello (see p.314), it consists of a shallow dome hovering over a bronze statue of Thomas Jefferson, the author of the Declaration of Independence and the third US president. The interior walls, encircled by an Ionic colonnade, are carved with Jefferson's words, and an inscription around the frieze reads "I have sworn upon the altar of God eternal hostility against every form of tyranny over the mind of man."

The **Tidal Basin**, which fills most of the space between the Lincoln and Jefferson memorials, was created in order to prevent the western end of the Mall, including the spots where the two memorials sit, from being inundated by Potomac floods. The reflections off it are especially pretty in spring (usually late April) when the rows of Japanese cherry trees come out in full bloom.

The Smithsonian Institution

The cream of Washington DC's remarkable panoply of historical artefacts and fine art works come under the general auspices of the **Smithsonian Institution**, which holds the US national collections of eveything under the sun. Endowed by an Englishman – James Smithson, bastard son of the first Duke of Northumberland, who never even visited the US – the Smithsonian was established in 1846 "for the increase and diffusion of Knowledge". This broad brief is reflected in its impressive range of research centres and museums, nine of which line up along the Mall, while four are located just north.

The original home of the Smithsonian, the 1849 Norman-style fortress known as **The Castle**, stands on the Mall halfway between the Capitol and the Washington Monument. It was at first devoted to scientific research, but as the Smithsonian became more of a museum, the sheer accumulation of stuff necessitated the construction of the various other buildings along the Mall. The old Castle is now the Smithsonian headquarters and main **visitor centre** (☎357-270); pick up the latest details on all the Smithsonian galleries at the hi-tech information desk. The ornate tomb of James Smithson is in an alcove just off the Mall entrance, and a lovely flower-filled garden (daily 7am–9pm) fronts the Castle on the south side. To get a feel for the days when this was known as "the nation's attic", take a look in the adjacent **Arts and Industries Building** at the hundreds of objects – including a steam locomotive and Samuel Morse's original telegraph – sent here for safekeeping after the 1876 Centennial Exhibition in Philadelphia.

Admission to all the galleries is **free**.

National Air and Space Museum

South side of the Mall between Fourth and Seventh streets SW; closest Metro *L'Enfant Plaza*. Daily summer 10am–7.30pm, otherwise 10am–5.30pm. ☎357-1400.

The **National Air and Space Museum**, DC's most popular attraction, is among the world's most visited museums, drawing nearly ten million people every year. Though most of them will seem to be here on the day you come, the hangar-like modern building can accommodate everyone without feeling crowded, and you can always see the hundreds of **historic aircraft** close up. Hanging from the rafters in the main entrance gallery, the **Milestones in Flight** collection includes the handmade plane in which the **Wright Brothers** made the first powered flight in 1903; **Charles Lindbergh's** *Spirit of St Louis*, in which he made the first solo transatlantic crossing; and the sleek black **X-15**, the world's fastest plane. Pick up a cassette-tape tour ($2.50) of the rest of the museum, or just wander around past Pershing and SS-20 ballistic missiles, various interactive computer exhibits, a mock-up of the Skylab space station – and the only touchable **moon rock** on earth, brought back by the Apollo astronauts.

The museum also shows a rotating programme of super-large-screen **IMAX** movies, for $2.25 each. All have some connection with flying; the most spectacular, *The Dream is Alive*, was shot from an orbiting space shuttle.

National Museum of Natural History

North side of the Mall between Ninth and 12th streets NW; closest Metro *Smithsonian*. Daily 10am–5.30pm. ☎357-2747.

The imposing three-storey entrance rotunda of the **National Museum of Natural History** feels like the busiest and most boisterous crossroads in all of DC, with troops of screeching school kids chasing each other non-stop around the African elephant. Hundreds of other stuffed animals, tracing evolution from fossilised four-billion-year-old plankton to dinosaurs' eggs and beyond, are on display in the rest of this huge museum – pick up floor plans and guides at the information desk at the elephant's feet. However, little seems to have changed since the 1950s. The museum's old-fashioned, Eurocentric ideology is evidenced by its treatment of pre-Columbian cultures: Inca and Mayan artefacts, and an extensive array of items from Pueblo and other native Southwest desert cultures, are displayed alongside bison, bighorn sheep and other once-wild things.

Upstairs are hundreds of creepy crawling critters – lizards, snakes, tarantulas and the like – as well as an **Insect Zoo**, filled with hundreds of bugs, which, should you so desire, you can play with. There's also a truly exceptional array of gemstones, including the legendary 45-carat **Hope Diamond**, which once belonged to Marie Antoinette.

National Museum of American History

North side of the Mall between 12th and 14th streets NW; closest Metro *Smithsonian*. Daily, summer 9.30am–7pm, otherwise 9.30am–5.30pm. ☎357-1481.

If you like kitsch, you won't want to miss the bizarre melange of cultural artefacts at the **National Museum of American History**. George Washington's wooden teeth, Muhammad Ali's boxing gloves, and the ruby slippers Judy Garland wore in the *Wizard of Oz* are set amongst didactic displays tracing the country's development. It's not so much a centre for the scholarly study of history as a sanctuary for vanishing Americana, incorporating Model T Fords, old post offices, and even a restored, turn-of-the-century ice cream parlour, which still serves up banana splits.

As you enter from the Mall, a hilariously over-the-top patriotic sound-and-light display showcases the battered flag that inspired the US national anthem – the **Star-Spangled Banner** itself. Every hour on the half-hour the curtain is raised to expose the 30-by-45ft red-white-and-blue emblem, which survived the British bombing of Baltimore harbour during the War of 1812. On the upper floor, **"After the Revolution**: Everyday Life in America 1790–1860" looks at the farm-based rural and agricultural society of the early US; across the hall, **"Field to Factory**: Afro-American Migration, 1915–1940" examines the mass movement of African-Americans from southern farms to the war-time industries of northern cities. The top floor galleries have the oddest display of objects, from political memorabilia (much of it over a century old) to stamp and coin collections, old TV sets, and typewriters.

Hirshhorn Museum

South side of the Mall between Seventh and Ninth streets SW; closest Metro *L'Enfant Plaza*. Daily 10am–5.30pm. ☎357-3235.

Next to the Air and Space Museum, and housed in the most clearly modern building on the Mall – a windowless cylinder poised on fifteen-foot stilts above a concrete plaza, it looks like a spaceship poised for takeoff – the **Hirshhorn Museum** holds the Smithsonian's extensive collection of late-nineteenth and twentieth-century art. From the main entrance on Independence Avenue, escalators climb to the upper floor galleries, where major works by Picasso, de Kooning, Mondrian, Pollock, Matisse and many more are on display. The gallery downstairs hosts travelling exhibitions, and highly rated films are shown in the evenings (☎357-1300 for details).

The Hirshhorn also has a stimulating collection of modern **sculpture**, displayed in an open-air garden across Jefferson Drive on the Mall side of the museum. Alongside assorted Moores, Rodins, Smiths and Malliols are two expressive abstract figures by Marino Marini, and a stalwart *Yucatan Woman* by Mexican sculptor Francisco Zuniga. The landscaped garden, sunk below ground level to spare Congress members from having to look at modern art, is also a nice place for a picnic lunch.

National Museum of African Art

South side of the Mall at 950 Independence Avenue SW; closest Metro *Smithsonian*. Daily 10am–5.30pm. ☎357-4860.

Filling the eastern half of the Mall's newest and most attractive building, the **National Museum of African Art** holds over six thousand sculptures and artefacts, both spiritual and functional, from the numerous tribal cultures of sub-Saharan Africa. The permanent collection ranges from Nigerian carved-ivory cult figures to Zairean mother-and-child fertility fetishes and puppet heads from eastern Mali. Around half the space is devoted to changing exhibitions on specific regions, and the gift shop sells woven and dyed fabrics and clothes as well as books and postcards.

Sackler Gallery

South side of the Mall at 1050 Independence Avenue SW; closest Metro *Smithsonian*. Daily 10am–5.30pm. ☎357-2104.

The angular and pyramidal counterpart of the curved and domed African Art museum – built together in 1987, the two are linked by an aseptic rooftop flower garden – the **Sackler Gallery** contains artworks and devotional objects from Asia and the Middle East. You'll find delicate translucent jade dragons and three-thousand-year-old bronzes from China; stone deities from India and Tibet; and lushly illustrated early Islamic texts from Iran, gorgeously coloured in gilt, silver and crushed stone pigments.

Freer Gallery

South side of the Mall, Jefferson Drive at 12th Street SW; closest Metro *Smithsonian*. Closed since 1988, the gallery is due to re-open in 1992. ☎357-2700.

From the day it opened in 1923, the **Freer Gallery** has been one of the more unusual Smithsonian museums. Put together and paid for by railroad millionaire Charles Freer, it revolves around over one thousand prints, drawings and paintings by London-based American artist **James McNeil Whistler** – the largest collection of his works anywhere – but also includes Chinese jades and bronzes, Byzantine illuminated manuscripts, Buddhist wall sculptures and pieces of Persian metalwork, all collected by Freer under Whistler's tutelage. Among other works are pieces by Whistler's contemporaries Winslow Homer, Albert Pinkham Ryder and John Singer Sargent.

Besides his portraits and landscapes, Whistler himself is represented by an entire room – the **Peacock Room**. Its original owner commissioned Whistler to execute a painting for the mantlepiece; the artist later covered the walls and furnishings with blue and gold painted peacock feathers. His patron hated it, so Freer bought it and shipped it over from London (he also kept live peacocks in the museum's central courtyard).

If all goes according to plan, a construction project will by mid-1992 have restored and modernised the very attractive skylit Freer galleries, linked them to the Sackler via an underground passage, and added an additional underground exhibition space.

National Museum of American Art

G Street between Seventh and Ninth streets; closest Metro *Gallery Place*. Open daily 10am to 5.30pm. ☎357-3111.

Separated from the main Mall galleries, the **National Museum of American Art** doesn't get nearly the traffic of the other museums, but it's perhaps the most worthwhile of all. Not only does it tend to mount the most thought-provoking shows – in the summer of 1991 an exhibition examining the romantic distortion and outright deceit (not to mention racism) underlying early images of the American frontier earned it national notoriety – its galleries are also pleasant places to be in their own right.

When it opened in 1829, the museum was known as the National Gallery of Art – Andrew Mellon later usurped that name. Since 1968, it has shared the Greek Revival-style **Old Patent Office** with the National Portrait Gallery (see below). Works range from Revolutionary portraits and genre scenes to WPA-style social realism and contemporary works by Helen Frankenthaler, Willem de Kooning, Robert Rauschenberg and Clyfford Still. The more modern pieces are displayed on the top floor in the vaulted and colonnaded **Lincoln Gallery**, which in 1865 hosted President Lincoln's post-Civil War Inaugural Ball and is still one of DC's most celebrated interior spaces.

National Portrait Gallery

F Street between Seventh and Ninth streets NW; closest Metro *Gallery Place*. Daily 10am–5.30pm. ☎357-2920.

The **National Portrait Gallery**, which shares its premises with the Museum of American Art, is pretty much what you'd expect: a set of paintings, sculptures and photographs of famous and not-so-famous people. Highlights include Gilbert Stuart's half-finished portrait of Founding Father George Washington, a Degas portrait of Mary Cassatt, a collection of Matthew Brady's Civil War photographs and a wall-full of *Time* magazine covers.

Renwick Gallery

Pennsylvania Avenue at 17th Street NW; closest Metro *Farragut West*. Daily 10am–5.30pm; ☎357-3111.

Housed in the red brick 1870s French Empire-style building that was the original home of the Corcoran Gallery (see p.296), the **Renwick Gallery** devotes itself to American

decorative arts and crafts. The building itself is a noteworthy piece of architecture –
from the inscription above the entrance, which simply reads "Dedicated to Art", it's
packed with ornate stone and woodwork. A few of the rooms, notably the **Grand
Salon**, are decorated as they would have been during the Victorian era; others hold
travelling exhibitions of contemporary crafts, and the fairly small permanent collection
is made up of mostly modern jewellery and furniture.

Other Museums and Attractions

While one could quite easily spend a good week wandering around the Smithsonian,
the national collections are by no means the only worthwhile museums in DC – or, for
that matter, along the Mall.

The large **National Gallery**, at the foot of the US Capitol, is, despite the name and
the high-profile location, actually an independent concern; it's also the best art museum
in the city, and one of the top ten in the world. Besides further top-quality art galleries,
you can tour various **federal buildings** – to watch the FBI track down criminals, or
count brand-new dollar bills as they roll off the presses – and venture out to see
Nixon's famous pandas at the **National Zoo**, or honour the nation's dead, including the
Kennedy brothers, at **Arlington National Cemetery**.

National Gallery of Art

North side of the Mall between Third and Seventh streets NW; closest Metro *Archives*. Mon–Sat
11am–5pm; Sun 11am–6pm. ☎737-4215.

The visually stunning **National Gallery of Art**, the nearest of the Mall museums to
the Capitol, is not in fact a government institution. One of the very finest art galleries in
the US, it does, however, deserve its name. It owes its prominence to the efforts of
industrialist **Andrew Mellon**, who bought the building and donated most of the paintings (many were purchased from the cash-poor post-revolutionary government of the
USSR, where they had previously hung in the Hermitage). His family have continued
as benefactors, raising countless millions to build the new **East Building** in 1978;
Walter Annenberg, whose multimillion-selling, mind-contracting *Reader's Digest* magazine helped to fund Ronald Reagan's rise to political stardom, was also a major patron.

The original neo-classical gallery, designed by John Russell Pope in 1941, is now
called the **West Building** and holds the bulk of the permanent collection. From its
domed central rotunda, where you can pick up a floor plan and gallery guide, a vaulted
corridor runs the length of the building, making it easy to keep your bearings.
Galleries to the west on the main floor display major works by Renaissance masters,
arranged by nationality: half a dozen Rembrandts fill the **Dutch** gallery, Van Eyck and
Rubens dominate the **Flemish**, and El Greco and Velazquez face off in the **Spanish**.
Downstairs, smaller galleries hold a broader range, including a rotating display of
drawings and watercolours by van Gogh, Cezanne and others, collected by Armand
Hammer. The other half of the West Building holds an exceptional collection of nineteenth-century **French** paintings – Gauguin, Renoir, van Gogh, Manet, Monet *et al*. At
either end of the building, skylit, fountain-filled **Garden Courts** make an ideal place to
rest weary feet.

The triangular **East Building** houses twentieth-century paintings as well as changing exhibitions. Like the Guggenheim in New York, the attention-grabbing spatial
choreography of the architecture ends up overpowering the works of art. You emerge
from under the oppressively low entrance into a central atrium, from where an escala-
tor, literally carved out of a forty-foot granite wall, climbs to the main galleries – which,
squeezed into the corners, seem like an afterthought. The underground concourse
which links the two buildings contains a good bookshop, an espresso bar and a large
cafeteria – topped by pyramidal skylights and bordered by a glassed-in waterfall.

Corcoran Gallery of Art

17th Street between E Street and New York Avenue NW; closest Metro *Farragut North* or *Farragut West*. Tues, Wed & Fri–Sun 10am–4.30pm, Thurs 10am–9pm. ☎638-3211.

Just down the street from the White House, the **Corcoran Gallery** is one of the oldest and most respected art museums in the US; at least it was, until it bowed to Jesse Helms and cancelled the 1989 retrospective of Robert Mapplethorpe's photography. Especially strong in American art – from frontier artists like Remington and Bierstadt, to portraiture by Mary Cassat and Thomas Eakins and modern works by the likes of Warhol and Rothko – it also includes a sampling of Dutch masters, medieval tapestries and French Impressionist paintings.

Phillips Collection

1600 21st Street at Q Street NW; closest Metro *Dupont Circle*. Tues–Sat 10am–5pm, Sun 2–7pm. ☎387-2151.

The **Phillips Collection**, one of the country's most extensive assemblies of modern paintings, starts off with a variety of proto-modern painters such as El Greco and Turner, before hurrying via French Impressionism to the real heart of the show – hundreds of works by Picasso, Matisse, Kandinsky, van Gogh, Rothko, O'Keeffe, Klee and many others. The building adds to the experience: part is displayed in the Phillips ornate 1890s mansion, the rest in a 1960s modern purpose-built gallery space, all of it recently renovated. A popular series of free concerts takes place on Sunday evenings at 5pm in the ornate music room (☎387-2151 for details).

National Museum of Women in the Arts

1250 New York Avenue NW; closest Metro *Metro Center*. Mon–Sat 10am–5pm, Sun noon–5pm. ☎783-5000. Admission $4.

Housed in a converted Masonic Temple, the **National Museum of Women in the Arts** has, since it opened in 1987, been the country's only museum dedicated to women artists. Though it includes hundreds of works by painters no one has ever heard of, that is of course partly the point – its curators were inspired by the fact that, as recently as twenty years ago, not one female artist was mentioned in the main American art history textbook. It also includes sculptures by Barbara Hepworth and Camille Claudel (Rodin's mistress and assistant) and paintings by Helen Frankenthaler, Georgia O'Keeffe, Mary Cassatt and Elaine de Kooning – and has one of the best museum cafes in DC, the *Palette Cafe* on the upper floor.

National Archives

North side of the Mall at Seventh Street and Constitution Avenue NW; closest Metro *Archives*. Daily, summer 10am–9pm, otherwise 10am–5.30pm. ☎501-5240.

On display inside the impressive neo-classical Greek Temple of the **National Archives** are the three short texts upon which the United States is founded: the **Declaration of Independence**, the **Constitution**, and the **Bill of Rights**. These three original sheets of parchment (the three further pages of the Constitution are not on display), drafted respectively in 1776, 1787 and 1789, are now held in helium-filled glass cases, which drop underground in case of fire or threat. You can look at them as long as you like, but if there's a crowd (there usually isn't) you have to shuffle on past.

As well as a copy of the **Magna Carta**, dating from 1297, the archives hold exhibitions and serve as the official repository of all US national records – census data, treaties (including the surrender of Japanese in World War II), passport applications, as well as genealogical records – most of which are held in storage. You may want to search out the so-called **Watergate Tapes**, which led to the downfall of President Richard Nixon; a shuttle bus will take you to where they're held (☎703/756-6498 for details).

The FBI

On Pennsylvania Avenue between Ninth and Tenth streets NW, just north of the Mall; closest Metro *Federal Triangle*. Hour-long tours, Mon–Fri 8.45 am–4pm. ☎327-3447.

A fortress-like modern building on Pennsylvania Avenue holds the headquarters of the FBI – the **Federal Bureau of Investigation**, the nation's elite law-enforcement organisation. Set up in 1908, the FBI came into its own chasing bootleggers and bank robbers like Al Capone and Machine Gun Kelly during the Thirties. Hordes of visitors queue outside, sometimes for well over an hour, to join tours through displays of the famous gangsters and dangerous Communists and subversives from whom the FBI shields the American people (they kept extensive files on Dr Martin Luther King, Jr). Ideology aside (the FBI has only just begun to emerge from the shadow of its longtime führer, J Edgar Hoover), the tour tells all about fingerprinting, ballistics testing and other crime-fighting techniques. What really brings the crowds in, however, is the culminating display of sharpshooting and firepower: agents blast away at cut-out targets with a battery of small arms and automatic weapons.

The Bureau of Printing and Engraving

One block south of the Mall at 14th and C streets SW; closest Metro *Smithsonian*. Mon–Fri, 9am–2pm. Closed for the entire week around Christmas. ☎447-0193.

In most ways, a tour of the **Bureau of Printing and Engraving** is like visiting any other printing plant. The difference here is that the presses are cranking out millions of dollars in currency every day, nearly $100 billion every year. It's a surprisingly low-tech operation: the bills come off in huge sheets, which are sliced up into single bills by ordinary paper cutters, checked for defects and loaded into large wheelbarrows. The Bureau also produces all US postage stamps. A short film explains the basics of intaglio printing, and you can watch it all happen from a glassed-in upstairs gallery.

The National Zoo

3000 Connecticut Avenue; closest Metro *Woodley Park/Zoo*. Daily, summer 8am–8pm, otherwise 8am–6pm. ☎673-4717.

At the **National Zoo**, just a short walk from the Metro, lush trails lead past credible and comparatively humane simulations of the natural environments of over three thousand creatures. Its stars are the **pandas**, *Ling Ling* and *Hsing Hsing*, given to the US by the People's Republic of China during Richard Nixon's 1972 visit; you can usually only see them at feeding times (11am & 3pm). The zoo also has the expected menagerie of monkeys and chimps, birds and bees, and lions and tigers (including rare white tigers).

Arlington National Cemetery

Across the Potomac River in Arlington, Virginia; closest Metro *Arlington Cemetery*. Daily, summer 8am–7pm, otherwise 8am–5pm. ☎1-703/692-0931.

A poignant contrast to the grand monuments of the national capital is provided by the endless sea of headstones on the hillsides of **Arlington National Cemetery**. The country's most honoured final resting place was first used during the Civil War, when the grand mansion at the top of the hill, and all the surrounding land, belonged to **Robert E Lee**, leader of the Confederate forces. Nearly 200,000 US war dead lie in neat rows of identical white stones, while the **Tomb of the Unknown Soldier** remembers thousands more whose bodies were never recovered or identified. An eternal flame marks the grave of **President John F Kennedy**, near his brother Robert; other well-known names include boxer Joe Louis, diplomat John Foster Dulles, and Pierre L'Enfant, whose gravesite offers a superb view over the Mall and the District he designed.

Unless you have strong legs and lots of time the best way to see the vast cemetery is by Tourmobile (see p.286), which leaves from the visitor centre at the entrance. You can also walk here from the Lincoln Memorial across the Arlington Bridge.

Washington Accommodation

Most DC **hotels** cater to business travellers and political lobbyists, and during the week are quite expensive. At weekends, however, many cut their rates by as much as fifty percent – for a list of properties contact the **Promote DC** office (☎724-4091 or ☎1-800/422-8644) and ask for a copy of *Washington Weekends*.

Washington also has a number of **B&B** agencies, offering comfy doubles from around $65 a night: try *B&B Ltd* (☎328-3510) or the *B&B League* (☎363-7767). There's no good **camping** anywhere near DC, but besides the **youth hostel**, a few DC **universities** offer cheap rooms in summer. You have to arrange these well in advance: contact *Catholic University* (☎635-5277) or *Georgetown University* (☎687-3999) for details.

Allen Lee Hotel, 2224 F St NW (☎331-1224 or ☎1-800/462-0186). Slightly faded but clean downtown hotel, two blocks from *Foggy Bottom* Metro. Doubles from $35.

Adams Inn, 1744 Lanier Place NW (☎745-3600). Small, friendly hotel in lively Adams-Morgan neighbourhood. Doubles from $55, including breakfast.

Connecticut-Woodley Guest House, 2647 Woodley Rd NW (☎667-0218). Pleasant small guest house opposite the *Sheraton Washington* and near the zoo. Doubles $51–65.

Harrington Hotel, 1100 E St NW (☎628-8140 or ☎1-800/424-8532). Large, refurbished older hotel, halfway between the Capitol and the White House. Doubles from $65.

Hay-Adams Hotel, 1 LaFayette Square NW (☎638-2260 or ☎1-800/332-3442). Beautiful and very expensive hotel overlooking the White House. Stop in for a drink if you can't afford $175 a night.

International Guest House, 1441 Kennedy St NW (☎726-5808). Small, homey boarding house, with rooms for $20 a night, $125 a week.

Kalorama Guest House, 1854 Mintwood Place NW (☎667-6369). Cosy, nicely furnished rooms spread around six houses in the lively Adams-Morgan neighbourhood. Doubles from $45.

Quality Hotel Central, 1900 Connecticut Ave NW (☎332-9300 or ☎1-800/465-4329). Well-placed modern hotel, near Dupont Circle. Doubles from $75 at weekends, $99 midweek.

Tabard Inn Hotel, 1739 N St NW (☎785-1277). Very pleasant small hotel, two blocks from *Dupont Circle* Metro. Doubles with shared bath from $65, including breakfast.

University Inn Hotel, 2134 G St NW (☎342-8020 or ☎1-800/842-1012). Older hotel, four blocks from the White House. Doubles with shared bath cost from $50.

Washington International AYH Hostel, 1009 11th St NW (☎737-2333). Huge (250 beds), clean and very central, three blocks north of *Metro Center*. AYH/IYHA members only, $13 a night.

Eating

Just as the faces in government change with every election, so too do **restaurants** come and go more quickly in Washington than just about anywhere else in the US. Within this constant flux a few longstanding favourites endure; and certain neighbourhoods – Dupont Circle, 18th Street and Columbia Road in **Adams-Morgan**, and M Street in **Georgetown** – always seem to hold a good range of dining options. It's often said, not entirely in jest, that the best restaurants tend to come from the "trouble spots" of the world – Vietnam in the 1970s, Afghanistan and Ethiopia in the 1980s, and most recently Central America. The cafes in the main museums are good for downtown lunch breaks.

Austin Grill, 2404 Wisconsin Ave NW (☎337-8080). Popular Georgetown Tex-Mex joint, with great chili and margaritas.

AV Ristorante, 607 New York Ave NW (☎737-0550). Huge, ever-popular downtown trattoria, serving up great pizzas and daily Italian specials for under $10.

Bacchus, 1827 Jefferson Place NW (☎785-0734). Somewhat pricey but very good downtown Lebanese restaurant, with excellent hummus and tangy kebabs.

Cities, 2424 18th St NW (☎328-7194). Trendy bistro-style cafe. Good pizzas plus an ever-changing menu of international foods on an outdoor terrace overlooking the Adams-Morgan streetlife parade.

Dancing Crab, 4611 Wisconsin Ave NW (☎244-1882). Unpretentious seafood cafe, specialising in Chesapeake Bay softshell crabs – all you can eat for around $15.

El Caribe, 1828 Columbia Rd NW (☎234-6969). Excellent, very authentic Latin American food for around $20 – try the seafood appetizers before tucking into the hearty stews and casseroles.

Mr Smith's, 3104 M St NW (☎333-3104). Casual and somewhat chaotic Georgetown burger bar.

Red Sea, 2463 18th St NW (☎483-5000). Cheap and plentiful portions of spicy Ethiopian food in crowded Adams-Morgan cafe.

Saigonnais, 2307 18th St NW (☎232-5300). Excellent, beautifully presented Vietnamese food in cosy, warmly lit Adams-Morgan townhouse.

Entertainment and Nightlife

With five different theatre spaces, the **Kennedy Center** (☎467-4600), next to the Watergate complex along the Potomac River, hosts most of the capital's high-brow cultural events, as well as nightly screenings organised by the **American Film Institute**. The *Arena Stage*, Sixth Street and Maine Avenue SW (☎488-3300), puts on contemporary plays and performance pieces, as does the *Church Street Theater*, 1742 Church Street NW (☎298-9000). *Woolly Mammoth*, 1401 Church Street NW (☎393-3939), and *Source Theatre Company*, 1815 14th Street (☎462-1073), are other companies worth seeking out. For half-price day-of-show theatre tickets, call ☎TIC-KETS.

Check the free weekly *CityPaper* for up-to-date listings of music, theatre and other events in the DC area – as well as good alternative features and reporting.

Bars and Live Music Venues

Not surprisingly, in view of the transient nature of much of the DC population, the **bar and cafe** scene is less developed than in more settled cities. Peak times for drinking tend to be the rush hours, and comparatively few people who work in the District during the week venture back into town at the weekend. However, things are slowly improving, and in the well-worn haunts of collegiate **Georgetown** and **Dupont Circle** you should be able to pass a pleasant evening or two.

The Bayou, Wisconsin Ave and K St (☎333-2897). Georgetown's leading headbanger hangout.

dc space, 433 Seventh Ave NW (☎347-1445). Artsy, downtown bar with the longest Happy Hour in DC; it's also a mostly rock-oriented nightclub.

The Dubliner, 520 N Capitol St NW (☎737-3773). Bare-bones Irish bar, with Harp and Guinness on draught and no end of boisterous conversation.

15 Min, 1030 15th Street NW (☎408-1855). Live bands; indie rock and dance music.

J Paul's, 3218 M St NW (☎333-3450). Huge and always lively Georgetown pub.

Kelly's Irish Times, 14 F St NW (☎543-5433). Half a block west of Union Station, this crowded but comfortable pub has a good range of beers and above-average bar food.

Kilimanjaro, 1724 California St NW (☎328-3838). Restaurant and nightclub; reggae and world beat.

Mr Eagan's, 1343 Connecticut Ave NW (☎861-9609). Halfway between a honky-tonk and an Irish pub, with the cheapest drinks near Dupont Circle.

Old Ebbitt Grill, 675 15th St NW (☎347-4800). Very plush, old-style downtown tavern, with an immaculate mahogany bar, gilt mirrors and stylish clientele.

P Street Station, 2161 P St (☎293-1293). Friendly, gay-orientated Dupont Circle bar with pool tables, huge jukebox and seven-hour-long Happy Hour.

Quigley's, 223 Pennsylvania Ave SE (☎544-6600). Retro-1920s saloon for the Capitol Hill singles crowd.

The Tombs, 1226 36th St NW (☎337-6668). Cosy, publike room, popular with Georgetown University students.

Cafes

Afterwords Cafe, 1517 Connecticut Ave NW (☎387-1462). Located in the back of Kramerbooks, DC's best bookshop, and serving up the District's best cappucino.

Au Pied au Cochon, 1335 Wisconsin Ave NW (☎333-5440). Casual and comfortable Georgetown coffee shop, open 24 hours a day.

Patent Pending, Museum of American Art, 8th and G St (☎357-2700). Located just off the sunny central courtyard in the ornate old Patent Building, with good pastries and sandwiches.

Patisserie Cafe Didier, 3206 Grace St NW (☎342-9083). Outrageously good cakes and pastries, washed down with piping hot teas and coffees. Just off Wisconsin Ave in the heart of Georgetown.

Vie de France Cafe, 1615 M St NW (☎659-0992). One of a chain of low-priced, lunchtime cafes featuring fresh-baked croissants.

Listings

Boat and Bike Rental If you want to cycle or cruise along the Potomac River or the historic C&O Canal both *Thompson's Boat Center*, Rock Creek Parkway at Virginia Ave NW (☎333-4861), near the Watergate complex, and *Fletcher's Boat House*, 4940 Canal Roads NW (☎244-0461), rent out touring bikes as well as range of rowboats and canoes.

Canal Boat Tours Mule-drawn canal boats, with costumed National Park Service guides, follow the old C&O Canal from 30th and M streets in Georgetown on a 90min narrated cruise ($5; ☎472-4376).

Disabled Visitors To get *Access Washington: A Guide for the Physically Disabled* , call ☎547-8081.

Events Line ☎737-8866 for taped listings of DC happenings.

Physicians Home Service ☎331-3888 for medical house calls to your hotel.

Post Office Across from Union Station on Massachusetts Ave and Capitol St NE (☎682-9595). Mon–Fri 8am–8pm, Sat 8am–2pm. Zip code 20002.

Sports The Washington Redskins football team, one of the best in the NFL, play at RFK Stadium (☎547-9077); every game is a sell-out, though, and seats are expensive and very hard to come by. Joggers, frisbee and softball players swarm over the Mall in summer months, and there are some good cycling paths along the Potomac (see above).

VIRGINIA

Travelling through **VIRGINIA**, the oldest, largest and wealthiest of the American colonies and the single most powerful influence on the early United States, is a non-stop history lesson. Pretty and largely rural it may be, but the past predominates; wherever you go you're pointed toward this or that painstakingly restored two-hundred-year-old building, where something or other happened some long time ago. The more you know about it all, the more rewarding Virginia is to visit, but it can get a bit ridiculous after a while, counting the historical plaques which mark every spot where George Washington slept, Thomas Jefferson thought, or Robert E Lee tied his horse to a tree.

Virginia's recorded history began at **Jamestown**, just off the Chesapeake Bay, with the establishment in 1607 of the first successful British colony in North America. Though the first colonists hoped to find gold, it was **tobacco** which made their fortunes. The native strain – used for hundreds of years by Virginia's aboriginal population, of whom almost no trace remains – was too strongly flavoured for European tastes, but when a smoother, more palatable variety was introduced in 1615 by John Rolfe – coincidentally the same man whose shipwreck on Bermuda had inspired Shakespeare's *The Tempest* – tobacco quickly become the colony's major cash crop. Before long vast plantations, owned by a very few aristocratic families, had sprung up along the many broad rivers that flow into the Chesapeake Bay. To grow and harvest tobacco required an immense amount of land – so the Indians had to go – and intensive labour – so the plantation owners brought in **slaves** from Africa. By the end of the seventeenth century, enslaved African-Americans accounted for nearly half of the colony's 75,000 people; a hundred years later, there were over 300,000 of them.

Virginians had an enormous impact on the foundation of the nascent United States: George Mason, Thomas Jefferson, and James Madison wrote the Declaration of Independence and the Constitution, and four of the first five US presidents were from Virginia. However, by the mid-1800s the state was in decline, its once fertile fields depleted by overuse and its predominantly rural, agrarian economy increasingly eclipsed by the urban and industrialised North.

As the confrontation between North and South over slavery and a host of related economic and political issues grew more divisive, Virginia was caught in the middle, both geographically and ideologically. Though this slaveholding state initially voted against secession from the Union, it joined the Confederacy when the **Civil War** broke out, providing its military leader, Robert E Lee, and its capital, Richmond. Four long years later Virginia was ravaged, its towns and cities wrecked, its farmlands ruined, and most of its youth dead. Since then it has never regained its early prosperity, nor its prominence in national affairs.

Richmond itself was largely destroyed in the war; today it's a small city, with some excellent museums, which makes the best starting point for seeing Virginia. The bulk of the **colonial** sites are concentrated just to the east, in what's known as the **Historic Triangle**. Here the remains of **Jamestown**, the original colony, **Williamsburg**, the restored colonial capital, and **Yorktown**, site of the final battle of the Revolutionary War, lie within half an hour's drive of each other.

Another historic centre, Thomas Jefferson's **Charlottesville**, sits at the foot of the gorgeous **Blue Ridge Mountains**, an hour west of Richmond. An exceptionally attractive small college town in its own right, it's also within easy reach of the natural splendours of **Shenandoah National Park** and the small towns of the western valleys. **Northern Virginia**, often visited as a day out from Washington DC, holds a number of famous restored homes , and several preserved Civil War **battlefields**.

Getting Around Virginia

Virginia's historic riches are not difficult to explore. *Amtrak* serves most cities (and the Historic Triangle) and *Greyhound* reaches dozens of smaller towns. If you've got the time, there's ample opportunity for **cycling**, whether on quiet country roads or up in the mountains, and **hiking** or **walking** tours are also worth thinking about.

Northern Virginia

Northern Virginia, almost all of which lies within commuting distance of Washington DC, holds some of the country's most exclusive suburbs – McLean and the rest of Fairfax County, for example, house quite inordinate numbers of US senators. This is the anglophile heartland of Virginia's landed gentry – it's often called the "Hunt Country" for its love of horses and fancy-dress blood sports – with well-preserved eighteenth- and nineteenth-century stately homes, weaver's cottages, churches, barns and taverns tucked away along the quiet backroads. It's all very popular with tourists, nowhere more so than **Mount Vernon**, the longtime home of George Washington. During the Civil War, **Fredericksburg** to the south witnessed the battles of Chancellorsville, Spotsylvania and the Wilderness, while **Manassas** to the west was the site of the bloody battle of Bull Run.

Mount Vernon – George Washington's Home

Set on a shallow bluff overlooking the broad Potomac River, **Mount Vernon** (daily, summer 9am–5pm, otherwise 9am–4pm; $5) is among the most attractive historic houses in the US. The country estate of **George Washington** has been maintained virtually intact since his death in 1799, with its eight-thousand acres of landscaped and planted grounds. Besides illuminating the life and times of the leader of the revolution-

---

The telephone **area code** for northern Virginia is ☎703.

ary armies, and the first US president, Mount Vernon also allows an eye-opening look into the aristocratic way of life of the colonial gentlemen who founded the USA.

A small museum gives an overview of Mount Vernon's history; in the house itself, the furnishings and decoration reflect Washington's preference for plain living, but few items – a reading chair with a built-in fan, and a key to the destroyed Bastille, presented by Thomas Paine on behalf of Lafayette – give much of a sense of his character. The four-posted bed upon which he died stands in an upstairs bedroom; he and his wife Martha are buried in a simple tomb on the south side of the house.

The plain brick 1755 **Gunston Hall**, home of Washington's contemporary **George Mason**, stands just around a bend in the river, ten minutes' drive south along Hwy-1 at the east end of Hwy-242 (daily 9.30am–5pm; $4). It was Mason's revolutionary idea "that all men are by nature equally free and independent and have certain inherent rights", which Jefferson incorporated into the Declaration of Independence. Mason was later one of the main authors of the US Constitution, which he refused to sign because it neither included a Bill of Rights nor abolished slavery. Unlike Washington and Jefferson, Mason eschewed public power, preferring to stay here with his family – which is understandable once you've seen the place, one of the most impressive pieces of architecture in Virginia. Most of it was designed and constructed by William Buckland; the masterful interiors, particularly in the stately drawing room, feature some beautiful carved ornament. The house fronts onto a large formal garden, and the extensive grounds are in turn surrounded by two riverfront state parks and wildlife refuges.

Manassas Battlefield National Park

One of northern Virginia's most affecting historic sites spreads on grassy green hills at the western fringes of the Washington DC suburban belt, just off the I-66 freeway. Though the modern world is just outside its boundaries – after a lengthy court battle, developers were prevented in 1991 from building a tract of battle-view homes on its fringes – wandering or driving through **Manassas Battlefield National Park** can't help but produce a chilling sensation. You don't have to know the details of what happened here to feel the numinous power of these brooding hillsides.

Soon after the first shots were fired at Fort Sumter, the first major land battle of the Civil War, known as the **Battle of Bull Run**, was fought here on the morning on July 21 1861. Expecting an easy victory, some 25,000 Union troops attacked a Confederate detachment controlling a vital railroad link to the Shenandoah Valley. The rebels proved powerful opponents, their strength in battle earning their commander, General Thomas Jackson, the famous nickname "Stonewall". A small visitor centre at the entrance has displays describing how the battle took shape, as well as detailing the other battles fought here over the course of the war.

Fredericksburg

Only a mile off the I-95 freeway, and easy to reach via mainline *Amtrak* trains and *Greyhound* buses, **FREDERICKSBURG** – the biggest city between Washington DC and the Virginia capital, Richmond – still retains a good deal of its historic feel. In colonial days, Fredericksburg was an important inland port, loading tobacco and other plantation products onto boats that sailed down the Rappahonock River. Dozens of eighteenth- and nineteenth-century buildings along the waterfront now hold antique stores and secondhand booksellers. The **visitor centre** at 706 Caroline Street (☎373-1776 or ☎1-800/678-4748) has maps of walking tours.

Two blocks away, in the 1816 town hall, the **Fredericksburg Area Museum**, 907 Princess Anne Street (Mon–Sat 9am–5pm, Sun 1–5pm; $2), has a broad range of displays tracing local history from Native American settlements to the present day. The **Rising Sun Tavern**, by the river at 1306 Caroline Street, was built in the mid-1700s by George Washington's brother Charles. By the end of the century it had been changed

NORTHERN VIRGINIA AND RICHMOND/303

into a coaching inn, and has since been restored into a small "living history" museum (daily 9am–5pm; $3), in which costumed "serving wenches" show you around a collection of pub-games and ancient pewterware. They don't, however, serve food or drink anymore, except for the glass of spiced herbal punch you get on the tour.

Fredericksburg's important strategic location made it vital during the **Civil War**, and the land around the town was heavily fought over. Over 100,000 men lost their lives in the major battles of Fredericksburg, Chancellorsville, Spotsylvania, and countless other bloody skirmishes. The **Fredericksburg National Battlefield Park**, on LaFayette Boulevard south of town, has a number of informative exhibits, and rents three-hour audio tours ($2.50 for tape and player) of the various battlefield sites.

Modern Fredericksburg gets a lot of weekend-escape trade, and so has several good places to **eat** and **drink**. The closest contemporary equivalent to the bawdy *Rising Sun* is probably the *Irish Brigade*, 1005 Princess Anne Street (☎371-9413), a lively sandwich and burger bar with draught Harp and Guinness, and nightly folk and R&B. Also worth a visit is the wood-panelled colonial *Seafood Emporium*, 715 Caroline Street (☎371-0300), with excellent clam chowders; the *Windsor Tavern and Tea Room*, 200 Hanover Street (☎371-6073), does a lovely afternoon tea, and has steak-and-kidney pies in its late-opening pub. Apart from modern **motels** – of which the best sited is the friendly, $50-a-night *Colonial Inn*, 1707 Princess Anne Street (☎371-5666) – places to stay tend toward pricier but nice **B&Bs** like the *Richard Johnson Inn*, 711 Caroline Street (☎899-7606).

Richmond and the Tidewater

At the very heart of Virginia, **Richmond** and the **Chesapeake Bay tidewater** are, in many ways, where the US was born. Not only does this fairly compact area hold some of the most important surviving colonial-era sites in the US, it is also where the strength of the nation was tested by the traumatic Civil War. The greatest interest is to be found in the compact **Historic Triangle**, east of Richmond; after which the Atlantic coast beyond comes as something of a disappointment.

Richmond and Around

Founded in 1737 at the furthest navigable point on the James River, **RICHMOND** remained a small outpost until just before the end of the colonial era, when independence-minded Virginians, realising that their capital at Williamsburg was open to British attack, shifted it here, fifty miles further inland. The move to Richmond failed to offer much protection – the city was raided many times and twice put to the torch, once by troops under the command of Benedict Arnold.

For the next 75 years Richmond flourished, its population reaching 100,000 by the time of the Civil War. Although, just a month before, Virginia had strongly opposed secession from the Union, voting two-to-one against, when war broke out Richmond was named the **capital of the Confederacy**. The massive **Tredegar Iron Works** – now being restored as a riverfront museum – became the main engine of the Confederate war machine. For four years the city remained the focus of Southern defences and Union attacks, but despite an almost constant state of siege – General McClellan came within six miles of the capital as early as 1862, and General Grant steamrollered toward it remorselessly through the last months of the war – it held on until the very end. It was less than a week after the fall of Richmond, on April 3 1865, that General Lee surrendered to General Grant at Appomattox, a hundred miles to the west.

The telephone **area code** for Richmond and the Tidewater is ☎804.

After the war, Richmond was devàstated. Much of its downtown was burned, allegedly by fleeing Confederates who wanted to keep its stores of weapons, and its warehouses full of valuable tobacco, out of the victors' hands. Rebuilding, however, was quick, and the city's economy has remained among the strongest in the South. **Tobacco** is still a major industry – machine-rolled cigarettes were invented here in the 1870s, and Marlboro-makers **Phillip Morris** run a huge manufacturing plant just south of downtown. In the mornings you can smell the sweet earthy aroma of the drying leaves. Richmond is also a leading **banking** centre, home to one of only fourteen branches of the Federal Reserve Bank, and has all the modern office towers of a major American city, as well an extensive inventory of architecturally significant older buildings.

Arrival, Information and Getting Around

Richmond is served by *Amtrak* (☎264-9194), pulling in to 7519 Staples Road, five miles northwest of downtown, and *Greyhound* (☎353-8903), who stop just off I-64 at 2910 N Boulevard, also a good way from the centre. The large **airport** ten miles east of downtown is served by major carriers like *American, Delta* and *United*.

Coming by **car**, Richmond is about two hours' drive from Washington DC via I-95, which cuts right through the east side of downtown; **Main Street** runs east–west parallel to the James River, with bigger **Broad Street**, US-60, another two blocks inland.

There's a large **visitor centre** (☎358-5511 or ☎1-800/365-7272) near the *Greyhound* station at 1710 Robin Hood Drive, and a smaller but more central office at 300 E Main Street (☎782-2777).

Most of Richmond is compact and easily walkable, but to get to outlying places (like the stations or the Fine Art Museum) you might want to take a *GRTC* **bus** ($1; ☎358-GRTC). The **Historic Richmond Foundation**, 2407 E Grace Street (☎780-0107), runs walking and van **tours** of the city.

Downtown Richmond

Richmond's **downtown** centres on a few blocks rising up from the James River to either side of Broad Street. Modern office towers front onto a riverside park, while up the shallow hill in the **Court End** district, dozens of well-preserved antebellum homes provide a gracious background to some important museums and historic sites.

The **Virginia state capitol** (daily 9am–5pm; free), which has been in use since 1788 as the seat of the state and – during the Civil War, Confederate – government, is the downtown focal point, visible from all over Richmond and offering a sweeping view from its columned portico. Thomas Jefferson had a hand in the design, modelling it after his favourite building, the Roman ruin of Maison Carré in Nimes, France. The domed central rotunda holds a life-sized marble statue of George Washington, the only one done from life, and busts of Jefferson and the seven other Virginia-born US presidents line the walls. Likenesses of famous Virginians, including a solemn bronze Robert E Lee, fill the adjacent **Old House Chamber**, the largest room in the Capitol and the place where Aaron Burr was tried and acquitted of treason in 1807.

Just two blocks north of the Capitol on 12th Street, the **Museum of the Confederacy**, 1201 E Clay Street (Mon–Sat 10am–5pm, Sun noon–5pm; $4), gives a surprisingly even-handed history of the Civil War, starting with a brief description of the 1850s abolitionist and states rights movements but concentrating on the various battles, from Fort Sumter to Appomattox, and on the personalities of the Confederate leaders. Next door, the so-called **White House of the Confederacy** (same hours; $4), a neoclassical mansion where Jefferson Davis lived while president of the Confederacy, has recently been restored to its 1860s appearance.

Two blocks to the west, the 1812 **Wickham House** now forms part of the **Valentine Museum** (Mon–Sat 10am–5pm, Sun noon–5pm; $3.50), at 1015 E Clay Street. This neoclassical monolith houses a small local history museum, focusing on the experience of working-class and black Americans, as well as an extensive array of furniture and pre-Civil War clothing – whalebone corsets and other *Gone with the Wind* period costumes.

A little further west, beyond the Convention Center complex on Sixth Street, is a neighbourhood of early nineteenth-century houses, many of them fronted by ornate wrought-iron balconies similar to those in the French Quarter of New Orleans. Known as **Jackson Ward**, and filling a dozen blocks around First and Clay streets, this has been the centre of Richmond's African-American community since well before the Civil War, when Richmond had the largest free black population of any US city. Plans are in the works to open a black heritage museum by mid-1992 (details on ☎780-9093), but the one site here now is the **Maggie L Walker House**, 110 E Leigh Street (Wed–Sun 9am–5pm; free), which traces the working life of the physically disabled black Richmond woman who, during the 1920s, founded and ran the first non-white-male-owned bank in the US, now the Consolidated Bank and Trust.

Shockoe Bottom, the Poe Museum and Church Hill

A short walk southeast from the Court End district, a very different neighbourhood allows a glimpse at another side of the Richmond story. Split down the middle by the raised I-95 freeway, the increasingly gentrified (and regularly flooded) riverfront warehouse district of **Shockoe Bottom** still holds a few palpable reminders of Richmond's industrial past, in and among restaurants and nightclubs. From **Shockoe Slip**, a prettified old wharf rebuilt in the 1890s after being destroyed in the Civil War, Cary Street runs east along the waterfront lined by forbidding brick warehouses known as **Tobacco Row**.

Nearby, in Richmond's oldest building, an appropriately gloomy 250-year-old stone house at 1914 E Main Street serves as the **Edgar Allan Poe Museum** (Tues–Sat 10am–4pm, Sun–Mon 1.30pm–4pm; $5). Poe spent much of his life in Richmond, and considered it his hometown; after his mother died in 1811 when Edgar was three years old, he was raised by foster parents before leaving for the University of Virginia at age eighteen, and later returned to write the *Narrative of Arthur Gordon Pym* while working on the Richmond-based magazine *Southern Literary Messenger*.

Church Hill, a few blocks northeast, is one of Richmond's oldest surviving residential districts, with dozens of well-maintained eighteenth-century houses looking out over the James River. Capping the hill at the heart of the neighbourhood, **St John's Church** (Mon–Sat 10am–3.30pm, Sun 1–3.30pm; $2 donation), 2401 E Broad Street, which dates back to 1741, is best known as the place where, during a March 1775 debate on whether the Virginia colony should raise a militia against the British, **Patrick Henry** made the impassioned plea: "Is life so dear, or peace so sweet, to be purchased at the price of chains of slavery? I know not what course others may take, but as for me, give me liberty or give me death". His speech is re-enacted by an actor every Sunday at 2pm, after the morning's religious services.

The Virginia Museum of Fine Arts and the Science Museum

The newest and most opulent of Richmond's neighbourhoods, called the **Fan District** because its tree-lined avenues fan out at oblique angles, spreads west from the downtown area, beyond Belvedere Street (US-1). Lined by garish turn-of-the-century mansions, the Fan District's broadest street, **Monument Avenue**, was laid out in 1889 as a symbol of the city's post-Reconstruction recovery, and is marked every few hundred yards by large-scale memorial statues honouring Civil War figures Jeb Stuart, Robert E Lee, Jefferson Davis and Stonewall Jackson.

South of Monument Avenue, at 2800 Grove Avenue, stands the **Virginia Museum of Fine Arts** (Tues–Sat 11am–5pm, Sun 1–5pm; $2 donation). Paul Mellon donated an extensive collection of Impressionist and Post-Impressionist paintings, displayed alongside American paintings ranging from George Catlin's romantic images of Plains

Indians to the Pop Art creations of Roy Lichtenstein and Claes Oldenburg in the vast new West Wing. Other galleries contain such diverse items as Frank Lloyd Wright furniture, Lalique jewellery, and Hindu and Buddhist sculpture from the Himalayas, but perhaps the popular part of the museum, and its one world-class collection, is the array of over three hundred jewel-encrusted **Fabergé eggs**, crafted in the 1890s for the Russian tsars.

Accommodation
Finding well-priced **accommodation** in Richmond isn't difficult, with no shortage of anonymous downtown hotels catering to the business and government trade. You can get a feel for the old city by staying the night in a **B&B** in one of the historic quarters; a good range, starting under $50 a night, is offered by the *Bensonhouse of Richmond* reservation service (☎648-7560 or ☎353-6900).

The Berkeley Hotel, 1200 E Cary St (☎780-1300). Upmarket but not outrageously pricey small hotel on historic Shockoe Slip; doubles from $69 to $100.

Caitlin-Abbott House, 2304 E Broad St (☎780-3746). Small B&B on Church Hill, across from St John's Church, with doubles from $55.

Holiday Inn Midtown, 3200 W Broad St (☎359-4061). Good location, near the Fan District and Fine Arts Museum; standard doubles from $50.

Jefferson Sheraton, 201 E Franklin St (☎788-8000 or ☎1-800/325-3535). Beautifully maintained grand hotel, with fountain-filled lobby and spacious rooms; doubles from $150 per night.

Linden Row Inn, 100 E Franklin St (☎783-7000). Historic red brick Georgian terrace houses converted into comfortable modern hotel; doubles from $70.

Massad House Hotel, 11 N Fourth St (☎648-2893). Cheap but cheerful older hotel in Court End district; doubles $38.

Eating
Richmond has a good choice of eating options at either end of the price spectrum, but not much in between.

Bill's Barbecue, 3100 N Blvd (☎355-9745). Great breakfasts and huge portions of barbecued chicken and ribs, plus delicious fresh pies. Seven other locations around Richmond.

Commercial Cafe, 111 N Robinson St (☎353-7110). Burgers, ribs and hickory-smoked chicken in stylish, Fan District surroundings.

Morton's Tea Room, 2 E Franklin St (☎648-7062). Homestyle southern food – Virginia ham and collard greens and the like – at low prices.

Peking Pavilion, 1302 E Cary St (☎649-8888). Very good, inexpensive (especially at lunchtime) Shockoe Slip Chinese place.

Strawberry Street Cafe, 421 N Strawberry Street (☎353-6860). Casual and comfortable Fan District neighbourhood cafe – mainly quiches, pastas and salads.

Third Street Diner, Third and Main St (☎788-4750). All-American diner, open daily 7am–2am, 24hr Fri and Sat.

Drinking and Nightlife
Richmond's main drinking and nightlife spots are concentrated around the riverside Shockoe Slip and Shockoe Bottom areas just east of downtown, where you'll find the likes of the *Bird in Hand*, 1718 E Main Street (☎788-1101); the singles-scene *Shockoe Slip Cafe*, 1218 E Cary Street (☎343-1757); or *Matt's British Pub*, 109 S Twelfth Street (☎644-0848) with nightly music and comedy. In the Fan District, look out for the *Paradise Cafe*, 2229 W Main Street (☎358-6759) or the *Stonewall*, 1520 W Main Street (☎359-6324).

TheaterVirginia (☎367-0840), at 2800 Grove Avenue in the Museum of Fine Arts, is Richmond's best bet for live **theatre**. For music and other events check out the listings in the free weekly *Night Moves* newspaper.

The Historic Triangle: Jamestown, Williamsburg, and Yorktown

The **Historic Triangle**, on the thin peninsula that stretches east of Richmond between the James and York rivers, holds by far the richest concentration of colonial-era sites in the US. **Jamestown,** founded in 1607, was Virginia's first settlement; **Williamsburg** is an animated if theatrical resurrection of the colonial capital; and it was at **Yorktown** that American independence from the English crown was finally secured. All three sites are within an hour by car, bus or train from the capital.

The I-64 freeway is the quickest way to cover the fifty miles from Richmond to Williamsburg, but once you're in the area the best way to get around is along the lushly landscaped **Colonial Parkway**, which winds west to Jamestown and east to Yorktown, twenty miles end-to-end. Most of the area's numerous tourist facilities – this is the most-visited destination in the state – are to be found around Williamsburg. We've listed a few suggestions under "Historic Triangle Practicalities" on p.311.

Jamestown National Historic Site

The first successful English colony in the New World, **JAMESTOWN** was established as a commercial venture, sponsored by King James I but paid for and owned by the **Virginia Company**. On April 26 1607 the colonists, thirty adventure-minded aristocrats and seventy-five indentured servants, arrived at the mouth of the Chesapeake Bay after four months at sea, and within two weeks established a fortified settlement upon a low-lying island forty miles up the James River.

Despite the fact that Jamestown was intended to be self-supporting, not one of the party had any experience of farming or fishing – their leader, **John Smith**, wrote in 1608 that "though there be Fish in the Sea, and Foules in the ayre, and Beasts in the woods, their bounds are so large, they are so wilde, and we so weake and ignorant, we cannot much trouble them". The Virginia Company continued to send new recruits, but the loss of life was extreme: of more than seven thousand settlers who came to Jamestown in its first decade, six thousand perished within a year of arriving.

What saved Jamestown, besides the provisions brought by new settlers, was **tobacco**: by 1619 the colony was shipping some twenty tons a year back to England. As it expanded, the colony began to encroach upon the **Powhatan** Indians, who until then had been fairly peaceable. In 1622 and again in 1644 provocations caused the Powhatan to attack the Jamestown colonists, killing some five hundred settlers each time. The most serious damage to Jamestown, however, was caused by the colonists themselves, when they burned the fort to the ground in 1675 to protest the lack of protection offered them by the crown. Rather than rebuild the tiny island outpost, by the end of the 1600s the capital and most of the commercial activity had been shifted inland to Williamsburg, and Jamestown slowly disappeared.

The one bit of seventeenth-century Jamestown to survive, protected within the **Jamestown National Historic Site**, is the fifty-foot tower of the first brick church, built in 1639 – the rest was destroyed by fire in 1698. Around it are sundry unearthed foundations, as well as numerous memorial shrines and monuments.

From the **visitor centre** (daily 9am–5pm; $5 per car), where artist's drawings and audio-visual exhibits endeavour to conjure up the past, a footpath leads down to the river, where the remains of the original fortress, now underwater, are vaguely visible.

Jamestown Settlement

Next to the authentic site of Jamestown, the state of Virginia has created **Jamestown Settlement** (daily 9am–5pm; $7, $9.50 with Yorktown Victory Center, see p.310), a complex of museums and full-size replicas which make the details of what went on here that much clearer. A short film dramatising Jamestown's early days is shown continuously, while museum displays explore Europe's needs for colonies, document-

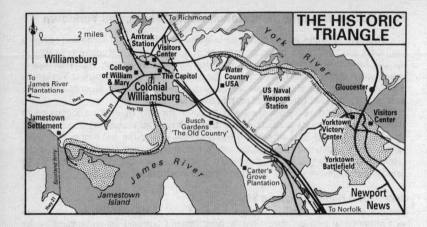

ing the economic and social conditions, in England especially, which lead to the founding of Jamestown. There's also an informative section dealing with the Powhatan, an
Algonquin-speaking tribe who controlled most of tidewater Virginia.

Behind the museum, two groups of reconstructed buildings are inhabited by interpretive guides, dressed in period costumes. In the **Powhatan Village**, women wearing
buckskins practice weaving and pottery, while in the larger and more convincing
replica of **James Fort**, some fifteen thatched, wattle-and-daub buildings – all built
using period tools – act as blacksmith shops, a storehouse, and a church. Full-sized
replicas of the three **ships** that carried the first settlers here – the *Godspeed* (which
retraced the route from England in 1985), the *Susan Constant* and the *Discovery* – are
moored below on the James River.

Williamsburg

After mosquito-plagued Jamestown burned down, in 1699 the colonial capital was
moved inland to a small village known as the Middle Plantation, quickly re-christened
WILLIAMSBURG in honour of King William III. To reflect the increasing wealth of
the colony, a grand city, centring upon a mile-long, hundred-foot-wide avenue, was laid
out. Suitable buildings were constructed, beginning with the **capitol** in 1704 and culminating in the opulent **Governor's Palace** in 1720. By the mid-1700s tobacco-rich
Virginia was the most prosperous of the American colonies, and Williamsburg was its
largest city, though with some two thousand residents it was not on the scale of
Philadelphia, New York or Boston. Williamsburg remained the seat of colonial government, and emerged as one of the leading centres of **revolutionary thought**: at the
College of William and Mary, George Wythe, Thomas Jefferson, James Monroe and
George Mason argued the finer points of law and democracy, while in the capitol, and
in the many raucous taverns surrounding it, firebrand politicians like Patrick Henry
held forth on the iniquities of colonialism and organised the first resistance to British
rule. When the Revolutionary War broke out, the government moved to the more-
defensible Richmond, and Williamsburg slowly faded from view, becoming a quiet
Virginia town, all but unrecognised for its place in American history.

Fortunately, many of the colonial structures survived intact until the 1920s, when oil
baron **John D Rockefeller** answered the pleas of a local priest, W A R Goodwin, to
support Williamsburg's restoration. (Goodwin, who considered that cars were going to
ruin American towns, and that the men who were making millions out of the car indus-

try might feel guilty about this, had initially approached Henry Ford, who sent him packing.) Over the ensuing years, Rockefeller, with Goodwin acting as his agent, spent some $90 million buying and restoring the surviving fragments to their original condition, in many cases rebuilding replicas from scratch. In 1934 **Colonial Williamsburg** opened as the first theme park in the US to use American history for amusement, with costumed guides as interpreters. While you have to buy a (very expensive) ticket to look inside most of the buildings – see below – the entire historic area, which includes many fine gardens, is open all the time, and you can wander freely down the cobbled streets and across the lush green commons. Cars, fortunately, are banned, and Williamsburg as a whole is a remarkably pleasant – if very crowded – place.

From the Wren Building on the William and Mary campus, built in 1716 at the west end of Williamsburg and now separated from the historic area by a mock-colonial shopping centre (and car park), **Duke of Gloucester Street** runs east through the historic area to the rebuilt Capitol. The first of its eighteenth-century buildings, a hundred yards along, is the **Bruton Parish Church** (Mon–Sat 9am–5pm, Sun noon–5pm; donations). Built as an Anglican church in 1715, when all white Virginians were required by law to attend services at least once a month, the church, now Episcopalian, is where Goodwin was priest. Behind it, the broad **Palace Green** spreads north to the rebuilt Governor's Palace (see below). West of the church, the **courthouse** – built in 1770 and still in use when Rockefeller bought it – and the octagonal **Powder Magazine** stand facing each other in the midst of the Market Square. Further along, **Chowning's Tavern**, a reconstruction of an alehouse that stood here in 1766, is one of four functioning pubs run by Colonial Williamsburg. Thomas Jefferson rented a room in the (no longer used) **Market Square Tavern** across the street as a law student.

Various other buildings along Duke of Gloucester Street house blacksmiths' shops, printers or milliners, open only to Colonial Williamsburg ticket-holders. At the east end of the street, fife-and-drum corps and members of the militia assemble in front of the reconstructed capitol (see below) before the evening's march through town.

Colonial Williamsburg

To set foot inside any of the more than two hundred assorted buildings that have been restored or rebuilt as part of **COLONIAL WILLIAMSBURG**, you need first to buy a ticket, either from the main **visitor centre** (daily 8.30am–8pm; ☎220-7643 or ☎1-800/HISTORY) off the Colonial Parkway, or from a smaller office at the west end of Duke of Gloucester Street. The **Basic Ticket** ($21) is good for four days and gets you into almost everything except the Governor's Palace (which costs $13 on its own) and the Wallace Gallery ($7.50); the **Royal Governor's Pass** ($24.50) covers the Governor's Palace as well, and the **Patriot's Pass** ($28) gives you unlimited access to everything in Williamsburg for an entire year and entitles you to an introductory guided tour. There's an additional charge for most of the special entertainment and educational events offered by Colonial Williamsburg, such as staged trials in the courthouse ($7), evening dances ($5), and candlelight walking tours ($7).

A visit to Williamsburg can get pretty expensive, but so long as you can avoid the overcrowded peak summer months, it's money well spent. The meticulously restored buildings and the various interpretive activities and crafts workshops – ranging over thirty colonial trades, from apothecary to wig-making – are both entertaining and true to life. As Rockefeller's overly tidy influence has waned (his idea of restoration was to make everything look like new), Williamsburg has tried to come to grips with the less savoury realities of colonial life. Thus people who used to be referred to as servants are now acknowledged to have been slaves – fully half of Williamsburg's population was African-American, and their lives and conditions are well covered. On another level, houses and outbuildings, formerly repainted every year, are now left to age naturally, and once-manicured lawns are now allowed to get (slightly at least) overgrown.

The real architectural highlight is the **capitol**, at the east end of Duke of Gloucester Street. The current building, a 1945 reconstruction of the 1705 original, has an open-air ground-floor **arcade** which links two keyhole-shaped wings. The east wing housed the elected, legislative body of the colonial government, the **House of Burgesses**, while the other held the chambers of the **General Court** – where alleged felons, including thirteen of Blackbeard's pirates, were tried. The eleven justices of the General Court, all of whom were appointed by the King, served as a second legislative body, much as the US House and Senate work today; if the two became deadlocked, they'd meet jointly in a conference chamber bridging the two wings. Just north of the capitol is the old **Public Gaol**, built in 1701 and in use until 1910.

A number of fully stocked and fairly tacky gift shops along **Duke of Gloucester Street** have been done up as Olde Worlde apothecaries and silversmiths. The **Raleigh Tavern** was where the independence-minded colonial government re-convened after being dissolved by the loyalist governors in 1769 and again in 1774; the original tavern burned in 1859. Considering that most Virginians of the time, even well-to-do landowners, lived in one- or two-room log cabins, the imposing two-storey **Governor's Palace** at the north end of the Palace Green, with its grand ballroom and opulent furnishings, must have served as a telling declaration of the power vested inside.

The smaller of the two conventional museums in Williamsburg, the recently expanded **Abby Aldrich Rockefeller Folk Art Center** on the south side of town, has an intriguing collection of household implements, children's toys, and general bric-a-brac as well as fascinating paintings and sculptures by so-called primitive or natural artists. The other, the **DeWitt Wallace Decorative Arts Gallery** ($7.50), features fine furniture, as well as porcelain figurines and painted portraits. Its modern galleries are entirely underground; the entrance is through the reconstructed facade of the **Public Hospital**, two blocks south of Bruton Parish Church. The first madhouse in North America, the hospital now has reconstructions of the wire cages in which many early inmates were kept, as well as other exhibits tracing the evolution of the treatment of mental illness in the US.

Yorktown Battlefield

YORKTOWN, along the York River on the north side of the peninsula, is not much of a town, but gave its name to the decisive final battle of the **Revolutionary War**. The least extensive (and least visited) of the Historic Triangle sites, Yorktown was little more than farmland when, on October 18 1781, overwhelmed and besieged British (and German) troops under the command of Cornwallis surrendered to the joint American and French ground and naval forces commanded by George Washington. At the heart of the battlefield, a **visitor centre** (daily 9am–5pm; free) has informative interpretive displays, racks of military artefacts, and a short audio-visual presentation on the war. The **Siege Line Overlook** on the roof gives good views of strategic points, and maps ($1) and a cassette-taped tour ($2) are available if you want to explore in greater detail.

The **Moore House**, where the British surrender was agreed, survived later Civil War battles (and eventual use as a barn) before John D Rockefeller bought it and had it restored; it stands along the York River, a mile east of the visitor centre.

Yorktown Victory Center

Though Yorktown survived the battle more or less unscathed – the fighting took place on open fields to the east, and in the waters of the Chesapeake Bay – much of the town was destroyed by fire in 1814, and very little of substance survives from the colonial days. Many of the surviving homes are privately owned, and not open to visitors. To make up for this, as at Jamestown the state of Virginia has constructed a mini-theme park – this time a re-created Continental Army encampment – as part of the **Yorktown Victory Center** (daily 9am–5pm; $6.50, $9.50 with Jamestown Settlement), west of the battlefield on US-17. It's not as extensive or convincing as the one at Jamestown, but the museum is if anything even better, focusing on the tobacco wealth of now-vanished York River towns and discussing both sides, British and American, of events leading up to the Revolution. A final gallery deals with the course and impact of the war itself.

Historic Triangle Practicalities

Of the three main sites, only Williamsburg is easily reached without a car. *Amtrak* **trains** and *Greyhound* **buses** stop at the **Transportation Center**, on Boundary Road two blocks from the Governor's Palace. Once there, the Colonial Parkway makes an excellent cycling route to Jamestown or Yorktown, but there's no other transport available; rent a **bike** from *Bikesmith* of Williamsburg (☎229-9858).

Considering the wealth of historic structures, it's surprising how few characterful hotels or B&Bs there are. However, good-value packages, with meals, two nights' lodging, and admission are available through Colonial Williamsburg, from around $150 per person – some provide accommodation in restored eighteenth-century homes within the historic area. Otherwise **places to stay** around the Historic Triangle are generally anodyne and rarely cheap; if you get stuck, the *Williamsburg Hotel/Motel Association* (☎220-3330 or ☎1-800/446-9244) will try to find you a bed at no extra charge. Around Williamsburg there are lots of $50-a-night motels – the *Bassett Motel*, 800 York Street (☎229-5175), and the *Econo Lodge*, 505 York Street (☎220-3100), are just a few blocks from the capitol – as well as a number of "Guest Homes", where you get your own room in someone's house. One of the best of these is *Mrs Carter's*, 903 Lafayette Street (☎229-1117), a short walk to the historic area, where doubles cost a very reasonable $30 a night. For a change of pace, the *Duke of York Motel*, 508 E Water Street in Yorktown (☎898-3232), has beachfront doubles along the York River from a bargain $35 a night.

Places to **eat** are, not surprisingly, often overpriced and less than enthralling, though the various Olde Worlde restaurants and taverns along Duke of Gloucester Street, operated by Colonial Williamsburg and featuring basic pub food as well as strolling entertainment, can be fun if you're in the mood. If not, head just west of the historic area to the **Merchants Square** shopping mall. The *Trellis Cafe* (☎229-8610) serves a range of fresh sandwiches, salads and light nouvelle lunches (as well as pricey dinners) in very pleasant surroundings, and the bare-bones cafeteria-style *A Good Place to Eat* churns out good cheap' breakfasts and burgers. Dozens of diners and fast-food places line Richmond Road (US-60) west of Williamsburg, but there's not much anywhere else.

The Atlantic Coast: Norfolk and Virginia Beach

One of the busiest of the East Coast ports, **Norfolk** sits at the point where the Chesapeake Bay empties into the Atlantic Ocean. Virginia's sole heavily industrial centre isn't by any stretch of the imagination a very pretty place, but it does have a rich maritime and naval heritage, as well as an excellent art gallery, the Chrysler Museum.

Fifteen miles east of Norfolk, along the open Atlantic Ocean, low-key **Virginia Beach** draws summer sun-seekers to the state's only real resort, surrounded by broad beaches and tidal marshlands. The rest of Virginia's Atlantic coast is on its isolated and sparsely populated eastern shore, packed full of bizarre place names – Nassawadox, Assawoman and Accomac, as well as Modest Town and Temperanceville. Its one really remarkable destination is **Chincoteague**, an island refuge straddling the Maryland border that's part of the Assateague National Seashore (see p.337).

Norfolk

A strategic location at the broad mouth of the Chesapeake Bay, and an extensive deep-water harbour, made colonial **NORFOLK** the main American port for trade with England and the West Indies – in the mid-eighteenth century it was the largest city in

Virginia. After being burned by the British in 1775, and suffering naval bombardments during the Civil War, Norfolk never regained much character, and despite recent efforts to redevelop its waterfront the modern city is little more than a supply depot for the vast naval shipyards. Along with Hampton and Newport News on the north side of the James River, Norfolk is home to the largest naval base outside the USSR, and carriers, cruisers and all manner of grey steel behemoths go steaming past on their way to the various dry-docks and shipyards.

A small **ferry** (11am–11pm; 75¢) shuttles from Town Point Park at the heart of the downtown waterfront across the harbour to the historic Portsmouth neighbourhood, where brick-paved streets are lined by dozens of eighteenth- and nineteenth-century houses. Another place to while away a couple of hours is the **Chrysler Museum** (Tues–Sat 10am–4pm, Sun 1–5pm; $3 suggested donation), half a mile north of the downtown waterfront. The collection of car magnate Walter Chrysler, Jr, who was on drinking terms with Picasso, includes a little bit of everything, from ancient Greek statuary to French Impressionist paintings to Franz Klein abstractions and Mayan funerary objects. The museum also holds one of the few Bernini sculptures in the US, and has a world-class collection of Tiffany and Lalique glassware.

Two blocks from the harbour, amidst the car parks and vacant lots of downtown, the **Douglas MacArthur Memorial** in the former Norfolk City Hall on Bank Street (Mon–Sat 10am–5pm, Sun 11am–5pm; free) houses the mortal remains and personal papers of the controversial old soldier. Norfolk, being such a strong Navy town, is an unlikely final resting place for MacArthur, the flamboyant US general who lead Allied forces in the Pacific during World War II and, as head of the occupying forces, wrote the modern Japanese Constitution. MacArthur was relieved of his command during the Korean War, apparently because of his alarming desire to bomb China. Objects in the Memorial include his trademark corncob pipe and dark glasses.

From **Patrick Henry International Airport**, twelve miles north of the city, the *Airport Shuttle* ($10; ☎857-1231) will bring you to downtown; *Amtrak*, stopping at the *Holiday Inn–Waterside*, 700 Monticello Street, and *Greyhound* serve Norfolk as well. Along with the highway motels, **accommodation** options include the modern *YMCA*, 312 W Bute Street (☎622-6328), with clean doubles and free use of the gym for $20 per night (men and women) across from the Chrysler Museum. The $120-a-night *Omni Waterside*, 777 Waterside Drive (☎622-6664), has views over the harbour and naval yards, while **B&B** doubles at the quaint *Glen Coe*, 222 North Street in Portsmouth (☎397-8128), cost from $65 a night. Norfolk's **visitor centre** is at 26 E Plume Street (☎441-1852 or ☎1-800/368-3097). **Eat** burritos, pizza or other international fast food at the *Portside Food Hall* across from the Portsmouth ferry landing, or Cajun-style seafood at the *Mason Dixon Grill*, 210 York Street downtown (☎623-3872).

Virginia Beach

Not as huge and frenzied as Ocean Beach in Maryland, nor as wild and open as the Outer Banks of North Carolina, both in character and geography **VIRGINIA BEACH** is about halfway in between the two. The state's only summer resort has all the usual beachfront hotels and motels, as well as a boardwalk strip of bars, restaurants and nightclubs, but it also has some long stretches of comparatively untouched golden sands, especially in **False Cape State Park**, which stretches from Virginia Beach to the North Carolina border.

During the day at least, there's not a lot to do apart from lie in the sun and play in the waves: Virginia Beach is one of the main East Coast surfing centres, hosting the summmer-long *Billabong* competitions. You can rent surf, skim and boogie boards from the *17th Street Surf Shop* on Pacific Avenue (☎425-9707). Away from the sands, most of the action is along Atlantic Avenue, the beachfront main drag, especially the few blocks around 24th Street.

Virginia Beach has one great boon for **budget travellers** – *Angie's Guest Cottage B&B AYH Hostel*, 302 24th Street (☎428-4690). Just a block from the beach, and with dorm rooms for $11 ($14 non-AYH members) and B&B doubles from $45, the hostel is open all day, and they'll pick you up from the bus or *Amtrak* station (at 1900 Pavilion Avenue). *Carolina Trailways*, the local *Greyhound* affiliate, drops off at 1017 Laskin Road (☎422-2998), off 31st Street. Hostellers and others congregate most nights at the *Jewish Mother*, 3108 Pacific Avenue (☎422-5430), a daytime deli and late-night beer bar with free live music; *Chicho's*, 2112 Atlantic Avenue (☎422-6011), is another popular eating and drinking spot. The **visitor centre** (☎425-7111 or 1-800/446-8038) is located at the east end of I-44, half a mile west of the beach on 21st Street.

Charlottesville and the Shenandoah Valley

The densely forested four-thousand-foot peaks of the Blue Ridge Mountains form a definite barrier between the history-rich worlds of tidewater Virginia to the east and the rougher river-and-valley country to the west. In between the two, at the geographical centre of the state, the friendly, manageably small college town of **Charlottesville** holds two great monuments to the mind of **Thomas Jefferson**. To the west, the northern **Blue Ridge Mountains**, crowned by the dense forests of **Shenandoah National Park**, run south to Tennessee, culminating in 5729ft Mount Rogers. On the far side of the mountains, the lush Shenandoah Valley was a vital battleground during the Civil War; since then little seems to have changed.

The main highway, I-81 through the Shenandoah Valley, is joined in the north by I-66 from Washington DC and in the middle by I-64 from Richmond through Charlottesville. Numerous scenic routes are slower but more worthwhile, such as **Skyline Drive** and the **Blue Ridge Parkway**, which weave along the four-hundred–mile mountain crest. You'll definitely need a car to get the most out of it, though cycling is a good option along the many back roads, and, for hikers, the **Appalachian Trail** runs right down the middle. There are plenty of roadside motels so you needn't be too concerned about advance planning – it's a great place for aimless exploration.

Charlottesville

If you only have a couple of days to see Virginia, **CHARLOTTESVILLE**, seventy miles west of Richmond, should be near the top of your itinerary. Abounding in history, and holding some of the finest examples of early American architecture, it is at once small enough to feel comfortable in and large enough to have good restaurants and night-spots. Its compact, low-rise centre is criss-crossed by magnolia-shaded streets, and makes a fine place to amble around, particularly the six pedestrianised blocks of **Main Street**, site of the nightly town promenade. However pleasant the town, the compelling attraction is the legacy of **Thomas Jefferson**, whose home and final resting place, **Monticello**, stands atop a hill just east of town, overlooking the beautifully landscaped neo-classical campus of the University of Virginia.

The University of Virginia
Though he wrote the Declaration of Independence and served as the third US president, Thomas Jefferson took more pride in having established the **University of Virginia** than in any of his other achievements, and if you're able to visit you may well share his view. In 1976 the University of Virginia was officially designated the greatest

---

The telephone **area code** for Charlottesville is ☎804; for the Shenandoah Valley, it's ☎703.

piece of architecture in the US, but the university also reveals the ideology of its patron, who besides designing every building down to the most minute detail also planned the curriculum and selected the faculty. Uniquely for universities of the time, which functioned primarily as seminaries, it was not rooted in religious training – Jefferson having been one of the prime proponents of the separation of church from the affairs of state – but emphasised instead a broadly based liberal arts education.

The highlight and architectural focus is the red-brick and white-domed **Rotunda**, modelled on the Pantheon and completed in 1821 to house the university library and classrooms. A basement gallery tells the story of the university, while upstairs three elliptical classrooms are linked by a voluptuous central hall. A staircase winds up to the **Dome Room**, where, in place of the planetarium Jefferson wanted to install, Corinthian columns rise to an ocular skylight.

From the Rotunda, where 45-minute guided tours (daily 10am–4pm; free) of the campus begin, twin colonnades stretch along either side of a lushly landscaped quadrangle, linking together a string of single-storey student apartments and taller pavilions, in which professors live and hold tutorials. While the overall feel is harmonious, each individual block is unique, the differing facades and rooflines designed to show off the various orders and styles of neoclassical architecture.

Parallel to the quadrangle buildings, two further rows of dormitory buildings, the East and West Ranges, front on to serpentine walled gardens. **Edgar Allan Poe** stayed in one of these rooms while studying at the University of Virginia in 1826, but was forced to drop out after his stepfather cut off his allowance, apparently because Edgar had lost all his money gambling. His room – Number 13, of course, in the West Range – is now restored to how it would have looked when Poe was here, and is virtually the only campus interior, apart from the Rotunda, which you can visit.

Monticello – Thomas Jefferson's Home

One of America's most familiar buildings – it graces the back of the nickel coin – **Monticello**, three miles southeast of Charlottesville on Hwy-53, was the home of **Thomas Jefferson** for most of his life. A visit provides a distinctive insight into the mind and personality of the most intriguing of America's Founding Fathers. Surrounded by acres of beautifully landscaped hilltop grounds with fine views out over the Virginia countryside, Monticello is a handsome house, whose symmetrical brick facade, centred upon a white Doric portico, belies the quirky irregularities of the interior – furnished as it was when Jefferson lived, and died, here.

To see Monticello you have join one of the **guided tours** (daily 9am–5pm; $7) which leave continuously from the carpark at the bottom of the hill. There's often a queue, especially on weekends, so try to get there as early as possible in the morning. From the outside, Monticello looks like an elegant, Palladian-style country home, but as soon as you enter the domed entrance hall, with its funhouse mirror – which reflects an upside-down image – and displays of fossilised bones and elk antlers (from Lewis and Clark's epic 1804 journey across North America, which Jefferson sponsored as president), you begin to get a sense that Jefferson was a somewhat more bizarre character than the sober statesman portrayed by most histories. His love of gadgets marked him as something of an eccentric: the weather vane over the front porch is connected to a dial, so he could see which way the wind was blowing without having to step outside, and the house is filled with odd little contraptions such as the elaborate dual-pen device Jefferson used to make automatic copies of all his letters. Jefferson's **private chambers** are also on the tour: he slept in a tiny alcove linking his dressing room and his study, and would get up on the right side of the bed if he wanted to make some late-night notes, on the left if he wanted to get dressed.

The upstairs rooms, where Jefferson's daughter and twelve grandchildren lived, are not, as yet, open to the public, but from the grounds around the house you can start to see how Monticello, a 5000-acre plantation, really functioned. Extensive flower and vegetable gardens spread to the south and west, and a dank passage runs under the house from the kitchen and beer cellar (Jefferson was a keen home-brewer) to the remains of Mulberry Row, Monticello's **slave quarters** – Jefferson, who called slavery an "abominable crime", owned almost two hundred of his fellow human beings. At the south end of Mulberry Row, a grove of ancient hardwood trees surrounds Jefferson's grave, marked by a simple stone obelisk; a footpath beyond winds back down to the bottom of the hill.

Charlottesville Practicalities

Amtrak trains from DC stop in Charlottesville at 810 W Main Street, and *Greyhound* pulls in a few blocks away at 310 W Main Street (☎295-5131). Once you arrive, you can get around on foot or, better, by renting a **bike** for $10 from *Blue Wheel*, 19 Elliewood Avenue (☎977-1870). The well-signed Charlottesville/Albemarle County **visitors bureau** (☎977-1783) is just south of I-64.

For its size, Charlottesville has quite a broad range of **accommodation**. The usual motels line Emmet Street (US-29) at the west end of town, the cheapest being the $40-a-night *Econo Lodge*, 400 Emmet Street (☎296-2104) and the nicest the $85-a-night *Sheraton* (☎973-2121) a mile north. **B&B** is available for around $50 in private homes through *Guesthouses* (☎979-7264) and at the *200 South Street Inn*, 200 South Street (☎979-0200).

The best **eating** and **drinking** is to be had near the university and in the downtown mall. Tucked away behind the row of pizza and burger places like *The Virginian*, 1521 W Main Street (☎293-2606), across from the campus, *Martha's Cafe*, 11 Elliewood Avenue (☎971-7530), serves up spinach lasagnes, crab cakes and Bass Ale on draught on a leafy front patio. In the downtown area, *Millers*, 109 W Main Street (☎971-8511), specialises in grilled meats and fish dishes and has live jazz most nights, and the *C&O Restaurant*, 515 E Water Street (☎971-7044), housed in an old railroad station, has bistro-style food in the humming bar and more upscale French nouvelle cuisine in the upstairs dining room. Virginia's best selection of wines and beers, plus a range of light meals, is on tap at the *Court Square Tavern*, 500 Court Square (☎296-6111), two blocks north of the mall.

As a college town, Charlottesville isn't short of **nightlife**, whether at cafes like the *Roasted Bean*, 110 N Fourth Street (☎977-JAVA), or in its two main nightclubs, *Zippers*, 1202 W Main Street (☎295-7060), and *Trax*, 127 S Eleventh Street (☎295-TRAX), both of which have nightly live bands.

Shenandoah National Park

SHENANDOAH NATIONAL PARK, which contains seemingly endless acres of dark forests, rocky deep ravines and precipitous, surging waterfalls, has one of the most unusual histories of any US national park. Far from being untouched for the past three hundred years, this "natural" landscape was created when hundreds of small family farms and homesteads were bought up by the state and federal governments during the Depression, and the land left to revert to its natural state.

One of the most scenic byways in the US, **Skyline Drive** is a thin ribbon of pavement curving along the crest of the Blue Ridge Mountains. It starts just off I-66 near the town of **Front Royal**, 75 miles west of DC, and winds south through the park giving great views over the Piedmont to the east and lovely Shenandoah Valley to the west.

The views are especially fine, and the crowds especially large, in the autumn, but any time of year you can get the best of the park's open spaces by following one of the many **hiking trails** that split off from the ridge. One favourite leaves from the parking area of *Big Meadows Lodge* (see over) in the southern half of the park and winds along to tumbling **Dark Hollow Falls**; another, leaving Skyline Drive at milemarker 45, climbs up a fairly treacherous incline to the top of **Old Rag Mountain** for 360° views out over the whole of Virginia and the Allegheny Mountains in the west. More ambitious hikers, or those who want to spend the night out in the backcountry, head for the **Appalachian Trail**; details on any of these hikes, or the required free overnight camping permit, can be picked up at either of the **visitor centres** (☎999-2266), located along Skyline Drive four miles beyond the north entrance and at milemarker 50, in the middle of the park.

Two rustic **lodges**, both near the middle of the park, offer food and beds. The northernmost and oldest, *Skyland Lodge*, opened in 1894, has cabins and more modern hotel rooms as well as a large restaurant with panoramic views; *Big Meadows Lodge*, ten miles south, has similar facilities, and is just next to the larger visitor centre. Prices vary from under $40 to over $100, depending upon type of room and time of year; for details contact *ARA Services* (☎743-5108 or ☎1-800/999-4714).

The Shenandoah Valley

While Skyline Drive and the Blue Ridge Parkway make an undeniably pretty route along the mountaintops, the small and characterful towns of the **Shenandoah Valley** down below are as rich in human history as any in Virginia. Many were left in ruins after the war, but have since been restored to their proud antebellum state, and numerous memorials, monuments and cemeteries line the back roads, surrounded by spacious horse farms and apple orchards.

Given its strategic importance and fertility, the Shenandoah Valley was inevitably one of the most fought-over battlegrounds in the Civil War, changing hands over seventy times at a cost of some 100,000 dead and maimed. The whole bloody story is told in evocative detail in the small but outstanding **museum** (daily 9am–5pm; $4) at the **New Market Battlefield**, just off I-81, thirty miles south of the I-66 junction. This was the scene of the legendary 1864 confrontation that involved a company of fourteen-year-old cadet-soldiers from the Virginia Military Institute.

Besides its Civil War history, the northern Shenandoah Valley also holds half a dozen of Virginia's many underground **limestone caverns**. All are privately owned and cost $4 to $10 to enter. You'll no doubt see billboards advertising each one as the best: the largest is **Luray Caverns**, twelve miles east of New Market. Further south, off Hwy-250 northwest of the town of Staunton, the **Museum of Frontier American Culture** (daily 9am–5pm; $4) brings to light how the various immigrants who settled here melded their traditions to develop a joint American culture. Most of the exhibits have to do with farming techniques and other somewhat mundane activities, but it's all engagingly presented and well worth a look.

Lexington

Though one of the region's smaller towns, **LEXINGTON**, in the heart of the Shenandoah Valley, definitely has the most to offer to visitors. From horse-drawn carriages parading along its quiet, brick-paved streets, to the fine rolling countryside all around, Lexington makes a great place to sit back and relax or, if you prefer, delve deep into Civil War and other military arcana at its small museums and memorials.

The most engaging of these, the **Lee Chapel** (Mon–Sat 9am–5pm, Sun 2–5pm; free), is on the attractive colonnaded campus of Washington and Lee University, a short walk north of the town centre. A commodious and sombre building, the chapel is named in honour of Confederate General Robert E Lee, who taught here after the Civil War. Behind the pulpit is a marble statue of Lee in repose, surrounded by an array of authentic battle flags; along with many members of his family, Lee is interred downstairs in the chapel crypt, and his trusted horse *Traveller* is buried just outside.

On the comparatively bland but formidable campus of the **Virginia Military Institute**, just east of the Lee Chapel, the Military Museum (Mon–Sat 9am–5pm; free) tells the story of the state-supported, male-only military academy which was founded in 1836 and has the dubious claim to fame of being the only university in US history to have sent its entire student body into battle. If possible, time your visit to coincide with the 4pm Friday full-dress parade – a bit like the changing of the guard, American-style – held on the field in front of the museum.

At the opposite end of the parade ground, the **George C Marshall Museum** (Mon–Sat 9am–5pm, Sun 2–5pm; free) documents the life of World War II US General and later Secretary of State George Marshall, whose plan for the reconstruction of post-war Europe earned him the Nobel Peace Prize in 1953.

The **Stonewall Jackson House**, 8 E Washington Street (Mon–Sat 9am–5pm; $3), is where the noted Confederate general and Virginia Military Institute philosophy professor lived for fifteen years before his death at the battle of Chancellorsville. His spartan brick townhouse is furnished as it was in the years before the war, and Stonewall himself is buried, along with hundreds of his fellow soldiers, in the Stonewall Jackson Memorial Cemetery off S Main Street.

Even if you're not thrilled by war stories, Lexington still makes a good stop, with its dozens of fine old homes; pick up a walking tour map and helpful hints from the **visitor centre** (daily 9am–5pm; ☎463-3777), 102 E Washington Street. The *Virginia House*, 722 S Main Street (☎463-3643), hard to find on the south side of town, serves up some of the best down-home **southern cooking** in the state; if your taste tends toward tofu, you'll probably prefer *Sprouts Natural Deli*, 110 W Washington Street (☎463-1163), across from the Washington and Lee campus. A block away stands Lexington's one remarkably cheap **place to stay**, Ms Ruth Rees' $5-a-night *Tourist Home*, 216 W Washington Street (☎463-3075); aside from the usual motels along the highways, another option is the comfy *Asherowe B&B*, 314 S Jefferson Street (☎463-4219).

WEST VIRGINIA

People who live in **WEST VIRGINIA** are only half joking when they call it the Ireland of the US. Generally poor and almost entirely rural – with the lowest per capita income, and the lowest crime rate, of any US state – it shares a similar history of exploitation by outside powers, with **timber** and **coal-mining** companies taking advantage of the rich natural resources while giving little in return. But, quite apart from the almost Third World deprivation which endures in some areas (and which, along with John Denver songs and the barefoot hillbillies supposed to inhabit its backwoods reaches, still colours most outsiders' preconceptions of the state), West Virginia is also, in places at least, an incredibly beautiful land, holding the longest whitewater rivers and most extensive wilderness areas in the eastern US. The extreme topography which has historically kept its inhabitants isolated from the outside world now makes it a popular destination for hikers and outdoors enthusiasts, and the moonshiners of old have been replaced by ski instructors and mountain bike guides.

After it hived itself off from Confederate Virginia in the middle of the Civil War – a separation which the other Virginia has yet to recognise officially – it took many years for West Virginia to develop a political and economic identity of its own. Around the turn of the century, when railroads from the East Coast first reached into the mountainous interior, timber companies clear-cut stand after stand of forest, setting up a succession of mill towns, each of which was dismantled in its turn when they moved on somewhere new – **Cass**, now preserved within the Allegheny National Forest, is one of the few that was left intact. Later on, coal-mining conglomerates, especially in the

The telephone **area code** for the entire state of West Virginia is ☎304.

south, perfected the "company town" approach, wherein the basic practice was to pay workers a little bit less each month than the amount they owed for their company-provided food and lodging. Coal companies still exert immense power in West Virginia, but the real key to the state's future prosperity is tourism, which in places now accounts for over half their income.

The most popular destination, the restored 1850s town of **Harpers Ferry**, is barely in West Virginia at all, standing just over the broad rivers which form its Maryland and Virginia borders. To the west, the **Allegheny Mountains** stretch for over 150 miles; more than a million acres of hardwood forest rival New England for brilliant autumn colour. West Virginia's oldest and most attractive town, **Lewisburg**, sits just off I-64 at the mountains' southern foot, while the capital, **Charleston**, lies in the comparatively flat Ohio River valley of the west.

Getting Around West Virginia

With its many mountains and rivers making straight, flat roads virtually non-existent, getting around West Virginia is as much a part of its attraction as is any specific destination – a bike and a stout pair of legs, or a motorcycle, would be ideal, but a car or some form of your own transport is pretty much necessary if you really want to see the state. *Greyhound* is basically useless, and *Amtrak*, apart from serving Harpers Ferry from Washington DC, has only one, albeit spectacular, route across the state, running through the New River Gorge to the capital, Charleston.

Harpers Ferry and Around

HARPERS FERRY, a ruggedly sited eighteenth-century town now restored as a national historic park, is many people's first and only look at West Virginia. It climbs up steep hillsides above the confluence of the Potomac and Shenandoah rivers, many of its forty-odd brick and stone buildings dating from the days when George Washington set up the country's first **national munitions factory** here to arm the young Republic. Throughout the mid-1800s Harpers Ferry was a thriving industrial complex, home to some five thousand workers and linked with the capital by the B&O Railroad and the Chesapeake & Ohio Canal, but after suffering the ravages of the Civil War and a series of torrential floods it was all but abandoned, the empty shells of its homes and factories slowly becoming overgrown by the dense forest which covers the surrounding hills. Almost all of Harpers Ferry has since been reconstructed as an outdoor museum, with a stunning combination of historical importance and natural beauty.

However pretty Harpers Ferry is – and in the autumn, when the leaves blaze with colour, it's hard to imagine a more picture-perfect setting – it's the town's unique place in US history that attracts most visitors. Like most mid-Atlantic towns, it had its share of Civil War experiences, but the years immediately before the outbreak of war are what is remembered here: specifically, anti-slavery revolutionary (and borderline psychotic) **John Brown**'s raid on the huge US arsenal. In the hope of fomenting a widespread slave revolt, Brown and 21 other abolitionist radicals, including two of his sons and five black men, seized the munitions factory and its large store of weapons on the night of October 16 1859. They held out for two days before US troops, under the command of Robert E Lee, stormed the buildings, killing many of the raiders and capturing Brown, who was taken to nearby Charles Town, tried, and convicted of treason and hanged. The near-rebellion rocked the already fragmented nation, and is seen as the clearest foreshadowing of the Civil War which broke out just sixteen months later.

Harpers Ferry was devastated during the Civil War – the arsenal buildings were burned in 1861 to keep the weapons out of Confederate hands, and in 1862 Stonewall Jackson captured the town and 12,500 Union soldiers – and it never really got back on its feet. Enough of the original buildings and cobbled streets survive to give a good sense of how things used to be, and the restoration project has so far managed to re-create the townscape without making it feel too much like a theme park.

Seeing Harpers Ferry

As the only public transport to Harpers Ferry, a **train** from DC, arrives at the awkward hour of 7pm, almost everyone who comes here drives. Parking is virtually banned in the old town area, so your point of arrival is likely to be the large **visitor centre** (daily 9am–5pm) along US-340, where you'll be expected to pay the $2 per person, $5 per car entry fee. Shuttle buses from there take you down to the old town, dropping off outside the balconied old **Stagecoach Inn**, at the end of gas-lit Shenandoah Street in the heart of the restored area; inside there's an information desk with maps and a small book-shop. Across the street, in the **Master Armorer's House**, a series of displays will tell you everything about gun-making; adjacent buildings include a restored blacksmith's shop, a general store and a tavern, often peopled with costumed guides who act out and describe events from the town's history.

John Brown's **fort** – actually the armoury's engine room where he and his raiders were captured – originally stood directly across from the tavern, and has been rebuilt a block away, near the point where the rivers meet. Other structures along **High Street** house exhibits on the Civil War and local black history, and between them a set of stone steps climbs up through the residential area to the **Harper House**, built in 1782 and preserved as a typical worker's rooming house of the period.

A footpath continues uphill past overgrown churchyards hemmed in by dry-stone walls to **Jefferson Rock**, a huge grey boulder giving a great view over the two rivers – Thomas Jefferson said that the outlook was worth a voyage across the Atlantic. If you're in the mood for a longer hike, two trails lead onwards into the surrounding forest: the **Appalachian Trail** continues from Jefferson Rock across the Shenandoah River into the **Blue Ridge Mountains** of Virginia, while the **Maryland Heights Trail** makes a four-mile round-trip around the headlands across the Potomac River.

Around Harpers Ferry

Among small towns worth seeing nearby is **Charles Town**, four miles south of Harpers Ferry on US-340, where John Brown was tried and hanged; the **Jefferson County Museum** (Mon–Sat 10am–4pm; free), on the corner of Washington and Samuel streets, tells the story of his trial, conviction, and execution, and remembers his last words: "I, John Brown, am now quite certain that the crimes of this guilty land will never be purged away but with blood." The cosy village of **Shepherdstown**, along the Potomac ten miles to the north, is prettier and better for wandering, its quaint ancient shops and cafes looking across the river to Maryland's bloody **Antietam Battlefield** (see p.331).

Further afield, and of more salubrious interest, is the old spa town of **Berkeley Springs**, now preserved intact as a state historic park, thirty miles west of Harpers Ferry on Hwy-9, seven miles south of I-70. The nearest early America ever came to having resorts like Bath in England, Berkeley Springs was a favourite summer retreat of the colonial elite – George Washington and Lord Fairfax were among the regulars who came here to "take the waters" – and assorted massage and steam bath treatments are still available in its many health farms. In summer, you can soak yourself in the old **Roman Baths**, in active use since 1815 and now run by the state. The town's **central square** is leafy and green, with footpaths fanning out in all directions, one climbing the hill up to **Berkeley Castle**, a fortress-like mid-Victorian folly above the town that origi-nally held a large ballroom and is now used mostly for weddings.

Harpers Ferry Practicalities

As it's a popular day out from Washington DC (and also further-flung places like Pittsburgh and Philadelphia), Harpers Ferry is well prepared for tourists, with a number of Olde Worlde **cafes** lining High Street up from the historic area – both the *Mountain House Cafe* (☎535-2339) and the *Garden of Food* (☎535-2202) are good and relatively inexpensive. If you want to **spend the night**, dozens of amiable $65-a-night B&Bs are sprinkled around the region, like the *Highlawn Inn*, 304 Market Street (258-5700), or the *Manor Inn*, 415 Fairfax Street (☎258-1552), both in Berkeley Springs. In Harpers Ferry itself, the 100-year-old *Hilltop House Hotel and Restaurant* on Ridge Street (☎535-2132 or ☎1-800/338-8319) may be showing its age, but still has reasonable prices (doubles $55) and the best views. Cheaper beds can be had at the *Comfort Inn* (☎535-6391 or ☎1-800/228-5150) on US-340, and there's lots of **camping** along the Potomac River in the C&O Canal Historic Park. The **park visitor centre** has further details, as does the Jefferson County tourist bureau (☎535-2627 or ☎1-800/848-TOUR) across US-340.

The Allegheny Mountains

Considering that it's the most extensive wilderness area on the East Coast, within a few hours' drive of a dozen big cities, surprisingly few people have heard about, much less bother to visit, the backcountry reaches of the **Allegheny Mountains**, West Virginia's segment of the Appalachian chain. The entire 140-mile crest is protected as part of the **Monongahela National Forest**, within which numerous state parks highlight the most spectacular sights. There are no cities and few towns, public transport is non-existent and not much goes on after dark – to give an idea of how rural it is, whole counties do without a single traffic light – but if you like to backpack, ski, cycle, climb, canoe or just wander around the great outdoors, the Alleghenies are well worth a look. For maps and more detailed information, contact the state tourist office (see p.18) or the Monongahela National Forest, 200 Sycamore Street, Elkins, WV 26253 (☎636-1800).

Blackwater Falls, the Canaan Valley and Seneca Rocks

Some of the most beautiful stretches of the Monongahela National Forest are in the northern corner of the state, where the thundering torrents of the **Blackwater Falls** pour over a sixty-foot limestone cliff before crashing down through a steeply walled canyon. South from here spreads the dense maple, oak, walnut and birch forest of broad **Canaan Valley**, while to the east rise the barren sub-arctic highlands of the **Dolly Sods Wilderness**, the whole area criss-crossed by hiking, cycling and skiing trails.

Rising up at the far end of the Canaan Valley, the state's highest point, the 4861ft **Spruce Knob**, stands out over the headwaters of the Potomac River. Even more impressive views can be had from the top of **Seneca Rocks**, eight miles to the northwest, whose one-thousand-foot limestone cliffs are commonly considered to present the most challenging rock-climb on the East Coast. There's a good trail around the back of the North Peak if you want to take the easy way up, and the helpful **visitor centre** (daily 9am–5.30pm in summer, Sat & Sun only in winter; ☎257-4488) here, at the junction of US-33 and Hwy-28, has details of outdoor recreation opportunities in the entire region.

The old logging town of **Davis** (population 868), just east of US-219 at the north end of the Canaan Valley, makes a good base from which to tour the area, with a couple of **places to stay** – the *Bright Morning Inn* (☎259-5119) on Williams Avenue doubles as the town cafe, and the *Davis Inn* (☎259-5142) has basic motel rooms for around $30. Among local **outdoor guides and outfitters**, the *Blackwater Outdoor Center* (☎259-5117) runs rafting, caving and rock-climbing trips; *Blackwater Bikes* (☎259-5286) rent out mountain bikes and offer off-road tours; and *Timberline Resort* (☎866-4801) has the state's largest downhill ski area. For more information, contact the Tucker County **visitor centre** (☎259-5315 or ☎1-800/782-2775).

Elkins and the Augusta Festival

One of the few ways visitors can experience the vibrant folkways of the West Virginia mountains is by taking part in the summer-long **Augusta Festival**, an annual celebration of arts, crafts and Appalachian culture. Held throughout July and August, just west of the Canaan Valley in **ELKINS**, the biggest town in northern West Virginia, the festival offers public workshops in such diverse down-home pursuits as banjo-playing, blacksmithing, quiltmaking and folk dancing, and after dark performers get together for a nightly hoe-down, featuring storytellers, bluegrass bands and general good times.

Find out more from the **Augusta Heritage Center**, part of Davis and Elkins College, 100 Sycamore Street, Elkins, WV 26241 (☎636-1903), or stop into the *Starr Cafe and Bookshop*, 224 Davis Avenue (☎636-7273) in the centre of town.

Pocahontas County

The southern half of the Monongahela National Forest is contained within hilly **Pocahontas County**, known as "the birthplace of rivers" because it holds the headwaters of the Greenbrier, Cheat, Gauley and other great West Virginia rivers. Like most of the Alleghenies, it's a mountainous, fairly inaccessible region – two roads, US-219 and Hwy-92, wind north-to-south, with a handful of narrow tracks twisting between them – offering outstanding outdoor recreation as well as endless scenic vistas.

Besides gorgeous scenery, Pocahontas County is also home to the **Cass Scenic Railroad**, a restored, steam-powered logging railroad built in 1902. Running on narrow-gauge tracks, the chugging *Shay* locomotive carries visitors up to the top of 4842ft Bald Knob on a converted logging train, starting at the old lumber-mill village of **CASS**, five miles west of Hwy-28 near the town of **Greenbank** (Tues–Sun at 11am, 1pm and 3pm, summer only; $8; ☎456-4300). Cass has been preserved in its entirety as a historic park, where you can wander around the old loggers' cabins and company store, or stay the night in the cosy *Shay Inn B&B* (☎456-4652), for $45.

If you're feeling energetic, walk the five miles downhill from Cass along the tracks to the start of the cycle-friendly **Greenbrier River Trail**, which follows the river and the railroad grade for 75 miles, coming out near the town of Lewisburg (see below). Another way to go is to rent a **mountain bike** from *Elk River Touring Center* (☎572-3771), fifteen miles north of **Marlinton**, the county seat, off US-219 in the hamlet of **Slatyfork**, and set off into the mountains. They also run shuttle service to the trailheads and organise backcountry cycling trips and ski tours in winter, and they have a year-round $45-a-night **hotel** with a hot tub and good-value restaurant. Pocahontas County **tourist bureau** (☎799-4636 or ☎1-800/336-7009) can help out with maps.

The other main attraction in this part of the Alleghenies is the birthplace of **Pearl S Buck**, author of *The Good Earth* and the only American woman to win the Nobel Prize for Literature. Her home at **Hillsboro**, on US-219 halfway between Marlinton and Lewisburg, is packed with memorabilia of her West Virginia upbringing; various special events are planned for 1992, the centenary of her birth.

Lewisburg and the Greenbrier Resort

Located just off I-64 on the southern edge of the Monongahela National Forest wilderness, **LEWISBURG** is the archetypal West Virginia town, its few square blocks of old buildings surrounded by rich pastureland, with good roads allowing quick access to the wilder mountain reaches. Originally a frontier outpost during the Indian Wars of the 1770s, Lewisburg was greatly prized during the Civil War for its location at the head of the Greenbrier Valley, but nowadays its attractions are those of a classic American small town, where everyone seems to know everyone else, and where the houses and shops have remained in the same hands for generations.

Washington Street, the four-block business district, is lined on both sides by brick-fronted early nineteenth-century houses, and makes for pleasant wandering; if you want to pick up on local colour, stop in at no. 106, which has been a two-chair barber shop for over a hundred years. A block away, in a small park at 200 N Jefferson Street, stands the oldest surviving structure in Lewisburg, a rough-hewn limestone shed built in 1770 to protect the still-flowing freshwater spring.

The **visitor centre**, at 105 Church Street (☎645-1000), hands out walking tour maps of the town, and can suggest driving tours around Greenbrier Valley. They also can put you in touch with various cosy **hotels**, such as the $55-a-night *General Lewis Inn*, 301 E Washington Street (☎645-2600), and suggest places to **eat**, like the innovative and inexpensive *Blue Moon Cafe* at 110 S Jefferson Street (☎645-4548).

Just east of Lewisburg, outside the faded spa of **White Sulphur Springs**, some two dozen US presidents – plus vice-president **Dan Quayle**, who goes whitewater rafting on nearby Gauley River – have escaped the pressures of politics in *The Greenbrier* (☎536-1110 or ☎1-800/624-6070). The grandest, plushest and most expensive hotel in West Virginia, it's five-star all the way, from the pillared entrance hall to the 6500 acres of lush grounds and golf courses. Needless to say it's incredibly pricey; stop in for a drink or a fine meal (or just to gape) if you can't afford the $250-a-night (and up) room rates.

The New River Gorge

One of West Virginia's most spectacular river canyons, the **New River Gorge**, lies just thirty miles west of Lewisburg along I-64. Now protected as a national park, and stretching for over fifty miles, the thousand-foot cleft was carved through the limestone West Virginia mountains by the New River – despite its name, one of the oldest rivers in North America. Apart from one daily train (see below), there's no easy access to most of the gorge – to see it, you have to get out on the water, with the help of any of over fifty professional rafting companies – but visitor centres located near the most impressive spots give details of recreation opportunities. Just off US-19 in **Fayetteville**, the new **Canyon Rim Visitor Center** sits alongside the New River Gorge Bridge, a single-span steel arch that rises nine hundred feet above the river; the smaller **Grandview Visitor Center** is located at an elbow bend in the river, five miles north of I-64 near Beckley.

Fortunately for car-less travellers, *Amtrak* trains from Washington DC pass right through the gorge on one of the most stunning railway journeys in the East. Though the ride itself is memorable enough, for a close-up look you can get off at the southern end of the gorge at the turn-of-the-century railroad town of **HINTON**. It's the train's only stop, and is a fascinating, if somewhat dilapidated remnant of the glory days of railroads. This almost perfectly preserved purpose-built company town – the National Park Service intends someday to restore it as a living museum – is beautifully sited, its brick-paved streets angling up from the water and lined by dozens of grand civic buildings as well as row after row of slowly decaying workers' houses. A walking tour map of Hinton is available from the Chamber of Commerce, 206 Temple Street (☎466-5420).

Although the town has definitely seen better days, Hinton still makes a workable base for visitors to the gorge, with a pair of $30-a-night **motels**, the *Coast-to-Coast* (☎466-2040) and the *Sandman* (☎466-1700), and a couple of riverfront taverns on Hwy-20 just south of town. Local **river-rafting** firms include *New River Tours* (☎466-2288 or ☎1-800/292-0880) and *Cantrell Canoes* (☎466-0595).

Charleston

After leaving the gorge, the New River flows west into the Ohio and eventually the Mississippi River, but not before passing through **CHARLESTON**, West Virginia's state capital and largest city. Charleston just isn't a place many people set out to visit, mainly because there's not very much to see or do: the riverfront **state capitol**, designed by Lincoln Memorial architect Cass Gilbert and completed in 1932, is pleasant enough, and on the grounds there's a small monument to black activist Booker T

Washington, but nothing really grabs you. The **West Virginia Cultural Center** (Mon–Fri 9am–9pm, Sat, Sun 1pm–9pm; free), next to the capitol, showcases traditional West Virginia culture, especially during the annual **Vandalia Festival**, Appalachia's largest celebration of folk arts and crafts, held every Memorial Day weekend and highlighted by live bluegrass music and lively tall-tale-telling contests.

MARYLAND

From its foundation as the sole Catholic colony in strongly Protestant America, to its role as the northernmost slave state, not to mention its irregular topography, **MARYLAND** has always been unusual. Even within its relatively small area, it has something of a split personality, ranging from its bustling urban centre, **Baltimore**, to Appalachian hill country and sleepy fishing villages arrayed around the historic and geographic heart, the **Chesapeake Bay**. Once one of the most productive fishing areas in the world, the Chesapeake has recently been brought back from the brink of complete annihilation due to pollution and overfishing – its abundant oyster stocks are a thing of the past, but its other delicacies, **soft-shell blue crabs**, are more plentiful than ever – and now supports a diverse, decentralised economy, buoyed by the hundreds of weekend sailors who cruise from one to another of its colonial-era towns.

Maryland's heritage isn't quite as impressive as Virginia's, and it has nowhere near as many historic sites. The state provided some of the most fearless fighters during the Revolutionary War, but few battles were fought on its soil. Maryland's main claim to fame occurred during what the Americans call the War of 1812 – a last-ditch effort by British military to wrest back the colonies, in which they burned much of Washington DC. One of the main British aims in this attack, which actually took place in 1814, was to destroy the shipyards at Baltimore. The British forces failed, having been held off by a small fort at the harbour's mouth; the fort's resistance inspired an onlooker, Francis Scott Key, to write the words to the **Star-Spangled Banner**, which has since been adopted as the US national anthem.

Maryland's largest city is the busy port of **Baltimore**, a quirky and engaging metropolis that has a couple of very good museums and an extensive and enjoyable urban waterfront. **Western Maryland** stretches for over a hundred miles to the Appalachian foothills, its rolling farmlands noteworthy chiefly for the Civil War battlefield at **Antietam**. Just twenty miles south of Baltimore, along the Chesapeake Bay, sits picturesque **Annapolis**, which stakes a claim to being the oldest city in the US – founded in 1649, it has served as Maryland's capital since 1694. Some of Maryland's most worthwhile destinations, from the pretty fishing and yachting town of **St Michaels** to the untouched wilderness of **Assateague Island**, are across the Chesapeake Bay on the eastern shore, connected to the rest of the state by the US-50 bridge but otherwise still a world apart – except for the sprawling summertime resort of **Ocean City**.

Getting Around Maryland

While it's not all that easy to do, the best way to get around Maryland is by **boat**, sailing around the gorgeous Chesapeake Bay. If you lack either the money or the good luck (chancing upon a skipper who needs a crew, for example), you can hop aboard the *Chesapeake Flyer* **catamaran** (☎639-7241) which cruises the bay from Baltimore to Annapolis and eastern shore towns of St Michaels and Rock Hall. **Cycling** is also a good option, especially on the eastern shore, where the roads are wide shouldered and little travelled, winding through cornfields from one colonial-era hamlet to another – the state tourist office (see p.18) puts out an excellent free map of the safest and most scenic routes. Otherwise, you're likely to be getting around by car – the only useful **public transport** in the state is between Baltimore and Annapolis.

Baltimore

I would never want to live anywhere but Baltimore. You can look far and wide, but you'll never discover a stranger city with such extreme style. It's as if every eccentric in the South decided to move north, ran out of gas in Baltimore, and decided to stay.

John Waters, *Shock Value*

BALTIMORE is among the more enjoyable stops on the East Coast. It may not have a Golden Gate Bridge or a Statue of Liberty, or even a Liberty Bell, but its closely knit neighbourhoods and historic quarters provide an engaging (and comparatively inexpensive) backdrop to many diverse attractions – like the **National Aquarium**, showpiece of the resurrected Inner Harbor **waterfront** – and top-rated **museums**, which cover everything from fine arts to black history to urban archaeology. That Baltimore has been home to such diverse figures as writers Edgar Allan Poe and Anne Tyler and civil rights activists Frederick Douglass and Thurgood Marshall goes some way in explaining its sometimes bizarrely varied character, but it's still hard to pin down exactly what makes it such an engaging city to visit, and to live in.

Arrival and Information

The spacious and modern **Baltimore–Washington International Airport** (BWI), ten miles south of the city centre and 25 miles northeast of Washington DC, is one of the busier East Coast hubs, with flights from all over the US and around the world. *Airport Shuttle* vans ($5) into Baltimore stop outside the terminal every twenty minutes and take around half an hour to reach downtown. **Taxis** cost around $20. *Amtrak* **trains** from the north stop every hour or so at the restored **Pennsylvania Station**, half a mile north of downtown at 1525 N Charles Street (☎539-2112), while *MARC* commuter trains (☎859-7400 or ☎1-800/325-RAIL) from DC stop at BWI airport before continuing on into the Camden Yards station south of downtown. *Greyhound* pulls in on the west side of downtown at 210 W Fayette Street (☎744-9311 or ☎931-4000).

Pick up free maps and the thrice-yearly *Quick City* visitors guide at the **Baltimore Area Convention and Visitors Association**, 1 E Pratt Street (☎837-4636 or ☎1-800/282-6632), across from the Inner Harbor, or their booths at the airport and train station.

Getting Around

Because the city is so compact – everything of interest is within a mile of the centre – you could get around quite happily on foot. If the weather's bad, or you get worn out, motorised **trolleys** (Mon–Sat 11am–7pm; 25¢) cruise the city on two circuits, one up and down Charles Street from Penn Station to the Inner Harbor, and another east from downtown to Fell's Point. A **water taxi** ($3.25 for an all-day pass) nips between the Inner Harbor and Fell's Point. The city-operated *MTA* bus, subway and light-rail system is more useful for commuters than for visitors, but runs 24 hours and costs $1. **Taxis** include *Yellow Cab* (☎685-1212) and *Diamond Cab* (☎947-3333).

Downtown Baltimore

When the whole of **downtown Baltimore** burned to the ground in 1904, everything from the waterfront to Mount Vernon was destroyed, except for the domed 1867 **City Hall**, three blocks east of Charles Street, the main business strip. Though Baltimore quickly rebuilt, the downtown area never recovered much character, and it's unlikely you'll want to spend much time here. That said, a few very different sorts of places give

The telephone **area code** for Baltimore is ☎410.

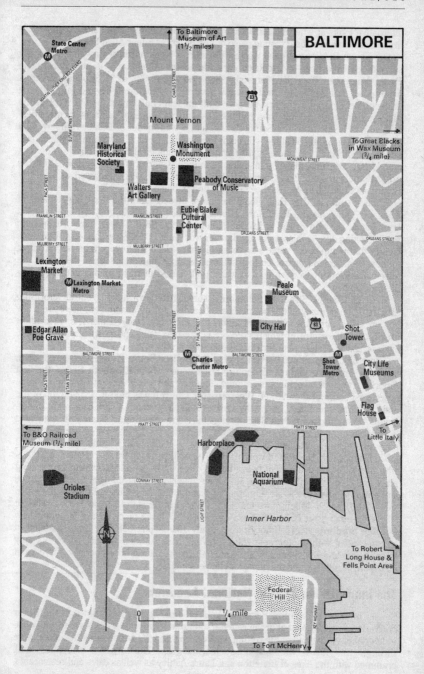

BALTIMORE

State Center Metro

To Baltimore Museum of Art (1½ miles)

MARTIN LUTHER KING BOULEVARD

EUTAW STREET

CHARLES STREET

Mount Vernon

To Great Blacks in Wax Museum (¾ mile)

Maryland Historical Society

Washington Monument

MONUMENT STREET

PACA STREET

Walters Art Gallery

Peabody Conservatory of Music

FRANKLIN STREET

FRANKLIN STREET

Eubie Blake Cultural Center

ORLEANS STREET

ORLEANS STREET

MULBERRY STREET

MULBERRY STREET

ST PAUL STREET

Lexington Market

Peale Museum

Lexington Market Metro

CHARLES STREET

ST PAUL STREET

City Hall

Shot Tower

Edgar Allan Poe Grave

Shot Tower Metro

City Life Museums

BALTIMORE STREET

BALTIMORE STREET

Charles Center Metro

PACA STREET

EUTAW STREET

LIGHT STREET

Flag House

To B&O Railroad Museum (½ mile)

PRATT STREET

PRATT STREET

To Little Italy

Harborplace

Orioles Stadium

CONWAY STREET

National Aquarium

LIGHT STREET

Inner Harbor

N

To Robert Long House & Fells Point Area

0   ¼ mile

Federal Hill

KEY HIGHWAY

To Fort McHenry

alternative looks at what makes Baltimore tick, from old industrial sites to America's first museum and the final resting place of horror writer Edgar Allan Poe.

Downtown Baltimore's most worthwhile stop, a block north of City Hall, is usually surrounded by a fleet of armoured cars (the *Brinks-Mat* garage is next door). The **Peale Museum** (Tues–Sat 10am–5pm, Sun noon–5pm; $2), at 225 Holiday Street, is living proof that Baltimore's taste for the bizarre goes back well beyond John Waters, or even Poe. Housed in the first purpose-built museum building in the US, it traces the history of museum-making, from eighteenth-century European "cabinets of curiosities" – shrunken heads from the South Pacific, and a wax model of Daniel Lambert, who died in 1809 weighing 53 stone – through the hyper-hype of P T Barnum's freak shows, and ends with the more didactic displays of anthropological tidbits – Native American and African artefacts, mainly – installed by founder Charles Willson Peale in 1814. His original museum didn't survive long, and the building was later used as an early Baltimore City Hall as well as the country's first public school for black children.

A block south of City Hall, along Baltimore Street, stand the decaying remains of what was known as the **Baltimore Block,** the East Coast's largest red light district. Looming at the end of the strip, the 215ft red-brick **Shot Tower** (daily 10am–4pm; free), looking like a misplaced lighthouse, was built in 1828 as part of a munitions factory that pumped out some six thousand tons of lead shot every year: tiny drops of molten lead became nearly perfect spheres as they plummeted from the top of the tower, dropping into a deep pool of water that caused them to solidify without losing their ideal shape.

West of Charles Street is Baltimore's somewhat down-at-heel central **shopping** district. Though many of the premises are boarded up and abandoned, there are a few holdouts, including the oldest and loudest of the city's covered markets, **Lexington Market**, at the centre of which *Faidley's* is the best (and cheapest) place to sample oysters, clams, crabs and other Chesapeake Bay produce.

Three blocks up, at 600 N Paca Street, the **Mother Seton House** (Sat–Sun 1–4pm; free) is a small, late eighteenth-century brick house where **Elizabeth Seton**, the first American woman to achieve sainthood, founded the Daughters of Charity Catholic order. Just south of the market, **Westminster Church** was built in 1852 on top of the main Baltimore cemetery, and many ornate tombs now stand in dark catacombs underneath. Among the prominent Baltimoreans buried here is **Edgar Allan Poe**, who lived in Baltimore for three years in the 1830s, marrying his 13-year-old cousin and beginning a career in journalism before moving on to Richmond, Virginia (see p.305 and p.326 for more on his life and works). In 1849, while passing through Baltimore, Poe – who had an obsessive fear of being buried alive – was found incoherent in a polling place and died soon afterwards. In 1875 his remains were moved from a pauper's grave and entombed within the stone memorial that stands along Green Street on the north side of the church. Much more fun than either of these is the narrow brick rowhouse where baseball great **Babe Ruth** was born in 1895, just a block east of the brand-new **Orioles Stadium** at 216 Emory Street (daily 10am–5pm; $3). The house is filled to bursting point with photographs, film clips and baseball memorabilia, which not only trace the life and achievements of the much-loved home-run hitter, but also serve as an enjoyable introduction to the game and its personalities.

The Inner Harbor and the National Aquarium

Sooner or later, if you're in Baltimore you're bound to be drawn down to the **Inner Harbor**, a success story of urban regeneration that leaves other cities green with post-industrial envy. Instead of the rotting wharves and derelict warehouses that stood here through the 1970s, the sparkling steel-and-glass **Harborplace** shopping mall, crammed with the likes of Benetton and Laura Ashley as well as cafes and restaurants, is now the city's pride and joy, swarming day and night with tourists and locals. Unlike Covent Garden, or Faneuil Hall in Boston, nothing here dates from before the rebuilding, but it's still quite an enjoyable place, the waterfront promenade enlivened by busking guitar players and the occasional fire-eating juggler.

To lend an air of authenticity, remnants from the city's proud maritime past have been assembled in the Inner Harbor, including the graceful **USS Constellation** (daily 10am–6pm; $2), an eighteenth-century, Baltimore-built frigate that was the US Navy's first ship. Another collection of ships – a Coast Guard cutter that survived Pearl Harbor, a Chesapeake Bay lightship, and a World War II submarine – make up the less-than-riveting **Baltimore Maritime Museum** (daily 9.30am–5pm; $3) on the next pier.

The National Aquarium

Far and away the biggest tourist attraction in Baltimore – on national holidays it rivals Florida's Walt Disney World as the most popular destination in the US – the **National Aquarium** (Mon–Thurs 9am–5pm, Fri–Sun 9am–8pm; $8.95) is certainly well worth seeing, so long as you avoid the weekend throngs. The main exhibition building, a rather grey, 1970s concrete space with a confusing jumble of escalators and ramps, rises in levels from a tankful of bat rays past a simulated South Pacific reef up to the rooftop rainforest garden, which emphasises the importance of the rainforest ecosystem in the greater scheme of things. From here, another ramp winds down past the **Open Ocean Exhibit**, which features a number of slow-moving sharks.

While the displays in the main building are generally educational if not all that innovative or thought provoking, the separate **Marine Mammal Pavilion**, at the end of an adjacent pier, is a lot more entertaining: this is where the aquarium's trained **dolphins** and beluga **whales** are put through their paces. Half-hour shows are given every ninety minutes, with the best views to be had from either side, where transparent acrylic panels allow you to watch the animals above and below the water as they perform a standard array of tail-walking, breaching, and spitting water into the audience.

Incidentally, despite the "national" in its name, this is a privately run, profit-making institution – a clever Maryland politician had a special decree passed in Congress so that it could be called the National Aquarium.

Mount Vernon

Baltimore's high-brow heart is just north of downtown on the shallow rise known as **Mount Vernon**, where a couple of good museums sit among rows of eighteenth-century brick townhouses. Baltimore's most elegant quarter takes its name from the country home of the first US president, George Washington, whose likeness tops the 165ft marble column of the **Washington Monument** at the centre of the district at Charles Street and Monument Place. Next to the aspirational spire of the sham-Gothic Mount Vernon Methodist Church, the monument is set in a small leafy park, and you can climb to the top for a great view over the city.

At the foot of the monument, the solemn stone facade of the Peabody Conservatory of Music hides one of the city's best interior spaces: the beautiful, skylit atrium of the **Peabody Library** (Mon–Fri 9am–3pm; free). Five tiers of intricate, wrought-iron balconies rise above ground floor displays of over a hundred sixteenth-century books, including a wonderfully illustrated 1555 edition of Boccaccio's *Decamarone* and a 1493 printing of the *Nuremburg Chronicles*. Two blocks west of the monument, the **Maryland Historical Society museum** (Tues–Sat 10am–5pm, Sun 1–5pm; $2.50) has a fairly tame collection of portraits of Maryland society and documents tracing local history, though its antique-filled chambers do give a strong sense of the maritime wealth created here through nineteenth-century trade. A small room off the lobby holds some nifty models of Chesapeake Bay boats, and upstairs the "War of 1812 Gallery" displays the original manuscript of the lyrics to the *Star-Spangled Banner*.

Walters Art Gallery

Baltimore's best museum, the **Walters Art Gallery** (Tues–Sun 11am–5pm; $3, free Wed), on Charles Street a block south of the Washington Monument, provides a comprehensive survey of art from ancient statuary up through French Impressionist painting. Its core is a large sculpture court, modelled upon an Italian Renaissance palazzo, beyond which a series of modern galleries show off Greek and Roman antiquities, medieval illuminated manuscripts, Islamic ceramics and some very fine Byzantine silver. The top floor has the oddest organisation, with pre-Columbian stone carvings displayed in a narrow corridor, at the end of a grand hall filled with late nineteenth-century paintings, including Manet's beer-drinking *At the Cafe*.

Almost everything on show was bought by William Walters, one of the first and foremost US collectors of **Chinese** and **Southeast Asian** art. The newly restored **Hackerman House** holds some especially fine pieces, including a roomful of Chinese jade figurines, a Ming dynasty handscroll, some lovely Japanese prints and a pair of polychrome and gilt temple doors, carved to look like peacock feathers. The prime exhibit is a seventh-century lacquered wood statue of a surprisingly svelte Buddha – perhaps the oldest such image in the world.

The City Life Museums, Little Italy and Fells Point

A quarter of a mile east of downtown and the Inner Harbor, across the busy Falls Expressway, four small city-operated museums at 800 E Lombard Street, known collectively as the **Baltimore City Life Museums**, delve into some less frequently charted corners of history (Tues–Sat 10am–4pm, Sun noon–4pm; $4, free Sat morning). The luxurious 1820s **Carroll Mansion**, home of Charles Carroll, a signatory of the US Declaration of Independence, contrasts with the **1840 House**, a reconstructed working-class cottage in which costumed guides gives demonstrations of the domestic life of the time. The **Courtyard Exhibition Center** traces the various strands involved in the revitalization of Baltimore's declining waterfront, and the **Center for Urban Archaeology** has practising archaeologists on hand to talk about the various digs going on in the Baltimore area. The nearby but separate **Flag House** and **1812 Museum** (Mon–Sat 10am–4pm; $2) was where Mary Pickersgill in 1813 sewed the 30-by-45-foot US flag which inspired Francis Scott Key to write the *Star-Spangled Banner*. The actual banner is now in the Museum of American History in Washington DC, but the house is full of various patriotic tributes.

The densely tangled streets of **Little Italy**, a still strongly Italian neighbourhood, spread to the south and east. Besides dozens of usually very good Italian restaurants and cafes, the area also holds some of Baltimore's trademark stone-fronted rowhouses, almost all of them with highly polished marble steps. As a sort of traditional local substitute for air-conditioning, in the heat of summer people move their furniture outdoors, thereby turning each entire street into an extended front room.

Beyond Little Italy, and separated from the renovated waterfront of the Inner Harbor by acres of derelict wharves and warehouses, stands Baltimore's oldest and liveliest quarter, **Fells Point**. Projecting into the main harbour, the deepwater frontage of Fells Point made it the heart of the city's extensive shipbuilding industry; the shipyards are long gone, but the many old bars and pubs have hung on to form one of the best nightlife districts in the country (see below for details). Specific places of interest are hard to pinpoint, though the **Pink Flamingoes** junk shop owned and run by Edith Massey, inspiration for many of director John Waters' stranger films, was at 728 S Broadway, a block from the water; it's now a novelty shop specialising in Divine memorabilia.

Around Baltimore

The **B&O Railroad Museum** (Wed–Sun 10am–4pm; $4) at 901 W Pratt Street, just half a mile west of the Inner Harbor, should not be missed by anyone with even a passing interest in early railways. Founded in 1827, the B&O grew into the first large-scale railway in the US, its trains running all over the eastern seaboard. The museum, housed in an 1830 passenger station and adjacent roundhouse, is the largest in the country, with dozens of ornate carriages, including some wacky parasol-covered early models, and row upon row of locomotives, from steam engines to sleek 1940s diesels.

Perhaps the most unusual museum in Baltimore, in ethos and effect if not in presentation, is about a mile northeast of the centre, in an old fire station off Broadway at 1601 E North Avenue. The **Great Blacks in Wax Museum** (Tues–Sat 9am–6pm, Sun noon–6pm; $4.50) uses wax models to illustrate the role of black people throughout history, from Egyptian pharaohs and early Muslims through to more contemporary leaders such as Martin Luther King, Jr, Marcus Garvey and Malcolm X. The models are posed in prop-filled dioramas – Rosa Parks being dragged off a Montgomery bus, for example, stands across from a pair of Jim Crow-era drinking fountains, a spotless enamel one labelled Whites Only and a rusty spigot for Coloured People – and the displays are elaborated with extensive written descriptions. Upstairs, figures in the Maryland Room include Baltimore-born ragtime piano player and composer Eubie Blake, and blues diva Billie Holiday, who was born and raised on Dallas Street just around the corner.

Further out on the north side, at the top of Charles Street about two miles from downtown (bus #3), are the pseudo-classical modern galleries of the **Baltimore Museum of Art** (Tues, Wed & Fri 10am–4pm, Thurs 10am–9pm, Sat & Sun 11am–6pm; $2, free Thurs). As well as a number of Italian and Dutch Old Master paintings by the likes of Botticelli, Raphael, Rembrandt and Van Dyke, there's also an overview of contemporary art, highlighted by Gilbert and George's *Hellish* self-portrait. The standout is the Cone Collection of works by Delacroix, Degas, Cezanne and Picasso, with over a hundred drawings and paintings by Henri Matisse.

Baltimore Accommodation

Apart from an attractive and central **youth hostel**, and the usual **motels** along the interstates, there are few cheap places to stay in Baltimore. However, **B&B** is a viable option – *Amanda's B&B Reservation Service* lists rooms in private homes for $45 per night and up, as does the *Maryland Reservation Center* (☎269-7550 or ☎1-800/654-9303) – and there are a number of inns around the historic waterfront area of Fells Point.

Admiral Fell Inn, 888 S Broadway (☎522-7377). Nicely restored historic hotel in the heart of Fells Point, with doubles from $90.

Baltimore International Youth Hostel, 17 W Mulberry St (☎576-8880). $10-a-night dorm beds in historic downtown brick rowhouse. There's an 11pm curfew, and you have to be out by 9am.

Celie's Waterfront B&B, 1714 Thames St (☎522-2323). Small Fells Point inn, right on the water; doubles from $70.

Comfort Inn, 24 W Franklin St (☎727-2000 or ☎1-800/228-5150). Recently modernised Mount Vernon hotel with mid-week doubles from $49.

Radisson Lord Baltimore Hotel, 20–30 W Baltimore St (☎539-8400). Plush downtown hotel, two blocks from the Inner Harbor, with doubles from $95.

Eating

Baltimore, long known as **Crab City**, has dozens of reasonably priced, fresh **seafood** places, as well as the usual range of diners and over a dozen good restaurants side by side in Little Italy, just east of the Inner Harbor. Restaurants tend to be unpretentious and family orientated, and prices lower than elsewhere.

Bertha's, 734 S Broadway (☎327-5795). Casual but stylish seafood restaurant, tucked away behind a tiny Fells Point bar.

Da Mimmo, 217 S High St (☎727-6876). Intimate, romantic Little Italy cafe, with live piano music and wide-ranging menu. Main dishes $9–15.

Faidley's, in Lexington Market (☎685-6169). Always crowded fresh oyster, clam and crab cake stand in boisterous downtown market. Fresh-shucked oysters (6 for $6), and $1.50 beers.

Louie's Bookstore Cafe, 518 N Charles St (☎962-1224). Busy Mount Vernon bar which also does a range of good $6–10 meals. Open late, with regular live music.

Luigi Petti, 1002 Eastern Ave (☎685-0055). Newish Little Italy trattoria, with sunny terrace.

Obrycki's, 1727 E Pratt St (☎732-6399). Baltimore's best and longest established fish restaurant, with delicious fresh crabs. Closed in winter.

John Steven Ltd, 1800 Thames St (☎276-9497). Fresh seafood, including good sushi – $5 for 6 pieces – in homey Fells Point pub.

Women's Industrial Exchange Restaurant, 333 N Charles St (☎685-4388). Excellent value 1940s cafe with full breakfasts for under $2, huge plates of chicken gumbo for $4, and great crab cakes.

Drinking and Nightlife

Baltimore's waterfront **Fells Point** neighbourhood may well have the densest assembly of drinking places in the US: one bar after another lines up along Broadway and the many smaller side streets, almost all of them featuring some sort of entertainment, usually live bands, and on summer nights the pavements are packed solid with revellers. The city's high-brow culture is concentrated northwest of the centre, along Mount Royal Avenue, where both the **Meyerhoff Symphony Hall** (☎783-8000) and the **Lyric Opera House** (☎685-5086) are located.

For a full rundown of what's on and where, pick up a copy of the free *City Paper*, available at book and record stores all over town.

Bars and Live Music Venues

Buddy's Jazz Pub, 313 N Charles St (☎332-4200). Evening jazz, for the price of a drink or two.

Cat's Eye Pub, 1730 Thames St (☎276-9085). Cosy bar with a good range of beers.

Louie's Bookstore Cafe, 518 N Charles St (☎962-1224). Downtown bar with live music.

Max's, 735 S Broadway (☎675-6297). Small but usually lively haunt that pulls in the likes of Jonathan Richman.

Mount Royal Tavern, 1204 W Mount Royal Ave (☎669-6686). Welcoming bar, popular with art students as well as night-capping musicians.

Old Oak Tavern, 641 Montford Ave (☎675-2565). Friendly gay and lesbian bar, a few blocks east of Fells Point, with oak panelling and pool tables.

Wharf Rat Bar, 801 S Ann St (☎276-9034). Another well-stocked and convivial bar.

Western Maryland

Stretched between West Virginia and the razor-straight Pennsylvania border, western Maryland ranges for some two hundred miles east–west, but is in places well under five miles across. The one sizeable town, **Frederick**, is equidistant from Baltimore and DC at the junction of I-70 and I-270, and in general the further west you go, the more mountainous and backwoodsy the feel – parts have much more in common with its Appalachian neighbours than with the rest of the state.

Though the countryside is very pretty, specific points of interest are few: apart from the Civil War battlefield at **Antietam**, west of Frederick, the best reason to come here is to cycle or hike along the footpath of the restored old **Chesapeake and Ohio Canal**, which winds along the Maryland side of the Potomac River from Washington DC for over 180 miles to the town of **Cumberland** in the western mountains.

Frederick and Around

One of the first towns settled in northwestern Maryland, **FREDERICK**, on I-70 an hour west of Baltimore, was laid out in 1745 by German farmers lured from Pennsylvania by the promise of cheap fertile land. It grew to become a main stopover on the route west to the Ohio Valley, and the bulk of today's tidy town survives from the early 1800s. A **visitor centre** (☎663-8703) at 19 E Church Street has walking tour maps of the town, pointing out such places as the **Schifferstadt House** (Tues–Sat 10am–4pm, Sun 1–4pm; $2), just off US-15, a stonewalled farmhouse built in 1753 and largely unaltered since. The other main local landmark is the **Barbara Fritchie House**, a tiny cottage along Carroll Creek on the west side of town, where according to a romantic poem popular with turn-of-the-century schoolchildren, 95-year-old Barbara Fritchie defiantly waved the US flag while Confederate soldiers marched through town. When Winston Churchill passed through here, he stopped at the house and recited the poem from memory.

Camp David, the mountain retreat used by US presidents since FDR, which was where Jimmy Carter brought Menachem Begin and Anwar Sadat together in 1978 to sign the historic Camp David accords between Israel and Egypt, is hidden away in the mountains north of Frederick. Nearby **Cunningham Falls State Park** and the **Catoctin Mountain Park** both hold endless hardwood forests – great for fall colour – in the midst of numerous preserved remnants of early homesteaders. Pick up details on **hiking** and **camping** in the two parks at the main visitor centre (daily 9am–5pm; ☎663-9388), off Hwy-77 two miles west of US-15.

Besides being a nice detour off the highway, Frederick is a good base for exploring places such as **Antietam** (see below) and **Harpers Ferry** in West Virginia (see p.318). There are **motels** along both I-70 and US-15, and in town the *Tyler Spite House*, 112 W Church Street (☎831-4455), is a pleasant **B&B** in an elegant 1814 mansion. For a bite to **eat**, try the soups and steaks at the *Brown Pelican*, 5 E Church Street, or the burgers and steamed crabs at *Cactus Flats*, off US-15 three miles north of town.

Antietam National Battlefield

The site of the bloodiest single battle in the Civil War, **Antietam National Battlefield** spreads over unaltered farmlands outside the whitewashed and balconied village of **Sharpsburg**. Here, fifteen miles west of Frederick, on the morning of September 17 1862, in an effort to consolidate rebel gains after their victory at Manassas, 40,000 troops faced a Union army twice that number. Hours later, some 25,000 from both sides lay dead or dying. The fiercest fighting, and the worst bloodshed, occurred in cornfields to the north; Union General Joseph Hooker recorded: "In the time that I am writing, every stalk of corn in the northern and greater part of the field was cut as closely as could have been done with a knife, and the slain lay in rows precisely as they had stood in their ranks a few moments before."

The battle continued throughout the day without a clear result, and though far from decisive – Gettysburg was fought the following summer, and the war dragged on for another two and a half years – the Confederate lack of success lost them the support of their erstwhile ally Great Britain, while the Union performance encouraged Lincoln to issue the Emancipation Proclamation. At the **visitor centre** (daily 9am–5pm; ☎432-5124), a mile north of Sharpsburg off Hwy-65, you can pick up a brochure and driving tour map of the park, and interpretive displays describe the progress of the battle. Numerous plaques and memorials have been constructed around the fields, but otherwise the site, with its various farm buildings and country churches, is unchanged, and the entire park serves as a mute but evocative memorial to the conflict.

The telephone **area code** for all Maryland outside Baltimore is ☎301.

Cumberland and the C&O Canal

The only large town in the far west of Maryland, **CUMBERLAND** started life as a coal-mining centre in the late 1700s. Often confused with Daniel Boone's Cumberland Gap in southwest Virginia (see p.381), this Cumberland was also an important trans-Appalachian crossing, but its main place in history is as the terminus of the ill-fated C&O (Chesapeake and Ohio) Canal, an impressive engineering feat begun in 1813 but not completed until 1850, by which time the railroads had already made it obsolete.

The **Western Maryland Station Center** (Wed–Sat 10am–5pm, Sun & Tues 1–4pm; ☎722-8226), beside the canal, can provide information on hiking, cycling, canoeing and camping; in summer, the **Western Maryland Scenic Railroad** ($9.50; ☎689-6668) runs historic trains from the station on scenic two-hour rides through the surrounding mountains.

Annapolis and Southern Maryland

While Baltimore has grown into the state's largest and busiest city, **Annapolis**, Maryland's colonial and current capital, has remained more or less unchanged. Before the US broke free from English rule, this was considered to be one of the most genteel and attractive colonial centres, and though its time-worn streets are now always crowded – every year over five million tourists descend upon this city of 35,000 – Annapolis is still among the more engaging small US cities. Its once-vital Chesapeake Bay **waterfront** now has little of the feel of colonial maritime life, but the real attractions of Annapolis, among its wanderable narrow streets, include fine homes, the Beaux Arts campus of the US Naval Academy, and the beautiful state capitol.

If you like the look of Annapolis, and want to get a better feel for the Chesapeake Bay region away from the crowds, head south to places like **St Mary's City** – the first capital of Maryland, completely reconstructed in the 1960s – or **Solomons Island**, one of many small Chesapeake Bay towns that seem unaltered for decades.

Annapolis

At the centre of **ANNAPOLIS**, overlooking the town's baroque web of streets, the **Maryland State House** (daily 9am–5pm; free) was completed in 1779 and soon after served as an early capitol of the United States. The **Old Senate Chamber**, to the right of the grand entrance hall, is where the Treaty of Paris was ratified in 1784, officially ending the Revolutionary War; a statue of George Washington stands on the spot where he resigned his commission as head of the Continental Army, and various displays document the role Annapolis played in the life of the young republic. Free guided tours are given on the hour, or you can wander around on your own, perhaps stopping in to listen to the proceedings of Maryland's current crop of legislators, who hold court from January to April in the more modern wing to the north of the old building. Also on the grounds of the State House is the cottage-sized **Old Treasury Building**, built in 1735 to hold colonial Maryland's currency reserves.

Many grand late eighteenth-century brick homes line the streets of Annapolis, but for substance and grace none surpasses the **Hammond-Harwood House** (Tues–Sat 10am–5pm, Sun 2–5pm; $3), two blocks west of the State House at 19 Maryland Avenue off King George Street. The warm red-brick Palladian villa, which consists of two symmetrical wings connected by a central hall, was built in 1774 to the designs of William Buckland, and is most notable for its beautifully carved decorative woodwork, especially evident in the intricate front doorway. Despite its architectural harmony, the house has had an unfortunate history, the original owner becoming so obsessed with its construction that his fiancée left him, breaking his heart and causing his untimely death at age 38; the architect Buckland also died in mysterious circumstances, before the house was completed.

Another historic Annapolis mansion, the 1765 **Paca House**, 186 Prince George Street (Tues–Sat 10am–4pm, Sun noon–4pm; $4), was a downmarket rooming house until the 1960s; it was restored to its period appearance in time for the 1976 Bicentennial, and boasts a splendid formal garden (a car park twenty years ago), which you can peer into from King George Street. Besides such elite manors, dozens of pastel eighteenth-century clapboard cottages and commercial structures, inhabited by dock-workers until the 1960s but now firmly in the realm of upper-class holiday homes, fill the narrow streets that run down to the waterfront. Of those that have escaped the gentrifi-ers, the **Tobacco Prise House**, 4 Pinkney Street (Sat & Sun 10am–4pm; $2), is a colo-nial tobacco warehouse that now sets out to explain the handling and storage of the valuable leaves. Further along, the **Shiplap House**, 18 Pinkney Street (daily 11am–4pm; free), was built in 1715 as a tavern; now it's a small museum of Annapolis history, with a herb garden behind containing assorted medicinal plants grown in colonial times.

The Waterfront and US Naval Academy

Although few colonial sites survive along the modern **Chesapeake Bay waterfront** to give a sense of the port's former maritime strength, the rebuilt 1850s dockside city market, the **Victualling Warehouse**, at 77 Main Street facing the Market Space (daily 11am–4pm; $2), is an early nineteenth-century replacement of a colonial warehouse used by the revolutionary army. Across the square, the **Middleton Tavern**, once an inn and later a general store, is now one of Annapolis's better places to eat (see below).

The rest of the waterfront is pleasant enough for an afternoon's wandering, espe-cially on summer weekends when the harbour and bay are full of clanging halyards and billowing sails. In among the boat supply shops and harbourside bars, the grey stone walls of the **US Naval Academy** (Mon–Sat 9.30am–5pm; free) seem designed to exacerbate the sensory deprivation endured by the over 4000 crew-cut young men and a handful of women (all of whom line up in formation outside **King Hall**, the dining commons, every day at noon) who spend four strictly disciplined years here before embarking on careers as naval officers. Various monuments and memorials are designed to instil naval pride and devotion to duty: a marble column commemorates five officers killed during the US invasion of Tripoli in 1804, and the foremast of the battleship *Maine*, whose destruction in Havana harbour set off the Spanish-American War, stands at the tip of the campus, where Spa Creek enters the Severn River. A small museum holds models of various British and US warships and other naval memora-bilia. Guided tours of the Academy ($2) leave hourly from the visitor centre in Ricketts Hall, near the main gate at the end of Randall Street, a block east of the City Dock.

Practicalities

Compared to the rest of Maryland, Annapolis is easy to reach, on *Greyhound*, *MTA* buses and, someday soon, on light rail from Baltimore. By road it's about half an hour from Washington (via US-50) or Baltimore (via Hwy-1), though parking can be difficult. A trolley bus (25¢) loops around the small and very walkable central area. Various organisations offer **walking tours**, the best being those given by Historic Annapolis (☎267-8149); if you'd rather see it on your own, the **visitor centre** (☎268-8687) at the end of the City Dock has free maps as well as tons of practical information.

Finding a **place to stay** is not usually a problem, though prices are fairly steep. There's a free accommodation bureau (☎1-800/848-4748), or you can choose from among **B&Bs** like the *Scot-Laur Inn*, 165 Main Street (☎268-5665), the best deal for anything characterful, with centrally located double rooms going from $60 including a full breakfast; the pricier *Prince George Inn*, 232 Prince George Street (☎263-6418); or the small and gay-friendly *Casa Bahia*, 262 King George Street (☎268-3106). Dozens of motels are to be found along US-50 on the west side of town.

Food and **drink**, as you might expect, are plentiful and very good: the no-frills *Chick and Ruth's Delly*, 165 Main Street (☎269-6737), does big breakfasts and has a booth on permanent reserve for the Maryland governor; the ritzier *Harry Browne's*, 66 State Circle (☎263-4332), is popular with politicos and expense-accounting lobbyists. For a bit more history, the waterfront *Middleton Tavern*, 2 Market Space (☎263-3323), is in one of the city's oldest buildings, and you can people-watch from the sunny porch while tucking into $6 plates of fish and chips. The *King of France Tavern* in the historic *Maryland Inn*, 16 Church Circle (☎263-2641), is good for drinking and listening to live jazz, while *Marmaduke's*, 301 Severn Avenue (☎269-5420), is a waterfront bar popular with the yachting brigades, who turn out to watch videos of themselves racing around the bay.

Southern Maryland

The little-visited back roads (there are no big roads) of **southern Maryland** in many ways resemble the agricultural Deep South. All along both main roads, US-301 from Baltimore and Hwy-2 from Annapolis, lush fields of corn and tobacco, dotted with ageing wooden barns, fill the arable lands in scattered parcels, and narrow, tree-lined country lanes open suddenly onto rivers or the broad Chesapeake Bay.

Solomons Island

Towns in southern Maryland are few and far between, but a couple are worth searching out. The old shipbuilding community of **Solomons Island**, sixty miles south of Annapolis via Hwy-2, is not actually an island but a narrow two-mile peninsula between the Patuxent River and Back Creek Bay. The entire waterfront is dotted with homely **B&Bs** like the *Back Creek Inn* (☎326-2022) and numerous fresh seafood **restaurants** – the *Lighthouse Inn* on the bay side, and *Solomon's Pier* across the road both have sunny outdoor decks – but the best reason to stop is the **Calvert Marine Museum** (daily 10am–5pm; $3), on Hwy-2 at the north end of town. This focuses specifically on the Patuxent River, and on the unique estuarine ecosystem of the Chesapeake Bay tidal areas. Its two protected marshland wildlife areas, one saltwater and one freshwater, can be explored on raised walkways. Inside the main building, exhibits follow the development of local boat-building and commercal fishing, and dozens of historic boats are on show. In summer, an old oyster buy-boat, the *William B Tennison*, leaves from the museum dock on hour-long **cruises** (daily at 2pm; $4) around the bay.

St Mary's City and Point Lookout State Park

It's not really historic, nor even much of a city, but the reconstructed village of **ST MARY'S CITY** is well worth a look, if only for its lovely position. Set on a broad Potomac cove near the southern tip of the Maryland peninsula, twenty miles south of Solomons Island and just over an hour from Washington DC, St Mary's City is a small-scale but credible reconstruction of Maryland's first colonial capital, established here in 1634 before being moved to Annapolis sixty years later. The entire complex, including a working tobacco plantation and a replica of the tiny ship on which the first colonists arrived from England, is run as a sort of theme park, complete with costumed tour guides (daily 10am–5pm; $4). Its main feature is a 1934 rebuilding of the long-vanished **State House**, where in 1689 Protestant rebels seized control of what had been a Catholic-run colony, but it's all a bit too manicured to give much sense of history. Nearby, and much more fun, the *Farthing's Ordinary* is a mock **tavern** selling hearty soups and sandwiches for around $6.

South from St Mary's City, the very tip of the southern Maryland peninsula was used during the Civil War as a **prisoner-of-war camp** for rebel forces captured at the battle of Gettysburg. In just over a year, from March 1864 to June 1865, over four thousand died due to the appalling conditions, including some seven hundred Union guards. Most of the Confederate soldiers were buried in a mass grave, now marked by a granite obelisk; the actual camp (the ramparts have been reconstructed and there's a small and somewhat gruesome museum) was a mile south. The point where the Potomac flows into the Chesapeake is a good place to watch the sun rise or set.

The Eastern Shore

Maryland's **eastern shore**, the broad peninsula that protects the Chesapeake from the open Atlantic, is a compelling and addictive region, with miles of back roads perfectly suited to aimless exploration and sudden discovery, coming across the odd wooden farmhouse or tobacco barn standing forlornly in the middle of a field, or an old sailboat tied up to an apparently decrepit dock that springs to life when the fishing craft return. The US-50 bridge, built across the Chesapeake Bay in the early 1960s, may have made the eastern shore more accessible, but it hasn't affected its air of somnolence. While US-50 races down the centre of the peninsula to the beach resort of **Ocean City**, away from the highway quiet country lanes lead to two-hundred-year-old waterfront towns like **Chestertown**, **St Michaels** and **Oxford**.

Chestertown and Rock Hall

A stopping place for travellers since colonial days, when it was a prime Chesapeake port, **CHESTERTOWN** is the northernmost centre on the eastern shore. Stretching west along High Street from the Chester River, it's surprisingly intact, with its fine old riverfront homes, a courthouse square lined with ornate wooden cottages, and a generally langorous feel that makes it a popular weekend escape from Baltimore or DC. Many of the old houses, like the *Widow's Walk Inn*, 402 High Street (☎778-6455), have been converted into $80-a-night **B&Bs**, while others now house top-rated **restaurants** like the *Feast of Reason*, 203 High Street (☎778-3828), and the swanky dining room of the *Imperial Hotel* (☎778-5000) across the street. The **visitor centre**, 118 N Cross Street (☎778-0416), has details of walking and cycling tours.

To the west of town, fifteen miles of country lanes lead down to the wharves and dockside restaurants of **Rock Hall**, an old Chesapeake Bay fishing port where you can watch the day's catch being unloaded while munching on crab legs at the bare-bones *Waterman's Crabhouse* (☎778-1803) on the main pier. The *Chesapeake Flyer* catamaran service lands here (see p.323), and bikes are available for rent from the marina office.

St Michaels

Always a contender for prettiest harbour on the Chesapeake Bay, tiny **ST MICHAELS**, twelve miles west of US-50 on Hwy-33, is also one of the Chesapeake's oldest ports. Founded during the mid-1600s, it grew into one of colonial America's prime ship-building centres; its fast sloops and shallow-draught "bugeyes" evaded British blockades during the Revolutionary War. Once Baltimore had risen to prominence as the main Chesapeake port, St Michaels languished, but since the early 1960s it has been rediscovered, its many old buildings now gentrified into art galleries, boutiques and cosy **B&Bs** like the *Hambleton Inn*, 202 Cherry Street (☎745-3350), and its wharves and docks filled with weekend sailors and fronted by restaurant-cum-bars like the *Town Dock* (☎745-5577) or *Longfellow's* (☎745-2624), both at the end of Mulberry Street.

Despite the touristy nature of St Michaels' recent revival, some corners have survived intact, especially the old town green, **St Mary's Square**, a block off the main Talbot Street on Mulberry Street. To get a clear sense of the human and natural history of Chesapeake Bay, head north along the docks to the extensive modern **Chesapeake**

Bay Maritime Museum (daily 9am–6pm; $5). Focusing on the bay's economic and military value, it revolves around the restored **Hooper Strait Lighthouse**, at the foot of which float a few Chesapeake Bay sailboats – designed to make the most of the bay's shallow waters. Nearby, some two hundred other boats include a Native American dugout canoe, while in the museum workshop skilled artisans and legions of volunteers restore and maintain historic boats using painstaking traditional techniques.

Tilghman Island

If you want to see the real, workaday Chesapeake, **Tilghman Island**, west from St Michaels across the Knapps Narrows drawbridge, is home to most of the Chesapeake's working skipjack fleet. Partly in response to the continued depletion of oyster stocks, and also to help preserve a dying tradition, the government has made it illegal to harvest oysters except from small, graceful and hopelessly outmoded sailing boats called **skipjacks**, of which around thirty are still in use. Most are moored at **Dogwood Harbor**, on the east side of the island; during the autumn and winter harvest, they can be seen unloading at the *Harrison Oyster Packing Company*, at the foot of the bridge. You can buy oysters fresh off the boat, or sample them and other local delicacies at two very good restaurants on either side of the bridge: the *Bay Hundred* (☎886-2622) and the more upscale *Bridge Restaurant* (☎886-2500).

Oxford

Just west of US-50, or seven miles south of St Michaels via country lanes and the **Tred-Avon Ferry** – which first crossed in 1683 and has been in continuous service since 1836 – the leafy waterfront hamlet of **OXFORD** seems to have slumbered peacefully since colonial days. Along with Annapolis, this was one of two ports of entry for all colonial Maryland, a role remembered by the reconstructed one-room **Customs House** next to the ferry landing on the north side of town. After the US won its independence, Oxford was all but forgotten; its full-time population is under a thousand, and there's hardly any tourist trade. Wandering around the quiet streets, however, or along the lengthy riverfront promenade, can be quite relaxing and enjoyable. The *Town Creek* (☎226-5131) is a friendly inexpensive **seafood restaurant** with a large deck right on the main harbour, at the end of Tilghman Street; the ancient *Robert Morris Inn*, on Morris Street at The Strand (☎226-5111), named for the Oxford man who personally financed the Continental army during the Revolutionary War, has rooms from $80 a night as well as James Michener's favourite crab cakes. In the larger but less interesting US-50 town of **Easton**, the ancient *Bishop's House B&B*, 214 Goldsborough Street (☎820-7290), provides a comfortable $60-a-night alternative to the highway motels.

Ocean City

With over ten miles of broad Atlantic beach, a boisterous boardwalk amusement park and around half a million visitors every weekend, **OCEAN CITY** is Maryland's number one summer resort. No matter how you get here, down the coast from Delaware or across the rural eastern shore along US-50, its tower-block hotels and urban overcrowding will come as a shock. If you're after a quiet weekend by the sea, avoid it like the plague; Ocean City is as close as the US comes to Benidorm and Torremolinos. If you like to spend as much time in bars and nightclubs as you do on the sands, or have a soft spot for tacky seaside resorts, on the other hand, it may be just what you're looking for.

Ocean City might be good for a day out, or even a long weekend away from home or work, but it's hard to imagine anyone wanting to stay very long. It is, at least, easy to reach; *Carolina Trailways* **buses** from DC end up at the southern end of town at Second Street and Hwy-1 (☎289-9307). Places to **stay** are plentiful except on summer weekends, and off-season rates are at least half prime-time ones, but pleasant accommodation is rare indeed. For a **motel** near the bus station and boardwalk, try the $40-a-night *Oceanic*

(☎289-6494 or ☎1-800/638-2106) at the south end of Baltimore Street. Alternatives range from the faded seaside grandeur of the *Commander Hotel* on the boardwalk at 14th Street (☎289-6166 or ☎1-800/543-6986), with doubles from $60, to the gleaming marble and glass of the $120-a-night *Cocoanut Mallory*, 60th Street and The Bay (☎524-5500 or ☎1-800/767-6060). If you get stuck, the **Chamber of Commerce**, on Hwy-1 at 40th Street (☎289-8181 or ☎1-800/62-OCEAN), can usually help out.

Apart from the boardwalk fast-food joints, and the national franchises along Hwy-1 (there are three all-night *McDonalds*, for example), Ocean City has few good **eating** options. The *Angler Restaurant*, on the bay at Talbot Street (☎289-7424), has fresh seafood and an all-you-can-eat salad bar; it also has nice beers, wild tropical cocktails and nightly live bands. Other **nightspots** include the *Big Kahuna Surf Club*, 18th and Hwy-1 (☎289-6331), and the all-ages *Nite Lite*, Boardwalk and Worcester (☎289-6313).

If you find yourself here in the peak of summer and want to escape the crowds, head just down the coast to **Assateague Island National Seashore** – a twenty-mile stretch of protected and entirely undeveloped beach and marshland. There's a visitor centre at the end of Hwy-611, five miles south of Ocean City, and **camping** right on the beach at Assateague State Park (☎641-2120). The best **lodging** is to be found near the southern half of Assateague Island, across the Virginia border in the tiny hamlet of **Chincoteague**, where the *Main Street House B&B*, 704 N Main Street (☎1-804/336-6030), and the *Anchor Inn*, 534 S Main Street (☎1-804/336-6313), both have rooms from $50 per night.

DELAWARE

Though **DELAWARE** has its beauty spots – including some of the mid-Atlantic's best beaches – its tourist boards and PR people have their work cut out for them. About the only images potential visitors have of the state are negative: Delaware is known for the massive chemical plants of the **Du Pont Corporation**, scattered about its northern half, and for **Dover Air Force Base**, where throughout the Vietnam War, and more recently during the conflict in the Persian Gulf, all US war dead have arrived back on American soil. It also has a reputation for tolerating shady **business** practices – fully half of America's largest companies have their official bases in the tiny state, thanks to the permissive tax, banking and incorporation laws (there's no sales tax either).

None of the above is likely to make you want to visit, so instead Delaware's promoters emphasise its **past** – for example, as the first ex-colony to ratify the Constitution, it claims the title of **America's First State**. Dutch whalers established a settlement at the mouth of the Delaware Bay in 1631, and soon after the Swedes built a larger colony at present-day **Wilmington**. The two groups fought among themselves until the British took over in 1664. Delaware was part of neighbouring Pennsylvania – Philadelphia is only ten miles north of the present, arching state border – until hiving itself off in 1776.

Much of Delaware's fortunes (and misfortunes) since then can be traced directly to the Du Pont family, who, fleeing the wrath of revolutionary France, set up a gunpowder mill that became, and has remained, the main supplier of conventional explosives to the US government. After World War I, the Du Ponts went public and made millions in the stock market frenzies of the Roaring Twenties, since when the company has diversified, its labs inventing such modern essentials as nylon and cellophane.

The Du Ponts built huge mansions for themselves in the **Brandywine Valley** north of Wilmington, near the old colonial capital, **New Castle**, a perfectly preserved eighteenth-century village on the Delaware Bay, just five miles south of I-95. Further south, **Dover**, the capital, won't detain you long, but beyond here the small and amiable resorts of **Lewes** and **Rehoboth Beach** mark the northern extent of over twenty miles of unspoiled Atlantic beaches.

> The telephone **area code** for the entire state of Delaware is ☎302.

Getting Around Delaware

Apart from Wilmington, which is on the main East Coast **train** and **bus** lines, Delaware is hard to get around without a car. *Greyhound* services are limited to a summer-only route from DC to **Rehoboth**, and local transport is non-existent.

I-95 and the New Jersey Turnpike converge at Wilmington, from where US-13 runs a hundred miles south through the state. More often called the **Du Pont Highway**, US-13 was paid for and constructed by the industrialists so that they could ride in comfort between their Wilmington mansions and Dover. Hwy-1 cuts off from Dover along the Atlantic, and a direct car and passenger **ferry** connects Cape May, the southern tip of New Jersey, and Lewes, at the mouth of the Delaware Bay (see p.341).

Wilmington and Around

WILMINGTON may not be the most compelling place in America, but this much-maligned, medium-sized city can make for a refreshing break from the tourist trail: not only does it boast the excellent **Delaware Art Museum** and some pretty waterside parks, but the surrounding **Brandywine Valley** holds the manor homes and gardens (and factories) of the First State's First Family, the Du Ponts, all open to the public and providing an inside look at America's de facto aristocracy.

If you arrive in Wilmington by **train**, on the *Amtrak* line between New York and Washington, you'll pull in to the quirky 1907 terracotta station on the somewhat dodgy south side of the city. From here, the two main streets, Market and King, run north for about a mile to the Brandywine River, their partly pedestrianised lengths holding a standard array of shops and other small businesses, as well as a handful of restored eighteenth-century rowhouses clustered around the **Old Town Hall**, 512 Market Street. The faceless grey monoliths that tower over the cityscape house the headquarters of hundreds of national companies.

A short walk north of the **downtown** commercial district, at the top end of Market Street, **Brandywine Park** comes as a welcome relief from the concrete pavements, its grassy knolls lining both banks of the Brandywine River. In the residential districts to the north are some of the city's oldest and poshest houses, many dating from the Revolutionary War, when Wilmington's flour mills fed the American forces. The nearby **Delaware Art Museum** (Tues 10am–9pm, Wed–Sat 10am–5pm, Sun noon–5pm; free), 2301 Kentmere Parkway, has a good range of works by American painters like Thomas Eakins, Winslow Homer and Edward Hopper, as well as a comprehensive collection of English Pre-Raphaelite painting and drawing.

Most of Wilmington's surprising number of important colonial sites are hidden away amidst the decrepit and heavily industrialised **waterfront** to the east of downtown. A poorly signed "historic Wilmington" loop runs past blocks of brick rowhouses mixed in with 1950s housing estates and numerous scrap metal yards, stopping first at the foot of Seventh Street, where a small monument marks the site of Delaware's first European colony, **Fort Christina**, set up by Swedish settlers in 1638. Nearby, at 606 Church Street, the **Old Swede's Church** is one of the oldest houses of worship in the US, built in 1698 and still retaining its impressive black walnut pulpit.

The **tourist office** at 1300 Market Street (☎652-4088) downtown has walking and driving tour maps and practical information, but unless you want to **eat** at the excellent *Waterworks Cafe*, 16th and French Street in Brandywine Park (☎652-6022), or blow $150 on a night at the splendidly ornate *Hotel Du Pont* (☎594-3100 or ☎1-800/441-9019), which fills an entire block of Market Street, there's no great reason to linger.

The Du Pont Mansions

Various generations of the Du Pont family built a handful of opulent homes in the rural Brandywine Valley northwest of Wilmington. To learn how their fortune was made, stop first at the **Hagley Museum** (daily 9.30am–5pm, Jan–March weekends only; $8), off Hwy-141 just north of Wilmington. Pierre Du Pont, the patriarch, was minister of finance to Louis XVI, but the museum begins with the foundation in 1802 of a small water-powered **gunpowder mill** along the banks of the Brandywine River. Mirroring the development of nineteenth-century American industry, the complex grew over the next hundred years to include ever-larger steam-powered and eventually electrically powered factories – almost all of which are still in working order.

You get an idea of the wealth and power the family garnered by visiting **Nemours Mansion** just a mile up the road. This enormous pink palace (tours every two hours, Tues–Sat 9am–3pm, Sun 11am–3pm; $7) was thrown up by Alfred Du Pont in 1910, modelled upon the family's ancestral home in France and surrounded by a 300-acre, Versailles-style formal garden. Two miles northwest, off Hwy-52, the one-time du Pont family estate of **Winterthur** (Tues–Sat 9.30am–5pm, Sun noon–5pm; $9, gardens only $4) has evolved into the country's finest museum of early American **decorative arts**. Since 1927, when Henry Du Pont took over the twelve-room cottage as a home for himself and his collection of antique furniture, Winterthur has grown into a vast private museum, each of its 200 rooms showcasing the decorative style of a particular era and culture. Ranging from the simplicity of a Shaker cottage to a beautiful three-storey eliptical staircase taken from a North Carolina plantation home, the various pieces of furniture, textiles, silverwork and paintings – all of which were made in America between 1640 and 1840 – are a rich catalogue of the diversity of American applied arts.

New Castle

Delaware's magnificently preserved first capital, **NEW CASTLE** – certainly among the prettiest places in the state – fronts the broad Delaware River, just six miles south of Wilmington via Hwy-141. Founded in the 1650s by the Dutch intent on expanding from their colony at New Amsterdam, and taken over by the British in 1664, New Castle was the main stopping point between the larger cities of Baltimore and Philadelphia. Though it was largely bypassed when railways and highways replaced the riverboats, it has somehow managed to survive intact, its quiet cobbled streets and immaculate eighteenth-century brick houses shaded by ancient hardwood trees.

The heart of New Castle is the tree-filled **Town Green**, spreading east from the shops of Delaware Street. Laid out in 1655 by Peter Stuyvesant, the green is dominated by the stalwart tower of the **Immanuel Episcopal Church**, built in 1703 and bordered by tidy rows of two-hundred-year-old gravestones. Its pristine white interior, however, is more recent, now reconstructed after a disastrous 1980s fire. On the west edge of the green, the **Old Court House** was built in 1732 and served as the first state capitol. Its dainty cupola was the centrepoint from which surveyors determined the state's curved northern border, drawn up when Delaware seceded from Pennsylvania in 1776.

Fine colonial houses fill the few blocks around the Town Green – the largest, and the only one regularly open to the public, being the **George Read II House** (Tues–Sun 10am–4pm, Jan & Feb Sat & Sun only; $4), two blocks south along the river at 42 The Strand. Built between 1797 and 1804, and restored in the 1970s, the sumptuously detailed house has marble fireplaces, brightly painted walls, elaborately carved woodwork and some of the finest plasterwork ornament of the Federal period. The spacious gardens behind were laid out in 1847 to the picturesque designs of Andrew Jackson Downing. The large houses across the street, backing on to the Delaware River, also date from the early nineteenth century, and many are now run as B&Bs.

New Castle Practicalities

Many visitors are content to see New Castle, just off the interstate, as a day out from Washington DC or Philadelphia, but there's enough to merit a longer trip. Comfortable **B&Bs** line the Delaware riverfront, varying from the homey hospitality of the *River House*, 21 The Strand (☎328-2323) to the more luxurious trappings of the *Jefferson House*, 5 The Strand (☎323-0999). There's good beer and pub-grub at the popular *Green Frog Tavern*, 114 Delaware Street, while more refined tastes will enjoy the historic *David Finney Inn*, 216 Delaware Street (☎322-6367), one of the state's best restaurants, just off the Town Green.

For further information, or to pick up a copy of the self-guided walking tour map, call in at the **visitor centre** at 220 Delaware Street (☎322-9802).

Dover

DOVER, the capital of Delaware, is pretty much a non-event as far as tourism goes. Located in the mostly agricultural centre of the state, just west of US-13 , it's basically a very small town, its low-rise business district hemmed in by blocks of suburban detached houses. South of **Lockerman Street**, the main route through town, a few, strangely somnolent governmental buildings centre upon the 1792 **Old State House**, its old legislative chambers now restored as a museum (Tues–Sat 10am–4.30pm; free) and furnished with early American antiques. To the west, around the oval **Town Green**, lawyers and insurance shops have taken over historic buildings such as the *Golden Fleece Tavern*, where Delaware's early legislators agreed to ratify the Constitution.

A short walk west of the green, the small **Delaware State Museum** (Tues–Sat 10am–4.30pm; free) is worth a look not for its fairly tedious displays of anthropological detritus – Native American shell necklaces, wooden water pipes from early Wilmington and the like – but because a small building across the graveyard holds the **Johnson Memorial**. One of the country's largest and most enjoyable collections of **phonographs**, dedicated to the memory of Dover-born engineer Eldridge Reeves Johnson, who helped to invent the *Victrola*, the memorial is laid out like a 1920s music shop. Dozens of "talking machines", from early wind-ups to prototype jukeboxes, play original period recordings, and comical photographs document early, pre-electric recording techniques – entire orchestras crowd together around huge megaphones. Pride of place goes to a painting of a dog, *Nipper*, listening to a *Victrola*, an image made immediately familiar as "His Master's Voice". In 1929 Johnson sold the rights to his machine, and to his trademark dog, to RCA for $29 million.

Every Tuesday and Friday for over fifty years, **Spence's Bazaar**, two blocks south on Queen Street at New Burton Road, has hosted a free-for-all **flea market**. All of Dover turns out, including dozens of local **Amish**, who ride here in their ancient horse-drawn buggies to sell home-grown fruits and vegetables. Though it's not nearly as well known as the Amish community of Lancaster County (see p.121), the area around Dover has nearly as large a population, concentrated in the farmlands to the west of town; happily for them, their presence has yet to become a tourist attraction.

Practicalities

Most of Dover's **restaurants** and **hotels** are concentrated on Lockerman Street and State Street in the town centre, just north of the Town Green. State Street in particular holds the *Dinner Bell Inn* at no. 121 (☎678-1234) and the more pub like *W T Smithers* (☎674-8875) across the street. US-13 highway also has some **budget accommodation**, such as the $40-a-night *Comfort Inn* (☎674-3300) two blocks south of Lockerman Street. A **visitor centre** (☎736-4266) next to the Old State House has the usual tourist information.

The Delaware Coast

The thirty-mile-long **Delaware coast** is one of the little-known jewels of the East Coast. Its one built-up resort, **Rehoboth Beach**, is a traditional seaside town, packed solid in summer and offering all the usual amenities, and the fishing community of **Lewes** is attractive and historic, but what really sets the area apart is the ease with which you can find long stretches of sand to yourself. For every developed stretch, about ten times more has been preserved as open space, most extensively at **Delaware Seashore State Park**, which stretches south from Rehoboth to the Maryland border.

Lewes

Whether you come down Hwy-1, or cruise across on the ferry from Cape May, New Jersey, **LEWES** makes a good introduction to the Delaware coast. Its natural harbour at the mouth of the Delaware Bay has attracted seafarers ever since a Dutch whaling company set up a small colony here in 1631. Lewes' current role as a summer resort hasn't obscured its substantial history, outlined in the mock-Dutch **Zwaanendael Museum** (Tues–Sat 10am–4.30pm, Sun 1.30–4.30pm; free), in the heart of town on Savannah Road at Kings Highway. The **tourist office** (☎645-8073) next door, housed inside a gambrel-roofed 1730s farmhouse, has walking tour maps of the rest of the town, pointing out the handful of eighteenth-century houses and outbuildings collected from around the area to form the **Lewes Historical Complex** on Front Street three blocks north. Along the canal, keep an eye out also for the **Overfalls Lightship**, which lit the entrance to Delaware Bay until 1961, and the array of cannons, one said to be from an old pirate ship, that are lined up along the top of **Memorial Park**.

Though Lewes can justly boast of being "the First Town in the First State", most people come here for the **beach** rather than history. There's an extensive strand along the usually calm Delaware Bay at the foot of the town, while **Cape Henlopen State Park**, a 3000-acre open space where the bay meets the open ocean just a mile east of the town centre, is even better, and has the biggest sand dunes north of Cape Hatteras.

Except on peak summer weekends, Lewes is quiet enough to mean you should have no trouble finding a room in **motels** like *Vesuvio's* (☎645-2224) or *The Captain's Quarters* (☎645-7924), both on Savannah Road near the water. Most of the **restaurants**, not surprisingly, feature seafood, the local favourite being *The Angler's* (☎645-9931), along the Lewes–Rehoboth Canal. You can **walk** almost everywhere in the compact centre, or rent a **bike** for $12 per day, $29 per week from *Lewes Cycle Sport*, 514 Savannah Road (☎645-4544). For a nice day out, or a possible next leg of your journey, take the **ferry** ($5 per person, $20 per car; ☎645-6313) across the Delaware Bay to the pleasant Victorian beach resort of **Cape May**, New Jersey (see p.138). It leaves every couple of hours from a terminal very near the town centre, and takes seventy minutes.

Rehoboth Beach

There's a non-stop parade of motels and shopping malls along the six miles of Hwy-1 linking Lewes with **REHOBOTH BEACH**, Delaware's largest and liveliest beach resort. Crowded all summer, but nearly empty the rest of the year, Rehoboth – the town started life as a Methodist revival camp, and attracts so many escapees from DC that it's known as the Nation's Summer Capital – is more family orientated than other beach towns, lacking the nightlife of Ocean City but making up for it with miles of clean and uncrowded **sands**.

Rehoboth has less of a history than Lewes, though its wooden **boardwalk** is one of the last on the East Coast. It stretches along the Atlantic to either side of Rehoboth Avenue – always "The Avenue" – and acts as the main drag, its four short blocks clogged with souvenir shoppers browsing though the usual array of T-shirts and seaside tat. Most of the **restaurants** and **nightspots** are concentrated here, with *Thrashers French*

Fries stands mixed in with the mock-Caribbean beach shack decor of the *Back Porch Cafe*, 59 Rehoboth Avenue (☎227-3674), and boardwalk burger bars like *Obie's-by-the-Sea*, three blocks north; after dark, the action shifts to the Anglophile environs of the *Country Squire*, 19 Rehoboth Avenue, which has the largest beer selection for miles.

Apart from the peak times of July and August, you shouldn't have much trouble finding a bed in one of Rehoboth's many **motels**: the *Sandcastle*, 61 Rehoboth Avenue (☎227-0400 or ☎1-800/372-2112), or the *Admiral*, a block south at 2 Baltimore Avenue (☎227-2103 or ☎1-800/428-2424) are right off the boardwalk, or if you want to avoid the crowds try *Adams Oceanfront*, a mile south of the centre at 4 Read Avenue in **Dewey Beach** (☎227-3030). Prices at all of the above places start at around $35 a night for a double, rising to upwards of $100 on summer weekends. For more information, contact the **Chamber of Commerce**, 501 Rehoboth Avenue (☎227-2233 or ☎1-800/441-1329).

South of Rehoboth, **Delaware Seashore State Park** stretches for miles along a thin sandy peninsula, split by Hwy-1 and bound on the east by the Atlantic and on the west by various freshwater marshlands. There's little here apart from beachfront carparks until you approach the Maryland border, where the concrete tower blocks of Bethany Beach do little to prepare you for the Costa del Sol-like concentrations of hotels and condos in **Ocean City**, ten miles further along (see p.336).

travel details

TRAINS

Routes (all *Amtrak*)

• Frequent trains – roughly forty services per day – connect **Washington DC** with **New York**, via **Baltimore** and **Philadelphia**. Eight continue to **Boston**, and one to **Montréal**.

• One daily from **Washington DC** to **Chicago**, via **Pittsburgh** and **Cleveland**.

• The daily *Crescent* train goes from **Washington DC** to **New Orleans**, via **Manassas**, **Charlottesville** and **Atlanta**. A connecting service leaves Charlottesville on Sun, Wed & Fri at 4.30pm, to Chicago via **White Sulphur Springs**, **Hinton** and **Charleston** in West Virginia.

• Six trains daily run south from **Washington DC** to **Fredericksburg** and **Richmond**; two, the *Silver Star* and the *Silver Meteor*, continue to **Miami**, Florida, and one, the *Carolinian*, continues to **Charlotte**, North Carolina.

• One train daily runs from **Richmond** via **Williamsburg** to **Newport News**, where a connecting bus goes on to **Virginia Beach**.

Journey Times

From Washington DC to Baltimore 50min; Philadelphia 1hr 40min; New York 3hr; Boston 8hr 30min; Montréal 20hr 30min; Chicago 17hr; New Orleans 25hr; Charlottesville 2hr 30min; Atlanta 13hr 30min; Fredericksburg 1hr 10min; Richmond 2hr; Charlotte 9hr 30min; Miami 23hr.

From Richmond to Williamsburg 1hr 15min; Virginia Beach (via connecting bus) 3hr.

From Charlottesville to Hinton 4hr; Charleston 6hr 30min.

BUSES

From Washington DC to Richmond/ Williamsburg/ Norfolk/ Virginia Beach (5 daily; 2hr/3hr/4hr 30min/ 5hr); to Baltimore (8 daily; 1hr 10min).

From Richmond one a day at 11.45 am to Charlottesville/ Lexington/ Lewisburg WV/ Charleston WV (1hr/3hr/ 5hr/ 8hr).

From Baltimore there are frequent services to Philadelphia (1hr 45min) and New York (4hr 30min).

FERRY

Chesapeake Flyer (☎639-7241 or 1-800/689-7320) runs a high-speed catamaran ferry service across the Chesapeake Bay from **Baltimore** and **Annapolis** to **Rock Hall** and **St Michaels**.

CHAPTER SIX

THE SOUTH

As Mark Twain put it in 1882, "In the South, the (Civil) war is what AD is elsewhere; they date everything from it". Five generations later, the legacies of years of slavery and the "War Between the States" are still evident throughout the southern heartland states of **NORTH CAROLINA, SOUTH CAROLINA, GEORGIA, KENTUCKY, TENNESSEE, ALABAMA** and **MISSISSIPPI**. The war is the focus point for countless museums and shrines, and the Confederate "Stars and Bars" flag is more conspicuous in some places than the Stars and Stripes.

It's not, however, an area that's entirely stuck in its ways. Quite whether the "New South" is all that different from the old is a matter for debate; but the last few decades have unquestionably seen the influx of high-tech industries, the emergence of liberal white politicians such as Jimmy Carter, and the growth of dynamic urban centres such as the go-ahead black city of **Atlanta**, the birthplace of Dr Martin Luther King Jr and the venue for the 1996 Olympics. It took suffering and bloodshed to effect the changes of the Fifties and Sixties, but relations between black and white have improved – and are essentially better than in many large cities elsewhere in the country.

The South has never been one uniform, homogenous unit; even during the Civil War there were substantial pockets of pro-Union support, particularly in the mountains. Today the culture and make-up of the overwhelmingly black Mississippi Delta or South Carolina are markedly different from the white hill farms in Kentucky and Tennessee, where prohibition is still enforced. Likewise, the sun belt industries of North Carolina and northern Alabama are far removed from the rural backwaters of southern Georgia.

However, the region still exhibits distinct social traits – particularly fundamentalist religious views and authoritarian values – that set it apart from the rest of the country. Life in the countryside is conducted at a slow, laid-back pace, with a code of rather quaint manners that contrasts starkly with the impersonal edge of the bigger cities. The much-vaunted **southern hospitality** is conspicuous everywhere, even if it remains unfortunately tempered by the continuing presence of rednecks, or good ole boys: a subclass of whites who don't take kindly to strangers.

The most exciting aspect of the southern heritage is undoubtedly its **music**. Hundreds of thousands of fans make pilgrimages each year to the country and blues meccas of **Nashville** and **Memphis**, the homelands of Elvis Presley, Robert Johnson, Dolly Parton and Otis Redding, and the hillbilly barn dances in Appalachia or the blues jook-joints of the Mississipi Delta and South Carolina. The southern experience is also reflected in a rich regional **literature**; its communities and people well documented by the likes of William Faulkner, Carson McCullers, Alice Walker, Eudora Welty and the one-book-wonders Margaret Mitchell and Harper Lee.

Although consisting mostly of undulating, sun-scorched hillsides broken by occasional forests, the southern scenery does hold some surprises. Among the highlights are the misty Appalachian **mountains** of Kentucky, Tennessee and North Carolina, the subtropical **beaches** and tranquil **barrier islands** along both the Atlantic and Gulf coasts, and the river road through the tiny settlements of the flat Mississippi Delta.

During July and August, the **temperature** is mostly a very humid 90°F; virtually every motel, bar, restaurant and museum is air-conditioned, but you might want to schedule your visit a little either side of these months. On the coast, where the beaches offer a cheaper and less crowded alternative to neighbouring Florida, the main season

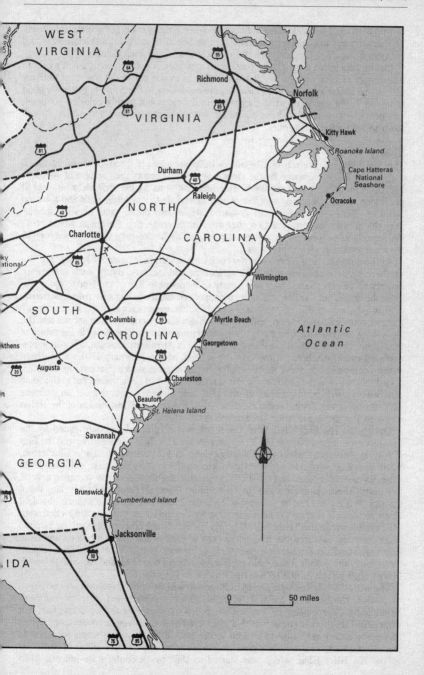

is from Memorial to Labor Day, and outside of these dates many attractions are closed. The autumn colours in the mountains (just as beautiful and a lot less expensive and congested than New England) are at their most stunning during October.

Public transport through the large rural expanses is poor. In any case, it's best to take things at your own pace – you'll find things to see and do in the most unlikely places – so hiring a car is a good idea. **Accommodation** in the South is generally good value, while its varied **cuisine** includes the delicious but highly calorific soulfood, excellent cheap seafood and the ubiquitous grits (maize porridge) and catfish (which has a sort of mild trout flavour).

History

The **Spanish** and **French** had begun to build settlements throughout the South as early as the 1520s. However, by the early seventeenth century their sphere of influence had been reduced to present-day Florida and Louisiana by the **British**, who steered the region towards a role as supplier of **raw materials** to its **cotton** mills and **tobacco** factories. Both climate and soil favoured staple agriculture, and massive labour-intensive **plantations** started to spring up. No self-respecting European would cross the Atlantic to pick cotton on a plantation, so the big landowners turned to **slavery** as the most profitable source of labour.

As the South became increasingly set in its ways, with little incentive to diversify, the northern states surged ahead in both agriculture and industry. By the early nineteenth century the southern economy was clearly subservient to that of the North: the South grew the crops, but northern factories monopolised the more lucrative **manufacturing** of finished goods. Southern politicians and plantation owners accused the North of political and economic aggression, and felt that unless slavery continued to spread into the Territories and even the free states, they would progressively lose all say in the future of the nation. The election as president in late 1860 of **Abraham Lincoln**, a hardline pro-northern candidate, brought the crisis to a head, and in February 1861 six southern states broke away to form the Confederate States of America. **Secession** radically upped the stakes in the controversy. Most northerners had been indifferent to the issue of slavery – even Lincoln, as late as mid-1861, said "I have no purpose . . . to interfere with slavery in the States where it exists" – but the potential destruction of the Union was seen as a far more serious – and treacherous – threat.

During the resultant **Civil War**, the South was outgunned and outmanned by the vast resources of the North. The Confederates fired the first shots and scored the first victory in April 1861 when the Union garrison at Fort Sumter (outside Charleston, South Carolina) surrendered. The Union was on the military defensive until mid-1862, when its navy blockaded the coast of Georgia and the Carolinas and occupied several key ports. Then Union forces in the west, under Generals Grant and Sherman, swept through Tennessee, and by the end of 1863 the North had taken Vicksburg, the final Confederate-held port on the Mississippi, as well as the strategic mountain-locked town of Chattanooga on the Tennessee–Georgia border. Grant proceeded north to Virginia while Sherman captured the transport nexus of Atlanta and began a bloody and ruthless march to the coast, burning everything in his way. With 228,000 men dead (a quarter of the South's adult white male population), defeat was total, and General Robert E Lee surrendered on April 9 1865 at Appomattox in Virginia.

The war was followed by a period of **Reconstruction**, when the South was occupied by Union troops. The political administrations imposed and run by northern Republicans ("carpetbaggers" or "scalawags") were characterised by corruption, but what galled southerners most was that blacks were also involved in government. When this probationary era came to an end in the mid-1870s, southern states returned to Democratic Party control; black politicians were intimidated out of office, in particular by the **Ku Klux Klan**, which was started in 1865 by ex-Confederate officers. "**Jim**

Crow" segregation laws were imposed – which amounted to a system of apartheid – and poll taxes, literacy tests and property qualifications disenfranchised virtually all blacks (and many poor whites).

The war had left the South in chaos; its towns had been destroyed and, with the abolition of slavery, the plantations were no longer viable. Instead the economy turned to **sharecropping**, a crude barter system under which landowners provided their tenants with land, housing and even food and implements, the cost of which was later deducted (along with a high rate of interest) from the sale of crops. Most farms were too small to be economical and sharecropping encouraged production of cash crops rather than food. As a result, the freed slaves benefited little from the abolition of the "peculiar institution": thousands were forced into debt, and and there were mass migrations to cities like Memphis and Atlanta, and to the North.

After the uncertainties of Reconstruction, industrial growth accelerated (the impetus coming ironically from northern investors who took advantage of the cheap land and labour), but by the time of the 1929 stock market crash the South still lagged well behind the North. During the **Depression**, the suffering of the region was exacerbated by the fact that its people were so poor to begin with. Roosevelt's New Deal programme, particularly the establishment of the TVA (see p.385) and road-building works, helped to alleviate immediate hardships and lay down an infrastructure to aid economic recovery, and the war effort during the early Forties stimulated industrial growth. Since the Sixties, foreign companies, particularly Japanese, have opened thousands of new factories in the South, attracted by the anti-union "Right to Work" statutes upheld by most states. What was the "Cotton Belt" now likes to go under the high-tech label of the "Sun Belt", but an overall lack of agricultural and industrial diversification still means that huge parts of the South remain overwhelmingly and disturbingly poor.

The political and legal advances made in Roosevelt's New Deal also started a more liberal trend in federal law-making. A groundbreaking 1954 Supreme Court ruling outlawed segregation in schools, but individual states in the South were at best very slow to effect the required changes. The **civil rights movement** was effectively started when blacks campaigned for the implementation of desegregation in education, and soon expanded to encompass demonstrations and protests against racial barriers in other areas of life, such as the Montgomery bus boycott and the Greensboro lunch counter sit-in. Before civil rights legislation was finally imposed in the late Sixties, southern whites, led by fire-eating politicians, put up a bloody resistance to social change, and left behind a catalogue of murder, attacks and harassment – particularly in Mississippi and Alabama.

The civil rights years left a marked effect on **party politics** in the South. Since the Civil War the region had voted almost en bloc for the **Democrats**, but as that party has become more identified with liberal reforms, greater government intervention and, especially, racial integration, there has been a marked shift towards the Republican Party, especially in presidential elections. Right-wing politicians have been forced to search for a party political home; Strom Thurmond of South Carolina and the equally vitriolic George Wallace campaigned for the US presidency under the banners of small segregationist parties, while the leading demagogue in the South today, Senator Jesse Helms of North Carolina, is a Republican. Nevertheless, many unreconstructed backwoodsmen still fight for white supremacy under the umbrella of the Democratic Party.

The plight of **Native Americans** is often the forgotten chapter of southern history. Colonial powers at best tolerated the Indians, for the most part peaceful, agrarian tribes, and used them as allies in their imperialist wars with each other. However, after the Revolution, pressure from plantation owners and small farmers led to the forced removal in the 1830s of the "five civilised tribes" – the Cherokee, Creek, Choctaw, Chickasaw and Seminole – to malarial Oklahoma. Today only a few thousand Native Americans live in the South.

NORTH CAROLINA

NORTH CAROLINA, though the most industrialised of the southern states, remains relatively rural and poor, with just six million people spread over an area larger than England. It suffered heavily during the **Civil War**, and **Reconstruction** brought mixed fortunes: although the Democrats regained control in 1870, they ran a liberal administration and were effective in stamping out the Ku Klux Klan. Since then there have been parallel traditions of radical black, and white racist, activity. **Greensboro**, for example, where **Jesse Jackson** served his political apprenticeship, was the site of the 1960 lunch-counter sit-in by black students, and also of the Greensboro Massacre of 1979 when Klansmen opened fire on a Communist Workers Party demonstration, killing five people, but were acquitted in the courts. The state's politics, particularly in rural areas, reflect the anti-gay, anti-union views of its senior senator, **Jesse Helms**, the unofficial leader of the US far right. This may be changing, however, after the very nearly successful attempt to unseat Helms in 1990 by **Harvey Gantt**, the black mayor of Charlotte.

Geographically, North Carolina breaks down into three distinct areas: running from east to west, the coast, the Piedmont and the mountains. For visitors, the **coast** is much the most promising, with good beaches, beautiful landscapes and a fascinating history. The inner coast consists largely of the less developed **Albemarle Peninsula**, with colonial Edenton nearby. The **Piedmont** is dominated by manufacturing cities. **Raleigh**, the state capital, and its twin city, **Durham**, home of prestigious Duke University, have little to recommend them. **Charlotte** bills itself as the next boom city of the South, but for the moment it's a boring mix of downtown skyscrapers and suburban malls. In the **mountains**, one of the most stunning stretches of Appalachia, the only towns of any size, Boone and Ashville, are linked by the spectacular **Blue Ridge Parkway**, while **Great Smoky Mountains National Park** overlaps the border with Tennessee.

Getting Around North Carolina

North Carolina's major **airports** are at Raleigh-Durham, a hub for *American Airlines*, and Charlotte, which offers a few transatlantic flights each week. Charlotte, Raleigh-Durham and Greensboro are served by *Amtrak* **trains**, but unfortunately there is no coastal route. Plenty of buses run within the Piedmont; schedules are much less frequent in the mountains and along the coast, both of which are best explored by car. The state has a good network of **cycling** routes along quiet country roads; for information contact the Dept of Transportation, 1 S Wilmington Street, Raleigh (☎733-2804).

The North Carolina Coast

The North Carolina **coast**, which ranges through salt marshes, beaches, barrier islands and estuaries, holds most of the state's more interesting **historic sites**. The continent's earliest English colonists vanished inexplicably from **Roanoake Island** in 1590; just over three centuries later, the Wright brothers achieved the first powered flight at **Kitty Hawk**. The **Outer Banks**, the long reef of barrier islands which stretch down from Virginia, are in parts tacky and elsewhere beautifully unspoiled.

Edenton and the Albemarle

The huge and generally relaxed **Albemarle Peninsula** remains largely unexploited. Local towns try to make much of their **colonial history** – this was the first part of North Carolina to have permanent European settlements, around the end of the seventeenth century – but often there's not a lot left to see, except for restored eighteenth-century buildings that get a bit similar after a while.

The telephone **area code** for the coast and the northern Piedmont is ☎919.

Edenton

EDENTON, set along a beautiful Albemarle-Sound **waterfront** roughly forty miles back from the ocean and the same distance south of the Virginia border, was established as North Carolina's first state capital in 1722. A major centre of unrest in the American Revolution, it remained a prosperous port until the early nineteenth century, when it began to fade. Today Edenton feels frozen some time around 1961.

As you stroll around the town – possibly aided by the self-guided walking tour issued by the **Barker House Visitor Center** (Mon–Sat 9am–4.30pm, Sun 2–5pm; ☎482-3663) – you'll come across an exceptional number of colonial and pre-Civil War **houses**, and the magnificent wooden **Cupola House**. St Paul's Parish Church, and the Georgian Chowan County Courthouse overlooking the waterfront are fine mid-seventeenth-century structures. The **main street** is also interesting in an offbeat way: Victorian facades, old-fashioned drugstores selling home-mixed sodas, and Fifties chrome signs.

The visitor centre also puts on a narrated slide show on the region, good on colonial history if not so explicit about slavery. There's no mention of the remarkable **Harriet Jacobs**, a slave who ran away from her master after being sexually harassed and hid for seven years in her grandmother's attic. She finally escaped to the North through various ruses including disguising herself as a male sailor, and was eventually reunited in Boston with the two children she had had by a white man in Edenton. She wrote this amazing story as *Incidents in the Life of a Slave Girl*, which became one of the most famous published slave narratives of the nineteenth century. Unfortunately, none of the buildings mentioned in the book is still standing, although you can get an idea of where places were from the map in the recent Harvard UP edition (1987).

Edenton isn't a bad place to **stay** while you explore the rest of the coast. B&Bs such as the *Trestle House Inn* on Soundside Road (☎482-2282) start at around $65 per night, while cheap **motels** include the *Coach House Inn* (☎482-2107) and the *Colonial Motel* (☎482-8010) on Broad St/US-17 north, both with rooms from around $35. The *Colonial Motel* also has a good inexpensive all-you-can-eat **buffet** of Southern food.

Exploring The Albemarle

Albemarle **plantation** life can be sampled at **Hope**, the home of a state governor and US senator of the revolutionary and Federal period, David Stone. It's off Hwy-308, a few miles west of **Windsor**, about 25 miles southwest of Edenton (March to late Dec Mon–Sat 10am–4pm, Sun 2–5pm; $5). The house, built in 1803, is classic Southern myth. White, with a double balcony at the front, it's all rather idyllic – though there's no mention of the slaves flogged, chained and sold by Stone to build his retreat.

You can get a better idea of slave life at **Somerset Place State Historic Site**, a plantation 25 miles southeast of Edenton on US-64 (summer Mon–Sat 9am–5pm, Sun 1–5pm; winter Mon–Sat 10am–5pm, Sun 1–4pm; free). This is how the lowland plantations must have looked, with fields dissolving into marshland beyond huge oaks. The wooden shacks of the slaves' quarters have gone, although you can see the foundations of the tiny shed-sized slave "hospital". A descendant of slaves from here is now the director of the site.

There's a **campground** at the neighbouring **Pettigrew State Park** on Phelps Lake (☎797-4475; $6). Even if you don't stay, take time to go down to the tiny museum at the water's edge, which has an interesting display on local Native Americans. It includes a couple of 400-year-old dugout canoes raised from the lake; others have been found that have been dated to well over 2000 years ago.

The southern shore of the Albemarle has less to see, although it's pretty and unspoiled. The Memorial Museum in the city hall at **Belhaven**, 25 miles east of

Washington, (daily 1–5pm; free), houses an engaging collection of anything and every-thing, from dressed fleas (as silly as it sounds) to old tools and militaria. There's a **campground** a couple of miles east (☎943-2849; $12 per tent) and a **motel** in Swan Quarter.

The surrounding marshy countryside and tree-lined roads make for a pleasant drive, and **Lake Mattamuskeet Wildlife Refuge**, off Hwy-94 on the causeway across the lake or off US-264 near New Holland, is an amazing sight in winter, when thousands of swans migrate here from Canada.

The Outer Banks

The **OUTER BANKS** are a series of long sand bars, sprinkled with sea oats, that stretch around 180 miles from the Virginia border to Cape Lookout, near Beaufort; a great place to wander along at your own speed, although unfortunately there's no public transport apart from the ferries between islands and to the mainland.

The main road from the north, US-158, crosses from the mainland on a low bridge to the southern half of **Bodie Island**; there's a roadside **visitor centre** as soon as you get onto the island (☎261-4644). South along US-158 and the parallel shoreline Beach Road, the seaside towns of Kitty Hawk, Kill Devil Hills and Nag's Head are strung out without a break, and the fine warm-water **beaches** are lined with motels and fast-food places mixed in with the huge holiday "cottages".

Kitty Hawk and Roanoke Island

The **Wright Brothers National Memorial** (daily summer 9am–7pm; winter 9am–5pm; ☎441-7430), just off the main road at **KITTY HAWK**, commemorates the **first ever powered flight**, on December 17 1903. A museum records the brothers' various experiments; after several years of trials with kites and gliders, visiting the Outer Banks for a few weeks at a time and living in makeshift shacks on the beach, they finally shook hands before launching their powered plane on a cold December morning. As one of the local lifeboatmen acting as ground crew remarked, "we couldn't help notice how they held on to each other's hand, sort o' like folks parting who weren't sure they'd ever see one another again." Wilbur asked the men "not to look too sad, but to . . . laugh and holler and clap . . . and try to cheer Orville up when he started." The phlegmatic Orville recorded the historic moment of take-off in his diary: "the machine lifted from the truck . . . I found control of the front rudder quite difficult . . . the machine would rise suddenly to about 10 ft and then as suddenly, on turning the rudder, dart for the ground . . . time about 12 seconds."

ROANOKE ISLAND, between Bodie Island and the mainland via US-64/264 and another bridge, was the **first English settlement** in North America, founded by **Sir Walter Raleigh** in 1585. The colonists survived initial difficulties with weather, disease and Indians, and were joined by one hundred more settlers brought over by John White in 1587. When White returned three years later, however, all trace of the colony had disappeared, except for the one mysterious word "Croatoan" carved on a tree. Theories as to the fate of the "Lost Colony" have varied, although it was and is gener-ally assumed that the settlers were massacred by hostile Indians – a key piece of early anti-Indian mythology. A rather fanciful but happier version has it that settlers and Indians banded together and marched inland, forming what is now the small and very racially mixed Lumbee tribe in southwest North Carolina.

Nothing authentic survives of Roanoke, but **Fort Raleigh**, three miles north of **Manteo** off US-64, is a conjectural reconstruction of the colonists' earthwork fort (daily summer 9am–8.15pm; winter 9am–5pm; free). Its museum is quite good on local Indian interaction with colonists. In Manteo, *Elizabeth II* is a reconstruction of **Raleigh's ship** (April–Oct daily 10am–6pm; Nov–March Tues–Sun 10am–4pm; $3).

The *Nettlewood Motel*, at Mile 7 on Beach Road in Kill Devil Hills (☎441-5039) charges around $40 for a double in summer, less out of season. Also on Beach Road in Kill Devil Hills, the *Mex-Econo* (☎441-8226) – a Mexican restaurant with surf-punk decor, spraypainted toilets and good, cheapish food – doubles as a night-time music venue where punk and guitar rock bands play almost every night.

Cape Hatteras National Seashore

CAPE HATTERAS NATIONAL SEASHORE stretches south onto **Hatteras** and **Ocracoke** islands, with wonderful unspoiled beaches on its seaward side. Most tourists just drive straight through on Hwy-12, and even in high season you can pull off the road and walk across the dunes to deserted beaches. The salt marshes on the western side are also beautiful, and at the northern end of Hatteras island the **Pea Island National Wildlife Refuge** has trails and observation platforms from which you can see a wide variety of birdlife. Over 600 ships have been wrecked along this treacherous stretch of coast since the sixteenth century. At the south end of Hatteras island, near the early nineteenth-century **Cape Hatteras Lighthouse**, a visitor centre (daily 9am–5pm, free; ☎987-2394) holds displays on the island's maritime history.

If you want to stay on Hatteras, there are **motels**, food shops and rather second-rate **restaurants** in the fly-blown settlements along Hwy-12; the *Ocean Aire* (☎987-2244; Easter–Nov only) in **Rodanthe** has rooms from $45 in summer. **Camping** is best, however, at one of the summer-only National Park Service campgrounds, near **Salvo**, **Buxton** and **Frisco**. These operate on a first-come, first-served basis, and tend to fill up, but you can usually find space – Ocracoke and Bodie island ranger stations at the entrances to the seashore keep daily lists of what's available (or call ☎473-2111).

Ocracoke Island

OCRACOKE ISLAND (pronounced *oke-ruhcoke*), forty minutes by ferry from Hatteras, is just as beautiful. The village of **Ocracoke**, at its southern tip, despite the crowds of tourists, somehow seems to have hung on to a least a bit of its village atmosphere, especially on the back lanes. There's nothing in particular to see, except perhaps for the harbour and squat brown lighthouse (you can't go in), and the tiny British cemetery where several sailors killed offshore during World War II are buried. You can see all this on a **trolley tour** from the *Trolley Stop* restaurant (on Hwy-12 as you come into the village; ☎928-1111; $3.50), although it's nicer just to walk or cycle – there are several **bike rental** places.

The many **hotels** and **B&Bs** in Ocracoke village get full in summer, and aren't particularly cheap; prices drop in September as elsewhere on the Outer Banks. The laid-back *Lightkeeper's Inn*, just off the harbour near the lighthouse (☎928-1821), charges $45 for a double all year, and the small *Sand Dollar Motel* (☎928-5571) is very reasonable. As for **food**, the *Trolley Stop* (☎928-4041) is about the cheapest; the *Back Porch*, on the main street (☎928-6401), is more reliable. There's a fairly isolated Park

---

OCRACOKE FERRIES

In summer, **ferries** between Ocracoke and Hatteras leave both islands on the hour and half hour all day, slightly less frequently before 7am and after 6.30pm. The crossing takes forty minutes, although you may have to wait to get on in a car as there's limited space and it's loaded on a first-come, first-served basis.

Ferries from Ocracoke also go south down the coast to **Cedar Island** (2hr 15min; 8 daily each way in summer, 4 in winter), and to and from **Swan Quarter**, on the Albemarle (2 per day all year; 2hr 30min). Both require motorists to reserve in summer; at short notice you should get the day you want, if not the time. Call the port from which you want to leave: Ocracoke – ☎928-3841; Cedar Island – ☎225-3551; Swan Quarter – ☎926-1111.

Service **campground** a few miles north, which tends to be the first of the Outer Banks sites to fill up (you can reserve through *Ticketron*), and a couple of commercial camp-grounds in the village, including *Beachcomber's Campground* (☎928-4031).

Cape Lookout National Seashore

The mainland between Cedar Island and Beaufort is a rural backwater, sparsely settled and hardly touched by tourists. It's reasonably attractive to wander around, but towns such as **Davis** and **Smyrna** don't have any accommodation, and the most likely reason to pass through is to get to the all but deserted **CAPE LOOKOUT NATIONAL SEASHORE**, which stretches south of Ocracoke Island along two undeveloped Outer Banks, with no roads or habitation (park headquarters in Beaufort, ☎728-2121). Its few visitors share a total of around 55 miles of beach along both islands, with the marshes on the landward side supporting rich and unusual plant and bird life adapted to the harsh, salty conditions.

At the northern tip of the **north island**, across from Ocracoke, stand the pretty, strangely eerie ruins of the abandoned village of **Portsmouth**, whose last two resi-dents only left in 1971. The main ferry for the island, from **Atlantic** (Morris Marina, 3 per day each way; $12 return; ☎225-4261) lands fifteen miles south of Portsmouth, which you can only reach on foot. Two boatmen also carry groups of three or more travellers to or from Ocracoke (Rudy Austin at ☎928-4361, or Dave McLawhorn at ☎928-5921; $15 per person). **Cabins** on the island, operated by the ferry company, cost around $10 per person; otherwise there's only primitive **camping**, with neither drink-ing water nor food available.

The **south island** is served in summer by two private ferries each way per day from Davis ($12 return; call Mr Alger Willis at ☎729-2791). Here, too, the ferry company manages some wood **cabins** (the smallest sleeps 4 people; all work out to $10 per head if full). Camping is as primitive as on the north island, but the ferry will buy food for you on the mainland and bring it across (at a 25 percent surcharge), and water supply and showers are supposedly being laid on near the ferry landing. Another ferry runs to the southern tip of the south island from low-key Harker's Island, south of Smyrna, to within two miles of Cape Lookout itself and its lighthouse (*Carteret Boat Tours*, ☎728-3866; $12 return).

Shackleford Island, which does not form part of the National Seashore, is rather more varied, with high sand dunes roamed by wild horse, and dwarf forests of trees hanging on in the harsh environment. Several places in Beaufort offer trips out – *Beaufort Tours* charge around $10 per person for a three- to four-hour trip (☎728-7827). They also do trips out to Carrot Island, in front of Beaufort harbour, for $5.

Beaufort

BEAUFORT, about 150 miles southeast of Raleigh just beyond the end of US-70, is probably the nicest of North Carolina's seaside towns; a relaxing place to hang out and drink cold beer, or just sit around on the waterfront. The **Maritime Museum** has good displays on local ecology and shipping history (Mon–Fri 9am–5pm, Sat 10am–5pm, Sun 2–5pm; free). In the restored area on Block Turner Street, off the waterfront, you'll find handsome **old houses**, an apothecary's shop, and the city jail. The main house serves as the town **visitor centre** (Mon–Sat 9.30am–4.30pm; ☎728-5225).

B&Bs along Ann Street – which was named for Queen Ann, and still boasts an elm tree sent by her personally – include the forty-room *Beaufort Inn* at no. 101 (☎728-2600), where doubles start at $45 in winter and $80 in summer, and the more friendly and inti-mate Victorian *Captains' Quarters* at no. 315 (☎728-7711), which ranges seasonally from $50 to $100 and has a wraparound verandah. There are cheaper motels and places to eat in **Morehead City**, a couple of miles down the coast, or in the Bogue Bank resorts.

The Beaches

South of Beaufort, the quality of the beaches along the twenty-mile offshore **Bogue Bank** ensures that they are always pretty crowded, especially at **Atlantic Beach** at the east end and marginally less so at **Emerald Isle**, to the west. On **Bear Island** to the south, though – reached by a summer-only ferry ($2) which operates a strict quota as to the number of passengers allowed in any one day – the stunning **Hammocks Beach State Park** offers high sand dunes, a wooded shore and perfect beaches. The entrance is two miles west of **Swansboro**; you have to register at the small park centre if you want to **camp** ($4; ☎326-4881). No camping is permitted on the few days around each full moon when **loggerhead sea turtles** come ashore to lay their eggs.

On the far side of the Camp Lejeune US Marine base, **Topsail Island**, yet another sand bar of resorts, is considerably less built up than Bogue Bank, presumably because its beaches aren't quite as good. **Surf City** and **Topsail** are both slightly run-down family resorts, with lots of cheap and rather shabby motels (cheaper out of season) and campgrounds. Public beach access points are signposted from the main road, but in practice you can get down at lots of other places.

South on the mainland the resorts get bigger and more crowded, but are still fairly manageable. At the tip of the peninsula near Kure, **Fort Fisher State Historic Site** commands a spectacular rocky site overlooking both the sea and the mouth of the Cape Fear River. A free museum focuses on its days as a Confederate stronghold during the Civil War (Mon–Sat 9am–5pm, Sun 1–5pm).

Wilmington

Though it's the largest place along the North Carolina coast, **WILMINGTON**, set back along the Cape Fear River fifty miles short of the southern border, has a welcoming down-home feel. During the Civil War, it was briefly the Confederacy's most important harbour, exporting cotton all over the world. "**Blockade-runners**" would attempt to outrun the Union navy, racing into the safety of Fort Fisher's guns. It was a stronghold of radical politics when, to the horror of the Democratic elite, a "Fusionist" (Republican-Populist-black) governor was elected in 1896. (Electoral fraud and intimidation ensured that the state did not have another Republican governor until 1980.) In a furious racist backlash, dozens of blacks were murdered by white mobs in the **Race Riot** of 1898.

Despite its traumatic history, Wilmington today is an attractive and friendly town, with a historic district that feels genuinely lived-in. The extravagant houses and ornate City Hall demonstrate its former wealth, while the cobbled streets of the **waterfront**, now lined with rather upmarket cafes and restaurants, are nice, if a bit too picturesque for their own good. Incidentally, much of the movie *Teenage Mutant Ninja Turtles* was filmed in Wilmington.

At 814 Market Street, the free **New Hanover County Museum** (Tues–Sat 9am–5pm, Sun 2–5pm) gives a reasonable account of local history, but barely touches on the Race Riot, nor on the more recent jailing of ten black civil rights activists on trumped-up arson charges. Before their pardon by President Carter, the "Wilmington Ten" were described by Amnesty International as "the most visible political prisoners in the US".

Practicalities

Wilmington's visitor centre is at 24 West Third Street (☎341-4030). The **bus** station is at 201 Harnette Street, a mile north of downtown off Third Street (☎762-6625). B&Bs such as the *Worth House*, 412 S Third Street (☎762-8562), charge from $70 in summer; there are cheaper **motels** on US-17 at the edge of town: *Motel 6* (☎467-6171) costs around $30, the *Comfort Inn* (☎763-3318) is more like $40. The nearest **campground** is *Camelot Campground*, seven miles north on US-17 (☎686-7705; $13 per tent).

Away from the waterfront, the town has a fairly thriving local nightlife – even a small gay scene. As far as **food** is concerned, suffice it to say that a recent survey showed that Wilmington's residents spend more per capita every year on fast food than the citizens of any other American town – almost $600 per head.

The North Carolina Piedmont

North Carolina's **Piedmont** is a fairly industrialised area of textile and tobacco towns, mostly in decline. Even close to the towns it can still be very rural, little changed since the 1950s and intensely conservative – it produced Senator Jesse Helms, as well as the turn-of-the-century novelist and white supremacist Thomas Dixon, who used it as the setting for his hugely successful books *The Leopard's Spots* (1902) and *The Clansman* (1905) – the latter adapted by Griffith for his epic film glorifying the Klan, *Birth of a Nation* (1916). Other writers – including Thomas Wolfe, while living in Chapel Hill – have concentrated more on the upheavals of industrialisation and on working-class life.

Charlotte

More than anywhere else in the region, **CHARLOTTE** can genuinely claim to have made it, a financial and transport centre which has become the largest city in the state. It has been "boosted", in much the same way as Atlanta (see p.367), by ambitious businessmen and city leaders who like to project the image of a sophisticated, fast-lane cultural metropolis, but in fact it's somewhat soulless – it could be anywhere. Served by direct *US Air* flights from London, however (see p.4), it does make a less abrasive point of arrival in the country than the larger cities of the north.

Downtown Charlotte, known as "uptown", is an unlovely mass of skyscrapers and concrete. The medium-sized **Mint Museum**, three miles east at 2730 Randolph Road on bus #15 (Tues 10am–10pm, Wed–Sat 10am–5pm, Sun 1–6pm; $2), has a good array of Indian and African art plus historical items. The **Spirit Square Arts Center**, 110 E Seventh Street (☎372-9664), has more art, and stages performances by the city's theatre company and symphony orchestra. **Discovery Place**, 301 N Tryon Street (Mon–Sat 9am–6pm, Sun 1–6pm; $4), is a kids-oriented science museum with an indoor rainforest.

Carowinds Theme Park (early June to mid-Aug Sun–Thurs 10am–8pm, Sat 10am–10pm; late March to early June Sat & Sun 10am–8pm; $17.95), ten miles south of Charlotte on I-77, is a vast conglomeration of uninspired but quite enjoyable Americana. As well as roller coasters and other rides, Carolinan theme areas include "Blue Ridge Junction", about the mountains, and Plantation Square, a reconstruction of Charleston's antebellum waterfront. The nearby **Heritage USA** (daily 10am–midnight; free) is owned by the **Praise the Lord** organisation, the far-right-wing Christian fundamentalist lobby founded by Reaganite televangelist Jerry Falwell. PTL took it over, along with the Inspirational Network broadcasting company, from Jim and Tammy Bakker in 1987, after Bakker was unseated (and jailed for forty years) following allegations of sexual misconduct and, later, fraud. As it was little short of a shrine to Bakker, Heritage USA's future is now uncertain. This dire collection of tobacco and alcohol-free restaurants, TV studios and trinket shops also includes the transplanted birthplace of Billy Graham.

Practicalities

Charlotte's **airport** (☎359-4000) is five miles west of town on Wilkinson Boulevard or I-85. **Buses** connect it with the city during rush hours (6–9am & 3–6pm; 70¢) and **taxis** cost about $11. Coming by **rail**, the *Amtrak* station is at 1914 Tryon Street; *Greyhound/Trailways* is at 601 W Trade Street (☎527-9393). The **visitor centre** is at the corner of Church and Sixth streets (Mon–Fri 8.30am–5pm; ☎371-8700).

The telephone **area code** for Charlotte and the mountains is ☎704.

Most of Charlotte's identical **hotels** are aimed at the conference trade. The cheaper ones are concentrated away from the centre, on I-85 and I-77. The two *Econo-Lodges*, near the airport off I-85 on Little Rock Road (☎394-0172), and four miles north off I-85 on Sugar Creek Road (☎597-0470), both have doubles from $40, and there's a cheaper *Motel 6* near the airport at 3433 Mulberry Church Road (☎394-0899). Of the city's **restaurants**, the *Bayou Kitchen*, 1958 E Seventh Street (☎332-2256), serves reasonable and moderately priced Cajun food, with live folk music, while *La Paz*, 23 Fenton Place (☎372-4168), is an excellent if crowded Mexican. *Calabash Cove and 42nd St Oyster Bar*, three miles east at 2920 Central Avenue (☎535-0248), is a good place to sample North Carolina fried seafood. There's also a fairly active **music** scene; good live jazz can be heard at *The Jazz Cellar at Jonathan's*, 330 N Tryon Street (☎332-3663), set in an expensive downtown restaurant, and country music just south of the city at *Lil' Gilleys*, 2740 Carowinds Boulevard (☎548-1324). For full listings, get hold of the *Charlotte Observer*.

The North Carolina Mountains

In the distinctive North Carolina **mountains**, local cultural traditions include **bluegrass** music, as played by Doc Watson (from Deep Gap) and Earl Scruggs, and **snake handling**, practiced by certain evangelical sects. It's a very poor region; the backroads, north of Asheville, are notable for grinding poverty set amidst stunning mountain views – families of grubby white children playing outside what are little more than shacks, and dilapidated trailer homes everywhere.

The Blue Ridge Parkway

The scenic **Blue Ridge Parkway**, which runs across northwestern North Carolina from Front Royal, Virginia (see p.315), to Cherokee at the gateway to the Great Smoky Mountains National Park, was mostly built in the 1930s by Roosevelt's Civilian Conservation Corps volunteers. It's closed to lorries and farm vehicles, and makes very easy driving, with superb views and numerous state-run campgrounds and short hiking trails all along its length. The peak tourist season is October, when the leaves turn, but it only gets really crowded at one or two hyped beauty spots, and the colours are simply breathtaking. Almost all the landscape is wooded, and most of the trees are deciduous, turning a range of colours from bright yellow and gold through browns to vivid red.

Boone

BOONE is the most obvious northern base for exploring the mountains, though the town itself, home to the Appalachian State University, holds little of interest. The backroads are pretty, dotted with occasional offbeat settlements, like **Valle Crucis** on US-194, where the *Mast General Store* still operates much as it did when first established in 1883. Commercial attractions in the area tend towards the tacky, such as the miniature *Tweetsie Railroad* or corny *Mystery Hill* house of optical illusions, both out on US-321.

A reasonable town **bus**, *AppalCART*, operates all over Boone and out along US-321 south (red route), from a station on Winkler's Creek Road also used by *Greyhound* and *Trailways*, Boone's only long-distance public transport connection. The **visitor centre** (☎264-2225) is south of town on US-321, which here is Blowing Rock Road. Of cheap **motels** nearby, the *Elk Motel* (☎264-6191) charges around $40 in summer; the more central *Boone Trail Motel* (☎264-8839), on US-421 as you come into town from the east, is similarly priced. Places to **eat** along Bowling Rock Road include *Shadracks* (☎264-

MOUNTAIN ACTIVITIES

Organised **outdoor pursuits** available along the Blue Ridge Parkway include excellent **whitewater rafting** and **canoeing**, most of it on the Nolichucky River near the Tennessee border south of Johnson City, TN, but also on the Watauga River and Wilson Creek. Among the many companies running trips are *Wahoo* (☎1-800/444-7238), based near Boone, and *High Mountain Expeditions* (☎295-4200) in Blowing Rock. Expect to pay $15–20 for a half day, $40 for a full day (safety equipment included), according to the exact length and difficulty of your trip.

In winter, this is also a fairly big area for **skiing**, with a number of slopes and resorts, particularly around **Banner Elk**, about twelve miles southwest of Boone. Resort accommodation is expensive, lift passes less so ($15–25 for each weekday). *Appalachian Ski Mountain* (☎1-800/322-2373) is near Blowing Rock, and *Ski Beech* (☎1-800/222-2293) at Beech Mountain; you can pick up full lists at visitor centres. A few places also offer **cross-country skiing**, at around $40 for a day tour.

1737), good for moderate-price barbecues, and with live bluegrass music at weekends, and the *Tumbleweed Grille* across from the ASU baseball field (☎264-7111), which serves reasonable, filling and cheap Mexican food. Next door, the *Klondike* (☎262-5065) is a basic but lively student bar. At weekends the *Depot St Music Hall*, 110 S Depot Street (☎262-5483), puts on live rock, with jazz on Sunday.

South Along The Parkway

Eight miles south of Boone, the town of **BLOWING ROCK** is a pleasant if touristy resort just south of the Parkway. The "Blowing Rock" itself (daily 8am–7pm; $3) is a bit silly, named for the implausible legend that says objects such as lovelorn Indians which fall from it will be blown back up by the wind – but the views are amazing. At the nearby **Parkway Craft Center** (☎295-7938), you can see traditional folk crafts being made. The **visitor centre** (☎295-7851) is on the main street, as well as standard-priced **motels** such as the *Boxwood* (☎295-9984). Just north of town, the *AYH*-affiliated **hostel** at the **Blowing Rock Assembly Grounds** (☎295-7813; $8) is a favourite haunt of Christian groups; the cheapest of the local **campgrounds** is at **Julian Price Park** on the Parkway (☎963-5911; $9). At *Woodland's*, on Hwy-12, the pork barbecue is excellent; it's also a good spot to drink beer, as is the back porch of *Holley's* (☎295-7661).

Holley's has a fine view of **Grandfather Mountain** (5964ft), fifteen miles further down the Parkway. The mountain is privately owned and a bit overpriced (daily summer 8am–8.30pm; winter 9am–4pm; $8.50), but the views from the top and from the suspension bridge between the peaks are about as good as they get. There are captive bears and other animals in habitat settings, and you can watch hang-gliders launch from the top. In the second week in July, the **Highland Games** and "Gathering of the Clans", consists of distantly Scottish Americans dressing up in kilts and pretending to have just come in off the bonnie braes.

This stretch of the Parkway has a number of short and easy **trails**, signposted from laybys and scenic "overlooks" in various places. The trail half a mile or so up to **Rough Ridge**, near milepost 301, gives you particularly good views east. Rough Ridge is one of several access points to the 11.5-mile **Tanawha Trail**, which runs back along the ridge above the parkway from Linn Cove to Julian Price Park. Even a short trail will give you a good idea of the mountain forest environment, with the lush and dense forests, fast rivers and occasional rock outcrops offering views out over the mountainsides. A longer backpacking trip, though, is really the best way to see the mountains. Be sure to equip yourself with one of the various large-scale Forest Service maps, widely available in camping stores. It's not difficult walking, although trails aren't always that well maintained and you can get lost rather easily in the woods.

One of the best walks is through the **Linville Gorge Wilderness**, a couple of miles outside Linville Falls village. The high and spectacular **Linville Falls** themselves are at one end of the wilderness. To reach the trails down into the gorge, carry on up the dirt road from the falls car park: a number run down off it at intervals. The **Linville River** at the bottom has some perfect, long, deep swimming pools, while the views from the mountains along either side of the gorge are really breathtaking, over 2000ft down to the river below. Be warned that ascents are steep, and some of the fainter paths are near-jungle. You can also climb **Hawksbill** or **Table Rock** mountains from the nearest unsurfaced Forest Road, which leaves Hwy-181 south of the village of Jonas Ridge (sign-posted "Gingercake Acres", with a small low sign to Table Rock).

The unremarkable but amiable villages of **Linville** and **Linville Falls** have the usual **motels** and restaurants; Linville Falls also holds a **campground** (☎765-2681), and *Spears Restaurant* (☎765-2658) is worth a detour for its hickory-smoked pork barbecue.

The views from the Parkway in the **Mount Mitchell State Park** area, south towards Asheville, are tremendous. Sadly, however, this is largely because as you approach the summit of Mount Mitchell – the highest point in the eastern US, at 6684ft – the trees have been ravaged by acid rain from coal-burning industries in the Chattanooga Basin to the west, and the large barren patches leave the horizon clear.

Twenty miles southeast of the Parkway on US-64/74, the natural rock tower of **Chimney Rock** sticks out from the almost-sheer side of Hickory Nut gorge (8.30am–6pm; $7). A lift takes you to the top, after which you can clamber over smaller nearby formations and walk out along the impressive cliffs, all on steps or protected walkways. A waterfall drops 400ft from the western end of the gorge.

Asheville

The modest provincial centre of **ASHEVILLE**, at the southern end of the mountains, makes an alternative base to Boone. The **Biltmore Estate** – the largest private mansion in the US – is worth a look, although you may well find it prohibitively expensive (daily 9am–5pm; $18.95). The entrance is a couple of miles south of downtown on Biltmore Avenue, just north of I-40. Built in the late nineteenth century by George Vanderbilt, it's a wildly over-the-top piece of nouveau-riche folly, loosely based on Loire chateaux. From the self-indulgent Victorian chic of the indoor palm court and banquet hall to the stately landscaped gardens, the whole thing's doubtless a monument to American Euro-snobbery and the inequities of nineteenth-century capitalism (not to say twentieth, with the entrance fee), but it's all quite entertaining nevertheless.

Asheville's *Greyhound/Trailways* terminal (☎253-5353) is inconveniently located, two miles out of downtown on bus #13 or #14. There's a **visitor centre** downtown at 151 Haywood Street (☎258-6111), where you can find out about the numerous local summer music and craft festivals. The **Mountain Dance and Folk Festival**, in August, features bluegrass and traditional dancing. As for sleeping and eating, there are plenty of **motels** and fast-food places in town and around the interstates. The *Interstate Motel*, 37 Hiawassee Street (☎254-0945), and *American Court Motel*, 85 Merrimon Avenue (☎253-4427), are both cheap and central. The nearest **campground** to town is *Bear Creek RV Park*, 81 S Bear Creek Road, off I-40 to the west (☎253-0798). *Stone Soup*, 50 Broadway Street (☎255-7687), is a co-operative soup and sandwich place, closed in the evenings; in fact nightlife is pretty quiet, although *Bill Stanley's Barbeque and Bluegrass* at 20 S Spruce Street (☎253-4871), something of a local institution, is a good barbecue joint where you can hear live bluegrass and see "clogging" (clog-dancing).

The hugely enjoyable **Black Mountain Folk Festival**, held in mid-May, fourteen miles east on I-40 (1 bus a day), showcases traditional Appalachian and world folk music and usually attracts major European and African musicians. *McDibb's Traditional Music Cafe*, 119 Cherry Street in Black Mountain (☎669-2456), is a good place to hear folk and blues year-round.

Great Smoky Mountains National Park

Most of the tourists who come to North Carolina's mountains head west of Asheville to the **GREAT SMOKY MOUNTAINS NATIONAL PARK**, the most visited national park in the US. The park straddles the border with Tennessee, and is covered in more detail – with a map – in our Tennessee section on p.387. In summer and autumn, the North Carolina approaches to the park are every bit as clogged with traffic as those in Tennessee, and all accommodation can be booked up weeks in advance.

The largest of the possible bases is **CHEROKEE**, where a few Cherokee managed to hang on when the tribe was "removed" along the Trail of Tears to Oklahoma in 1838 (see p.390). Now known as the "Eastern Band of the Cherokee Nation", they have a small reservation on the edge of the park, which derives its main income from tourism. As a result, Cherokee itself is a mass of fast-food restaurants, cornily named motels and tacky gift shops, where the sentimentalised presentation of Indians as noble savages all but equates them with the bears of the park as just another novelty for tourists.

Away from the kitsch and cliche, however, the **Museum of the Cherokee Indian** at the north end of town (summer Mon–Sat 9am–8pm, Sun 9am–5pm; otherwise daily 9am–5pm; $3.50) has good archaeological displays and sections on Cherokee arts and history. You can hear taped Cherokee folk tales, and spoken Cherokee, still widely used on the reservation. *Qualla Arts and Crafts* (☎497-3103), across the street, is a Cherokee-run co-operative selling traditional crafts, principally basketwork. Nearby, the **Oconaluftee Indian Village** (summer daily 9am–5.30pm; $7) is a reconstruction of a mid-eighteenth-century Cherokee village. Amid the log cabins, you can see demonstrations of weaving and basket-making, as well as crafts and skills that have long since died out, such as dugout canoe construction and blowpipe hunting.

Cherokee is not much of a place to stay, without a single passable place to eat, and is unbelievably dead between about October and March. Of its many motels, the central *Thunderbird Motel* (☎497-2212) is about the cheapest at $40 for a double, and is perfectly adequate. Being on an Indian reservation, the whole town is dry.

The **Oconaluftee visitor centre**, the headquarters of the North Carolina side of the park, is a short way out of Cherokee along US-441 (summer 8am–7pm; spring and autumn 8am–6pm; winter 8am–5pm; admission to the park is free; ☎497-9146). Besides good displays on Appalachian farming life, there's a re-creation of a **pioneer village**.

Southwestern North Carolina

West of Asheville, and south of the national park, you come to a number of spectacular **waterfalls**. **Looking Glass Falls**, about twelve miles south of the Parkway on US-276, is in a particularly beautiful section of the **Pisgah National Forest**. The falls drop 85 feet, and there's a great (albeit very cold) swimming hole at the bottom. **Connestee Falls**, a few miles south on US-276 towards Brevard, is a double waterfall, even higher. Unbridled optimists can pay to pan for **gemstones**, particularly rubies, at outwashes of the numerous gem mines near the 250ft **Cullasaja Falls**, further west on US-64.

The far west corner of the state is famous for its superb **whitewater**, primarily on the **Nantahala River**. You can go canoeing or rafting between the "put-in" at Nantahala and the point where US-19 enters the **Nantahala Gorge**, seven miles north at Wesser. Masses of guided raft expeditions charge around $25 for a three-hour trip; one company, *Nantahala Outdoor Center* (☎488-6900), also runs a **youth hostel** (☎488-2175; $8). *Nantahala Rafts* (☎1-800/245-7700) is based a couple of miles south by the river.

West of the Nantahala, off US-129 almost in Tennessee, **Joyce Kilmer National Forest** is worth a final detour. It's one of the last remaining stands of unlogged virgin forest in the southeast, and some hardwood trees have grown to a huge size. There's no camping there, but there are a few places back south on US-129.

SOUTH CAROLINA

Politics in the relatively small state of **SOUTH CAROLINA**, the first to secede from the Union in 1860, have traditionally been conservative. Reconstruction was mired in some of the worst Klan violence anywhere in the South and turn-of-the-century demagogues like Senator Ben Tillman and Governor Cole Blease openly espoused lynching and enforced "Jim Crow" laws with particular zeal. It contains two of the country's most right-wing minor universities – the football-fixated Clemson and the Christian and puritanical Bob Jones University in Greenville, a training ground for the fundamentalist right. Yet as elsewhere in the South, such politics have coexisted alongside radical black politics and culture, and while South Carolina remains, with Mississippi, one of the poorest and most rural states, African-Americans (over half the population) have made considerable gains in employment and education since the Sixties.

On the whole, South Carolina – for the most part rolling Piedmont and flat rural coastal plain – is one of the least interesting states in the South, and would hardly be worth visiting at all if it were not for its glorious **coast**. The grand old peninsular port of **Charleston** is arguably the most elegant city in the US, with beautiful buildings and magnificent tree-lined avenues. It's also a fun place at night. A series of restored plantations stretch as far north as **Georgetown**, after which comes the poseur's paradise of **Myrtle Beach**. South of Charleston is a fascinating subtropical coastline of **sea islands**, great beaches, marshes and lush palmetto groves. The islands preserve the traces of a virtually independent black culture (featuring a unique patois), from the days of early settlement when slaves escaped the mainland plantations.

Although the **Piedmont** industrialised at the same time as Georgia and North Carolina, it lacks their economic diversity, and is more depressed and more than a bit depressing. The main textile centres of **Greenville** and **Spartanburg** are soulless, and the state capital, **Columbia**, is devoid of noteworthy sights, though a few small surrounding towns like Sumter and Camden, both rich in antebellum buildings, are more appealing. Elsewhere, the eastern coastal plain is flat, rural and poverty-stricken, while in the west, the mountain area is very small and hardly more than foothills at that.

Getting Around South Carolina

Charleston has South Carolina's biggest **airport**, with flights to and from major towns on the east coast. Three *Amtrak* routes cut through the state, stopping at Greenville and Clemson in the west, Columbia and other towns in the centre and Charleston on the coast. Most **buses** run along I-85 en route between Charlotte, North Carolina and Atlanta. A less regular service operates along the coast, with Myrtle Beach and Charleston the major stops.

KUDZU

The western Carolinas are badly afflicted by **kudzu**, a leafy climbing vine introduced from Japan in 1876 for decoration and for shade. Its use was encouraged by the federal government from the 1930s to stop soil erosion. Unbelievably, it can grow as much as a foot a day in hot weather, and eventually kills trees by cutting off the sunlight. Now a major problem throughout the southeast, it has covered about two million acres of forest. In places it's amazing, totally carpeting whole stands of trees and telegraph poles and wires. South Carolina folk poet James Dickey's poem *Kudzu* portrays it as a mysterious, evil invader from the east:

> *In Georgia, the legend says*
> *that you must close your windows*
> *at night to keep it out of the house*
> *the glass is tinged with green, even so . . .*

Myrtle Beach and the North Coast

The kindest thing to say about **MYRTLE BEACH**, twenty miles down the coast from the border with North Carolina, at the centre of the fifty-mile "Grand Strand", is that it is unforgettable. It's the kitschiest, most sustained splurge of urban beachside development on the east coast, packed out from late spring through to late summer – even though the beach itself really isn't anything special.

Droves of students, decked out in brightly coloured "jams" and swilling huge quantities of beer, come here from universities all over the South during mid-term vacation breaks (if you've seen the movie *Shag* you'll know what to expect), as do thousands of families from the eastern US. For their delectation, there are dozens of theme parks and crazy golf courses – not to mention the usual *Believe It Or Not* museum and the Waccamaw Pottery and Outlet Park, probably the largest concentration of tasteless ceramics in the world – as well as innumerable bars, discos and fast-food places, ranging from "family restaurants" to brazen studenty pick-up joints. You can buy sunglasses, T-shirts, fireworks and beer practically 24 hours a day.

Practicalities

Greyhound **buses** from Charleston and Wilmington come in to Myrtle Beach at Ninth Avenue N (closed 2.30–7pm daily, and after 2.30pm on Saturday; ☎448-2471). Transport in the beach areas is provided by *Coastal Rapid Public Transit* buses (75¢ one-way).

The **visitor centre** at 13th Avenue N, on the corner with King's Highway (☎672-7444), can provide events listings and details of accommodation – though there's no great reason to choose any one of the countless **motels** over the rest. The waterfront *La Roca Motel*, 1708 Ocean Boulevard (☎448-3341), has doubles from $36 in summer; *King's Road Lodge*, 1205 N King's Highway (☎448-1625), is handy for *Greyhound* and charges more like $45. If you want burgers, standard diner meals or any one of a zillion varieties of ethnic fast food, you'll have no problem finding somewhere. Well prepared **seafood** can be had at the classier *Sea Captain's House* at 3002 N Ocean Boulevard (☎448-8082), or at a number of similar establishments in **Murrells Inlet**, further south.

Myrtle Beach calls itself the "Camping Capital of the World"; most of the commercial **campgrounds** are concentrated along King's Highway (US-17 Business), where just south of town you'll find the vast (and pretty hellish) campground at **Myrtle Beach State Park** (☎238-5325).

South to Charleston: the Plantations

The **waterfront** of **GEORGETOWN**, the first town beyond Myrtle Beach to be anything more than a beach town, is a refreshing and dignified contrast, while the main street has a rather time-warped, late-1950s feel. There are several fine antebellum and eighteenth-century houses: ask at the **visitor centre**, 600 Front Street (☎1-800/777-7705), for a self-guided walking tour sheet. The **Rice Museum** under the clock tower on Front Street (Mon–Fri 9.30am–4.30pm, Sat 10am–4.30pm, Sun 2–4.30pm) tells how the cultivation of rice briefly flourished on the coast during the slavery period. **Rooms** at the *Best Western Carolinian*, 706 Church Street (☎546-5191), start around $60.

Just north out of Georgetown on US-17, the first right turning after the bridge leads to the **Belle W Baruch Plantation** (daily 10am–5.30pm, tours Thurs only; $3). Though now fairly overgrown, the plantation is practically unique in that its original "**slave street**" is still standing, complete with wooden shacks and church. It serves as a powerful reminder of the brutal basis of antebellum southern prosperity and gentility.

The telephone **area code** for the entire state of South Carolina is ☎803.

Hopsewee Plantation, once the home of Thomas Lynch, a signatory of the Declaration of Independence, is twelve miles south on US-17 (March–Oct Tues–Fri 10am–5pm; $5). It's an especially grand mansion set in stunning Spanish-moss-draped grounds; however, clouds of large and ferocious mosquitoes drift up from the adjacent river, so think twice before going in summer. The mosquito-free and less manicured **Hampton Plantation State Park**, further south, eight miles off US-17 on Hwy-857, is probably closer to the look of a typical plantation. The grounds (Thurs–Mon 9am–6pm) are pretty, but the house (Mon–Fri 1–4pm, Sat 10am–3pm, Sun noon–3pm; $1) is most impressive, a huge eighteenth-century neoclassical monolith, its white exterior restored but the inside still bare. As yet, there are no interpretive displays here.

The plantation is isolated in the heart of the dense **Francis Marion National Forest**, badly damaged by Hurricane Hugo in September 1989. It's a heavily black area, particularly known for its sweetgrass basket-weaving. This craft originated with the slaves in West Africa, using tight bundles of grasses to make intricate baskets and pots. You can see baskets being made at roadside stalls here, as well as in Charleston, but in view of the enormously time-consuming work they're far from cheap.

Further south, beyond the forest a few miles north of Charleston, is the much-publicised **Boone Hall Plantation** (spring and summer Mon–Sat 8.30am–6.30pm, Sun 1–5pm; autumn and winter Mon–Fri 9am–5pm, Sun 1–4pm; $6). A visit is a sanitised and annoying experience: the plantation may date from the late seventeenth century but the house is a twentieth-century reconstruction, with tours conducted by hapless young women in Southern belle costumes. The grounds are more interesting, with a long tree-lined drive, and another rare slave street, this time of small mid-eighteenth-century brick cabins that housed privileged slaves – domestic servants and skilled craftsmen.

Charleston

CHARLESTON, one of the most elegant cities in the US, spreads way beyond its original confines on the tip of a peninsula between the Ashley and Cooper rivers, roughly one hundred miles south of Myrtle Beach and north of Savannah. Few other places can match its concentration of over 1500 historic buildings in four square miles; the one drawback is that the city is well aware of just how special it is, and it is probably more expensive to visit than anywhere else in the South.

Founded in 1670, Charleston swiftly boomed as a **port** serving the southern plantations. It became the region's dominant town, a commercial and cultural centre which right from the start had a mixed population, with immigrants including French, Germans, Jews, Italians and Irish as well as the English majority. There was a sizeable **free black** community too, and its then unusually urban density allowed an anonymity and racial openness which, while still dominated by slavery, went a lot further than the rest of the South. Nevertheless there was still slave unrest, culminating in the abortive Veysey slave revolt of 1823, after which the city built the Citadel armoury and later the military university to control future uprisings.

The **Civil War** started on Charleston's very doorstep, at Fort Sumter in the harbour. Fire swept through the city, destroying large chunks, in 1861; more damage was inflicted when it was taken by Union troops in February 1865. The decline of the plantation economy and slump in cotton prices led to an economic crash after the war, made worse by a catastrophic earthquake in 1886. As the upcountry industrialised, capital steadily deserted the city, and it didn't really recover until World War II restored its importance as a port and naval base. Since then, a steady programme of preservation and restoration – not helped by the devastation of Hurricane Hugo in 1989 – has made **tourism** Charleston's main focus. Despite the crowds, however, it has kept its atmosphere – perhaps a tad artificial, but captivating for all that.

Arrival, Getting Around and Information

Charleston International Airport is about ten miles north of downtown, off I-26; a $13 taxi ride. Both *Amtrak* – 4565 Gaynor Avenue, eight miles north of downtown – and *Greyhound* – stranded at 3610 Dorchester Road, out near I-26, by the closure of its former downtown depot (☎744-4247) – are in inconvenient and potentially dangerous locations. **Public transport** isn't bad, however. *SCE&G* buses cover most areas, including the *Amtrak* and *Greyhound* terminals, for 75¢, and the *Downtown Area Shuttle* (*DASH*) runs through downtown south of Cannon Street (every 15min, Mon–Fri 8am–5pm only; 75¢). The many available **guided tours** include *Gray Line* (☎722-4444). You can rent **bikes** from *The Bicycle Shoppe*, 283 Meeting Street (☎722-8168).

Charleston's new **visitor centre**, which gives out lots of discount coupons, can be found at 375 Meeting Street, opposite the Charleston Museum (daily 8.30am–5pm; ☎722-8338). The **post office** is at 11 Broad Street (☎745-4359; zip code 29401).

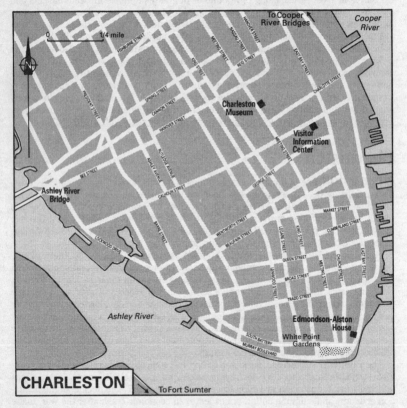

The Town

Charleston's **historic district** is fairly self-contained, bounded by Calhoun Street on the north and East Bay Street, by the river. It's best taken in by strolling around at your own pace – though that pace can get pretty slow at midday in high summer, when the heat is intense. Attractive spots to pause in the shade at such times include the new **Waterfront Park** along Concord Street, and **White Point Gardens**, by the Battery on the tip of the peninsula, which has good views out across the water and a breeze even in summer. Further around, the southern end of the docks was the setting for Dubose Heyward's novel of black waterfront life, *Porgy*, dramatised by Gershwin in his opera *Porgy and Bess* (1935). The market along Market Street is inevitably overcommercial, but it's still fun. The **Preservation Society visitor centre**, 147 King Street (daily 9am–5pm; ☎723-4381), has displays on the restoration of the city since the 1930s, plus information on walking tours. They also show *Dear Charleston*, an interesting documentary in which Charlestonians talk about the town (on the hour, 10am–4pm except at 1pm; $3.25).

Most of the city's fine **houses** are private, and can only be admired from the outside. You're not necessarily missing all that much; the appeal of those that you can get into doesn't take all that long to pall. The late nineteenth-century **Calhoun Mansion**, 16 Meeting Street, is one of the most over-the-top, with its ornate plaster and woodwork, hand-painted porcelain ballroom chandeliers and similar extravagances (daily 10am–4pm; $5). The **Edmonston-Alston House**, 21 E Battery Street, is an 1828 Greek revival mansion (Mon–Sat 10am–5pm, Sun 2–5pm; $4); a $6 combination ticket also gets you into the **Nathaniel Russell House**, 51 Meeting Street, noted for its daring flying staircase (same hours). More varied is the **Charleston Museum**, 360 Meeting Street (Mon–Sat 9am–5pm, Sun 1–5pm; $4), a slightly ragbag collection of city memorabilia.

No **black history** seems to be covered in Charleston now, the slave museum having closed down. The temple-like museum above the entrance to the market is on the site of the slave block; rich Charlestonians gathered on the cobbles below to buy the human cargo off the slave ships.

The very first shots of the Civil War were fired on April 12 1861 at **Fort Sumter**, on a small island some way out from Charleston, where the rivers meet the Atlantic. Once South Carolina had announced its secession, the federal government was faced with the decision whether to attempt to re-provision its forts in the south. The commander of Fort Sumter, Major Robert Anderson, requested supplies in early 1861; when a relief expedition was sent, Confederate General Pierre Beauregard demanded the fort's surrender. In one of the ironies that so characterised the war, General Beauregard, who personally co-ordinated the bombardment, had been the star pupil of artillery classes at West Point taught by Major Anderson himself. After a relentless barrage, the garrison gave in the next day, becoming the first prisoners of the war. The fort was retaken by Union troops on Good Friday 1865, the very day of Lincoln's assassination.

Fort Sumter today is an impressive site, with a good **museum** and guided tours. **Boats** leave from the Municipal Marina, off Lockwood Boulevard (spring and summer daily at 9.30am, noon & 2.30pm; ☎722-1691; $7.50 for boat and fort).

Accommodation

Though Charleston isn't cheap, and **accommodation** options are limited if your budget's tight, it's really worth trying to stay within walking distance of downtown. As well as hotels, a lot of grand historic district houses serve as **B&Bs**, with prices starting at around $65. Agencies include *Charleston Society B&B*, 84 Murray Boulevard (☎723-4948), and *Historic Charleston B&B*, 43 Legare Street (☎722-6606). Further out, there are concentrations of $35-a-night **motels** around US-17 in West Ashley and Mount Pleasant, and along I-26 in North Charleston. Valuable discount coupons can be picked up at visitor centres all over the state.

Days Inn Historic District, 155 Meeting St (☎722-8411). Downtown hotel with rooms from $60.

Heart of Charleston, 200 Meeting St (☎723-3451). Central rooms from around $57.

Motel 6, 2058 Savannah Hwy (☎556-5144). Four miles out; doubles from just under $40.

Rutledge Guest House, 114 Rutledge Ave (☎722-7551). The only cheap place in the historic district, on the west side. Nice double rooms in the three houses start at $47.50; smaller student rooms are $37.50, or $15 (minimum of two days) per person if shared. Friendly atmosphere.

Eating

Eating in Charleston can be expensive; most places in the **historic district** serve over-priced and not terribly distinguished seafood. **Mount Pleasant** and **West Ashley** have a lot more options, though they're not much cheaper; there are rock-bottom diners galore north of downtown, but it's not a great area to find yourself at night.

Aaron's Deli 213 Meeting St (☎723-6000). An excellent New York-style Jewish deli with great sandwiches, open until late and with acoustic folk some nights.

Gaulart and Maliclet, 98 Broad St (☎577-9797). Very nice and not too expensive French bistro.

Henry's, 54 N Market St (☎723-4363). Competitively priced and innovative seafood, very flash decor, and live jazz at weekends.

Joe's Seafood Emporium, 130 Mill St, Mt Pleasant (☎884-3410). Good, fresh food, and cheaper than some of the more pretentious grills around Mount Pleasant.

Kaspers, 72 State St (☎722-7138). Tiny, very cheap diner with good food.

The Magic Wok, 219 Meeting St (☎723-8163). A reasonable, cheap and friendly Chinese.

Pinckney's, 18 Pinckney Street (☎577-0961). Well prepared and inexpensive seafood.

Nightlife and Entertainment

Charleston has quite a dynamic **nightlife**, with a wide choice of **music**, **clubs** and **bars**. It also puts on a lot of festivals – check with the visitor centre, pick up the free monthly listings paper *Omnibus*, or call the *Arts Line* (☎727-8327). The major **Spoleto Festival**, featuring many arts but concentrating mainly on classical music, is held from late May until early June. The **Maja Arts Festival**, in the first half of October, is an interesting African/Caribbean festival of theatre, dance and film, all events free or cheap.

Black Market Cafe, 2 Guignard St (☎722-4220). Small downmarket venue, featuring good blues and bluegrass.

Cumberlands, 26 Cumberland St (☎577-9469). A nice bar and deli which puts on blues and folk.

Deja Vu, 525 E Bay St (☎722-5994). Mixed gay bar.

Louis Charleston Grill at the *Omni Hotel*, 130 Market St (☎722-4900). Surprisingly good jazz in rather synthetic surroundings.

Myskyns, 5 Faber St (☎577-5595). Lively and unpretentious place which attracts some big blues, reggae and African artists, as well as more local rock.

Soft Rock Cafe, 139 Calhoun St (☎577-6219). Rock and acoustic acts in friendly atmosphere.

Out from Charleston

The **river road**, Hwy-61, leads **north** from Charleston along the Ashley River, past a series of magnificent plantations – though all are a bit expensive and very poor on anything grittier than their slave masters' furniture and dining habits. **Drayton Hall**, closest to Charleston, is a particularly fine mid-seventeenth-century Georgian mansion (daily March–Oct 10am–5pm; Nov–Feb 10am–3pm; $6). **Magnolia Plantation and Gardens** is nearby, with stunning ornamental gardens, particularly in spring when the azaleas are blooming (daily 8am–8pm; $7). The **Audubon Swamp Garden** (daily 8am–dusk; $3.50) here is an interesting preservation of a local swamp, complete with such wildlife as alligators, with flowers added. Across the Ashley River, **Charlestowne Landing** is a state park (daily summer 9am–6pm; winter 9am–5pm; $5), with a restored waterfront and a replica of a seventeenth-century merchant ship.

South of Charleston, **beaches** such as **Isle of Palms** and **Sullivan's Island** are heavily used by Charlestonians at weekends. The further you get from town, the more likely you are to find a stretch to yourself. The Mount Pleasant bus from Calhoun Street runs to both Isle of Palms and Sullivan's Island. If you want to stay, there are plenty of motels and eating places, and the odd decent bar – the *Windjammer*, 1008 Ocean Boulevard, Isle of Palms (☎886-8596), is a popular bar with live rock at weekends; *Bert's Bar*, 2209 Middle Street, Sullivan's Island (☎883-9318), is similar.

The Sea Islands

South of Charleston towards Savannah, the coastline, staggeringly rich in seafood, dissolves into marshy, small islands. **Edisto Island**, south of US-17 on Hwy-174, is typical: huge live oaks festooned with great drapes of Spanish moss line the roads, there are bright green marshes with rich bird life, and wide beaches on the seaward side. If you want to stay, there are no cheap motels, but there's a **campground** at **Edisto Beach State Park** (☎869-2156), near a great beach lined with palmetto trees and other semi-tropical plants.

BEAUFORT (pronounced *Byoofort*), the biggest town, has a few old houses but a slightly weird Southern atmosphere, with some strong racial tensions and the baleful proximity of Parris Island US Marine Base, notorious for the brutality of its training regime, as mythologised in Kubrick's Vietnam film *Full Metal Jacket*. The **visitor centre** at 1006 Bay Street (☎524-3163) has details of tours around the small historic district, and discount coupons for the many **motels** out on US-21 – *Lord Careret Motel* (☎524-3303) and *Scottish Inns* (☎524-3166), are among the cheapest, with doubles from $35. The *Greyhound* **bus** station is two miles north of town on US-21 (☎524-4646).

St Helena Island

Across the bridge to the southeast of Beaufort, **ST HELENA ISLAND** is among the least spoiled of the eastern sea islands. The **landscape** is gorgeous: amazing Spanish moss and enormous, wide views out across bright marshes, and small shrimp and oyster fishing communities. Occasionally you see what looks like a fleet of ships in the middle of a field, only to realise that it's actually bright green marsh reeds, and the boats are anchored in a small salt creek hidden by the vegetation.

This is an area of strong **black communities**, descended from slaves, who were given parcels of land when they were freed by the Union army in February 1865, and speak a dialect known as *gullah*, an Afro-English patois with many West African words. There's not much for an outsider to see of this culture, although you do occasionally hear *gullah*, or more often the distinctive West-Indian-style local accent. A **Gullah Institute** at the Penn Center, part of a National Historic District, off US-21, contains the **school** started for freed slaves by Charlotte Forten, a black Massachusetts teacher. Forten remarked that "I have never seen children so eager to learn . . . the majority learn with wonderful rapidity. Many of the grown people are desirous of learning to read. It is wonderful how a people who have been so long crushed to the earth . . . can have so great a desire for knowledge, and such a capability for attaining it." The school was an important retreat for civil rights leaders in the 1960s, used by Dr Martin Luther King Jr's SCLC and others. The white building set back from the road is a **museum** (Mon–Fri 9am–5pm; $1) containing fascinating turn-of-the-century pictures of black fishermen and farmers, plus old tools and shrimp nets, and rattlesnake skins. Nearby, off US-21, is the ruined black **Church of Ease**, amongst thick Spanish moss, with seashell-adorned interior walls.

St Helena's main **beach**, at **Hunting Island State Park** on the east shore, is simply superb. It can get crowded, but it's idyllic: soft white sand, wide and gently shelving, lined with palmettos, palm trees and sea oats, and with incredibly warm water. Pelicans come in to feed, particularly in the early morning, and the shrimp fleet sails past soon after. There's a large **campground** here (☎838-2011), though there are few other places to stay. Occasional roadside restaurants sell excellent fresh **seafood**. The "shrimp burger" at the *Shrimp Shack* (☎838-2962), to the east near Hunting Island, has to be seen to be believed.

There's little more of interest as you head south to Savannah. The last sea island, the resort and retirement complex of **Hilton Head Island**, is really one huge golf course.

GEORGIA

Compared to the rest of **GEORGIA**, the largest of the southern states, the bright lights of its capital **Atlanta** are a wild aberration. Apart from some beaches and towns on the highly indented coastline, this overwhelmingly rural state is composed of slow, easy-going settlements where the best, and sometimes the only, way to enjoy your time is to sip iced tea, and have a chat on the porch.

Settlement in Georgia, the thirteenth British colony (named after King George II), started at **Savannah** in 1733, intended as a haven of Christian principles for poor Britons, with both alcohol and slavery banned. However, under pressure from planters, **slavery** was introduced in 1752, and by the time of the **Civil War** almost half the population were black slaves. Little fighting took place on Georgian soil until Sherman's troops marched in from Tennessee, burned Atlanta to the ground and laid waste to all property on the way to the coast. The economy successfully re-established itself after the war; Atlanta rose from the ashes to become the communications centre of the South, and attracted substantial investment in the latter years of the nineteenth century.

Today, bustling **Atlanta**, the venue for the 1996 Olympics, stands as the unofficial capital of the South. The city where **Dr Martin Luther King Jr** was born, preached, and is buried is held up as a role model for other cities with large black populations – though for all the undeniable progress, it has the highest levels of urban poverty in the country apart from Newark and more violent crime per capita than any US city.

The major tourist destination to rival Atlanta is the **Georgia coast**, stretching south from beautiful old **Savannah** via the **sea islands** to the semi-tropical **Okefenokee Swamp**, slightly inland near the Florida state line. However, several areas of interest lie within an hour's drive of the capital. To the **northwest**, the Appalachian foothills are particularly fetching in autumn, while sixty miles **east** is **Athens**, home to the huge University of Georgia campus. This pleasant if predictable college town is packed with bars and venues featuring progressive Southern guitar rock, as played by bands such as **REM** and the **B-52's**. **South Georgia** is more famous for its people than places to see. **Otis Redding**, **James Brown**, **Little Richard** and the **Allman Brothers** were all born or grew up in the area, while former president and peanut farmer **Jimmy Carter** came from the small town of Plains. The largest communities are the dull army centre of **Columbus** and the textile town of **Macon**.

Getting Around Georgia

Though Georgia's main points of interest are easily accessible, intrastate transport is poor. *Amtrak* **trains** from Washington DC to New Orleans and Florida call at Atlanta and Savannah respectively. **Bus** services in most areas are very patchy and infrequent though there are regular connections between Atlanta and the major cities, and Savannah is served several times a day by buses along the coast. Atlanta has the largest passenger **airport** in the world; Savannah also has a reasonable service.

The telephone **area code** for Atlanta and northern Georgia is ☎404.

Atlanta

ATLANTA is a relatively young city: it was only incorporated in 1847, and was a small transport centre until the Civil War, when its accessibility made it a good site for the huge Confederacy munitions industry – and consequently a major target for the Union army. The **Atlanta Underground** was built at that time, a small network of streets below ground in the centre of town, safe from bombardment. Nevertheless, in 1864

Sherman's army **burned** the city, an act immortalised in *Gone with the Wind*. Recovery after the war took just a few years: Atlanta was the archetype of the aggressive, urban, industrial "New South", furiously championed by **"boosters"** – newspaper owners, bankers, politicians and city leaders. Industrial giants who based themselves here included **Coca-Cola**, source of a string of philanthropic gifts to the city – most recently the Woodruff Arts Center. **Black** immigration to Atlanta was also heavy, leading to the establishment of a thriving community centred around Auburn Avenue.

The "booster" tradition has continued to the present, peaking spectacularly in 1990 when Atlanta won the right to host the 1996 **Olympics**. The characters – politicians and pressmen – have changed little. The bid to convince the world of Atlanta's prosperity and cosmopolitan sophistication was led by city fathers like ex-mayor **Andrew Young** and flamboyant Cable News Network owner **Ted Turner**, and the celebrations of huge crowds in the restored Underground when the news came through were self-consciously beamed around the world by Turner.

Today, Atlanta seems at first glance a typical huge American city: a population of 2.5 million, with the usual traffic congestion, racially segregated neighbourhoods cut off from each other by roaring freeways, bright lights, and enclave mentality. That said, the city maintains a distinctively Southern character. It also has its share of urban **problems**. Racial tensions in particular, glossed over by the semi-official saying that Atlanta is "too busy to hate", are and always have been close to the surface. Despite having a black mayor as early as 1974 (Maynard Jackson – now back in office) and later the nationally prominent Andrew Young, little has improved for poor blacks in the city.

Arrival, Getting Around and Information

The colossal **Hartsfield International Airport** (☎530-6600) is a few miles south of downtown Atlanta, just inside I-285 ("the perimeter"). Road **shuttle** services such as the *Atlanta Airport Shuttle* (☎525-2177) run into the city for around $12, and it is also the southern terminus of one of the two **subway** lines, half an hour's ride from downtown. The *Amtrak* station is at 1688 Peachtree Street, just north of downtown. It's too far to walk in: take bus #23 to the Arts Center subway, N5 on the northern line). Greyhound **buses** arrive downtown at 81 International Boulevard (☎522-6300).

The subway and the wide network of **buses** are run by the *Metropolitan Area Rapid Transit Authority* (*MARTA*), and are clean, reliable, and pretty safe, operating until midnight on Sunday and 1am on other days. Each trip costs $1, or a week's unlimited travel is $9. Route maps are available from the central intersection at Five Points. **Bikes** can be rented from *Skate Escape*, 1086 Piedmont Avenue NE (☎892-1292).

One good way to see the neighbourhoods of Atlanta is on a **walking tour** with the *Atlanta Preservation Center* – suite 401, 140 Peachtree Street (☎522-4345) – who run tours of the various districts at 11am each Saturday, and various other times.

The CVB's **visitor centre** is at suite 2000 in the Harris Tower of the Peachtree Center, 233 Peachtree Street (Mon–Fri 9am–5pm; ☎659-4270); there's a subsidiary one in the Underground. The main **post office** is at 3900 Crown Road (Mon–Fri 7.30am–5pm; ☎525-2228; zip code 30321).

The City

Downtown Atlanta is for the most part an uninspiring concentration of glitzy skyscrapers, with the usual nineteenth-century mock-Classical **State Capitol** just to the south (tours Mon–Fri at 10am, 11am, 1pm & 2pm). The much-hyped **Atlanta Underground**, opened in 1989 on the site of the original Civil War complex but no longer actually underground, is more of a showpiece for visitors than a genuine centre for the city, though it does have a few fun restaurants and clubs. The **World of Coca-Cola** pavilion (Mon–Sat 10am–9.30pm, Sun noon–6pm; $2.50), with its "special look at those unforgettable commercials" and array of merchandise, does little to relieve the air of unreality.

You can get much more of a feel for the history of Atlanta by heading half a mile east (on bus #3) to the **Auburn Avenue** neighbourhood. In its 1920s heyday "**Sweet Auburn**" was a prosperous area of black-owned businesses and jazz clubs, but since the Depression it has declined, and it hasn't yet manage to reincarnate itself as a living monument to black culture and heritage.

Several blocks have been designated as the **Martin Luther King Jr National Historic Site**, in honour of its most illustrious native son, who won the Nobel Peace Prize at a time when he was being actively persecuted by agents of the US government. King's **birthplace** still stands at 501 Auburn Avenue (daily summer 10am–4.30pm; otherwise 10am–3.30pm; free), and the **Ebenezer Baptist Church**, where he was pastor, is at nos. 407–13; both are now a bit run-down.

Auburn remained the base for King's breathtakingly courageous campaigning during the Sixties, and his Southern Christian Leadership Conference (SCLC) still has its headquarters on Auburn Avenue. After his assassination in Memphis in 1968 (see p.401), King was brought home to be buried in what is now the **Martin Luther King Center for Nonviolent Change**, at 449 Auburn Avenue. The privately run African-American Panoramic Experience (**APEX**) at 135 Auburn Avenue (Tues & Thurs–Sat 10am–5pm, Wed 10am–6pm; Aug also Sun 1–5pm; $2) has an interesting collection on black history, including a reconstruction of a 1920s drugstore and an African art gallery.

East of Auburn Avenue, around the junction of Euclid and Moreland avenues, is the **Little Five Points** district, center of the city's alternative community. There are some fun psychedelic clothes and secondhand record stores there, as well as more bars and clubs. By way of contrast, just a few blocks north at 1 Copenhill Avenue, the **Carter Presidential Center** houses a small museum on the years the former Georgia state governor spent as president, together with his collected papers. It's rather ponderously reverential; how you feel about it, of course, depends on your feelings about the man, but the films of him speaking are reasonably interesting (Mon–Sat 9am–4.45pm, Sun noon–4.45pm; $2.50).

Back in central Atlanta, a short way north of the Underground, the **Atlanta Public Library** at Carnegie Way and Forsythe Street (Mon & Fri 9am–6pm, Tues–Thurs 9am–8pm, Sat 10am–6pm, Sun 2–6pm) has a room devoted to *Gone with the Wind* author and Atlanta native **Margaret Mitchell**, with various memorabilia. The novel (1936) and film (1939) helped perpetuate and reinforce popular images of the genteel plantation South – not least, of course, the burning of Atlanta. Mitchell herself is buried in the Victorian Oakland Cemetery, near the Auburn district.

The **Fox Theater** at 660 Peachtree Street at Ponce de Leon (☎881-1977) should not be missed. It's a wildly over-the-top Art Deco theatre/cinema with a strong Moorish theme, still putting on fairly mainstream theatrical shows. Unless you go to see one of these, the only way to get in is on an organised tour. Another mile or so north, in **midtown**, the huge **Woodruff Arts Center** at 1280 Peachtree Street hosts interesting exhibitions and performances. Next door, the futuristic main branch of the **High Museum of Art** (Tues–Sat 10am–5pm, Wed 10am–9pm, Sun noon–5pm; $4) has excellent contemporary and non-Western galleries – particularly strong in African art – and a variety of exhibitions, tours, films and lectures.

Even further out to the north, at 3101 Andrew Drive in the upmarket suburb of Buckhead, the museum of the **Atlanta Historical Society** (Mon–Sat 9am–5.30pm, Sun noon–5.30pm; $6) provides reasonable coverage of black and women's history. The long-term exhibits include *Atlanta Resurgens*, which features short videos of Atlantans talking on subjects like "What is Atlanta's Image?". Every half-hour there are tours of two houses in the extensive grounds: the **Swan House**, a rather ponderous 1920s mock-classical mansion, and the **Tullie Smith Farm**, an antebellum farmhouse and garden.

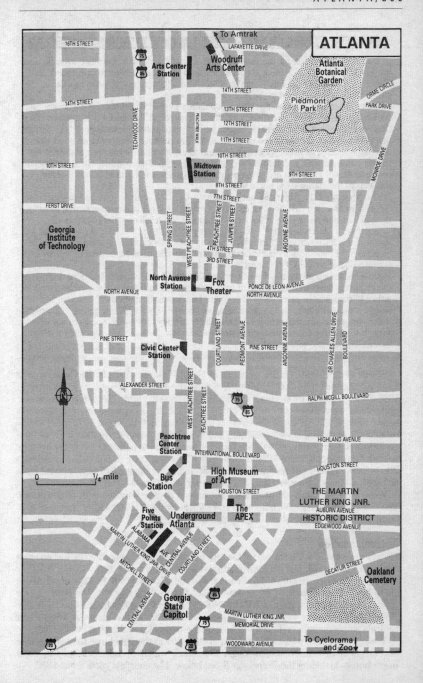

THE BURNING OF ATLANTA AND THE MARCH TO THE SEA

In summer 1864, following the comprehensive Confederate defeats of Spotsylvania and the Wilderness in May, Union **General William Tecumseh Sherman** invaded north Georgia. Outflanking the much smaller Confederate forces, he laid siege to Atlanta; the city eventually surrendered at the start of September.

Sherman announced that the entire population of the city must leave forthwith, and declared that he would burn such of their property as he deemed necessary. The Confederate commander, General Hood, powerless to resist, expostulated: "sir, permit me to to say that the unprecedented measure you propose transcends, in studied and ingenious cruelty, all acts ever before brought to my attention in the dark history of war. In the name of God and humanity, I protest." Sherman responded: "In the name of common sense, I ask you not to appeal to a just God in such a sacreligious manner . . . talk thus to the marines, but not to me."

On November 16, Sherman put a torch to the city, and set out on his notorious "**March to the Sea**". As he later exulted, "behind us lay Atlanta, smouldering in ruins, the black smoke rising high in the air, and hanging like a pall over the ruined city."

Sherman's March is widely seen as an early example of total war; some say that he invented the *Blitzkrieg* which the Nazis were to copy. His explicit intention was to "make Georgia howl", via the systematic destruction of agricultural and industrial resources and terrorisation of civilians. One Georgia woman noted in her diary that "there was hardly a fence left standing all the way from Sparta to Gordon. The fields were trampled down and the road was lined with carcasses of horses, hogs and cattles that the invaders, unable either to consume or carry away with them, had wantonly shot down, to starve out the people . . . the dwellings that were standing all showed signs of pillage, and on every plantation we saw . . . charred remains." It was the final body blow to the Southern war effort; though the Confederate armies struggled on for a few more months after Sherman took Savannah, their fate was sealed.

South of downtown, on the west side of Grant Park (bus #97), is the **Cyclorama**, a huge circular painting (50ft by 900ft) depicting the Battle of Atlanta. It was painted in 1885–86 by a group of German and Polish artists, for purely commercial purposes: cycloramas were mobile, travelling around the country as entertainment in the days before movies. You sit inside the circle of the painting and the whole auditorium slowly rotates. It's surprisingly well-presented and interesting; both the painting itself and the accompanying museum and exhibits treat the war from the point of view of the average soldier (May–Sept 9.30am–5.30pm; Oct–April 9.30am–4.30pm; $3.50). Adjacent **Atlanta Zoo** is in the process of spending millions of dollars on upgrading, with "natural habitat" surroundings (summer 10am–5.30pm, otherwise 10am–4.30pm; $6.75).

West End, Atlanta's oldest quarter but now in decline, is also south of downtown. You can visit the *Wren's Nest*, home of *Br'er Rabbit* author Joel Chandler Harris, at 1050 Gordon Street SW (Tues–Sat 10am–5pm, Sun 2–5pm; $3).

Accommodation

Hotels in downtown Atlanta, one of the biggest convention cities in the US, feel no great need to offer special deals to individual travellers. If you're not happy to spend $50 or more on a room, there are very few central options. Motorists will find the usual chains along the interstates around the perimeter, but that's a long way out. The *B&B Atlanta* agency, 1801 Piedmont Avenue NE (☎875-0525), has **B&B** rooms from around $55. The closest **campground** to town is *Arrowhead Campsites*, at the giant Six Flags Over Georgia amusement park, four miles beyond the perimeter to the west (☎948-7302).

Young travellers who call in person at the CVB in the Peachtree Center can take advantage of the "International Youth Program", which co-ordinates beds in eight major hotels, including the *Travelodge* listed below. The cheapest costs around $30.

Barclay Hotel, 89 Luckie St NW (☎524-7991). Cheap, quiet downtown hotel, behind the Peachtree Center. Doubles from around $55.

Bessie's B&B, 223 Ponce de Leon Ave (☎875-9449). Beautifully converted former bordello with B&B doubles from $80.

Travelodge, 1641 Peachtree Street NE (☎873-5731). Downtown doubles, very near *Amtrak*, from $50.

YMCA, 22 Butler Street (☎659-8085). Near downtown in the Auburn Avenue area. Not very salubrious, this isn't a great neighbourhood at night, and you can't reserve. Men-only accommodation at $17.50 single plus $5 key deposit.

Eating

Although Atlanta's **restaurants** aren't cheap on average, there's a huge range of ethnic foods and settings. Apart from the Underground, the two big nightlife neighbourhoods are **Virginia-Highland,** east of downtown with Little Five Points on its eastern edge, and the glitzier **Buckhead**.

Addis, 453 Moreland Ave (☎523-4748). Excellent, well priced Ethiopian food in Virginia-Highland.

The Atomic Cafe, 1655 McLendon Ave (☎377-6068). Artists' and beatniks' vegetarian coffeehouse, just east of Little Five Points. Particularly good for breakfast.

Auburn Ave Rib Shack, 302 Auburn Ave (☎523-8315). Good cheap ribs and soul food, very near the King Center.

Burton's Grill, 1029 Edgewood Ave (☎525-9439). Excellent black soul food diner, east of Auburn Ave, south of Little Five Points. Some of the greasiest and best fried chicken around, and the most heavyweight peach cobbler. Breakfast too. From only $3.

Caramba Cafe, 1409D N Highland Ave (☎874-1343). Family-run Virginia-Highland Mexican restaurant with superb food and moderate prices.

Caribbean Sunset, 60 Upper Alabama St (☎659-4589). Good Jamaican food in the Atlanta Underground, but not especially cheap at $15 upward. Cocktails and live reggae too.

Cha Gio, 996 Peachtree St at 10th St (☎885-9387). Midtown's best Vietnamese food.

Khun Nara, Monroe Drive and 8th St (☎872-2699). Superb midtown Thai restaurant; moderately priced at around $10–18.

Majestic Diner, 1031 Ponce de Leon (☎875-0276). Very cheap Virginia-Highland 1920s diner, crowded even at 5am for authentic white country cooking. Wear polyester or leather to fit in.

Touch of India, 962 Peachtree St (☎876-7777). Some of the best Indian food in town, at good prices in a nice midtown setting.

The Varsity, 61 North Ave (☎881-1706). Vast and usually very full drive-in restaurant in midtown: a true 1950s throwback where you can eat for well under $10.

Nightlife and Drinking

Atlanta is a place where you can have a very good time; it's well worth budgeting to blow some money hopping between its bars and clubs. The **Atlanta Underground** complex comes into its own at night; otherwise the main concentrations are in **Virginia-Highland** and the more upmarket **Midtown**, the centre of Atlanta's thriving **gay and lesbian** scene. Up-to-the-minute listings for all venues can be found in the free weekly *Creative Loafing*, available from street newspaper boxes.

The Armory, 836 Juniper St (☎881-9280). Hardcore gay leather cocktail bar/disco, in midtown.

Atkins Park, 794 N Highland Ave (☎876-7249). Original Twenties decor in a lively Virginia-Highland neighbourhood bar. A bit overpriced, but a great place to hang out.

Blind Willie's, 828 N Highland Ave (☎873-2583). The best blues venue in town, with appearances by major artists, this Virginia-Highland hangout is also a lively bar.

Blues Harbor, 10 Kenney's Alley–Underground (☎524-3001). Good blues bar, if a bit expensive.

Cotton Club Revue, 1021 Peachtree St (☎674-2523). Midtown's major venue for live rock music.

Euclid Avenue Yacht Club, 1136 Euclid Ave (☎688-2582). Classic neighbourhood bar in Little Five Points. Fine pork barbecue and brunswick stew.

Limerick Junction, 824 N Highland Ave (☎874-7147). Partially gay Irish bar in Virginia-Highland; lively, with live folk and (often dreadfully kitschy) Irish music; decent Guinness.

The Masquerade, 695 North Ave (☎577-8178). Weird punk/metal/goth hangout in midtown: a series of three clubs – Heaven, Hell and Purgatory – in one building, with bars and discos.

Miss Kitty's Saloon and Dancehall, 121 Central Ave–Underground (☎524-4614). Fun downtown bar with live country and western music.

R. J.'s Wine Bar, 870 N Highland Ave (☎875-7775). Reasonably priced wines, and some rare American "microbrewery" beers, amid innovative industrial decor in Virginia-Highland.

The Stein Club, 929 Peachtree St NE (☎876-3707). An Atlanta institution since the 1960s, a huge, smoky, friendly downtown dive.

Taco Mac, 1006 N Highland Ave (☎873-6529). Fun, studenty Virginia-Highland bar, with large selection of beers and excellent spicy chicken wings.

Weekends, 1022 Peachtree St (☎875-5835). Lively gay disco club, clientele a complete mix.

Stone Mountain

Just half an hour's drive east of Atlanta, **Stone Mountain State Park** (daily 6am–midnight; $5 per vehicle) centres around a huge dome of granite, about half a mile long. You can walk up it in around 45 minutes, or take a cable car ($2.50), and there are various train rides, fast-food joints and so on, but most visitors come to see the massive 90x190ft relief of Confederate Civil War "heroes" Jefferson Davis, Robert E Lee and Stonewall Jackson. Work on the colosssal sculpture was started in 1924 by Gutzon Borglum, who went on to carve Mount Rushmore in South Dakota (see p.586), but it was not completed until 1970. Concessions and gift shops down below supply endless quantities of souvenir kitsch, and there's a spectacular nightly laser son et lumière in the summer (at 9pm; free with entrance to park). There's **camping** at the *Stone Park Campground* (☎498-5710).

North from Atlanta: the Mountains

Atlanta is a short drive from some spectacular Appalachian mountain scenery, at its best in October when the autumn leaves turn gold and red. **DAHLONEGA**, forty miles northwest of Atlanta on US-19, makes a good general base for the area. It was the site of the first gold rush in the US, in 1828, although the native Cherokees had panned for gold long before then. Over $6 million of gold coin was minted here before the Civil War; the mining industry more or less died out later in the nineteenth century. An interesting **Gold Museum** is housed in the handsome county courthouse on the main square (Tues–Sat 9am–5pm, Sun 2–5.30pm; $1.50). You can also pan for gold at various small mines in the area, although you're hardly likely to make your fortune. The town hosts one of Appalachia's biggest annual **bluegrass** festivals, in the third week of June.

Dahlonega's **visitor centre** is across from the courthouse (☎864-3711). The *Smith House* at 202 S Chestatee Street (☎864-3566) has comfortable double rooms from $55, and serves excellent food. Alternatively, you can **camp** and rest up at local state parks, such as **Amicalola Falls State Park**, twenty miles west (☎265-2885; also cabins at $45 double). The falls are impressive and easily accessible, and there are a lot of trails. One goes 7.5 miles north to **Springer Mountain**, the southernmost point of the often superb 2000-mile **Appalachian Trail**.

As you drive through the mountains on the secondary roads, you come across endless hairpins and narrow passes; Hwy-348 goes up a particularly impressive pass at the White County line, crossed by the Appalachian Trail at the top. The towns and villages are disappointing, though, either unremarkable or overrun by kitsch. **HELEN**, about 35 miles northeast of Dahlonega, has been turned into a pseudo-Bavarian "theme village", full of fake half-timbered houses and gift shoppes. The *Motel Alpenhüf* on Unicoi Street (☎1-800/535-8678) has rooms from $40; you might conceivably get a kick out of eating at the *Spaghetti Haus*. **CLAYTON**, near the borders of North and South Carolina, offers the *Small Motel* (☎782-6488), also with doubles for $40.

This area is particularly famous for its **waterfalls**: most are fairly inaccessible, and you'll need a vehicle and some patience finding your way on dirt forest roads, but they're worth the effort. Among the best are **High Shoals Falls** and **Duke's Creek Falls**, both off Hwy-75 between Helen and Hiawassee. Visitor centres in Clayton and elsewhere can supply a good leaflet with directions on how to get to them, as well as details of **whitewater rafting** expeditions on the Chattooga River in the far northeastern corner of the state. Half-day trips for beginners cost around $30, or a little more at weekends, and there are harder routes and overnight trips if you have canoeing experience. Companies include *Wildwater Ltd* (☎1-800/451-9972) and *Nantahala Outdoor Center* (☎1-800/232-7238).

Savannah

SAVANNAH, just inside the border with South Carolina, is the natural starting point for explorations of the short **Georgia coast**. In its own right it has a much more genuine feel to it than downtown Charleston, to which it's often compared. There's a fair amount to see, and the heart of the Historic District holds a busy, heavily black downtown and lots of good night-time hangouts.

Savannah was founded in 1733 as the first settlement of the new British colony of Georgia; with the advent of slavery, plantation agriculture thrived, and it became a major export centre, at the end of important railway lines by which **cotton** was funnelled from far away in the South. Sherman arrived here in December 1864 at the end of his march to the sea, but left the city intact and set to work apportioning land to freed slaves. This was the first recognition of the need for "reconstruction", but such concrete economic provision for slaves was rarely to occur again.

The plantations foundered after the Civil War; cotton prices slumped, and Savannah went into decline. There was little industry beyond the port, and as that fell into disuse and decay so, too, did Savannah's graceful town houses and tree-lined boulevards. It was not until the 1950s that local citizens started to organise what has been, on the whole, the successful restoration of their town.

Arrival, Getting Around and Information

Savannah's **airport**, served by several major airlines, is five miles west of the city. The **bus station** (☎232-2135) is just north of downtown at 610 E Oglethorpe Avenue, while the **railway station** is about three miles from the centre, at 2611 Seaboard Coastline Drive. It isn't served by buses; a taxi in costs about $6.

To **get around** in town, *Chatham Area Transit* (*CAT*) operate a reasonable **bus** network. Route maps are available from the **visitor centre**, 301 Martin Luther King Jr. Drive (☎944-0456), which also has discount accommodation coupons and maps for city walking tours. You can rent **bicycles** at the *Hyatt Regency*, 2 W Bay Street (☎233-3957), and the *Desoto Hilton*, 15 E Liberty Street (☎232-4624). All kinds of **tours** cover the centre, by **minibus** (1hr for $5-7 per person, 2hr for $9-11) or horse-drawn **carriage**. *Gray Line Tours* at 215 W Boundary Street (☎236-9604) also run further afield.

The **post office** is at 2 N Fahm Street (Mon-Fri 8.30am-5pm; ☎235-4646; zip code 31402).

The telephone **area code** for Savannah and the Georgia coast is ☎912.

The Town

The best way to get a feel for downtown Savannah is simply to wander around – making sure, of course, not to spend too long out in the blistering summer heat and humidity. There are plenty of shady parks in the squares that dot the grid layout (and usually over-blown statues, too; General James Oglethorpe, leader of the first settlement expedition, is in Chippewa square). The whole of the city centre forms the **Historic District**, while down by the Savannah River is the now rather commercialised **waterfront**.

Most visitors to Savannah take in one or two of the town's old **mansions**, such as the classic British Regency-period **Owens-Thomas house**, at 124 Abercorn Street (Tues–Sat 10am–5pm, Sun & Mon 2–5pm; $3). You can get a better historical overview, however, at the **Savannah History Museum**, in the restored Central of Georgia Railroad Station at 303 Martin Luther King Drive, behind the visitor centre (daily 9am–5pm; $3). They show a couple of theatre presentations, and have informative displays.

Savannah is one of the few places in the southeast with a decent **black history museum** – albeit very short of funds – at the King-Tisdell Cottage, 514 E Huntingdon Street (Mon–Fri 10.30am–4.30pm, Sat & Sun 1–4pm; free, but make a donation), with a friendly and knowledgeable staff. Documentary material illustrates the history of slaves and free blacks before the Civil War, and of the freedmen after, commemorating the fact that Savannah was the site of Sherman's famous **"Field Order #15"**, which granted each freed slave forty acres of land and a mule. The museum also operates black heritage tours of the town which it is hoping to extend. These are currently a bit difficult to catch: Wednesday and Saturday only, with 24 hours' notice. If you have your own car, the guide will drive with you and it costs $6 per person; if not, then it's $9 per person, with a minimum of five people. The two-hour tour takes in the **Second African Baptist Church**, where Field Order #15 was signed; the poor black **Yamacraw** neighbourhood, the centre of a thriving free black community of workers, small businessmen and artists before the war but now sadly run-down and depressed; and the 1777 **First African Baptist Church**, the oldest black church in North America. You can visit the latter, at 23 Montgomery Street, on your own if you can't catch a tour: it's only open Friday 10am to 2pm, but they're quite helpful if you call (☎233-6597) to arrange a time for the pastor to open up the church for you (make a donation).

Accommodation

As well as the cheap **hotels** on and around Boundary Street near the *Greyhound* station, and the chain **motels** further out on Ogeechee Road (US-17), Savannah has a good number of central **B&Bs** in elegant private houses. Call in at the visitor centre first to collect discount coupons. The nearest **campground** is six miles southeast, at **Skidaway Island State Park** (☎598-0393); a barrier, or "sea" island with an interesting combination of salt and freshwater habitats.

Bed and Breakfast Inn, 117 W Gordon St (☎238-0518). B&B from $40 for a double – reservations essential.

Days Inn, 201 W Bay St (☎236-4440). The most affordable hotel in the historic district, at around $55 double.

Quality Inn, 231 W Boundary St (☎232-3200). Motel near *Greyhound*, $35 or so with discount vouchers.

Thunderbird Inn, 611 W Oglethorpe Ave (☎236-4440). Basic rooms opposite *Greyhound*, from $37.

Eating

Savannah has a great number of **restaurants**, though many of the seafood places on the riverfront are overpriced and almost entirely devoid of atmosphere. One alternative worth considering is to use one of the many reasonable (a bit downmarket maybe, but with a great early-Sixties feel) **lunch counters** in downtown shops such as *Fabers* or *McCory's Discount Store*, on the corner of Bull and W Broughton streets.

Dockside Seafood, 201 W River St (☎236-9253). Traditional seafood beside the river, in an eighteenth-century ships' chandlery built from ballast stone.

Mrs Wilkes' Boarding House, 107 W Jones St (☎232-5997). Savannah's most famous eating place; fairly cheap and filling Southern breakfasts and lunches in a family-run restaurant.

Savannah Bistro, 309 W Congress St (☎233-6266). A place to come if you have a bit of spare cash. Its delicious Cajun and far-Eastern influenced dishes are worthy of far more expensive restaurants.

The Shrimp Factory, 131 E River St (☎236-4229). On the riverfront, with some good and unusual shrimp dishes, moderate to expensive.

W. G. Shuckers, 225 W River St (☎236-1427). A reasonably laid-back oyster bar and seafood place beside the river, moderately priced.

Wall's BBQ, in between Price and Houston in the alley between York and Oglethorpe (Thurs–Sat only). Tiny and spartan, with good soul food. It's difficult to spend more than $5.

Bars, Clubs and Music

Savannah has good nightlife, with a slightly more laid-back atmosphere than Charleston, let alone Atlanta – though for some reason it's particularly strict about demanding ID for proof of age. Everything is fairly close together, in the Market-River district. The city also hosts a reasonable **jazz festival** in late September or October each year. For information on this or other jazz events/venues, contact the *Coastal Jazz Association* at ☎232-2222.

The Bottom Line, 206 W Julian St (☎232-0812). Be-bop, traditional and big-band jazz in the market, with moderate cover charge.

Congress St Station, 121 W Congress St (☎233-2259). Attracts a younger and more studenty crowd, and tends to feature progressive rock and college bands.

Crystal Beer Parlor, 301 W Jones St (☎232-1153). An enjoyable bar in which to spend an evening, with reasonable and moderately priced food.

Emma's Piano Bar, 224 W Bay St (☎232-1223). Old-fashioned night out, listening to Emma play some of the 6000 songs she knows by heart. $5 cover, knocked off the price of your drinks.

Malone's, 27 Barnard St (☎234-3059). Club with disco and live jazz and rock, and a younger crowd; extremely lively, crowded, and a lot of fun.

Miss Billies, 34 Montgomery St (☎236-1492). Rock and punk bands, with Caribbean food and obstreperous bouncers.

Who's Who, 217 E Bay St (☎232-9432). Good gay venue, usually dominated by men.

Out from Savannah

The main beach for Savannah is at **Tybee Island**, eighteen miles east of the city on US-80: a reasonable beach, and not too overdeveloped. There is plenty of cheapish **accommodation** should you want to stay – the brand-new *Ocean Plaza Inn*, 15th Street (☎786-7664), starts at $40 – as well as the odd reasonable bar. *Spanky's Beachside* at 404 Butler Ave (☎786-5526) has live rock and "beach music" at weekends. There is, however, no public transport to Tybee. **Fort Pulaski National Monument**, off US-80 nearby, is probably the most interesting of several forts in the area (daily summer 8.30am–6.45pm; winter 8.30am–5.15pm; $1). An impressive Confederate stronghold, it was nevertheless taken by Union troops, the first masonry fortress to be pierced by rifled cannon fire.

Nearer the city, eight miles out on Skidaway Road on bus #16, **Wormsloe State Historic Site** (Tues–Sat 9am–5pm, Sun 2–5.30pm; $1.50) is the site of an eighteenth-century defensive plantation. All that is left now are the ruins of the fortified house of British settler Noble Jones, but the "tabby" ruins (a kind of primitive concrete) are quite atmospheric, rather overgrown with palms and lush forest. There's also a good film shown at the museum on the early settlement of Savannah, with some displays of archaeological finds.

Brunswick and the Southern Coast

BRUNSWICK, the one sizeable settlement south of Savannah, makes an obvious base for exploring the offshore **Sea Islands**. It's not in itself very exciting, although the shrimp docks are quite interesting when the catch is brought in. Its cheap **motels** cost around $30 – the **visitor centre** (daily 9am–5pm; ☎264-5337) will give you a list – and at more upmarket **B&Bs** such as the central *Rose Manor Guest House*, 1108 Richmond Street (☎267-6369), rooms start at $50. Dorm beds at the welcoming *Hostel in the Forest*, nine miles west of town on US-84 (☎264-9738), cost just $6.

The **Hofwyl-Broadfield Plantation**, ten miles north of Brunswick on US-17, gives a vivid idea of life under slavery (Tues–Sat 9am–5pm; $1.50). There's a good exhibit on the rice cultivation that made the planters so fabulously wealthy, and you can see the surprisingly modest plantation house where their descendants lived until the 1970s. Occasional **gospel** concerts are held here on summer Saturdays, with soul food on sale.

The Sea Islands

Several of the **SEA ISLANDS**, off the coast north of **Darien**, were divided after the Civil War between freed slaves (see also p.365). They remained poor, agricultural communities, however, and little now remains from those years for an outsider to see.

The **southern islands** are the most developed, all with swanky resort pretensions. This is largely due to **Jekyll Island**, bought in 1887 for use as an exclusive club by a group of millionaires whose wildly over-the-top "village" is still standing (daily summer 10am–4pm; winter 9.30am–2pm; $2). Jekyll is the one island to hold much **accommodation**: mostly expensive, with the *Clarion-Buccaneer Beach Resort*, 85 Beachview Drive (☎635-2261), about the cheapest, starting at $50. There's a **campground** a little further north (☎635-3021; $10), near the nesting sites of loggerhead turtles.

Most of the bigger **St Simon's Island** is still a pleasant landscape of marshes and live oaks covered with Spanish moss. At the (free) Sea Island Festival here in late August, you can hear traditional music and see folk crafts being made (☎638-9014). **Fort Frederica National Monument**, seven miles north of the causeway (daily summer 8am–8pm; winter 8am–5pm; $1.50), was built in 1736 by General Oglethorpe, as the largest British fort in North America; now it's an atmospheric ruin.

To the south, **Cumberland Island** is a stunning wildlife refuge of marshes, beaches and semitropical forest, with the odd deserted planter's mansion, and wild horses. You can get there by ferry from the village of St Mary's to the south near the Florida border (out at 9am and 11.45am, returning at 10.15am and 4.45pm, taking 45min; $7.50).

Okefenokee Swamp

Rural south Georgia, inland from the coast, is quiet, agricultural, and not very interesting. The one exception is the **OKEFENOKEE SWAMP**, a dense semitropical swamp stretching over thirty miles down to Florida. It holds an astonishing profusion of luxuriant plants and trees, as well as something like 20,000 alligators, over thirty species of snakes, and bears and pumas. You can only get in at the **Okefenokee Swamp Park**, a private charity-owned concession at the northeast end, on Hwy-177, off US-23/1, not served by public transport (summer 9am–6.30pm; otherwise 9am–5.30pm; $7; ☎283-0583). Included in the fee are a half-hour boat trip through the swamp, a serpentarium, a good interpretive centre on wildlife, an observation tower, reconstructed pioneer buildings – and a lot of disconcertingly large alligators.

Unlovely **WAYCROSS**, ten miles north, holds **motels** such as the *Pinecrest* (☎283-3580), where doubles start at $25. The **Okefenokee Heritage Center** (Mon–Sat 10am–5pm, Sun 2–4pm; $4) has slightly erratic displays on the history of the swamp.

KENTUCKY

Two hundred years after it was wrested from the Indians, **KENTUCKY** still hasn't quite made up its mind as to whether it belongs in the North or the South. Both the rival presidents in the Civil War, Abraham Lincoln and Jefferson Davis, were born here, and divisions were acute between slave-owning farmers and the merchants who depended on trade with the nearby cities of the industrial north. Officially neutral, seventy thousand Kentuckians joined the Union army and forty thousand the Confederates. After the war Kentucky sided with the South in its hostility to Reconstruction, and since then it has remained solidly Democrat.

Kentucky's rugged beauty is at its most appealing in the mountainous **east** and the small historic towns of the **Bluegrass Downs**, with visits enlivened by the varied attractions of bourbon whiskey, thoroughbred horses and bluegrass music. **Louisville**, home of the **Kentucky Derby**, is a busy manufacturing and arts centre; the more reserved **Lexington**, eighty miles east, is a major horse-breeding marketplace.

Getting Around Kentucky

Kentucky's limited **public transport** can be a real headache. There's a full *Greyhound* service along the interstates south of Louisville and Lexington (and both have surprisingly good city transport), but a lot of ground is left uncovered. *Amtrak* doesn't operate here at all. **Cycling** is a pleasant and manageable option; if you're **driving**, be sure to keep small change for the tolls on the state highways. Lexington has its own small airport, but it's also within easy reach of the airport for Cincinnati, Ohio, which is in Covington, Kentucky (see p.226). Louisville is served by the larger Standiford Field.

Lexington, The Bluegrass and East Kentucky

The fertile **Bluegrass Downs**, just eighty miles across, form the base of America's thoroughbred racing industry, with **Lexington** quietly prospering at its heart. The name comes from the unique steel-blue sheen of the buds in the meadows, only visible in early morning during April and May. Kentucky's first white pioneers, who trekked in the 1770s through the 150 miles of wilderness now called the **Daniel Boone National Forest**, were amazed to find this "Eden" deserted while the Indians lived in much less attractive terrain. Anthropologists have now discovered that the area's twelfth-century inhabitants were plagued by fatal bone diseases, due to mineral deficiencies in the soil.

Around modern Lexington are some of the oldest towns west of the Alleghenies. However, alongside the fine scenery of the **Natural Bridge** and **Cumberland Gap** districts, eastern Kentucky also suffers from acute rural poverty.

Lexington

The productivity of the bluegrass fields has kept **LEXINGTON**'s economy ticking over since 1775, though its lack of a navigable river always made its traders vulnerable to competition from Louisville. Eighty miles east of Louisville and ninety south of Cincinnati, it still retains large numbers of fine antebellum houses. However, its current affluence dates from after World War I, when smoking caught on internationally and Lexington emerged as the world's largest burley **tobacco** market. Despite a population now exceeding 200,000, the city maintains an almost rustic atmosphere, with its most conspicuous activity the **horse** trade.

The telephone **area code** for Lexington and eastern Kentucky is ☎606.

Arrival and Information

Lexington's **airport** is six miles west of town on US-60W, near Keeneland racetrack (handy for the private jets of the horse-breeders). *Greyhound* (☎255-4261) drop passengers off about a mile from downtown at 477 New Circle Road – take bus #6. *Lex-Tran* (☎252-4936) operates a relatively good service to the University and suburbs, including a free downtown trolley, but you need a car to reach the horse-related attractions. The **visitor centre** is at 430 W Vine Street (☎848-1224).

Downtown Lexington

The plush hotels, glass office blocks, skywalks and shopping malls of Lexington's city centre, set in a dip on the Bluegrass Downs, crowd in on fountain-filled **Triangle Park**. Despite its age, the city lacks buildings of historical interest; the early merchants threw up mostly functional structures, preferring to get on with making money. The red-brick ivy-covered buildings of small 1780 **Transylvania University** are behind the Courthouse at N Broadway and Third Street (the name means "across the woods", an appropriate description of Kentucky at the time). At the other side of downtown, the **Art Museum** on the sprawling University of Kentucky campus displays contemporary American art and Indian artefacts (Tues–Sun noon–5pm; free).

Lexington's horses

Along **Paris** and **Ironworks Pikes**, northeast of Lexington, in an idyllic Kentuckian landscape, sleek thoroughbred horses cavort in bluegrass meadows. Some farms are still staked out by miles of immaculate white-plank fences, though most now use the cheaper but much less attractive black creosote to protect the wood. You can watch the horses' early-morning workouts at **Keeneland racecourse** to the west (April–Oct daily dawn–9.30am; free), after a super-cheap breakfast at the adjacent *Keeneland Kitchen*. Tasteful dark-green grandstands emphasise the crisp white rails around the one-mile oval track, and the absence of a public address system makes for a unique race-day atmosphere; thousands of puzzled voices, trying to work out which horse is which, break into cheers as they hurtle into the final furlong (April & Oct daily 1pm; $2–5).

Tours of horse farms used to be very popular, but owners have become reluctant to let the public get too close to these shy creatures. One exception is **Spendthrift Farm**, seven miles out at 884 Ironworks Pike (via I-75 Exit 120), which commands stud fees of up to $20,000 for its thirty stallions. Between February and June, visitors come specifically to watch the horses "at stud" in a special viewing gallery. Tours are free but you should tip the groom (Mon–Sat 10am–2pm; ☎255-2003).

The enjoyable **Kentucky Horse Park** is a little further along at 4089 Ironworks Pike (May–Oct daily 9am–5pm; Nov–April Wed–Sun only; $7.95). Its museum traces the uses to which horses have been put throughout history, from Roman chariot races through cavalry regiments, commercial haulage and modern sports. The 1032-acre park also features live specimens of over thirty different breeds, and a working farm.

Accommodation

Even the cheapest of Lexington's **hotels** and **motels** charges upward of $35 per night. If you're stuck, *Dial-A-Accommodations* (☎233-7299) help to find rooms. The best **campground** (☎233-4303) is at the Horse Park.

Kimball House Motel, 267 S Limestone St (☎252-9565). Ten-room downtown boarding house with antique-furnished rooms. $25–35.

La Quinta, 1919 Stanton Way (☎231-7551). Handily placed at the I-75/I-64 intersection. $52.

University of Kentucky (☎257-3721). Rooms during the summer for around $20; a few are also available during the academic year.

YMCA, 239 E High St (☎255-9622). Dingy downtown men-only location, often fully booked. Single rooms $20–30.

Food

Lexington's large student population means it has several lively youth-oriented **eating places**, besides the steakhouses catering for the horse crowd and expense-account conventioneers. Fast-food cafes, open until early evening, fill the third floor of central **Festival Market** at Vine and Limestone streets.

Alfalfa, 557 S Limestone St (☎253-0014). Hippyish cafe, near the University of Kentucky. A wide range of international, mostly vegetarian dishes. Lunch specials $2.50–5, evening meals under $10.

De Sha's, 101 N Broadway (☎259-3771). *The* downtown place to be seen eating. Seafood and steak dishes in nice surroundings, if a bit pricey. Reservations required.

High on Rose Cantina, 301 E High St (☎252-9498). All-purpose diner serving good-value Tex-Mex food and beer, to a backdrop of loud music, until 1am.

Ramsey's Diner, 496 E High St (☎259-2708). Very popular and atmospheric. Tasty sandwiches, burgers and meals for $4–8. After 10.30pm cheap snacks are available from the bar, open until 1am.

Nightlife

A Baptist-inspired 1am curfew on bars and clubs restricts Lexington's nightlife somewhat, though at the weekend there are a few lively bars at the back of Festival Market, such as the *Cheapside* at 131 Cheapside (☎254-0046). *The Bar*, 224 E Main Street (☎255-1551), and *Metro*, 156 E Main Street (☎254-9881), are popular downtown **gay** bars.

Bluegrass Country

Apart from the horse farms directly to the north of Lexington, most places of interest lie to the south, such as the fine old towns of **Danville** and **Harrodsburg**, and the marvellously restored **Shaker Village**. After approximately forty miles the meadows give way to the striking **Knobs** – random lumpy outcrops, shrouded in trees and wispy low-hanging clouds, that are the eroded remnants of the Pennyrile Plateau.

Shaker Village at Pleasant Hill

The Utopian settlement of **PLEASANT HILL**, hidden among the bluegrass hillocks near Harrodsburg, twenty-five miles west of Lexington on US-68, was established by Shaker missionaries from New England around 1805. Within twenty years, five hundred villagers were producing seeds, tools and cloth, for sale as far away as New Orleans. During the Civil War, Union and Confederate troops alike were billeted upon the pacifist Shakers. Numbers thereafter declined until the last member died in 1923. A non-profit organisation has since 1961 returned the village to its nineteenth-century appearance. (Daily summer 9am–5pm; winter hours vary; $6.50.)

The central Shaker values of absolute celibacy, hygiene, simplicity and communal ownership have left their mark on the 27 grey and pastel-coloured dwellings. Women and men entered the symmetrical dwellings via different doors; pegboards on the walls were used to hang chairs while the rooms were swept. There are demonstrations of broom-making, weaving, quilting and other traditional crafts, and the *Trustees Office Inn* houses a superb **restaurant** specialising in boiled ham, lemon pie and other Kentucky favourites (☎734-5111). You can also **stay** here; rooms with reproduction Shaker furniture range from $35 to $85 and should be reserved well in advance.

Berea

Thirty miles south of Lexington, just off I-75 in the foothills where Bluegrass meets Appalachia, the unique **BEREA COLLEGE** gives its 1500 students free tuition in return for work in any of 120 crafts ranging from needlework to wrought ironwork. Founded in 1855 by abolitionists as a vocational college for the young people of East Kentucky – both white and black – it was forcefully shut down four years later by mobs opposed to the board's support for John Brown's raid at Harper's Ferry (see p.318).

The **Appalachian Museum** on Jackson Street relates the story of the region's people (Mon–Sat 9am–6pm, Sun 1–6pm; closed Jan). Free campus tours leave from *Boone Hall Tavern*, a student-run hotel and restaurant (☎986-9358) at Main and Prospect streets, taking in the student art gallery and the sales room (Mon & Wed–Sat). The college's national reputation has also attracted many private art and craft galleries to the small town of BEREA.

Daniel Boone National Forest

Almost the entire eastern length of Kentucky is taken up by the steep slopes, narrow valleys and sandstone cliffs of the unspoiled **DANIEL BOONE NATIONAL FOREST**. Few Americans have been mythologised quite as much as **Daniel Boone**. As far as can be ascertained, Boone was one of Kentucky's earliest fur-trapping pioneers, in 1767. Of the many tales of his encounters with Shawnee Indians, the most famous is that of the time he was captured and initiated as *Sheltowee*, or Big Turtle. Learning of Shawnee plans to attack pioneer communities, Big Turtle escaped just in time to warn and defend the good citizens of his own settlement at **Boonesborough**, southeast of Lexington. But all did not end happily ever after. Through failure to legalise land claims, Boone lost practically all of the land in Kentucky he had claimed for himself and his sponsors. The resultant animosity forced the ageing frontiersman to press further west to Missouri in 1798, where he died in 1820 aged eighty-six.

Natural Bridge and around

The geological extravaganza of the **Red River Gorge**, sixty miles east of Lexington via the Mountain Parkway, is best seen by taking a thirty-mile loop drive from the **Natural Bridge Resort Park** on Hwy-77 near the village of Slade. Natural Bridge itself is a large sandstone arch surrounded by steep hollows and exposed clifflines; for the best panoramic view, continue to the solid span of **Sky Bridge**, which stretches along the top of a thin ridge. As well as hiking trails, canoeing, fishing, rock-climbing and camping, there's cottage **accommodation** in the park's secluded *Hemlock Lodge* ($70).

For all its natural beauty, the **Snakey Hollow** area shows rural deprivation at its starkest. Some tourists, kitted out in expensive walking gear with cameras at the ready, come here to see whether Hollywood images of backwardness, incest and violence square up in real life. Whatever your intentions, it's surely best not to holiday on the misery of others, and to leave such communities undisturbed.

Towards the Southeast

In 1940, "Colonel" Harlan Sanders opened a small diner at the back of a filling station in tiny **CORBIN**, ninety miles south of Lexington on I-75. His **Kentucky Fried Chicken** empire has since spread to over 58 countries. The original 100-seat restaurant, at the junction of US-25E and US-25W, has been restored with 1940s decor and memorabilia (☎528-2163). The bespectacled Sanders (1890–1980) was not a soldier, but a member of the Honorable Order of Kentucky Colonels, a kind of minor knighthood.

STEARNS, fifty miles southwest of Corbin on Hwy-92, is a classic former mining-company town, one of many such in the Appalachians, in which the company owned every building – shops, church, Sheriff's office and all. As one Thirties writer put it, "with their unpaved streets and unpainted buildings (they) come into view like blighted spots on the land, with all the inconveniences and few if any of the comforts of modern towns of equal size." The **Stearns Museum** at 1 Henderson Street (mid-April to Oct Wed–Sun 10am–5pm) takes a sanitised look at this history. The highlight for visitors is the eleven-mile trip on the **Big South Fork Scenic Railway** (mid-April to early Nov daily 11am & 3pm; ☎1-800/462-5664), which traverses deep woodlands and descends a rugged 600-ft gorge to **Blue Heron**, another former mining community.

On the tri-state border of Kentucky, Tennessee and Virginia, the **Cumberland Gap National Historic Park** is one of the most visited parts of Boone Forest. A natural passageway used by migrating deer and bison, it served as a gateway to the west for Boone and other pioneers. **Pinnacle Overlook**, a 1000-ft lookout over the three states, is near the visitor centre (☎248-2817) on US-25E in **Middlesboro**.

Just outside the forest boundaries on the Virginia border, there are plenty of coalfields and lumber forests, but few people. The high death toll in underground mines and the ecological disasters of strip-mining have drawn national attention, particularly during the violent struggles of the Thirties in places such as **Harlan County**, where striking miners were killed and evicted from their homes by armed company men.

Louisville, Central and Western Kentucky

In heavily rural Kentucky, the manufacturing giant of **Louisville** stands out, with its lively cultural and racial mix. Only occasionally does it bother with the laid-back southern image other parts of the state are so keen to promote. In the **southern** hinterland, numerous small towns retain their tree-shaded squares and nineteenth-century town houses – and their strict Baptist beliefs – and the endless caverns of **Mammoth Cave National Park** attract spelunkers and hikers in their thousands. The west, where the Ohio River meets the Mississippi, is flat, heavily forested and generally less attractive.

Louisville

LOUISVILLE, just south of Indiana across the Ohio river, is firmly embedded in the American national consciousness for its multimillion-dollar **Kentucky Derby**. The horse race attracts over 500,000 fans each year to this cosmopolitan and well-diversified industrial city, which still bears the traces of the early French settlers who came upriver from New Orleans. A third of the USA's bourbon is made here, and it's also home to the giant Philip Morris company – manufacturers of *Marlboro* cigarettes – which until recently was the target of an acrimonious national boycott, spearheaded by Louisville's gay community, for its backing of far-right politicians like Jesse Helms.

Louisville's history revolves around a perennial rivalry with Cincinnati, a mere one hundred miles upstream. For example, despite being pro-Union during the Civil War, it promoted itself thereafter – erecting Confederate statues, and so on – as the place for southern business to invest, as opposed to Midwestern Yankee cities like Cincinnati.

As well as a lively arts scene and lots of citywide festivals, Louisville boasts an unrivalled network of public parks, many designed by Frederick Law Olmstead. One native son who took advantage of the recreation facilities was three-times world heavyweight boxing champion **Muhammad Ali**, who used to do his early-morning roadwork in the scenic environs of Chickasaw Park.

Arrival and Information

All major US airlines fly into **Standiford Field Airport** (☎367-4636), five miles south of downtown on I-65; take bus #2 or pay a $13 cab fare. *Greyhound* terminates at fairly central 720 W Muhammad Ali Boulevard (☎585-3331). An excellent **bus** service (60¢) makes getting around easy. Some routes operate as late as 2am, and downtown **trolleys** run from 7.30am to 6pm. The **visitor centre** at 400 S First Street provides a good range of maps and information (Mon–Fri 8.30am–5pm, Sat 8.30am–3pm; summer also Sun 11am–3pm; ☎582-3732; ☎1-800/633-3384 in KY; ☎1-800/626-5646 outside KY).

The telephone **area code** for Louisville, central and western Kentucky is ☎502.

Central Louisville

Downtown Louisville rolls gently down towards Main Street, then abruptly lunges down to the river. **Riverfront Plaza**, between Fifth and Sixth streets, is a prime observation point for the natural **Falls of the Ohio** and the bizarre **Louisville Falls Fountain**, which every fifteen minutes sprays water from an offshore barge 375 feet into the air to form a coloured fleur-de-lys, and otherwise looks like a wonky sewage unit discharging into the river. The *Belle of Louisville*, a 1914 steam **stern-wheeler**, leaves nearby for daily cruises during summer (daily 2pm; $7; ☎625-2355).

The most impressive modern structure along Main Street, where skyscrapers blend in with early nineteenth-century warehouses, is the extravagantly marbled **Humana Building** at no. 500. These lavish offices, complete with 2000-year-old Roman statues, are the headquarters of a giant hospital group; testimony to the amount of money that can be made out of healthcare. Free tours take place on Saturday morning from 10am to 1.30pm, the 25th-floor terrace providing a great view of the Ohio (☎580-3606).

The sizeable **J B Speed Art Museum** at 2035 S Third Street, in the University of Louisville campus, displays extensive collections of art and sculpture from medieval to modern times, featuring works by Picasso, Rembrandt, Rubens, Monet and Henry Moore (Tues–Sat 10am–4pm, Sun 1–5pm; $2 donation, students free).

Louisville's Horses: the Kentucky Derby

The **Kentucky Derby** is one of the world's premier horse races; it's also, as gonzo journalist Hunter S Thompson put it, "decadent and depraved". Since 1875, the leading lights of Southern society have gathered for an annual orgy of betting, haute cuisine and mint juleps in the plush grandstand, while tens of thousands of the beer-guzzling proletariat cram into the infield.

The two-week **Kentucky Derby Festival** – parades, beer, concerts, bourbon, galas, and more beer – leads up to Derby Day on the first Saturday in May. Apart from the $20 infield tickets available on the day – offering virtually no chance of a decent view – all seats are sold out months in advance. The race itself, traditionally preceded by a mass drunken rendition of *My Old Kentucky Home*, is run over a distance of one and a quarter miles, lasts barely two minutes, and offers close to a million dollars in prize money. Only during the Superbowl do television commercials cost more.

Thoroughbreds also race at **Churchill Downs**, three miles south of downtown at 700 Central Avenue, in May, June and October ($1.50; ☎636-4400), and there's harness racing at **Louisville Downs**, 4520 Poplar Level Road ($2; ☎964-6415), most of the year.

The excellent hands-on **Kentucky Derby Museum**, next to Churchill Downs (#4 bus), will appeal to horse-racing ignoramuses and enthusiasts alike. Admission includes a tour of the racetrack, and a magnificent audio-visual display captures the Derby-Day atmosphere on a 360° screen (daily 9am–5pm; $3).

Accommodation

Most of the year, Louisville's **accommodation** is plentiful and reasonably priced, though of course it's incredibly booked up for the Derby Festival. *Kentucky Homes*, 1431 St James Court (☎635-7241), is a **B&B** reservation service. You can **camp** just over the river in Indiana at the central *KOA*, 900 Marriot Drive, Clarksville ($15; ☎812/282-4474), or occasionally at the University (☎588-6691) during festivities.

Days Inn, 101 E Jefferson St (☎585-2200). Near downtown. Indoor and outdoor pools. Around $50.

Emily Boone Home Hostel (AYH), 1027 E Franklin St (☎585-3430). Just east of the centre among the shotgun houses of Butchertown. $7 plus twenty minutes of chores. Reservations essential.

Galt House, 140 Fourth St (☎589-5200). Huge riverside hotel. Faded grandeur but lots of character. At quiet times some rooms go for $50.

Motel 6, 3304 Bardstown Rd (☎456-2861). Seven miles from downtown, near #17 bus route. $28.

Travelodge, 401 S Second St (☎583-2841). Downtown. $41, including breakfast.

Eating

Louisville's **restaurants** cater for all tastes, though downtown prices are fairly high.

Baja Bay, 1801 Bardstown Rd (☎459-6398). The best Tex-Mex in town. Try the white chili, a delicious blend of white beans, chicken, onions, cheese and sour cream. Entrees $7–11.

Dietrich's, 2862 Frankfort Ave (☎897-6076). Atmospheric converted picture house in the Crescent Hill district. Inventive seafood and meat choices cooked on a wood-burning grill. Entrees $6–20.

Lilly's, 1147 Bardstown Rd (☎451-0447). Avant-garde decor and a regularly-changing menu, strong on veal and seafood. Most main courses cost around $10–12.

Old Spaghetti Factory, 235 W Market St (☎581-1070). Downtown's best value, with main dishes all under $7. Antiques and curiosities give this big-chain restaurant an individual feel.

Nightlife and Entertainment

The **Kentucky Center for the Arts** (☎584-7777 or ☎1-800/283-7777), prominent downtown between Fifth and Sixth avenues and fronted by several outlandish sculptures, is Louisville's main venue for high culture. As for **drinking** and **live music**, the two-mile strip around Bardstown Road and Baxter Avenue (bus #17) is punctuated by fun bars and restaurants. Louisville enjoys a lively **gay** scene with the best clubs on the eastern edge of downtown.

Anthony's By The Bridge, 131 W Main St (☎584-7720). Sixty-nine different beers, acoustic/blues music, comedy on Friday and Saturday, and decent pasta dishes for around $8.

Butchertown Pub, 1335 Storey Ave (☎583-2242). Ever-popular live music pub in the Butchertown district near downtown. Cover under $3. Take #15 bus.

Connections, 130 S Floyd St (☎585-5742). The pick of Louisville's gay scene. At weekends this giant club, complete with terrace garden, holds over 2000, playing house and hi-energy.

Phoenix Hill Tavern, 644 Baxter Ave (☎589-4957). Premier live music venue. Cover $2–3.

Out From Louisville

South from Louisville to Tennessee, **central Kentucky** offers great scope for a one- or two-day driving tour. There's small-town charm in **Bardstown** and Abraham Lincoln's birthplace of **Hodgenville**, while the top natural attraction is the amazing **Mammoth Cave National Park**, the largest underground cave system in the world.

Kentucky's **western** stretches don't compare with the ruggedness of the east for scenic beauty; all the significant lakes were created by damming its rivers and much of the land is scarred by stripmines, oilfields and commercial forests. There's little of real interest here except for the **Land Between The Lakes** recreation area, squeezed between Kentucky and Barkley lakes, overlapping the Tennessee border.

Fort Knox

Legendary **FORT KNOX** straddles 100,000 acres either side of US-31W, thirty miles southwest of Louisville. The bomb-proof **Bullion Depository**, surrounded by security fences, machine-gun turrets, patrol guards and huge floodlights, stores nine million pounds of the federal gold reserve behind doors weighing twenty tons apiece. No visits are allowed, and you can only stop by the roadside for a maximum of five minutes.

Bardstown and Bourbon Distilleries

Forty miles south of Louisville on US-31E, attractive **BARDSTOWN** is the place to get acquainted with Kentucky **bourbon whiskey**, created in earliest pioneer days, so the story goes, when Elijah Craig, a Baptist minister, added corn to the usual rye and barley. Named for Bourbon County near Lexington, Kentucky's whiskey soon gained a national reputation, thanks to crisp limestone water and the skills of small-scale distillers. Under federal law, corn must make up at least 51 percent of all solid ingredients, and the drink must mature for two years in new oak barrels with charred interiors.

Get into the spirit at Bardstown's free **Oscar Getz Museum of Whiskey History**, 114 N Fifth Street (May–Oct Mon–Sat 9am–5pm, Sun 1–5pm; otherwise times vary). Fourteen miles west at **CLERMONT**, you can tour **Jim Beam's** famous plant (Mon–Sat 9am–4.30pm, Sun 1–4pm; free; ☎543-9877). **Maker's Mark Distillery**, a small family-run operation twenty miles south of Bardstown near **LORETTO**, is an out-of-the-way collection of beautifully restored black, red and gray plankhouses, in which whiskey is still made manually (Mon–Sat 10.30am–3.30pm; closed Sat during Jan & Feb; free; ☎865-2881). However, you shouldn't expect a sample at either distillery. Like most of rural Kentucky, the area is **dry**.

Abraham Lincoln Birthplace

On February 12 1809, **Abraham Lincoln**, the sixteenth President of the USA, was born in a one-room log cabin in the frontier wilds, son of a wandering farmer and, if some accounts are to be believed, an illiterate and illegitimate mother. The original dirt-floored hut, three miles south of **HODGENVILLE** on US-31E, is now enclosed in a granite and marble Memorial Building with 56 steps, one for each year of Lincoln's life. The family moved in 1811 to **Knob Creek**, seven miles east of town, where Lincoln's earliest memory was of slaves being forcefully driven along the road. Little Hodgenville, which the Lincolns left in 1816 for Indiana, doesn't overplay the presidential connection, and its homely cafes make it a good place to stop.

Mammoth Cave National Park

The three hundred miles of labyrinthine passages and domed caverns of **MAMMOTH CAVE NATIONAL PARK** lie halfway between Louisville and Bowling Green, ten miles off I-65 (exits 48 or 53). An amazing range of geological formations, carved by acidic water trickling through limestone, includes a bewildering display of stalagmites and stalagtites, a huge cascacde of flowstone known as **Frozen Niagara**, and **Echo River**, 365 feet below ground, populated by a unique species of colourless and sightless fish. Among traces of human occupation are Native American artefacts, a former saltpetre mine, and the remains of an experimental tuberculosis hospital built in 1843 in the belief that the cool atmosphere of the cave would help clear patients' lungs.

To protect the stone, access to the caves is by guided tour ($3.50–$25); tickets from the **visitor centre** (☎758-2251), or *Ticketron*. Book ahead, especially in summer. The temperature in the caves is a constant 54°F, so be sure to take a sweater or jacket.

The park's attractions are by no means all subterranean. The scenic **Green River** cuts through densely forested hillsides and jagged limestone cliffs; you can hire canoes, but for a more leisurely trip take the *Miss Green River II* **cruise boat** ($4). **Camping** is free in the backcountry, while cottage **rooms** in the *Mammoth Cave Hotel* (☎758-2225) cost $30 and upwards.

The privately owned caves all around, many of which ruin the sights with garish light shows, and the "attractions" in nearby Cave City and Park City, are best ignored.

Bowling Green and Around

BOWLING GREEN's main claim to fame is as the only place where you can buy a drink between Louisville and Nashville, just sixty miles further southwest. It's a lively enough place, though, and offers a treat for **sports car** enthusiasts. One-hour tours of the **General Motors Corvette Plant**, on Louisville Road, off I-65, take a step-by-step look at the manufacture of one of the great symbols of the American Dream (Mon–Fri at 9am & 1pm; free; ☎745-8419; reservations advisable).

There's another former **Shaker settlement**, with crafts displays, ten miles west of Bowling Green on US-68, in **SOUTH UNION** (April–Nov Mon–Sat 9am–5pm, Sun 1–5pm; ☎542-4167). The 1869 *Shaker Tavern*, a mile or two away on Hwy-73, serves traditional Kentucky recipes such as chess pie (reservations ☎542-6801).

TENNESSEE

TENNESSEE, one of the most visited states in the US, divides into three distinct regions. A shallow rectangle, only one hundred miles from north to south, it stretches 450 miles from the Appalachians to the Mississippi. The mountainous **east**, which remained largely isolated until the middle of this century, shares its top attraction with North Carolina – the peaks, streams and meadows of **Great Smoky Mountains National Park**. The fine plantation homes and tidy old towns of **Middle Tennessee**'s rolling farmland reflect the more comfortable lifestyle of its pioneers. If this is the heart of the Bible Belt, then **Nashville**, the state capital and **country music**'s mecca, is its buckle. Down in the southwest corner, the Mississippi riverport of **Memphis**, Tennessee's largest city, is another magnet for music fans, both for its blues heritage and its pivotal role in the legend of **Elvis**.

Tennessee's first white settlers, most of them British Protestants, appeared from across the mountains in the 1770s, to settle in the hills and hollows of the Appalachians. Initially relations with the **Cherokee** were good. However, demand for land increased, and confrontations throughout the state culminated in 1838 with the forced removal of the Indians on the "Trail of Tears". One of the main congressional opponents of this process was **Davy Crockett**, more familiar as the heavy-drinking hunter in a coonskin cap who figures in many a tale of pioneer hardship. When **Civil War** came, the plantation owners of the west manoeuvred Tennessee into the Confederacy, against the wishes of the non-slaveholding smallhold farmers in the east. The last state to secede became the primary battlefield in the west, the site of 424 battles and skirmishes.

Despite a rate of economic development to rival any in the country, soil erosion and farm mechanisation led to a mass migration to the cities in the years before World War I. The fundamentalist beliefs of these transplanted hill-dwellers (whose folk and fiddle music served to spark Nashville's country scene) influenced a **prohibition** movement which kept all Tennessee bone-dry until 1939, and still sees a majority of counties forbidding the sale of alcohol. The New Deal of the Thirties brought significant benefits. In particular, the **Tennessee Valley Authority**, created in 1933, harnessed the flood-prone Tennessee River, providing much-needed jobs and cheap power, and ignited the transition from an agricultural to an industrial economy.

Getting Around Tennessee

For such a popular tourist destination, Tennessee has disappointing **transport** connections. *Amtrak* only calls at Memphis, and while *Greyhound* provides a reasonable service to major towns and cities, travelling by bus through the small towns in the east is very difficult. The **airports** at Memphis and Nashville have extensive connections throughout the USA, but few flights beyond. Chattanooga and Knoxville have regional airports. If you cherish a fantasy of travelling **by boat** along the Mississippi, unfortunately only luxury craft make the trip these days, at prohibitive prices (see p.398).

Eastern Tennessee

Until the creation of the TVA, the opening of Great Smoky Mountains National Park and the building of the interstate highways, life had continued in the remote hills and valleys of eastern Tennessee in much the same way as it had ever since the arrival of the first pioneers. Now visitors flock here for its endless expanses of natural beauty; and as a result, especially in autumn, the Smokies can get very clogged with traffic. Most communities are small, and either over-touristed or just bland. The two main cities, modern **Knoxville** and picturesque **Chattanooga**, have much in common, including healthy post-World War II industrial growth, thanks to cheap TVA power.

The telephone **area code** for eastern and central Tennessee, including Nashville, is ☎615.

Knoxville

Surrounded by the hillbilly wilderness of the Great Smoky, the Cumberland and the Blue Ridge mountains, **KNOXVILLE**, the original capital of Tennessee, is a growing conurbation of 180,000. Modern skyscrapers, older brick buildings and a riverfront at the bottom of steep bluffs, combine to give **downtown** an attractive edge, but specific places of interest are thin on the ground. On the northern fringe, the **Old City**, centred on Central and Jackson streets, is a rejuvenated area of shops, galleries, restaurants and nightspots in Victorian warehouses along narrow cobbled streets and railway arches.

On the western edge of downtown, the **World's Fair Park** is dominated by the futuristic **Sunsphere**, a huge glass ball mounted on a round concrete tower. The **Knoxville Museum of Art**, in the park at 410 Tenth Street, features a small permanent collection of paintings and a cleverly designed sculpture garden focused on a 200-year-old elm tree. Follow Cumberland Avenue up a few blocks and you come to the large, leafy campus of the University of Tennessee. Lined with bars and diners, frequently bedecked in the orange colours of the Volunteers football team, the campus has two theatres and the free **Frank H McClung Museum** at Circle Park, which features displays on the city's archaeology, art and history.

Practicalities

Greyhound buses stop in the Old City on North Central Street (☎522-5141); *K-Trans* city buses run a free trolley to the campus. The **visitor centre** is at 500 Henley Street (☎523-7263). The *Best Western Campus Inn*, 1706 W Cumberland Avenue (☎521-5000), is a comfortable, fairly central place to stay for $40 and up, though rooms anywhere in the city tend to be fully booked when the Tennessee Volunteers are playing at home.

Knoxville's favourite **restaurant**, the rib-specialists *Calhoun's*, overlooks the river downtown at 400 Neyland Drive (☎544-0349), and, in the Old City, the *131 Deli and Sidewalk Cafe* (☎523-4131) sells really tasty sandwiches. *Planet Earth* (☎522-2737) on West Jackson Street is a popular **bar** with live guitar bands most evenings. On campus, Cumberland Avenue offers a range of cheap eating options and lively drinking holes.

Oak Ridge

Twenty-five miles west of Knoxville, **OAK RIDGE** was hastily erected in 1942, on a site hacked out of thick forest, to manufacture the enriched uranium used in the atomic bombs dropped on Hiroshima. Its very existence was not officially admitted until 1949. Many of its original barracks and dwellings still stand, giving the place an eerie feel.

Towards the Great Smoky Mountains

The most common way to approach the Smokies from the west is on US-441 via the small market centre of **SEVIERVILLE**, which evokes days gone by with its wooden-floored general stores and small cafes serving mountains of southern food to hungry farmers. A statue of the county's best-known citizen, **Dolly Parton**, stands on the lawn outside the courthouse. Sevierville merges almost seamlessly into the six-mile strip of motels, fast-food outlets and souvenir shops at **PIGEON FORGE**. This dry town, firmly geared toward the family market, is the home of **Dollywood** (see box).

Five miles further along US-441, a heavy layer of kitsch all but submerges the genuine Germanic heritage of the more upmarket, "wet" tourist town of **GATLINBURG**. The long narrow main street is packed to the point of claustrophobia with gimmicky souvenir shops, wax museums, and stalls selling sickly-sweet taffy.

<table>
<tr><td colspan="2" align="center">**DOLLYWOOD**</td></tr>
</table>

Born in 1946, one of twelve children, **Dolly Parton** lived in several modest homes around Pigeon Forge, the most isolated of them two miles from the nearest neighbour and over four miles from the mailbox. As a child she sang every week on local radio, before leaving for Nashville on the day she finished at Sevier County High School. Her first success, duetting with Porter Wagoner, came to an acrimonious end in the early Seventies, but she scored a major country hit in 1976 with *Jolene*. She then crossed over to a poppier sound, and into Hollywood films like *9 to 5* and *The Best Little Whorehouse in Texas*. Her songs have been acclaimed for their readiness to address issues like rural poverty, and refusal to tag along with the Nashville stereotype of subservient females.

Dollywood, Dolly Parton's "homespun fun" **theme park**, is an enjoyable blend of old-time mountain heritage and the glitz and glamour of its celebrity shareholder. With its rustic buildings and free-running hens, it's a showcase for Appalachian **crafts**, where one can watch the manufacture of everything from lye soap to horse-drawn carriages. Highlights include a scenic five-mile **steam-train** trip through the foothills of the Great Smokies, the "only Dolly Parton museum in the world", and music shows starring lesser-known Partons. Dolly herself occasionally uses an apartment on site.

Dollywood is at 700 Dollywood Lane at the north end of Pigeon Forge (May–Oct & Xmas, as a rule 9am–9pm but considerable variations; $16.50; ☎428-9488). Local **radio station** *WDLY*, on 105.5, is another Dolly Parton enterprise.

Practicalities

Accommodation prices in the foothill towns fluctuate seasonally, ranging from $20 to $80. Motels in **Sevierville** are often cheaper; try the *Mize Motel* (☎453-4018), one mile south at 804 Parkway, for around $40. Rooms at the *Parkview* in **Pigeon Forge**, 901 S Parkway (☎453-5051), are usually about $40; the comfortable, friendly *Shula Inn*, 1001 N Parkway (☎453-2700), costs a little more. If you prefer neon lights to wilderness trails, you can camp at the *Smokies Campground*, 705 S Parkway (☎453-4129).

Gatlinburg tends to be the most expensive, but *Bales* at 118 Bishop Lane (☎436-4773) and *Conner*, Rte 2 River Road (☎436-5147), are motels with rooms under $50. It is, however, the best choice for **food**. *Linebergers* (☎436-9284), at traffic light #8 on the Parkway, is strong on seafood and vegetable dishes. A good **breakfast** place in Pigeon Forge is the *Smoky Mountain Pancake House* at 301 N Parkway (☎453-1827).

Great Smoky Mountains National Park

The northern boundary of the **GREAT SMOKY MOUNTAINS NATIONAL PARK**, which stretches for seventy miles along the Tennessee–North Carolina border (see also p.358), is just two miles south of Gatlinburg on US-441. Don't expect immediate tranquillity, however: the roads, particularly in autumn, can be lined almost bumper-to-bumper with cars. The Smokies, within a day's drive of the major urban centres of the East Coast and the Great Lakes, attract over 9 million visitors per year, more than twice as many as any other national park. These heavily contorted peaks are named for the **bluish haze** which hangs over them, made up of moisture and hydrocarbons released by the lush vegetation (a mature tree emits up to 900 gallons on a summer day). Since the Sixties, **air pollution** has been adding sulphates to the filmy smoke, and has cut back visibility by thirty percent. More than 120 tree species and over 1400 flowering plants clothe the mountains and meadows in colour from early spring to late autumn. Sixteen peaks rise above 6000 feet, their steep elevation accounting for dramatic changes in climate.

The most popular **times to visit** are between late March and mid-May, to see the delicate spring flowers, and during the second half of October when the hills are shrouded in a magnificent canopy of glaring reds, subtle yellows and faded browns. During June and July, rhododendrons blaze fiercely in the sometimes stifling summer heat.

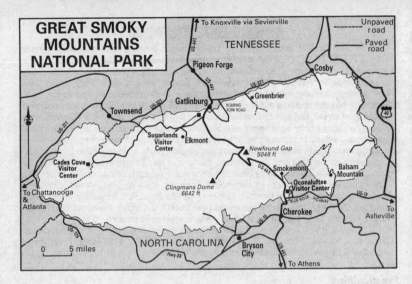

Just inside the park on US-441, the main artery running through to North Carolina, **Sugarlands visitor centre** (summer 8am–7pm; autumn and spring 8am–6pm; winter 8am–5pm) is a very useful source of leaflets covering hiking trails, driving tours, forests and wildlife. From here it's a ten-mile drive to Newfound Gap on the state line, with a seven-mile spur road winding its way up to **Clingman's Dome**, at 6643ft the highest point in the park and in all Tennessee. A spiral path here climbs up to an observation tower affording a panoramic, though hazy, view of the mountains.

The scenic **Little River Road** branches off back at Sugarlands towards **Cade's Cove**, where another visitor centre (with the same hours) is situated halfway round an eleven-mile driving loop, in summer and autumn always jam-packed with cars. Along the route, deserted barns, homesteads, mills and churches stand as a reminder of the farmers who carved out a living from this wilderness, before having to move out when National Park status was conferred in 1934. Quieter **Hwy-321**, on the other side of Sugarlands, branches off onto a gravel road towards the beautiful Greenbrier area.

If you really want to get away from it all, escape onto the nine hundred miles of **hiking** trails. On the Appalachian Trail, you can now only camp in designated areas, caged-in behind iron bars to keep out the bears.

Practicalities

Hikers intending to stay out overnight require **backcountry permits**, available from visitor centres. The park also has ten developed **campgrounds**, of which the three most popular – *Cades Cove*, *Elkmont* and *Smokemont* – are always fully booked. Reserve through *Ticketron* if you want a space in summer or autumn. Only two places within the park boundaries offer **lodgings**. To reach *Le Conte Lodge* (☎436-4473), on the slopes of Mount Le Conte in the vicinity of Newfound Gap, you have to walk – a five- to eight-mile trek. Overnight accommodation costs from $35 to $40, including dinner and breakfast. The *Wonderland Club Hotel* (☎436-5490), near the *Elkmont* campground, affords a little more luxury than the lodge for $61 per night, though as its lease expires shortly its future must be in doubt. For details of the North Carolina side of the park, see p.358.

On Saturday, from dawn until 10am, the Cades Cove loop is reserved for **cyclists**. Bikes can be rented at the *Cades Cove Campground* (☎436-5615).

Chattanooga

Few cities can be so identified with a song as is **CHATTANOOGA**, in the southeast corner of Tennessee. Visitors brought up on Tex Beneke and Glenn Miller's *Chattanooga Choo-Choo* will be let down to find that there is no longer even an *Amtrak* service, but the town continues to celebrate its railroad history, and has plenty more to offer besides – not least its beautiful location on a deep bend in the Tennessee River, walled in by tree-covered mountains on three sides. This setting led John Ross, of mixed Scottish and Cherokee ancestry, to found a trading post here in 1815, and its strategic importance made it a great prize during the Civil War; victories here were the springboard for Sherman's march through Georgia (see p.370).

The centrepiece of Chattanooga's twenty miles of reclaimed riverfront is the **Ross's Landing** public park at the bottom of Broad Street, where the **Tennessee Aquarium** opens in 1992, with five levels of tanks tracing the aquatic life of the Mississippi from its Tennessee tributaries to the Gulf of Mexico. Cruises on the *Southern Belle* **riverboat** (☎266-4488), from the bottom of nearby Chestnut Street, include the daunting experience of bobbing around in the bottom of a huge lock on Chickamauga Lake.

A few blocks from the river, the **Chattanooga Regional History Museum** at 400 Chestnut Street (Tue–Fri 10am–4.30pm, Sat & Sun noon–4.30pm; $2) takes a people-centred look at the area's rich history, with displays on its steel, soft-drink bottling and power industries, and on the Cherokee. A short walk further along are the grand old turn-of-the-century buildings of the lively business district, centred on Market and Broad streets. None is more eye-catching than the recently restored *Tivoli Theatre* at 709 Broad Street, whose flashing lights stand out like a beacon at night.

Two miles in from the river is the **Choo-Choo complex**, where the 1909 Beaux-Arts style **Southern Railroad Terminal**, at 1400 Market Street (☎266-5000), is today a *Holiday Inn*, the *Chattanooga Choo-Choo Hotel*. The impressive high-domed waiting room serves as the lobby, leading through to the former platform area where restored carriages act as hotel suites. Several gift shops and cafes share space with a steam engine similar to the original Choo-Choo (which was the name given by the local paper to the first passenger train to come in from Cincinnati in 1880). You're free to roam around; admission to the world's largest model railway display, on site, is $1.50.

The only opportunity to ride on a real **steam train** in Chattanooga these days is to take the **Tennessee Valley Railroad** along a stunning six-mile route that crosses the river, goes through deep tunnels and turns round on a giant turntable. The two main stations, restored to their 1930s look, are at 2200 N Chamberlain Avenue in east Chattanooga, and 4119 Cromwell Road (I-75 exit 4 to Hwy-153), though some weekend routes pick up at the Choo-Choo. For full schedules call ☎894-8028.

Practicalities

A taxi downtown from Chattanooga's municipal **airport**, three miles east, costs around $10. *Greyhound* offers connections to Nashville, Knoxville and Atlanta (☎267-6531). The **visitor centre**, 1001 Market Street (☎756-8687), provides the usual range of help, along with a useful guide for travellers with disabilities. Good value **places to stay** downtown include the *Best Western* at 901 Carter Street (☎266-7331) and *Days Inn* at 401 West M L King Blvd (☎265-8571), both for $45. Nearby **camping** is available at *KOA Lookout Mountain* (☎404/657-6815) and *Raccoon Mountain Campground*, Rte 4, Cummings Highway (☎821-9403).

For a **breakfast** special, treat yourself to the $6 buffet in the elegant black walnut-panelled dining rooms of the *Radisson Read House* at 827 Broad Street (☎266-4121). The *Pickle Barrel* (☎266-1103) on Market Street, opposite the Civic Forum, does good-value pub lunches. At night, the place to go is *Michelangelo's Blues Club* (☎267-7843) in downtown Miller Plaza, where live blues, jazz and rock are on offer for a $5 cover.

THE CHEROKEE NATION AND THE TRAIL OF TEARS

During the eighteenth and early nineteenth centuries, the **Cherokee** were the most powerful Indian tribe in the tri-state region of Tennessee, Georgia and North Carolina. They forged close links with white pioneers, adopting white methods in schooling and agriculture, intermarrying – and owning African slaves. The only Native Americans to develop their own written language, they had a regular newspaper, *The Cherokee Phoenix*. They even supplied soldiers for Andrew Jackson's US forces against the Creek Indians and the British in 1814, hoping to buy influence with the federal government.

Thirteen years later, against a background of aggressive territorial claims by settlers, they produced a written constitution modelled on that of the USA, stating their intention to continue to be a self-governing nation. John Ross, founder of Ross's Landing, and at most one-eighth Cherokee, was elected as the first Principal Chief in 1828 in an effort to appease and negotiate with national and state governments over their lands. However, as white demand for land increased, their former ally **Jackson**, now US president, was pressurised by the Georgians into "offering" the Cherokee western lands in exchange for those east of the Mississippi. Although the tribal leadership refused, a minority faction accepted, giving the government the get-out clause they wanted. The Cherokee were ordered to leave within two years and 14,000 of them were forcefully removed to Oklahoma in 1838 along the horrific **Trail of Tears**: 4000 died of disease or exposure on the way. In the meantime, their land was sold by lottery and Ross's Landing was renamed Chattanooga. One thousand Cherokee managed to avoid removal by escaping into the mountains, and their descendants now occupy a small reservation in North Carolina.

The **Red Clay State Historic Park**, twenty miles east of Chattanooga off Hwy-317, recounts the old Cherokee way of life, with replica houses, tools and household implements. Its balsamic Sacred Council Spring was a meeting place for Cherokee elders.

Lookout Mountain

Three miles from downtown is the prominent landmark of **Lookout Mountain**. From 3917 St Elmo Avenue, on the #14 bus route, the glass-roofed, trolley-style cars of the world's steepest **incline railway** grind their tentative way to the top through a narrow gash in the lush forest, tackling gradients of up to 72.7 percent (daily; $5; ☎821-4224). Once there, a walk of a few hundred yards past exclusive homes takes you to **Point Park**, and the only statue in the country to show Union and Confederate soldiers shaking hands. This is part of the Chickamauga and Chattanooga National Military Park, covering several sites around the city and in nearby Chickamauga, Georgia. A short, steep, walking trail descends several tiers of steps to an overlook affording a not-to-be-missed view of the city and the meandering Tennessee River.

Nashville

Set amid the gentle hills and fertile farmlands of central Tennessee, **NASHVILLE** attracts six million people each year – a mixture of devoted fans and the just plain curious – to immerse themselves in **country music**. They come to enjoy themselves, and the city makes sure that they do, offering not just the relatively mainstream **Opryland**, **Country Music Hall of Fame** and **Grand Ole Opry**, but all the wonders of "Tacksville". To make the most of Nashville, you need to abandon any idea of detachment, and get out there among the nightspots and gift emporia, joining the quest for souvenir T-shirts, stetsons, rattlesnake belts and photos of your favourite star.

However, there is a real city beneath the rhinestone glitter. Nashville has been the leading settlement in middle Tennessee since **Fort Nashborough** was established in 1779. State capital since 1843, it is now the **financial** and **insurance** centre of the mid-south as well as developing a fast-growing **manufacturing** base. Giant *Nissan* and

Saturn motor plants have recently been attracted to its immediate hinterland, and rapid growth since World War II has transformed a once-compact city into a sprawling conurbation stretching out in all directions along the undulating roads, here known as **pikes**.

For all its blue-collar "Nash-Vegas" image, Nashville has maintained a strong reputation for **learning** since planter times, and is home to sixteen higher education establishments, including Vanderbilt University and the renowned black colleges of Fisk University and Meharry Medical School. The city likes to see itself as the "Athens of the South" – and, endearingly, has built a replica of the Parthenon to bolster its claim.

The other conspicuous element in Nashville's make-up is **religion**. There are over seven hundred churches, more per capita than anywhere else in the country. But what really earns it the tag of "Protestant Vatican" is the proliferation of colleges for training preachers and missionaries, church administrative offices and Bible-publishing plants.

Arrival and Information

Nashville International Airport is eight miles southeast of downtown. Buses into town (weekdays 6.15am–10.30pm; weekend times vary) take around thirty minutes and cost 85¢. Taxis are quicker but will set you back up to $20. *Greyhound* buses arrive in a seedy part of downtown at 200 Eighth Avenue South (☎256-6141); there's no *Amtrak* service. *Metropolitan Transit Authority* (☎242-4433) **buses** run until 11pm to most parts of the county, departing from the transit mall on Deaderick Street. **Trolleys** cover the entire downtown area plus Music Row for a fare of 25¢. Places of interest in Nashville are so far apart that it's worth thinking about renting a **car**, though the one-way system can be maddening, and the roads change name without warning. *Grand Ole Opry Tours* (☎889-9490), *Gray Line* (☎883-5555) and *Stardust* (☎244-2335) all offer **coach tours**. Expect to pay $16 for a three-hour trip, not including admission to attractions.

If you're on foot, it's a bit of an effort to get to the main **Tourist Information Center** (☎259-4747), across the bridge on Interstate Drive at Exit 85, off I-65. However, the **Chamber of Commerce Office** at 161 Fourth Avenue North (☎259-4755) has a well-stocked rack of maps and leaflets. The **post office** is downtown at 921 Broadway (Mon–Fri 8am–6pm, Sat 8am–noon; ☎251-5321; zip code 37202).

The City

Downtown Nashville looks much like any other regional business centre, dominated by office blocks and parking lots. It's perfectly possible to spend a busy day here without coming into contact with country music. A good starting point – though it borders on a rough part of town – is **Riverfront Park** at First and Broadway, a thin stretch of grass and terracing dipping down to the Cumberland River. A replica of the wooden **Fort Nashborough** stands on a promontory above the river as a monument to the city's founders of 1779 (Tues–Sat 9am–4pm; donation). Overlooking all proceedings from First Avenue, a row of craggy Victorian brick warehouses runs right through to Second Avenue where their cast-iron frontages house restaurants, bars and shops. During the religious revival of the Thirties, these streets were packed every Sunday for "free for all preachings", when zealous fundamentalists would proclaim their own brand of theology from atop any convenient box, cart or wall.

A few blocks away, the **Tennessee State Museum** at 505 Deaderick Street (Mon–Sat 10am–5pm, Sun 1–5pm; free) does a worthy job of relating the state's history. It's strongest on the Civil War, highlighting the hardships of the ill-clad, ill-fed soldiers, of whom 23,000 out of 77,000 died at Shiloh alone. Other displays focus on frontier life and on black Tennesseans, looking at slavery, Reconstruction, the founding of the Ku Klux Klan and the civil rights movement. In a city where you can pay $5 to see a few old cars or the stage costumes of country stars, it's good to find something like this for free.

Marking downtown's northern boundary at Sixth and Charlotte, the resplendent **Tennessee State Capitol**, modelled on an Ionic temple, looks out across the city from its hilltop perch. Earlier this century, this area was yet another "Hell's Half Acre", notorious for its drinking holes, gambling clubs, sex shows and dope dens; it's considerably tamer now, housing hotels and a huge State Museum/Performing Arts complex.

Ten minutes' walk north of the Capitol, the **Museum of Tobacco Art and History** at 800 Harrison Street (Tues–Sat 10am–4pm; free) takes an excellent look at what it calls the "truly American commodity". An international collection of advertisements spans a century, alongside elaborate snuff boxes, meerschaum pipes and spittoons. Exhibits trace the use of tobacco ever since Columbus found Native Americans smoking, chewing and snorting it in 1492. Although run by the small US Tobacco Company, the museum doesn't set out to glorify the whole sordid business.

At the 1897 Tennessee Centennial Exposition, the Nashville exhibit, entitled "Athens of the South", featured a full-size replica of the **Parthenon** made out of wood and plaster. This proved so popular with Nashville residents that the present permanent structure, in the middle of **Centennial Park** southwest of downtown at West End and 25th avenues, was built in 1931. It may be familiar to movie-goers from the finale of Robert Altman's not-always-flattering *Nashville*. This impressive edifice is now the home of Nashville's premier **art museum** (Tues, Wed, Fri & Sat 9am–4.30pm, Thurs 9am–8pm; $2.50). The lower level contains American paintings; the upper hall is dominated by a 42-ft replica of Phidias' statue of Athena holding Nike (the goddess of victory).

Just across West End Avenue, weatherbeaten Gothic structures sit alongside more modern utilitarian buildings on the campus of prestigious **Vanderbilt University**. This bastion of conservatism was one of the very few colleges to witness student demonstrations in *support* of American aggression in Vietnam.

Of the many buildings erected by Nashville's antebellum elite, none was more elaborate than **Belmont Mansion**, one mile southeast of the Parthenon at 1900 Belmont Boulevard (June–Aug Mon–Sat 10am–4pm; otherwise Tues–Sat 10am–4pm; $3). This 36-room 1850 Italianate villa looks out across ornamented gardens that once contained a bear house and a lake stocked with alligators.

Country Music Nashville

The status of Nashville as country music's capital city dates back to the Twenties, and the arrival of thousands of migrants fleeing rural poverty. The music they brought with them, rooted in the folksongs of Tennessee's first Irish and British settlers, soon mutated in the urban environment into something new, incorporating elements of Tin Pan Alley musicals, religious hymns and songs from ex-slaves.

As radios and record players became widely available for the first time, the **recording industry** began to take off, and Nashville became the obvious geographical base for the musicians of the mid-south. Radio station WSM had championed the country sound since 1925, and its live weekly Grand Ole Opry concerts (see box) spearheaded the city's burgeoning **live music** scene.

The first big commercial boom came in the decade of prosperity after World War II. Nashville proliferated with recording studios, publishing companies, artists' agencies and associated trade. The big labels recognised that a large slice of the (white) record-buying public wanted something a bit safer than rockabilly. The clean-cut, middle-of-the-road, easy-listening **Nashville Sound** they came up with, pioneered by Patsy Cline and Jim Reeves, remains country's dominant force, thanks to artists like Barbara Mandrell and Kenny Rogers. Not that the clean-cut image always holds true; the concentration of stars and music-biz executives has turned Nashville into a downmarket Hollywood, with lifestyles to match (memorably exposed in Randall Reise's book *Nashville Babylon*).

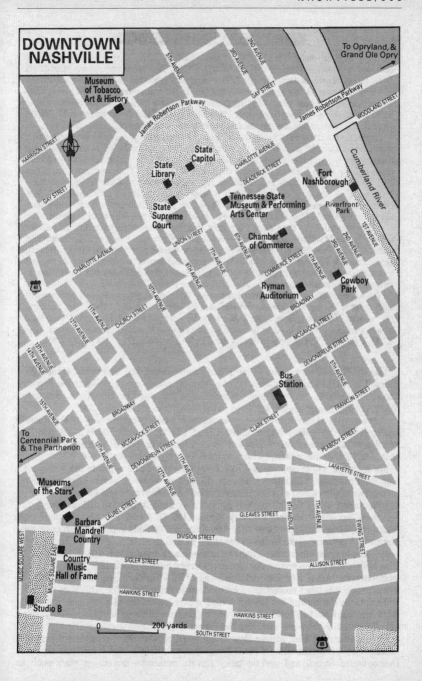

THE GRAND OLE OPRY

Nashville's radio station WSM ("We Shield Millions", the slogan of its insurance-company sponsor) first broadcast on October 5 1925. Two years later, at the start of his *Barn Dance* show, compere George D Hay announced "for the past hour we have been listening to music taken largely from Grand Opera, but from now on we will present *The Grand Ole Opry*". This piece of slang became the name of America's longest-running radio show, still going out to millions every Friday and Saturday evening on WSM-AM (650m); the original hillbilly jam session has become country music's elite showcase.

By the time it moved in 1943 to the **Ryman Auditorium**, the former tabernacle which was to be its home for thirty years, the show had long outgrown the WSM studios. During these years it acquired its make-or-break reputation; up-and-coming singers could only claim to have made it if they had gone down well at the Opry. The thousands of hopefuls who tried to get on the show included Elvis Presley, who was advised by an Opry official in 1954 to stick to truck-driving. The first appearance of **Hank Williams**, in 1949, commanded an unequalled six encores. Within four years, the Opry audience were singing his evangelical *I Saw The Light* on the news of his drink- and drug-induced death.

In the Seventies the show moved on again, this time to a new purpose-built 4424-seater theatre in the **Opryland** theme park – one of many Opry spin-offs, including hotels, TV stations and a record label. Among more than sixty stars currently on the Opry roster are old-timers like Roy Acuff and Minnie Pearl, perennial superstars like Loretta Lynn, and current country chart-toppers such as Reba McEntire, Randy Travis and Ricky Skaggs (whose other commitments mean they don't appear here all that often).

Throughout the year, two performances on Saturday night and one on Friday night feature up to twenty acts. During the summer, an extra Friday-night show, and matinees on Tuesday, Thursday, Saturday and Sunday offer fewer artists. **Tickets** are not too hard to get, especially if you book in advance. Evening shows cost $12–14; matinees are $10–12. Contact the ticket office at 2808 Opryland Drive, Nashville TN 37214 (☎889-3060).

Though Nashville's country scene is both conspicuous and accessible, submerging yourself in it takes time and quite a lot of money; prices are set at what the industry knows enthusiastic fans will pay. In addition to the daytime attractions mentioned below, country music venues are listed in the "Nightlife" section on p.396.

Downtown at 116 Fifth Avenue, you can take a twenty-minute tour of the **Ryman Auditorium**, the former home of the Grand Ole Opry (daily 8.30am–4.30pm; $2). You'll see the wooden church pews of the auditorium proper, as well as the dressing rooms and the well-worn stage where so many country greats performed.

For a surreal photo opportunity, stop by at **Cowboy Park** opposite the honky-tonk bars on Broadway. This former derelict site is now home to seven brightly painted "urban cowboy" sculptures made from recycled household cans and boxes.

Blue route trolleys along Broadway run just over a mile southwest of downtown to the excellent, but often crowded, **Country Music Hall Of Fame**, at 4 Music Square East (daily, June–Aug 8am–8pm; Sept–May 9am–5pm; $6.50). This is packed with costumes, guitars and personal possessions of the stars, including Elvis' gold-laden Cadillac, with forty coats of paint containing crushed diamonds and oriental fish scales. Film and TV clips help to clarify the arcane distinctions between hillbilly, rockabilly, honky-tonk and western swing. Admission also includes a tour of RCA's historic **Studio B**, preserved as it was when the label moved to more modern premises in 1971. The likes of Willie Nelson, Dolly Parton and Jim Reeves recorded here, as did the Monkees and the Everly Brothers, and Elvis laid down over 200 tracks. You can follow in their footsteps by trying out all sorts of instruments, including the indispensable dobro (steel guitar).

The surrounding area, **Music Row**, is the heart of Nashville's recording industry. A minute's walk from the Hall Of Fame brings you to a strip of garish souvenir shops on Demonbreun Street, and several tacky private museums honouring stars such as

Waylon Jennings, Elvis Presley and Hank Williams Jnr. These places charge you to see personal mementoes and rubbish that the stars don't want to keep in their homes; it costs $7, for example, to visit **Barbara Mandrell Country** at 1510 Division Street.

A similar assortment of "museums" and gift shops, **Music Village**, can be found in the small town of **Hendersonville**, eighteen miles north of Nashville. This is near Old Hickory Lake, where nouveau-riche country stars have built their own luxury shoreside enclave, abandoning uncomfortable attempts to live in select Nashville suburbs such as Belle Meade. Tour buses bring thousands of fans to see the homes and possessions of stars like Johnny Cash, Willie Nelson and Conway Twitty.

Opryland

Nine miles northeast of downtown Nashville on Briley Parkway, just off the I-40E loop. Daily Memorial Day to Labor Day; weekends only late March–May & Sept–early Nov. Usual summer hours 9am–9pm, otherwise considerable variation – call ☎889-6700. $19.95 admission includes rides but not paddlesteamer trips ($12.95 extra) or Opry Theater tickets (see box).

There's nothing all that "country" about **Opryland**. It's basically a standard **theme park** where the staff happen to wear gingham instead of cartoon costumes. The twenty-one **rides** included in the price are not exceptional, though the roller coaster *Chaos* is worth trying, and there's a plethora of shooting galleries, shops and fast-food stalls – even a studio to make your own country tape – to keep you spending. Twelve stages offer music fans very professional but utterly sanitised family shows of mainstream jazz, gospel, rock'n'roll and, of course, watered-down country music.

To the north of the park, on McGavock Pike in **Music Valley**, a colony of parasitic attractions – a wax museum, a "cars of the stars" place, and so on – has sprung up around the opulent 1900-room *Opryland Hotel* (☎889-1000; rooms $130–2000 per night).

Accommodation

It's usually possible to find a reasonably priced **place to stay** in Nashville. The cheapest **motels** are a couple of miles north of downtown, off the I-65 Trinity Lane/Brick Church Pike exit. Two companies offering **B&B** reservations are *B&B Hospitality Tennessee*, PO Box 110227, TN 37222 (☎331-5244), and *B&B of Middle Tennessee*, PO Box 40804, TN 37204 (☎297-0883).

The cheapest (and nearest to Opryland) of the **campgrounds**, ten miles northeast in Music Valley, is *Fiddlers Inn Campground*, 2404 Music Valley Drive (☎885-1440).

Cabot Lodge, 1111 Airport Center at Donelson Pike North (☎883-1366). Eleven miles east of downtown, off I-40, convenient for the airport and Opryland. Spacious rooms for $55.

Days Inn Downtown/Convention Center, 711 Union St (☎242-4311). Excellent location in the centre of downtown. Rooms cost anywhere between $45 and $90. Usually has good weekend rates.

Econolodge Near Opryland, 2460 Music Valley Drive (☎889-0090). Just about the cheapest motel you'll find in this elite area, with doubles for $35–60.

Hampton Inn, 1919 West End Ave (☎329-1144). Clean, comfortable lodgings in the pleasant Vanderbilt University area, one mile west of downtown and six blocks from Music Row; $55.

Travelodge Downtown, 800 James Robertson Pkwy (☎244-2630). Situated at the north end of downtown, behind the state capitol; $40.

Tudor Inn Downtown, 750 James Robertson Pkwy (☎244-8970). Works out slightly cheaper than the neighbouring *Travelodge* , with doubles in the $30–40 bracket.

Eating

Nashville is all but taken over by fast-food and family-eating chains, but you should be able to dig up something of interest, particularly among the cheap diners around Vanderbilt University. Otherwise you might have to rely on the large **food mall** on the top floor of Church Street Shopping Center between Seventh and Eighth avenues.

Crawdaddy's, 14 Oldham St (☎255-5434). Large downtown riverfront establishment with outdoor seating, specialising in Cajun seafood. Good for lunch ($4–8), though the dinner menu is dearer.

Laurell's Raw Bar, 123 Second Ave (☎244-1230). Excellent selection of fresh seafood dishes; the menu often includes exotic crustaceans. Entrees from $6 to $22.

Old Spaghetti Factory, 160 Second Ave (☎254-9010). With its turn-of-the-century decor, this pasta chain is one of downtown's best-value places. Main dishes around $7, but be prepared to queue.

Rotier's, 2413 Elliston Place (☎327-9892). A basic, good-value, no-frills diner near Vanderbilt, strong on tasty southern-style dishes, including a great choice of filling vegetable plates.

Satsuma Tea Room, 417 Union St (☎256-5211). A downtown tradition popular with office workers and tourists. Tasty homemade breads and desserts with lunches under $5. Mon–Fri 10.45am–2pm.

Windows on the Cumberland, 112 Second Ave (☎244-7944). Reasonably priced daytime vegetarian cafe serving sandwiches, baked potatoes, beans'n'rice and salads.

Nightlife

Of all Nashville's varied country music venues, the main ones to **avoid** are the tacky tourist-bus-plagued clubs along the much-hyped and sleazy downtown **Printers' Alley**. The **honky-tonks** on Broadway, between Second and Fourth avenues, are more genuine and down-to-earth, though best avoided if you're on your own. Dine-and-dance places like the *Stock Yard* offer good-quality mainstream country music (and more tour-bus crowds); up-and-coming progressive country bands play smaller venues like the *Bluebird Cafe*. Every June, the **Fan Fair** is a week-long series of concerts and opportunities to meet the stars (contact 2804 Opryland Drive, Nashville TN 37214; ☎889-7502).

For **listings** of upcoming gigs and events, see the free weekly *Nashville Scene*, Thursday's *Nashville Banner*, or Friday's and Saturday's *Tennessean*. If you're looking for music other than country, **Second Avenue** is a popular downtown hangout for both locals and tourists, offering everything from bluegrass to funk and punk, and various haunts of interest can be found around Vanderbilt campus.

Nashville's prime venue for theatre, dance and classical music is the **Tennessee Performing Arts Center** at 505 Deaderick Street (☎741-2787). Its **symphony orchestra** also puts on weekend concerts in **Centennial Park**, at West End and 25th avenues by Vanderbilt University, between June and August. Foreign and avant-garde **films** are shown at the *Sarratt Cinema* (☎322-2425) on the Vanderbilt campus.

Bluebird Cafe, 4104 Hillsboro Rd (☎383-1461). A small intimate cafe, six miles west of downtown, which has become *the* place to see the latest honky-tonk and new country artists. Early evening entertainment is free, but a cover of around $6 is charged after 9.30pm.

Ernest Tubb's Record Store Midnight Jamboree, 2414 Music Valley Drive (☎889-2474). A live radio show, recorded every Saturday from midnight to 1am in a wooden hut next to the shop. Ernest Tubb, pioneer of the gutsy, bluesy honky-tonk style, has passed the show on to his son, Justin. Genuinely promising newcomers as well as major Opry stars. Free.

Exit/In, 2208 Elliston Place (☎321-4400). Very popular venue near Vanderbilt putting on all sorts of rock and guitar bands, plus the occasional big name. Cover $3–6.

Grand Ole Opry, 2808 Opryland Drive (☎889-3060). See box.

Mere Bulles, 152 Second Ave (☎256-1946). Loud, lively jazz-funk cafe-bar. Usually no cover.

Nashville Palace, 2400 Opryland Drive (☎885-1540). Opposite *Opryland Hotel*. Resident country bands, and Opry acts on summer Mondays. A good insight into mainstream Nashville. Cover $3–5.

Station Inn, 402 12th Ave S (☎255-3307). Very popular bluegrass and acoustic venue, a mile south of downtown. Slightly above-average cover of $4–8, but free jam sessions every Sunday night.

Stock Yard/Bull Pen, 901 Second Ave (☎255-6464). Spacious dine-and-dance country venue serving huge steaks, and frequented by the stars – no surprise as it's owned by Buddy Killen, President of *Tree International*, country music's largest publishers. As good a place as any to submerge yourself in the rhinestone scene.

Windows on the Cumberland, 112 Second Ave (☎244-7944). Live acoustic, singer-songwriter and world music Thurs–Sat, plus good Sunday-afternoon jazz sessions.

World's End, 1713 Church St (☎329-3480). The city's friendliest gay club, for men and women.

South from Nashville

As you head southeast from Nashville, large nineteenth-century plantation homes line US-31 between suburban Brentwood and the historic town of **FRANKLIN**, eighteen miles out. One of the bloodiest battles of the Civil War occurred here on November 30 1864, when 8500 men fell in less than an hour. Despite forcing the Union troops back to Nashville, huge losses meant that the southerners could not follow up their victory. Among several strategic buildings open for visits is **Carnton Mansion** (☎794-0903), about a mile southeast of the town on Hwy-431, a former Confederate hospital where bloodstains are still visible on the floor. The town's entire fifteen-block centre, now full of antique and speciality shops, is listed in the National Register of Historic Places.

Jack Daniel's at Lynchburg

The change-resistant village of **LYNCHBURG**, seventy miles southeast of Nashville, is home to **Jack Daniel's Distillery** (daily 8am–4pm; free). Founded in 1866, this is the oldest registered distillery in the country (hence the famous *No 1* appellation). Entertaining seventy-minute tours lead you through every step of the sour-mash whiskey-making process – but you can't actually sample the stuff, as you're in a dry county.

Lynchburg itself is a pretty hamlet, laid out around a red-brick courthouse, with a number of old-fashioned stores. One enjoyable throwback is *Miss Mary Bobo's Boarding House*, which serves southern dinners at a single 1pm sitting (Mon–Sat; reservations essential; ☎759-7394).

Western Tennessee

The western third of Tennessee occupies a low plateau edging down towards the Mississippi River, along which floods and underground seepage have produced swampy marshlands. As a result, bar a pair of tiny hamlets, the only settlement on the Tennessee side of the Mississippi is the port and agribusiness centre of **Memphis**, birthplace of urban blues. Apart from Memphis, the two main sites of interest, **Shiloh National Military Park** and the nature reserve of **Reelfoot Lake**, lie in opposite corners well over one hundred miles apart. The only other conurbation of any size is industrial **Jackson**, home of the legendary train driver Casey Jones.

Memphis

The cotton-trading capital of the Delta, **MEMPHIS**, two hundred miles east of Nashville and three hundred south of St Louis, is one of the great romantic destinations of the South. Pilgrims come from all over the world to celebrate the city which virtually invented blues, soul and rock'n'roll – to see **Elvis Presley's** Graceland and to walk down Beale Street; but while the home of *Sun Records* and *Stax* is proud of its musical heritage, thankfully it doesn't hype it to the same extent as Nashville or New Orleans.

Although the pallor of the Mississippi and the dull downtown office blocks don't make Memphis an immediately attractive city, it exudes a small-town southern warmth and friendliness. Downtown sights include the 321-ft **Great American Pyramid** and the new **National Civil Rights Museum**, built on the spot where Martin Luther King was shot. There always seems to be some **festival** going on, the biggest and best being the month-long **Memphis in May**, when the Barbecue Cookout Competition attracts over 10,000 pork-eaters, many dressed as hogs.

The telephone **area code** for Memphis and western Tennessee is ☎901.

THE MISSISSIPPI RIVER

> I do not know much about gods; but I think that the river
> Is a strong brown god – sullen, untamed and intractable.
>   St Louis-born T S Eliot, *The Four Quartets*

North America's principal waterway, the **Mississippi River**, starts just ninety miles south of the Canadian border at Lake Itasca, Minnesota, and winds its way 2348 miles to the Gulf of Mexico, taking in over one hundred tributaries on the way and draining all or part of 31 US states and two Canadian provinces.

One of the busiest commercial rivers in the world, it's also one of the most unconventional. Only by quirk of history does it bear the name Mississippi; if the upper Mississippi had not been discovered and charted first, geographers might well have designated the 1403-mile longer Missouri-Mississippi fork as the main stream. Instead of widening towards its mouth, like most rivers, the Mississippi grows narrower and deeper. Its "**Delta**", over three hundred miles upstream from its mouth, is not a delta at all but an alluvial flood plain. On the other hand, its estuary deposits, which extend the land six miles out to sea every century, are comparatively paltry; Gulf currents disperse the sediment before it has time to settle.

The Mississippi is also, in the words of Mark Twain, who spent four years as a river boat pilot, "the **crookedest** river in the world." As it weaves and curls its way extravagantly along its channel it straightens and shortens itself by cutting through narrow necks of land leaving behind oxbow lakes, meander scars, cutoffs and marshy backwaters. A bar could operate one day in Arkansas and then find itself in dry Tennessee the next, thanks to an overnight cut-off.

A more serious manifestation of the Mississippi's power is its propensity to **flood**. Although the river builds its own natural levees, artificial embankments help further to safeguard crops and homes; the entire area from Cape Girardeau, Missouri, to the sea is now virtually walled in. You can even drive along the top of the larger ones, and at times of low water some serve as makeshift beaches.

It's no longer feasible to sail Twain's route for yourself. However, **riverboat excursions** are available in most sizeable river towns. Longer cruises, from two to twelve nights, on the luxurious *Delta Queen* and *Mississippi Queen* paddlewheelers are expensive; contact the *Delta Queen Steamboat Company*, 30 Robin Street Wharf, New Orleans, LA 70130 (☎1-800/543-1949).

Culturally and geographically, Memphis has more in common with the deltalands of Mississippi and Arkansas than with the rest of Tennessee. Founded in 1819 and named for Egypt's ancient Nile capital, the fortunes of Memphis paralleled those of **cotton**. A major port and trading centre before the Civil War, the city was plunged into economic chaos when the Confederate defeat ended the slave trade. Things were exacerbated by three severe yellow fever epidemics, but an excellent location on the Mississippi River, and good railroad connections, ensured that Memphis bounced back. It became a major stopping-off point for **black migrants** escaping the poverty of the Delta, and many stayed, significantly shaping the city's identity and culture. Memphis today exploits its geographic position to the full, as one of the nation's leading distribution centres, its second-largest inland port, and home of the huge *Federal Express* company.

Arrival and Information

Memphis International Airport is ten miles south of downtown. No buses go direct to downtown, which is a long and complicated trip. The *Yellow Cabs* **limo/van** service (☎477-7700) costs $6, **taxis** around $13–16 (agree the fare before getting in).

Greyhound **buses** stop at 203 Union Avenue at Fourth Street downtown (☎523-7676), while the *Amtrak* station at 545 S Main Street is in a particularly seedy and unsafe area on the southern edge of downtown. *Memphis Area Transit Authority* **buses** cover nearly

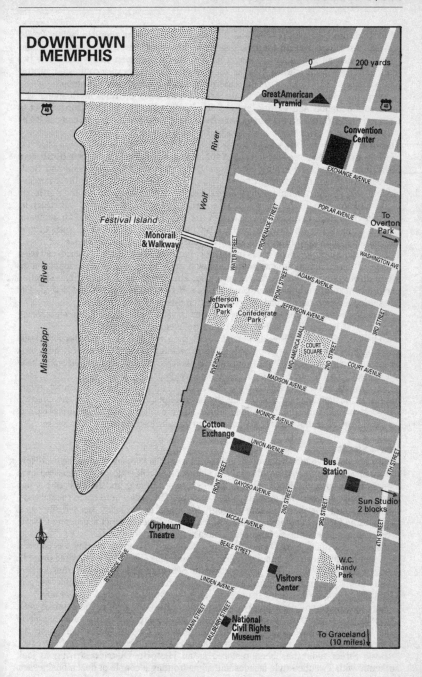

DOWNTOWN MEMPHIS

0   200 yards

Great American Pyramid

Convention Center

EXCHANGE AVENUE

POPLAR AVENUE

To Overton Park

WASHINGTON AVE

River

Wolf

Festival Island

Monorail & Walkway

PROMENADE STREET

WATER STREET

FRONT STREET

ADAMS AVENUE

Mississippi River

Jefferson Davis Park

Confederate Park

JEFFERSON AVENUE

MID-AMERICA MALL

COURT SQUARE

3RD STREET

2ND STREET

COURT AVENUE

RIVERSIDE

MADISON AVENUE

MONROE AVENUE

Cotton Exchange

UNION AVENUE

Bus Station

Sun Studio 2 blocks

FRONT STREET

GAYOSO AVENUE

2ND STREET

3RD STREET

4TH STREET

MCCALL AVENUE

Orpheum Theatre

BEALE STREET

W.C. Handy Park

RIVERSIDE DRIVE

LINDEN AVENUE

Visitors Center

MAIN STREET

MULBERRY STREET

National Civil Rights Museum

To Graceland (10 miles)

all parts of the city, but are slow and infrequent; an excellent phone-in facility (☎274-MATA) can advise you on the quickest route. *Showboat* buses, decorated as paddle-wheelers, visit all tourist attractions, at 95¢ per trip or $2 for an all-day pass. The two main east–west roads in town, **Poplar** and **Union** avenues, get very congested; **motorists** will often find it quicker to take a more circuitous route via the I-240 loop.

Memphis' **visitor centre**, 207 Beale Street (☎526-4880), provides invaluable advice on accommodation and getting around. The **post office** is at 555 Third Street at Calhoun Street (Mon–Fri 8.30am–5.30pm, Sat 10am–2pm; ☎521-2140; zip code 38101).

The Riverfront

Since its major businesses moved out to suburban malls during the Sixties, **downtown Memphis** has lacked a central retail area. Developments in the Riverside and Beale Street areas have, however, revitalised things. The latest addition to the Memphis skyline, the 32-storey stainless-steel **Great American Pyramid**, marks the north end of downtown. Two-thirds the size of the Great Pyramid, this surreal construction, completed in 1991, is a symbolic link with the Nile Delta. You can take an inclinator ride up its flanks, or go inside to find a 22,000-seat theatre, as well as all sorts of food concessions and family attractions, many worked around Egyptian themes.

Boats and monorail trains cross from the Pyramid to **Mud Island** (considered such an eyesore in 1917 that the city voted to blow it up), where several performance areas are dedicated to all forms of American music. The musicians in the big band section play in front of the original **Memphis Belle**, a B-17 bomber from World War II. The Mississippi River Museum had yet to open when this book went to press.

Paddlewheelers offer tours of the harbour for $3.50 or ninety-minute sightseeing trips at $6.50, leaving Riverside Drive at Monroe Avenue (☎527-5694).

In between Riverside Drive and Front Street, the small tree-shaded **Jefferson Davis** and Confederate Parks are popular lunchtime meeting places. When the Union took Memphis during the Civil War, thousands of dismayed residents watched from these sites as seven out of eight Confederate gunboats were sunk.

The imposing buildings of **Cotton Row**, about halfway along Front Street, might have seen busier days, but this is still the largest spot cotton market in the country. The Cotton Exchange Building at 84 S Front Street contains a small historical exhibit on the cotton trade, but visitors are not allowed into the trading area.

Beale Street

Beale Street began life as one of Memphis' most exclusive residential enclaves, before the moneyed elite moved out during the yellow fever epidemics to be replaced by a diverse ethnic mix of blacks, whites, Greeks, Jews, Chinese and Italians. But it was Beale's **black culture** that gave the street its fame. This was where black roustabouts, deckhands and travellers passing through Memphis immediately headed for; rural blacks came for the bustling Saturday market; and, in times of strict segregation, Beale acted as the centre for black businesses, financiers and professionals.

As the black main street of the mid-South, Beale in its Twenties heyday was jammed with vaudeville theatres, concert halls, bars and jook-joints (mostly white-owned). Along with the frivolity came a reputation for heavy gambling, voodoo, murder and prostitution. One appalled evangelist proclaimed that "if whiskey ran ankle deep in Memphis . . . you could not get drunker quicker than you can on Beale Street now."

Although Beale still drew huge crowds in the Forties, the drift to the suburbs, and, ironically, the success of the **civil rights** years in opening up the rest of Memphis to black businesses, almost killed it off. The **bulldozers** of the late Sixties spared only the *Orpheum Theatre* and a few commercial buildings between Second and Fourth streets.

Beale Street today has been restored as an **Historic District**, striving to look authentic with Twenties-style facades and signs fronting a couple of dozen businesses.

Its empty open spaces make it feel a bit like a film set but, dominated once more by shops, clubs and cafes, it offers a lot to see during the day.

A nine-foot bronze **statue of Elvis Presley** marks Beale's western end, at the junction with Main Street. Fans traditionally drop their business cards into his guitar. A few yards down at no. 152, the excellent **Center for Southern Folklore** (Mon–Sat 9am–5.30pm, Sun 1–5.30pm) is not what you might expect. Without a Confederate flag or picture of Dolly Parton in sight, this oral-history project celebrates the music, food, storytelling and crafts of the people of the mid-South, with great archive film. There's a very good gift shop, and the staff are happy to advise on gig venues and places to see.

A Schwabs Dry Goods Store, at no. 163, looks much as it must have done when it opened in 1876. An incredible array includes such voodoo paraphernalia, familiar from the blues, as *Mojo Hands* and *John The Conqueroo*, as well as 99¢ neckties and Sunday School badges. To the east, tree-shaded **Handy Park** echoes day and night to jamming blues musicians. The **Blues Foundation**, annual promoters of the National Blues Music Awards, is based at no. 352, the tiny former home of **W C Handy**, who was in 1910 the first man to publish blues tunes (often blues in name only; see p.415).

Ten minutes' walk from Beale, **Sun Studio** at 706 Union Avenue (daily 9am–7pm; $4) was where Elvis, Johnny Cash and others cut their first records (see box). "Tours" (sic) of its single room, just eighteen feet by thirty feet, last twenty minutes, featuring tapes of what went on during the legendary recording sessions. Sun Records moved out in 1959; the studio was restored in 1987, and has since been used by artists such as U2.

The National Civil Rights Museum

450 Mulberry Street. Mon & Wed–Sat 10am–5pm, June–Aug Sun 1–6pm, Sept–May Sun 1–5pm. $5; free Mon 3–5pm. ☎521-9699.

The **National Civil Rights Museum**, a few blocks south of Beale Street, has been built around the remains of the *Lorraine Motel*, where **Dr Martin Luther King Jr** was assassinated by James Earl Ray on April 4 1968, at a time when the ghettos of the nation were literally aflame. In increasingly hard-line speeches, Dr King had explicitly linked black poverty with military spending in Vietnam. He was killed by a single bullet the evening before he was due to lead a march in Memphis in support of a strike by black sanitation workers. Protestors have charged that Memphis' role in Dr King's death can only ever be a source of shame and not a tourist attraction, and that his memory would have been better served if the site had been turned into a training centre for unemployed blacks.

That said, Dr King's room, and the balcony where he was shot, make a powerful focus for displays that span the years of struggle, from the initial legal triumph of *Brown vs Topeka Board of Education*, via the bus boycotts, freedom marches, student sit-ins and voter registration campaigns, to King's death and beyond. A large bronze sculpture in the foyer, *Movement to Overcome*, represents a mass of individuals united in a common struggle: a pertinent reminder of the mass strength of the movement in a museum which inevitably revolves around one remarkable man.

Graceland

3765 Elvis Presley Boulevard (☎332-3322 or ☎1-800/238-2000). Daily May 8am–6pm; June–Aug 8am–7pm; Sept–April 9am–6pm. Combined ticket to all the .tractions $15.95; house tours only $7.95. Nine miles from downtown, on bus route #13 from Third & Union. Reservations are recommended, especially during Aug (Graceland, PO Box 16508, Memphis TN 38186-0508).

When the 22-year-old **Elvis Presley** bought **Graceland** for $100,000 in 1957, it was considered one of the most desirable properties in Memphis. Since then, the neighbourhood has become distinctly less exclusive. The main thoroughfare, now known as **Elvis Presley Boulevard**, is lined for miles with motels, fast-food joints, souvenir shops and other eyesores catering to the various needs of the 600,000 devotees who each year queue up to get a glimpse inside the house where Elvis died.

THE SOUND OF MEMPHIS

Since the start of this century, Memphis has been a meeting place for black musicians from the Mississippi Delta and beyond. During the Twenties, its downtown pubs, clubs and street corners were alive with the sound of the blues. **Jug bands**, in which singers were given a bass accompaniment by blowing across the neck of a jug, were a speciality. Several songs by **Gus Cannon's Jug Stompers** – such as *Walk Right In* – became hits for white artists during the folk revival of the Sixties. Guitarist **Memphis Minnie**, **Bukka White** and **Memphis Slim** appeared at nightspots like *Mitchell's Hotel* and *Pee Wee's Saloon*, all long since defunct. After World War II, young musicians and radio DJs experimented by blending the traditional blues sound with jazz, adding electrical amplification to create **rhythm'n'blues**. Pioneers included **Bobby Bland** and **B B King**.

White promoter Sam Phillips started **Sun Records** in 1953, employing Ike Turner as a scout to comb the Beale Street clubs for new talent. Among those whom Turner helped introduce to vinyl were his own girlfriend Annie Mae Bullock (later **Tina Turner**), **Howlin' Wolf**, and **Little Junior Parker**, whose *Mystery Train* was Sun's first great recording. Phillips was in business to make money, saying "If I could find a white boy who could sing like a nigger, then I could make a million dollars." Sure enough, in 1954, during a coffee break, he overheard a young white man who had hired the studio to record a disc for his mother – **Elvis Presley**. Phillips dropped his black artists right away, signing other white **rockabilly** singers like **Carl Perkins** and **Jerry Lee Lewis** to make classics such as *Blue Suede Shoes* and *Great Balls of Fire*. Elvis was soon sold on to RCA (for just $35,000), and didn't record in Memphis again until 1969, when with songs like *Suspicious Minds* he produced the best material of his later career.

In the Sixties and early Seventies, Memphis' **Stax Records** provided a rootsy alternative to the poppier sounds of Motown. This hard-edged **southern soul** was created by a multiracial mix of musicians, Steve Cropper's fluid guitar complementing the blaring Memphis Horns. The label's first real success was *Green Onions* by studio band **Booker T and the MGs**; further hits followed from **Otis Redding** (*These Arms Of Mine*), **Wilson Pickett** (*Midnight Hour*), **Sam and Dave** (*Soul Man*) and **Isaac Hayes** (*Shaft*). The label eventually foundered in acrimony; the last straw for many of its veteran soulmen was the signing of the British child star Lena Zavaroni for a six-figure sum.

Memphis has been renowned for its **gospel** music since the Thirties, when Rev Herbert Brewster wrote Mahalia Jackson's *Move On Up A Little Higher*. The consummate soul stylist **Al Green**, who achieved chart success for **Hi Records** with *Let's Stay Together* and *Tired Of Being Alone*, now sings only gospel music following a religious revelation. When he's in town, Rev Al Green preaches on Sunday at 11am at the Full Gospel Tabernacle, 787 Hale Road (phone ahead to check; ☎396-9192). Uplifting gospel sounds can also be heard at the Mississippi Boulevard Christian Church, 205 E Raines Road (☎345-1312), every Sunday at 8am and 11am.

Though always referred to as a mansion, Graceland can in reality seem disappointingly small. It's hard to get an accurate feel of its size and layout, as the rooms where Elvis' housekeeper still lives, along with the entire upstairs, are out of bounds to visitors. The interior, designed by Elvis and his wife Priscilla (star of *Dallas*), is a frozen tribute to the taste of the Seventies. Choice moments include the **Jungle Room** with its carpeted ceiling, and the ugly combination of mirrors, navy and lemon in the **TV Room**, which is fitted with three screens so Elvis could watch three football games at once. The lengthy **Hall of Gold**, crammed with platinum, gold and silver records, is followed by the **Trophy Room** containing Elvis' stage costumes, outfits from some of his 31 films, and his extensive gun collection. The picture of Elvis painted by the tour-guides is of the supremely talented entertainer, crack karate expert, patriotic soldier and churchgoing family man; there's no mention of the problems and pressures of his later days. The **Meditation Garden** outside, where Elvis (Jan 8 1935–Aug 16 1977), his mother Gladys, his father Vernon, and his grandmother are buried, is usually the scene of a mass cry-in.

The ninety-minute tours start in **Graceland Plaza** across the road. A fleet of mini-buses, departing every few minutes, ferries visitors to the house, sweeping past the fieldstone fence known as the "**Wall of Love**", festooned with tens of thousands of messages from fans. In the Plaza itself, you can see the **Elvis Presley Automobile Museum** and board his fully customised **aeroplane**, the *Lisa Marie*.

Midtown and East Memphis

The mile-long, heavily wooded expanse of **Overton Park** lies three miles from down-town (#50 bus) on Poplar Avenue, just before East Parkway. Its two main attractions are the wide-ranging **Memphis Brooks Museum of Art** (Tues–Sat 10am–5pm, Sun 11.30am–5pm; $2, free Fri) and the **Memphis Zoo and Aquarium** ($3.50, free Mon 3.30–5pm). **Overton Square**, the city's top suburban entertainment, dining and shop-ping district, is within walking distance. Just past East Parkway, the **Memphis Pink Palace Museum and Planetarium** at 3050 Central Avenue (Tues–Sat 9.30am–4pm, Sun 1–5pm; $3, free Thurs 5–8.30pm) centres on the pink marble mansion of Clarence Saunders, who founded America's first chain of self-service **supermarkets**, *Piggly-Wiggly*, in 1916. As well as a walk-through model of the first store, complete with original packets and prices, an audio-visual programme traces the history of Memphis, with some interesting material on the anti-union activities of "Boss" Crump, whose crooked political machine ran the city from 1909 until the early Fifties.

Accommodation

Downtown Memphis has a few reasonably cheap **places to stay**, though if you're unlucky, and don't have a car, you may be stuck with a long bus journey out to the suburbs. The **visitor centre** (see p.400) offers good advice, and is particularly helpful at busy times such as the anniversary of Elvis' death in mid-August and the Church of God in Christ convention in late October.

B&B in Memphis (PO Box 41621, TN 38174; ☎726-5920) runs a reservation service, with rooms in the $36–55 range. The closest **campground** is the *Elvis Presley Blvd RV Park*, 3971 Elvis Presley Boulevard (☎332-3633), three blocks south of Graceland.

Admiral Benbow Inn, 1220 Union Ave (☎725-0630). Basic motel in midtown Memphis at I-240, with rooms for around $40.

Days Inn–Downtown, 147 Union Ave (☎527-4100). A prime location, with rooms often under $45.

Journey's Inn, 3222 Airways Blvd (☎332-3800). By the airport, but also handy for Graceland. Offers a high standard of comfort and service for only $40.

Lowenstein-Long House, 1084 Poplar Ave (☎527-7174). Victorian mansion just over a mile from downtown. (Bus #50 from Third and Poplar.) Hostel beds for $10 (*AYH* members) or $13.

River Place Inn, 100 N Front St (☎526-0583). Some rooms below $50, though the usual midweek price is closer to $75.

Wilson World, 3677 Elvis Presley Blvd (☎332-1000). New hotel, right across from Graceland, with fridge and microwave in every room; $45.

Eating

Memphians are fond of their food, claiming to be the **pork barbecue** capital of the world with over 100 specialist restaurants. There is also a good selection of reasonably priced soul-food cafes. **Downtown** has a reasonably good choice (including some pass-able cafes on Beale Street); for a bit of variety, try **Overton Square** in midtown.

Buntyn's, 3070 Southern Ave (☎458-8776). Ever-popular, super-cheap, soul-food cafe, six blocks west of Memphis State University. The decor has barely changed since 1927. Mon–Fri 11am–8pm.

Doe's Eat Place, Beale St (☎526-3637). New branch of *Greenville*, Mississippi's famous delta soul-food restaurant. Lacks the down-to-earth ambience of the original, but the giant steaks, tamales and all the trimmings are just as good.

Little Tea Shop, 69 Monroe Ave, downtown (☎525-6000). Unusual soul-food cafe, serving a health-conscious version of what is traditionally a very fatty type of food. Lunches cost around $5.

Molly's La Casita, 2006 Madison Ave, Overton Sq (☎726-1873). The city's favourite Mexican restaurant, with good food at reasonable prices. Go for the half-price margaritas on Monday.

The North End, 346 N Main St (☎526-0319). More of a pub than a restaurant, specialising in delicious wild-rice dishes, burgers and tamales for under $5. Just one dessert, a delicious hot fudge pie. Open until 3am daily, happy hour 4–7pm. Live blues 10pm–2am Wed–Sun; $2 cover Fri only.

Paulette's, 2110 Madison Ave, Overton Sq (☎726-5128). An exciting fusion of American, French and Hungarian cuisine. Main courses $9–19.

Public Eye, 17 S Cooper St, Overton Square (☎726-4040), and 111 Court Ave, downtown (☎527-5757). Superb pork ribs and very cheap lunch specials.

The Rendezvous, General Washburn Alley, 52 S Second St (☎523-2746). The most famous and highly regarded of Memphis' many pork barbecue joints. Huge helpings and a nice atmosphere.

Nightlife and Entertainment

The **live music** scene in Memphis doesn't match up to the days when the likes of Johnny Ace, Bobby Bland or Sam and Dave were based here, but plenty of places still uphold the blues and soul tradition. The two main concentrations of nightspots are at **Beale Street**, now pulling in tourists largely on the strength of its past, and **Overton Square**, three miles east of downtown.

The beautifully restored *Orpheum Theatre*, at Main and Beale streets (☎525-3000), puts on a year-round programme of Broadway shows, opera, ballet and classic films. *Playhouse on the Square* at 51 S Cooper Street (Sept–July; ☎726-4656) in Overton Square is home to Memphis' only theatre company, while *Theater Works*, 414 S Main Street (☎526-1066), promotes performing and visual arts productions. The **Overton Park Shell** puts on a free film show and rock band every summer Monday night.

The best sources for **listings** are the free weekly *Memphis Flyer*, Friday's *Memphis Commercial Appeal*, and the community **radio** station WEVL (FM90, daily 6am–2am).

B B King's Blues Club, Beale St (☎527-5464). New in 1991, but already the best known club in the city. Blues seven nights a week with occasional appearances by the proprietor.

Green's, 2090 E Person Ave (☎274-9800). Unpretentious neighbourhood venue with live blues until 2.30am every Fri and Sat. $3 cover.

Huey's, 1927 Madison Ave (☎726-4372). Popular Overton Square venue with live jazz on Sunday afternoon, followed by an out-of-town blues band in the evening.

King's Palace, 162 Beale St (☎521-1851). Live jazz/blues seven nights a week. $4 cover at weekend; $2 during the week. No connection with B B's club.

Kudzu's, 603 Monroe Ave (☎525-4924). Live blues downtown, Mon & Thurs. Free.

New Daisy Theatre, 330 Beale St (☎525-8979). Visiting rock bands on Fri and Sat.

Poplar Lounge, 2563 Poplar Ave (☎324-1233). Packed out every Wed for long-running resident R&B band, The Cut-Outs.

Rum Boogie Cafe/Blues Hall, 182 Beale St (☎528-0150). Usually one of Beale Street's most crowded venues, with resident blues bands every night 9pm–1.30am. $4 cover.

Shiloh National Military Park

Approximately 110 miles east of Memphis and twelve south of Savannah, via US-64 and Hwy-22, **SHILOH NATIONAL MILITARY PARK** commemorates one of the most crucial battles of the Civil War. After victories at Fort Henry and Fort Donelson, General Grant's confident Union forces were all but defeated by a surprise early-morning Confederate attack on April 6 1862. A stubborn rump of resistance held on until around 5pm, and the Confederates elected to finish the task off the next morning rather than launching a twilight assault. However, Grant's decimated regiments were bolstered by the overnight arrival of new troops, and instead it was their dawn initiative which forced the tired and demoralised Confederates to retreat.

Shiloh was the first encounter on a scale that became common as the war continued, putting an abrupt end to the romantic innocence of many a raw volunteer soldier. Over

20,000 men from the two sides were killed or wounded. Even the Union's war-toughened General Sherman spoke of "piles of dead soldiers' mangled bodies . . . without heads and legs . . . the scenes on this field would have cured anyone of war."

The **visitor centre** displays artefacts recovered from the battlefield and shows an informative twenty-minute film. A self-guided ten-mile driving tour takes in the **National Cemetery**, whose moss-covered walls contains thousands of unidentified graves (daily summer 8am–6pm; otherwise 8am–5pm; free; ☎689-5275).

Reelfoot Lake

Surrounded by a thick growth of oak and cottonwood trees, woven together by wild grape vines, the eighteen-mile **REELFOOT LAKE** in the northeastern corner of Tennessee has its own strange beauty. It was created by the New Madrid earthquakes between December 1811 and March 1812. The ground sank, huge trees snapped in half and the Mississippi was even forced to flow northwards for two days, filling the depression in a series of gigantic waves.

Between December and March, the Reelfoot Lake State Park organises trips to catch a glimpse of the national bird, the migratory **bald eagle**. The park's **visitor centre** (☎253-7756) is five miles east of **Tiptonville** on Hwy-21 on the lake's south shore. The *Blue Bank Motel* (☎253-6878), in between the two, has comfortable rooms for $30 to $50, and there are **campgrounds** in the park. The nearby *Boyette's Dining Room* (☎253-7307) is good for reasonably priced ham, chicken and catfish a la mode.

ALABAMA

Just 250 miles from north to south, **ALABAMA** ranges from the fast-flowing rivers, waterfalls and lakes of the **Appalachian** foothills to the subtropical bayous and white beaches of the **Gulf Coast**. Most of its industry is concentrated in the **north**, around the rejuvenated former steel city of **Birmingham**, and **Huntsville**, home of the nation's space programme. The sun-scorched farmlands of middle Alabama envelop sober **Montgomery**, the state capital. Away from the French-influenced coastal strip around attractive **Mobile**, the relatively homogenous white population has developed a fundamentalist Protestant outlook which fuels right-wing segregationist politics. The most famous of Alabama's breed of fire-eating demagogues was **George Wallace**, the four-times state governor who received ten million votes in the 1968 presidential election.

During the **civil rights** struggle, repressive Alabama witnessed the Montgomery bus boycott, the 1963 Birmingham riots and the murder-marred 1965 battle to get rid of racist voting restrictions in rural **Selma**. Times have moved on. The achievements of the thousands of campaigners are now celebrated in tourist-board handouts, and even Wallace renounced his racist views, courting – and winning – black votes in his successful campaign for governor in 1982. Even so, Alabaman blacks – a quarter of the population – still conspicuously lack political and commercial power.

Getting Around Alabama

Considering its rural nature, **public transport** is relatively good in Alabama. A daily *Amtrak* service between Birmingham and Mobile calls at Montgomery and several small towns, while the New York–Atlanta–New Orleans train stops at Anniston, Birmingham and Tuscaloosa. *Greyhound* serves the major towns and cities. Mobile, Montgomery, Huntsville and Birmingham all have small airports.

The telephone **area code** for the entire state of Alabama is ☎205.

Northern Alabama

Northern Alabama, on the trailing edges of the Appalachians, is brightened up by the mountain lakes, rivers and canyons of the Tennessee River Valley. The area's first white settlers were small farmers who had little in common with the big plantation owners further south, and made various localised attempts to disassociate from the Confederacy during the Civil War. Just after the war, substantial mineral finds led to an industrial boom which peaked in the early Thirties.

Huntsville

Many southern cities aspire to blend the old with the new, but few achieve it so dramatically as **HUNTSVILLE**, just over a hundred miles south of Nashville just inside the Alabama border. Its sleepy centre still recalls the days when it was dominated by cotton merchants and railroad owners. The **Huntsville Depot Transportation Museum**, 320 Church Street (Tues–Sun 10am–5pm; $2.50), has an absorbing account of the city's railroad and commercial history. An excellent **trolley service** tours the town (50¢ for an all-day ticket), taking in historic **Twickenham** – the community's original name in 1808, before anti-British sentiment in the run-up to the 1812 War dictated that it should be renamed for its first settler, a Virginian named John Hunt.

Time was when Huntsville was content to be known as the "Watercress Capital of the World"; the great leap forward came just after World War II, when the Army decided to consolidate its **rocket and missile** research efforts in the city. Spearheading the project were **Dr Wernher von Braun** and 118 other German scientists, who came to Huntsville after a token period of rehabilitation. Von Braun's contribution of the V-2 ballistic missile to the Nazi war effort is ignored by the city, which prefers to laud his later space-age achievements, such as **Saturn V**, which launched the first Americans on the moon, and **Explorer I**, the nation's first satellite.

The world's largest space museum, the **Space and Rocket Center**, is five miles west of downtown on Hwy-20, off I-65 (daily summer 8am–7pm; otherwise 9am–6pm; $10.95). It contains a mind-boggling array of technological exhibits, hands-on displays, and weightlessness simulators, as well as a giant Omnimax screen showing breathtaking pictures taken by astronauts. Outdoors, in the surreal Rocket and Space Shuttle parks, redundant rockets protrude skywards in the blazing Alabama sunshine. The 120-yard, four-storey Saturn V rocket is laid on its side to emphasise its immensity; the 98-ton full-size replica of the Pathfinder Space Shuttle is of similar proportions.

Practicalities

Huntsville's **visitor centre** is at 700 Monroe Street (Mon–Sat 9am–5pm; ☎533-5723). The *Hilton*, 401 Williams Avenue (☎533-1400), occasionally has rooms for $49; otherwise various chain **motels** on the outskirts cost $30 or less. Among the varied **restaurants**, *Bubba's*, at 105 Washington Street (☎534-3133), has burgers and ribs all day.

Birmingham

The rapid transformation of farmland into the city of **BIRMINGHAM** began in 1870, when two railroad routes met in the Jones Valley, a hundred miles south of Huntsville. What attracted speculators was not the land but what lay under it – a mixture of iron ore, limestone and coal, perfect for the manufacture of iron and steel. Heavy industry looked capable of indefinite expansion, until it was brought to an abrupt halt by the Depression. Today iron and steel account for only a few thousand jobs, but new service and medical industries have helped transform this once smog-filled metropolis to the extent that it has been selected by *Newsweek* as one of the top ten cities to live in the USA.

Being known as the "Pittsburgh of the South" might seem like faint praise; however, Birmingham also earned the label of the "Johannesburg of America" for the brutality and intolerance of its police force. An intense civil rights campaign in 1963 was the turning point, setting Birmingham on the road to smoother race relations, enhanced by the election of its first black mayor in 1979.

Arrival and Information

Birmingham Airport is just three miles from downtown, but it's not served by buses; *Yellow Cabs* are on ☎252-1131. *Amtrak* pulls in at 1819 Morris Avenue, downtown, and the *Greyhound* station is at 19th Street (☎252-7171), between Fourth and Fifth avenues – a rough area at night. Public transport is poor; most of the attractions are well strung out, so you need a car to see the city properly. **Visitor centres** are located at the airport (☎254-1640) and at 1201 University Boulevard (☎254-1654) on the university campus.

The Town

Downtown Birmingham extends north from the railroad tracks at Morris Avenue to Tenth Avenue North, bounded to east and west by 25th and 15th streets. The landscaped greenery of 20th Street, overlooked by a collection of early skyscrapers, is not enough to save these one-hundred-plus blocks from anonymity, with shopping now firmly anchored in the malls and suburbs.

The concrete colossus of the Birmingham-Jefferson Civic Center, at 22nd Street and Tenth Avenue North, contains the **Alabama Sports Hall of Fame**, a tribute to sporting greats such as 1936 Olympic hero **Jesse Owens**, Le Roy "Satchel" Paige, the first black baseball player to appear in the World Series, and boxer Joe Louis. There's even a space for former governor George Wallace on the rather flimsy excuse that he was state amateur boxing champion (Tues–Sat 10am–6pm; $2). Weave your way past the monotonous white-walled legal buildings to the nearby **Museum of Art**, 2000 Eighth Avenue North, which is strong on Oriental art, American landscapes and Wedgwood pottery (Tues, Wed, Fri & Sat 10am–5pm, Thurs 10am–9pm, Sun 1–5pm; free).

A few blocks from the edge of downtown at First Avenue North and 32nd Street, the massive sheds and tall chimney stacks of **Sloss Furnaces**, which produced pig iron to

---

CIVIL RIGHTS IN BIRMINGHAM

In the first half of 1963 civil rights leaders chose Birmingham as the target of the "Project C" (for confrontation) campaign, which aimed to force businesses to integrate lunch counters and employ more blacks. In the face of threats from Police Chief "Bull" Connor that there would be "blood running down the streets of Birmingham", a rolling programme of pickets, sit-ins and marches sparked wholesale arrests. Over 2000 protestors, including Dr Martin Luther King Jr, filled the jails beyond capacity. While in prison, King was branded by a group of local white clergymen as an extremist; his reply, "Letter from a Birmingham Jail", is a classic of protest literature.

Violent clashes continued, but Connor's decision to use high-pressure hoses, cattle-prods and dogs on a march by local children acted as a potent catalyst of support. Pictures of snarling Alsatians sinking their teeth into the flesh of schoolkids were transmitted throughout the world; the resultant pressure led to an agreement between civil rights leaders and businesses in June 1963. Success in Birmingham sparked demonstrations in 186 other cities, which culminated in the 1964 Civil Rights Act prohibiting racial segregation.

The headquarters for the campaign, the 16th Street Baptist Church, between Sixth and Seventh avenues, was the site of a sickening Klan bombing on September 15 1963, which killed four young black girls attending a Bible class. Open daily, the church contains a small shrine dedicated to the murdered girls, along with a stained-glass memorial window donated by the principality of Wales. A bronze statue of Dr King stands across the road from the church in Kelly Ingram Park, site of many huge rallies during the Sixties.

feed the city's mills and foundries from 1882 until 1971, symbolise Birmingham's industrial past. Self-guided tours through the boilers, stoves and casting areas vividly portray the harsh working conditions endured by the ex-slaves, prisoners and unskilled immigrants. The dark redundant buildings themselves are awesome enough, but when you imagine the searing heat, cramped space, the heavy loads and the putrid gaseous emissions, it's easy to appreciate why one former Sloss worker claimed "if mules had to do this work they would have banned it" (Tues–Sat 10am–4pm, Sun noon–4pm; free).

Atop **Red Mountain**, four miles south of downtown, a 55-ft iron statue of Vulcan, Roman god of the forge, stands as a monument to the city's heavy industry. The largest cast-iron statue ever made, this was Birmingham's exhibit at the 1904 World Fair in St Louis. The chubby rust-coloured figure, perched high up on its 124-foot pedestal, looks rather insignificant from ground level, but it's worth winding your way up the steep, verdant mountain road to relax in the peaceful grounds, or ride to the top of the tower for a superb panoramic view of the Jones Valley (daily 8am–10.30pm; $1).

Accommodation

Many of Birmingham's wide range of places to stay offer advantageous weekend rates. The nearest place to **camp** is the *Birmingham South KOA* (☎664-8832), eight miles south in Pelham, off I-65S.

Econolodge, 2224 Fifth Ave N (☎324-6688). The best value in downtown at around $35.

Sheraton Civic Center Plaza, 901 21st St N (☎322-1234). Downtown rooms for $40 on weekends.

Campus Inn, 800 11th St S (☎933-1900). Just south of downtown; $40.

Motel Birmingham, 7905 Crestwood Blvd (☎956-4440). Pleasant rooms for $40, though a little far out, past the airport on I-20 Montevello Exit.

Eating and Drinking

The best bet in Birmingham is to ignore downtown in favour of **Five Points South**, at the foot of Red Mountain, two miles below downtown. Its narrow streets and alleys, packed with bars and restaurants, throng with crowds of revellers every weekend.

The Back Alley, Cobb Lane at 20th St S & 13th Ave (☎933-6211). Attractive restaurant famed for its desserts, on a cobbled lane in Five Points South. Main courses are mostly under $10.

Bogue's, 3028 Clairmont Ave (☎254-9780). Fantastic soul-food cafe near Five Points South offering superb value. Open during the week until 2pm and for morning brunch only at the weekend.

Cosmo's Pizza, 2012 Magnolia Ave (☎930-9971). A lively standard-priced pizza parlour popular with students and situated in the Art Deco Pickwick Plaza in Five Points South.

Manhattan, 2000 Second Ave (☎251-1832). Popular diner open for breakfast and lunch, offering good value gyros, falafel, burgers, salads and soup.

West of Birmingham

Just west of Birmingham city limits, I-20/59 passes **BESSEMER**, a likeable small town founded in 1887 by industrialists who called it after Sir Henry Bessemer, the English engineer who perfected the steel-making process. The **Hall of History Museum** in the 1916 Southern railroad depot, 1905 Alabama Avenue, displays Native American artefacts alongside exhibits from the industrial pioneer years (Tues–Sat 10am–4pm; free).

TUSCALOOSA, home of the lively main campus of the University of Alabama, but little else of interest, lies 32 miles southwest of Bessemer. If you're hungry, combine eating with a view of the Black Warrior River at *Henson's Cypress Inn*, 501 Rice Mine Road N (☎345-6963), which specialises in keenly priced seafood dishes and steaks.

Sixteen miles south on US-69, the **Mound State Monument** preserves twenty earthen mounds, carpeted in lush grass, with the largest supporting a rebuilt Native American temple. An estimated three thousand people lived here on the banks of the Black Warrior during the twelfth century; the on-site museum exhibits items found in burial grounds including jewellery, ceremonial vessels and a few skeletons.

South Central Alabama

The **southern** portion of Alabama – memorably depicted in Harper Lee's powerful child's eye view of racial conflict, *To Kill a Mocking-Bird* – is still comprised mostly of small, sleepy, god-fearing rural communities. Only **Montgomery**, the state capital, with a population of just over 200,000, achieves metropolitan status. It lies in the heart of the **Black Belt**, which was originally named for the rich loamy soil, but is these days more usually taken to refer to the region's ethnic make-up. Cotton was the major earner here until 1915, when a boll weevil infestation ended its dominance. Now it has been supplanted (officially) by soybeans, corn and peanuts – though surveys suggest that the leading cash crop is, in fact, marijuana.

Montgomery

MONTGOMERY, 90 miles south of Birmingham and 160 west of Atlanta, has always cut a conservative edge. Its Black Belt position made it a natural political centre for the plantation elite, leading to its adoption as state capital in 1846 and temporary capital of the Confederacy fifteen years later. Despite its administrative importance, Montgomery is strangely quiet, largely because many businesses have relocated to the suburbs. Most neighbourhoods are either exclusively white or totally black; integration sadly does not appear to be on the social agenda, in the city that saw the first successful mass civil rights activity in 1955–56, when a bus boycott ended segregation on public transport.

Arrival and Information

Dannelly Field Airport (☎281-5040) is fifteen miles from downtown on US-80. Amtrak stops at Commerce and Coosa streets by Riverfront Park, while the Greyhound station is even more conveniently located at 210 S Court Street (☎264-4518). All places of interest downtown are easily walkable, though there is a handy downtown trolley route. The **visitor centre** is in a grand mansion house at Madison and N Hull streets (☎262-0013).

The City

Downtown Montgomery bears conspicuous reminders of white supremacism. The Confederate flag still flies, albeit alongside the Stars and Stripes, over the white-domed Greek Revival **State Capitol**, high on a hill at the top of Dexter Avenue. A bronze star marks the spot where Jefferson Davis was sworn in as President of the Confederacy on February 18 1861 – an occasion on which his Vice-President proudly proclaimed that this government was "the first in the history of the world, based upon this great physical and moral truth . . . that the Negro is not equal to the white man". Other "attractions" in this vein include the **Alabama Department of Archives and History**, next door, notable only for the lavish use of marble in its interior (Mon–Fri 8am–5pm, Sat & Sun 9am–5pm; free) and the **First White House of the Confederacy**, 644 Washington Avenue, the temporary home of Jefferson Davis, now crammed with sentimental Confederate oddments (Mon–Fri 8am–4.30pm, Sat & Sun 9am–4.30pm; free).

On a different note, Montgomery was jammed with thousands of mourners in 1954 for the funeral of 29-year-old country star **Hank Williams**, who died of a heart attack on his way to a concert on the night of New Year's Eve 1953. An Alabama native from Butler County, Williams was as famous for his drink- and drug-related lifestyle as he was for writing honky-tonk classics like *Your Cheating Heart* and *I'm So Lonesome I Could Cry*. His hit single at the time of his death was *I'll Never Get Out of This World Alive*. The **Hank Williams Memorial**, a large white marble headstone complete with song lyrics and an image of the singer, dominates the Oakwood Cemetery Annex, 1304 Upper Wetumpka Road, on the edge of downtown.

CIVIL RIGHTS IN MONTGOMERY

During the Fifties, Montgomery's **bus system** – as was the norm in the South – was a miniature model of segregated society. Though the regulation that ordered blacks to give up seats to whites had often come under attack from black organisations, it was not until the Women's Political Council (WPC), a group of middle-class black women, made it their central campaign issue that protests really gathered momentum. When black activist **Rosa Parks** was arrested on December 1 1955 for refusing to give up her seat, a mass boycott of all Montgomery buses was called by the WPC for the following Monday. Black workers were asked to walk to work and lifts were arranged for those who lived too far away, in black-owned taxis that agreed to charge the same 10¢ fare as buses. Over ninety per cent of black travellers supported the call and the Montgomery Improvement Association (MIA), set up to co-ordinate activities, elected the 27-year-old **Dr Martin Luther King Jr** as its chief spokesperson. Despite personal hardships, bombings and jailings, the boycott continued for eleven months, when the US Supreme Court ruled in November 1956 that segregation on public transport was illegal.

King remained pastor at the small brick **Dexter Avenue King Memorial Baptist Church**, 454 Dexter Avenue (Mon–Fri 8.30am–noon & 1–4.30pm; call ahead on ☎263-3970), until his move to Atlanta in 1960. A mural stretching the length of a basement wall chronicles his role in the movement from Montgomery to his assassination in Memphis. The upstairs sanctuary, much the same as it was during his ministry in the late Fifties, contains the pulpit from which he used to preach. One block away at the corner of Washington and Hull, in front of the Southern Poverty Law Center (a civil rights group that specialises in helping victims of racial attacks and monitors activities of the Klan), the deeply moving **Civil Rights Memorial** consists of a black granite table that records the names of forty martyrs murdered by white supremacists and police. Cool water is pumped slowly and evenly across it, and the wall behind is engraved with the quote used so often by Dr King, "(we will not be satisfied) until justice rolls down like waters and righteousness like a mighty stream."

Reminiscent of the grounds of a large English stately home, the stunningly landscaped **Blount Cultural Park** has, since opening in the mid-Eighties, given some substance to the city's claim of being a regional centre for the arts. Situated off Woodmere Boulevard, ten miles southeast of the city, it's home to the Alabama Shakespeare Festival (☎277-2273), who also perform contemporary works in the sumptuous Renaissance-style *Carolyn Blount Theatre* (Ms Blount's husband provided the entire funds for the park). The equally slick **Montgomery Museum of Fine Arts** (Tues, Wed, Fri & Sat 10am–5pm, Thurs 10am–9pm, Sun noon–5pm; free) spans more than 200 years of American art through paintings, watercolours and drawings.

Accommodation

There are several good-value places to stay in and around downtown Montgomery, with the usual motel names all sitting alongside the highways.

Capitol Inn, 205 N Goldthwaite St (☎265-0541). Well-kept establishment on a small hill, a fifteen-minute walk from downtown. $35.

Red Bluff Cottage, 551 Clay St (☎264-0056). Hospitable B&B, with good food, near the *Capitol Inn*. Around $50.

Town Plaza Motel, 743 Madison Ave (☎269-1561). Conveniently located, but very basic. $28.

Whitley Hotel, 231 Montgomery St (☎262-6461). Twenties decor, comfortable rooms. $45 and up.

Eating and Drinking

Downtown Montgomery is dotted with cheap cafes selling burgers or soul food; a few miles away, the suburb of **Cloverdale** offers a good selection of eating places covering every price range. Especially in the centre, things get pretty quiet at night.

Corsino's, 911 S Court St (☎263-9752). Small, family-run pizza parlour, open until 9.30pm.

Farmers' Market Cafe, 315 N McDonough St (☎262-9163). Just off downtown, next to the busy marketplace; the best place for southern-style breakfast in Montgomery. Mon–Fri, 5am–2pm.

Kat & Harri's, 1061 Woodley Rd, Cloverdale (☎834-2500). The pick of the suburban nightspots, though only really lively on Fri or Sat.

Martin's, 1716 Carter Hill Rd, Cloverdale (☎265-1767). The city's favourite place for home cooking; nothing over $6. Closes 7.45pm, not open Sat.

Montgomery Marina, 617 Shady St (☎259-5490). Unpretentious cafe and bar, pleasantly located about a mile from downtown on the banks of the Alabama River.

Vintage Year, 405 Cloverdale Rd, Cloverdale (☎264-8463). Reservations are necessary at one of Alabama's most highly rated restaurants. The haute cuisine will set you back at least $30.

Selma

The neat market town of **SELMA**, set deep in Black Belt country, fifty miles west of Montgomery, played host to some of the most notorious events of the civil rights era. In the early Sixties only 156 out of 15,000 blacks adults in the county were able to vote, the worst statistics in the whole of the South, so Selma was an ideal choice as the focal point for a national campaign to achieve voting rights for blacks. Demonstrations, meetings and attempts to register were repeatedly met by police violence, but the murder of a local black protestor, Jimmy Lee Jackson, by a state trooper prompted the decision to organise the historic **march from Selma to Montgomery** to put pressure on segregationist Governor George Wallace. On the "Bloody Sunday" of March 7 1965, six hundred marchers set off across the steep incline of the imposing, narrow, steel-framed **Edmund Pettus Bridge**. As the march went over the apex of the bridge, a line of state troopers fired tear gas without warning, lashing out at the panic-stricken demonstrators with nightsticks and cattleprods. This violent confrontation, broadcast all over the world, is credited with having directly influenced the passage of the **Voting Rights Act** the following year. Outside the 1965 campaign headquarters at the **Brown Chapel AME Church**, 410 Martin Luther King Street, a bust of Dr King is part of a monument to the struggle. Plans are currently under way to designate the entire route of the march as a National Historic Trail.

Downtown and the Historic District

Lined with independently owned stores and cafes, **Broad Street** is the town's busy main thoroughfare, running into the wide riverfront **Water Avenue**, which still feels set in the Forties with its frontier-style shopfronts, seed warehouses and garages. Just a few blocks away stand the beautiful homes of the town's Historic District.

Selma's history stretches back well before the Sixties; its huge arsenal and shipbuilding plant were prime targets for Union troops who looted and burned most buildings in March 1865. One of the few remaining plantation homes is **Sturvidant Hall**, 713 Mabry Street (Tues–Sun 9am–4pm; $4), an attractively furnished house with an accessible cupola tower and lovely grounds.

Practicalities

Unfortunately, downtown Selma is totally devoid of places to **stay**, with the only options being a number of small independently owned motels on the outskirts of town, or the *Holiday Inn* (☎872-0461), three miles west on US-80, for $50 a night. The pick of the **soul-food restaurants** is the *Downtowner*, 1114 Selma Avenue (☎875-5933), open for breakfast and lunch; *Major Grumbles*, 1 Grumbles Alley (☎872-2006), is a slightly upmarket riverside pub with hot sandwiches for around $6 (try the almondine flounder special). Montgomery's **visitor centre**, at 2207 Broad Street (☎875-7485), provides self-guided tour brochures for both the Historic District and black heritage sites.

Tuskegee

TUSKEGEE, forty miles east of Montgomery, off I-85 on US-29, has played a seminal role in black history as the home of **Tuskegee University**, one of the earliest black colleges, founded in 1881 by ex-slave **Booker T Washington**. He believed that blacks should work for advances in education and employment instead of campaigning for social equality with whites, and that voting rights were worth sacrificing for a share in economic growth. Adding a practical element to his theory of non-confrontation and self-improvement, the college concentrated more on crafts than academia.

Washington's controversial ideas catapulted him to national fame, and he was seen, by the white press at least, as the most influential black figure in the country around the turn of the century. His accommodationist approach aroused bitter opposition from black radicals like **W E B Du Bois**, who accused him of selling out to the white capitalists. However, with the virtual disenfranchisement of blacks in the South through property and literacy tests, and massively rising unemployment, Washington began to come closer to agreement with his detractors before his death in 1915.

Today the privately run 3500-student university is short of funds and very shabby; many of the original buildings built by students are still in use, and all roads and pathways, except for those used by Ronald Reagan during a presidential visit, are full of potholes and weeds. On campus, the **George Washington Carver Museum** catalogues the work of the Tuskegee agricultural scientist who promoted self-help programmes for black farmers but is best known as the inventor of more than 300 byproducts from the peanut and sweet potato (daily 9am–5pm; free).

The **visitor centre** (☎727-6390) is inside the museum, and *Dorothy Hall* (☎727-8753) on campus provides a cheap place to **stay** – though with nothing to see in the rest of the town, it's unlikely that you'll want to spend long in Tuskegee.

Alabama's Gulf Coast

Alabama's narrow share of the **Gulf coastline** is blessed with an abundance of fine white sand beaches, laundered by clear blue waters. The coast veers sharply inwards to accommodate the port city of **Mobile**, featuring hundreds of antebellum buildings in a tree-shaded centre. Away from the water's edge, agriculture, dominated by pecan, peach and watermelon growing, flourishes on the gently sloping coastal plain.

Mobile

The busy port and paper manufacturing city of **MOBILE** (pronounced *Mo-beel*) can trace its origins back to a French community founded in 1702. These early white settlers brought with them **Mardi Gras**, celebrated in Mobile continuously since 1704 – several years before New Orleans. Nowadays, festivities, including over fifteen parades and around thirty masked balls, start two weeks before the main celebrations on Shrove Tuesday.

Virtually every street is transformed in early spring by the delicate colours of azaleas, camellias and dogwoods: a beautiful complement to the many early eighteenth-century Spanish and Colonial-style buildings. Yet, despite this combination of bricks and bulbs, the city is unlikely to hold your attention for more than a day. Mobile survived the torches of the Union army during the Civil War, and possesses such a wealth of antebellum buildings that it's able to designate four sizeable areas as historic districts. Fanning out from Fort Conde, whose ramparts provide a good view of the city, the **Church Street Historic District** contains 59, mostly pre-Civil War, buildings. Also located within this district are two free museums, both worth a visit.

Glittering Mardi Gras costumes and lavish horse-drawn carriages are just some of the exhibits in the **History Museum,** 355 Government Street, while steam fire engines, resplendent in original livery, shining brass bells and trumpets, are the star attractions at the **Phoenix Fire Museum**, 203 S Clairborne Street. (Both museums Tues–Sat 10am–5pm, Sun 1–5pm; free; ☎434-7620).

Despite being largely dormant outside of Mardi Gras, downtown Mobile's lack of action is made up for by an amazing display of greenery, particularly down its main thoroughfare, Government Street, which is shaded by a canopy of adjoining oaks, and central Bienville Square, a popular eat-out lunch spot with free concerts every Wednesday during summer between 11am and 2pm.

Practicalities

Amtrak, 11 Government Boulevard, and *Greyhound*, 201 Government Boulevard (☎432-1861), are both in central downtown. Mobile's resourceful **visitor centre**, located in reconstructed Fort Conde, 150 S Royal Street (☎438-7304), can provide valuable discount vouchers for **accommodation**. The cheapest downtown place – which seems to change its name every year – is the *Oak Tree Inn*, 255 Church Street (☎433-6923), which costs around $35. The *Malaga Inn*, 359 Church Street (☎438-4701), is an 1862 twin town house, where huge rooms are great value at $48 to $56, and there's a good but expensive seafood restaurant. Mobile's finest hotel, *Stouffer's Riverview Plaza*, 64 Water Street (☎438-3719), has a great view of the port . At $89 and up it is firmly in the luxury category, though weekend rooms are around $59.

The *Back Porch*, 200 S Royal Street (☎432-5875), is a friendly lunchtime **cafe** serving cheap subs and a renowned red beans'n'rice, while *Wintzels' Oyster House*, 605 Dauphin Street (☎433-1004), serves good-value seafood platters in a determinedly eccentric atmosphere. At night, downtown Mobile is largely deserted; *G T Henry's Bar*, 462 Dauphin Street (☎432-0300), is a popular pub with a pool room, loud music by independent label bands, and a wide selection of beers.

Around The Bay Area

Twenty miles south of Mobile, off I-10, the 65 acres of landscaped colour that make up **Bellingrath Gardens** include a quarter of a million azaleas and thousands of other plants. Fifteen miles further south on Hwy-193 are the quiet beaches and undisturbed pine forest of sunny **Dauphin Island**, which has a campground (☎861-2742) on its western tip.

The *Mobile Bay Ferry* links Dauphin with the larger **Pleasure Island**, five miles away (adults $1; cars $9; ☎968-7511). The real gem here, and indeed on the entire Alabama Gulf Coast, lies twenty miles west, in the shape of **GULF SHORES**, a stunning **beach** where ultramarine waters sweep gently over blindingly snow-white sands, just beyond the junction of Hwy-59 and Hwy-182. Although it never really gets over-crowded, the beach is particularly busy on a Sunday, when young people from all over LA – Lower Alabama in this case – choose the resort in preference to the more expensive Florida Panhandle. A smattering of lively cafes specialise in freshly caught **shrimp**; the lurid *Pink Pony Pub* (☎948-6371) is the most popular place for refreshment and music.

Tourism is Gulf Shores' only trade; if you get bored with the beach and the bars, there's not a lot else to do. **Accommodation** is pricey and often booked up during summer weekends, though the *Port of Call Motel*, one mile west on Beach Boulevard (☎948-7739), has rooms for $45 to $65. Otherwise expect to pay in excess of $70 for a double, though you can **camp** three miles further east at the Gulf State Park Resort (☎948-6353). The Gulf Coast **CVB** (☎968-8832) on Hwy-59, near Gulf Shores, provides a full range of information.

MISSISSIPPI

When the cotton trade was at its peak, early in the nineteenth century – and slavery was as yet unchallenged – **MISSISSIPPI** was the nation's fifth wealthiest state. Ever since the Civil War, it has been the poorest, its dependence on cotton now a handicap which makes it forever victim to the vagaries of the commodities market.

In no other state was white resistance to black political participation so widespread and so violent as in Mississippi. At the start of the Sixties, no white man had ever been convicted of the murder of a black man in the state; as the widow of murdered civil rights leader Medgar Evers put it, the map of Mississippi was a map of atrocity, not geography. Not until the early Seventies did the church bombings and murders come to an end; no one could claim that racial tension does not exist, but matters have improved since the days of *Mississippi Burning*.

The only significant city in this largely flat state is the capital, **Jackson**. However, historic river towns like **Vicksburg** and **Natchez** provide good reasons to stay off the interstates, and **blues** fans will need no encouragement to go exploring sleepy **Delta** settlements such as Alligator or Yazoo City, in search of the old haunts of Robert Johnson and Muddy Waters.

Getting Around Mississippi

Although *Greyhound* serves most of Mississippi, including the Delta, only along the coastal stretch are services at all frequent. Jackson has the only **airport** of any size, and *Amtrak* passes through on the way between New Orleans and Memphis. Trips along the Mississippi itself tend to be run on expensive luxury cruisers (see p.398).

The Delta

> *That Delta. Five thousand square miles, without any hill save the bumps of dirt the Indians made to stand on when the river over-flowed.*
>
> William Faulkner, *Sanctuary*

"That Delta" is not in fact a delta at all; technically it's an alluvial flood plain, a couple of hundred miles short of the mouth of the Mississippi. The name is owed to its resemblance to the fertile Delta of the Nile (which also began at a city named **Memphis**); the extravagant meanderings of the river on its way down to **Vicksburg** deposit sufficient rich topsoil to make this one of the world's finest cotton-producing regions.

The Delta is a land of scorching sun, parched earth, flooding creeks and thickets of bone-dry evergreens, best seen at dawn or dusk when the glassy-smooth Mississippi waters reflect the sun and the foliage along the banks. Just to contain the sheer volume of water is a never-ending battle, with giant levees struggling to protect the farmland. The main thoroughfare south is the legendary **Highway 61**; but exploring is best on the backroads, characterised by roadside shacks, tiny churches and the sound of the blues.

Clarksdale

The flat expanse of **CLARKSDALE**, the first major town south of Memphis, may lack beauty, but it's *the* place to search out authentic blues music. You are greeted in the **Delta Blues Museum**, 114 Delta Avenue (☎624-4461), by a life-sized and lifelike figure of Muddy Waters. The museum celebrates the blues, and in particular ex-Clarksdale residents such as John Lee Hooker, Howlin' Wolf and Robert Johnson, through a great

The telephone **area code** for the entire state of Mississippi is ☎601.

THE DELTA BLUES

Even as recently as the turn of this century, the **Mississippi Delta** was known as "The Swamp". Much of it remained a dense and impenetrable wilderness of cypress and gum trees, roamed by panthers and bears, and plagued with mosquitoes. Bit by bit land had been cleared for cotton plantations, but, though the soil was fertile, white labourers could simply not be enticed to work in this god-forsaken backcountry. Since emancipation, the economy had come to depend on black **sharecroppers**, who would work an assigned portion of the land on a white-owned plantation in return for a share (often pitifully small) of the eventual crop. As a rule, the sharecropping lifestyle ensured long periods of poverty and debt interspersed with occasional windfalls; but in the Delta the returns tended to be greater than elsewhere, and blacks moved here from all over Mississippi.

In 1903, W C Handy, often credited as "the Father of the Blues" but at that time the leader of a professional ragtime and vaudeville orchestra, found himself waiting nine hours for a train in Tutwiler, fifteen miles southeast of Clarksdale. At some point in the night, a ragged-clothed black man carrying a guitar sat down next to him and began to play what Handy called "the weirdest music I had ever heard". Using a pocketknife pressed against the guitar-strings to accentuate his mournful vocal style, the man sang that he was "Goin' where the Southern cross the Dog".

This was the **Delta blues**, characterised by the interplay between words and music, with the guitar aiming to parallel and complement the singing rather than simply provide a backing. It was very much a local and place-specific music; the "Southern" and the "Dog" were both local railroads, which crossed a short way south at Moorhead. Though it was here in Mississippi that the blues achieved its greatest expression, it had not of course simply appeared from nowhere. The music combined elements of traditional African instrumental and vocal techniques with the "field hollers" chanted by nineteenth-century slaves, and the reels and jigs that were the basis of American popular entertainment.

Two men epitomise the Delta blues. One was **Charley Patton**, born in the hills just west of Jackson in April 1891. The classic itinerant bluesman, Patton moved from plantation to plantation and wife to wife – as his contemporary Son House put it, "Charlie hated work like God hates sin. He just natural born hated it. It didn't look right to him" – playing at Saturday-night dances with a repertoire that extended from rollicking dance pieces to documentary songs such as *High Water Everywhere*, which chronicled the bursting of the Mississippi levees in April 1927. The far more enigmatic **Robert Johnson** was rumoured to have sold his soul to the Devil in return for a few brief years of writing songs such as *Love In Vain* and *Stop Breakin' Down* (both later recorded by the Rolling Stones). His *Crossroads Blues* spoke of being stranded at night in the chilling emptiness of the open Delta; such themes of isolation were carried to almost metaphysical extremes in *Hellhound On My Trail* and *Me And The Devil Blues* – "you may bury my body down by the highway side / So my old evil spirit can catch a Greyhound bus and ride".

Both Patton and Johnson died in the 1930s. However, within a few years the Delta blues had been carried north to **Chicago** – by men such as **Muddy Waters**, once a tractor-driver on the Stovall Plantation, near Clarksdale, and **Howlin' Wolf**, brought up (along with Roebuck "Pops" Staples, of the Staples Singers) on Dockery's Plantation, between Clarksdale and Greenville (one of Patton's few long-term bases). Their electrified urban blues, rooted in the music of the Delta, was the most immediate ancestor of rock 'n'roll.

Getting to See Blues Events

Though the blues still play a prominent role in Delta life, managing to hear live music is rarely a straightforward business. Half the time nobody seems to know who is playing where, let alone when, and many of the venues don't have phones. On the whole, most of the "jookin" either gets done at weekends, or on the first and third days of each month, which are the usual paydays. Local radio stations may have details.

Nearly all the "jook joints" themselves are dark and rudimentary places, making few concessions to decor or comfort, but beer is usually very cheap and admission is often free. With public transport – even taxis – all but nonexistent, a car is essential.

collection of photos, instruments and personal possessions, as well as videos and record-ings. It has recently undergone a major expansion, thanks to a huge fundraising drive spearheaded by Z Z Top – ring for the current opening times. Blues fans should also call in at the **Stackhouse/Delta Record Mart**, 232 Sunflower Avenue (☎627-2209). The home of the *Rooster Blues* record label and a mail-order service, it is stuffed with obscure records, books and Delta crafts, and the staff are very useful for gig information.

Practicalities

Clarksdale's **accommodation** is concentrated along US-61, which in town is State Street. The most pleasant option, for around $45, is the *Comfort Inn* at no. 710 (☎627-9292); the *Southern Inn* (☎624-5558) and the *Beacon Inn* (☎624-4391) range from $22 to $35. Two cheap central **restaurants** are the *Lebanese Rest Haven*, 419 S State Street (☎624-9106), and *Fair's*, 227 Fourth Street (☎627-2747), which serves great soul food.

The most famous of Clarksdale's **jook-joints**, *Smitty's Red Top Lounge*, 377 Yazoo Avenue (☎627-4421), features live blues band most weekends. *Margaret's Blue Diamond Lounge*, Tallahatchie Avenue, off Fourth Street (no phone), usually has some-thing going on on a Saturday night; on Sunday afternoon, try *Red's South End Disco*, 395–397 Sunflower Street (no sign or phone).

Central Delta Towns

GREENVILLE, seventy miles south of Clarksdale, is the largest town on the Delta. Still an important riverport, it hosts the **Mississippi Delta Blues Festival** every September. Tree-lined avenues lead from the characterless outskirts into the business district, beyond which pallid warehouses stand in the shadow of a huge levee. Several of the flimsy shacks along **Nelson Street**, a run-down street in a potentially dangerous part of town, transform at night into blues joints. Booba Barnes, currently one of the Delta's top bluesmen, can usually be seen at the *Playboy*, at no. 928, on Friday and Saturday nights. The top place to **eat** – arguably in the entire Delta – is *Doe's* on the safer end of Nelson at no. 502 (☎334-3315). It's a real down-home spot; the decor, furnishings and cutlery may be mismatched, but the steaks and tamales are fantastic.

Fifteen miles east on US-82, **INDIANOLA** is the home of the largest catfish process-ing company in the world, *Delta*, a co-operative owned by 180 white farmers. Low wage levels have recently led to strikes and protests by the overwhelmingly black female workforce. B B King, who was born here, plays a home-town show once a year at the *Ebony Club*, 404 Hannah Street. The *Keyhole Inn* on Church Street also puts on blues.

For a look at the Delta's social and economic history, call in on **GREENWOOD**, a sleepy town of 20,000 people, forty miles east on US-82, and still the country's second largest cotton exchange after Memphis. Downtown is reminiscent of the days when cotton was king with the nineteenth-century offices of Cotton Row overlooking the shady Yazoo River along with the graceful mansions lining pretty Grand Boulevard. The **Cottonlandia Museum** (Tues–Sat 9am–5pm, Sun 1–5pm), two miles west of the town centre on US-49E, focuses on the history of the Delta agriculture and its workers.

Northern Mississippi

Cutting its way south through Mississippi, I-55 acts as an approximate boundary between the Delta and the luscious green forests of the northeast. Of the small northern market towns, the most appealing are **Holly Springs**, whose oak-lined streets emanate from a neat courthouse square, and the old-style shopping centre of **Columbus**. The only two places of major interest in the region are genteel **Oxford**, and tidy blue-collar **Tupelo**, birthplace of **Elvis Presley**.

Oxford

Twelve thousand residents and eleven thousand students enable **OXFORD**, an enclave of wealth in a predominantly poor region, to blend small-town charm with a busy nightlife. Its central square and leafy streets have a vaguely European air about them – the town called itself after the English city as part of its campaign to persuade the **University of Mississippi** – known as Ole Miss – to locate its main campus here.

It's difficult now to believe that the serene leafy campus was in September 1962 the site of the most bitter display of racial hatred ever seen in Mississippi. After eighteen months of legal and political wrangling, the federal court ruled that the black James Meredith should be allowed to enrol as a student at Ole Miss, which until then had been exclusively white. The news that Meredith had been sneaked into college by federal troops sparked a riot that by dawn had left three dead and 160 injured. Despite constant threats, Meredith graduated the following year, and in a snub to the racists wore a "NEVER" badge (the segregationist slogan of Mississippi Governor Ross Barnett) turned upside down when he went up to receive his papers. The **Blues Archive** (Mon–Fri 8.30am–5pm; ☎232-7753 in advance) on campus holds thousands of recordings and B B King's personal memorabilia, while the **Center for the Study of Southern Culture** looks at southern folkways and lifestyle (Mon–Fri 8.15am–4.45pm; free).

From Ole Miss, a ten-minute walk through lush Bailey Woods leads to secluded **Rowan Oak**, the former home of novelist **William Faulkner**, preserved as it was on the day he died in July 1962 (Mon–Fri 10am–noon & 2–4pm, Sat 10am–noon, Sun 2–4pm; free). The fictional Deep-South town of Jefferson, where the Nobel prizewinner set his major works, was based heavily on Oxford and its environs.

Practicalities

Oxford's **visitor centre** (☎232-2149) is in the town square. **Accommodation** options include *Ole Miss Motel*, 1517 University Avenue (☎234-2424), where doubles cost around $30, and the *University Inn*, 2201 W Jackson Avenue (☎234-7013), which is about $10 more. Prices go up during graduation, the Faulkner Literary Festival each August, and on weekends of football games. You can **eat** good-value Mexican meals at *Cafe Ole*, 1612 University Avenue, or soul food at the *Beacon* one mile north on Hwy-7 (☎234-5041). **Nightlife** focuses on **Harrison Avenue**. Just off this street, the *Hoka* (☎234-3057) is a dilapidated shack housing a cheap cafe and a small theatre, which puts on bands or avant-garde movies every night. Across the yard, the *Gin Bar* (☎234-0024), in an old cotton warehouse, has live music at the weekend.

Tupelo

On January 8 1935, **Elvis Presley** and his twin brother Jesse were born in **TUPELO**, an industrial town in northeastern Mississippi. Jesse died at birth, while Elvis grew up to be a truck-driver. Their parents, Gladys and Vernon Presley, who lived in poor-white East Tupelo, found it hard to make ends meet. Such was the financial strain of rearing the young Elvis that his sharecropper father was reduced to forgery in a desperate attempt to raise cash, and was jailed for three years. The two-room home was repossessed, and the family eventually moved to Memphis in 1948.

Tupelo **CVB**, 712 E President Street (☎841-6521), has details of a four-mile driving tour which takes in Elvis' first school and the shop where he bought his first guitar. The town doesn't go in for overkill, however, and has few of the tacky gift shops, waxworks and so on that you might expect. The actual **Elvis Presley Birthplace**, 306 Elvis Presley Drive, more of an emotive shrine than a glitzy tourist stop, now stands in Elvis Presley Park, near a meditation chapel built with donations from fans (May–Sept Mon–Sat 9am–5.30pm, Sun 1–5pm; Oct–April Mon–Sat 9am–5pm, Sun 1–5pm; $1).

South Central Mississippi

South of the Delta, the swamps and bayous give way to steep loess bluffs marking the transition to the rich woodlands and meadows of central Mississippi. Each of its engaging towns – **Jackson**, **Vicksburg** and **Natchez** – teems with its own brand of history. Driving is a real pleasure in these parts, especially along the unspoiled Natchez Trace Parkway – devoid of trucks, buildings and neon signs – which runs through Jackson.

Jackson

JACKSON, halfway between Memphis and New Orleans at 200 miles from either, has been Mississippi's state capital since 1821. Only in this century, however, has it become the largest conurbation in the state. It's now a pleasant and hospitable community which is flourishing as a centre for health and technological industries.

Jackson's **Old Capitol**, at the top of Capitol Avenue, serves these days as the **State Historical Museum**, charting Mississippi's somewhat unenviable history. Look out for the excellent displays on civil rights and slavery, especially the chilling notices announcing slave auctions (Mon–Fri 8am–5pm, Sat 9.30am–4.30pm, Sun 12.30–4.30pm; free). The "new" **Mississippi State Capitol**, 400 High Street, built in 1903 as a Beaux Arts Classical showpiece, is a much more ornate structure. In true Mississippi rebel fashion, a gold-leaf covered eagle was deliberately perched on the roof looking away from Washington, the only one to do so in the entire US.

A block west, the **Smith-Robertson Museum and Cultural Center**, 528 Bloom Street, tells the story of black Mississippians from the introduction of the first slaves by the French in 1719 to the present day, focusing on the fortunes of the people of Farish Street, the oldest black neighbourhood in the city (Mon–Fri 9am–5pm; $1).

Practicalities

Greyhound **buses** from Atlanta, Dallas and Memphis arrive at 201 S Jefferson Street (☎353-6342); the **Amtrak** station is at 300 W Capitol Avenue. Jackson's regional **airport** is ten minutes east of downtown on I-20 – a $15 taxi ride or $9.50 via the 24-hour van service (☎957-6868). *JATRAN* runs a reasonable in-town bus service until 6pm.

Central **rooms** for between $30 and $35 can be had at the *Sun N Sand Motel*, 410 N Lamar Boulevard beside the Capitol (☎354-2501), and the *Wilson Inn*, 310 Greymont Street (☎1-800/333-9475). Options further out include the *Holiday Inn North*, 5075 I-55 North (☎366-9411), where nice rooms with use of a pool start at $50.

Downtown Jackson more or less closes down at 6pm, though one notable exception is *Hal & Mel's Restaurant & Oyster Bar*, at 200 Commerce Street by the Mississippi State Fairgrounds (☎948-0888), which specialises in New Orleans cuisine and puts on live bands at the weekend. Several bars in the suburbs serve quality food to the accompaniment of live music, such as *Poet's*, 1855 Lakeland Drive (☎982-9711), which does great things with redfish for $10.

Vicksburg

The historic port of **VICKSBURG**, straddling a high bluff on a bend in the Mississippi, is a hauntingly bare yet beautiful city of precipitous streets, steep terraces and wooded ravines. Tourism is the town's biggest industry, but its charm remains intact, especially along the riverfront, overlooked by imposing grey warehouses on which the names of their Victorian proprietors are now barely visible. There's a museum crammed with Civil War memorabilia, but the best way to spend time in Vicksburg is a cruise on the **Spirit of Vicksburg** riverboat, which departs from the bottom of Clay Street (daily May–Aug 10am & 2pm; Sept–April 2pm; $6).

During the Civil War, Abraham Lincoln labelled the bustling port of Vicksburg as the "key to the Confederacy". In the spring of 1863, after four attempts during the previous winter, Ulysses S Grant and his Union troops landed to the south, circled inland, and attacked Vicksburg from the east. The outnumbered Confederates, hemmed in by gunboats on both the Mississippi and Yazoo rivers, refused to give in. After a 47-day siege, the town surrendered on the Fourth of July 1863 – a holiday it declined to celebrate for the next hundred years. **Vicksburg National Military Park** (daily 8am–5pm; $3 per car; ☎636-0583), entered on US-80 (Clay Street) just northeast, preserves the main battlefield. The topography and presentation of the site is nothing short of breathtaking. Rippling green hillsides are pock-marked with trenches, and every twist in the sixteen-mile road seems to be punctuated by a refurbished cannon or by one of over 1600 elaborate monuments. Also in the park are the remains of the cumbersome **USS Cairo**, one of the Union Navy's ironclad fighting ships, which came to grief during the campaign on the Yazoo River, and the **Vicksburg National Cemetery**, in which 13,000 of the 17,000 Union graves are simply marked "Unknown".

Practicalities

Vicksburg's **visitor centre**, opposite the entrance to the Military Park (☎636-9421), can provide details on **accommodation**. The *Economy Inn*, 4216 Washington Street (☎638-5750), offers the only river view for $35; motels nearer the battlefield range from the clean and cheap *Hillcrest*, 4503 Hwy-80 E (☎638-1491), costing $23, to the comfortable $50 *Park Inn International*, 4137 I-20 Frontage Road (☎638-5811). The central *Cherry Tree Cottage*, 2212 Cherry Street (☎636-7086), is a **B&B** charging $60. You can **camp** at the *Battlefield KOA Campground*, 4407 I-20 Frontage Road (☎636-2025). The *New Orleans Cafe*, 1100 Washington Street (☎638-8182), serves sandwiches and burgers; the *Top O' The River*, 4150 Washington Street (☎636-6262), does great catfish dinners.

Natchez

Greek revival mansions with meticulously maintained gardens abound in **NATCHEZ**, a river town which still conjures up a plantation atmosphere – a legacy of pre-Civil War days when, at one time, more than half of the millionaires in the entire United States lived here. Fourteen homes stay open all year round, including elaborate octagonal **Longwood**, 140 Lower Woodville Street (daily 9am–5pm; $5), with a huge dome and an abundance of snow-white arches and columns. Each year in late March, early April and October most of the rest can be seen on tours, often led by women wearing massive hoopskirts, known as the **Natchez Pilgrimage**.

Natchez is so rich in antebellum architecture that it is easy to overlook its earlier history. By the mid-sixteenth century, local Native Americans had built a flourishing commercial empire, which they defended in bitter running battles with the French some two hundred years later. The **Grand Village of the Natchez Indians**, 400 Jefferson Davis Boulevard, features an archaeological site and a small museum (free).

Down below the town proper, the raucous Natchez-under-the Hill landing was once known as the "Sodom of the Mississippi"; these days it's considerably more refined, and, with its spectacular river view, it's one of the most pleasant districts of town. The *Jubilee* **riverboat** (☎647-6742) runs daily sightseeing tours.

Practicalities

The Natchez **CVB** is at 311 Liberty Road (☎446-6345 or ☎1-800/547-6724). Places to **stay** include *Days Inn*, 109 US-61 S (☎445-8291), and *Best Western*, US-61 at the junction with US-65 (☎442-1691), both costing around $40 a night. The *Ramada Hilltop*, 130 John R Junkin Drive (☎446-6311), is a bit more expensive at $60, but could be worth it if you get a river view. Many of the antebellum mansions do B&B from $75 per night.

Mississippi's Gulf Coast

Mississippi's hundred-mile strip of **coast** is utterly unlike the rest of the state, culturally as well as physically – a strong Mediterranean (Catholic) heritage is conspicuous amid the subtropical beauty. Some of the towns are scarred by hurricanes, but the **beaches** are often superb. Along the **Gulf Islands National Seashore**, four beautiful barrier islands boast brilliant white sand and crystal-blue waters, while the twenty-six-mile artificial **Harrison County Beach** runs parallel with the busy coast road between **Biloxi**, the major resort, and laid-back **Pass Christian**. The weather is usually good for bathing at least one month to either side of the main Memorial to Labor Day season, though some swimmers find the muddy waters of the Mississippi Sound off-putting.

Biloxi

Plastic, neon-lit **BILOXI** (pronounced *Bi-lux-i*), sprawling alongside a busy four-lane highway, cannot claim to be the prettiest resort in the world. But it's inexpensive compared to its Florida neighbours, it's just a short drive from New Orleans, and has sufficient diversity to satisfy beach-poseurs, bus loads of elderly visitors and legions of blue-collar families. Biloxi was already attracting wealthy visitors by the mid-nineteenth century, but tourism has never been its only source of income. Its first **cannery** opened in 1881, and Biloxi sees itself as rivalling Baltimore as the "seafood capital of the world". Numerous plants line the bayou at the rear of the city, along with a massive USAF base.

Away from the shabby **Main Street, Old Biloxi**, at the far end of Lameuse Boulevard, consists of narrow lane-like streets of turn-of-the-century stuccoed buildings, in a tree-shaded tranquillity that seems miles from the hustle and bustle of busy US-90. Directly across the highway, shrimp and oyster fleets unload the day's catch at the **Small Crafts Harbor**. You can also hire boats to go fishing or to visit **Deer Island**, a long thin stretch of windblown trees and shrubs half a mile offshore. Seventy-minute shrimping tours cost $7 (times vary; ☎374-5718). A mile further west, a glut of tacky shops selling T-shirts, seashells, trinkets and other ephemera mark the approach to the most popular stretch of **Harrison County Beach**, in front of the *Biloxi Hilton*.

Five miles from Main Street, the compact white Louisiana-style raised cottage of **Beauvoir** was the final home of Jefferson Davis, the only President of the Confederate States of America. At the end of the Civil War, Davis was arrested trying to escape to Mexico and jailed on charges of treason. On his release two years later, he accepted an invitation from a friend to stay at Beauvoir, eventually buying the property and living here until his death in 1889. The home and beautiful wooded grounds have been turned into a shrine run by the Sons of Confederate Veterans, whose political perspective is heavily apparent in the displays, but the museum section gives a brilliant insight into what life was like for the ordinary Civil War soldier, the amputation kit being one of the most gory reminders. The actual home contains such Davis memorabilia as the 1978 joint resolution of Congress which posthumously restored his US citizenship ($4; daily 9am–5pm; ☎388-1313).

West Ship Island

Considered by *USA Today* to be one of the top ten beaches in the country, the barrier island of **West Ship** was only created in 1969, when the 200mph winds and thirty-foot tide of Hurricane Camille ripped what was previously Ship Island in half. It's basically one giant sandbank, dotted with inland ponds (home to a family of alligators), marshlands, sand dunes and warm tidal pools. Everywhere you come across delicate wispy sea oats; there's a heavy fine for even touching these, as their elaborate root structure is all that holds the island together.

The small, idyllic **beach** boasts fine white sand, free showers and a reasonable cafe, though umbrella and deckchair hire is expensive at $12 per day. D-shaped Fort Massachusetts alongside was built in 1859, and captured by the Union Navy early in the Civil War. Free tours give a wonderful panoramic view from its grass-topped roof.

West Ship is the only barrier island with a regular **ferry** service; boats from *David M's* on the Loop cost $11, take seventy minutes, and leave at 9am and noon each day during summer, arriving back at 3.45 and 6.45pm (☎432-2197). Ferries from Gulfport Yacht Harbor, at the intersection of US-90 and US-49 (☎864-1014), operate the same schedules during the summer, plus daily trips during spring and autumn.

Practicalities

Biloxi's **visitor centre** is at 710 Beach Boulevard at Main Street (☎435-6248). *Greyhound* **buses** from New Orleans and Mobile come in at 322 Main Street (☎436-4336). *Coast Area Transit* (☎896-8080) runs a reasonable hourly service taking in other coastal towns. An all-day pass on the *Beachcomber* line costs $2.

The cost of a **room** in Biloxi varies considerably according to season; it's well worth shopping around. The most convenient area to stay is the **Loop**, where I-110 intersects US-90 five minutes from Main Street. The *Buena Vista Beach Club*, 911 Beach Boulevard (☎432-5511), in an ideal location with a good pool and bar, charges $70 to $80; the nearby *Sun Tan Motel*, 780 Beach Boulevard (☎432-8641), is cheaper at $45 a night. There are also several places around the $40–60 mark near the *Hilton*, including a very good *Travelodge*, 2030 Beach Boulevard (☎388-5531). The most central place to **camp** is *Biloxi Beach Campground*, 1816 Beach Boulevard (☎432-2755).

Among places to **eat** in the Loop are the *Pier* (☎374-1242), behind the *Buena Vista*, for a choice of cheap lunch specials, or *Baricev's*, 633 Beach Boulevard (☎435-3626), which serves delicious stuffed flounder. At *Mary Mahoney's Old French House*, 138 Rue Magnolia (☎374-0163), a sumptuous meal in very tasteful surroundings will set you back around $20 to $30. Two miles east of the Loop, the unglamorous *Fisherman's Wharf*, 315 Beach Boulevard (☎436-4513), does superb mullet dishes.

The Loop is liveliest at **night**, and with most places charging no cover, it is possible to wander around and see what takes your fancy. Popular haunts include the bar at the *Biloxi Hilton*, 2060 Beach Boulevard (☎388-7000), and *Gorenflo's*, just before the Ocean Springs Bridge, where you drink outdoors and listen to live R&B. *Le Bistro*, 222 Pat Harrison Avenue (☎388-9366), is Biloxi's only **gay** club, playing the best dance music in town.

Out from Biloxi

Six miles east of Biloxi, the attractive tree-canopied **Ocean Springs** village, dotted with art, craft and clothes shops, is well worth exploring. The **visitor centre** of the Gulf Islands National Seashore at 3500 Park Road (☎875-7320) offers informative film shows, exhibits, nature trails and marsh tours of **Davis Bayou**, where, with luck, you might catch a glimpse of an armadillo.

To the west, Biloxi blends almost imperceptibly into unspectacular **Gulfport**, the area's main business centre, and then **Long Beach**, whereof the amazing **Friendship Oak** (free) on the University of Southern Mississippi's Gulf Coast Campus has a sixteen-foot trunk, limbs five feet in diameter and a set of stairs built into its centre. **Pass Christian**, twenty miles from downtown Biloxi, is noted for a fine display of live oaks. This serene town hasn't let 150 years of tourism dent its Old South atmosphere.

travel details

TRAINS
Routes

• Four trains daily connect **New York City** and **Washington DC** with **Selma**, North Carolina. Two of those follow the coast all the way to Florida, calling at **Charleston** and **Savannah**. One follows an **inland** route to Savannah via **Raleigh**, and Camden and Denmark in South Carolina, the other continues through North Carolina to **Raleigh** and **Charlotte**.

• One train daily between **New York City**, **Washington DC** and **New Orleans** calls at **Charlotte**, **Atlanta**, and **Birmingham**. Birmingham has one daily connection with the Alabama coast at **Mobile**, via **Montgomery**.

• One train daily each way between **Chicago** and **New Orleans** stops at **Memphis** and **Jackson**. There are connecting services between **Memphis**, **St Louis**, and **Kansas City**.

• **Nashville** is not served by trains.

Journey Times

From Charlotte: to Raleigh 3hr 45min; Washington DC 9hr; New York 14hr.

From Atlanta: to Clemson 2hr 20min; Greenville 3hr; Charlotte 5hr 30min; Greensboro 7hr 30min; Washington DC 14hr; New York City 18hr; Birmingham 3hr 20min; Tuscaloosa 5hr 20min; New Orleans 7hr 30min.

From Savannah: to Charleston 1hr 30min; Raleigh 6hr 30min; Washington DC 11hr; New York City 15hr 20min; Jacksonville FL 2hr 30min; Orlando FL 5hr 30min.

From Memphis: to Chicago 11hr; Jackson 4hr 30min; New Orleans 8hr; St Louis 8hr; Kansas City 13hr.

From Birmingham: to Montgomery 2hr; Mobile 5hr 45min.

BUSES

From Atlanta: to New Orleans (7 daily, 9hr); Birmingham 5, 2hr 30min); Montgomery (5, 3hr); Charlotte (1, 5hr); Washington DC (2, 14hr).

From Savannah: to Jacksonville (10; 3hr); Charleston (3; 2hr 30min); Washington DC (6, 17hr).

From Louisville: to Indianapolis (6 daily, 2hr); Cincinnati (7, 2hr); Chicago (2, 6hr); Nashville (10, 3hr); Lexington (2, 1hr 30min).

From Lexington: to Cincinnati (7 daily, 1hr 30min); Knoxville (7, 3hr).

From Nashville: to Atlanta (7 daily, 7hr 30min); Washington DC (7, 16hr); Memphis (9, 4hr); Knoxville (6, 4hr).

From Memphis: to New Orleans (5 daily, 11hr); Jackson (1, 4hr 30min); Oxford (1, 1hr 30min); Tupelo (1, 2hr 30min); Birmingham (1, 5hr 30min).

From Jackson: to Dallas (4 daily, 10hr); Montgomery (7, 7hr); Vicksburg (6, 1hr); Biloxi (2, 4hr).

From Biloxi: to New Orleans (12 daily, 1hr 45min); to Mobile (12, 1hr).

CHAPTER SEVEN

FLORIDA

Brochure images of tanning flesh and Mickey Mouse give an inaccurate and incomplete picture of **FLORIDA**. Although the aptly nicknamed "sunshine state" is indeed devoted to the tourist trade, it's also among the least-understood parts of the US, with much that the travel agent never reveals: forests and rivers; deserted strands filled with wildlife; modern cities and primeval swamps. In many respects, too, Florida is still evolving. A thousand people a day move to the state, now the fourth most populous in the nation. Changing demographics have begun to erode the traditional Deep South conservatism: the new Floridians tend to be a younger, more energetic breed, while Spanish-speaking enclaves provide close ties to Latin America and the Caribbean – links as influential in creating wealth as the recent arrival of the film industry in central Florida, fresh from Hollywood.

The essential stop is **Miami**, whose cosmopolitan nature is enriched by the Hispanic half of its population. From Miami, it's a simple journey south to the **Florida Keys**, a hundred-mile string of islands known for sports fishing, coral-reef diving, and the town of **Key West**, legendary for its sunsets and anything-goes attitude. North from Miami, much of the **east coast** is disappointingly urbanised, albeit with miles of unbroken beaches flowing alongside. The residential stranglehold is finally escaped further north, where communities become subservient to the local sands (as epitomised by the annual student Spring Break frenzy that rips through **Daytona Beach**).

In **central Florida** the terrain turns green, though the sole upset to the largely rural idyll could hardly be a bigger one: **Walt Disney World**, where tourism is practised on the scale of the infinite. If the upfront commercialism disappoints you, skip north to the forests of the **Panhandle**, Florida's link with the Deep South, or to the towns and beaches of the **west coast**, which should be savoured while progressing steadily south to the **Everglades**, an alligator-filled swathe of sawgrass plain – as definitive a statement of Florida's natural beauty as you'll encounter.

It makes little difference **when** you visit; warm sunshine and blue skies are a fact of life. Florida does however split into **two climatic zones**: subtropical in the south and warm temperate in the north. Anywhere south of Orlando has very mild winters (November to April), with warm temperatures and low humidity. This is the peak tourist season, when prices are at their highest. The southern summer (May to October), on the other hand, sees extremely high humidity – the rewards for braving the mugginess are lower prices and fewer tourists. Winter is the off-peak period north of Orlando, and while snow has been known to fall in the Panhandle, daytime temperatures are generally akin to a good British summer. The northern Florida summer is when the crowds arrive, and when the days – and the nights – get hot and sticky.

History

The **first European sighting** of Florida, just six years after Christopher Columbus located the "New World", is believed to have been made by John and Sebastian Cabot in 1498, when they spotted what is now Cape Florida, on Key Biscayne in Miami. At the time, the area's 100,000 inhabitants formed several distinct **tribes**: the Timucua across northern Florida, the Calusa around the southwest and Lake Okeechobee, the Apalachee in the Panhandle and the Tequesta along the southeast coast.

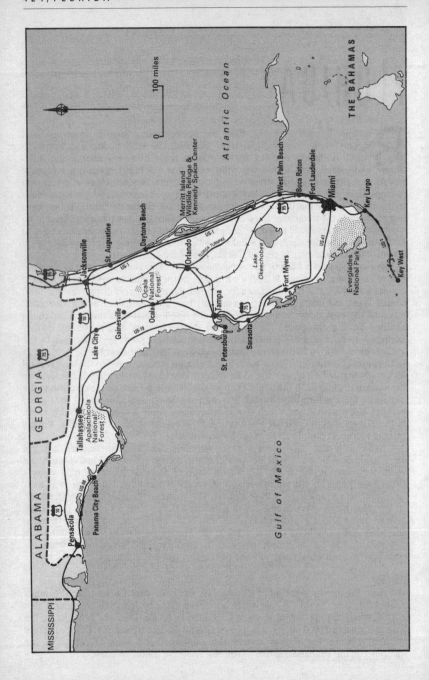

In 1513, a **Spaniard**, Juan Ponce de León, sighted land during *Pascua Florida*, the Festival of the Flowers, and named what he saw *La Florida* – or "Land of Flowers". Eight years later he returned with a mandate from the Spanish king to conquer and colonise the territory, the first of several Spanish incursions prompted by rumours of gold hidden in the north of the region. When it became clear that Florida did not harbour stunning riches, interest waned; but the arrival of French Huguenots in 1562 forced the Spanish into a more determined effort at settlement. Three years later, **Pedro Menéndez de Avilés** founded St Augustine – the longest continuous site of European habitation on the continent. In 1586 St Augustine was razed by a British naval bombardment led by Francis Drake. The ensuing bloody confrontation for control of North America was eventually settled when the British captured the crucial Spanish possession of Havana, and Spain willingly parted with Florida to get it back. By this time, aboriginal Floridians had been largely wiped out by disease, and Florida's Indian population was becoming composed of disparate tribes arriving from the west, collectively known as the **Seminoles**, who were generally left undisturbed in the inland areas.

Following American independence, when Florida was returned to Spain, the US began to think in terms of controlling the state. In 1814 a US general, Andrew Jackson, marched south, killing hundreds of Indians and triggering the **First Seminole War** – on the pretext of subduing the Seminoles but with the actual intention of taking the state. Spain formally **ceded Florida to the US** in 1819, with Jackson sworn in as Florida's first American governor and Tallahassee selected as the new administrative centre. Eleven years later, the **Act of Indian Removal** decreed that all Native Americans in the eastern US should be transferred to reservations in the Midwest. Most Seminoles were determined to stay and the **Second Seminole War** broke out, with the Indians steadily driven south, away from the fertile lands of central Florida and into the Everglades, where they eventually agreed to remain.

Florida **became a state** on March 3 1845, coinciding with a period of material prosperity as the first railways arrived. Aligning itself with the Confederacy in the run-up to the **Civil War**, Florida's primary contribution to the war effort was the provision of food – a foretaste of its post-war economic role when finally re-admitted to the Union. As northern speculators began to invest in Florida, articles extolling the virtues of its climate as a cure for all ills began appearing in the country's newspapers. These early efforts to promote Florida as a **tourist destination** brought in the wintering rich: Henry Flagler opened luxury resorts on the northeast coast and extended his Florida East Coast Railroad south, giving birth to communities such as Palm Beach. Henry Plant connected *his* railway to Tampa, turning it into a thriving port city. Florida's climate enabled citrus fruits to be grown during the winter and sold to the cooler north, and the state became a major supplier of beef to the rest of the US. In the rush of prosperity that followed World War I, everyone in America wanted a piece of Florida, and chartered trains brought in thousands of eager buyers. But most deals were paper transactions, with buyers paying a small deposit into a bank, and in 1926 – when they began to default – banks went **bust**. The **Wall Street Crash** proceeded to make paupers of the millionaires whose investments had helped shaped the state.

What saved Florida was **World War II**. Thousands of troops arrived to guard the coastline, empty tourist hotels provided ready-made barracks, and – most importantly – the soldiers got a taste of Florida that would entice many of them to return. In the mid-Sixties, the state government bent over backwards to help the Disney Corporation turn a sizeable slice of central Florida into **Walt Disney World**, the biggest theme park complex ever known. Its enormous commercial success helped solidify Florida's place in the international tourist market: directly or indirectly, one in five of the state's twelve million inhabitants now earns a living from the tourist trade.

Behind the optimistic facade, however, lie many **problems**. There's a broadening gap between the relative liberalism of the big cities and the arch-conservatism of the

Bible Belt rural area: while Miami promotes its multicultural make-up, the Ku Klux Klan holds picnics in the Panhandle. In 1976, Florida became the first state to restore the death penalty, "the ultimate deterrent", while the gun laws remain notoriously lax. And the multimillion-dollar **drugs trade** shows few signs of abating – at least a quarter of the cocaine entering the US is said to arrive via Florida. **Racial issues** continue to be vexed, too, with tension on several fronts: between Anglo-Americans and nouveau-riche Cubans, blacks and whites, blacks and Hispanics, police and the inner-city poor. However, increased protection of the state's **natural resources** has been a more positive feature of the last decade and impressive amounts of land are under state control – overall, wildlife is less threatened now than at any time since white settlers first arrived.

Getting around Florida

Distances in Florida are surprisingly short, and with a **car** you'll have few problems: crossing between the east and west coasts takes only a couple of hours, and even the longest possible trip – between the western extremity of the Panhandle and Miami – can be done in a day. **Public transport**, on the other hand, requires adroit forward planning. *Greyhound* **buses** link all the major towns and cities, but sadly, many rural areas and some of the most enjoyable sections of the coast are off-limits. Florida's **railways** were built to service the boom towns of the Twenties, and consequently some present-day rural nooks have rail links as good as the modern cities. However, on no route are there more than two services a day, and in some areas, *Amtrak* buses have replaced the trains. The southeast coast boasts a new elevated **Tri-Rail** system, ferrying commuters between Miami and West Palm Beach, with almost all services running during rush hours – meaning a very early start or an early evening arrival.

In practice then, non-drivers should plan carefully and make judicious use of rented **bicycles**. Although cycling is seldom a good way to get around the cities, there are miles of marked cycle paths along the coast, and a number of long-distance bike trails cross the state's interior. Forget **hitching**: it's potentially very dangerous (especially for women) and is illegal in Miami (where, if you did hitch, you'd be lucky to live to regret it) and on the outskirts of many other cities.

MIAMI AND MIAMI BEACH

Far and away the most exciting city in Florida, **Miami** is a stunning and often intoxicatingly beautiful place. Awash with sunlight-intensified natural colours, there are moments – when the downtown skyline glows in the warm night and the beachside palm trees sway in the evening breeze – when a better-looking city is hard to imagine. Even so, people, not climate or landscape, are what make Miami unique. Half of the two-million population is Hispanic, the vast majority Cubans. Spanish is the predominant language almost everywhere, and news from Havana, Caracas or Bogota frequently gets more attention than the latest word from Washington.

The city is no melting pot, however. Since the black ghettos first erupted in the Sixties, violent expressions of rage – most recently among Haitians and Puerto Ricans – have been a regular feature of Miami life. Though 1980 saw the highest murder rate in the country, in the last ten years it has smartened itself up considerably. One factor in that revival, strangely, has been *Miami Vice*, a TV cop show less about crime than designer clothes and fabulous subtropical scenery. The newly restored Art Deco district of **Miami Beach** – a long strip of land separating mainland Miami from the ocean – became a regular backdrop on the fashion pages of glossy magazines.

The telephone **area code** for Miami and Miami Beach is ☎305.

Just a century ago Miami was a swampy outpost of mosquito-tormented settlers. The arrival of the railway in 1896 gave Miami its first fixed land-link with the rest of the continent, and literally cleared the way for the Twenties property boom when entire communities appeared almost overnight. In the Fifties, Miami Beach became a celebrity-filled resort area, just as thousands of Cubans fleeing the regime of Fidel Castro began arriving in mainland Miami. The Sixties and Seventies brought decline, though with the strengthening of Latin American economic links and the upsurge in tourism, the city is now enjoying a burst of affluence. As Hispanic immigration into the US re-shapes the demography of the nation, today's Miami could well be a foretaste of tomorrow's US.

Arriving, Information and Getting Around

Miami International Airport is six miles west of the city; local bus #7 runs downtown. Taxis cost $15 to downtown or $20 to Miami Beach, while the 24-hour *Airporter, SuperShuttle* and *Red Top* minivans will deliver you to any address in Miami for $8 to $15. Four daily *Greyhound* buses on the Miami–Key West route connect the airport with Coral Gables and Miami Beach. All other **Greyhound** services into Miami stop downtown, at 99 NE Fourth Street (☎374-7222). The **train** station, 8303 NW 37th Avenue, is seven miles northwest, with an adjacent *Metrorail* stop providing access to downtown Miami and beyond; bus #L stops here on its way to Central Miami Beach. The **Tri-Rail** links with the *Metrorail* at 1149 E 21st Street, also seven miles northwest of downtown.

For free maps and information, use the **Greater Miami Convention and Visitors Bureau**, 701 Brickell Avenue (Mon–Fri 9am–5pm; ☎539-3000), near downtown. The **post office** in downtown Miami is at 500 NW Second Avenue (zip code 33101).

City Transport

Driving around Miami is the most practical way to get about, and the major car rental firms have desks at the airport. However, **bus** routes do cover the entire city – there are usually two services an hour between 6am and 7pm on weekdays, fewer at weekends; on busy routes, such as Miami–Miami Beach, buses run until 10pm or 11pm. The flat-rate single-journey bus fare is $1; transfers cost 25¢ extra.

Metrorail trains (5.30am–midnight) run along a single line between the northern suburbs and South Miami; useful stops are Government Center (for downtown), Coconut Grove, and Douglas Road or University (for Coral Gables). Single-journey fares are $1. Downtown Miami is also ringed by the **Metromover** (flat fare, 25¢), a daytime monorail loop that doesn't cover much ground but gives a bird's-eye view.

For regular public transport use, buy a one-month **Metropass** – $50 from any shop displaying the *Metro-Dade Transit* sign. **Information** and free **route maps and timetables** can be had at the *Transit Service Center* (daily 7am–6pm; ☎638-6700) inside the Metro Dade Center in downtown Miami.

Taxis, Cycling and Tours

Taxis are abundant, and the trip from downtown to Coconut Grove or Miami Beach is about $8. *Central Taxicab* (☎534-06940) and *Metro Taxi* (☎888-8888) are fairly reliable. Otherwise, get the free leaflet, *Miami on Two Wheels,* from the CVB and **rent a bike** for $12–25 per day from one of several outlets: at Miami Beach, try *Miami Beach Cycle Center,* 923 W 39th Street (☎531-4161).

For an informed stroll, take one of **Dr Paul George's Walking Tours** ($13; ☎375-1625), or try the shorter **Art Deco walking tour** of South Miami Beach, which begins each Saturday at 10.30am from the Art Deco Welcome Center, 661 Washington Avenue ($5; ☎672-2014). The ninety-minute **Old Town Trolley Tour** leaves from the Bayside Marketplace every thirty minutes (daily 10am–4pm; $7).

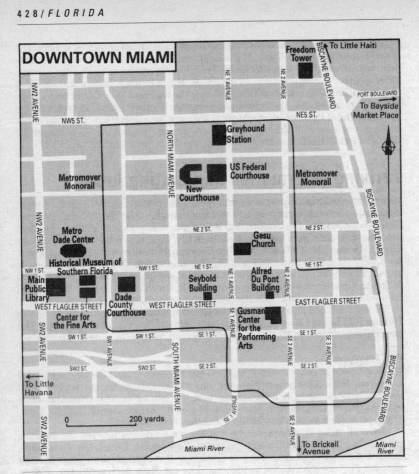

DOWNTOWN MIAMI

The City

Many of **MIAMI**'s districts are officially cities in their own right, and each has a background and character very much its own. The obvious starting point is **downtown Miami**, the small, bustling nerve centre of the city, overlooked by futuristic office buildings. Beyond downtown, Miami spreads out in a broad arc to the west and south. **Little Havana** is still one of the most intriguing areas, rich with Latin American looks and sounds, and immediately south the spacious boulevards of **Coral Gables** are as impressive now as they were in the Twenties, when the district set new standards in town planning. South of downtown, **Coconut Grove** is currently Miami's trendiest quarter, with a plethora of neatly appointed streetside cafes to linger in. Make time, too, for **Key Biscayne**: a smart, secluded island community with some beautiful beaches, five miles off the mainland but easily reached by causeway. In varying degrees, all twelve miles of **MIAMI BEACH** are worth seeing – it's excellent for sunbathing and swimming throughout – but only **the South Beach** will hold your attention for long. Here, rows of tastefully restyled Thirties Art Deco buildings have become the chic gathering places for the city's fashionable faces.

Downtown Miami

Don't try to relax in **DOWNTOWN MIAMI**: humanity storms down its short streets, rippling the gaudy awnings of cut-price electronics, clothes and jewellery stores, easing up only to gulp down a spicy snack and a mango juice from a roadside fast-food stand. Since the early Sixties, the predominantly Spanish-speaking businesses of downtown's square mile have reaped the benefits of any boost in South or Central American economies. Only some solid US public architecture and whistle-blowing traffic cops remind you that you're still in Florida and not on the main drag of a Latin American capital.

Nowhere is better for a first taste of downtown Miami than **Flagler Street**, very much the loudest, brightest, busiest strip. Four forbidding Doric columns mark the entrance to the **Dade County Courthouse**, at 73 W Flagler Street. Built in 1926 on the site of an earlier courthouse – one-time venue for public hangings – this was for fifty years Miami's tallest building, its night-time lights showing off a distinctive ziggurat peak. There's little inside the courthouse worth passing the security check for; cross SW First Avenue instead towards the **Metro-Dade Cultural Center**, an ambitious attempt by the architect Philip Johnson to create a post-modern Mediterranean-style piazza. Art shows, historical collections and a library frame the courtyard, but Johnson forgot the power of the south Florida sun: rather than pausing to rest and gossip, most people scamper across the open space towards the nearest shade. Facing the plaza, the **Historical Museum of Southern Florida** (Mon–Wed, Fri & Sat 10am–5pm, Thurs 10am–9pm, Sun noon–5pm; $3) provides a comprehensive peek into the multifaceted past of south Florida. The Seminole section in particular has a strong collection of artefacts.

The Eighties saw the destruction of the decaying buildings beside **Biscayne Boulevard** (part of Hwy-1), on the western edge of downtown, to make way for the **Bayside Marketplace** (Mon–Sat 10am–10pm, Sun noon–8pm), an oversized, pink-coloured shopping mall, enlivened by buskers and food stands. In case you've ever wondered, it was just to the south, on the yacht-filled marina of Bayfront Park of the Americas, that *Miami Vice*'s Sonny Crockett moored his floating home.

Across Biscayne Boulevard, the **Freedom Tower** earned its name by housing the Cuban Refugee Center in the 1960s. Between December 1965 and June 1972, ten planes a week brought over 250,000 Cubans to Miami, allowed to leave the island by Fidel Castro. While US propaganda hailed them as "freedom fighters", most of the arrivals were simply seeking the fruits of capitalism, and, as Castro astutely recognised, any that were seriously committed to overthrowing his regime would be far less troublesome outside Cuba. Most of those who left Cuba this way got their first taste of US bureaucracy at the Freedom Tower – a 1925 building modelled on a Spanish bell tower.

Little Haiti

Roughly a third of Miami's 170,000 **Haitians** live in what's become known as **LITTLE HAITI**, a two-hundred-block area that centres on NE Second Avenue, north of 42nd Street (buses #9 or #10 from downtown). Aside from hearing Haitian Creole on the streets, you'll notice the brightly coloured shops, offices and restaurants. The recently opened *Caribbean Marketplace*, 5927 NE Second Avenue, is an entertaining attempt to satiate tourists' curiosity – proffering a mouth-watering array of tropical fruits and Haitian delicacies, such as fried goat.

South of Downtown: the Miami River and Brickell Avenue

Fifteen minutes' walk from Flagler Street, the **Miami River** marks the southern limit of downtown. At the turn of the century, the millionaire oil baron Henry Flagler extended his railway, which had opened up Florida's east coast, to reach Miami from Palm Beach. His *Royal Palm Hotel* (on the site of today's *Hotel Inter-Continental*) did much to put Miami on the map. One of the landowners was William Brickell, who ran a trading post on the south side of the river, an area now dominated by **Brickell Avenue** – *the* address in 1910s Miami. While the original grand homes have largely disappeared, money is still the avenue's most obvious asset: its half-mile parade of **bank buildings** is the largest grouping of international banks in the US. The rise of the banks was matched by new condominiums of breathtaking design and expense a few blocks further along, which include the most stunning modern building in Miami: **the Atlantis**, at no. 2025, finished in 1983, whose focal point is a gaping square hole through its middle.

Little Havana

The impact of **Cubans** on Miami, unquestionably the largest and most visible ethnic group in the city, has been incalculable. Unlike most Hispanic immigrants to the US, who trade one form of poverty for another, Miami's first Cubans had already tasted the good life when they arrived during the late Fifties and were soon enjoying more of the same here. Some now wield considerable clout in the running of the city.

The initial home of the Miami Cubans was a few miles west of downtown in what became **LITTLE HAVANA**, whose streets, if the tourist brochures are to be believed, are filled by old men in *guayaberas* (billowing cotton shirts) playing dominoes, and exotic restaurants whose walls vibrate to the pulsating rhythms of the homeland. Naturally, the reality is quite different: Little Havana's parks, memorials, shops and food stands all reflect the Cuban experience but the streets are quieter than those of downtown Miami (except during the Little Havana festival in early March). There isn't a great deal actually to see; the appeal of the place is almost all atmosphere.

The neighbourhood's main strip, SW Eighth Street, or **Calle Ocho** (a direct Spanish translation), offers most to see: tiny cups of Cuban coffee are consumed from street-side counters, the odours of cigars being rolled and bread being baked periodically waft across the pavement, and shops sell *santeria* (a Voodoo-like religion of African origin) ephemera beside six-foot-high models of Catholic saints.

The most pertinent place to begin is between Twelfth and Thirteenth avenues, where the simple stone **Brigade 2506 Memorial** remembers those who died at the Bay of Pigs on April 17 1961, during the abortive invasion of Cuba by a group of US-trained Cuban soldiers. Depending on who tells the story, the action was either merely ill-conceived, or else highlighted the lack of commitment to Cuba by the US. Veterans of the landing gather here for each anniversary: a strange sight of middle-aged men dressed in combat fatigues making all-night-long pledges of patriotism. A few yards

---

CUBANS IN MIAMI

During the mid-Fifties, when opposition to Cuba's Batista dictatorship began to assert itself, a trickle of Cubans started arriving in a predominantly Jewish section of Miami called Riverside. The trickle became a flood when Fidel Castro took power, and the area became Little Havana, populated by the affluent Cuban middle classes who had most to lose under communism. The second great Cuban influx into Miami was quite different, the **Mariel boatlift** bringing 125,000 islanders from the Cuban port of Mariel to Miami in May 1980. These arrivals were poor and uneducated, and a fifth of them were fresh from Cuban jails – incarcerated for criminal rather than political crimes. Bluntly, Castro had dumped his misfits on Miami.

Many Miami Cubans still see themselves as exiles – though few would seriously think about returning, whatever regime governed Cuba. Within the complexities of **exile politics**, passions run high. In Miami, Cubans have been killed for being *suspected* of advocating dialogue with Castro, and the Museum of Cuban Arts and Culture (1300 SW Twelfth Street) was bombed in 1989 for displaying the work of Castro-approved artists. It's hard to see the feud ending until the more fanatical factions die out, Castro himself expires, and Cuba emerges from its isolation from the rest of the world.

away is the **Maximo Lopez Domino Park**, filling a corner of Fourteenth Avenue, to which entry to the open-air tables is (quite illegally) restricted to men over 55; one place where you *will* see old men in *guayaberas* playing dominoes.

Coral Gables

All of Miami's constituent cities are fast to assert their individuality, but none has a greater case than **CORAL GABLES**, south of Little Havana. Twelve square miles of broad boulevards, leafy side streets and Spanish and Italian architecture form a cultured setting for a cultured community. Coral Gables' creator was a local aesthete, **George Merrick**, who raided street names from a Spanish dictionary to plan the plazas, fountains and carefully aged stucco-fronted buildings. Following the first land sale in 1921, $150 million poured in, which Merrick channelled into the biggest advertising campaign ever known. But while Coral Gables took shape, the Florida property boom ended. Merrick was wiped out; he died as Miami's postmaster in 1942. Coral Gables never lost its good looks, and remains an impressive place to explore. Merrick wanted people to know they'd arrived somewhere special, and eight grand **entrances** were planned on the main approach roads (though only four were completed).

The best way into Coral Gables is along NW 22nd Street. Once across Douglas Road, this becomes the **Miracle Mile**, conceived by Merrick as the centrepiece of his city's business district. Dominated by department stores, travel agents, and a staggering number of bridal shops, the Miracle Mile (actually only half a mile long) becomes increasingly exclusive as you proceed west – note the arcades and balconies, and the spirals and peaks of the **Colonnade Building**, no. 133–169, completed in 1926 to accommodate George Merrick's office. Further west, along Coral Way, the **Coral Gables House**, no. 907 (Sun & Wed 1–4pm; $1), was Merrick's boyhood home, restored in the 1970s. In 1899, when George was 12, his family arrived here from New England to run a 160-acre fruit and vegetable farm. The farm was so successful that the house quickly grew from a wooden shack into an elegant dwelling of coral rock and gabled windows (a combination that inspired the name of the future city).

Merrick's crowning achievement was the **Biltmore Hotel**, 1200 Anastasia Avenue, wrapping its broad wings around the southern end of De Soto Boulevard, its 26-storey tower visible across much of low-lying Miami. Everything about the *Biltmore* was over-the-top: 25ft-high fresco-coated walls, vaulted ceilings, immense fireplaces and custom-loomed rugs. In 1986, $40 million was spent on restoration, but the company involved collapsed and the great building remains closed, with no definite future.

Coconut Grove

A stamping ground of down-at-heel artists and writers through the Sixties and Seventies, **COCONUT GROVE** has been turned by a business-led revitalisation into a hangout for the glitterati: art galleries, fashionable cafes and restaurants, and towering bay-view apartments mark its central section. But Coconut Grove also retains much of value from its formative years. A century ago, a strange mix of Bahamian salvagers and New England intellectuals laid the foundations of a fiercely individual community, separated from the fledgling city of Miami by a dense wedge of tropical foliage.

In 1914, farm machinery mogul James Deering blew $15 million on recreating a sixteenth-century Italian villa within this jungle. A thousand-strong workforce completed his **Villa Viscaya**, 3251 South Miami Avenue (daily 9.30am–4.30pm; $8), in just two years. Deering's madly eclectic art collection, and the concept that the villa should appear to have been inhabited for 400 years, results in a thunderous clash of Baroque, Renaissance, Rococo and Neoclassical fixtures and fittings, and even the landscaped **gardens**, with their fountains and sculptures, aren't spared the pretensions. Vulgar as it is, Villa Viscaya is one of Miami's better sights, and is rightly one of the most visited. **Guided tours** leave frequently from the entrance loggia and provide solid background, after which you're free to explore at leisure.

Hints of major money in the district give way to blatant statements of wealth the closer you get to central Coconut Grove. The marina on **Dinner Key** sports lines of $100,000 yachts, and the neighbouring **Coconut Grove Exhibition Center** is usually consumed by top-of-the-range car and interior furnishing shows. It was at the Dinner Key Auditorium (a forerunner of the Exhibition Center) in 1969 that rock legend **Jim Morrison**, singer with the Doors, dropped his leather trousers to expose his private parts during the band's first – and last – Florida show, bringing the band more infamy than they knew what to do with.

Key Biscayne

A compact, immaculately manicured community, decorated by rows of coconut palms, **KEY BISCAYNE**, five miles off mainland Miami, is a great place to live – if you can afford it. The moneyed of Miami fill the island's upmarket homes; Richard Nixon had a presidential winter house here. The only way onto Key Biscayne is along the four-mile **Rickenbacker Causeway** ($1 toll), a continuation of SW 26th Road just south of downtown, which soars high above Biscayne Bay, giving a gasp-inducing view of the Brickell Avenue skyline. As well as by car, you can cross by bike, bus (#B), or on foot.

Crandon Park Beach, a mile along Crandon Boulevard (the continuation of the main road from the causeway), is one of the finest landscaped beaches in the city. Three miles of yellow-brown beach line fringe this grassy, palm-dotted park, and give access to a sandbar enabling knee-depth wading far from shore.

Crandon Boulevard terminates at the entrance to the **Bill Baggs Cape Florida State Recreation Area**, four hundred wooded acres covering the southern extremity of Key Biscayne. An excellent swimming **beach** lines the Atlantic-facing side of the park, and a boardwalk cuts around the wind-bitten sand dunes towards the **Cape Florida lighthouse**, built in the 1820s. Only with the ranger-led **tour** (daily except Tues at 10.30am, 1pm, 2.30pm & 3.30pm; $1) can you climb through the 95ft-high structure – attacked by Seminoles in 1836 and nobbled by Confederate soldiers to disrupt Union shipping during the Civil War – which now serves as a navigational beacon.

Miami Beach

A long slender arm of land between Biscayne Bay and the Atlantic Ocean, three miles off mainland Miami, **MIAMI BEACH** was an ailing fruit farm in the 1910s when its Quaker owner, John Collins, formed an unlikely partnership with a flashy entrepreneur called Carl Fisher. With Fisher's money, Biscayne Bay was dredged. The muck raised from its murky bed provided the landfill to transform this wildly vegetated barrier island into a carefully sculptured landscape of palm trees, hotels and tennis courts.

Occupying the southernmost three miles, the one genuinely exciting part of Miami Beach is the **SOUTH BEACH**, with its pastel-coloured Art Deco buildings. The hundreds of these late-Thirties gems, concentrated between 5th and 23rd streets, are best assessed along **Ocean Drive**, where a line of revamped hotels have made much of their design heritage. Swarms of photographers and film crews zoom in on what has become – thanks to the visuals of *Miami Vice* and the fashion photography of Bruce Weber – the hottest high-style backdrop in the world.

Socially, the South Beach is unsurpassed. By day, ravers soak up the rays on the beach; by night, the ten blocks of Ocean Drive are the heart and soul of the biggest party in Miami, as chic terrace cafes spill across the specially widened sidewalk. Just a few blocks from Ocean Drive, the streets are much less photogenic, still bearing the scars of the poverty-stricken Seventies. Provided you stick to the main streets and exercise the usual caution, however, none of the South Beach is unduly dangerous.

Accommodation

Though Miami's small size means that you can stay just about anywhere and not feel isolated, most **hotels** and **motels** are on **Miami Beach**, an ideal base for nightlife and beachlife. Reckon on spending from $40–75 during the summer, and $60–85 during the winter. **Downtown Miami** has few affordable rivals to the expense-account chain hotels; **Coral Gables** is appealing but seldom cheap; and the stylish high-rises of **Coconut Grove** are a jet-setters' preserve. Budget alternatives include a couple of **bed and breakfast inns**, and the **youth hostel** in Miami Beach. Contact the *Bed and Breakfast Company*, PO Box 262, South Miami 33243 (☎661-3270), and note that B&B space is always at a premium, so make a booking as far ahead as possible.

Colony Hotel, 736 Ocean Drive, South Miami Beach (☎673-0088). Beautifully refurbished Art Deco delight. Singles and doubles from $95.

Double Tree at Coconut Grove, 2649 S Bayshore Drive, Coconut Grove (☎1-800/528-0444). Elegant high-rise, a 15-min walk from the area's cafes and bars. Singles $120, doubles $130.

Gables Inn, 730 S Dixie Hwy, Coral Gables (☎661-7999). Basic but clean; singles and doubles $45.

The Golden Sands, 6910 Collins Ave, Central Miami Beach (☎1-800/932-0333). Mostly filled by package-holidaying Europeans, but likely to have cheap deals. Singles $55, doubles $60–70.

Hostel International of Miami Beach, at the *Clay Hotel*, 406 Española Way, South Miami Beach (☎534-2988). Dorm-beds for $10 ($13 for non-IYHA-members). Also private rooms in the hotel proper; singles $20, doubles $28.

Hotel Place St Michel, 162 Alcazar Ave, Coral Gables (☎444-1666). Small, romantic hideaway, with pastel decor and European antiques. Rate includes breakfast. Singles $90, doubles $105.

Howard Johnson, 200 SE Second Ave, downtown (☎1-800/654-2000). Standard chain-hotel but the lowest-priced rooms this close to the heart of downtown Miami. Single $90, double $100.

Leonard Beach Hotel, 54 Ocean Drive, South Miami Beach (☎532-2412). Stamping ground of crazed artists and bohemians, with strong gay patronage. Singles $35, doubles $40.

Park Central, 640 Ocean Drive, South Miami Beach (☎538-1611). Among the best of the Art Deco piles, retaining ceiling fans alongside regular air conditioning. Single and doubles $85–135.

Riverparc, 100 SE Fourth St, downtown Miami (☎374-5100). A good choice, delectably positioned beside the Miami River. All rooms are suites with small kitchens. From $90.

Eating

Apart from seafood – every bit as good as you'd expect so close to tropical waters – **Cuban** food is what Miami does best, and a meal in one of the innumerable family-run diners will be a fraction of the price of an identical meal at one of the fancier Cuban restaurants (mostly in Little Havana and Coral Gables) now being discovered by the nation's food critics. **Haitian** cooking is the current city rage, while the strong Caribbean and Latin American elements in the city are further acknowledged by Argentinian, Jamaican, Nicaraguan and Peruvian cooking.

Aux Palmistes Chez Julie, 6820 NE Second Ave, Little Haiti (☎759-8527). Where Little Haiti dines on home-cooked fried pork, goat and fish. Closed Mon.

Ayestaran, 706 SW 27th Ave, Little Havana (☎649-4982). Long a favourite Cuban restaurant among those in the know, especially good value for its $5 daily specials.

Bimini Grill, 620 NE 78th St, downtown (☎758-9154). Florida bayou-style food in a wooden shack on a river bank: barbecued meats and Caribbean conch fritters among the treats.

Captain Dick's Tackle Shack, 3381 Pan American Drive, Coconut Grove (☎854-5871). In the shadow of Miami City Hall: filling seafood and salads all at rock-bottom prices.

Don't Say Sandwich to Me, 1331 Washington Ave, Miami Beach (☎532-6700). Serves every quick eat imaginable – and cheap beer after 4pm. Cheap Sunday brunch, too. Open 24 hours.

El Corral, 3545 Coral Way, Coral Gables (☎444-8272). An appealingly priced Nicaraguan eatery where anything that isn't beef isn't taken seriously – carnivores' heaven.

El Inka, 1756 SW Eighth St, Little Havana (☎845-0243). The city's oldest and best Peruvian restaurant, famed for its spicy meats and seafood, and doing extraordinary things with squid.

News Café, 800 Ocean Drive, Miami Beach (☎538-6397). Fashionable sidewalk cafe with front-row seating for the South Beach promenade. Weekends open 24hrs.

Rita's Italian Restaurant, 7232 Biscayne Blvd, downtown (☎757-9470). Family-run Italian diner with check tablecloths, hearty portions and good prices – and an owner inclined to burst into song.

Sundays on the Bay, 5420 Biscayne Blvd, Key Biscayne (☎361-6777). The biggest and most enjoyable brunch in Miami; make a reservation to avoid queueing.

Versailles, 3555 SW Eighth St, Little Havana (☎444-0240). Chandeliers, mirrored walls, a great atmosphere, and wonderful inexpensive Cuban food.

Wolfie's, 2038 Collins Ave, Miami Beach (☎538-6626). Long-established deli drawing late-night clubbers – served generous helpings by waitresses with beehive hairdos. Open 24 hours.

Drinking, Nightlife and Entertainment

Miami folk usually **drink** in restaurants, clubs and discos, but some of the bars and pubs listed below are suited to an early-evening tipple, and others make prime vantage points to watch the city's posers come and go. Miami's **clubs** are rated as among the hippest in the world; the novelty may soon fade, but for the time being there's an air of excitement. The **salsa** or **merengue** (a slinky dance music from the Caribbean) clubs, hosted by Spanish-speaking DJs, are especially worth tracking down.

Miami is virtually impossible to **get around** at night without a car or taxi, but most of the action takes place at the walkable South Beach. The Friday issue of the *Miami Herald* carries comprehensive weekend entertainment **listings**; the free weeklies *New Times* and the *South Beach Antenna* are more reliable on local cafes and clubs. The key source of **gay and lesbian info** is the free *TWN* (*The Weekly News*), available from many of the bars and clubs around Coconut Grove and the South Beach.

If you fancy the local **sports** scene, the *Miami Dolphins*, Florida's only professional football team, play at the Joe Robbie Stadium, sixteen miles northwest of downtown Miami (box office Mon–Fri 10am–6pm; ☎620-2578).

Bars and pubs

American Classics, at the *Quality Inn*, 8701 Collins Ave, Miami Beach (☎865-6661). A classic-car fanciers' spot; snuggle down inside booths that once formed part of Fifties American autos.

Bayside Seafood Restaurant, 3501 Rickenbacker Causeway, Key Biscayne (☎361-0808). Friendly beer-drinking crowd beside the bay.

Coco Loco's, in the *Sheraton*, 495 Brickell Ave, near downtown Miami (☎373-6000). No better place to round off a day downtown; pricey drinks, but for a dollar you help yourself to a big buffet.

Coyote, at the *Leonard Beach Hotel*, 54 Ocean Drive, Miami Beach (☎538-6955). Tiki bar by the ocean, favoured hangout of artily inclined South Beach gays.

Firehouse Four, 1000 S Miami Ave, downtown (☎379-1923). Filled by day with expense-account eaters, in the evening Miami's oldest fire station building makes a fine spot for a drink.

Monty's Bayshore Restaurant, 2560 S Bayshore Drive, Coconut Grove (☎858-1431). Drinkers often outnumber the diners, drawn here by the gregarious mood and the views across the bay.

Rolo's, 38 Ocean Drive, Miami Beach (☎532-2662). Over a hundred international beers to sample in the company of a tanned, surfing crowd.

Shagnasty's Saloon & Eatery, 638 S Miami Ave, near downtown Miami (☎381-8970). The hip yuppie's happy-hour hangout, with free appetisers and many discounted drinks.

Clubs and discos

Bonfire, 1060 NE 79th St, Little Haiti (☎756-0200). Smooth and danceable salsa. Wed–Sun; $2–5.

Club Boomerang, 323 23rd St, Miami Beach (no phone). The coolest and most crowded club on the South Beach, with a Sixties vibe and silver/gold walls. Thurs–Sun; cover $5.

Club Passion, 1235 Washington Ave, Miami Beach (☎531-8080). Cavernous disco often with live bands, laser lights, and many drinks specials; $5–15.

Club Tipico Dominicano, 1344 NW 36th St, Little Havana (☎634-7819). Top merengue DJ hosting the sessions Fri–Sun; $5.

Rockers Café, 216 Española Way, Miami Beach (☎537-7701). Top-notch reggae disco except on Fri and Sat which see hip-hop and Deep House sounds respectively; free–$5.

Warsaw Ballroom, 1450 Collins Ave, Miami Beach (☎1-800/9-WARSAW). While not exclusively gay, this is the busiest and biggest gay disco in town; lesbian night Wed.

Live music

In a city that still goes crazy over the studio-based latin-pop of local girl Gloria Estefan, you might not expect to find a **live music** scene at all in Miami. In fact, an impressive number of **venues** – many of them poky clubs or the back rooms of restaurants – host bands throughout the week. **Reggae** is strong; Miami has a sizeable Jamaican population, and there are regular appearances by local as well as flown-in acts.

Aux Palmistes Chez Julie, 6820 NE Second Ave, Little Haiti (☎759-8527). Great live Haitian music from 10pm to 4am on Fri & Sat. Free–$5.

Hungry Sailor, 3064½ Grand Ave, Coconut Grove (☎444-9359). Reggae bands fill the tiny corner stage of this would-be English pub almost every night. Free–$2.

Peacock Café, 2977 McFarlane Rd, Coconut Grove (☎442-8833). Back-room lounge features jazz, blues and occasional rock acts. Cover varies.

Rockers Café, 216 Española Way, Miami Beach (☎537-7701). Big names from Jamaica, top Miami talent, and, when there's no live band, a rootsy reggae disco. Free–$20.

Tobacco Road, 626 S Miami Ave, downtown Miami (☎374-1198). Earthy R&B from some of the country's finest exponents. Free–$5.

THE FLORIDA KEYS

Fiction, films and folklore have given the **Florida Keys** – a hundred-mile string of islands running from the southeastern corner of the state to within ninety miles of Cuba – an image of glamorous intrigue that they don't really deserve. Instead, fishing, snorkelling and diving dominate, and are ruthlessly hawked at every opportunity. Here and there some idiosyncratic history rears its head, and there are terrific untainted natural areas, particularly the **Florida Reef**, a great band of living coral just a few miles off the coast. But the various keys are really only stops on the way to fascinating **Key West**, once the richest town in the US and the final dot of the North American continent before a thousand miles of ocean. Here you'll find plenty of congenial bars in which to waste away the hours, watching the famous spectacular **sunsets**.

Travelling through the Keys could hardly be easier. There's just one route all the way through to Key West: the **Overseas Highway (US-1)**. The road is punctuated by **mile markers (MM)** – posts on which mileage is marked, starting with MM127 just south of Miami and finishing with MM0 in Key West. The motels and restaurants strung along the highway often use the mile markers as addresses.

Key Largo

The first and largest of the keys, **Key Largo** is also the dullest, though it does boast a fine opportunity to visit the Florida Reef, at the **John Pennecamp Coral Reef State Park** at MM102.5 (daily 8am–sunset; cars $2, passengers, pedestrians and cyclists $1) in North Key Largo. This is a protected 78-square-mile section of living coral reef, which experts rate as one of the most beautiful in the world. Certainly, the eulogistic descriptions you'll hear are rarely exaggerations. If possible, take the **snorkelling tour**

The telephone **area code** for the Florida Keys is ☎305.

(9am, noon & 3pm; $18–20), or the **guided scuba dive** (10am & 1pm; $30), though less demanding is the **glass-bottomed boat tour** (9am, noon & 3pm; $11–12).

Even from the glass-bottomed boat, you're virtually certain to spot lobsters, angelfish, eels and jellyfish along the reef, and shoals of silvery minnows stalked by angryfaced barracudas. The reef itself is a delicate living thing, composed of millions of minute coral polyps extracting calcium from the sea water and growing from one to sixteen feet every 1000 years. Sadly, it's far easier to spot signs of death rather than life: white patches show where a carelessly dropped anchor, or diver's hand, has scraped away the protective mucus layer and left the coral susceptible to terminal disease.

Key Largo and Tavernier

South of the park, the people of Rock Harbor recognised a good thing when they saw one and changed the name of their community to **KEY LARGO** after the success of the 1948 film in which Humphrey Bogart and Lauren Bacall grappled with Florida's best-known features – crime and hurricanes. Yet the movie's title was chosen for no other reason than it suggested somewhere exotic, and the film, though set here, was almost entirely shot in Hollywood. This being the case, the real town of Key Largo is totally boring; if you want a place to stop, keep moving ten miles on to the far more homely **TAVERNIER**. Here, the **Harry Harris Park**, off the Overseas Highway along Burton Drive, often has free live music at weekends around its picnic tables.

If you're going to explore North Key Largo and the Coral Reef State Park at length, you'll have to sleep and eat in either Key Largo town or Tavernier. The **Florida Keys Welcome Center**, 103400 Overseas Highway (Mon–Sat 9am–5pm; ☎1-800/822-1088) has more information. Local **motels** offer diving packages as well as rooms: try *Economy Efficiency*, 103365 Overseas Highway (☎451-4712), $25 to $35 with a two-night minimum; *Sea Farer*, MM97.8 (☎852-5349), beach cottages from $40 to $50; or the *Hungry Pelican*, MM99.5 (☎451-3576), from $35 to $40.

The Middle and Lower Keys

Once over Long Key Bridge, you're into the **Middle Keys**, a sensible base for seeing the Keys without uprooting yourself too often. The largest of several islands, Key Vaca holds the nucleus of the area's major settlement, **MARATHON**. On first sight it's a town as uninspiring as Key Largo, but it does at least have a couple of small **beaches**. Sombrero Beach, along Sombrero Beach Road (off the Overseas Highway near MM50), has good swimming waters and shaded picnic tables; Key Colony Beach four miles north is prettier and quieter.

Marathon has several well-equipped **resorts**, such as *Sombrero*, 19 Sombrero Boulevard (☎1-800/433-8660), or *Banana Bay*, 4590 Overseas Highway (☎1-800/488-6636), and there's a good supply of cheaper **motels**, too, in the neighbourhood. For **eating**, *Herbie's*, 6350 Overseas Highway, is justly busy on account of its inexpensive seafood, while *Porky's Too BBQ*, MM45, provides platefuls of beef and chicken.

The Lower Keys

Starkly different to their northerly neighbours, the **Lower Keys** are quiet, heavily wooded and predominantly residential. Built on a limestone rather than a coral base, these islands have a flora and fauna that's very much their own.

The first place of consequence you'll hit after crossing Seven Mile Bridge is **Bahia Honda State Recreation Area** (daily 8am–sunset; cars $2; passengers, pedestrians and cyclists $1), one of the Keys' prettiest places. Its lagoon has a beckoning natural **beach** and two-tone ocean waters. The best diversion, though, is a visit to **Looe Key Marine Sanctuary**, signposted from the Overseas Highway on Ramrod Key – a five-square-mile protected reef area, in every part the equal of the John Pennecamp Coral Reef State Park (see p.435). The **sanctuary office** (Mon–Fri 8am–5pm; ☎1-800/942-5397) can provide free maps, but to visit the reef you'll need the services of a dive shop; the nearest is the neighbouring *Looe Key Dive Center* (☎1-800/942-5397).

The main Lower Keys settlement is **Big Pine Key**, where you'll find the **Chamber of Commerce**, at MM31.9 (Mon–Fri 9am–5pm, Sat 9am–3pm; ☎872-2411). Of the **motels**, *Looe Key Reef Resort*, MM27.5 (☎872-2215), is ideal for visiting the marine sanctuary, and costs upwards of $55. The **B&Bs** ($80 a night) along Long Beach Drive on Big Pine Key make a cosy alternative, but book early: *Deer Run*, MM32.5 (☎872-2015), *Barnacle*, MM32.5 (☎872-3298), and *Casa Grande*, 33MM (☎872-2878).

Key West

Much closer to Cuba than mainland Florida, **KEY WEST**'s links with the rest of the US often seem very tenuous indeed. Famed for their tolerant attitudes and laid-back life-styles, the thirty thousand islanders seem adrift in a great expanse of sea and sky, and – despite a million tourists per year – the place resonates with an individual spirit that hits you the instant you arrive. Yet as wild as it may at first appear, Key West today is far from being the dropouts' mecca that it was just a decade ago. Much of the sleaziness has been brushed away through a steady process of restoration, setting the course for the advent of a sizeable holiday industry. But Key West is still resolutely non-conformist – a deliciously seductive place – and in particular, the liberal manners have stimulated a large **gay** influx. The sense of isolation from the mainland is best appreciated by adjusting to the mellow pace: amble the streets, make meals last for hours, and pause regularly for refreshment in the numerous bars.

Arriving and Getting Around

Both the **Welcome Center** on North Roosevelt Boulevard (daily 9am–5pm; ☎296-4444) and the **Greater Key West Chamber of Commerce**, 402 Wall Street (Mon–Fri 8.30am–5pm, Sat & Sun 9am–5pm; ☎294-2587) can give precise dates for Key West's annual **festivals**, the best being the *Old Island Days* (Jan–March) celebrating Key West's history, the *Conch Republic Celebration* in April, and the *Fantasy Fest* in late October, a gay-dominated version of Mardi Gras. A number of weekly **free publications** list current events, like *Island Life* and the gay-oriented *What's Happening*. The **Greyhound** station is at 615½ Duval Street (☎296-9072); confusingly, its entrance is on Simonton Street, a block east of Duval Street itself.

It's best to see the narrow streets of the mile-square Old Town – which contains virtually everything that you'll want to see – by **walking**. You could do it on foot in little more than a day, though dashing about isn't the way to enjoy the place. **Bikes** can be rented from *Bubba's*, 705 Duval Street, or the youth hostel (see p.439).

Around the Old Town

Anyone who saw Key West two decades ago would now barely recognise the Old Town's main promenade, **Duval Street**. Teetering just on the safe side of seedy for many years, much of the street has been transformed into a tourist strip of boutiques and beachwear shops. It's never boring, and the mile-long swathe it cuts right through the Old Town makes it easy to regain bearings after exploring the side streets.

The **Wrecker's Museum**, 322 Duval Street (daily 10am–4pm; $2), gives some background to the industry on which Key West's earliest good times were based: salvaging cargo from foundering vessels. Judging by the choice furniture that fills the house, Captain Watlington, the wrecker who lived here from the 1830s, did pretty well. Further up, at 516 Duval Street, the **San Carlos Opera House** (daily 9am–5pm; $3) has played a leading role in Cuban exile life since it opened as the San Carlos Institute in 1871. Financed by a grant from the Cuban government, the present building dates from 1924 and holds a commendable account of Key West history and Cuban life in the town. Across its grounds are spread soil from Cuba's six provinces, and a cornerstone which was taken from the tomb of Cuban independence campaigner, José Martí.

You'll know when you get near the southern end of Duval Street because everything, whether house, motel, filling station or restaurant, advertises itself as "the Southernmost . . .". Accurately, the **southernmost point** in Key West, and consequently in the continental US, is to be found at the intersection of Whitehead and South streets, and there's a daft-looking buoy to mark the spot.

In the early 1800s, thousands of dollars' worth of salvage was landed at the piers, stored in the warehouses, and flogged at the auction houses on **Mallory Square**, just west of the northern end of Duval Street. By day, the square is a plain souvenir market, with overpriced ice cream, trinkets and T-shirts, but at night there's a tourist-oriented (but fun) **sunset celebration**, when buskers and fire-eaters create a merry backdrop to the sinking of the sun. More entertaining than the square during the day is the small gathering of sea life inside the adjacent **Key West Aquarium**, 1 Whitehead Street (daily 10am–6pm, winter until 7pm; $5), where porcupine fish and longspine squirrel fish leer out from behind glass. Small sharks are known to jump out of their open tanks during the **guided tours**, conducted roughly every two hours.

In **Mel Fisher's Treasure Exhibit**, 200 Greene Street (daily 10am–6pm; $4), not far from the aquarium, an impressive emerald cross, a liftable gold bar, and countless vases and daggers are displayed alongside the obligatory cannon, pulled up from two seventeenth-century wrecks. Fisher was running a surf shop in California before he arrived in Florida armed with ancient Spanish sea charts and, in 1985, discovered the *Neustra Señora de Atocha* and *Santa Margarita*, both sunk during a hurricane in 1622, forty miles southeast of Key West. The haul was said to be worth millions of dollars.

For all the atmosphere of the streets and alleys, Key West's most popular tourist attraction is the **Hemingway House**, at 907 Whitehead Street (daily 9am–5pm; $5). The compulsory half-hour **guided tours** deal, sadly, more in fantasy than fact: although Ernest Hemingway owned this large, vaguely Moorish house for thirty years, he lived in it for barely ten, and even the authenticity of the furnishings is disputed by his former secretary. Hemingway bought the house in 1931, when it was seriously run-down, and some of the writer's most acclaimed novels, such as *For Whom the Bell Tolls* and *To Have and Have Not*, were produced in the study (in an outhouse which Hemingway entered by way of a rope bridge). Divorced in 1940, Hemingway boxed up his manuscripts and moved them to a back room at the original *Sloppy Joe's* (see opposite) before heading off for a house in Cuba with his new wife, journalist Martha Gellhorn.

Accommodation

It's essential to make a **reservation** in Key West during winter, either by calling the place directly, or by booking through the free *Key West Reservation Service*, 628 Fleming Street (daily 9am–5.30pm; ☎294-7713).

Blue Parrot Inn, 916 Elizabeth St (☎296-0033). Guest house with rooms for $35–40.

Caribbean House, 226 Petronia St (☎1-800/543-4518). Relaxed hotel. Rooms are $40–80.

Cypress House, 601 Caroline St (☎294-6969). Best of the predominantly gay male guest houses, though *Big Ruby's* at 409 Applerouth Lane (☎296-2323) is a close second. $50–75.

Key West Hostel, 718 South St (☎296-5719). Youth hostel; members $12, others $15.

Marlinn, 811 Simonton St (☎296-3336). Well-priced guest house. Rooms $50–70.

Southern Cross, 326 Duval St (☎1-800/533-4891). Dowdy hotel, bang in the centre of town, with rooms from $40–80.

Sweet Caroline, 529 Caroline St (☎296-5173). A women-only guest house, for $40–55.

Tilton Hilton, 511 Angela St (☎294-8697). Hostel accommodation for $30 per night.

Eating

In Key West, it's de rigeur to sample **conch fritter** – it turns up on most menus, although the stand on the corner of Duval and Fleming streets does the best in town for under two dollars. Also, if you've not tried it before, don't leave without tasting **Cuban food**, as there are several excellent restaurants in town.

La Bodega, 829 Simonton St. Mega-sized lunchtime sandwiches.

The Buttery, 1208 Simonton St. Good Florida seafood served in French style. A little pricey.

Café Marquesa, 600 Fleming St. Fiery but affordable specialities from the culinary hot spots of South and Central America.

La Cubanita, 601 Duval St. Decently priced Cuban lunches and dinners.

Dim Sum, 613 Duval St. Spicy dishes from all points east for upwards of $15 a head.

Pigeon House Patio, 301 Whitehead St. Here you'll get a wide-ranging, high-quality menu, and a piano player worth heckling.

Two Friends, 512 Front St. Well-priced steaks, seafood and Dixieland jazz in cosy surroundings.

Drinking and Nightlife

The anything-goes nature of Key West is exemplified by the **bars** which make up the bulk of the island's nightlife. Gregarious, rough-and-ready affairs, often open until 4am and with regular live music, the best bars are grouped around the northern end of Duval Street, no more than a few minutes' stagger from one another.

Bull & Whistle Bar, 224 Duval St. The upstairs balcony overlooks the Duval Street crowds.

Captain Tony's Saloon, at 428 Greene St. Site of the original *Sloppy Joe's* (see below), and once a Hemingway haunt: now reasonably untouristy and likeable.

Greene Parrot, 400 Southard St. A ramshackle and fun bar.

Havana Docks, at the *Pier House Hotel*, 1 Duval St. Come here for fabulous views of the sunset.

Margaritaville Café, 500 Duval St. Owned by legendary Florida balladeer, Jimmy Buffett, this rowdy place keeps the alcohol and music flowing.

Sloppy Joe's, 201 Duval St. The town's busiest bar, where a manic throng crashes elbows to live sounds. Hemingway drank here in the late Thirties.

THE EAST COAST

Stretching from the northern fringe of Miami to the very northeastern edge of the state, the Atlantic **east coast** runs for over three hundred miles – largely the sun-soaked Florida of popular imagination, with palm-dotted beaches and warm ocean waves. That said, the first fifty-odd miles of coast are deep within the sway of Miami – back-to-back conurbations often with little to tell them apart. **Fort Lauderdale**, at least, is certainly distinctive, though its reputation for rowdy beach parties is now well out of date. Further north, **Boca Raton**'s hallmark is the Mediterranean Revival architecture seen also in nearby **Palm Beach**, inhabited almost exclusively by multi-millionaires. North of here, though, much of the coast is still substantially free of commercial exploitation – with the single exception of the **Space Coast** centring on the **Kennedy Space Center**. Beyond the excesses of **Daytona Beach**, evidence of

Florida's early European landings are plentiful and are nowhere better displayed than in the comprehensively restored **St Augustine**, where Spaniards established North America's earliest foreign settlement.

By car, the scenic route along the coast is **Hwy-A1A**, which sticks to the ocean side of the **intracoastal waterway**, formed when the rivers dividing the mainland from the barrier islands were joined and deepened during World War II.

Fort Lauderdale

A thinly populated riverside trading camp at the turn of the century, seven miles of palm-shaded white sands and a low-budget Hollywood film later conspired to turn mild-mannered **FORT LAUDERDALE** into a town with a global reputation for rumbustuous beachlife. The 1960 teen-exploitation movie, *Where the Boys Are*, instantly made Fort Lauderdale the US's number one Spring Break venue, drawing hundreds of thousands of students to a frenzy of under-age drinking and lascivious excess. Not surprisingly, this hindered the town's chances of attracting regular tourists, and in the late Seventies the local authorities enacted strict laws to restrict boozing and wild behaviour around the beach. Fort Lauderdale was left dominated by a mix of wealthy retirees and affluent yuppies, desperate to play down the beach-party tag and play up the town's settler-period history.

Anonymous bank buildings and tall glass-fronted offices make a uninspiring initial impression, but lately a multimillion-dollar effort has prettified **downtown Fort Lauderdale** with parks and promenades, linked by the pedestrian **riverwalk** along the north bank of the New River. You can follow the riverwalk to the **Historic District**, where the 1907 **King-Cromartie House** features many then-futuristic fixtures – including the first indoor bathroom in Fort Lauderdale, gleefully pointed out by the period-attired tour guides. To give perspective on the old buildings, the **Historical Society Museum**, 219 SW Second Avenue (Tues–Sat 10am–4pm, Sun 1–4pm; donations), mounts temporary displays and stocks historical books and pamphlets.

Like most, though, you've probably come for the **beach** and its bars, and the action there is still what Fort Lauderdale does best, even if the glory days have been and gone. Leave downtown along **Las Olas Boulevard**, lined by trendy shops, art galleries, restaurants. Once across the arching intracoastal waterway bridge, about two miles on, you're within sight of the ocean and the mood changes appreciably. Where Las Olas Boulevard ends, **beachside Fort Lauderdale** begins – T-shirt, sunscreen and swimwear shops are suddenly everywhere. Along the seafront, **Ocean Boulevard** bore the brunt of Spring Break partying, but only a few beachfront bars suggest the carousing of the past. The sands, though, are by no means deserted or dull – and still get a fair number of whooping students each spring.

Practicalities

All the public transport terminals are in or near downtown: the *Greyhound* **bus** station is at 515 NE Third Street (☎305/764-6551), the **train** and *Tri-Rail* stations two miles west at 200 SW 21st Terrace (☎305/464-8251) – take buses #9, #10 or #81 to the centre. While downtown, get information from the **Convention and Visitors Bureau**, 500 E Broward Boulevard (Mon–Fri 8.30am–5pm; ☎305/765-4466).

The handiest **local bus** service is #11, which runs twice hourly along Las Olas Boulevard between downtown Fort Lauderdale and the beach. Or use the **Water Taxi** (☎305/565-5507), a small boat which will deliver you almost anywhere along Fort Lauderdale's many miles of waterfront; single journeys are $4, an all-day ticket $11.

From May to November, $35-a-night rooms can be found in the cluster of beachside **motels** lining Bayshore Drive and Birch Road; expect to pay $50 to $60 any other time.

Try *Cadillac*, 3101 Bayshore Drive (☎305/467-0568), or *Elton Motel*, 400 N Birch Road (☎305/564-0618). Or use one of the two **youth hostels**: the beachside *Sol Y Mar*, 2839 Vistamar Street (☎305/566-1023; members $12, others $15), or, by US-1, the *International Youth Hostel*, 905 NE 17th Terrace (☎305/467-0452; members $7, others $8). For **eating**, check out *Café 66*, 2001 SE Seventeenth Street, for salads and pasta; *15th Street Fisheries*, 1900 SE Fifteenth Street, for fresh seafood; or *Japanese Village*, 716 E Las Olas Boulevard, for some Far Eastern creations.

Boca Raton

BOCA RATON (literally "the mouth of the rat"), twenty miles north, is populated by the top executives of the numerous local hi-tech companies, such as IBM. More noticeably, it has an over-abundance of Mediterranean Revival architecture, a style prevalent here since the Twenties and kept alive all over the **downtown** area by strict building codes. The town's new structures are compelled to use arched entranceways, fake bell towers and red-tiled roofs whenever possible; which may be too contrived for comfort, but it certainly stands out.

It all goes back to **Addison Mizner**, the "Aladdin of architects" (see the box overleaf), who swept in to Boca Raton on the tide of the Florida property boom, bought 1600 acres of farmland and began selling plots of a future community. Mizner envisioned gondola-filled canals, a luxury hotel, and a great cathedral, but his plan was nipped in the bud by the economic crash and he went back to Palm Beach with his tail between his legs. Bankruptcy notwithstanding, the few buildings he completed left an indelible mark. The million-dollar *Cloister Inn* grew into the present $200-a-night *Boca Raton Resort and Club*, a pink palace of marble columns, sculptured fountains, and carefully aged wood, which can be viewed on guided tours (Dec–April; $4; ☎407/395-8655).

Boca Raton's most explorable **beachside** area is **Spanish River Park** (daily 8am–sunset; cars $2, pedestrians and cyclists free), a couple of miles north of downtown. Most of these fifty acres of vivid vegetation and high-rise greenery are only penetrable on trails through shady thickets.

The **Chamber of Commerce**, 1800 N Federal Highway (Mon–Fri 9am–5pm; ☎407/395-4433), supplies the usual details. The best value **motels** near the beaches, at $45–60, are *Shore Edge*, 425 N Ocean Boulevard (☎407/395-4491), and *Ocean Lodge*, 531 N Ocean Boulevard (☎407/395-7772). You'll save money by sleeping inland at the *Econo Lodge*, 2899 N Federal Highway (☎1-800/624-3606), which charges around $38.

Palm Beach

A small island town of palatial homes and gardens, and streets so clean you could eat your dinner off them, **PALM BEACH** has been synonymous for nearly a century with the kind of lifestyle only limitless loot can buy. The nation's nobs began wintering here in the 1890s, after Henry Flagler brought his East Coast railway south from St Augustine and built two luxury hotels on this then-secluded, palm-filled island. Since then, tycoons, sports aces, aristocrats, rock stars and CIA directors have flocked here, eager to become part of the Palm Beach elite and enjoy its aloofness from mainland – and mainstream – life. Joe Kennedy – father of John, Robert and Edward – bought the so-called Kennedy Compound here in 1933, the focus in 1991 of much prurient interest as the scene of the events which led to the trial of his grandson William Kennedy Smith, who was acquitted of sexual battery.

Summer in Palm Beach is very quiet – and easily the least costly time to stay overnight – but the place gets into motion between November and May. The winter months

ADDISON MIZNER: ARCHITECT OF PALM BEACH

A former miner and prize-fighter, **Addison Mizner** was an unemployed architect when he arrived in Palm Beach in 1918. Inspired by the medieval buildings he'd seen around the Mediterranean, Mizner built the **Everglades Club**, at 356 Worth Avenue – the first public building in Florida in the Mediterranean Revival style. The success of the club, and the house he subsequently built for society bigwig Eva Stotesbury, won Mizner commissions all over Palm Beach as the wintering wealthy decided to swap suites at one of Henry Flagler's hotels for a "million-dollar cottage" of their own.

Brilliant and unorthodox, Mizner's loggias and U-shaped interiors made the most of Florida's pleasant winter temperatures, while his twisting staircases to nowhere became legendary. Mizner used untrained workmen to lay crooked roof tiles, sprayed condensed milk onto walls to create an impression of centuries-old grime, and fired shotgun pellets into wood to imitate worm holes. By the mid-Twenties, Mizner had created the Palm Beach Style, and he later fashioned much of Boca Raton.

see a whirl of elegant balls, fund-raising dinners and charity galas, as well as the polo season – watching a chukka or two is the only time Palm Beach denizens show themselves in the less particular environs of West Palm Beach (on the mainland).

The main residential section of Palm Beach – **the town** – is where you should spend most of your time. Start by strolling by the designer stores and high-class art galleries on **Worth Avenue**, on the southern boundary of town. It's cruised by Rolls Royces, Mercedes and Jaguars, and filled by some of the most upmarket shops and restaurants anywhere in the US. The most appealing aspect of the street is its **architecture**: stucco walls, Romanesque facades, and passageways leading to small courtyards where miniature bridges cross non-existent canals and spiral staircases climb to the upper levels.

Along **Cocoanut Row**, the white Doric columns fronting **Whitehall** (Tues–Sat 10am–5pm, Sun noon–5pm; $5) make it the most overtly ostentatious home on the island: a $4-million wedding present from Henry Flagler to his third wife, Mary Lily Kenan. As in many of Florida's first luxury homes, the interior design was pillaged from the great buildings of Europe: among the 73 rooms are an Italian library, a French salon, a Swiss billiard room, a hallway modelled on St Peter's, and a Louis XV ballroom. All are stuffed with ornamentation, but they lack aesthetic cohesion. Informative 45-minute **free guided tours** depart continuously from the 110-ft hallway, and will leave you giddy with the tales of the earliest Palm Beach excesses.

Practicalities

Even by walking – much the best way to view the moneyed isle – you'll get the measure of Palm Beach in a day. Either drive in along Hwy-A1A from the south, or arrive on foot using one of the two bridges over Lake Worth from West Palm Beach, which is the the nearest **bus** and **train** stop.

The **Chamber of Commerce**, 45 Cocoanut Way (Mon–Fri 9am–5pm; ☎407/655-3282) provides free maps and reliable information. However, you'll need plenty of money to **sleep** in Palm Beach: $200 a night is not an uncommon asking price. Between May and December, *The Chesterfield*, 363 Cocoanut Row (1-800/CHESTR-1), the *Colony*, 155 Hammon Avenue (☎1-800/521-5525), and *The Plaza Inn*, 215 Brazilian Avenue (☎1-800/832-8666), have rooms for $70 to $80; during the winter, the same rooms are around $120. It's far cheaper to stay outside Palm Beach and visit by day.

As for **eating**, *TooJay's*, 313 Poinciana Place, is a bakery and deli with omelettes under $6; *Green's Pharmacy*, 151 N County Road, has a steady supply of diner food; and *Testa's*, 221 Royal Poinciana Way, does exquisite seafood and pasta. If money is no object – and you're dressed to kill – make for *Café L'Europe*, 150 Worth Avenue. Spend less than $50 each in this super-elegant French restaurant and you'll still be hungry.

The Space Coast

The so-called **SPACE COAST**, the base of the country's space industry, occupies a flat, marshy island bulging into the Atlantic. Many visitors are surprised to find that the land from which the Space Shuttle leaves earth is also a sizeable wildlife refuge.

The Kennedy Space Center

Justifiably the biggest attraction in the area, the **Kennedy Space Center** is the nucleus of the US space programme: it's here that space vehicles are developed, tested, and blasted into orbit. Confusingly, the first launches were from the US Air Force base on Cape Canaveral (renamed Cape Kennedy from 1963 to 1973), from which unmanned satellites are still sent up. After the space programme was expanded in 1964, the centre of activity became Merritt Island, between Cape Canaveral and the mainland.

Arrive early at **Spaceport USA** (daily 9am–6pm; free), reached via Hwy-405 from Titusville or Hwy-3 off Hwy-A1A, to avoid the crowds (thinnest on weekends and during May & Sept). The **museum** has everything you might expect: actual mission capsules, space suits, models of satellites, the Viking craft used on Mars, a replica space shuttle flight deck. The firework-like rockets which launched the early space shots stand outside the museum in the **Rocket Garden**. Next door, the **Galaxy Theater** runs a 37-minute *IMAX* movie ($2.75), with dramatic shots from an orbiting space shuttle.

The **"Red" bus tour** (two hours long; $4) is the only way to see the rest of the Merritt Island space complex; buy tickets for it as soon as you arrive. It first crosses the "crawlerway" – the huge tracks along which the space shuttles are wheeled to the launch pad – on the way to the 52-storey **Vehicle Assembly Building** where the shuttles are assembled and fitted with their payloads. With luck, a door may be open and you'll get a slight sense of the innards of what, in terms of volume, is among the world's largest structures. The most impressive part of the bus tour is, perversely, also the most contrived: a simulated Apollo countdown and take-off watched from behind the blinking screens of a mocked-up control room.

For the dates and times of **launches** from the Space Center, phone ☎1-800-SHUTTLE; free passes can be reserved on ☎407/452-2121 (8am–4pm). Almost as good a view can however be had from anywhere within a forty-mile radius of the Space Center.

Staying over: Cocoa Beach

Unquestionably the best base from which to see the Space Coast, **COCOA BEACH** is just a few miles south on a ten-mile strip of shore washed by some of the biggest surfing waves in Florida. **Motel** bargains include *Gateway to the Stars*, 8701 Astronaut Boulevard (☎407/783-0361), at $30 – a price matched in summer by the *Econo Lodge*, 5500 N Atlantic Avenue (☎1-800/446-6900), otherwise $10 to $15 dearer. Of the rest, *Motel 6*, 3701 N Atlantic Avenue (☎407/783-3103), is $35 a single, $6 for each extra person; the *Wakulla Motel*, 3550 N Atlantic Avenue (☎407/783-2230), $40 to $55.

Merritt Island Wildlife Refuge

NASA doesn't have Merritt Island all to itself, but shares it with the **Merritt Island National Wildlife Refuge** (daily 8am–two hours before sunset; free), which allows alligators, armadillos, racoons and bobcats – and one of Florida's greatest gatherings of bird life – to live out their primeval existence beside some of the human world's most advanced technology. Winter is the **best time to visit**, when the island's skies are alive with tens of thousands of migratory birds from the frozen north, and mosquitoes are nowhere to be found. At any other period, and especially in summer, the island's Mosquito Lagoon is worthy of its name; bring ample insect repellent.

Seven miles east of Titusville on Route 406, the six-mile **Black Point wildlife drive** gives a solid introduction to the basics of the island's ecosystem; pick up the informative free leaflet at the entrance. Be sure to do some walking within the refuge, too. Off the wildlife drive, the five-mile **Cruickshank trail** weaves around the edge of the Indian River; or drive a few miles further east along Route 402 – branching from Route 406 just south of the wildlife drive – and tackle the half-mile **Oak Hammock trail**, or the two-mile **Palm Hammock trail**, both accessible from the same car park.

Daytona Beach

The consummate Florida beach town, with rows of T-shirt shops, amusement arcades, wall-to-wall motels and barroom G-string contests passing for high culture, **DAYTONA BEACH** owes its existence to twenty miles of light brown sand where the only pressure is to strip off and enjoy yourself. Each March and April, Daytona is invaded by half a million college kids going through the Spring Break ritual of underage drinking and libido liberation, and by thousands of leather-clad motorcyclists arriving for the early-March Bike Week races at the Daytona International Speedway racetrack. Although costs are higher than usual – and beer, food and accommodation are known to run out – Daytona during Spring Break is an experience few forget. Arriving at any other time, however, reveals Daytona's truer nature: a down-to-earth resort, much smaller and milder-mannered than its downmarket reputation would suggest – but with little to see beyond its famous sands.

Without a doubt, the best thing about Daytona Beach *is* the seemingly limitless **beach**: 500-foot wide at low tide and fading dreamily into the heat haze. Pioneering auto enthusiasts such as Louis Chevrolet, Ransom Olds and Henry Ford came to Daytona's firm sands during the early 1900s to race prototype vehicles beside the ocean. The land speed record was regularly smashed, five times by millionaire British speedster Malcolm Campbell who, in 1935, roared along at 276mph.

When high speeds made racing on Daytona's sands unsafe, the solution was to build the **Daytona International Speedway**, about three miles west of downtown along Volusia Avenue (bus #9) – an ungainly configuration of concrete and steel which has done much to promote Daytona's name around the world. Opened in 1959, it has a capacity of 150,000 and hosts eight major race meetings each year, starting in early February with the **Sunbank 24**, a 24-hour race for GT prototype sports cars. A week or so later begin the qualifying races leading up the biggest event of the year, the **Daytona 500** stock-car race in mid-February. Tickets (the cheapest are $20–25 for cars, $10–15 for bikes) for this sell out well in advance, and you should book accommodation at least six months ahead; for **information** and ticket details: ☎904/253-6711.

Though it can't capture the excitement of a race, the guided minibus **tour** (daily 9am–5pm except on race days; $1) is the only way to get in without buying a ticket, and to witness the remarkable gradient of the curves, which help make this the fastest – 180mph is not uncommon – racetrack in the world.

Practicalities

As Ridgeway Avenue, **US-1** steams through mainland Daytona, passing the *Greyhound* station at no. 138 S (☎904/253-6576). By car, keep to **Hwy-A1A** (known as Atlantic Avenue), which enters beachside Daytona. **Local buses** (☎904/761-7700) connect the two (no night or Sunday services); the bus terminal is at the junction of Palmetto and Volusia avenues in mainland Daytona. A "trolley" runs along the beach.

From mid-May to November, scores of small **motels** on Atlantic Avenue slash their rates to $20 or $30 a room; these rates go up by $10 from December to February, and soar to $60 in March and April. Any of the following makes a good beach base:

Cardinal, no. 738 (☎904/255-6591); *Daytona Shores Inn*, no. 805 (☎904/253-1441); and *Robin Hood*, no. 1150 (☎904/252-8228). The big and superbly positioned **youth hostel** at 140 S Atlantic Avenue (☎904/258-6937) charges members $12, others $15.

A couple of good places for **lunch** include *Julian's*, 88 S Atlantic Avenue, a dimly lit mock-Tahitian lounge with great food, or *Lighthouse Landing*, beside the Ponce Inlet Lighthouse, for fresh fish dishes. For **dinner**, *Gringo's*, 701 N Atlantic Avenue, has decent Mexican fare and *Aunt Catfish's*, 4009 Halifax Drive, offers Southern-style seafood. The nucleus of the **beachside action** is *Penrod's on the Beach*, 600 N Atlantic Avenue, with bars, discos and live music. Simply for a **drink**, the *Boothill Saloon*, 318 Main Street, and *Froggies*, 800 Main Street, are enjoyable, or try *The Oyster Pub*, 555 Seabreeze Boulevard, where there's beer, dirt-cheap oysters and a loud jukebox.

St Augustine

Few places in Florida are as immediately engaging as **ST AUGUSTINE**, which has the size and even some of the looks of a small Mediterranean town. The oldest permanent settlement in the US, with much from its early days still intact, its narrow streets are lined by carefully renovated reminders of Florida's European heritage, while just across the bay are two alluring lengths of beach.

Ponce de León touched ground here in 1513, but it wasn't until Pedro Menéndez de Avilés put ashore on St Augustine's Day in 1565 that European settlement began. The first of many battles with the British came when Sir Francis Drake's ships razed St Augustine in 1586, but Spanish control was only relinquished when Florida was ceded to Britain in 1763. By then the town was an important social and administrative centre, soon to be capital of East Florida. Subsequently, Tallahassee (see p.463) became capital of a unified Florida, and St Augustine's fortunes waned. Expansion largely bypassed the town – a fact inadvertently making possible the **restoration programme**, which has turned this quiet community into the finest historical showcase for miles around.

Arriving and information

The *Greyhound* station, 100 Malaga Street (☎904/829-6281), is a fifteen-minute walk from the centre. St Augustine is best seen **on foot**, but if you're in a hurry, the **sight-seeing train** (tickets from 170 S Marco Avenue; daily 8am–5pm; $7) makes an hour-long circuit of the main landmarks. Not having a car won't cause any problems in St Augustine itself, but getting to the beaches means either a two-mile hike, renting a **bike** from *Buddy Larsen's*, 130 King Street (☎904/824-2402), or calling a **taxi** (☎904/824-8161) – there's no public transport. The **visitor centre**, 10 Castillo Drive (daily 8.30am–5.30pm; ☎904/824-3334), shows a free film on the history of the town, and can fill you in on the area's numerous local festivals. Harbour **cruises** ($6) leave five or six times a day from the City Yacht Pier, near the foot of King Street.

The Old Town

St Augustine's historic area – or **Old Town** – along St George Street and south of the central plaza, carries the well-tended evidence of the Spanish period. St Augustine is small, but there's a lot to see: an early start, around 9am, will give you a lead on the tourist crowds and should enable a good look at almost everything inside a day.

Given the fine state of the **Castillo de San Marcos** (summer daily 9am–6pm; winter 9am–5.15pm; $1; free guided tours hourly), on the northern edge of the Old Town beside the bay, it's difficult to credit that the fortress was started in the late 1600s. Its longevity is down to its design: a diamond-shaped rampart at each corner maximised firepower, and fourteen-foot-thick walls reduced vulnerability to attack. Inside, there's not a lot beyond a small museum and echoing rooms to admire, but venturing along the 35ft-high ramparts gives an unobstructed view over the city.

The eighteenth-century **City Gate** marks the entrance to **St George Street**, once the main thoroughfare and now a tourist-trampled pedestrianised strip. A fair-sized plot at the corner of St George and Cuna Streets is taken up by the **Spanish Quarter Living Museum** (daily 9am–5pm; $2.25). In its eight reconstructed homes and workshops, volunteers disguised as Spanish settlers go about their daily tasks at spinning wheels, anvils and foot-driven wood lathes. It's not at all bad, but try to visit early in the day; crocodile lines of camera-wielding tourists substantially lessen the effect.

In the sixteenth century, the Spanish king decreed that all colonial towns had to be built around a central plaza. St Augustine was no exception: St George Street runs into **Plaza de la Constitucion**, a marketplace from 1598. On the north side of the plaza, the **Basilica Cathedral of St Augustine** (Mon–Fri 5.30am–5pm, Sat & Sun 5.30am–7pm; free) adds a touch of grandeur, although it's largely a Sixties remake of the late eighteenth-century original.

Tourist numbers lessen as you cross **south of the plaza** into a web of quiet, narrow streets, jus as old as St George Street. At 4 Artillery Lane, the **Oldest Store Museum** (summer Mon–Sat 9am–5pm, Sun 10am–5pm; rest of the year Mon–Sat 9am–5pm, Sun noon–5pm; $3) does an excellent job of recreating a general store of the 1880s, filled to the rafters with foods and drinks, medicinal potions, and oversized consumer essentials like cigar moulders and wooden washing machines.

Close by, at 20 Aviles Street, the **Ximenze Fatio House** (March–Aug, Thurs–Sat & Mon 11am–4pm, Sun 1–4pm; free) was favoured by travellers who predated the town's first tourist boom, drawn by the airy balconies added to the original structure, which was built in 1797 for a Spanish merchant. More substantial history is unfurled a ten-minute walk away at the **Oldest House**, 14 St Francis Street (daily 9am–5pm; $5), which is indeed the oldest house in town, and was occupied from the early 1700s by the family of an artillery hand at the castle.

The beaches

Some fine **beaches** lie just a couple of miles from the Old Town. On weekends, the locals descend in droves. Across the bay, **St Augustine Beach** is family terrain, but here also the **Anastasia State Recreation Area** (daily 8am–sunset; cars $2, passengers, cyclists and pedestrians $1) offers a thousand protected acres of dunes, marshes and scrub, linked by nature walks. In the other direction (take May Street, off San Marco Avenue), **Vilano Beach** pulls a younger crowd.

Accommodation

Most of St Augustine's visitors stay between February and October, when costs will be $10 to $20 above the winter rates. Many restored inns in the Old Town offer **bed and breakfast**, and there are cheap **motels** outside the centre along San Marco Avenue.

American Inn, 42 San Marco Ave (☎904/829-2292). The least expensive motel on the edge of the Old Town, with rooms from just $25.

Anchorage Motor Inn, 1 Dolphin Drive (☎904/829-9841). Across the bay from the Old Town, a waterside location for $30–45.

Carriage Way, 70 Cuna St (☎904/829-2467). One of the Old Town's best-priced B&Bs, from $50.

Kenwood Inn, 38 Marine St (☎904/824-2116). $50-a-night B&B accommodation in the Old Town.

Vilano Beach Motel, 50 Vilano Rd (☎904/829-2651). This laid-back motel is one of the best beach bargains, a great base for enjoying the North Beach. Rooms from $35.

Youth Hostel, 32 Treasury St (☎904/829-6163). The town's only hostel accommodation, very near the plaza. Members $10, others $13.

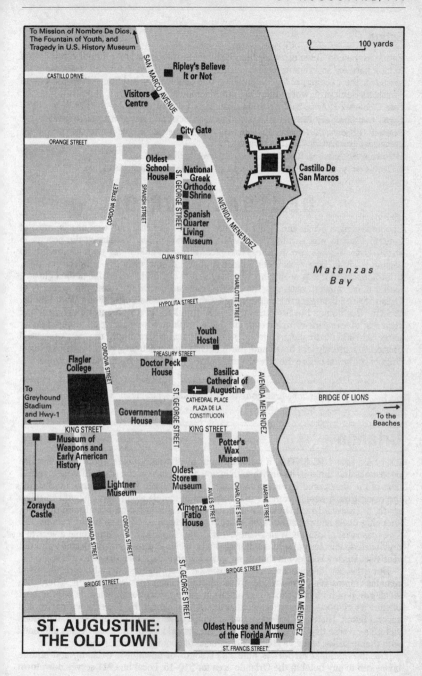

To Mission of Nombre De Dios,
The Fountain of Youth, and
Tragedy in U.S. History Museum

0   100 yards

CASTILLO DRIVE

SAN MARCO AVENUE

Ripley's Believe
It or Not

Visitors
Centre

City Gate

ORANGE STREET

Castillo De
San Marcos

Oldest
School
House

National
Greek
Orthodox
Shrine

Spanish
Quarter
Living
Museum

CORDOVA STREET

SPANISH STREET

ST. GEORGE STREET

AVENIDA MENENDEZ

CUNA STREET

Matanzas
Bay

CHARLOTTE STREET

HYPOLITA STREET

Youth
Hostel

TREASURY STREET

Flagler
College

Doctor Peck
House

CORDOVA STREET

Basilica
Cathedral of
Augustine

AVENIDA MENENDEZ

BRIDGE OF LIONS

To
Greyhound
Stadium
and Hwy-1

CATHEDRAL PLACE
PLAZA DE LA
CONSTITUCION

To the
Beaches

Government
House

ST. GEORGE STREET

KING STREET   KING STREET

Museum of
Weapons and
Early American
History

Potter's
Wax
Museum

Oldest
Store
Museum

Lightner
Museum

Zorayda
Castle

Ximenze
Fatio
House

AVILES STREET

CHARLOTTE STREET

MARINE STREET

GRANADA STREET

CORDOVA STREET

ST. GEORGE STREET

BRIDGE STREET

BRIDGE STREET

AVENIDA MENENDEZ

**ST. AUGUSTINE:
THE OLD TOWN**

Oldest House and Museum
of the Florida Army

ST. FRANCIS STREET

Eating

Eating in the Old Town is pricier than it should be, particularly for dinner – you'll need to look hard for an evening meal under $15. Many Old Town cafes and restaurants are closed in the evening, but you can solve this problem by heading across the bay to Anastasia Boulevard, where there are several good places.

Café Camacho, 11 Aviles St. Cut-rate breakfasts and good-sized lunches.

Gypsy Cab Company, 828 Anastasia Blvd. Greek and Italian food served in Art Deco style.

Scarlett O'Hara's, 70 Hypolita St. Tasty soups and salads in the Old Town, and open in the evening for excellent fried crayfish suppers.

O'Steen's, 205 Anastasia Blvd. Fish and shrimp feasts until 8.30pm.

El Toro Con Sombrero, 10 Anastasia Blvd. Fast-food Mexican, jumping until 1am.

CENTRAL FLORIDA

Encompassing a broad and fertile expanse between the east and west coasts, most of **central Florida** was farming country when vacation-mania first struck the beachside strips. Over the last two decades, this picture of tranquillity has been shattered: no section of the state has been affected more dramatically by modern tourism. Contradictory as it may seem, the most visited part of Florida is also one of the ugliest: a clutter of freeway interchanges, motels and billboards, arching around the small city of **Orlando**. The blame for the vulgarity lies with Orlando's near-neighbour, **Walt Disney World**, which since the Seventies has sucked millions of people into the biggest and cleverest theme park complex ever created – involuntarily sparking off a tourist-dollar chase of Gold Rush magnitude on its outskirts. Encouragingly, the rest of central Florida is markedly less brash and, north of Orlando particularly, rural towns like Ocala still typify Florida before the arrival of the highways and made-to-measure vacations.

> The telephone **area code** for Orlando and central Florida is ☎407.

Orlando

It's ironic that **ORLANDO**, a quiet farming town twenty years ago, now has more people passing through its environs than any other place in the state. Although reminders of the slow-paced Florida of an earlier era are easy to find in and around the city, the closest most people come is to the strings of motels along Hwy-192, fifteen miles south, or **International Drive**, five miles southwest – a brand new boulevard of hotels, shopping malls and restaurants, so short of character it could be moulded from plastic. The reason is, of course, Walt Disney World, which pulls 25 million people a year to a previously featureless plot of scrubland. It's possible to pass through Orlando and not visit Walt Disney World, but there's no way you can escape its influence.

Nevertheless, despite enormous expansion over the last decade, Orlando itself remains impressively free of the gross commercialism that surrounds it. There is a small group of high-rise banks and offices in the compact downtown area but the bulk of the city comprises smart residential districts enhanced by recreational **parks** and several **lakes**. Historical left-overs and art collections spread through several sections will fill a diverse day – and, for anyone whose knowledge of the state begins and ends with theme parks, will give at least a brief taste of genuine Florida living.

The international **airport** is nine miles south of downtown Orlando, and shuttle buses run to any hotel in the Orlando area for $10–15. Local bus #11 serves downtown

Orlando (until 7.40pm Mon–Sat; 6.20pm on Sundays and holidays). A taxi to down-town, International Drive or the motels on Hwy-192 costs around $40. **Bus and train** arrivals are downtown, at the *Greyhound* terminal, 300 W Amelia Street (☎843-7720), or the train station, 1400 Slight Boulevard (☎1-800/872-7245). The **visitor information center**, 8445 International Drive (daily 8am–8pm; ☎351-0412), is where you should pick up the free *Official Visitor's Guide to Orlando*.

Getting around: visiting the theme parks

Local **buses** converge on the downtown Orlando terminal between Central and Pine streets: useful **routes** are #11 to the airport (a 45-min journey) and #21 to International Drive, where you can catch a **shuttle bus** to Walt Disney World. Run by private com-panies, these connect the main accommodation areas with Walt Disney World, Sea World and Universal Studios – phone at least a day ahead to be picked up. *Rabbit Bus* (☎291-2424) charges $7 return to Walt Disney World, $5 to Sea World and Universal Studios; or try *Mears Transportation Service* (☎423-5566). If you don't rent a car, **taxis** are the only way to get around at night – try *Yellow Cab* (☎699-9999).

Accommodation

If you're going to Walt Disney World, Orlando is the obvious base. The only budget choices are two hostels in **downtown Orlando**, which is where you'll have to stay if you're dependent on public transport. Scores of plain but cheap motels are lined **along Hwy-192** between Walt Disney World and Kissimmee. Most package tourists end up in pricey chain hotels on **International Drive**; independent travellers who show up on spec during the slow winter periods may find some bargains.

Aloha, 4643 Hwy-192 (☎396-1340). One of the lowest-priced motels along this strip.

Davis Brother Motor Lodge, 6603 International Drive (☎1-800/722-2900). All the regular comforts at $55–70 a night.

Econo Lodge, 8738 International Drive (☎1-800/321-2429). Rooms usually between $55 and $70.

Harley Hotel, 151 E Washington Street (☎1-800/321-3232). A restored downtown hotel, strong on rustic atmosphere, from around $60.

King's Motel, 4836 Hwy-192 (☎1-800/432-9928). Cheap highway motel, from $25 a night.

Orlando Heritage Inn, 9861 International Drive (☎1-800/282-1890). Pseudo-Victorian style at $70–100 a night.

Plantation Manor, 227 N Eola Drive (☎843-8888). Downtown hostel, where beds in small dorms are $12, and singles or doubles $26.

Travelodge, 409 N Magnolia Street (☎423-1671). Rooms for IYHA members at $15 per person.

Eating

The only problem with **eating** in the Orlando area is wading through the choices. Downtown and its environs holds the pick of the locals' haunts, while tourist custom around International Drive results in a glut of overpriced eating places, but spread among them are some inexpensive all-day buffets and serious gourmet restaurants.

Arabian Nights, 6225 W Hwy-192 (☎1-800/553-6116). Reservations essential at this "show restau-rant", where the four-course rib dinner comes with chariot racin₃ and Arabian horse dancing.

El Bohio Café, 5756 Dahlia Drive. Excellently priced Cu⊦⌐ ₁ lunches, a couple of miles out of downtown.

Lilia's Philippine Delights, 3150 S Orange Ave. Downtown Filipino food; the menu includes a whole roast pig!

Ming Court, 9188 International Drive. World-class Chinese food, at $20–40 a head depending how restrained you are.

Le Peep, 250 S Orange Ave. Good soups, pancakes and sandwiches.

Royal Orleans, at the *Mercado* mall, 8445 International Drive. Cajun and creole cooking at its spicy best.

Walt Disney World

As significant as air conditioning in making the state what it is today, **WALT DISNEY WORLD** turned a wedge of Florida cow fields into one of the world's most lucrative vacation venues within ten years. The immense and astutely planned empire also pushed the state's media profile through the roof: from being a down-at-heel mixture of cheap motels, retirement homes and clapped-out alligator zoos, Florida suddenly became a showcase of modern international tourism.

Whatever your attitude to theme parks, there's no denying that Walt Disney World is the pacesetter: it goes way beyond Walt Disney's original "theme park" – Disneyland, which opened in Los Angeles in 1955 (see p.753) – delivering escapism at its most technologically advanced and psychologically brilliant across an area twice the size of Manhattan. In a crime-free environment where all-American values dominate and the concept of good clean fun finds its ultimate expression, Walt Disney World often makes the real world – and its problems – seem like a distant memory. It's not cheap, and there are times when you'll feel like a cog in a vast machine, but Walt Disney World, with ruthless efficiency, always delivers what it promises.

Costs may come as a shock, especially to families (who should note that Walt Disney World as a whole is much less geared to kids than might be expected), but the admission fee allows unlimited access to all the shows and rides in the particular park – and you'll need *at least* a day to go on everything in each of the three main ones. There's a strict embargo on bringing **food and drink** into the parks, where restaurants and snack bars are plentiful but pricey. The four or five **hotels** within Walt Disney World itself are also expensive (from $200 a night), and require reservations made well in advance.

Seeing Walt Disney World: the main parks

Walt Disney World's three main theme parks are quite separate entities. The **Magic Kingdom** is the Disney park everyone imagines, where Mickey Mouse mingles with the crowds – very much the park for kids. Recognisable for its giant, golfball like geosphere, **EPCOT Center** is Disney's celebration of science and technology: boring for young kids, it's a sprawling area that involves a lot of walking. The newest and most easily assimilated of the three, **Disney-MGM Studios**, suits almost everyone; its special effects are enjoyable even if you've never seen the movies they're based on. Doing justice to all three parks will take at least four days – one day should be set aside for rest – and you shouldn't tackle more than one on any single day. If you only have one day to spare, pick the park that appeals most and stick to it.

The **busiest periods** are mid-February to August, and from Christmas Day to New Year's Day. The slowest months are January, September, October and November. The **busiest day** is Tuesday, with Friday and Sunday the least crowded. Provided you **arrive early** at a park (say, 8am) you'll easily get through the most popular rides before the mid-afternoon crush. For details of **getting there from Orlando**, see "Orlando" above.

Opening times and tickets; and Pleasure Island

Each park is **open** daily from 9am to 11pm between February and August, from 9am to 9pm throughout the rest of the year, with extended hours on holidays. A **one-day ticket** costs $33 (under tens $26; children under three free) from any park entrance, and allows *entry to one park only*, with unlimited passouts. For seeing more than two of the parks, use one of the **passports**, which permit entry to all three parks and free use of the shuttle buses. **Four-day passports** cost $111 (children $88); **five-day passports** cost $145 (children $116).

THE WORLD OF WALT DISNEY

When brilliant illustrator and animator Walt Disney devised the world's first theme park, LA's Disneyland (see p.753), he left himself with no control over the hotels and restaurants which quickly engulfed it, preventing growth and racking off profits Disney felt to be rightly his. Determined not to let that happen again, the Disney corporation secretly bought up 27,500 acres of central Florida farmland, acquiring by the late Sixties a site a hundred times bigger than Disneyland. With the promise of a jobs bonanza for Florida, the state legislature gave the corporation the rights of any major municipality: empowering it to lay roads, enact building codes, and enforce the law with its own security force.

Walt Disney World's first park, the Magic Kingdom, which opened in 1971, was a huge success. Unveiled in 1982, the far more ambitious EPCOT Center represented the first major break from cartoon-based escapism, but its rose-tinted look at the future received a mixed response. Partly due to this, and some cockeyed management decisions, the Disney empire (Disney himself died in 1966) faced bankruptcy by the mid-Eighties. Since then, clever marketing has brought the corporation back from the abyss, as it aims to increase Walt Disney World's 100,000 daily visitors and stay ahead of its rivals.

The **car parks** (fee $3) are enormous, so make at least a mental note of where exactly you're parked to save hours of embarrassed searching later on. The complex **transportation system** using buses and a monorail is chiefly designed to zap people from the Disney hotels to the various parks; if you've arrived under your own steam it's only likely to be of use for reaching **Pleasure Island** in the evening (exit 26B off I-4). It's free to walk around this fantasy abandoned island, with its mixture of themed bars and nightclubs, but drinks are dear and to go inside any of the nightclubs – which are open from 7pm until 2am – you'll need a $11.95 **ticket** from one of the booths at the entry points, which lets you wander in and out of them all.

The Magic Kingdom

Anyone who's been to Disneyland will recognise much of the **Magic Kingdom**; like the original Disney theme park, it divides into four sections (in declining order of merit: *Adventureland, Tomorrowland, Fantasyland* and *Frontierland*). Some rides are identical to their Californian forebears; some are greatly improved. And, like its older relative, the only way to deal with the place is enthusiastically. Jump in with both feet and go on every ride you can – and never stop to think how stupid it all is.

The ride with the cleverest special effects also has the fastest-moving queues, so you should hold back from joining the **Pirates of the Caribbean** – a hair-raising boat ride through a pirate attack on a Caribbean island – until the mid-afternoon crowds jampack everything else. **Space Mountain** offers a gut-churning trip around distant galaxies on a ferocious switchback – not for nothing are people with weak hearts steered towards the less frenetic runaway train of **Big Thunder Mountain Railroad**. Elsewhere, the most bizarre sight comes with the **Tropical Serenade**, where The Enchanted Tiki Birds – "AudioAnimatronic" robots of birds, flowers and Tiki-god statues – sing and whistle through a programme of South Seas musical favourites.

EPCOT Center

Even before the new Magic Kingdom opened, Walt Disney was developing plans for **EPCOT Center**, or Experimental Prototype Community of Tomorrow, conceived in 1966 as a real community experimenting and working with the new ideas and materials of the technologically advancing US. The idea failed to shape up as Disney had envisioned: EPCOT didn't open its gates until 1982, when global recession and ecological concerns had put paid to utopian notions based on the infallibility of science. One drawback of this park is simply its immense size: twice as big as the Magic Kingdom and very sapping on the feet.

Inside the unmissable 180-ft geosphere (unlike a semicircular geodesic *dome*, the geo*sphere* is completely round) is *Future World*, a reminder of the park's original concept, detailing the history and possible advances to be made in agriculture, transport, energy and communications. The best of the rides here – all corporately sponsored, so don't expect any mention of alternative power or global warming – are **Universe of Energy**, a venture into the dinosaur-era, when fossil fuels were being formed; **Wonders of Life**, a fantastic voyage through the body's immune system; and **The Living Seas**, Disney's retort to Sea World (see below), the world's largest artificial saltwater environment, occupied by a multitude of dolphins, sharks and sea lions.

Disney-MGM Studios

When the Disney corporation began making films and TV shows for adults – most notably *Who Killed Roger Rabbit* – they also set about devising a theme park to entertain adults as much as kids. Buying the rights to the Metro-Goldwyn-Mayer (MGM) oeuvre of films and TV shows, Disney acquired a vast repertoire of instantly familiar images to mould into shows and rides. Opening in 1990, **Disney-MGM Studios** served to mute the opening of Florida's Universal Studios (see below), and at the same time found an extra use for the real film studios based here – the people you'll see labouring over storyboards aren't there for show, they are genuinely making films.

If you arrive early, avoid a long wait in the sun later on by going straight on the two-hour **Backstage Tour**, visiting film production facilities and venturing around Disney's animation studios: the interest level fluctuates but you won't have had your money's worth if you miss it. The same applies to the **Indiana Jones Stunt Spectacular**, re-creating – and explaining – many of the action-packed set pieces from the Spielberg films. **Star Tours**, a flight-simulator trip piloted by *Star Wars* characters R2D2 and C-3PO, is the most physical ride in the park by a long way – passengers' seatbelts are carefully checked before lift-off. For laughs, go to **Superstar Television**, which plucks volunteers from the crowd to read the news, appear in *The Lucy Show* or team up with *The Golden Girls* – one place in Walt Disney World where the fun is spontaneous.

Universal Studios and Sea World

If you've spent time at Walt Disney World and enjoyed it, you'll find it hard to resist the other two attractions in the Orlando area, which sit either side of the International Drive visitor information center on the way back towards downtown Orlando.

Universal Studios

Half a mile north of Exit 30B off I-4. Summer daily 9am–7pm; winter 9am–9pm. $29, two-days for $49.

All the predictions suggest that Florida will be the US moving-image capital of the next century. The opening of **UNIVERSAL STUDIOS** in 1990 did nothing to dampen such speculation. Florida's Universal, like its competitor Disney-MGM, is a working studio, filling more than four hundred acres with the latest in TV and movie production technology and already turning out major features such as Ron Howard's *Parenthood*, *Psycho IV*, and a bunch of tedious US sitcoms. As a theme park, however, Universal is still struggling to justify the hype which surrounded its opening. Overall, the rides are more spectacular than those at Disney-MGM, with less emphasis on movie nostalgia – but the park has a less homely feel and only the very energetic can take it all in inside a day.

Street sets – such as New York's East Side – create a striking backdrop to the park, whose strongest special effects are found with **Ghostbusters** and the much better **Earthquake**, a ride in a San Francisco subway train that starts with gentle rocking and builds to an 8.3 Richter-scale quake complete with heaving streets and the approach of a gigantic tidal wave. Elsewhere, there are attempts to demystify production techniques, the most successful being **Alfred Hitchcock: The Art of Making Movies**, exploring some of the visual tricks employed by Hitchcock, with intriguing glimpses of some of Hitch's better films.

Sea World

6227 Sea Harbor Drive. Daily 9am–7pm. $25.50.

SEA WORLD, the cream of Florida's sizeable crop of marine parks, should not be missed. To see it all and get value for money, you'll need to allocate a whole day; pick up the free map and show schedule at the entrance. The big event is the *Shamu* show – twenty minutes of tricks performed by a playful killer whale. With substantially less razzmatazz, plenty of smaller tanks and displays explain more than you need to know about the undersea world. Among the highlights, the **Penguin Encounter** attempts to re-create Antarctica with scores of waddling birds scampering over an iceberg; the occupants of the **Dolphin Pool** assert their advanced intellect by flapping their fins and drenching passers-by; and **Sharks!** includes a walk through a glass-sided tunnel, offering the closest eye-contact you're ever likely to have with a shark and live to tell the tale.

THE WEST COAST

In three hundred miles from the state's southern tip to the border of the Panhandle, Florida's **west coast** embraces all the extremes. Buzzing, youthful towns neighbour placid fishing hamlets; mobbed holiday strips are just minutes from desolate swamplands. Surprises are plentiful, though the coast's one constant is proximity to the Gulf of Mexico – and sunset views rivalled only by those of the Florida Keys.

The largest city, **Tampa** won't unduly detain you, though it does have more to offer than its corporate towers initially suggest – not least its long-established Cuban community. For the mass of visitors, though, the Tampa Bay area begins and ends with the **St Petersburg beaches**, whose miles of sea, sun and sand are undiluted vacation territory. South of Tampa, a string of barrier-island beaches runs the length of the Gulf, and the mainland towns which provide access to them – such as Sarasota and Fort Myers – have enough to warrant a stop. But really, the best move is inland, to the **Everglades National Park**, explorable on simple walking trails, by canoeing, or by spending the night at backcountry campgrounds with only the alligators for company.

The telephone area code for Tampa, the west coast and the Everglades is ☎813.

Tampa

A small city with an infectious, upbeat mood, you'll only need a day to explore **TAMPA** thoroughly; but you'll depart with a lasting impression of a city on the rise. The business hub of the west coast, Tampa has been one of the major benefactors of the recent flood of money into Florida – of which it lavishes an impressive amount on a cultural diet envied by many of its larger rivals. In spite of this, Tampa gets scant regard from most visitors, who aim straight for the Gulf coast beaches half an hour's drive west and miss out totally on its urban energy.

Tampa began as a small settlement beside a US army base built to keep an eye on local Seminoles during the 1820s. In the 1880s the railway arrived, and the Hillsborough River on which the city stands was dredged to allow sea-going vessels to dock. Tampa became a booming port, simultaneously acquiring a major tobacco industry as thousands of Cubans moved north from Key West to the new cigar factories of neighbouring Ybor City. The Depression saw off the economic surge, but the port remained one of the busiest in the country and tempered Tampa's post-war decline. While the social problems that blight any US city are evident, there seems little to stand in the way of Tampa's continued emergence as a forward-thinking and financially secure community.

Arriving, information and getting around

The city's **airport** (☎267-3400) is five miles northwest of downtown: local bus #30 is the quickest connection, or use the *Central Florida Transit* minivans ($10; ☎276-2730). If you're heading for St Petersburg use the around-the-clock *Limo Inc* buses (☎1-800/283-6817); flat fare to any coastal accommodation is $10.25. **Taxis** (try *United*, ☎253-2424, or *Yellow*, ☎253-0125) to downtown or a Busch Boulevard motel cost $12 to $15; to St Petersburg or the beaches, $25 to $35. All the major **car rental** companies have desks at the airport. *Greyhound* **buses** terminate downtown at 610 Polk Street (☎229-2174); **trains** arrive at 601 Nebraska Avenue (☎221-7600).

In downtown Tampa, get general information from the **visitor centre** at 111 Madison Street (Mon–Sat 9am–5pm; ☎1-800/44-TAMPA). The **Ybor City Chamber of Commerce** is at 1513 Eighth Street in Ybor City (Mon–Fri 9am–5pm; ☎248-3712).

Although both downtown Tampa and Ybor City are easily covered on foot, to travel between them without a car you'll need to use **local buses** (☎254-HART), whose routes fan out from Marion Street in downtown Tampa. Useful numbers are #8 to Ybor City and #30 to the airport. Rush-hour commuter buses run **between Tampa and the coast** – #100 to St Petersburg and #200 to Clearwater. Alternatives are the numerous daily *Greyhound* buses or the twice-daily *Amtrak* bus.

Downtown Tampa

Upright office towers are proof of **downtown Tampa**'s prosperous present. Aside from riverside warehouses in various states of dilapidation around the northern end of the pedestrianised **Franklin Street** (once the district's main drag and still the best place to get your bearings), recalling the city's past is largely left to plaques detailing everything from the passing through of sixteenth-century explorer Hernando de Soto to the site of Florida's first radio station. None of the contemporary buildings in downtown Tampa better reflects the city's striving for cultural articulacy than the **Tampa Museum of Art**, on the banks of the Hillsborough River at 601 Doyle Carlton Drive (Tues, Thurs & Sat 10am–6pm, Wed 10am–9pm, Sun 1–5pm; free). The highly regarded museum specialises in classical antiquities and twentieth-century American art: selections from the permanent modern stock are cleverly blended with prime loaned specimens of recent US painting, photography and sculpture.

Further south, you'll feel like an insignificant speck at the feet of the city's tallest structures. For a better view of them – and their surrounds – make the short monorail ride (from the top of the Fort Brooke Parking Garage on Whiting Street) to **Harbor Island**, a large shopping mall on a small island dredged from the Hillsborough Bay. From here you'll see the silver minarets, cupolas and domes on the far side of the river, sprouting from the main building of the University of Tampa – formerly the **Tampa Bay Hotel**, and financed by steamship and railway magnate Henry B Plant. To reach it, walk across the river on Kennedy Boulevard and descend the steps into Plant Park.

The structure is as bizarre a sight in today's Tampa as it was on its opening in 1891, when its five hundred rooms looked out on a community of just seven hundred souls. Plant had been buying up bankrupt railways since the Civil War, steadily inching his way into Florida to meet his steamships unloading at Tampa's harbour, and was wealthy enough to put fantasies of creating the world's most luxurious hotel into practice without worrying about the cost. But lack of care for the fittings (the hotel was only used during winter and left to fester during the scorching summer), and Plant's death in 1899, hastened its transformation from the last word in comfort to a pile of crumbling plaster. The city authorities bought it in 1905 and halted the rot, leasing it to the fledgling Tampa University 23 years later. In a wing of the main building, the **Plant Museum** (Tues–Sat 10am–4pm; $2) holds what's left of the hotel's furnishings, which were largely the fruits of a half-million-dollar shopping trip across Europe and Asia by Plant and his wife.

A few strides from the museum, the former lobby makes a popular rendezvous for the university's 2000 students. You can roam around much of the building at will, but the details only fall into place on the **free guided tour**, departing from the lobby at 1.30pm on Tuesday and Thursday (Sept–May only).

Ybor City

In 1886, as soon as Henry Plant's ships ensured a regular supply of Havana tobacco into Tampa, cigar magnate Don Vincente Martinez Ybor cleared a patch of scrubland three miles northeast of present-day downtown Tampa and laid the foundations of **YBOR CITY**. Around twenty thousand migrants, mostly Cuban, settled here and created a Latin American enclave, producing the top-class hand-rolled cigars that made Tampa the "Cigar Capital of the World". However, mass-production, the popularity of cigarettes, and the Depression proved a fatal combination for skilled cigar makers: as unemployment struck, Ybor City's tight-knit blocks of cobbled streets and red-brick buildings became surrounded by drab low-rent neighbourhoods.

Over the last few years, efforts to mould Ybor City into a tourist attraction have saved many older buildings from dereliction. As yet, visitors are too few to over-commercialise the place: shops still sell hand-rolled cigars, and the smell of Cuban bread and freshly brewed coffee are never far off. Take it in by strolling the ten blocks of Seventh and Eighth avenues east of Thirteenth Street. The **Ybor City State Museum**, 1818 Ninth Avenue (Tues–Sat 9am–noon & 1–5pm; 50¢), helps you grasp the main points of Ybor City's creation and its multi-ethnic make-up. The factory where the cigar-rolling took place is now converted into shops, restaurants and snack bars as **Ybor Square**, 1901 Thirteenth Street (Mon–Sat 9.30am–5.30pm, Sun noon–5.30pm). Standing on the factory's steps in 1893, the Cuban poet and independence fighter José Martí called for "money, machetes and manpower" for the country's anti-Spanish struggles – expatriate cigar workers responded by contributing ten percent of their earnings.

Accommodation

Tampa is not generously supplied with low-cost **accommodation**; you'll almost certainly save money by sleeping in St Petersburg or at the beaches. There are some good deals, though, in the **motels** along Busch Boulevard, six miles north.

Days Inn, 515 E Cass St (☎1-800/678-DAYS). The cheapest place in downtown Tampa, but a gloomy choice; around $50.

Gardens View, 2500 Busch Blvd (☎933-3958). Regular motel for $35–55 a night.

Golden Key, 2523 Busch Blvd (☎933-6760). Rooms from $35–55 depending on the season.

Hampton Inn, 4817 W Laurel St (☎878-0778). Best value near the airport. Around $50 a night.

Riverside, 200 N Ashley Drive (☎1-800/AT TAMPA). The better and brighter downtown hotel, where arriving on spec on a quiet day should secure a double for around $90.

Eating

Choice and quality are features of Tampa **eating**, though in downtown you'll need to be content with the basic lunchtime sandwich stops servicing office folk. Ybor City, not surprisingly, is the place to go for Cuban food.

Café Creole & Oyster Bar, 1330 Ninth Ave, Ybor City. This cafe excels in spicy Cajun dishes – try the filling gumbo seafood soup.

Columbia, 2117 Seventh Ave, Ybor City. Refined Spanish and Cuban food, served in the same place since 1905.

JD's, 2029 E Seventh Ave, Ybor City. Low-priced Cuban meals.

New Soul Sandwich Shop, 518 N Willow Ave. Southern staples, like fried chicken and collard greens, added to the standard sandwich fillings.

Silver Ring, 1831 E Seventh Ave, Ybor City. The *Silver Ring* has been serving simple but authentic Cuban sandwiches for nearly fifty years.

Nightlife

Many live music venues and nightclubs have tempting **drink** reductions, although the most cost-effective way to booze is at the **happy hours** all over the city – just watch for the signs. For **nightlife listings**, read the free *Creative Loafing* and *Tampa Tonite*, or buy the Friday edition of the *Tampa Tribune*.

Comedy Corner, 3447 W Kennedy Blvd. Long-running comedy club; cover charge is $3–10.

Skipper's Smokehouse, 910 Skipper Rd. Tampa's most dependable venue for live blues and reggae.

Three Birds Bookstore and Coffee Room, 1518 Seventh Ave, Ybor City. A hangout of Tampa's coffee-drinking literary crowd; poetry readings on Thursday and Saturday.

Thunder Bay Café, 8829 W Hillsborough Blvd. An unusual promise – rock bands at low volume.

Yucatan Liquor Stand, 4811 W Cypress Blvd. The best venue for late-night rowdy drinking.

St Petersburg

Declared the healthiest place in the US in 1885, **ST PETERSBURG**, twenty miles from Tampa on the eastern edge of the Pinellas peninsula, wasted no time in attracting the recuperating and the retired, at one point putting five thousand green benches on its streets to take the weight of elderly backsides. By the early 1980s, few people under the age of fifty lived in the town, and no one was surprised when it became the setting for the 1985 movie *Cocoon*, in which a group of local geriatrics magically regain the vigour of their youth. Right now, St Petersburg itself seems to be emulating them. The average age of its residents has been almost halved, the revamped pier is a great place for open-air socialising, and – most remarkably of all – the town has acquired a major collection of works by Salvador Dali: reason enough to be in St Petersburg, if only as a day's break from the St Petersburg Beaches, nine miles west.

Few places make a less likely depository for a huge museum of works by Dali than St Petersburg, but the **Salvador Dali Museum**, 1000 S Third Street (Tues–Sat 10am–5pm, Sun noon–5pm; $5), stores more than a thousand paintings from the collection of a Cleveland industrialist who struck up a friendship with the controversial artist in the Forties. **Free tours** begin whenever sufficient people gather, and trace a chronological path around the works, from early experiments with Impressionism and Cubism to the seminal Surrealist canvas, *Persistence of Memory*.

Once you've dealt with Dali, it's the quarter-mile-long **pier**, jutting from the end of Second Avenue N, that's the centre of gravity in town. It often features several browsable arts and crafts exhibitions, and you'll find stacks of tourist literature at a desk near the inverted-pyramid-like building at its head, whose five storeys are packed with restaurants, shops and fast-food counters. At the foot of the pier, the **Historical Museum** (Mon–Sat 10am–5pm, Sun 1–5pm; $2) modestly recounts St Petersburg's early twentieth-century heyday as a winter resort; pick up their free *Historic Downtown Walking Tour* brochure, which pinpoints some of the town's older buildings within easy reach.

Practicalities

The *Greyhound* **bus** station is at 180 Ninth Street (☎898-1496); the **train** station, 3601 31st Street (☎522-9475), is two miles west of downtown. There are no trains between Tampa and St Petersburg, just an *Amtrak* bus link. The **Chamber of Commerce and Visitors Center** is at 100 Second Avenue N (Mon–Fri 9am–5pm; ☎821-4069).

Sleeping in St Petersburg can be less costly than doing so at the beaches. There are two **youth hostels** (members $10, others $13): *St Petersburg International Hostel*, 215 Central Avenue (☎822/4095), and the *St Petersburg AYH Hostel*, 326 First Avenue (☎822-4141). **Motels** can be exceptionally cheap, too – under $30 during the summer, under $40 in winter. Of dozens along Fourth Street, the closest to the centre are *Banyan*, no. 610 N (☎822-7072), *Landmark*, no. 1930 (☎895-1629), and *Kentucky*, no. 4246 (☎526-7373). For an excellent and inexpensive seafood meal, head for *Fourth Street Shrimp Store*, 1006 Fourth Street N, or the innovative *Seabar*, 4912 Fourth Street, where you select your meal from the display and have it cooked to your desire.

The St Petersburg Beaches

Drab suburbs stretch west from St Petersburg, covering virtually all of the Pinellas peninsula, a bulky thumb of land poking between Tampa Bay and the Gulf of Mexico. Framing the Gulf side of the peninsula, a 25-mile chain of barrier islands form the **St Petersburg Beaches**, one of Florida's busiest coastal strips. When the resorts of Miami Beach lost their allure during the Seventies, the St Petersburg Beaches grew in popularity with Americans, and more recently they've become a major destination for package-holidaying Europeans. The sands are broad and beautiful, the sea is warm, and the sunsets are fabulous – but in no way is this Florida at its best or most diverse.

All **buses** to the beaches originate in St Petersburg at the **Williams Park terminal**, at the junction of First Avenue N and Third Street N; there's an information booth there for route details.

The southern beaches

In twenty-odd miles of heavily touristed coast, only **PASS-A-GRILLE**, at the very southern tip of the barrier island chain, has the look and feel of a genuine community – two miles of tidy houses, cared-for lawns, small shops, and a cluster of bars and restaurants. On weekends, informed locals come to enjoy one of the area's liveliest set of sands. A mile and a half north of Pass-a-Grille, the **Don Cesar Hotel**, 3400 Gulf Boulevard (free guided tours on Fri at 11.30am), is a grandiose pink castle, filling seven beachside acres. Opened in 1928, its glamour was short-lived; during the Depression part of the hotel was used as a warehouse, and later as the spring training base of the New York Yankees baseball team. The building received a $15 million rejuvenation during the Seventies, and regained its function as a hotel – a base for anyone with upwards of $150 a night to spare (and where much of Robert Altman's movie *Health* was shot).

Keeping to Gulf Boulevard brings you into the main section of **ST PETERSBURG BEACH**, uninspiring rows of hotels, motels and eating places grouped along Gulf Boulevard. Further north, **TREASURE ISLAND** is even less varied tourist territory, culminating in the wood-walled, tin-roofed shops of **John's Pass Village**, 12901 Gulf Boulevard. Immediately north, Gulf Boulevard crosses an arching drawbridge into **MADEIRA BEACH**, which is essentially more of the same – although, if you can't make it to Pass-a-Grille, the local beach justifies a weekend fling.

The northern beaches
Much of the northern section of Sand Key, the longest barrier island in the St Petersburg chain and one of the wealthier portions of the coast, is taken up by stylish condos and time-share apartments. It ends with the pretty **Sand Key Park**, where tall palm trees frame a scintillating strip of sand. Among the nearby high-rises which somewhat mar the view is the *Sheraton Sand Key Resort*, venue of the liaison between TV evangelist Jim Bakker and model Jessica Hahn in 1987, which led to the fall from grace of the media preacher and, for a time, greatly boosted the hotel's custom.

Sand Key Park occupies one bank of Clearwater Pass, across which a belt of sparkling white sands characterises the holiday town of **CLEARWATER BEACH**, whose streets still retain an endearing small-town feel. There are regular bus links between Clearwater Beach and the mainland town of Clearwater – across the two-mile causeway – where you'll find connections to St Petersburg and a *Greyhound* station.

Beach practicalities
Hotels here tend to be filled with package tourists, and are always pricier than the **motels** that line mile after mile of Gulf Boulevard – typically $35 to $50 in winter, $10 to $15 less during the summer. Remember, too, that you'll pay $5 to $10 extra for a room on the beach side of Gulf Boulevard compared to an identical room on the inland side. Pass-a-Grille makes the best base: choose between the *Keystone Motel*, 801 Gulf Way (☎360-1313); *Pass-a-Grille Beach Motel*, 709 Gulf Way (☎1-800/544-4184); and *Quebec Apartments*, 1107 Gulf Way (☎360-1333).

It's easy to find a decent place to **eat** around the beaches, and anywhere along Gulf Boulevard can oblige. In particular, a couple of hotel restaurants offer lunch and dinner buffets, like *Howard Johnson's*, 6100 and 11185 Gulf Boulevard, and *Breckinridge*, 5700 Gulf Boulevard. But the best-value buffet food is at *The Bank 1890s*, 11595 Gulf Boulevard, where the three daily sittings are priced at $4 to $10.

Sarasota

Rising on a gentle hillside beside the blue waters of Sarasota Bay, **SARASOTA** is one of Florida's better-off and better-looking towns, and also one of the state's leading cultural centres. It's home to numerous writers and artists, and the base of several respected performing arts companies. Despite periodic conservative flappings, the community is far less stuffy than its wealth, and the abundance of Neoclassical statues, fountains and manicured lawns decorating it, suggest. Downtown Sarasota itself has less impact than the Ringling estate on the town's northern edge – home of the art-loving millionaire from whom modern Sarasota takes its cue – and the barrier island beaches, a couple of miles away across the bay.

Northern Sarasota: the Ringling house and museums
Don't fail to tour the house and art collections of **John Ringling**, a multimillionaire who gave Sarasota a taste for fine arts that it's never lost. One of the owners of the fantastically successful *Ringling Brothers Circus*, which toured the US from the 1890s,

---

The telephone code for the Sarasota area is ☎813.

Ringling acquired a fortune estimated at $200 million. Recognising Sarasota's investment potential, Ringling built the first causeway to the barrier islands and made this the winter base for his circus. His greatest gift to the town, however, was a Venetian Gothic mansion and an incredible collection of European Baroque paintings, displayed in a purpose-built museum beside the house.

To get to the **Ringling house and museums** (daily 10am–6pm, Thurs 10am–10pm; $6), three miles north of downtown Sarasota beside US-41, use **buses** #2 or #10. Begin your exploration by walking through the gardens to the former Ringling residence, **Ca' d'Zan** ("House of John", in Venetian dialect), a gorgeous piece of work serenely situated beside the bay and – unlike contemporary mansions elsewhere in Florida – a triumph of taste and proportion. On trips to Europe to scout for new circus talent, Ringling became obsessed with Baroque art and acquired more than five hundred old masters: a gathering now regarded as one of the finest collections of its kind in the US. To display the paintings, a spacious **museum** was built around a mock fifteenth-century Italian palazzo. As with Ca' d'Zan, the very concept seems absurdly pretentious but, like the house, the idea works; the architecture matches the art with great aplomb. Five enormous paintings by Rubens, commissioned in 1625, and the painter's subsequent *Portrait of Archduke Ferdinand*, are the highlights, though there's also a wealth of talent from Europe's leading schools of the mid-sixteenth to mid-eighteenth centuries.

The Sarasota beaches

Increasingly the stamping ground of European package tourists, spilling south from the St Petersburg Beaches, the white sands of the **Sarasota beaches** are gradually losing much of their scenic appeal to towering condos. For all that, they're worth a day of anybody's time, with the two islands on which they lie, Lido Key and Siesta Key, reachable by car and buses from the mainland. There is, however, no direct link between them.

The Ringling Causeway – take buses #4 or #18 – crosses the yacht-filled Sarasota Bay from the foot of Main Street to **Lido Key** and flows into **St Armands Circle**, a glorified roundabout ringed by upmarket shops and restaurants. Continuing south along Benjamin Franklin Drive are the island's most easily accessible beaches, ending after two miles at the more attractive **South Lido Park** (daily 8am–sunset; free), a belt of dazzlingly bright sand beyond a large grassy park.

The bulbous northerly section of **Siesta Key**, reached by Siesta Drive off US-41 about five miles south of downtown Sarasota (bus #11), holds the bulk of the tadpole-shaped island's residents, on streets which twist around a network of canals. To escape the crowds at **Siesta Key Beach**, beside Ocean Beach Boulevard, continue south past Crescent Beach, and follow Midnight Pass Road for six miles to **Turtle Beach**, a small body of sand which has the islands' only campground.

Practicalities

In downtown Sarasota, *Greyhound* **buses** stop at 575 N Washington Boulevard (☎955-5735), and the *Amtrak* bus from Tampa pulls up at the **local bus terminal** on Lemon Avenue, between First and Second streets (where you catch the buses out to the Ringling house or the beaches). A good way to explore the town and the islands is by **renting a bike** for $25 a week (or $10 a day) from *Sarasota Bicycle Center*, 4048 Bee Ridge Road (☎377-4505). Call at the **Chamber of Commerce**, 1551 Second Street (Mon–Fri 9am–5pm; ☎955-8187), for the customary discount coupons and leaflets.

On the mainland, **motels** run the length of US-41 between the Ringling estate and downtown Sarasota, typically charging $25 to $40. Prices are higher at the beaches, with the lowest rates on Lido Key at the *Gulf Side Motel*, 138 Garfield Drive (☎388-2590), and the *Lido Apartment Motel*, 528 S Polk Drive (☎388-1004).

Fort Myers

FORT MYERS, fifty miles south, may lack the élan of Sarasota, but it's nonetheless one of the up-and-coming communities of the southwest coast, having recently undergone considerable expansion. Fortunately, most of the growth has occurred on the north side of the wide Caloosahatchee River, which the town straddles, allowing the traditional centre, along the waterway's south shore, to remain relatively unspoiled.

Once across the Caloosahatchee River, US-41 strikes **downtown Fort Myers**, picturesquely nestled on the river's edge, where the community first took root and now very much the commercial base. You'll need to look to the creditable exhibitions of the **Fort Myers Historical Museum**, 2300 Peck Street (Tues–Fri 9am–4.30pm, Sat & Sun 1–5pm; $2), for thorough insights into the past, which include the exploits of Doctor Franklin Miles, the local man who developed *Alka Seltzer*.

In 1885, six years after inventing the light bulb, **Thomas Edison** collapsed from exhaustion and was instructed by his doctor to find a warm working environment or face an early death. Vacationing in Florida, the 37-year-old Edison bought fourteen acres of land on the banks of the Caloosahatchee River and cleared a section of it to spend his remaining winters (he lived to be 84) at what became the **Edison Winter Home**, 2350 McGregor Boulevard (guided tours every half-hour; Mon–Sat 9am–4pm, Sun 12.30pm–4pm; $6), a mile west of downtown. Edison's house (which you can only glimpse through the windows) is an anticlimax, its plainness probably due to the fact that he spent most of his waking hours inside the **laboratory**, attempting to turn the latex-rich sap of *solidago Edisoni* (a strain of goldenrod weed which he developed) into rubber. When the tour reaches the engrossing **museum** the full impact of Edison's achievements becomes apparent: a design for an improved ticker-tape machine provided him with the funds for the experiments which led to the creation of the phonograph in 1877, and financed research that resulted in the incandescent light bulb. Here, too, you'll see some of the ungainly cinema projectors derived from Edison's *Kinetoscope* – which brought him a million dollars a year in royalties from 1907.

The Fort Myers beaches

Still being discovered by the holidaying multitudes, the **Fort Myers beaches**, fifteen miles south of downtown, are appreciably different in character from the west coast's more commercialised beach strips, with a cheerful seaside mood that's worth getting acquainted with. Accommodation is plentiful on and around Estero Boulevard – reached by San Carlos Boulevard, off McGregor Boulevard – which runs the seven-mile length of **Estero Island**. Most activity revolves around the short fishing pier and the **Lynne Hall Memorial Park**, at the island's northern end.

Estero Island becomes increasingly residential as you press south, Estero Boulevard eventually swinging over a slender causeway onto the barely developed **San Carlos Island**. A few miles ahead, at the **Carl Johnson Park** (daily 8am–5pm; $1.50), a footpath picks a trail over a couple of mangrove-fringed islands and several mullet-filled creeks to **Lovers Key**, a spectacularly secluded beach. If you don't fancy the half-mile walk, a free trolley will transport you between the park entrance and the beach.

Practicalities

To get from downtown to the beaches, take any bus to the Edison Square mall, then use #50 to Summerlin Square, from where a trolley continues to Estero Island and Carl Johnson Park (no local public transport on Sun). The *Greyhound* station is at 2064 Victoria Avenue (☎334-1011), just south of the downtown **chamber of commerce**, at 1365 Hendry Street (Mon–Fri 9.30am–5pm; ☎332-3634).

Accommodation costs in and around Fort Myers are low between May and mid-December, when $10 to $20 gets lopped off the standard rates. Downtown, look along

First Street – *Sea Chest*, no. 2571 (☎332-1545) and *Ta Ki-Ki*, no. 2631 (☎334-2135) are the cheapest at $40 to $60 – and there are many more along Cleveland Avenue. At the beaches, try Estero Boulevard and be prepared to spend $70, though in midweek you might find cheaper deals at *Beacon*, no. 1240 (☎463-5264); *Gulf*, no. 2700 (☎463-9247); or *Laughing Gull*, no. 2890 (☎463-1346).

The Everglades

Whatever scenic excitement you might anticipate from one of the country's more celebrated natural areas, there's nothing to herald your arrival in the **EVERGLADES**, seventy miles south of Fort Myers – one of the natural world's most remarkable ecosystems. From the monotonous course of US-41, the most dramatic sights are small pockets of trees poking above a completely flat sawgrass plain. Yet these wide open spaces resonate with life, forming part of an ever-changing ecosystem, evolved through a one-off combination of climate, vegetation and wildlife.

Appearing as flat as a table-top, the oolitic limestone on which the Everglades stand actually tilts very slightly towards the southwest. For thousands of years, water from summer storms and the overflow of nearby Lake Okeechobee has moved slowly through the Everglades towards the coast. The water replenishes the sawgrass, growing on a thin layer of soil formed by decaying vegetation, and gives birth to the algae at the foot of a complex food chain which sustains much larger creatures, most importantly **alligators**. After the floodwaters have reached the sea, drained through the bedrock or simply evaporated, the Everglades are barren except for the water accumulated in ponds – or "gator holes" – created when an alligator senses water and clears the soil covering it with its tail. Besides nourishing the alligator, the pond provides a home for other wildlife until the summer rains return. **Sawgrass** covers much of the Everglades but where natural indentations in the limestone fill with soil, fertile tree islands – or "**hammocks**" – appear, just high enough to stand above the flood waters.

Several **Native American tribes** once lived hunter-gatherer existences in the Everglades; the shell mounds they built can still be seen in sections of the park. In the nineteenth century, Seminoles, fleeing white settlers from the north, also lived peaceably in the area. By the late 1800s, a few towns had sprung up, peopled by settlers, who, unlike the Indians, looked to exploit the land, rather than live in harmony with it. As Florida's population grew, the damage caused by hunting, road building, and draining for farmland gave rise to a significant **conservation** lobby. In 1947, a section of the Everglades was declared a National Park, but unrestrained commercial use of nearby areas continues to upset the Everglades' natural cycle. The 1500 miles of canals built to divert the flow of water away from the Everglades and towards the state's expanding cities, the poisoning caused by agricultural chemicals from local farmlands, and the broader changes wrought by global warming, could yet turn Florida's greatest natural asset into a wasteland.

The Everglades National Park

Throughout this century the Everglades' boundaries have steadily been pushed back by urban development, and the **Everglades National Park** bestows federal protection to only a comparatively small section around Florida's southeastern corner. It's in the park that the vital links holding the Everglades together become apparent: the all-important cycle of wet and dry seasons; the ability of alligators to discover water and dig for it with their tails; the tree islands which provide sanctuaries for animals during the floods; and the forces, such as human demands for farmland and fresh water, which threaten to tear them apart.

Everglades City and around

Purchased and named in the Twenties by an advertising executive dreaming of a subtropical metropolis, **EVERGLADES CITY**, a few miles south off US-41 along Route 29, now has a population of just under five hundred. Most who visit are solely intent on diminishing the stocks of sports fish living around the mangrove islands – the aptly titled **Ten Thousand Islands** – arranged like jigsaw-puzzle pieces around the coastline.

For a closer look at the mangroves, which safeguard the Everglades from surge tides, take one of the park-sanctioned winter-only **boat trips** (departures half-hourly 9.30am–4.30pm; $9) from the dock on Chokoloskee, a blob of land – actually an Indian shell mound – marking the end of Route 29. The dockside **visitor center** (daily 8.30am–5pm; ☎695-3311) provides details on the cruises and the excellent ranger-led **canoe trips** (winter Sat at 10am). In Chokoloskee, you can rent an RV by the night for $25 to $30 at *Outdoor Resorts* (☎695-2881), or get a cottage in the grounds of the *Everglades Gun & Lodge Club*, 200 Riverside Drive (☎695-4211), for around $50.

The Miccosukee Indian Village and Shark Valley

Driven out of central Florida by white settlers, several hundred Seminole Indians retreated to the Everglades during the nineteenth century, and their descendants – the **Miccosukee** – still live here, though the coming of US-41 brought a fundamental change in their lifestyle as they set about grabbing their share of the tourist dollars. Four miles east of Forty Mile Bend, the **Miccosukee Indian Village** (daily 9am–5pm) symbolises their uneasy compromise. In the souvenir shop, good quality traditional crafts and clothes stand side-by-side with blatant tack, and in the "village" (entry $5), men turn logs into canoes and women cook over open fires. It's such a contrived affair that anyone with an ounce of sensitivity can't help but feel uneasy.

A mile east of the Indian Village, **SHARK VALLEY** (daily 8.30am–6pm; cars $3, pedestrians and cyclists $1) epitomises the Everglades' "River of Grass" tag. From here, dotted by hardwood hammocks, the sawgrass plain stretches as far as the eye can see. Aside from a few simple walking trails close to the **visitor centre** (winter daily 8.30am–5.15pm; reduced hours during summer; ☎305/221-8776), you can see Shark Valley only from a fourteen-mile loop road, ideally covered by renting a **bike** ($1.50 an hour). Alternatively, a highly informative two-hour **tram tour** (winter hourly from 9am; summer at 9am, 11am, 1pm & 3pm; $6) stops frequently to view wildlife – but won't allow you to linger in any particular place, as you'll certainly want to do.

Flamingo

The **Flamingo** section of the park – the entire southerly portion – holds virtually everything that makes the Everglades tick: spend a day or two here and you'll quickly grasp the fundamentals of its complex ecology. From the **park entrance** (always open; cars $5, pedestrians and cyclists $2), the road passes the **main visitor centre** (daily 8am–5pm; ☎305/247-6211) and continues for 38 miles to the tiny coastal settlement of **FLAMINGO**, perched on Florida's southern tip, a former fishing colony now comprising a marina, hotel and campground. A century ago, the only way to get here was by boat – it was so remote it didn't even have a name until the opening of a post office made one necessary. Then "Flamingo" was chosen, due to the abundant roseate spoonbills – pink-plumed birds which the locals failed to identify correctly as they killed them for their feathers.

Flamingo now does a brisk trade servicing the needs of sports fishing fanatics. On land, the **visitor centre** (daily 8am–5pm; ☎695-3101) and the marina of the *Flamingo Lodge*, the park's only hotel, are the activity bases. From the marina, the informative **backwater cruise** (daily at noon & 3pm; $9; reservations on ☎305/253-2241) makes a two-hour foray around the mangrove-enshrouded Whitewater Bay.

Park practicalities
US-41 skirts the northern edge of the park, providing the only land access to the Everglades City and Shark Valley park entrances, and to the Indian Village. To reach the Flamingo entrance, you'll need to touch the edge of Miami and head south. There's **no public transport** along US-41, or to any of the park entrances. **Entering the park** is free at Everglades City; at Shark Valley and Flamingo you'll pay $3 and $5 respectively per car. Tickets are valid for seven days.

The park is **open all year**, but the most favourable time to visit is **winter** (Nov–April), when the receding floodwaters cause wildlife to congregate around gator holes, ranger-led activities are frequent and the mosquitoes are bearable. In **summer** (May–Oct), afternoon storms flood the prairies, park activities are substantially reduced and the mosquitoes are a severe annoyance.

There are two well-equipped **campgrounds** at Flamingo, and many backcountry spots (free, but you need a permit, issued at the visitor centres) on the longer walking and canoe trails. Spare space at Flamingo (which fills quickly) can be checked on the board just inside the park entrance. The only **rooms** within the park are at *Flamingo Lodge* (☎695-3101 or ☎305/253-2241), for seasonal rates upwards of $55 to $85; make a reservation months in advance if arriving between November and April.

THE PANHANDLE

Rubbing hard against Alabama in the west and Georgia in the north, the long, narrow **Panhandle** has much more in common with the states of the Deep South than with the rest of Florida. City sophisticates have countless jokes lampooning the folksy lifestyles of the people here, but you won't get a true picture of Florida without seeing at least some of the Panhandle. Indeed, a century ago, the Panhandle *was* Florida. At the western edge, **Pensacola** was a busy port when Miami was still a swamp. Fertile soils lured wealthy plantation owners south and helped establish **Tallahassee** as a high-society gathering place and administrative centre – a role which, as the state capital, it retains. But the decline of cotton, the chopping down of too many trees, and the coming of the East Coast railway eventually left the Panhandle high and dry. Much of the inland region still seems neglected, and the **Apalachicola National Forest** is perhaps the best place in Florida to disappear into the wilderness. The **coastal Panhandle**, on the other hand, is enjoying better times, and though there are rows of holiday hotels, much is still untainted, with miles of blindingly white sands.

Tallahassee and Around

State capital though it is, **TALLAHASSEE** is a provincial city of oak trees and soft hills that won't take more than two days to explore in full. Briefcase-clutching bureaucrats set the mood around its small grid of central streets, where you'll find plentiful reminders of Florida's formative years. When Florida was incorporated into the US, Tallahassee was made its administrative base – the local Native Americans, the Tamali tribe, being unceremoniously dispatched to make room for the trio of log cabins in which the first Florida government sat in 1823. However, Tallahassee's own recent fortunes have been hindered by the lightning-paced development of south Florida, and – oddly distanced from most of the people it now governs – the city remains a conservative place.

A fifty-million-dollar eyesore dominates the square mile of **downtown Tallahassee** – the vertical vents of the towering **New Capitol Building**, at the junction of Apalachee Parkway and Monroe Street (Mon–Fri 8.30am–4.30pm; free). The seat of Florida lawmaking consequently resembles a gigantic air-conditioning machine. Florida's growing

The telephone **area code** for Tallahassee, and the rest of the Panhandle, is ☎904.

army of bureaucrats had previously been crammed into the ninety-year-old **Old Capitol Building** (Mon–Fri 9am–4.30pm; free) that stands in the shadow of its replacement. Altogether on a more human and welcoming scale, it's hard to credit that the Old Capitol's walls once echoed with the decisions that shaped modern Florida, though proof is provided by the absorbing exhibits contained within the side rooms.

For a more rounded history – easily the fullest account of Florida's past anywhere in the state – visit the **Museum of Florida History**, 500 S Bronough Street (Mon–Fri 9am–4.30pm, Sat 10am–4.30pm, Sun noon–4.30pm; free). Detailed accounts of Paleo-Indian settlements, and the significance of their burial and temple mounds – some of which have been found on the edge of Tallahassee – are valuable tools in comprehending Florida's prehistory, and the imperialist crusades of the Spanish are outlined with copious finds. There's disappointingly little on the nineteenth-century Seminole Wars – one of the bloodier skeletons in Florida's closet – though there's much on the turn-of-the-century railways that made Florida a winter resort for wealthy northerners.

Arrival and Information

The *Greyhound* **bus** terminal is at 112 W Tennessee Street (☎222-4240), within walking distance of downtown and opposite the local bus station. You can get a **free ride** into downtown Tallahassee from the bus station with the **Old Town Trolley**, which runs to the Civic Center (near the New Capitol Building) and back at fifteen-minute intervals on weekdays (7am–6pm). Otherwise, downtown Tallahassee is best seen **on foot**, though for **car rental**, try *Alamo*, 1720 Capitol Circle (☎576-6009) or *Ugly Duckling*, 2611 W Tennessee Street (☎575-3002) as well as the usual outlets.

The **Chamber of Commerce**, 100 N Duval Street (Mon–Fri 8.30am–5pm; ☎681-9200), and the **visitor centre**, 200 W College Boulevard (daily 8am–5pm; same phone number) have stacks of leaflets relating to the city and the surrounding area. For material covering the whole state, use the **Florida Information Center** (Mon–Fri 8.30am–4.30pm) on the ground floor of the New Capitol Building.

Accommodation

Finding **accommodation** in Tallahassee is only problematic during the sixty-day sitting of the state legislature from early April, and on autumn weekends when the Seminoles football team are playing at home. If you can't avoid these periods, book well ahead. The cheapest **hotels** and **motels** are on N Monroe Street about three miles from downtown Tallahassee; staying in downtown is dearer.

Econo Lodge, 2681 N Monroe St (☎1-800/446-6900). Typical for this street; around $30 a night.

Holiday Inn, 316 W Tennessee St (☎1-800/HOLIDAY). Cheapest regular hotel choice in the downtown area; $50–60 a night.

Osceola Hall, 500 Chapel Drive (☎222-5010). $25-a-night rooms in summer on the Florida State University campus.

Super 8, 2702 N Monroe St (☎386-8818). Regular motel facilities for $30 a night.

Eating

With so many politicos passing through, there's plenty of good **food** in Tallahassee; the presence of 25,000 students at its two universities keeps it affordable.

Andrew's Adams Street Café, 228 S Adams St. Stylish lunch cafe.

Andrew's Second Act, 102 W Jefferson St. Pricey evening meals in a classy restaurant.

Barnacle Bill's, 1830 N Monroe St. Low-cost seafood, in a riotous atmosphere. Live Fifties music.

China Garden, 220 W Tennessee St. Chinese lunch and dinner buffets for $5–6.

Mom and Dad's, 4175 Apalachee Parkway. Delicious and well-priced homemade Italian food.

Drinking and entertainment

Bolstered by the students, Tallahassee has a strong nightlife, with a leaning to social **drinking** and **live rock music**. There's also a fair amount of **drama**, headed by the student productions at the *University Theater*, on the FSU campus (☎644-6500), and the *Tallahassee Little Theater*, at the corner of Thomasville and Betton roads (☎224-8474).

Andrew's Upstairs, 228 S Adams St. Hosts modern jazz combos.

Calico Jack's, 2745 Capitol Circle. Beer, oysters, and rock'n'roll records in a less student-dominated environment.

Halligan's, 1700 Halstead Blvd. Popular for its pool tables and chilled mugs of beer.

The Moon, 1020 E Lafayette St (☎878-6900 for recorded info). Big name live bands appear here.

The Warehouse, 706 W Gaines St. Intimate venue, mixing rockabilly, avant-garde music and performance art.

Wakulla Springs

Fifteen miles south of Tallahassee on Hwy-61, **Wakulla Springs State Park** (daily 9am–5.30pm; cars $2, passengers, pedestrians and cyclists $1), holds what is believed to be one of the biggest and deepest natural springs in the world, pumping up half a million gallons of crystal-clear pure water from the bowels of the earth every day – though it would be difficult to guess that from the calm surface.

It's refreshing to **swim** in the cool liquid, but to learn more about the spring, take the fifteen-minute **glass-bottomed boat tour** ($4), and peer down to the swarms of fish hovering around the 180ft-deep cavern through which the water comes. Half-hour **river cruises** ($4) bring glimpses of some of the park's legged inhabitants: deer, turkeys, herons and egrets – and the inevitable alligators – among them. If *déjà vu* strikes, it may be because a number of movies have been shot here, including several of the early Tarzan movies and parts of *The Creature from the Black Lagoon*.

The Apalachicola National Forest

With swamps, savannahs and springs dotted liberally about its half-million acres, the **APALACHICOLA NATIONAL FOREST** is the inland Panhandle at its natural best. Several roads enable you to drive through a good-sized chunk, with many undemanding spots for a rest and a snack, but to see deeper into the forest you'll have to make an effort: exploring unhurriedly and at length, following one of the hiking trails, taking a canoe on one of the rivers, or simply spending a night under the stars at one of the basic campgrounds. Driving through the forest on Hwy-65, or around it on Hwy-319, you'll eventually pass the large and forbidding area believably called **Tate's Hell Swamp**. This is a breeding ground for the deadly water moccasin snake, and gung-ho locals sometimes venture into the swamp hoping to catch a few snakes to sell to the less reputable zoos; you're well advised to stay clear.

The main **entrances** to the forest are off Hwy-20 and Hwy-319; three minor roads, highways 267, 375 and 65, form cross-forest links between the two. **Accommodation** is limited to camping and, with the exception of Silver Lake (nine miles east of Tallahassee; $4), all the campgrounds are free with basic facilities.

Panama City Beach

An orgy of motels, go-kart tracks, mini-golf courses and amusement parks, **PANAMA CITY BEACH** is entirely without pretensions, capitalising as blatantly as possible on the appeal of its 27-mile beach. The whole place is as commercial as hell, but with the shops, bars and restaurants all trying to undercut one another, there are some great bargains to be found – from T-shirts and cut-price sunglasses to cheap buffet food. Throughout the lively summer (the so-called "100 Magic Days"), accommodation costs are high and advance bookings essential. In winter, prices drop and visitors are fewer; most are Canadians and – increasingly – northern Europeans, who have no problems sunbathing and swimming in the cool temperatures.

Getting a tan, running yourself ragged at beach sports, and going hammer-and-tong at the nightlife are the main concerns in Panama City Beach – you'll be regarded as a very raw prawn indeed if you go around demanding history, art and culture. If you get restless, try go-karting (around $3 for ten laps), one of the amusement parks (usually $10 for a go-on-everything day ticket), a fishing trip (take your pick of the party boats on the Thomas Drive marina, around $20 a day) or scuba-diving (several explorable shipwrecks litter the area; details from any of the numerous dive shops).

Practicalities

Greyhound **buses** stop at the Exxon station, 17325 W Hwy-98 (☎235-8999), leaving a fifteen-minute walk to the nearest motels. Travelling by bus, however, you may well end up in Panama City (917 Harrison Ave; ☎785-7861), eight miles east of Panama City Beach, in which case you'll need to use one of the four daily *Greyhound* services linking the two towns.

Places to stay are plentiful, but fill with amazing speed, especially on weekends. As a very general rule, **motels** at the eastern end of the beach are smarter and slightly pricier than those in the centre, and those at the western end are quiet and family-oriented. The cheapest places to **eat** are the buffet restaurants on Front Beach Road, charging $4 to $10 for all you can manage. Or try one of the regular **lunch or dinner** restaurants, like *Hickory Key*, 4106 Thomas Avenue, known for its barbecued meats and formidable seafood platter, and *Shuckum's Oyster Pub*, 15618 W Hwy-98. Really to get into the swing of things, visit one of the two beachside **nightlife** fleshpots, *Club La Vela*, 8813 Thomas Drive, or *Spinnaker*, 8795 Thomas Drive, each of which has dozens of bars, several discos, live bands, and a predominantly under-25 clientele.

Pensacola and Around

Tucked away at the western end of the Panhandle, you might be inclined to overlook **PENSACOLA**, built on the northern bank of the broad Pensacola Bay and five miles inland from the nearest beaches, particularly as its prime features are a naval aviation school and some busy dockyards. Pensacola is, however, an historic centre: occupied by the Spanish from 1559 – only the hurricane which ended their settlement prevented it becoming the oldest city in the US – it repeatedly changed hands between the Spanish, French and British before becoming the place where Florida was officially ceded by Spain to the US in 1821.

Pensacola was already a booming port by the turn of the century, when the opening of the Panama Canal was expected to boost its fortunes still further. The many new buildings which appeared in the **Palofax District**, around the southerly section of Palofax Street, in the early 1900s – with their delicate ornamentation and attention to detail – reflect the optimism of the era. Between 1870 and 1930, Pensacola's professional classes took a shine to the area just across Wright Street from Palofax called **North Hill**, commissioning elaborate homes in a plethora of fancy styles. Strewn across the fifty-block area are Neoclassical porches, Tudor-Revival cottages, low-slung California bungalows, and the rounded towers of the finest Queen Anne homes – though as none is open to the public, the best way to see them is with the historical tour (see opposite).

In earlier times, Native Americans, pioneer settlers and seafaring traders had gathered to swap, sell and barter on the waterfront of the **Seville District**, about half a mile east of Palofax Street. Those who did well took up permanent residence, and many of their homes remain in fine states of repair, forming – together with several museums – the **Historic Pensacola Village** (Easter to Labor Day Mon–Sat 10am–4.30pm, Sun 1–4.30pm; rest of the year Mon–Sat 10am–4.30pm; $3). One payment secures admission to all of the museums and former homes in an easily navigated four-block area.

Around Pensacola: Santa Rosa Island

On the other side of the bay from the city, the glistening beaches of **Santa Rosa Island** (the barrier island that runs sixty miles from Fort Walton) are ideal for sunbathing, and an endless row of windswept sand dunes demands investigation. **PENSACOLA BEACH** in particular has everything you'd want from a Gulf coast beach: mile after mile of fine white sands, rental outlets for water-sports equipment, a busy fishing pier and a sprinkling of motels, beachside bars and snack stands. It's hard to beat for uncomplicated oceanside recreation, but while sunning yourself, don't ignore what lies a short way west. At the **GULF ISLANDS NATIONAL SEASHORE**, on Fort Pickens Road (9am–sunset; cars $3, pedestrians and cyclists free), vibrant white sands are walled by a nine-mile-long stretch of high, rugged dunes and the only reminder of civilisation is a foliage-encircled campground.

Practicalities

At the foot of the three-mile Pensacola Bay Bridge into the city (on the city side), the **visitor centre** (daily 8.30am–5pm; ☎1-800/343-4321) is packed with the usual worthwhile handouts. An hour-long **historical tour** (Mon–Sat at 10am & 1pm; $7.50; ☎934-4200) departs by van from here. The **Greyhound** station is seven miles north of the city centre at 505 W Burgess Road (☎476-4800); bus #10 links it to Pensacola proper. **Local buses** serve the city but not the beach; the main terminal is at the junction of Gregory and Palofax streets.

Plenty of **budget chain hotels**, all $30 to $50 a night, line N Davis Boulevard and Pensacola Boulevard, the main approach roads from I-10. Of the central options, cheapest is the *Seville Inn*, 221 E Garden Street (☎1-800/277-7275), $25 to $40; the *Travelodge*, 200 N Palofax Street (☎1-800/255-3050), and *Days Inn*, 710 N Palofax Street (☎438-4922), are slightly dearer. **At the beach**, the lowest prices are $40 to $50 at *Barbary Coast*, 24 Via De Luna (☎932-2233), *Gulf Aire*, 21 Via De Luna (☎932-2319), and *Mai Kai*, 731 Pensacola Beach Boulevard (☎932-2089).

travel details

TRAINS
Routes

• Three *Amtrak* trains daily arrive in **Jacksonville** from **New York** and **Washington DC**. Two connecting services per day continue to **Orlando** and **Tampa**, and another two continue to **Palm Beach** and **Miami**.

• *Amtrak* buses to **St Petersburg** connect with trains at **Tampa**.

• Passengers **with cars** only can use *Amtrak's* daily *Auto Train* from Lorton, Virginia (just south of Washington DC) to Sanford, north of Orlando.

• *Tri-Rail* trains run from **Miami** to **Fort Lauderdale**, **Boca Raton**, and **West Palm Beach** around ten times daily.

Journey Times

From Miami: Fort Lauderdale 34min; Boca Raton 1hr; West Palm Beach 1hr 40min; Ocala 5hr 53min; Washington 22hr; New York 29hr.

From Orlando: Tampa 2hr 17min.

From Tampa: Clearwater 35min; Clearwater Beach 50min; St Petersburg 30min; Sarasota 1hr 35min.

From Sanford: Lorton 17hr 30min.

BUSES

From Miami to Daytona Beach (7 daily; 8hr 55min–9hr 50min); Fort Lauderdale (19 daily; 1hr); Fort Myers (5 daily; 5hr 35min); Key West (2 daily; 4hr 30min); Orlando (7 daily; 6hr 45min); Sarasota (5 daily; 7hr 35min); St Petersburg (3 daily; 9hr 50min); Tampa (5 daily; 9hr 45min–10hr 35min); West Palm Beach (12 daily; 2hr 30min).

Local *Greyhounds* from downtown Miami to Coral Gables (8 daily; 30min); Miami Beach (7 daily; 45min–1hr 15min); Miami West (18 daily; 15–45min); North Miami Beach (18 daily; 20–45min).

Florida Keys: two daily *Greyhound* buses run from Miami to Key West, down the Overseas Highway, a 4hr 30min trip, with scheduled stops in North Key Largo (Central Plaza, 103200 Overseas Highway); Marathon (6363 Overseas Highway;); Big Pine Key (MM30.2); Key West (615½ Duval Street).

From Fort Lauderdale to Boca Raton (4 daily; 50min); Walt Disney World (1 daily; 4hr 41min); West Palm Beach (13 daily; 2hr).

From West Palm Beach to Tampa (2 daily; 6hr); Walt Disney World (1 daily; 3hr 46min).

From Cocoa to Daytona Beach (6 daily; 1hr 40min).

From Daytona Beach to Orlando (12 daily; 1hr 15min); St Augustine (5 daily; 35min).

From Orlando to West Palm Beach/Fort Lauderdale/Miami (7 daily; 3hr 45min/5hr 20min/5hr 55min); Kissimmee (2 daily; 30min); Ocala/Tallahassee (4 daily; 1hr 30min/5hr 30min); Sea World/EPCOT Center/Disney-MGM/Magic Kingdom (1 daily; 20min/40min/55min/1hr 5min); Tampa (5 daily; 3hr 15min).

From Tampa to Sarasota/Fort Myers/Fort Lauderdale/Miami (5 daily; 1hr 35min/2hr 5min/7hr 5min/8hr 55min); St Petersburg (15 daily; 35min); Clearwater (6 daily; 30min); Tallahassee (4 daily; 6hr 35min); West Palm Beach (1 daily; 6hr).

From Tallahassee to Panama City Beach (3 daily; 2hr 30min); Pensacola (5 daily; 2hr 35min); Miami (4 daily; 11hr 55min); Tampa (4 daily; 5hr); Orlando (4 daily; 6hr 30min); New Orleans (6 daily; 8hr 30min).

From Panama City Beach to Panama City (4 daily; 30min); Pensacola (4 daily; 2hr 15min).

From Pensacola to Tallahassee (5 daily; 4hr 25min); New Orleans (8 daily; 4hr 15min).

CHAPTER EIGHT

LOUISIANA

S wathed in the romance of pirates, voodoo and Mardi Gras, **LOUISIANA** is undeniably special. Its history is barely on nodding terms with the view that America was the creation of the Pilgrim Fathers; its way of life is proudly set apart. This is the land of the rural French-speaking **Cajuns** (descended from eighteenth-century French-Canadian refugees), and the haughty **Creole** aristocrats of jazzy, sassy **New Orleans**. (The term Creole covers those born in the state to non-Anglo colonists, famed in days gone by for their glittering masked balls, family feuds and duels, as well as native-born French-speaking slaves.) **North Louisiana** – Protestant Bible Belt country, complete with cotton fields, southern belles, and fine old plantation homes – is more "Southern" than the marshy bayous, shaded by ancient cypress trees and laced by wispy trails of Spanish moss, of Catholic **south Louisiana**. Louisiana's spicy homecooked **food**, almost weekly **festivals**, and lilting French-based dialect – and above all its music (**jazz**, **R&B**, **cajun** and its bluesier black counterpart, **zydeco**) – draw from all these cultures.

The **French** first settled Louisiana in 1682, braving swamps and plagues to harvest the abundant cypress, but the state was sparsely inhabited before its first permanent settlement, the trading post of **Natchitoches**, was established in 1714. In 1764, Louis XV

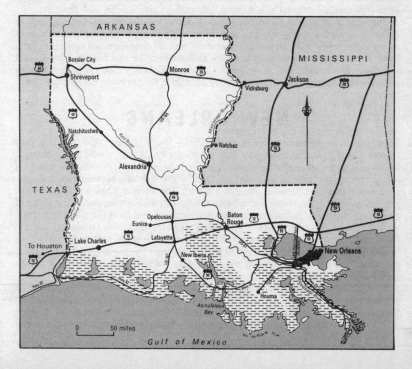

secretly handed all French territory west of the Mississippi to his **Spanish** cousin, as a safeguard against the British, and Louisiana remained Spanish until it was ceded to Napoleon in 1801, under the proviso that it should never change hands again. Just two years later, Napoleon needed cash and struck a bargain with Jefferson, known as the **Louisiana Purchase**. This sneaky agreement handed over to the US all French lands between Canada and Mexico, from the Mississippi to the Rockies, for a total cost of $15 million. The subsequent "Americanisation" of Louisiana was much resisted by the proud Creoles, and the state eventually joined the Confederacy in 1861. There were, however, important differences between Louisiana and other slave-driven Southern states. Here slavery was more in the West Indian mould than the Anglo-American. The **Black Code** of Louisiana, established by the French, upheld by the Spanish and then effectively broken by the Americans, gave slaves rights unparalleled elsewhere, including permission to marry, meet socially and take Sundays off. The black population of New Orleans in particular was renowned as exceptionally literate and cosmopolitan.

Louisiana was economically rather than physically scarred by the Civil War, with few important battles being fought on its soil, and in time it recovered, benefitting from rich **agricultural** land, the mighty Mississippi River and offshore **oil**. Today **tourism** is crucial, but despite rabid commercialism, Louisiana stays unique; one can only hope that the alarming but fortunately unsuccessful attempt in late·1991 of the openly racist David Duke (see p.485) to become state governor will not have lasting effects on its intriguing and compelling mix of upbeat, quirky, laidback ease.

Getting Around Louisiana

Louisiana is crossed east–west by two major interstates, I-20 in the north and I-10 in the south. New Orleans is very much the hub, served by I-55 and I-59 from Mississippi. I-49 sweeps across southeast to northwest, connecting Cajun country with the north.

The main international **airport** is in New Orleans; various regional airlines, such as *L'Express*, serve the rest of the state and surrounding areas. *Greyhound* **buses** connect all the major towns with the rest of the country, and are supplemented by smaller local lines. Three *Amtrak* **trains** daily link New Orleans with the east and west coasts, and with the north central states. As well as the Mississippi's bridges and causeways, **ferries** cross the river at both New Orleans and St Francisville, further north in Cajun country.

NEW ORLEANS

There's a whole lot more to **NEW ORLEANS** – the "Big Easy", the "city that care forgot" – than its tourist image as a non-stop party city. At once sordid and sublime, it reels along under an infuriating double think. In between having enormous amounts of fun, you're always liable to be pulled up short by the divisions between rich and poor (and more explicitly, between white and black). The **French Quarter**, for example, playground of the city, teems with white tourists, with blacks relegated to the status of musicians, doormen, and waiters; and a mere stone's throw from the partying and the money-making, on Canal Street or in Lafayette Square, black New Orleanians line the street begging. Even so, the city's vitality and *joie de vivre* are real, buffeted but not beaten by the vagaries of commercialism and poverty. The melange of cultures and races that built the city still gives it its heart. It may not be "easy", exactly, but it's quite unlike anywhere else in the States – or in the world.

New Orleans began life in 1718 as a set of shacks on a disease-ridden marsh. Its prime location led to rapid development, and with the first mass importation of African **slaves** as early as the 1720s its unique demography began to take shape. The **French** and **Spanish** colonists were initially fierce rivals, but economic necessity soon forced them to learn to live together.

NEW ORLEANS

By the end of the eighteenth century, the **port** was flourishing, the haunt of smugglers, gamblers, prostitutes, pirates and escapees from the French Revolution and West Indian slave rebellions. New Orleans was thus already a diverse and many-textured city when it experienced two quick-fire changes of government, passing back into **French** control in 1801 and then being sold to **America** under the **Louisiana Purchase** two years later. This heralded the most bitter transition in the city's history, literally splitting it into two sections. The Americans who migrated here in droves were seen as crass and uncouth by the Creoles and hated by the blacks, upon whom they placed previously unknown restrictions. Unwelcome in the French Quarter, the newcomers were forced to settle in the areas known now as the **Central Business District** and the Garden District. Canal Street divided the two sectors, and even today the median strip in the middle of the main roads is called "the neutral ground".

Creoles and Americans came together briefly in 1815, defeating the British in the **Battle of New Orleans** which ended the War of 1812 and secured American supremacy in the States. The victorious general, **Andrew Jackson**, became a national hero; his army was made up of pirates (supplied by the notorious **Jean Lafitte**, previously a sworn enemy of the Americans), slaves, Creoles and Native Americans.

New Orleans then embarked upon a **"Golden Age"** which lasted until the Civil War. The city boomed as a finance centre for the cotton-producing South, as well as trading in tobacco, cotton and indigo. The flood of immigrants included Irish, Germans, and

Sicilians (by 1890, New Orleans was famed as the American seat of the **Mafia**, still a tangible presence today). However, the Union troops who occupied the city and sealed off the Mississippi until 1872 isolated it from its markets. As the North industrialised, and other southern cities grew, the fortunes of New Orleans took a downturn. The coming of **rail**, especially, which diminished the importance of the river, and the abolition of **slavery**, both marked the end of the glory days.

Jazz exploded into the bars and the bordellos at the turn of the century, and, along with the development of **Mardi Gras** as a tourist attraction, breathed new life into the city. Even so, it was the less romantic duo of **oil** and the **petrochemical** industry that really saved the economy – until the slump of the 1950s pushed New Orleans well behind other US cities. The oil crash of the early Eighties gave it yet another battering, but battle-scarred New Orleans remains, against the odds, simply irresistable.

One word of warning: due to its swampy climate, New Orleans can be unbearably **hot**; if you can, it's well worth trying to avoid coming in **summer**, the off-season.

Arrival, Information and Getting Around

One of New Orleans' many nicknames is "the **Crescent City**", for the way it nestles between a bend in the Mississippi River and the southern shore of Lake Pontchartrain. This makes its layout somewhat confusing, with streets twisting to follow the curve of the river. Locals often use the terms riverside, lakeside, uptown (or upriver), and downtown (or downriver) as directions; just remember that **upriver** from Canal Street (the widest main street in the nation) is south, **downriver** is north. **Uptown** includes the Garden District, the two universities, and Carrollton. The Central Business District (CBD) and the French Quarter (or Vieux Carré), the main tourist area, are both **downtown**.

New Orleans International **Airport** (☎464-0831 or ☎729-2591) is twelve miles northwest on I-10. There's a visitor centre (10am–10pm) in the baggage claim area. **Taxi** fares into town are around $20 (*United Cabs* are on ☎524-9606), but *Airport Rhodes* **buses** (☎469-4335) will take you to your hotel (tickets, $7, available in the baggage claim area or from the bus driver). A **public bus** from the airport goes to the downtown side of Tulane Avenue (daily 6am–6.30pm; every 10min 6–9am and 3–6pm, every half-hour otherwise; $1.10; ☎737-9611).

Greyhound (☎525-4201) comes in next to *Amtrak* (☎528-1610) at 1001 Loyola Avenue, near the Superdome. This area, ten minutes from Canal Street, is dangerous at night; catch a taxi.

Getting Around

Although New Orleans is easy to walk around – the French Quarter is definitely best enjoyed by a leisurely stroll – its **public transport** is good. The *Regional Transit Authority* (Plaza Tower, 101 Dauphine St, Mon–Fri 8.30am–5pm; 24-hr route information ☎569-2700) runs **buses** from Canal Street across the city well into the night, some routes continuing until 3.30am. Fares range from 80¢–$1. An *Easy Rider* shuttle bus runs through the CBD from the Convention Centre to the Superdome, stopping along Poydras and Canal streets (Mon–Sat 6.30am–6.30pm; 30¢). The **St Charles streetcar** (a National Historic Monument) rumbles from Canal Street, along St Charles Avenue in the Garden District, to Audubon Park, 24 hours a day. Settling back on the old wooden benches next to an open window is an ideal way to do a city tour on the cheap (80¢ each way). Seven other streetcars run along the riverfront, and for a mere 60¢ you can also catch the **Vieux Carré minibus** through the Quarter (5am–7pm). *VisiTour*

The telephone **area code** for New Orleans is ☎504.

CITY TOURS AND RIVER CRUISES

Gray Line (☎587-0865) and *New Orleans Tours* (☎592-0560) organise similar **bus tours** of the city itself (2hr; around $15), the plantations (7hr; $31), and New Orleans' nightlife (2hr 30min; $33). The *Friends of the Cabildo* lead two-hour **walking tours** from the Presbytere in Jackson Square (Tues–Sat 9.30am & 1.30pm, Sun 1.30pm; $7 – no reservations required).

One pleasant, if overpriced, way to while away a few hours is on a **river cruise**. The *Creole Queen* paddlewheeler and *Cajun Queen* riverboat (☎524-0814) leave from Riverwalk Mall on Canal Street; trips include excursions to Chalmette Plantation ($12), and 8pm Dixieland jazz dinner cruises ($34; $18 without dinner). *Natchez* (☎586-8777), from Toulouse Street wharf, has a summer Saturday evening moonlit cruise at 10pm, a buffet cruise for $29.75, and a 6.30pm jazz cruise.

---

passes, available from major hotels, entitle you to unlimited travel on all streetcars and buses ($3 per day, $6 for three days).

Around Jackson Square on the river, **horse-drawn carriages** give narrated rides through the Quarter, but the price ($8) and the unhappy horses, decked out in funny hats, can be a turn-off. Instead, join locals on the **commuter ferry** crossing from Canal Street to suburban Algiers, for a good view of activity on Old Man River. A night ride makes a cheap alternative to "romantic" moonlit paddle boat cruises; you save about $35, but miss out on the live jazz accompaniment.

Bicycles can be rented from the *St Charles Guest House* and the *Marquette House Youth Hostel* (see p.479).

Information

For detailed information on the city, and excellent self-guided walking tours, drop in at the **New Orleans Welcome Centre** in the French Quarter at 529 St Ann Street (daily, summer 10am–6pm, winter 9am–5pm; ☎566-5031).

The official **post office** is at 701 Loyola Avenue (Mon–Fri 8am–4.30pm, Sat 8am–1pm; ☎589-1112; zip code 70140), but an equivalent service is offered in the French Quarter by *French Quarter Postal Emporium*, 940 Royal Street (Mon–Fri 9.30am–6pm, Sat 10am–3pm; ☎525-6651).

The City

New Orleans' spiritual centre is the surprisingly small **French Quarter**, site of the city's original settlement. Upriver (but still downtown) is the **CBD**, the early "American section" and the city's financial centre, spreading from Canal Street to Howard Avenue and including, towards Lake Pontchartrain, the gargantuan Superdome. The **Garden District**, uptown, offers a quite different taste of New Orleans.

The French Quarter

Breathtakingly beautiful, depressingly tacky, the **French Quarter** is the heart of New Orleans. Each block, with its overhanging lacy ironwork balconies, pastel stucco walls, shutters and high-walled cobbled courtyards, smacks of history and legend. Official tours are useful for orientation, but it's most fun simply to wander – and you'll need a couple of days at least to do it justice, absorbing the jumble of sounds, people, sights and smells. Early morning, in the pearly light from the river, is a good time to explore, as sleepy locals wake themselves up with strong coffee in the neighbourhood cafes, shops crank open their shutters, and all-night revellers stumble home. You can almost feel the

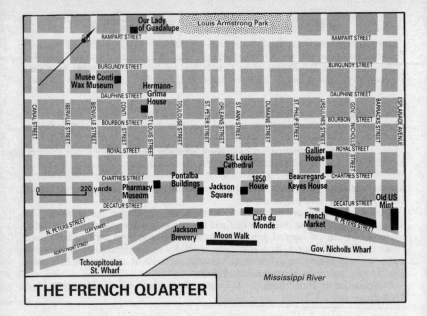

THE FRENCH QUARTER

build-up of adrenaline, and when the first plaintive trumpet moans through the air, it's as if a morning bell has sounded. New Orleans puts on its party face and the day begins.

The Quarter is laid out in a grid, with central **Jackson Square** facing the Mississippi. The architecture is predominantly Spanish colonial, with a strong Caribbean influence, and dates from the end of the eighteenth century, after most of the original French buildings had been devastated by two great fires in 1788 and 1794. Today the Quarter is home to offices, shops, galleries, restaurants, bars and apartments.

Jackson Square

Jackson Square, as the *Place d'Armes* once used for public meetings and executions, is now a well-kept park where artists, horse-drawn carriages and buskers congregate to entertain picnicking office workers and tourists, presided over by an equestrian statue of Andrew Jackson himself.

The **St Louis Cathedral**, in the middle of Chartres Street facing the river, is the third church on this spot, built in 1794 after the first two were destroyed by fire and hurricane. Its design is Spanish, with a grand gold and wooden altar, on which Jackson is said to have laid his sword in thanks for victory at the Battle of New Orleans. Devout worshippers stream in, illustrating New Orleans' claim to be the most Catholic city in America. The stately Spanish structure with an impressive ironwork balcony next door is the **Cabildo**, seat of the first Spanish government. After the Louisiana Purchase, which was signed in a room on the second floor, it was used as the city hall and state supreme court, and rebuilt in 1851 to look more French. Today it is part of the State Museum. Sadly, this grand old building had to be closed after being damaged by fire in 1988; at the time this book went to press it was due to re-open shortly. On the other side of the cathedral, at 751 Chartres Street, is the **Presbytere**, bought from the Church by the city in 1853, and now part of the **State Museum**, exhibiting antique portraits, musical instruments, maps, toys, and decorative art (Wed–Sun 10am–5pm; $3; ☎568-6968).

The smart red three-storey **Pontalba Buildings** on St Peter and St Ann streets bordering the Square were designed in 1850 by the eccentric Baroness Pontalba (who donned trousers to oversee the work at every stage). Planned as both business and residential units to draw activity back into the Quarter, which had been hard hit by American success in the CBD, they are a source of much pride to the city. The **1850 House** at 523 St Ann Street has been restored to display the ostentatious tastes of a well-to-do Creole family (Wed–Sun 10am–5pm; $3).

Decatur Street and Esplanade Avenue

For good views of the **Port**, cross Decatur Street to the **Moon Walk**, a wooden promenade where buskers serenade you as you gaze over the river. Downriver along Decatur Street is the **French Market**, a marketplace since the 1720s which is now filled with bric-à-brac, and, directly behind it, the old **Farmer's Market**, selling fresh fruit and vegetables 24 hours daily. The weekend flea market is full of bargain oddities, as are many of the vintage clothes shops opposite on Decatur Street. Look out for *Noney's*, 1224 Decatur Street, with quirky antiques and bulging bags of colourful Mardi Gras beads. *Jazzrags* nearby at no. 1232 sells quality secondhand clothes at low prices.

Continuing downriver, you'll come to the outer boundary of the Quarter, **Esplanade Avenue**, a broad oak-lined boulevard with several grand nineteenth-century Creole mansions. The **Old US Mint**, on its 400 block, houses the **Jazz Museum**, tracing the history of the music that New Orleans calls its own, through photographs, old letters and adverts, with a lively jazz soundtrack and videos. A Mardi Gras exhibit explains the complexities of the carnival, with lots of old costumes, and the original 1906 "Streetcar named Desire" stands in the grounds (Wed–Sun 10am–5pm; $3).

Along Chartres and Royal Streets

A left turn at the 600 block of Esplanade Avenue brings you to the **Old Ursulines Convent** at 1114 Chartres Street. Built in 1750, this is the only remaining example of French colonial architecture in the States, and quite possibly the oldest building in the whole Mississippi valley. The **Beauregard-Keyes House** opposite at no. 1113 (Mon–Sat 10am–3pm; $4) owes its name to Confederate General Pierre **Beauregard**, who ordered the first shot of the Civil War at Fort Sumter, and rented a room here when desperately poor and unemployed in later years, and to local novelist Frances Parkinson **Keyes**. She refurbished this "raised cottage", (with the basement on the ground floor), as her winter home in the 1940s. Her novels – including *Madame Castel's Lodger*, about the "Beauregard period", which features the house itself – are on sale.

A block north at 1132 Royal Street, the **Gallier House**, dating from 1860, is a great little museum, demonstrating such typical features of French Quarter residences as the outdoor cistern and cooling system, and the safe for storing tea and coffee – precious commodities of the time. The view across the French Quarter from the lacy iron balcony upstairs, where you're left in peace after the tour to linger and sup free coffee, is superb. (Mon–Sat 10.30am–3.45pm, Sun noon–3.45pm; $4.)

Behind St Louis Cathedral, the small iron-fenced garden of **St Anthony's Square** was the scene of numerous celebrated duels in the 1830s. The narrow lane alongside (lined with pavement artists) is known as **Pirate's Alley**, and is one of the many supposed locations of secret meetings between Jean Lafitte and Andrew Jackson to plan the Battle of New Orleans in 1815. It's highly unlikely that this is true – the road was only constructed in 1831 – but it's one of those stories that New Orleanians so love.

The scholarly **Historic New Orleans Collection** at 533 Royal Street looks quite appropriate amongst all the antique shops and posh art galleries. Exhibits in the dignified 1792 building, one of the few survivors of the 1794 fire, include old maps, drawings and documents relating to the Louisiana Purchase (Tues–Sat; $2). A free gallery focuses on local art and culture.

MACABRE NEW ORLEANS

Voodoo

Voodoo was brought to New Orleans by early African slaves, for whom Catholicism provided good cover for praying to their own gods. French and Spanish authorities tried to suppress what they saw as subversive devil-worship, but under American rule, partly due to the lifting of a ban on importing slaves from Haiti and the West Indies, voodoo flourished. As the weekly slave gatherings at **Congo Square** (now Louis Armstrong Park), with dancing, singing and weird ceremonies, turned into a tourist attraction for whites, the authentic worship of African gods shifted underground. The fascination and repulsion felt by the white community for this sexual, exotic, snakeworship were fuelled by frequent reports of white women dancing naked at rituals. New Orleans' most famous voodoo priestess was **Marie Laveau**, of mixed African, white, and Native American blood, who prepared spells for all walks of New Orleans life – wealthy Creoles and Americans as well as slaves. Although she died in 1881, her legend persists, with her grave(s) frequently visited (see below) and her memory revered.

The Historic Voodoo Museum at 723 Dumaine Street contains various ceremonial objects, paintings, spells and *gris-gris* – pouches carried for good luck, filled with amulets, charms and herbs. (Daily 10am–dusk; $3.)

Psychic readings are widely available; they're fun, but can be pricey. Try at the tiny *Marie Laveau's House of Voodoo*, 739 Bourbon Street (☎581-3751), *Voodoo Macumba*, 813 Toulouse Street (☎588-1462), or *Bottom of the Cup*, 616 Conti Street (☎524-1557).

The Cities of the Dead

So much of New Orleans is at, or below, sea level that early settlers who buried their dead found that the corpses would gruesomely float to the ground. Graves began to be placed, Spanish-style, in above-ground vaults, surrounded by small fences and gardens. The **cemeteries** grew to resemble cities, laid out in "streets" and taking on an eerie appearance as the tombs crumbled, tilted over and fell apart. This creepiness isn't totally imaginary, either, though muggers, rather than ghosts, haunt the cemeteries today. Exploring should never be done alone. There are plenty of special guided tours, and nearly all the city tours (see p.473) include a quick trip around one of the graveyards.

St Louis Cemetery No 1, at 400 Basin Street between Toulouse and St Louis streets, is the oldest city of the dead. This small graveyard dates from 1788, and is full of crooked mausolea jutting into narrow, twisting pathways. Its spook value is enhanced by Marie Laveau's grave, covered with red brick-dust crosses. If you turn around and knock on the slab three times, and mark a cross on her tomb with the brick provided, her spirit will grant you any favour. Mysteriously, they say, the grave is always in immaculate condition, compared to the decay that surrounds it.

St Louis No 2, at N Claiborne Avenue and Bienville Street, is more orderly, with many well-kept graves in Greek Revival style. Marie Laveau is supposedly buried here, too, and another vault daubed with red crosses marks the spot. This one grants the wishes of any woman seeking a husband.

St Louis No 3, at 3421 Esplanade Avenue, is a peaceful burial ground mostly used by religious orders; all the priests of the diocese are buried here, and fragile angels balance on top of the tombs.

A Haunted House

The striking grey and black **LaLaurie Home** at 1140 Royal Street is New Orleans' most famous **haunted house** (though not open to the public). It belonged to socialite Delphine LaLaurie, who although seen whipping a young slave on the roof was merely fined when the same girl "fell" from the roof to her death. Whispers about her cruelty were horribly verified when neighbours rushed in after a fire in 1834, to find slaves choked by neck braces, handcuffed and immobile, locked in a dingy attic. The next day an angry mob gathered outside the house. Delphine escaped in a carriage, and fled to France, as her home was ripped apart. Many claim to have heard the hissing of a whip and ghostly moans from the building at night; some have seen a little girl stumble across the rooftop . . .

Less learned, but just as informative, is the **Pharmacy Museum**, a block away at 514 Chartres Street, tracing the history of medicine from the twelfth century (Tues–Sun 10am–5pm; $1). This quirky little place, in an old apothecary, is full of hand-carved rosewood cabinets, cluttered with intriguing dusty phials, ancient lotions, potions and powders. Shelves heave with *gris-gris*, jars of leeches for blood-letting (to remove excessive irritability) and Creole "female tonics" (used to cure "all the various form of female weakness"), as well as adverts for *7-Up*, the most popular drink during the Depression due to its high lithium content. There is also a stunning red marble soda fountain.

Exchange Alley, in the 600 block (between Chartres and Royal streets) of Conti Street just west of the Pharmacy Museum, was another of the city's favourite duelling spots, known in the 1830s as the "street of the fencing masters". Many of these duelling teachers also hired themselves out as assassins, working by provoking their prey into unwinnable duels, and consequently the street saw some pretty bloody goings-on.

Bourbon Street

If you continue lakeside, and cross Royal Street once more, Conti Street will lead you up to **Bourbon Street**, the most famous – and tackiest – street in the city. Lined with strip joints, neon bars and souvenir shops, with a couple of great bars (see p.483), it is in fact one of the least worthwhile streets of the Quarter. Half a block north at 820 St Louis Street, the restored 1831 **Hermann-Grima House** illustrates the lifestyle of middle-class Creoles in the city's Golden Age (Mon–Sat 10am–3.30pm; $3; ☎525-5661). Cookery demonstrations are held in the kitchen every summer Thursday.

Quiet **Dauphine Street**, just north, home to a large gay community, has a peaceful atmosphere that welcomes tourists without being touristy. By following it a block west and then turning north you'll come to the **Musee Conti Wax Museum** at 917 Conti Street (daily 10am–5pm; $5), which tells the story of New Orleans through lurid tableaux, including voodoo, gambling and jazz, and a waxwork house of horror, with much shrieking and wailing. **Our Lady of Guadalupe** church at 411 N Rampart Street, on the corner of Conti Street, is notable for its statue of "Saint Expedite", mysteriously delivered here in a crate simply stamped *expedite*. There's a jazz mass held every Saturday night, but take care when walking around here after dark, especially near **Louis Armstrong Park**, sadly one of the most dangerous areas in the city.

Outside the French Quarter

The unattractive riverside skyscraper at 2 Canal Street is the **World Trade Centre**, which has an observation deck on the 31st floor and a slide show about New Orleans (daily 9am–5pm; $2). Also on the river, the impressive **Aquarium of the Americas**, near the Canal Street wharf, has a climate-controlled Amazon rainforest and Caribbean reef. Its exotic sea creatures include killer sharks that zoom towards those who dare to cross the glass underwater tunnel (daily 9.30am–9pm; $7.50).

During the Civil War, the (then incomplete) **Customs House** at 423 Canal Street (Mon–Fri 9am–4.30pm) was headquarters to Union General Butler, known scornfully as "Spoons" Butler for his kleptomaniac habit of stealing the cutlery from his hosts. Finally completed in the 1880s, it has a huge marble hall on the second floor, in which fourteen towering columns of white Italian marble support the dazzling white and gilt ceiling.

The **St Charles streetcar** from Canal Street offers a leisurely trip to many of New Orleans' sights. **Lafayette Square** was the American version of the *Place d'Armes*, now filled with winos despite all the city's efforts to clear them out. It doesn't look much, but has been the site of some pretty dramatic events, including acting as a military camp in an 1858 mini-Civil War between Creoles and Americans battling over city elections. A few hundred yards away, the **Confederate Museum** at 929 Camp Street tells the story of the Confederacy cogently and poignantly (Mon–Sat 10am–4pm; $3).

The Garden District and Audubon Park
The grand residential **Garden District**, two miles upriver from the French Quarter,
was built in the 1840s by rich Americans, who loved to display their wealth through
spacious landscaped gardens, as opposed to the cramped confines of the Creole courtyards in the Quarter. Tropical bushes and magnificent oaks flourish in the fertile soil,
while the ornate buildings, raised to avoid water damage, evoke the Deep South in a
profusion of porches, columns and balconies. Look out for the **Brown House** at 4717
St Charles Avenue, and the 1941 replica of **Tara**, the house in *Gone with the Wind*, at
no. 5705. You can't miss the **Wedding Cake House** at no. 5809. It suits its name, an
ostentatious Colonial-Greek Revival building, with balconies, cornices and lots of
columns. The Welcome Centre provides a self-guided walking tour, but the homes are
only open to the public during the Spring Fiesta (see festivals, p.482).

Peaceful **Audubon Park** is full of lagoons, ancient oaks overhung with wispy
Spanish moss, palms and fountains, with a swimming pool, jogging paths and bikes for
the more active. New Orleanians are justifiably boastful about the spectacular
Audubon Zoo at 6500 Magazine Street behind the park, which features a white tiger,
white alligators, and reconstructions of a Louisiana swamp, as well as Australian and
African habitats (daily all year 9am–4.30pm, Sat & Sun 9am–5.30pm in summer; $6).
You can walk through the park to the zoo, or take a shuttle bus from the park gates.
The **Pitot House** is within walking distance at 1440 Moss Street. This West Indies-
style plantation house on the Bayou St John is the only remaining of its kind in the city,
and is furnished with antiques (Wed–Sat 10am–3pm; $3).

Approaching Lake Pontchartrain
The lakeside edge of the CBD would be pretty lifeless without the magnificent home of
the New Orleans Saints football team, the **Superdome**. At 680ft in diameter, 27 storeys
high, and covering 52 acres, this is one of the largest buildings in the world. You can't
really conceive of its hugeness until you venture inside (tours 10am, noon, 2pm, & 4pm;
$4; ☎587-3810). This area, though safe enough in the day, is dangerous at night.

Even further towards the Lake is New Orleans' 1500-acre **City Park**, site of the
Dueling Oaks, under which Creoles and Americans met at dawn to defend their
honour. The nearby **New Orleans Museum of Art**, surrounded by lagoons, has works
by Degas, Picasso, and Dufy, Rodin sculptures, pre-Columbian pieces from Central
America, and some Fabergé jewelled eggs (Tues–Sun 10am–5pm; $4).

The Chalmette Plantation
The **Chalmette Plantation** (☎589-2636), six miles downriver from Canal Street, is the
site where Jackson's ragbag army defeated the British in 1815. There isn't much to show
for it, apart from bare fields and the simple Beauregard plantation home. Jean Lafitte
National Historical Park rangers provide a self-guided walking tour, and give talks in the
small visitor centre four times daily. The plantation can be reached on a steamboat
excursion or from Hwy-46, and is open from 9am until 5pm daily.

Accommodation

Room rates in New Orleans, never low, increase considerably for Mardi Gras, the Jazz
Festival, and the Sugar Bowl, when reservations should be made as much as a year
ahead. Even during the off-season it's a good idea to call before you arrive; this is not a
city in which you'd want to be stranded overnight. Summer accommodation is available
at **Tulane** (27 McAlister Drive, ☎865-5426) and **Loyola** (6363 St Charles Ave, ☎865-
3735) universities. Both are on the St Charles streetcar line, the former offering
doubles with bath and kitchenette for $35, the latter with doubles from $50.

Bed and breakfast inns in old Creole cottages or townhouses are some of the most beautiful, and cheapest, lodgings in the city. Contact *New Orleans B&B*, PO Box 8128 (☎822-5046), or *B&B Inc*, 1360 Moss Street, Box 52257 (☎525-4640), which can root out quaint and affordable guest houses for as little as $35. Outside the French Quarter, try Prytania Street, near St Charles Avenue. The **Welcome Centre** in Jackson Square (see p.473) offers a room booking service.

French Quarter

Chateau Motor Hotel, 1001 Chartres St (☎524-9636). Basic rooms lacking the more elegant touches of other French Quarter hotels, with a pleasant outdoor cafe. Doubles $60–75.

French Quarter Maisonettes, 1130 Chartres St (☎524-9918). Peaceful, popular B&B. Courtyard with fountain, tropical plants and climbing vines. Hospitable hostess. $45–55, booking essential.

Hotel Villa Convento, 616 Ursulines St (☎522-1793). Simple guest house in old Creole townhouse, rooms from $50, breakfast included.

Hotel Provincial, 1024 Chartres St (☎581-4995). Quite luxurious; antique-filled rooms $65–95.

Outside the Quarter

The Frenchmen, 417 Frenchmen St (☎948-2166). Two 1860 townhouses on the very fringes of the French Quarter. Rooms overlook a pretty courtyard, pool and patio. Free full breakfast. $68–108.

Hummingbird Hotel and Grill, 804 St Charles Ave (☎561-9229). $30, with discounts for students. Popular 24-hr local restaurant on the ground floor.

La Salle Hotel, 1113 Canal St (☎523-5831). Near the French Quarter on the city's main thoroughfare. Cheap student rates. Clean rooms from $32, $45 with bath. Seedy area at night.

Marquette House Youth Hostel, 2253 Carondelet St (☎523-3014). Antebellum house one block from streetcar in the Garden District. Functional rooms go for $27 with membership, $30 without. Rooms with bathroom and kitchen are $39, or $45 non-members. Dormitory beds $10, $13 for non-members. Reservations recommended, and for Mardi Gras should be paid in full well in advance.

St Charles Guest House, 1748 Prytania St (☎523-6556). Friendly local owners, and bohemian clientele. Pool and palm-lined terrace. Doubles $45–60, or $30–45 without bath.

YMCA, 936 St Charles Ave (☎568-9622). Co-ed dormitory, or double rooms (no showers) from $31.

Eating

Eating out in New Orleans is delectable, a big occasion that can last the whole night. The food is a spicy and substantial mix of French, Spanish, African and Cajun; it's also delightfully cheap. The mainstay of most menus are **gumbo** – a thick soup of seafood, chicken, and vegetables (*gumbo* is the Bantu for okra, a prime ingredient) – and **jambalaya**, a paella again containing seafood, chicken, sausage and vegetables. Many dishes are served *etouffé*, literally "smothered" in a spicy tomato sauce.

It's still just about possible to distinguish Cajun from Creole dishes, although differences have become blurred over the years. **Creole** food derives from the French and Spanish colonists and their black slaves. A lot of it, like red beans and rice (Monday's lunch), shows a strong Caribbean influence. **Cajun** food is more countrified, based upon the *roux*, a tasty brown sauce, and using shallots, parsley, peppers, pork and garlic. Dishes that were originally designed to use up leftovers can look vile, so "Cajun" restaurants often prettify original recipes. Much that claims to be Cajun – for example, blackened and deep fried dishes – simply isn't. The increasingly rare turtle soup, however, is.

The swankiest New Orleans restaurants, the "Big Five" – *Antoine's, Arnaud's, Brennan's, Commander's Palace* and *Galatoire's* – serve Creole haute cuisine, often accompanied by live jazz in a formal setting. All but *Galatoire's* are very expensive by the city's standards ($30–50), but the food is exquisite. It's even more fun, and considerably cheaper, however, to root out home cooking in small local places. At the other end of the scale, but equally unmissable, are the *Lucky Dogs* **hotdog carts,** featured in John

Kennedy Toole's sleaze farce *A Confederacy of Dunces*. These obscene giant hotdogs, shoved by some of the city's most eccentric characters, are a much-loved institution, and can be seen being trundled through the French Quarter at all hours.

Other specialities are **po-boys**, french-bread sandwiches crammed with oysters, shrimp or almost anything else, along with a lot of spicy sauces, and **muffulettas**, the Italian version, stuffed full of aromatic meats and cheese and dripping with olive dressing. Once looked down on as "trash" food, but now a favourite delicacy, **crawfish** look like baby lobster and are served in everything from omelettes to bisques.

Finally, European-influenced New Orleans is probably *the* American city for **coffee**. The stuff is drunk in copious amounts, fresh, strong and aromatic.

French Quarter

Acme Oyster House, 724 Iberville St (☎522-5973). Fresh oysters shucked on marble counters. Increasingly popular with tourists for its authentic atmosphere but still a favourite with local police officers and business people. $7 for a large plate of oysters, fries and salad; seafood po-boys for $5.

Back to the Garden, 207 Dauphine St (☎524-6915). Quiet little vegetarian lunch spot serving good salads, soups and quiches, an oddity in a city which rarely bothers with health consciousness.

Cafe du Monde, 800 Decatur St (☎561-9235). Everyone goes here for the *beignets* (crispy doughnuts without the hole, smothered in icing sugar) and *café au lait*. Completely overrun by tourists, but an unavoidable part of your stay in New Orleans. Open 24 hours.

Cafe Sbisa, 1011 Decatur St (☎561-8354). Casual old restaurant frequented by local intelligentsia, with delicious seafood ranging from $10 to $25, and nightly jazz pianist.

Central Grocery, 923 Decatur St (☎523-1620). Old Italian deli; the best muffulettas in New Orleans.

Esmerelda's, 219 Dauphine St (☎529-5741). A real find. Homestyle lunches (red beans and rice, smothered okra with shrimp), and breakfasts (hash browns, eggs, grits, sausage). Nothing over $4.

Gumbo Shop, 630 St Peter St (☎525-1486). Old-fashioned but touristy, in one of the oldest buildings in the Quarter. Huge seafood gumbos and jambalayas, also sandwiches and po-boys.

Johnny's Po-boy, 511 St Louis St (☎524-8129). Family-owned restaurant serving huge po-boys, a fantastic gumbo (with garlic bread) and all day breakfasts to friendly locals. Unbelievably cheap.

Kaldi's Coffeeshop, 941 Decatur St (☎586-8989). Fresh brewed coffees, including Ethiopian decaf and iced Venetian *creme caffe*, exotic teas, piles of books and magazines, and a trendy student and gay clientele. One of the nicest ways to spend a New Orleans afternoon, sitting at the open window overlooking the French Market. Live music Thurs–Sun when local musicians play for tips.

Molly's at the Market, 1107 Decatur St (☎525-5169). Dark bar and cafe with a neighbourhood feel, frequented by politicians, media celebs, and regulars who never seem to leave. Po-boys, snacks, all-you-can-eat shrimp for $8.95, full meals with free bread pudding and whiskey sauce.

Palm Court Jazz Cafe, 1204 Decatur St (☎525-0200). Adjacent to the warehouse of the Jazz Foundation building. Blues, jazz (mostly traditional), or folk requests from the Foundation's record collection, played over a cheap dinner of shrimp, jambalaya or chicken. Closed Mon and Tues.

Outside the Quarter

Albertos, 611 Frenchmen St (☎949-5952). Creole cuisine with Italian flair; lots of seafood pasta dishes. A 24-hour bar, but the restaurant itself closes at 11pm. Dinner won't cost more than $12.

Chez Helene, 1530 W Robertson St (☎947-9155). Creole soul food at reasonable prices, including fried chicken, corn bread and red beans and rice.

Mother's, 401 Poydras St (☎523-9656). One of New Orleans' greatest – and cheapest – institutions. Exposed brick walls, formica tables and concrete floors, and some of the best food in town. Mountainous po-boys, gumbo, red beans and rice, and traditional hash browns and sausage. Try the shrimp *etouffée* omelette for Sunday breakfast, or the turtle soup for weekday lunch.

Mystery Street Cafe, 3201 Esplanade Ave (☎947-6117). Mostly French food, extremely reasonably priced, with a popular Sunday brunch from 10.30am–3pm, for $7.50.

PJ's Coffee and Tea, 7713 Maple St (☎866-9963). Uptown coffee shop favoured by "intellectuals" reading, writing, and loafing about. Wide variety of exotic teas and coffees.

Ye Olde College Inn, 3016 S Carrollton Ave (☎866-3683). Oysters, red beans and rice, and fried chicken for around $5.

Entertainment and Nightlife

New Orleans positively reels under the energy of its ever-present **live music**. From the most lonesome busker, through the shiny uptown jazz bands to the big-name Neville Brothers, music remains integral to the economy and the ideology of the city.

To try and decide what to do on any given night, you could be terribly organised, checking in the *Lagniappe* supplement of the *Times-Picayune* on Friday, or in the monthly listings papers *Offbeat* and *Wavelength*, and asking in French Quarter record shops (*Hot Wax*, 722 Orleans Street, is especially recommended). You could just as well, on the other hand, take pot-luck. Nothing compares with wandering into a local bar for a quick drink, only to be overwhelmed by the superb music coming from the unprepossessing band in the corner.

One of the most exciting features of New Orleans nightlife is that doors are always open, and with 24-hour drinking licences common, the music often doesn't get going until around midnight. Sleazy Bourbon Street strip clubs and hip uptown blues bars alike, everything can be seen – and heard – from the streets. If you hear something you like, but don't want to pay the cover charge – low or nonexistent in bars, but as much as $10 in some clubs – you can just stand outside with a "beer to go" from another bar. New Orleans is not, however, a place to skimp on entertainment. Saving money by missing out on some of the best music you'll ever hear in your life is simply a false economy.

Jazz

It is generally agreed that **jazz** was born in New Orleans, shaped early this century by the twin talents of **Louis Armstrong** and **Joe "King" Oliver** from a diverse heritage of African and Caribbean slave music, Civil War brass bands, plantation spirituals, black church music and work songs. It suits the city well: hard to define, improvisational, and ranging from melancholic to jubilant, upmarket to downright seedy.

In 1897, New Orleans' council, unable to control the city's prostitution, gambling and drinking, decided to restrict the bordellos and saloons to an area skirted by Iberville and Lower Basin streets, named **Storyville** after the mayor. This soon filled with newly arrived ex-plantation workers, seamen and gamblers, and from the "mood setting" tunes played in the brothels, to bawdy saloon gigs, there was plenty of opportunity for musicians to develop personal styles. Children too young to enter the bars set up makeshift "spasm bands" in the streets. Their legacy lives on in the streetwise ragamuffins on every corner, tap dancing, shoe-shining and playing trumpet.

Jazz was originally looked down upon by the white establishment as the "filthy" music of poor blacks, and Storyville was officially closed in 1917. Many jazz artists left the city, or gave up playing altogether, during the Depression (King Oliver died an impoverished janitor); but in the Fifties, the city fathers literally changed their tune, and began to promote jazz as a tourist attraction. The double-edged nature of the music – indigenous and authentic, and at the same time a commercial construction – persists. The quality ranges from **good** to **exceptional**; badly played jazz is almost nonexistent, and, thankfully, the best is not confined to the tourist traps.

Jazz funerals still occur – decorous and haunting affairs, with dirges and farewell hymns expressing intense grief, followed by a burst of musical joy at the prospect of eternal life. They mostly occur in the poorest neighbourhoods, off the beaten track, but they are, along with brass band street parades, announced on WWOZ Radio (90.7 FM). There's also a weekly **jazz mass** at the Lady of Guadalupe church (see p.477), and a **jazz tour** offered by the Louis Armstrong Foundation from the *Hotel Le Meridien* (daily 9am, noon, & 3pm; $15; ☎527-6703).

MARDI GRAS

New Orleans' **Mardi Gras** (French for *Fat Tuesday*) began in the 1740s with grand balls marking the end of Carnival season, on the eve of Lent. As befits its origins in the *Carnelevamen*, the debauched "farewell to flesh", however, from early days it was known for cavorting, outrageous costumes, drinking and general bacchanalia. It has developed into a unique celebration, inextricably linked with the city's social structures. Although it is the busiest tourist season – it's practically impossible to find a room in New Orleans around the end of February – Mardi Gras is not held for commercial reasons; it's a party held by New Orleans for New Orleans, with tourists as unofficial guests.

It was the birth of the **krewe** system – with the unexpected appearance in 1857 of a stately moonlit procession calling itself the *Krewe of Comus, Merrie Monarch of Mirth* – that really gelled Mardi Gras, bringing together the populist street festivities and the elite social functions. Initiated by a group of Anglo-Americans, the idea of secret carnival clubs was taken up enthusiastically by New Orleans aristocracy. About sixty different krewes now equip colourful floats, leading processions on different – usually mythical – themes. These themes, and the identity of the King and Queen (usually an older, politically powerful man and a young debutante), are completely unknown outside the krewes until the Big Day. Not all krewes are aristocratic; there are women-only krewes, "populist" ones open to anyone who could afford to join, and also three important **black** groups. The best known is **Zulu**, established in 1909 when a black man mocked Rex, King of Carnival, by dancing behind his float with a tin can on his head. They now parade in grass skirts and war paint. The eerie torch carriers of **Comus** parade at night, hooded and in flowing smocks, sparking bitter debate about whether the servile role demeans blacks, and the **Mardi Gras Indians** dance and chant in elaborate feather headdresses.

One important Mardi Gras ritual is the flinging and catching of **"throws"**. Beads, beakers and doubloons (toy coins marked with the insignia of individual krewes) are scattered amongst street revellers. Souvenirs vary in worth; the cheap and colourful strings of beads that adorn balconies everywhere are least valuable, while the coconut handed down from the float of the Zulu krewe is worth its weight in gold.

The **gay** community also has a lot of fun during Mardi Gras. Subversive gay parades and balls parody the "straight" Carnival, and the French Quarter is dominated by elaborate gay fancy-dress competitions.

The two weeks leading up to Mardi Gras are filled with processions, parties and balls, but excitement reaches fever pitch on the Tuesday itself, after a great free public masked ball in the Spanish Plaza the night before. Shambolic walking clubs, floatless, open the day, playing raucous jazz as they stride through the city. Zulu arrives at 9am, Rex appears before lunch, and the dramatic torchlit parade of Comus is the grand finale. By midnight, the police are clearing away die-hard revellers, and repentance can begin.

OTHER NEW ORLEANS FESTIVALS

French Quarter Festival, in early April. The Quarter is even more alive than usual, with jazz competitions, tours of private patios, free concerts, talent contests and a giant jazz brunch in Jackson Square.

Jazz and Heritage Festival, held at the end of April and start of May at the Fairgrounds Race Track. Ten outdoor stages host traditional jazz, R&B, gospel, African, Caribbean, Cajun, blues, ragtime, folk, bluegrass and country music, with evening performances at the *French Quarter Storyville Jazz Hall*, a marquee on the river, and the *Theater of the Performing Arts*, 801 N Rampart St (☎522-0592). Hundreds of unofficial street bands, local arts, crafts and food. Contact PO Box 53407, New Orleans, LA 70153 (☎522-4786).

La Fête, in June/July. Food festival, with stalls all over town selling Cajun and Creole food from the simple to the outlandish.

Spring Fiesta, on the first Friday after Easter. The only time of the year when many of New Orleans' private homes are open to the public. Tours through plantation homes, French Quarter Creole cottages and patios, and Garden District mansions, many of them conducted by the owners. Public classical concerts and opera are held all around town.

Jazz venues

The Columns Hotel, 3811 St Charles Ave (☎899-9308). Comfy yuppie bar, with good modern jazz.

The Famous Door, 339 Bourbon St (☎522-7626). One of Bourbon Street's oldest authentic clubs.

Gazebo Cafe and Bar, 1018 Decatur St (☎522-0862). Jazz on the patio daily and nightly.

Glass House, 2519 S Saratoga St (☎895-9279). Lively neighbourhood bar specialising in excellent young brass bands (such as *The Dirty Dozen* and *Rebirth*). This area is not safe at night – take a taxi.

New Storyville Jazz Hall, 1104 Decatur St (☎525-8199). Family place, with top-quality Dixieland bands, and occasional contemporary sets. Street musicians play on Sunday evenings. Cover varies.

Petroleum Lounge, 1501 St Philip St (☎523-0248). Authentic local bar, featuring New Orleans brass bands, and a brass band jukebox. Frequented by local music celebs. $3 cover, first drink free.

Preservation Hall, 726 St Peter St (☎522-2238 day, ☎523-8939 night). Not a bar or club, more like a shabby front room. No seats, drinks or air-conditioning, but long lauded as the best, if not the only, place to hear traditional jazz. Always full of smug tourists, with queues hours before the doors open at 8pm. Inside it's a zoo; old black musicians playing in an atmosphere kept deliberately derelict to titillate tourists. The $2 cover and the lengthy set (until well after midnight) are the main bonuses.

Other Live Music

Despite its heavy investment in traditional jazz, New Orleans is by no means just a jazz city. The **"New Orleans sound"** is characterised by the soulful R&B feel of the much-loved Neville Brothers, as well as the Cajun, gospel, blues, zydeco and rock, that play all over, all the time. **Blues** has always been big in this boozy, dreamy city, though influenced more by neighbouring Texas than the country blues of the Mississippi delta. Piano blues lived alongside jazz in Storyville, and was continued by Tuts Washington and Professor Longhair. Look out especially for blues shouter J Monque D, who howls down the walls of many an uptown bar, and two exceptional women blues singers: Irma Thomas, whose set always includes *You can have my husband, but please don't mess with my man*, and the powerful gospel and blues fusion of Marva Wright.

Bars and live music in the French Quarter

Absinthe Bar, 400 Bourbon St (☎525-8108). Tiny dark bar with the original fixtures of the first New Orleans absinthe bar (nearby at 240 Bourbon St, but a lot less lively), including a marble absinthe fountain and ancient ceiling fans. Great jazz and R&B. Small cover Fri & Sat.

Lafitte's Blacksmith Shop, 941 Bourbon St (☎523-0066). Dim and ancient wooden bar frequented by artists and writers (how they see by the candlelight remains a mystery). A front for Lafitte's plottings, unchanged since the eighteenth century. A far better Hurricane rum cocktail than *Pat O'Brien's* (see below) and, in the evenings, the enormously popular Miss Lily Hood, piano singer.

The Mint, 504 Esplanade Ave (☎525-2000). Rumbustious gay bar, with rowdy sing-alongs, ragtime piano, and drag acts. Cover around $2.

Napoleon House, 500 Chartres St (☎524-9752). Once the home of Mayor Girod, who schemed with Jean Lafitte to rescue Napoleon from St Helena in 1821. A civilised bar, with taped classical music, fading Napoleonic memorabilia, old wooden tables on the street and delicious muffulettas.

Pat O'Brien's, 718 St Peter St (☎525-4823). Famous for inventing the sickly sweet Hurricane and for its noisy piano bar. Push your way to the front, request a song from the two warring piano players (who know every song ever written), and brace yourself for a raucous night. Open until 4am.

Rhythms, 227 Bourbon St (☎523-3800). Formerly the *Bourbon Street Gospel and Blues Club*, and featuring just that. Regular shows from the outstanding Marva Wright and Irma Thomas. $3 cover.

Bars and live music outside the Quarter

Benny's Bar, 938 Valence St (☎895-9405). Authentic, seedy local blues bar, also putting on R&B and reggae bands. Music starts after midnight. No cover charge.

Cafe Brazil, 2100 Chartres St (☎947-9386). Self-consciously bohemian bar on the fringes of the Quarter, with bluegrass and gospel on alternate Sundays, jazz jam and movies on Wednesday, and a cappella, jazz, gospel or blues nightly. Good coffee bar and art gallery during the day.

Jimmy's, 8200 Willow St (☎866-9549). Very noisy student club. Only charges for big-name acts.

Lion's Den, 2655 Gravier St at Broad Ave (☎822-9591). Owned by R&B singer Irma Thomas who performs on Sunday evenings. Dodgy area; take a taxi.

Maple Leaf Bar, 8316 Oak St (☎866-9359). Shabby, friendly, cheap bar with superlative Cajun, zydeco and blues. Chess and darts, poetry readings on Sunday afternoon and Cajun dance lessons.

Muddy Water's, 8301 Oak St (☎866-7174). Blues, R&B, and good $2 meals. Many people, including the patrolling police, wander all night between this and the *Maple Leaf* opposite. Cover $5.

Snug Harbor, 626 Frenchmen St (☎949-0696). Excellent, intimate, jazz club, with a hassle-free atmosphere. Two shows a night, 9 and 11pm. Full meals and a friendly bar open long after the live music stops. Cover $5–10, but it's OK to sit and hear the music from the bar. Charmaine Neville's R&B act, with exceptional saxophonist and drummer, is an essential New Orleans night out.

Tipitina's, 501 Napoleon Ave (☎895-9144). Famed venue, named for a Professor Longhair song. An unpretentious and friendly hall hosting the smallest Cajun bands to the biggest acts. The Neville Brothers recorded a live album here. Joyful Sunday afternoon Cajun dances, $4 with free jambalaya.

The Warehouse Cafe, 636 Tchoupitoulas St (☎586-1282). More of a warehouse than a cafe, with a trendy clientele and eclectic live music.

CAJUN COUNTRY

Cajun country stretches across southern Louisiana from **Houma** in the east, via **Lafayette** and Opelousas, into Texas. It's a region best enjoyed away from the larger towns, by visiting its many old-style hamlets, which despite modernisation can still be found, cut off from civilisation in soupy bayous, coastal marshes, and inland swamps.

Cajuns are descended from the French colonists of Acadia, part of Nova Scotia which was taken over by the British in 1713. The Catholic Acadians, who had quietly fished, hunted and farmed for more than a century, refused to renounce their faith and swear allegiance to the English king, and in 1755, the British brutally expelled them all, separating families and burning towns. About 2500 ended up in French Louisiana, where they were given land and enabled to set up small farming communities, making it possible to rebuild the culture they had left behind. Hunting, farming and trapping, they lived in relative isolation until the 1940s when major roads were built, immigrants from other states poured in to work in the **oil** business, and accordionist Iry Lejeune popularised **Cajun music** nationally. Since then, the poignant history of the Cajuns has continued to be one of struggle. Towns like **Lafayette** have been hard hit by the oil slump, while the rapid erosion of coastal wetlands threatens the existence of Houma and Morgan City, and the silting up of the Atchafalaya Basin is having adverse effects on fishing and shrimping.

The popular image of the Cajuns as partying, funloving people, who welcome strangers, is borne out at the many local dances, or *fais-do-dos*. These singing, dancing celebrations are held with an unremitting frequency, providing a chance to listen to some of the best story-tellers in the world, and absorb the uniqueness of their culture. The French creole dialect of the older inhabitants, with its strong African and English influences, has primarily been kept alive by music (after Roosevelt's administration decreed that all American children should speak English in schools, French was practically wiped out in Louisiana). The favourite Cajun phrase, *lache pas la patate* – "don't let go of the potato" – is an encouragement not to give up that suits this enduring and endearing culture to a tee.

Although **Baton Rouge**, the capital of Lousiana, is not strictly speaking in Cajun country, heading out this way from New Orleans, via the **plantations** on the banks of the Mississippi, makes a good approach.

The telephone **area code** for Baton Rouge is ☎504; for Cajun country and northern Louisiana it's ☎318.

Northwest from New Orleans: Plantation Country

The fastest roads out from New Orleans towards the west are the major I-10 and US-61; but a far more interesting route is to follow Hwy-18 beside the Mississippi as it winds its way through flat fertile farmland, next to an immaculate grass-covered levee. The French farmers of the early plantations – or rather, their slaves – could load cotton, sugar or indigo onto riverboats berthed virtually at their front doors. Several large and very spectacular homes still survive, as restaurants, inns, or private residences.

The road out from New Orleans runs at first in the shadow of giant oil and chemical plants, prodigious sugar refineries, and even a nuclear power station at Taft, before emerging to pass levee-side clusters of small houses, tiny stores and pristine white churches. After twenty-five miles you come to the **San Francisco House** (daily, 10am–4pm; $5), two miles south of **Reserve**, built in the "Steamboat Gothic" style, with rails, awnings and pillars designed to recreate the ambience of a Mississippi showboat. The elaborate external detail is matched by a lavish interior featuring Victorian furniture, decorative ceilings, marble work and cypress mouldings.

Eighteen miles south of Baton Rouge on the west bank, **Nottoway** is the largest surviving plantation home in the South, a huge white Italianate edifice of 64 rooms, 200 windows, and 165 doors. Tours cost an extortionate $8 but you can get a peep from the road (daily, 9am–5pm). The house is also used as an inn and restaurant.

Baton Rouge

When French explorers first came upon the site of **BATON ROUGE** in 1699, they found poles smeared in animal blood to designate the separate hunting grounds of the Houmas and Bayougoulas Indians. The area on these shallow bluffs therefore appeared on French maps as *Baton Rouge*, meaning "red stick". Now capital of Louisiana and the country's fifth biggest port, Baton Rouge is an extremely easy-going city for its size. It must also be one of America's greenest conurbations, its avenues canopied in oak and elm. Little happens in the central downtown section, but several parts of towns are worth strolling around.

Louisiana State Capitol

Surrounded by fifty acres of showpiece gardens, the magnificent Art Deco **Louisiana State Capitol** serves as a monument to **Huey Long**, the "Kingfish". The larger-than-life state governor ordered its construction in 1931 and was assassinated in its corridors just four years later. Long was first elected governor in 1928 after a vehemently anti-big-business campaign and swiftly concentrated virtually all power in his hands. His massive programme of public works included financing charity hospitals by heavy taxes on the big oil and gas corporations. Variously labelled a demagogue, communist and even fascist, he set himself apart from other southern populists of the time by refusing to exploit the race issue. Just as his appeal – with slogans like "Every Man a King" – began to reach national proportions, with a bid for the presidency in the offing, he was shot by a local doctor whose exact motives remain unknown.

Other controversial figures to have worked in the building include the segregationist country singer Jimmie Davis, better remembered for writing *You Are My Sunshine* and riding his horse up the steps of the capitol than for any political skills and more recently David Duke, the former Grand Wizard of the Ku Klux Klan who was elected as a state representative in 1989 and was the Republican nominee for governor in 1991.

Tours of this stunning building, with its huge murals and sculptures, are enlivened by the intensity and maverick nature of Louisiana politics. Guides point out stray bullets in the marble pillars of the ground-floor corridor, and a pencil embedded in the ceiling of the legislative chamber by an exploding bomb. Long decreed that nothing in

JIMMY SWAGGART'S BATON ROUGE

Beside I-10 from New Orleans as it enters Baton Rouge, the giant electronic message *THE LORD IS MY SHEPHERD* welcomes you to the home of the Jimmy Swaggart Bible College. Once characterised by perpetual construction and overflowing car parks, its concrete campus has been a quieter place since its founder broke the seventh commandment with Debra Murphree, a New Orleans prostitute, in 1988. Threatened with excommunication by his Assemblies of God Church, this self-styled "old-fashioned, Holy Ghost-filled, shouting, weeping, soul-winning, gospel-preaching preacher" – a cousin of Jerry Lee Lewis – was back in the pulpit within three months. In October 1991, however, he managed to compromise himself again with a Californian call-girl, and his career is back in jeopardy.

Before his misdemeanour, Swaggart's programmes were beamed to 145 countries and attracted over $140 million in annual donations. Such popularity spawned an extravagant lifestyle, manifested by his lavish home off I-10 Highland Exit, across from the exclusive *Louisiana Country Club* and near the lurid pink shell of *Ralph and Kakoo's Seafood Restaurant*, where he dines almost every night.

Baton Rouge could be taller than the 450ft capitol, so its 27th-floor observation deck is the city's best vantage point to look out over miles of greenery and the sluggish Mississippi (daily, 8am–4pm; free).

The Riverfront

Mark Twain referred to Baton Rouge's **Old State Capitol** (in use 1850–1931) as "that monstrosity on the Mississippi". A grey crenellated structure on a lumpy mound overlooking the river, penned in by an ugly wrought-iron fence, it looks like a cross between a castle and a cathedral, without the particular merits of either. Inside, a chunky iron staircase spirals up towards an elegant glass dome which casts splashes of coloured light onto the central hall. Plans are underway to develop a museum of Louisianan government (Mon–Sat 9am–4.30pm, Sun 1–4.30pm; free).

One-hour harbour tours on the *Samuel Clemens* **riverboat** leave from the end of Florida Boulevard, passing under the Baton Rouge Bridge. This was perhaps the most ingenious of Huey Long's constructions; his stipulation that it should have a clearance of just 65ft ensured that big boats could go no further north, and thereby boosted the port trade of Baton Rouge several times over.

Practicalities

Regular *Greyhound* **buses** to Baton Rouge come in at 1253 Florida Boulevard, near downtown (☎343-4891). Except for the #7 route to LSU, the local buses provided by *Capital City Transportation* (☎336-0821) are very infrequent.

Full **information** on the town, including accommodation and restaurants, is available at the **visitor centre** in the Capitol (daily, 8am–4.30pm; ☎383-1825). **Downtown** offers few places to stay; the most convenient is the comfortable *Ramada Hotel*, 1480 Nicholson Drive (☎387-1111), charging roughly $55 per night. This is halfway between the centre and the elegant shady campus of **Louisiana State University**, a mile south, which itself offers rooms for $40 (☎387-0297). *Motel 6*, 10445 Rieger Road (☎291-4912), is well out along I-10 but costs only $26. If you want to **camp**, the nearest site is *KOA* at 7628 Vincent Road in Denham Springs, off I-12 (☎664-7281) .

At the *Frostop Drive Inn*, 402 Government Street (☎344-1179), you can gulp burgers and dogs, washed down with frozen root beer, amid Fifties decor and jukebox sounds. It's also worth the trip out to *Phil's Oyster Bar*, 5162 Government Street (☎924-3045), where the speciality is super-fresh oysters, and Cajun and pasta dishes cost less than $10. Lots of cheap food joints line the Highland Avenue border of LSU, and on the campus itself you can eat cheaply and well in the Union building.

Lafayette and Around

LAFAYETTE, 130 miles northwest of New Orleans on I-10, is geographically central in Cajun country, and is the key city for its **oil** business. Originally named Vermilionville, after the orangey bayou nearby, it was renamed in the 1880s when the railroad came to town. Today Lafayette is a surprisingly quiet place, a city with a small-town feel, with absolutely no "downtown". It does claim, however, two excellent historic reconstructions of early Cajun settlements, and some good restaurants – and makes the best base for exploring the Cajun swamps and bayous.

Arrival, Information and Getting Around

Greyhound arrives in Lafayette at 315 Lee Avenue (☎235-1541), and *Amtrak* a few blocks north at 133 E Grant Street. The **bus** system (400 Dorset St; ☎261-8570) doesn't really cater for visitors, running infrequently, and not at all on Sundays, so your best bet is to rent a car (*Thrifty* is at 401 E Pinhook Road; ☎237-1282), or take a **tour** with *Acadiana To Go*, 619 Woodvale Avenue (☎981-3918), or *Allons à Lafayette*, 127 Baudoin Street (☎269-9607). If you need a taxi, try *Cajun Cabs* (☎235-7515). The Lafayette Parish **CVB** is at 1400 N W Evangeline Thruway (daily 9am–5pm; ☎232-3808).

The Town of Lafayette

In the centre of Lafayette, such as it is, stands the Romanesque **St John's Cathedral**, 914 St John Street, and the old **cemetery**, full of crumbling raised graves, where Jean Mouton, the town's Cajun founder, is buried. Opposite is the ancient gnarled **St John Oak**, whose magnificent branches, one of which weighs 72 tons, spreads over 150 feet. Three blocks north, at 1122 Lafayette Street, the small **Lafayette Museum** was the "Sunday home" – used as a townhouse after mass before the family returned the fifteen miles to their plantation – of Jean's son Alexandre, Louisiana's first Democratic governor. It is filled with Mouton family memorabilia and Cajun Mardi Gras costumes. (Tues–Sat 9am–5pm, Sun 3–5pm; $3).

The quirky-looking red-brick **Old City Hall** at 217 Main Street now houses *CODOFIL*, the organisation dedicated to the preservation of Louisiana French; the concrete monstrosity across the road is the new City Hall. The campus of the **University of Southwestern Louisiana**, south of the centre, boasts a swamp – complete with alligators, turtles, water birds and tattered Spanish moss – next to the Student Union.

The great energies Lafayette has put into boosting tourism since the oil slump have created two excellent reconstructions of early Cajun communities. **Vermilionville** at 1600 Surrey Street across from the airport is the easier to reach. This impressive living-history exhibition on the Bayou Vermilion explores the culture of Cajuns, Native Americans and Creoles. Plantation slave buildings sell coffee, beignets, and *boudin* (spicy smoked sausage), and stage cookery demonstrations. A large barn serves as a theatre, with storytellers, dances, plays, lectures, and noisy *fais-do-dos*, and you can buy good Cajun lunches at the restaurant next door. Costumed craftspeople explain their work in Cajun French, and a simple chapel and cemetery host lectures on religious traditions, from voodoo to the *traiteurs*, Cajuns believed to have passed healing powers from generation to generation (Mon–Thurs 9am–5pm, Fri–Sun 9am–9pm; $8; ☎233-4077).

Lafayette's other folk-life museum, the **Acadian Village** at 200 Greenleaf Road, depicts Cajun life along the bayous. It too is a good venue for festivals and celebrations. Original structures – homes, stores, and a chapel – line a sluggish bayou set in gardens and woodlands, and are filled with traditional furnishings and crafts. The gift shop sells books, prints, crafts and food (daily 10am–5pm; $4).

Accommodation

Cheap **rooms** are easy to find in Lafayette. Chain hotels line Evangeline Thruway just south of I-10, and US-90 and Hwy 182 towards New Iberia. Cajun **B&Bs** are especially welcoming, and reasonably cheap, but you must book ahead (contact *Southern Comfort B&B Reservation Service*, 2856 Hundred Oaks, Baton Rouge; ☎504-346-1928). There's **camping** at *Acadiana Park Campground*, 1201 E Alexander Street (☎234-3838), north-east of town, and at *KOA Lafayette*, five miles west on I-10.

Bois des Chenes, 338 N Sterling St (☎233-7816). Two miles from I-10, B&B in the carriage house of an 1821 plantation home. $65, with a bottle of wine and breakfast. Reservations required.

Days Inn, 1620 N University Ave (☎237-8880). Comfortable, very big rooms from $35, northwest of town.

Hotel Acadiana, 1801 W Pinhook Rd (☎233-8120). Luxury hotel near the airport and Vermilionville, with rooms starting at $53.

Mouton Manor, 310 Sidney Martin Rd (☎237-6996). 1806 Cajun plantation house north of town, in lovely three-acre setting, surrounded by pecan trees. Rooms start at $55.

Ramada Inn, 2501 S E Evangeline Thruway (☎234-8521). Comfortable rooms from $49, just south.

Eating In and Around Lafayette

Learning to **cook**, for a Cajun, is a rite of passage as important as one's first fishing trip or *fais-do-do*. Eating is inseparable from dancing and music; evening – or afternoon, or even morning – entertainment revolves around local family-run restaurants which act as impromptu dance-halls (see opposite). If you don't feel like dancing yourself, you can just watch, while downing a delicious seafood dinner.

Cajun food is characterised by its use of anything going (they say a true Cajun cooks every part of a pig but its squeal). Basic, one-pot cooking it may be, but it's impossible to eat badly – and hard to spend over $15. Cajuns eat out all the time – Lafayette sells more restaurant food per person than any other city in America. At lunchtime, takeaway *boudin* goes down a treat, as do finger-licking Cajun specialities like rich pork cracklin washed down with cold beer. Some of the restaurants below are a short drive out from town, but are well worth the cab fare if you have no car.

Bayou Boudin and Cracklin, Bayou Teche, Hwy 94 (☎332-6158). Restored nineteenth-century Cajun country house selling cheap *boudin*, cracklin', hogshead cheese and crawfish balls, all prepared on the spot from traditional recipes. Also does good po-boys and dinners during the week.

Poche's, 3015-A Main Highway, Poche Bridge (☎332-2108). Out-of-the-way little Cajun fast-food place selling great *boudin* and cracklin', weekday lunches, and Sunday barbecue dinners.

Poor Boy's Riverside Inn, 240 Tubing Road, Lafayette (☎837-4011). Good Cajun food in refined atmosphere, with bright decor. Catfish, crawfish, alligator and gumbo are all reasonably priced.

Prudhommes Cajun Cafe, 4676 N E Evangeline Thruway, Lafayette (☎896-7964). Run by the sister of New Orleans chef Paul Prudhomme. Down-to-earth and deservedly popular country restaurant; exquisite shrimp *etouffé*, jalapeno cornbread, banana bread and sweet potato muffins. From $7.

Touring Cajun Country

GRAND COTEAU, off I-49 ten miles north of Lafayette, is a picture-perfect little town, with whitewashed buildings – including a dazzling white chapel – and prettily winding roads. Since 1866, when a dying woman was miraculously healed by the intercession of a saint, in the **Academy of the Sacred Heart** on Church Street, devout Cajun Catholics have come here on pilgrimage. You can tour the old classrooms of this beautifully columned former school, and follow a long path through the ornate gardens, canopied by huge old oaks (Mon–Fri 10am–3pm, weekends 1–4pm; $5).

The 1831 **Chretien Point Plantation**, just east of Sunset, seventeen miles northwest of Lafayette on I-10, is Louisiana's oldest Greek Revival building. Its main stair-

CAJUN MUSIC

Cajuns enjoy nothing better than "passing a good time", and you may run into a dance or *fais-do-do* at any time of day. **Cajun music** is a jangling and infectious melange of accordion, violin and triangle, with traces of country, swing, jazz and blues. **Zydeco** is similar, but more blues-based, and more often played by black musicians. The nasal singing bears only a passing resemblance to the language spoken in France. Music is never performed without space for **dancing**; everyone from the smallest child to the most aged grandparent joins in, and locals are always willing to tutor those unsure of the two-step. Venues include restaurants, (see opposite), simple dance halls, record shops and the streets themselves. Ask around or just stop where you hear the festivities.

Downtown Alive!, Jefferson St, Lafayette (☎268-5566). Free street dances, including well-known Cajun and zydeco artists, Fridays, 5.30–8pm, April–June and Sept–Nov only.

El Sid O's Zydeco Club, 1523 Martin Luther King Drive, Lafayette (☎235-0647). Dances Fri– Sun. Great house bands.

Mulate's, 325 Mills Ave, Breaux Bridge (☎332-4648). Touristy but fun Cajun restaurant. Seafood dinners under $15, big-name Cajun and zydeco music for no extra charge. Dancing nightly, and daily at noon. 15min from Lafayette on Hwy 94, a mile off I-10.

Prejean's, 3480 US-167 N, Lafayette (☎896-3247). Unfussy restaurant. A separate oyster bar serves reasonably priced fish and alligator to a lively local crowd. Dancing begins at 7pm.

Randol's, 2320 Kaliste Saloom Rd, Lafayette (☎981-7080). Locally famed dance hall serving fresh seafood dinners. Their nightly *fais-do-dos* are occasionally televised.

Rendezvous des Cajuns, live Cajun/zydeco radio and television show, Liberty Center for Performing Arts, Second St and Park Ave, Eunice (☎457-6575). North of Lafayette in Evangeline Parish, every Saturday 6–8pm; also joke tellers and recipes.

Savoy Music Center Accordion Factory, Eunice, on US-190 west of Opelousas (☎457-9563). A popular Cajun record shop, producing accordions in its back room. Lively Saturday morning jam sessions, starting at about 9am.

Slim's Y-Ki-Ki, Washington Rd, Opelousas (☎942-9982). Black Cajun music and dancing.

CAJUN FESTIVALS

Cajun **festivals** (genuinely lively and enthusiastic local events, not concocted to attract tourists) are held almost daily, it seems, to celebrate anything from frogs to new harvests. They're a wonderful way to experience the food and music of the region, although for some of the larger events, it's a good idea to book a room in advance; the rest of the world is catching on to the fun, and Lafayette, especially, gets crowded.

Mardi Gras. Second only to the New Orleans bash, this pre-Lenten party begins on the Saturday before "Fat Tuesday", with street dancing. Cajun Mardi Gras differs from its New Orleans city cousin; although there are private balls and parties, it is a far more pagan affair. In the rural villages around Lafayette, like Eunice, Church Point and Mamou, the *Courir du Mardi Gras* sees masked horsemen in colourful capes gallop through the countryside led by a captain, who gathers ingredients for the community Mardi Gras gumbo from the neighbours.

Festival International de Louisiane, 3rd week of April. Huge festival in Lafayette, with participants from all over the French-speaking world. Particular emphasis on indigenous music and food.

Festivals Acadiens and **Jambalaya du Musique**, 3rd week of Sept. Based at Lafayette's Acadian Village. Cajun, zydeco and traditional French bands play all day. (☎232-3737).

Zydeco Festival, Saturday before Labor Day at the Southern Development Farm, Hwy 167 before Opelousas. Zydeco performers play "black Cajun" music. (☎942-2392).

Cajun Heritage and Music Festival, 2nd weekend of Oct. The Acadian Village is alive with music, auctions, storytelling, and Native American chanting.

Louisiana Yambilee, last week in Oct. Opelousas, yam capital of the world, goes all out to celebrate the sweet potato. Food stalls, sweet potato auctions, music, *Miss Yambilee* and *Lil Miss Yum Yum* contests.

case was the model for Tara in *Gone with the Wind*. Mrs Chretien, left alone to run the plantation after her husband's death in 1832, was very much in the Scarlett O'Hara mould. She scandalised the community by drinking, smoking, gambling and sitting with the men after dinner, and once shot an intruder – as seen in *Gone with the Wind* – whose ghost roams the corridors. Bullet holes in the front door date from 1863, when Mrs Chretien's son showed a Masonic sign to an attacking Union general, who thereupon directed fire safely over the roof. Though some outbuildings were destroyed, the house and its inhabitants remained unharmed (daily 10am–5pm; $4; ☎233-7050).

Predominantly French-speaking **OPELOUSAS**, twenty miles north of Lafayette on I-49, was the boyhood home of Jim Bowie, Texas Revolutionary hero and inventor of the Bowie knife. The **Jim Bowie Museum**, 220 Academy Street, is filled with his personal possessions (Mon–Fri 8am–4pm; free). Opelousas' two other great claims to fame are as the birthplace of the great zydeco musician **Clifton Chenier** and – less trendily – as **yam** capital of the world.

St Martinville

Old **ST MARTINVILLE** on the Bayou Teche, just off US-90 a dozen miles south of Lafayette, was a major port of entry for exiled Acadians. The **Evangeline Oak**, on Port Street where it meets the bayou, marks where Emmeline Labiche, the inspiration for Longfellow's *Evangeline*, disembarked after her hard journey from Nova Scotia, only to hear that her lover was engaged to another. This little country town was known as "le petit Paris", filled with French Royalists fleeing the Revolution and re-creating a glittering city life of soirees and balls. It was later decimated by yellow fever, fire and hurricane, and now it's just a peaceful hamlet, kept going by day-trippers from Lafayette.

The St Martin de Tours **Catholic Church** at 103 Main Street contains a gold and silver sanctuary light and intricate carved font said to have been gifts from Louis XVI and Marie Antoinette. Behind the church, on the left, the **Evangeline Monument** was donated by the producers of the 1929 movie *The Romance of Evangeline*, and is based on Dolores del Rio, its star. North of town on Hwy 31, a large park on the bayou contains a **Creole Plantation House** (☎394-3754), made with the bousillage mixture characteristic of early Louisianan buildings, and held together by wooden pegs.

SWAMP TOURS

Swamp tours are available from many landings in the **Atchafalaya Basin**. Any expectations of cutting through uncharted jungle, or glimpsing remote forgotten swamp communities, will be rudely confounded. The basin is an eerie place; almost all its cypresses were harvested last century, and now just the twisted silhouettes of their stumps poke out of the sluggish waters. Cars cut right across on the enormous concrete I-10, and most of the old houseboats have been abandoned, or are used for weekend retreats. There is, however, plenty of wildlife, including sunbathing alligators and scores of fishing boats. Tours are conducted by Cajuns who see the basin as more than just a tourist attraction, and give fascinating personal commentaries for people they feel are really interested.

Angelle's Atchafalaya Tours, Whiskey River landing, Henderson. About twenty minutes from Lafayette along I-10 and then on hwys 347 and 332, this quiet landing is run by the Angelle brothers, who also own the restaurant (and informal dance hall) on the bank. Taking a 2-hr Sunday afternoon tour and then returning to eat fresh crawfish at a *fais-do-do* is a wonderful way to spend the day. (Daily 10am, 1pm and 3pm, extra 5pm tour in the summer; no reservations are required; $7; ☎228-8567.)

McGee's Basin Swamp Tours (☎228-8519). Tours leave McGee's Landing, on Route 5 in Breaux Bridge (a favourite fishing spot) at the same times as the *Angelle* tours, for $8.50.

Annie Miller's Terrebonne Swamp and Marsh Tours (☎504-879-3934). 3-hr boat trips through the wildlife of the bayou. Two trips daily, March–Oct, from Miller's Landing on Big Bayou Black, in Houma (pronounced *Homer*), an oyster and shrimp fishing centre on the soggy Bayou Terrebonne.

Avery Island and Morgan City

AVERY ISLAND, seven miles southwest of the pretty bayou town of NEW IBERIA, is not an island at all; it's the tip of a massive salt dome. The hot chili peppers that go to make **Tabasco sauce** grow here, and the sauce is still prepared from a family recipe in the *McIlhenny* factory (Mon–Fri 9am–4pm, Sat 9am–noon; free). The steamy 200-acre **Jungle Gardens** close by are full of exotic camelias, azaleas and irises, and serve as a sanctuary for blue herons, black ibises and snowy egrets (daily 9am–5pm; $4.50).

MORGAN CITY, about thirty miles southwest of well-preserved FRANKLIN on US-90, was where the first *Tarzan* was filmed in 1917. It's shown daily at the *Turn of the Century House*, 715 Second Street, which also contains period furnishings and Mardi Gras costumes (Mon–Fri 9am–5pm, weekends 1–5pm; $2). The town is a fishing centre, with many surrounding bayous, rivers and lakes, and hunting in the forests and sugar fields. Daily guided walking tours of **Heritage Park**, an outdoor swamp museum, trace the settlement of the Atchafalaya Basin.

NORTHERN LOUISIANA

North Louisiana is at the heart of the region known as the **Ark-La-Tex**, a blend of the cotton fields, Bible Belt mentality and soft drawl of the Deep South, with the ranches and oil (and passion for country and western music) of Texas, and hilly Arkansan forests (resplendent in the autumn). **Shreveport**, its key city, has more in common with, say, Tyler, Texas, than New Orleans. Having been settled by the Scottish and Irish after the Louisiana Purchase, the area is strongly Baptist, with less of a penchant for fun than south Louisiana. At least it shares its profusion of **festivals**; Shreveport's **State Fair** is a real c'n'w hoedown, with rodeos and big-name country performers.

Natchitoches

Tiny **NATCHITOCHES** (pronounced *Nakitish*), in the sleepy cotton fields of the Cane River, is the oldest European settlement in Louisiana, having begun life as a French trading post in 1714. Something of a Catholic oasis in a Protestant desert, it was swiftly fortified when its Spanish and Native American customers started to combine aggression with commerce. The town made an appropriate setting for the 1988 movie *Steel Magnolias*, centring on the lives of a group of strong women. Don't mistake the genteel groups lunching downtown for bored small-town housewives; they provide much of the town's energy, in the tradition of their formidable ancestors. **Kate Chopin** – whose nineteenth-century novel *The Awakening*, about a married woman's desire for independence, shocked the nation – lived in nearby Cloutierville, where a museum is dedicated to her.

The town

With its lovingly restored Creole architecture, Natchitoches' exquisite **Front Street** on the river looks a lot like New Orleans' French Quarter. The lacy iron balconies, spiral staircases and cobbled courtyards are complemented by friendly old-style stores such as *Kaffies* haberdashers. The 1717 **Immaculate Conception Catholic Church**, on the corner of Second and Church streets, has many of its original French features, including glass chandeliers and a hand-carved font. A nearby **Starwalk** commemorates celebrities with local connections, such as the *Steel Magnolias* cast, John Wayne and Clementine Hunter (see below). **Fort St Jean**, on Mill and Jefferson Streets, is a five-acre reconstruction of the town's 1716 fort, with rough wooden and adobe buildings, all enclosed by tall wooden fencing (Wed–Sun; $2).

Practical details

Natchitoches lies seventy miles southeast of Shreveport, on Hwy 6 off I-49. *Greyhound* comes in on the west side of town, on Caspari Street near the university, but there's no public transport or taxi; to avoid being stranded the car-less should reserve accommodation in advance at a **bed and breakfast** inn, and arrange to be collected. One of the most welcoming is the *Fleur de Lis*, 336 Second Street (☎352-6621; prepaid reservations only), with its romantic verandah and huge communal breakfasts; the *Jefferson House*, 229 Jefferson Street (☎352-3957) by the river is also nice. Both offer rooms from $55.

The **visitor centre**, 781 Front Street (Mon–Sat 9am–5pm, Sun 10am–2pm; ☎352-8072) provides self-guided walking and driving tours, will put you in touch with tour companies, and can help find accommodation. Good places to **eat** include the chintzy *Just Friends* at 746 Front Street (☎352-3836), and *Lasyone's Meat Pie Kitchen* (☎352-3353), around the corner at 622 Second Street. Lasyone, the chef, happily chats to customers gobbling his special meat pies (spicy, flaky and lightly fried), red beans and sausage, fresh corn bread and rich cream pies. Come early for dinner; it closes at 7pm.

The Cane River Plantations

The rural **Cane River roads** are dotted with ramshackle houses and small farms. As you drive past the dungareed farmers sitting on porches, and the women hanging out washing, you'll come across many **plantation homes**, some overgrown and in sad disrepair, others beautifully restored and well-kept.

Melrose, sixteen miles south of Natchitoches on Hwy 119, has a romantic history. It was granted in 1794 to Marie Coincoin, a freed slave, by her owner, Claude Metoyer – the father of ten of her fourteen children. By the 1830s, the slave-operated plantation had grown to 12,000 acres, and Coincoin was able to buy freedom for two of her children and one of her grandchildren. At the turn of the century, "Miss Cammie" Henry turned the crumbling Melrose into an arts community, visited by writers such as John Steinbeck and William Faulkner. In the 1940s a black field worker, **Clementine Hunter**, started to paint vivid images of rural life, using left-over materials. She lived to be over one hundred, and her works are on show in the upper storey of the 1800 **African House**, which resembles a Congo mud hut and was used as the slave jail. A short film about Melrose is shown in the **Big House** – a typical plantation home, part brick, part wood.

Shreveport

SHREVEPORT, in Louisiana's northwest corner, was established in 1839, after Henry Miller Shreve had spent seven years clearing a 160-mile logjam which clogged the Red River. Built on land "given" by the Caddo Indians to Shreve's business partner Larkin Edwards (or so he claimed), it was a prosperous cotton, lumber and oil port until the River rebelled, silting up so seriously that it was no longer navigable.

Despite the depression caused by the oil slump, Shreveport remains the hub of the Ark-La-Tex, flying the flags of all three states. Links with Texas are especially strong, with streets named for the Southern volunteers who passed this way heading for the Texan Revolution. In 1873 there was even a short-lived bid to annex Shreveport and all the land west of the Red River to the Lone Star state.

This city of steakhouses, cowboy boots and Stetsons has always tapped its feet to country music, and in the 1930s and 1940s was home to radio's **Louisiana Hayride**. The show is now broadcast on the first and third Saturday of every month from the auditorium of the *Airline High School* in **Bossier City** just across the river, otherwise notable for its restaurants and the new thoroughbred racetrack of Louisiana Downs. There's little excitement in Shreveport today, though great energies are going into revitalisation, and there's hope of clearing the river for barge traffic once more.

Arrival, Information and Getting Around

Shreveport Regional Airport is five miles southwest of downtown, where *Greyhound* arrives on Fannin Street (☎424-4061). The city bus system, *Sportrans*, is little use for seeing the scattered attractions, running every half-hour to Bossier and the shopping malls, but few places else. The **Convention and Tourist Bureau**, 629 Spring Street (Mon–Fri 8am–5pm; ☎222-9391), has an historical walking tour of the downtown area.

The City

Downtown Shreveport aims to focus activity on the green riverfront, but for most of the year it offers little more than pleasant views and walks. There are, however, some lively annual festivals, such as the two-day **Festa Italiana** in October, a celebration of Italian food and culture which includes the *La Gran Del Naso Piu Grandios*, when large noses compete on their character, shape, size and appearance. At the beginning of October, the eight-day **Red River Revel** incorporates classical and country music, clogging and street entertainment.

At 525 Spring Street, the **Spring Street Museum** features nineteenth-century clothes, maps, newspapers and decorative arts (Sun 1.30pm–4.40pm; $1). Three blocks further from the river, on Court House Square, is the **Caddo Parish Courthouse**. A monument outside marks the spot where Shreveport's Confederate flag was lowered in June 1865, marking the end of the Civil War.

The doughnut-shaped Thirties building in the State Fairground is the disappointingly old-fashioned **Louisiana State Museum**, which has a large collection of artefacts from nearby Poverty Point, an ancient pre-Caddoan settlement thought to be the earliest community in the Mississippi valley (Tues–Sat 9am–4.30pm; free).

Southeast of downtown, on the campus of Centenary College, the small **Meadows Museum of Art** exhibits the works of Jean Despujols, who was commissioned in the 1930s by the French Society of Colonial Painters to travel through Indochina. He spent twenty months painting priests, chiefs and young men and women; his diaries, which are apparently a bit raunchy, are as yet unpublished. The paintings, though, make interesting ethnographic records (Tues–Fri 1–5pm, Sat & Sun 2–5pm; free).

An interesting view of nineteenth-century local life can be had at the **Pioneer Heritage Center**, on the campus of Louisiana State University at 8515 Youree Drive. Costumed guides give tours through five restored buildings and give demonstrations of making cypress shingles, bricks and lye soap. One small area concentrates on folk medicine and local home remedies (Sun, March–Dec 1.30–4.30pm; $1).

The fifty or so gardens of the **American Rose Center** (☎938-5402), sixteen miles west of the city, contain thousands of species of rose and hundreds of other shrubs and flowers. Its winding paths, shaded by towering cypress trees and dotted with statues and gazebos, have a prevailing sense of peace. Open all year, the gardens are best visited during the blooming season, April to October (daily 10am–6pm; $3).

Accommodation

Shreveport's **accommodation** options are uninspiring but adequate. The cheapest are near the airport on Monkhouse Drive, or on I-20 around downtown, though in the eagerness to attract conventions, even upmarket hotels are quite reasonably priced. If you're **camping**, try *Randy's KOA Shreveport/Bossier*, 6510 W 70th Street (☎687-1010), where tent sites, with toilets, pool, laundry and shower facilities, go for $11.10.

Chateau Suite Hotel, 201 Lake St (☎222-7620). Luxury hotel just off I-20 downtown. Doubles from $60, suites for $72. River views, a pool, and free transportation to the airport and bus station.

Days Inn, 4935 W Monkhouse Drive (☎636-0080). Doubles for around $40, with cheaper winter rates. Free transportation to bus station and nearby airport.

North Market Inn, 1906 N Market St (☎424-6621). North of downtown, with a pool. Rooms for $50.

Eating

Shreveport's cuisine pilfers elements from Southern, Tex-Mex, and Louisiana cooking. This results in delicious dishes like shrimp with guacamole and side plates of fluffy cornbread, as well as the usual gumbo and jambalaya. Catfish is also popular.

The Acadiana Cafe, 4100 Barksdale Blvd (☎746-9461). Simple wooden Bossier City restaurant serving excellent – and very cheap – Cajun and Creole food. Seafood platters $8, crawfish dinner $7.

The Centenary Oyster House, 1309 Centenary Blvd (☎221-7596). Gourmet burgers and raw oysters at reasonable prices. Live weekend entertainment, open Mon–Sat until 2am.

City Grille, 211 Texas St (☎221-3685). Downtown pastel-and-pine yuppie lunch place. Great, innovative, nouvelle Southwestern cuisine ranging from $5 pasta lunches to $16 dinners.

Don's Seafood, 3100 Highland Ave (☎865-4291). Cajun seafood dishes, crawfish, gumbo and red beans and rice, at remarkably low prices.

Smith's Cross Lake Inn, 5301 S Lakeshore Drive (☎631-0919). Unprepossessing restaurant, but popular for great views overlooking the lake, singing waiters, and steak and seafood.

Nightlife and Entertainment

Shreveport has a rich musical heritage (blues singer Leadbelly and country star Hank Williams Jr were born here), and its music scene remains vibrant: bluesy, distinctly country, and quite different from the Cajun or jazz heard in south Louisiana. During its many festivals, the city kicks up a party spirit that rivals even that of the jubilant south. Look out for the black-oriented **Good Times Festival** in mid-June, with jazz, blues and gospel music, art exhibitions and food stalls.

Ark-La-Tex Round-up, 4725 Greenwood Road (☎861-1539). Live music every first and third Sat.

Cowboy's, 1005 Gould Drive (☎746-4400). Authentic live c'n'w club in Bossier.

Enoch's Cafe, 1911 Centenary Blvd (☎222-9942). Shack-like venue, serving Cajun food and featuring regional musicians, poetry readings and lively blues jams. Open until 1am Mon–Sat.

Strand Theater, 619 Louisiana Ave (☎226-1481). Restored 1920s theatre; blues, jazz, comedy and drama.

travel details

TRAINS

Routes

• The *Sunset Limited* departs **New Orleans** three times weekly for **New Iberia** and **Lafayette**, and onwards to Los Angeles.

• The *City of New Orleans* arrives in **New Orleans** from Chicago every afternoon.

• The *Crescent* makes a daily run from New York to **New Orleans**.

There are three connecting buses to **Baton Rouge**; two arrive daily from New Orleans (in the afternoon and evening), and one comes in three times a week from Lafayette.

Journey Times

From New Orleans: New Iberia 2hr 36min; Lafayette 3hr 18min; Lake Charles 4hr 44min; Baton Rouge 1hr 50min (*Amtrak* bus); Chicago 19hr.

BUSES

From New Orleans to Baton Rouge (15 daily; 1hr 50min); New Iberia (8; 2hr); Lafayette (8; 3hr); Lake Charles (9; 4hr).

From Shreveport to Marshall, Texas (7 daily; 30min).

From Lafayette to New Iberia (10 daily; 1hr).

CHAPTER NINE

TEXAS

Still cherishing the memory that from 1836 to 1845 it was an independent nation in its own right, **TEXAS** stands out as different from the rest of the United States. While its sheer size – eight hundred miles from east to west and nearly a thousand from top to bottom – gives it a great geographical diversity, its shared history, culture and ideology bind it firmly together. Independence is key to the Texan mentality; from the overriding distrust of government – any government – to the absence of unionised labour. As the anti-litter campaign has it, "Don't mess with Texas".

Preconceived ideas about what exactly is "Texan" are soon shattered. Each of the major tourist destinations has its own distinct character. Hispanic **San Antonio**, for example, with its Mexican population and historic importance, has a laid-back feel absent from the big-city neurosis of **Houston** or **Dallas**, while trendy **Austin** revels in a lively music scene and intellectualism found nowhere else.

Regional differences are vast. The swampy, forested **east** is more like Louisiana than the pretty **Hill Country** or the agricultural plains of the **Panhandle**, and the tropical

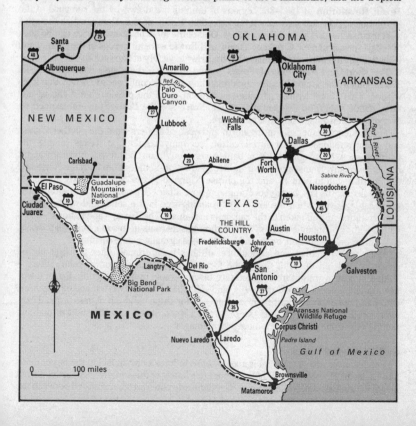

Gulf Coast has little in common with the mountainous **deserts** of the west. Changes in **climate** are equally dramatic; snow is common on the Panhandle, whereas the humidity of Houston, in particular, is only made bearable by non-stop high-power air-conditioning.

One thing shared by the whole of Texas is the constant boasting – everything has to be bigger and better than anywhere else. Such chauvinism is tempered somewhat by the state's melting-pot of cultures. The much-cited Texan **friendliness** is not imaginary; to be unwelcoming would simply be unpatriotic. Texas is, after all, named for an Indian word meaning friend, *tejas*, and a visit here, especially to the Panhandle, or the smaller communities of the Hill Country, isn't for those who want to be alone.

History

Early inhabitants of Texas included the Caddo in the east, and nomadic Coahuiltecan tribes further south. The **Comanche**, who arrived from the Rockies in the 1600s, soon found themselves fighting bloody wars with the **Spanish**, who came in search of gold. In the 1700s, threatened by French hopes of westward expansion from Louisiana, the Spanish began to build **missions** and forts. When Mexico won its independence from Spain in 1821, Texas was part of the deal. At first, the Mexicans were keen to open up their land, and offered generous incentives to settlers. Stephen Austin ("the father of Texas") proceeded to establish Anglo-American colonies in the Brazos and Colorado River valleys. However, the Mexican leader Santa Anna soon became alarmed by Anglo aspirations to autonomy, and his increasingly tight restrictions led to the eight-month **Texan Revolution** of 1835–36. Legions of tourists are drawn by the romance of the Revolution to **San Antonio**, site of the legendary **Battle of the Alamo**, which though a military disaster presaged independence. One of the most obvious legacies can be seen in today's street names: Crockett, Travis, and Bowie were all heroes at the Alamo, and Houston was the general who finally led the army to victory at San Jacinto.

The short-lived **Republic of Texas** served to define the state's identity. In 1845, Texas joined the Union on the understanding that it could secede whenever it so wished. This is still written into the constitution, as is the proviso that it can, at any time, divide itself into five separate states. You'll see the **Lone Star** emblazoned on everything from advertising to architecture.

The influence, especially in the north and east, of settlers from the southern states and their attendant slave-centred cotton economy resulted in Texas joining the **Confederacy**. No major Civil War battles were fought on Texan soil, however, and it remained relatively unscathed. During Reconstruction, settlers from both the North and the South began to pour in, and the phrase "Gone to Texas" was familiarly applied to anyone fleeing the law, bad debts or unhappy love affairs. This was also the period of the great cattle drives, when the longhorns roaming free in the south and west of Texas were rounded up and taken to the railroads in Kansas. The Texan – and national – fascination with the romantic myth of the **cowboy** has its roots in this era, and still prevails; today his regalia – Stetson, boots and bandana – is virtually a state costume.

Along with ranching and agriculture, **oil** has been crucial. After the first big oil strike in 1901, on the Gulf Coast, the focus of the Texan economy – and culture – shifted almost overnight from agriculture towards rapid industrialisation. Boom towns flew up as pioneers chased the wells, and millions of dollars were made as ranchers, who had previously thought their land only fit for cattle, sold out at vast profit. Texas today produces one third of all the oil in the United States, and the sight of nodding pump jacks is one of the state's most potent images.

Getting Around Texas

Texan distances are so vast that it makes sense to have a **car**; in fact in the larger cities like Dallas or Houston it is all but essential (curiously in this largely "dry" state, it's not illegal to drink alcohol while driving). **Greyhound** routes are concentrated between the major cities of the east, though buses also connect the Gulf Coast, the Rio Grande valley, West Texas and to a lesser extent the Panhandle to the rest of the state. There are two main **Amtrak** routes. The *Sunset Limited*, between New Orleans and LA, passes through Houston, San Antonio, and El Paso three times weekly, while the *Texas Eagle* links Chicago and LA daily via these cities, as well as Dallas/Fort Worth and Austin. **Flying** saves time and can be extremely cheap; look out for price wars between airlines such as *Southwest, Chapparal* and *Texas*. Over thirty cities have airports.

Where Texas really falls down is on **public transport** within the cities themselves. It's proved very difficult to encourage mass transit in a state where long distances – in Houston many people travel at least twenty-five miles to work – and low petrol prices make the love affair with the car almost inevitable.

Hitching is not to be encouraged. **Cycling**, too, isn't really viable – distances are too far and Texan drivers too unfamiliar with the concept of sharing the roads. Recreational cycling within cities is more feasible; in Austin and San Antonio it's even possible to use a bike as your sole form of transport.

SOUTHERN TEXAS
AND THE GULF COAST

The coastline of south Texas curves from Beaumont (the site of the first major oil strike in Texas) on the much-touristed **Gulf Coast**, down past the urban monster of Houston, to culminate at the Rio Grande Valley, the border with Mexico. The whole region is dominated by **Houston** – physically, as it sprawls ever further outwards, and culturally. Houston's great wealth and cosmopolitan significance have led to a thriving arts scene, but ultimately it overpowers, rather than relates to, the rest of the region.

Geographically and culturally, this area has two distinct faces. To the east are the seaside resorts of the prairie, rolling away from the hills and forests of east Texas. Much of the coast is feeling the strain of rapid property development and commercialisation, but there are still unspoilt stretches along the **Padre Island National Seashore**. In the south, a Hispanic influence spreads north from the fertile Rio Grande Valley. The border towns here have little charm except as points of entry to Mexico for cheap shopping and entertainment. A hot, swampy climate is one factor uniting south Texas. Houston, especially, is unbearable in the summer, one reason for the mass exodus to the coast.

Houston

HOUSTON is an ungainly beast of a city, the fourth largest in the US, crazed and confused by overdevelopment during the oil boom and then traumatised by the sudden slump of the early Eighties. It's a suffocating place, choking on appalling traffic congestion, and facing crime rates shooting as high as its surreal space-age downtown skyline. Yet for all this, its sheer energy, its relentless Texan pride, and above all its refusal to take itself totally seriously, give it a perverse appeal. That Howard Hughes came from Houston makes absolute sense; eccentric, domineering and sordid, the millionaire typified all that makes the city intriguing.

There is no good reason why Houston exists at all; it was founded on a muddy mire in 1837 by two brothers from New York who hoped it would become the capital of the new Republic of Texas. For all their wild claims about its potential as a port, and its (imaginary) urban attractions, the more promising site of Austin was made capital in 1839. However, by then drunken and diseased Houston had somehow established itself as a commercial centre. Oil – discovered in 1901, and, like the city itself, unpredictable and

> The telephone **area code** for Houston is ☎713.

heading for obsolescence – became the foundation, along with cotton and real estate, of vast private fortunes. However, the contradictions of urban life are still writ large, and abject poverty (not least among the blacks who migrated here from the rural South in the 1960s) coexists with the ostentatious wealth.

Arrival, Information and Getting Around

Downtown Houston is at the intersection of interstates 10 (San Antonio–New Orleans) and 45 (Dallas–Galveston), with most of what you'll want to see encircled by Loop 610, now being widened on the west to include the huge Galleria mall. **Houston Intercontinental Airport** (☎230-3000), 25 miles north, is linked by a half-hourly *Express Bus* ($8.50), which drops off at the *Hyatt Regency* in the centre, the Medical Centre to the south, and the Galleria. Taxis cost from $26 to $45. **Hobby Airport** (☎643-4596), nine miles north, just west of I-45, has information centres in each terminal, and the van ride into town costs $5. The downtown **tourist office** is at 3300 Main Street (Mon–Fri 8.30am–5pm; ☎620-6609), and the main **post office** is at 4021 Franklin Street (☎227-1474; zip code 77052).

Amtrak arrives at 902 Washington Avenue, near the post office. Have your camera ready for a splendid view of the downtown skyline, though the station itself is small, isolated, and barely served by taxis. Try to arrive here, or at the large and modern *Greyhound* terminal (2121 Main St; ☎222-1161 or ☎759-6581), during daylight.

City Transport

There are few options for non-drivers in Houston. The *Metro Buses* are predominantly for commuters, **taxis** (most reliable firm – *Yellow Cabs*, ☎236-1111) are expensive, and the humid climate and huge distances make walking unappealing. However, in the face of crippling traffic congestion, efforts are being made to encourage mass transit. Furious debates are raging about the possible construction of an underground rail system – though many claim that the plans serve property and business interests rather than potential users. Maps of the city's **bus** routes can be had from downtown *Metro Ride Stores*, at Fannin and Capitol streets, or 912 Dallas Avenue (Mon–Fri only). Local fares are 70¢, and express services (along the freeways) cost $1, while the downtown *Texas Special* shuttle bus costs 25¢ a ride. Full information is on ☎635-4000.

Gray Line Tours run daily **coach tours**, at 10am, for $20 (602 Sampson St; ☎223-8800). *Citiwalks* (3131 Timmons Ave; ☎963-0807) arrange downtown tunnel **walks**.

The City

It's demoralizing and unwise to try and see too much of Houston in one go; best to concentrate on **downtown** or the **Museum District**, which can be walked around at leisure. Houston's human face is most evident in the **Montrose** area, on the way to yuppification but still home to eccentrics and bohemians.

Downtown

Since the oil crisis in the early Eighties, the frenzy of skyscraper-building has slowed down; but Houston's dramatic skyline defiantly stands as an unforgettable monument to an earlier age of arrogant certainty. Observation floors on the **Texas Commerce Tower**, 600 Travis Street, and the **Texaco Plaza** offer views of the seemingly endless plateau over which the city is spread.

Most people escape the heat by staying underground, in the four miles of air-conditioned **tunnels** entered from the *Hyatt Regency* or the Main Street banks. Don't bother to explore these, however; they're a confusing and unaesthetic way for visitors to get around, despite the city's pride in their shops and restaurants. One consequence of this subterranean world is a surreal, dreamlike isolation above ground, as the plate-glass towers shimmer with reflections of the modern sculptures scattered at every turn (such as the Miros outside the Texas Commerce Tower).

Nestling below the skyscrapers, **Sam Houston Historical Park** at 110 Bagby Street contains restored structures such as a church and shop, while **Market Square** features some of the original buildings at the heart of the early city, including the 1860 Creole *La Carafe*, at 813 Congress Street. Once a trading post, it is now a laid-back bar complete with shadowy corners and old wooden floors.

Even if you can't afford one of the performances in the **Theater District**, west of Milam Street between Preston and Rusk streets, visit the **Wortham Theatre**, 500 Texas Street (☎237-1439), which houses the city's opera and ballet. The beautifully sculpted interior, perfect acoustic systems and secluded private bars take the breath away, as does the knowledge that the whole set-up cost $70 million – a sum raised in its entirety in 1987 before the theatre was even built.

The Museum District and the Rice University Area

Five miles southwest of downtown, the quiet and leafy Museum and Rice districts, with boulevards lined by huge oaks, are enjoyable to explore on foot. There are students everywhere, cycling, walking or just lounging on the grass, and several good book-shops. Metro buses from downtown are #65 Bissonet, #70 University, #8 South Main Street and #9 Med Centre.

The **Menil Collection**, at 1515 Sul Ross, is housed in an airy and naturally lit building designed by Renzo Piano, who also contributed to the Pompidou Centre in Paris. Oil millionaires Jean and Dominique de Menil collected a superb array of works, ancient and modern, with Picasso, Léger and Magritte well represented (Wed–Sun 11am–7pm; free). A short way east, the minimalist Ecumenical **Rothko Chapel** at 1409 Sul Ross (daily 10am–6pm) was designed in 1971 as a space for meditation, and contains fourteen abstract paintings by Mark Rothko – though many deride its resemblance to a nuclear bunker. The broken obelisk in the small park outside is dedicated to Martin Luther King Jr.

At the intersection of Bissonet Street with Main Street, the **Museum of Fine Arts** features an eclectic collection from all eras (Tues, Wed, Fri & Sat 10am–5pm, Sun 12.15–6pm; $3, free Thurs 5–9pm). Crane your neck upwards from the Matisses and Rodins in the pine-shaded **Cullen Sculpture Garden** outside (daily, 9am–10pm; free) to the downtown skyline. In a city with no zoning regulations, such architectural incongruity springs on you constantly.

Hermann Park, three miles south of downtown, is a pleasant green space, though best avoided at night. The **Museum of Natural Science** here (Mon–Sat 9am–6pm, Sun noon–6pm; free Thurs from 9am–noon) includes informative exhibits on regional natural history, an IMAX theatre, and a stunning gem collection. There's also a good coffee shop and a fountain shaped like Texas.

The Galleria and Around

The ultra-modern **Galleria** shopping centre lies just west of the loop, on Westheimer Road. With over three hundred smart shops, cinemas, restaurants, a skating rink and a glass-floored jogging track, this hypermall pays homage to Houston's love affair with modern architecture, international style and Texan tack. Across the way, a waterfall-sized fountain cascades outside the black glass **Transco Tower**, looming breathtakingly high when lit up at night.

Montrose

Bohemian and fun **Montrose** begins at the junction of Smith and Elgin streets. It's all quirky sleaziness, abounding with tattoo parlours, vintage clothing stores, art galleries, and junk shops full of barbed-wire cactii and other curiosities. Unfortunately, plans are underway, spearheaded by a group of wealthy young Texans, to redevelop this as "the Old Westheimer District", erecting old-fashioned gas street lamps and other such unnecessities. The teenagers that once cruised the streets on Saturday night have been cleared away, and the strip joints closed down, but this has long been the base for a very visible and strong gay community; and there remains a high concentration of gay bars and clubs.

Accommodation

There's little call for budget accommodation in central Houston, where most visitors have cars; cheap hotels are concentrated near the Astrodome and outside the Loop, and motorists should try I-45, or the Katy or Southwest freeways.

You might also arrange **bed and breakfast** accommodation in advance; the human touch can be welcome in a city this potentially alienating. As well as the places listed below, try *B&B Texas Style*, 4224 Red Bird Lane, Dallas TX 75237 (☎214/298-8586), or the *B&B Society of Texas*, 8880 B-2 Bellaire, #284, Houston TX 77036-4900 (☎771-3919), which has over twenty houses in Houston, starting at $45.

Days Inn Downtown, 801 Calhoun St (☎659-2222). A modern and very central tower hotel. Rooms are $70–90, and there's a full free breakfast and buffet table.

The Highlander, 607 Highland St (☎861-7545). Almost downtown, in the northwest of the city, with rooms from $42.

Houston Hostel, 5530 Hillman St #2 (☎926-3444). $7 for a bed in a tiny mixed dorm, four miles from the downtown bus terminal. Laundry and lockers.

Perry House Houston International Hostel, 5302 Crawford St (☎523-1009). Near the museums in a pleasant neighbourhood. Beds for around $10, but you should call to reserve.

Sara's Bed and Breakfast, 941 Heights Blvd (☎868-1130). Less than four miles northwest of downtown, near Memorial Park. A chintzy Victorian house with a fine view of downtown Houston, serving continental breakfasts on the porch. Rates begin at $45, double or single.

YMCA, 1600 Louisiana St (☎659-8501). Downtown beds for $15 and a $2 key deposit.

Eating

There's plenty of variety in Houston's **food**; the large immigrant population has left its mark. Look out for Mexican, Vietnamese and even Indian restaurants, and the many good delis – such as the eight outlets of *Antone's Deli* – serving huge salads and sandwiches with an international flavour.

A Moveable Feast, 2202 W Alabama Ave (☎528-3585). Ideologically sound vegetarian food in the medium dinner price range.

Andy's Home Cafe, 1115 E 11th St (☎861-9423). Good late night Tex-Mex food, and huge breakfasts at reasonable prices.

Ba Le, 2800 Travis St (☎520-1965). An enormous and exotic Vietnamese sandwich with coffee at this downtown location costs under $5.

Bombay Grill, 3640 Hillcroft St (☎977-1272). Excellent Indian food, especially the good-value buffet lunch and vegetarian choices. Lunch 11am–2pm, dinner 5.30–10.30pm.

Cafe Express,1800 S Post Oak Rd (☎963-9222), and 3200 Kirby Rd (☎522-3994). California-style fast food with good sandwiches at low prices, and tangy blackcurrant iced tea for under a dollar.

La Jaliscience, 1308 Montrose Blvd (☎524-8676). Gathering place for families, yuppies and Houston hipsters; very cheap food. Open until 3am during the week, 4am at the weekend.

Treebeards, 315 Travis St (☎225-2160), and 1100 Louisiana St (☎752-2601). Downtown Cajun lunches, Mon–Fri 11am–2pm. Cheap and tasty specials popular with business types.

Entertainment and Nightlife

There's no shortage of things to do in Houston; just check the listings in the free *Houston Press*, or the more alternative *Public News*, and you'll find everything from feminist events to Pakistani costume shows. Head outside the Loop for **country and western** music; most urban Houstonians are too hip to hoe down. The **Main Street Theater**, in the Rice Village, presents comedy, classics and experimental works, at 2540 Times (☎524-6706), while **Miller Outdoor Theatre** in Hermann Park, at 2020 Hermann Drive (☎520-3290), has free symphony concerts, ballet and opera on summer evenings, and a Shakespeare Festival around the end of July. The **Alley Theatre** at 615 Texas Avenue (☎228-8421) offers last-minute discount seats, and *Showtix* (☎552-1882), in the *Houston Sports Exchange Store* in the Galleria, has half-price theatre, dance and music tickets.

Bars and Clubs

Axiom, 2425 McKinney Ave (☎224-1240). The club of the moment, offering multimedia art/video/ music performances. The *Lysergic Shindig* night is open-mike night.

Bon Ton Room, 4216 Washington Ave, between downtown and Memorial Park (☎863-0010). Good live R&B, plus some of the best Cajun and zydeco musicians around (significant in Houston since a wave of migration from rural Louisiana in the early 1960s).

Etta's Lounge, 5120 Scott St (☎528-2611). Old blues bar, south of downtown.

House of Eden, 3232 Travis St (☎529-8184). House music club, Sundays 10pm until sunrise.

The Last Resort, 1403 Nance St (☎226-8563). East of downtown, in an arty and isolated area. Once a house of ill repute; knock twice on the closed door to get in. Good cheap Tex-Mex food and live bands in the back garden; but you can just drink all night if you prefer.

Listings

American Express First West Building, 1307 Travis St, ☎658-1114.

Astrodome 8400 Kirby St at Loop 610 S. Gigantic covered stadium which pioneered *Astroturf*; home to basketball's *Rockets*, football's *Oilers*, and baseball's *Astros*. Tickets ☎799-9555, tours ☎799-9595.

Chemist 24-hr *Cunningham Pharmacy*, 6033 Airline Drive, ☎697-3261.

Currency Exchange *Texas Foreign Exchange Inc*, 1130 Travis St, ☎654-0999.

Gay Switchboard ☎529-3211, 3pm–midnight.

Medical Emergencies General Hospital, Ben Traub Loop, ☎791-7300.

Rape Crisis ☎528-7273, 24-hr.

Ticketron 2990 Richmond Ave, ☎526-6557. Ticket outlets throughout Houston.

Western Wear Store *Just Boots*, 5705 Richmond Ave, ☎977-8077. Discount boots and cowboy gear, in the northeast of the city.

Around Houston

Houston's double-edged status as having both historical importance and all the trappings of a twenty-first-century "space city" is neatly demonstrated with two possible excursions, both about twenty miles south of the city.

San Jacinto Battleground State Historical Park

San Jacinto Battleground, 21 miles southeast of Houston, was the site of a fifteen-minute fight, two months after the Alamo in 1836, in which the Texans all but wiped out the superbly trained Mexican army. Its focal point is the tallest **monument** in the world (570ft, topped by a 35ft Lone Star); but from the observation deck ($2) there's little to see but miles of flat land. The **Museum of History** inside is more interesting, and includes the stirring and emotive 35-minute film show *Texas Forever!* (daily, park 8am–7pm, museum 9am–6pm; ☎479-2421).

NASA

NASA has been controlling space flight from 25 miles south of Houston since the launch of Gemini 4 in 1965. As a working facility, it's not really geared to tourists; all tours are self-guided, although you are rushed through the (tiny) Mission Control Room itself with a quick-fire lecture. Tours start at the visitor centre (daily 9am–4pm; free; ☎483-4321); try on space helmets, and inspect moonrocks and various remarkably cranky-looking rocket replicas, then join astronauts and scientists in the unremarkable but cheap cafeteria, and stock up on tacky space-age presents at the gift shop.

By **car** from Houston, take I-45 south to NASA/Alvin, go three miles east on NASA Road 1, and the gate is on the left. **Bus** #246 Bay Area-NASA via 245 Edgebrook bus from downtown runs to the Space Center (every 50min, Mon–Fri only, 7.45am–2.25pm outwards, 9am–3.30pm back, journey time 1hr).

The Gulf Coast

You only have to look at the number of condominium developments along the **Gulf Coast** to see that this is a major tourist destination. The climate ranges from balmy at **Galveston** to subtropical at the Mexican border, but everywhere it's windy; **Corpus Christi** rivals Chicago as gustiest city in the States, and devastating hurricanes in the early 1900s all but ruined the traditional economy. The fierce tide, progressively eating the beaches away, must place tourism itself in jeopardy; but for the moment, Galveston offers history, shopping and low-key relief from uptight Houston, while Corpus Christi to the south makes the best base for the beaches of Padre Island National Seashore. Rockport, a weathered resort on Hwy-35, is convenient for the Aransas National Wildlife Refuge, sheltering endangered whooping crane, armadillo and alligators.

Galveston

In 1890 **GALVESTON** was a thriving port, far larger than Houston; many newly arrived European immigrants chose to stay here in "the Queen of the Gulf". The building of Houston's Ship Canal, after the hurricanes of 1900 killed over six thousand people and washed away much of the land, left the coastal town to fade slowly away. Its recent revitalisation as a historic district and beach resort has renewed spirits somewhat, but just beneath the pastel prettiness of the restored Victorian architecture and the relentless positivism of the inhabitants is a deathly stillness, as if the place is holding its breath, waiting to see if this time it can succeed without calamity or disaster.

Galveston's old Santa Fe depot at 25th Street and the Strand is now a **Railroad Museum**, displaying steam trains, Pullman cars and endless artefacts relating to train travel (daily 10am–5pm; ☎765-5700). Eerie white statues stand around in the waiting room; pick up a telephone and listen to their conversations. It's a skilful evocation of a lost era, fascinating to a society in which many people have never travelled by train.

In town, the **Strand**, once "the Wall Street of the Southwest", has been fitted with gaslights, upmarket shops, restaurants and galleries. Old houses are everywhere, such as the grotesque Victorian **Bishop's Palace**, 1402 Broadway Avenue (☎762-2475), with its stained glass, mosaics, and marble; the antebellum **Ashton Villa**, 2328 Broadway Avenue (☎762-3933), which shows a film about the 1900 hurricane; and the 1839 **Samuel May Williams Home**, 3601 Avenue P (☎765-1839).

The **beaches** of Seawall Boulevard are a constant reminder of Galveston's struggle simply to exist: murky, rocky, and protected behind a ten-mile-long seawall from the ever-encroaching tides and the threat of further hurricanes. **Stewart Beach Park**, the most convenient beach for the seawall, gets very crowded; free ferries run to the quieter beaches of the **Bolivar Peninsula** from the eastern end of Seawall Boulevard.

Practicalities

Greyhound takes about an hour and a half to cover the fifty miles from Houston, arriving at 4913 Broadway Avenue ($4 by cab from the centre). There is no *Amtrak* service, but the vintage and expensive *Texas Limited Train* makes two-hour trips from Houston to the Railroad Museum (Houston ☎526-1709 or Galveston ☎765-5700). A five-mile **trolley** system links the **visitor centres** at 2014 The Strand (daily 9.30am–5.30pm; ☎765-7834) and 21st Street and Seawall Boulevard (☎763-4311) with all the points of interest, at $2 for the round trip or $4 for a narrated tour (Thurs–Tues, 10am–5pm).

Rooms in Galveston are pricey in summer and at weekends, but there are bargains to be found at other times. The normal $50 rate at the *Commodore on the Beach*, 3618 Seawall Boulevard (☎763-2375), for example, can drop much lower, while doubles at the upmarket *Holiday Inn on the Beach*, 5002 Seawall Boulevard (☎740-3581) come down to $50 during the week. *Hazlewood House* at 1127 Church Street (☎762-1668) is the cheapest of the bed and breakfasts, with rooms from $55; the same phone number serves as a general B&B reservation service.

Nightlife in Galveston doesn't amount to much, though there's high-quality, if expensive, theatre at *The Grand 1894 Opera House*, 2020 Post Office Street (☎765-1894). Otherwise, catch up on some sleep, or put all your energies into having a good meal out. One of the best seafood **restaurants** is *Gaido's Seaside Inn* at 3828 Seawall Boulevard (also rooms $35–70; ☎762-9625). *Yaga's Cafe*, 2314 The Strand (☎762-6676) serves delicious Caribbean-style seafood, chicken and veggies, amid embarrassingly racist decor, and has live music at night. The *Country Morning Bakery* at 101 21st Street (closed Mon; ☎763-1617) is good for weekday lunches.

The telephone **area code** for Galveston is ☎409; for Corpus Christi it's ☎512.

Corpus Christi

The unabashed resort town of **CORPUS CHRISTI** is reached along the coast on Hwy-35 from Houston or Galveston, or on I-37 from San Antonio. Originally a rambunctious trading post, it too was hit by a fierce hurricane, in 1919, but managed to pick itself up, shake itself down and industrialise. It's now a centre for naval air training, petroleum and ranching; apart from fishing, sailing and water sports, there's not a great deal to do. If you're tiring of the outdoor life, the impressive collection of the **Art Museum of South Texas**, 1902 N Shoreline Boulevard, includes Monet and Picasso, while the **Corpus Christi Museum**, 1900 N Chaparral Street, specialises in hands-on natural history exhibits and naval aviation. Both museums are free, but closed on Mondays.

Practicalities

Greyhound arrives at 702 N Chaparral Street, downtown (☎882-2516). The **Visitors Information Centre** (Mon–Fri 8.30am–5pm; ☎882-5603) is at 1201 N Shoreline Boulevard, in the centre of all tourist activity, about a mile south of downtown. Daytime **buses** operate downtown (no service Sun). A **trolley** runs from the motels on Shoreline Boulevard to the large Padre Island and Sunrise shopping malls, fare 50¢.

Cheap **motels** line Leopard Street in the northwest, but these aren't very convenient without use of a car. Along Shoreline Boulevard, the *Sand and Sea Budget Inn* at no. 1013 N (☎882-6518) costs from $27, while bay-view rooms at the *Quality Inn Bayfront*, no. 411 N (☎884-4815) start at around $32. Doubles from $55 can be had at the beachside *Best Western Sandy Shores Resort*, 3200 Surfside Road (☎883-7456). *The Lighthouse* at 444 N Shoreline Boulevard (☎883-3982) does good **seafood**, pricier than in downtown but in a nicer location. The *Downtown Cafe*, 510 N Chaparral Street (☎884-8385), has live bands at weekends.

South Towards Mexico

The disconnected islands of **Padre Island National Seashore** stretch just offshore for 110 miles south of Corpus Christi, almost down to the Mexican border. The frontier between **Brownsville** and **Matamoros** is not, however, very interesting; for a brief taste of Mexico, head almost due west from Corpus one hundred miles to **Laredo**. US-83 runs along the Rio Grande between Brownsville and Laredo. Away from the coast, the fertile landscape begins to dry out and citrus groves give way to the brush and mesquite of a region of huge ranches, where Mexican *vaqueros* (cowboys) once held sway.

Padre Island National Seashore and Brownsville

Padre Island National Seashore is not quite as unspoilt these days as its reputation might suggest, with its ranks of condos advancing steadily, but it remains a good destination for bird-watching, beachcombing and camping. Pick up details at the Park HQ, on the main route out from Corpus Christi, at 9405 S Padre Island Drive (Mon–Sat 8.30am–4.30pm; ☎937-2621). Infrequent buses run from Corpus Christi to the tip of Padre Island, and there is a shuttle service into the park (☎949-8850). Entry is $3, but there's free camping on the beaches to the south. Note that an impassable canal divides the island, meaning that the pricier and much more touristed **Padre Island** in the south can only be accessed from the mainland.

Brownsville, just across from South Padre Island, is a scruffy semitropical resort, populated by elderly Texans on their winter holidays, where you'll hear more Spanish spoken than English. To cross the border into **Matamoros**, pick up a tourist card from the Mexican Consulate at 10th Avenue and Washington Street, then walk across the bridge at International Boulevard (a *Maxi-Taxi* costs 25¢). It's standard to give a small bribe before you're let through. Wealthier than Brownsville, and considerably larger, the Mexican city is not terribly inspiring, but it has a good market, Mercado Juarez, on calles 9 and 10, and an untouristy Main Plaza at Calle 5, dominated by the cathedral.

Laredo

The dusty and poverty-stricken smuggling centre of **Laredo** has seen greater days. Santa Anna marched his troops through here in 1836, and in 1840, the city was the centre of Zapata's Mexican separatist protest. The capitol of his short-lived Republic of the Rio Grande still stands on Zaragoza Street (Tues–Sun 10am–noon and 1–5pm; free). San Agustin Plaza, the site of the original Spanish settlement, has now been

---

A MEXICAN BORDER CROSSING

It's an easy walk across the bridge from San Agustin Plaza in Laredo (on payment of a small toll) to the typical Mexican border town of **Nuevo Laredo**; so easy that this is the most popular crossing along the entire frontier, with most trippers coming simply for evening meals and weekend shopping. There is a lively atmosphere, with all the tourist shops and restaurants concentrated near the bridge, on "the strip", Avenida Guerrero. Most take American dollars, and bargaining is acceptable at some of them.

Seven blocks down Avenida Guerrero, the Main Plaza is the social centre of town. The *Cadillac Bar*, Avenida Ocampo and Calle de Belde, was the first of its **bars** and **restaurants** to encourage tourism here, serving drinks to Texans escaping Prohibition. It's a bit tacky now; better to head for *Nuevo Leon*, 508 Avenida Guerrero, for *cabrito* (barbecued goat), guacamole and cold beer, or further off the beaten track to the faded but authentic *Rincon del Viejo* at 4834 Avenida Gonzalez, which offers *cabrito*, *fajitas* and *alambres*, and occasional mariachi shows. As a whole though, Nuevo Laredo lacks real charm, and can be particularly depressing after dark; have a meal, but give the nightlife a miss.

As with all border crossings, expect to undergo full immigration procedures when you attempt to re-enter the United States.

restored with cobbled streets and Victorian buildings, as has El Mercado, on San Agustin Avenue, the former hub of downtown activity.

Greyhound arrives at Matamoros Street and Santa Ursula Avenue downtown (☎723-4324), *Trailways* at Washington Street and San Agustin Avenue. The visitor centre is at 2310 San Bernardo Avenue (Mon–Fri 8am–5pm; ☎722-9895). Cheap **motels** in town include *Siesta Motel*, 4109 San Bernando Avenue (☎723-3661), with rooms from $36, and *La Quinta*, 3600 Santa Ursula Avenue (☎722-0511), from $44. At lunchtime, *La Posada Dining Room*, 1000 Zaragoza Street (☎722-1701) offers a big buffet and good steaks, the sometimes-rowdy *Unicorn Restaurant and Pegasus Bar*, 3810 San Bernardo Avenue (☎727-4663) serves an eclectic menu, and *El Meson de San Agustin*, 908 Grant Street (☎722-9727) specialises in Oaxaquenan dishes.

CENTRAL TEXAS

Central Texas stretches from the prairies of the northeast through the green and fertile Hill Country into the chalky limestone landscape of the west, and includes two of Texas' most pleasant cities: **San Antonio** and **Austin**. Austin in particular, the capital city and home to the progressive University of Texas, helps to give the region an intellectual and political feel uncharacteristic of the rest of the state.

Agriculture has been the mainstay of the economy here ever since the resistant Comanche population was finally packed off to reservations in the 1840s. The slave-driven cotton plantations of the south and east have gone, but the small communities set up by Polish, Czech, Norwegian and Swedish immigrants in the **Hill Country** maintained, even until very recently, the traditions, architecture and languages of their homelands. Great cattle drives came trampling through after the Civil War, and played a large part in the development of San Antonio.

San Antonio

With neither the twenty-first-century skyline of an oil town, nor the tumbleweed-strewn landscape of the Wild West, **SAN ANTONIO** looks nothing like the stereotyped image of Texas; but it has been pivotal in the state's history. Standing at a geographical crossroads, it encapsulates the complex social and ethnic mixes of all Texas. Although the Spanish and the Germans, among others, have made strong contributions to its architecture, cuisine and music, the predominant influence has to be Mexican. Abundant Tex-Mex restaurants, the prevalent Catholicism, a Mexican university campus, and Levi's billboards in Spanish all attest to a long history of "Texican" culture.

San Antonio is most famous for the legendary **Battle of the Alamo** in 1836, when the Mexican General Santa Anna, seeking to curb the aspirations of Anglo-American pioneers in Mexican-controlled Texas, wiped out a band of Texan volunteers: thus the claim to be "birthplace of the revolution", borne out by its role during Texas' ten subsequent years of independence. After the Civil War, it became a hard-drinking, hard-fighting "sin city", at the heart of the Texas **cattle** empire. Drastic floods in the 1920s left it riddled with slums, poverty and crime, but the sensitive WPA programme which revitalised two of its prettiest sites, **La Villita** and the **River Walk**, laid the foundations for a future as a major tourist destination. San Antonio is now the ninth largest city in the US, with a population of over a million, and receives 10.5 million visitors each year, but it retains an unhurried, organic feeling, thanks to a winning combination of small-town warmth, respect for diversity and a self-confidence rooted in its own history.

The telephone **area code** for Laredo, San Antonio and Austin is ☎512.

Arrival, Information and Getting Around

International flights land at **San Antonio International Airport** (☎821-3411), just north of the relatively small I-410 loop which encircles most of the sights. An express van service runs the twenty-minute journey downtown ($6; every 15min 6am–6.45pm, every 45min 6.45pm–midnight). Taxis cost about $12 (*Yellow Cabs*, ☎226-4242). *Amtrak* serves San Antonio at 1174 E Commerce Street. *Greyhound/Trailways* (☎270-5800) arrive at 500 N St Mary's Street, and is supplemented by the regional *Kerrville Bus Co*, based at 1430 E Houston Street (☎226-7371).

Pick up information on **city transport** from the **visitor centre** at 317 Alamo Plaza downtown (daily 9am–5.30pm; ☎299-8155), or call the *VIA Metropolitan Transit Service* (☎227-2020). **Buses** are reliable and cheap – 40¢ for any travel within the I-410 loop, but many routes stop at 5pm. Five downtown **trolley** routes serve all the major attractions for a mere 10¢. Bus **tours** such as those run by *Gray Line* (☎227-5371/☎240-2826) are only really of much use as a convenient way of seeing the most distant missions.

More strictly pleasurable ways of getting around include renting a **bicycle** from *Bike San Antonio*, 210 Navarro Street (daily 8am–7pm; ☎225-7045), or taking a trip on the **river taxi**, 430 E Commerce Street (☎222-1701).

The main **post office** is at 615 E Houston Street, next to the Alamo.

The Alamo and the Other Missions

The Alamo is the most famous – for reasons which have nothing to do with its original purpose – of a trail of Catholic missions established by the Spanish along remote stretches of the San Antonio River early in the eighteenth century. For a real sense of early Spanish influence in Texas, it's important to make an effort to get out and see all the missions. Each was laid out like a small fortified town, with the church as aesthetic and cultural focus. The goal was to strengthen Spanish control by "converting" the Coahuiltecan Indians – in practice, using them as workforce and army. The missions flourished from 1745 to 1775, but couldn't survive the ravages of disease and attack from Apaches and Comanches, and fell into disuse early in the nineteenth century.

The Alamo

All that is left of the great landmark of the **Alamo** is a large arched shrine, with a facade of delicately carved sandstone, smack in the centre of downtown San Antonio. The first of the Spanish missions, established as San Antonio de Valero in 1718, it only became known as the Pueblo del Alamo in 1801, after secularisation, when it was named for the hometown of a Spanish cavalry unit which used it as a base. The **Battle** for which it has been immortalised in film and song occurred on March 6 1836, when all of the 189 men who had held out for thirteen days against Santa Anna's vastly superior Mexican troops were massacred. They consisted of a few native – Hispanic – Texans, and a majority of volunteers (adventurers like Davy Crockett and Jim Bowie, and aspiring colonists from other states), dreaming of Texan autonomy and driven by the battle cry of "Victory or Death".

A constant stream of bus tours makes visits crowded and hectic; but they're also crucial to understanding all the pride and stubbornness of Texas. The **museum** of battle memorabilia is full of undeniably emotive stuff, such as the poignant letters sent by soldiers preparing to die (Mon–Sat 9am–5.30pm, Sun 10am–5.30pm; free). At the **Rivercentre Mall**, the Battle is re-enacted on a six-storey, Texas-scale IMAX screen; fact and sentiment may converge, but it is a callous viewer who feels no lump in the throat at the rousing patriotism of the finale. Take time also to sit in peace amongst the pecan trees and oaks in the four-acre Alamo grounds, away from the downtown commotion just outside the walls.

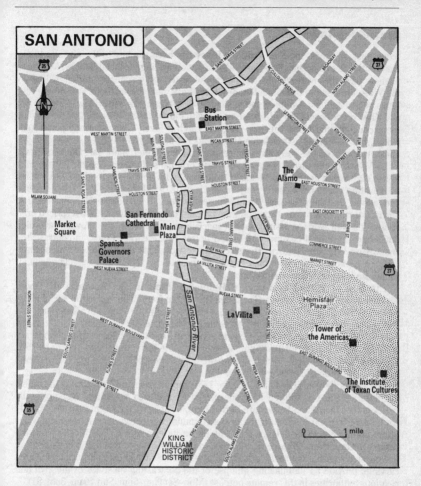

The Other Missions

The **Mission Trail** runs nine miles south along the river from Alamo Street, down S St Mary's Street and onto Mission Road, and can be reached by bus #42. Each of the remaining four missions has been restored to act as an interpretive centre illustrating some aspect of mission life (all free, daily summer 9am–6pm, winter 8am–5pm), while the churches themselves still serve active parishes.

At **Mission Concepcion**, 807 Mission Road (☎229-5732), the exhibits concentrate on the religious function of the missions; scraps of original frescoes can still be seen, along with bullet holes from rougher days. The 1721 **Mission San Jose**, 6539 San Jose Drive (☎229-4770), notable for its beautiful carved-stone ornamentation (especially the ornate "Rose Window"), holds a Mariachi Mass at noon on Sunday. Of the two smaller and more isolated missions, **Mission San Juan**, 9101 Graf Road (☎229-5734), has displays on the mission as economic centre (as well as a unique delicate bell tower), while **Mission San Francisco de la Espada**, 10040 Espada Road (☎627-2021), looks back on its educational role.

Around the Town

Since mission times, the **San Antonio River** has been the key to the city's fortunes. Destructive floods in the 1920s, and subsequent oil drilling, reduced its flow, leading to plans to pave the river over. Instead, a careful landscaping scheme, started in 1939 by the WPA, created the Paseo del Rio, or **River Walk**, now the aesthetic and commercial focus of San Antonio. Cobbled paths, shaded by cypress, oak and willow, wind for two and a half miles beside the jade-green water, with much of the city's eating and entertainment concentrated along the way. You can catch a River Taxi at various points (see p.506), but walking is as much fun and cheaper, watching as the river slowly changes character between the lively Rivercentre Mall and the quieter, more parklike outskirts.

La Villita ("little town") was San Antonio's original settlement, occupied in the mid-to late eighteenth century by Mexican "squatters" with no titles to the land. Only when its elevation enabled it to survive fierce floods in 1819 did this rude collection of stone and adobe buildings become suddenly respectable. It is now a National Historic District, turned over to an "arts community", and consisting mostly of overpriced craft shops. It's well worth a visit though, especially at dusk when the crowds have died down and the muted colours, smells and noises evoke earlier times. In contrast, the small **King William Historic District** southwest contains the elegant late-nineteenth-century homes of German merchants. A surprise in this Mexican-feeling city, it remains a fashionable residential area.

The best of several museums in **Hemisfair Plaza** is the **Institute of Texan Cultures**, 801 S Bowie Street (Tues–Sun 9am–5pm; free). This maps the social histories of thirty diverse "Texan" cultures, with especially pertinent Afro-American and Native American sections. Guided tours help to alleviate the intimidating scale of the place. Also in the Plaza are the **Mexican Cultural Institute**, filled with contemporary Mexican art (Tues–Fri 10am–7pm, weekends noon–6pm; free), and the ugly 750ft **Tower of the Americas**, which but for the observation deck at the top (daily 10am–11pm; $1.75) is devoid of interest.

Across the river at 115 Main Plaza, the 1731 **San Fernando Cathedral** is the oldest cathedral in the US, though it's underplayed as a tourist attraction. Nobody really believes that the Alamo heroes are buried here, whatever they might say, and visually it's uninspiring; but its importance to the community is paramount. A Mariachi Mass offers the chance to experience local culture on its own terms. Two blocks west, the **Spanish Governors Palace** at 105 Plaza de Armas housed Spanish officials during the mission era. It's not really a palace, but its period furnishings and ornate wooden carvings provide an illuminating glimpse of the contrasting lifestyles of the civil and religious authorities in this remote outpost (Mon–Sat 9am–5pm, Sun 10am–5pm; $1).

Market Square, a couple of blocks further on, dates from 1840, and with its outdoor restaurants and bustle is still at the heart of the city's life. Fruit and vegetables are on sale early in the morning, while the shops are a compelling mix of colour and kitsch. Indoors it supposedly resembles a traditional Mexican market, selling gifts, jewellery and oddities. Some of the shops are great, even if the air-conditioning, piped music, and indignant refusal of the shopkeepers to engage in haggling do little to convince you of the authenticity of the venture.

About two miles south of the city, the surreal **Buckhorn Hall of Horns** at the *Lone Star Brewery*, 600 Lone Star Boulevard, is a monument to Texan excess. During San Antonio's heyday as a cowtown, cowboys, trappers and traders would bring in their horns to the Buckhorn Saloon in exchange for a drink. Thousands are now on display, mounted as trophies, chandeliers and chairs, along with endless cases of Lone Star memorabilia, a Hall of Fins and Feathers, and a wax museum. The $3.50 admission includes two complimentary glasses of the "National Beer of Texas". Lovers of kitsch will find it a bargain (daily 9.30am–5pm; ☎226-8301).

It's also worth getting to the **McNay Art Museum**, 6000 N New Braunfels Avenue, at US-81 Austin Highway (Tues–Sat 9am–5pm, Sun 2–5pm; free). This exquisite Moorish-styled villa was built in the Fifties to house the art collection of millionairess and folk artist Marion McNay, which includes Gothic and Medieval works as well as Post-Impressionists. Its garden is a haven of tranquillity. Buses #11(Nacogdoches) or #14(Thousand Oaks) serve the museum from downtown.

Accommodation

The luxury of a moonlit amble along the river back to your hotel is one of the best reasons for visiting San Antonio, so it's worth making a determined effort to stay in the centre. However, downtown is monopolised by luxury hotels, and a car is virtually a prerequisite for finding budget lodgings. There are clusters of reasonably priced **motels** (rooms $30–50) just north of Brackenridge Park on Austin Highway, or, convenient for the airport, on I-35 north towards Austin.

With enough notice, *Bed and Breakfast Hosts*, 166 Rockhill (☎824-8036), can arrange rooms in a castle, a Victorian residence in the King William District, or in less pricey alternatives, for $29 to $65 single, $36 to $90 double (deposit often required).

Alamo Travelodge, 405 Broadway (☎222-1000). Four blocks from the Alamo. Facilities include bar, restaurant and pool. Doubles from $48.

Alpha Hotel, 315 N Main Ave (☎223-7764). The cheapest downtown accommodation, near Market Square, with minimal facilities. Doubles $25–30. No credit cards.

Bullis House Inn International Hostel, 621 Pierce St (☎223-9426). Across from Fort Sam Houston, two miles northeast of the centre (by bus #11). Singles for non-members $19–55, doubles $25–59. A good place to meet people, with pool and kitchens. Call ahead to reserve in summer.

Coliseum Inn, 365 N Pan Am Expressway (☎225-8000). Functional double rooms go for $39.95, just across the road from the hostel.

Downtowner Motel, 902 E Houston St (☎227-6233). Behind the Alamo, with a pool. Doubles $48.

Navarro Hotel, 116 Navarro St (☎224-0255). Across from La Villita and Hemisfair Plaza. Doubles $26. No credit cards.

Eating

Not surprisingly, San Antonio has good **Tex-Mex** food in all price ranges. Many visitors head straight for the Mexican restaurants of the Paseo del Rio; however, charming as it is to eat al fresco beside the river, don't be seduced to such an extent that you never venture above ground. Even downtown, there are many good, local, cheap eating places. Downstairs at the **Rivercentre Mall** is packed with fast-food stalls from Greek through baked potatoes to *Dairy Queen*, but in a city with so much more going for it, these are only recommended when time or money are at a premium.

A H Burritos, 516 Houston St. A pleasant surprise, two doors down from *Woolworths* in the shadow of the Alamo. Fine breakfasts of huevos rancheros, while for dinner, shrimp and steak are the most expensive items, at $6 each.

Casa Rio, 430 E Commerce St (☎225-6718). The nicest place to eat on the River Walk, with excellent cheap Mexican food (a huge "deluxe dinner" costs $5.95).

The Guenther House, 129 E Guenther St (☎227-1061). Delicious cookies and cakes from 75¢, in a cool green flour-mill-cum-museum in the King William District. Good breakfasts and lunches.

La Margarita, 120 Produce Row in the Market Square (☎227-7140). The world's best chicken fajitas, sizzling with onions and peppers, and mountains of guacamole. Pretty special margaritas, too. Dinner is $6 – or nearer $10 if you want a tune from a strolling mariachi.

El Mirador, 722 S St Mary's St (☎225-9444). Wonderful Mexican breakfasts and lunches for under $5. Specialities include *xocetl* (chicken broth) and *Azteca* (spicy tomato) soups. Closed Sun and Aug.

Mi Tierra, 218 Produce Row (☎225-1262). A bustling old market building, across the alley from *La Margarita*, and open 24 hours. Midnight snacks, or full meals. Bar until 2am.

Entertainment and Nightlife

With its abundance of picturesque settings, San Antonio is a great city for **festivals**. During the **Texas Folklife Festival** in Hemisfair Plaza every August, ten stages reflect the huge diversity of music to be found in Texas, ranging from gospel to Lebanese. The **International Conjunto Festival**, each May at the *Guadalupe Cultural Arts Centre* on Guadalupe Street (☎271-9070), west of downtown, celebrates the German/ Mexican country music of south and central Texas.

Check in the free weekly *Current* for details of gigs, films and events, plus money-off vouchers and freebies. There's often live jazz, flamenco or rock in the restaurants along the **River Walk**. Otherwise, **N St Mary's Street** (just beyond the bus station towards the art museum) is the main strip for college nightclubs and bars. The outdoor **Arneson River Theater**, opposite La Villita, at which the river separates the audience from the stage, has live music during the summer.

The Blue Bonnet Palace, 16842 I-35 N Schertz, TX 78154 (☎651-6702). A bit of a trek, north of the airport, but very popular, with country bands 9pm–2am on Fri and Sat. The highlight is the live bull-riding rounds at 10pm and 11.30pm – real urban cowboy stuff.

The Menger Hotel, 204 Alamo Plaza (☎223-4361). The most famous hotel in Texas during the great cattle drives; Teddy Roosevelt came here in 1898 to recruit his "Rough Riders" for the Spanish-American War. Inexplicably furnished to replicate the tap-room at the House of Lords, today the *Roosevelt Bar* is a good place for a cold beer, if you can stand the crowds.

St Mary's Bar and Grill, 3000 St Mary's St (☎737-3900). $3 for R&B, Fri and Sat.

Tycoon Flats, 2926 St Mary's St (☎737-1929). A variety of live music with no cover charge.

Austin

AUSTIN was only a tiny community on the verdant banks of the (Texas) Colorado River when Mirabeau B Lamar, president of the republic, suggested in 1839 that it would make a better **capital** than swampy and disease-ridden Houston. Early building had to be done under armed guard, as angry Comanche watched from the surrounding hills, but despite its perilous location, the city thrived.

These days it wears its status as capital of Texas very lightly; sightseeing rates as a low priority against simply hanging out. This laid-back and progressive city has been a haven since the Sixties for artists, musicians and writers, and an air of creativity hangs over the place. Many visitors come specifically for the **music**. Local musicians are renowned for their innovative re-workings of Texas' country, folk, and R&B heritage, often severing their rural roots to use Austin's enthusiastic environment as a spring-board to national recognition. During the mid-Eighties it was the launchpad of the "New Country" sound, exemplified by Steve Earle and Lyle Lovett, and today musicians hungry for fame tumble out of buses from West Texas or the Panhandle at the weekend to play their hearts out at any of hundreds of live venues.

Austin is one of the few cities in the state where walking, cycling, and reading on the grass are more common than driving around in big cars. It may not have completely avoided the usual problems of urban growth – until recently it was Texas' fastest-growing city, and ugly suburbs have shot up to threaten its small-town feel – but it feels beautifully safe for visitors, even women travelling alone. The presence of the vast UT campus adds to the atmosphere, even if the students' demented support of the "Longhorns" football team can get wearing.

Within the city limits the great park system offers numerous hiking and biking trails, while the two lakes snaking through the centre make wonderful swimming holes. Looking further afield, Austin makes a fine base for exploring the green **Hill Country** that rolls away to the west.

Arrival, Information and Getting Around

Austin spreads about twenty miles north–south and eighteen miles east–west, severed by I-35 (between Dallas and San Antonio) to the east. The Colorado River runs south of downtown. Flights come in conveniently close to downtown, at the **Municipal Airport** on I-35 and Airport Boulevard, east of Guadalupe Street and the university.

Greyhound, 916 E Koenig Lane (☎458-5267), and *Amtrak*, 250 N Lamar Boulevard, are both some way out of the centre. You can catch buses from the Highland Mall a few blocks east of the *Greyhound* station. **Taxis** are reliable and cheap; if you can't hail one down or find a rank, try *American Cars*, ☎452-9999.

Walking is an easy and pleasant way of getting around, and Austin also has a good **mass transit** system – currently free, though unfortunately that may well change soon. The *Capital METRO* bus runs downtown, crosstown and through the campus, with extra university shuttle routes – distinguishable by the longhorn emblem beside the route number – during term time. Services run from 6am until midnight, Monday to Saturday, and until 8pm on Sunday, and schedules are available from the METRO Information Center at Fifth Street and Congress Avenue (in front of the NCNB building), as well as at local kiosks, from grocery stores, and on campus. The *Dillo Express*, also run by *METRO*, is a downtown **trolley** system, running every fifteen minutes between 7am and 7pm on weekdays. *Rose Maries Tours* (☎441-0790) run **tours** of the city and Hill Country excursions. **Bicycles** can be rented from *University Schwinn*, at 2901 N Lamar Boulevard (Mon–Fri 10am–7pm, Sat 10am–6pm; ☎474-6696).

The **visitor centre** is at 412 E Sixth Street (Mon–Fri 8.30am–5pm, Sat–Sun 1–5pm; ☎478-0098), and there's a State Tourist Information Center (daily 8am–5pm) in the foyer of the state capitol. The **post office** is at 300 E Ninth Street.

The Town

The Texas **State Capitol**, between 11th and 14th streets, is taller than the national capitol in Washington, with a pink granite dome that dominates the downtown skyline. The chandeliers, carpets and even the door hinges of this colossal building are emblazoned with lone stars and "TEXAS" motifs (daily 8.30am–4.30pm; public tours every 15min; free). The nearby **Texas State Library** and **Governors Mansion** both contain displays on Texan history. **Congress Avenue**, which slopes south from the capitol down to the river, is worthy of a stroll; at no. 1006 the *Old Bakery and Emporium*, built as a Swedish bakery in 1876, houses a craft shop and hospitality desk.

Sixth Street, running west from I-35 to Congress Street (also known as Old Pecan Street), is the focus of much of the city's nightlife, as well as featuring many renovated buildings, galleries and shops. The *Women and their Work Gallery*, at 1137 W Sixth Street, is particularly good, although not all of the work in its temporary exhibitions is by women. *Grove Drug Store*, 209 E Sixth Street, is Texas' oldest drug store, complete with original soda fountain and faded shopfront. Between Fifth and Sixth streets, just west of Lamar Boulevard, is the magnificent 600-year-old **Treaty Oak**.

Two interesting museums in the east of the city are the **George Washington Carver Museum** of local black history at 1165 Angelina Street (Tues–Thurs 10am–6pm, Fri & Sat noon–5pm; free), which each Saturday hosts free concerts, and the **Elizabet Ney Museum** at 304 E 44th Street. This latter, a German-influenced building in a leafy historic residential area, preserves the last studio, with maquettes and finished marbles, of Austin's most celebrated sculptress (Wed–Sat 10am–5pm, Sun noon–5pm; free).

Zilker Park, across the river from the *Amtrak* station and southwest of the centre, is one of the best of the many fine parks in the city, a perfect retreat on sweaty Austin afternoons. One of its main attractions is the spring-fed (and freezing cold) **Barton Springs**

Pool, shaded by pecans (April–Oct, Mon & Fri 8am–7.30pm, Tues–Thurs, Sat & Sun 8am–9pm; $1.75). Also in Zilker Park you'll find hiking and biking trails, a miniature railroad winding beside the river (daily 10am–dusk; $1.25), and, to the west, the wildlife garden of the **Austin Nature Center** (Mon–Fri 8am–5pm, Sat 10am–5pm; free).

In the northwest of the city, overlooking Lake Austin, sits the **Laguna Gloria Art Museum**, 3809 W 35th Street (Tues–Sat 10am–5pm, Sun 1–5pm, and 5–9pm on Thurs when admission is free; $2 at all other times; ☎458-8191). This beautiful 1916 villa belonged to Clara Driscoll, who at 22 bought the Alamo for the Daughters of the Republic of Texas. It now features changing exhibits of twentieth-century art, and has a replica of the Rose Window at the San Jose Mission in San Antonio. Don't miss **Mayfield Park** next door, a peaceful idyll complete with waterlilies and stroppy peacocks. **Mount Bonnell**, further north on the Colorado River, gives quite spectacular views over the city and surrounding countryside.

Around the University

Having its own oil well (the drilling rig *Santa Rita No 1* is on San Jacinto Boulevard) has made the **University of Texas** one of the world's richest universities. Its unparalleled collection of manuscripts by contemporary authors is available to scholars amid tight security in the greenhouse-like library; stories abound of the sums lavished to acquire work from relative unknowns who might some day achieve fame. One of Austin's grimmest memories is of the day in 1966 when a gunman climbed the campus administration building, the **UT Tower** on Guadalupe Street, to take potshots at passing pedestrians. Best just to look rather than enquire if you want to make any friends here. Student-guided tours of the campus and its museums leave the information centre in the main building twice daily on weekdays and once on Saturday.

Guadalupe Street itself, on the west edge of the campus running north from Martin Luther King Boulevard to 24th Street, is known as the Drag, and is the focus of much student activity; vintage clothes shops, bookshops and restaurants abound. Joe Ely, one of Austin's many adoptive rock'n'roll sons, even wrote a song about it – *Down on the Drag*. In summer, there's a *Peoples Renaissance Outdoor Market* at 23rd Street.

The **LBJ Library and Museum**, on the northeast edge of the campus at 2313 Red River Street, traces the career of the brash and egotistical Lyndon Baines Johnson from his origins in the Hill Country to the House of Representatives, the Senate and the White House. The curious circumstances of his first senatorial election in 1948 (confirmed only after some "overlooked" votes – all written in the same hand – were found three days after his opponent had been elected) go unmentioned. John Kennedy is said to have made Johnson his vice-president to avoid his establishing a rival power base; but in the aftermath of Kennedy's assassination, Johnson's administration (1963–68) was able to push through a far more radical programme than Kennedy ever attempted. Johnson's nemesis, Vietnam, is presented here as an awful mess left by Kennedy for him to clear up, at the cost of great personal anguish. There's a replica of the Johnson Oval Office at the White House, as well as a wonderfully corny set of political campaign memorabilia from Roosevelt to Bush; some of the badges are on sale.

Accommodation

I-35 and Congress Avenue are the cheap hotel strips, but bed and breakfasts are better options; there are good ones in most areas of the city.

Austin International AYH Hostel, 2200 S Lakeshore Blvd (☎444-2294). Southeast of downtown (bus #7 Duval from *Greyhound*) beside Town Lake. $8 per night for members.

Carringtons Bluff, 1900 David St (☎479-0638). Very central and very nice countrified bed and breakfast, a block from Lamar at Martin Luther King Blvd, with rooms from $49–59.

Crest Hotel, 111 E First St (☎478-9611). Central location, airport shuttle, rooms $45–55.

La Prelle Place Bed and Breakfast, 2204 Lindell Ave (☎441-2204). Rather far south, but on the right side of the town lake for hike and bike trails and Barton Springs. Rates start at $49. Reservations and one night's deposit required.

Woodburn House, 4401 Avenue D (☎458-4335). B&B in the leafy Hyde Park area, within walking distance of the university. $55 double. Reservation and deposit required.

Eating

Radical Austin has many more vegetarian and wholefood restaurants than is usual in Texas; even chicken-fried steak can be found prepared healthily. Add this to the fact that sitting on your own reading a book over your meal is not seen as aberrant behaviour, and you have a city in which eating out can be a real pleasure. Plenty of cheap and good restaurants near the university cater to the student population, especially along Guadalupe Street – look for the crowds. If, on the other hand, you get sick of the sight of UT students, try along Lamar Boulevard beyond the *Amtrak* station for good local restaurants.

The Broken Spoke, 3201 S Lamar Blvd (☎442-6189). Neighbourhood country and western joint. No-nonsense waitresses slap down excellent chicken-fried steaks for around $5.

Good Eats Cafe, 1530 Barton Springs Rd (☎476-8141). High-quality healthy home-cooking, from around $3. The restaurant also organises early-morning walking groups in the area.

Jane's Restaurant, Guadalupe St at 35th St (☎458-6326). Quiet local diner with a clientele intent on the serious home-cooking.

Matt's El Rancho, 2613 S Lamar Blvd (☎462-9333). Huge, rowdy Mexican restaurant with very mixed crowd. Food is authentic and cheap. Long queues, but great margaritas.

Mothers Cafe, 4215 Duval St (☎451-3994). Healthy international vegetarian food; delicious enchiladas, noodles and crepes. Traditional Southwestern breakfasts include unbeatable banana and walnut pancakes. Bookish clientele and chirpy waiters.

Ruby's BBQ, W 29th St at Guadalupe St (☎477-1651). Reasonably priced barbecue and Cajun food, behind *Antone's Blues Club*. Open for live blues until 3.30am on Fri and Sat.

Threadgill's, 6416 N Lamar Blvd (☎451-5440). An Austin institution since Kenneth Threadgill was given the first licence to sell beer in the city after Prohibition. Real home-cooking at bargain prices, with free seconds of wonderful vegetables like black-eyed peas and okra. Lively atmosphere, with occasional live fiddle music, folk, or country and western bands. A must.

Uptown Enchilada Bar, 1702 Lavaca St (☎477-7689). The usual Mexican choices, with a Sunday $5 "all you can eat" buffet from 4.30–10pm.

West Campus Cafe, 26th St and Rio Grande Ave (☎480-9011). Open 24hr for homestyle Southwestern cooking from around $5. Abundant *Grateful Dead* memorabilia, and live music at weekends.

Wokaholic, 121 W Fifth St and Colorado St (☎320-0555). Cheap Chinese lunch and dinner buffet.

Nightlife

The only problem you'll have with Austin **nightlife** is being spoilt for choice; there are so many bars and clubs in such a relatively small area. In **Sixth Street** in particular, virtually every building houses a club or a bar. Two excellent local newspapers, the *Daily Texan*, the UT paper (Thursdays), and the *Austin Chronicle* (Fridays) carry listings and news of community and cultural issues.

There's always something going on at the **university** campus. Big names in drama and dance appear in the **Performing Arts Center** at 23rd Street and E Campus Drive, (☎471-1444); smaller-scale theatre (☎471-1444) and free classical concerts (☎471-5401) take place in the **College of Fine Arts**. In town, *Synergy Studio* at 150 W Fifth Street (☎322-0227) puts on performance art and contemporary dance. Two of the best venues to see **independent movies** are *Austin Media Arts*, 2118 Guadalupe Street (☎459-5875) and the *Dobie Cinema* at 2021 Guadalupe and 21st streets. The *Velveeta Room*, 317 E Sixth Street (☎469-9116), puts on **comedy** on Wednesday and Thursday nights.

Live Music

Although Austin's folk revival in the Sixties attracted sufficient attention to propel **Janis Joplin** on her way from Port Arthur, Texas, to stardom in California, the city first achieved prominence in its own right as the centre of **"outlaw country"** music in the Seventies. **Willie Nelson** and **Waylon Jennings**, disillusioned with Nashville, spearheaded a movement which reworked sentimental country and western with an incisive injection of rock'n'roll. The audiences in Austin, far removed from the hard-drinking honky-tonk crowds of West Texas, provided an environment which encouraged and rewarded risk-taking and experiment. These days the **"Austin sound"** is a melange of country, folk, blues, psychedelic and "alternative" influences, very much reliant on acoustics and guitars.

The tradition of black Texas bluesmen such as Blind Lemon Jefferson and Blind Willie Johnson still lives on; *Antone's Blues Club* on Guadalupe Street is the place to hear **live blues**, while the enthusiastic and knowledgeable staff in *Antone's Record Store*, opposite, can provide advice on what to see on any given night. **Folk** music, traditional or with a punk twist, is also thriving, with an annual folk festival at Rod Kennedy's *Quiet Valley Ranch* in Kerrville (☎257-3600).

If you feel like **dancing**, two modern clubs are *Sanitarium*, 705 Red River Street (☎477-6626), and *Boathouse*, 407 Colorado Street (☎474-9667).

Antone's, 2915 Guadalupe St (☎474-5314). Hot, sweaty and crowded; the best blues club in the city, with big-name national and local acts nightly.

The Broken Spoke, 3201 S Lamar Blvd (☎442-6189). Neighbourhood restaurant and stomping country music venue, with all the trappings but well away from the centre. The barn-like dance hall regularly attracts the best Texan acts on the circuit. Dancing begins at 9pm.

Cactus Cafe, Texas Union, 24th St and Guadalupe St (☎471-8228). One of Austin's favourite venues. Consistently good country, rock and folk music; regular showcases for new acts.

Cap'n Tom's Bar B Q, 1800 N Lamar Blvd (☎834-1858). Regular bluegrass and fiddle-playing jams, a long way from downtown.

Carlins, 416 E Sixth St (☎473-0905). Live R&B, soul, blues and jazz, 9.30pm–2am.

Continental Club, 1315 S Congress Ave (☎441-2444). Huge variety of live music, with the "Blue Monday" night attracting many surprise guest stars.

The Green Mesquite, 1400 Barton Springs Road (☎479-0485). Somewhat inaccessible, but with nightly live bluegrass, folk and R&B. Barbecue and beer on tap.

Liberty Lunch, 405 W Second St (☎477-0461). A must: *the* club for the best and hippest local and national acts.

The Ritz Theatre, 320 E Sixth (☎477-2123). Live bands and vintage movies.

Top of the Marc, 618 W Sixth St (☎472-9849). Exclusively jazz, conveniently sited above a deli.

La Zona Rosa, 612 W Fourth St (☎482-0662). Tex-Mex, acoustic and rockabilly, with Mexican food.

The Hill Country

The rolling hills, lakes and valleys of the **HILL COUNTRY**, north and west of Austin and San Antonio, were inhabited mostly by Apache and Comanche until after statehood, when German and Scandinavian settlers arrived. Many of the log-cabin farming communities they established are still here, such as **New Braunfels** (famous for its sausages and pastries) and **Luckenbach**. You may still hear German spoken, and German influence is felt in local food and music; *conjunto*, for example, is a blend of Tex-Mex and accordion music.

The whole region is a popular Texan retreat and resort area, with some wonderful hill views and lake swimming, and a lot of good places to camp. Among its numerous state parks is the **Lyndon B Johnson State and National Historical Park**, about fifty miles west of Austin on US-290, preserving LBJ's birthplace (1908) and the ranch house where Lady Bird Johnson still lives. A Living History Farmstead depicts German family life in the early 1900s. Johnson's boyhood home is at **Johnson City**, fourteen miles further east; for a good lunch, stop off here at the *Hill Country Cupboard*, at the junction of US-281 and US-290.

Fredericksburg

FREDERICKSBURG, smack in the middle of the Hill Country, might at first glance look like a pastiche of a German village, overrun by Biergartens and gingerbread cottages. In fact at core it's still pretty much the town founded by six hundred enterprising Germans in 1846. They managed to make – and, uniquely, keep – treaties with the local Comanche, and their community, based on hard work and perseverance, survived through epidemics and civil war.

The main activities Fredericksburg has to offer are wandering around Main Street's galleries, craft shops and antique stores, or sitting in the numerous twee tea rooms and Biergartens. Some of the old buildings are worth looking out for, such as the quirky limestone and pink granite *Bank of Fredericksburg*, and there are also two good museums. Several original structures make up the **Pioneer Museum** at 309 W Main Street, including a church and a store (summer Mon & Wed–Sat 10am–5pm, Sun 1–5pm; winter weekends only). The **Nimitz Hotel**, 340 E Main Street, with its looming tower that looks like a steamboat, was once the last hotel on the military road to California. Now it's a museum honouring Fleet Admiral Nimitz, the grandson of the hotel's original owner, and commander of the Naval forces in the Pacific in World War II (daily 8am–5pm; $2). One of its major exhibits, a Japanese midget submarine used in the attack on Pearl Harbor, is due to be returned to Honolulu shortly.

Practicalities

Like the rest of the Hill Country, Fredericksburg has no *Greyhound* or *Amtrak* service; if you're not on a coach tour, you'll have to drive, via US-290 from Austin or US-87 from San Antonio. The **Convention and Visitors Bureau** (☎997-6523), in the Market Square at 112 W Main Street, can provide details of the cheap **hotels** along E Main Street. The *Best Western Sunday House*, 501 E Main Street (☎997-4484), is one of the more luxurious options, with a pool; rooms are around $42. **Bed and breakfast** is big business in historic Fredericksburg; try the lodging service at 102 S Cherry Street, off W Main Street (☎997-4712), or at *Terrill's B&B*, 242 W Main Street, Apt A (☎997-8615). There's **camping** in the Lady Bird Johnson Municipal Park, three miles southwest on Hwy-16 S, or in the Enchanted Rock State Natural Area, detailed over the page.

Plenty of **restaurants** and bakeries line Main Street, most of them catering to the hordes of day-trippers and doing cheap lunch specials. *The Fountain*, 240 W Main Street, specialises in Texas' own scrumptious *Blue Bell* ice cream, while *Fenner and Beans*, 294 E Main Street, serves sturdy German meals, barbecue and chili – but closes at 8pm.

Luckenbach

LUCKENBACH, about ten miles southeast of Fredericksburg, has become a national joke since Willie Nelson and Waylon Jennings recorded the song *Let's go to Luckenbach, Texas* ("where ain't nobody feelin' no pain") in the Seventies. Its charm is that nothing happens, apart from a bit of guitar-picking and card-playing, and the occasional dance. Call the *General Store* (☎997-3224) – which, as virtually the only building in town, acts as bar, post office and dance hall – to see what may or may not be happening. To reach Luckenbach, drive east from Fredericksburg along US-290 and then south on RR 1376; that there are no signs is all just part of the fun.

Enchanted Rock State Park

Eighteen miles north of Fredericksburg, more than one thousand acres of hills and streams lying in the shadow of a 500ft dome of pink granite have been designated as **ENCHANTED ROCK STATE PARK**. The Comanche attributed magical powers to the rock; in fact its nocturnal creaks and groans are due to contraction after the day's heat. In 1841, Texas Ranger Jack Hays, renowned for his brutality, fought with Indians on its summit. Nowadays crowds of visitors huff and puff their way up there for some truly wonderful views. The park (☎915-247-3903) is open for day use 8am–10pm and there is plenty of **camping** in the tent area near the car park, as well as primitive camping spaces for backpackers along the four-mile Loop Hiking Trail. There are no facilities for vehicular camping.

NORTH AND EAST TEXAS

Early immigration into north and east Texas, during the days of the Republic and following the devastation of the Civil War, was largely from the southern states. In the 1930s, the northeastern oil fields near **Tyler** (a drab town only redeemed by its beautiful rose gardens) proved to be the richest ever found in the USA. The whole region is now predominantly agricultural, with logging important in the densely forested east. The grand exception is, of course, the **Metroplex**, as the area which includes **Dallas** and **Fort Worth** is known. The main tourist attractions and cultural life of the region are concentrated here; but if you enjoy exploring small-town America, and have a car, the north and east can yield more subtle pleasures. Fans of the Wim Wenders movie will want to check out **Paris, Texas**, northeast on US-82, and four **National Forests** in the east offer unsurpassed opportunities for outdoor living: Angelina, Davy Crockett, Sabine, and Sam Houston. The forest supervisor (☎713-632-4446) in Lufkin, midway between Davy Crockett and Angelina on US-59, has details of free and private **camping** facilities.

East Texas

The tall pine forests of east Texas bear more relation to neighbouring Louisiana than to the rest of the state; while undeniably Texan, the locals also identify themselves culturally and geographically with the adjacent corners of Arkansas and Louisiana – the "Arklatex". Thus you'll find jambalaya and gumbo in restaurants along with more standard Texan dishes. Burial sites and reconstructed dwellings of the sophisticated Caddo Indians, who were here as early as 800 AD, can be seen at the **Caddoan Mounds**, six miles southwest of **Alto** on Route 21.

Big Thicket National Preserve

The **BIG THICKET NATIONAL PRESERVE**, south of the Piney Woods on US-96, is a remarkable composite of natural elements from the southwestern desert, central plains and Appalachian mountains, with some swamps and bayous to boot. Once the area offered ideal refuge for outlaws, runaway slaves and gamblers; now it just hides a huge variety of plant and animal life, including deer, alligator, armadillo, possums, hogs and panthers, and over three hundred species of birds. Wild flowers, orchids and towering trees share space with cactii and yucca.

Check in at the Visitors Centre, south of Angelina National Forest on FM 420 off US-69, just south of Wildwood, before entering the site; casual rambling isn't allowed, and hiking or canoeing is best done with the Preserve guides. There is primitive **camping** in designated areas.

Nacogdoches

NACOGDOCHES, north of Angelina National Forest on US-59, claims to be the oldest town in Texas. One of the first five Spanish **missions** in the state was established here in 1716, to keep a watchful eye on the French in Louisiana, and a pyramidal **Caddo Indian Mound** in the 500 block of Mound Street testifies to more ancient history. Among several small historical museums, the *Adolphus Sterne House*, 211 S LaNana Street, illustrates early pioneer life.

La Hacienda, 1411 North Street (☎409/564-6487), serves cheap Mexican **food** in a prairie-style ranch home, and the *Holiday Inn* at 3220 North Street (☎409/564-0261) has double **rooms** from $46. The Chamber of Commerce is on ☎409/564-7351.

Dallas

Contrary to popular belief, there's no oil in the glitzy status-conscious city of **DALLAS**. Since its foundation in 1841 as a prairie trading post, successive generations of **entrepreneurs** have amassed their wealth here through trade and finance, using first cattle and later oil reserves as collateral. One early group of European settlers, the Socialist Réunion co-operative of the 1850s, had to pack up and move on due to an inability to adapt to local farming methods. They did, however, leave a legacy of arts and **high culture**, on which the city still prides itself.

The power of **money** in Dallas was clearly demonstrated in the late 1950s, when its financiers threw their weight behind integration. Potentially racist restaurant owners or bus drivers were pressurised not to resist the new policies, and Dallas was spared major upheavals. Rioting, after all, would have been bad for business. The city's image was, however, catastrophically tarnished by the **assassination** of President Kennedy in 1963, and it took the building of the giant DFW airport in the Sixties, and the twin successes of the *Dallas* TV show and the Cowboys football team in the Seventies, to restore confidence. Then boom turned to crash once more. Unemployment, a losing team and the demise of the Ewings – not to mention an appalling crime rate – have all taken their toll, but the indomitable entrepreneurial spirit remains.

Competitive with Houston, and smug about its cowtown neighbour Fort Worth, Dallas boasts of its "sophistication" and its "old" wealth. Ultimately, however, it is a strait-laced town, with the largest Baptist church in the world, and hordes of street preachers roaming the downtown area. "Fashion" here means haute couture; there are few signs of innovative street style. For all that, there is still fun to be had if you know where to look – especially in the alternative **Deep Ellum** district, where the restaurants and nightlife are superb.

Arrival, Information and Getting Around

Dallas is served by two major **airports**. **Dallas/Fort Worth** (DFW; ☎574-6701), as big as Manhattan and the world's second busiest airport, is exactly midway between the two cities. Shuttle buses to Dallas leave every thirty minutes for $8; taxis cost around $20 (☎574-5878 for both). **Lovefield** lies about nine miles northwest of Dallas (☎670-7275).

Dallas proper is circled by inner loop 12 (or Northwest Highway) and the outer loop I-635 (which becomes LBJ Freeway). A **car** makes sense in a city this size, though the main sights of downtown's Central Business District are easy to tour on foot. Get hold of the CVB's **walking** guide from the **visitor centres**, at 603 Munger Street, in the West End Marketplace (Mon–Sat 11am–8pm, Sun noon–8pm), at 1201 Elm Street (Mon–Fri

The telephone **area code** for Dallas is ☎214.

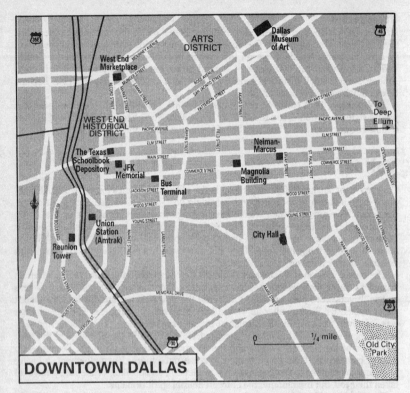

DOWNTOWN DALLAS

8.30am–5pm), and in *Amtrak*'s 1916 Union Station, west of downtown at 400 S Houston Street (daily 9am–5pm). *Greyhound* is at 205 S Lamar Street (☎655-7000); use the coffee shop in the station if you've got a long wait, as the surrounding area is a bit seedy.

Downtown, *Hop-a-buses* (which for no obvious reason look like frogs, or rabbits – complete with big floppy ears) operate for a 75¢ fare until 10pm on weekdays and 6pm at weekends, linked to the *DART Bus Service* (☎979-1111). The *McKinney Trolley* runs from McKinney Avenue, a strip of bars, clubs and restaurants north of downtown, to the Arts District downtown (one-way fares 50¢, day passes $2; Mon–Thurs 10am–10pm, Fri & Sat 10am–midnight; ☎855-0307). *Gray Line Tours* (☎824-2424) do all-day ($32, including Southfork) and half-day ($17) **city tours**, and *Longhorn Tours* (☎228-4571) have a four-hour trip to the Mesquite Rodeo (Fri & Sat evenings, April–Sept) for $21. You can rent **bikes** from *Bicycle Exchange*, 11716 Ferguson Road (☎270-9269).

The **post office** is at 400 N Ervay Street; zip code 75201.

The City

Downtown Dallas is a hymn to commerce. Many of its skyscrapers are landmarks in themselves; at night the red neon *Mobil Pegasus* on the 1921 Magnolia Building appears to soar over the city, while over two miles of green neon delineate the 72-storey NCNB Texas Plaza. The original **Neiman Marcus** department store, set up in 1907 by brother and sister Carrie Neiman and Herbert Marcus, and famed for its glamorous Christmas catalogue, is still there on Main Street, an inspiration to all keen young business people

(Mon–Sat 10am–5.30pm). One small refuge is the quiet **Thanks-Giving Square** (weekdays 9am–5pm, weekends 1–5pm), with its meditation garden, descending walkways, fountains and chapel – though even here pealing bells boom out at regular intervals. South of the square on Ervay Street looms the precarious upside-down pyramid of **City Hall**, possibly familiar as the police station in the film *Robocop.*

North of the West End, the **Arts District** boasts the wide-ranging collection of the **Museum of Art**, 1717 N Harwood Street (Tues, Wed, Fri & Sat 10am–5pm, Thurs 10am–9pm, Sun noon–5pm). This is free, except for the Reves Collection of Impressionists, Post-Impressionists, and decorative arts ($3, free after 5pm on Thursday). Two blocks east, the magnificent **Morton H Meyerson Centre** is the home of the symphony orchestra. The vast geometries of glass, onyx and wood inside cost $80 million, as the tour guides won't let you forget.

Local yuppies and tourists flock to the restored red-brick warehouses of the **West End Historical District**, on the site of the original 1841 settlement, for its eighty shops and fifty restaurants. Apart from the potential for cheap eating, it's a little too commercial and squeaky clean to hold much interest.

The city's first park, **Old City Park**, 1717 Gano Street, at I-30 and Harwood Street, is now a cultural and historical museum as well as a popular recreational area, charting the history of Dallas from 1840 to 1910 through buildings which include farmhouses, a bank, a train station, a store, a church, and a schoolhouse (daily dawn–dusk; free; tours Tues–Sat 10am–3pm, Sun 1.30–3.30pm; $4).

Dallas' hippest district, **Deep Ellum**, five blocks east of downtown between the railroad tracks and I-30 at Elm and Main streets, has been the stamping ground for the terminally trendy for about five years. Famous in the Twenties for its jazz and blues clubs (and supposedly named by Blind Lemon Jefferson), the old warehouse district now accommodates avant garde galleries, theatres, street-hip clothes shops and many excellent restaurants and clubs. To the despair of its original inhabitants – note the

---

THE ASSASSINATION OF PRESIDENT KENNEDY

It was 12.30pm on November 22 1963, as John F Kennedy greeted the crowds of Dallas from his ceremonial motorcade, when the shots rang out over Dealey Plaza which killed the president and ended the "Camelot" era.

Within hours, a gunman's nest was discovered in the nearby Texas Schoolbook Depository, and one of its employees, **Lee Harvey Oswald**, was arrested. Two days later, he in turn was shot and killed in a Dallas police station by nightclub owner **Jack Ruby**, who said he wanted to spare Kennedy's wife Jackie from having to testify at Oswald's trial. The **Warren Commission** which first investigated the assassination concluded that Oswald had acted alone, but **conspiracy** theories have flourished ever since. Most accept that Oswald (an ex-marine who defected to Russia and returned with a Russian wife) fired the shots, but see him as the fall guy in a larger plot, variously attributed to the Mafia, anti-Castroists, Cuba, the KGB and even US government agencies. Claims by witnesses to have heard shots on the famous **Grassy Knoll** on the north side of Elm Street remain unsubstantiated, and Senate inquiries were finally closed down by the Justice Department in 1988, arguing that there was no "persuasive evidence" of any plot.

Dealey Plaza, a small park on the triple underpass marked with a plaque, is one block east of the Dallas Historical Plaza, where an open cenotaph enclosing an eight-foot black marble square stands as the **Kennedy Memorial**. The **Texas Schoolbook Depository** itself, at 411 Elm Street, now houses a **museum**, *The Sixth Floor*, showing film of the event (Sun–Fri 10am–6pm, Sat 10am–7pm; $4). Displays build up a suspenseful narrative, with the infamous images of Kennedy crumpling into Jackie's arms left until the end, at which point there's likely to be much sobbing from moved visitors. The "nest" has been recreated and, whatever you feel about Oswald's guilt, it is undeniably chilling to look down at the streets below and imagine the mayhem they must have seen that day.

Yuppies go home graffiti – prices are rocketing as the area goes mainstream. However, its sense of rebellion and nonconformity makes a great antidote to the prevalent stuffiness of Dallas. The adjacent **State Fair Park**, built to house the Texas Centennial Exposition in 1936, still hosts the State Fair each October. It's a gargantuan oddity, featuring fine Art Deco sculpture and architecture (all bedecked with endless Lone Stars), and home to several museums.

Southfork Ranch, former TV home of the *Dallas* soap's wheeling and dealing Ewing clan, lies northeast of Dallas, beyond I-635 on Parker Road at **Plano**. This working ranch has been kitted out as a museum in which you can see the gun that shot JR, and have your photo taken – wearing a Stetson – at JR's desk (daily 9am–dusk, tours every 15min; ☎442-6536). The Ranch House itself is surprisingly small – all the interior scenes were shot in California, and the exterior views used a very wide angle lens. Non-motorists can only get to the ranch on special bus tours, though real fans may need more time to pore over the exhibits. Be sure to call ahead; the facility may well close altogether.

Accommodation

Rooms are very expensive in Dallas, though special **weekend** deals can be found at the posh downtown hotels. Chain **motels** are concentrated out on the freeways, a long way from central Dallas. There's **camping** in the pretty *Lewisville Lake Park* on the Kingfisher Trail, a mile east of I-35 in Lewisville. **Bed and breakfast**, from $50 single, can be arranged through *B&B Texas Style*, 4224 W Red Bird Lane (☎298-5433).

AYH Hostel, 1451 E Northgate St, Irving (☎438-6061). Out in the suburbs, two bus rides (#202 and #306) from downtown; but at $12 for non-members, possibly worth the effort.

Best Western Market Centre, 2023 Market Centre Blvd (☎741-5041). Two miles from downtown, with doubles $65–70. Complimentary breakfast.

Dallas Budget Inn, 4001 Live Oak St (☎826-7110). Reasonably close to downtown, with shabby rooms from $25.

Econolodge, 9356 LBJ Freeway (☎690-1220). Standard motel rooms from $37.

Holiday Inn Downtown, 1015 Elm St (☎748-9951) and **Holiday Inn Park Centre**, 8102 LBJ Freeway (☎239-7111). Neither is cheap – *Downtown* doubles are $82–104, *Park Centre* $64–78 – but both do weekend specials starting at $49.

Park Cities Inn, 6101 Hillcrest Ave, across from the university (☎521-0330). Doubles $54–68, weekends $44. Free continental breakfast and coffee.

Eating

The cheaper and less pretentious of Dallas' five thousand restaurants are concentrated in **Lower Greenville Avenue** and **Deep Ellum**; even the excellent New American cuisine here won't break the bank, though you'll pay at least $10 for a sizeable meal.

Aw Shucks, 3601 Greenville Ave (☎821-9449). Cheap and cheerful fresh oysters, catfish and shellfish. Highly recommended.

The Butcher Shop Steakhouse, 808 Munger St (☎720-1032). Cook your steak, chicken or fish to your own taste, around an open charcoal pit. From around $5.

Deep Ellum Cafe, 2706 Elm St (☎741-9012). The first restaurant in the area. Very popular, serving delicious New American food for around $10.

Good Eats, Market St and Ross Ave, in the West End (☎744-EATS). Healthy and delicious Texan home-cooking. Plenty of fresh veg, and a sumptuous banana cream pie.

Tejas Cafe, 2909 McKinney Ave (☎871-2050). Happy hour with free buffet weekdays 4–7pm. Specialities include blackened fajitas, and there's an outside patio overlooking the trolley.

Tolbert's, 1800 N Market St (☎969-0310). X-rated chili in the West End (claimed as the standard by which to judge all others), plus Tex-Mex and vegetarian options, all for under $6.

Zodiac Restaurant, inside *Neiman Marcus* on Main St (☎741-6911). Worth the $10–15 to see wealthy female Dallas socialites "doing lunch" during long-haul shopping trips.

Nightlife and Entertainment

The place to head for more alternative entertainment in Dallas has to be **Deep Ellum**; downtown nightlife is pretty formal. Mainstream attractions include the **Symphony Orchestra** at the showpiece *Morton H Meyerson Center* (☎692-0203), and the **Black Dance** company in the Twenties *Majestic Theater* at 1925 Elm Street (☎871-2376). In June and July, there are free **Shakespeare in the Park** performances in Fair Park (☎954-0199). Check out also the huge Art Deco **Granada Cinema and Drafthouse** at 3524 Greenville Avenue (☎823-9610), which has its own restaurant and bar.

Copious listings can be found in the *Dallas Observer* every Thursday, or the music-oriented *Buddy* and *Funky Times*. There's a special events information line on ☎746-6679, a blues hotline on ☎521-BLUE, and a jazz hotline on ☎744-BBOP.

Arcadia, 2005 Greenville Ave (☎826-7554). Big-name bands.

Cowboys, 7331 Gaston Ave at Garland Road, east of Greenville (☎321-0115). Large honky-tonk with some big-name country acts, Tues–Sun 4pm–2am. Free dancing lessons Sun 4–7pm.

Dada, 2720 Elm St (☎744-DADA). Famed Deep Ellum club where Edie Brickell and the New Bohemians began their days. Acoustic jam Sun 3–9pm, live bands and club nights.

Dallas Alley, 2019 Lamar St in the West End (☎988-9378). One cover charge (around $8) gets you into nine clubs and five live venues, including the R&B club *Froggy Bottoms*.

Dick's Last Resort at Ross Ave and Record St (☎747-0001). Accompanies messy barbecue with noisy Dixieland jazz in the West End. 11am–2am. No cover.

diva, 2556 Elm St (☎741-5010). Thurs 10pm–2am, Fri and Sat 10pm–4am; no cover until 11pm, with 75¢ draft beer all night. Alternative music, mostly from the early Eighties.

Exodus, 210 N Crowdus St (☎748-7871). Reggae club in Deep Ellum.

Farley's Garage Bar, 2642 Main St (☎742-5000). Downtown blues.

Schooners, 1212 Skillman at Live Oak St (☎821-1934). East of Greenville Avenue, blues club famed for its jamming sessions.

Listings

American Express Renaissance Tower, 1201 Elm St, ☎748-8606.

Gay Hotline ☎368-6283, daily 7.30pm–midnight.

Ranches Cowboy cook-offs, recreation areas, hay rides, and other special attractions. *Chaparral Ranch*, ☎817-430-8846; *Texas Lil's Diamond A Ranch*, in nearby Justin, ☎817-430-0192; *Wagon Wheel Ranch*, 353 State Rd, Coppel, ☎462-0894.

Six Flags over Texas Massive theme park with over one hundred rides, and the tallest wooden roller-coaster in the world. Halfway between Dallas and Fort Worth in Arlington, ☎817-640-8900, $19.95 for one day.

Sports Information The Cotton Bowl, ☎638-BOWL, in Fair Park; Dallas Cowboys, ☎556-2500; Mesquite Championship Rodeo, 1818 Rodeo Drive, Mesquite, ☎285-8777.

Fort Worth

Yes, Dallas does have something Fort Worth doesn't have – a real city thirty miles away.
Amon Carter, publisher, philanthropist, Fort Worthian

FORT WORTH, often dismissed as some kind of poor relation of Dallas, in fact has a rush and energy lacked by its stuffier neighbour thirty miles to the east. Unashamed of its origins as a lawless frontier cowtown, this is one of the most "Western" cities in Texas. In the 1870s it was the last stop on the great cattle drive to Kansas, the **Chisholm Trail**; when the railroads arrived, it became a livestock market in its own right, while remaining a haven for cowboys and outlaws. The **cattle** trade is still the major industry, centred on the redeveloped **stockyards**, but the city can also pride itself on a thriving cultural life. Unlike the more anxious Dallas, Fort Worth doesn't feel the need to brag about its many excellent **museums**. For a place so **wealthy** (the grand **Western Hills** area has proportionately more millionaires than any other US locale), it's surprisingly laid-back. It is a truly cosmopolitan city, comfortable with itself, where cowboys and roustabouts will happily down a few beers with modern jazz fans.

Arrival, Information and Getting Around

The main road between Fort Worth and Dallas, **I-30**, cuts the city east–west; loop 820 encircles it. An airport express **bus** (☎334-0092) runs to and from DFW Airport, seventeen miles northeast (see p.517). The city's public transport system, **The T**, also operates **free buses** downtown, running north on Throckmorton Street and south on Houston Street (Mon–Fri 6am–8pm, Sat & Sun 6am–5pm; ☎870-6200). *Amtrak* services run daily to Houston and Chicago from 1501 Jones Street.

There are three **visitor centres**: in the **Stockyards** at 121 E Exchange Avenue (Thurs–Mon 10am–5pm), **downtown** at 309 Main Street, and in the Science Museum at 1501 Montgomery Street. The downtown and stockyard areas are well patrolled and safe to walk around after dark; if you'd prefer a **taxi**, call *American Cab Co* on ☎429-8829.

The City

The chief focus of downtown fun in Fort Worth is **Sundance Square**, a brick-paved area of shops, restaurants and bars, ringed by glittering skyscrapers and tangibly pervaded with a genuine enthusiasm for the town's rich history. Notice the carvings of longhorn skulls everywhere, and the many trompe l'oeil murals – especially the Chisholm Trail mural on Fourth Street between Main and Houston streets. Naming the square after the Sundance Kid isn't particularly appropriate; he, and such other outlaws as Bonnie and Clyde, would have spent their time a few blocks to the south, just north of I-30 at the city's original settlement. Even into the 1950s **"Hell's Half Acre"** was renowned for bawdy lawlessness; these days sadly it's much less exciting. Various – very worthwhile – downtown walking tours start from here (ask at visitor centres).

In the **Cattlemans Museum**, west of downtown at 1301 W Seventh Street (☎332-7064), the changing economic face of the cattle trade is traced from the days of open range, via the great cattle drives, to modern ranching and latterday cowboys – with some good stuff on early women pioneers.

The **Cultural District**, two miles west of downtown, is an impressive area of museums and art galleries. The finest collection is at the **Modern Art Museum**, 1309 Montgomery Street (Tues–Sat 10am–5pm, Sun 1–5pm; free; ☎738-9215), specialising in abstract twentieth-century works. The **Kimbell** and **Amon Carter** museums at 3333 and 3501 Camp Bowie Boulevard, respectively, are also interesting. The latter has some great photographs of Western landscapes.

However, museums, no matter how good, aren't necessarily what you want from a cowtown. The ten-block **Stockyards Area**, two miles from downtown, is a glorious evocation of the days when Fort Worth's stockyards spread over 100 acres and this was "the richest little city in the world". It's much more than a cynical creation for cowboy-hungry tourists. Look out over the wooden sidewalks and old shopfronts, listen to the bellows of the rodeo cattle, and you can almost see the dust rising and the snorting herds being driven through. Along with the restaurants and bars, there are shops to have western-wear fetishists in heaven. Look out for *Fincher's* rodeo equipment store and *M L Leddy's* saddle shop, or check out the *Maverick Trading Post*. Packed with cowgirl regalia and jewellery, and with a bar serving the coldest beer in town, the store encourages you to drink first and buy later; this is not a good idea.

The telephone **area code** for Fort Worth is ☎817.

Ideally, you should get to one of the **cattle auctions** held at 12.30pm on Mondays in the huge 1902 **Livestock Exchange Building** at 131 E Exchange Avenue. If you miss that, the **Stockyards Museum** here has historical displays on the area, and provides maps. Walking tours leave each Wednesday at 11am.

Accommodation

Fort Worth is blessed with plenty of reasonably priced accommodation, even downtown. South Fort Worth yields many cheap motels – especially along the South Freeway, but isn't very convenient for any of the things you'll want to see.

Days Inn, 600 Commerce St (☎332-6900). Excellent location, footsteps away from Sundance Square and the bus station, with rooms from $51.

Great Western Inn, 1815 E Lancaster St, near downtown (☎877-3500), and at 913 E Northside Drive (☎332-9693). Downtown rooms $27–32; further north, $22–40.

Holiday Inn Midtown, 1401 S University Drive (☎336-9311). West of town, $50–57.

Miss Molly's Bed and Breakfast, 109 W Exchange Ave (☎626-1522). Old bordello in the Stockyards, if you can't resist cowboy kitsch and have a little extra money. $60–115.

Park Central Hotel, 1010 Houston St (☎336-2011). Centrally located, convenient for downtown and Sundance Square; $43–49.

Western Hills Motel, 6651 Camp Bowie Blvd (☎732-7741). Near Cultural District; $24–28.

Eating

If you love steak, Fort Worth is the place. Meat here is hefty, fresh, and prepared with a lot of tender loving care, especially in the stockyard area, where the many good home-cooking cafes are frequented as much by cattle ranchers as by visitors. Vegetarians will do less well; try the more upmarket restaurants downtown.

Cattleman's Steak House, 2458 N Main St (☎624-3945). Dim lighting, wall-sized portraits of prize steers. A Fort Worth institution for its steaks and margaritas. Dinner is around $10.

Juanita's, 115 W Second St (☎335-1777). Downtown Mexican restaurant with an uptown feel; specialities include quail in tequila. Lunch specials on weekdays for under $5.

Owen's Family Restaurant, 1700 S University Drive (☎336-6644). Very cheap home cooking.

The Star Cafe, 111 W Exchange Ave (☎624-8701). Famed for its gruff service, sumptuous steaks grilled in lemon butter – and remarkable low prices.

Nightlife and Entertainment

You'd be hard pushed not to find something to your taste amidst Fort Worth's late-night drinking and carousing. Bar crawling is safe and fun, and there's a great mix of live music venues (though the pick-up joints in the stockyards are well worth avoiding). Call ☎548-7337 for a telephone **listings** guide.

As well as the regular cowboy venues below, the **Chisholm Trail Round Up** (second weekend in June), and **Pioneer Days** (three days in late September) are two hugely enjoyable annual western-style celebrations in the stockyards. *Cowtown Coliseum* holds championship **rodeo** on Saturday evenings (April–Sept only).

Billy Bob's, 2520 Rodeo Plaza (☎624-7117). Sun noon–7pm, Mon noon–5pm, Tues–Sat noon–2am; rodeos Sat 9 and 10pm. The largest honky-tonk in the world, down in the stockyards, with **live** bull-riding, pool tables, bars, restaurants and shops, and big-name oncerts.

The Caravan of Dreams, 312 Houston St (☎877-3000). Superb jazz club and experimental theatre. A beautiful building, with great murals and a rooftop bar and greenhouse. This friendly and stylish club has become hugely popular and regularly attracts big names.

Johnnie High Country Music Review, Will Rogers Auditorium, 3301 W Lancaster St (☎481-4518). $7.50; Sat 7pm. Popular cowboy cavortings.

The White Elephant, 106 E Exchange Ave (☎624-1887). $2 cover on Friday; Fri and Sat noon–2am, Sun–Thurs noon–midnight. Notoriously wild and authentic stockyards saloon; prop yourself up at the long wooden bar and listen to cowboy singer Don Edwards.

Towards the Panhandle

Routes west from central Texas lead you through the state's "backyard", where farm-lands and rough-cut juniper-covered hills give way to treeless sandy landscapes. Of the towns, only **Abilene** on I-20 towards Lubbock, and **Wichita Falls** on US-287 to Amarillo, near the border with Oklahoma, are even marginally interesting enough to be possible stopovers for long-distance drivers. In theory, this is rich oil-bearing land, but the cities have taken a battering since the slump.

Abilene and Sweetwater

ABILENE has a certain curiosity value as an oppressively God-fearing Bible city, though that's no great incentive to get off one of the six *Greyhound* buses which pass through each day. If you have to stay, the *Royal Inn*, 5695 First Street (☎915-692-3022), has doubles from $40, as well as a pool and a steakhouse.

Dozy **SWEETWATER**, further west on I-20, began as a general store for buffalo hunters in 1877, and is now notable for its **rattlesnake round-up** on the second week-end of March, when you can try fried snake (tough but tasty), or buy a transparent toilet seat with a rattler coiled in it. There are motels along Georgia Street; the *Holiday Inn* (☎915-236-6887) has rooms from $42.

Wichita Falls

The only pretty thing about **WICHITA FALLS** is its name; it's an unromantic and heav-ily industrial city. **Motels** such as *Best Western* (☎817-723-5541; $26–34) and *La Quinta* (☎817-322-6971; $34–44) line US-287. The city's **restaurants** are uninspired, though *Luby's* at 1801 Ninth Street serves good food for about $5, until 8pm. The fifty-foot **water-falls** to the north, once home to Wichita Indians, were reconstructed in 1987 after being washed away earlier this century. Fifteen miles southeast, **Lake Arrowhead** (which is dotted with large oil derricks) offers **camping** facilities along with nature trails.

THE PANHANDLE

The inhabitants of the **PANHANDLE**, the southernmost portion of the Great Plains, call it "the real Texas"; it certainly fulfils the fantasy of what Texas should look like. When Coronado's gold-seeking expedition passed this way in the sixteenth century, they drove stakes into the ground across the vast and unchanging landscape, despair-ing of otherwise finding their way home. Hence the name *Llano Estacado*, or staked plains, which still persists today.

Once the buffalo – and consequently the Indians as well – were driven away from what was seen as perilous and uninhabitable frontier country, the Panhandle began, around the 1870s, to yield its great **natural resources**. Helium – especially in Amarillo – and oil, as well as **agriculture**, have brought wealth to the region, and some of the world's largest **ranches** have been established.

Though there are few specific tourist attractions, there is a rural charm and quirki-ness far removed from the touristed cities to the east. **Music** has a particular signifi-cance in a region famous for songwriters such as Buddy Holly, Roy Orbison and Joe Ely; while most musicians relocate to cosmopolitan music centres like Austin, they don't forget – and are not forgotten by – their birthplace. Above all, it is the fiercely proud and exceptionally hospitable **people** of the Panhandle, still facing hardship and struggle in their battles with the elements, that make it special, along with the starkly romantic landscape, strewn with tumbleweeds and mesquite trees – and, of course, those big, big skies.

Lubbock

LUBBOCK is the largest city in the Panhandle, and has long served as the centre for its commerce and transportation, roughly one hundred miles northwest of Abilene and the same distance south of Amarillo. At first this was cattle-grazing land, but the discovery of copious underground water made agriculture profitable. The prosperity of the city was built on cotton; in recent years government restrictions have hit prices hard, and the days of self-sufficient farming look numbered. You may, however, still see solitary cotton fields defiantly standing on the outskirts, where stubborn farmers have refused to sell out.

With its fields, farms, lumpen bungalows and faceless block buildings, Lubbock is relentlessly ordinary-looking, its muted downtown area dotted with fading Fifties shopfronts. Which is not to say that it's dull; though Southern Baptism has left its mark and this is officially a "dry" city, drinking and dancing are not seen as sinful. Lubbock has a definite panache, and a pervasive sense of fun which can't just be put down to the students from Texas Tech.

Arrival, Information and Getting Around
Loop 289 circles all of Lubbock proper, with the **airport** (☎762-6411) just a few minutes north. I-127 slashes through the loop west of downtown, north to Amarillo and south to Tahoka. The two main roads crossing the city east to west are Broadway and Fourth Street, while University Avenue and Avenue Q run north to south.

Greyhound **buses** come in downtown at 1313 13th Street (☎765-6644). The **citibus** system, downtown at 801 Texas Avenue (☎762-0111), runs extensive commuter routes within the loop, which stop at around 6pm and don't run on Sundays or holidays. Fares are 75¢, and buses can be flagged down on any street corner. You'll need a car to travel outside the loop. Lubbock's **visitor centre** is at 14th Street and Avenue K (☎747-5232).

The Town
Downtown Lubbock, and the university, are on the northern side of town. Few buildings of interest survive, thanks to the construction boom of the 1950s and a tornado in 1970. However, you can get a stimulating overview of local history at the **Ranching Heritage Centre**, Fourth Street and Indiana Avenue (Mon–Sat 10am–5pm, Sun 1pm–5pm; free). Over thirty original ranch buildings, from simple cowboy huts to grand overseers' houses, are set in a harsh landscape spiked with cactii and mesquite. There's an excellent museum on pioneer and cowboy history, and demonstrations on making such items as lye soap, sourdough or quilts. The adjacent **Texas Tech Museum** (closed Mon) has further southwestern displays and a room of Buddy Holly memorabilia.

Nearby, the **Lubbock Lake** archaeological site has yielded an impressive array of artefacts spanning 1200 years. It's open daily 8am–5pm, until 8pm in July and August, but unless you take a guided tour (Sat 9am–noon; $1) it may not seem much more than a dry gravelly site buzzing with gigantic Texan insects. As indeed may **Prairie Dog Town**, in Mackenzie State Park, where six hundred determined little critters are attempting to re-populate the world and gain their revenge for the attempts of government officials and irate ranchers in the 1930s to poison them into extinction. A prairie dog is a kind of fat barking hamster with a waggly tail; this cute and intelligent lot seem to be enjoying themselves immensely.

Three miles east of the loop on Hwy-1585, the *Llano Estacado* **winery** started as the hobby of two university professors. It might look incongruous, set amidst scrubby

---

The telephone **area code** for the Panhandle, including Lubbock and Amarillo, is ☎806.

BUDDY HOLLY

Lubbock's greatest claim to world fame is as the birthplace of Charles Hardin Holley on September 7 1936. Inspired by the blues and country music of his childhood – and a seminal encounter with the young Elvis Presley, gigging in Lubbock at the Cotton Club – **Buddy Holly** was one of the first great rock'n'roll singer-songwriters. The Holly sound, characterised by steady strumming guitar, rapid drumming, and his trademark hiccoughing vocals, was made famous by hits such as *Peggy Sue*, *Rave On*, *Not Fade Away*, *Oh Boy!* and *That'll Be The Day*; but Buddy himself was killed at the age of 22 by the Iowa plane crash of February 2 1959 ("the day the music died"), which also claimed the Big Bopper and Ritchie Valens.

An eight-foot bronze **Buddy Holly Statue**, on 8th Street and Avenue Q, towers over a **Walk of Fame**, of plaques to local performers like Roy Orbison and Waylon Jennings (the bassist for Buddy's final concert). Other sites around town include:

Buddy's birthplace, 1911 Sixth St. Now a vacant lot.

J T Hutchinson Junior High School, 3102 Canton Ave. Buddy and friend Bob Montgomery performed here in the sixth grade. Souvenirs are on sale.

Lubbock High School, 2004 19th St. Buddy and Bob, who graduated in 1955, won the school's "Westerners Round Up" with *Flower of my Heart*.

Tabernacle Baptist Church, 1911 34th St. A percentage of Buddy's royalties still go to the church which saw his baptism, wedding, and funeral.

Radio Station KRLB, 6602 Quirt Ave. Opened in 1953, this was the first full-time country music station in the States. Buddy and Jack Neal had their own show.

Fair Park Coliseum, Tenth St and Ave A. Where Buddy opened shows for Bill Haley and Elvis Presley. His "discovery" here in 1955 led to a contract with Decca.

Home of Buddy Holly in 1957, 1305 37th St. Now a private home.

Buddy Holly's grave, in Lubbock cemetery at end of 34th Street. Take right fork inside the gate, and the grave is on the left, halfway down the road.

Contact Bill Griggs at the Buddy Holly Memorial Society (PO Box 6123, Lubbock, Texas 79493), or subscribe to their *Rockin' 50s* magazine, for more information.

pastureland and cotton fields, but its success has led Lubbock to pin great hopes on the potential of wine to revitalise and diversify its flagging economy. Visitors are given a guided tour and free tasting – many cautious Texans, brought up on beer, don't like paying for an unfamiliar drink until they've tried it. Europeans, who are looked on as connoisseurs, can expect to be questioned on your favourite vintage during the sociable and informal tasting sessions (Mon–Sat 10am–4pm, Sun noon–4pm; ☎745-2258).

Accommodation

As prices are very reasonable in this region, and hotel rooms are plentiful, there should be no problem finding somewhere to stay.

Astro Motel, 501 Ave Q (☎762-8726). Archetypal motel, with paddling-pool size "swimming pool" and interesting inhabitants. Very cheap, with doubles from $25.50–28.50.

The Lubbock Inn, 3901 19th St (☎792-5181). A pool with waterfalls, and free breakfast, in the $40–60 price range.

La Quinta Motor Inn, 601 Ave Q (☎763-9441). Free coffee, adjacent to a 24hr restaurant, and just across from the Buddy Holly Statue. Doubles $52.

Travelers Inn, 714 Ave Q (☎765-8847). Dirt-cheap doubles at $21–23.

Eating

Lubbock has a surprising variety of eating places, with good barbecue and Tex-Mex and even some New American restaurants. However, many of even the most upmarket restaurants close before 10pm.

The Depot, 19th St and Ave G (☎747-1646). In the old Santa Fe train depot. It looks a bit formal, but there are always a lot of students, waiters and customers around. The food is very good, verging on the cordon bleu, especially their huge Sunday brunches starting at $4.95.

Grapevine Cafe, 2407b 19th St (☎794-1415), behind *Burger King*. Alternative music, trendy waiters, and excellent food (innovative pasta and crepes). The healthy specials start at $4.50.

River Smith's Chicken and Catfish, Fourth St and Ave U (☎765-8164). Cheap and cheerful family restaurant. Large catfish sandwich costs $3.50. Also an oyster bar and "lite menu".

Santa Fe, Fourth St and Ave Q (☎763-6114). Bulging enchiladas, gargantuan burritos and all the standard Tex-Mex favourites, in an unrowdy family atmosphere. From about $5.

The County Line, half a mile west of I-27 in Escondido Canyon (☎763-6001). Mediterranean decor, Forties music, and the best barbecue in Lubbock, with a $13.95 all-you-can-eat plate.

Entertainment

The best entertainment the Panhandle has to offer is at its **annual events**. **Rodeos** are always rip-roaring fun; the Texas Tech holds one each October in Fair Park, and the **ABC Rodeo** is at Lubbock Municipal Coliseum every spring. The twirling contests, bull riding, big-name country performers and livestock exhibits at the **Panhandle South Plains Fair** in Fair Park in late September and early October make it the most important fair in the region.

There isn't a great deal of **nightlife** in Lubbock; the *Lubbock Avalanche-Journal* carries listings. As well as the places listed below, thanks to the Texas Tech there are several student haunts such as *The Warehouse*, opposite the *Depot* on 19th Street, which puts on live jazz, Tex-Mex and country. The Tech itself has its own venues for comedy, theatre and music – information on ☎742-3341.

Midnight Rodeo, S Loop 289 and University Ave (☎745-2813). Until 2am nightly, closed Mon. Huge c'n'w club, complete with pool tables, lanky cowboys and coiffed Texan belles. Great fun, even for a woman on her own.

Rosie's Bar & Grill, 3703b Ave Q (☎747-3848). Tex-Mex music at the weekend.

Jiggers Up, 4802 Ave Q (☎744-5061). Country jam sessions on Sunday evenings.

Amarillo

AMARILLO may seem cut off from the rest of Texas, up in the north of the Panhandle, but it stands on one of the great American cross-country routes – I-40, once the legendary **Route 66** – roughly three hundred miles east of Albuquerque and 250 miles west of Oklahoma City. *Amarillo* is the Spanish for "yellow" – the name comes from its characteristic yellow soil. An early promoter of the city was so delighted with its potential – as a site for lucrative buffalo hunting (for those who braved the Apache and Comanche threat) and as excellent ranching land – that he painted all the buildings bright yellow.

Today, sitting on ninety percent of the world's helium and hosting a world-class cattle market, Amarillo is a prosperous but surprisingly uneventful city, with little to interest the traveller. The small **"old town"** consists of a few tree-lined streets and some staid old homes; the antique shops along **Sixth Street** (which is the old Route 66, known here as "Old San Jacinto") serve equally well as museums of pioneer life. Following Sixth Street ten miles west onto I-40 brings you to **Cadillac Ranch**. An extraordinary vision in the middle of nowhere, ten Cadillacs stand upended in the soil, their tail fins demonstrating the different Cadillac designs from 1949 to 1963. Some of the time they're crumbling with rust and defaced with graffiti (encouraged by the designer, eccentric helium millionaire Stanley Marsh III Marsh, on whose land the cars are planted); sometimes they're shiny blue or red after having been painted for a photo shoot.

Amarillo is also host to the stompingest, snortingest **livestock auction** in Texas, at 100 Manhattan Street, on the east side of town. Tours run every day except Sunday, and the auction proper is held weekly (details on ☎373-7464).

Practicalities

There is no **public transport** to speak of in the city, but car drivers will find it easy enough to navigate. *Greyhound* comes in downtown at 700 S Tyler Street (☎374-5371). Visitor information is at 1000 Polk Street (☎374-1497).

Innumerable cheap **hotels** are concentrated along I-40. For luxury, *Harvey Hotel*, 3130 I-40W (☎358-6161), is good value, with singles going for $75, doubles $85. More standard is the *Quality Inn-West*, 2801 I-40W (☎358-6161), with doubles from $42. Texana fans will love the tongue-in-cheek western camp of the *Inn of the Big Texan*, 7701 I-40E on exit 73 (☎372-5000), which has rooms from $35 to $43. It's also home to the *Big Texan Steak Ranch* (☎372-7000). As well as fried rattlesnake and buffalo chili (even some vegetarian options), there's the 72oz steak challenge: if you can eat it all, you get it free. The cheap food and beer (served in cowboy-boot-shaped glasses) is accompanied by strolling country musicians, and they also have a rifle range. Other popular Amarillo **restaurants** include the lively *Chili's Grill and Bar*, 3810 I-40W (☎379-6118), serving good burgers, Tex-Mex favourites, and delicious fresh grilled tuna, and the *Iron Horse Cafe*, 401 S Grant Street (☎373-1591), which does daily lunch specials for around $5.

Ranches Around Amarillo

The need to diversify to ensure their survival has led several of the grand old **ranches** of the Panhandle to turn to tourism. If you want to play cowboys for a while, a visit can be great fun. Some of the ranches just open for the day; others provide accommodation and full board as well, which can work out to be quite expensive. The ranchers who entertain you are often natural showmen and women, whose welcome is utterly genuine; but most of your hosts won't deny that they'd rather be working the animals for real than running a theme park.

At **Bootsteps Guest Ranch** (5 miles west of Amarillo on I-40, then 6 miles north to Patrick Pass; ☎1-800/692-1338), the attractions include horse-drawn hay rides, goat milking, horseshoe tossing and cow-chip throwing, with a flapjack breakfast or barbecue on arrival, for $17.50. **Cal Farleys Boys Ranch** (40 miles northwest on US-385; ☎373-6411) is a little different. It's a non fee-paying community for "troubled boys" to live, work and be schooled as "fine young Americans". They're quite happy to greet impromptu guests, and you can join them at meal times, but this is a working community, not just for show, and it's considerate to call ahead. Entry is free.

TASCOSA nearby is a ghost of an early cattle town that died along with the cattle trails. You can now see a small schoolroom, the Boothill graveyard and the old courthouse, which houses a museum.

Canyon

The one "sight" in the former cattle town of **CANYON**, fifteen minutes south of Amarillo on I-27, is a must. The **Panhandle-Plains Historical Museum** has exhibits of restored pioneer buildings, artefacts of the Plains Indians, histories of Texas ranching, natural history displays, and a collection of Western art. Even the history of the oil and gas industry is made interesting – a difficult feat. The museum is nominally free, but you'll be asked for a donation. The lumber-built *Hudspeth House* at 1905 Fourth Avenue (☎655-9800) makes a good base for Palo Duro Canyon, with **rooms** for $36–75. For **food**, head for the *Cowboy Cafe*, on 15th Street and Hwy-60, with giant cowboy "Tex" standing outside.

Palo Duro State Canyon Park

The stunning **PALO DURO CANYON**, twelve miles east of Canyon and twenty miles southeast of Amarillo, is one of Texas' best-kept secrets. Plunging 1200 feet from rim to floor, it splits the plains wide open and offers breathtaking views and colours, especially at sunset. In the spring, the whole chasm is scattered with foliage and flowers. Pillars of sturdy sandstone loom over the flame-coloured rocks, which Coronado's explorers gave the name of "Spanish Skirts" on account of their stripy, flounced appearance.

The **Park** itself is located in the most scenic part of the sixty-mile canyon (entrance $2 per car; visitor centre daily, 8am–5pm; interpretive centre Wed–Sun 11am–7pm, June–Aug). You can explore the depths by **train** (the *Sad Monkey Railroad* runs daily April–Sept, at weekends all year; ☎488-2222) or on **horseback**, though backpackers and hikers may want to escape the tourist busloads by following the Prairie Dog Town fork into more remote sections of the park. There are over a hundred **campgrounds**, with varying fees; advance reservations are recommended (☎488-2227). The *Goodnight Trading Post* (☎488-2760) sells snacks. The Convention and Visitors Council in Amarillo organise a special $19 half-day tour between May and September, which includes breakfast (and cow-chip throwing) at the *Figure 3 Ranch* on the rim of the Canyon.

You may usually balk at heart-warming middle-of-the-road musicals, but the outdoor performance *TEXAS!* has an undeniable pull, with the dramatic prairie sky as a ceiling, a 600ft cliff as a backdrop, and thunder and lightning special effects. The view of history may be a little less than progressive, but it's a spectacular way to spend an evening in an area not exactly throbbing with nightlife (Mon–Sat at 8.30pm, June–August; tickets cost from $6; pre-show chuckwagon barbecue at 6.30pm, another $6; ☎655-2181).

WEST TEXAS

WEST TEXAS is the stuff of Wild West fantasy: parched deserts, ghost towns, looming mesas, and above all the sense of utter isolation. Although the area south from the Panhandle down to Del Rio on the Rio Grande is, for convenience, also known as West Texas, the fantasy really begins west of the River Pecos; you can drive for hours without a sign of life to reach **El Paso**, Texas' shabby westernmost city. Most travellers only venture into the desolation to explore **Big Bend National Park**, nearly three hundred miles southeast of El Paso in the curve of the Rio Grande. The only towns of any size on the way, Fort Stockton and Alpine, have little charm except as stopping-off points.

Minimal rainfall and harsh land were not the only hindrances to settlement. The **Apache** and **Comanche**, though accustomed in the 1820s to trading with Mexican *comancheros*, were infuriated when hapless white pioneers began to trickle in during the 1830s. With their horsemanship and ability to find the scarce water supplies, the Indians posed a real threat; upon statehood, federal money helped to set up a string of cavalry forts to protect Mexican and Anglo settlers from attack. As trading posts and cattle ranges began to spring up after the Civil War, the paramilitary **Texas Rangers** were sent out on violent vigilante missions. Eventually, as in the Panhandle, a brutal programme of buffalo slaughter, supported by the US Army, starved the Indians out. Not long afterwards, **oil** hit West Texas and boomtowns appeared, with all the attendant lawlessness, gun-slinging and brawling.

Big Bend National Park

The Rio Grande, flowing through 1500ft gorges, makes a ninety-degree bend south of Marathon, to form the southern border of **BIG BEND NATIONAL PARK**. The Apache, who forced the Chisos Indians out three hundred years ago, told that this hauntingly beautiful wilderness was used by the Great Spirit to dump all the rocks left over from the creation of the world. A breathtaking million-acre expanse of pine-forested mountains and cactus-dotted desert, Big Bend has been home to prospectors and smugglers, a last frontier for the true-grit pioneers at the end of the nineteenth century who took advantage of the rich cinnabar deposits for mercury mining. Today there is camping in specific areas, and some trailer parks, but much of the Park remains barely charted territory, the ruins of primitive Mexican and white settlements testament to its power to defeat earlier visitors. Wild animals have fared somewhat better; coyotes, roadrunners and peccary (a particularly stupid breed of bristly black pig) all roam free, and you may come across the paw prints of panthers. The contrasts in topography and temperature result in dramatic juxtapositions of desert and mountain plant and animal life. Despite the dryness, pretty wild flowers and blossoming cactii, including the peyote, erupt into colour each April.

Alpine

You can't follow the Rio Grande by road from east or west into Big Bend. The nearest town of any size to the park is **Alpine**, a college town on US-90 at the edge of the desert, about sixty-five miles northwest of the northernmost tip of the Park. Most travellers make this their last stop at civilisation, to stock up on supplies – especially gas and water for desert survival – and to get a night's sleep. What (minimal) action there is in town is concentrated on the campus of Sul Ross University. The **Museum of the Big Bend** is worth a look for its exhibits relating to Indian life and European settlement of the area. The *Sunday House Inn* (☎837-3363), a mile east on US-90, has **rooms** from $42. *Amtrak* serves Alpine three times a week, en route between El Paso and east Texas, but Big Bend itself is not accessible by any public transport. There is car rental in Alpine. To continue on to the park, take US-90 east, and turn onto US-385 to Marathon.

Into the Park

From Alpine, as the mountains begin to tower above, it is about 38 miles south to the park headquarters at **Panther Junction**, where you pay the $5 entrance fee and must collect your wilderness permit for overnight stays. There is a daytime **gas** station at the Junction. Camping is on a first-come first-served basis. The park administration building (daily, 8am–7pm; ☎477-2251) contains orientation exhibits.

The **Chisos Basin**, about seven miles off the connecting road within the park, has a visitor contact station, a store and post office (May–Oct 9am–8.45pm, Nov–April 9am–5.30pm), and a **motel**, the *Chisos Mountains Lodge* (reservations essential; ☎477-2291). Doubles go for $65, and there's a cafe (dinner runs $5–12; closes at 7.30pm). There are 63 camping sites available in the Basin (for $5), with toilets, running water and cooking grills. There is no garage or service station.

Rio Grande Village, twenty miles southeast of Panther Junction, has another visitor center, hot shower facilities in the grocery store, camping ($5), and a laundry. There is also another daytime **gas** station, and primitive camping facilities (with pit toilets) for when the main camping area is full, at a cost of $3.

There are primitive campgrounds at **Castolon** too, and you can fill up on gas between 10am and 6pm. There are free primitive campgrounds along the thirty-six marked hiking trails. These have no facilities and you'll need a wilderness permit, map, compass, torch and first-aid kit before being allowed to venture onto the trails.

If you're feeling brave enough to navigate the wild currents of the Rio Grande, *Far Flung Adventures*, based in nearby **TERLINGUA** (west of the park off FM 170) offers

---

The telephone **area code** for West Texas, including El Paso, is ☎915.

one-day narrated **raft trips**, including lunch, for $65 (☎371-3489.) **Horse rides** are available from *Desert Walkers*, of Terlingua ($25 for a half day; ☎371-2364), and *Chisos Remuda Saddle Horses*, in the Chisos Basin (half-day $20, full-day $45; ☎477-2374).

Langtry

For a taste of the peculiar logic which ran the semimythical Wild West, head for tiny **LANGTRY**, where the River Pecos meets the Rio Grande. The *Lily Saloon* here, with its famed slogan "Law West of the Pecos", was where **Judge Roy Bean**, the first "JP" of rowdy Pecos County, carried out his arbitrary and individualistic form of lawkeeping. Among his memorably dubious fines was a round of drinks for the "jury" (in fact, the drinkers at the bar). The Judge Roy Bean Interpretive Center is open daily from 8am until 5pm (☎291-3340).

El Paso

Back when Texas was still Tejas, **EL PASO** was the main crossing on the Rio Grande. It still plays that role today, its 600,000 residents joining with another 1.2 million across the river in **CIUDAD JUAREZ**, Mexico, to form the largest binational (and bilingual) megalopolis in North America. It's not an especially pretty place – massive Southern Pacific railyards fill up much of the downtown area, belching smelters of poisonous copper mills line the riverfront, and the giant Fort Bliss military base, where NATO pilots and Patriot missile units are trained, fills out the northern reaches – but you may well find yourself here on your way to New (or Old) Mexico or Arizona. The **downtown** area, just off I-10 around Main and Santa Fe streets, has a few fairly grand turn-of-the-century buildings like the *Paso del Norte Hotel* at 101 S El Paso Street, and there's a small but ambitious **Americana Museum** (Tues–Sat 10am–5pm; free) in the Convention Center complex on Santa Fe Street, but otherwise there isn't all that much to see or do.

It's the US–Mexico border that defines the city and gives El Paso what character it has. In times past outlaws and exiles from one side of the border would take refuge across the river, and these days the traffic is still considerable and not entirely uncontroversial. Manual workers come north to find undocumented jobs, and US companies secretly dump their toxic waste on the south side. The border itself, defined by the Rio Grande, has caused its share of disagreements: the river changed course quite often in the 1800s, and it was not until the 1960s, when it was run through a concrete channel, that it was made permanent. An attractive park, the **Chamizal National Memorial** (daily 8am–5pm; free) on the east side of downtown off Paisano Drive, has a small museum discussing the history of cross-border disputes, and throughout the summer hosts a variety of fiestas and cultural events. The **Cordova Bridge** heads acoss the river into Mexico, where there's a larger park and a number of good museums; there are no formalities, so long as you have a multiple-entry visa for the US and don't travel more than 25 miles south of the border.

Practicalities

One reason to come to El Paso is for its **airport**, one of the busiest in the southwestern US and a handy and often cheap starting point. *Sprint Airport Shuttle* vans ($10) connect it with the downtown area. *Greyhound* **buses** stop at 111 San Francisco Avenue (☎544-7200) in the centre of El Paso, while *Amtrak* **trains** pull in to the Daniel Burnham-designed Union Station at 700 San Francisco Avenue (☎545-2247) slightly to the west. The atmospheric *Gardner Hotel* – where John Dillinger stayed in the 1920s – has $13 hostel beds and private **rooms** from $20 to $30 at 311 E Franklin Street (☎532-3661); there are dozens of $30-a-night **motels** along I-10. For more information on El Paso and its Mexican neighbour, contact the downtown **visitor centre** (☎534-0653 or ☎1-800/351-6024) at 5 Civic Center Plaza in the Convention Center complex. For some of the best **Tex-Mex food** anywhere, call in at *Forte's Mexican Elder*, 321 Chelsea Street (☎772-0066), just east of downtown, where a tableful of chili-charged enchiladas and rellenos costs around $7. El Paso is also the home of *Tony Lama*, makers of top-quality **cowboy boots**, available at substantial discounts at 204 Mills Street (☎532-6052).

After dark, strut on down to *Dallas Nightclub*, 1840 N Lee Trevino Drive, to meet the cowboy or cowgirl of your dreams or just imbibe the $1 margaritas. Some of the region's best nightlife is across the border in **Ciudad Juarez**: the Hemingwayesque *Kentucky Club Cantina*, 629 Avenida Juarez just south of the Santa Fe Street bridge, or the more touristy *Chihuahua Charlie's*, 2525 Triunfo de la Republica near the Plaza de Toros Monumental (the main bullfight arena), are both tried and tested haunts.

travel details

TRAINS
Routes

• Three trains per week between New Orleans and LA connect **Houston**, **San Antonio**, **Alpine** and **El Paso**, also stopping at Del Rio and Sanderson.

• One train daily connects **San Antonio** to **Austin**, **Fort Worth** and **Dallas**, winding into Chicago through Arkansas and Missouri.

• One train daily runs between **Dallas** and **Houston**, continuing to Chicago by the same route.

Journey Times

From Houston: San Antonio 4hr 30min; Alpine 12hr 30min; El Paso 15hr 30min.

From San Antonio: Austin 2hr 30min; Fort Worth 7hr; Dallas 9hr.

From Austin: Dallas 6hr; San Antonio 2hr 30min; El Paso 7hr.

From Dallas: Houston 6hr.

BUSES

All the below are *Greyhound* services.

From Houston to Galveston (6 daily; 1hr 30min); Corpus Christi (4; 3hr); Dallas (5; 5hr); San Antonio (7; 3hr 45min); Laredo (1; 6hr 30min); El Paso (4; 15hr).

From Laredo to El Paso (1 daily; 12hr); San Antonio (1; 3hr).

From San Antonio to Corpus Christi (4 daily; 3hr); Austin (6; 2hr 30min); Dallas (6 daily; 7hr); El Paso (4; 11hr).

From Austin to Dallas (6 daily; 5hr); Houston (11; 4hr).

From Dallas to Fort Worth (12 daily; 50min); Abilene (12; 4hr 30min); El Paso (12; 13hr).

From Amarillo to Oklahoma City (5 daily; 5hr); Albuquerque (5; 5hr).

From El Paso to Abilene (6 daily; 11hr); Fort Worth (6; 15hr).

CHAPTER TEN

THE GREAT PLAINS

The **GREAT PLAINS**, defined here as stretching west of the Mississippi River through **ARKANSAS, OKLAHOMA, MISSOURI, KANSAS, IOWA, NEBRASKA,** and **NORTH** and **SOUTH DAKOTA,** are lumped together in the popular imagination as an unappealing expanse of unvarying flatness and conservative "Mid American" values, a huge national joke to be passed through as fast as possible. Once, however, this was the **West,** a vast empty canvas on which outlaws, fur-trappers, buffalo hunters and cowboys painted their dreams. In the 1870s, the wide open range of the lone prairie, which had originally been known as the **Great American Desert** but was now promoted as a bountiful Garden of Eden, inspired such fascination that General Custer was moved to call it "the fairest and richest portion of the national domain". As well as the main routes west (the Oregon and Santa Fe trails through Missouri and Kansas), the Plains were criss-crossed by the Pony Express, cattle trails and railroads. Today the massive Gateway Arch in **St Louis** celebrates the traders, explorers and pioneers who followed their destinies further and further west.

Early maps show the "Desert" as uninterrupted by towns or roads; even today there are fewer towns, spaced further apart, on the plains than anywhere else in the nation, and the population has steadily dropped since the 1930s. One sinister note echoes through this openness and emptiness: most of the nation's **nuclear missiles** – marked by unprepossessing concrete blocks fenced into empty fields – sit patiently beneath a land already ravaged and destroyed by greed.

For the plains, today so apparently uneventful, share a trauma-scarred history. The systematic destruction by white settlers of the awesome herds of **bison** presaged the virtual eradication of the **Plains Indians**. Reservations, agencies and "assigned lands" dwindled as the natural resources of the area attracted white settlement; after 1874, when **gold** was discovered in the Black Hills, the fate of the Native Americans was practically sealed. However, thanks to warrior heroes like **Crazy Horse** and **Sitting Bull**, the struggle for control of the plains was by no means as easy as the Hollywood Westerns imply. Today the region is troublingly ambivalent about this history: its many museums and monuments to the Native Americans can seem as much a veiled celebration of, as an apology for, the destruction of their culture.

The plains are more comfortable, however, playing **cowboys**, priding in a romantic myth of the Wild West and flaunting sanitised versions of wicked old cowtowns like **Deadwood** in South Dakota, **Dodge City** (once called the "Beautiful, Bibulous Babylon of the Frontier") in Kansas, and **Fort Smith**, at the start of the trail to California, on the Arkansas/Oklahoma border. **Calamity Jane, Wild Bill Hickok, Billy the Kid** and **Annie Oakley** all left their mark here when this was the wild frontier, and today, in the sandy scrublands of northern Nebraska, you can still see real cowboy and cattle country.

After Reconstruction, Southern blacks came here in search of an egalitarian future, and black colonies sprang up all around the region. The dreams soon died, though, and there are few black faces to be seen nowadays. There is, however, more evidence of nineteenth-century **Russian** and **German** settlement; many of the oldest families on the plains are descendants of Mennonites who escaped religious persecution in the 1870s, bringing with them new farming methods that heralded the region's great agricultural prosperity. The Great Plains still provide the nation with much of its food, and export two-thirds of the world's **wheat**, seas of which can be seen waving over the flat

fields of Iowa, Nebraska and Kansas. The economy has also been dependent on **oil**, especially in Oklahoma, and **gold** in the Dakotas.

Defining the geographical limits of the Plains is difficult, and the term itself is almost a misnomer – there are vast flat expanses and long, long uninterrupted roads, but there are also canyons, forests, and splashes of unexpected colour, and two of the nation's mightiest rivers, the **Missouri**, which weaves its course southeast from North Dakota, and the **Mississippi**, which it joins at St Louis. Since the 1950s, the mining of the underground Ogallala aquifer from Nebraska to Oklahoma has transformed much that was once dusty desert into verdant fields; the consequences of overuse (assuring the depletion of the reservoir in another fifty years) remain to be seen.

The woods, caves and springs of the **Ozarks** in Missouri and Arkansas, which nurture a practically autonomous hillbilly culture, the lakes and mountains of Arkansas, the startling lunar landscapes of South Dakota's **Badlands**, and stately **Mount Rushmore** are the region's most touristed areas. Otherwise, there are few immediate attractions and only a handful of cities of any real charm; drama comes instead in the form of unpredictable **weather**. Freak blizzards, dust storms, lightning storms and the notorious "twister" tornados are not uncommon, and have carved much of the region's identity, with images of the devastating Thirties' dustbowl Depression (when topsoil was whisked as far away as Washington DC) as potent as the Technicolour fantasy of Dorothy and Toto being swept up from Kansas by a tornado to the land of Oz.

A **car** is practically obligatory in the plains, where distances are long, roads straight and seemingly endless, and the sparse population is scattered. The main routes (I-94, I-90, I-80, I-70, I-40) cross east–west, making it frustratingly difficult to travel north–south. *Greyhound* **buses** travel the interstates, often bypassing the small towns which provide a real sense of the region. Subsidiary bus lines include *Iowa Lines* in Arkansas and *Jack Rabbit* in South Dakota, as well as the *Jefferson Line*, which covers Iowa, Kansas, Missouri, Oklahoma and Arkansas. True to their image as a crossroads rather than a destination, the plains are crossed by *Amtrak* **trains** almost exclusively at night, with Oklahoma and South Dakota not covered at all. St Louis, Missouri, is the major **airport**, while Wichita, Kansas, is a regional hub.

ARKANSAS

Historically, **ARKANSAS** belongs very much to the American South. It sided firmly with the Confederacy in the Civil War, and its capital Little Rock was the scene in 1957 of one of the most notorious flashpoints of the struggle for civil rights. Geographically, however, it marks the beginning of the Great Plains. Unlike the other southern states, on the far side of the Mississippi River, Arkansas remained very sparsely populated until almost a century ago. Westward expansion was blocked by the existence of the Indian Territory in what's now Oklahoma, and it was not until the railroads opened up the forested interior during the 1880s that settlers in any numbers strayed from their small riverside villages. Only once the Depression and mechanisation had forced thousands of farmers to leave their fields did Arkansas begin to develop any significant industrial base. The national prominence given by Governor Bill Clinton's run for the Presidency in 1992 belies Arkansas' continuing low position on most socio-economic indicators.

Though Arkansas encompasses the **Mississippi Delta** in the east, oil-rich timberlands in the south, and the sweeping **Ouachita Mountains** in the west, the cragged and charismatic **Ozark Mountains** in the north are its most scenic asset. Sleepy **Little Rock** is its only sizeable conurbation, and, except for the nearby spa town of **Hot Springs**, the main attraction for tourists are the uncrowded parks and unspoiled rivers.

"Arkansas" is a distorted version of the name of a small Indian tribe; the state legislature declared once and for all in 1881 that the correct pronunciation is *Arkansaw*.

Getting Around Arkansas

It's extremely difficult to venture beyond Little Rock and Hot Springs by public transport. *Greyhound* runs intermittent services, while *Amtrak* cuts diagonally east–west through the state, calling at Little Rock, which also holds the only sizeable **airport**. To see the Ozarks you'll need a car.

> The telephone **area code** for the entire state of Arkansas is ☎501.

Eastern and Southern Arkansas

What's surprising about the eastern Arkansas deltalands is that they are far from totally flat: **Crowley's Ridge**, a narrow arc of wind-blown loess hills, breaks up the uniform smoothness, stretching 150 miles from southern Missouri to the likeable rivertown of **Helena**. Despite scenic rivers and sleepy bayous, the pine-clad woodlands of the Gulf Coastal Plain in southern Arkansas are of little real interest.

Helena

The small Mississippi port of **HELENA**, roughly sixty miles south of Memphis, was once the shipping point for Arkansas' cotton crop. Mark Twain described it as "occupying one of the prettiest situations on the river", and it still retains a flavour of the Old South. Stately plantation mansions line the surrounding roads while **Cherry Street**, the main thoroughfare parallel to the levee, is fronted by well-preserved stores.

Musicians among Helena's large black population have ensured that the town is an important stop on the itinerary of **delta blues** enthusiasts – it's no great distance from Clarksdale, Mississippi (see p.414). Home of radio station KFFA (1360m), which broadcasts the long-running *King Biscuit Time Show* every weekday from 12.15 to 12.45pm, Helena also hosts one of the country's leading blues festivals every October. During the rest of the year, you can hear live blues at *Bubba Sullivan's Blues Corner*, 105 Cherry Street (no phone). The **Delta Cultural Center**, celebrating the blues tradition, is due to open shortly. The **visitor centre**, 111 Hickory Hills Drive (☎338-8327), has details on other attractions and **accommodation**; the Edwardian *B&B*, 317 Briscoe Street, near the river (☎339-9155), is a great place to stay for $60.

Central and West Arkansas

Quiet **Little Rock** stands right in the middle of the state, just fifty miles west of the rejuvenated spa town of Hot Springs, which marks the eastern gateway to the remote **Ouachita Mountains**. The rippling farmland of the **Arkansas River Valley** is sandwiched in by the Ouachita crests on the south side and the craggy ridges of the Ozarks to the north. Mining and logging communities dot the east–west-running roads, and former frontier towns like **Fort Smith** and **Van Buren** retain their Old West flavour.

Little Rock

The geographical, political and financial centre of Arkansas, **LITTLE ROCK** is at the meeting point of its two major regions, the northwestern hills and the eastern delta. Forever associated with the confrontations in 1957 at its Central High School (see box), Little Rock today has a relaxed and open feel to it, but considering it's a capital city, there's disappointingly little to see and do.

CONFRONTATION AT LITTLE ROCK

In 1957, Little Rock unexpectedly became the battleground in the first major conflict between state and federal government over **race relations**. At the time, the city was generally viewed as progressive by southern standards. All parks, libraries and buses were integrated, a relatively high thirty percent of blacks were on the electoral register and there were black police officers. However, when the Little Rock School Board announced its decision to phase in **desegregation** gradually – the Supreme Court having declared segregation of schools to be unconstitutional – James Johnson, a candidate for state governor, started a campaign opposed to interracial education. Johnson's rhetoric began to win him support, and the incumbent governor, **Orval Faubus**, who had previously shown no interest in the issue, jumped on the bandwagon himself.

The first nine black students were due to enter Central High School that September. The day before school opened, Faubus reversed his decision to let blacks enrol "in the interest of safety", only to be overruled by the federal court. He ordered state troopers to keep out the black students anyway; soldiers with bayonets forced Elizabeth Eckford, one of the nine, away from the school entrance into a seething crowd, from which she had to jump on a bus to escape. As legal battles raged during the day, at night blacks were subject to violent attacks by white gangs. Three weeks later, President Eisenhower somewhat reluctantly brought in the 101st Airborne Division, and amidst violent demonstrations the nine were at last able to enter Central High. Throughout the year, they experienced immense intimidation; when one retaliated, she was expelled. The graduation of James Green, the oldest, at the end of the year, seemed to put an end to the affair but Faubus, up for re-election, renewed his political posturing by closing down all public schools in the city for the 1958–59 academic year – and thereby increased his majority.

The school itself is an enormous brown crescent-shaped structure, more like a fortress, at 1500 S Park Avenue, about a mile from the Capitol on bus route #9.

The cream-coloured **Old State House Museum**, 300 W Markham Street, surrounded by smooth lawns and shaded by evergreens, backs onto the Arkansas River, which served as the main means of transportation for early politicians. Inside, displays cover all periods of Arkansas history, but the most impressive rooms are the two senate chambers, restored to their original grandeur and uncluttered by any exhibits (Mon–Sat 9am–5pm, Sun 1–5pm; free). The pleasant thin strip of greenery, benches and fountains of **Riverfront Park** run for several blocks behind the museum. A commemorative sign marks the actual "little rock" for which the city is named, which is just as well or you could easily miss it. A French explorer in 1722 called it "La Petite Roche" to distinguish it from a larger outcrop upstream. The *Spirit* **paddlewheeler** sets out on one-hour cruises from just across the river (Tues–Sat 2pm; $5).

Practicalities

Little Rock Airport lies two miles east of downtown on I-440; *Southwest Airlines* (☎374-1221) frequently offer round trips from Dallas for as little as $39. *Greyhound* (☎372-1861) arrives at 118 E Washington Street in North Little Rock. *Amtrak* (☎372-6841) enjoys a more central location at Markham and Victory streets. **Taxis** don't pick up on the street, so call *Black and White* (☎374-1163); downtown to the airport costs around $7, to *Greyhound* at most $5. The **CVB** is at Markham and Main streets (Mon–Fri 9–11.30am & 12.30–3.30pm; ☎376-4781).

Finding a **room** in downtown Little Rock should be no problem. The *Econolodge*, 322 E Capital Street (☎376-3661), is very basic, but has a pool and costs only $35, while the *Quapaw Inn*, 1868 S Gaines Street (☎376-6873), is a very nice B&B charging $50 to $60 per night. *Cajun's Wharf*, 2400 Cantrell Road (☎375-5351), a popular riverside **restaurant** in the warehouse district, serves reasonably priced Cajun-style seafood and doubles as a live music venue. *Juanita's Cantina*, 1300 S Main Street (☎372-1228), is an atmospheric and imaginative Mexican place which also puts on live bands. Little Rock's finest eating is at the *Cafe St Moritz*, 225 E Markham Street (☎372-0411), where the Swiss chef conjures up great continental seafood and superb desserts. Main courses in the evening cost between $7 and $16.

Hot Springs

Fifty miles southwest of Little Rock, the spa town of **HOT SPRINGS** nestles in the heavily forested Zig Zag Mountains on the eastern flank of the Ouachitas. Its thermal waters have been attracting visitors since Native Americans used the area as a neutral zone to settle disputes. Early settlers fashioned a crude resort out of the wilderness, and after the railroads arrived in 1875 it became a European-style spa. During the town's heyday in the Twenties and Thirties, the mayor reputedly ran a gambling syndicate worth $30 million per annum, and punters included Al Capone and Bugs Malone. However, Hot Springs' popularity waned when new cures for arthritis appeared during the Fifties, and all but one of the bathhouses closed down.

Downtown Hot Springs is crammed into a looping wooded valley that between Fountain and Reserve streets is only wide enough to accommodate Central Avenue. Eight magnificent buildings here, behind a lush display of magnolia trees, elms and verdant hedgerows, make up Bathhouse Row. Between 1915 and 1962, the grandest of them all was the **Fordyce Bathhouse**, which reopened in 1989 as the **visitor centre** for **Hot Springs National Park** – the only national park to fall within city limits. Its interior is a strange mixture of the elegant and the obsolete; the heavy use of marble, mosaic-tile floors and the stained-glass ceiling of the Sun Room lend it a decadent feel, while a glimpse at the archaic equipment in the gym shows just how far advanced sports equipment has become (daily 9am–5pm; free; ☎623-1433).

It's still possible to sample the old-time style and luxury of Hot Springs by taking a **bath**. The only establishment on Bathhouse Row still open for business is the *Buckstaff* (☎623-2308), where a thermal mineral bath costs $9.50. Full bathing facilities are also available at several of the town's hotels. To taste the water, which lacks the strong sulphuric taste often associated with thermal springs, fill up a container at the drinking fountain at Central and Reserve streets.

To the rear of the *Fordyce*, two small **springs** have been left open for viewing. The **Grand Promenade** from here is a half-mile red and yellow brick walkway overlooking downtown. Trails of various lengths and severity lead up the steep slopes of **Hot Springs Mountain**. A short drive or testing two-and-a-half-mile hike through dense woods of oak, hickory and short-leafed pine takes you to the summit where the observation decks of **Mountain Tower** offer superb views of the town, the Ouachitas and surrounding lakes (daily summer 9am–9pm; other months vary; $2.25).

Practicalities

Greyhound (☎623-6390) operate infrequent **buses** from the capital and from Dallas, six hours away. Providing you are in central accommodation, most places of interest will be within walking distance, though *Hot Springs Intracity Transport* buses provide a reasonable hourly service to most parts of the city. **Bikes** can be rented from *Bikes Etc*, 312A Whittington Avenue (☎623-BIKE).

Hot Springs' **visitor centre** is at Central and Reserve streets (☎624-3383). Luxury **accommodation** comes surprisingly cheap in Hot Springs. Dominating the town centre, the elegant twin-towered *Arlington Resort/Spa* at Central Avenue and Fountain Street (☎623-7771) has rooms from only $50. The *Downtowner Motor Inn*, 135 Central Avenue (☎624-5521), has seen better days but is still good value at $35. The *Park Avenue Motel*, 415 Park Avenue (☎623-4623), is one of several neighbouring motels costing as little as $20. Prices rise by up to fifty percent during high season, between

February and April. The nearest place to **camp** is *Gulpha Gorge Campground* in the National Park, two miles from downtown on Hwy-70B, off Hwy-70 East.

Hidden among the usual holiday-town family **restaurants** is the morning-only *Pancake Shop*, 216 Central Avenue (☎624-9465), whose stuffed pancakes make a filling start to the day. The excellent *New Orleans Cafe,* two doors down at no. 210 (☎624-3200), serves everything from Cajun breakfasts to very cheap seafood in the evening.

Western Arkansas

West of Hot Springs, US-270 cuts through the heart of the Ouachita (*Wash-i-taw*) Mountains, unique to the continent in that they run east–west rather than north–south. On its way to Oklahoma, the road passes over uneven crests separated by wide valleys speckled with tiny communities, so isolated that, in the Thirties, hill-dwellers supposedly spoke a form of English similar to that used during Elizabethan times. Separating the Ouachita range from the northerly Ozarks, the **Arkansas River Valley**, a natural east–west path for bison, was used for centuries by Native Americans and white hunters before steamboats arrived in the 1820s.

Fort Smith

Now an industrial city of 70,000 people, **FORT SMITH**, on the Oklahoma border, maintains a pronounced western feel. Until Charles Isaac Parker was appointed district judge in 1875, this was a rowdy pioneer town, uncomfortably close to lawless Indian Territory, a sanctuary for robbers and bandits. Parker recruited 200 marshals, who undertook the dangerous task of riding out into the territory to round up the fugitives. Known as the "Hanging Judge", in 21 years Parker sentenced 160 to death and saw 79 go to the gallows. **Fort Smith National Historic Site** on Rogers Avenue features remains of the original fort, Parker's courtroom, the dingy basement jail and a set of gallows (daily 9am–5pm; $2). **Old Main Street** in **Van Buren**, on the opposite bank of the Arkansas River, is a stretch of over seventy restored buildings that has been used in numerous westerns.

Places to **stay** in Fort Smith include the central *Days Inn*, 301 N 11th Street (☎783-0271), for $40; *Motel 6*, 6001 Rogers Avenue (☎484-0576), and *Regal 8*, 1021 Garrison Avenue (☎785-2611), cost less than $30. For tasty home-cooked Italian food, try *Taliano's*, 201 N 14th Street (☎785-2292), where meals are between $5 and $10.

The Ozark Mountains

Although the highest peak fails to top 2000 feet, the **Ozark Mountains**, which extend beyond northern Arkansas into southern Missouri, are characterised by severe steep ridges and jagged spurs. Hair-raising roads weave their way over the precipitous hills, past rugged lakeshores and pristine rivers. When ambitious speculators poured into Arkansas in the 1830s, those who missed the best land etched out remote hill farms that represented no gain on what they had left behind in Kentucky or Tennessee. They remained utterly isolated until the last few decades; the Ozarks have now become the fastest-growing rural section of the US, a major tourist and retirement destination. Much-needed cash has flooded in, bringing with it the cafes and souvenir shops that have converted centres such as Harrison into identikit American towns.

The word *Ozark* is everywhere, used to entice tourists into music shows or gift emporia which owe more to Nashville or Taiwan than to these mountains. With all the hype, it's getting increasingly difficult to tell the genuine article from imitations, which is a good reason for visiting the state park at **Mountain View**, a serious attempt to preserve traditional Ozark skills and music. The most visited town in the region,

Eureka Springs, just inside the Missouri border, is a pretty mountainside Victorian spa town, though not one where you should expect to find out much about Ozark life.

Mountain View

Roughly sixty miles due north of Little Rock, the state-run **Ozark Folk Center**, two miles north of the town of **MOUNTAIN VIEW** on Hwy-14, is a living history museum that attempts to show how life used to be in these remote hillsides, not reached by paved roads until the Fifties. Different homestead skills are displayed in reconstructed log cabins, while folk musicians and storytellers perform throughout the park. Every night of the week live Ozark music concerts are held at 7.30pm (mid-April to early Nov daily; craft displays $4.75, concerts $5.25; ☎269-3851).

   Rooms at the *Lodge* (☎269-3871) in the Center's grounds cost $45; the *Dogwood Motel*, one mile east of the town on Hwy-14, costs $40. For Saturday night entertainment, it's hard to beat the friendly jam sessions in Mountain View's town square.

   The spectacular **Buffalo National River** – a prime destination for whitewater canoeing – flows across the state north of Mountain View. It can be seen at its best around **Pruitt Landing**, thirteen miles south of unremarkable **Harrison**.

Eureka Springs

Picturebook **EUREKA SPRINGS**, set on steep mountain slopes in Arkansas' northeastern corner, began life a hundred years ago as a health centre. As that role declined, its striking location turned it into a regular tourist destination, given a particularly tacky edge by its specialising in weddings and honeymoons. Despite the abundance of tourist shops, Eureka Springs is nonetheless an enjoyable place to stroll around, filled with tasteful Victorian buildings. A ride on the **Eureka Springs and North Arkansas Railway** through lush wooded Ozark valleys is an excellent way to appreciate the area's beauty. Rolling stock includes a magnificent "cabbage-head" woodburning locomotive, and trips depart on the hour from the depot at 299 N Main Street (mid-April to Oct daily 10am–4pm; ☎253-9623).

   The Ozarks' position in the Bible Belt is underlined by an incredible religious complex, three miles east, which includes the seven-storey **Christ of the Ozarks** – a surreal statue of a bemused-looking Jesus with a sixty-foot arm span – a **Bible Museum** and a **Sacred Arts Center**. Strangest of all is the **New Holy Land** theme park, through which minibuses whisk visitors past scaled-down versions of the Sea of Galilee, the River Jordan and other holy places. Elna M Smith, whose Foundation runs the whole show, was so worried that the historic sites of the Middle East would be destroyed by war that she decided to build replicas in the Ozarks, safe from Arab attack. At 8.30pm, two-hundred-plus actors re-enact Christ's last week on earth in the **Great Passion Play** in a 4400-seater amphitheatre (May–Oct Tues, Wed & Fri–Sun; $8–11; ☎253-9200). *Gray Line Bus Tours* provide transport to the site, picking up at most motels ($3; ☎253-9540).

Practicalities

Accommodation prices in Eureka Springs vary considerably according to season, but you can usually find an inexpensive place to stay just over a mile from downtown on US-62E; *Razorback Lodge* (☎253-8952), for example, costs $24 to $32. At the more central *Best Western Eureka Inn* (☎253-9551), at the junction of US-62 and S Main Street, comfortable rooms cost $60. The local **visitor centre** is nearby (☎253-8737).

   The *Eureka Egg Roll Emporium* at Basin Park on Spring Street (☎252-8029) does cheap lunch specials while *Joe's Mexican Restaurant*, 179 N Main Street (☎253-9617), serves red snapper and seafood dishes for between $5 and $10. Just off the well-worn tourist paths, *Chelsea Corner*, 10 Mountain Street, off Spring Street (☎253-6723), sells standard-priced burgers and sandwiches and has live music most evenings.

OKLAHOMA

Ridiculed by the rest of the nation as boring, and forever the butt of jokes at the expense of the "Okies", **OKLAHOMA** has had a traumatic and far from dull history. In the 1830s, all this land, held to be useless, was set aside as **Indian Territory**; a convenient dumping ground for the so-called Five Civilised Tribes who blocked white settlement in the southern states. The Choctaw and Chickasaw of Mississippi, the Seminole of Florida, and the Creek of Alabama were each assigned a share, while the rest (though already inhabited by indigenous Indians) was given to the Cherokee from Carolina, Tennessee and Georgia, who followed in 1838 on the four-month trek notorious as "the Trail of Tears" (see p.390). Today the state has a large Indian population – *oklahoma* is the Choctaw word for "red man" – and even the smallest towns tend to have museums of Native American history.

Once white settlers realised that Indian Territory was, in fact, well worth farming, they decided to stay. The Indians were relocated once more, and in a manic free-for-all scramble in 1889, entire towns sprang up literally overnight. Those who jumped the gun and claimed land illegally were known as Sooners; hence Oklahoma's nickname, the **Sooner State**. White settlers didn't have an easy life, however, facing, after great oil prosperity in the Twenties, an era of unthinkable hardship in the Thirties. The desperate migration, when whole communities fled the dust bowl for California, has come to encapsulate the worst horrors of the Depression, most famously in John Steinbeck's novel (and John Ford's film) **The Grapes of Wrath**, but also in Dorothea Lange's haunting photos of itinerant families, hitching and camping on the road, and in the sad yet hopeful songs of Woodie Guthrie. Since the slump of the early Eighties, the region is facing another crisis, and its major downtown areas are uncannily still.

Oklahoma is not the flat and unchanging expanse of popular imagination. Most of its places of interest, such as attractive **Tulsa**, lie in the hilly wooded northeast; only the sparse and treeless west is devoid of appeal, on the far side of the central "tornado alley" prairie grassland which holds the state's hard-hit capital, **Oklahoma City**. The lakes and parks of the south, which bears more than a passing resemblance to neighbouring Arkansas (complete with mountains, foliage and bluegrass music), have made tourism Oklahoma's second industry after oil.

Getting Around Oklahoma

Car travel is the only rational way to explore Oklahoma, which has no *Amtrak* service. *Greyhound* **buses** speed along I-35 and I-40, which converge on Oklahoma City, but public transport within the towns is minimal. Tulsa and Oklahoma City have reasonably sized airports. **Route 66**, which passes through both on its way from Missouri to Texas, is no longer a national highway, but if you have plenty of time (and sturdy tyres; much of the road is in a bad way), makes an interesting alternative to the interstates. A booklet available at the Tulsa CVB details the small communities and ghost towns en route.

Eastern Oklahoma

Eastern Oklahoma includes the "Green Country" of the northeast, patterned with the foothills of the Ozarks, and woods, streams, lakes and rivers that make it a popular camping destination. Art Deco **Tulsa** is its cultural centre; **Tahlequah** and **Pawhuska** are the capitals of the Cherokee and Osage nations respectively.

The telephone **area code** for Tulsa and eastern Oklahoma is ☎918.

Tulsa

Tulsa is a good-looking city, thanks in part to the striking Art Deco architecture that dates from its Twenties heyday as an immensely wealthy oil town. Despite – or possibly because of – its pleasant atmosphere, two excellent museums, and thriving high arts scene, it does, however, tend towards nouveau-riche smugness. The overriding Bible-Belt mentality is hard to ignore; even in the hip *Tulsa Press* a regular feature reviews local churches, whimsically named *Pew View*.

Arrival, Information and Getting Around

Tulsa International Airport (☎838-5000) lies just minutes east of downtown. Hwy-169 from Kansas City skirts its east side; I-244, which gives access from the south, is also the main route east–west across town. *Greyhound* comes in downtown to 317 S Detroit Avenue. The **CVB**, 616 S Boston Avenue (☎585-1201), provides a self-guided walking tour of downtown – such as it is – as well as schedules for the rudimentary local **bus** system, which runs (if you're lucky) every half-hour until 6pm. A free **trolley** also serves downtown (11.30am–1.30pm & 4.30–6.30pm).

The Town

Downtown Tulsa's most obvious landmark is the ornate Art Deco **Union Depot**, on the First Street and Boston Avenue Overpass, built in the early Thirties to encourage the flagging economy and now housing offices. The **320 Boston Building** on Boston Avenue, known in the Twenties as the "Oil Bank of America", is worth a look for its huge brass doors, stone archways, gargoyles and hand-painted ceilings. Further along the other side of the road, the **Philtower**, 527 S Boston Avenue, is another distinctive Twenties skyscraper. It has a green and red tiled sloping roof and crouching gargoyles, a lobby richly decorated in brass and marble, and a small gallery of Tulsa history. **Lyon's Indian Store**, on the southwest corner of Seventh and Main streets, is an old trading post selling authentic Native American goods, including feather headdresses, bead work, rugs and jewellery. Over thirty tribes from around the state sell their stuff here; though not cheap, it's worth a rummage. The huge and gloriously over-the-top Art Deco **Boston Avenue Methodist Church**, 1301 S Boston Avenue – at 255 feet high, it's practically cathedral-sized – offers good views of the city from its fourteenth storey, and free Sunday tours after the 10.55am service.

Outside downtown, to the south, the 75ft **Creek Council Oak**, 18th Street and Cheyenne Avenue, marks the spot where the Creek Indians ended their tortuous migration from Alabama in 1836, and founded Tulsa on the Arkansas River. The tree became a tribal meeting site, used ceremonially until 1896. The airy and stylish **Philbrook Art Center**, 2727 S Rockford Road, in the house of oilman Waite Phillips in the well-heeled Mapleridge residential area, is a Florentine-style mansion set in Gatsbyesque acres. Though displays include Native American pottery, African sculpture, Chinese jades and Renaissance paintings, the house itself is every bit as decorative as the art, with ostentatious marble floors, indoor fountains and sweeping staircases. The gardens, with crumbling paths, pretty fountains and fantastic hill views are also worth exploring (Tues, Wed, Fri & Sat 10am–5pm, Sun 1–5pm, Thurs 5–8pm; free tours Thurs, Sat & Sun).

Oral Roberts University, 7777 S Lewis Avenue, is a must for kitsch junkies. University, hospital and television station all in one, the concept was inspired by visionary Oral Roberts – who back in 1987 announced that God had decided to "call him home" unless he could raise 4.5 million dollars before a certain deadline. Roberts retreated to a lonely vigil at the top of his **Prayer Tower**, a kind of B-movie space ship; he got his money (or God's; the distinction was unclear), though his credibility was dented when the tower was struck by lightning at the crucial moment. You can now see a sycophantic exhibition, complete with heavenly choir, on the great man's life (Mon–

Sat 9am–5pm, Sun 1–5pm). There's an 80ft-high pair of hands in prayer on the grass outside the **City of Faith Medical Centre**, where a multimedia "journey through the Bible" (the first eight books of it) runs every twenty minutes from 10.30am until 4.30pm.

The **Gilcrease Museum**, 1400 Gilcrease Museum Road, just northwest of downtown, is set in the gently rolling **Osage Hills**, with a fine vista from the back and good view of downtown from the front. Thomas Gilcrease, of Indian heritage, grew very rich after oil was found on his land. His private collection of western art includes Native American works, as well as excellent Remingtons, Russells and Morans (Mon–Sat 9am–5pm, Sun 1–5pm; free tours daily at 2pm).

To experience some of Tulsa's cowboy history, make for the **Ted Allen Ranch**, seven miles west of town along 181st Street at 19600 S Memorial Drive, Bixby. This working horse ranch opens daily at 9am; activities include riding, overnight campouts, moonlit hayrides and rodeos. Call to see what's on offer (☎366-3010); prices vary. There's a music show and chuckwagon supper (steak, beans, baked potato and coffee) each Friday and Saturday at 7.30pm, from April to September, for $15. The band is good, with the fastest fiddle-playing and throatiest yodelling this side of Missouri, and Ted Allen's laconic humour makes it all great fun.

Accommodation
Most of Tulsa's **budget hotels** are outside downtown, along **East Skelly Drive** forking southwest from I-44, and around I-44 and I-244 in general. There's **camping** at the *KOA*, 139 East Avenue (☎266-4227). For details of **B&Bs**, contact *Ozark Mountain Country B&B*, Box 295, Branson, MO 65726 (☎417/334-4720).

Best Western Trade Winds East, 3337 E Skelly Drive (☎743-7931). Comfortable rooms for $55.

Crosswinds, 8201 E Skelly Drive (☎665-6800). $40, with free breakfast and popcorn.

Lexington Hotel Suites, 8525 E 41st St (☎627-0030). Luxury doubles $49–69, with breakfast.

Thrifty Inn, 6030 E Skelly Drive (☎665-2630). $35, with free breakfast.

Eating
Tulsa's **restaurants** are diverse and scattered; good, if sometimes expensive, options can be found along **E 15th Street** and **S Peoria Avenue**.

Back Bay Gourmet, 1536 E 15th St (☎584-2300). Costs up to $20, but it's a bit special. Items on the varied menu include goat cheese won ton with basil chili sauce.

Chimi's, 1423 E 15th St (☎587-4411). Good down-home Mexican restaurant.

15th Street Grill, 1542 E 15th St (☎587-4411). Art Deco seafood and pasta joint. Lunch $5–8.

Metro Diner, 3001 E 11th St (☎592-2616). Fifties-style diner east of down-town, serving good home-baked pies and chicken fried steaks, as well as great ice cream sodas.

The Orange Blossom Cafe, 3523 S Peoria Ave. Hip hangout on the main stretch along the river. Homemade soups and chocolate cake, plus choc fudge coffee. Live jazz Fri & Sat.

Nightlife and Entertainment
There is even less to do in downtown Tulsa after dark than during the day; **15th** and **Cherry streets** just south, and S Peoria Avenue by the river, are much more lively. If you visit in September, try to catch the **Chili Cookoff and Bluegrass Festival**, featuring spicy chili competitions, clogging, and bluegrass gigs. Newssheets like the **Monthly Uptown News**, *Tulsa World* and *Tulsa Press* (the "teepee") carry full nightlife listings

Club One, 3200 S Riverside Drive (☎743-1665). R&B during the week, All Star Blues jam Wed.

Discoveryland, ten miles west on W 41st St (☎245-6552). Rodgers and Hammerstein's *Oklahoma!* performed outdoors Mon–Sat, June–Aug. Pre-show barbecue at 5.30pm. Show $11, dinner $6.50.

Joey's Blues Bar, 6825 S Peoria Ave (☎481-8787). Favourite blues venue.

Spotlight Theatre, 1381 Riverside Drive (☎587-5030). Art Deco building that for forty years has hosted the melodrama *The Drunkard*, accompanied by pretzels and sandwiches, every Sat.

The Sunset Grill, 3410 S Peoria Ave (☎744-5550). Hip live bands, free beer on Sunday 8–9pm.

Claremore

Thirty miles northeast of Tulsa on Route 66, **CLAREMORE**, the birthplace of **Will Rogers**, populist comedian, journalist and Twenties film star, is a shrine to a man being slowly forgotten as his films are no longer seen. His career began with a vaudeville show which included lassooing a horse and its rider, while giving a witty commentary, and he was renowned for his pithy and good-natured one-liners. When he died in a plane crash in 1935 there was a nationwide thirty-minute silence. One of his most famous statements, "I never met a man I didn't like", is inscribed on his statue at the **Will Rogers Memorial**, on Will Rogers Boulevard on Hwy-88, which displays his possessions, such as his "gag book", together with stills and clips from his films.

Bartlesville

For forty miles north of Tulsa, the monotony of the plains is relieved only by clumps of spindly scrub oaks. Then comes the quiet town of **BARTLESVILLE**, dominated by the extraordinary **Price Tower**, designed by Frank Lloyd Wright in 1956 – an ugly cantilevered green oddity at Sixth and Dewey streets, which resembles a tall tree. The **Frank Phillips Home**, 1107 S Cherokee Avenue, built in 1908 by the founder of **Phillips Oil**, displays oil wealth at its very gaudiest, with gold taps, mirrored ceilings and marble floors. More impressive is his **Woolaroc Ranch** (named for the many *woo*ds, *la*kes and *roc*ks in the area), thirteen miles southwest on Hwy-123, now a wildlife refuge and museum of western art and history, set in four thousand acres in the Blackjack Hills. Over 60,000 artefacts from prehistory to the early twentieth century are scattered through seven huge rooms, roughly in chronological sequence. Paintings and decorative art line the walls, from Native American works to the epic western paintings of Remington and Russell, while artefacts of various tribes, pioneers and cowboys are gathered in too great an abundance to take it all in. Look out especially for the 95-million-year-old dinosaur egg, exquisite Navajo blankets, gruesome scalps taken by Indians and Buffalo Bill's weathered saddle (Tues–Sun 10am–5pm; $3).

If you want to **stay**, the *Travelers Motel*, 3105 Frank Phillips Boulevard (☎333-1900), has rooms from around $25 with continental breakfast. Doubles at the *Ramada Inn*, 1410 SE Washington Boulevard (☎333-8320), cost around $50.

Tahlequah

Forty-five minutes' drive south from Tulsa on Hwy-51, **TAHLEQUAH** is the capital of the **Cherokee** nation, formed in 1839 when the Trail of Tears finally reached its end. The sophisticated Cherokee had a written constitution, published the first newspaper in Indian Territory (in both Cherokee and English) and set up the Cherokee female seminary, the first higher education school for women west of the Mississippi. It stands today on the campus of **Northeastern State University** on Hwy-82, which has more Native American students than any other academic institution in the US.

Tahlequah itself is uncommercialised, and the **Cherokee Heritage Centre**, three miles south at Tsa-La-Gi, presents Native American life to curious tourists with more dignity than might be expected. In the museum, artefacts illustrate the area from prehistory to the present, including wooden ceremonial masks, and a display on the Cherokee alphabet (Mon–Sat 10am–5pm, Sun 1–5pm; $2.50). A reconstructed seventeenth-century Indian village gives arts and crafts demonstrations (May–Aug Mon–Sat 10am–5pm, Sun 1–5pm; $3.50), and a "Trail of Tears" drama is put on in the summer ($8).

In the winter, the place is pretty much dead; in summer it's not a bad idea to take a **room** in the *Tahlequah Motor Lodge*, 2501 S Muskogee Avenue (☎456-2350), or the *Lodge of the Cherokees*, south on Hwy-62 (☎456-0511), which both cost from $40. The *Restaurant of the Cherokees* (also ☎456-0511) specialises in traditional smoked dishes.

Muskogee

The Creek Indians, relocated to **MUSKOGEE** in the 1830s, established the town as the central meeting place of the Civilised Tribes; Indian leaders gathered here in 1905 to draw up a plan for a separate Native American state, which was never to be. The arrival of the railroad in the 1870s and the discovery of oil in 1903 both guaranteed that the town would be usurped by white settlers. The **Five Civilised Tribes Museum**, Honor Heights Drive, Agency Hill, tells the Native Americans' story through costumes, documents, photographs and jewellery, with a reconstructed trading post and a print room (Mon–Sat 10am–5pm, Sun 1–5pm; $2). Muskogee is an appealing place, and a good base for the crystal-clear **Lake Tenkiller**, thirty miles southeast on US-64. Surrounded by woods, cliffs and quiet beaches, the lake is perfect for fishing, boating, swimming and scuba diving, and has camping facilities, but is (unsurprisingly) heavily touristed.

Oklahoma City and Westwards

If you're heading west, your last stop in Oklahoma is likely to be the capital, **Oklahoma City**, smack in the centre of the state. Beyond that, the Great Plains stretch in all their emptiness, the endless horizons broken only by small agricultural communities. The **southwest** is the most densely populated, as it is crossed by the two main routes to Texas – I-40 west to Amarillo, and I-44 south to Wichita Falls – to the north, in the **Oklahoman Panhandle**, ranches and tiny hamlets are the only signs of life.

Oklahoma City

OKLAHOMA CITY was created in a matter of hours on April 22 1889, after a single gunshot signalled the opening of the land to white settlement. What was barren prairie at dawn was by nightfall a city of ten thousand. In 1911, the capital was moved here from nearby Guthrie, and in 1928 oil was discovered. Sitting on one of the nation's largest oilfields, the city was brought up short by the slump in the Eighties. However, it is also the largest stocker and feeder cattle market in the world, and is trying to revitalise its pitifully depressed economy by developing tourism, aided by the presence of the unmissable **National Cowboy Hall of Fame**.

Arrival, Information and Getting Around

Will Rogers World Airport, 6100 Terminal Drive (☎681-5311), lies southwest of the city, within about fifteen minutes of the hotels and motels. Public transport, far from adequate, is based at the Mass Transit Bus Terminal, 20 W Reno Avenue (☎235-7433), southeast of the Myriad Gardens and north of I-40. Buses run daily except Sunday until 6pm. You can rent **bikes** from *Miller's Bicycle Distribution*, 739 Asp Avenue (☎321-8296). The **visitor centre** is downtown at 4 Santa Fe Plaza (Mon–Fri 8am–4.30pm; ☎278-8912), just around the corner from *Greyhound* at 427 W Sheridan Avenue, while the **post office** is at 320 SW Fifth Street (Mon–Fri 8.30am–5.30pm, Sat 9am–noon; ☎278-6246; zip code 73125).

The Town

Urban renewal in Oklahoma City's drab **downtown** has not yet quite taken off, although the renovated warehouses of **Bricktown**, on Sheridan Avenue east of the Santa Fe Railroad, are developing into a reasonable eating and nightlife centre. The

The telephone **area code** for Oklahoma City and western Oklahoma is ☎405.

city's skyscrapers are low-key and old-fashioned, and there is no real sense of commercial activity; even in the middle of the day it can be depressingly quiet.

Myriad Gardens on Sheridan Avenue, prettily landscaped with hills, gardens and waterways, give great views across to the brick-towered downtown skyline, and on a sunny day the **Crystal Bridge** tropical botanical garden, in a glass tube in the middle of the park, abounds in garish exotic blooms.

As well as a couple of historical museums, the **Capitol Complex**, just north of downtown, includes the unprepossessing **Capitol**, which makes up for its lack of the usual dome by having a working oil well in its grounds. The **Heritage Hills** area nearby, where the cattle barons, oil millionaires and bankers used to live, is now run-down and seedy in parts, with many buildings abandoned. Of the two of its mansions open to the public, the Victorian-style **Overholser Mansion**, 405 NW 15th Street, is to be preferred to the **Oklahoma Heritage Center**, 201 NW 14th Street, only because the latter holds the unrelentingly tedious "Oklahoma Hall of Fame" portrait gallery.

Two much quirkier attractions lie in the northeast of the city. **Enterprise Square USA**, 2501 E Memorial Road between I-35 and Eastern Avenue, is an outrageous barrage of propaganda about the glories of free enterprise – and a hallucinogenic nightmare to boot. Giant consumer products loom above your head, the George Washingtons on huge dollar bills sing the national anthem with eyes rolling and heads bobbing, and a crazed "government" computer becomes more and more manic until threatening to self-destruct (moral – don't let government interference obstruct freedom of choice). Some highly complicated computer games gauge how successful you have been in soaking up the principles. Different "careers" with guidance notes are available; fragile egos should beware, it's a blow to go bankrupt setting up your gardening business when the eight-year-old on the next computer is happily balancing the economy (Mon–Fri 9am–4pm, Sat 9am–5pm, Sun 1–4pm; $4).

The **National Cowboy Hall of Fame**, ten minutes' walk south at 1700 NE 63rd Street, is a real treat. Sitting atop Persimmon Hill overlooking Route 66, it combines "high art" and popular art in one loving collection. In the works of Remington and Russell – rugged landscapes, stoical cowboys with horses or in comradely groups – the link between Western art and Western movies is very clear. The paintings look like film stills, and with titles like *Waiting for Trouble*, evoke the cinema's endlessly reworked myths of the West. There are also large exhibitions of contemporary Native American work, much of it colourful, bitter and subversive. Actor John Wayne's collection is a delight for the cowboy fetishist, and the Western Performers Hall of Fame pays homage to movie cowboys and gals in hilariously reverent oil paintings and eclectic bunches of movie memorabilia. The poignant *End of the Trail* sculpture, 18ft high, portrays an Indian slumped exhausted – or dead – over his horse. In the garden, dotted with horse graves, corny epigraphs send the much-loved deceased beasts to "Hoss Heaven" (daily summer 8.30am–6pm; winter 9am–5pm).

Oklahoma City's **Stockyards**, in the southwest on Agnew Avenue and Exchange Street, are worth a visit, though vegetarians and animal-lovers should steer clear. This is the real thing, stomping, snorting and smelly, with scrawny animals shunted in and out of tiny pens for auction. The roughnecks that spend their lives here, smoking, chatting, even sleeping, take no apparent notice of the quick-fire auctioneer, but nonetheless millions of heads of cattle per year are bought and sold, and it can make addictive entertainment. Sales begin at 8am Monday to Thursday, and fizzle out by early afternoon.

Accommodation

Rooms are very cheap; try along the interstates, especially S I-35, for chain motels. B&Bs are a good deal, but even the downtown luxury hotels can be affordable.

Best Western Saddleback Inn, 4300 SW Third St (☎947-7000). Three blocks northeast of I-40, on the west side of town. $52–67. Pseudo-Indian decor, but luxurious touches like poolside service.

Country House, 10101 Oakview Rd (☎794-4008). B&B near Lake Draper in the far southeast of the city. Two rooms, $35 and $45.

Howard Johnson West, 400 S Meridian Ave (☎943-9841). Doubles $46–60, breakfast included.

Ramada Inn South, 6800 S I-35 (☎631-3321). Directly east of the airport, with functional rooms from $36. The adjoining cafe does a good breakfast and is a favourite with motorists.

The Sheraton Century Centre, 1 N Broadway (☎235-2780). Downtown luxury hotel. $65–90.

Eating

Not surprisingly, **beef** is good in Oklahoma City, especially around the stockyards. The restaurants of **Bricktown**, the restored warehouse area, are popular with the after-work and singles crowd, and there are cheap places all along I-40.

Applewoods, 4301 SW Third St (☎947-8484). Famed in the city for its good steaks and all-you-can-eat apple fritters. They're greasy and rich, but fill you up. Lunch from $4, dinner from $9.

The Cattlemen's Cafe, 1309 S Agnew Ave (☎236-0416). Cattlemen from the adjacent stockyards eat in a comfortable publike atmosphere. The restaurant, which has served beautiful steaks since 1910, was allegedly won in a crap game in 1946. Lunchtime specials under $5.

Molly Murphy's House of Fine Repute, I-40 and Meridian Ave. Fancy-dressed staff shout at and humiliate customers, who are expected, each time *Car Wash* is played, to leap up, gather at the salad bar (a 1962 Jag) and groove on down. Even so, the food is good, with fish, chicken, steaks and burgers, and you might manage to hide behind a beleaguered birthday group. Dinner around $10.

Piggy's, 303 E Sheridan Ave (☎232-3912). Good plain barbecue and beans in Bricktown, accompanied by a lively, youthful Dixieland house band. Dinner with two side orders comes to $7.45.

Pump's, 5700 N Western Ave (☎840-4369). Cheap Mexican food, omelettes and sandwiches in an old gas station. Happy hour 4–6pm, and two-for-one beer 9.30pm–midnight.

Nightlife and Entertainment

Oklahoma City can be pretty dodgy at night, especially in the isolated downtown; it's a long way from the cutting edge as regards live music or dancing. **Norman**, home to the University of Oklahoma, has campus nightlife, but it's a thirty-minute drive south. Wednesday's *Oklahoma Gazette*, along with lively articles, carries good listings.

Black Liberated Arts Center, 1901 N Ellison Ave (☎528-4266). Northwest of downtown, a variety of black theatre and musical events during the winter season.

Jokers Comedy Club, 2925 W Britton Ave (☎752-5270). Comedy shows nightly.

O'Briens Piano Bar, 104 E Sheridan Ave (☎235-3434). Bricktown dive based on the famous New Orleans bar of the same name, with a quarter of its entertainment value and a millionth of its clientele. However, it has good boozy karaoke nights, and everyone tries very hard to have fun.

Oklahoma Opry, 404 W Commerce Ave (☎632-8322). Authentic c'n'w shows, Sat at 8pm.

Guthrie

GUTHRIE, thirty miles north of downtown Oklahoma City on I-35, was the capital from statehood in 1907 until 1911. Today the 1400-acre **Guthrie Historical District** forms a remarkably complete collection of restored Victorian architecture. The **State Publishing Museum**, 301 W Harrison Avenue, exhibits printing technology from the earliest newspaper printed in Oklahoma Territory, and the ornate Doric **Scottish Rite Masonic Temple**, 900 E Oklahoma Avenue, the largest Masonic complex in the world, features hundreds of bright stained-glass windows. Guthrie is also home to the **Lazy E Arena**, four miles east of downtown, a huge site which hosts world champion rodeos and roping competitions, as well as big-name concerts (☎282-3004).

Guthrie has two good **B&Bs**. The *Stone Lion Inn*, 1016 W Warner Avenue (☎282-0012), has rooms from $50 to $75; *Harrison House*, 124 W Harrison Avenue (☎282-1000), in Guthrie's first bank building, charges from $50 to $85. The *Town House Motel*, two blocks east of US-77 at 221 E Oklahoma Avenue (☎282-2000), has doubles for $31. The local Chamber of Commerce is at 223 South First Street (☎282-1947).

MISSOURI

The state of **MISSOURI**, where the forest meets the prairie and the Mississippi River meets the Missouri River, has just two significant cities. Dominant **St Louis** sits midway down its eastern fringe, **Kansas City** is almost directly across on the western border. The pair are linked by I-70, but there's not much in between to warrant stopping off. In contrast, the **south** features the beautiful hillsides, streams and ragged lakes of the **Ozark Mountains**, while in the **east**, numerous small river towns including Mark Twain's **Hannibal** and serene **Ste Genevieve** brighten up the course of the Mississippi. The **northwest**, home of the Pony Express and the outlaw Jesse James, still manages to strike up images of frontier times.

Although the first French colonists honoured the claims of local Native Americans, such as the original Missouri, when the area was sold to the US in 1803 as part of the Louisiana Purchase the Indians were driven west by a great rush of settlers. In the 1840s and 1850s immigrants from Germany and Ireland flooded into the east. They outnumbered their pro-slavery predecessors and swung the balance in favour of staying in the Union during the Civil War. However, Confederate guerilla forces attracted considerable support among the western slave-owners. Meanwhile Missouri, and St Louis in particular, was establishing itself as an important gateway to the West.

Today, the "**Show Me State**" (so called because of the supposed scepticism of the typical Missourian) retains a conservative air, particularly in the rural areas where its Democratic party stalwarts have more in common with their colleagues in the Deep South than with the Jesse Jackson wing of the organisation.

Getting Around Missouri

The central corridor between St Louis and Kansas City is well served by *Greyhound*, and *Amtrak* runs a daily service. Infrequent *Greyhound* buses run through the southeast, to Springfield and a few Ozark towns, though to see the mountains and the river towns in the north, you'll need a car. St Louis and Kansas City have major **airports**.

Eastern Missouri

The Mississippi River defines Missouri's eastern border, taking in the major tributaries of the Missouri, Ohio, Illinois and Des Moines rivers. Innumerable towns sprang up along the river, their hopeful aspirations reflected by such classical names as Alexandria, Antioch and Athens. **Hannibal**, the boyhood home of Mark Twain and setting for his most famous novels, is the largest in the northeast, while Gallic-influenced **Ste Genevieve** is the prettiest in the south. All have, however, decreased in size as the state's major city, **St Louis**, achieved pre-eminence. Away from the river the land rises to the **Ozark Plateau**, whose deep green valleys are cut by swift clear streams.

Hannibal

HANNIBAL might well have been just another medium-sized river settlement, had not Samuel Langhorne Clemens, who renamed himself **Mark Twain** after the cry of pilots on the Mississippi, spent his boyhood here. Although Hannibal does have other industries, downtown is little more than a Twain theme park, with Twain-related attractions such as museums, donkey rides and wax displays. Businesses include the

The telephone **area code** for St Louis and eastern Missouri is ☎314.

Clemens Hotel, Tom'n'Huck Motel, Injun Joe Campground and even the *Mark Twain Roofing Company.*

What Twain actually felt about his own town is largely unknown. He wrote surprisingly little about it in his extensive non-fiction works, though you could say he spoke with his feet when he left for good at seventeen to become a journeyman printer, riverboat pilot, journalist and writer. Those of his books most specifically set in Hannibal, however – the *Adventures of Tom Sawyer* and the sequel *Adventures of Huckleberry Finn* – provide vivid accounts of what it was like for a boy to grow up in this often rowdy frontier riverport.

Hannibal is shambolically picturesque. Squeezed in between two steep bluffs – Tom Sawyer's "**Cardiff Hill**" to the north and **Lover's Leap** to the south – the once-busy **riverside** is now largely quiet except for the occasional creaking of a crane loading grain or cement. Antique, souvenir and gift shops line the north end of **Main Street**, near the short cobbled incline of **Hill Street**, among whose original buildings are Twain's father's law office, the home of the real-life Becky Thatcher (Sawyer's first love) and the **Tom Sawyer Boyhood Home** where Twain himself lived between 1844 and 1853. Adjoining the home, memorabilia at the **Mark Twain Museum** includes first editions, letters, photos, original artwork and one of his trademark white suits (daily summer 8am–6pm; rest of year times vary; $2.50; ☎221-9010).

Practicalities

Motel rates in Hannibal vary wildly according to season. The very central *Best Western Hotel Clemens*, 401 N Third Street (☎248-1150), with a pool and breakfast, is good value at $45 to $65, while the basic *Mark Twain Motor Inn*, 612 Mark Twain Avenue (☎221-1490), on the edge of downtown, costs $30 to $55. You can **camp** at the shaded *Mark Twain Campground* (☎221-1656), a mile south of the town on Hwy-79.

For delicacies like Tom Sawyer burgers or Huck Finn shakes, try the *Mark Twain Family Restaurant*, Third and Hill streets (☎221-5300). *Kelly's Etc*, 306 N 3rd Street (☎248-1266), which also serves a full range of cheap meals, is the best of the downtown **bars**. The **CVB** is at 320 Broadway (☎221-8300).

South to St Louis

For fifty miles south of Hannibal, Hwy-79 offers one of the most **scenic drives** along the Mississippi, almost continuously broken by thin, elongated, thickly wooded islands and bounded by towering limestone bluffs. Various riverports en route lost their function when railroads took away their river trade. The market town of **LOUISIANA** has coped better than others, maintaining a remarkably intact Victorian streetscape. **Riverview Park**, at Moyes and Main streets, overlooks the Mississippi; rooms at the nearby *Rivers' Edge Motel*, by the Hwy-54 bridge (☎754-4522), cost $40.

St Louis

Perched just below the confluence of the Mississippi and Missouri rivers, around three hundred miles south of Chicago and north of Memphis, cosmopolitan **ST LOUIS** (pronounced, whatever any song might say, as *Lewis*) possesses a vaguely European air, thanks to its history and highly developed cultural infrastructure. Any city capable of producing the two greatest poets of the twentieth century – Chuck Berry and T S Eliot – must have a whole lot going for it.

St Louis was founded in 1764 by the French fur trader **Pierre Laclede**, but the American immigration that followed its sale to the US under the Louisiana Purchase extinguished most of the refined air it had gained during French and Spanish rule. It subsequently acquired a crucial role as the major gateway for pioneers on the wagon trails westward. Transportation – first steamboats, then trains and now air haulage – has always been at the basis of its considerable industrial strength.

However, life has not always been a smooth trip for St Louis. The city's downtown area reached its nadir during the Seventies, gaining a national reputation for scruffiness and crime, but the past decade has seen a remarkable turnaround. Once a blight on the landscape, the revitalised **riverfront** now holds some of the city's top attractions, including the magnificent **Gateway Arch** and the restored warehouses of **Laclede's Landing**.

Try not to leave without sampling some of the **suburbs**. To the west lie arty **Central West End** and studenty **University** (or "U") **City**, on either side of prodigious **Forest Park** with its museums and playing fields. The more blue-collar **southside** features the markets, antique shops and jazz pubs of **Soulard** and the Italian shops and cafes of the **Hill**. Directly across the river in Illinois, **East St Louis**, once the stomping ground for jazz stars like Miles Davis and John Coltrane, these days has little to offer visitors.

Arrival and Information

Lambert-St Louis International Airport is ten miles southeast of downtown – $20 by taxi or $1 by bus. Some *Greyhound* **buses** call at the aiport, though the main terminal is downtown at 809 N Broadway (☎231-7800). *Amtrak* stops at 550 S 16th Street, at Market Street downtown. The *Bi-State Transit System* (☎231-2345) operates the *Levee Line*, a free downtown service between the riverside and 18th Street. Buses also go to all of the city's suburbs, but services are slow and infrequent. You can rent a **bicycle** from any of five branches of *Touring Cyclist* (☎739-4648).

The city's main **visitor centre** is in the Mansion House at 445 North Memorial Drive, near the riverfront (daily 10.30am–4.30pm; ☎241-1764 or ☎1-800/247-9791). The **post office** is at 1720 Market Street (Mon–Fri 7am–5pm; ☎436-5255; zip code 63166).

The Riverfront

The one-and-a-half-mile cobbled granite **wharf** along the Mississippi used to lie in the shadow of a dense tangle of warehouses and factories. When river trade decreased these became an embarrassing eyesore. Most were ripped down, but some of the better structures, between Eads and Martin Luther King bridges, have been restored to form **Laclede's Landing Historic District**, their cast-iron facades now fronting antique shops, office suites, restaurants and live music venues. On the **waterfront** itself, where thousands of roustabouts handled cargoes of cotton and ores, a collection of permanently moored craft house museums, theatre shows, a heliport and even a floating *Burger King*. **Cruises** aboard replica steamboats leave from under the Gateway Arch (April–Nov daily; frequent departures 10am–5pm; 1hr $6.50, 2hr $9.50; ☎621-4040).

Ten minutes' walk south, over thirty blocks of derelict buildings were ripped down to clear space for the **Jefferson National Expansion Memorial**, dedicated to the US president who negotiated the Louisiana Purchase and thereby opened up the west, and to the pioneers who journeyed along the Oregon and Santa Fe trails. Its highlight, the **Gateway Arch**, was completed in 1965, a 630-foot stainless steel parabola of quite majestic symmetry; in technical terms it's a weighted catenary curve, an outline formed by a heavy cable hanging freely from two points. The arch is at its most striking when its gleaming coat catches a stray reflection – perhaps a rich red sunset or a firework display. In less than thirty years, the unusual monument has been universally adopted as the city's emblem, used in all sorts of corporate logos and insignia.

So long as you're not claustrophobic, it's fun to take the **tram ride** up the hollow curving leg of the Arch. Tiny, windowless, five-seater capsules carry you on a stuttering four-minute ride to a viewing gallery, repeatedly stopping and starting to shift position so that you don't arrive at the top upside down. Unfortunately, after such an epic ride, the aerial view is disappointing. Lengthy queues build up during summer, but you can

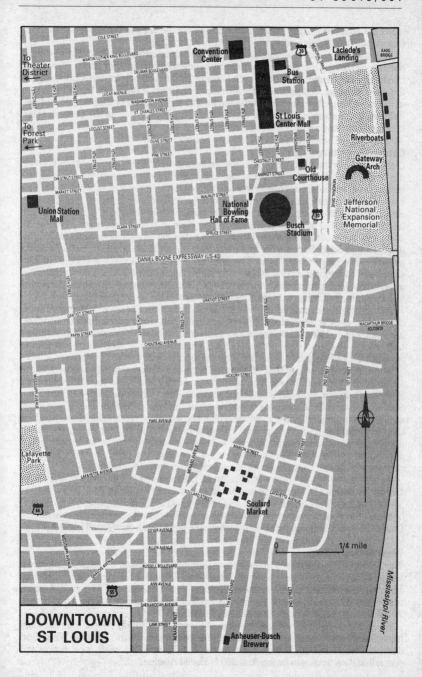

DOWNTOWN ST LOUIS

pick up a numbered ticket earlier in the day and come back at the allotted time (daily summer 8.30am–9.10pm; otherwise 9.30am–5.10pm; $2.50).

In a massive bunker beneath the Arch, the **visitor centre** (☎425-4465) screens a riveting film about the construction of the monument and another on the Lewis and Clark Expedition, which set off from St Louis in 1804 to explore the Missouri River and the water communications to the Pacific Ocean. It returned two years later with details of trade routes, Native American settlements and observations of animal and plant life. Exhibits in the spacious **Museum of Western Expansion** recount the story, drawing heavily on the pair's very readable journals.

Central Downtown

One block from the Arch along St Louis' main east–west thoroughfare, Market Street, the stately **Old Courthouse Museum** traces the development of the city and the settling of the West through excellent old photographs (daily 8am–4.30pm; free). The two courtrooms that housed the trial of **Dred Scott** have been restored. Scott, a black slave, argued that having spent time with his owner in non-slave Illinois and Wisconsin, he had the right to be set free. His case was upheld in 1850, but overturned two years later. On appeal, the Supreme Court, dominated by pro-slavery southern judges, declared that Scott, born a slave in a slave state, might like any other chattel be taken anywhere his master chose to go. The decision, which meant that the US Constitution saw slaves as legitimate personal property, sent shock waves through the corridors of government, and hastened the onrush of Civil War. Scott himself, by now a nationally known figure, was voluntarily freed by his new owner, but died a year later.

A couple of blocks away, bounded by Walnut, Broadway, Spruce and Seventh streets, the circular **Busch Stadium** stands out amongst acres of car parks. Each of its 54,000 gleaming red and blue seats provides an unobstructed view of St Louis Cardinals **baseball** games (daily tours $2.50; ☎241-3900). Underneath the stadium, the **St Louis Sports Hall of Fame** highlights the greats associated with this sports-mad city.

The **National Bowling Hall of Fame**, Eighth and Walnut streets, is devoted to the favourite sport of such diverse figures as Martin Luther and TV cartoon fallguy Homer Simpson (summer Mon–Sat 9am–7pm, Sun noon–7pm; otherwise Mon–Sat 9am–5pm, Sun noon–5pm; $3). It succeeds in utterly capturing your attention, even if you know nothing about the game. The most absorbing section is the remarkable display tracing the history of the sport from ancient Egyptian times to the present. Bowling was not always the slick commercial sport it is today; excessive betting on games got it denounced by the church in fifteenth-century Germany and, three centuries later, the behaviour of drunken fans led to all alleys being shut down in London.

Further along Market Street at 18th Street, the focal point of the giant Romanesque **Union Station** is a 230-ft clock tower. Closed as a railway station in 1971, it now houses a hotel and two floors of shops, cafes and bars, with an artificial lake, where you can rent boats, at the rear. Downtown's other main concentration of retail outlets is at the **St Louis Centre**, Washington and Sixth streets, the largest city centre mall in the US.

West of Downtown

The **Theater District**, three miles west of downtown, is staked out with ornate street lamps along Grand Avenue between Lindell and Delmar boulevards. Bright posters advertise the current shows at the **Fabulous Fox Theater**, 527 N Grand Avenue, where you can have a look at its magnificent Siamese-Byzantine interior and massive Wurlitzer organ (tours Tues, Thurs & Sat; ☎534-1678).

About a mile further west, on the edge of Forest Park, trendy shops, wine bars and turn-of-the-century mansions line the leafy thoroughfares of the **Central West End** district. One of the city's best **bookstores**, *Left Bank Books*, with good fiction and secondhand sections, can be found at 399 N Euclid Avenue.

THE POETS OF ST LOUIS

Thomas Stearns Eliot, who as a naturalised Englishman won the Nobel Prize for Literature in 1948, was born in St Louis on September 26 1888. His family were Unitarian aristocrats who traced their ancestry back to the earliest days of settlement in New England; his grandfather, the Rev William Eliot, founded St Louis' Washington University. Eliot lived in the city until he was seventeen, and went to school at Smith Academy on Union Avenue, a period which he later referred to as one of the happiest of his life. The "Prufrock" of his first major poem, *The Love Song of J Alfred Prufrock*, was a St Louis furniture dealer; "the yellow fog that rubs its back upon the window-panes" was the smog drifting across the Mississippi from the city's factories.

Once Eliot moved to Boston, to attend Harvard University, and then on to Europe, he rarely returned, and he deliberately threw off his drawling St Louis accent. The house in which he was born, at 2635 Locust Street, has long since been torn down, and the only memorial to him in the city is the incongruous brass star set into the sidewalk of Delmar Boulevard as part of the St Louis Walk of Fame.

Another honoree of the Walk of Fame, **Chuck Berry**, first saw the light of day on October 18 1926 at 2520 Goode Avenue – hence his most famous song, *Johnny B Goode*. Berry played his earliest gigs at the *Cosmopolitan Club* at 17th and Bond streets in East St Louis. Initially seen as a bizarre hybrid, a black hillbilly singing country and western songs, within a few months of his first recording for *Chess Records* in Chicago (*Maybellene*, in 1955) Chuck Berry's blend of razor-sharp lyrics and incisive guitar (not to mention his legendary business acumen) had made him the definitive rock'n'roll songwriter.

The decision to site **Forest Park** four miles directly west of downtown (#93 bus) aroused much criticism during the 1870s, opponents claiming that its inaccessibility would mean the park was merely going to be a pleasure ground for the rich who had homes in the area. Larger than New York's Central Park, it contains just as many things to do, though busy roads spoil any sense of tranquillity.

Standing on Arts Hill in the central west section of the park, the striking Beaux-Arts **St Louis Museum of Art** is the only remaining structure from the World's Fair held here in 1904. It sets itself an ambitious brief to cover international art from prehistoric times to the present, but none of its galleries can be considered as weak points or fillers. It houses one of the most extensive collections of **German Expressionism** in the world, devoting an entire gallery to the powerful, spiralling and jagged images of Max Beckmann, and its **pre-Columbian artworks** cover every significant style, medium and culture from Mexico to Peru. Daily tours of the highlights start at 1.30pm (Tues 1.30–8.30pm, Wed, Thurs, Sat & Sun 10am–5pm, Fri 10am–8.30pm; free).

In addition to almost three hundred animals in its "cageless displays", **St Louis Zoo** features the "Living World" educational exhibit in which Charles Darwin has evolved into an animatronic robot giving synopses of his theories (daily 9am–5pm; free).

The main strengths of the **History Museum**, on the northern fringe of the park, are the thematic collections of old pictures of St Louis documenting river life, black music in the city and Charles Lindbergh's 1927 flight in the *Spirit of St Louis* (sponsored by the city's aircraft industry) from New York to Paris (Tues–Sun 9.30am–4.45pm; free).

Southside

The tens of thousands of Germans who came to St Louis in the mid-eighteenth century settled mostly in the **southside**, which has retained a noticeable Teutonic influence. They were skilled **brewers**; only one of the breweries they opened from the 1850s onwards still stands, but it does happen to be the largest in the world. The **Anheuser-Busch** plant, at Broadway and Pestalozzi, produces a sizeable proportion of the company's 1100 million-plus cases of beer each year including *Budweiser* and *Michelob*.

The buildings themselves are architecturally interesting: over one hundred intricate red-brick structures. Free **tours** last eighty minutes; they're mostly company PR but it's still good fun, and at the end you get two glasses of the company product before being shunted into the gift shop (summer Mon–Sat 9.30am–4pm; otherwise Mon–Fri only).

Red, white and green fireplugs let you know that you're in the nearby thirty-square-block **Hill** district, a working-class **Italian** community made up of small, neat homes. At its heart, **St Ambrose Church** displays a statue of Italian immigrants; all around, the aroma of freshly baked bread drifts out of the small speciality bakeries that share the area with one-room grocery stores and dozens of restaurants.

Further west at 4344 Shaw Boulevard, the 79-acre **Missouri Botanical Gardens** are a haven of peace and tranquillity, just a few hundred yards from busy I-44. The gardens contain everything from a magnificent Japanese Garden surrounding a small lake and adorned with stepping-stones, arched bridges and wooden teahouse, through scented, rose and English woodland gardens to the Climatron, a huge greenhouse that re-creates a tropical rainforest complete with waterfalls and cliffs. (Summer Sun–Tues, Thurs & Fri 9am–8pm, Wed & Sat 7.30am–8pm; otherwise Sun–Tues, Thurs & Fri 9am–5pm, Wed & Sat 7.30am–5pm; $2, free until noon Wed & Sat.)

Accommodation

Nearly all **rooms** in downtown St Louis are expensive during the week, but even the swanky hotels do good weekend specials. The *B&B Greater St Louis Reservation Service*, PO Box 30069, MO 63119 (☎961-2252), provides rooms from $40 to $85. The closest **camping** is at the *St Louis RV Park*, 900 N Jefferson Avenue (☎241-3330).

Forest Park Hotel, 4910 W Pine Blvd (☎361-3500). Comfortable rooms in a building that's getting on a bit in years but is well maintained. Close to the park with pool, sauna and bar. $55–65.

Huckleberry Finn Youth Hostel, 1904–6 S 12th St (☎241-0076). Dormitories and single rooms. On the edge of a dodgy area, so it's best to take #13 bus. $10 *AYH*, $13 non-members.

Motel 6, 4576 Woodson Rd (☎427-1313). Good value, with outdoor pool. Close to the airport. $34.

Red Roof Inn, 5823 Wilson Ave (☎645-0101). No-frills budget option in midtown, reasonably near Forest Park and the Hill. $38–44.

Thrifty Inn, 1100 N Third St (☎421-6556). The cheapest downtown option. Double rooms for $48.

Washington University, Big Bend and Wydown blvds (☎889-5050). Rooms on campus between June and mid-August for around $16 per person. Ideal for U City shops and Forest Park.

Eating

Italian eating places, ranging from the humble salami seller to five-star establishments where a meal will set you back $100, dominate St Louis cuisine. Most of the clean, friendly **Irish** pubs serve beef sandwiches and stew. For a wide selection of ethnic foods, go to **Delmar Boulevard** in University City, which offers a choice of African, Middle Eastern, Chinese, Indian, Jamaican and many others. More expensive cafes can be found in **Laclede's Landing**, downtown, and the **Central West End**.

Duff's, 392 N Euclid Ave, Central West End (☎361-0522). Small, relaxed, moderately priced restaurant. The menu bears a heavy flavour of France. Good homemade desserts and Sunday brunch.

John D McGurk's Irish Pub, 1200 Russell Blvd at 12th St, Soulard (☎776-8309). Fresh-baked soda bread, corned beef'n'cabbage, Irish stew and imported Guinness are just some of the things to tempt you to this cheery bar/cafe with live Irish music every night.

O'Connell's Pub, 4652 Shaw at Kingshighway (☎773-6600). The best burgers in the city, and the beef sandwiches aren't bad either. Near the Hill district.

Red Sea, 6511 Delmar Blvd, U City (☎863-0099). Cheap and cheerful Ethiopian restaurant; *berbere* sauce with everything. The decor is basic and the service slow, but the food's great.

Rigazzi's, 4945 Daggett Blvd, the Hill (☎772-4900). Popular trattoria, famous for "frozen fish bowls" of beer. Over thirty different pasta dishes, all at $7, plus pizzas, veal, chicken and steak entrees.

Saleem's, 6501 Delmar Blvd, U City (☎721-7947). "Where garlic is king" and St Louisans reckon you get the best ethnic food in the city. Lebanese and continental menu; reasonably inexpensive.

Sunshine Inn, 80 N Euclid Ave, Central West End (☎367-1413). Innovative vegetarian menu. Great salads made even better by their unusual dressings. Main courses around $5–8.

Nightlife

The highest concentration of bars and clubs in downtown St Louis can be found in **Laclede's Landing**, where there's jazz, blues, rock and reggae on offer every night. Some of the outlying districts are well worth checking out in the evening; these include the Loop in **U City**, whose bars and cafes are not just popular with students, the slightly more upmarket cafes and wine bars of **Central West End** and the unpretentious jazz pubs in **Soulard**. Every spring, the four-day Mid-America Jazz festival brings the top names together for performances all over St Louis.

Don't forget also to check out what's on in the **Theater District**, centred on North Grand Boulevard in midtown. All listings can be found in the excellent weekly free paper the *Riverfront Times*.

Blueberry Hill, 6504 Delmar Blvd, U City (☎727-0880; band info ☎726-0066). Crammed full of memorabilia, with the downstairs dedicated to Elvis and a jukebox acclaimed as the best in the country by *Cashbox* magazine. Live entertainment every weekend, good drinks and burgers at any time.

Cicero's Basement Bar, 6510 Delmar Blvd, U City (☎862-0009). Downstairs club putting on jazz fusion, acoustic and "alternative" music.

Dub Club, 214 Morgan St, Laclede's Landing (☎231-CLUB). Small venue playing mostly reggae music with many live acts.

Hilary's, 1015 Russell, Soulard (☎421-3126). Set in a former residential property, this cosy pub venue provides an intimate setting for live jazz every night of the week and Saturday afternoon.

Muddy Waters Saloon, 724 N First St, Laclede's Landing (☎421-5335). Jazz/blues club.

South of St Louis

The French and German heritage of tiny **STE GENEVIEVE**, sixty miles south of St Louis, is conspicuous through its architecture, cafes and festivals, though its graceful old French homes, characterised by vertical log construction, are under constant threat from flooding. The central *Ste Genevieve Inn*, Main and Merchant streets (☎883-3562), offers rooms for $30 to $42, while interesting Amish variations on catfish, chicken and seafood are on the menu in the *Anvil Saloon*, 46 S 3rd Street (☎883-7323).

Fifty-five miles downriver, **CAPE GIRADEAU** looks down on the Mississippi from a rocky ledge. Among the antebellum and Victorian buildings of the town centre is the *Port Cape Giradeau*, 19 N Water Street (☎334-0954), which serves tasty ribs. The *Cape Budget Inn* at I-55 exit 96 (☎334-0501), with indoor and outdoor pools, is good value at $35 per night. The road continues south to Arkansas from here through reclaimed swamplands, rich in wheat, corn and melons, but little else.

Kansas City and Around

KANSAS CITY, 250 miles due west of St Louis, straddles the state line between Kansas and Missouri. On the more interesting Missouri side, set in pretty countryside near the Lake of the Ozarks, hundreds of fountains, boulevards, and Art Deco and Mediterranean-style buildings, and the slow but encouraging revitalisation of downtown, are unusual and welcome features in a Midwestern city. Kansas City, Kansas, on the other hand, is a dull sprawl of suburbs that deserves little, if any, attention.

Kansas City was a convenient stopping point for 1830s wagon trains on the main routes west. Its consequent prosperity (and rough and tumble "sin city" image) lasted well into the 1850s, but was brought to an abrupt end by the Civil War. However, in the 1870s, the coming of the railroads revived its fortunes, effecting a major boom in livestock packing and the development of the famous stockyards.

Thanks to the notoriously corrupt Mayor Pendergast, an outrageous figure with whom the city still has a love-hate relationship, its many jazz clubs were permitted to sell alcohol during Prohibition. As in Chicago and New Orleans, speakeasies, brothels and gambling dens went hand in hand with some superlative **jazz** – and, to a lesser extent, blues – spawning the careers of Count Basie, Duke Ellington and, in the Fifties, Charlie Parker. Kansas City's jazz scene is currently enjoying a resurgence, and plenty of good clubs and live venues cater for die-hard fans.

Arrival, Information and Getting Around

From **Kansas City International Airport** (☎243-5200), twenty-five miles northwest of downtown, a convenient forty-minute **shuttle bus** (☎243-5950) heads to major downtown hotels ($11) and the *Greyhound* station ($9), every half-hour from 5.45am until 11.30pm. The equivalent **taxi** ride costs around $25.

The *Greyhound* terminal itself is well out from the centre of town at 12th Street and Troost Avenue, and rather isolated (☎698-0080). *Amtrak* is in the old Union Station at 23rd and Main streets opposite the Crown Center. *Metro Buses*, 1350 E 17th Street (☎221-0660), run more than 35 **bus** routes, including one to Independence, MO, with extensive downtown coverage (Mon–Fri 6am–6pm). Five **trolleys** run a continuous loop between downtown, the Crown Center, Westport, and the Country Club Plaza ($3 round trip). *Gray Line*, 1212 E Tenth Street (☎471-5996), does a two-hour **city tour** for $10, starting at 10am, and a three-hour tour of "Truman country" for $15.

Kansas City's **visitor centre** is at 1100 Main Street (Mon–Fri 8.30–5pm; ☎221-5242); its **post office** at 315 W Pershing Road (Mon–Fri 8am–6.30pm, Sat 8am–12.30pm; ☎374-9275; zipcode 64108).

The telephone **area code** for Kansas City and around is ☎816.

The City

Kansas City is doing a good job of reinvigorating its **downtown**, putting the commercial and residential needs of its citizens first. There are few tourist attractions, but some good bars and restaurants. Most sights lie further south, though wandering past the restored lofts and small businesses of the **Garment District**, between Sixth and Ninth streets, makes a nice route to **City Hall**, 414 E 12th Street, a fine Art Deco building with an observation deck on its thirtieth floor (Mon–Fri 8.30am–4.15pm; free.)

The **18th and Vine Heritage District**, south of I-70 as it sweeps east–west, was the hub of the city's 1920s **jazz scene**. There's not much to see now, except a depressing series of empty lots and some good clubs, but plans are underway to revitalise the area. The **Black Archives of Mid America**, 2033 Vine Street, is a gallery of black arts, painting and sculpture, with extensive research facilities (Mon–Fri 9am–4.30pm; 50¢).

Although the once huge Kansas City cattle market has dwindled considerably, the **Stockyards** at Genessee Avenue and 17th Street, just south of downtown on bus route #12, still hold auctions (Tues–Thurs) and special events throughout the year.

The sprawling concrete **Crown Center**, on Grand and Pershing roads, funded by *Hallmark Cards*, calls itself "a city within a city", with apartments, shops, restaurants, offices and hotels. Its splendidly awful **Hallmark Visitors Center** has an interesting display on the history of design, tracing styles of greetings cards alongside political and cultural changes, and demonstrating printing processes and hand decoration, but it's a strain to keep a straight face at the sentiment that cards are "messengers of the heart" which "aid humans in their love for one another" (Mon–Fri 9am–5pm, Sat 9.30am–4.30pm; free). Nearby **Union Station** is a Kansas City landmark; huge, and still riddled with the bullet holes from a Pretty Boy Floyd shoot-out. Across from the Crown Center and Union Station at 100 W 26th Street, the tall skinny **Liberty Memorial** commemorates World War I, with a small museum and a life-scale representation of a trench. There's a good view from its 217ft observation deck (Tues–Sun 9.30am–4.30pm; 50¢).

Westport, between 39th and 45th streets, is an attractive district of good restaurants, cafes and trendy shops that was the original jumping-off point for the Santa Fe Trail. Stop off for a drink at the oldest building in the city, *Kelly's Westport Inn*, 500 Westport Street, a shabby but friendly red brick bar. Beginning at 47th and Main streets, the elegant Country Club Plaza dates from the early Twenties. Tree- shaded and upmarket (with branches of *Gucci* and *Saks*), its tiling, mosaics, fountains and orange trees evoke the streets of Spain, and the replica of a Sevillan tower completes the effect. A self-guided walking art tour of the Plaza, available from the CVB, identifies the many murals, tile works and sculptures.

The extensive **Nelson Atkins Museum of Art**, 4525 Oak Street, has superb Oriental exhibits, plus Van Goghs, Monets and Rembrandts, with twelve Henry Moore sculptures on the grounds (Tues–Sat 10am–5pm, Sun 1–5pm; $3, free on Sat). The pretty **Toy and Miniatures Museum**, south at 5235 Oak Street, includes an offbeat collection of antique toys, games and puppets (Wed–Sat 10am–4pm, Sun 1–4pm; $2.50).

Quiet **Loose Park**, at 51st Street and Wornall Road, was the site of the 1863 Battle of Westport, a comprehensive Confederate defeat. The park now belies its violent history with an attractive rose garden, jogging paths and a lake.

The **Kansas City Museum**, in the north of the city near the Missouri River, is worth the trek (or take bus #30) ten blocks north of Independence Avenue to 3218 Gladstone Boulevard, if only for the ice creams from its restored 1910 drug store. You can also see Native American artefacts and costumes, vintage photographs, and a Planetarium (Tues–Sat 9.30am–4.30pm, Sun noon–4.30pm; $3.50).

Independence and Liberty

Bus #24 goes to the small town of **INDEPENDENCE**, ten minutes east of the city, which was the scene of violent battles in the 1830s between the polygamous **Mormons** and hostile Anglo-American settlers, who reacted to the growth of the religious group by burning down their houses and instigating armed raids on Mormon communities; eventually the Mormons migrated en masse to Utah.

Independence is, however, most famous as the former home of President Harry S Truman. The **Truman Library** on US-24 and Delaware Street includes a reconstruction of his White House office, and chilling documents pertaining to the development of the atomic bomb (daily 9am–5pm; $2). The Victorian **Truman Home**, a mile south at 219 S Delaware Street, is decorated as it was when used as the summer White House (tours 8.30am–5pm; $1). The 1859 **Marshal's Home and Jail Museum**, 217 Main Street, has restored dungeon-like cells that incarcerated such villains as Confederate guerilla leader Quantrill, and a museum of regional history with exhibits on early settlers, the Mormons and slavery (Mon–Sat 10am–5pm, Sun 1–4pm; $2).

If this has developed your taste for criminal history, head for **LIBERTY**, fifteen miles from the centre of Kansas City. The **Jesse James Bank Museum**, on the Old Town Square, is where James staged the first ever daylight bank robbery in 1866. There's lots of Jesse James memorabilia, and you can see the vault and the safe that he raided, along with some dusty relics of early banking (daily 9am–5pm; $1.75).

Accommodation

Kansas City's cheapest hotels lie along the interstates or out towards Independence, but there are some reasonable central options. For **B&B**, contact Diane Kuhn or Edwina Monroe, *Kansas City B&B*, Box 14781, Lenexa, KS 66215 (☎913/268-4214).

There's **camping** at *Kansas City East KOA*, Box 191, I-70 at Oak Grove exit (☎625-7515), or thirteen miles from downtown in a 1500-acre wooded area containing a 330ft lake: *Wyandotte County Park*, on N Hwy-5 at 91st Street (☎229-0550).

Best Western Seville Plaza, 4309 Main St (☎561-9600). Doubles $50–55. Good central position.

Comfort Inn, 801 Westport Rd (☎931-1000). Doubles $55–64. Free continental breakfast; near the lively Westport district.

Days Hotel, 1215 Wyandotte Ave (☎471-1333). Doubles $54–64, in a downtown location which can feel a bit isolated at night.

Hotel Savoy, 219 W Ninth St (☎891-7788). Bed and breakfast doubles for $60 in an 1888 building.

Rodeway Inn, Sixth and Main streets (☎842-9060). Doubles $60. Coin laundry and 24hr cafe.

Eating

Barbecue, once the unfashionable food of the poor, is big news in Kansas City; cheap, cheerful, hickory-smoked and served with a variety of tasty sauces. The many good **steak** restaurants tend to be duller, and more expensive. Restaurants in the **Crown Center** are quite good but overpriced; many require formal dress. The **Plaza** has some great restaurants, but again, they're not that cheap; relaxed **Westport** is a better bet.

Annie's Santa Fe, 100 Ward Parkway (☎753-1621). Popular Mexican restaurant in the Plaza area, decorated with Hopi and Navajo crafts. Dinner $4.50–8.

Arthur Bryant's, 1727 Brooklyn Ave (☎231-1123). *The* place for barbecue, a mile east of downtown in a desolate area. The largest portions you will ever see of barbecue and beans; the $5 combo plate easily feeds two hefty appetites. The murky bottles in the window contain the crucial sauces. This is serious business – be sure not to dawdle in the queue, as novices are given short shrift.

Fedora Cafe and Bar, 210 W 47th St (☎561-6565). Bistro-style eating in the Plaza, with Italian food and discreet classical music. Seafood and pasta costs around $4 for lunch, $8 for dinner.

The Golden Ox, 160 Genessee Ave (☎842-2866). Next to the stockyards. The cheap cafe does steak lunches, while the adjacent restaurant has pricier evening meals.

Prospect of Westport, 4109 Pennsylvania St (☎753-2227). Fresh fish and pasta. Dinner $5–20.

Stanford and Sons, 504 Westport Rd (☎756-1450). Lively and popular Westport spot. Dinner costs $4–15, and there's a comedy club adjacent every night except Sunday.

Nightlife and Entertainment

Check out the reviving **jazz** and **blues** scene in Kansas City, especially the authentic dives where you'll hear wonderful jamming sessions into the early hours. Friday's *Kansas City Star* has detailed listings, as does *Pitch*, a free monthly. For more information, call *The Kansas City Jazz Embassadors* (☎942-3349); *The Blues Society* (☎531-7557); or the *Jazz Hotline* (☎931-2888). Many clubs also feature rock and R&B, so call in advance if only jazz will do.

Downtown is otherwise pretty dead by mid-evening, and most people head to **Westport** for nightlife from country and western to alternative rock. In the summer, big-name bands play **free concerts** in the square at Crown Center; bring your own picnic and booze, and get there early for a good position. Showtime is 8pm Friday.

The Auditorium Bar and Grill, 217 W 14th St (☎421-8483). Good atmosphere and a good bar, with occasional jazz one-nighters.

Birdland, 1600 E 19th St (☎842-8463). Seedy and authentic jazz club, in historic 18th and Vine area.

Blayneys, 415 Westport Rd (☎501-3747). Live music in the cellar, with blues every Monday.

Club Eblon, 1601 E 18th St (☎221-6612). Nicely restored jazz club in the 18th and Vine district.

The Grand Emporium, 3832 Main St (☎531-1504). R&B, blues, reggae and jazz with Cajun and Jamaican food. Voted the best blues club in America by the National Blues Foundation.

Kikis Bon Ton Maison, 1515 Westport Rd (☎931-9417). Cajun food, plus Cajun and zydeco music.

The Mutual Musicians Foundation, 1823 Highland Ave (☎421-9229). National Historic Landmark in the 18th and Vine district. Fierce jam sessions begin at 1.30am Fri & Sat, musicians competing in a frenzy for hours. It can get a bit rough, and is not recommended for women alone.

The Phoenix Piano Bar and Grill, Eighth St and Central Ave (☎472-0001). Downtown piano jazz.

The Tuba, 333 Southwest Blvd (☎471-6510). Small club, with restaurant, live music Tues–Sat, jazz on Sat evenings.

St Joseph

Twenty-eight miles north of Kansas City, **ST JOSEPH** (commonly known as St Joe) boomed as a supply depot for the California Gold Rush, and today is still a thriving manufacturing town with a number of beautiful parks and fine Romanesque homes. For a brief eighteen months, starting in 1860, it was the home of the legendary **Pony Express**, which delivered mail all the way to Sacramento, California, by continuous horseback relay. The Pony Express was a financial disaster, driven out of business by its inability to compete with the transcontinental telegraph, but riders such as Buffalo Bill Cody and Pony Bob Haslam became some of the most colourful figures of the Wild West. The full story is told at the **Pony Express Museum**, 914 Penn Street, attractively set in the company's original stables (April–Sept daily; $2).

The larger **St Joseph Museum**, 11th and Charles streets, houses an exceptional collection of Native American artefacts, with interesting displays on the history of the west, the Civil War and outlaws including the Jesse James gang (April–Sept daily; Oct–March Tues–Sat; $2). It was in St Joseph, on April 3 1882, that the notorious **Jesse James** was shot in the back by Robert Ford, one of his own gang members. James' exploits have been romanticised by countless books and films, portraying him as a latterday Robin Hood figure; in fact, he spent most of the Civil War riding with a band of Confederate guerillas. After hostilities ended he claimed that persecution of his family forced him to become an outlaw; among his exploits was the first ever train robbery, in 1873. The **Jesse James Home**, a one-storey frame cottage, is at 12th and Penn streets (April–Oct daily; Nov–March Tues–Sat; $2).

Among **motels** on or near I-29, the *Drury Inn*, 4213 Frederick Boulevard at exit 47 (☎364-4700), has doubles from $50. *Barbarosa's* at 4804 Frederick Avenue (☎232-0221) serves cheap home-cooked Mexican food.

Southwest Missouri – Ozark Country

There's little to see **south of Kansas City** before the **Ozark Mountains**. Occupying most of southern Missouri and northern Arkansas (see p.539), the area remained frontier territory until the timber companies moved in at the end of the century. When they moved on, the hill-dwellers were left to eke out a living from the denuded terrain. Terrible droughts forced many to leave for the cities. For those who remained, fishing resorts and tourist attractions supply some work, though the region remains poor and economically backward. None of the Ozark peaks is particularly high, but the roads through switch, dip, climb and swerve to provide stunning views of steep hillsides, thick with oak, elm, hickory and redbud and quite resplendent in autumn.

SPRINGFIELD, the gateway to the Ozarks 170 miles south of Kansas City, is blighted by mile after mile of shopping malls, car showrooms, places to eat and vast hospital complexes. If you want to stop over, try the excellent downtown *Walnut Street Inn*, 900 E Walnut Street, and *Cottage Inn* a few doors along (☎864-6346 for both), offering bed and imaginative breakfasts for $50 to $90.

The resort of **BRANSON** nestles in beautiful Ozarks scenery around Table Rock Lake and Lake Taneycom, forty miles south of Springfield on US-65. A major centre for **live country music**, its twenty-one different theatres and numerous smaller venues total around 30,000 seats, a figure said to exceed even that of Nashville. The biggest mainstream country names play at the **Roy Clark Celebrity Theater** (☎334-7535), while stars such as Boxcar Willie, Mel Tillis and Mickey Gilley have their own venues. Branson is, however, geared wholeheartedly towards the family market; you won't find anything remotely progressive or avant-garde. **Motel** prices change radically according to season, but the *Paramount Motor Lodge* (☎334-2111) on the US-65 Business route usually has nice rooms for under $40.

KANSAS

Today's cutesy, gingham-pinafore image of **KANSAS**, immediately associated with *Little House on the Prairie* and *The Wizard of Oz*, is a far cry indeed from the troubled history which made it known as "bleeding Kansas". It took three hundred years after Coronado came in search of gold in 1541 before pioneers established trails across the region, and Kansas' bid for statehood in 1861 is often cited as the catalyst for the Civil War. The 1854 Kansas-Nebraska Act, which gave both territories the right to self-determination over slavery, led to fierce clashes between Free Staters and pro-slavery forces. Runaway slaves from the south were given passage through the area, aided by abolitionist John Brown, and Kansas eventually joined the Union as a free state.

After the war, the mighty cattle drives from Texas made towns like **Abilene**, **Wichita** and **Dodge City** centres of the "**Wild West**". The debauched, male image of the West, spawning heroes like Wyatt Earp and Wild Bill Hickok, is, however, challenged in Kansas, which as well as being the first state to give women the vote in municipal elections, boasts the nation's first female mayor and senator, as well as aviatrix Amelia Earhart and the battling Prohibitionist Carry Nation.

In 1874, Mennonite immigrants from Russia brought the grain that was to transform the state into the bountiful "bread basket" which today harvests most of the nation's wheat. However, only in the west of the state do miles of golden corn sway in Kansas' infamous gusty wind. The green and hilly northeast, patterned with woods and lakes, is home to the capital city **Topeka**, liberal university town **Lawrence**, and, straddling the border with Missouri, Kansas City's dull suburbs. The wild and sparse northwest is pioneer country, while the once-wicked cowtown **Dodge City** is in the southwest. **Wichita**, Kansas' largest city, lies in the south central area.

Getting Around

Greyhound **buses** run to all Kansas's main cities, supplemented by erratic smaller companies; service to the west and southwest is especially poor. *Amtrak* **trains** head east–west through the centre of the state, calling at Lawrence, Topeka, Newton (for Wichita, but without a connecting service), Dodge City and Garden City. Wichita has the state's biggest **airport**.

East Kansas

Undulating **east Kansas** is laced with rivers, lakes and parks. The **northeast**, crossed in the 1840s by the Oregon, Santa Fe and Smoky Hill trails, and claiming both the state capital **Topeka**, and **Lawrence**, home to the University of Kansas, is more heavily visited than the southeast, where the major sight is TV's *Little House on the Prairie*, just south of Independence on SW US-75.

Lawrence

LAWRENCE, a mellow town on the Kansas River, lies roughly halfway between Kansas City and Topeka. Tree-lined streets, a welcoming historic downtown and an aura of old-hippy artsiness make it an appealing destination, with a cultural energy due in part to the State University and a long history of liberalism and intellectualism. Founded by the New England Emigrant Aid Company in 1854 and a centre of Free State activities, Lawrence was the site of a violent Civil War skirmish in 1863, when Missourian Confederate guerilla leader **Quantrill** led about 300 men on the town, killing over 150, wounding hundreds more, and setting much of the place alight. Rebuilding was quick, however, as evidenced by the limestone and brick buildings that you see today.

> The telephone **area code** for Lawrence and east Kansas is ☎913.

Lawrence is a delight to walk around, with or without the CVB's walking-tour maps. **Downtown**, centred on **Massachusetts Street**, is a rare town centre with a human face. Quiet out of season, it hots up in the summer when day-trippers from less congenial big cities come for its vintage shops and arts and crafts centres. The tantalisingly scatty **Elizabeth Watkins Community Museum** (Tues–Sat 10am–4pm, Sun 1.30pm–4pm; free), 1047 Massachusetts Street, is an eclectic assortment of Lawrence memorabilia with an enthusiastic, makeshift feel. Photographs and old documents demonstrate the town's black history, from the influx of southern blacks during and after the Civil War to civil rights clashes in the 1960s and a statue of gay black poet Langston Hughes, who spent five years of his childhood here. All this plus an extensive **barbed wire** collection, old toys, a restored barbershop and a "Kansas All Sports Hall of Fame".

Kansas University campus is on a steep, tree-covered grassy bank known as **Mount Oread**, dotted with old limestone red-roofed buildings. On Jayhawk Boulevard along the crest of the hill, Romanesque Spooner Hall houses a **Museum of Anthropology**; amongst its artefacts are a totem pole, Aboriginal bark paintings, Eskimo fishing equipment and African thrones (Mon–Sat 9am–5pm, Sun 1–5pm; free). In nearby Dyche Hall, the **Museum of Natural History** holds a chronological historic panorama of North American plants and animals, and an exhibit on the Battle of Little Bighorn which features Custer's beloved, enormous – and now stuffed – horse, *Comanche* (Mon–Sat 8am–5pm, Sun 1–5pm; $2). Also on campus, the **Spencer Art Museum**, opposite the union on Mississippi Street, specialises in world art, with an Oriental gallery, Old Masters and Pre-Raphaelites. Graphic art from the Sixties include some Warhols, and exceptional photographs, from Diane Arbus' disturbing portraits to Weegee's documentary exposes of New York City life. Its gift shop does a great line in surreal and offbeat postcards (Tues–Sat 8.30am–5pm, Sun noon–5pm; free).

Practicalities

Amtrak comes into Lawrence at 413 E Seventh Street, and *Greyhound* to the tiny hut at 1401 W Sixth Street (☎843-5622). The **CVB** is downtown at Eighth and Vermont streets (Mon–Fri 8.30am–5pm; ☎865-4411). Public transport is provided by the kitsch Fifties-style *Lawrence Bus Co*; in term-time routes run throughout the city from 7am until 6pm, but in summer there's only a shuttle bus between the university and downtown.

Rooms can be found near the bus station for between $30 and $40 at the *Virginia Inn*, 2907 W Sixth Street (☎843-6611), or the *Westminster Inn*, 2525 W Sixth Street (☎841-8410). Both these places are adequate but dull; if you have a little extra money, head instead to the lovely *Eldridge Hotel*, at Seventh and Massachusetts streets (☎749-5011). Twice burned down by pro-Slavery forces, the present hotel has been restored to an evocative faded elegance. Suites with kitchen facilities go for $55.

Lawrence is a good place for **vegetarian** and **health food**. The *Yellow Sub* (☎841-3268), and, next door, the *Glass Onion* (☎841-2310), both on campus at 12th Street and Mount Oread, serve lunch in a laid-back atmosphere with sweeping views. Downtown, the *Paradise Cafe*, 728 Massachusetts Street (☎842-5199), does veggie burgers, soups and salads; meat lovers can fill up with the hickory smoked barbecue at *Buffalo Bob's Smokehouse*, 719 Massachusetts Street (☎841-6100). *Tin Pan Alley*, 1105 Massachusetts Street (☎749-9756), can get rowdy, but is deservedly popular for its Mexican food.

Lawrence's **nightlife** is dominated by students. Two popular bars on Massachusetts Street are the *Jazzhaus*, at no. 926 (☎749-3320), and the *Kansas Sports Bar and Grill*, no. 701 (☎749-5011). *Liberty Hall*, at no. 642 (☎749-1912), had a long history as a social and political centre, and housed Lawrence's first newspaper, until it was burned down by pro-slavery agitators in 1856. Today it puts on art-house films, plays and concerts.

Topeka

Industrial **TOPEKA**, the state capital, is twenty-five miles and a whole world away from Lawrence, east on US-40. Created as a railway terminus, it is still reliant on the offices and machine shops of the railroad, as well as steelworks, printing, meatpacking and tyres. If you must stop here, take a look at the State Capitol, on a twenty-acre square in the heart of the city at Tenth and Harrison streets. Its sky-blue dome rises over 300 feet, and it is decorated inside with seemingly hundreds of different kinds of marble. The **Kansas Museum of History**, 6425 SW Sixth Street, includes a Wichita Indian grass lodge, a Cheyenne tepee, prairie displays and a covered wagon (Mon–Sat 9am–4.30pm, Sun 12.30–4pm; free). Topeka is home to the **Menninger Clinic and Foundation**, a research and treatment centre for mental illness; its museum, 5600 W Sixth Street, has a huge collection of Sigmund Freud's papers (Mon–Fri 8.45am–4.30pm).

You'd do better to stay in nearby Lawrence, but if you find yourself in Topeka, there are cheap **motels** along US-75, which becomes Topeka Avenue as it runs north–south through the town, and on I-70 to the west. More pleasant (and more expensive) is the *Heritage House B&B*, 3535 SW Sixth Street (☎233-3800), with rooms from $55.

West Through Kansas

Further west across Kansas, three towns re-create the state's Wild West heritage, although only in the westernmost, **Dodge City**, does the scrubby landscape conform to the cowboy-movie image. **Abilene**, if less famous than Dodge City, has as many outlaw and gunslinging stories, and **Wichita**, about 200 miles southwest of Kansas City, holds an excellent, authentic reconstruction of frontier days in its Cowtown Museum.

Abilene

Like all the old cattle-trail cowtowns, **ABILENE**, ninety miles west of Topeka on I-70, claims to have been the riproaringest of the lot. The *New York Tribune* seemed to agree, writing in the 1860s that "There is no law, no restraint in this seething cauldron of vice and depravity." The railhead at the end of the Chisholm Trail, Abilene shipped more than a million Longhorns east between 1867 and 1871, when legendary lawman Wild Bill Hickok became its marshall. By that time the unruly behaviour was already dying down, and today there is little left to remind you of those wild days. Abilene is a centre of wheat production, which now prefers to stress its connections with president Eisenhower. The **Eisenhower Center**, 201 SE Fourth Street, includes Dwight's boyhood home, with its original furnishings, the obligatory film show, murals in the lobby depicting the high points of his life, and copies of presidential papers in the library. The former president and his wife are buried in the meditation chapel (daily 9am–5pm).

As for rough and tumble cowboy history, **Old Abilene Town**, SE Sixth and Kuney streets, is a replica of the town during the cattle boom, complete with stagecoach rides. Gunfights are held on Sunday at 2.45pm and 4pm, with Can Can dancers at 2.15pm and 3pm (daily March–Sept 8am–8pm; Oct & Nov 10am–5pm; donation).

Practicalities

Abilene's **visitor centre** is at 201 NW Second Street (☎263-2231). Most of its cheap **motels** are on Hwy-15 around the junction with I-70. The *Diamond*, closer to the centre of town at 1407 NW Third Street (☎263-2360), has cheap rooms ($18–27), minimal facilities and free transportation to the *Greyhound* depot.

> The telephone **area code** for west Kansas, including Wichita and Dodge City, is ☎316.

Wichita

WICHITA, about 140 miles southwest of Topeka on I-35, is the largest city in Kansas, severed by the Arkansas River, which forks just north of downtown into the Big and Little Arkansas rivers (incidentally, Kansans take umbrage if you pronounce it *Arkansaw*; pronounce it here the way it is spelt). Originally settled by the Wichita Indians (in whose language the name means "painted faces'), who by 1865 had been relocated to Oklahoman Indian Territory, Wichita grew up as a stop on the Chisholm Trail. Its glory days were to be short-lived, however, as farmers, angry about the damage done by stampeding cattle, erected fences which forced the drives onto different trails further west, creating new cowtowns like Dodge City. Today three of the world's major aircraft producers are based here, and although downtown is wilting a little, Wichita remains attractive and cheeerful, kept buoyant by its rich arts scene.

Arrival, Information and Getting Around

Domestic flights arrive at the **Mid-Continent Airport**, five miles southwest of downtown on Hwy-54 W (Kellogg Drive). *Amtrak* stops at **Newton**, a small Mennonite town twenty-five miles north, with a bus connection to Wichita throughout the day; *Greyhound* comes in to 312 Broadway Avenue, two blocks east of Main Street. City transport is poor: Starline **buses** (Mon–Sat 7am–6pm; ☎265-7221) run slow and unreliable commuter services from the suburbs. The friendly **CVB** is in the heart of downtown on the corner of Douglas Avenue and Main Street (Mon–Fri 8am–5pm; ☎265-2800).

The City

Downtown Wichita is a rapidly emptying casualty of the exodus to the suburbs, enlivened mainly by the profusion of public art and sculpture, which pop up unexpectedly all over the place, in tree stumps and empty lots. The exceptional **Wichita-Sedgwick County Historical Museum**, 204 S Main Street, is in the distinctive **Old City Hall**, a heavy stone building, decorated with turrets, gargoyles and arches, known locally as "The Palace of the Plains". The cosy interior is crammed with exhibits on everything from the Wichita Indians through decorative art to Carry Nation, whose initial zeal for singing hymns to errant drunks grew into a campaign against everything from tobacco to corsets. In her last attack on a saloon, her female bar owner opponent gave as good as she got, and a violent fight ensued (Tues–Fri 11am–4pm, Sat & Sun 1–5pm; $1).

Across from the former Union Station, the **Great Plains Transportation Museum**, 700 E Douglas Avenue, is a train-spotters' delight, packed with steam train memorabilia (Sat 9am–3pm). The now-seedy **Eaton Hotel**, 525 East Douglas Avenue, is not recommended as somewhere to sleep, but when known as the *Carey Hotel* was one of the many places in which Carry Nation caused havoc. The stately church with vivid stained-glass windows at 601 N Water Street houses the **First National Black Historical Society of Kansas**, an eclectic antidote to more mainstream views of Great Plains history, with details on Buffalo Soldiers, inventors and early black Wichitans, and some African art (Mon & Fri 10am–2pm, Sun 2–6pm; free).

The **Riverside** area is a stretch of parkland with walking and bike trails and some excellent museums, including the **Mid-America All-Indian Center and Museum**, 650 N Seneca Drive (May–Sept Mon–Sat 10am–5pm, Sun 1–5pm; Oct–April Tues–Sat 10am–5pm, Sun 1–5pm; $1.75). The 44ft **"Keeper of the Plains"** statue, facing east at the confluence of the Little and Big Arkansas rivers, was designed in the 1970s by a Kiowa-Comanche artist, Blackbear Bosin, and dedicated by Native Americans and city officials smoking the peace pipe. It's an eerie sight at dusk, reaching into the sky with some unknown offering. The museum itself is small, with changing exhibits of traditional and contemporary Native American art: clothing and beadwork, pottery and baskets, paintings and prints. On Tuesday lunchtimes they serve cheap and delicious

Indian tacos and fry bread. **Old Cowtown**, 1871 Sim Park Drive, is an outside exhibit re-creating the buildings of 1870s Wichita. Looking and feeling like a movie set, the area includes – along with some docile Longhorns – the city's first one-room jail, a school room, a store, a smithy and old homes. In the low season, however, it's a ghost town (daily 10am–5pm; until 6pm Sat & Sun in summer; $3).

To the north of the city, the surreal geodesic **Pyradomes**, 3100 N Hillside Avenue, house the Garvey Center for the Improvement of Human Functioning, which aims, by using holistic medicine, to find a cure for cancer by the year 2000. It's all very worthy, but weird: road signs, for example, tell you to "de-stress to 25". Tours include a video show and individual sample "nutrient profiles" (daily at 1.30pm; $4; ☎682-3100).

Accommodation

Cheap **lodgings** in Wichita are plentiful: near the airport on W Kellogg Drive/Hwy-54W, along the thoroughfares entering and leaving town, and even around the centre. The nearest **camping** is at the *USI Campgrounds*, 2920-1 E 33rd Street (☎838-8699).

Days Inn, 221 E Kellogg Drive/Hwy-54 (☎267-9281). Downtown doubles from $50 with breakfast.

Park Inn International, 1000 N Broadway (☎267-6211). Northeast of town. Doubles $45–50, heated pool, whirlpool and adjacent cafe.

The Residence Inn, 120 W Orme St (☎263-1061). A block south of Kellogg Drive, suites with fireplaces and balconies go from $70, including pool, whirlpool, laundry and free breakfast.

The Wichita Royale, 125 N Market St (☎263-2101). Doubles from $65. Pool and free breakfast.

Eating and Drinking

Downtown, though filled with good places to **eat**, has fewer options for drinking or clubbing. Nightlife revolves around wine bars and private clubs. Wichita's latest excitement is the recently legalised gambling at the **Greyhound Park**, north on I-135 at the Kansas Coliseum (1.15pm & 7.30pm; $3, plus $1.50 to get into the restaurant or deli; ☎755-4000, ☎755-1212 for dinner reservations).

Art Museum Cafe, 619 Stackman Drive (☎268-4961). Sadly only open until 1.30pm Tues–Fri and for Sunday brunch until 2pm; delicious full set meals for under $5, and lovely river views.

Doc's Steakhouse, 1515 N Broadway (☎264-4735). North of downtown. Exceptional steaks; cheap, cheerful and popular.

The Old Mill Tasty Shop, 604 E Douglas Ave (☎264-6500). Great food in a historic building complete with marble soda fountain. Try the wild mushroom strudel or any of the fish dishes.

The Two Feathers, 108 E Second St (☎262-8300). Tasty *fajitas* and southwestern food in a lively setting, with live music on Fri and Sat evenings.

Dodge City

DODGE CITY, 150 miles west of Wichita, is perhaps the most famous of all America's cowtowns. It has certainly been committed to celluloid more times than any other, in great Thirties westerns like *My Darling Clementine* and *Dodge City*. However, this wildest of Wild West cities had a raucous heyday of only a decade, from 1875 until 1886. Established in 1872 with the Santa Fe Railroad, which transported the hides of the millions of buffalo that roamed the plains, by 1875 the town of traders, trappers and hunters had to find a new economic base – all the buffalo had been exterminated. The era of the great cattle drives was already under way, and Dodge City became a raucous den of iniquity where gambling, drinking and general lawlessness were the norm. Such wickedness led inevitably to gunfights galore, and the notorious Boot Hill cemetery was kept busy by charismatic lawmen such as sheriff Bat Masterson and marshalls Wyatt Earp and Doc Holliday.

Dodge City today is rather more staid, content to replay its movie image in the relatively small and touristy **Historic Front Street**, where you'll find, along with the old jail, a schoolhouse and a smithy, plenty of "authentic" Western entertainment: stage-coach rides, medicine shows, gunfights and melodramas, and dancing at the **Long Branch Saloon**. The **Boot Hill Museum**, 500 Wyatt Earp Boulevard, is on the site of the original Boot Hill graveyard. **Hardesty House**, the home of an early cattle baron, has been restored to its original grandeur (summer daily 8am–8pm; winter Mon–Sat 9am–5pm, Sun 1–5pm).

Other sights in town include the **Home of Stone**, 112 E Vine Street, an emotive memorial to pioneer mothers, often forgotten amid the macho Wild West myth-making. The house looks pretty much as it would have in 1881, with a lot of domestic memorabilia from early plainswomen (June–Sept Mon–Sat 9am–5pm, Sun 1–5pm). **El Capitan**, at Second Street and Wyatt Earp Boulevard, is a massive bronze Longhorn, facing south towards an identical north-facing statue in Abilene, West Texas. Together they mark the beginning and the end of the cattle drives.

Practicalities

Greyhound **buses** from Wichita arrive twice daily at 910 E Wyatt Earp Boulevard (☎225-1617). *Amtrak* comes in right to the town centre, at Central and Front streets, in the historic Santa Fe Station. Call the **CVB** (☎227-2176) for advice or information, or drop in at Fourth and West Spruce streets, a block north of Front Street. There is no public transport in town, but *Gunsmoke Historical Tours* give trips to historical sites and a Western clothing store for those who want to play cowboys. They also do tours of a working Longhorn ranch and around Dodge City itself. You can get tickets from the booth on the Boot Hill parking lot, from which the buses also depart.

Cheap **hotels** and **restaurants** line Wyatt Earp Boulevard, which isn't very conven-ient for the town centre. For **rooms**, the *Astro*, 2200 Wyatt Earp Boulevard (☎227-8146), has doubles from $30, with free transportation to the train and bus stations, and the *Dodge House Inn Motel*, at no. 2408 (☎225-9900), has rooms from $21 to $52, with free breakfast and a coin laundry. Both the *Dodge House Inn* and the *Golden Corral*, at no. 700 (☎227-7455), have good steak-and-seafood **restaurants**. The *Western Inn Motel*, two miles east of town on US-50 (☎225-1381), is opposite the bus station, with rooms for $28 to $47. **Camping** is an option for the carless; the *Gunsmoke Campground* on W Hwy-50 is three miles west of Front Street (☎227-8247), and the *Water Sports Campground Recreation*, 500 Cherry Street, stands beside a lake south of Front Street (☎225-9003).

IOWA

Stand on two phone books anywhere in Iowa and you get a view
Bill Bryson, *Lost Continent*

Nothing about **IOWA** truly stands out: its overwhelmingly uniform 55,000 square miles don't even manage to be completely flat, they just wobble up and down a little. The state is the very essence of smalltown America, close to the geographical centre of the mainland US, and coming 25th out of fifty states in size, population and level of personal income. Even the cities seem to be villages grown large.

Iowa's history, too, has been uneventful. It was opened for settlement after the Black Hawk Treaty of 1832, a rather one-sided exercise in negotiations with the Sauk Indians, conducted after many of their number had been chased down and slaughtered in neighbouring Wisconsin and Illinois. The migrants from northern Europe who replaced them did little to ignite political fire, being more concerned with the agricul-tural development that saw Iowa become the **"Foodbasket of America"** – a role which might make it a good place for farmers, but holds little promise for travellers.

Getting Around Iowa

Greyhound calls on all Iowa's major towns, with frequent services along I-80. *Amtrak's* east–west route misses the cities, stopping instead at a number of small communities in the south of the state. The only sizeable **airport** is in Des Moines.

The telephone **area code** for eastern Iowa is ☎319

Eastern Iowa

Eastern Iowa, in the Mississippi River hinterland, is liberally sprinkled with **agribusiness** towns that display the continuing influence of their central and northern European pioneers, plus a number of **religious** communities – Amish, Mennonite and the Amana Colonies. All are easily accessible from **Iowa City**, the state's brightest spot and home to a huge university and lively nightlife. Riverside towns like northerly **Dubuque** and **Burlington**, near the Missouri state line, have been enlivened since 1991 by the introduction of **gambling**, though so far low-stake poker and roulette games can only be played on board Mississippi River paddlewheelers, which come decked out in less-than-authentic Mark Twain-era trimmings.

Dubuque and Cedar Rapids

In both appearance and age, **DUBUQUE** stands out from other Iowa communities. This handsome town, overlooked by rocky bluffs on the Mississippi around 150 miles west of Chicago, was founded as the first white settlement in Iowa by French-Canadian leadminers in 1788. In the nineteenth century it became a boisterous riverport and logging centre. Many buildings from this era still stand, but the companies occupying the premises are now concerned with meatpacking and other food industries.

The quaint downtown **Ice Harbor** is the departure point for the *Dubuque Casino Belle* (☎583-1761), though you'll need a significant amount of luck on the machines and gaming tables to cover the $30 price of a lunch or dinner cruise. If you prefer to see the high-banked Mississippi without the company of croupiers, *Roberts River Rides* offer ninety-minute **paddlewheeler cruises** (May–Oct daily; $6; ☎583-1761).

Close to the harbour, **cable-cars** grind their way in summer up the at-times sheer bluff from Fourth Street to residential Fenelon Place, for a fine view across the Mississippi to Illinois and Wisconsin. The *Julien Inn*, 200 Main Street (☎556-4200), is a comfortable downtown place to stay, charging $40 to $70.

Seventy miles southwest, **CEDAR RAPIDS**, home of Quaker Oats, is Iowa's industrial leader. In the late 1840s, a meatpacking boom lured thousands of Czechs here. The **Czech Village** on 16th Avenue SW features the excellent bakery *Sykora's*, gift shops, traditional houses and a small museum of national costumes and pioneer artefacts. The **Museum of Art**, 410 Third Avenue SE, boasts a comprehensive collection of paintings by Grant Wood, best known for his woozy, pastel depictions of Thirties farmlife (Tues, Wed, Fri & Sat 10am–4pm, Thurs 10am–7pm, Sun noon–3pm; $2). Good **rooms** at the *Village Inn Motor Hotel*, 100 F Avenue NW (☎366-5323), are around $45.

The Amana Colonies

The **AMANA COLONIES** spread out from the intersection of US-151 and Hwy-220 (just off US-6), midway between Cedar Rapids and Iowa City. Now packed with sightseers, they were founded in 1855 by the Community of True Inspiration, a group of pacifist German refugees (not linked to the Amish or Mennonite orders) who believed that

God spoke through prophets – themselves, for example – rather than ordained ministers. Members led a simple collective lifestyle: each family lived in its own home, but they all ate together and shared profits from the farms. During the Depression, communal ownership became increasingly difficult to maintain, and in 1932 stock was redistributed between all the adults. However, they did keep up their commitment to close family ties, a sense of community and religious principles. On Sunday mornings, you can still see women church members wearing the traditional black cap, shawl and apron, with men dressed in equally sombre attire. Church services for visitors, held in English, take place at 10am each Sunday in Middle Amana.

The largest of the seven separate villages in this immaculately serene valley, where neat plank fences divide up the rolling meadows, is **AMANA**, whose twee streets are lined with several restaurants and craft shops, a brewery, winery, woollen mill and a small museum (☎622-3567). Picturesque **HOMESTEAD** is enhanced by a walking trail around the dam on a scenic bend of the Iowa River, which was built centuries ago by Indians to concentrate fish into one area and thus allow them to be caught more easily.

Practicalities

The **visitor centre** for the Colonies is near the junction of US-151 and Hwy-220 (☎622-3828). They do not use conventional addresses, but most points of interest are well signposted. Among cheap, wholesome places to eat old-style German **food** are the *Amana Bread & Pastry Shop* (☎622-3600) in Amana village, and *Hahn's Hearth Oven Bakery* in Middle Amana. For a mid-priced sit-down meal, the *Colony Market Place Restaurant* (☎622-3225) in South Amana offers sausages of every imaginable variety.

Iowa City

IOWA CITY, on I-80, 55 miles west of the Mississippi, is refreshingly young at heart. Its restored gold-domed **Old Capitol** is a reminder of the days when it was the state capital, before government was transferred to the more central Des Moines. To placate residents, the state **university** was established here. The arty shops and sidewalk cafes of the compact, partly pedestrianised downtown touch the east end of the university grounds, but its red and grey buildings, closeted by tall dark trees, remain aloof from the rest of the town.

Greyhound stops at 404 E College Avenue (☎337-2127), just off downtown. The CVB is at 325 E Washington Street (☎337-6592). The most central place to stay is *Iowa House*, a nice comfortable hotel in the Union building (☎335-3513) with large doubles for $50 a night. The tidy *Wesley AYH Hostel*, 120 N Dubuque Street (☎338-1179), also handy for downtown, costs $10 (members and students only). Inexpensive motels in **Coralville**, to the west, include the clean *Capri*, 705 Second Street (☎354-5100), charging $26 to $35. Good cheap **food** isn't hard to find. The trendy *Kitchen*, 9 S Dubuque Street (☎337-5444), serves fresh pasta and Cajun dishes for around $5. Next door is *Mickey's* (☎338-6860), a friendly, dimly lit Irish bar with good burgers.

Midwest Old Threshers Heritage Museum

Old Threshers Road, Mount Pleasant. June–Aug daily 9am–4.30pm, mid-April to mid-Oct Mon–Fri 9am–4.30pm; $2.50; ☎385-3937.

The excellent **Midwest Old Threshers Heritage Museum** is just south of the small manufacturing town of MOUNT PLEASANT (served by *Amtrak*), eighty miles south of Iowa City. Its major strength is that its resources are devoted to the maintenance of its hundred fully-operative steam engines, three hundred tractors and a host of other antique farm equipment rather than attempting to make the place more aesthetically pleasing. Located in two huge barns, the museum contains vastly informative displays on the influence of electricity on farming, and on the important economic role played by women. It also runs the **Museum of Repertoire Americana**, stacked with memorabilia from the days before television when travelling tent shows and opera companies provided the only rural entertainment.

Central and Western Iowa

Pigs outnumber people in central Iowa. The only city amongst the cornfields, state capital **Des Moines**, struggles to lift the monotony with a few attractions and some good places to eat. The humdrum west has little to offer; Omaha and Lincoln, just over the state line in Nebraska, make more appealing destinations (see p.570).

Des Moines

DES MOINES, near the centre of Iowa amid tree-covered hills at the confluence of the sluggish Des Moines and Racoon rivers, owes its origins to a military fort set up in 1843 to protect pioneers. It had already grown into a trading centre for the region's farmers by the time the eighteen-year-old Frederick Hubbell arrived in 1855; within a decade he had founded the Equitable Life and Insurance Corporation to service their need for investment capital. Other companies soon realised the potential of agrarian business and today the city is the world's third largest **insurance** centre, behind London and Hartford, Connecticut.

Among illustrious former denizens of Des Moines are **Ronald Reagan**, who began his career as a sportscaster on Radio WHO, and **John Wayne**, born and raised in nearby Winterset.

Arrival and Information

Des Moines's *Greyhound* station (☎243-5211) is just northwest of downtown at 1107 Keosauqua Way. From the very efficient transfer mall at Sixth and Walnut streets, you can get a *MTA* bus practically anywhere in the city. The **visitor centre** (☎244-2444) is close at hand in the Skywalk complex.

The Town

The steel and glass skyline of **downtown Des Moines**, most of which shot up during the Eighties, is testimony to its ever-growing insurance trade. Towering above all is the boxy, 44-storey **801 Grand** building, headquarters of the *Principal Financial Company*. However, for such a fast-track financial centre, the streets are curiously empty. Pedestrians instead use the **Skywalk**: a three-mile network of air-conditioned corridors linking twenty blocks of offices, banks, car parks, restaurants, hotels and cinemas.

Most businesses stand on the west bank of the Des Moines River, which cuts downtown in two. In 1857, a group of speculators attempted to shift the commercial hub to the east side by bribing commissioners to site the **State Capitol** at E Ninth Street and Grand Avenue. Their hopes of huge spin-offs were dashed when the nationwide financial crash later that same year saw property prices collapse. As a result, the five-domed Italian Renaissance-style mass, on the crest of a steep hill, is now detached from the commercial heart of the city. A short walk downhill, displays in the futuristic pink and brown **Iowa State Historical Building** at E Sixth and Locust streets (and topped by a strange neon figurine) cover Indian civilisation, pioneer times and the development of Iowan farming (Tues–Sat 9am–4.30pm, Sun noon–4.30pm; free).

The telephone **area code** for central and western Iowa is ☎515.

Three miles west, the **Des Moines Art Center** at 4700 Grand Avenue is housed in a trio of buildings designed by Eliel Saarinen, I M Pei and Richard Meier. Matisse, Picasso and Renoir are represented alongside twentieth-century American artists such as Wood, Hopper and O'Keeffe. The most dynamic exhibits are in the mixed media wing, especially the giant disturbing Anselm Keifer canvas (Tues, Wed, Fri & Sat 11am–5pm, Thurs 11am–9pm, Sun noon–5pm; $2, free daily until 1pm & all day Thurs).

Accommodation

Downtown Des Moines caters mostly for insurance company business, but still offers some fairly inexpensive places to stay.

Best Western Starlite Village, 929 Third St (☎282-5251). Reasonable downtown rooms for $60.

Hotel Fort Des Moines, Tenth St and Walnut Ave (☎243-1161). Grand old historical downtown hotel. The standard room rate is around $100, though $55 specials are frequently on offer.

Motel 6, 4817 Fleur Drive (☎287-8961). Clean rooms near the airport; $32.

YMCA, 101 Locust St (☎288-0131). Men-only downtown rooms; some need sprucing up. $19.50.

YWCA, 717 Grand Ave (☎244-8961). Clean dorm-style rooms for women in a safe part of downtown; $8.50 per night with discount for weekly stays.

Eating, Drinking and Nightlife

That Iowans eat well is reflected in the quality – and quantity – of food on offer in Des Moines **restaurants**. A cruising craze – known as "Slooping the Loop" – means that Des Moines is not just another quiet prairie town at night.

Battani's, 210 Fourth St (☎244-4773). Locals' favourite downtown pizzeria.

French Quarter Bar & Restaurant, 100 Court Ave (☎246-9820). The New Orleans-style cuisine is pricey, as are the drinks, but the Fri–Sun jazz sessions ($1 cover) usually make a visit worthwhile.

Juke Box Saturday Night, 208 Third St (☎243-0707). Favourite gathering place for young Des Moines with guitar bands at the weekend and cheap entry.

Julio's, 308 Court Ave (☎244-1710). Lively, reasonably priced Tex-Mex cafe.

Kaplan Hat, 307 Court Ave (☎243-1414). Art Deco restaurant noted for its doorstopper sandwiches, blue plate specials and, most of all, its stuffed pork chops for $9–12.

Stella's Blue Sky Diner, 400 Locust St, in Capitol Square building (☎246-1953). Kitsch Fifties-style diner decked out in lurid pinks, turquoises and yellows. Burgers and fries ($3.50) washed down with divine chocolate, peanut butter and banana malts. Mon–Sat 8am–6pm; a must for lunch.

Out From Des Moines

Ten miles west of downtown Des Moines (I-80 exit 125), the 600-acre **Living History Farms** in **Urbandale** traces the evolution of agriculture on the plains. Self-guided tours lead from the oval bark homes of an eighteenth-century Ioway Indian settlement, through an 1850s homestead, to a look at the high-tech methods of today (May–Oct Mon–Sat 9am–5pm, Sun 11am–6pm; $7). Next to the entrance, the *Iowa Machine Shed Restaurant*, 11151 Hickman Road (☎270-6818), pays homage to the Iowa farmer, dispensing colossal portions of salad, meat loaf, chops and assorted sandwiches, mostly for under $7.

In the sleepy, run-down town of **WINTERSET**, twenty-five miles southwest of Des Moines, the modest former home of the local pharmacist at 224 S Second Street now serves as a museum to his son, Marion Robert Morrison, born in 1907, who grew up to become Hollywood hardman **John Wayne**. His first lead role was in 1930 but real stardom didn't come for another nine years, when he played the Ringo Kid in the John Ford classic, *Stagecoach*. Three more decades passed before Wayne claimed his one and only Oscar as Rooster Cogburn, the drunken one-eyed marshal in *True Grit*. Among the photos, personal belongings and movie mementoes is a glowing personal endorsement of the "Duke" from his buddy Ronald Reagan, who shared his political views, if not perhaps his acting abilities (daily April–Dec 10am–5pm; Jan–March noon– 5pm).

NEBRASKA

For the early pioneers, heading west during the Gold Rush, **NEBRASKA** was just another dreary expanse of prairie to get through as fast as possible. Most transcontinental travellers still choose to avoid this ultra-flat and sparsely populated state, but it does hold some places of interest. The problem is that they are hundreds of miles apart, separated by an underwhelming drive along I-80.

The eastern fringe holds commercial **Omaha** and the livelier state capital, **Lincoln**. To the west, in the **Panhandle**, the livestock-rearing flatlands are briefly interrupted by giant sand hills and valleys, broken by towering rocky columns and hemmed in by sheer-faced buttes. This area was still embroiled in vicious and bloody battles against Native Americans long after eastern Nebraska had been settled; from the first serious uprising in 1854, it was 36 years before the US Army could make white control unchallengeable. Close to the South Dakota state line, **Fort Robinson**, where Crazy Horse was murdered, remains one of the West's most evocative historic sites.

Without any navigable rivers, Nebraska had to rely on the railroads to help populate the land. During the 1870s and 1880s, rail companies, encouraged by grants that allowed them to accumulate one sixth of the state, laid down such a comprehensive network of tracks that virtually every farmer was within a day's walk of the nearest halt. Thus the buffalo-hunting country of the Sioux and Pawnee was turned into high-yield farmland, which today has few rivals in terms of cattle and grain production.

Getting Around Nebraska

Airports at both Omaha and Lincoln offer reasonable domestic links. *Greyhound* operates almost exclusively along I-80 with *Amtrak* **trains**, travelling through the night, following a similar route. Be prepared for long bouts of boredom on a cross-state drive.

Eastern Nebraska

The silt-laden **Missouri River** separates eastern Nebraska from both Iowa and Missouri on the far side. This stretch of the "Big Muddy" offers few natural ports, and **Omaha** remains the only riverfront community of any size. **Lincoln**, 58 miles southwest, is the state's capital and seat of its university.

Omaha

Although **OMAHA**, Nebraska's largest and most easterly city, is visibly a prosperous place, with a great zoo, several museums and parks and a thriving entertainment district, the atmosphere remains sedate and predominantly suburban. As a major terminus on the first transcontinental railroad, Omaha made a logical alternative to distant Chicago as a marketplace for Wyoming and Nebraska ranchers to sell their herds of cattle. By the turn of the century massive stockyards spread along the southern edge of town, and the city still handles well over one million head of livestock per year.

The broad sweeping thoroughfares of **downtown Omaha** have been all but killed off by the drift to the malls, though the cobbled streets of the **Old Market** district hold a few interesting craft shops, bars and cafes. The *Antiquarian Bookstore*, 1215 Harney Street (☎341-8077), is packed with dusty volumes (and local bohemians).

Displays in the **Western Heritage Museum**, 801 S Tenth Street, fail to live up to the huge 1929 Art Deco Union Pacific station in which it's housed. Some fascinating

The telephone **area code** for Omaha and eastern Nebraska is ☎402.

exhibits cover the city's at-times turbulent labour history (Mon–Sat 10am–5pm, Sun 1–5pm; closed Mon out of season; $3). For an absorbing, albeit biased, look at the impact of the railroad on the Great Plains, call in at the small **Union Pacific Railroad Museum**, 14th and Dodge streets (Mon–Fri 9am–5pm, Sat 9am–1pm; free). Pride of place is taken by a huge stuffed **buffalo**; millions of these beasts were wiped out as the railroads pressed westwards, but Union Pacific suggest they had to be exterminated because they were prone to charge passing trains. A section of Abraham Lincoln's funeral carriage and a giant model train set occupy other parts of the room, and push-button video screens show hilarious old UP singalong TV commercials.

The **Great Plains Black Museum**, in the city's predominantly black north side at 2213 Lake Street (Mon–Fri times vary; ☎345-2212), presents the history of black people on the prairies. The most interesting exhibits cover blacks in the frontier army. In the main recently freed slaves, who could find no work in the Deep South after the Civil War, they were often sent as advance parties in to the most hostile and dangerous regions; it was Native American warriors who first called them "buffalo soldiers", because of their tightly curled hair and the colour of their skin. The Black Muslim leader **Malcolm X** was born in Omaha in May 1925, though his family moved to Michigan immediately thereafter, in the face of Ku Klux Klan death threats to his father, a preacher who followed the back-to-Africa teachings of Marcus Garvey.

The **Henry Doorly Zoo**, 3701 S Tenth Street (daily April–Oct 9.30am–7pm; Nov–March 9.30am–6pm; $7), is one of best small-city-zoos in America. It started off with two buffalo borrowed from Buffalo Bill. Now it features a gigantic free-flying aviary, some rare white Siberian tigers and a magnificent bear canyon, as well as the new **Lied Jungle**, an indoor rainforest housing tropical wildlife from South America, Asia and Africa. An elevated walkway, with a real swaying rope bridge, leads you into a world populated by species such as the aptly named Howler monkeys, pygmy hippos, gibbons, leopards, crocodiles, leopards, parrots and butterflies.

Practicalities

Omaha's *Greyhound* station is at 16th and Jackson streets (☎341-1900); *Amtrak* (☎342-1501), whose trains arrive and depart very late at night, is at Ninth and Pacific streets.

The **CVB**, at 1819 Farnham Street (☎444-4660), has discount vouchers for **motels**, which are mostly located out towards the airport. At the cheapest of the lot, the *Motel 6* at 10708 M Street (☎331-3161), doubles are just $33, but it's six miles from downtown and not on any bus route. *Econolodge*, 221 Douglas Street (☎345-9565), at the edge of downtown, costs $45; the *YMCA*, 430 S 20th Street (☎341-1600), has private hostel-style rooms for $20, plus $10 key deposit.

Downtown's **Old Market** district, centred on Tenth and Howard streets, has the liveliest **restaurants** and **bars** (though if you fancy a steak you should head out to the stockyards). The *Indian Oven*, 1010 Howard Street (☎342-4856), is a superb and very welcome **Indian** restaurant, where excellent paneer and vegetable dishes start at well under $7, while *Trini's*, 1020 Howard Street (☎346-8400), is a good cheap Mexican. The *Howard Street Tavern*, 1112 Howard Street (☎341-0433), is a reliable live music venue.

Lincoln

Were it not for Omaha, 58 miles northeast, **LINCOLN** would be in the back of beyond; the next major point of civilisation to the east is Denver, Colorado, 480 miles further along I-80. As tiny Rochester, it was selected to be **state capital** in 1867 – on the condition that it change its name to Lincoln in honour of the recently assassinated president. Such was the disappointment in the territorial seat of government, Omaha, that state officials had to smuggle documents, books and office furniture out of the city in the middle of the night to avoid armed gangs. This town of 170,000 now serves as an oasis of culture for a large chunk of the Plains. At night, when the students emerge, downtown comes into its own, packed with cafes, bars, cinemas and theatres. O Street is the main drag, with 13th and 14th streets containing most of the good bars and places to eat, though the entire downtown, including the capitol and campus, is easily walkable.

Dwarfing the rest of **downtown**, the central tower of the 1932 **Nebraska State Capitol**, 1445 K Street, protrudes 400 feet into the sky. Topped by a twenty-foot statue of a sower on a pedestal of wheat and corn, its remarkable phallic appearance – an adventurous departure from the usual architecture of state capitols – has prompted the nickname "penis of the prairies". For once there's no golden dome, and the superb iridescent murals in the foyer are a welcome alternative to old portraits, flags and emblems. From the fourteenth-floor observation deck you can survey the flatness of the surrounding farmland (Mon–Fri 8am–5pm, Sat & hols 10am–5pm, Sun 1–5pm; free).

Twelve thousand years of life on the plains are covered at the **Museum of Nebraska History**, 15th and P streets, where the displays focus more on anthropology than history (Mon–Sat 9am–5pm, Sun 1.30–5pm; free). The Elephant Hall, a gallery of towering mammoth, mastodon and four-tusker skeletons, is the highlight of the **U of M State Museum** at 14th and U streets (Mon–Sat 9.30am–4.30pm, Sun & hols 1.30–4.30pm; $1). A few blocks away, the **Sheldon Memorial Art Gallery**, 12th and R streets, traces the development of American art, and has a twenty-piece sculpture garden (Tues–Sat 10am–5pm, Thurs & Sat also 7–9pm, Sun 2–9pm; free). Marking the northern end of campus, the 76,000-seater **Memorial Stadium** (tickets ☎472-3111), at the end of Vine Street, is where the brutal "Big Red" Cornhuskers invariably thrash the footballing opposition.

Practicalities

Lincoln's *Greyhound* station is downtown at 940 P Street (☎474-1071), while *Amtrak* passes through 201 N Seventh Street at crazy early-morning hours. *Lincoln Transystem* (☎476-1234) runs good local buses. The **visitor centre** is at 1221 N Street (☎476-7551).

Except on football weekends, central **accommodation** is not hard to find. The large *Clayton House Hotel*, Tenth and O streets (☎476-0333), next to the *Greyhound* station and very close to the bars, may be a bit scruffy but it's excellent value at $45, while the *Cornerstone* **AYH Hostel**, 640 N 16th Street (☎476-0355), on the edge of campus, offers basic members-only dormitory lodging for $5. Two miles from downtown, the *Senate Inn*, 2801 West O Street (☎475-4921), has comfortable rooms for $35–40.

Valentino's, 13th & Q streets (☎475-1501), is a good Italian **restaurant**; the casual *Julio's*, 132 S 13th Street (☎477-5122), which has nice cheap Tex-Mex food, puts on live jazz at weekends. *The Zoo*, 136 N 14th Street (☎435-8754), is the top venue in town for blues, jazz and touring bands, adjacent to *O'Rourkes Lounge*, a raucous well-priced bar. Students flock to *Duffy's Bar*, 1412 O Street (☎474-3543), for beef stew and beer.

Western Nebraska

After the unerringly flat journey across Nebraska, the far west comes as a refreshing change. In the **Panhandle**, as it's often called, wave upon wave of rumpled sandy hills, with a thin coating of prairie grass, back off towards the horizon like a sea in constant turmoil. Early mapmakers saw this as the Great American Desert, and it remained barren until massive irrigation work at the start of this century enabled agricultural settlement. In the northwest the sand hills yield to classic John-Ford-style western scenery: pancake-flat valleys, criss-crossed by dry meandering river beds and corralled by crusty, contorted bluffs under a seemingly constant shadow of fast-moving clouds.

The telephone **area code** for western Nebraska is ☎308.

Chimney Rock and Scottsbluff

The much-painted and photographed **Chimney Rock**, which rises almost five hundred feet above the North Platte River thirteen miles west of **Bridgeport** on Hwy-92, served as an Oregon Trail landmark to show that the prairies were coming to an end. Twenty-five miles further west, **SCOTTSBLUFF** is the commercial centre for the farmlands of western Nebraska; its well-kept *Lamplighter Motel*, 606 E 27th Street (☎632-7108), charges less than $40 per room. On Hwy-92, near the 800-foot rugged bluff of the **Scottsbluff National Monument**, southwest of town, the **Oregon Trail Museum** (daily 8am–4.30pm) relates the experiences of the early travellers; in places around here you can still see the ruts left by their covered wagons.

Fort Robinson State Park

Some eighty miles north of Scottsbluff, just west of **Crawford** village, **Fort Robinson State Park**, beside 1000-foot crenellated cliffs in the inhospitable White River Valley, stands as a sad reminder of the brutality of the Indian Wars. It was from here that the US Army campaign to rid the gold-rich Badlands of the native Sioux was co-ordinated (see box below). Today, it's a sort of cross between a dude ranch, a mini-college campus and a living history village; the fact that it has been cosmeticised to the point where the brochures highlight its family-oriented leisure pursuits just helps to make the memories of the obliteration of an entire way of native life that much more poignant.

Restored fort buildings contain period furnishings, and two small museums exhibit army and Indian artefacts. *Fort Robinson Lodge* (☎665-2660), in the park, has good rooms for around $30, and its restaurant serves buffalo dishes for under $10.

CRAZY HORSE

The life of Oglala Sioux leader **Crazy Horse** is shrouded in confusion, misinterpretation and controversy. So thoroughly did the most enigmatic figure in Plains Indian history avoid contact with whites outside of battle that no photograph or even sketch of him exists; unlike other Indian chiefs, he refused to visit Washington DC or talk to reporters.

Crazy Horse earned his title as a youth, after he single-handedly charged rival Arapahoe and took two scalps. The finest moment in a brilliant military career came in June 1876 when he led a thousand warriors in inflicting a stinging defeat on the superior forces of General George Crook at the **Battle of the Rosebud River**. Only eight days later Crazy Horse headed the attack at the **Battle of Little Bighorn**, where Custer and his entire company were killed (see p.628).

After Little Bighorn, US Army efforts to round up the Indians redoubled. Crazy Horse managed to stay ahead of the whites until May 1877, when he surprised friend and foe alike by leading 900 of his people into Fort Robinson. They gave up their weapons and Crazy Horse, keen to stay in his native land (unlike Sitting Bull, who had retreated to Canada), demanded that the buffalo grounds along the Powder River should remain in Indian hands. Tensions at Fort Robinson rose after a rumour went round the barracks that the Sioux chief had come to the army camp to murder General Crook. Crazy Horse was arrested on September 5 1877 and, during a tussle outside the fort jail, he was bayoneted three times, dying the next morning.

Quite why this undefeated warrior should have surrendered without a fight, and whether he fell victim to a deliberate assassination, remain unclear. What is certain is that his death signalled the closing chapter of the Indian Wars. The Oglala Sioux were forcibly moved to the poor hunting country of Missouri, and settlers immediately swept in their thousands into western Nebraska, South Dakota, Wyoming and Montana.

Crazy Horse was buried by his family in an unmarked grave in an out-of-the-way creek called **Wounded Knee** – the very place where thirteen years later three hundred Sioux men, women and children were slaughtered in the bloody finale to over half a century of barbarism (see p.583).

NORTH DAKOTA

NORTH DAKOTA has no instantly recognisable national landmarks, nor is the state's history particularly lurid or glamorous. It seems like somebody's quiet afterthought, a place to pass through. Grain silos loom on the horizon; the haystacks resemble bread-loaves. In the summer, with the sun baking in a defiantly blue sky and the wind raking strong fingers through tall fields of golden wheat and flax, North Dakota epitomises all things rural American. Charming, picturesque – and a bit maddening.

It was the Homestead Act of 1862 that made the Dakota Territory so attractive to settlers. The influx of Europeans led to a population and agricultural boom that lasted into this century. As in South Dakota, the fertile eastern portion is more thickly settled than the west, where vast cattle and sheep ranges predominate. From **Fargo**, the major eastern city, I-94 passes through the central capital of **Bismarck**, and on to the **Bad Lands** of the west, an area cherished by President Theodore Roosevelt. Though the national park bearing his name is a key destination, Roosevelt would surely not be pleased that the west's oil and coal reserves continue to be mined, despite environmentalists' warnings about the disfiguring damage being done to the earth.

Getting Around North Dakota

Amtrak run one train per day in each direction between Fargo and Williston in the northwest, via Grand Forks. **Greyhound** is the major interstate coach operator.

East of the Missouri

North Dakota has far more land east of the big winding **Missouri River**, its uneven dividing line, than west. The **Red River Valley**, the state's furthest eastern strip, has some of the nation's richest soil and two notable cities, **Grand Forks** and **Fargo**.

Pelicans, geese, swans, prairie chickens and ring-necked pheasants live off the sloughs and potholes of the rolling, glaciated prairie of south-central North Dakota, while lakes and woodland dominate the north and the Canadian border. **Fort Totten Indian Reservation** at Devils Lake is midway between the Turtle Mountains and Grand Forks. The low-slung Turtles are topped by Lake Metigoshe and the International Peace Garden (more of a political symbol than a compelling sight). The northeast corner of the state is graced by Icelandic State Park and North Dakota's first permanent white settlement, **Pembina Historic Site** (1801).

Grand Forks

GRAND FORKS sits eighty miles north of Fargo at the confluence of two rivers. Even before its founding a hundred years ago, fur traders had used the area as a convenient stopping place for resting and bartering during their travels between Winnipeg, 145 miles north, and Minneapolis/St Paul, just over 300 miles southeast. It's an easy-going, small, outdoorsy city, with nineteen parks and several tree-lined avenues of fine homes. The compact, user-friendly downtown sports an Art Deco cinema (the *Empire*, 400 Demers Avenue) and a handful of idiosyncratic bars and cafes that spill over the bridge into East Grand Forks, Minnesota.

The **visitor centre** is housed in a converted railway depot at 202 N Third Street (☎746-0444 or ☎1-800/866-4566). *Greyhound* is a bit out of the way at 1325 Demers Avenue (☎775-4781); *Amtrak* is at no. 5555. *Triangle Transportation* (☎218/773-2631) runs coaches into Minnesota out of East Grand Forks from 1611 Central Avenue NW.

The telephone **area code** for the entire state of North Dakota is ☎701.

Downtown's *Best Western Town House*, 710 First Avenue N (☎746-5411), has doubles for $55 to $65. About $10 cheaper, the *Fabulous Westward Ho* on Hwy-2 (☎775-5341) features among its kitschiest decor an outdoor swimming pool shaped like a cowboy boot. The nearby *Super 8*, 1122 N 43rd Street (☎775-8138), has rooms for $38–41. Reservations are necessary at *Lord Byron's*, 521 S Fifth Street (☎775-0194), the city's sole B&B. No smoking, kids, pets or credit cards, but a substantial breakfast is guaranteed in this big, comfy 1897 house with rooms costing $60–70.

Sanders 1907, 312 Kittson Avenue (☎746-8970), is a handsome hole-in-the-wall **restaurant** with a limited, eclectic European menu costing $8 to $10. *The Pantry*, 109 N Third Street (☎746-6695), has sit-down meals and takeaway sandwiches ($5 and up), while the lurid *Red Pepper*, on the edge of town at 1011 University Avenue (☎775-9671), serves cheap Mexican takeaway, subs and baked potatoes until 1.30am.

Fargo

FARGO, North Dakota's largest city, is parenthesised by the smaller townships of West Fargo and Moorhead, Minnesota, just across the Red River. It's a clean, green valley city, family-oriented, conservative and collegiate, with twenty thousand students attending the three schools within its purlieus. The best sight of the **downtown** district is the *Fargo Theatre*, 314 Broadway Avenue, a vaudeville-cum-movie-palace circa 1926. Even if you don't go inside the auditorium to catch a stage show or film, check out the sleek Art Moderne lines of the mirrored lobby with its white baby grand piano. Each April and October the management programmes silent film classics to the accompaniment of an all-wind Wurlitzer pipe organ exhumed from beneath the stage.

Apart from shopping or accommodation, the sole reason to venture into **WEST FARGO** is **Bonanzaville, USA** (late May–late Oct Mon–Fri 9am–8pm, Sat & Sun 9am–5pm; $4). This flavoursome pioneer village and museum, at exit 85 off I-94, commemorates the bonanza farming era of the 1880s. An indoor museum (Tues–Fri 9.30am–4pm off-season) features an international collection of **salt and pepper shakers**. Beyond this, nearly four dozen mostly genuine buildings have been transplanted here and stuffed with memorabilia and antiques; it's like stepping onto a film studio back-lot, with a soundtrack of mellow old-fashioned music playing on the loudspeakers.

Moorhead's top attraction is the **Heritage Hjemkomst Center**, 202 First Avenue N (Mon–Wed, Fri & Sat 9am–5pm, Thurs 9am–9pm, Sun noon–5pm; $3.50). The roof, resembling a circus big top, is shaped to fit the mast of a replica of a ninth-century **Viking sailing vessel**. Builder Robert Asp's dream was to sail the 76-foot *Hjemkomst* (pronounced *yem-komst*, it's the Norwegian word for homecoming) 1300 miles from Duluth, Minnesota, through the Great Lakes to New York City harbour, and a further 3900 miles to Bergen, Norway. He died of leukaemia, leaving it to a dozen-strong crew, including four members of his own family, to make the journey in 1982. It's a tale of stubborn vision, courage and goodwill guaranteed to tug at even the stoniest heart.

Practicalities

Fargo-Moorhead's **visitor centre** (☎237-6134) is at 1220 Main Avenue. *Greyhound* is very central at 402 NP Avenue, and *Amtrak* trains come in at 420 Fourth Street.

Rooms at the downtown *Radisson Hotel*, 201 N Fifth Street (☎232-7363 or ☎1-800/333-3333), start at $86, but there are plenty of cheaper inns and motels, particularly where I-29 and I-94 meet. *Super 8*, 3518 Interstate Boulevard (☎232-9202), costs around $35; *Days Inn*, 901 38th Street SW (☎282-9100), upwards of $39. *Bohligs*, 1418 S Third Street (☎235-7867), a simple and slightly run-down B&B in a family home, charges $35 to $45. The restaurant, nightclub and casino *Broadway*, 22 Broadway Avenue (☎237-6161), is a staple of Fargo's downtown scene, with eclectic decor, a casual atmosphere and affordable prices. *Passages*, in the *Radisson*, is a more sedate dining alternative.

Devils Lake

The town of **DEVILS LAKE**, ninety miles west of Grand Forks on Hwy-2, shares its name with the state's largest natural body of water, which has four state parks and five private campgrounds on its 300 sprawling and irregular miles of shoreline. Downtown holds a smattering of historic nineteenth-century buildings and a few rough and ready bars. Most of the **accommodation** is strung along Hwy-2, like for example the *Artclare Motel*, where rooms are roughly $28 (☎662-4001). *Woodland Resort*, on the west side of Creel Bay about eight miles from town (☎662-5996), is an attractive year-round facility with a good restaurant and cabins going for $299 weekly. Boats and pontoons can be hired there or across the bay at *Creel Bay Marina* (☎662-4786) on Lakewood Beach.

At **Fort Totten Indian Reservation**, fourteen miles south of town, the Fort itself, also known as Cavalry Square, is one of the best preserved frontier military posts (mid-May to mid-Sept daily 8am–5pm). The thrilling **Fort Totten Days Pow-wow and Rodeo** takes place annually during the last weekend in July (daily admission $3, $5 for all three days). It's a peaceful but impassioned, alcohol-free, multitribal party in which hundreds of dancing contestants of all ages compete for cash prizes. Their gorgeous costumes, decorated with bells, beads, feathers and bits of metal can take months to fashion. Singers sit in a circle, chanting and wailing in unison, and beating out a rhythm on a big drum, while the dancers tap, stomp and lurch around a long, semi-enclosed oval of earth. Stalls sell food, clothing and gifts. Demonstrations of rodeo skills such as calf and goat roping, barrel racing and saddle bronc riding are accompanied by the sexist patter of the male announcer, and some clowns whose job it is to keep the livelier animals from stomping the humans. Bring your beer belly, toy pistol and cowboy boots.

The West

Anyone with a hankering to play cowboy could do worse than follow in the footsteps of **Theodore Roosevelt**, who once said "I never would have been President if it had not been for my experiences in North Dakota". Roosevelt initially came to the state in search of spiritual and physical renewal after the deaths (on the same day) of his mother and first wife. He dubbed what he discovered during his few years in this "grimly picturesque" area, with its clear skies, panoramic views and weird, colourful land forms, a "perfect freedom". The national park named after him is the choicest destination in the **North Dakota Bad Lands** (distinct from South Dakota's Badlands) that dominate the state's western half.

The region's other prominent natural feature, the **Missouri River**, wriggles like a giant raggedy worm out of Montana, down past the capital, **Bismarck**, and into South Dakota. En route it is transformed into Lake Sakakawea, a virtual inland sea nearly two hundred miles long that's the state's premier water playground. The US Corps of Discovery, better known as the Lewis and Clark Expedition, explored the Missouri at President Thomas Jefferson's behest in 1804–06. Scenic state highways 1804 and 1806 follow the expedition's trail; I-94 (east–west) and US-85 (north–south), however, provide more direct access to the area's most popular sights.

Bismarck and Mandan

The West seems to begin as soon as you cross the Missouri River from **BISMARCK**, a capital city with a small-town feel, to Mandan. Both were founded in 1872, Bismarck as a military camp to protect railroad crews from hostile Indians and outlaws. Its original name, Edwinton, was changed by the secretary of the Northern Pacific Railroad, both in honour of German Chancellor Otto von Bismarck, and in hopes of attracting overseas investment, given the growing number of German immigrants settling in the area.

The scheme failed, but the name stuck. The city survived an early lawless period (present-day Fourth Street was once dubbed "Murderers' Gulch") and a major fire to become first the territorial and then the state capital.

Contemporary Bismarck is pretty much contained within the oblong between I-94 in the north and Business 94, or Main Street, to the south. Locals are particularly proud of their nineteen-storey limestone **Capitol Building**, dating from the mid-1930s and set at the crest of a public park. The interior, a model of spatial economy and marbled, Art Deco elegance, is open for free guided tours weekdays, year-round. Across the street, the superb **North Dakota Heritage Center** (Mon–Thurs 8am–5pm, Fri 8am–8pm, Sat 9am–5pm, Sun 11am–5pm) divides the state's past into six sections, starting with the dinosaurs, designed and presented in a way that makes history resonate. Look for the bison robe painted by the celebrated warrior Sitting Bull, and the bison "smell box".

The major reason to venture into **MANDAN** is **Fort Lincoln State Park**, five miles south of downtown via Hwy-1806, the centrepiece of which is the **Custer House** (May–Sept 9.30am–8.30pm; $3), an admirable reconstruction of the 1874 original designed by the brutally ambitious, indefatigable Lieutenant Colonel himself. The guided tour supplies nuggets of quirky information about him (he loved to eat raw onions, and wore wigs of his own ginger-coloured hair to fancy dress balls), his devoted wife Libbie and their household prior to his death at Little Bighorn, Montana, in 1876. Nearer the river are five earthlodge reconstructions on the site of the once-vast On-a-Slant village occupied by the Mandan (or River Dweller) tribe from about 1610 to the late 1700s. The lodges, site and adjacent historical museum are all somewhat run-down. The quiet riverside **campground** (☎663-9571) costs $9 to $12. Be sure to make it up to the bluff above the village, where there are fine views of the Missouri and several re-created block houses recall the Park's infantry-post days.

Practicalities

Bismarck's *Greyhound* terminal (☎223-6576) is at 1237 W Divide Street, off I-94, exit 35; its **visitor centre** is at 523 N Fourth Street (Mon–Fri 8am–5pm; ☎222-4308). The small but conveniently located city-centre *Fleck House*, 122 E Thayer Avenue (☎255-1450), has rooms for $32 to $42. **Mandan**'s *Days Inn*, I-94, exit 31 (☎663-0001), costs $37 to $41. For **camping** off the beaten track, try the excellent *Cross Ranch State Park* (☎794-3731), thirty minutes north of Bismarck on route 112A. Overlapped by a 6000-acre Nature Preserve, the park features sixteen miles of trails and a primitive log cabin furnished with antiques (rentable May–Sept Mon–Thurs, $25 per night for up to five people). Campsites cost $5 to $8, plus $2 vehicle fee.

Dining and **nightlife** are plentiful in Bismarck. *Peacock Alley*, Fifth and Main streets (☎255-7917), is in a downtown hotel that was once the headquarters of the progressive Non-Partisan League. Its Cajun, Italian and American cuisine costs $9 and up, but the classy adjoining bar has lunches for under $7 and a $2 burger special. *Fiesta Villa* (☎222-8075), across the street in a converted railway depot, features a patio, live music and an extensive South of the Border menu for $5 to $8. The *Drumstick*, 307 N Third Street (☎223-8444; closed Sun), is a classic low-cost greasy spoon rightly proud of its home cooking and 24-hour breakfasts. In Mandan, the *Drug Store and Soda Fountain*, 316 W Main Street (☎663-5900), is a good place to grab a cheap lunch and an ice cream.

Theodore Roosevelt National Park

The **THEODORE ROOSEVELT NATIONAL PARK** is split into north and south units approximately seventy miles apart, the area between comprising a checkerboard of federal, state and privately owned territory. Exploring the park's 110 acres can be compared to going into different rooms: from desert to woods to mountains. Vehicle and pedestrian fees are $3 and $1 respectively, May to October, daylight hours.

Your first taste of the larger, more popular southern unit is likely to be at the breath-taking **Painted Canyon**, seven miles east of the town of **Medora** off I-94, exit 8. Here and elsewhere in the park, the land is like a sedimentary layer cake that for millions of years has been beaten by hard, infrequent rains, baked by the sun into a rainbow of hues and cut through to the base by erosive streams and rivers. A mile-long nature hike begins at the end of the canyon's boardwalk.

The southern unit's main **visitor centre** in Medora (June–Aug 8am–8pm; otherwise 8am–4.30pm; ☎623-4466) runs tours, nature walks and campfire programmes in high season. Out back, the simple cabin was used by the young Roosevelt while a partner in the Maltese Cross Ranch (free guided tours daily until 4.15pm). A highlight of the southern unit's scenic 36-mile **loop road** is the sublime view from **Wind Canyon**, ten miles out of Medora. Peaceful *Valley Ranch* (☎623-4496), six miles from Medora and a mile from the park's *Cottonwood Campground* ($7 fee), arranges **horseback tours** in summer, including one to the Park's petrified forest.

The northern unit, off Hwy-85 near **Watford City**, receives only a tenth as many visi-tors and is on the whole less spectacular, though its fifteen-mile scenic drive ends at **Oxbow Overlook**, a magnificent cul de sac. Its visitor centre is open daily between May and September (9am–5pm), and on weekends and limited holidays the remainder of the year. *Squaw Creek Campground* operates on a first-come, first-served basis. Either unit is at its subtlest at sunrise or sundown, the best times to observe such fauna as elk, antelope, bison and several fascinating, closely knit **prairie dog** communities.

If you've time to spare, take Hwy-85 from Watford City the forty-six miles to Williston, from where it's another twenty-four miles southwest on Hwy-1804 to **Fort Union** (June to mid-Sept 8am–8pm; otherwise 8am–5.30pm). Located near the confluence of the Yellowstone and Missouri rivers, and established by John Jacob Astor's American Fur Company, this was the territory's pre-eminent trading centre in the first half of the nine-teenth century. Inside the sturdy palisade walls are an Indian trade house, a pristine reconstruction of the **French Colonial Bourgeois House** ("bourgeois" being the title given to the fort's resident manager) and a lot of history, much of it imparted in a free half-hour tour given daily at 10am, noon, 2 and 4pm. The rangers at this National Historic Site don't shy away from telling the truth – for example, how the white fur trad-ers made a 200 to 2000 percent profit in their dealings with the Indians.

Medora

MEDORA, the southern gateway to Theodore Roosevelt National Park, languished in obscurity until the early Sixties, but has become one of North Dakota's principal attrac-tions, an inoffensively touristy place with enough to keep you busy, and reasonably interested, for a day. The story of its founding is cinema or at the very least TV mini-series material, focusing on the fortunes of a young, trailblazing French aristocrat impressively named Antoine Amedee Marie Vincent Manca de Vallombrosa, the Marquis de Mores. His wife, Medora von Hoffman, was a New York banker's daughter whom he'd met and wed in Paris. After moving to America and studying the cattle indus-try, the Marquis decided that the ideal place to create the meatpacking capital of the west was in North Dakota Territory, at the confluence of the Little Missouri River and the Northern Pacific Railroad. Using investment capital from his father-in-law, in 1883 he bought some land and created his own town from scratch, naming it after his wife. Within four months, he was supplying refrigerated beef, as opposed to live cattle, to the east. Established meat companies and livestock markets, however, resisted and even sabotaged the Marquis' innovations, and within three years of its inception, his ambi-tious scheme was washed up. He, his family and retinue of servants moved away from Medora, leaving behind a 26-room red-roofed frontier ranch home known somewhat misleadingly as the **Chateau** (8.30am–5.20pm high season; $2), an empty meatpacking plant (only the smokestack of which still stands), a town of over eighty buildings, and an aura of faded dreams. Shortly thereafter, the Marquis went to India to hunt tigers, and was later killed, just before his 38th birthday, trying to forge a French-Moroccan alliance. Photos of the maverick man himself, in the visitor centre below the chateau, show a dashing but silly buckskinned Euro-cowboy toting a Winchester (he was a crack shot) and sporting a supercilious expression.

Elsewhere in town, the biggest noise is the **Medora Musical** (Mon–Fri 7.30pm, Sat & Sun 7pm; $9.50–10.50), a pseudo-western, super-Americana variety show staged beneath the stars in a vast, modern amphitheatre. If a man balancing on a board balanced on a bowling ball to a cover version of the *Hawaii Five-O* theme is your idea of a great time, book on ☎623-4422.

The Medora Foundation has a monopoly on **accommodation**, operating the *Rough Riders Hotel* (rooms $55) and the *Medora* ($48) and *Badlands* ($33–50) motels. The last two, open seasonally, have outdoor pools. Make reservations for all three on ☎623-4422, or ☎223-4800 off-season. The *Medora Campground* (☎623-4435) has sites for tents, vans, pick-ups and RVs ($3–14.50). Prices are comparable on the southeast side of town at *Red Trail* (☎623-4317; summer only), where there's free live country music.

Don't expect gourmet **dining** in Medora. The Musical hosts a beef-heavy "pitchfork fondue" most nights prior to the performance. The dining room at the restored *Rough Riders Hotel* serves reliable meals daily until 9pm. The nearby *Chuckwagon Cafeteria* offers cheap filling grub between 7am and 7.30pm. The high fluoride content of Medora's **water** means it tastes terrible out of the tap. Buy it bottled at the old but immaculate *Joe Ferris' General Store* (8am–8pm), named after one of Roosevelt's partners and the only place in town to stock up on groceries and drugstore goods.

SOUTH DAKOTA

The wide-open spaces of the Great Plains roll away to infinity to either side of I-90 in **SOUTH DAKOTA**. Vast numbers of high-season visitors speed straight through on this road to the spectacular **southwest**, site of the **Black Hills**, the adjacent **Badlands**, and that most patriotic of icons, **Mount Rushmore**. The plains are at their most fertile east of the Missouri River, which flows unevenly down through the centre of the state before veering to the southeast, bordering Nebraska.

Time and Hollywood have mythologised the larger-than-life personalities for whom the Dakota Territory served as a stomping ground; **General Custer** and **Crazy Horse** battled here for supremacy over the Plains, while **"Wild Bill" Hickok** and **"Calamity Jane"** were denizens of the once-notorious Gold Rush town of Deadwood.

The **Sioux**, or Dakota, tribes dominated the plains from the eighteenth century, having gradually been pushed westwards out of the Great Lakes by the encroaching whites. To these nomadic hunters, unlike the gun-toting Christian settlers and federal politicians, the concept of owning the earth was utterly alien. They fought hard to keep their land, and themselves, free: the Sioux are the only Indian nation to defeat the United States in war and force it to sign a treaty (in 1868) favourable to their race. Even so, they were compelled to relinquish the sacred Black Hills, and ultimately the choice lay between death or confinement on reservations. For decades Indian history and culture was outlawed; until the 1940s it was illegal to teach or even speak Lakota, the Sioux language. More Sioux live on South Dakota's six reservations now than dwelt in the whole state during pioneer days, but their prospects are often grim. Thanks to the Hills, South Dakota is the country's leading **gold**-producing state, but the Indians are the most neglected, impoverished American minority. Nowhere is the sorrowful legacy of injustice better symbolised than at **Wounded Knee**, on the Oglala Sioux reservation **Pine Ridge** – scene of the infamous 1890 massacre by the US Army, and also of a prolonged "civil disturbance" by the radical American Indian Movement in 1973.

Kevin Costner's award-winning film *Dances With Wolves*, most of it shot in South Dakota, has boosted the state's tourism image while pricking liberal white America's collective conscience. The lead character's ramshackle outpost was built on a ranch northeast of Rapid City, not far from the airport; the Sioux village he finds was located along the Belle Fourche River about fifteen miles east of Sturgis; and the winter camp seen at the film's conclusion was in Spearfish Canyon. The buffalo hunt, however, was filmed state centre on the Triple U Standing Butte Ranch near Fort Pierre.

Native American traditions are publicly celebrated at **pow-wows**, tribal gatherings of music, dance and socialising, held usually in summer on the reservations; the state tourist office (see p.18) can supply dates and locations. Apart from pow-wows, summers in South Dakota are typically taken up with historical celebrations, *volksmarches* (a friendly sort of community walking exercise), ethnic festivals and rodeos. The state has 170 parks and recreation areas in which to hike and camp. In winter, downhill skiing is limited to Terry Peak or Deer Mountain in the Black Hills; cross-country and snowmobiling are more prevalent.

Getting Around South Dakota

You'll be hard put to see much of South Dakota without a car. *Amtrak* routes bypass the state entirely, while *Greyhound* and *Jack Rabbit* (☎1-800/759-8687) **coach** lines serve points between the two largest cities, Rapid City and Sioux Falls, where the two major airports are also located.

The telephone **area code** for the entire state of South Dakota is ☎605.

East of the Missouri

For tourists, little in **eastern** or **central** South Dakota constitutes the essential. **Sioux Falls**, the state's biggest city, is faceless but handy. As one of the country's quietest and smallest capital cities, **Pierre** has its charms. **Mitchell** has a few sights, such as its Corn Palace and a doll museum, to satisfy both specialists and curiosity-seekers. **Yankton**, comfortably ensconced along the Missouri River across from Nebraska, is a gem-like historic town with the excellent Lewis and Clark Recreation Area on its doorstep. Nearby **Vermillion** is home to the exceptional Shrine to Music Museum. About sixty miles northwest of Sioux Falls, **De Smet**, known as "Little Town on the Prairie" thanks to Laura Ingalls Wilder, author of a well-loved series of autobiographical books about prairie life from a child's perspective (though the TV location is in Kansas; see p.560). De Smet's annual Wilder Pageant (the last weekend in June and the first two in July) is held on grounds overlooking the Wilder homestead. You can tour eighteen sites mentioned in her books. The Historical Festival held for two days in early June at **Fort Sisseton** (25 miles west of I-29, in the northeast) is a re-creation of 1860s life as experienced at a frontier post, complete with infantry drills, music, food, crafts and an Indian teepee village. It's representative of what you'll find east of the Missouri: smatterings of history, pretty scenery and homely pride.

Mitchell

Mitchell makes a mildly diverting stop on the long ride across South Dakota via I-90. The **Corn Palace** at 604 N Main Street (summer daily 8.30am–10pm, winter Mon–Fri 8.30am–5pm) has been humorously pegged as "the world's largest birdfeeder"; the first Corn Palace was built in 1892 to encourage settlement and to display products of the rich local soil. Topped with brightly painted onion-shaped domes and minarets like some kitsch Moorish transplant to the American cornbelt, the exterior of this sports and performance auditorium is decorated annually (at a cost of about $35,000) with large murals depicting hunting, fishing, farming and other outdoor scenes. The artists' materials consist exclusively of native corn, grains and grasses of varied but entirely natural colour, all grown by specially commissioned local farmers. Their designs are mounted on roofing paper attached to wooden panels, then sprayed with preservatives and repellents to ward off birds, squirrels and insects. Further examples of this rural folk art are inside the Palace, along with photos of the building spanning the century.

In the **Enchanted World Doll Museum** (daily summer 8am–8pm; spring and autumn 8am–5pm; $2.50), in a mock-medieval castle across the street from the Palace, more than 4000 dolls from nearly 150 countries are on view. It's much less twee and far more interesting than you might expect. Highlights include several schizoid two- and three-faced dolls, a salt-carved Shirley Temple, Japanese Beatles circa 1964, a dried fruit, veg and nut family, the first bent-limbed doll (Kaiser Wilhelm, 1903) and, for fans of modern fairy tales, Princesses Di and Fergie.

There are other ways to while away a few hours in Mitchell: a gallery devoted to the work of a Yanktonai Sioux painter, a pioneer museum and a prehistoric Native American village. The *Best Western* (☎996-5536) and *Super 8* (☎996-9678) chain **motels** are both at the junction of I-90 and Hwy-37, with rooms ranging from $34 to $48. The chef-owned *Town House*, 103 N Main Street (☎996-4615), is a good place to grab a meal. Mitchell's **visitor centre** (☎996-7311) is located in the Corn Palace.

The Badlands and Black Hills

The **Badlands** and **Black Hills** are two of the most dramatic, mysterious, and legend-impacted tracts of land in the US. For the whites, they encapsulate a wagonload of American notions about heritage and the taming of the West. To Native Americans they are ancient, spiritually resonant places. Physically they're endlessly pleasing and intriguing. The science-fiction severity of the Badlands resists conversion into easy tourist palatability. The bigger, friendlier Black Hills can be more actively experienced (hiking trails, mountain lakes and streams, scenic highways), and exploited for entertainment and profit (via dozens of physical, historical and plain commercial attractions, and the mining of gold and other metals).

The Badlands

The **WHITE RIVER BADLANDS** could be considered a pocket-sized cousin of Arizona's Grand Canyon. But look past the family resemblance and you'll see that what's most impressive about the "Badlandscape" is not its scale, as at the Canyon, but rather its sheer strangeness. More than 35 million years ago this area of southwest South Dakota was a saltwater sea, later a marsh. The remains of such prehistoric mammals as sabre-toothed tigers and three-toed horses sank into the marsh, to be covered with white volcanic ash (fossil specimens can be seen free of charge in the Museum of Geology at South Dakota School of Mines and Technology, Rapid City). The terrain dried as it evolved, and became unable to support the deep-rooted shrubs or trees that might have preserved it. The erosion that commenced a few million years ago is slowly eating away layers of sand, silt, ash, mud and gravel, to reveal rippling gradations of earth tones and pastel colours. The friable earth is carved into all manner of shapes: pinnacles, precipices, pyramids, knobs, cones, ridges, gorges or, if you're feeling poetic, lunar sandcastles and cathedrals. The Sioux dubbed these incredible contortions of nature *Mako Sica*, literally "land bad"; early French trappers echoed that with *Mauvaises Terres à Traverser*, or "bad lands to travel across"; they were also once

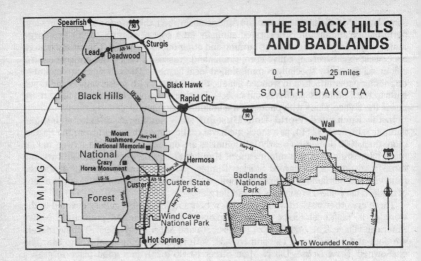

aptly described as "hell with the fires out". Despite this daunting reputation, many species of wildlife are at home here, while on average a million visitors pass through each year. The Badlands' rainbow colours are most vibrant just after a rainfall.

About one tenth of the Badlands – the most fantastic bits – were declared a National Monument in 1939, and a **National Park** nearly forty years later. The park is open year-round, its two most accessible entrances being at exits 131 (Northeast entrance) and 109–110 (Pinnacles entrance), off I-90. The charge is $4 per vehicle, late May until early September; often there is no fee in winter. Visitors can backpack or climb just about anywhere. Information on numerous trails is available from **Cedar Pass Visitor Center** (summer 7am–dusk; otherwise 8am–4.30pm; ☎433-5361), five miles from the Northeast entrance. State Hwy-240 connects the two park entrances, a forty-mile black-topped loop that includes nine scenic overlooks.

If you want to **stay** in the Badlands themselves, a double at *Cedar Pass Lodge* (mid-April to Oct; ☎433-5460), operated by the Oglala Sioux, costs $36. Prices are comparable at the *Badlands Inn* (mid-April to mid-Nov; ☎433-5401), but *Badlands Budget Host Motel* (June to mid-Sept; ☎433-5335 or ☎1-800/999-6116) has the best deal at $30. There is a handful of seasonal **campgrounds**, both in the park and in Wall.

Wall

The town of **WALL**, eight miles north of the Badlands, looks like nothing special, yet thanks to **Wall Drug**, begun modestly in 1931 as a "mom and pop" shop on Main Street, it's known around the world. You'll know about Wall long before you reach exits 109 or 110 off I-90. *"Just ahead"*, *"Here comes"*, *"Next 2 exits"*, *"Last chance"* say the hoardings near to Wall, but several hundred are spread throughout the neighbouring states.

In 1936, Ted and Dorothy Hustead made a last-ditch effort to rescue their 600-square-foot pharmacy (half of it living quarters) from financial failure by planting hand-made hoardings on the nearby highway, offering free ice water to all comers. The turn-around was immediate. Today they and their offspring manage an irresistibly kitschy emporium where over two hundred employees serve up to twenty thousand visitors per day. You can fill up on steaks'n'cakes in the 520-seat cafe-cum-Western art gallery, or simply drink one of the five thousand glasses of ice water dispensed daily. There's free coffee and doughnuts for Vietnam veterans, honeymooners, hunters, snowmobilers, skiers, missile crews and other privileged groups. For decades the Husteads have been giving away stick-on sheets plugging *Wall Drug*, ensuring free advertising all over the globe, from London's underground to the South Pole; the *Drug* has the snapshots to prove it. Just about every available wall or floor space is taken up with photos, artwork, memorabilia, stuffed and mounted animals (including the facetious "jackalope"), manne-quins and mechanical displays like the Cowboy Orchestra and the Chuckwagon Quartet – Ronald Reagan is an unmistakeable member of the latter. The merchandise runs a gamut from quality (7000 pairs of boots, an excellent bookshop specialising in Western lore, and a complete trail outfitters) to junk (anyone for a rattlesnake mould?). Most of all, there's the crackpot cornucopia atmosphere of this ultimate family store, a downmar-ket, down-home Disneyland blatantly trading on American nostalgia.

There's absolutely no reason to **spend the night** in Wall, but if you're stuck try the *Best Western Plains Motel*, 712 Glenn Street (☎279-2145), which has rooms for $48 to $68, or the *Super 8* next door(☎1-800/843-1991), where prices range $30 to $53. If you're hungry there's home cooking at the *Elkton House* (☎279-2152), at I-90 and Hwy-240, and dining and cocktails at the *Cactus Restaurant Lounge* on Main Street (☎279-2561).

Wounded Knee

No other atrocity against Native Americans, perhaps, is so potent and poignant as the massacre at **WOUNDED KNEE**. On December 29 1890, the US Army delivered a *coup de grace* to the vestiges of Plains Indian resistance, killing several hundred unarmed Sioux men, women and children. Most were **Ghost Dancers**, followers of a messianic cult who believed that by ritualistic, trance-inducing dancing and singing they could recover their lost land, ancestors and way of life. The carnage may have been an impul-sive but inevitable act of retaliation for the Battle of Little Bighorn, in Montana in 1876, when the Seventh Cavalry led by George Custer were soundly defeated by Crazy Horse, Sitting Bull and their fellow tribesmen (see p.628). It was triggered by a misunderstand-ing during a tribal round-up. A deaf Indian, asked to surrender his rifle along with his peers, instead held it above his head, shouting that he'd paid a lot for it. An officer grabbed at the gun, it went off, and the troops started shooting. "I can still see the butch-ered women and children lying heaped and scattered along the crooked gulch," the holy man Black Elk recalled more than forty years later, "as plain as when I saw them with eyes still young. And I can see that something else died there in the bloody mud . . . People's dreams died there . . . The nation's hoop is broken and scattered."

The victims' shabby collective gravesite is in a desolate spot at the bottom of **Pine Ridge Indian Reservation**, above US-18 not far from the state border. There's not a lot to see – a commemorative sign and a stone monument surrounded by a chain-link fence. But there's also something intangible, a feeling of grief and anger that permeates the Indian nations. The mass murder at Wounded Knee has left an indelible scar on all First Americans. Eighty-three years later, members of the radical American Indian Movement (AIM) grabbed headlines by occupying Wounded Knee in a dispute over a federally imposed tribal government. Violence spread on the reservation, with armed FBI agents and a special paramilitary unit dispatched to rout AIM and its sympa-thisers. More peaceably, the *Sitanka Wokiksuye* movement began in the mid-1980s. A more pragmatic version of Ghost Dancing, it involves an annual pilgrimage in which an ever-growing number of Indians brave the often harsh winter weather, travelling to Wounded Knee on horseback to release symbolically the spirits of their dead ancestors and thereby mend the sacred hoop of the Sioux nation. It's difficult to say what influ-ence, if any, the movement has had in Washington DC, but moves are afoot to desig-nate the gravesite a national monument.

Pine Ridge, the second largest reservation in the United States, overlaps with the Badlands. It is also located in the nation's poorest county. Its prefab and mobile homes blend sadly and uneasily with the surrounding dry grasslands, rocky bluffs and tree-lined creeks. **Red Cloud Indian Mission School**, a few miles west of the town of Pine Ridge on US-18, holds an Indian art show each summer featuring work by thirty different tribes. The school has a permanent display of star quilts (a Sioux tradition), paintings and a gift shop (all open Mon–Fri 9am–5pm, Sat & Sun by appointment). The **Oglala Nation Fair**, the first weekend in August, includes a pow-wow and rodeo. For details, contact the Oglala Sioux Tribe, Pine Ridge, SD 57770 (☎867-5771).

The Black Hills

The **BLACK HILLS**, roughly a hundred miles long and varying from forty to sixty miles wide, occupy some 6000 square miles between the Belle Fourche River in the north and the Cheyenne to the south. For many nations of Sioux, their value was and still is immeasurable. The Hills are "the heart of everything that is", a kind of spiritual safe, a place of gods and holy mountains where warriors went to speak with *Wakan Tanka* (the Great Spirit) and await visions. They were dubbed *Paha Sapa*, or Black Hills, even though they are actually mountains (the highest, Harney Peak, rises over 7000ft), and the blue spruce and Norway pine trees that cover them only appear to be black from a distance. These timbered, rocky outcroppings rise like an island from a sea of lower rolling hills and flat grain-growing plains.

Thinking the Hills were worthless, the United States government drew up a treaty in the mid-nineteenth century that gave them and most of the land west of the Missouri River to the Indians. All such treaties were destined to be broken when the discovery of gold turned the Indians' Eden into the white man's Eldorado, and fortune-hunters came pouring in. The story has an incomplete postscript: in 1980, the US Supreme Court ordered the federal government to pay the Sioux $105 million in **compensation** for the illegal seizure of the Hills in 1877. After heated debate amongst Indian representatives this settlement was rejected and a steering committee subsequently formed to campaign for the return of the Hills themselves to the tribes. The legal battle continues today, often hindered by a lack of consensus amongst the Native Americans.

The Hills today combine tourism with conservation. The danger of the whole area being reduced to a back-to-nature theme park hasn't always been avoided, as evidenced by the number of T-shirt stores, pseudohistorical wax museums, cowboy supper shows, water slides and so on. But the marketing and merchandising aren't so extensive as to rob the Hills of all their beauty or dignity.

Using your own vehicle is much the best way to explore the Hills, though *Gray Line* (☎342-4461) is one of the more reliable of several companies operating all-day (and night-time) **tours** out of **Rapid City**, a reasonably diverting urban gateway on the Hills' central eastern edge. A clutch of towns in the north – **Sturgis**, site of a mammoth annual motorcycle rally; **Spearfish**, which hosts the Black Hills Passion Play; the glorified gambling den **Deadwood**; and the mining centre **Lead** – are of more than passing interest, while the southern section has **Custer State Park**, home to the largest herd of American bison, **Wind Cave National Park**, and the prehistoric bones and mineral waters of **Hot Springs**. No place in the Hills is much more than ninety minutes from the four presidential heads carved into **Mount Rushmore**, but even more remarkable is **Crazy Horse Mountain**, the world's most ambitious work-in-progress.

Finally, a word about **gold**. Numerous outlets sell the area's distinctive grape-leaf design. The Hills variety has a frosted finish and comes in three shades – yellow, green and pink; the last two are alloys, made by mixing gold with silver and copper or zinc.

Deadwood and the North Hills

The northern portion of the Black Hills is mainly a loop of mountain communities linked by scenic drives. Aspen, birch and white spruce spread over the towering limestone cliffs above the nineteen-mile **Spearfish Canyon National Scenic Highway**.

Part of US-14A, the road follows Spearfish Creek down into the Hills and around to Lead and Deadwood, passing Bridal Veil and Roughlock Falls.

Still nurturing its reputation as one of the West's wildest Gold Rush towns, **DEADWOOD** is one of the few cities in the US to be entirely designated a National Historic Landmark. Its Main Street lies at the bottom of a gulch, the rest of the town dribbling along up the steep sides of the canyon. Gold was discovered here, 42 miles northwest of Rapid City, in 1876. Within a year six thousand gold-diggers swarmed in to stake their claims. At its peak the population included con artists, outlaws and other dubious frontier types. Among them were James Butler, aka **Wild Bill Hickok** – sometime spy, scout, bullwhacker, stagecoach driver, sheriff and gambler, who spent only a few weeks in Deadwood prior to his murder by a young drifter named Jack McCall – and Martha **"Calamity Jane"** Canary Burke, a coarse illiterate alcoholic, whose checkered career included stints as dishwasher, muleskinner, scout, prostitute, nurse and Wild West Show performer. She died penniless in 1903, her last wish to be buried beside Hickok high up above town in Mount Moriah Cemetary. A sign near their neighbouring graves reads, "Pard, we will meet again in the happy hunting ground to part no more".

Gambling was outlawed in Deadwood in 1889, the year South Dakota achieved statehood. That didn't stop betting parlours and brothels from flourishing well into this century. Now the old ghosts of Deadwood's raunchy past have been revitalised. In the late 1980s the snappily titled "Deadwood You Bet" committee started pushing a gaming proposal through the local, county and state-wide legislatures; the people of South Dakota voted it into legality in 1989. Deadwood, with a residential population of only 2000, is now a boomtown again, but at a cost. Arrests are up 250 percent, and the economy is almost totally based on gaming. Real estate prices have soared so high that no non-gambling business can afford to be on Main Street, where the action is, without hauling in fleets of insidious one-armed bandits.

A visit to Deadwood is nevertheless essential, if only to see that Sin City can flourish even in a God's Country like the Black Hills. Topping the list of places to **stay** is *Adams House*, 22 Van Buren Street (☎578-3877), an antique-stuffed Victorian B&B, where rooms in summer cost $80 to $90. Lodgings at the historic *Franklin Hotel*, 700 Main Street (☎578-2241), are $48 to $68, depending on whether you stay in the old hotel or the modern motor inn across the road. *Deadwood Gulch Resort*, which offers rooms for $49 to $54, is on US-85 south (☎578-1294). The local **Chamber of Commerce** is at 735 Main Street (☎578-1876).

Even teetotallers should check out the massive carved oak **bar** at the *Bodega*, 662 Main Street (☎578-1996), where meals are available from 11am until 11pm daily. *Saloon #10*, 657 Main Street (☎578-3346), has decent grub, sawdust floors and lots of memorabilia and taxidermy. Above the door is the chair in which the poker-playing Hickok was supposedly sitting when shot dead while holding two aces, a pair of eights and the nine of diamonds, forever after christened the Dead Man's Hand. His assassin was captured across the street at **Goldberg's Grocery**, once the oldest grocery west of the Missouri until taken over by slots; the place is redeemed by its old-fashioned soda fountain, a splendid 32-foot Italian green marble counter.

Custer State Park and the South Hills

The southern Black Hills encompass lower foothills and wooded pastureland; from a purely physical standpoint, their attractions are more enticing than those in the north. The sublime scenery of **Custer State Park** ($6 per vehicle, valid for 5 consecutive days, May–Sept), covering 73,000 acres in the eastern central section, below Mount Rushmore, is highlighted on three routes.

The **Needles Highway** (Hwy-87, open mid-April to mid-Oct) winds for fourteen miles through pine forests and past the eponymous jagged granite spires, up to the park's higher elevations. A 6400-foot summit faces **Harney Peak**, the state's highest point at

THE BISON OF THE GREAT PLAINS

It has been estimated that the Great Plains were in the fifteenth century covered by at least sixty million shaggy, short-sighted **bison** (popularly known as buffalo, a corruption of the French *boeuf*). Apart from eating their flesh, the Native Americans used the fur and hide for clothing and shelter, the bones for toys, weapons and utensils, and the droppings for fuel. Eliminating the bison en masse, as the white man did, was a mercilessly effective way of depleting the Indians as well. By 1910 there were less than a hundred head left.

Custer State Park was instrumental in helping to raise that meagre number to today's national count of 55,000. The 1500 bison occupying the park now constitute the country's largest publicly owned herd. As North America's biggest mammal, the bison is not to be trifled with. An average bull can stand six feet high at the hump, weigh up to a ton and live up to a ripe old twenty-five years. It can outrun a horse and turn on a dime.

The bison are free to roam where they please until the first Monday in October, when the park stages its annual **round-up**. Clustered behind fences at select vantage points, the public is welcome to witness one of the Midwest's more thrilling occasions. Modern technology has invaded cowboy territory. Helicopters, jeeps and pick-up trucks, as well as riders on horseback, steer the often recalcitrant herd down a six-mile "corridor" and into a series of pens. There the calves are branded and vaccinated, and the whole herd sorted in order to determine which 500 will be auctioned off on the third Saturday in November. Proceeds from the sale account for twenty percent of the park's annual revenue.

7200 feet. Look out for **Needle's Eye**, a gap in one of the pinnacles that measures three to four feet wide and fifty to sixty feet long. The seventeen miles of **Iron Mountain Road** (US-16A) run up and over the 5500ft **Iron Mountain**. This engineer's nightmare is a sightseeing motorist's delight, with three pig-tailed bridges, and a trio of one-lane tunnels – cleverly designed by park founder Peter Norbeck to frame the distant Rushmore monument. This route is especially popular with the park's famous "begging burros", tame and disarming four-legged panhandlers who stick their snouts through the windows of passing vehicles in search of a hand-out. The eighteen-mile **Wildlife Loop** wraps around the park's southern edge. Sunrise and sunset are prime times to spy such critters as elk, mountain goats, antelope, deer and coyote.

Tucked up in the northwest corner on its own manmade lake, *Sylvan Lake Resort* (☎574-2561) is open year-round. The warm wood and thick stones of the main building ($59–72 for one bed) exude a relaxed, Thirties-style sumptuousness. The 31 adjacent cabins (starting at $62), spread out beneath the pines, are just as comfy. The *Lakota Dining Room* serves acceptable meals for $10 to $15. Reservations at the park's other resorts can be made on ☎1-800/658-3530. Prices at all three for two persons staying in a variety of lodge rooms, hotel units and cabins start at $55. The best-known is the *State Game Lodge*, just east of the Peter Norbeck **visitor centre** (☎255-4464) on Hwy-16A. Custer State Park also has ten **campgrounds** (☎255-4000).

The small community of **Custer**, five miles west of the park on US-16, is a good touring base. The *Bavarian Inn* (☎673-2802), also on US-16, has classic German dining and rooms for $26 to $54. The **Chamber of Commerce** (☎673-2244) is at 447 Crook Street.

Mount Rushmore National Monument

America's two largest stone carvings are a mere seventeen miles apart, spitting distance when you consider the scale on which they're conceived. The better-known **Mount Rushmore National Monument**, 24 miles southwest of Rapid City off US-16A (☎574-2523), originally dubbed The Shrine of Democracy, is the linchpin of the Hills tourist circuit. Only New York City's Statue of Liberty rivals it as a globally recognised symbol of American aspirations and ideals. In 1923, state historian Doane Robinson suggested to sculptor Gutzon Borglum that the imposing fingers of granite known as the Needles might be suitable material for a dramatic patriotic sculpture. They discussed depictions of such heroic figures of the West as Lewis and Clark, Buffalo Bill Cody and various Sioux Indians. Borglum, Idaho-born and of Danish descent, special-ised in colossal groups, such as his carving of the leaders of the Confederacy in Stone Mountain, Georgia (see p.372). He opted for a nearby mountain named after New York attorney Charles E Rushmore, upon which he would fashion the faces and heads of four certifiably great American presidents: **George Washington, Thomas Jefferson, Abraham Lincoln** and Borglum's buddy, **Theodore Roosevelt.**

Borglum talked, dreamed and worked big. "American art ought to be monumental in keeping with American life" he opined. Sixty when the project began in 1927, he died, $200,000 in debt, just a few months prior to its final dedication fourteen years later. His son Lincoln carried on. Inclement weather and uncertain funding had meant that the actual sculpting time was about six and a half years. The total cost of $989,000 included contributions from state residents, hence the not inaccurate notion that Rushmore was "paid for with schoolkids' pennies". Half a million tons of rock were removed to reach the softer, more malleable granite from which the heads were drilled and chiselled into recognisability. Ninety percent of the carving, however, was done with dynamite.

The Big Four gaze out impassively, cheek by jowl, arguably a greater engineering feat than an artistic one. Each head is about sixty feet from chin to crown. (The Statue of Liberty's head is only seventeen feet.) Lincoln, Borglum's favourite, has an eighteen-foot-long nose, the glint in each eleven-foot-wide eye is thirty inches, and his mole is sixteen inches in diameter. If he and his fellow presidents had been done full-figure to scale, they'd stand 465ft tall and be able to stride across the Potomac River in Washington DC without getting their knees wet. Rumours about expanding the monu-ment to include other presidents (Franklin Delano Roosevelt, Eisenhower, Truman, Kennedy, Reagan) or American icons like John Wayne, Elvis Presley and even Mickey Mouse seem unlikely at best, sacrilegious at worst.

The best time to view Rushmore is probably dawn or dusk – less people, good light-ing. By congressional decree, there is no admission charge. The nearest town is the tourist trap **Keystone**, where the **Rushmore-Borglum Story** (mid-April to mid-Oct daily 8am–10pm; $4.50) provides background information on the monument and its maker. The *Best Western Four Presidents*, Hwy-16A (May to mid-Nov; ☎666-4472), has **rooms** for $40 to $77. The nearby *Kelly Inn* (☎666-4483 or ☎1-800/635-3559) charges $53 to $60 in high season. *Spokane Creek Resort* (☎666-4609, off-season ☎343-5158), ten miles south on Hwy-16A, has campsites starting at $9 and cabins from $24. *Ruby House Restaurant and Red Garter Saloon*, Main Street (☎666-4404), formerly a bordello, serves decent **food** for $7 to $13. *Powder House Lodge* (☎666-4646), on US-16, features buffalo steaks in its rustic restaurant.

Crazy Horse

Korczak Ziolkowski worked briefly on Rushmore in 1939. Less than a decade later, with just $174 to his Polish name and pushing forty, the Boston-born orphan moved permanently to the Black Hills to undertake a vastly more ambitious scheme of his own – the **Crazy Horse Mountain Memorial**, on US-16-385, six miles north of Custer (☎673-4681). The self-taught sculptor had accepted Lakota Chief Henry Standing Bear's invitation to carve a memorial to the heroes of the Indian people. His subject, the revered warrior Crazy Horse, on horseback, so appealed to Ziolkowski that he decided to make his monument the biggest statue in the world. The work begun on Thunderhead Mountain in 1948 didn't stop with his death in 1982. His wife and most of their ten children (and doubtless their children's children) continue to realise his vision. The monument is still very much in the process of becoming itself; at present it looks like a ruin in reverse, even though 8.3 million tons of rock have been blasted and bulldozed so far. The twenty-foot scale model in the courtyard of the **visitor centre** is thirty-four times smaller than the end result, which will be 563ft high and 641ft long. An estimated four thousand people could stand atop the Indian's outstretched arm. They say all four Rushmore heads can fit in Crazy Horse's head, from which will jut a 44-foot-high stone feather. Nor do the plans stop with the carving: Ziolkowski's descendants hope to build a North American Indian museum, university and medical training centre on the land stretching between the current visitor centre and the monument.

Ziolkowski himself raised and spent $4 million on the project. His belief in free enterprise means that Crazy Horse has received no federal or state funds, instead relying entirely on admissions and contributions. The site, open dawn to dusk year-round, is free to Indians. Non-Indians over six pay $4 each, car-loads are let in for $10. It's a bargain. Apart from the monument, the premises contain a superb collection of Indian artefacts and crafts, several rooms devoted to Ziolkowski's life and work, and an excellent gift shop. Coffee and souvenir stones are free. On the first weekend in June, the public is invited to walk to the top of the mountain and see the work close-up.

travel details

TRAINS
Routes
• One daily train between **Chicago** and **Texas** in each direction calls at **St Louis** and **Little Rock**.

• The *Southwest Chief* between **Chicago** and **Los Angeles** passes through Missouri and Kansas, stopping once daily each way at **Lawrence**, **Topeka**, **Newton** (for **Wichita**, but without a special connecting service), **Dodge City** and **Garden City**. However, the first stop at which it is feasible to disembark is Newton, at 5am; the earlier stops will leave you stranded in the middle of the night. Similarly, trains travelling east towards Kansas City leave from Newton at 3.25am and from Dodge City at 12.45am.

• A more northerly route between **Chicago** and **Los Angeles** passes through Iowa and Nebraska, calling once daily at **Omaha**, **Lincoln**, **Hastings**, **Holdrege** and **McCook**.

• Trains between **Chicago** and the **Northwest** pass even further north, across North Dakota, stopping at **Fargo**, **Grand Forks** and **Minot** among others.

• **Oklahoma** and **South Dakota** have no train service.

Journey Times
From St Louis: to Chicago 6hr 30min; Memphis 8hr; Little Rock 8hr; Dallas 15hr.

From Omaha: to Chicago 9hr (arr 11.29pm, dep 7.04am), Lincoln 1hr and Denver 8hr (both arr 6.39am, dep 11.44pm).

From Lincoln: to Chicago 10hr and Omaha 1hr (both arr 12.49am, dep 5.39am), Denver 6hr 45min (arr 5.29am, dep 1.04am).

From Grand Forks: to Chicago 15hr; Seattle 27hr.

BUSES
All **Greyhound** unless otherwise indicated.

From Little Rock: to Memphis (4 daily; 2hr).

From Tulsa: to Oklahoma City (8 daily; 2hr); Dallas (6; 7hr).

From St Louis: to Kansas City (6 daily; 4hr 30min); Tulsa (9; 8hr 30min); Chicago (5; 4hr 30min; Memphis (5; 5hr 30min).

From Kansas City: to Chicago, (6 daily; 11hr)

From Des Moines: to Omaha (6 daily; 2hr 30min); Kansas City (4; 4hr); Minneapolis (2; 5hr); St Louis (6; 9hr); Chicago (9; 9hr); Tulsa (4; 7hr); Oklahoma City (5; 10hr).

From Iowa City: to Des Moines (6 daily; 1hr 30min); Chicago (6; 7hr 30min).

From Omaha: to Kansas City (3 daily; 4hr 30 min), Chicago (8 daily; 9–12hr), Denver (4 daily; 12hr); Rapid City (*Arrow Stage Lines*; 3, 13hr).

From Lincoln: to Omaha (6 daily; 1hr), Chicago (6 daily; 10–12hr).

From Bismarck: to Minneapolis (2 daily; 10hr); Billings (2; 12hr).

From Rapid City: *Powder River* to Cheyenne (2 daily; 8hr 30min) and Billings (2; 9hr); *Jack Rabbit Buses* (2; 1hr 30min).

CHAPTER ELEVEN

THE ROCKIES

E xploring the Rocky Mountain states of **COLORADO**, **WYOMING**, **MONTANA** and **IDAHO** could literally take forever. Stretching over one thousand miles from the virgin forests on the Canadian border to the desert of New Mexico, America's rugged spine encompasses an astonishing array of **landscapes** – geyser basins, lava flows, arid valleys and huge sand dunes – each in its own way as dramatic as the magnificent white-topped peaks. The geological grandeur is enhanced by **wildlife** such as buffalo, bears, moose and elk, and the conspicuous legacy of the miners, cowboys, outlaws and Native Americans who fought over the area's rich resources during the nineteenth century.

Apart from the **Anasazi** cliff-dwellers, who lived in southern Colorado until around 1300 AD, most **Native Americans** in this region belonged to nomadic hunting tribes. They inhabited the eastern extremities of the Great Plains, the richest buffalo-grazing land in the continent. Spaniards, groping through Colorado in the sixteenth century in search of gold, were the first whites to venture into the Rockies. But only after the territory was sold to the US in 1803 as part of the **Louisiana Purchase** was it thoroughly charted, starting with the **Lewis and Clark** expedition which traversed Montana and Idaho in 1805. As a result of their reports of copious quantities of game, the fabled "**mountainmen**" had soon trapped the beavers to the point of virtual extinction. They left as soon as the pelt boom was over, however, and permanent white settlement did not begin until gold was discovered at Denver in 1858. Within a decade, speculators were plundering every accessible gorge and creek in the four states in the search for valuable ores. When the construction of transcontinental rail lines and the establishment of vast cattle ranches to feed the mining camps dictated the slaughter of millions of buffalo, conflict with the Indians became inevitable. The **Sioux** and **Cheyenne**, led by brilliant strategists such as Sitting Bull and Crazy Horse, inflicted decisive victories over the US Army, most notably at Little Bighorn – "**Custer's Last Stand**". However, a massive military operation cleared the region of all warring Indians by the late 1870s.

The bulk of those who replaced the Indians saw the Rockies strictly in terms of profit: they came, took what they wanted and left with little concern for what lay in their wake. Most of the small communities in this isolated terrain remain exclusively dedicated to coal, oil or some other single commodity. All too often the uncertain tightrope walk between boom and bust is evident in their run-down facades.

Each of the four states has its own distinct character. **Colorado**, with fifty peaks over 14,000 feet, is the most mountainous and the most highly populated – friendly, sophisticated **Denver** is the only major metropolis in the Rockies. It's also the most visited, in part because it's that much more accessible, but the numbers remain low enough not to detract from its role as a summer paradise for cyclists and whitewater enthusiasts, and home to the best ski resorts in the country. Less touched by the tourist circus is vast, brawny **Montana**, where the "Big Sky" looks down on a glorious verdant manuscript scribbled over with gushing streams, lakes and tiny communities.

Away from gurgling, spitting **Yellowstone**, adjacent **Grand Teton** park and the nearby Bighorn Mountains, there's little to see among the vast stretches of scrubland which fill the rest of **Wyoming**, the country's least populated state. **Idaho**, the most rugged, rocky and inhospitable of the Rocky Mountain states, has some outstanding sights, but is just too desolate and remote to attract much attention.

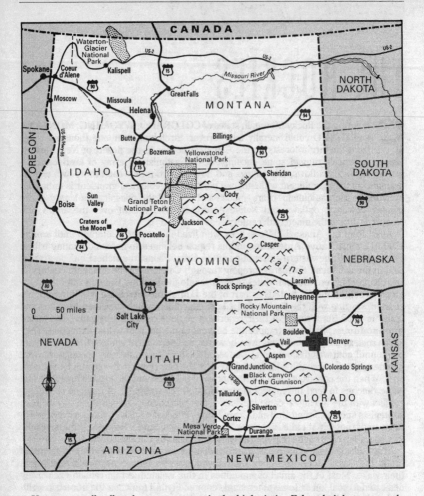

You can usually allow for temperatures in the high sixties Fahrenheit between early June and early September, though in the mountains you have to be prepared for wild local variations – and, of course, the higher you go the colder it gets. The altitude is high enough to warrant a period of acclimatisation; the intensity of the sun at these elevations should also be borne in mind. Spring (the "mud season"), when the snow melts, is the least attractive time to visit the Rockies, and while the delicate golds of quaking aspen trees light up the mountainsides in autumn, things are generally a bit cold for enjoyable hiking or sports. Most **ski** runs are open by late November and operate well into March. The coldest month is January, when temperatures of -50°F are common.

Attempting to rush around every national park and major town is a sure way to miss out on one of the Rockies' real delights – coaxing a car along the tight switchback roads that wind up and over precipitous mountain passes. At some point it's worth forsaking motorised transport, to see at least some of the area by **bike**; the Rockies contain some of the most rewarding and challenging cycling terrain on the continent.

COLORADO

COLORADO is one of the least homogenous of the United States, ranging from the flat and endless plains of the east to the colossal mountains of the west. In the north, **Native Americans** hunted and trapped in lush mountain valleys in summer, and returned to the prairies for the winter; in the south, the Anasazi of Mesa Verde grew corn on their isolated mesas and shared in the great early civilisation of the southwest.

Different parts of what's now Colorado accrued to the US at different times; the east and north were acquired under the **Louisiana Purchase** in 1803, while the south was won forty years later in the war with **Mexico**. (Mexican land grants were honoured by the Americans, which accounts for the still-strong Hispanic influence in the region.) Gold-hungry Spaniards came through in the sixteenth century, and Colonel Zebulon Pike ventured into the mountains in 1806, but the Native American way of life only became seriously threatened with the discovery of **gold** west of Denver in 1858. (At that time Colorado was still part of Kansas Territory; it became a territory in its own right in 1861, and a state in 1876.) The distractions of the Civil War gave the Indians the opportunity to fight back, but they were soon overwhelmed. From then until the end of the century, Colorado boomed; the quantities of gold and silver extracted from the mountains do not really compare with the riches found in California, but they were sufficient to fuel a rip-roaring frontier lifestyle. At first, too, absentee landlords attempted to exploit massive **ranches** on the plains, but their complete disregard for conservation ensured that the droughts and storms of 1886 and 1887 swept away the topsoil.

For the modern visitor, the obvious first port of call is **Denver**, at the edge of the eastern foothills of the Rockies and much the biggest city in a 600-mile radius. Nearby to the north are the go-ahead college town of **Boulder** and the spectacular **Rocky Mountain National Park** – not all that diffferent from the rest of the mountain range, but no less worth seeing for that. Much of **central** Colorado is now prime skiing country, with the exclusive resorts of **Aspen** and **Vail** the most popular destinations. To the **southwest**, untouched old mining towns can be explored along the **San Juan Skyway**, while **Mesa Verde National Park** preserves perhaps the most impressive of all the cliff cities left by the ancient Anasazi.

Getting Around Colorado

Much the biggest **airport** in Colorado is in Denver – in fact, it will soon have the largest airport in the world. Shuttle buses radiate from there to all the main towns and ski resorts – as do commuter-style aircraft. Denver itself is also a major hub for *Greyhound* **buses** to all neighbouring states. *Amtrak* **trains** run straight across the middle of Colorado, timed in both directions to pass through magnificent Glenwood Canyon in hours of daylight, but little more useful in terms of getting from A to B than the hugely enjoyable *Durango & Silverton Narrow Gauge Railroad* in the southwest.

Colorado is also one of the best destinations in the world for **cyclists**, hosting numerous championships. The State Department of Highways (4201 E Arkansas Ave, Denver, CO 80222) produces excellent maps and guides to cycle routes in the state.

Denver

Its skyscrapers marking the final transition between the Great Plains and the American West, **DENVER** stands at the threshold of the **Rocky Mountains**. Despite being known as the "Mile High City", and serving as the obvious point of arrival for travellers heading into the mountains, it is itself uniformly flat. The majestic peaks are clearly visible, but they only begin to rise roughly fifteen miles west of downtown, and Denver has, during the last century, had plenty of room to spread itself out.

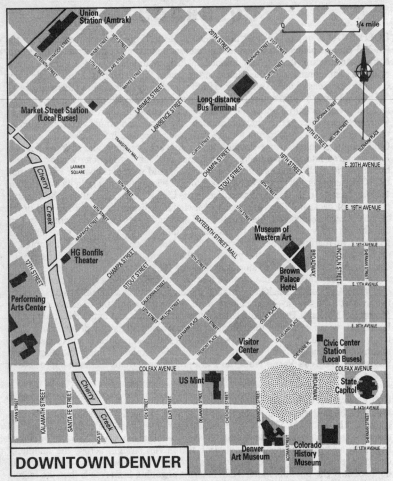

DOWNTOWN DENVER

Mineral wealth has always been at the heart of the city's prosperity, with all the fluctuations of fortune that entails. Though local resources have been progressively exhausted, Denver has managed to hang on to its role as the most important commercial and transportation nexus in the state. Its original "foundation" in 1858 was pure chance; this was the exact spot where small quantities of **gold** were first discovered in Colorado. There was no significant river, let alone a road, but prospectors came streaming in, regardless of prior claims to the land – least of all those of the **Arapahoe Indians**, who had supposedly been confirmed in their ownership of the area by the Fort Laramie Treaty of 1851. Various communities had their own names for the city; with the judicious distribution of whiskey, one faction persuaded the rest to agree to "Denver" in 1859. The hope was to ingratiate themselves with the governor of the Kansas Territory, James Denver; but as it turned out, he had already resigned. The newspaperman Horace Greeley passed through in the early days, and described the place as a "log city of 150 dwellings, not three-fourths completed nor two-thirds inhabited, nor one-third fit to be".

There was actually very little gold in Denver itself; the infant town swarmed briefly with disgruntled fortune-seekers, who de-camped when news came in of the massive gold strike at Central City. Denver survived, however, prospering further with the discovery of **silver** in the mountains. All sorts of shady characters made this their home; "Soapy" Smith for example (see p.874) acquired his nickname here, selling bars of soap at extortionate prices under the pretence that some contained $100 bills. When the first railroads bypassed Denver – the death knell for so many other communities – the citizens simply banded together and built their own connecting spur.

These days, Denver is a welcoming and enjoyable city to visit. Tourism is based on getting out into the wide open spaces rather than on sightseeing in town, but somehow its isolation, a good six hundred miles from any conurbation of even vaguely simlar size, gives its two-million population a refreshing friendliness; and in a city which is used to providing its own entertainment there always seems to be something going on. Denver may perhaps be less the loose-living city Kerouac wrote about in *On The Road*, and more the Eighties oil-boom metropolis familiar from *Dynasty*, but as its recent acquisition of a major-league baseball team confirms, it's still a place where things happen.

Arrival and Information

Though Denver's **Stapleton International Airport**, eight miles from downtown, is the fifth largest in the world, it's no longer considered big enough – work is underway to replace it with the world's biggest, twenty-six miles out. For the moment, *RTD* **buses** A and B from Stapleton serve downtown and Boulder, while a **taxi** into town will come to around $15, with tip. Several companies operate direct buses to other parts to Colorado. Both *Skiers Connection* (☎1-800/824-1104 or ☎343-6000) and *Vans to Vail* ($30; ☎1-800/222-2112 or ☎476-4467) run eight times daily to **Vail**. *Charles Limousine* runs to **Estes Park** (6 daily; $18; ☎1-800/950-DASH or ☎586-5151). *Airport Express* have nine daily services to **Colorado Springs** and **Fort Collins** ($25; ☎599-0505), as well as **Cheyenne** and **Laramie** in Wyoming ($30 & $35; ☎482-0505), and *Resort Express* connects with **Silverthorne** in Summit County (6 daily; $30; ☎1-800/334-7433 or ☎468-7600).

Amtrak **trains** arrive on the northwest side of downtown Denver at the old **Union Station** on Wynkoop Street, and the *Greyhound* **bus terminal** is every bit as close to the action at 1055 19th Street (☎292-0652; fares and schedules on ☎292-6111). *Gray Line* run **tours** of Rocky Mountain National Park, as well as Denver itself (☎289-2841).

The best place to pick up **information** about the city is the **Denver Metro CVB**, near the Capitol at 225 W Colfax Avenue (summer Mon–Fri 8am–6pm, Sat 9am–5pm, Sun noon–4pm; otherwise Mon–Fri 8am–5pm, Sat 9am–1pm; ☎892-1112), though there's also an informal morning-only advice centre for travellers arriving at the *Greyhound* terminal. The main downtown **post office** is at 1823 Stout Street (Mon–Fri 8am–5pm; zip code 80201); a 24-hour postal service is available at the **Terminal Annex**, 1595 Wynkoop Street (☎297-6325).

Getting Around

Downtown Denver is fairly easily negotiated on foot, with the occasional help of the very regular **free buses** up and down the 16th Street pedestrian mall at its heart. *RTD* local **buses** (☎299-6000), including the frequent services to Boulder and Golden, and also to the airport, radiate from the underground **Market Street Station** at Market and 16th streets. The two main areas outside the city centre that you might wish to visit are **City Park**, on the airport bus route, and **Cherry Creek** mall, which is served by buses #1, #2 and #3 (every half-hour during the day, then hourly until 11pm).

The telephone **area code** for Denver and northern Colorado is ☎303.

The City

Though oil money brought a hectic spate of high-rise construction in the early Eighties, creating the "17th Street canyon", **downtown Denver** remains recognisable as the gold-rush town of the 1860s. It's very easy to pick out the oldest sections on a map; though an endless regimental grid stretches for miles in all directions, at its very heart one small area of tightly packed streets stands at a sharp angle to the rest. Much of the day-to-day activity of Denver takes place along **16th Street** here, which but for its free buses is a pedestrian zone; however, the shops are not especially stimulating, and it holds nothing of any great historical interest.

For a quick appreciation of Denver's geographical position, head for the **State Capitol**. The thirteenth of the steps leading up to its entrance carries a plaque to denote that it is exactly one mile above sea level; turn back and look west, and you get a commanding view – zealously protected by building regulations – of the Rockies swelling on the horizon. The Capitol is a rather predictable copy of the one in Washington DC, but the free tours (Mon–Fri 9am–3.30pm) are pleasantly informal, and you can climb its dome for an even better view. The world's entire supply of red onyx was used to make its wainscoting.

Civic Center Park, right in front of the Capitol, contains two of Denver's finest museums. The **Art Museum** at 100 W 14th Avenue (covered in grey glass tiles) has paintings from around the world, but it's most noteworthy for its superb examples of Native American craftwork, with some marvellous pieces by the Plains Indians and also the Hopi. Some of the pre-Columbian art from central America – particularly the extraordinary Olmec miniatures – is also quite spectacular (Tues–Sat 10am–5pm, Sun noon–5pm; $3.50, free Sat; live jazz until 8pm every Wed). The most interesting features of the **Colorado History Museum** at 1300 Broadway are to be found in the downstairs galleries. Several dioramas, made under the auspices of the WPA in the Thirties, show historical scenes in fascinating detail, starting with the Anasazi of Mesa Verde, and following up with trappers meeting with Indians at a "fair in the wilderness" in the early 1800s, and a model of Denver in 1860. An exhaustive archive of **photographs** of the early West showcases the work of W H Jackson, who died at the age of 99 in 1942 (Mon–Sat 10am–4.30pm, Sun noon–4.30pm; $3.50).

A couple of blocks behind the Capitol to the west stands the Victorian home of **"Unsinkable Molly Brown"**, at 1340 Pennsylvania Street. The ephemera of her daily life would be of marginal appeal, were it not for the fact that she survived the *Titanic* disaster – as immortalised in the movie musical starring Debbie Reynolds (June–Aug Tues–Sat 10am–4pm, Sun noon–4pm; rest of the year closed Mon and slightly shorter hours; $4).

Free tours of the **US Mint** on Cherokee Street to the east enable you to see millions of fresh coins come gushing from the presses in a flurry of flashing metal; the inevitable greedy daydreams are held in check once you notice the machine-gun turrets on the exterior, mounted at the height of the Depression (May–Aug Mon–Fri 8am–3pm; Sept–April Mon–Fri 8.30am–3pm).

It was in the **Larimer Square** district, now found between 14th and 16th streets, not far from Union Station, that William Larimer put up Denver's original log cabin. That burned down in a general conflagration within a few years, whereupon a city ordinance decreed that all new construction should use brick. Larimer Square has been restored to its late Victorian appearance, providing a small-scale focus for shops, bars and restaurants.

Many of the paintings at the **Museum of Western Art** at 1727 Tremont Place are of historic rather than artistic significance, though some stimulating works by Georgia O'Keeffe hang alongside the usual pieces by Frederick Remington et al (Tues–Sat 10am–4.30pm; $3). The building itself was once Denver's leading brothel, discreetly connected by an underground passage to the grand triangular *Brown Palace Hotel* across the road.

The city's black community is most prominent in the old **Five Points** district, northwest of downtown, where the **Black American West Museum** at 3091 California Street provides ample evidence of an enduring black presence. Perhaps one third of all cowboys are thought to have been black, many of them slaves freed by the Civil War who left the South and found work as cattle hands (Wed–Fri 10am–2pm, Sat noon–5pm, Sun 2–5pm; $2.50).

Two or three miles east of downtown en route to the airport, the enormous **City Park** is home to the **Denver Museum of Natural History**, 2001 Colorado Boulevard (daily 9am–5pm; $5). As with many such museums, its brief extends beyond the (very good) dinosaur exhibits and wildlife displays to include anthropological material on Native Americans, which, though fascinating, does seem rather out of place. There's also a large **zoo** nearby (daily summer 10am–6pm; winter 10am–5pm; $5).

Denver's most popular shopping centre these days is the newly renovated and very glitzy **Cherry Creek Mall**, a few miles southeast of downtown. Opposite its main entrance is one of the best **bookstores** in the US, the *Tattered Cover Bookstore* at 2955 E First Avenue (☎322-7727), which spreads over four extremely well stocked floors.

Finally, twenty miles west of downtown, high above the *Coors*-brewery town of Golden, **Buffalo Bill's Grave and Museum** on Lookout Mountain is the final resting place of William Cody, famed frontiersman, buffalo-hunter, army scout and showman who died in Denver in 1915 (see also p.618). The museum features posters, rifles, clothing, paintings and Indian artefacts relating to Cody's career (May–Oct daily 9am–5pm; Nov–April Tues–Sun 9am–4pm; $2).

Accommodation

For a city of its importance, Denver has a remarkable quantity of cheap central **accommodation**, ranging from hostels to motels and homely B&Bs. If you have a little more money, there are also various grand historic downtown hotels. Two specialist **agencies** with a selection of reasonably priced properties in Denver and throughout Colorado are *B&B Colorado*, PO Box 12206, Boulder, CO 80303 (☎1-800/373-4995) and *B&B Rocky Mountains*, PO Box 804, Colorado Springs, CO 80901 (☎719/630-3433).

Broadway Plaza Motel, 1111 Broadway (☎893-3501). Downtown motel with doubles from $30.

Denver International Youth Hostel, 630 E 16th Ave (☎832-9996). Four blocks from State Capitol, dorm beds for $7.

Melbourne Hotel and Melbourne International Hostel, 607 22nd St (☎292-6386). Easy walking distance from the centre; dorms from $10, single rooms from $20 and doubles from $25. No curfew.

Motel 6, 12020 E 39th Ave (☎371-1980). Standard motel just off I-70 at Peoria, three miles from the airport. Doubles from $30.

Oxford Alexis Hotel, 1600 17th St (☎628-5400). Grand traditional Western hotel, where rooms start at $125.

Queen Anne Inn, 2147 Tremont Place (☎296-6666). Central and very hospitable B&B; each of the ten rooms in this nineteenth-century house is tastefully decorated to an individual theme. Doubles $70–120.

The Standish, 1530 California St (☎534-3231). Very central doubles from as little as $20.

Eating

As well as plenty of Western-themed steak and barbecue places, Denver has a cosmopolitan selection of international restaurants, particularly Mexican. Of the several distinct districts where restaurants tend to congregate, **Larimer Square** is probably the most easily accessible on foot, and has a wide enough selection to suit most tastes.

Brick Oven Beanery, 1007 E Colfax Ave (☎860-0077). Self-service restaurant offering good solid food at knock-down prices.

Casa Bonita, 6715 W Colfax Ave (☎232-5115). Absolutely wild Mexican place. Gunfights, cliff divers, abandoned mines to explore . . . the only weak link is the food itself, but it's all a lot of fun, especially if you have kids in tow, and far from expensive.

Denver Firefighters Museum and Restaurant, 1326 Tremont Place (☎892-1100). Unusual lunch-only venue; quality standard meals in a building jammed with ancient fire engines.

Dozens, 13th Ave and Cherokee St (☎572-0066). Excellent breakfasts and lunches, not far from the Capitol.

Fouchers Creole Cafe, 2005 E 17th Ave (☎388-6503). Family restaurant, with down-home Creole cooking at reasonable prices.

Green's Natural Foods Cafe, 320 E Colfax Ave (☎831-1315). Innovative and very cheap vegetarian specialities, as well as organic meat dishes and healthy seafood.

Josephina's, 1433 Larimer Square (☎623-0166). Busy Italian restaurant with lively bar.

La Bonne Soupe, 1512 Larimer Square (☎595-9169). Bistro-style French restaurant; good food, well prepared.

Paramount Cafe, 511 16th St (☎893-2000). Basic cheap American food, with lunch specials. In summer, you can sit out on the patio right on the 16th Street mall, and watch the world go by.

Seoul Food, 701 E 16th Ave (☎837-1460). Bright-lights Korean diner, authentic and good value.

Nightlife and Entertainment

Denver's pride and joy is the ultra-modern **Denver Center for the Performing Arts** on 14th and Curtis streets, which hosts nightly musical, dramatic and other performances (information on ☎893-4000, tickets on ☎893-4100). Facilities in the complex include three **theatres**, as well as the **Symphony Hall** (which is in the round, giving it superb acoustics).

The remarkable **Red Rocks Amphitheater** (☎694-1234), twelve miles west of downtown Denver, has been the setting for thousands of rock and classical concerts; U2 recorded their massively successful *Under a Blood Red Sky* album here. This 9000-seater venue is squeezed between two 400-foot red sandstone rocks that seem to glow in early morning and late evening. The park is open free of charge during the day.

Plenty of smaller-scale gigs take place in town. Consult Friday's free *Westword* newspaper, or the "Weekend" section in the *Denver Post* for listings. Each May, Civic Center Park in front of the Capitol sees the **Capitol Hill Peoples' Fair**, while in August **A Taste of Colorado** is a heady outdoor mix of food and live music.

Following in the successful footsteps of the *Wynkoop* (see below), **brew-pubs** are starting to spring up all over the city. Since October 1991, however, the latest thing to do of an evening has been to head west out of Denver into the cradle of the Colorado Gold Rush, **Central City**. This small community, whose narrow streets cling to the steep hillside, has just legalised **gambling**, and is currently booming once again. So far it's reasonably low-key, geared around slot machines rather than serious casino games, but all sorts of bars and restaurants are beginning to appear.

Bars and Music Venues

El Chapultepec, 20th and Market St (☎295-9126). Tiny venue with live jazz every day.

Herman's Hideaway, 1578 S Broadway (☎778-9916). Rock club; mostly mainstream but consistently interesting.

Jimmy's Grille, 320 South Birch (☎322-5334). Live reggae Wed–Sat every week.

Ruby, 708 E 17th Ave (☎831-8990). Eclectic live music from all over the world.

Wynkoop Brewing Co, 1634 18th St (☎297-2700). Colorado's first brew-pub; good home-brewed beers and a lively atmosphere, opposite Union Station. They also serve bar food, and downstairs *Jazz Works* puts on live jazz and other music.

Northern Colorado

The major attractions for visitors in the immediate area of Denver is **Rocky Mountains National Park** to the northwest. Though on the map the distances involved may not look that great, it would be a mistake to attempt to see the whole park on a day trip from Denver. Segments of the loop drive this involves can be very slow and laborious, and in a single day it's more realistic just to dip a few miles into the park's eastern fringes. Which is not to say that the full circuit is not worth attempting, so long as you allow yourself enough time; an evening in **Boulder** is always time well spent, while approaching the park via its western entrance at Grand Lake gives you the opportunity to visit the old mining towns of **Central City** (see opposite) and attractive **Georgetown**.

Boulder

BOULDER, just 27 miles northwest of Denver on US-36, is one of the liveliest college towns in the country, filled with a young population which seems to divide its time between phenomenally healthy day-time pursuits and almost equally unhealthy night-time activities. It was founded in 1858 by a prospecting party who felt that the nearby Flatiron Mountains, the first swell of the Rockies, "looked right for gold"; in fact they found little, but the community grew anyway.

While the actual town of Boulder isn't a destination which repays all that much exploration, it makes an excellent place to return to each night after a day in the mountains. Downtown centres on the pedestrian mall of **Pearl Street**, lined with all sorts of cafes and stores – including several places where you can hire mountain bikes. At the *Boulder Arts and Crafts Cooperative* at no. 142 (☎443-3683), seventy artists take it in turns to sell each others' work. The most obvious short excursion is to drive or hike up nearby Flagstaff Mountain, for views over town and further into the Rockies; any road west joins up with the Peak to Peak Highway which heads through spectacular scenery to Estes Park and Rocky Mountain National Park.

The adventurous **University of Colorado** is a dependable source of entertainment and culture. Its mid-April Conference on World Affairs attracts an eclectic and surprisingly high-powered assortment of world figures to a sort of free-for-all think tank, while it plays host each summer to the Colorado Music Festival, in the Chautauqua Auditorium (☎449-1397), and the Colorado Shakespeare Festival (☎492-8181).

Practicalities

Local and long-distance **buses** come into Boulder at the Transit Center, 14th and Walnut streets (☎778-6000); there are regular services to Denver and its airport (half-hourly 8am–6pm, hourly 5–8am & 6–11pm). The hospitable **visitor centre** is at 2440 Pearl Street (Mon 9am–5pm, Tues–Fri 8.30am–5pm; ☎442-1044).

Few **rooms** at the showcase *Hotel Boulderado*, 2115 13th Street (☎442-4344), cost much under $100 per night, but even if you're not staying it's an atmospheric place to wander into for a drink, and to listen to the free evening jazz. The *Foot of the Mountain*, 200 Arapahoe Avenue (☎442-5688), is a friendly **motel**, nine blocks from downtown beside Boulder Creek, where log-cabin-style accommodation starts at $50. In summer only, there's a welcoming **youth hostel** at 1107 12th Street near the campus (☎442-9304); dorm beds cost $12, and you can also get single ($22) and double ($26) rooms.

You won't have any problem finding **bars** and **restaurants** downtown, especially around the Pearl Street area. *Sushi Zanmai*, 1221 Spruce Avenue (☎440-0733), is a friendly good-value sushi place, with karaoke and live music; the *Siamese Plate*, 1575 Folsom Avenue (☎447-9718), serves superb and well-priced Thai meals. The *Walrus Cafe*, 1911 11th Street, is a late-opening bar with cheap food.

Rocky Mountains National Park

You don't have to go to **ROCKY MOUNTAINS NATIONAL PARK** to appreciate the full splendour of the Rockies; it is simply one small section of the mighty range, measuring roughly twenty-five miles by fifteen miles. A tenth of the size of Yellowstone, it attracts the same number of visitors – around three million per year – and with the bulk of those coming in high summer, the one main road through the mountains can get incredibly congested. However, it is undeniably beautiful, straddling the Continental Divide at elevations often well in excess of ten thousand feet. A full third of the park is above the tree line, and large areas of snow never melt; the name of the **Never Summer Mountains** speaks volumes about the long, empty expanses of arctic-style tundra. Lower down, among the rich forests, are patches of lush greenery; you never know when you may stumble upon a sheltered mountain meadow flecked with colourful flowers. Parallels with the European Alps spring readily to mind – helped, of course, by the heavy-handed Swiss and Bavarian themes of the motels and restaurants in the vicinity.

This is not an area where humans have ever made their homes, though it lies on the route of old Indian trails, and the Ute would come here to hunt in summer. Early white mining ventures came to nothing, and the region was dedicated as a national park in 1915. The original proposal was for it to be much bigger, extending from Wyoming to Pikes Peak; the existing boundaries were drawn up as a compromise, after long negotiations with Colorado's powerful logging and mining interests.

The easiest **approach** to the park is from the **east**; you have barely penetrated the foothills of the Rockies by the time you arrive at the gateway town of **ESTES PARK**, 65 miles northwest of Denver (and 90 miles southwest of Cheyenne). At the end of the nineteenth century, Estes Park belonged to the Irish Earl of Dunraven, who made illegal use of frontmen to buy up all the surrounding land as his private hunting preserve; once he was squeezed out, the town took on the more democratic function it still serves, of efficiently providing visitors with food, lodging and other services. In itself, Estes Park is not an attractive place, but its presence does at least ensure that all the necessary evils of mass tourism in the area are confined into one neat valley. The park headquarters and main **visitor centre** (information on ☎586-2371, weather on ☎586-2385) is a couple of miles north of Estes Park on US-36. Admission is $5, though as ever a *Golden Eagle* pass (see p.37) is a good investment.

The **western** entrance, 85 miles from Denver, is reached by turning north off I-70 onto US-40; a small detour beyond the junction takes you to the former pit community of **GEORGETOWN**, where over 200 Victorian buildings line the immaculate streets. The **Georgetown Loop Railroad** departs from 100 Loop Drive on a tortuous six-mile trip, at one point spiralling over itself to gain elevation (summer daily 10am–4pm; $10; ☎569-2403). US-40 itself negotiates **Berthoud Pass** en route to **GRAND LAKE**, a whole lot lower-key than Estes Park. Startlingly, it's a **yachting** centre, high in the mountains; it has a smaller but perfectly adequate selection of accommodation and restaurants. One mile north of town, you come to the **Kawuneeche Visitor Center** (☎627-3471).

Exploring the Park

The showpiece of the park is **Trail Ridge Road**, which connects Estes Park and Grand Lake. This 45-mile stretch of US-34, said to be the highest highway in the world, affords a succession of tremendous views, and several short trails leave parking lots along the way. There are no services en route, and rangers advise that you allow three to four hours' driving time. The road is normally kept open between Memorial Day and mid-October; at other times there is no way to cross the park. As the winter progresses and the snow falls, it is blocked progressively lower down, but you can always expect to get as far as **Many Peaks Curve** from the east or the **Colorado River Trailhead** from the west.

Even more so than most national parks, this one is best appreciated by getting out of your car and **hiking**; the road itself is just too busy. Recommending any one trail above another is futile, as it depends so much on how many people are around; enquire at one of the visitor centres when you arrive. While a hike on the tundra is (literally) the high spot of any visit, the ecosystem is so delicate that, if you do so, it is essential to stay on the paths. You should also be aware of quite how delicate your own system is at this altitude: the slightest exertion can strain even the healthiest constitution.

Between June and September, the informative **Alpine Visitor Center**, halfway along Trail Ridge Road at Fall River Pass, marks the centre of the park; the rangers here put on a twice-weekly educational puppet show for kids. You can also drive in here in summer along the unpaved **Old Fall River Road**, the first road to be built in the park. This runs through the bed of a valley carved by glaciers into a U-shape, so it doesn't have open mountain vistas, but it's much quieter than the Trail Ridge, and there's far more chance of spotting **wildlife**. Animals roaming the park include moose, coyote, mountain lions, beavers (often seen at work in the rivers), and a total population of perhaps thirty brown bears, which with a plentiful natural food supply tend to avoid contact with humans. The central and southern tracts of this wilderness are all but impenetrable; only a well-planned hiking expedition can get you into the remoter forests and valleys.

Just inside the park, near the Estes Park entrance, a spur road, open year-round, leads south to two small and pristine alpine lakes. To ease the traffic in summer, a free and very regular **shuttle bus** from the Glacier Basin parking area runs the last few miles up to **Bear Lake** (8am–5.30pm), which is the park's single most definitive viewpoint, with the mountains framed to perfection beyond the cool still waters. **Sprague Lake**, lower down, has been landscaped to provide access for disabled visitors; a dead-level paved path encircles the shore, while the free **Handicamp** campground is exclusively for the use of wheelchair-bound travellers (contact the park HQ for details).

Park Practicalities

If you're not driving yourself, **public transport** to Estes Park from Denver includes the *Estes Park Bus Company* (☎586-8108) and *Charles Limousine* service from Stapleton airport (6 daily; $18; ☎1-800/950-DASH or ☎586-5151). However, you can't expect to see the place on foot, so you'll either have to pick up a **tour** from Estes Park, which with admission (not always included in the quoted price) should cost around $20, or do the whole thing from Denver, with *Gray Line* for example (☎289-2841).

The only accommodation within the park boundaries is in the five official **campgrounds**, at Moraine Peak, Glacier Basin, Aspenglen, Longs Peak and Timber Creek. All of these fill up early each day, and it's advisable in summer to make reservations through *Ticketron*. Longs Peak imposes a maximum stay of three days, the rest allow one week. For **backcountry camping** you need a free permit, again valid for a maximum of seven days in summer (☎586-4459).

Lodges and **motels** abound in and around **Estes Park**; the Chamber of Commerce has full details (☎1-800/443-7837). At the *Alpine Trail Ridge Inn*, 927B Moraine Avenue (☎1-800/223-5023 or ☎586-4585), and the *Best Value Budget Inn*, 760 S Saint Vrain Avenue (☎1-800/726-7325 or ☎586-4451), rooms start at $50 in summer. *Emerald Manor*, 441 Chiquita Lane (☎586-8050), is a self-styled "Irish B&B", where antique-filled rooms with mountain views cost from $60. There's also a summer-only *AYH* **youth hostel** a little way out of town, the *H Bar G Ranch* (☎586-3688), where dorm beds in cabins looking over the mountains cost $9. Call ahead if you need to be picked up from the bus. The relaxed *Friar's* at 157 W Elkhorn Avenue (☎586-2806) has a good selection of **food** at all prices, but with so many other possibilities you're spoiled for choice.

Grand Lake, too, has a **youth hostel** in summer; as well as its budget dorms, the *Shadowcliff*, high on Tunnel Road (☎627-9966), also has motel rooms from around $45. For **eating**, the down-home *Mountain Inn* at 612 Grand Avenue (☎627-3385) is reliable.

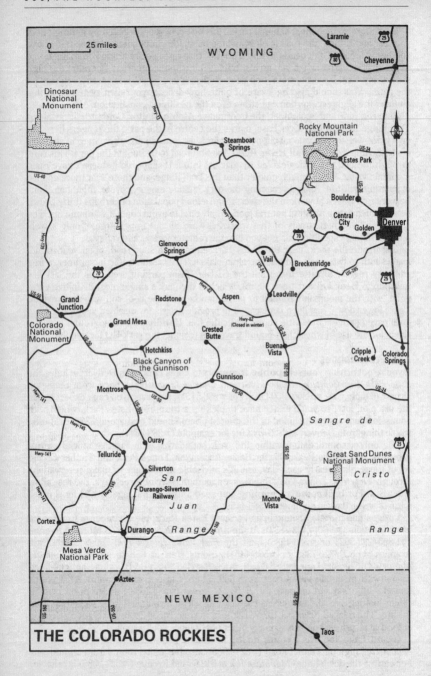

THE COLORADO ROCKIES

Central Colorado

West out of Denver, I-70 travels 275 miles to the Utah desert, through a patchwork of granite peaks, wide locked-in valleys and red sandstone cliffs. This splendid scenery, once home to cowboys, outlaws and miners, is now enjoyed to the full by legions of **hikers, skiers** and **cyclists**. The sheer numbers of tourists and athletes can be a bit offputting at times, but it's always possible to find a small mountain road and escape the crowds that flock to resorts such as **Vail** and **Aspen**. The two finest spectacles of all are the **Colorado National Monument**, a deep multicoloured canyon just outside Grand Junction in the far west, and the brooding **Black Canyon of the Gunnison**.

Colorado Springs

Seventy miles south of Denver on I-25, **COLORADO SPRINGS**, the second largest city in the state, was originally developed in 1871 as a genteel vacation spot by railway tycoon William Jackson Palmer. He attracted so many English gentry to the town that it earned the nickname of "Little London". Despite sprawling for the best part of ten miles alongside I-25, modern Colorado Springs, a bastion of conservatism compared to liberal Denver, still retains much of Palmer's vision. Contributing factors include a high military presence, a number of fundamentalist religious organisations, the exclusive Colorado College and a well-to-do Anglo-American community.

The major attraction within the city limits is the **Garden of the Gods**, an incredible sculpted giant red sandstone rockery on the west edge of town off US-24W, Ridge Road Exit. It epitomises the concept of drive-through scenery: motorists can whisk through on a figure-of-eight circuit, and never bother get out of their vehicles. These gnarled, twisted and warped rocks were lifted up at the same time as the nearby mountains, but have since been shaped by erosion into finely balanced overhangs, jagged pinnacles, massive pedestals and mushroom formations. Among outstanding features are **High Point**, which has the best view, **Balanced Rock** and the **Central Garden**. The **visitor centre** has details of hiking trails (daily, summer 9am–5pm; winter 10am–4pm).

At the **Pro Rodeo Hall of Fame**, 101 Pro Rodeo Drive, off I-25 Exit 147 (daily summer 9am–5pm; otherwise 9am–4.30pm; $4), videos and displays explain the sport's various disciplines. Free ninety-minute tours of the **US Olympic Complex**, 1750 E Boulder Street, take you round the training facilities for thirteen sports, and include a film on America's Olympic Games history (Mon–Sat 9am–4pm, Sun noon–4pm). The **US Air Force Academy**, just north off I25 Exit 156B, puts on a hugely popular parade ground-show every weekday at 12.10pm when the 4400 cadets march to lunch. Of more interest, even to those not of a military bent, is the **NORAD** (North American Aerospace Command), buried deep inside Cheyenne Mountain behind 25-foot-thick doors. Built to withstand nuclear attack, the whole facility, a key element in the controversial "Star Wars" programme, is built on metal springs. Tours are conducted every Saturday morning, but tend to be booked up well in advance (☎554-3841).

Practicalities

Colorado Springs' **visitor centre** is at 104 S Cascade Street (☎635-1632). *Greyhound* (☎635-1505) stops at 327 S Weber Street downtown. Getting around without a car can be frustrating: the attractions are spread out and there's only a commuter bus service. Tours with *Gray Line*, 322 N Nevada Avenue (☎633-1747), cost between $25 and $40.

Accommodation is easy to find. The best value downtown is the oldish but clean *Dale Motel*, 620 W Colorado Avenue (☎636-3721), at $30 to $60, though the spacious

The telephone **area code** for Colorado Springs and central Colorado is ☎719.

Heartstone Inn B&B, 506 N Cascade Street (☎473-4413) doesn't overcharge at $80 to $120 a night. The *Garden of the Gods Motel*, 3704 W Colorado Avenue (☎475-9450) offers motel rooms for $50, dorm beds for $9.50 ($7 *AYH* members) and a $15 campground.

Characterful places to **eat** downtown include the *Red Top*, 1520 S Nevada Avenue (☎623-2444), a Fifties-style diner famous for its six-inch burgers; *Dale St Cafe*, 1125 E Dale Street (☎578-9898), a favourite for cheap pizza and pastas; and the excellent vegetarian *Olive Branch*, Boulder and Tejon streets (☎475-1199). Out in Old Colorado City, four miles west, the family-owned *Henri's Mexican*, 2427 W Colorado Avenue (☎634-9031), pulls in the crowds for home-style food and superb margaritas. Nearby, one of the best **bars** in the city, *Meadow Muffins*, 2432 W Colorado Avenue (☎633-0583), is festooned with movie memorabilia and serves good burgers, sandwiches and salads.

Pikes Peak

Though there are thirty taller mountains in Colorado alone, **Pikes Peak**, just outside Colorado Springs to the west, is probably the best known – largely because the view from its summit inspired Katherine Lee Bates to write the words to *America The Beautiful*. The 14,110-foot peak was first mapped by Zebulon Pike in 1806. He never climbed it himself, but a decade later another army expedition did, and by the end of the century wagon trails had been built to take rich tourists like Ms Bates to the top. In 1929 it took Bill Williams, a Texan, twenty days and 170 changes of trousers to scale the mountain, pushing a peanut with his nose.

You can reach the top by a long **hike**, or by a difficult **toll road** ($5) which is not at all enjoyable for the driver. The thrilling **Pikes Peak Cog Railway** grinds its way up an average of 847 feet per mile on its ninety-minute journey to the summit; from 11,500 feet onwards it crosses a barren expanse of tundra, scarred by giant scree flows. From the bleak and windswept top, it's possible to see Denver seventy miles north, and the endless prairie to the east, while to the west mile upon mile of giant snowcapped peaks rise into the distance. The train leaves from 515 Ruxton Avenue, **Manitou Springs**, six miles west of Colorado Springs (mid-June to Oct; $21, reservations advised; ☎685-5401).

The Cripple Creek Area

Fifty miles or so out from Colorado Springs, the much-chronicled gold camp of **CRIPPLE CREEK** nestles in a grim volcanic bowl on the west flank of Pikes Peak. It was named for a calf that broke its leg trying to jump over a tumbling stream, and a cowhand, Bob Womack, was in 1891 the first to discover gold on this poor cattle-raising land. Elated by his find, he sold his share for $500 and spent the lot on whiskey. Others were more fortunate: a total of over 500 million dollars worth of gold was extracted. By the turn of the century 25,000 people lived in a town boasting eight newspapers, numerous banks, several splendid hotels, department stores, elegant homes and even a stock exchange – as well as the less salubrious hallmarks of a typical mining settlement.

Today the main street of this isolated outpost backs onto a forbidding rocky plateau, and most of its Victorian buildings have fallen silent. Dust storms come howling through, and a herd of donkeys, descended from former pit animals, roams wild. Things may change, however, with the decision in late 1991 to grant casino licences.

Scenic four-mile steam trips on the **Narrow Gauge Railway**, Fifth and Car streets (June to mid-Oct daily 10am–5pm; $6; ☎689-2640), trundle past many abandoned mines. One mile north on Hwy-67, ex-miners take you a thousand feet underground to see gold veins in **Mollie Kathleen's Mine** (daily 9am–5pm; $7; ☎689-2466). The grand old *Imperial Hotel* (☎689-2922) is a unique place to **stay**, for a modest $55 a night.

Six bumpy miles south, the less lavish **Victor** is where most of the miners who worked in Cripple Creek lived. *Zeke's*, 108 Third Street (☎636-3091), serving delicious chili and cold beers, is the best place for a meal in either town.

Summit County

The mixture of purpose-built ski resorts, old mining towns, snow-crested peaks, alpine meadows and crystal lakes that make up **Summit County** lie just off I-70, around seventy miles west of Denver. **BRECKENRIDGE**, whose streets are lined with beautifully restored, brightly painted Victorian houses, shops and cafes, stands head and shoulders above the other areas. In summer, you can get a good view of the area, sandwiched between the Continental Divide and the Ten Mile and Gore ranges, from the top of the **Super Chair** ride (daily 10am–4pm; $4; ☎303/453-5000). For an exciting descent, ride a **toboggan** down the dry **Super Slide** (summer daily 10am–5pm; $4.50).

Frisco, stretching out sedately along a quiet valley overlooking the calm Dillon Reservoir, is the only other centre to hold much interest; the exclusive resorts of **Keystone** (where you can ski at night) and **Copper Mountain** both lack atmosphere.

Practicalities

Accommodation in Summit County is relatively cheap. The *Fireside Inn*, 114 N French Street, Breckenridge (☎453-6456), is a cosy B&B with rooms for $30 in summer (winter $52) and dorm beds for $12 (winter $20). Rustic *Breckenridge Mountain Lodge*, 600 S Ridge Street (☎453-2333), has rooms from $25 in summer and $35 in winter. The pick of the budget **motels** on Frisco's Main Street, *Frisco Lodge* at no.321 (☎668-0195), offers a hot tub and practical advice on outdoor activities. Summer rates are only $28 ($30–45 en suite); in winter, rooms cost $28 to $50 ($35–80 en suite).

The *Gold Pan*, 105 Main Street, Breckenridge (☎453-5499), is the place to go for a **meal**. The only spot you could get a drink in Colorado during Prohibition, it serves up good-value Mexican food and burgers, and has a lively bar. *Fatty's*, 106 Ridge Street (☎453-9802), is excellent for cheap pizza and pasta, and *Shamus O'Toole's Roadhouse Saloon*, 115 Ridge Street (☎453-2004), is good for a beer. In **Frisco**, drinking goes on each morning in the dark wooden interior of the *Moosejaw*, 208 Main Street (☎668-3931), until 2am, and if you're hungry it's hard to find a better burger.

Leadville

Standing at an elevation of over 10,000 feet, eighty miles west of Denver, **LEADVILLE** is the highest incorporated city in the US, with a magnificent view across to broad-shouldered, ice-laden, mounts **Elbert** and **Massive**, Colorado's two highest peaks. As you approach from the south, your first impression is of giant slag heaps and disused mining sheds, but don't let this put you off: Leadville is rich in character and romance.

Tales and fables abound of gunfights over plots, miners dying of exposure and even graveyards being excavated to get at the seams. One legendary figure was **Horace Tabor**, a storekeeper who grubstaked goods to prospectors in exchange for a share in profits if they hit lucky. Tabor's gamble paid off – two prospectors developed a silver mine that produced $20 million inside a year, and he collected a one-third share. With the aid of some nifty stock exchange dealings, he amassed a huge fortune, and left his wife to marry local waitress "Baby Doe" McCourt. The socialite wedding of 1883 was attended by US President Chester Arthur. By the time of his death in 1899, Tabor was financially ruined. Baby Doe took his dying injunction to "hold onto the Matchless" – his only remaining mine – literally. She died there, emaciated and frostbitten in a crude wooden shack, 36 years later. The **Matchless Mine** itself is still there, just a couple of godforsaken wooden outhouses two miles out of town on Seventh Street ($2).

There are no fewer than eight museums in town, including the National Mining Hall of Fame, but the contents of all put together would only make one good collection. A better way to spend your time is on a **rafting** or **mountain biking** expedition. *Tenth Mountain Sports*, 112 E Seventh Street (☎486-2202), rent equipment for both. The same company also do good deals on **ski** hire; Leadville is a handy base for **SKI Cooper**, just ten miles north, where learning to ski is remarkably cheap. Lift tickets cost $18, and two-hour lessons are just $15 (☎486-3684).

Practicalities

Leadville's **visitor centre** is at 809 Harrison Avenue (☎486-3900). If you want to **stay**, the landmark *Delaware Hotel*, 700 Harrison Avenue (☎486-1239 or ☎1/800-748-2004), costs only $40 to $50 for a double with breakfast, while B&B at the more intimate *Leadville Country Inn*, 127 E Eighth Street (☎486-2354 or ☎1/800-748-2354), is $47 to $67. There are two very good Mexican restaurants in town – the *Grill*, 716 Elm Street (☎486-9930), and the spartan *Cantina*, one mile south on Hwy-24 (☎486-9927), which features traditional dancing at the weekend. For large portions of American family-style food, head for the *Golden Burro*, 710 Harrison Avenue (☎486-1239).

Among Leadville's great **bars**, the *Pastime Salon*, 120 W Second Street (☎486-9986), housing an 1870s Chinese bar, offers a great mountain view from its patio, and serves delicious wings and burgers, while the wood-panelled *Silver Dollar Saloon*, 315 Harrison Avenue (☎486-9914), of similar vintage, is filled with Irish memorabilia.

Aspen

Coffee-table magazines might have you believe that a toll gate outside **ASPEN** only admits film stars and the super-rich. This elite **ski resort**, two hundred miles west of Denver via Leadville, is indeed home to the likes of Cher, Jack Nicholson, Goldie Hawn and John Denver, but it's a perfectly affordable place for anyone to come in summer – unless you're on an absolute shoestring budget. Visiting in winter takes considerably more cash, though you can still save money by bunking up in a dorm and skiing the less expensive Aspen Highlands slopes.

From inauspicious beginnings in 1879, this pristine mountain-locked town grew quickly to become the world's top silver producer. By the time the silver market crashed some fourteen years later, it had acquired tasteful residential palaces, grand hotels and an opera house. By 1930 the population had slumped to less than seven hundred. Ironically, it was the anti-poverty WPA programme that gave the struggling community the cash to build its first crude ski lift in 1936. Entrepreneurs, impressed by the varied terrain and plentiful snowfall, saw the opportunities for a resort, and the first chairlift was dedicated on Aspen Mountain in 1947. Since then, three more mountains have opened for skiing, and the jet set arrived in force during the Sixties.

Development is a burning political issue in Aspen; tight architectural constraints have been put on businesses (*McDonalds* are not allowed to have a neon sign), but the last decade has seen yet more tacky Scandinavian-style lodges and condo blocks.

Arrival and Information

In winter, **Independence Pass** on Hwy-82, which provides the quickest access to Aspen, is closed, and the detour through Glenwood Springs adds an extra seventy miles to the trip from Denver. The **airport** (☎920-5380) is four miles north of town on Hwy-82; if you fly into Denver on *Continental* or *United*, it only costs another $40 or so to get here. In winter there are eight flights per day from Denver, and around three per week from Chicago, Dallas and LA; in summer, there are just two per day from Denver. The bus fare into town is $1. Once in Aspen, there's no problem **getting around**; the *Roaring Fork Transit Agency* (daily summer 7am–midnight; winter 7am–1am) charges nothing for journeys within the town and also serves outlying places.

Aspen's main **visitor centre** is in the Wheeler Opera House, 320 E Hyman Avenue (☎925-1940). An excellent source of local gossip, news, and food and drink offers, is the free *Aspen Daily News* ("If you don't want it printed, don't let it happen").

The Town and the Mountains

There's not all that much to do in Aspen, apart from sitting around the pedestrianised streets and watching the world go by, though there are some good shops and galleries to browse in. The best account of Aspen's mining past is to be had at the **Aspen Historical Society**, 620 W Bleeker Street (Tues–Sun 1–4pm; $3).

Three of Aspen's four mountains are run by the **Aspen Ski Co** (a division of *20th Century Fox*): **Aspen Mountain**, looming over downtown, is for experienced skiiers only; **Buttermilk** is best for beginners, with an excellent ski school; and the wide-open runs of **Snowmass**, though mostly for intermediate skiiers, feature a kids' area. Daily ski-lift tickets cost $40; savings can be made on multiple purchases. The other mountain, **Aspen Highlands**, can't boast the same high-tech lifts or as many celebrities, but is cheaper at $34 per day, and holds free schools for beginners every Monday. **Rental** of skis, boots and poles usually costs around $15 a day; *Snowmass Sports* in Silvertree Plaza, Snowmass Village (☎923-3567), have a good reputation. It's also worth considering **buying** equipment; the new shops are expensive, but the rich – who can't be seen in anything but up-to-the-minute ski-wear – sometimes leave their gear behind; *Gracy's*, 202 E Main Street (☎925-5131), is the place to pick up bargains.

Cycling is the main summer pursuit, with road bikes more popular than fat-wheelers; one popular ride climbs to the top of Independence Pass and then races down again. *The Hub*, 315 E Hyman Avenue (☎925-7970), has a wide choice of bikes for $22 a day; *Timberline*, 204 S Galena Street (☎925-9237), is the cheapest for mountain bikes at $17. Most of the bike shops also rent out rollerblades – *the* thing for local poseurs.

The **Roaring Fork River**, surging out of the Sawatch range, is excellent for kayaking and rafting, but sections can be dangerous and each summer sees a few fatalities. *Blazing Paddles* (around $40 for a half-day float trip; ☎925-5651) are not the cheapest company but they do have a good safety record.

If you fancy **walking** in the mountains, a **Gondola** climbs from 601 Dean Street (Fri–Wed 9.30am–3pm; $12; ☎925-1220 ext 3598) to the summit of Aspen Mountain for terrific views of the valley. Even more alluring is the countryside around the twin purple-grey peaks of the **Maroon Bells**, fifteen miles southwest, soaring magnificently above the dark blue Maroon Lake. The road is closed to all traffic between 8.30am and 5pm, except for overnight campers with permits, travellers with disabilities, and *RFTA* buses which leave every half-hour from downtown ($3.50 return). Details on hiking are available from the ranger office, 806 W Hallam Street (☎925-3445).

Accommodation

Aspen Central Reservations (☎1–800/262-7736 or ☎925-9000) run a superb service, and don't mind if you ask for the cheapest available room. Rates vary considerably even in winter; the least expensive times to come are in the "value seasons" (last week in Nov, first two weeks of Dec & first two weeks of April). Between mid-December and January 4, you'll do well to find a double for under $100, unless you book well in advance. Money can be saved by renting a **condo**, or **camping**; the ranger office (☎925-3445) can advise on free wilderness sites and **campgrounds** such as *Maroon Creek* or several smaller places out towards Independence Pass, costing around $6 a night.

Christmas Inn B&B, 232 W Main St (☎925-3822). Friendly, family-run motel, two minutes' walk from downtown. Free continental breakfast, free ski shuttle. Summer $48–70; winter $60–90.

Innsbruck Inn, 233 W Main St (☎925-2980). Opposite the *Christmas Inn*, with just that little bit more luxury. Buffet breakfast, pool and free shuttle to ski slopes; summer $62–100, winter $95–190.

Mountain Chalet, 333 E Durant Ave (☎925-7797). Downtown dorm beds for $28 in summer, $30–45 in winter. Motel rooms range $50–130 and $90–150 in summer and winter respectively.

St Moritz Lodge and Hostel, 334 W Hyman Ave (☎925-3220). Rooms for $62 in summer, $80–160 in winter. The hostel accommodation is not great, but costs just $24 (summer) and $28–40 (winter).

Tyrolean Lodge, 200 W Main St (☎925-4595). Motel near downtown; summer $45, winter $50–66.

Eating and Drinking

Many of Aspen's eighty cafes and restaurants charge over $20 for an entree, but good budget places exist and competition is keen.

Boogie's Diner, 534 E Cooper Ave (☎925-6610). Fifties-style diner above a trendy T-shirt store. 1lb-burgers with all the trimmings for $9.95; blue plate specials like meat loaf and mash for around $6.

Cooper St Pier, 500 E Cooper St (☎925-7758). Lively bar and cafe offering daily specials, plus burgers, fries and drink for $3.95. Popular evening hangout for young people.

Explore Booksellers and Coffeehouse, 211 E Main St (☎925-5336). Great wholefood and dessert menu at reasonable prices to an accompaniment of classical music. Open daily 10am–midnight.

Little Annie's, 517 E Hyman Ave (☎925-1098). Lively, popular and unpretentious. Potato pancakes ($4) and hearty stews ($5) for lunch. Huge trout, chicken, beef or rib dinner platters for $12.

Woody Creek Tavern, Woody Creek (☎923-4585). Seven miles north of Aspen along Hwy-82, right on River Road and then first left. Cult bar where ranch hands and rock stars shoot pool, drink imported beers and eat Tex-Mex food. The regular haunt of gonzo journalist Hunter S Thompson.

Entertainment and Nightlife

Going out in Aspen, the capital of après-ski, is fun all year round and needn't be expensive, certainly by big city standards. Look in the free papers for details of special offers. In summer, downtown hosts several top-notch festivals. The **Aspen Music Festival**, between late June and late August, features international artists and conductors (☎925-9042), while July and early August see the **DanceAspen** festival. The major winter carnival, mid-January's **Winterskol**, includes sporting events, parades and concerts.

Jerome Bar, 330 E Main St in the *Jerome Hotel* (☎920-1000). Grand historic bar; drink and mingle with the well-heeled hotel guests.

Legends of Aspen, 325 E Main St (☎925-5860). Popular sports-type bar opposite the *Jerome*, usually offering good-value drinks specials.

Paradise Club, 450 S Galena St (☎925-5886). Aspen's top live music venue. Usually free before 10pm with reasonable drink prices.

Shooters, 210 S Galena St (☎925-4567). Swinging country and western below the *Hard Rock Cafe*.

Vail

Compared to most other Colorado ski towns, **VAIL**, one hundred miles west of Denver off I-70, is a new creation. Only a handful of farmers lived here before the resort, a collection of fake Tyrolean-style chalets and concrete-block condominiums, opened in 1952. It became famous during the Ford administration as the western White House (Gerald Ford and his wife still live here, hosting annual celebrity golf and skiing competitions) and in 1989 it played host to the World Alpine Ski Championships.

According to *SKI* magazine, Vail is the top **ski** destination in the US – but not for its aesthetic beauty. What lures the ultra-rich (there's even more conspicuous wealth here than in Aspen) is the exceptional quality of snow, the variety of the terrain and the huge number of lifts (expensive at $40 a day). There's also an exciting 3000-foot **bobsleigh run** for a reasonable $12 per person. Vail has recently become a popular **mountain bike** centre, with trails catering for all abilities. The best option is to take the gondola from Lionshead centre (mid-June to Aug 10am–4.30pm; $15) and ride down the mountain or climb right to the top over very tough terrain.

Practicalities

Vail spreads out for eight miles along the narrow valley floor, centred successively from east to west around Vail Village, Lionshead, Cascade Village and West Vail. Beaver Creek, home of the Fords, lies a further ten miles west. The entire Vail complex is pedestrianised; there's no charge for using the car parks in summer and *Vail Buses* run a free year-round shuttle service.

For information on skiing and accommodation, contact *Vail Associates* (☎476-5601), or call into a **visitor centre** at either Vail Village or Lionshead. Finding an affordable place to **stay** can be a real problem. The best bets are probably in **West Vail**, where the *Roost Lodge* (☎476-5451) costs $50 to $60 in summer, $65 to $110 in winter, and *Days Inn* (☎476-6317) charges $52 to $85 in summer, $70 to $150 in winter. In **Vail Village**, the main social centre, prices are higher. The best value is *Tivoli Lodge* (summer $60–75, winter $100–150), while the *Mountain Haus* (summer $90–125, winter $125–infinity) is pretty sumptuous and not bad value. You can make bookings for both through the *Vail Resort Asociation* (☎1-800/525-3875). One particularly nice alternative is the *Eagle River Inn*, 145 N Main Street (☎827-5761 or ☎1-800/344-1750), a B&B decked out in tasteful Santa Fe style in the hamlet of **Minturn**, seven miles south of Vail on US-24. It costs $79 in summer, $89 to $155 in winter.

Eating out can also prove expensive. *Jackalope* in West Vail Mall (☎476-4314) is a lively bar and pool hall serving basic Mexican and American food, with complete dinners for $7. *Vendetta's*, 291 Bridge Street in Vail Village (☎476-5070), offers fine Italian lunch specials at $6, pasta dinners for $9 and entrees at $12 to $15.

Nightlife revolves around **The Circuit** on Bridge Street, Vail Village. Most people tour between the bars and discos; the checklist of places to see and be seen includes *The Club* (live music), the *Red Lion* (Brit-style pub), upstairs at *Vendetta's* (the ski patrol hangout) and *Nick's*, below *Russell's Restaurant*, which plays reasonable dance music.

Glenwood Springs

Busy – if not downright hectic – **GLENWOOD SPRINGS** sits at the end of impressive Glenwood Canyon, 125 miles west of Denver and within easy striking distance of Vail and Aspen. Long used by the Ute Indians as a place of relaxation, the **hot springs** here were the target for unscrupulous speculators who broke treaties and established resort facilities in the 1880s. The sulphurous smell that hits you on the north side of the river emanates from **Glenwood Hot Springs Pool**, 410 N River Street. Billed as the "world's largest outdoor mineral hot springs pool", it's a great spot to wind down, with an exhilarating hydrotube water slide (daily summer 7.30am–10pm; winter 9am–10pm; $6).

Some of the west's most colourful characters came here in the early days, including Dr John R **"Doc" Holliday**, a dentist better known as a gambler, gunslinger and participant in the gunfight at the OK Corral (see p.674). A chronic tuberculosis sufferer, Holliday came to the springs for a cure but died just a few months later in November 1887 at the age of 35. He is buried on a bluff overlooking the town in the picturesque Linwood Cemetery. In the paupers' section, you can find the grave of Harvey Logan, alias bankrobber Kid Curry, a member of Butch Cassidy's notorious gang.

Rafting along a fairly placid twenty-mile stretch of the Colorado River is a popular local activity. *Rock Gardens*, at the I-70 No Name (No. 119) exit (☎945-6737), charge $28 for a half-day trip. **Hiking** trails past streams and waterfalls criss-cross the White River National Forest which surrounds the town, while the nearby family-oriented *Ski Sunlight* complex offers some of the cheapest **skiing** in the region (☎945-7491).

Practicalities

Amtrak arrives at 413 Seventh Street in Glenwood Springs, having followed a very scenic route through the canyons, gorges and valleys of central Colorado. *Greyhound*, travelling along the less-inspiring I-70, stops close to downtown. The **visitor centre** can be found at 1102 Grand Avenue (☎945-6589). **Rooms** at the *Cedar Lodge Motel*, 2102 Grand Avenue (☎945-6579), cost a reasonable $42 to $60. The *Daily Bread Cafe & Bakery*, downtown at 729 Grand Avenue (☎945-6253), serves up delicious fresh breads, pastries, soups and salads. A little further out, the *19th Street Diner*, 1908 Grand Avenue (☎945-9133) offers cheap American and Mexican meals, with a good bar open until 1am.

The Black Canyon Of The Gunnison

Several western canyons exceed the Black Canyon in overall size. Some are larger; some are narrower; and a few have walls as steep. But no other canyon in North America combines the depth, narrowness, sheerness and sombre countenance of the Black Canyon.

US Geology Field Report

The **BLACK CANYON OF THE GUNNISON NATIONAL MONUMENT**, around eighty miles south of Glenwood Springs, or two hundred miles due west of Colorado Springs on US-50, holds none of the beauty of the magnificent gorges of Utah or Arizona – and at 2900 feet, it's less deep than many other canyons throughout the Rockies.

It is, however, absolutely eerie. The eleven-mile dirt road which leads to the **north rim** from Crawford, thirteen miles south of Hotchkiss on Hwy-92, is a hauntingly quiet trip through deeply rutted scrubland; hawks, turkey vultures and bald eagles are more commonly sighted than people. From the ranger office at the rim, other dirt roads lead to several vertigo-inducing overlooks, where you have to crane your neck to see the gloomy Gunnison far below. The only sound is the ceaseless roar of the river. If you're more ambitious, and brave, you can hike down to the bottom where the canyon walls are just forty feet apart; this takes a full day, as the climb back up is very demanding.

Most tourists plump for the tamer scenery and more accessible views of the **south rim**, fourteen miles east of **Montrose**, via Hwy-50 and an unpaved road. The **visitor centre** at 2233 E Main Street here (☎249-7036) can advise on **camping** on both rims.

Grand Junction

GRAND JUNCTION, 246 miles west of Denver on I-70, is often neglected as a destination, even though its immediate environs abound with outdoor opportunities, and within a fifty-mile stretch you can trace the transition from fertile delta to full-blown desert. Another town which sprang into life in the 1880s with the arrival of the railroads, it now makes its living primarily through the oil and gas industries. Although initial impressions are bound to be unfavourable – an unsightly sprawl of factory units and salesyards lines the I-70 Business Loop – downtown is much better, with leafy boulevards encircling a small, tree-lined, historic and retail district.

The **Dinosaur Valley Museum**, 362 Main Street (summer daily 9.30am–5.30pm; winter Tues–Sat 10am–4.30pm; $3.50), houses reconstructed reptiles along with a vast assortment of giant bones dug up in the surrounding area. They can also advise on self-guided tours of excavation sites at Dinosaur Hill on the west side of town.

Grand Junction offers a wide range of **cycling** terrain, from canal paths to rigorous mountain trails. Bikes can be hired from the *Bike Peddler*, 701 First Street (☎243-5602). There's great **hiking** beside the rippled, purple-grey **Book Cliffs**, paralleling the town on the north side, whose subtle changes of colour throughout the day are a delight.

Practicalities

Amtrak stops at Second and Pitkin streets. *Greyhound* buses serve Durango, Denver and Salt Lake City from 230 S Fifth Street (☎242-6012). The **visitor centre**, 759 Horizon Drive (☎243-1001), provides a very helpful service. Budget **motels** on the interstate offer rock-bottom rates, while the downtown *Two Rivers Inn*, 141 N First Street (☎245-8585), the *Friendship Inn Motel*, three miles out at 733 Horizon Drive (☎245-7200), and the friendly *Gate House B&B*, 2502 N First Street (☎242-6105), all charge between $32 and $62. The *Hotel Melrose*, 337 Colorado Avenue (☎242-9636), close to both *Amtrak* and *Greyhound*, charges $16 per person for a room without bath ($25 en suite).

You can **eat** well for under $10 at the *River City Cafe & Bar*, 748 North Avenue (☎245-8040), while the *Good Pasture* in the *Friendship Inn Motel* looks like another boring family diner, but serves a very health-conscious and good-value menu.

Colorado National Monument

Millions of years of wind and water erosion have carved the big and brightly coloured rock spires, domes, arches, pedestals and balanced rocks that lie within the sheer-walled canyon of the **COLORADO NATIONAL MONUMENT**, just four miles west of Grand Junction. This painted desert of warm reds, stunning purples, burnt oranges and browns is also home to a high arid vegetation of piñon pine, yucca, sagebrush and Utah juniper. There's an entry fee of $3 per car, good for seven days.

The 23-mile **rim drive** (a 39-mile round trip from Grand Junction) twists and curves along the top of the canyon. Numerous overlooks, the best on the western half, provide great photo spots, though few visitors find the most magnificent of all, the **Book Cliff View**, or the **Parade of the Monoliths**, just off the rim road at the sign for Window Rock Trail. Short hikes include the one-hour **John Otto's Trail**, which leads to a dramatic overlook of several monoliths; longer trails get right down to the canyon floor.

If you want to **camp**, there are sites at the *Saddlehorn Campground* in the park ($6) or you can pitch a tent anywhere more than a quarter of a mile off the road.

Grand Mesa

The **GRAND MESA**, thirty miles east of Grand Junction on Hwy-65, via I-70, is the largest flat-topped mountain in the world at 10,000 feet. Around 600 million years ago a 400-foot lava flow capped the surface where it now stands. Erosion has worn down the surrounding sedimentary rock, but the lava cap has preserved the mountain's original height. In one sense, it feels like an island in the sky; on the other hand, it's almost too big to give the impression of a mountaintop, and to see its proper definition you have to go thirty miles away to the Utah state line. However, those who ascend the twisting Hwy-65 to the plateau can't fail to be moved by the tranquil landscape, covered by pine and aspen groves with over 200 lakes, all coloured by the reflections of shoreline trees. **Lands End Road**, an eleven-mile dirt track, comes out to a stunning panorama from thick forest on the left to desert on the right, with lakes, plains, sand hills and smaller mesas in between, and the snow-crested San Juan peaks far off in the background.

There are pretty campgrounds on the east side near Alexander Lake (details from the ranger office; ☎242-8211), as well as a motel and basic cafes. Just at the bottom of the Mesa, five miles north of **Cedaredge**, the *Llama's B&B* on Hwy-65 (☎856-6836) offers wonderful hospitality, fantastic breakfast served on a sun deck and a chance to meet some llamas.

Southwest Colorado

The high mountain passes of southwest Colorado are classic mining territory; dotted through the valleys you'll find all sorts of well-preserved late Victorian frontier towns. As the pioneers moved in, first illegally and then backed by the US government, they drove the Ute Indians away into the poorer land of the far southwest.

The San Juan Skyway

From Durango, the main town of southwest Colorado, the dramatic **SAN JUAN SKYWAY** completes a loop of over two hundred miles through the mountains, north along US-550 and then back via Hwy-145 and US-160. The stretch immediately north of Durango is known as the **Million Dollar Highway**, for the amount of gold in the gravel that was used in its construction. It makes its way over stunning high passes, such as the 11018-ft **Red Mountain Pass** (which really is red, thanks to mineral deposits), passing abandoned mine workings and rusting machinery in the most unlikely and inaccessible spots.

Durango

DURANGO, named for Durango Mexico and now twinned with it, too, was founded in 1880 as a rail junction for the gold-rush community of Silverton, 45 miles further north. The **steam trains**, which still run the same spectacular route through the Animas Valley, remain the foundation of Durango's tourist economy; the **Durango & Silverton Narrow Gauge Railroad** runs up to four return trips daily between May and October, from a depot at the south end of town. Tickets should be reserved, at the very least two weeks in advance, from the office at 479 Main Avenue ($40 return; ☎247-2733).

There's not very much to see in the town itself. It makes a good base for Mesa Verde (see below), but otherwise the main activity is all kinds of outdoor pursuits. Durango is a sometime host of the World Mountain Bike Championships; you can try out the gruelling circuits for yourself on a bike hired from *Hassle Free Sports*, 2615 Main Avenue (☎259-3874).

Durango's **visitor centre**, near the train station (☎247-0312 or ☎1-800/525-8855), has full lists of **accommodation**. Rooms at the *Strater Hotel*, the town's best known landmark, at 699 Main Avenue (☎247-4431; ☎1-800/247-4431 out of state), start at around $70. Among innumerable **motels** along Main Avenue heading north, the *Siesta* at no. 3416 (☎247-0741) and the *Silver Spur*, no. 3416 (☎247-5552), both charge well under $30. The *Scrubby Oaks*, three miles east at 1901 Florida Road (☎247-2176), is a good-value mountain-view **B&B** charging from $35 to $60. There are plenty of places to **eat**; *B W Shay's*, at 948 Main Avenue (☎247-4144), serves good Mexican and American food.

Silverton

Journey's end for the narrow-gauge railroad comes at **SILVERTON**, spread across a small flat valley but surrounded by high mountains. It's one of the most atmospheric of Colorado's mountain towns, with the false-front stores along Blair Street recalling the days when Bat Masterson was the city marshal (even if they are now mostly T-shirt emporia).

Few people come here as anything more than day-trippers, so to spend a night in Silverton is to step back a century. Its two main **accommodation** options are both only open in summer: the *Wyman Hotel*, 1371 Greene Street (☎387-5372), offers a distinct touch of luxury for around $50, while the *Alma House*, 220 E Tenth Street (☎387-5336), starts at $35. The *French Bakery*, 1250 Greene Street (☎387-5423), serves food from sandwiches through to full meals.

Telluride

TELLURIDE, 120 miles northwest of Durango on Hwy-145, is another former mining town, which in the 1880s was briefly home to the young Butch Cassidy. He returned to hold up the San Miguel Valley Bank in June 1889, and got away with $20,000. Telluride these days has found its fortune as a ski resort, but it has done so without losing its character – the wide main street, with low-slung buildings to either side, still heads directly up towards a stupendous mountain view. Healthy young bohemians with few visible means of support seem to form the majority of the population.

Accommodation is much cheaper in summer than during the skiing season, though prices do go up for the Bluegrass Festival in June, the Jazz Festival at the beginning of August, and the Film Festival at the start of September. *Telluride Central Reservations* (☎728-4431 or ☎1-800/525-3455) co-ordinates reservations for all lodging in town; of specific places, the 1895 *New Sheridan Hotel*, 231 W Colorado Avenue (☎728-4351), has basic rooms from $30 and a good bar downstairs, which they're planning to turn into a brew-pub, and the *Victoria Inn*, 401 W Pacific Avenue (☎728-6601), has doubles from $44. *Eddie's Cafe* at 300 W Colorado Avenue (☎728-5335) serves good Italian **food**. There's no public transport to or around Telluride, but you can hire **bikes** from *Olympic Sports*, 150 W Colorado Avenue (☎728-4477).

Cortez

The town of **CORTEZ**, in the far southwest corner of Colorado, consists basically of one long stretch of highway (US-160), roughly 25 miles up from the **Four Corners Monument** which marks the meeting place of Colorado, New Mexico, Arizona and Utah. Its primary function is an overnight stop for travellers heading to or from the canyonlands of northern Arizona, being very handy for visitors to Mesa Verde National Park. Nothing in town commands much attention, though the giant **Sleeping Ute Mountain** to the southwest, visible from all over, makes a dramatic backdrop, looking uncannily like a warrior god asleep with his arms folded across his chest.

The **Colorado Welcome Center** at 928 E Main Street (☎656-3414 or ☎1-800/346-6528) can provide information on the entire state. Cheap **motels** include *El Capri* at 2110 S Broadway (☎565/3764), from $40, and the *Arrow*, 440 S Broadway (☎565-7778), which starts at around $35. *Stromsted's Restaurant*, 1020 S Broadway (Hwy-666; ☎565-1257) is a classy and convivial place to **eat**.

Mesa Verde

MESA VERDE NATIONAL PARK, the only national park in the US exclusively devoted to archaeological remains, is set high in the plateaux of southwest Colorado, entered off US-160 halfway between Cortez and Mancos. It's an astonishing place, so far off the beaten track that its extensive **Anasazi ruins** were not fully explored until 1888.

Between the time of Christ and 1300 AD, Anasazi civilisation expanded to cover much of the area now known as the "**Four Corners**" district. Their earliest dwellings were simple pits in the ground, but before they vanished mysteriously from history they had developed the architectural sophistication needed to build the extraordinary complexes of Mesa Verde. Most of the best preserved Anasazi relics are in the modern states of New Mexico, Arizona and Utah; see p.657 for more background information, and a full list of other sites which can be visited.

Mesa Verde today is a densely wooded plateau, cut at its southern edge by sheer canyons which divide the land into narrow fingers. The Anasazi are thought to have been the only inhabitants the region has ever had; no one has lived here since the thirteenth century, and neither have any traces been found of a human presence before 500 AD. The people who built their first pithouses here in the sixth century were already skilled potters leading a stable agricultural lifestyle; they owned domesticated turkeys and grew corn. After several hundred years, they moved off the mesa tops and began to construct spectacular multistorey apartments and entire communities, nestling in rocky alcoves high above the canyons. Quite why they did so is not clear; the Round Towers in the Cliff Palace, for example, cannot have served as lookouts, while Spruce Tree House could hardly have been built for defence, as it's simply not defensible at all. Neither is it known why they eventually left; elsewhere there are signs that the Anasazi were violent displaced by marauding newcomers, but at Mesa Verde the soil may just have become too depleted for them to stay on.

Touring the Park

The road up from the park entrance twists and climbs for around fifteen miles – giving dramatic views along the way – before reaching the main **Far View Visitor Center** (daily 8am–5pm; ☎529-4461). Just beyond this, the road divides to the two main constellations of remains: Wetherill Mesa to the west, and Chapin Mesa further south.

Wetherill Mesa, which is only accessible in summer, is a tortuous twelve-mile drive. Ruins such as the Long House are said to be more authentic than those elsewhere in the park, having been "re-stabilised" in recent years rather than subjected to the extensive rebuilding of the more famous sites earlier this century; but on the other hand they're less dramatic, and a lot more difficult to reach.

A couple of miles down the road from the visitor centre towards Chapin Mesa, you pass **Far View** itself on the left. This mesa-top pueblo, thought to have been abandoned in the early 1200s, depended for its water supply on nearby **Mummy Lake**, an artificial reservoir ninety feet across by twelve feet deep, holding half a million gallons, which was fed by a five-mile canal.

The **museum** at the park headquarters, as you come onto **Chapin Mesa**, contains excellent displays on the Anasazi – although unfortunately many artefacts from Mesa Verde were shipped away by plundering archaeologists at the turn of this century. **Spruce Tree House** here is the only ruin which can be seen in winter. In summer, a one-way driving loop takes you past the **Square Tower House**, the unfinished mesa-top **Sun Temple**, and on to the **Cliff Palace**. The largest Anasazi cliff dwelling to survive, this once housed over two hundred people; now its adobe towers, smoothly blending in with the surrounding rock, provide a haunting evocation of a lost and little-known world. You can sit and dream for hours. Ladders lead down from the main plaza into circular kivas. Inside some of the structures, fading Anasazi murals can still be discerned.

Visiting **Balcony House**, further on, involves scrambling thirty feet up a ladder and through a narrow tunnel – and, once you're there you find yourself teetering above a steep drop into Soda Canyon. Unless you share the fearless Anasazi attitude to heights, you might prefer to give this fascinating fortress-like edifice a miss.

Park Practicalities

Mesa Verde can get very crowded in high summer; the best times to visit are in May, September and October. The park and the museum stay open all year round, though most of the sights are inaccessible, as detailed above, and the concessions such as gas, food and lodging only operate between mid-May and mid-October.

Most visitors stay in nearby towns such as Cortez or Durango; the only **rooms** available in the park itself – and the cheapest is $80 – are at *Far View Motor Lodge*, at the summit of Navajo Hill near the visitor centre (Box 277, Mancos, CO 81328; ☎529-4421). The ranger at the park entrance knows if rooms are available. You can **camp** at the first-come, first-served *Morefield Campground*, four miles up from the entrance (☎529-4421), and there are also several commercial campgrounds nearby.

Greyhound **buses** will theoretically drop passengers at the park entrance, but that's very little help when it comes to seeing the ruins themselves; if you don't have your own transport, you'd do best to take one of the many daily **coach tours** from Durango.

WYOMING

Pronghorn antelope all but outnumber people in arid, windswept **WYOMING**, the ninth largest but least populous state in the union, with just 460,000 residents. Above all, this is classic **cowboy country** – the inspiration behind *Shane*, *The Virginian* and countless other western novels – where the days of the open range are evoked by rodeos, country and western dance halls and ranchwear stores. The state emblem, seen everywhere, is a hat-waving cowboy astride a bucking bronco.

Any journey through **southern Wyoming** will involve long stretches of boredom – the genial capital, **Cheyenne**, and, to a lesser extent, the nearby ranching and college town of **Laramie**, are about the only worthwhile ports of call. **Northern Wyoming** is, however, a different matter. Close to three million tourists per year head for its western corner to explore the simmering geothermal landscape of **Yellowstone National Park**, and the craggy mountain vistas of the adjacent, and equally outstanding, **Grand Teton National Park**. Wedged in between Yellowstone and South Dakota to the east are the helter-skelter **Bighorn Mountains**, likeable old west towns such as **Buffalo** and the otherworldly outcrop of **Devils Tower**.

The meagre supply of buffalo in early Wyoming caused fierce intertribal wars over hunting grounds and kept the number of **Native Americans** down to 10,000. However, Sioux, Cheyenne and Blackfoot combined in staunch resistance to pioneer intrusion, inflicting notable defeats on the US Army before it could clear the way for white settlement in the 1870s. The cattle ranchers and sheep-farming homesteaders who followed engaged in violent **range wars** over grazing rights to the wiry grasslands.

Unlikely as it may seem, this rowdy, heavily male-dominated state was the first to grant all women the vote in 1869 – a full half-century before the rest of the country. This was thanks not to a mass suffragist movement, but to skilful lobbying by a handful of women who persuaded the territorial governor that enfranchising women would be excellent for public relations, thus attracting more settlers and hastening statehood, which depended upon population. A year later Wyoming appointed the country's first women jurors, and the "Equality State" also elected the first female US governor in 1924.

The absence of rivers to irrigate farmland has effectively put a lid on agricultural and population growth. Any weatherbeaten, Wrangler-clad stranger is more likely, these days, to be an oil roustabout than a genuine cowboy, fuel and mineral extraction having replaced livestock as the mainstay of the economy in the early part of this century.

Getting Around Wyoming

One daily *Amtrak* **train** crosses southern Wyoming in daylight hours in each direction. *Greyhound* **buses** operate along I-80 through the south, and to the western entrance to Yellowstone Park. The rest of the state is covered by regional bus companies; it takes considerable time and planning to get where you want to go. Once in the towns, public transport is virtually nonexistent: only Jackson operates a very limited service. The only **airport** of any size is at Cheyenne. **Cycling** across northern Wyoming can be great fun, though check the contours for the easiest way over the Bighorn Mountains.

South and Central Wyoming

State capital **Cheyenne** is the only town of real note in the lower two-thirds of Wyoming. It's surrounded by rich prairie, a surprising contrast with the uninspiring jumble of scrubland, mountain and desert which characterises most of the region. The city has closer economic ties with Omaha or Denver than with the rest of Wyoming – a point which the more northerly oil city of **Casper** was keen to stress in various unsuccessful bids to become the seat of government. West of Cheyenne, smaller **Laramie** possesses an agreeable frontier feel, but lacks real spark. The spectacular wilderness of the **Wind River Range**, accessible from **Pinedale** and **Lander**, accounts for most of the west central portion of the state. The bleak and barren southwest corner holds least interest.

Cheyenne

With its ranchwear shops and honky-tonk saloons, **CHEYENNE** looks at first like an overgrown cowboy town. But a quick walk round reveals a much more diverse community, shaped by railroads, state politics, and even nuclear arms. When the tracks of the Union Pacific Railroad reached this site in 1867, the company had to use soldiers to drive out the "**Hell on Wheels**" brigade, a brutal roadshow of gamblers, moonshiners and hard-drinking gunmen who kept one jump ahead of the railroads, claiming land and then selling it for huge profit before moving on to the next proposed terminal.

Union Pacific's sprawling yards and fine old terminus now mark the eastern edge of downtown. Ever since a fort was established to guard the railroad, Cheyenne has had a

The telephone **area code** for the entire state of Wyoming is ☎307.

high military presence. The long-standing installation at the western edge of town was massively expanded in 1957 to house the first US intercontinental ballistic missile base.

The **approach** into Cheyenne, dropping into a wide dip in the plains, leaves the longest-lasting memories for most travellers. With the snow-crested Rockies looming in the distance and short, sun-bleached grass encircling the town, the sky suddenly appears gargantuan, dwarfing the the city's leafy suburbs and everything else below it.

The nine-day **Cheyenne Frontier Days** festival in late July celebrates **cowboy culture**, with its showpiece the world's largest outdoor **rodeo**; there are also concerts by top country stars, parades, chuckwagon races, air shows and free pancake breakfasts. For the rest of the year, you'll have to make do with the **Old Cheyenne Gunfight**, at Sixteenth and Carey streets (summer Mon–Fri 6pm, Sat "high noon"; free), in which gunslingers act out incidents from the town's turbulent first decade.

Sixteenth Street is the retail and entertainment heart of Cheyenne. Five minutes' walk north up leafy Capitol Avenue near the unspectacular Wyoming State Capitol, the **Wyoming State Museum**, at Central Avenue and 24th Street, takes a sober look at Wild West history (Mon–Fri 8.30am–5pm, Sat 9am–5pm; summer also Sun 1–5pm; free). The **Cheyenne Frontier Days Old West Museum**, five minutes' drive from downtown at Eighth and Carey streets, is more lighthearted, telling how the railroad came to town, with some great old engines (June–Aug Mon–Sat 8am–7pm, Sun 10am–6pm; Sept–May Mon–Fri 9am–5pm, Sat & Sun 11.30am–4.30pm; $2).

Practicalities

Greyhound **buses** (☎634-7744) run east and west along I-80 and south to Denver, while *Powder River* (☎635-1327) buses travel through eastern Wyoming to Montana and South Dakota. Both companies share the depot at 1503 S Capitol Avenue, a two-block walk from the **visitor centre**, 301 W Sixteenth Street (☎778-1401), which operates a ninety-minute **trolley tour** of Cheyenne for $5.50.

Places to **stay** are inexpensive, except during the Frontier Days, when prices double. Motels in the $25–30 range line up along West Lincolnway (a continuation of Sixteenth Street), but the best value can be found downtown in the *Historic Plains Motel*, 1600 Central Avenue (☎638-3311), where the large, clean rooms are a bargain at $27 to $32 a night. For **camping**, the *Restway Travel Park*, six miles east of downtown at 4212 Whitney Road (☎634-3811), offers good facilities for $13.

Cheyenne has no shortage of diners serving cowboy-sized breakfast and lunches, such as the excellent *Driftwood Cafe*, 200 E 18th Street (☎634-5304). *Los Amigos*, 620 Central Avenue (☎638-8591), offers tasty home-style Mexican food, and the best c&w sounds can be heard at the spacious *Cowboy South*, 312 S Greeley Highway (☎637-3800).

Laramie

LARAMIE lies fifty miles west of Cheyenne on I-80, or slightly further via the spectacular Happy Jack Road (Hwy-210), which slices through plains studded with bizarrely shaped boulders and outcrops. The town itself at first seems typical of rural Wyoming, but behind the Victorian facades of the quaint downtown lurk record stores championing rock music, cafes specialising in vegetarian dishes and a good number of second-hand bookshops – all unusual for the heart of rodeo land. This is all due to the University of Wyoming, whose campus spreads east from the town centre.

The ambitious **Wyoming Territorial Park** project is west of town at 975 Snowy Range Road (June–Aug daily 11am–8pm; otherwise times vary; $5.95). The centrepiece of this living history park is the old territorial **prison**, a touch over-restored but holding informative displays on the Old West, women in Wyoming and huge mugshots of ex-convicts, among them Butch Cassidy. The famous bandit was incarcerated here for eighteen months from 1896, after being arrested for cattle-rustling.

Practicalities

Laramie's **Greyhound** station, 1358 N Second Street (☎742-0896), is a five-minute walk north from downtown. Cheapest overnight stays are at the downtown *Travel Inn*, 262 N Third Street (☎745-4853), and *Motel 6*, 621 Plaza Lane (☎742-2307), both $26 to $29. The best of several Mexican **cafes** is *El Conquistador*, 110 Ivinson Avenue (☎742-2377), while for a few dollars more you can choose from a healthfood and nouvelle menu at *Jeffrey's Bistro*, 123 Ivinson Avenue (☎742-7406). During term time, Laramie possesses a moderately lively nightlife. Students, yuppies and bikers pack out the frontier-style *Buckhorn Bar*, 114 Ivinson Avenue (☎742-3554); the friendly *Cowboy Saloon*, 108 S Second Street (☎721-3165), is a fun place to go and see some c&w bands.

West from Laramie

Crossing southern Wyoming on I-80 produces few high points. However, just outside Laramie, **Hwy-130** dips into the huge wind-gouged bowl of **Big Hollow** before passing through rustic Centennial to start the steep climb up **Medicine Bow Mountains** – known locally, and more descriptively, as the Snowy Range. Overlooks at the top of the 10,847-ft Snowy Range Pass present picturesque alpine lakes and meadows, tight against steep mountain faces.

Sixty-five miles out from Centennial, stylish **Saratoga** is hemmed in by the Snowy and Sierra Madre ranges. The **Hobo Hot Springs** on Walnut Avenue is a free outdoor pool fed by 114°F water from the town's springs. Easily the best place to stay is the old brick *Wolf Hotel*, 101 Bridge Street (☎326-5525), whose antique-furnished rooms cost $25 to $40. *Wally's*, 110 Bridge Street (☎326-8472), serves up great pizzas, vegetarian food and a mean steak sandwich.

Once Hwy-130 loops back onto I-80, twenty miles north of Saratoga, there is nothing much before the state line with Idaho. **Rawlins**, one hundred miles west of Laramie, offers little more than clean, $30 rooms in the *Hi-Top Motel*, 713 W Spruce Street (☎324-4561), and an excellent Mexican cantina, *Rose's Lariat*, 410 E Cedar Street (☎324-5261).

Fifty miles west of Rawlins, the brick-red **Red Desert** stretches to the horizon on either side of the interstate. From here on, the depressed towns show tell-tale signs of recent oil and mineral busts. **Rock Springs** stands out merely because it is even more ugly than the rest. However *Greyhound* drops off here for connections via the *Rock Springs–Jackson Bus Line*, 913 Second Street (☎362-6161), to Jackson, a gateway town for Grand Teton and Yellowstone national parks. If you need to stay overnight, the *Lamplighter Motel*, beside the *Greyhound* depot at 1004 Dewar Drive (☎362-6673), has reasonable rooms for $35, and the nearby *Kilpeppers* serves good family-style meals.

The Wind River Range

Roads to Grand Teton and Yellowstone national parks from southern Wyoming skirt the **Wind River Mountains**, the state's longest and highest range, with some challenging backpacking terrain. No roads cross the the mountains, so you'll have to choose whether to see them from the east or west sides. The latter is less convenient to get to, but has the better scenery and trails.

Lander on US-287 offers best access on the east. The ranger office at 600 N US-287 can advise on trails and dirt roads that edge into the foothills towards **Sinks Canyon State Park**, where the Popo Agie River plunges underground, only to re-emerge half a mile later in a gigantic spring. Places to stay in town include dorm beds for $5 at *Ma's Boarding House* on Mortimer Lane (☎332-3123) and rooms at the *Teton Motel*, 586 Main Street (☎332-3582), for $28.

Right at the northern end of the range on US-287 is the former logging town of **Dubois**, fifty miles south of Grand Teton National Park. When its final sawmill closed in 1987, Dubois started a concerted drive to attract some of the passing tourist trade. It's certainly a cheaper place to stay than Jackson (see p.626), though there's little to do in the evening except watch country crooners in the local bars. There's recommended budget accommodation at the *Branding Iron Motel*, 401 Ramshorn (☎455-2893), where cabins with kitchenettes cost $30. Close by, *Whisker Pete's Cafe* does good breakfasts.

On the west side, tiny, well-to-do **Pinedale** on US-191 offers unrivalled access to the mountains. Once an important logging centre, it now attracts second-home-owners and legions of backpackers. A sixteen-mile road winds out of town past Fremont Lake to Elkhart Park, from where some good trails lead past beautiful Seneca Lake and along rugged Indian Pass to the glaciers and 13,000-ft peaks. Call into the ranger office at 210 W Pine Street (☎367-4326) for ideas on hiking and sightseeing. *Rock Springs–Jackson Bus Line* serve Pinedale once a day. Clean basic **rooms** are available at the *Sundance Motel*, 148 E Pine Street (☎367-4336), for $30. Try the *Wrangler Cafe*, 310 E Pine Stree,t for breakfast, or the burgers and Mexican food at the *Corral Bar*, 30 W Pine Street.

Casper

Dreary **CASPER** is an unlikely place to visit, but it's a good 150 miles from anywhere of similar size, and the surrounding small towns are even duller. The centre of Wyoming's oil region, its fortunes since 1890 have been dictated by the commodities market, with the population fluctuating between periods of high and low demand. Likewise, the town's appearance varies depending on whether it is a time of boom or bust. Right now the economy is ticking along rather well, though with the exception of a couple of retail blocks along E Second Street downtown still hasn't shaken off the signs of harder times.

Powder River Transportation **buses**, serving Cheyenne, Billings and Rapid City, pull in at 315 N Walcott Street (☎266-1904). The **visitor centre** is a couple of blocks north at 500 N Center Street (☎234-5311). Casper's **motels** charge agreeably low rates, though you should look at rooms in the cheaper places before paying. The downtown *Galley Motel*, 310 N Center Street (☎234-4330), is clean and costs $20; the *Showboat Motel*, 100 West F Street (☎235-2711), with its flashing neon lights and waterbeds, is the kitsch option for $35 a night. There's **camping** across the river from the massive oil refineries at *Fort Caspar Campground*, 4205 W Thirteenth Street (☎234-3260), or high up on nearby Casper Mountain (☎234-6821). The *Cheese Barrel*, 544 S Center Street (☎235-5202), serves great breakfasts, sticky cheese bread, soups and sandwiches. *Bosco's*, 847 A Street (☎265-9658), is good for reasonably priced Italian food.

Northwest and North Central Wyoming

Cutting across northern Wyoming is more than a handy route between the **Black Hills of Dakota** and **Yellowstone National Park**; it also happens to be the most interesting and varied part of the state. The surreal volcanic monument of **Devils Tower**, the abrupt **Bighorn Mountains** and the desertscape of the **Bighorn Basin** are the major natural attractions in a land steeped in the history of Indian wars, outlaw activity and pioneer hardships. Small towns such as unassuming **Buffalo** and more commercialised **Cody**, originally developed by William "Buffalo Bill" Cody, are potential stopovers.

Devils Tower

Congress designated **DEVILS TOWER** the country's first national monument in 1906, but it took Steven Spielberg's inspired use of it as the alien landing spot in *Close Encounters of the Third Kind* to make this supernatural-looking six-hundred-foot volcanic outcrop a true national icon. Plonked on top of a thickly forested hill, itself a full six hundred feet above the banks of the peaceful Belle Fourche River, it resembles a giant wizened tree stump; but, painted ever-changing hues by the sun and moon, it can be hauntingly beautiful. Sioux legend has it that the tower was formed after three young girls jumped on top of a boulder to escape a vicious bear. They were rescued when the great god, seeing their plight, made the rock rise higher and higher; the bear's desperate efforts to climb up scored the sides of the column.

Four short trails loop the tower, beginning from the **visitor centre** (daily summer 8am–7.45pm; otherwise 8am–4.45pm; ☎467-5501) at its base. The entrance fee per car is $3, and you can camp for $6 a night – arrive early or you'll end up paying more than twice that at one of the nearby commercial campgrounds.

Buffalo

Snuggled among the southeastern foothills of the Bighorn Mountains, **BUFFALO**, 130 miles west of Sundance, is a quiet, attractive town, unaffected by the bustle of the nearby I-90/I-25 intersection. Although **Main Street**, now lined with frontier-style shops and businesses, was an old buffalo trail, the town's name in fact comes from an early resident's home city of Buffalo, New York. The **Jim Gatchell Museum**, 10 Fort Street, stacked full of Old West curiosities pertaining to soldiers, ranchers and Native Americans, is well worth a visit (June–Aug daily 9am–8pm; free).

Buffalo's **visitor centre**, 55 N Main Street (☎684-5544,) provides an excellent information service on the entire tri-state area. Decent **rooms** at the *Mountain View Motel*, 585 Fort Street (☎684-2881), cost $33; the clean, but tastelessly decorated *Canyon Motel*, 997 Fort Street (☎684-2957), charges $20 to $30. The *Breadboard*, 57 S Main Street (☎684-2318), sells very cheap sandwiches, and *Steve's*, 820 N Main Street (☎684-5111), serves exquisite gourmet seafood and beef dishes for a very reasonable $8 to $12.

Fort Phil Kearney

Seventeen miles north of Buffalo, off I-90, is the site of **Fort Phil Kearney**. Though only operative from 1866 to 1868, it was the bloodiest of the western army forts, repeatedly stormed by Sioux, Apache and Cheyenne. There's nothing left of the actual fort – jubilant Sioux burned it down after it was abandoned by treaty in 1868 – but the **museum** tells the story of the 1866 **Fetterman Massacre**, one of the most famous clashes of the Plains Indian wars. Captain William Fetterman (who bragged that with eighty men he could whip any Indians in battle) was ignoring strict orders when he was lured by a small party of Sioux directly into the path of over a thousand warriors. Fetterman and all of his eighty soldiers were killed, the first time the US Army had suffered a defeat from which there were no survivors. Monuments marking this and other battlesites can be found within a few miles of the museum (summer daily 8am-6pm; free).

Through the Bighorn Mountains

Of the three possible routes through the **Bighorn Mountains**, US-14A from **Burgess Junction**, fifty miles west of Victorian **Sheridan**, is the most spectacular. The massive and heavily wooded Bighorns suddenly burst out of the plains to a height of over 9000 feet; the loftiest peaks, protruding above the timberline, seem strikingly bald beside their dark-coated neighbours. The road edges its way up lofty Medicine Mountain, where the mysterious **Medicine Wheel** (the largest monument of its kind that's still intact) is laid out on the windswept, western peak. The original purpose of these flat stones, placed in a geometrically perfect circle, is unknown; the "wheel" has 28 spokes and a circumference of 245 feet. Local Indian legends offer no clues, though the pattern implies that the builders were sun-worshippers or early astronomers.

The route down the west side, with gradients of ten to twenty percent and three awesome runaway truck ramps, is said to have cost more to build per mile than any other road in America. Tight hairpin bends, passing what seem like almost vertical drops, keep the driver's eyes off the magnificent overlooks, but the most spectacular view is near the bottom when the road belches you out into the fifty-mile **Bighorn Basin**. The first sight of this ultra-flat, sparsely vegetated valley, walled in by precipitous mountains on three sides and ragged foothills to the north, is enough to make you think you've uncovered a land that time forgot.

Cody

CODY was the brainchild of investors who in 1896 persuaded "Buffalo Bill" Cody to get involved in their development company. They named the settlement after him, knowing that the approval of the most famous man in the west would attract homesteaders and visitors alike. During summer, tourism is big business, but underneath all the Buffalo Bill-linked attractions and paraphernalia, Cody still manages to retain the feel of a rural western settlement. It's certainly not a place where you would have expected avant-garde painter **Jackson Pollock** to have been born and brought up.

The main reason to visit is the huge Buffalo Bill Historical Center, though other enticements include a good nightly rodeo, float trips down the Shoshone River (*Cody Rapid Transit*; ☎587-3535) and an array of souvenir and ranchwear shops along the wide dusty main thoroughfare of Sheridan Avenue.

BUFFALO BILL

The exploits of **William Frederick "Buffalo Bill" Cody** seem today so far-fetched that it's easy to think of him as a mythical character from the wildest Wild West fiction.

When just eleven years old, the murder of his father left him as family breadwinner, forcing him to get a job as an army despatch rider. After escaping ambush on an early mission, Cody attained regionwide fame as the "Youngest Indian Slayer of the Plains". Four years later he was once again the most youthful in his trade, this time as a rider for the **Pony Express**, delivering mail by horseback to the West Coast.

After a stint fighting for the Union in the Civil War, Cody found work – and a lifelong nickname supplying buffalo meat to railroad workers laying the transcontinental lines. He killed over 4200 animals in just eighteen months, before rejoining the army in 1868 as its chief scout. In the next decade, he achieved the rank of colonel, a Congressional Medal of Honour and a remarkable record of never losing any troops in ambushes at a time when the Plains Indian Wars were at their peak. As a scout, Cody joined battles such as the 1877 encounter with Sioux forces when he killed – and scalped – Chief Yellow Hand.

By the late 1870s, Cody's adventures were reported widely in the eastern press and with the Indian Wars all but over he found no shortage of work guiding Yankee and European gentry on buffalo hunts. He referred to the vacationers as "dudes", and was probably the first to use the term "dude ranch", which he applied to his camps. From the theatrical productions which he laid on for his rich guests developed the world famous **Wild West Show**. First staged in 1883, these spectacular outdoor carnivals usually consisted of a re-enactment of a famous Indian battle (a favourite was Custer's Last Stand featuring many of the Sioux who had been present at Little Bighorn), trick riders, a herd of buffalo, some clowns and exhibition shooting and riding by the man himself. The show spent ten of its thirty years in Europe, helping to make Buffalo Bill, as one historian put it, "the most famous and recognised man in the world". Dressed in the finest silks and sporting a well-groomed goatee, Cody entered the realms of high society, staying in the finest hotels and dining with heads of state; Queen Victoria was so enthusiastic in her admiration of him that rumours circulated of an affair between them.

In later life, a mellowing Cody played down his past activities, to the point of urging the government to respect all Indian treaties and put an end to the wanton slaughter of buffalo and game. Although the Wild West Show was reckoned to have brought in as much as one million dollars per year, his many investments failed badly, and, in January 1915, a penniless 69-year-old Buffalo Bill died at his sister's home in Denver. His grave can be found atop Lookout Mountain, outside Golden, Colorado (see p.595).

Buffalo Bill Historical Center

720 Sheridan Ave. June–Aug daily 7am–10pm; other months vary; $7; ☎587-4771.

One of the nation's most comprehensive collections of western Americana, the giant **Buffalo Bill Historical Center** comprises several distinct museums. Biographic artefacts from William Cody's various careers help the **Buffalo Bill Museum** to chronicle the years of the Pony Express, Civil War, Indian Wars and wild west shows. Guns, gifts from European heads of state, billboards, clothes and dime novels lurk in dozens of cabinets while a stagecoach, two stuffed buffalo and a replica stage fill the rest of the space.

A display of Ghost Dance shirts add a tragic element to the **Plains Indian Museum**. In the late 1880s, Native Americans, recognising that they could not defeat whites by force of arms, adopted a non-violent religious doctrine that involved singing and dancing until they slumped into trance. They believed that by so doing they would hasten the day when all whites would be buried by a heaven-sent fall of soil and that their dead warriors, along with huge herds of buffalo, would return to the Plains. Instead, the US Army condemned Ghost Dances as unacceptable shows of resistance, and mobilised troops to disrupt ceremonies. The rest of the museum focuses on craftwork rather than history, providing an interesting look at Native Americans living in the west today.

Bierstadt, Catlin and Moran are among the top names featured in the beautifully laid-out **Whitney Gallery of Western Art**, but the contrasting styles of Frederic Remington and Charles M Russell command most attention. The propagandist Remington dwells on conflict, depicting the Indian as a savage in the path of progress, while Russell's work shows a consistent respect for Native American life.

Yellowstone National Park

YELLOWSTONE NATIONAL PARK is quite literally phenomenal. Into an area roughly sixty miles by fifty miles are crammed more than half the **geysers** in the world (including the celebrated Old Faithful), plus thousands of other **hot springs**, gurgling **mud pools**, hissing **fumaroles** and whole mountainsides murmuring with **steam vents**. Add to that a **waterfall** twice as high as Niagara, an awe-inspiring **canyon**, the continent's largest **alpine lake**, and **wildflower meadows** that are home to abundant wildlife, and it all seems too good to be true.

On the other hand, when you take into account the presence of 2.5 million tourists per year, a legion of recreational vehicles clogging the roads, poor-value lodgings and overpriced food, the whole scenario becomes a lot less appealing. But if you allow yourself to get frustrated by these drawbacks, you'll be missing something very special. The key to appreciating Yellowstone is to take your time, and to plan carefully; above all, try to allow for a stay of at least three days.

Arrival and Information

Two of the five main **entrances** to Yellowstone National Park are in Wyoming, at **Cody** in the east and **Grand Teton National Park** to the south. The others are in Montana: **West Yellowstone** (west), **Gardiner** (north) and **Cooke City** (northeast). Admission to the park – $10 per car ($4 for each pedestrian or cyclist) – is good for seven days, and includes entry to Grand Teton National Park. See p.37 for details of the *Golden Eagle* pass, which saves on admission to national parks.

To get to Yellowstone by **bus**, take *Karst Stage* (☎406/586-8567) from Bozeman, via West Yellowstone or Gardiner; *Powder River Transportation* (☎1-800/442-3682) from Jackson, Cody or West Yellowstone; or *TW Services* (☎344-7311) from West Yellowstone or Billings. *Greyhound* also run as far as West Yellowstone (☎406/646-7666).

The **park headquarters** are at **Mammoth Hot Springs** near the north entrance. The main switchboard (☎344-7381) can connect you with visitor centres, help with

A BRIEF HUMAN HISTORY OF YELLOWSTONE

Native Americans shunned what is now **Yellowstone National Park** as the self-evident abode of evil spirits. The first white man to come was **John Colter** in 1807. His descriptions of "Colter's Hell", packed with exploding geysers and seething cauldrons, were widely ridiculed. However, as increasing numbers of trappers, scouts and prospectors hit upon Yellowstone, the government eventually decided to send out survey teams in 1870. Just two years later, Yellowstone was set aside as the first **national park,** in part to ensure that its natural assets were not stripped away by hunters, miners or lumber companies.

Management of the park during the early years was beset by problems; Congress may have shown enthusiasm for protecting the area, but it allocated no money for development. Among untoward incidents, irresponsible tourists stuck soap down the geysers, ruining the intricate geothermal plumbing; bandits preyed on stagecoaches carrying rich excursionists; and there was even a dramatic incursion by the Nez Perce Indians (see p.640), who raced through the park and killed two tourists along the way. Congress took the park out of civilian hands in 1886, and put the army in charge. By the time they handed over to the newly created National Park Service in 1917, the ascendancy of the automobile in Yellowstone had begun.

Since then, conflict has raged between the need for tourist facilities and the survival of the park's ecosystem and wildlife. One disturbing episode involved the relaxing of regulations regarding the feeding of bears, who became so reliant on tourists that many forgot, or never learnt, how to forage in the wild. Such close contact with humans produced inevitable maulings, a far cry from the friendly image of TV's *Jellystone* bears, Yogi and Boo Boo. Since the reversal of this policy, bears have gone back deep into the wilderness in search of food, and are now seen much less often.

The huge fires that razed 36 percent of the park in 1988 once again pushed Yellowstone's environmental policies onto centre stage. President Reagan expressed dismay that this natural asset was being allowed to burn, but environmentalists and park authorities maintained that the natural fire programme was essential to maintain the forest's ecocycle. The tourists' response was to vote with their wheels: the scarred and devastated mountainsides attracted double the usual number of park visitors in 1989.

camping queries and provide information for travellers with disabilities. Tune into 1606 AM for weather information, and consult the *Yellowstone Today* freesheet for schedules of activities and current regulations. National Park Service leaflets (25¢ each) cover the important landmarks, and help in working out what to see.

All **visitor centres**, located approximately every twenty miles along the main **Loop Road**, issue backcountry **hiking permits** and have guides on hand for disabled travellers. Each centre hosts a comprehensive exhibit on a different aspect of the park, covering natural and human history (Mammoth Hot Springs), geothermal activity (Old Faithful and Norris), wilderness areas and the 1988 forest fires (Grant Village), wildlife (Fishing Bridge) and geology (Canyon).

Only as a last resort should you see Yellowstone from the confines of a **tour bus**. *TW Services* operate all-day tours costing $18 to $28; *Gray Line* (☎406/646-9374) and *Powder River* run similar excursions from West Yellowstone.

Touring the Park

All of Yellowstone's major sights lie within a few hundred yards of the 142-mile **Loop Road**, a figure-of-eight circuit fed by roads from the five entrances. Virtually every feature is labelled and signposted, so you could in theory race around as many as possible, but you'll get more out of a visit, even if you're short on time, if you choose one or two areas to explore thoroughly. The **speed limit** on the Loop Road is a radar-enforced 45mph, though the traffic makes journey times hard to predict.

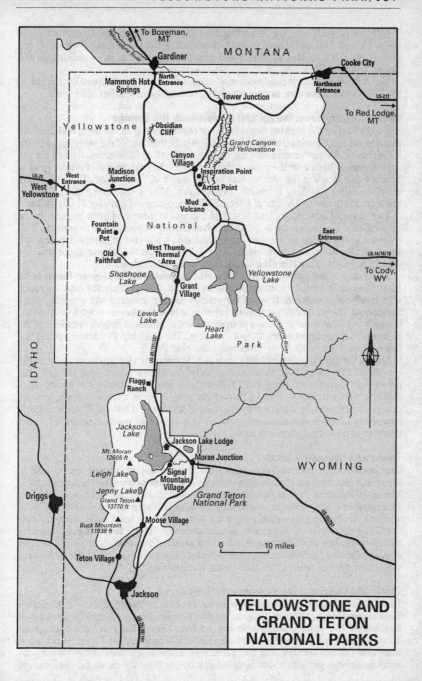

YELLOWSTONE AND GRAND TETON NATIONAL PARKS

Only in the early morning is **cycling** bearable or safe; there are no mountain bike trails. Though you can expect to **walk** considerable distances along the canyon and geyser trails, it's an idea to leave backcountry hiking for the more exciting **Grand Teton National Park** – which doesn't have the mosquitoes.

The following account runs clockwise around the Loop Road, from Old Faithful to the Yellowstone Lake area, both of which lie in the southern reaches of the park.

Geyser Country: From Old Faithful to Mammoth Hot Springs

Although neither the highest, largest or most regular geyser in the park, **Old Faithful** remains the most popular, erupting more frequently than any of the other big geysers. It "performs" for the camera-clicking masses every 45 to 84 minutes – you'll find an approximate schedule in the nearby visitor centre – and taking a seat on the rows of benches that face it is the obvious way to start a visit to Yellowstone. The first sign of activity is water splashing repeatedly over the rim. After several minutes, a column of water begins to rise to a height of 100 to 180 feet, spurting out a total of 11,000 gallons.

Two miles of boardwalks lead from Old Faithful to dozens of other geysers in the Upper Basin. If possible, try to get there when **Grand Geyser** is due to explode. This colossus blows its top on average just twice a day, for twelve to twenty minutes, in a series of four powerful bursts which climb to 200 feet. At the far end of the trail, the deep blue colour of the **Morning Glory Pool** is caused by algae.

Thirty miles north of Old Faithful, the less crowded **Norris Geyser Basin** is for many visitors the most exciting thermal area of all. It's certainly the most compact, with hundreds of different types of hot springs hissing, gurgling and steaming away. **Steamboat**, the world's tallest geyser, forces near-boiling water over 300 feet in the air, but only functions once or twice a year, whereas the whirlpool-pattern eruptions of the **Echinus Geyser** occur every 35 to 75 minutes. The **Evening Primrose Spring** is a flower-shaped crater filled with iridescent yellow mud.

One of the park's strangest landscapes is at **Mammoth Hot Springs**, at the northern tip of the Loop Road. A vapour-shrouded mountain looms over the perfectly preserved red-roofed US Army **Fort Yellowstone**, laden with terraces of barnacle-like deposits. These terraces – tinted a marvellous array of greys, greens, yellows, browns, oranges and greens by algae – are composed of travertine, a form of limestone which, having been dissolved and carried to the surface by boiling water, is deposited as tier upon tier of cascading, steaming stone.

Tower and Roosevelt Areas

Compared to the rest of Yellowstone, the **Tower** and **Roosevelt** areas, east of Mammoth Hot Springs, contain comparatively few things to see. The main landmark is **Mount Washburn**, the park's highest peak, whose lookout tower can be reached by an enjoyable all-day hike or a gruelling cycle ride. From Tower Junction, US-212 wanders out to the east entrance through serene, uncrowded **Lamar Valley**, which bears tell-tale signs of aggressive glacial scouring. The **Lamar River** meanders aimlessly through wildflower meadows, where herds of moose and buffalo can be seen grazing against a marvellous mountain backdrop. The road rises out of the park alongside the ice-packed peaks of the **Beartooth Mountains**.

The Grand Canyon of the Yellowstone River

The Yellowstone River roars and tumbles for 24 miles between the sheer golden-hued cliffs of the 1540-foot **Grand Canyon of the Yellowstone**, its course punctuated by two narrow but striking **waterfalls**: the 109-foot **Upper Falls** and the thunderous **Lower Falls**, plummeting 308 feet. Both rims of the canyon offer superb vistas, short trails and intense scenery, but the north side is the more popular, as tourists can combine sightseeing with a visit to the nearby burger bars, ice cream parlours and gift

---

WINTER IN YELLOWSTONE

Blanketed in four feet of snow between November and April, Yellowstone takes on a whole new appearance: a silent and bizarre world where waterfalls freeze in mid-plunge, geysers blast towering plumes of steam and water into the cold, crisp air, and buffalo, beards matted with ice, stand round in huddles. During snowfall, all roads except between Mammoth Hot Springs and Cooke City are shut, and the only places to stay are at Mammoth Hot Springs and Old Faithful.

Winter vacationing in Yellowstone, and with it another intense environmental debate, took off in a big way in the Sixties, when the park allowed snowcoaches and snowmobiles for the first time. **Snowcoaches**, which look like bloated 2CVs on bulldozer tracks, leave from Flagg Ranch at the southern entrance, West Yellowstone and Mammoth Hot springs to tour the west side of the park. Trips cost from $52 to $72 and are operated by *TW Services*. *Alpen Guides* (☎406/646-9591) run similar, slightly cheaper, excursions out of West Yellowstone. **Snowmobiling** is a great way to see the park but rental, generally cheapest in West Yellowstone, costs upwards of $70 a day. Much less expensive is **cross-country skiing**; there are several miles of groomed trails, again on the park's west side.

---

shops. If you want to see some bears, try to get to the viewing area at the intersection of the Tower and Northern Rim roads at dawn or dusk.

On the south rim, **Artists' Point** looks down 700 feet to the river, swirling between mineral-stained walls. Nearby, Uncle Tom's Trail descends deep into the canyon, to a gently vibrating, spray-covered platform right in the face of the Lower Falls. A few miles south, the river widens to meander over tranquil, marshy **Haydn Valley**. Buffalo, elk and deer congregate here, so it's an unsuitable place to go on foot.

By way of vulgar contrast, the seething rumblings and sulphurous stench of the **Mud Volcano** area make it the moodiest and ugliest of the park's thermal regions. A one-mile boardwalk winds through gurgling pools of sickly brown and yellow mud, past trees that have been steamed to death, to the bleak, barren shores of Sour Lake – an unnerving sight at the best of times, at dusk it makes a chemical waste dump look appealing.

Accommodation in the Park

In what must amount to a licence to print money, *TW Recreational Services Inc* (Yellowstone Park, WY 82190-9989; ☎344-7311) operate all accommodation within the park. Reservations, strongly recommended during July and August, are absolutely essential over public holiday weekends.

Although you can get better value outside the park, staying inside its boundaries can be relaxing; none of the rooms has a TV, and only a few après-hike revellers stay up past midnight. Every location has a lodge building offering dining facilities (closing at 9.30pm) and sometimes a laundromat, grocery store, gift shop and gas station.

Canyon Lodge Cabins. Half a mile from the Grand Canyon of the Yellowstone. $45–70, all en suite.

Grant Village. On the southwest shore of Yellowstone Lake. The park's most modern facility, completed in 1984 – though the rooms are still quite spartan. $56–60.

Lake Yellowstone Hotel and Cabins. Rooms in this grand Colonial-style hotel cost $65–220. Dark and dingy en-suite cabins are $52 a night. In the evening, the *Sun Room*, looking out over the lake, makes a great place for a relaxing drink.

Mammoth Hot Springs Hotel & Cabins. Right at the north end of the park. Hotel rooms are $32–52 en-suite cabins $50 and *Rough Rider* cabins, without shower or toilet, cost $25.

Old Faithful Inn and Lodge. Not surprisingly, a very popular location. Rooms in the wonderful-looking inn, said to be the world's largest log building, run from $36 right through to sumptuous suites for $170. *Rough Rider* and en-suite cabins cost $22 and $35 respectively.

Roosevelt Lodge Cabins. The cheapest place to stay in the park at $20 for a rustic shelter that has no bedding. *Rough Rider* and en-suite cabins run from $22 to $52.

Accommodation in Gateway Towns

The small towns just outside the park's western and two northern gates offer better choice and value, as well as bars and cafes that stay open to reasonable hours. **West Yellowstone**, the largest, at the west entrance, is disfigured by T-shirt shops, gift stores and fast-food joints, though the surrounding Gallatin and Targhee national forestlands are well worth exploring. The hamlet of **Gardiner** lies next to the northwest entrance, just five miles from Mammoth Hot Springs, while the one-street villages of **Silver Gate** and **Cooke City** lie three and ten miles respectively from the northeast entrance on US-212; the latter has a slightly better choice of motels and places to eat.

The two most developed towns in the region are both in Wyoming, but lie farther afield – Jackson (see p.626) is seventy miles south and Cody (p.618) 52 miles east.

All motels listed below are in Montana, for which the area code is ☎406.

Alpine Motel, US-212, Cooke City (☎838-2371). Basic but clean rooms for $32.

Alpine Motel, 120 Madison Avenue, West Yellowstone (☎646-7544). No-frills lodgings. Around $30.

Al's Westward Ho Motel, 16 Boundary Street, West Yellowstone (☎646-7331). Clean, basic rooms, some with kitchenette, for $30–35.

Blue Haven Motel, Gardiner (☎848-7719). Basic cabins with kitchenettes for $33.

Brandin' Iron Motel, 201 Canyon Street, West Yellowstone (☎646-9411). Bright new motel with hot tubs; around $45.

Hillcrest Motel, on US-89, Gardiner (☎848-9353). All rooms have kitchenettes, but are a little pokey. Nevertheless, it's hard to complain about the $30 tariff.

Hoosier's Motel, US-212, Cooke City (☎838-2241). Immaculate modern motel. $36–50.

Parkview Cabins, US-212, Silver Gate (☎838-2371). Plain cabins for $30, or $36 with kitchenette.

Westernaire Motel, Gardiner (☎848-7397). Good standard accommodation for $52 a night.

West Yellowstone International Hostel and **Madison Hotel**, 139 Yellowstone Ave, West Yellowstone (☎646-7745). Friendly hosts, clean rooms and low prices make this old wooden hotel a great place to stay. Dorm beds $13, hotel rooms $28–35. Summer only.

Camping

The **National Park Service** (☎344-7381) operates eleven **campgrounds** in the park. All operate on a first-come, first-served basis, except for **Bridge Bay**, where reservations can be made through *Ticketron* (☎1-800/452-1111). With a total of less than 2000 spaces, it's best to turn up very early in the morning. Fees are $6 to $10 per night.

Mammoth Hot Springs is the only campground open year round; most of the others operate between late May and September. In the northeast of the park, Slough Creek, Tower Fall and Pebble Creek are all small, very scenic and extremely popular locations. You can also camp at Madison, Norris, Indian Creek, Lewis Lake and Grant Village, which has the best shower and laundry facilities. Due to prowling bears, spaces at Canyon Village and Fishing Bridge are restricted to hard-sided vehicles.

To camp in the **backcountry** you need a wilderness permit, free from visitor centres or ranger stations. Camping is also available at commercial grounds in the gateway towns, and in neighbouring National Forests such as Gallatin (☎344-7381) to the northwest and Shoshone (☎527-6241) to the east.

Eating

Snack bars and **restaurants** inside the park are expensive; even buying food at the general stores can work out pricey. The gateway towns hold few culinary delights, but do offer cheaper prices and more variety. In West Yellowstone, the *Running Bear Pancake House*, 538 Madison Avenue, is good for breakfast, and the down-home *Thiem's Cafe*, 38 Canyon Street, does the best lunches. The huge salad bar at the *Town Cafe* in Gardiner provides a welcome chance to eat your fill, while the stylish *Beartooth Cafe* in Cooke City is probably the best place for breakfast, burgers and inexpensive dinners in any of the peripheral towns.

Grand Teton National Park and Jackson Hole

GRAND TETON NATIONAL PARK, which stretches for fifty miles between Yellowstone and Jackson, is less congested and every bit as dramatic as its better known neighbour. Visiting here should be more than an afterthought on the route out of Yellowstone. Though not especially high or extensive by Rocky Mountain standards, these sheer-faced cliffs make a magnificent spectacle, rising abruptly to tower 7000 feet above the valley floor. A string of gem-like lakes is set tight at the foot of the mountains; beyond them lies the broad, sagebrush-covered **Jackson Hole** (a "hole" was the pioneers' term for a flat, mountain-ringed valley), broken by the winding Snake River. At the southern end of the valley, once-attractive Jackson is blighted by pricey motels, glitzy shops and the rhinestones and rattlesnake boots of fake cowboys.

Shoshone Indians knew the mountains as the *Teewinot* ("many pinnacles"), but the present name, meaning big bosom, was given by lonesome French-Canadian trappers in the 1830s. After Congress set the mountains aside as a national park in 1929, it took another 21 years of legal wrangling for Grand Teton to reach its current size – local ranchers protested that the economy of Jackson Hole would be ruined if any further land was turned over for tourist use. Meanwhile, John D Rockefeller Jr bought up a large swathe of Jackson Hole and offered it to the government for free. Congress eventually accepted the gift, thus ensuring that the land would remain unspoiled – and that Rockefeller, as owner of the *Grand Teton Lodge Company*, would be the exclusive operator of park concessions.

Sights and Activities

Roads in Grand Teton were designed with an eye to the mountains, affording stunning views at every turn. Two excellent side trips are the **Jenny Lake Scenic Loop**, leading to a face-to-face encounter with towering, partly hunchbacked **Grand Teton Mountain**, and the narrow track up to the top of **Signal Mountain**, which gives a fine view of the main Teton block and Jackson Hole.

Hiking trails, too, have been laid out so that no time is wasted in getting to the highlights. One easy and popular walk is along the sandy beaches of **Leigh Lake**, where the imposing 12,605-foot **Mount Moran** bursts out dramatically from the lake shores. Also very accessible are the cascading **Hidden Falls**, reachable by a two-mile walk along the south shore of Jenny Lake; it's more fun to take the shuttle boat ($3.50 return) across the lake, and walk the remaining 800 yards. For the more adventurous, the rocky nine-mile trail from Hidden Falls through the U-shaped **Cascade Canyon** leads to aptly named **Lake Solitude**. Another strenuous hike, and an excellent way to reach treeline in a short distance, is the five-mile trail from **Lupine Meadows**, just south of Jenny Lake, skirting small glacial pools like Amphitheater and Surprise lakes.

Cycling is a particularly good way to see the park; rent a bike down in Jackson, or from *Dornan's* in Moose (☎733-3314). To admire the scenery of the Teton from **water**, take a float trip along the Snake River (see Jackson) or rent a rowing boat from either Colter Bay (☎543-2811) or Signal Mountain marinas (☎543-2831). In winter, all hiking trails are open to cross-country **skiiers**, and **snowmobiles** can be rented, none too cheaply, from various outlets in Jackson.

Practicalities

Shuttle buses to the park run from Jackson and Yellowstone. The **visitor centres** are just off the main road in **Moose** (☎733-2880) to the south, and at **Colter Bay** (☎543-2467), halfway up, on the east shore of Jackson Lake. A 24-hour recorded message (☎733-2220) and the free *Teewinot* newspaper give details of ranger-led activities. The entrance fee of $10 per car ($4 for each pedestrian or cyclist) also covers Yellowstone.

Rooms and services within the park are managed by the *Grand Teton Lodge Co* (PO Box 240, Moran, WY 83013; ☎543-2811), and reservations are more or less essential during summer. The comfortable cabins at *Jackson Lake Lodge* occupy a prime location but cost $90; the more utilitarian *Colter Bay Village Cabins* will set you back $28, or $50 en suite. On the park perimeter, the basic *Atkinson's Motel* in Moran (☎543-2442) has rooms for $32, and a few motels in Jackson (see below) charge less than $50.

All the five park **campgrounds** work on a first-come, first-served basis. During July and August they fill to capacity; visitor centres or entrance stations can advise on availability. Individual campgrounds tend to fill as follows: Jenny Lake (8am), Signal Mountain (10am), Colter Bay (noon), Lizard Creek (2pm) and Gros Ventre (evening). For backcountry camping, you need a permit from the Moose ranger station (☎733-2880).

Snack bars, general stores and restaurants in the park charge the prices you would expect from a monopoly operation, so it's best to bring your own food. *Dornan's* (☎733-2415), however, just outside the southern entrance in Moose, serves all-you-can-eat pancake breakfasts for $5 and rib dinners for $10. For the ultimate in relaxation, have an early-evening drink in *Jackson Lake Lodge*'s *Blue Heron Lounge*, where you can recline in comfortable chairs and watch the ever-changing blues, greys, purples and warm pinks of Mount Moran through huge picture windows.

Jackson

JACKSON is tucked in at the end of Jackson Hole, ten miles from the park's southern gate. Hunched around a tree-shaded square, marked by an arch of elk antlers at each corner, the Old-West-style boardwalks of **downtown** front designer clothes shops, craft shops and over thirty galleries. Despite its conspicuous opulence and fabricated Old West image, Jackson is a good base for rafting, biking, horse-riding and exploring the two national parks. You might in any case have to stay here if park accommodations are full. Every evening in summer, except Sundays, there's an amateurish re-creation of an Old West shootout in the town square. Time is better spent visiting the **National Elk Refuge** on the north edge of town, where you can take a horse-drawn sleigh ride among a 10,000-strong herd of elk ($7; ☎733-9212).

Dozens of companies in Jackson offer **float trips** on the Snake River. *Fort Jackson Float Trips*, 315 W Broadway (☎733-2583), do good-value five-hour trips for $28 including lunch, while daily rental prices for rafts, kayaks, tubes and bikes at *Leisure Sports*, 1075 Hwy-89S (☎733-3040), are quite reasonable. Horse rides at the *OK Corral Ranch* (☎733-6556), ten minutes' drive south on Hwy-191, cost as little as $12 for two hours.

Chairlift rides up the 7751-foot Snow King Mountain depart from Snow King Avenue, six blocks from the town square (summer daily 10am–6pm; $4; ☎733-5200). Alternative ways to get back down are hiking, cycling or the thrilling **Alpine Slide** ($4 a go). Out at **Teton Village**, aerial **trams** swoosh their way 10,536 feet up to the top of Rendezvous Mountain for a spectacular panorama of the valley and mountain ranges (June–Aug 9am–7pm; May & Sept 10am–5pm; $14; ☎733-2292).

Coach tours are available from *Gray Line*, 330 N Glenwood Street (☎733-4325), who whisk you through both Teton and Yellowstone parks on a brisk one-day drive for $40. *Powder River Tours*, 565 N Cache Street (☎733-2136), which spends a full day in the Tetons, with a boat trip on Jenny Lake, for $36, is a better option.

Practicalities

Jackson has reasonable public transport. *START* buses (☎733-3135) run to Teton Village Ski Resort, twelve miles northwest, while the *Grand Teton Lodge Company* (☎733-2811) and *Powder River* (☎733-2136) operate services to Grand Teton National Park; the latter continue to Yellowstone. *Jackson–Rock Springs* vans (☎733-3135) connect with Rock Springs, 165 miles southeast, the closest *Greyhound* stop to the park.

The **visitor centre** is at 532 N Cache Street (☎733-3316), next to the Bridger-Teton National Forest Headquarters (☎733-2752), which provides details of hiking and back-country camping. Most **accommodation** in Jackson costs the wrong side of $70, though budget motels include the *Snow King Lodge*, 470 King Street ($35–46; ☎733-3480), *Woods Motel*, 120 N Glenwood Street (☎48; ☎733-2953), *Ranch Inn*, 45 E Pearl Street ($50; ☎733-6363), and the *Hitching Post Lodge*, 460 E Broadway ($55–65; ☎733-2606). During winter, motel rates are generally 25 percent cheaper.

Jackson also has two **hostels**. The *AYH Hostel* (☎733-3415), out in Teton Village Ski Resort, charges $15 for a dorm bed, while the central *Bunkhouse in the Anvil Motel*, 215 N Cache Street (☎733-3668), offers beds in a clean forty-person dorm for $16. The closest **camping** is at the *Jackson Hole Campground* (☎733-2927), off West Broadway.

Good-value places to **eat** include the *Bunnery*, 130 N Cache Street (☎733-5474), for great breakfasts, stuffed omelettes and sandwiches under $5, and *Pedro's*, 139 N Cache Street (☎733-9015), serving cheap Mexican food al fresco. A fancier choice is the Art-Deco *Cadillac Grill*, Cache Street (☎733-3279), which, in addition to huge burgers for under $6, offers buffalo, wild boar, caribou, antelope and seafood entrees for $12 to $20.

If you enjoy western-themed **nightlife**, the antique-laden *Mangy Moose* (☎733-4913) in Teton Village is good for rock and reggae, and the glitzy *Million Dollar Cowboy Bar*, 25 N Cache Street (☎733-2207), has saddles for seats. On the other hand, *Spirits of the West*, 385 W Broadway (☎733-3853), is a good local bar.

MONTANA

MONTANA is Big Sky country. The entire state is blessed with a huge blue roof, which perfectly complements its beautiful **west**. A magnificent northernmost cap for the US Rockies, this is a region of snowcapped summits, turbulent rivers, spectacular glacial valleys, heavily wooded forests and sparkling blue lakes, at their most dramatic in Glacier National Park. By contrast, the **eastern** two-thirds is high prairie: sunparched in summer and wracked by icy blizzards each winter.

Preconceptions of a desolate land populated by cowpunchers are soon shattered; each of Montana's small cities has its own proud identity: the university and sawmill community of **Missoula**, for example, possesses a high-culture feel absent from the heavily Irish, copper-mining town and union stronghold of **Butte**, while state capital **Helena** still harks back to its prosperous gold mining years.

Those who first braved this inhospitable terrain and unpredictable weather did so in the hope of profit. The fur-trappers and gold miners soon moved on, but as white settlers invaded Indian hunting grounds, conflict was inevitable. A key plank of the army strategy was to starve the Indians into submission: "For the sake of a lasting peace let them [professional hunters] kill, skin and sell until the buffalo are exterminated. Then your prairies can be covered by the speckled cow and the festive cowboy," declared General Philip Sheridan. By the late 1870s most of Montana had been cleared for settlement and the buffalo had been reduced from around twenty million to just a few hundred.

The speckled cow and festive cowboy were not in for an easy time. The horrendous winter of 1886 wiped out many herds, and the "sodbusters" who planted wheat in the wake of bankrupt ranchers often fared little better. Plagues of grasshoppers, droughts, falling wheat prices and erosion of the topsoil caused farms to fail everywhere in the Twenties, during which time Montana was the only state to record a population decline.

Wheat has since made a revival, and now, with lumbering and coal mining, forms the base of Montana's economy. Another significant money-earner is tourism, though the harsh climate restricts the season to the months between June and September.

The telephone **area code** for the entire state of Montana is ☎406.

Getting Around Montana

Considering Montana's size and sparse population, transport connections are reasonable. *Amtrak* **trains** cross the north, stopping at Glacier National Park. *Greyhound* and several regional **bus** companies serve towns on I-90 and I-15. The larger towns offer at least some public transport, though they are quite easily negotiated on foot.

The best way to get around is by car. You can cover this huge state relatively quickly on the interstates, and if you get bored, don't worry: practically every exit in western Montana leads to areas of mountain solitude, interesting landmarks or small communities. *Delta Airlines* offer the most **flights** to Montana, landing in seven towns. Western Montana is great **cycling** territory; the best source of special maps is the *Bikecentennial* organisation, whose national headquarters are in Missoula (see p.633).

Eastern Montana

Before ranchers and farmers settled the flat prairie of **eastern Montana**, it was prime **buffalo** territory: one early traveller waited three nights while a massive herd crossed his path. Native Americans fought hard to hold onto their land; the crushing defeats they inflicted on the US Army include the legendary victory at **Little Bighorn**.

The eastern Montana plains are intermittently broken by mountains, of which the most impressive are the icy **Beartooth Range**, crammed between the village of Red Lodge and Yellowstone. Don't expect much from the region's towns; most are lazy farm supply centres, and down-at-heel **Billings**, Montana's largest city with a population of just over 70,000, doesn't have much more to offer.

Custer Battlefield National Monument

56 miles southeast of Billings; entrance 2 miles east of I-90 on US-212. Visitor centre and museum: daily summer 8am–7.45pm, otherwise 8am–4.30pm; ☎638-2622. Battlefield: daily 8am–dusk; $3 per car, though free passes are available for the cemetery only.

In June 1876 massive US Army detachments were sent to southeastern Montana to subjugate the Sioux and Cheyenne. A key unit in the campaign was the crack **Seventh Cavalry**; at its head was the flamboyant, gung-ho **General George Armstrong Custer**.

Few, if any US soldiers have achieved the fame or opprobrium of Custer. During an erratic career, he graduated last in his class at West Point in 1861; was made the US Army's youngest ever major general by the end of the Civil War; was suspended for a year for ordering the execution of soldiers who deserted a forced march he led through Kansas primarily so that he could see his wife; and earned notoriety in the West for allowing his charges to murder unarmed Indians, such as in the 1868 slaughter of almost one hundred Cheyenne women and children.

On June 25 1876, Custer's was the first unit to arrive in the **Little Bighorn Valley**. Instead of waiting for reinforcements, he decided to seek glory by razing an Indian teepee village along the Little Bighorn River. Custer expected to be met by a force of 800 warriors, and divided his 600-strong command to form a three-pronged attack. Without checking on the progress of his two advance flanks – which had in fact been obliged to retreat – Custer's party charged the Indian camp to administer the coup de grace. Before they got there, at least 2000 Sioux and Cheyenne rode out from either side of a ravine and encircled the soldiers. Custer's men dismounted to attempt to shoot their way out, but they were overwhelmed by the sheer Indian numbers. The battle, which lasted less than an hour, left no white survivors; the last man to fall was Custer – "the Long Hair stood like a sheaf of corn with all the ears fallen around him", according to Sitting Bull, commander of the victorious Native American forces.

Custer's Last Stand was the most decisive Indian victory in the West. The battle was also the final great show of resistance by Native Americans. An incensed President

Grant called it a massacre, and piled maximum resources into a military campaign that brought about the effective defeat of all Plains Indians by the end of the decade.

You can see the battlefield on a five-mile self-guided car tour, or on a narrated bus tour ($2). The focal point is the **cemetery**, dominated by a tall sandstone obelisk above the mass grave of all the 265 soldiers who died (except for Custer, who lies in West Point Military Academy). Dioramas in the visitor centre outline the battle, and clumps of white marble tablets denote the places where the troops are believed to have fallen.

Hardin

Thirteen miles northwest of the Custer Battlefield, the small town of **HARDIN** is the main trading centre for the Crow Indian Reservation. Much of its income comes from tourists seeking authentic Indian artefacts and other western mementoes. Each year, on the weekend closest to the battle's anniversary of 25 June, Hardin hosts the **Little Bighorn Days** festival, centred around re-enactments of Custer's Last Stand at a site eight miles west of the town (*not* at the original battlefield). Other activities include Indian dancing, downtown parades, dinner dances and a rodeo.

The cheapest place to **stay**, at under $40 a night, is the budget *Western Motel* at the junction of Hwy-313 and W Third Street (☎665-2296); the comfortable *American Inn Motel*, at the I-90 city centre exit (☎665-1870), and the central *Lariat Hotel*, 709 N Center Avenue (☎665-2863), both charge around $45.

Billings

By Montana standards, **BILLINGS** is a big city. Its dramatic setting, bounded on its north and east sides by the 400-foot crumpled sandstone cliffs of the **Rimrock**, certainly makes it something more than a pockmark on the prairie. The town itself, however, consists largely of run-down housing estates, and a city centre whose shops have transferred out to the malls. Scarring its west side are the tracks and warehouses of the Northern Pacific Railroad, whose president, Frederick Billings, gave the city its name.

On the Rimroad, right by Logan Airport, the free **Peter Yegen Jr Museum** is a fascinating jumble of exhibits devoted to eastern Montana pioneers. Among the cabinets of weapons, clothes, fossils and domestic equipment are real oddities like a stuffed two-headed calf and a display of the dozens of types of barbed wire homesteaders used to fence off their lots – much to the chagrin of the ranchowners who coveted the grazing space (Mon–Fri 10am–5pm, Sun 2–5pm).

The **bus station** in Billings, served by *Greyhound* from towns along I-90 and I-15, and *Powder River*, north from Wyoming, is at 2501 First Avenue (☎245-5116). The *Best Western Ponderosa Inn*, next door at 2511 First Avenue North (☎259-5511), provides acceptable **rooms** for $40. All the usual motel chains line up along I-90, off exit 446, such as *Motel 6* (☎252-0093), at $32. Downtown, *Casey's Golden Pheasant*, 109 N Broadway (☎256-5200), is a jazz/blues bar serving good Cajun food; *Pug Mahon's*, 3011 First Avenue North (☎259-4190), pulls in the crowds for Irish cooking and Guinness.

Red Lodge and the Beartooth Scenic Highway

The village of **RED LODGE**, sixty miles south of Billings at the foot of the awesome Beartooth Mountains, makes for an altogether more pleasant stop. Shops, cafes and bars line the main thoroughfare of Broadway. You can get good Mexican food and cocktails at *Bogart's*, 11 S Broadway (☎446-1784), or stock up on French bread sandwiches and pasties at the *City Bakery*, 104 S Broadway (☎446-2100). The *Carbon County Coal Co*, 119 S Broadway (☎446-3333), has live music most nights.

The majority of **motels** group round the south side of town, but few match the prices at the extremely central, big red *Pollard Hotel*, 2 S Broadway (☎446-2860), whose clean rooms, sauna and whirlpool make it worth the $35 or $45 rates. You can camp at the *KOA* (☎446-2364), two miles north of the town, for around $15.

During winter, Red Lodge acts as a base for skiiers using Red Lodge Mountain (☎446-2610 or ☎1-800/444-8977), six miles west on US-212, where ski lifts are $22 a day (half-price Mon & Tues from early Jan).

Red Lodge looked to face extinction in 1924, when its largest coal mine closed, but its future was secured by the construction of the 65-mile **Beartooth Scenic Highway** through the mountains to Cooke City (see p.624) at the northeastern entrance to Yellowstone National Park. Other roads in the Rockies may be higher, but none gives quite such a top-of-the-world feeling as this succession of tight switchbacks, steep grades and exciting overlooks such as the 10,940-foot **Beartooth Pass**. Even on a hot summer day it's incredibly chilly on top, where the springy tundra turf is always covered with snow that (due to algae) turns pink when crushed. All around are gem-like corries, deeply-gouged granite walls, stretches of scree and huge blocks of roadside ice.

Western Montana

The **western** third of Montana sees the state at its best – terrific mountain scenery, bountiful outdoor opportunities and bustling communities that destroy the myth that "Smalltown USA" is boring. The only mining camps of the 1860s gold rush to grow into substantial permanent settlements were state capital **Helena** and craggy working-class **Butte**, which made most of its money from copper. Between them they conjure up more of a feel for the rambunctious times, the lust for profit and the post-bust hardships of the mining era than a visit to all of the hyped-up ghost towns in the Rockies combined.

Bozeman

Pretty, tree-lined **BOZEMAN** lies deep in the lush Gallatin Valley, 142 miles west of Billings and a mere eighty miles north of Yellowstone. Founded as an agricultural community in 1863, it's the only sizeable town in Montana not to owe its roots to mining, railroading or lumbering. The absence of slag heaps, shabby warehouses or railyards gives Bozeman a more attractive feel than most Montana towns: the smart-looking shops along the busy Victorian Main Street just beg to be window-shopped.

South of downtown, as Montana State University peters out into a beautiful wilderness in the shadow of the Rockies, the huge **Museum of the Rockies** at S Seventh Avenue and Kagy Boulevard (summer daily 9am–9pm; otherwise Mon–Sat 9am–5pm, Sun noon–5pm; $4) holds dinosaur finds, exhibits of Indian weapons and a fine selection of western landscape paintings. There's also a **planetarium**.

Bozeman is well placed for those in search of outdoor activities. The ranger office, 601 Niles Avenue (☎587-6920), provides details of local walking trails, and *Chalet Sports* at Main and Willson streets (☎587-4595) rent out mountain bikes and ski equipment.

Practicalities

Greyhound and *Rim Rock Stages* operate along the interstates from 625 N Seventh Street (☎587-3110), while *TW Services* puts on one bus per day to Yellowstone (see p.619). The **visitor centre** is at 1205 E Main Street (☎586-5421).

Of places to **stay** within easy walking distance, the *Royal 6 Motel* (☎587-3103) and the *Rainbow Motel* (☎587-4201), at 310 and 510 N Seventh Avenue, both have rooms for $35. There's **camping** eleven miles from downtown at the *KOA*, 133 Lower Rainbow Road (☎586-6492), next to the Bozeman Hot Springs bathing pools.

Homely *Colombo's* at 1003 W College Avenue (☎587-5544) serves affordable feasts of spaghetti, pizza and Italian lunch specials. In the downtown *Baxter Hotel*, 105 W Main Street (☎586-1314), the *Bacchus Pub* serves gourmet burgers and fine soups such as wild rice, bacon and cheese with mountains of bread for around $5.

Butte

Eighty miles west of Bozeman, copper-mining **BUTTE** is bunched on a steep, almost treeless hillside. Massive black headframes of long-abandoned pits soar up among paintbare homes, stark grey business premises, and a ring of surface workings and dirty-yellow slag heaps. The disorderly landscape is so ugly, it's captivating.

Exploration of this friendly town soon reveals a community rich in ethnic and trade union culture. Among the young men from all over the world who came to work the mines, the **Irish** were so dominant that the local rug trader, Mohammed Akran, changed his name to Mohammed Murphy. Butte still hosts the biggest St Patrick's Day celebrations in the Rockies: an estimated 40,000 customers pass through the famous old *M&M Bar* every March 17. Another group of immigrants to leave their mark came from **Cornwall**; the traditional pastie is still served in most cafes.

From its early days, Butte has stood out as the "Gibraltar of Unionism" in the anti-union West. Miners were quick to realise their collective strength. Demands for a minimum wage and an eight-hour day were soon met, and it became impossible to get work without a union card. Such confidence bred radicalism, and Butte miners sent the largest delegation to the founding convention of the International Workers of the World (the "Wobblies") in 1906. But the consolidation of mining operations under the huge Anaconda Company, and inter-union rivalries led to frustration, rioting and incidents like the dynamiting of the Miners Union Hall in 1914 and the public hanging of an IWW organiser by vigilantes three years later. Unions in Butte remain well-organised, but aspirations of revolution have long since disappeared.

From the vantage point of the town's only significant clump of greenery, reached by climbing West Park Street, you can examine the ecological disaster down below. Carry on a few yards to the excellent, free, volunteer-run **World Museum of Mining**, packed with memorabilia from the boom years including safety equipment, union banners, portraits of the copper barons and cabinets of rock samples. The 37-building **Hell Roarin' Gulch** here re-creates a cobbled-street mining camp, complete with saloon, bordello, church, schoolhouse and Chinese laundry. Looming above is the blackened headframe of the Orphan Girl mineshaft, around which lie battered ore wagons and rusted tools (summer 9am–9pm otherwise 10am–5pm; closed Dec–March).

The town's largest mine, the grotesque 2500- by 1800-yard **Berkeley Pit**, was abandoned in 1983, but today you can see the partly water-filled mess from a viewing platform on Continental Drive. A recorded message details the history of Butte's mining operations (summer 8am–9pm; free). At night floodlights illuminate the 90-foot **Our Lady of the Rockies** statue. Built entirely by voluntary labour, it was set in place on top of the Continental Divide, some 3500 feet above Butte, by helicopter.

Practicalities

Greyhound and *Intermountain Transit* **buses** drop off in downtown Butte. In summer, regular ninety-minute **trolley tours** of town ($5) leave from the **Chamber of Commerce**, 2950 Harrison Avenue (☎494-5595), out on the "Flat" by the interstate near the chain **motels**. The efficiently run *Best Western Butte Plaza*, 2900 Harrison Avenue (☎494-5595), has good rooms, a large swimming pool and a gym for $59 per night. Downtown, the motels are a bit rougher round the edges, though the clean, family-run *Eddy's* at Front and Montana streets (☎723-4364) is great value at $20.

Gamer's Confectionery, 15 W Park Street (☎782-7367), is a great spot for breakfast, pot pies and pasties, where you ring up the sale yourself and take the change in the antique cash register. Savings on decor and a huge custom allow the roomy *M & M Bar*, 9 N Main Street, to serve bottled beer at $1 and the cheapest grease-laden breakfasts in town. The recently refurbished *Silver Dollar Saloon*, 133 S Main Street (☎782-7367), the most sumptuous bar in Butte, features live jazz and blues most nights.

Helena

In 1864 a party of disheartened prospectors working over the present site of **HELENA**, more or less halfway between Yellowstone and Glacier national parks, decided to have one final dig along a likely-looking ravine. They struck lucky on what is now **Last Chance Gulch** – the town's attractive, fountain-lined main street.

More than $20 million of gold was extracted from the area, but Helena managed to maintain a rather orderly appearance: prospectors who hit it rich decided to stay in this town set neatly at the foot of two rounded mountains with a fine view out over the golden-brown **Prickly Pear Valley**. At one time it was the richest community per capita in the country; over fifty millionaires lived here, and the palatial residences they built still enhance the west side of town.

The architectural highlight is the massive neoclassical **State Capitol**, atop a small hill surrounded by lawns at Sixth and Montana avenues. Inside, huge murals by "cowboy artist" C M Russell depict scenes from Montana history. You can see more of his work at the free **State Historical Museum**, 225 N Roberts Street, as well as a gallery of early photographs of pioneer life (summer Mon–Fri 8am–6pm, Sat & Sun 9am–5pm; otherwise Mon–Fri 8am–5pm, Sat 9am–5pm). The majestic red-tiled spires of the **Cathedral of St Helena** rise 230 feet at 530 N Ewing Street; elaborate Bavarian stained glass, white marble altars and gold leaf decorate the interior.

Sixteen miles north of Helena off I-15, you can take a two-hour **boat tour** through the **Gates of the Mountains**. This dramatic stretch of the Missouri River was named by Meriwether Lewis (of the Lewis and Clark expedition), who thought it the most spectacular sight he had seen on his mammoth journey (daily June–Sept; $6.50; ☎458-5241).

Practicalities

Helena's bus station, 5 W Fifteenth Street (☎442-5860), is used by *Greyhound*, *Rim Rock* and *Intermountain*, who between them offer connections to all major Montana towns. There's a **visitor centre** at 201 E Lyndale Street (☎442-4120).

Two very cheap, basic hotels can be found downtown on N Last Chance Gulch. The $15 rooms in the *Iron Front Hotel* at no. 415 (☎443-2400) are clean but come without a bath or shower. En-suite facilities at the *Park Hotel* at no. 432 (☎442-0960) cost $20. For more comfort, try the *Sanders B&B*, 328 N Ewing Street (☎442-3309), with its antique furnishings and gourmet breakfasts; prices range from $45 to $70.

Also on Last Chance Gulch, *Bert and Ernies*, no. 361 (☎443-5680), is a well-priced and classy **restaurant**. One of the best **bars** in town is the *Windbag Saloon*, no. 19 (☎443-9669), a big old barn of a place that serves a reasonable pint of Guinness.

Missoula

Blue-collar and academic cultures converge in **MISSOULA**, framed by the Bitteroot and Sapphire mountains, to produce one of the most vibrant and friendly small towns in the country. It's a town of contrasting faces – truck salesyards and bookstores, continental cafes and gun shops – where nearly everyone seems to be connected to either the city's huge sawmills or the 10,000-student University of Montana.

A good first port of call in Missoula is the **Chamber of Commerce** office, across the river from the campus, at 825 E Front Street (☎543-6623). Among the **walks** detailed on their *Trails Missoula* leaflet for hikers is one which leads from here up **Mount Sentinel**, embellished by a huge concrete letter "M". From the top you can get a great view of the surrounding area, especially the rugged Hellgate River canyon. Other worthwhile trails traverse the **Rattlesnake Wilderness**, which, despite its name, has no serpents. The most developed of three small **ski** areas nearby is the **Snowbowl**, twelve miles northwest, which boasts a summer **chairlift** ($5; $2 for bikes; ☎549-9777).

MISSOULA AND BIKES

Missoula has enjoyed close ties with **cycling** ever since 1896 when the town's army fort became home to the 25th Infantry Bicycle Corps. The unit was founded to test the military potential of bikes as a means of transporting troops in mountainous regions. Its tasks included a 1900-mile ride to St Louis, where the army decided against the use of cycles and the soldiers journeyed back to Missoula by train.

Today Missoula is one of the best cities for cycling in the country, offering dozens of great road and dirt bike routes. The council even employs a bicycling co-ordinator (☎523-4626), but the best source of information and trail maps is *Bikecentennial*, 113 W Main Street (☎721-1776; see also p.27). The *Braxton Bike Shop*, 2100 South Avenue W (☎549-2513), rents out good-quality cycles and can also advise on routes.

Free guided tours of the US Forest Service **Aerial Fire Depot and Smokejumper Center**, ten miles out of town on US-93, look at the methods used to train smokejumpers, the highly trained firefighters who parachute into forested areas to stop the spread of wildfires. A small visitor centre features pictures, dioramas and videos about the work of smokejumpers (mid-May to mid-Sept; call for times; ☎329-4900).

Missoula is home to a surprising number of **authors**, among them crime writers James Lee Burke and James Crumley, and several good bookstores. *Freddy's Feed and Read*, for example, 1221 Helena Avenue (☎549-2127), is a fine deli which also sells a wide selection of fiction and unexpected titles.

Practicalities

Greyhound, *Rim Rock Stages* and *Intermountain* share the **bus depot** at 1660 W Broadway (☎549-2339). **Motels** along East Broadway, which runs for a mile between downtown and the campus, include the *Downtown Motel* at no. 502 (☎549-5191), which costs $32. *Goldsmith's B&B Inn*, 809 E Front Street (☎721-6732), on the riverbank across from campus, serves award-winning food and provides comfortable rooms for $50. The *Birchwood AYH Hostel*, 600 S Orange Street (☎728-9799), charges $6 a night and has lots of space for cycles.

For some of the best Italian **food** in the northern Rockies, join the inevitable queue at *Zimorino's Red Pies Over Montana*, 424 N Higgins Street (☎728-6686); try the white pizza or any of the numerous pastas and speciality sauces. The *New Pacific Grill*, 100 E Railroad Avenue (☎542-3353), produces inventive American dishes like the jalapeno-fuelled *Violence Chicken* for $8.50, while cheap and filling Greek salads and kebabs are the specialities at *Zorba's*, 420 S Orange Street (☎728-9259).

Bars and Entertainment

When Milo Milodragonovitch, the heavy-drinking, coke-snorting private eye in James Crumley's *Dancing Bear*, was left battered and bleeding miles from Missoula, he was consoled by the knowledge that soon he would be back in what he considered to be "the town with the best bars in a state of great bars". It's hard to argue with either claim.

The bar that Milodragonovitch uses as an impromptu office is based on *Charley B's*, 428 N Higgins Street – a dark, dingy, no-frills local. On the walls are dozens of black and white photos of all the regulars, with silver stars stuck on those who have passed away. Another rough and ready joint is the *Top Hat*, 134 W Front Street (☎728-9865), which features live rock and rockabilly bands most nights. The *Rhinocerous* (*Rhinos*), 158 Ryman Avenue (☎721-6061), attracts students and yuppies, as does the *Ironhorse Pub*, 100 E Railroad Avenue (☎721-8705), which sells own-brand ales in the former rail station. Other bars worth checking out are the sporty *Union Club*, 208 E Main Street (☎728-7980), and the *Missoula Club*, hiding behind a neon "Burgers and Beer" sign at 139 W Main Street (☎728-3740).

Glacier National Park

Two thousand lakes and a thousand miles of rivers, threading between thick forests and glorious meadows, weave a blue and green carpet below the tightly packed peaks of **GLACIER NATIONAL PARK** – a haven for bighorn sheep, mountain goats, grizzly bears and mule deer. Though the park still holds 50 small glaciers, its name comes from the fact that these immense valleys were carved by huge flows of ice, millennia ago. The crisp air, freezing waterfalls and year-round snow combine to give the impression of being very close to the Arctic Circle; in fact, the latitude here is lower than London.

Arrival and Information

Visitor centres can be found at the park's **western** (Apgar) entrance, twenty miles east of **Whitefish** (see below), just 35 miles south of the Canadian border, and the main **east** gate at **St Mary**, seventy miles west of **Shelby**. There's also another at the top of Logan Pass on the Going-to-the-Sun road, which is the one through road between the two entrances. The park itself is open all year round, though the road is usually only passable between mid-June and mid-October. There's an entrance fee of $5 per car, good for seven days; all park information is on ☎888-5441.

Glacier is linked with the adjacent and much smaller Waterton Lakes National Park (☎403/859-2224) in Canada to form the **Waterton-Glacier International Peace Park**. However, both parks operate their own fees and regulations and to get to Waterton you'll have to pass customs and pay an extra $4 a day (or $9 for four days).

Amtrak **trains** stop at East Glacier and Essex on the southern border of the park and at West Glacier, a short walk from the west gate. *Intermountain* **buses** (☎563-5246) operate fairly frequent buses during summer from Missoula, Kalispell, Whitefish, and, on the east side of the park, Great Falls.

Seeing the Park

Driving the fifty-mile **Going-to-the-Sun road** from west to east (which can take several hours) creates the illusion that you will be climbing forever. After a stealthy ascent of the foothills, when the road appears to be heading straight into the huge bare mountain that fills the entire windscreen, each successive hairpin confronts you with a new colossus. At the east end of ten-mile **Lake McDonald**, the road starts to climb in earnest. Snowmelt from waterfalls gushes across the road, spilling over the sheer drops on the other side. The winding route nudges over the **Continental Divide** at **Logan Pass** (6680ft) – a bewildering area where the peaks that looked so unscaleable from the valley floor are now mere hillocks of ice. Four miles on, there's an overlook at **Jackson Glacier**, one of the few glaciers visible from the roadside. Once you get down to the east gate, continue for about five miles southeast on US-89 for a stunning view of the start of the Great Plains, which stretch 1600 miles east to Chicago.

Good short **trails** start from **Avalanche Creek** on the west side of Going-to-the-Sun. The **Trail of the Cedars** leads through dark forest to a wall of contoured vivid red sandstone, from where a four-mile path continues gently uphill, past several waterfalls, to glacier-fed **Avalanche Lake**. Another popular trail begins at Logan Pass, traversing beautiful wildflower meadows framed by craggy peaks en route to serene **Hidden Lake**. At **Swiftcurrent Lake**, north of the east entrance, an easy two-mile trail runs along the lakeshore, and an exciting nine-mile trail heads to **Iceberg Lake**, so called for the blocks of ice that float on its surface even in midsummer.

Cycling in Glacier, assuming you have the appropriate sprockets and calf muscles, can be tremendous fun. However, the roads are narrow and winding, and bikes are banned in July and August from sections of Going-to-the-Sun road during peak hours.

Tour boats explore all of the large lakes, charging $6 for one-hour trips, including sunset cruises on Lake McDonald and St Mary's Lake. You can also rent canoes, rowboats and outboards. The lakes, teeming with cutthroat trout, are excellent for **fishing**; regulations are outlined in a free pamphlet available from visitor centres.

Both *Glacier Raft Co* (☎888-5454) and *Wild River Adventures* (☎888-5539), based outside the west gate, offer half-day ($29) and full-day ($54 including lunch) **float trips** down the middle fork of the Flathead River, which runs along the park boundary.

Park Practicalities

All **accommodation** within the park is run by *Glacier Park Inc* (May–Sept, East Glacier Park, MT 59434, ☎226-5531; otherwise Station 1210, Greyhound, Phoenix, AZ 85077, ☎602/248-6816). Most rooms cost over $80, though the *Swiftcurrent Motor Inn* on the upper east side costs $55 (basic cabins $23), the *Rising Sun Motor Inn*, seven miles in from the east gate at St Mary's, around $60, and the *Village Inn* at the west gate $70.

Just outside the western entrance, the *ApgarVillage Lodge* (☎888-5484) has clean rooms for $45 to $60. An unusual place to stay on the southern boundary is the *Izaak Walton Inn* at **Essex** (☎888-5700), halfway between the east and west gates. *Amtrak* stops at the front door of this grand 1939 building, originally used to house railway workers charged with keeping the lines clear in winter. Rooms cost between $65 and $85, including breakfast. There are two **youth hostels** in the area: the *North Fork AYH* in **Polebridge** (☎756-4780 or ☎756-5174), thirty miles north of the west gate on a gravel road, and *Brownie's Grocery & AYH Hostel*, 1020 Hwy-49 (☎226-4426), near *Amtrak* in the village of East Glacier Park.

The park's eleven **campgrounds**, all first-come first-served, fill up by late morning during July and August; ask at any visitor centre for locations and availability. Most are open from late May to mid-September, though you can camp at *Apgar* or *St Mary* at any time of the year. For overnight backpacking, get a free permit from any visitor centre.

There are only a few places to eat in the park, and in any case it's best to bring your own food, as what's on sale is pricey and bland.

Alternative Bases: Kalispell and Whitefish

Thirty miles southwest of Glacier park, and fifteen miles north of Flathead Lake, largish **KALISPELL** has been successful in cornering a significant portion of the tourist trade en route to Glacier. There's not much to do here, but in high season it may be the closest place you'll get to stay to the park. The *Best Western Outlaw Inn*, 1701 US-93S (☎755-6100), and the venerable *Kalispell Hotel*, First and Main streets (☎752-5145), are the stylish options for around $65 a night. The clean and central *Four Seasons Motel*, 350 N Main Street (☎755-6123), represents good value at $45. The cheapest places to stay are *Motel 6*, 1540 US-93S (☎752-6335), for $33, and the *AYH* **hostel**, 2155 Whitefish Stage Road (☎756-1908), for $8 ($10 in winter). For **food**, try the breakfasts or salads with purple sauce at *Sky Jordan*, 127 N Main Street (☎752-6170), or the pizzas and sandwiches in the grand old-fashioned *Moose's Saloon*, 173 N Main Street (☎755-2337).

A more pleasant stop is the resort and lumbering village of **WHITEFISH**, seventeen miles north, though accommodation here is more limited. Hacked out of thick forests, it lies on the south shore of beautiful Whitefish Lake in the shade of the *Big Mountain Ski Resort* (☎862-3511). The narrow roads round the lake and foothills deserve to be **cycled**; bikes can be hired from *Glacier Cyclery*, 336 Second Street (☎862-6446).

The least expensive **motels** in Whitefish are the *Downtowner*, 224 Spokane Avenue (☎862-3511), and the *Mountain Holiday*, one mile south on US-93, both for around $50. For good steak and seafood dinners ($10–14), go to the lively *Stumpjumpers* bar, 115 Central Avenue (☎862-4979), which also has a cheaper bar menu. The *Buff Cafe*, 514 Third Street and Sebastian's, 214 Central Avenue, does $3 lunch specials.

Amtrak drops off downtown on Central Avenue, while *Intermountain* **buses** (☎563-5246) call in on their way between Missoula and Glacier National Park during summer.

IDAHO

Forbidding, desolate **IDAHO**, the last of the fifty states to be explored by whites, lacks the rich Wild West heritage of its neighbours. In 1805, **Lewis and Clark** declared the mountain ranges of mid-Idaho – untraversed by road even today – as the most difficult leg of their mammoth journey from St Louis to the Pacific. Reports of game animals in such numbers as to be tripping over each other attracted the usual legions of itinerant trappers, but the gold rush of the 1860s and white pressure for land hastened the violent end of traditional life: the first major battle between whites and Native Americans left four hundred Shoshoni men, women and children dead along the Bear River in 1863, and by the end of the 1870s the "Indian problem" had been eradicated. Irrigation programmes in the 1880s – partly instigated by Mormons from Utah – transformed the scrubland of southern Idaho into fertile fields, though the influence of the Latter Day Saints waned after polygamy was banned and they were disqualified from voting.

Idaho's odd jigsaw-piece shape represents the land left over in 1890 after the boundaries of Washington, Oregon and Montana had been fixed. This political carve-up left it as a state of two very distinct halves, separated by wilderness. The heavily forested **north**, interspersed with glacial lakes now fronted by resorts like **Sandpoint** and **Coeur d'Alene**, has always had strong trading links with Spokane in Washington, while the farmland of the south looks rather to state capital Boise and Salt Lake City in Utah.

While Idaho's licence plates may boast of "Famous Potatoes", only in the south is the land suitable for growing vegetables. The rest of the state is dominated by no fewer than 81 mountain ranges, interspersed with virgin forests and lava plateaux. Natural wonders in its five-hundred-mile stretch include **Hell's Canyon**, America's deepest river gorge, and the black, barren **Craters of the Moon**. But much of the scenery can seem too bleak, too isolated and too intense for many, and with a marked absence of urban centres (pleasant Boise being the only real exception), a poorly-planned trip through Idaho could prove to be a long and lonesome experience.

Getting Around Idaho

Bus services between north and south Idaho are nonexistent, and a car is essential for extensive travel. *Amtrak* cuts two routes through the state. Sandpoint is the only stop on the northern line, though Spokane is not far across the border. Boise and other smaller towns are served on the southerly route between Portland and Salt Lake City. Boise also has a regional **airport**, though Spokane and Salt Lake City can be more convenient for destinations in northern and southern Idaho respectively.

Southern Idaho

To drivers on the interstates, southern Idaho appears to consist of little more than miles of vegetable fields and a few rocky or sandy desert stretches; only state capital **Boise** provides any urban interest. A trip into the interior along US-20, however, brings you to the spectacular ragged outcrops of the **Sawtooth Mountains**. During summer, the much-hyped **Sun Valley** ski resort is a good base for cyclists and canoeists, and has the only good bars and restaurants in this remote zone.

Some 45 miles west of Idaho Falls on US-20, the unassuming red-brick Experimental Breeder Reactor No 1 (**EBR-1**) – in lay terms, the **world's first nuclear power station** – stands just south of the 890-square-mile Idaho National Engineering Laboratory (aka nuclear waste dump). Now decommissioned, it's a free museum.

The telephone **area code** for the entire state of Idaho is ☎208.

Craters Of The Moon National Monument

The eerie **CRATERS OF THE MOON NATIONAL MONUMENT** is around ninety miles west of Idaho Springs, less than twenty miles beyond Arco. At first sight, it looks like a sooty-black wasteland, but closer inspection reveals a surreal cornucopia of lava cones, buttes, craters, caves and splatter cones. Here and there, sagebrush clings to the bleak soil, and trees have been battered by the fierce winds into bonsai-like contortions. All these features were formed without the aid of a volcano as such; instead, for 13,000 years, lava oozed from a gaping wound in the earth's crust. Activity finally ceased just two thousand years ago.

The park **visitor centre** is on US-20 (daily 8am–6pm; ☎527-3257); entrance is $3 per car, and spaces at the *Lava Flow* **campground** are $5. Ranger-led activities include enjoyable and free ninety-minute **cave tours** (summer daily 9am, 11.30am, 2pm & 4pm). If you're doing a self-guided tour, stick to the trails, as the rocks are razor-sharp and can reach temperatures of 200°F.

Sun Valley

Technically, **Sun Valley**, in the centre of southern Idaho, 150 miles west of Idaho Falls and a similar distance east of Boise, is just the name of a ski resort, which came into being in the Thirties as a scheme by the Union Pacific Railroad to promote its new northern line. The name was chosen because the snow stayed even when the bright winter sun radiated temperatures of 70°F; early brochures showed skiiers descending Baldy Mountain stripped to the waist. More recently, the tourist boards have latched onto the snazzy title and made it the common label for the entire Wood River Valley area.

To enjoy the resort itself, you need to have a couple of hundred bucks to spend on food and board. But the old sheep-ranching village of **KETCHUM**, half a mile west, is something of an oasis of nightlife in this otherwise thinly populated zone. Up to a point, it resembles the Colorado ski towns, though summer trade is nowhere near as busy.

Practicalities

Ketchum's **visitor centre** is at no. 400 on the short Main Street (☎726-3423). *Sun Valley Stages* (☎622-4200) run regular buses from Boise, and there's a free in-town service between 7.30am and 10.30pm. Two good central **accommodation** options on Main Street, both of which cost around $52 in summer ($70 in winter), are the comfortable *Lift Tower Lodge* (☎726-5163) and the well-appointed *Ketchum Korral Motor Lodge* (☎726-3510).

Louie's, Sun Valley Road and Leadville Street (☎726-7775), cooks up great pizzas, and *Desperado's*, 211 Fourth Street (☎726-3068), serves fish burritos ($4.50) and other cheap Mexican food. The village also has a number of decent drinking spots. The most popular place to **drink** is *Grumpy's*, two blocks up Warm Springs Road, easily distinguished by the "Sorry We're Open" sign. The *Elephant's Perch*, 220 East Avenue (☎726-3497), rents out sports equipment of all kinds.

The best place to **camp** in the region is in the wilderness of the **Sawtooth National Recreation Area** to the north. Pick up details of primitive sites and hiking trails at its headquarters (☎726-8291), eight miles out of Ketchum

Boise

Anywhere in the US, the strikingly verdant community of **BOISE** (pronounced *Boyzee*) would come across as a bustling and likeable small city; located in arid southwestern Idaho, it's all the more appealing. The town straddles I-84, just 350 miles from Salt Lake City to the southeast and a trifling 490 miles from Seattle in the northwest.

The town grew up under the protective wing of Fort Boise, established in 1862 for the benefit of pioneers using the Oregon Trail. After adapting (or misspelling) the name originally given to the area by French trappers – *les bois*, the woods – the earliest residents boosted the town's appearance by planting hundreds more trees. Today Boise acts as a trading centre for southern Idaho farms, with other jobs coming from government business, education and manufacturing.

To explore Boise's compact, friendly **downtown**, start from the central **State Capitol** at Jefferson Street and Capitol Boulevard. This squat replica of the national Capitol exhibits gemstones such as the star garnet, found only in Indo-China and Idaho. **Old Boise Historic District**, nearby, is a once-elegant area of brick houses currently undergoing exetensive restoration. The **Idaho Basque Museum and Cultural Center** at 607 Grove Street is located in a former boarding house that for many years acted as home for Basque immigrants newly arrived from northern Spain. They came to central Idaho, with its similarly rocky terrain, to employ their shepherding skills. The museum traces the Basque cultural heritage, and hosts regular traditional dance nights (May–Sept Tues–Sat 10am–5pm; Oct–April Thurs–Sat 11am–3pm).

It's impossible not to be impressed by the contrast between the urban greenery and the humpy desert hills all around. The city is rightly proud of the **Greenbelt**, almost ten miles of paths that criss-cross the sluggish, brown **Boise River** to link nine separate parks. In Julia Davis Park, the **Idaho Historical Museum** chronicles the experience of the Chinese miners of the 1870s and 1880s, who picked over mines long since abandoned by whites. The state legislature, controlled by unreconstructed Confederates who had fled the South after the Civil War, did nothing to stamp out endemic racial violence, and forced the Chinese to pay $4 a month, a considerable amount at the time, just to live in the Territory (Mon–Sat 9am–5pm, Sun 1–5pm).

The **Old Idaho Penitentiary** nestles beneath desert hills at 2445 Old Penitentiary Road, off Warm Springs Avenue (daily summer noon–5pm; otherwise noon–4pm; $3). This imposing sandstone-walled citadel feels like a desolate outpost, despite being just a mile from downtown. Constructed in 1870 to hold bandits, robbers, rustlers and other western desperadoes, it remained open until 1974. Self-guided tours take you through the cramped solitary confinement unit, and the gallows room where the last hanging in Idaho was carried out in 1957. Restoration work has sensibly avoided trying to make this brutal prison look more palatable. A small museum on site displays confiscated weapons and mugshots of former inmates, including one Harry Orchard who blew up the state governor in 1905 and served out his sentence here, dying in 1954 aged 88.

Practicalities

Greyhound **buses** stop at 1212 W Bannock Street (☎343-7531) and *Amtrak* pulls in at 1701 Eastover Terrace; both are on the edge of downtown.

The **visitor centre** is at 100 N Ninth Street (☎344-7777). **Rooms** in the *Idanaha Hotel*, 928 Main Street (☎342-3611), a downtown landmark topped by a castellated mansard roof and black corner turrets, are a real bargain at $49 to $54. Further out, the *Capri Motel*, 2600 Fairview Avenue (☎344-8617), and the nicer *Seven K Motel*, 3633 Childen Boulevard (☎343-7723), both charge a little over $30. A prime site to **camp** is the *AOK Americana Kampground*, 3600 Americana Terrace (☎342-9691) – a little expensive at $16 but right in the heart of town, across the river from Ann Morrison Park.

When it comes to **eating**, *Louie's*, 620 W Idaho Street (☎344-5200), is good for inexpensive pasta and pizzas. The *Piper Pub & Grill*, Eighth and Main streets, serves reasonable burgers and bar food on its outdoor terrace. *Christina's*, Fifth and Main streets (☎385-0133), is a first-class bakery with great pastries and tasty lunches; try the atomic taco. *Pengilly's*, 513 Main Street (☎345-6344), is the town's most atmospheric **bar**. Incidentally, downtown Boise is caught up in an incredible **cruising** craze, and resounds to the screeching of hundreds of cars until the early hours at weekends.

Northern Idaho

The wilderness peaks and pinnacles of the Sawtooth, Salmon River and Clearwater mountains make travelling through the heart of Idaho impossible. There are only two routes from south to north: up the eastern fringe from Idaho Falls, or, more enjoyably, along US-95 via Hwy-55 out of Boise. At first barren and infertile, not until just before Lewiston does the scenery unfold into superb pastoral farmland. The Nez Percé hunted buffalo, gathered berries and fished here for hundreds of years, until gold was discovered and they were forced to beat a bloody retreat.

The heavily forested far north of the Idaho Panhandle is broken by hundreds of deep glacial lakes, the largest of which have resort towns like Coeur d'Alene and Sandpoint. While not major destinations, they can make good one- or two-day stops.

Hell's Canyon Region

From the busy but not overcommercialised little watersports resort of **McCall**, 110 miles north of Boise, Hwy-55 climbs steadily to merge with US-95 and follow the turbulent **Little Salmon River**. Just south of the hamlet of Riggins, thirty miles on, comes the only good opportunity to see **Hell's Canyon** from Idaho. With an average depth of 5500 feet this is the deepest river gorge in the USA, though its low-relief formation, hemmed in by a series of gradually ascending false peaks, means that it lacks the impact of the steep-walled Grand Canyon. Nevertheless, it is impressive, with Oregon's Wallowa and Eagle Cap ranges rising behind it and the river glimmering far down below. Hwy-241 leads towards the overlooks; the final few miles of dirt road require a four-wheel drive vehicle and permission from the forest ranger office (☎628-3916). The canyon is also accessible by road from Oregon (p.863) and by boat from Lewiston.

Riggins itself reclines in a steeply rising T-shaped canyon. This is prime **whitewater rafting** country, and outfitters, spread along a one-mile stretch of the one-street village, outnumber cafes and shops. The Chamber of Commerce (☎628-3456) has details. From Riggins, US-95 heads north along the Salmon River Valley for 30 miles to the rumpled terrain around **White Bird**, the start of Nez Percé Indian country (see overleaf).

There are two possible reasons to visit industrial **LEWISTON**, 110 miles north of Riggins. The first is to drive down the old road into town from the top of Lewiston Hill, just north. What seems like an intricate network of roads criss-crossing a series of mounds is, in fact, a single tarmac ribbon, which twists and turns for several miles down the steep hillside – although as the crow flies the distance is no more than a mile.

The other reason to subject yourself to the nasty smells emanating from the local paper mills is for the fantastic journey down Hell's Canyon on the Salmon River. Boats sail past abandoned mine shafts and Indian caves, with mountain goats, bobcats, snakes and various birds of prey adding further interest. Of the various outfitters, *Snake River Adventures*, 227 Snake River Avenue (☎746-6276), offer the best value with a 180-mile round trip from 7.30am to 5pm costing $65 including lunch. Contact the visitor centre, 2207 E Main Street (☎743-3531), to check other prices.

Moscow

The thirty miles of US-95 between Lewiston and **MOSCOW** wind through the beautiful rolling hillsides of the fertile Palouse Valley – a patchwork of green lentils, bright yellow rape, soft white wheat and (100-foot-thick) black topsoil. Roadside red barns and farmhouses complete a marvellous rural picture.

With only 10,000 year-round residents and a similar number of University of Idaho students, Moscow is a friendly, culturally rich town which makes a good overnight stop. Bookshops, galleries, bars and sidewalk cafes line up along tree-shaded, part-

THE NEZ PERCÉ INDIANS

The first whites to encounter the **Nez Percé Indians** were the weak, hungry and disease-ridden Lewis and Clark expedition in 1805. Though the Native Americans had the explorers at their mercy, they gave them food and shelter, and cared for the animals until the party was ready to carry on westward.

Relations between the Nez Percé (so called by French-Canadian trappers for their shell-pierced noses) and whites remained excellent for over half a century – until the discovery of gold, led the government to persuade some renegade Nez Percé to sign a treaty in 1863, taking away three-quarters of tribal land. As settlers started to move into the hunting grounds of the Wallowa Valley in the early 1870s, the majority of the Nez Percé, under the leadership of **Chief Joseph**, refused to recognise the agreement. In 1877, after much vacillation, the government decided to enact its terms, and gave the tribe thirty days to leave. The Indians asked for more time to round up their livestock and avoid crossing the Snake River at a dangerous time; the general in charge refused.

The ensuing tensions resulted in skirmishes which caused the deaths of a handful of settlers – the first whites ever to be attacked by Nez Percé – and a large army force began to gather to round up the Indians. Chief Joseph thereupon embarked upon the famous **Retreat of the Nez Percé**. Around 250 warriors (protecting twice as many women, children and old people) outmanoeuvred army columns many times their size, launching frequent guerilla attacks in a series of hair-breadth escapes. After four months and 1700 miles, the Nez Percé were cornered just thirty miles from the relative safety of the Canadian border. Chief Joseph (reportedly) made his much-quoted speech of surrender:

Hear me my chiefs! I am tired. My heart is sick and sad. From where the sun now stands I will fight no more forever.

The Indians had been told that they would be put on a reservation in Idaho; instead, they were taken to Oklahoma, where marshy land caused a malaria epidemic. Chief Joseph died in 1904 on the Colville reservation in Washington, but decades later the Nez Percé were allowed to return to the northwest, where today some 1500 live in a reservation between Lewiston and Grangeville – a minute fraction of their original territory.

The **Nez Percé National Historic Park**, containing 24 separate sites, is spread over 12,000 square miles of north central Idaho. At the visitor centre in **Spalding**, ten miles east of Lewiston, the Museum of Nez Percé Culture is good on arts and crafts but weak on history; the heavily ravined **White Bird Battlefield**, seventy miles further south on US-95, was where the Indians inflicted 34 deaths on the US Army at no cost to themselves in the first major battle of the retreat. Further exhibits on Nez Percé history can be found in the Wallowa County Museum in Joseph, Oregon (see p.863).

pedestrianised **Main Street**, the only shopping thoroughfare. Theatre, music and avant-garde cinema are on offer throughout the year, while summer sees a sprinkling of big-budget arts festivals.

The town's name might raise a few eyebrows, but it's pretty ordinary compared to the first settlers' choice of Hog Heaven. A proposal to rename it Paradise was seen as a trifle over-the-top; the present title comes from one early resident's home town in Pennsylvania.

Practicalities

The *Royal Motor Inn*, 120 W Sixth Street (☎882-2581), which doubles as the *Greyhound* stop, has decent **rooms** for $30. For a bit more comfort, try the *Mark IV Motor Inn*, 414 N Main Street (☎882-7557), which has a nice pool and charges $40 to $60.

Moscow's several likeable **coffeeshops** often feature live acoustic and classical music in the evening. *Mikey's Gyros*, 527 Main Street (☎882-0780), offers cheap, simple Greek food, while *Cafe Spudnik*, 215 Main Street (☎882-9257), is popular for its international cuisine – a good meal should cost under $10.

Coeur d'Alene

When US Army Chief of Staff William Tecumseh Sherman set up camp in 1877 on the present site of **COEUR D'ALENE** (ninety miles north of Moscow on US-95), he found the sparkling blue lake, surrounded by wildflower borders and lush forest, so appealing that he ordered a fort to be built here. Another large structure now stands on the beautiful shoreline of long, narrow Lake Coeur d'Alene; looking not unlike an office block, the phenomenally expensive **Coeur d'Alene Resort** (*Condé Nast* called it the best resort in inland America; it boasts the world's only floating golf green) completely dominates downtown. Not surprisingly, it's a bitter local debating point.

Downtown is unremarkable, verging on the tacky with its sidewalk cafes and pricey shops. Directly east of the Resort, a small public beach backs onto a balmy park area. Scenic **lake cruises** leave from the City Dock by the resort (summer daily 1.30pm, 4pm & 6pm; $8.50; ☎765-4000). You can also see the lake on a twenty-minute **sea plane flight** from here, for $25 (☎664-2842).

Greyhound use the **bus station** at 1923 N Fourth Street (☎664-3343), a mile north of downtown. There's a **visitor centre** at Front Avenue and Second Street (☎664-3194). You can get central **rooms** at *El Rancho Motel*, 1915 Sherman Avenue (☎664-8794), or *Lake Drive Motel*, 316 Lake Drive (☎667-8486), for $30 to $40. The unpretentious B&B *Sleeping Place of the Wheels*, two miles from downtown at 3308 Lodgepole Road (☎765-3435), costs just $35 ($22 for one person). The *Third Street Cantina*, 201 N Third Street (☎664-0581), serves Mexican-style fish dishes; *Natural Food & Restaurant*, Third & Lakeside streets (☎664-0581), does vegetarian lunches. For beer brewed on the premises, call in at the friendly *T W Fisher's Brew Pub*, 204 N Second Street (☎664-BREW).

East from Coeur d'Alene on I-90

Fifty miles along the interstate towards Missoula, Montana (see p.632), the run-down streets, thrift shops and basic bars of **WALLACE** evoke images of its silver-mining days. The 75-minute **Sierra Silver Mine Tour** leaves by trolley car from 420 N Fifth Street every half-hour, on a fun trip which takes you a thousand feet underground (summer daily 9am–4pm; $6). The *Silveradough Bakery* on Bank Street serves large lunches for just $4. In summer 1991, the FBI seized all the slot machines and gaming tables in town in a much-publicised raid.

NAZIS IN THE NORTHWEST

The beauty and remoteness of the intermountain west has recently come to appeal to that section of American society that believes the Second Coming and/or nuclear holocaust is just around the corner. Throughout the region, tiny "post-Nam" sects, armed to the teeth and with a distinct dislike for being disturbed, have taken to the woods.

The largest and most public of the various right-wing, survivalist, fundamentalist Christian – or just plain cranky – sects is the **Aryan Nations**, led by Rev Richard Butler, who are based in a ranch ten miles northwest of Coeur d'Alene, near Hayden Lake. They hope to establish an all-white region in the states of Washington, Oregon, Idaho and Montana, and each year play host to the Aryan Nations World Congress, attended by Klan hierarchy and representatives of most North American far-right groups.

According to journalist Stephen Singular (see "Contexts"), the Aryan Nations' idea of revolt goes no further than "going into the woods and shooting at pictures of Menachem Begin and at six-pointed stars". More eager for a white revolution were the paramilitary **Bruders Schweigen** (Silent Brotherhood), who met at the ranch but left to establish themselves in Metaline Falls in Washington. Their strategy was to assassinate prominent Jews and "Zionist collaborators in the US government;" they got no further than murdering anti-fascist Denver DJ Alan Berg (subject of Oliver Stone's *Talk Radio* movie) before all their members were rounded up in an intensive FBI manhunt.

Sandpoint

Forty-four miles north of Coeur d'Alene in the shadows of the spiky Selkirk Mountains, **SANDPOINT**, northern Idaho's most attractive resort, is at the northwestern end of Lake Pend Orielle (pronounced *Pon-duh-ray*). Smaller and less commercialised than Coeur d'Alene, Sandpoint's lazy downtown is brightened by Cedar Street Bridge Public Market, a covered mall of stalls, shops and cafes overlooking placid Sandy Creek.

The *Lakeside Inn* (☎263-3717), right beside the lovely white sandy beach, charges $50 to $60; the *K2 Motel*, 501 N Fourth Street (☎263-3441), $32 to $50. Savings can be made by taking a dorm bed for $10 at *Whitaker House B&B*, 410 Railroad Avenue (☎263-0816). *Amtrak* passes through early in the morning in both directions.

travel details

TRAINS

Routes

• One daily train travels each way between **Chicago** and **Seattle** via **Denver**, southern Wyoming – where it calls at Borie (for **Cheyenne**) and **Laramie** – and southern Idaho towns including **Boise**.

• Another daily train each way between **Chicago** and **Seattle**, on a shorter route parallel to the Canadian border, stops at several Montana towns including **Shelby** and **West Glacier** (plus three other stops in Glacier Park vicinity) and Sandpoint, Idaho.

• One daily train each way between Chicago and Los Angeles calls at **Denver**, **Glenwood Springs**, **Grand Junction** and **Salt Lake City**. The westbound train leaves Denver at 9.40am; the eastbound train leaves Grand Junction at 11.40am.

• Another daily train each way between **Chicago** and **Los Angeles** takes a southern route through New Mexico and Arizona, calling at **Lamar**, **La Junta** and **Trinidad** in southeastern Colorado.

Journey Times

From Denver: Borie 2hr; Laramie 3hr; Boise 22hr 40min; Portland 33hr; Seattle 37hr; Glenwood Springs 6hr 30min; Grand Junction 8hr 30min; Salt Lake City 13hr 30min; Omaha 8hr; Chicago 17hr.

From West Glacier: Sandpoint 3hr; Spokane 5hr; Seattle 13hr 30min; Minneapolis 8hr 30min; Chicago 29hr 30min.

BUSES

All *Greyhound* unless otherwise stated.

From Denver to Cheyenne (4 daily; 3hr); Glenwood Springs (4; 3hr 30min); Grand Junction (4; 5hr 30min); Salt Lake City (4; 12hr); Colorado Springs (8; 1hr 30min); Salt Lake City (5; 12hr); Kansas City (3; 15hr); St Louis (3; 21hr); Amarillo (3; 11hr); Dallas (3; 20hr 30min); Taos (1; 9hr); Santa Fe (4; 8hr 30min); Las Vegas (3; 15hr 30min); Chicago (3; 25hr).

From Grand Junction to Colorado Springs (1; 8hr 30min); Dallas (1; 23hr 30min).

From Cheyenne to Laramie (2 daily; 1hr); Rock Springs (2; 6hr 30min); by *Powder River Transportation* to Casper (2; 4hr); Buffalo (2; 7hr); Sheridan (2; 7hr 30min); Billings (2; 10hr).

From Sheridan by *Powder River Transportation* to Cody (1 daily; 4hr); Yellowstone Park (1; 5hr 30min).

From Billings to Bozeman (3 daily; 2hr 30min); Butte (3; 5hr); Helena (2; 7hr); Missoula (3; 9–11hr); *Rim Rock* buses run similar schedules.

From Bozeman to West Yellowstone (2 daily; 2hr), and by *Karst Stages* (2; 2hr) and *TW Services* (1; 2hr); *TW Services* to Yellowstone Park (2; 2hr).

From Butte to Missoula (2 daily; 2hr 30min). Also by *Intermountain Transport* to Helena (2; 1hr); Great Falls (2; 2hr); Glacier Park East (2; 5hr 30min, summer only).

From Missoula to Coeur d'Alene (2 daily; 4hr 30min); Spokane (2; 5hr 15min). By *Intermountain Transportation* to Kalispell (2 daily; 3hr); Whitefish (2; 3hr 30min); Glacier Park West (2; 4hr 15min, summer only).

From West Yellowstone to Salt Lake City (1 daily; 7hr 30min).

From Boise to Portland (2 daily; 9hr); Seattle (3; 12hr); Salt Lake City (2; 8hr 30min); by *Sun Valley Stages* to Sun Valley (2; 2hr 30min).

From Coeur d'Alene by *Empire Lines* to Sandpoint (1 daily; 1hr).

CHAPTER TWELVE

THE SOUTHWEST

The four sparsely populated Southwest desert states of **NEW MEXICO**, **ARIZONA, UTAH** and **NEVADA** are extraordinary, unforgettable, and absolutely unique. They stretch from Texas to California across an elemental landscape ranging from towering monoliths of stark red sandstone to snow-capped mountains, on a high desert plateau which repeatedly splits open to reveal deep yawning canyons. The raw power of the scenery, uninterrupted from horizon to horizon, is overwhelming, and it is complemented by the emphatic presence of numerous Native American cultures and the palpable legacy of America's Wild West frontier.

Among the earliest inhabitants were the mysterious **Anasazi**; the remains of their cliff palaces and cities, scattered throughout the region, display an architectural sophistication to rival their contemporaries, the Maya of Mexico. The Anasazi abandoned all their settlements around seven hundred years ago, but the **Pueblo** people of New Mexico and the **Hopi** in Arizona still follow much the same peaceful lifestyle, in more or less the same places, and are thought to be their direct descendants.

More war-like tribes, such as the **Navajo** and the **Apache**, began to migrate to the Southwest early in the sixteenth century. They adopted local agricultural and crafts techniques and appropriated vast tracts of territory, which they in turn soon found themselves having to defend against bands of European immigrants. The first such, in 1540, was a party of **Spanish** explorers led by Coronado, who spent two years searching for the mythical El Dorado-style Seven Cities of Cibola. A hundred years later Spanish friars returned to establish Catholic missions, many of which are still intact. Although the religion took a strong hold, particularly in New Mexico, white American traders had already come to dominate the region's economy by the time the newly independent Republic of **Mexico** superseded Spain in 1820. Thirty years later, following war with Mexico, the **United States** took over the entire Southwest, and large numbers of outsiders began to pass through on their way to Gold Rush California.

Thereafter, increasingly violent confrontations took place between the US government and the Native Americans. The entire Navajo Nation was rounded up and forcibly removed to the barren plains of eastern New Mexico in 1869 – though it was eventually allowed to return to northeastern Arizona – and the **Apache**, under warrior chiefs Cochise and Geronimo, fought extended battles with the US cavalry. Though the nominal intention was to open up Indian lands to American settlers, few such groups ever succeeded in extracting a living from this harsh terrain.

One exception were the devout and hardworking **Mormons** (or Church of Christ of Latter Day Saints). Fleeing religious persecution elsewhere in the US, they established from the late 1840s onwards what amounted to an independent nation in the alkaline basin of Utah's Great Salt Lake, with outlying communities all over the Southwest. Even here they met with resistance, and until the Civil War intervened, there was a real possibility that the US might declare war on them. They now amount to seventy percent of the state's population, and remain in virtual control of the Utah government.

Despite their common heritage, each of the four Southwestern states remains quite distinct. **New Mexico** bears the most obvious traces of long-term settlement, the Indian Pueblos of the north co-existing alongside major towns, laid out around spacious plazas, which clearly retain their Spanish colonial identity. In **Arizona**, the history of the Wild West is more conspicuous, in towns such as Tombstone, site of the

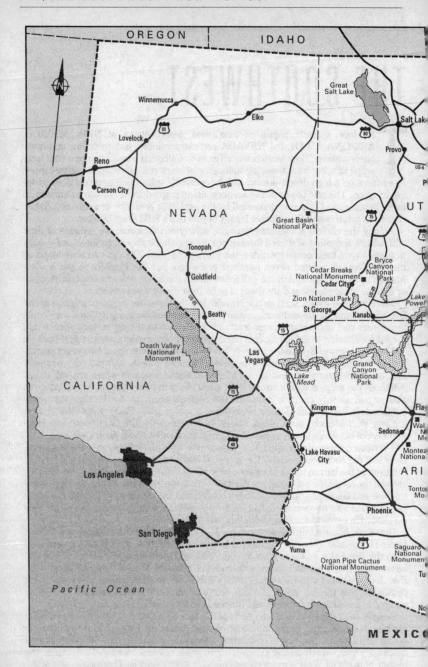

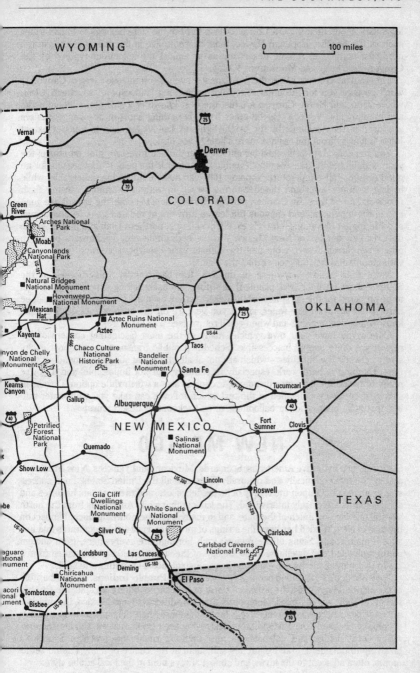

legendary shootout at the OK Corral. Over a third of the state belongs to Indian tribes such as the Apache, Hopi and Navajo, most of whom live in the red-rock lands of the northeast corner, on remote desert mesas or amidst the splendour typified by the **Canyon de Chelly** and **Monument Valley**.

The canyon country of northern Arizona – even the immense **Grand Canyon** – won't prepare you for the uninhabited but compelling landscape of **southern Utah**, where **Zion** and **Bryce Canyon** are just the best known of a string of national parks and monuments. **Nevada**, on the other hand, is nothing short of desolate; gamblers are lured in their millions by the bright lights of **Las Vegas**, and to a lesser extent Reno, but away from the casinos there's little to see or do.

You can count on warm sunshine anywhere in the Southwest for nine months of the year, with incredible sunsets most evenings. Summer is the peak tourist season, for no good reason – air temperatures topping 100° can make outdoor life unbearable, while in late summer awesome thunderstorms sweep in without warning, causing flash floods and forest fires. By October, perhaps the best time to come, the crowds are gone and in the mountains and canyons the leaves turn bright red and gold. Winter brings snow to higher elevations – there's excellent skiing in northern Utah and in the Sangre de Cristo mountains of New Mexico – while springtime sees wildflowers bloom in otherwise barren desert. Note that the climate varies sharply according to elevation, with mountains often 30° cooler than the plains.

More than almost anywhere in the US, the backcountry wildernesses of the Southwest are ideal for (well-planned) **camping** and backpacking expeditions. It's vital to be prepared for the harshness of the desert, where even the most basic needs can be hard to fill; always carry water, and if you venture off the beaten track let someone know where you're going and when you'll return (see p.38 for more).

Unless you have your own vehicle, many of the most fascinating corners of the region are quite simply inaccessible. Scheduled public transport runs almost exclusively between the big cities – which are not at all where you should be spending your time. Hitching is hard work, especially in summer, but not impossible, and if you're ready to tackle the immense distances, cycling is also a worthwhile option. Dozens of specialist companies, detailed in the text which follows, can take you whitewater rafting, mountain biking, hot air ballooning, or on backcountry desert tours.

NEW MEXICO

Settled in turn by Native Americans, Spaniards, Mexicans and Yankees, **New Mexico** is among the most ethnically and culturally diverse of all the United States. Each successive group has built upon the legacy of its predecessors, and their various histories and achievements are closely intertwined. The late-coming white Americans from the north are still outsiders in much of the state, and in many ways their only significant impact on the face of New Mexico has been the strings of motels and fast-food restaurants that line all the main roads. Signs of the region's rich heritage are everywhere, from ancient pictographs and cliff dwellings to the design of the state's license plates, taken from a Zia Indian symbol for the sun – the one near-constant fact of life in this arid land.

New Mexico's indigenous peoples – especially the **Pueblo Indians**, clear inheritors of the city-building Anasazi – provide a sense of cultural continuity. Despite the **Pueblo Revolt** of 1680, which forced a temporary Spanish withdrawal into Mexico, the missionary endeavour here was in general less brutal than elsewhere. The proselytising padres eventually co-opted the natives without destroying their traditional ways of life, incorporating local deities and celebrations into Catholic ritual and practice. Somewhat bizarrely to outsiders, grand churches still stand at the centre of many Pueblo settlements, often adjacent to the kivas, and almost always built in the local adobe style.

The Americans who took over from the Mexicans in 1848 saw New Mexico as a useless wasteland, and left it relatively undisturbed in their eagerness to develop California. In fact, apart from a few mining booms and range wars – such as the so-called Lincoln County War which brought **Billy the Kid** to fame – New Mexico was more or less forgotten until the US finally got around to making it a state in 1912. During World War II, it was the base of operations for the top-secret **Manhattan Project**, which built and detonated the first atomic bomb, and since then America's premier weapons research outposts have been located here. But these activities are the exceptions to the rule, and by and large people here work close to the land, mining, farming and ranching, with tourism increasingly underpinning it all.

Northern New Mexico centres on the Rio Grande Valley, which contains some of the state's most magnificent landscapes, as well as its two finest cities – the artists' colony and winter resort of **Taos**, and **Santa Fe**, the capital. More than a dozen Pueblo villages can be found in the mountainous area between Taos and Santa Fe, while to the west lie the evocative Anasazi ruins at **Bandelier** and **Chaco Canyon**. Places of interest in the rest of the state are further-flung. The broad swath of **central New Mexico**, along the I-40 transcontinental highway – the successor of the old **Route 66** – pivots around the state's biggest city, **Albuquerque**, with the extraordinary mesa-top Pueblo village of **Acoma** ("Sky City"), an hour's drive to the west. The gigantic **Carlsbad Caverns** are the main attraction in wild and wide-open **southern New Mexico**, while here, as all over the state, you can still stumble upon old mining and cattle-ranching towns which have somehow hung on since the end of the Wild West.

Getting Around New Mexico

Public transport is rare in New Mexico; Santa Fe, for example, no longer has a rail service. *Amtrak* **trains** do, however, pass through Albuquerque, pit-stop for transcontinental *Greyhound* **buses** and site of the only major **airport**. Distances are such that **cycling** is viable only for the fittest of riders, and **hitch-hikers** may have to spend a long hard time stranded in the desert sun. A few companies offer guided **coach tours** in the Santa Fe and Taos area, but as usual, getting around is really best done by **car**.

> The telephone **area code** for the entire state of New Mexico is ☎505.

Northern New Mexico

The northern third of New Mexico, high in the sharp peaks of the Sangre de Cristo mountains, is definitely the choicest area on which to focus your attention. Ranging along the headwaters of the Rio Grande, the amiable frontier town of **Taos** was immortalised by Georgia O'Keeffe and D H Lawrence, but is probably best known for the remarkable multi-storey adobe apartments of neighbouring **Taos Pueblo**. Significantly bigger but far less attractive, 75 miles southwest, the state capital **Santa Fe** is the only real city in the region. Even so, with well under 100,000 residents it is hardly metropolitan in scale, and the narrow streets of its small historic centre, though regularly thronged with tourists lured by the high-profile hype, retain the feel of long-gone days.

An hour's drive west from Taos or Santa Fe brings you to **Bandelier National Monument**, where ancient cliff dwellings have been carved out of a volcanic tableland. In the midst of this forested plateau spreads the eerie Los Alamos National Weapons Lab, where much of the US nuclear arsenal is designed. Much further afield, but well worth an extended visit, **Chaco Canyon** holds the remains of one of the largest pre-Columbian cities in North America; the smaller **Aztec Ruins**, near the Colorado border in the north, are more easily accessible.

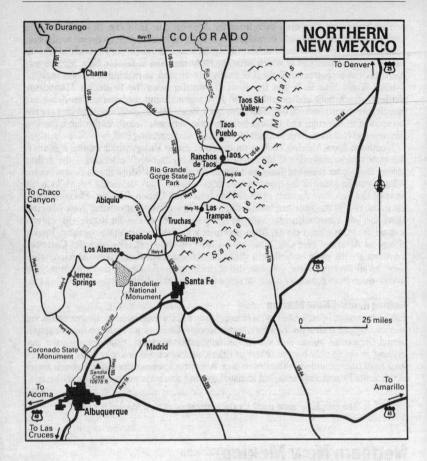

Taos

Part Spanish colonial outpost, part hangout for bohemian artists, and home to the most memorable of the Pueblo Indian villages, tiny **TAOS** has managed to retain its rough-hewn charms despite a constant stream of tourists. This attractively unpretentious town of less than five thousand people is made up of three separate communities: **Taos** itself, around the plaza; **Taos Pueblo** two miles north; and sprawling **Ranchos de Taos** five miles to the south. The landscape in which they stand is stunning, with the pine-forested Sangre de Cristo mountains rising high above dry, sunbleached foothills, undulating along the banks of the Rio Grande. Year-round the sun burns down with the magical New Mexico "light" that artists – and tourist boards – rave about: **Georgia O'Keeffe** did most of her signature desert abstractions around Taos, and spent the last fifty years of her life near Abiquiu, in the Rio Chama Valley forty miles to the west. **D H Lawrence**, who lived here in the 1920s, wrote "there are all kinds of beauty in the world, but for greatness of beauty I have never experienced anything like New Mexico"; a small shrine holding his mortal remains overlooks the upper Rio Grande, twenty miles northwest of town.

Arrival, Information and Getting Around

Greyhound (☎758-1144) arrive in Taos on Hwy-68, a mile south of downtown; *Faust Transportation* (☎758-3410 or ☎1-800/345-3738) run shuttles from Albuquerque airport for $30. Drivers are most likely to come in past the motels along Hwy-68 to the south; keep going, and park near the plaza or at Kit Carson State Park a hundred yards north.

Basic orientation can be had from an **information booth** (☎758-3873) in Taos' leafy and low-key plaza. Walking is the best way to get around the compact town centre, though in summer, the *Pride of Taos* open-air **trolley** ($1) loops around the plaza, Taos Pueblo and Ranchos de Taos, stopping at hotels and motels. Another option is to **rent a bike** from *Taos Trading Post*, 231 Paseo del Pueblo Sur (☎758-4293), two blocks south of the plaza on Hwy-68, or *Native Sons Adventures*, 813A S Hwy-68 (☎758-9342). In winter, **skiers** try their luck on the challenging slopes of the *Taos Ski Valley* resort (lift tickets $32; ☎776-2291) at Wheeler Peak, the highest point in New Mexico.

Taos Plaza

The old Spanish **plaza**, still at the heart of Taos, is now ringed by jewellery shops, art galleries and restaurants; all conform to the rounded brown adobe plaster of the predominant Pueblo motif. Specific sights are few – a small museum ($3) off the elderly lobby of the *La Fonda de Taos* hotel has a collection of sexy but amateurish paintings by D H Lawrence, and the tree-filled square itself is often animated by guitar-toting buskers – but the surrounding streets are perfect for an aimless stroll, and it's easy to spend half a day just mooching around. Some of the best places to eat or drink, as well as a number of top-notch art and crafts galleries, are on **Bent Street**, a block north of the plaza. *Moby Dickens* at no. 124 is a fine bookshop specialising in historic and contemporary Taos. Bent Street takes its name not from any irregularities, but from the first American governor of New Mexico, Charles Bent, whose house has been preserved as a museum of frontier Taotian life (daily 10am–5pm; $1).

Just east of the plaza, across Hwy-68 at the end of Taos' sole surviving stretch of wooden boardwalk, is the dusty but evocative adobe abode where mountain man and part-time US cavalry officer **Kit Carson** (see p.690) lived for some 25 years in the mid-1800s. It's now a rather flavourless museum, filled with saddles, rifles, and Wild West paraphernalia (daily 8am–6pm; $2.50). Two blocks south of the plaza on Ledoux Street, the much-restored 1790 house of artist and collector Ernest L Blumenshein, co-founder of the town's 1920s arts colony, displays paintings and furniture (daily 9am–5pm; $2.50).

Taos Pueblo and the Millicent Rogers Museum

The intact and flourishing community of **Taos Pueblo** is two miles north of the plaza, half a mile off Hwy-68. These multi-storey adobes have been continuously inhabited for some eight hundred years, and the imposing complex is the most impressive Native American structure still in use. Its 250 full-time residents have made few concessions to the modern world, living without toilets, running water, or electricity (although many others choose to live in newer homes nearby). For most of the year, their daily life continues with scant regard for the intrusion of tourists, but the pueblo is capable of putting on a spectacular show for its feast days and dances. These are held regularly throughout the summer; the biggest parties are the **Corn Dances** in June and July and the **Feast of San Gerónimo** at the end of September, when hundreds and even thousands of outsiders flock to join the general revelry. The pueblo governors regulate visitors; there's a $5 fee per car, and photography permits are $10 extra.

Two miles north of Taos Pueblo on Hwy-68, the **Millicent Rogers Museum** (summer daily 9am–5pm, otherwise Wed–Sun 10am–4pm; $3) shows off one of New Mexico's foremost collections of high-quality craftworks. Objects on display range from pre-Columbian Zuni and Hopi pottery to contemporary black-on-black pieces by noted Pueblo potter Maria Martinez, and beautiful Navajo blankets. Some of the most affecting exhibits trace the development of Spanish Colonial religious art in the heathen New World; the highlight is a seventeenth-century "Death Cart", in which a skeleton holding a bow-and-arrow rides in the back of an ornate funeral carriage.

Ranchos de Taos

Spreading south from the central plaza area, to either side of Hwy-68, the **Ranchos de Taos** were once the farms that fed the townspeople of Taos. Each rancho had its own main house, or hacienda; one has been restored as a museum of colonial life. The **Martinez Hacienda** (daily 9am–5pm; $2), two miles southwest of the plaza on Ranchitos Road, was built in 1804 by an early mayor of Taos. Two dozen thickly walled adobe rooms are wrapped around lushly landscaped patios and furnished to recreate the typical family home of landed Spanish gentry.

The massively buttressed adobe church of **San Francisco de Asis** turns its back to the passing traffic four miles south of the plaza on Hwy-68. It is one of colonial New Mexico's most splendid architectural achievements, with subtly rounded walls and corners disguising the underlying structural strength. The church was one of painter Georgia O'Keeffe's favourite subjects, but the neighbouring buildings – such as an old barn converted into a drive-through taco stand and liquor store – do little to enhance its situation. Once inside, however, there's a marvellously ornate reredos amidst the typically overwrought clutter of devotional objects and artworks.

Accommodation

Taos has accommodation to meet all needs. Three clean and pleasant **hostels** provide bare-bones bunks or simple rooms; a handful of anodyne **motels** line Hwy-68. For a few dollars more, you can avail yourself of atmospheric **B&B** inns or luxury hotels.

Abominable Snowmansion Hostel, in the mountains near Taos Ski Valley (☎776-8298). Dorm beds $12.50 a night, private rooms from $25; prices double during ski season.

Highlands-Taos International Hostel, on Hwy-64 two miles north of town (☎758-5537 or ☎758-1651). An easy walk to Taos Pueblo. Dorm beds for $12.50 a night, private rooms from $25.

Koshari Inn, off Kit Carson Road (☎758-7199). Inexpensive ($35 for a double room) and hospitable accommodations on the east side of town.

Mabel Dodge Luhan House, Morada Lane (☎758-9456). Good value and characterful rooms.

Plum Tree Hostel (☎758-4696). On Hwy-68 near Rio Grande Gorge State Park, 15 miles south of Taos, with dorm beds $12.50 a night and private rooms from $35.

Taos Super 8 Motel, 1347 S Hwy 68 (☎758-1088). Cheapest among the franchise motels lining Hwy-68 south of town, with doubles from $35 a night.

Taos Inn, 125 Paseo del Pueblo Norte (☎758-2233). Central Taos landmark, with the nicest rooms in town; doubles from $65 to well over $100. Their *Doc Martins* restaurant (no relation to the English bootmakers), serves expensive, immaculate grilled meats and other New Mexican favourites, while the *Adobe Bar* is a congenial drinking spot, with a huge roaring fire and free live music most nights.

Eating, Drinking and Nightlife

Taos is too small to have much nightlife, but for eating it caters to all tastes and budgets. Look out for the itinerant catering trucks which roam the streets, particularly along Hwy-68 south of the plaza, selling top-rate tacos, burritos and burgers.

Apple Tree Restaurant, 123 Bent Street (☎758-1900). Good, cheap Mexican and international food.

Bent Street Deli & Cafe, 120 Bent Street (☎758-5787). Just off the plaza. Airy, partly outdoor place for cheap breakfasts and lunches. A variety of Mexican food and two dozen sorts of sandwiches.

El Pueblo Cafe, north of the plaza at 625 Hwy-64 (☎758-2053). Near the turnoff for Taos Pueblo, a roadside shed that always draws crowds for its round-the-clock diner food.

Floyd's Lounge, 819 S Hwy-68 (☎758-4142). Scruffy bar; regular live bands and no frills.

Stakeout Grill and Bar, Outlaw Hill off Hwy-68. Well-hidden, unpretentious, and very popular restaurant in a truly stunning setting. Very big – and very good value – steak dinners. Only accessible by car; head four-plus miles south from Taos then climb east up a dirt track.

THE PUEBLOS AND THE PENITENTES

Two distinctive but interrelated groups, the native **Pueblo Indians** and the descendants of the early Spanish colonists, have together contributed much to the unique culture of northern New Mexico. At first, the people we now call Pueblo Indians welcomed the Spanish, but they soon came to resent the imposition of Catholicism and the virtual enslavement of Pueblo labourers. In the **Pueblo Revolt** of 1680, the various tribes banded together and ousted the entire colonial regime, killing scores of priests and soldiers and sending hundreds more south to Mexico. However, after the Spanish returned in 1693 the Pueblos showed little further resistance, and have co-existed surprisingly amicably ever since, accepting aspects of Catholicism – most pueblos have a large adobe church at the core – without giving up their traditional beliefs and practices.

All the pueblos, of which a dozen lie within an hour's drive of Taos or Santa Fe, have been modernised to some extent, but all proudly retain the "Old Ways". Saints' days, and even the Fourth of July, are celebrated with a strange combination of native traditions and Catholic rituals, featuring elaborately costumed dances and massive communal feasts. The most impressive – and most touristed – of the pueblos is at **Taos**, but many of the less well known ones are as worthwhile to visit, particularly if you're interested in the renowned Pueblo arts and crafts, especially fine pottery. At each pueblo, visitors are required to **register** at a visitor centre, and pay a fee, usually $3 to $5 to park plus $5 for a camera permit, but there's no extra charge for feast days or dances. Always behave respectfully when visiting – don't go "exploring" places which are off limits to visitors, such as shrines, kivas or private homes.

Among the more visitable of the pueblos are:

San Ildefonso Pueblo (☎455-2273), fifteen miles north of Santa Fe just west of US-84. The best museum, with exhibits of excellent black pottery, including museum-worthy pieces by Maria Martinez and Popvi Da which fetch thousands of dollars each. Main festivities include the large festival of Pueblo arts and crafts, held every July.

San Felipe Pueblo (☎867-3382), off I-25 ten miles north of Bernalillo along the banks of the Rio Grande. Scene of the renowned ceremonial Corn Dances on May 1.

Santa Clara Pueblo (☎753-7326), on Hwy-30 one mile west of Española. Not only some very fine pottery, but also the Puye Cliff Dwellings, an extensive (750-room) pre-Columbian ruin hollowed out of the cliffs above the village.

Nambe Pueblo (☎455-2036), thirty miles north of Santa Fe, then three miles east on Hwy-503. Among the most beautifully sited of the pueblos, which celebrates the Fourth of July with a staged ceremonial dance at the foot of cascading Nambe Falls.

The High Route

One of the most satisfying tours of the Pueblo region continues past Nambe Pueblo along what's known as "The High Route" between Santa Fe and Taos, taking you high into the pines and aspens of the Sangre de Christo Mountains, and passing by a number of pueblos as well as dozens of timeless devoutly Catholic villages still occupied by direct descendants of the Spaniards.

Chimayo, at the junction of Hwy-503 and Hwy-76 east of Española, holds one of New Mexico's best restaurants (see p.654) as well as its most famous Spanish colonial church, the 1816 adobe **Sanctuario de Chimayo**, a squat, twin-towered chapel, set behind an enclosed courtyard and filled with a mind-boggling array of devotional objects. A smaller chapel, facing the Sanctuario across a gravelled carpark, contains a small statue of *Santo Niño*, the Lost Child, to whom expectant mothers bring offerings such as tiny pairs of shoes. Higher up in the mountains, in the quiet hamlet of **Las Trampas**, another powerfully evocative adobe church, **San Jose de Garcia**, stands stern and imposing above the highway. If it's closed, ask for the caretaker in the small store opposite.

The surrounding hills, dotted with isolated, tin-roofed shacks and barns, are said to be the heartland of the secretive **Penitentes**, fanatical Catholics who, during Lent, form dawn processions along the ridges, flagellating themselves with yucca whips while chanting prayers.

Santa Fe

During the 1980s **SANTA FE** was the most stylish place in the US to be and be seen. What was once an honourable and well-meaning campaign to preserve the town's unique blend of Native American and Spanish traditions had grown into a frenzied promotion of Santa Fe chic, with upwards of a million and a half tourists every year descending upon the city of 65,000 residents. New hotels were built, old ones upgraded, and smart boutiques and art galleries that previously had branches only in New York or LA opened up outlets in Santa Fe, replacing hardware stores with international couture. But the early 1990s see a different Santa Fe; many of the shops and galleries that sprang up during the tourist boom have now gone, and Santa Feans at last have a chance to rediscover what it was people liked about their town.

And there is a lot to like about Santa Fe. In 1609, ten years before the Pilgrim Fathers arrived at Plymouth Rock, **Spanish missionaries** established Santa Fe as the northernmost capital of their colonial empire. It has been the capital of New Mexico ever since, and the adobe houses and baroque churches they laid out at the foot of the mountains survive fairly intact under the surface glitz of the modern American city.

The old central **plaza** is still the focus of town life – especially during the annual **Indian Market** on the third weekend in August, when buyers and craftspeople come from all over the world, and during the Labor Day weekend for the **Fiesta de Santa Fe** – but apart from an influx of art galleries and stylish restaurants, the web of narrow streets around it has changed little in the intervening years. Although when the Yankees took over in 1848 they neglected the adobes and chose to build in wood, many of the finer houses were saved, thanks in part to a 1930s campaign to promote respect for the region's Hispanic and Native American heritage. Since then almost every non-adobe structure within sight of the plaza, even the downtown *Woolworth's*, has been designed or redecorated to suit the city-mandated Spanish Revival mode, with oddly canted, rounded mud-coloured plaster walls supporting roof beams made of thick pine logs (called *vigas*). Santa Fe today, in fact – at least at its core – looks much more like its original Spanish self than it did a hundred years ago.

Arrival and Getting Around

For all its fame, Santa Fe is surprisingly far off the beaten path. There's no rail link, despite having the *Atcheson, Topeka and Santa Fe Railroad* named after it – *Amtrak* **trains** stop once a day in the town of **Lamy**, fifteen miles away, to be met by connecting buses – and the airport is served only by small commuter planes. The nearest major airport is at Albuquerque, an hour's drive away. *Shuttle Jack* (☎243-3244 or ☎982-4311) run **buses** from Albuquerque, and *Greyhound* has regular service from all over the Southwest to a terminal just south of the plaza at 858 St Michaels Drive (☎471-0008). If you **drive** in on I-25, you have to negotiate your way through a long sprawl of motels and fast-food restaurants to reach the centre of town.

It's just as well that almost everything to see in Santa Fe is within walking distance of the central plaza, because since 1990 there's been no public transport. However, coupons obtainable at the downtown public library on Washington Street, across from the Palace of the Governors, save fifty percent on **taxis** (☎989-1221 or ☎988-2090).

The **Santa Fe CVB** (Mon–Fri 9am-5pm; ☎984-6760 or ☎1-800/777-CITY), two blocks from the plaza at 201 W Marcy Street, has the usual ad-packed information.

The Plaza

One of the main models for Santa Fe's revived architectural unity fills the entire northern side of the plaza. The **Palace of the Governors** (daily 10am–5pm) is a low-slung, originally sod-roofed structure constructed in 1610 as the headquarters of Spanish colonial administration. The name is misleadingly grand for this humble edifice, but it's the oldest public building in the US, and makes the best first stop on a tour of Santa Fe. The arcaded adobe veranda along its front serves as a shaded market for local Indian crafts-sellers, and the well-preserved interior, organised around an open-air courtyard, houses part of the worthwhile **Museum of New Mexico**, most of which is clustered together a mile to the southeast. A two-day pass to all parts of the museum costs $5; each individual section costs $3.

On the plaza's northwest corner, and also part of the Museum of New Mexico, the **Museum of Fine Arts** (daily 10am–5pm) is one of the few major art museums to be started by artists, as opposed to educators or collectors, and focuses on painting and sculpture by mostly local artists. Many of the **Georgia O'Keeffe** paintings come from the artist's own collection, in her home and studio near Abiquiu, forty miles northwest.

The Churches of Santa Fe

After the plaza area, the most attractive corner of central Santa Fe is across the river, three blocks to the southwest along Guadalupe Street around the small but beautiful **Sanctuario de Guadalupe** (daily 9am–4pm; donations). Built at the end of the eighteenth century and recently restored, with a fine Baroque reredos, the shrine during Spanish and Mexican times marked the end of Camino Real highway from Mexico City. The surrounding neighbourhood was later to become the main point of arrival into Santa Fe for trains on the Denver and Rio Grande railroad. Old warehouses and small factory premises nearby, like the **Sanbusco Center** on Montezuma Avenue, have recently been converted to house boutiques, art galleries and restaurants.

If you follow the tiny Santa Fe River upstream, or walk two blocks east from the plaza, you approach a strange building looming at the top of San Francisco Street. **St Francis Cathedral**, the first church west of the Mississippi to be designated a cathedral, was built in 1869 by **Archbishop Lamy**. The French-educated Lamy, the title figure in Willa Cather's novel *Death Comes for the Archbishop*, had the building designed along elevated European lines, and it looks very out of place among Santa Fe's earthy adobes. Another nearby church, the **Chapel of Loretto**, a block away at the start of Old Santa Fe Trail, is known for its so-called Miraculous Staircase, built without nails or obvious means of support. During construction, the church's designer is said to have been killed by Lamy's cousin, and for years there was no way up to the choir loft. Then an unknown carpenter arrived, built the stairs, and disappeared.

Two blocks south, across the river along the Old Santa Fe Trail, is the ancient **San Miguel Chapel**. Only a few of the massive adobe internal walls survive from the original 1610 building, most of which was destroyed in the 1680 Pueblo Revolt. The chapel is the heart of the old *Barrio de Analco* workers' district, whose many 200-year-old houses now form one of Santa Fe's most appealing residential neighbourhoods.

The New Mexico State Museums

East of central Santa Fe, gallery-lined **Canyon Road** – which stakes a claim to being the oldest street in the US, dating from Pueblo days – heads up a steady but shallow incline along the river bed lined by dozens more fine adobes. A mile south along Camino del Monte Sol, on Camino Lejo two miles southeast from the central plaza, is Santa Fe's other concentration of museums. The main attraction here, the third part of the New Mexico Museum quartet, is the **Museum of International Folk Art** (daily 10am–5pm), which holds an astonishingly diverse range of artefacts from all corners of the globe – and sells many of them in its gift shop. One huge room contains detailed and colourful dioramas depicting life in virtually any country you might care to think of, while the recently opened Hispanic Heritage Wing is an engaging reminder of just how close New Mexico's ties have always been with Mexico itself. The **Museum of Indian Arts and Culture**, fourth of the four, sets out to provide insight into the ways of life followed by New Mexico's various Native American tribes – but is not as successful as the Indian Pueblo Cultural Center in Albuquerque (see p.660). The larger, private **Wheelwright Museum of the American Indian** (Mon–Sat 10am–5pm, Sun 1–5pm; $2 donation), designed to look like a Navajo hogan, stands behind the folk art museum. Its carefully chosen Anasazi ceramics in particular are quite exquisite.

Accommodation

Places to **stay** in Santa Fe don't come cheap, especially not during the peak summer months, when every bed in town can seem to be taken. **Cerrillos Road** (US-85), the main road into Santa Fe from I-25, holds most of the town's **motels** and its one **hostel**. Everything gets more expensive as you approach the centre, though **B&Bs** are an attractive alternative to the overpriced hotels around the plaza. If you get stuck, phone the CVB's **accommodations hotline** (daily 4pm–10pm; ☎986-0043 or ☎988-4252) or commercial agency *Santa Fe Central Reservations* (☎983-8200 or ☎1-800/982-7669).

Budget Inn, 725 Cerrillos Road (☎982-5952). The closest in of the chain motels. Doubles from $35.

El Paradero, 220 W Manhattan Ave (☎988-1177). Near the Guadalupe Street restaurant district, with B&B doubles from $65–125.

El Rey Inn, 1862 Cerrillos Road (☎982-1931). Most characterful and best value of the Cerrillos Road motels, and surprisingly stylish, with doubles from $45.

Grant Corner Inn, 122 Grant Ave (☎983-6678). Considerable luxury, and great breakfasts, just two blocks from the plaza. From $75.

Howard Johnson's, 4048 Cerrillos Road (☎473-4646). Spacious motel; fairly plush rooms from $60.

Santa Fe International AYH Hostel, 1412 Cerrillos Road (☎988-1153). Under a mile from the plaza, this is the cheapest place in town, with dorm beds for $11 and private rooms for $25.

Eating

Santa Fe has been one of America's culinary hotspots for at least the last decade, rivalling California Cuisine. Many of the newer restaurants will put a sizeable hole in your wallet, but you needn't break the bank to get a good meal. Some of the best places are collected along Guadalupe Street, five minutes' walk from the plaza.

Coyote Cafe, 132 W Water St (☎983-1615). Super-trendy, money's-no-object restaurant just off the plaza. Its open kitchen puts out delicious grilled meats and other trademarks of so-called "New New Mexican" cuisine; if you just want a taste, there's a cheaper rooftop bar and cafe upstairs.

Guadalupe Cafe, 313 Guadalupe St (☎982-9762). Central, good-value meals throughout the day.

Restaurante Rancho de Chimayo, Hwy-503, Chimayo (☎984-2100). The best traditional New Mexican restaurant around, in a quaint mountain village 25 miles north of Santa Fe (described in the box on p.651). Superb *flautas* and a mouthwatering *sopapilla* stuffed with meat and chilis in a gorgeous rambling adobe ranch house or, in summer, on a lovely sun-drenched outdoor patio.

Tecolote Cafe, 1203 Cerrillos Road (☎988-1362). Inconspicuous joint, a little way out from the centre. Its magnificent breakfasts (burritos, creamy eggs benedict) make a perfect start to the day.

Tomasita's, 500 Guadalupe St (☎983-5721), Another lively, unpretentious place, cranking out plate-fuls of tasty Mexican food, plus margaritas by the litre, inside the old railroad station.

Zia's, 326 Guadalupe St (☎988-7008). Flashy, high-tech diner. All American meats and fish dishes.

Nightlife and Entertainment

The CVB can give details about the well-respected *Santa Fe Opera* and the various local music and arts festivals, while the *Cinematheque*, in the Center for Contemporary Art, 291 Barcelona (☎982-1338), shows the most interesting films in New Mexico. Check the free weekly *Reporter* or the *Pasatiempo* section of the Friday *New Mexican* paper for up-to-date **listings**.

All the town's hotels and restaurants have their own **bars**, but straight drinking places are surprisingly few and far between. *Evangelo's*, 200 W San Francisco Street, is the only good bare-bones bar near the plaza, with a pool table and a jukebox. *Mr Rs*, 2911 Cerrillos Road (473-4138), puts on non-stop country music every night, and *Club West*, 213 W Alameda Street (☎982-0099), has live reggae, blues and bluegrass.

Bandelier National Monument

Cut into the forested mesas of the Pajarito Plateau, 35 miles northwest of Santa Fe, the **cliff dwellings** and Anasazi ruins of **BANDELIER NATIONAL MONUMENT** ($5 per car) are spread across fifty square miles of pine woods and deep stream-cut gorges. However, all its most important features are concentrated along a paved, mile-long loop trail through **Frijoles Canyon**, off Hwy-4 at the end of a narrow switchbacking road (which often gets congested in summer). The **visitor centre** at the start of the trail gives an excellent overview of the site, with displays of pottery and jewellery, models of the ruins, full-scale reconstructions of pueblo interiors and fascinating photographs of local Indian life at the turn of the century.

The ancient settlement at Bandelier – named for the amateur archaeologist Adolph Bandelier, who first publicised the place in the 1880s – dates from the very end of the Anasazi period (see p.657). It is thought that some time around 1300 AD various itinerant groups of Anasazi and other tribes, seeking sanctuary from drought and invasion, gathered here to build a community which amalgamated their assorted cultures. Quite possibly, the people of Bandelier were the direct ancestors of today's Pueblo Indians.

The first stop along the trail is the remains of **Tyuonyi**, a circular, multistoreyed village of some 400 rooms, of which only the ground floor and foundations survive. A side path leads up to dozens of **cave dwellings**, their rounded chambers scooped out of the soft volcanic rock; you can scramble up to, and even enter, some of them, to peer out across the valley. The main trail continues to the **Long House**, an 800-foot series of two- and three-storey houses built side by side against the canyon wall. Though most of the upper storeys have collapsed, you can still see the morticed holes that held up the roof beams; above these are rows of carved petroglyphs, mostly figures and abstract symbols. Half a mile beyond that, along the stream up the canyon, a reconstructed kiva sits in **Ceremonial Cave**, protected by a rock overhang 150 feet above the canyon floor. To reach it you have to climb a succession of rickety ladders and steep stairs cut into the crumbly rock – not for the faint-hearted.

Much less visited than Frijoles Canyon is the **wilderness** of the rest of the monument, open to more energetic hikers. A trail south of the visitor centre comes out after one and a half miles at the **Lower Falls**, at their best in late spring, and then carries on another ten minutes to the Rio Grande. Other routes lead to the **Stone Lions Shrine** and the **Painted Cave**; for all these, you need a (free) permit from the visitor centre. As well as backcountry sites, there's a very nice **campground** on Frijoles Mesa, just beyond the Hwy-4 turnoff, a half-hour hike up the Frey Trail from Frijoles Canyon.

Grayline run half-day **coach tours** to Bandelier from Santa Fe ($30; ☎983-9491), though you may well find that they don't allow you as much time here as you'd like.

Los Alamos

If you approach Bandelier from the east, you'll pass **Los Alamos National Laboratory**, the main US center for the research and development of **nuclear weapons** (as well as neurobiology, computer science, and solar and geothermal energy). Virtually all the work at this, one of the foremost scientific research establishments in the world, is military-based, and consequently most of the complex is off-limits – the small and over-simplified **Bradbury Science Museum** (Tues–Fri 9am–5pm, Sat–Mon 1–5pm; free) is the only part you can visit. What's both remarkable and unnerving about the place is that the people who work here seem oblivious to the fact that not every everybody has learned to love the Bomb. The local radio station (106.7FM – great Fifties' tunes) is called *KBOM*, and museum guides glow with excitement as they describe their weapons' devastating power. Judging by the visitors register, a sizeable percentage of visitors come here as a sort of pilgrimage from Hiroshima and Nagasaki.

Jemez Springs

The countryside to the west of Bandelier provides an unexpectedly lush counterpoint to the dry-as-dust terrain of most of New Mexico. Hwy-4 circles beyond Los Alamos through the gorgeous pinewoods and wide meadows of the **Jemez Mountains**, passing along the edge of the broad green expanse of **Valle Grande**. The geological forces which created this now-extinct volcanic caldera are responsible for numerous local **hot springs** that bubble up from underground at a sybaritically soothing 120°-plus.

Thirty miles from Bandelier, the tiny roadside hamlet of **JEMEZ SPRINGS** can offer a **hostel**-cum-B&B, the *Canyon Quarters* (☎829-3584), and good **food** at the *Chile Bowl Cafe and Motel* (☎829-3692) and *Los Ojos Restaurant and Saloon* (☎829-3547), complete with pool tables and cheap beers till 2am. The small Jemez State Monument ($2) protects the remains of **Jemez Pueblo**, one of the last holdouts against the colonial Spanish, half a mile north of the village, but the most appealing reasons to pass this way are further north along the lovely Jemez River. Just over five miles from the village, at the foot of the aptly named **Battleship Rock**, there's a fifty-foot-long pool of steaming clear water; a couple of miles further on, on a hillside promontory between mileposts 24 and 25, **Spence's Hot Spring** has to be one of the most beautifully sited natural springs in North America. At sunset especially it's irresistible. Half a dozen waterfall-connected pools provide a range of temperatures to suit any body, from the high 90s in the lower pools to a blissful 104° at the top; local custom calls for bathing suits on weekend nights, otherwise it's clothing optional. To get there cross the river over a fallen tree and then climb up the canyon, keeping to the left for about ten minutes' walk uphill.

Chaco Canyon

Protected by the US government as the Chaco Culture National Historic Park, the hundreds of **Anasazi ruins** dotted around **CHACO CANYON** include the remains of what's generally considered to be the **largest pre-Columbian city** in North America. To archaeologists, Chaco is the greatest architectural achievement of the Anasazi people. Enough is still standing to take your breath away, although scattered over 35 square miles of scrubby high-desert plains, the buildings are not as immediately striking or photogenic as those at Mesa Verde or Canyon de Chelly, and their isolation – two hours' drive from the nearest paved road, and without food or lodging – makes them the least visited of all the major Anasazi sites.

The park **visitor centre** (daily, summer 8am–6pm, otherwise 8am–5pm; ☎988-6727) is at the east end of Chaco Canyon. From there, an eight-mile paved road loops to the west around a circuit of the principal structures.The biggest and most intriguing of the lot, **Pueblo Bonito**, was during the eleventh century home to around a thousand people, and was the central focus for a much larger economic and political community of perhaps five thousand more, spread over the southern Colorado Plateau. Today the finely dressed stone walls and doorways of the semi-circular compound only hint at the former grandeur of this huge multistoreyed complex; a trail guide (50¢) explains the history and construction techniques, leading you through basement rooms into the two central courtyards, and the **great kivas** which were its religious and social focal point.

The smaller complex of **Chetro Ketl**, quarter of a mile to the east, was built slightly after Pueblo Bonito. It shows Chaco-style masonry construction at its most sophisticated, with horizontal rows of large, squared-off stones chinked with smaller, flatter stones and set into a bed of adobe mortar. Another sign of the Chacoans' engineering capabilities is the extensive system of **stone-built causeways** that reach out across the mesa tops to some 75 outlying communities, including one that stretched all the way to Aztec Ruins, 45 miles north (see below). All in all over four hundred miles of arrow-straight roads, averaging thirty feet in width, have been uncovered around the

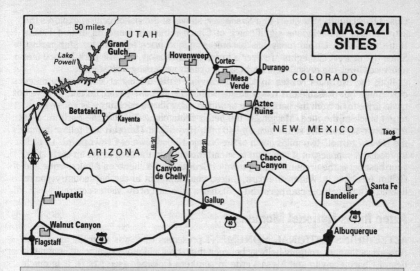

Few foreign visitors to the Southwest are prepared for the awesome scale and beauty of the desert cities and cliff palaces left by the ancient **Anasazi**. Signs of their civilization are to be found all over the high plateaus of what is now the **"Four Corners"** district, around the meeting point of the states of Colorado, New Mexico, Arizona and Utah.

The earliest humans reached the Southwest around 10,000 BC; the Anasazi made their first appearance as the **Basketmakers**, near the San Juan River, at about the time of Christ. Named for their woven sandals and bowls, they lived in pits in the earth, roofed with logs and mud. Over the course of a thousand years, the Anasazi adopted an increasingly settled lifestyle, becoming expert farmers and potters. Their first free-standing houses on the plains were followed by multistoreyed **pueblos**, in which hundreds of families lived in complexes of contiguous "apartments". The astonishing **cliff dwellings**, perched on precarious ledges high above remote canyons, which they began to build around 1100 AD, are an indication that things were going wrong; these were the first Anasazi settlements to show signs of defensive fortifications. A severe drought towards the end of the thirteenth century made competition for scarce resources even fiercer, as aggressors moved into the area. At this point the Anasazi disappear from history; it is thought that they moved eastwards and joined forces with other displaced groups in a coming-together which eventually produced the modern **Pueblo Indians**.

Among the most significant **Anasazi sites**, in the order they appear in this book, are:

Mesa Verde. Magnificent cliff palaces, high in the canyons of Colorado. See p.611.

Bandelier National Monument. Large riverside pueblos, and cave-like homes hollowed from volcanic rock. See p.655.

Chaco Canyon. The largest and most sophisticated free-standing pueblos far out in the desert. See p.656.

Aztec Ruins. Accessible ancient pueblo, notable for restored great kiva. See p.658.

Wupatki. Several small pueblo communities, built by assorted tribal groups. See p.682.

Walnut Canyon. Numerous canyon-wall houses above lush Walnut Creek. See p.682.

Canyon de Chelly. Superbly dramatic cliff dwellings in glowing sandstone canyon; now owned and farmed by the Navajo. See p.690.

Betatakin. Canyon-side community set in a vast rocky alcove in the Navajo National Monument. See p.694.

Grand Gulch Primitive Area. Barely explored ruins in the wilderness. See p.715.

Hovenweep. Enigmatic towers poised high above a canyon. See p.716.

Chaco backcountry; the short film *Sundagger*, shown at the visitor centre, explores the astronomical and religious significance of Chaco remnants found on distant Fajada Butte. Ironically, Chaco today has become a unique place to come for **star-gazing**. Since the nearest city lights are over a hundred miles away, and the park is 6000 feet above sea level, the crystal-clear night sky is usually swimming with stars.

Both the two main **routes to Chaco Canyon** entail driving at least twenty miles over rough but passable dirt roads. Roads within the park are paved; do not, however, try to drive to or from the park during or within a day after a rainstorm, as you're likely to get stuck in the mud. Marginally the better route comes in from the north or east from Hwy-44; from the south turn off I-40 onto Hwy-371 at **Thoreau** and follow it until the Hwy-57 turnoff, two miles north of the Navajo Nation town of **Crownpoint**. To pick up food and supplies, or if you want to spend the night in the area to get an early start, your best bet is the uranium mining town of **Grants**, on I-40 between Albuquerque and Gallup (see p.663). Within the park, unless you camp out in the backcountry you're limited to a fairly basic **campground** ($6), half a mile east of the visitor centre.

Aztec Ruins National Monument

AZTEC RUINS NATIONAL MONUMENT preserves what was basically an outlyer Anasazi settlement, roughly halfway between the larger and more significant communities of Chaco Canyon and Mesa Verde in southern Colorado (see p.657). It is much more accessible than Chaco, lying just off US-550. The main structure (misnamed Aztec by pioneer Americans) was an E-shaped compound of some 500 rooms; unlike other sites the **great kiva** here has been rebuilt and can be entered. Always circular in shape – modelled on the ancient pit-houses even when built above ground – kivas were strictly male preserves, often augmented by secret passageways so priests, and mysterious voices, could emerge from unexpected directions. Similarities between such kivas and modern Hopi practices are one reason for regarding the Hopi as descendants of the Anasazi. The nearby **visitor centre** (daily 8am–6.30pm) has a good range of Anasazi artefacts, and rangers lead walking tours of the ruins throughout the day.

In the town of **AZTEC**, you can grab an early breakfast or a steak dinner at the hearty *Aztec Restaurant*, 107 Aztec Boulevard (☎334-9586); rooms can be had at the $35-a-night *Enchantment Lodge*, 1800 W Aztec Boulevard (☎334-6143), or the cheaper *El Aztec Motel*, 221 S Main Street (☎334-6300).

Albuquerque and Central New Mexico

Little in central **New Mexico** can rival the attractions of the rest of the state. No Carlsbad Caverns draw in the tourists (see p.664), and no town has anything like the fashionable cachet of Taos or Santa Fe. Although to most travellers it's an area to be got through as quickly as possible, it does hold isolated pockets of interest, along with its scenery. Dozens of all-American small towns hang on to the last remnants of **Route 66**, the winding old "Chicago-to-LA" transcontinental highway which has by and large been bypassed by high-speed Interstate 40.

Albuquerque – far and away New Mexico's largest city, with a third of the state's population – sits pretty much dead centre, at the intersection of I-40 and I-25, the main north–south and east–west interstate highways. It's also a main stop on the *Amtrak* and *Greyhound* routes, and holds New Mexico's only major **airport**, so you're likely to find yourself here, if only on the way somewhere else.

The area **east of Albuquerque**, stretching along the I-40 corridor towards Texas, is among the most desolate parts of the Southwest, flat and dry and nearly devoid of interest to the casual traveller. One or two towns have enough of a claim to fame to deserve a quick detour off the Interstate, mostly due to some **Wild West** hero who passed through – Kit Carson and Billy the Kid, to name two. The mountainous region to the **west of Albuquerque** has more to see – not only **Acoma Pueblo**, the mesa-top community known as "Sky City" for its incredible position on a 500-foot-high desert tableland, but also the volcanic badlands of **El Malpais National Monument**.

East of Albuquerque: Tucumcari, Clovis and Fort Sumner

TUCUMCARI, the biggest town between Albuquerque and Amarillo, Texas, is typical of the eastern half of central New Mexico. Its long line of truckstops, diners, and motels have made it a favourite I-40 pit-stop, immortalised by Lowell George and Little Feat in the trucker's anthem *Willin'*, and by Frank Zappa in the movie *200 Motels*. At night, its neon signs rival the best of Las Vegas. During the day you can while away an hour at the mind-bogglingly bizarre Tucumcari Historical Research Institute Museum at 416 S Adams Street (Tues–Sat 9am–5pm, Sun 1-5pm; $2), which boasts one of the world's greatest collections of **barbed wire**. On a more practical level, *Greyhound* stops at 118 E Center Street (☎461-1350). If you want a bite to **eat**, *El Toro Cafe* makes a mean burrito at 107 S First Street (461-3328), or take your pick from any of a dozen burger joints and 24-hour coffee shops. The cheapest **rooms** are at the $18-a-night *Buckaroo Motel*, 1315 W Tucumcari (☎461-1650), or choose from the 2000-odd others lining this stretch of old Route 66.

CLOVIS, 85 miles southeast of Tucumcari on the Texas border, has twice shifted human history in its tracks. Once was at the very dawn of time; skeletons of hunters found here alongside mammoth and giant bison are the first known signs of a human presence in the Southwest. Just 12,000 years later, a bespectacled teenager, **Charles "Buddy" Holly**, nipped across from nearby Lubbock, Texas (see p.526) to record a few tunes with his band, the Crickets – *Peggy Sue*, *That'll Be the Day* and a dozen others. Norman Petty's small studios, which also gave Roy Orbison his first break, are now a museum, open irregular hours (☎763-3435). The midsized railroad and ranching community of Clovis, meanwhile, has lapsed into another 12,000-year slumber.

FORT SUMNER, sixty miles west of Clovis and 45 miles south of I-40, means different things to different people. To the Navajo, Fort Sumner was where frontiersman and US Army colonel **Kit Carson** dragged them to in 1864 after destroying their orchards and burning their villages in Arizona (see p.690). To Wild West fanatics, Fort Sumner is a pilgrimage spot because it holds the grave of legendary outlaw **Billy the Kid**, gunned down here by Pat Garrett in 1881. Both tales are told in the small **Fort Sumner Museum** (daily 9am–5pm; $2), two miles east of town on US-60, behind which a steel cage protects the tombstone of Billy the Kid from would-be memento seekers; a brass plaque nearby is all that marks the site of the vanished Army outpost.

Albuquerque

ALBUQUERQUE is the fastest-growing city in New Mexico, with a population of half a million, but it's not among the state's most attractive corners. Sprawling, disjointed and in places intimidating, it feels more like an overgrown highway town than the economic engine it really is. The recent spate of construction downtown has done little to focus or encourage civic pride, and there's still little to detain you more than a day at the outside. Which isn't to say there's nothing to see: the **Old Town** area retains its **Spanish plaza** intact, and the excellent **Indian Pueblo Cultural Center** is close at hand. Every October Albuquerque hosts the nation's largest **hot-air balloon** rally, attracting upwards of 100,000 people to its mass ascensions, and all year enjoyable day trips can take you up 10,000ft **Sandia Peak** for a stunning sunset view, or south to the ancient pueblos of **Salinas National Monument**.

Arrival and Information

As the only major airport for hundreds of miles, Albuquerque's **International Airport**, two miles south of the city centre, may well be your point of arrival in the Southwest. You can reach downtown via *Sun Tran* **buses** (60¢), or *Yellow Cab* (☎247-8888) and *Checker Cab* (☎243-7777) **taxis** (about $4). *Amtrak* **trains** (one daily from east and west) arrive at a small station behind the modern *Greyhound* terminal, 300 Second Street SW (☎247-3495), which has good-sized left-luggage lockers. Both terminals are in an otherwise abandoned area, five easy minutes' walk south of downtown.

A useful free listings-packed magazine, *The Art of Visiting Albuquerque*, is available from the main **tourist office** downtown at 121 Tijeras Street NE (Mon–Fri 8am–5pm; ☎243-3696 or ☎1-800/284-2282), or from the Old Town booth (Mon–Sat 10am–5pm, Sun 11am–5pm) opposite the west side of the plaza.

Old Town

Once you've cruised up and down **Central Avenue**, looking at the flashing neon and 1940s architecture of this twenty-mile stretch of Route 66 (regular *Sun Tran* buses do it all day for 60¢), most of what's interesting about Albuquerque is concentrated in **Old Town**, the recently tidied-up old Spanish heart of the city. The tree-filled **main plaza** is overlooked by the twin-towered adobe facade of **San Felipe de Neri church**, and circled by horse-drawn carriages that you can hop on for a short tour ($3). It's a very pleasant place to wander or have a meal, even if there's not a whole lot to do. One of the more bizarre of the many knick-knacky shops is the *Rattlesnake Museum* west of the plaza, with live rattlers on display (and rattlesnake curios on sale); also nearby is *Gus' Trading Post*, at 2026 Central Avenue, one of the best-value shops in the entire Southwest for buying the perfect bolo tie or other piece of Indian **jewellery**.

The one place worth spending some time, especially if you've got kids in tow, is the **New Mexico Museum of Natural History**, four blocks northeast of the plaza at 1801 Mountain Road NW (daily 10am–5pm; $3), which has full-scale, animated models of dinosaurs, a simulated volcanic eruption and a replica of an Ice Age snow cave, as well as an engaging, handleable collection of fossils and dinosaur bones. For a more up-to-date look at the local ecology, head two miles north from Old Town along Rio Grande Boulevard to the **Rio Grande Nature Center** (daily 10am–5pm). Informative displays describe Albuquerque's wildlife, and two short but much appreciated nature trails along the riverside feel far removed from the city.

Indian Pueblo Cultural Center

2401 12th Street NW, one block north of I-40. Daily 9am-5.30pm. $2. ☎843-7270 or ☎242-4943.

The **Indian Pueblo Cultural Center** is a stunning museum and crafts market owned and operated as a co-operative venture by the diverse Pueblo Indians of New Mexico. The modern building is modelled on traditional Pueblo architectural forms, organised in a horseshoe shape around a central courtyard where Pueblo dances are held every Saturday and Sunday at 11am and 2pm (April–Dec only; free).

As New Mexico's one major museum about Indians to be curated by Indians, the place has a clear and distinct point of view: *Our Land, Our Culture, Our Story*, as the sign at the entrance puts it. The shared Anasazi heritage which lies at the root of Pueblo culture is explained in detail, while the final few exhibits express the betrayal felt by the Native Americans when the Spanish strangers they welcomed and helped turned into conquerors and oppressors; in contrast to other msueums, history here ends with the Pueblo Revolt of 1680. Modern Pueblo life is discussed in a series of videotapes, and there's an outstanding selection of covetable pottery and jewellery both on display and on sale in the gift shop, with works from each of the Pueblo tribes (the Zia ceramics are a highlight). A good-quality **cafe** serves assorted Pueblo specialities.

Sandia Crest and the Turquoise Trail

The forested 10,500ft peaks of the **Sandia Crest** tower over Albuquerque to the east, affording particularly beautiful views from the top at and after sunset, when the city lights sparkle below. In summer it's a good 25° cooler up here than in the valley, and in winter you can go downhill or cross-country skiing (lift tickets $24 per day; ☎296-9585). If you don't want to drive the scenic but twisting twenty-mile route from Albuquerque, take the **Sandia Peak Aerial Tram** (daily 9am–9pm; $10; ☎298-8518), at 2.7 miles the world's longest single-span tramway, from the end of Tramway Road at the northeast edge of the city.

Sandia Crest also makes a good stop on the way to or from Santa Fe. Rather than take the I-25 freeway, detour along Hwy-14, the so-called "Turquoise Trail", which passes between the Sandia and Ortiz mountains through ghostly mining camps like **Golden** (site of the Wild West's first gold discovery) and the New Agey village of **MADRID** (pronounced *MAD-rid*), where since the mid-1970s a community of arts-and-craftsy ex-hippies has resurrected the shacks and company stores of an old coal-mining town, complete with an enterable mine shaft behind the lively *Mine Shaft Tavern*.

If you do drive the I-25 route, be sure to stop off along the way at **CORONADO NATIONAL MONUMENT**, just off the freeway eighteen miles north of Albuquerque. Named for the Spanish explorer who arrived in the area in 1540 (and who, in frustration at not finding any of the vast riches he was searching for, tortured and brutally murdered a number of local Indians), the monument contains a large **adobe pueblo** beside the Rio Grande, notable for its multihued interior murals.

Salinas National Monument

About an hour south of Albuquerque's city limits, off US-60 in the southern section of the Cibola National Forest, the **SALINAS NATIONAL MONUMENT** (daily 8am–5pm; free) preserves the remnants of three separate but interrelated pre-colonial Indian **pueblos**, and some of the oldest **missionary churches** in North America. The largest of the pueblos is 26 miles south along Hwy-14 from the monument's visitor centre in **Mountainair**; the impressive 300-room **Gran Quivira** is the only one to have been more than minimally excavated. The main feature of **Quarai**, located eight miles north of US-60 on Hwy-55, is the massive fortress-like stone church **Nuestra Senora de la Concepcion**, which stands above mounds of unexcavated ruins; **Abo**, the smallest and least interesting of the three sections, is just off US-60 nine miles west of Mountainair.

Accommodation

Central Avenue, the old Route 66 artery, holds the bulk of Albuquerque's budget **accommodation**; all along its twenty-mile stretch are the blinking neon signs of dozens of $25-a-night motels. There are also a few more upscale hotels downtown, and a number of national chains near the airport.

Albuquerque International Hostel, 1012 Central Ave SW (☎243-6101). Near Old Town, a mile west of downtown. Dorm beds for $9 and doubles for $22.

El Vado, 2500 Central Ave SW (☎243-4594). Classic Route-66-style motel near Old Town. From $32.

Monterey Motel, 2402 Central Ave SW (☎243-3554). Another Old Town motel. Rooms start at $37.

Barcelona Court, 900 Louisiana Ave (☎255-5566). Just off I-40, three miles east of downtown, this spacious family-orientated hotel includes full breakfasts and evening cocktails for $60 a night midweek. Each room has an en-suite kitchen.

Casas de Sueños, 310 Rio Grande Rd (☎247-4560). One of the most pleasant places to stay in all of New Mexico. Beautifully furnished, exotic and friendly B&B near Old Town. Doubles from $80.

Comfort Inn, 2300 Yale Road (☎243-2244). The best-value place to stay near the airport, with free airport shuttle and doubles for $50.

La Posada de Albuquerque, 125 Second St (☎242-9090). Historic, elegant downtown hotel, with doubles for $75.

Eating

Unfortunately for visitors, Albuquerque's **restaurants** are spread out fairly evenly over the hundred-square-mile city area, so you'll either have to take your chances in the city centre area or hop in the car and drive somewhere.

Artichoke Cafe, 424 Central Ave SE (☎243-0200). Good-quality breakfasts and lunches.

FoFo's, 107 San Pablo SE (☎255-6674). Tucked away on the east side of town, but worth searching out for its range of Jamaican specialities and Caribbean fish dishes and chilled *Red Stripe* beer.

Frontier Restaurant, 2400 Central Ave SE (☎266-0550). Basic diner food, open all day.

Garcia's Diner, 1736 Central Ave SW (☎842-0273). All-American meals near Old Town; good value but worth a look for the neon sign alone.

La Hacienda, 302 San Felipe St (☎243-3131). The best bet in Old Town, with an outdoor patio overlooking the plaza and good-value Mexican cooking.

Route 66 Diner, 1405 Central Ave NE (☎247-1421). East of Old Town, near the University of New Mexico, with standard diner food and a usually lively, late-night clientele.

Monte Vista Fire Station, 3201 Central Ave NE (☎255-2424). Upmarket haunt, housed in restored firestation, serving up fine grilled meats and fish.

Drinking and Nightlife

Unfortunately, most of the city's reputable bars and nightclubs are inside the larger chain hotels. For **dancing**, you can two-step with throngs of urban cowboys, or take your chance at a handful of comparatively fashionable downtown clubs.

Beyond Ordinary, 211 Gold St (☎764-8858). The only place in town where you can move to the groove of contemporary, almost underground sounds.

Caravan East, 7605 Central Ave NE (☎265-6993). Huge dance floor, alomst invariably packed with Stetsoned cowpokes and their partners.

KiMo Theatre, 419 Central Ave NW (☎243-4500). Art Deco landmark which puts on live bands.

Lobby Bar, inside the classic Spanish Revival hotel *La Posada de Albuquerque*, 125 Second St (☎242-9090). Spacious and far from anodyne bar, with occasional live jazz.

West of Albuquerque: I-40 to Arizona

Driving between Albuquerque and Arizona you could easily be so put off by the parade of billboards and hoardings offering cheap cigarettes and Indian jewellery that you'd miss out on some of central New Mexico's most interesting places, such as **Acoma Pueblo** and **El Malpais National Monument**, which lie just south of I-40.

Acoma Pueblo

The ancient mesa-top community of **ACOMA PUEBLO**, twelve miles off the interstate 55 miles west of Albuquerque, has been continuously inhabited for over 800 years, which makes it one of the oldest settlements in North America (rivalled by the Hopi Mesas – see p.692). Though it has become heavily dependent upon tourism – even hosting the Miss America swimsuit competition – its setting remains as dramatic as ever, and "Sky City" still has a certain aloof detachment from the modern world.

To see Acoma, you have to join one of the hour-long guided **tours** ($6, plus $5 for photo permit) that leave regularly from the small museum/gift shop at the base of the 350ft mesa, climbing to the top by bus. The main stop is at the **San Esteban del Rey** mission, a thick-walled adobe church completed in 1640. Its earthen-floored nave is capped by a roof made of pine logs, which are said to have been carried here from the top of Mount Taylor, twenty miles away, without once touching the ground. Catholicism did eventually take root among the Pueblo people, but tales of the early mission days often speak of the Spanish priests as harsh and unfeeling taskmasters, and many came to rather sticky ends. The sheer visual impact of the building is undeniable, but in part that's due to its sheer incongruity, and it's striking that the Acomans obviously never felt inclined to follow its architectural example. Instead they went on constructing the multistorey stone and adobe houses around which the tour then proceeds. Few of these are now lived in with any regularity, as most Acomans prefer to live down below where they can get electricity and running water – and jobs. Villagers do, however, come up here during the day to sell pottery and fry-bread.

If you choose not to take the bus back down, you can instead walk by the old path, scrambling over boulders and through narrow clefts and using toeholds and notches worn away since time immemorial. Away to the east, legend has it that the forbidding **Enchanted Mesa** once held its own Pueblo community; the only access to the top was via a system of ropes strung between the mesa itself and an adjoining rock pillar. When that pillar collapsed one day while the men were away from the village, the women and children were left stranded on the top, their cries for help fading as they starved away.

El Malpais National Monument

At its western edge, Acoma Pueblo is bounded by the barren badlands of **EL MALPAIS NATIONAL MONUMENT**, whose subsurface tunnels and tubes attract potholers and geology buffs, but hardly anyone else. Most of this remote land is accessible only by four-wheel-drive vehicles, in good weather, though you can get a good look at it by driving the one paved road, Hwy-117, which passes through the **Narrows**, a glossy black formation at the base of 500-foot sandstone cliffs. More ambitious visitors may want to hike the Zuni–Acoma Trail, a fifteen-mile round trip through four distinct lava flows, or explore the **Big Lava Tubes** further west.

You can get up-to-date information on El Malpais at the National Park Service office, 620 E Santa Fe Avenue (☎285-5406), along old Route 66 in **GRANTS**. Something of a thriving metropolis for these parts, Grants has a couple of good cafes – try the beefy *Sirloin Stockade* at 1140 E Santa Fe Avenue or the New Mexican specialities at nearby *Maria's Diner* – and half a dozen $25-a-night motels just off I-40, including *Travelodge* (☎287-2991) and *Motel 6* (☎285-4607). The comprehensive and enjoyable **New Mexico Museum of Mining** at 100 Iron Street (Mon–Sat 10am–4pm, Sun 1–4pm; $2) focuses on the local **uranium mines**, and gives you a chance to descend into one.

Gallup

Just half an hour from the Arizona border, 65 miles west of Grants, the famous **Route 66** town of **GALLUP** is a handy I-40 pitstop, but otherwise uninteresting. A five-mile line of the old Route 66 frontage contains some of the **cheapest motels** in the US, ranging from the $12.95-a-night singles of the *Ambassador*, 1601 Route 66 (☎722-3843), and the *Colonial*, 1007 Coal Street (☎863-6821), to the pricier national chains. Unless you're falling asleep at the wheel, the only place really worth stopping for in Gallup is the *El Rancho Hotel*, 1000 E Route 66 (☎863-4408), built in 1937 by the brother of D W Griffith as a home from home for the many Hollywood stars who needed a place to stay while filming nearby. Nowadays you can ogle their photos in the spacious Spanish Revival lobby, grab a bite in the cafe or spend the night in the *Ronald Reagan Room*, the *Marx Brothers Room* or the *Mae West Room* for a reasonable $45.

Gallup has evolved into a major commercial centre for the Navajo Nation and other nearby Native American communities, who come together here on the second weekend in August for the **Inter-Tribal Indian Ceremonial**, the largest such gathering anywhere. Four days of dances and crafts shows have as their highlight a Saturday morning parade through the town.

Zuni Pueblo and Inscription Rock

ZUNI PUEBLO, just off Hwy-602 35 miles south of Gallup, is the sole survivor of the quasi-historical golden "Seven Cities of Cibola" sought by Coronado – not that it ever had any gold. It's noted today for its immaculate mission church and elaborate masked dances, and for the intricate fetishes carved by Zuni craftspeople. Half an hour east of Zuni on Hwy-53, **Inscription Rock**, officially known as El Morro National Monument, is a sandstone cliff marked on by centuries of travellers from ancient Anasazi to conquistadores and modern Kilroys. If you want to stretch your legs, climb the mile-long trail to the top to see the extensive, recently excavated Anasazi ruins of **Atsinna**, which around 1300 AD was inhabited by some 1500 people.

Southern New Mexico

Most of the travellers who come to southern New Mexico are here to visit **Carlsbad Caverns National Park**. Crassly commercialised it may be, but, like the Grand Canyon, it's such an amazing geological spectacle that it should not be missed. To the northwest of Carlsbad, the **Sacramento** and **Jicarilla** mountains – home to the large Mescalero Apache reservation as well as some rough-and-ready resorts with alpine settings to match Taos – rise out of the desert plains once roamed by Billy the Kid and other Wild West heroes. West of the mountains spread the desolate dunes of the **White Sands**, half national park, half missile and bombing range, with the rolling hills of the **Rio Grande Valley** beyond. The little-visited southwest corner – just an hour west of El Paso, Texas, the region's only city, via the I-10 freeway – is among the most attractive reaches of the Southwest, with dozens more ghost towns and some fine scenery, plus the undisturbed pre-Columbian remains of the **Gila Cliff Dwellings National Monument.**

Carlsbad Caverns National Park

The limestone formations of **Carlsbad Caverns** may not quite warrant the reams of purple prose that have been written about them, but wandering through these swirling shapes of liquid rock does have a definite mesmeric effect. At least 250 million years of oozing dribbling water have transformed what was once a submarine limestone reef into a vast network of tortuous and eerie tunnels, punctuated by colossal lightless halls.

The national park consists of the two largest caves, with a separate admission fee for each one. Tickets for both are sold at the **visitor centre** (daily, summer 8am–7pm, otherwise 8am–5pm; ☎785-2232), seven miles west of US-62, which has a relief model and photographs of the caverns, a restaurant and fairly tacky gift shop, a creche and even a kennel. Most of the year, the only queues are first thing in the morning, when everyone tries to beat the rush. Guided tours are offered in winter; in summer you're on your own, though you can rent a radio (50¢) for a broadcast description of the various forms. Most days you'll find it cool (56°) and peaceful, even when it's 100° on the surface, but on summer holiday weekends the place can be maddeningly crowded.

Carlsbad Cavern (daily, summer 8.30am–3.30pm, otherwise 8.30am–2pm; $5) is the biggest of the lot – its underground rooms are hundreds of feet across, and high enough to hold a dozen Wembleys – and the easiest to get a look at. All its formations, however delicate, are a uniform stone grey; the rare touches of colour are provided by slight red or brown mineral-rich tinges. Early visitors were dropped down in buckets and guided through on ropes; nowadays you can walk a three-mile trail, known as the "Blue Tour", which winds steeply down from the mouth of the cave. Should you have mobility problems, or be short on time, a modern elevator descends straight to the half-mile-long **Big Room** (where there's a bizarre gift shop and cafeteria, 750 feet underground) – but if you take it, you're missing the best of the experience. All visitors are in any case obliged to ride the lift back out.

Carlsbad Cavern is closed to the public early in the afternoon, in time for the nightly aerobatics show put on by the **millions of migratory bats** that make their homes

here in summer, hanging upside down in the caves throughout the day. At dusk (or a bit later) black clouds of the little creatures ascend in spirals from the mouth of the caverns, right by the visitor centre, and spread out over the desert for their nightly feed, returning before dawn. Park rangers are on hand to give a free and informative "Bats aren't as bad as you think" presentation, and to answer questions.

The much less visited **New Cave**, 25 miles southwest of the visitor centre, can only be seen on a somewhat strenuous guided tour ($6.50, and you must have a flashlight and stout shoes; ring the visitor centre for times and reservations). It's much less developed, and will appeal to anyone wanting a bit of extra adventure. One especially beautiful cave, **Lechuguilla**, is so dangerous and difficult that it's off limits to all but the most expert cavers; others have to content themselves with the marvellous pictures of its delicate crystalline formations in the visitor centre.

Carlsbad Practicalities

No matter how you get to Carlsbad Caverns, you have to cross seemingly endless miles of the Llano Estacado, the deathly flat rangeland that covers southeast New Mexico and the Texas Panhandle (see p.524). The route from El Paso, Texas, has the distinct advantage of passing through **Guadalupe Mountains National Park**, a beautiful though little-visited complement to Carlsbad which offers superb camping.

There are quite a few motels on all the main roads, but the best **places to stay** are at the entrance to the park, right on US-285 in **WHITE'S CITY**. This is basically one big tourist complex (☎785-2291 or ☎1-800/CAVERNS) – three motels, a $10-a-night youth hostel, an RV park and a couple of restaurants – all owned and operated by the White family. *Greyhound* buses (operated by *T&NMO*) stop here three times daily; White's City run mini-van trips into the park ($7). The town of **Carlsbad** itself, 25 miles north of White's City, isn't worth the drive.

Ruidoso

The Sacramento, Capitan and Jicarilla mountains, which rise at the western edge of the Llano Estacado, 85 miles northwest of Carlsbad, form a rare respite from the scrubby flatness. Spread out along winding roads that cut through dense groves of pine, fir and aspen, the main town here, **RUIDOSO**, is the fastest-growing resort in the Southwest, with dozens of motels and mountain lodges lining the banks of the Ruidoso ("Noisy") River. It's especially popular with Texans, who flock here in summer for the refreshing cool mountain air (and to bet on the horses at Ruidoso Downs racetrack), and in winter to hit the 12,000ft slopes at **Ski Apache**, a downhill ski area owned and operated by the Mescalero Apache tribe.

Despite scores of $30-a-night **motels**, such as *Apache Motel*, 344 Sudderth Avenue (☎257-2986), and *Pines Motel*, 620 Sudderth Avenue (☎257-2334), Ruidoso can't always handle the demand for **rooms** on summer weekends. The best **food** is at *My Sister's Place,* 1501 Sudderth Avenue, or the *Circle J Barbeque*, 1845 Sudderth Avenue, and the **visitors bureau** is at 720 Sudderth Avenue (☎257-7395 or ☎1-800/253-2255).

Lincoln County

One of the most enduring of New Mexico's many legendary Wild West figures was a Brooklyn-born onetime busboy named William Bonney, better known as **Billy the Kid**. Many towns lay claim to him, but he first came to fame as an 18-year-old in the **Lincoln County War**, which erupted in 1878 in the frontier town of **LINCOLN** when rival groups of ranchers and merchants fought to gain control of the town and the hundreds of square miles of grazing lands that surround it. Today Lincoln, on Hwy-380 roughly halfway between Carlsbad and Albuquerque, is probably the best place to get a feel for those lawless years; the entire town, consisting of some two dozen frontier-era buildings along Main Street, has been preserved pretty much intact. There are two good museums: one inside the restored **Lincoln County Courthouse** at the west end of town tells all about Billy the Kid and his various jailbreaks and escapades, and a more modern one on the east side details local Native American cultures, with an eye-opening exhibit about the **Buffalo Soldiers**, a unit of black cavalrymen who were stationed at nearby Fort Stanton, fighting Apaches (see also p.571). Admission to the museums, along with other smaller displays in various houses and stores, costs $4. If you want to **stay** the night, the *Wortly Hotel* (☎653-4500) has doubles for $40, and serves good meals throughout the day.

West of Lincoln are the scenes of yet more violence – both natural and thermonuclear. **Valley of Fires State Park**, a six-mile-wide black lava flow, bordering US-380 west of the small town of Carrizozo, forms an incredible contrast with the bleached desert of the White Sands fifty miles to the south (see below). Across the desert thirty miles to the west, at the **Trinity Site**, the first **atomic bomb** was detonated on July 16 1945, blasting the sands below Ground Zero into a thick slab of radioactive glass. Anything that was here when the bomb exploded was either destroyed or has been dug up and carted away, so there's very little to see; in any event, the whole area is on the White Sands Missile Range, and is off limits except for twice-yearly tours.

The White Sands National Monument and Alamogordo

Filling a broad valley west of Ruidoso and the Sacramento Mountains, the **White Sands** are 250 square miles of glistening, three-storey high dunes, not of sand but of finely ground gypsum eroded from the nearby peaks. Unfortunately, most of the desert valley is under the control of the US military, who use it as a missile range and training ground for pilots, and as a landing site for the **space shuttle**; only the southern half of the dunes is protected within the White Sands National Monument. The best place to start is at the **visitor centre**, just off US-70, where there are displays on the uniquely evolved plants and animals that dwell here – it's not as lifeless as it first appears. An eight-mile paved road ($3) stretches into the heart of the dunes, where you can scramble around the sands. Don't forget to bring water.

ALAMOGORDO, which sits at the base of the Sacramento Mountains, sixteen miles east of the Monument along US-54, holds the nearest food and lodging options as well as a very tacky but barely memorable *International Space Hall of Fame*.

The Rio Grande Valley

From White Sands, US-70 heads southwest across the Tularosa Valley to **LAS CRUCES** – "the Crosses" – a large, modern farming community on the Rio Grande at the junction of I-10 and I-25. The town takes its name from the dozens of white crosses set up in the sands to mark the graves of early travellers killed by Apaches in 1830, but any real sense of its history is pretty well buried by motels and fast-food franchises.

North from Las Cruces towards Albuquerque, I-25 stretches for miles along the Rio Grande, passing a number of irrigation reservoirs and the elderly resort town of **TRUTH OR CONSEQUENCES**, which re-named itself after a 1950s TV show for the sake of a bit of fame. One of the few places here to tempt you off the highway is 120 miles north of Las Cruces, halfway to Albuquerque: the **Bosque del Apache Wildlife Refuge**, a great place for seeing migratory birds and the only place where you see the Rio Grande in its (relatively) natural state.

Mesilla

The little-changed Spanish colonial village of **MESILLA**, just south of I-10 two miles west of Las Cruces, was until the 1870s one of the Southwest's biggest towns, with upwards of eight thousand inhabitants. During the Civil War it even served briefly as the Confederate capital of New Mexico and Arizona, but it went into swift decline when the railroad bypassed it in favour of Las Cruces in 1881. A couple of good **restaurants** – the *Double Eagle* for steaks and *El Patio Cantina* for beers and Mexican food – are housed in old frontier buildings around the central plaza. Many of these adobes now house art galleries and souvenir shops, while the small **Gadsen Museum** (daily 9–11am & 1–5pm; $2.12), just east of Hwy-28 two blocks from the plaza, recounts the town's history and details the events leading up to the Gadsen Purchase in 1854, when the US bought 30,000 square miles of Mexican land west of the Rio Grande.

The Southwest Corner

I-10 heads west from Las Cruces across the wide open rangeland that fills out the southwest corner of New Mexico, also known as the "Bootheel" for the way it steps down toward Mexico. It's so sparsely inhabited, there are roughly three square miles per person. Towns are few and far between: **DEMING**, sixty miles west of Las Cruces, has a few motels and cafes and is one of two places where *Amtrak* trains stop. Even if you're racing through on the interstate, make time for the very good **Luna Mimbres Museum** (Mon–Sat 9am–4pm, Sun 1.30–4pm) which relates the region's Native American and Wild West past, and has a great show of minerals and gemstones. If you've got more time, check out **Rock Hound State Park** ten miles southeast of town, one of the few places in the Southwest where you are encouraged to take away stones such as agates, onyx and geodes. Thirty miles south of Deming, just on the US side of the Mexican border, **Pancho Villa State Park** is a sixty-acre desert botanical garden on the site where the thousand-strong forces of the outlaw Mexican revolutionary Pancho Villa did battle in 1916 against the US cavalry, after being chased out of Mexico by his erstwhile allies. It's a nice place to camp (except in summer, when it's baking hot), and you can cross over the border to sleepy **Las Palomas** for a *cerveza* or two.

The other main town in the southwest corner, **LORDSBURG**, on I-10 twenty miles before Arizona, has a line of petrol stations, cafes and motels but little else. Just two miles south sit the remnants of **Shakespeare**, one of the best preserved and most easily accessible of the area's dozens of **ghost towns**. To see it you have to join an (unfortunately rare) guided tour (every other Sat & Sun, 10am–2pm; $2; ☎542-9034).

Silver City

Rarely visited and almost entirely wilderness, the semi-arid forested volcanic **Mogollon** and **Mimbres mountains** soar above the high desert plain of southwest New Mexico to over 10,000 feet. But for a number of copper mines, the area is protected within the **Gila National Forest**. The mountains are some of the most remote in the US, little altered since the days when they were the homelands (and strongholds) of Apache warriors Cochise and **Geronimo** – who was born here at the headwaters of the Gila River.

Halfway up the mountains, the biggest settlement, **SILVER CITY**, lies 45 miles north of I-10 at the junction of US-180 from Deming and Hwy-90 from Lordsburg. The Spanish came here in 1804, sold the Mimbreño Indians into slavery, and opened the **Santa Rita copper mine**, just east of town below the Kneeling Nun monolith, but the town was re-established in 1870 as a rough-and-tumble silver camp – Billy the Kid spent most of his childhood here. A fine selection of ornate old buildings is scattered along avenues of elms and in the surrounding hills. The excellent **museum** at 312 W Broadway (Tues–Fri 9am–4.30pm, Sat & Sun 10am–4pm; donations) tells the boom-and-bust tales while quoting from Lewis Mumford, and holds fine specimens of Casas Grandes pottery, beautiful Navajo rugs, and basketry from all the major Southwest tribes. Three blocks east, the original Main Street was washed away in a great flood and has become the cottonwood-shaded **Big Gulch Park**. Bullard Street holds atmospheric saloons and cafes like the *Silver Cafe* and the *Corner Cafe*.

Just outside of town, the *Bear Mountain Guest Ranch* (☎538-2538) is the best **place to stay** in southwest New Mexico, with very pleasant rooms in a large 1920s ranch house (plus three full meals) for as little as $55 a night. Myra McCormick, who has run the place for 33 years, regularly guides bird-watching trips (warblers and Western Tanagers are often sighted – and heard – nearby) and can suggest or arrange a variety of multiday cycling, mountain-biking, or cross-country skiing tours of the surrounding area. If you just want a place to sleep, there are half a dozen motels along US-180.

Gila Cliff Dwellings National Monument

Beautiful, twisting Hwy-15 threads north from Silver City into the mountains, passing the picturesque old mining camp of Pinos Altos on its way to the **Gila Cliff Dwellings National Monument**. From a small visitor centre at the end of the road, a mile-long trail loops along a year-round stream before climbing the side of the canyon, where you get your first view of the substantial and only slightly restored **ruins**. All of these six cliff-dwellings, set back in deep caves some two hundred feet above the canyon floor, were abandoned about seven hundred years ago by their builders, the **Mogollon** people, who had lived here for just forty years. They may not be as architecturally impressive as those of Mesa Verde (see p.611), but exploring them alone – you can wander freely through the chambers, and the chances are there will be no one else around – really encourages you to imagine yourself as one of the original occupants.

The largest of the caves, near the end of the trail, holds some fifteen rooms, looking out at the cottonwoods and ponderosa pines of the canyon. The south-facing caves stay warm in winter, but are well enough shaded to keep cool in summer. Keep an eye out for the various pictograph figures above the cave entrances, before you climb down the wooden ladder and circle back down the cliff-face to the car park. There's **camping** nearby along the Gila River, and excellent hiking (and a couple of natural **hot springs**) in the adjacent Gila Wilderness Area.

ARIZONA

The tourism industry in **ARIZONA** has, literally, one colossal advantage – the **Grand Canyon** of the Colorado River. It's the single most awe-inspiring spectacle in a land of unforgettable geology, and one of the few places in the world which you absolutely *have* to see at least once in your life; but surprisingly enough the Grand Canyon is by no means the most interesting or memorable destination in the state. It's quite inhuman in scale, whereas other parts of Arizona have an abiding emotional impact precisely because of the sheer drama of human involvement in this forbidding but deeply resonant desert landscape.

Over a third of the state still belongs to the **Native Americans** who have lived here for centuries, and who outside the cities form the majority of the population. In the so-called **Indian Country** of northeastern Arizona, a sovereign state within the US, the reservation lands of the **Navajo Nation** hold the stupendous **Canyon de Chelly** and dozens of other marvellously sited **Anasazi ruins** as well as the stark rocks of **Monument Valley**. The Navajo surround the homeland of one of the most stoutly traditional and least reconstructed of all Native American tribes, the **Hopi**; even the most determinedly cynical of visitors is likely to be overwhelmed by the extent to which their ancient **mesa-top villages** remain distanced from the maelstrom of modern America. The third main tribal group are the **Apache**, in the harshly beautiful southeastern mountains; they were virtually the last of the Native Americans to give in to the overwhelming power of the white American invaders, and are now among the most prosperous of Arizona's native peoples.

Away from the reservations, **Wild West** towns like **Tombstone**, site of the famed gunfight at the OK Corral, give a clear sense of the state's characteristically rough-and-ready, pioneer mentality. Arizona was the last of the lower 48 states to join the Union, in 1912, and its current notoriety as one of two states – the other is New Hampshire – not to recognise Martin Luther King's national holiday owes a lot to its historical hard-nosed independence. One consequence of such anti-socialness is that Arizona's **cities** aren't much fun. **Phoenix**, the capital, is a city of well over a million souls scattered over a 500-square-mile morass of shopping malls and tract-house suburbs; **Tucson** is a bit more civil but still wears thin after a day or so.

Getting Around Arizona

Arizona is better served by public transport than much of the Southwest, but it can still be an effort to get around without a car. *Greyhound* **buses** stop at all the major cities and at most towns along the interstates, while *Amtrak* **trains** cross the state on two of their transcontinental routes; however, neither is of much use in getting to the back-country. The largest airport is at Phoenix, though a number of short-hop flights within the state – and to the Grand Canyon from Las Vegas – give surprisingly good value for money. The only worthwhile **coach tours** visit the area around Flagstaff.

> The telephone **area code** for the entire state of Arizona is ☎602.

Tucson, Phoenix and Southern Arizona

Most of Arizona's compelling attractions are in its northern reaches, but the **southern** half of the state holds ninety percent of its people, all its significant cities and several important historic sites. Apart from a couple of old Spanish missions, the bulk of what there is to see is frontier Americana, especially in **Tombstone**, in the southeast corner, perhaps the best known Wild West town, where a dozen saloons now serve tourists and local ranchers in relatively equal numbers. **Phoenix**, the state capital, is huge,

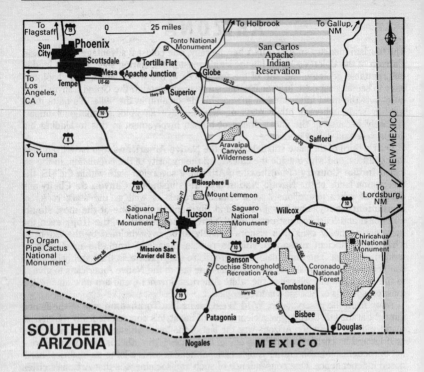

SOUTHERN
ARIZONA

sprawling and dull; **Tucson** makes a better base for visiting this part of the world, and for trips south of the border into Mexico. Though the open spaces of southern Arizona can be harsh and violent – most of the southwestern quarter, along the parallel I-8 and I-10 highways, is used by the US military as a bombing range – the bleakness is balanced somewhat by the many nature reserves which protect its amazing flora and fauna, such as the magical **Aravaipa Canyon Wilderness**, the remote **Organ Pipe Cactus National Monument** on the Mexican border, and **Saguaro National Monument** just outside Tucson.

Tucson

After serving as a colonial outpost under the Spanish and Mexicans, and then as territorial capital for both the US and Confederate governments, **TUCSON** (pronounced *too-sawn*) has grown into a modern mini-metropolis of nearly a million people without entirely sacrificing its historic quarters. Now equal parts college town and retirement community, it's one of the more attractive big cities of the Southwest – which admittedly isn't saying much. It does suffer from the same Sunbelt sprawl as Albuquerque and Phoenix, but it also has a wanderable centre, some enjoyable restaurants, and a pretty good nightlife, energised by the 35,000 students at the University of Arizona. It is also redeemed by having so much superb landscape within easy reach, from the forested flanks of Mount Lemmon to the rolling foothills of **Saguaro National Monument** with its giant cacti, real-life roadrunners and rare gila monsters. The **Arizona-Sonora Desert Museum**, which borders the western half of the monument, gives an excellent introduction to the natural life of the entire desert region.

Arrival and Information

Tucson is located right on the I-10 interstate, which winds from Dallas to Los Angeles. You can fly here from all over the US, though most flights go via Phoenix; **Tucson International Airport**, about eight miles south of downtown, is connected by regular *Sun Tran* **bus** #8 (60¢). *Amtrak* (☎623-4442) and *Greyhound* (☎792-0972) both stop in the centre of town, on Toole Avenue to either side of Congress Street, just off Broadway. Everywhere in town is pretty much within walking distance of the centre, though if it's too hot you might want to ride the **Fourth Avenue Trolley** (25¢) out to the university, a mile east of the city centre.

Tucson's **visitor centre**, at 130 S Scott Avenue downtown (Mon–Fri 8.30am–5pm, Sat & Sun 10am–3pm; ☎624-1889), has free maps and information. The *Southwest Parks Association* **bookshop**, three blocks away at 223 N Court Street (☎792-0239) in the El Presidio district, stocks Arizona's best selection of historical, hiking and wildlife guides.

The Town

Tucson has two main centres: the **historic core** along the (usually bone-dry) Santa Cruz River, bisected by Congress Street, and the quarter around the **University of Arizona** campus, a mile to the east. The city was founded in the late 1700s by Catholic missionaries who came from Mexico, then a Spanish colony, to convert the Pima Indians. Nothing very substantial remains from this era, but hundreds of artefacts have been collected and are now on display inside the many historic adobe homes in and around the **El Presidio** district of cafes, art galleries and B&Bs, two blocks north of Broadway. The oldest, **La Casa Cordova** on Meyer Street, dates from the 1850s, after Arizona was in US hands. Informative (and free) walking tours of the four-block district leave from the tree-shaded courtyard of the adjacent **Tucson Museum of Art**. This modern building, at 140 N Main Street (Tues–Sun 10am–4pm; $2, free Tues), holds exhibitions of contemporary painting and sculpture, mostly to do with the Southwest.

Three blocks south, in the middle of the Tucson Convention Center complex, a single hundred-year-old house is the sole survivor of a once-extensive neighbourhood of adobe homes torn down during the mid-1960s in the name of urban renewal. Known as the **Fremont House** (Wed–Sat 10am–4pm; free) because frontier American explorer John C Fremont lived in it for a few months in the 1870s, it belonged for many years to Leopoldo Carrillo, one of Tucson's wealthiest merchants. Though much restored, it still gives a vivid sense of the more civilised side of frontier life, from the high-quality furniture and the saguaro-rib ceilings to the fig-tree-shaded rear courtyard gardens.

Tucson's other main area of interest is around the University of Arizona, which spreads between Sixth Street and Speedway Boulevard a mile east of dowtown. The highlight is the **Arizona State Museum** (Mon–Sat 9am–5pm, Sun 2–5pm; free), where an exceptionally comprehensive assembly of Native American artefacts from the very earliest days traces the evolution of the various Southwest tribes. The campus also holds one of the world's finest photography archives. The **Center for Creative Photography** (Tues–Fri 10am–5pm; free) is a repository of the collected works (negatives, prints and journals) of Richard Avedon and Ansel Adams, among others. The **art museum** next door on Speedway Boulevard has some morbid Spanish retablos and assorted modern pieces, in particular some fine cubist sculpture by Lipchitz and Picasso.

Old Tucson and the Desert Museum

Twelve miles west of the university on Speedway Boulevard, en route to Saguaro, **Old Tucson** (daily 9am–5pm; $7.95) is an entertaining if contrived Wild West amusement center. It's built around a movie set and soundstage constructed for a 1930s Hollywood western, and later used for numerous TV shows and commercials. Nowadays you can ride a stagecoach or an old coal-fired steam train, and watch a bawdy music hall show in the saloon or a gunfight on Main Street.

Much more worthwhile, especially if you've got kids, is the **Arizona-Sonora Desert Museum** (daily 8.30am–5pm, longer in summer; adults $6, ages 6–12 $1), two miles further west in **Tucson Mountain Park**. Museum exhibits inside the Congdon Earth Sciences Center explain the geology and ancient history of the region, and a series of dioramas are filled with tarantulas, rattlesnakes and other creepy crawlers. Outside, bighorn sheep, mountain lions, jaguars and other rarely seen denizens of the desert prowl in credible simulations of their natural habitats, while hawks and bald eagles fly about in a large aviary. One of the best and most educational zoological centres in the US, the museum is as much an animal rescue centre as it is a zoo: almost all the animals you see had been injured in some way before ending up here, and would be unable to survive on their own in the desert.

Saguaro National Monument

Saguaro National Monument, part of which stretches north from the Desert Museum, gives you the chance to wander through weird forests of forty-foot, multi-limbed Saguaro (*SWAH-row*) **cacti**. It's divided into two separate sections. The smaller, more accessible (and much more popular) parcel, here on the northern slopes of Tucson Mountain, is ideal for visits of an hour or two, as you can drive through the best bits on a scenic nine-mile paved loop. The more remote section, seventeen miles east of Tucson in the **Tanque Verde** mountains north of I-10, is better if you have the time and inclination to backpack overnight: it has miles of trails, and the cacti look particularly strange by moonlight. **Visitor centres** (daily 9am–5pm) at the entrance to each of the areas make good first stops; a $3-per-car fee is collected at the eastern section only, and there's no water in either part.

Accommodation

Accommodation options in Tucson range from affordably bohemian downtown hotels to outrageously expensive dude ranches on the outskirts. Prices, especially in the upper echelons, fluctuate considerably – when the mercury rises, prices drop – and some places are open only in the peak winter and spring months. *Old Pueblo Homestays*, PO Box 13603 (☎790-2399), is an agency offering rooms in private houses from $40 a night.

The Arizona Inn, 2200 E Elm St (☎325-1541). Arizona's most comfortable and elegant resort, this desert oasis has been a winter favourite for numerous presidents, Rockefellers and the Duke and Duchess of Windsor. It remains surprisingly unstuffy – and not all that expensive. Doubles (in summer) from $70, including gourmet breakfast; in peak season (Jan–May) prices start at $100.

Congress Hotel, 311 E Congress St (☎622-8848). Very central and comfortably arts-orientated old downtown hotel, with hostel beds for under $15 and private rooms from around $35 a night.

Days Inn – Santa Rita, 88 E Broadway (☎622-4000). At the heart of downtown. Handy for the El Presidio district and Congress Street, but in itself fairly anonymous. Doubles from $45.

El Presidio Inn, 297 N Main St (☎623-6151). Nicely furnished Spanish colonial rooms in historic downtown home, from $50/double including full breakfast.

Triangle L Ranch, Box 900, Oracle (☎623-6732 or ☎1-800/266-2804). Set on the oak-shaded foot-hills of Mount Lemmon, 35 miles north of central Tucson and perfect for birdwatchers or just a quiet getaway. Double rooms in private cottages from $60 a night.

Eating

Food in Tucson is characterised by a predominance of good Mexican places, with a few more entertaining restaurants serving up Wild West cowboy food – huge steaks, burgers and bowls of chili. Most of the better places are downtown, but for budget meals try the various cafes in the student union on the University of Arizona campus.

Arizona Inn, 2200 E Elm St (☎325-1541). The traditional food you'd expect, in a lovely high-ceilinged room. Fresh and well prepared – the Caesar's salad is a life-preserver on a hot dry day.

Bowen and Bailey Cafe and Greengrocer, 135 S Sixth St (☎792-2603). Upmarket, European-style cafe-deli. Tasty pates and salads as well as more hearty dishes for breakfast, lunch and dinner.

Cafe Magritte, 254 E Congress St (☎884-8004). As you might guess, an arty cafe, with an eclectic – but not expensive – menu to match the offbeat clientele. Great desserts, coffees, and digestifs.

Courtyard Cafe, 186 N Meyer Ave (☎622-0351). Outdoor grill in historic El Presidio adobe courtyard, with good-value salads, burgers, beer and wine.

El Adobe, 40 W Broadway (☎791-7458). Longstanding local favourite for large portions of Mexican food and some of the Southwest's best margaritas.

Janos, 150 N Main St (☎884-9426). Tucson's trendiest hotspot, serving inventive cuisine in an immaculate El Presidio adobe home. Very expensive, dinner only, excellent desserts.

Ranchers Club, 5151 E Grant Rd (☎323-6262). Tucson's best (and biggest) cuts of beef – 48-oz steaks – carefully grilled over your choice of desert mesquite or subtle cherrywood flame, plus excellent soups and salads in classy but unpretentious surroundings.

Drinking and Nightlife

Nightlife in Tucson focuses on Congress Street downtown, with its gaggle of arty cafes and nightclubs. A handful of student places can be found near the university plus half a dozen country and western saloons on the outskirts. Most of the regular venues double as bars or restaurants. For a full rundown, check the listings in the free *Tucson Weekly*. The *Tucson Jazz Society* (☎743-3399) promotes gigs all over town.

Cafe Sweetwater, 340 E Sixth St (☎622-6464). Casual, thirty-something cafe and bar with regular live jazz.

Cushing Street Bar, 343 S Meyer (☎622-7984). Likely spot to catch good live music of all sorts, near the Fremont House.

The Green Dolphin, 95 N Park Ave (☎622-6099). Popular student rock venue.

Muddbugg's, 136 N Park Ave (☎882-9844). Live rock and R&B, near the university.

South to the Border: Tumacacori and Nogales, Mexico

South from Tucson, I-19 heads straight for the Mexican border, 65 miles away, passing some tangible reminders of the region's Spanish and Mexican heritage. The first of these, the pristine white **Mission San Xavier del Bac** (daily 9am–6pm; donations), lies just west of the freeway, five miles from downtown Tucson on the fringe of the vast arid plain of San Xavier Indian Reservation. Built in 1778 and definitely showing its age, the crumbling church is a curious mix of the baroque aspirations of the Catholic missionaries who designed it, and the folksy, handcrafted details of the Indians who built and have maintained it. The best time to come is on Sunday morning, when the congregation can be so big that many have to stand outside and listen through the darkened doorway.

In many ways an even more evocative memorial to the missionary effort, the massive adobe church at the heart of the **Tumacacori National Monument** was ravaged by the elements for almost a hundred years before the US government took steps to preserve it. The hulking structure, built around 1800, has been re-roofed and stabilised, but the internal walls have been left as they were found, the exposed, unplastered adobe of the more damaged parts pointing out the delicacy of the surviving, finely sculpted detailing. A very good museum is housed in the small **visitor centre** at the entrance, and a self-guided tour map ($1) tells the mission story.

Nogales, Arizona and Nogales, Mexico

Twenty miles south of Tumacacori, an hour from Tucson, sits the largest and most pleasant of the Arizonan–Mexican border towns, **NOGALES**. Promoted as "Ambos Nogales" (both Nogales), it seems to get the same number of people going each way – Mexicans coming north to stock up at *Safeway*, and gringos heading south to buy cheap beer and maybe a rug or a hammock. Though revolutionary bandit Pancho Villa used to hang out on the Mexican side, and iconoclastic jazz great **Charles Mingus** was born on the US side, there are no real sights; it's basically a lively, large-scale street market. Nogales is not nearly as seedy as Ciudad Juarez, and nowhere near as much a tourist rip-off as Tijuana; to get a brief taste of Mexico, it's not bad at all. Dollars are the most common currency, and there are few border formalities (though you must check that your visa status entitles you to re-enter the US). If you want to continue on south, get a tourist visa at the border crossing; trains and dozens of buses head to destinations throughout Mexico.

Patagonia and the Sonoita Creek Bird Sanctuary

A longer but much more beautiful route between Nogales and Tucson, Hwy-82 avoids the interstate by looping northeast from Nogales through the lush **Sonoita Valley** in the craggy mountains of the Coronado National Forest. At the end of a mile-long dirt road from Fourth Street in the dusty cattle-ranching town of **PATAGONIA**, the **Sonoita Creek Bird Sanctuary** is a dense stand of oaks and cottonwoods that's home to an amazing variety and density of songbirds and raptors, including finches, warblers, hawks, kestrels, woodpeckers and cardinals. The place is amazingly green throughout the year – in fact the Sonora is known as the greenest desert on earth. Twelve miles north of Patagonia, Hwy-83 veers off to the northwest to rejoin I-10 just east of Saguaro National Monument; Hwy-82 cuts east toward Tombstone, 35 miles away.

Tombstone and the Southeast Corner

Amongst thousands of acres of unspoiled and magnificent wilderness, southeast Arizona contains numerous well-preserved and highly atmospheric **ghost towns**. While I-10 buzzes along from the New Mexico border, the more scenic US-80 makes a grand tour of the region. Even if you're racing through this barren country, set aside an hour at least for the excellent **Amerind Foundation Museum** (daily 10am–4pm; $2), just off the interstate 65 miles east of Tucson at exit 318, for one of the best anthropological museums in the US, broad in scope and focusing in turn on the native cultures of the Southwest, the Pacific Northwest, and Central and South America.

Tombstone and Bisbee

From the I-10 truckstop of **Benson**, 45 miles east of Tucson, US-80 cuts off south 22 miles to the most famous Wild West town of all, **TOMBSTONE**. Known as "The Town Too Tough to Die", and fabled for its daily shootouts in the streets, Tombstone is so steeped in its own mythology that it's impossible to separate the facts from the tall tales, but whether you're a history buff or just want to play outlaw for a day it's still hard to beat. Tombstone only began life as a silver-boomtown in 1877, and by the end of the 1880s it was all but deserted again. However, on the day which gave it the notoriety which has kept it alive, its population stood at over ten thousand. It was 2pm on October 26 1881 when **Doc Holliday**, along with **Wyatt Earp** and his brothers Virgil and Morgan (who all served as local sheriffs), confronted a band of suspected cattle rustlers in the legendary **Gunfight at the OK Corral**. What exactly occurred is far from certain – apart from the fact that the showdown in fact took place on Fremont Street, a block from the OK Corral – but within a few minutes three of the suspects were dead. The Earps were accused of murder but charges were eventually dropped.

Much of the town, including the OK Corral, is preserved as a national historic site. Though dependent upon tourism, its dozen or so saloons, bars and cafes are also frequented by local cowboys and ranchers, giving the town an authentic edge to counter-balance its more contrived aspects – such as the wax dummies of the Earp brothers in the *Historama*, next to the OK Corral. The best time to visit is during **Helldorado Days** in late October, when the air is cooler and the sun less harsh, but the streets are full of gun-toting strangers acting out gunbattles and stagecoach robberies.

BISBEE, 25 miles south, has a similar murder-and-mayhem mythology, and it too has managed to keep going with most of its historic structures intact. Until 1974, Bisbee had one of the largest and most profitable **copper mines** in the world – over four million tons of high-grade ore were dug from its depths. A handful of spit-and-sawdust saloons and restaurants still line Brewery Gulch, the main drag, but Bisbee's centrepiece remains the grand old *Copper Queen Hotel*, 11 Howell Avenue (☎432-2216), with a plush bar, a shady pavement cafe, and double rooms from $45 a night.

From Bisbee, US-80 swerves to the east along the Mexican border to **DOUGLAS** (said to be one of the major throughways for drug traffickers and the slave-trade in illegal Mexican farm labourers) before circling northwards through the untouched mountain fastness of the Chiricahua and Pendregosa mountains. Apache warriors Geronimo and Cochise both availed themselves of this stark and often impassable terrain when escaping from the US cavalry, and the entire range is now kept in its natural state, within the **Coronado National Forest**. For details on hiking and exploring, contact the US Forest Service in Tucson at 300 W Congress Street (☎670-6483).

Southwest Arizona

There's virtually nothing in the vast desert plain of southwest Arizona to tempt you off the twin freeways that sprint to California. The US Army stages tank battles in its Yuma Proving Grounds between I-10 and I-8, while the Air Force drops bombs and tests Stealth technology in the more mountainous region bordering Mexico. The largest town, **YUMA** is little more than an oversized pitstop for freight trains and cross-country truckers, with 25 motels and a dozen diners along its Fourth Avenue. **Yuma Territorial Prison**, now a state park (daily 8am–5pm; $2) beside the Colorado River, was known a century ago as the "Hell Hole of Arizona", holding over a hundred of the Wild West's most violent criminals. Its first inmates were forced to build the adobe walls which later held them; there's a small museum, and you can wander around the grounds and cellblocks at will.

North of Yuma along the Colorado River, three **wildlife refuges**, the **Kofa**, **Cibola** and **Imperial**, line the banks of the Colorado River. Established to protect herds of mule deer and bighorn sheep as well as thousands of migratory Canadian geese, the parks aren't really designed for human visitors, and are virtually inaccessible without a four-wheel-drive vehicle. It is, however, worth making the effort to reach the 500-square-mile **Organ Pipe Cactus National Monument**, 55 miles south of the town of **GILA BEND**. Besides the unusual Organ Pipe, which grows in groups of tubular "pipes" from a shared root system, with a sweet fruit once prized by Native Americans, there are acres of spectacular saguaro, ironwood and other desert dwellers. Before you set off through the reserve, stop into the **visitor centre** (daily 8am–5pm), which will tell you what to look out for on the two scenic loops along good dirt roads, one of 21 miles up the Ajo Mountains and the other twice as long across the Puerto Blanco plain. The copper-mining company town of **AJO**, fourteen miles north of the park, holds the nearest food and lodging options.

Phoenix

The state capital and largest city in Arizona, **PHOENIX**, can't seem to rid itself of its reputation as the most unpleasant city in the Southwest – imagine Las Vegas without gambling, or LA without a beach, and you have a good idea what it's like. Founded in 1864, it was little more than a small farming town until the 1930s when the first tourists arrived to enjoy the (then) clean air and (very) warm weather – Phoenix in summer is the **hottest** city outside the Middle East, with daytime highs rarely dipping below 100°. At first a few winter resorts and dude ranches brought in vacationers from back

East, but the city really took off in the post-war, post-automobile era, and its population multiplied from 30,000 to some 600,000 between 1940 and 1975. Many of the immigrants were retirees, settling in pre-fab communities like **Sun City** on Phoenix's western edge.

Since then the Phoenix **sprawl** has engulfed the neighbouring communities of Scottsdale, Mesa, and Tempe to become the tenth largest city in the US, and there's no end in sight: Motorola, IBM and other high-tech firms have set up assembly plants on the still cheap land, and, following a lengthy legal battle with their Californian and Mexican neighbours, the city has recently completed an aqueduct from the Colorado River to secure its precious water supply. A nice but far from thrilling network of canals fans out across the desert, pleasant for cycling or strolling. Otherwise there are a couple of small museums, but Phoenix's main activity seems to be killing time beside the **pool** – its posh resort hotels must have the most extravagant swimming pools in the world – or popping into the many art galleries and upscale shopping malls.

Arrival and Information

Sky Harbor International Airport, just east of downtown, is a main hub for *America West* and many other airlines, receiving flights from all over the western US. Rent a car there, take **bus #13**, or ride *Super Shuttle* **vans** ($5) to the centre. *Amtrak* **trains** come into grungy old Union Station, on the south side of downtown at Fourth Avenue and Harrison Street (☎253-0121); *Greyhound* arrives at Fifth Avenue and Washington Street (☎248-4040), opposite the Civic Center. Getting around without a car isn't ideal – it can take hours to cross town – but it's not impossible: *Phoenix Transit Service* (*PTS*) has regular **buses** for 75¢ a ride or $2.50 all day; pick up a system map and other information from the **visitor centre** (☎254-6400) at Second Avenue and Adams Street in the Civic Center.

The city's relentless grid of streets does little to encourage casual strolling, but does make **orientation** quite straightforward: basically, numbered **avenues** (1st–115th and beyond) run north to south, intersected by east–west **streets** named for US presidents (Van Buren, for some reason, is the main one). Most of the main sights are within walking distance of the Civic Center.

Civic Center

Civic Center, long a black hole at the city centre, was the subject of a major international design competition some years ago, resulting in some attractive gateways and street lights but as yet no real change. Phoenix's two most worthwhile stops are on the north side of downtown, a few blocks up Central Avenue. At 1625 Central Avenue, the **Phoenix Art Museum** (Tues & Thur–Sat 10am–5pm, Wed 10am–9pm, Sun 1–5pm; $3, free Wed) bravely tries to trace the history of art, with a handful of forgettable paintings by middleweight Old Masters; it does better, not surprisingly, on Western art.

The **Heard Museum** at 22 E Monte Vista Road (Mon–Sat 10am–5pm, Sun 1–5pm; $3), three blocks north and a block east of Central Avenue, provides an excellent introduction to the craftswork of Arizona's many Indian reservations. It displays top-notch Navajo rugs and Hopi kachina dolls (some 400 of which were donated by arch-conservative Arizona senator Barry Goldwater), as well as the personal collection of Grand Canyon promoter Fred Harvey. Outside, in a peaceful sculpture garden full of primitive Olmec-style figures, are dozens of cacti, including agaves, ocotillos, prickly pears, and a statuesque saguaro.

West of Civic Center the sparkling copper dome of the disused **Arizona State Capitol** stands amidst the low-level sprawl. Inside it, a small **museum** (Mon–Fri 8am–5pm; free) illuminates the state's colourful – if often violent – history. In between Civic Center and the Capitol, at 1002 W Van Buren Street, the tiny **Arizona Museum** (Wed–Sun 11am–4pm; free) has enagagingly unpretentious exhibits tracing regional history from Anasazi days to statehood.

If Phoenix gets too hot to bear, the coolest place to beat the heat is on the east side of town at the *Island of the Big Surf* **water park**, at 1500 N McClintock Avenue (March–Sept only, Tues–Sun 8am–6pm; ☎947-7873), where you can ride five-foot waves or career down multistorey waterslides into a giant freshwater lagoon.

Accommodation

The nicest (and most expensive) of Phoenix's **hotels** tend to be in Scottsdale, away on its northeastern edge. A strip of **motels** lines Black Canyon Highway (I-17) on the north side of town, and there are a dozen more in the Mormon community of Mesa to the east side. The Phoenix visitor centre has a toll-free **hotline** for those wishing to book a room – ☎1-800/528-0483, or ☎1-800/992-6005 within Arizona.

Budget Lodge Motel, 402 W Van Buren St (☎254-7247). Reasonably attractive rooms from $29.

Howard Johnson Lodge, 124 S 24th St (☎244-8221). Standard doubles near the airport from $45.

Motel 6, 1511 S Country Club Drive (☎834-0066). $25 doubles in Mesa; also at 336 W Hampton Ave (☎844-8899).

FUTURISTIC VISIONS IN THE DESERT

Despite the general lack of aesthetic sensitivity in Phoenix, it has managed to attract some of the more visionary designers of the twentieth century, most notably **Frank Lloyd Wright**, who came to the city to work on the *Biltmore Hotel* and stayed for most of the next 25 years before his death in 1959. Though he travelled extensively, he generally wintered in Phoenix, working in his **Taliesin West** studio, at the northeastern edge of the Phoenix sprawl on 108th Street just north of Shea Boulevard. Now run by the Frank Lloyd Wright Foundation, it's an architecture school and a working design studio, with regular multimedia exhibits of the man's life and work. Hourly tours of the studio and grounds, including an unnecessarily saccharine hagiography, are offered throughout the winter and on request in summer (daily 10am–4pm; $5; ☎860-2700).

Less well known, but in many ways more compelling, is the **Cosanti Foundation**, four miles west of Taliesin at 6433 Doubletree Road (daily 9am–5pm; $3; ☎948-6145) in Paradise Valley. The buildings, designed by **Paolo Soleri**, an Italian-born ex-student of Wright, and constructed out of rammed earth and concrete, have a much more organic feel than Taliesin. Crafts workshops make bells and cast bronzes, and a small museum shows drawings and models of Soleri's life work – **Arcosanti**, a space-age, environmentally sensitive and in general unique project slowly but surely emerging from the desert just an hour's drive north, a mile east of I-17 at Cordes Junction.

Set on the rim of a beautiful high desert canyon, and designed to be (someday) an entirely self-sufficient community of 5000 people, Arcosanti is the clearest embodiment of **Arcology** – Soleri's ideal blend of architecture and ecology. Visitors come from all over the world for the three-hour guided tours of the complex given throughout the day ($5 donation; ☎632-7135), and an airy and spacious cafe serves healthy and tasty meals. Arcosanti hosts a very popular series of outdoor summer **concerts**, and you can **stay the night** for a very reasonable $15–25; if you like what you see, sign up for one of the month-long workshops and help out with the construction.

A futuristic enterprise of much more questionable intent is taking shape in the desert southeast of Phoenix, in a high-security compound off Hwy-77 near the town of **Oracle**. Rather than working to save the earth, a cultish group of retired actors and Sixties ex-radicals, financed by Texas tycoon Ed Bass, has constructed a space-age escape module named **Biosphere-2**. This veritable Noah's Ark, stocked with 4000 species of plants and animals, is designed to allow them and their investors to live happily ever after . . . on **Mars**. A small party of experimenters is currently sealed within the giant Plexiglas bubble for its first two-year trial. The site has become a popular tourist destination, offering a slide show and a brief guided tour (daily on the hour, 9am–4pm; $9.50; ☎896-2108 or ☎1-800/828-2462). A replica of the Biosphere is being built alongside for tourists to walk through, and there's talk of erecting a third Biosphere in Las Vegas.

Valley of the Sun International Hostel, 1026 N Ninth St above Roosevelt St (☎262-9439). Dorm beds for $11, 15-min walk from the Civic Center. Also bicycle rental for $5 per day.

YMCA, 350 N First Ave (☎253-6181). Grungy but central; single rooms for men and women, with shared bathrooms, for $20.

Eating

It might seem like heaven for **fast-food** fans, but by and large eating out in Phoenix is hard work and not much fun. Everything is hidden away in shopping malls, with no neighbourhood cafes and surprisingly few coffeeshops or diners. At least there are quite a few good **Mexican** places.

Baxter's, 4515 Cactus Road (☎953-9200). Good-value Western-themed barbecue joint.

Ed Debevic's, 2102 E Highland Ave (☎956-2760). Burgers-and-fries retro-Americana.

Julio's Barrio, 7243 E Camelback Road (☎423-0058). Good, inexpensive Mexican food in an upbeat 1930s Scottsdale diner.

La Pasadita, 1731 E Van Buren St (☎253-7237). East of the Civic Center; hard to beat for a lunchtime burrito.

The Orangerie, in the *Biltmore Hotel*, 24th St and Missouri Ave (954-2507). Extremely good but outrageously pricey restaurant in a resort hotel on the northeastern side of the city. Top quality, stylish American food in gorgeous Art Deco surroundings.

Nightlife and Entertainment

Not surprisingly, **nightlife** in Phoenix tends toward cowboy dance halls and Top 40 discos in the big hotels. One of the nicest **bars** in town is in the *Biltmore* (see above), but budget travellers stuck here for longer than expected will find hundreds of places to drown their sorrows.

For a rundown of **what's on** musically, pick up the free *New Times Weekly* in local record- or bookstores, or check out standbys like the *Sun Club*, 1001 E Eighth Street (☎968-5802), *Char's Blues*, 4631 N Seventh Avenue (☎230-0205) or the headbanging *Mason Jar*, 2303 E Indian School (☎956-6271). The *Scottsdale Center for the Arts*, 7383 Scottsdale Mall (☎994-2787), puts on a fairly upmarket series of jazz, ballet, and chamber music concerts, as well as weekend cinema classics.

East of Phoenix: The Superstition Mountains and Aravaipa Canyon

Whatever its faults, at least Phoenix lies within easy reach of the intriguingly named and haunting **Superstition Mountains** that rise to the east. The main route through the angular mountains, Hwy-88 (popularly known as the **Apache Trail**), is full of cars on a summer weekend; the road cuts off northeast from US-60 about ten miles east of downtown Phoenix. Despite the many dams along the Salt River it makes for a pleasant drive, and there are lots of picnic spots and campgrounds. The road turns to gravel just beyond the funky hamlet of **Tortilla Flat** (named after the Steinbeck novella), before reaching the cliff dwellings of **Tonto National Monument** (daily 8am–4pm; $3 per car), where the remains of a large pueblo built in the mid-fourteenth century by Salado Indians are preserved in the mouths of three distinct caves.

Hwy-88 rejoins US-60 at the old mining town of **GLOBE**, on the western edge of the two-million-acre Apache Indian Reservation. Globe has the small but diverting **Gila County Historical Museum**, 1330 N Broad Street (summer only, Sat & Sun 10am–5pm; free), and an art gallery inside the grand old County Courthouse on Broad at Oak streets, but is most worth a look during the **Apache Days** celebration on the third weekend in October, when Native Americans of all tribes come together for a three-day street fair. The *Ember Motel,* 1105 Broad Street (☎425-5736), has doubles (and a pool) for $30 a night, and *La Luz del Dia* bakery and cafe on Broad Street at Mesquite does tasty burritos made from fresh tortillas.

Aravaipa Canyon

The mountainous but generally featureless Apache Indian reservations stretch east of Globe nearly to the New Mexico border, while Hwy-77 heads south toward Tucson through the heart of Arizona's copper-mining territory. Some of the landscape is terribly scarred, but one of the prettiest spots in the entire state, **Aravaipa Canyon**, can be reached 46 miles south of Globe and then eleven miles east on a well-maintained, mostly dirt road. A wilderness area managed jointly by the US government and the Arizona Nature Conservancy, Aravaipa, with its numerous side canyons, forms a microcosm of the desert, ranging from saguaro cactus on sun-drenched hillsides to giant cottonwood trees along a deep gorge, carved from luminous red volcanic stone by the erosive effects of **Aravaipa Creek** – one of the few year-round desert streams. It's a great place to experience the desert in its wild state, but you need to come prepared. It has no trails, no established campgrounds, and no signs; but on the other hand there are rattlesnakes, scorpions, and the hot summer sun. In order to ensure solitude, only fifty people are allowed to be in the thirty-square-mile wilderness at any one time; get a permit ($1.50 a day), and more information by contacting the Bureau of Land Management, 425 E Fourth Street, Safford AZ 85546 (☎428-4040).

Central Arizona

The interstate I-40 crosses through the centre of Arizona, skirting the **Navajo Reservation** which fills the northeastern corner of the state. Though the narrow strip of land to either side can be extraordinarily beautiful, with double rainbows reaching across the desert plain and fiery dawns blazing along the horizon, it holds few specific places worth stopping for until you come to the **Flagstaff** area. Itself a pleasant town, Flagstaff makes a base for several interesting excursions – to ancient **Indian sites** and the New Age mecca of **Sedona**, but above all through the forests to the **Grand Canyon**. Beyond Flagstaff to the west, there is once again little of interest.

East of Flagstaff: Winslow, Holbrook and the Petrified Forest

The widely touted **Meteor Crater** (daily 8am–5pm; $6), six miles south of the interstate on a well-marked road 38 miles east of Flagstaff, might possibly have been interesting 22,000 years ago, when a meteorite blasted a huge hole, nearly a mile across and over 500 feet deep, into the scrubby plateau, but is only worth visiting today for those who are obsessed with astronauts. The private and unimaginative **Astronauts Hall of Fame** (daily, dawn to dusk; $6) commemorates the fact that the first men on the moon were trained on its other-worldly surface (and according to sceptics faked their entire mission here). You cannot hike into the actual crater.

Two old Route 66 towns, **WINSLOW** and **HOLBROOK**, are kept alive by transcontinental truckers. Each has a strip of motels – try the *Town House Lodge* in Winslow (☎289-4611) or the *Comfort Inn* in Holbrook (☎524-6131) – and not much else. Winslow is a bit more interesting (*Evelyne's Tavern* is worth checking out); Holbrook, 32 miles further east, is so dull that three of the four pages in its visitors guide carry TV listings.

The Petrified Forest and the Painted Desert

At **Petrified Forest National Park**, which straddles I-40 a dozen miles east of Holbrook and roughly a hundred miles from Flagstaff, a fossilised prehistoric forest of gigantic trees is gradually being unearthed by erosion. The original cells of the wood have been replaced by multicoloured crystals of quartz. Cross-sections, cut through with diamond saws and polished, look stunning, and can be seen in the two **visitor centres**, roughly thirty miles apart at the north and south entrances. On the ground, however, the trees are not really all that exciting: segmented, crumbling and very dark. Here and there rough concrete walkways have been laid over the terrain – and often over the tree trunks themselves. If you do want to see for yourself, the **Long Logs Walk** near the southern entrance is probably the best; but when all is said and done, they're still just a bunch of logs lying in the sand, even if they are stone logs.

The park's Indian **relics** include the reconstructed seven-hundred-year-old **Agate House** on Long Logs Walk, built entirely from petrified wood but somehow completely unatmospheric. Ten miles further on, one of the many petroglyph-covered rocks to be known as **Newspaper Rock** lies at the foot of a rocky incline. Close access is strictly forbidden, and in the absence of the official park telescopes you can just peer hopefully at the indistinct and undeciphered scribbles.

The northern section of the national park is renowned for its views of the **Painted Desert**, an undulating expanse of sand dunes which at different times of day take on different colours (predominantly blueish shades of grey and reddish shades of brown). It's a god-forsaken and eerie landscape, but not one that lives long in the memory compared to many of the other natural wonders of Arizona.

Flagstaff

Although some of its old streets are still redolent with Wild West charm, **FLAGSTAFF**'s real significance has always been as a centre for transport and trade. Its main thoroughfare, Santa Fe Avenue, was once Route 66, and, before that, the pioneer trail west. For more than a century, the Santa Fe Railroad has run right alongside, and trains still pull in at the wooden stationhouse right in the heart of town, a minute's walk from the helpful **visitor centre** at 101 W Santa Fe Avenue (Mon–Sat 8am–9pm, Sun 8am–5pm; ☎1-800/842-7293 or ☎774-9541).

The first white settlers arrived in 1876, lured from Boston by widely published accounts of mineral wealth and fertile land – and soon moved on, disappointed, towards Prescott. However, they stayed long enough to celebrate the centenary of American independence by flying the Stars and Stripes from a towering pine tree. This flagpole itself became a familiar landmark on the route west, and as the community grew it inevitably became known as Flagstaff. Right from the start, it was a cosmopolitan town, with a strong black and Hispanic population working in the (originally Mormon-owned) lumber mills and in the cattle industry, and Navajo and Hopi Indians heading in from their nearby reservations to trade.

Today, Flagstaff makes an ideal base for travellers, with hotels, restaurants, bars and shops aplenty within easy strolling range of the centre (and the food and lodging chains a couple of miles away beside the interstate). There's not all that much of interest in the town itself, but the countryside in every direction is very much worth exploring.

Flagstaff Public Transport – and Getting to the Grand Canyon

As the nearest town of any size to the Grand Canyon, seventy miles northwest (see p.695), Flagstaff remains the major junction for road and rail passengers. Though the Santa Fe Railroad is still busy with freight, the only passenger **trains** which stop here now each day are the 6.57am to Albuquerque and the 9.24pm to Los Angeles. *Greyhound* (☎774-4573) and *Nava-Hopi* (☎774-5003 or ☎1-800/892-8687) **buses** pull up at 399 S Malpais Lane, south of the tracks a few minutes' walk away. Both serve long-distance east–west routes and also run south to Phoenix via Sedona. Within town, *Pine Country Transit* **buses** are geared to suit residents rather than tourists, running through the suburbs, past the university, and up to the interstate.

To reach the **Grand Canyon**, unless you take an *America West* flight (at least one daily; ☎1-800/247-5692), you can either rent a vehicle or take the *Nava-Hopi* bus. At present three buses each day run to Grand Canyon Village ($14 single), at 7.10am,

8.45am, and 4pm; the first two run from both the *Amtrak* and *Greyhound* stations, the last from *Greyhound* only.

Both *Nava-Hopi Tours* and the slightly more energetic *Northern Arizona Wilderness Tours* at 284 Toho Trail (☎525-1028) run reasonably priced (if a bit hurried) daily **excursions** around the vicinity, as well as to Navajo and Hopi country and beyond.

The cheapest **car rental**, which shared between a group can cost less than the bus, is *Bargain Rent-a-Car* at 23 N Leroux Street (☎526-2323). Two shops rent out **mountain bikes** at $20 for one day, $10 per day long term: *Absolute Bikes*, 18 N San Francisco Street (☎779-5969), and *Cosmic Cycles*, 113 S San Francisco Street (☎779-1092).

The Museum of Northern Arizona

The exceptional **Museum of Northern Arizona** (daily, 9am–5pm; $3), three miles northwest of Flagstaff on US-180 but not on a local bus route, covers geography, flora and fauna, but places its main emphasis on documenting Indian life. It provides an excellent run-through of the **Anasazi** past and contemporary Navajo, Havasupai and Hopi culture, as well as actively encouraging the development of traditional and even new skills among Native American craftworkers. The exquisite inlaid silver jewellery now made by the Hopi stems, for example, from a museum-backed programme to find work for Hopi servicemen returning from World War II.

At all times there are marvellous pots, rugs and kachina dolls on display – and marvellous ones do exist, despite the low standards often seen elsewhere – but *the* time to come is for one of the Indian Craftsmen Exhibitions each summer. The **Zuni** show lasts for five days around Memorial Day weekend in late May; the **Hopi** one is on the weekend closest to July 4, and the nine-day **Navajo** event is at the end of July and the start of August, with every item for sale. There are also temporary shows of local (not always Indian) arts and crafts, and a well-stocked bookshop.

A **nature trail** runs through a small canyon next to the museum. On the road back towards town, the **Coconino Center for the Arts** is a gallery and concert hall specialising in works by local artists, while just behind it the co-operatively run **Art Barn** has a wide selection of crafts for sale.

Lowell Observatory

Astronomer Dr Percival Lowell established the **observatory** at the top of Mars Hill, a mile west of downtown Flagstaff, in 1894. Here he deluded himself that he'd discovered canals on Mars; but here too he performed the calculations which led to the discovery of the planet Pluto in 1930. Serious work continues, but there are daily guided tours at 1.30pm, and star-gazing sessions from 8pm to 10pm every Friday which provide an opportunity (weather permitting) to look through the original telescope (☎774-2096).

Flagstaff Practicalities

There are three very cheap and basic **hostels** right in the centre of town: *Weatherford Hotel*, 23 N Leroux Street (☎774-2731), *Du Beau Motel*, 19 W Phoenix Avenue (☎774-6731), and the summer-only *Downtowner*, 19 S San Francisco Street (☎774 8461), all provide dorm beds or small shared rooms at $10 to $12 per night per person. Cheap **motels** abound along the interstate in the Butler Avenue area. For greater comfort, try the *Ramada* at 2320 E Lucky Lane, costing around $55 (☎526-1150). **Campgrounds** are five miles north on US-89 – *Flagstaff KOA* (☎526 9926) – and three miles south on US-89A – *Fort Tuthill County Park* (☎774 5139).

For **food**, *Charley's Pub and Restaurant* in the *Weatherford Hotel* makes a classy if unlikely contrast with the hostel rooms upstairs, serving good cheap food accompanied by live music (cocktail piano at lunch, bands at night). San Francisco Street, south of the tracks and near the university, has largely been taken over by the alternative student crowd. The wholefood at the daytime-only *Morning Glory Cafe*, no. 115 (☎774-

9080) is cheaper though not to everyone's taste, while *Hassib's* at no. 211 (☎774-1037) does a variety of mid-Eastern and European dishes. *Dragons Plunder* at no. 217 is a lively secondhand **bookshop**, while the *Mad Italian* at no. 101 (☎779-1820) is a highly sociable **bar** with several pool tables.

Around Flagstaff

The area around Flagstaff is extraordinarily rich in natural and archaeological wonders, with three national monuments – **Sunset Crater, Wupatki**, and **Walnut Canyon** – within 25 miles. Of these, only Sunset Crater even has a campground, and none has indoor lodgings. The one alternative base to Flagstaff, Sedona (see below), is that bit further away and that bit more expensive, and there's no scheduled public transport, so if you don't have your own vehicle you'll have to take a guided tour.

Sunset Crater and Wupatki

The **San Francisco Volcanic Field** north of Flagstaff, of around 400 volcanoes, is prominent on the western horizon from the Hopi Mesas, and its peaks are said to be the home of their powerful kachina spirits. At certain times of year the Hopi make pilgrimages on foot from the mesas to shrines hidden in the mountains.

Several hiking trails lead into the San Francisco Peaks, and a chairlift operates through the summer (10am–4pm; ☎779-6127) from the **Fairfield Snowbowl** almost to the summit of Mount Agassiz (12,350 feet), though you can't hike any further from there. For a brief period each winter this becomes a mildly hectic ski area.

Some of the volcanoes are probably still active, though the most recent eruption was that of **Sunset Crater** (twelve miles from Flagstaff on US-89) in or around 1066 AD. In addition to the impression this made as a spectacle, it had a profound impact on local population and economy. Thick deposits of ash for miles around opened up previously infertile land to cultivation, accelerating if not triggering a landrush which threw different Indian cultures into contact and competition for the first time. The crater was named by John Wesley Powell for the many colours of its cone, which swells from a black base through reds and oranges to a yellow-tinged crest. It's now too unstable for walkers to be allowed onto the rim, but a trail passes through "Ice Caves" and lava tubes around its base. There's a **visitor centre** nearby (open all year, at least 8am–5pm; ☎527-7042), opposite the *Bonito Campground* (mid-May to mid-Oct).

A dozen miles further north, the ancient Indian ruins at **Wupatki National Monument** appear to show different tribal groups living side by side in harmony. The Sinagua were joined here by many others, including the Anasazi, after the Sunset Crater explosion. When the rich new soil created by the eruption had been exhausted, around 150 years later, they all moved on once more. The specific site known as Wupatki (*tall* or *big house*) is just the largest of innumerable sites here, standing proud on its natural foundations of red sandstone. Many others remain unexcavated; there may well be further finds as significant as the oval ball court, reminiscent of the great Mexican civilisations, discovered in 1965.

Walnut Canyon

Between 1100 and 1250 AD **Walnut Canyon**, ten miles east of Flagstaff just south of I-40, was home to a thriving Sinagua community, who lived in small family groups rather than in communal pueblos. Literally hundreds of their **cliff dwellings** can still be seen nestling beneath overhangs in the sides of the canyon. They simply walled off alcoves where the softer levels of the striated rock had eroded away, and then put up partitions to make separate rooms.

A large scenic window in the **visitor centre** (summer 7am–6pm, otherwise 8am–5pm; ☎526-3367) gives an excellent overall view. **Walnut Creek** itself, long since diverted to provide Flagstaff's drinking water, now runs very dry, but you can still see how fertile this valley must have been when the Sinagua first arrived. Trees cling to the porous rock to shade the ancient dwellings, and the vegetation thickens down to a valley floor dense with black walnut and oak. A short trail of steep steps leads down from the visitor centre and across a narrow causeway to an isthmus of rock high above a gooseneck of the creek. Along the path, you can go inside several Sinagua homes; note the T-shaped doorways, that could only be entered head first, and the ceilings blackened by the smoke of generations of fires. Lots of petroglyphs have been found in the other ruins visible to all sides of the canyon, though none remain on the trail.

Another trail follows the rim of the canyon. Its main purpose is as a less strenuous walk, leading to a picnic area and to some surface ruins (in the dissimilar pueblo style), though you could keep going to turn this into a lengthy hike. There is no accommodation, and only minimal snack food, available at the canyon.

Sedona and Red Rock Country

US-89A threads its way south from Flagstaff down **Oak Creek Canyon** to emerge after 28 miles at **Sedona**, on the threshold of the extraordinary **Red Rock Country**. Up from the valley rise giant mesas and buttes of stark red sandstone, where Zane Grey set a number of his Wild West adventures. The boom-and-bust mining town of **Jerome** looks down from a mountainside to the south, while back beside I-17 towards Phoenix are the haunting Sinagua ruins of **Tuzigoot** and **Montezuma Castle**.

Oak Creek Canyon

Claims that Oak Creek Canyon is a serious rival to the Grand Canyon are somewhat exaggerated. However, you *can* drive right through it, and with its sheer walls striped in vivid horizontal bands of colour, its sparkling streams and densely wooded glens, and its facilities for camping, eating and generally playing around, anywhere else in the world this would be an unmissable attraction.

Lookout Point, its northern end, appears suddenly a dozen forested miles out of Flagstaff. The road then drops sharply to run alongside **Oak Creek** itself. The lowest level in the rocks to either side, often obscured by maples, cedars, oaks and pine, is the bright red Supai sandstone. Above that rise layers of white sandstone, buff limestone, and finally black basalt, all testifying to a geological history which has fluctuated from harsh desert to sea bottom. Temperatures are cool enough to make fishing, picnicking and hiking expeditions welcome escapes. **Slide Rock State Park** ($5) is a natural waterchute, where families can swim and slide across smooth boulders set in the river bed. The absence of still water in Oak Creek means that it's almost insect-free.

The canyon floor is quite narrow, and has been heavily developed with leisure facilities, though at least careful landscaping makes most of these inconspicuous. Only those **campgrounds** which are at river (and road) level can stay open year-round; these include *Bootlegger* and *Pine Flat* (both ☎282-4119). *Don Hoel's Cabins* (☎282-3560) are well-equipped log cabins costing $42 to $65 per night. The most popular place to **eat** is *Garland's* (☎282-3343), which has a different very small menu each night, and tends to be booked up way in advance.

Sedona

SEDONA itself adds nothing to the beauty of the scenery. Architecturally, it's a real mess, with all manner of pseudo-historical buildings – such as Sacajawea Mall and the Sinagua Shopping Center – lining its narrow main road. Fifty years ago this was a small Mormon settlement, unmarked on most maps. Now it's a major artistic and spiritual community (and retirement centre) which many locals like to see as becoming "the next Santa Fe" (the response to which in Santa Fe is, "they're welcome").

An intriguing blend of influences is at work in Sedona. Since Page Bryant, author and psychic, "channelled" the information in 1981 that Sedona is in fact "the heart *chakra* of the planet", and pinpointed her first **vortex** (see box below), the town has achieved its own personal growth and blossomed as a focus for **New Age** practitioners of all kinds. Even the most hard-nosed commercial operation here can seem just a front for the real business of holding earnest conversations about the state of each other's psyches. At the same time, this is the heartland of support for former Arizona senator Barry Goldwater, the most right-wing Republican presidential candidate this century, so there's a strong element of "pay not taxes/take no welfare" mixed in too. The whole thing is kept ticking over by the very rich, who dominate the property market and expect to have their expensive tastes catered for.

Greyhound **buses** between Flagstaff and Phoenix stop in downtown Sedona, just before the road junction known as the "Y". Walking along the busy main street, you can hear the synchronised chirruping of the crickets in Oak Creek down below. One branch of town continues intermittently for several miles along US-89A, while a short way along Hwy-179 towards the interstate you come to the comparatively tasteful **Tlaquepaque** shopping centre. If you don't have much time to spend exploring, a cruise along US-89A enables you to see most of the sights, albeit from a distance; the best parts are south along Hwy-179 within Coconino National Forest. The closest **vortex** to town is on **Airport Mesa**; turn left up Airport Road from US-89A as you head south, about a mile past the "Y". The vortex is at the junction of the second and third peaks, just after the cattle grid. Further up, beyond the precarious airport, the **Shrine of the Red Rocks** looks out across the entire valley.

Sedona is not a cheap place to **stay**; you can get better deals at Cottonwood, Jerome and near Montezuma Castle (see p.686). In town, there are a number of luxury B&Bs;

VORTEX TOURS OF RED ROCK COUNTRY

What to a traditional tour guide is a big red rock called "Snoopy" or "Garfield" is to the enterprises below a "sacred energy area" or a "beacon vortex". Combining New Age mysticism with (a version of) Native American wisdom, a "vortex" is a point at which psychic energies can be channelled for personal and planetary harmony.

Huge crowds of alternative practitioners came to Sedona a couple of years back for the "Harmonic Convergence"; the one unsatisfied customer was the gentleman who brought his mouth-organ, under the impression that it was a harmonica convergence.

Dorian Tours (☎284-1650). The original vortex tour.

Earth Wisdom Tours (☎282-4714). From 1hr 30min up to a six-day earth medicine workshop.

Kachina Riding Stables (☎282-7252). Horseback trips, largely geared around eating (in traditional cowboy style).

Northern Light Balloon Expeditions (☎282-2274). Balloon trips with champagne picnics.

Pink Jeep Tours (☎282-5000). You can't miss this lot in downtown Sedona. Quite exceptionally garish "4-wheelin' vehicles", crunching around in 3hr off-road tours.

Sedona Adventures (☎282-4114). A 3hr "opportunity for a personal experience at a Sedona vortex", or up to 8hr honouring the living earth by bombing around in a jeep to sacred Indian sites. Also a "pampered camp-

ing experience" of three days and two nights: "spend quality time in nature, discovering your inner vision, with a master guide".

Sedona Llama Treks (☎284-0233). You don't actually ride the llamas, they just carry your lunch, with "chilled wines and outrageous desserts". You can stay out all night with one if you want.

Sedona Red Rock Jeep Tours (☎1-800/848-7728). 3hr Sacred Earth Tours. "Learn to smudge and walk in balance", to "work with crystals and . . . tap the energy of the earth's power spots to enhance personal growth" and "focus on the need to offer love and healing to our earth, as well as each other".

Sedona Source (☎1-800/359-5940) co-ordinate a whole trip, with accommodation, tours, flights, and alternative stuff.

Time Expeditions (☎282-2137). Up to 3hr in a jeep with an anthropologist.

contact the Chamber of Commerce near the "Y" (☎1-800/288-7336). What pass here for budget **motels**, all just north of the "Y" and with doubles for around $45, are the *Star*, 295 Jordan Road (☎282-3641), *Canyon Portal*, 210 N US-89A (☎282-7125) and *La Vista*, 500 N US-89A (☎282-7301). The nearest **camping** is in Oak Creek Canyon.

With **restaurants** of all styles and prices, you're spoilt for choice. Several of the more expensive are in Tlaquepaque; otherwise *Eat Your Heart Out* at 350 Jordan Road (☎282-1471) is recommended as an Italian and continental cafe, and *Food Among the Flowers* is a very reasonable vegetarian place at 2445 W US-89A (☎282-2334). This latter, well west of the "Y", shares its premises with *The Center in Sedona for the New Age* (☎282-1949). Nearby, the *Golden Word Book Centre* at 3150 US-89A (☎282-2688) is a **New Age bookshop**, with exclusive rights to Page Bryant's vortex revelations, as well as crystals and cassettes. Sedona's superb setting and New Age connections have put it on the circuit for big-name **musical** events, including the *Jazz On The Rocks* festival each September (☎282-1935).

As well as the *Greyhound* link, the *Sedona–Phoenix Shuttle* **bus** (☎282-2066) runs thrice daily; and five daily return **flights** to Phoenix are operated by *Air Sedona* (☎282-7935 or ☎1-800/535-4448). Two companies rent **bikes**: *Canyon Country Mountain Bikes*, at 245 N US-89A, inside *Sedona Sports* (☎282-6985), and *Sedona Mountain Bike Rental* at 376 Apple Avenue downtown (☎282-2164).

Jerome

The former mining town of **Jerome**, once the fourth largest community in Arizona, stands high above the Verde Valley on US-89A about thirty miles south of Sedona. It's conspicuous from quite a distance; an enormous letter "J" is etched deep into the hillside above it, and a large chunk of that hillside is missing altogether, having been blown apart for **opencast copper mining**. This land abounds in mineral wealth – thick veins of copper are interspersed with gold and silver, and an endless supply of limestone is still extracted for cement – but serious exploitation only started in 1876. The **United Verde** mine was partly financed by New Yorker Eugene Jerome (a cousin of Winston Churchill's mother, Jennie Jerome), who insisted that the new town bear his name. Until the current tortuous road was built, the only way up to Jerome was the precipitous railway connecting the mine with the world's largest copper smelter (the smokestacks are still there) at Clarkdale.

With its vastly disproportionate population of young males, Jerome was known as a hard-drinking and hard-living town. The young **Pancho Villa** started out in life by supplying its drinking water, using a relay of two hundred burros, and for a brief period the International Workers of the World (the "**Wobblies**") were a strong presence; several hundred miners and "outside agitators" were literally railroaded out of town in July 1917 and dumped unceremoniously in the remote deserts of southwest Arizona.

Harsh economic realities have always determined local fortunes. Plenty of copper remains in the earth; although the Depression hit hard, the mine was only closed when cheap imported copper in the early 1950s made it uneconomic to continue, and there's every possibility that as prices rise, it will re-open. To keep the mineral rights from reverting to the state, the present owners are obliged to keep on researching and prospecting; in fact they consistently do more than they have to, and have reportedly found enough gold to cover their expenses.

Even as recently as the 1970s, this was a **ghost town** in which it was possible to turn up and move into an empty house. Many who did so are still here, making a living from arts and crafts, and the town itself has made a dramatic recovery. It's a bit of a tourist trap, but is nonetheless fascinating to explore. The hillside is so steep that the stone houses (it was far too expensive to haul timber up here) tend to have two storeys at the front and four or five at the back. Under the repeated concussion of over 200 miles of tunnels being blasted into the mountainside, the whole town used to slip downhill at the rate of five inches per year, and the **Sliding Jail** on Hull Avenue came to rest 225 feet from where it was built.

The two old-style **hotels** on Jerome's Main Street – *Connor Hotel* (☎634-5792) at no. 168, and the *Miner's Roost* (☎634-5094) at no. 309 – charge $30 to $45 for a double room. Both have **bars**, and the latter also operates a **cafe**, *Betty's Ore House*. *Macy's European Coffee House* at no. 416 is another good small cafe. The *English Kitchen* (☎634-2132) has been at 119 Jerome Avenue since 1899. Under Chinese ownership, it was an opium den; later the Wobblies held their meetings downstairs. Now it's open for breakfast and lunch every day except Monday, and its terrace offers a commanding view of the valley. Many of the **shops** stock only tacky souvenirs, but interesting crafts showrooms on Lower Main Street include the *Knapp Gallery* and, next door, *Made in Jerome Pottery*.

Motels, and every fast-food outlet imaginable, can be found in **Cottonwood**, a big new retirement centre on the valley floor. The *Sundial Motel* at 1034 N Main St ($28; ☎634-8031) is on the one old street which survives amidst the sprawl.

Tuzigoot

Between Cottonwood and Clarkdale, at **Tuzigoot National Monument**, the roofless but impressive remains of a **Sinagua pueblo** stand forlorn on the crest of a long ridge. The ground floor alone had 77 rooms, and shows signs of repeated additions; this may have been a final enclave, where the Sinagua gathered against encroaching drought before abandoning the area early in the fifteenth century. Artefacts at the **visitor centre** (summer 8am–7pm; ☎634-5564) include turquoise mosaics and shell jewellery.

Montezuma Well and Montezuma Castle

Two further Sinagua sites constitute **Montezuma Castle National Monument**, very near I-17 forty miles south of Flagstaff and twenty miles from Sedona. **Montezuma Well** was once underground, but became a lake, 470ft across, when the rock above it caved in. A phenomenal 1.9 million gallons per day of precious water emerges from the depths, used by farmers today as it was by the Sinagua who built their homes around it in the thirteenth century. You can still see their irrigation ditches, now with solid linings formed by calcium deposits.

Five miles south, **Montezuma Castle** is a superbly preserved **cliff dwelling** in an idyllic setting just above Beaver Creek. Filling an alcove in the hillside with a wall of pink adobe, its five storeys taper up to fit the contours of the rock. Apparently the fingerprints of the masons are still visible on the bricks, and the sycamore beams are still firmly in place, but visitors are no longer permitted to climb up. The ruins of an even larger dwelling "next door", which was burned out around 1400, can be examined more closely. This had 45 rooms, as well as little "cupboards" recessed into the walls.

The **visitor centre** at the castle (summer 8am–7pm, otherwise closing earlier; ☎567 3322) has informative displays on the Sinagua, including a macaw skeleton which suggests trade with the Mexican civilisations thousands of miles to the south. There is no connection with the Aztec ruler Montezuma, though the well does appear on a deer-skin map which belonged to Cortes himself, so presumably his men passed this way.

Two motels at nearby **Camp Verde** charge around $30 per room; *Fort Verde* (☎567-3486) and *Chapparral* (☎567-3451). *Cliff Castle Lodge* (☎567-6611) on the approach road to Montezuma Castle is a luxury hotel built in what might conceivably have been Anasazi style, had the Anasazi ever felt the urge to build enormous hotels.

West of Flagstaff: I-40 to California

Everything along I-40 west of Flagstaff is dominated by the fact of being on the main route between Las Vegas and the Grand Canyon. The first town you reach, **WILLIAMS**, seems to exist solely to capture the passing tourist trade, though it livens up come winter, when the slopes of Mount Williams and the rest of the surrounding **Kaibab National Forest** offer good skiing, particularly for cross-country aficionados. Further west 45 miles, at the town of SELIGMAN, one of the longest surviving stretches of the old Route 66 heads off on a northern loop through the **Hualapai Indian Reservation** and a dozen quickly fading towns, **Peach Springs** in particular, that look straight out of *The Grapes of Wrath*. With its old diners and dusty grand hotels, it makes a great detour on what is otherwise a very dull drive; it also provides the best access to the less visited western reaches of the Grand Canyon, around emerald **Havasu Canyon** (see p.700).

Apart from needing to fill your tank, or fill up on fast food, there's little reason to stop at **KINGMAN**, the largest town in western Arizona, from where US-93 branches north to Las Vegas and I-40 continues to Los Angeles.

Lake Havasu City

Forty miles southwest of Kingman, ten miles from the California border, a detour south brings you to one of the more bizarre sights of the American desert – the old grey stone of **London Bridge**, reaching out to an artificial island across the stagnant waters of the dammed Colorado River at **LAKE HAVASU CITY**. It has to be said that it looks a hell of a lot better here in the middle of the desert, with the Chemehuevi Mountains as a backdrop, than it ever did between South London and the City. The resort's developer, Robert P McCulloch, bought the bridge (under the impression it was Tower Bridge – or so the story goes) for 2.4 million dollars in the late 1960s, and painstakingly shipped it across the Atlantic Ocean and much of the continental US chunk by chunk before reassembling it over a channel dug to divert water from Lake Havasu, creating an island on the other side of the bridge known as Pittsburgh Point.

One *Greyhound* **bus** daily stops outside *McDonalds*, 100 Swanson Avenue, on its way to Las Vegas. **Motels** are abundant; the *Windsor Inn Motel,* 451 London Bridge Road (☎855-4135), has rooms from $28, while *Pioneer Hotel of Lake Havasu,* 271 S Lake Havasu Avenue (☎1-800/528-5169), costs a little more ($40–60) but has its own casino. Among several good-value **restaurants** is *Shrugrue's* in the Island Fashion Mall at the end of London Bridge, which serves fresh fish, salads and pasta.

About twenty miles south of town, clearly signposted from Hwy-95, the **Colorado River Indian Reservation** (daily 8am–sundown; $3) has a collection of prehistoric giant rock figures, or *intaglios*, made by "carving" the desert floor, shedding the darker top layer of rock to reveal the lighter layers of sand beneath. The figures are so huge (up to 160 feet) that it's hard to tell what you're looking at, but gaze long enough and you can discern a four-legged animal, and a human and spiral design.

Northeastern Arizona: Indian Country

The deserts of northeastern Arizona, popularly known as **Indian Country**, hold some of the most fascinating **pre-Columbian ruins** in North America, in the most striking settings imaginable. The cliff palaces of **Canyon de Chelly**, and **Betatakin** and **Keet Seel** in the Navajo National Monument, are among the greatest architectural achievements of the **Anasazi**, made that much more special by the fact that the lands on which they stand are still lived in and worked by their heirs, the Navajo and Hopi.

The **Navajo Nation**, the largest Indian reservation in the US, fills most of the region, lapping over into western New Mexico and stretching to include the majestic sandstone pillars of Monument Valley in southernmost Utah. Historically, the migrant Navajo have been adept at absorbing other cultures, and in modern times they've embraced the American Way – driving pickup trucks and wearing baseball caps emblazoned with the names of their favourite tractor, fertilizer or football team. But to speak

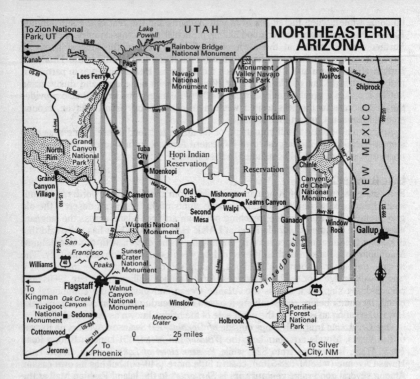

of them as constituting a separate and sovereign nation within the United States is not some polite fiction. You get a very real sense of travelling through a foreign country. The Navajo have their own police and legal system, and though everyone can speak English, Navajo is still the native tongue: a language so complex that it was used as a secret US military code during World War II. High-tech supermarkets mark their prices in Navajo, and the reservation has its own time zone; in frontier-style towns like Tuba City the time on the clock varies according to whether you're in an American or a Navajo district. Tune into the Navajo Nation **radio station**, KTNN 740AM, for a sometimes surreal sense of the Navajo-American melange.

While the Navajo were here long before the Spanish, let alone white Americans, it seems that to the **Hopi** people, who have lived for nearly a thousand years, high on multi-fingered mesas at the heart of what is now the Navajo reservation, they will always be interlopers. Far outnumbered by the Navajo, who began to encroach upon their territory around five hundred years ago and eventually surrounded them completely, the Hopi are renowned for their richly spiritual and anti-materialistic way of life, which they celebrate in elaborate dances and religious ceremonies, almost all of which are open to outsiders.

However much others may like to muse about the spirituality and more meaningful way of life of the Native Americans, the people here suffer from the same problems as everywhere in the modern world, if not worse. Unemployment is staggeringly high (upwards of fifty percent), poverty is rife (average income per family is around $6000 per year), and drug and alcohol problems take a heavy toll. Things may perhaps be slowly changing for the better; the provision of education, for instance, which until the

1960s was available almost exclusively through missionary schools which forced students to adopt their faith before they could study, is improving immensely. Also, for the Navajo in particular, money has begun to flow in from the (admittedly contentious) sale of the right to mine the valuable deposits of coal and uranium that lie beneath the bleak surface.

Visiting Indian Country can be fascinating and rewarding, but it's important to respect the people and places you encounter. The Anasazi have long since vanished – Native Americans come here from all over the Southwest and beyond to take pride in their heritage – but many of the relics they left behind are on land that is still of spiritual significance to their modern counterparts. Similarly, it is offensive to photograph or otherwise intrude upon peoples' lives without permission; the reason the Hopi, for example, banned photography was largely because it was such an interfering nuisance.

On a strictly practical note, you shouldn't expect extensive **tourist facilities**. Towns such as Tuba City, Kayenta, Chinle, the Navajo capital Window Rock, and the Hopi's Keams Canyon are mostly recent creations, established as outposts of the US government bureaucracy, with little to offer visitors beyond a handful of places to eat and even fewer hotels and motels. They only come alive during the annual tribal fairs and rodeos, which are great opportunities to sample delicacies like Navajo tacos, or to buy jewellery direct from craftspeople. At other times, you may well be better off staying near I-40 to the south, in Winslow or Holbrook.

Eastern Navajo Reservation

By the time white immigrants began to arrive in force, during the early nineteenth century, the Navajo – who call themselves *Dineh*, "The People" – had lived a settled lifestyle in Arizona for hundreds of years; within a generation they had lost almost everything. When the Yankees took over from the Mexicans, things just got worse, hitting bottom in 1864 when Kit Carson rounded up every Navajo he could find and forced them to move to Fort Sumner in the desolate plain of eastern New Mexico (see p.659). A few years later the Navajo were allowed to return, the US government granting them most of the vast acreage they hold today (lawsuits arising from territorial disputes with the Hopi dragged on until 1978 before eventually being decided in favour of the Hopi). Most of the 100,000 Navajo today are spread out on small holdings, working the land as shepherds and farmers, though many craftspeople also live by selling their wares from small stands set up along highways and in tourist stops.

The political centre of the Navajo reservation is far over on its eastern edge, along the New Mexico border. It was based for fifty years at Fort Defiance, the old US cavalry outpost, until in the 1930s **WINDOW ROCK** was established as a new capital. The seat of the Navajo Tribal Council, the elected governing body, it isn't, however, a great place to get a grasp of Navajo culture. Named for the natural stone arch on its northern side, Window Rock does at least have petrol stations, shops, and a $50-a-night **motel**, the *Navajo Nation Inn* on Hwy-264 (☎871-4108), and the adjacent **Navajo Tribal Museum** (free) gives the background on tribal history and displays a range of high-quality craftwork. The town was in the media spotlight in 1990 because of the illegal dealings of Peter MacDonald, the flamboyant ex-head of Navajo government convicted of extortion, bribery and embezzling over a million dollars in tribal funds.

Thirty miles west of Window Rock on Hwy-264, or 35 miles north of I-40 on US-191, sits the small village of **Ganado**, named after Chief Ganado Mucho ("Won a lot"), who in 1868 signed the treaty giving the Navajo the million-acre parcel they inhabit today. A mile west of the village, which sits astride the highway crossroads, is the **Hubbell Trading Post**. When the Navajo returned to the surrounding land after their incarceration at Fort Sumner, with their livelihood in tatters, it was mainly thanks to independent traders that they were able to survive the first few years and learn to adapt to the whites' dominion. **John Hubbell** encouraged the Navajo to develop their crafts skills, and provided them with food and supplies in exchange for their woven blankets and other crafts. By the 1880s his trading post here had become the main interface between the Navajo and the outside world. The buldings are preserved as they were then, with most of the place still functioning as a shop, and in the visitor centre next door Navajo artisans are at work amidst displays of historical photos and documents.

Canyon de Chelly

A short distance east of **Chinle**, another thirty miles north on US-191, twin sandstone walls emerge abruptly from the desert floor, climbing at a phenomenal rate to become the awesome thousand-foot cliffs of **Canyon de Chelly National Monument**. Between these sheer sides, the meandering course of the Chinle Wash can be discerned by its fringe of cottonwoods as it winds through grasslands and planted fields. Here and there a Navajo hogan stands in a grove of fruit trees, a straggle of sheep is penned in by a crude wooden fence, or ponies drink at the water's edge. And everywhere, perched above the valley on ledges in the canyon walls and dwarfed by the towering cliffs, are the long-abandoned adobe and stone dwellings of the Anasazi.

There are two main canyons, which branch apart a few miles upstream; Canyon de Chelly (a corruption of the Navajo *tségi*, and pronounced *de shay*) to the south and Canyon del Muerto to the north. Each twists and turns in all directions, scattered with vast rock monoliths, while several smaller canyons break away. The whole labyrinth threads its way upwards for thirty miles into the Chuska Mountains.

Visits are constrained by the nature of the terrain and by the fact that the monument retains great symbolic significance to the Navajo (despite the fact that they did not themselves build the cliff dwellings). There is no paved road, and you can only enter upon the canyon floor in the company of one of the many Navajo guides who daily career along the sandy river bed in four-wheel-drive jeeps and trucks.

History

The first known inhabitants of the canyon were the **Anasazi** Basketmakers, around 300 AD. During the next thousand years, before the Anasazi disappeared from history, they had advanced from living in pit houses dug into the soil to building elegant cliff dwellings, and developed fine pottery and weaving (for more on the Anasazi, see p.657). For some centuries thereafter, the Hopi came here to farm each summer, returning for the winter to the mesas to the east, but as time went by, Navajo migrants from the north and west eventually displaced the Hopi altogether.

From 1583 onwards, the Navajo were locked with the Spanish in a bloody cycle of armed clashes and slave raids. The US Army too failed in repeated attempts to dislodge the Navajo, though no treaty could restrain the rapacious pressure for land by New Mexican settlers, as well as Utes, Paiutes, Apaches and Comanches. The end appeared to have come with the brutal roundup and deportation (the "Long Walk") of the entire Navajo people, completed by Kit Carson in 1864 when he starved the last of them down from Navajo Rock and destroyed their homes, livestock, and, worst of all, their beloved peach orchards. So barbaric was their imprisonment at Fort Sumner, however, that Congress soon allowed them to return. To this day, twenty-five Navajo families still farm the Canyon de Chelly in summer, the matrilineal descendants of the women between whom it was re-apportioned in the 1870s.

The View from Above: The Rim Drives

Each of the two "rim drives" from the visitor centre is highly recommended for its succession of spectacular overlooks, which provide the only unaccompanied way to see the canyon. Allow two to three hours for each of the forty-mile round trips. In the past, thefts from cars have been a major problem, and it's wise to follow the prominent warnings.

The furthest point of the **South Rim drive** along Canyon de Chelly is the astonishing **Spider Rock**, twin eight-hundred-foot pinnacles of rock that reach to within two hundred feet of the canyon rim. At **Sliding House Overlook**, the Anasazi ruins seem to be sliding down the canyon walls towards the ploughed Navajo fields below. **White House Overlook** presents the highly photogenic White House Ruins, and is the only point from which you are permitted to hike alone into the canyon, taking perhaps 30 to 45 minutes to get down and a good hour to get back up. The trail itself is very safe, though it is frustrating at the bottom to find that you are forbidden to walk for more than a hundred yards in either direction. Be prepared to wade the wash, though there may be a rudimentary log walkway. **Junction Overlook** is at the meeting point of the two canyons; as you scramble across the bare rocks you can see Canyon de Chelly narrowing away, with a hogan immediately below.

The **North Rim Drive** runs twenty miles up Canyon del Muerto to **Massacre Cave**, where the Spanish expedition of 1805, led by Lieutenant Narbona, is thought to have killed around one hundred Navajo women, children and old men. The "cave" is just a pitifully exposed ledge, upon which the huddled group were easily picked off by the Spanish, using ricochets off the overhang above. Visible from **Mummy Cave Overlook** is the House Under The Rock, with its central tower in the Mesa Verde style – the single most striking ruin in the monument. There are two viewpoints at **Antelope House Overlook**. One is opposite Navajo Rock, the isolated natural fortress where the Navajo were besieged for three months in 1863, climbing by means of pole ladders drawn up behind them and using a human chain to carry water to the top. At the other viewpoint you see the ruins of Antelope House far below, and across the wash the Mummy Cave, where the embalmed body of an old man was found wrapped in golden eagle feathers.

In the small town of **TSAILE**, a short way beyond the monument along the North Rim Drive, the Navajo Community College has a stimulating Indian-run museum of ancient and modern cultures (Mon–Fri 8.30am–noon & 1–4.30pm; ☎724-3311). It is possible to hike into the Canyon del Muerto from this end, although you have to hire the necessary Navajo guides back in Chenle.

Into the Canyons

Tours of the canyon floor, organised by *Thunderbird Lodge* (see below), zigzag along the washes, which vary from two or three feet deep during the spring thaw to completely dry in summer. For most of the year, the tours are in open-top flatbed trucks, and the heat can be incredible; in winter they carry on in glass-roofed army vehicles with caterpillar tracks. To reach as far as Spider Rock, you have to take the full-day tour ($45), but the half-day trip at $28 still enables you to see a wide variety of sites and terrain.

Virtually all the ruins face south to catch the sun, with cold storage chambers deep in shady recesses. Many look more inaccessible than they were, due to rock falls and the erosion of toe- and hand-holds carved into the soft sandstone. The first stop on the tours is at the fenced-off **Antelope House Ruins** in Canyon del Muerto, made of shaped sandstone blocks around a central tower. The wall paintings here are not Anasazi, but were painted in the 1830s by the same Navajo as the "Spanish Mural" a little further along, showing a Spanish lieutenant, priest and troops advancing through the canyon. At the adjacent **Standing Cow Ruin**, a Navajo hogan is built on the foundations of an Anasazi kiva; when the Navajo first returned from Fort Sumner, in their urgent need for shelter they converted some Anasazi ruins for their own use.

The **White House Ruins** are a short distance up Canyon de Chelly. The ground-level buildings here used to be four storeys high, with ladders from the roof reaching up to those on the ledge above.

Practicalities

For the moment, Canyon de Chelly remains remarkably unspoiled. As well as being friendly and informative guides, the Navajo are excellent stewards of the monument. However, facilities are overstretched, and it's essential to book your **accommodation** well in advance. There are only two options, both of which cost around $65 per night: *Canyon de Chelly Motel* (☎674-5875) and *Thunderbird Lodge* (☎674-5841), very near the canyon entrance. The *Lodge* has a cheap and good cafeteria and a well-stocked gift shop, and arranges the standard sightseeing tours (if you take a tour on the day you leave, be sure to check out of your room first; they charge $5 per hour extra after 11am). The adjacent (free and minimally equipped) *Cottonwood Campground* has pleasant sites among the trees. For **food**, the *Canyon de Chelly Restaurant* nearer town has virtually the same menu as the *Thunderbird* cafeteria; at both places, the Navajo taco is the best value. Chinle itself is a brief nondescript straggle on the highway, with service stations, *Taco Bell*, *Kentucky Fried Chicken*, a post office and a laundromat.

The **visitor centre** (daily, May–Sept 8am–6pm, otherwise 8am–5pm; ☎674-5436) on the road out from Chinle has informative displays, and can provide guides for any unorthodox hiking or motorised expeditions. For a group, having your own personal guided tour need not be any more expensive. **Horseback** trips are provided by *Justin's Horse Rentals* (☎674-5678) and *Twin Trail Tours* (☎674-5985).

The Hopi Mesas

The **Hopi** people are virtually unique in the United States; they have lived continuously in the same place for over eight hundred years. Some invaders have come and gone in that time, others have stayed; but the villages on **First**, **Second** and **Third mesas** have endured, if not exactly undisturbed then at least unmoved.

One simple reason is that only the Hopi possess the art to support themselves in this unpromising environment. Although the mesa-tops themselves, six hundred feet from the desert floor, are all but barren, and rain is pitifully scarce, the **Black Mesa** to which they are attached is tilted at just the correct angle to deliver a tiny subterranean layer of water to the washes down below the villages. The Hopi can thus practice "dry farming", rigorously preserving enough precious liquid to grow their crops of corn, beans and squash on hand-tilled terraces. This is a way of life that has, however, been forced upon them; centuries ago, they would farm in summer as far afield as the fertile Canyon de Chelly, and return to the mesas in winter. Then the Navajo came and steadily cut them off from their grazing lands and pastures.

Each of the dozen or so settlements on the mesas centres around a **plaza**, where countless generations have built new houses on top of the old ones as they crumble into sand. Often the main entrance is via the roof, reached by a wooden ladder. A few buildings are now constructed of grey breeze-blocks, but still they blend almost imperceptibly with the ruins that trail away down the slopes. Many of the villages stand on open seams of coal – which is how the Black Mesa gets its name – and massive chunks of coal lie scattered around. Outhouses are dotted across the hillsides, and all waste was traditionally thrown over the edge of the mesa to tumble down and fertilise the terraces – a conservationist policy that works less well now that refrigerators and old bedsteads are being thrown over too.

There are now around ten thousand Hopi, about as many as there were in 1650, which constitutes a recovery from the early twentieth century when just 2500 were left. Visitors are treated with great hospitality, but the Hopi are clearly not interested in turning themselves into a tourist attraction. Accompanied tours of almost all the villages are permitted, though you don't actually see all that much apart from the houses themselves and the distant desert views unless there's a dance or ceremony going on (see box).

THE HOPI CALENDAR

Hopi spirituality, which sees human existence as a cyclical but essentially progressive passage along the road of life, has much in common with Tibetan and Hindu mysticism. Briefly, the Hopi believe that they have evolved through four distinct worlds. In each one, an initial state of innocence has given way to a time of forgetfulness and corruption, and the people have fanned out across the earth to search for the "Place of Emergence" into the next. Here in the fourth world, life is once more difficult, as each individual struggles towards a knowledge of his or her origins, only to be blocked by materialism and selfishness. Hopi mythology describes history as an endless series of migrations, within and between the successive worlds; many of the journeys described seem to correspond to actual geographical features of the Americas. The various partings and reunions that occurred in the current world before the Hopi settled into their present home account for the subdivision of the tribe into the dozen **clans**, each of which has its own clear secular and religious responsibilities.

Over and beyond the clans, the most important forces in Hopi religion are the **kachina** spirits. More akin to angels than to gods, these invisible life forces – who bring rain and crops, and ensure health and welfare, but also occasionally misbehave – are said to be present on the mesas for the first half of each year. Masked and costumed dancers take on the roles of the various kachinas in an elaborate **ritual calendar**, culminating in a sixteen-day sequence of ceremonies each July, once the corn has begun to sprout, when the kachinas return to their homes in the San Francisco Peaks, sixty miles to the west. Carved **dolls** modelled on the different kachina spirits are given to children; these are without religious significance, but have become very popular crafts objects.

Hopi **dances**, held in the central plazas of the mesa-top villages, take place throughout the year, usually at the weekend, so that those Hopi who live and work off the reservation can attend. The **Snake Dance**, in which members of the Snake clan dance with live snakes between their teeth, is held alternately in Shungopavi and Mishongnovi, and is usually closed to outsiders. Tourists who are prepared to maintain the appropriate distance – and don't attempt to take photographs – are, however, made welcome at most of the other dances. Specific timings tend not to be announced until a few days before the ceremonies take place; for information, contact the Cultural Center at Second Mesa.

Visiting the Hopi Mesas

The mesas are roughly fifty miles north of I-40, reached by Hwy-87 from Winslow or Hwy-77 from Holbrook. Hwy-264 runs east to west along the foot of the mesas, from the US Bureau of Indian Affairs outpost at **Keams Canyon** to the half-Hopi, half-Navajo town of **Moenkopi** (where Robert Redford filmed the Anasazi thriller *Dark Wind*).

The essential first stop, at the very heart of the mesas, is the **Hopi Cultural Center**, which serves as motel, restaurant, information centre, gift shop, and museum. This is the place to find out what's going on; the friendly staff are happy to volunteer details of forthcoming dances and events. Much of the **museum** (Mon–Fri 9am–5pm, Sat & Sun 9am–4pm, closed Sun in winter; $3) is devoted to describing various Hopi arts and crafts, with choice examples of pottery and silver overlay jewellery, a recent speciality. It also provides a lot of historical background – particularly to do with the long-running dispute with the Navajo – as well as brief descriptions of each of the mesa-top villages.

The most impressive of the Hopi villages, particularly if you can manage to be there at sunset, when the desert panorama seems set alight and the sacred San Francisco Peaks stand in sharp silhouette, is ancient **WALPI**. Standing all alone on a narrow mesa, connected to the other First Mesa villages by a neck of stone that drops straight down three hundred feet to either side, Walpi is the most unchanged of the Hopi villages, home to some 35 people who do without electricity or running water. To see it, take Hwy-264 to the modern town of **Polacca**, then drive a mile or so up the twisting paved road until it ends at the Ponsi Hall Community Center in the village of

Sichomovi. From the small museum, guides will take you on half-hour tours (9am–5pm; donations), taking in the recently stabilised main plaza, where the famed Snake Dances are held. Depending on the time of year, you'll either be in a group of twenty or so, or on your own, but be sure to ask the guide to point out the steep stairway that drops down to the cornfields four hundred feet below.

The best place to **stay the night** on the Hopi Reservation is the modern $60-a-night motel at the Hopi Cultural Center (☎734-2401); rooms are usually booked solid a week or more in advance, especially during the most popular festivities. In the cafeteria you can get good solid meals – or try **blue cornflakes** for breakfast. Fairly basic double rooms are available for $35 at the *Keams Canyon Motel* (☎738-2297), along Hwy-264 at the eastern edge of the reservation; there's a popular cafe here too, open until 9pm only and dishing up local-style fast food (including exceptionally tough mutton). Some Hopi have established a great rapport with the Rastafarians; top-name **reggae** bands regularly come from Jamaica to play here. No alcohol is sold on the reservation.

Navajo National Monument

Made up of three separate Anasazi sites spread over the forested Shonto Plateau in the northwest quarter of the reservation, the **Navajo National Monument** protects some of the largest and most beautifully sited cliff dwellings in Arizona. From behind the good **visitor centre** (daily 8am–5pm) at the end of paved Hwy-564, ten miles north of US-160, a short walkway crosses the plateau to a viewpoint where you can peer across a canyon to **Betatakin**, a 135-room masonry structure tucked away in a large natural alcove halfway up a 700-foot-high, brilliant red sandstone cliff. A powerful telescope on the overlook enables you to see the exceptionally well-preserved ruins in detail, looking as if they were abandoned just a few years ago. The ladders are new additions, but the visible roof beams are the original timber. To see Betatakin up close, you have to join one of the six-hour ranger-guided hikes (May–Sept only; daily 9am), which leave from the visitor centre. Numbers are limited, and no advance bookings are taken, so get here as early as possible on the day – or stay the previous night at the very attractive free **campground** in the forest next to the visitor centre.

The other two ruins within the monument are much more difficult to get a look at; in fact the small **Inscription House** ruin has been closed to visitors for many years because of its structural instability, and there are no plans to re-open it. During the summer you can still visit **Keet Seel**, one of the best-preserved Anasazi sites in the Southwest, though it's a sixteen-mile round trip from the visitor centre. The largest cliff dwelling in Arizona, consisting of over 150 rooms and four kivas, Keet Seel is well worth the effort it takes to reach, especially if you can stay the night at the small **campground** near the site. Horseback trips are also available for $40 per day, though all visitors must get a permit at least a day in advance (☎672-2366), and be escorted through the site by the park ranger. (The box on p.657 gives more background on the Anasazi.)

Practicalities

Most people pass through this area on their way to somewhere else, so there aren't many places to **stay**. **TUBA CITY**, to the west of the monument, has a $10-a-night **youth hostel** (☎283-6271), a short way east of the point where US-160 meets Hwy-264 from the Hopi Mesas, and the *Tuba City Motel* (☎283-4545), which costs around $50. It also hosts the three-day **Western Navajo Fair** each October. The coal and uranium mining town of **KAYENTA**, 22 miles northeast of the monument at the junction of US-160 and US-163, holds two $70 options: the *Wetherill Inn* (☎697-3231), and the *Holiday Inn* (☎697-3221), inside which there is a distinctive and good-value **restaurant**.

The road north to Kayenta beside the Black Mesa is paralleled by the railroad which carries coal from the mines up to the **Navajo Generating Station** at **Page** (see p.718).

Monument Valley

The bizarre fiery-red sandstone towers of **Monument Valley**, sharply outlined against the desert horizon as they loom over US-163 on both sides of the Arizona–Utah border, are one of the more unforgettable landmarks of the Southwest. This otherworldly skyline has been featured in countless Hollywood Westerns from *Stagecoach* onwards, but even such worldwide exposure can't dilute the visual impact of the red-rock buttes and jagged pinnacles. They are quite simply an amazing sight, especially at sunset when the rock seems to glow even more brightly than the sun itself.

The biggest and most impressive of the monoliths are a pair called **The Mittens**, one East and one West, each of which has a distinct thumb splintering off from its central bulk. The taller of the two rises a thousand feet above the valley floor, with sand dunes lapping at its base. Over a dozen other spires are spread around nearby, along with some rock art panels and an assortment of minor but nicely sited Anasazi ruins.

The whole Monument Valley area is on Navajo reservation land, this portion of which is set aside as the **Monument Valley Tribal Park**. Though you can see almost everything from the highway, the best views are to be had from the small **visitor centre** (daily, summer 7am–sunset, otherwise 7am–5pm; $2.50), a mile east of US-163 and surrounded by Navajo selling crafts and trinkets. If you're captivated and have the time and money to spare, you can see Monument Valley up close on **jeep** or **horse** tours, led by Navajo guides; a two-hour jeep trip costs from around $25 per person, and can be arranged at the visitor centre or through *Goulding's Lodge* (see below). Backpackers can wake up to the sight of Monument Valley, though you need to arrange for a guide to accompany you for the duration of your visit.

Practicalities

There's not much choice as far as sleeping and eating options go: right next to the visitor centre there's the very exposed *Mitten View* campground, which costs $10, and the only nearby place to stay indoors, *Goulding's Lodge* (☎801/727-3231), is over the Utah border, two miles west of US-163 on the road which extends from the Monument Valley visitor centre. *Goulding's* has been here since 1924, when it opened as a trading post; it's now a plush resort with pricey motel rooms (doubles are $85), a fairly good restaurant, and a general store and petrol station. They also offer guided tours. Twenty-five miles north, further into southern Utah, the San Juan River towns of **Bluff** and **Mexican Hat** (see p.716) also make good bases for visiting the area.

The Grand Canyon

Although three million people come to see the **GRAND CANYON OF THE COLORADO** every year, it remains beyond the grasp of the human imagination. No photograph, no set of statistics, can prepare you for such vastness. At more than one mile deep, it's an inconceivable abyss; at from four to eighteen miles wide it's an endless expanse of bewildering shapes and colours, glaring desert brightness and impenetrable shadow, stark promontories and soaring never-to-be-climbed sandstone pinnacles. Somehow it's so impassive, so remote; you could never call it a disappointment, but at the same time many visitors are left feeling peculiarly flat. In a sense, none of the available activities can quite live up to that first stunning sight of the chasm. The **overlooks** along the rim all offer views that shift and change unceasingly from dawn to sunset; you can **hike** down into the depths on foot or by mule, hover above in a **helicopter** or raft through the **whitewater rapids** of the river itself; you can spend a night at **Phantom Ranch** on the canyon floor, or swim in the waterfalls of the idyllic **Havasupai Reservation**; and yet that distance always remains – the Grand Canyon stands apart.

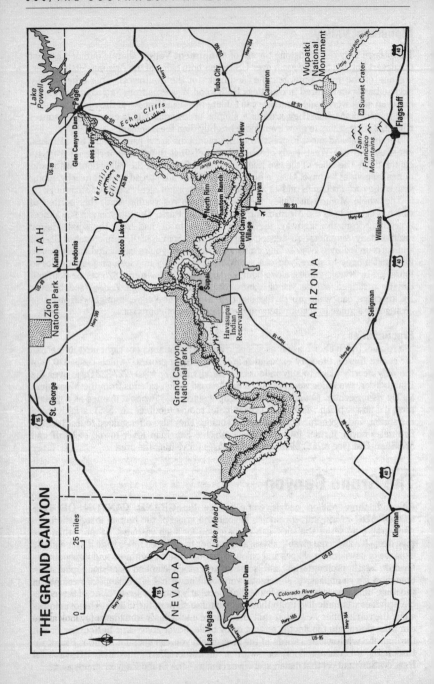

THE GRAND CANYON

0   25 miles

GEOLOGY AND HISTORY OF THE CANYON

Layer upon layer of different rocks, readily distinguished by colour, and each with its own fossil record, recedes down into the Grand Canyon and back through time, until the strata at the river bed are among the oldest exposed rocks on earth. And yet how the canyon was **formed** is a mystery. Satellite photos show that the Colorado actually runs through the heart of an enormous hill (what the Indians called the *Kaibab*, the mountain with no peak); experts cannot agree on how this could happen. Studies show that the canyon still deepens, at the slow rate of 50ft per million years. Its fantastic sandstone and limestone formations were not literally carved by the river; they're the result of erosion by wind and extreme cycles of heat and cold. These features were named – **Brahma Temple**, **Vishnu Temple**, and so on – by Clarence Dutton, a student of comparative religion who wrote the first Geological Survey report on the canyon in 1881.

It may look forbidding, but the Grand Canyon is not a dead place. All sorts of desert **wildlife** survive here – sheep and rabbits, eagles and vultures, mountain lions, and, of course, spiders, scorpions, and snakes. The **human** presence has never been on any great scale, but signs have been found of habitation as early as 2000 BC, and the **Anasazi** were certainly here later on. A party of **Spaniards** passed through in 1540 – less than twenty years after Cortes conquered the Aztecs – searching for cities of gold, and a Father Garcés spent some time with the Havasupai in 1776. **John Wesley Powell's** expeditions along the fearsome and uncharted waters of the Colorado in 1869 and 1871–72 were what really brought the canyon to public attention. A few abortive attempts were made to mine different areas, but facilities for tourism were swiftly realised to be a far more lucrative investment. With the exception of the Indian reservations, the Grand Canyon is now run exclusively for the benefit of visitors; although even as recently as 1963 there were proposals to dam the Colorado and flood 150 miles of the Canyon, and the Glen Canyon dam has seriously affected the ecology downstream.

Until the 1920s, the average **visitor** would stay here for two or three weeks. These days it's more like two or three hours – of which forty minutes are spent actually looking at the canyon. The vast majority come to the **South Rim** – it's much easier to get to by car, train, bus or plane, there are far more facilities (mainly at the Fred Harvey-owned **Grand Canyon Village**), and it's open all year round. There is another lodge and campground at the **North Rim**, which by virtue of its isolation can be a whole lot more evocative, but at one thousand feet higher this is usually closed by snow from mid-October until May. Few people visit both rims; to get from one to the other demands either a two-day hike down one side of the canyon and up the other, or a 215-mile drive by road.

Finally, be warned that there's an ever-increasing risk that on the day you come here the Grand Canyon will be invisible beneath a layer of **fog**; many people blame the 250 tons of sulphurous emissions pumped out every day by the Navajo Generating Station, seventy miles upriver at Page.

Grand Canyon Village

Grand Canyon Village is not a very stimulating place to spend any time. However, in the absence of significantly cheaper accommodation within fifty miles (for example, in **Tusayan** at the park entrance), there's little option but to stay here. The centrepiece is the magnificent **terrace**, in front of *Bright Angel Lodge* (usually the liveliest spot in town) and the black-beamed 1905 *El Tovar Hotel*, that gives many visitors their only look at the canyon – though the Colorado itself is too deep in the Inner Gorge to be seen from here. Further back are more lodges and gift shops, and employee housing, while about a mile east through the woods are the informative **visitor centre** (8am–dusk; ☎638-9304 for recorded information only), the **post office**, the **general store**, and the **campground**.

Getting To and From the Canyon

The most usual approach is by **road** from the south, turning off I-17 at either **Williams** or **Flagstaff**. The final twenty miles of the plain is covered by a thick ponderosa pine forest. The canyon itself is not visible from any distance – often not even from the rim road – so the restored **steam trains** which take 2hr 45min to run the 64 miles up from Williams have few scenic delights to offer. They pull in at the picturesque village station (April–Sept, departing Williams 9am & 10am, and the canyon 3.30pm & 4.30pm; otherwise 10am from Williams and 4.30pm from the canyon; no service Jan & Feb; return fare $50 adults, $25 children under 12; ☎1-800/THE-TRAIN).

Nava-Hopi buses start from *Bright Angel Lodge*, where you can buy tickets. Each day there's a direct service to Flagstaff at 9.45am, and one via Williams at 5.45pm (fare $14).

The **airport** is just outside the park at Tusayan; hourly shuttle buses run the seven miles to the village. *America West* (☎1-800/247-5692) fly to Flagstaff, Phoenix and Las Vegas; *Scenic Airlines* (☎1-800/634-6801) and *Air Nevada* (☎1-800/634-6377) operate to Las Vegas only. Planes no longer fly directly above the canyon, but the Las Vegas flights give a good view and for as little as $60 save an awful lot of time.

During high season (roughly May–Sept) free **shuttle buses** operate every fifteen minutes within the village itself, and along the West Rim Drive (which at those times is barred to motorists), stopping at the main overlooks.

Grand Canyon Accommodation and Food

The Fred Harvey company's monopoly on **accommodation** means that all the "lodges" in the village are at pretty similar prices, without any real budget alternative. (The youth hostel which formerly offered a few cheap beds was condemned as unfit for habitation in 1990, and there are no plans to re-house it elsewhere.)

In terms of seeing the canyon, it makes little difference where in the village you stay. Even in the "rim-edge" places – *El Tovar Hotel* ($90–222), and *Bright Angel* ($44–92), *Thunderbird* and *Kachina* lodges (both $81–87) – few rooms offer much of a view, and in any case it's always dark by 8pm. Further back are *Maswik Lodge* ($44–82; cabins can be shared between groups), and, near the visitor centre, *Yavapai Lodge* ($64–73). All **reservations** are handled by *Grand Canyon National Park Lodges*, PO Box 699, Grand Canyon, AZ 86023 (same-day ☎638-2631, advance ☎638-2401).

GRAND CANYON TOURS AND ENTERTAINMENTS

Fred Harvey do at least two short daily **coach tours** along the **rim** to the west and east of the village, a **sunset trip** to Yavapai point, and **mule** rides to Phantom Ranch. They also run a five-hour **Smooth Water River Raft Excursion** through Marble Canyon; whitewater rafting trips in the canyon proper (see below) are booked up literally years in advance, so this is probably your only chance of a trip along the river at short notice. Details from lodge Transportation Desks, or on ☎638-2401.

Unless otherwise specified, all these companies are in **Tusayan**, at or near the airport.

Airplane tours cost from around $45 for 30min ($30 child) up to as long as you like for as much as you've got:
Air Grand Canyon (☎1-800/AIR-GRAND or ☎638-2686); *Grand Canyon Airlines* (☎1-800/528-2413 or ☎638-2407); *Windrock Aviation* (☎1-800/24ROCKY or ☎638-9591).

Helicopter tours, from $75 for 30min:
AirStar Helicopters (☎638-2622); *Grand Canyon Helicopters* (☎638-2419); *Kenai Helicopters* (☎638-2412).

Wilderness River Adventures (Box 717, Page, AZ 86040; ☎1-800/528-6154 or ☎645-3279). 3–12 day **whitewater raft** trips through the canyon, by the operators of Fred Harvey's half-day trip detailed above.

Grand Canyon IMAX Theatre (summer 8.30am–8.30pm, winter less; $6 adults $4 kids; ☎638-2468). One of the most popular attractions, a 34-minute giant-screen film show of death-defying feats in and above the canyon.

Camping facilities (and a laundromat) are available at the *Mather* campground (☎638-7888) near the visitor centre, at least one section of which is open year-round. If you arrive on foot, you don't need a reservation; all vehicles (there's an RV park as well) should, however, check in well in advance. It's also possible to camp inside the canyon itself, if you first obtain a free permit from the **Backcountry Reservations Office** at the village campground – indeed you can camp anywhere in the national forest that is more than six hundred feet from a roadway.

Food, fortunately, is not always exorbitant. *Yavapai* and *Maswik* lodges have cafeterias, with a good basic range for $6 to $12, open until l0pm. *Bright Angel Lodge* has its own restaurant as well as the *Arizona Steakhouse*, both also open until l0pm, and both costing $15 to $30. At *El Tovar*, where the dining room looks right out over the canyon, the sumptuous menu is, however, enormously expensive. Breakfast is the most affordable; lunch and dinner can easily cost upwards of $40.

Along the South Rim

It's possible to walk along the South Rim for several miles in either direction from the village, the first few of them on railed and concreted pathways. The most obvious short excursions are to see the sun rise and set. At or near the village, the giant wall that reaches out in the west overshadows much of the evening view. If, however, you walk right out to Hopi Point at its end, looking down as you go onto the Bright Angel Trail as it winds across the Tonto Plateau, you may well see a magical **sunset**, with the Colorado – 350 feet wide at this point – visible way below.

The best place within walking distance to watch the **dawn** is Mather Point, a mile east of the visitor centre. Nearby, if you can tear your eyes away from its panoramic bay windows, the **Yavapai Geologic Museum** (9am–7pm in summer) has illuminating displays on how the canyon may have been formed.

Further dramatic views are available along the **East Rim Drive** – although unless you take an excursion you'll need your own vehicle to see them. **Desert View**, 23 miles out from the village, is at 7500 feet the highest point on the South Rim. Visible to the east are the vast flatlands of the **Navajo Nation**; to the northeast, **Vermillion and Echo Cliffs**, and the grey bulk of **Navajo Mountain** ninety miles away; to the west, the gigantic peaks of **Vishnu** and **Buddha Temples**. Through the plains comes the narrow gorge of the **Little Colorado**; somewhere in the depths, before it meets the Colorado itself, is the *sipapu*, the hole through which the Hopi believe that men first entered this, the Third World. The odd-looking construction on the very lip of the canyon is **Desert View Watchtower**, built by Fred Harvey in 1932 in a conglomeration of Native American styles (though a steel frame props it all up) and decorated with Hopi pictographs. It contains a gift shop, as does the general store a few yards away. Groups of tarantulas are often seen in the evenings at Desert View, scuttling back into the warmth of the canyon for the night.

Tusayan Ruin, three miles west of Desert View (and not to be confused with modern Tusayan) is a genuine Anasazi pueblo, though not comparable in scale to the relics elsewhere in this region.

Into the Canyon

A descent into the Grand Canyon offers something more than just another view of the same thing. Instead you pass through a sequence of utterly different landscapes, each with its own distinct climate, wildlife, and topography. It's a hostile environment, and one to be treated with respect. The basic rules are, first, that whatever time you spend hiking down, you should allow twice that to get back up again, and second, carry (and drink) at least one litre of water per person.

The temperature at river level is on average 20° higher than on the South Rim, and there's far less rain. The **ecology** down here is changing fast since Glen Canyon Dam was completed 25 years ago. Previously, up to a million tons of earth and rock hurtled past Phantom Ranch each day. Now it's more like 80,000; trees are establishing themselves that would previously have been swept away, and fish are becoming extinct.

There's only space here to detail the most popular **hiking trail**, the **Bright Angel**. Many of the others, such as the **Hermit**, date from the days prior to 1928, when the obstreperous Ralph Cameron controlled access to the Bright Angel and many other rim-edge sites by means of spurious mining claims, and Fred Harvey had to find other ways to get its customers down to the Colorado. These other trails tend to be overgrown now, or partially blocked by landslides; check before setting out.

Bright Angel Trail

The **Bright Angel Trail**, followed on foot or mule by thousands of visitors each year, starts from the wooden shack in the village which was once the Kolb photographic studio. Allowing four or five hours to hike the 9.6 miles down to **Phantom Ranch**, and another eight or nine to get back up again, you should think carefully before attempting the return trip in one day. Many hikers choose instead to go as far as **Plateau Point** on the edge of the arid Tonto Plateau, an overlook above the Inner Gorge from which it is not possible to descend any further. In summer, you can obtain water along the trail, and only need to carry one litre of water per person; in winter, when there is none, you should carry two.

The first section of the trail was laid out by miners a century ago, along an old Havasupai route. There are two short tunnels in its first mile. After another mile, the **wildlife** starts to increase (deer, rodents and the ubiquitous ravens), and there are a few **pictographs** which have been all but obscured by graffiti.

At **Indian Gardens**, almost five miles down, there's a ranger station and campground with water. Here the trails split, to Plateau Point or down to the river via the **Devil's Corkscrew**, constructed by the WPA in the 1930s. It leads through sand dunes scattered with cacti and down beside **Garden Creek** to the Colorado, which you then follow for more than a mile to get to Phantom Ranch.

Phantom Ranch

It's a real thrill to spend a night at the very bottom of the canyon, in the 1922 **Phantom Ranch**. You can only get there after an all-day hike on foot or mule, and in any case the $58 cabins are fully booked eighteen months ahead (though there may be $22 dorm beds available). All supplies reach Phantom Ranch the same way you do, so meals are expensive, a minimum of $10 for breakfast and $17 for dinner. Hikers must register with the *Bright Angel* transportation desk the day prior to their reservation, by 4pm, or on that day call ☎638-2631 ext 6576 to confirm. Do not hike down without a reservation.

The **suspension bridge** here was set in place in 1928 (hanging from twin cables carried down on the shoulders of 42 Havasupai). The delta of **Bright Angel Creek**, named by Powell to contrast with the muddy **Dirty Devil** stream a short way upriver, is several hundred feet wide here, and strewn with boulders. All the water used on the South Rim now comes by pipeline from the North Rim, and crosses the river on the 1960s Silver Bridge nearby. (Do not drink the water from any streams you pass, as it's swarming with illness-inducing bacteria.)

Havasupai

The **Havasupai Indian Reservation** really is another world. An anthropologist in the 1930s called it "the only spot in the United States where native culture has remained in anything like its pristine condition"; things may have changed a little since then, but the sheer magic of its turquoise waterfalls and canyon scenery make this a very special place. Traditionally, the Havasupai lifestyle was to spend summer on the canyon floor and winter on the plateau above. When the reservation was created in 1882, they were only granted land at the bottom of the canyon, and not until 1975 did the concession of an additional 251,000 acres up above make it possible for some to resume their ancient pattern.

Havasu Canyon is a side canyon of the Grand Canyon, about 35 miles as the raven flies from Grand Canyon village, but almost 200 miles by road. Turn off the Interstate at Seligman or Kingman, onto AZ-66 which curves north between the two, stock up with water and petrol, and then turn on to Arrowhead Hwy-18. The road ends at **Hualapai Hilltop**, an eight-mile hike from the village of **Supai**.

Plans to build a road – or even a tramway – down into the canyon have always been rejected, in part because much of the income of the five or six hundred Havasupai comes from guiding visitors on foot, mule or horseback. Beyond Supai the trail becomes more difficult, but leads to a succession of spectacular waterfalls, including **Havasu Falls**, one of the best for swimming, and **Mooney Falls**, which was named after an unfortunate prospector who dangled here for three days in the 1890s, at the end of a snagged rope, before falling to his death.

A **campground** (☎448-2121) stretches between Havasu and Mooney Falls, and in Supai itself *Havasupai Lodge* (☎448-2111) has doubles at $50, less in winter. There's a cafe and a general store, and the only post office in the US still to receive its mail by pack train. From time to time Supai is hit by freak floods – most recently on Labor Day 1990 – which can result in the temporary closure of the campground and hotel.

Around to the North Rim

The 215-mile route by road from Grand Canyon Village to the North Rim follows AZ-64 along the East Rim Drive to Desert View, then passes an overlook into the gorge of the Little Colorado, before joining US-89 after fifty miles at **CAMERON**. The *Cameron Trading Post* has the best selection of Native American crafts in the Grand Canyon area, and remains a trading centre for the Navajo Nation (with some of its business still conducted by barter). Its **motel** (☎679-2231) has single rooms at $29 and doubles from $41, and a cafeteria serves reasonable food.

Fifteen miles north of Cameron comes the junction with US-160, which heads northeast via **Tuba City** (where there's more accommodation; see p.694) towards Monument Valley and Colorado. Continuing north, after another forty miles of barren wasteland US-89 branches off to climb the mesa to the right, heading for Page and Glen Canyon Dam (see p.718).

Lee's Ferry

The direct route to the North Rim, now US-89A, crosses the Colorado at last over the single arch of Navajo Bridge, almost five hundred feet above the river. Until the bridge was completed in 1929, a ferry service operated at **LEE'S FERRY**, six miles north. This was established in 1872, at the instigation of the Mormon Church, by John D Lee, at the only spot within hundreds of miles to offer easy access to the banks of the river on both sides. The Colorado, however, could still be a raging torrent, and the crossing was carried out in both directions by casting out and struggling across while being swept downstream, in constant danger from currents and winds. Lee himself was on the run after the **Mountain Meadows Massacre** in Utah in 1857, when a wagon train of would-be settlers was slaughtered by an armed white band clumsily disguised as Indians. He remains a hero to some Mormons (a local plaque calls him "a man of good faith, sound judgment and indomitable courage"); those who have read Mark Twain's account of the massacre in *Roughing It* may disagree. He was finally apprehended and executed in 1877.

The ferry service was abandoned after a fatal accident in June 1928. A crucial piece of equipment needed to finish the bridge on the left bank was stranded on the right bank; the only way to get it across was to take it eight hundred miles by road, via Las Vegas.

Lee's Ferry is the launching point for **whitewater rafting** trips – boats setting off from here can't leave the canyon before Diamond Creek, twelve days away by muscle power – and the end of Fred Harvey's smooth water trips from Glen Canyon Dam (see p.718). It has a few relics of Lee's days, as well as a half-sunk steamboat, hauled from San Francisco in 1911 and abandoned as a failed experiment after only five trips. There's also a **campground** (☎355-2334), while back on US-89A beneath the red of the **Vermilion Cliffs** are three successive motels – *Marble Canyon Lodge* (☎355-2225; $51 double), *Lee's Ferry Lodge* (☎355-2223; $38), and *Cliff Dweller's Lodge* (☎355-2228; $48) – all with restaurants.

The turning south to get to the North Rim, off US-89A onto AZ-67, comes at **JACOB LAKE**, which has an *Inn* (☎643-7232; $53) and **campground**, but not much else. From here – along a road which is closed in winter – it's 27 miles on to *Kaibab Lodge* (☎638-2389) and another fourteen to the canyon itself.

The North Rim

The **North Rim** of the Grand Canyon is nothing like as developed for visitors as the south. It's higher, and bleaker, with a succession of viewpoints that offer a radically different perspective on the chasm below. Tourist facilities, concentrated at **Bright Angel Point**, open for the season in mid-May and remain in operation until the first major snowfall of winter, which usually comes towards the end of October. Prices for different grades of **accommodation** at the *Grand Canyon Lodge* range from $48 to $63 for a double; the cheapest deal is a *Pioneer Cabin* at $54 for four or five people. Advance reservations are essential; contact *TWA Services*, Box 400, Cedar City, Utah 84721 (☎801/586-7686). The *Lodge* has a restaurant, a general store, a post office and a gift shop, and its **information desk** (8am–6pm; ☎638-7864) co-ordinates **mule rides** along the rim or into the canyon, and **bus tours**. Just over a mile north is *North Rim Campground*, where spaces can be reserved – though it's not necessary for backpackers – through any *Ticketron* outlet, or on ☎340-9033.

UTAH

With the biggest, most beautiful and most pristine landscapes in North America, **UTAH** has something for everyone: from brilliantly coloured canyons, across endless desert plains, to thickly wooded and snow-covered mountains. This unmatched range of terrain, almost all of which is unspoiled (and unpopulated) public land, makes it *the* place to come for **outdoor pursuits** – from hiking to off-track mountain biking, whitewater rafting, and skiing.

The astonishing scenery of **southern Utah** means that it has more **national parks** than anywhere else in the US; there are serious proposals to turn the entire area into one vast national park. For the moment, only those places which are accessible on paved roads, such as **Zion** and **Bryce Canyon**, receive visitors in any numbers. Huge tracts of this empty desert, in which beautiful pre-Columbian pictographs and Anasazi ruins lie hidden, are all but unexplored. There are virtually no towns, let alone cities, and seeing the sights in safety requires a good degree of advance planning and self-sufficiency.

The rest of Utah, though not as spectacular, is far from dull. In the **northeast**, which has more in common with the Rockies than with the rest of the Southwest, the **Uinta** Mountains remain uncrossed by road and form one of the most extensive wilderness areas outside Alaska. The **northwest** is equally distinctive – flat and dry, with the exception of the alpine wall of the **Wasatch Front**, the granite mountains which tower over **Salt Lake City**. The state capital is a surprisingly attractive and enjoyable stopover – particularly if you're a skier: Alta, Snowbird, Park City and the other Utah resorts offer some of the best skiing in North America.

For all its natural beauty, most people's first image of Utah is of the **Mormons**. The state's earliest white settlers now constitute some seventy percent of its two million population. Led by Brigham Young, Mormons arrived in the Salt Lake area in 1848; ever since, they've multiplied and prospered without giving up any of their fundamentalist beliefs. The most visible sign of Mormon influence on Utah is in the layout of towns and cities – residential streets as wide as motorways, all numbered block-by-block according to the same logical but often ponderous system. You'll begin to notice more aspects the longer you stay here: the **drinking laws** for one are hilariously complicated (few places serve spirits, and those that do can only offer airplane mini-bottles for you to mix your own). The state may be notorious for its **reactionary politics** – in 1915 Utah convicted and executed labour organiser and songwriter **Joe Hill** on obviously trumped-up murder charges, and in 1990 passed a law declaring abortion a capital crime – but for those who toe the line the healthy Mormon lifestyle is responsible for Utah's having the highest birth rate and the longest life expectancy in the US.

Getting Around Utah

It's nearly impossible to get anywhere in Utah without your own **car**. *Amtrak* and *Greyhound* serve Salt Lake City and a few provincial towns, but practically nowhere else. However, a couple of firms offer **coach tours** of the national parks, and if you're feeling adventurous, southern Utah also has an unbeatable range of mountain-biking, river-rafting, even hot-air ballooning opportunities: see p.714 for a list of companies.

The telephone **area code** for the entire state of Utah is ☎801.

Southern Utah: the National Parks

There's nothing quite like **southern Utah** anywhere else in the world. In this infinite elemental landscape, hardly touched by civilisation, 11,000ft peaks, covered in dense stands of conifers, aspens and maples, rise above awesome sandstone canyons that have been carved like some intricate geological jigsaw puzzle into the fiery red desert by some of the mightiest stretches of America's most powerful rivers.

The southwestern national parks, **Bryce Canyon** and the overwhelming **Zion**, are the easiest to reach (just off I-15, the only interstate), and therefore can get crowded, but remain absolutely magnificent; to the east, **Capitol Reef**, **Canyonlands** and **Arches** national parks are drier, hotter and much harsher, with massive humps of bare stone standing out of the arid plateaus. Besides the national parks, there are dozens of smaller national monuments and state parks: Cedar Breaks, Kodachrome Basin, Newspaper Rock and Dead Horse Point, to name an evocative few.

If you've got the time, the very best way to experience the region is as the first explorers did: by **water**. Dozens of companies offer river-rafting trips, floating downstream, and camping out under the clear night sky to experience the sights, sounds and smells of the desert – we've listed a number of guides on p.714. It's a tough land, and a rough one for travellers: there are fewer roads here than anywhere else in the US, which means that almost nobody gets far into the deep backcountry, and even within the national park lands, overground access is more often than not limited to heavy-duty, high-clearance four-wheel-drive vehicles, **hikers** and, increasingly, to **mountain bikes**.

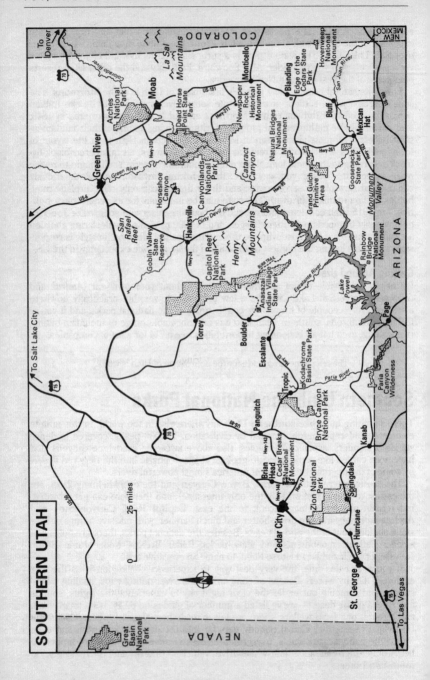

The Towns: St George and Cedar City

The two biggest towns in southern Utah, **St George** and **Cedar City**, are fifty miles apart on I-15 . They both make serviceable bases for seeing the region, and are reasonably pleasant places, if not ones that are likely to detain you for very long.

St George

ST GEORGE was the winter home of Brigham Young and other early Mormon leaders, who came to "Utah's Dixie" to bask in its comparatively mild climate. Set at the foot of a broad reddish-brown sandstone cliff, it's a pretty enough town, centring round the fine 1877 **LDS Temple** at 400 East and 200 South streets, the oldest still in use anywhere. The rest of the town holds quaint houses built by Mormon pioneers, including Brigham Young's much-restored **adobe house** on 200 North Street off Main Street; pick up a walking tour map there or at the **visitor centre** (Mon–Fri 9am–5pm; ☎628-0505) in the old **County Courthouse** at 97 E St George Boulevard.

Greyhound **buses** between Las Vegas and Salt Lake City stop outside the good-value *Trafalgar Restaurant* at 76 W St George Boulevard (☎673-2933); other central places to eat include the fancier *Gable House* at 290 E St George Boulevard (☎673-6796). There are **motels** aplenty, too: for rooms at $30 to $40, try the central *Dixie Palms*, 185 E St George Boulevard (☎673-3531) or the *Red Mesa*, 247 E St George Boulevard (☎673-3163). The Hwy-9 turnoff to Zion and Bryce is five miles north of town; *SAGA* (☎628-8000 or ☎1-800/634-3905) run guided **coach tours** through both parks from St George, the only way to get there without a car.

Cedar City

CEDAR CITY, 53 miles north of St George, is bigger, if not particularly more worthy of a stop. Founded as an iron-mining town in the late 1850s, it's now kept alive by the Southern Utah State College on its western fringe, and by the flood of tourists who come here to watch plays at the **Utah Shakespeare Festival**, held on the campus every summer (☎586-7880). The productions are enthusiastic if somewhat amateurish, but seats (and most of the town's motel rooms) are booked solid weeks in advance.

Main Street is handy for food and lodging. The *Sugar Loaf*, no. 261 S (☎586-6593), has Navajo tacos and standard coffee-shop meals; *Sullivan's* at no. 86 S (☎586-6761) is similar. Everything shuts at 9pm apart from *Ed and Deb's Truck Stop*, which has good 24-hour diner food just west of I-15 on the northern fringes of town. The cheapest **beds** are on Main Street south of town, where the *Astro Budget*, no. 323 S (☎586-6557); the *Thrifty*, no. 344 S (☎586-9416); and the *American Siesta*, no. 427 S (☎586-2700) all have swimming pools and doubles from around $30. Hwy-14 heads east from the town centre through the Dixie National Forest to Cedar Breaks and Bryce Canyon.

Zion National Park

ZION is the jewel in the crown of southern Utah parklands – indeed to many people it is the most beautiful of all the US national parks. The name, given by early Mormons who marvelled at its massive walls of stone, only hints at its stupendous display of river and rock. Zion isn't all that big – about a tenth the size of the Grand Canyon – but its sheer rock faces and dense riparian forests are if anything more memorable.

Until a few years ago the park was formally divided into two sections; in practice, it still is. The main part, **Zion Canyon** along the Virgin River, in the southeast corner, some 21 miles off I-15 via Hwy-9, holds the most impressive sights, and gets most of the tourist traffic. Hardly any visitors make their way to the **northwestern** section, the finger canyons of the **Kolob Plateau**, where cliffs of brilliant red sandstone soar hundreds and thousands of feet above maple- and aspen-lined stream valleys.

Zion Canyon

Zion Canyon is deservedly the most popular corner of the park, with its mighty walls of Navajo sandstone rising nearly half a mile above the groves of box elders and cottonwoods that line the loping Virgin River. A six-mile paved road runs along the river from the park entrance, giving good views of the **Court of the Patriarchs**, the **Great White Throne**, **Angel's Landing** and other piously named landmarks. It ends at the foot of the **Temple of Sinawava**, beyond which the paved and fairly flat Gateway to the Narrows trail continues on another half a mile up the canyon, to the point where the river fills the entire floor. It's a fine walk to the end of the trail and back, but at certain times of year (check with the visitor centre) determined hikers can continue on, wading through the chilly river thigh- or even neck-deep for some eight miles to reach **The Narrows**, where the canyon is only twenty feet across and the walls tower some eight hundred feet straight up. It's best done as an overnight trip, camping out in one of the many enticing side canyons that splinter off the main gorge.

Less ambitious walkers might prefer to wander up to **Weeping Rock**, an easy half-hour round trip from the road to a gorgeous spring-fed garden that dangles from a rocky alcove. From the same trailhead, a mile beyond *Zion Lodge*, a more strenuous and exciting route cuts through narrow **Hidden Canyon**, whose mouth turns into a waterfall after a good rain. Directly across from the lodge a short (two-mile round trip) and fairly flat trail winds up at the **Emerald Pools**, a series of three clearwater pools, the best (and furthest) of which has a small sandy beach at the foot of a gigantic cliff; at certain times of the year a broad waterfall sprinkles down over the trail.

The single best half-day **hike** climbs up to **Angel's Landing**, a narrow ledge of whitish sandstone protruding out some 1750 feet above the canyon floor. Starting on the same trail as for the Emerald Pools, the Angel's Landing trail switchbacks up sharply through the delightful coolness of **Refrigerator Canyon** before emerging on the canyon's west rim; near the end you have to cross a heart-stopping, five-foot neck of rock with sheer drops to either side (there's a steel cable to grab hold of). Allow two hours up and an hour back down for Angel's Landing; backpackers can continue another twenty miles to the gorgeous Kolob Canyons district (see opposite).

The high dry plateau above and to the east of Zion Canyon is a complete contrast to the lush Virgin River gorge. The most dramatic sight is the blind **Great Arch**, best seen from the turnouts before the mile-long tunnel, beyond which the **Canyon Overlook** nature trail gives a good introduction to the flora and fauna of the park, such as the speedy lizards which race from rock to rock. The road then climbs through smooth slickrock sandstone and bizarrely eroded **hoodoos**, passing the angular Checkerboard Mesa before heading on to the North Rim of the Grand Canyon (see p.702).

Practicalities

Located just beyond the park entrance, north of Springdale on Hwy-9, the **visitor centre** (daily, May–Sept 9am–9pm, otherwise 9am–5pm; ☎722-3256) has maps and information on hiking trails and weather conditions, and evening slide shows. The only **food and lodging** within Zion itself is at the *Zion Lodge* (May–mid-Oct only; doubles $85, dinners from $15; ☎586-7686), which tends to be booked up by tour groups. There's also a first-come, first-served **campground** ($6) just across the road from the visitor centre; get there early in the morning to be sure of a space in summer.

Much better than the in-park lodge is the $55-a-night *Cliffrose Lodge*, 281 Zion Park Boulevard ☎772-3234, set amongst the cottonwoods along the Virgin River half a mile south of the park entrance in the small town of **SPRINGDALE**. Elsewhere along Zion Park Boulevard (which doubles as Hwy-9), Springdale also holds *Flanigan's Inn*, no. 428 ($40 and up; ☎772-3244), and the cheaper *El Rio Lodge* at no. 995 (from $30; ☎772-3205), as well as **restaurants**; try the *Driftwood*, no. 1515, for breakfast, and *Sparky's*, in a converted church at no. 868, for lunch or a light dinner. For solid **Tex-Mex food** after a day on the trails, head to the *Bit and Spur Saloon* on the west edge of town at no. 1212; it's the liveliest **bar** in this corner of Utah, with the only good margaritas for miles.

The Kolob Canyons

Fewer than one in ten visitors to Zion make their way to the immaculate yet easily accessible **Kolob Canyons**, just three miles off I-15, twenty miles south of Cedar City. As in the rest of Zion, the focus is on **red rock canyons**, which here in the Kolob seem somehow redder, and the trees greener (and then in their turn redder, when the maples turn colour in autumn), than those down below.

The view from the five-mile paved road which heads up from the small but worthwhile **visitor centre** (daily 8am–4.30pm) is amazing, but hiking off along either of two main trails will give you a feeling for what makes this place so special. The first and shorter of the two starts two miles from the visitor centre and follows Taylor Creek on a five-mile round trip to **Double Arch Alcove**, a spectacular natural amphitheatre roofed by twin sandstone arches; there's also a small waterfall a quarter of a mile further along. The other trail starts from the north side of the parking area at Lee Pass, four miles beyond the visitor centre, and follows a well-marked route past LaVerkin Falls seven miles to **Kolob Arch**, the world's longest natural rock span at over 300 feet across.

Cedar Breaks National Monument

The shortest drive between southwest Utah's two national parks, along the Virgin River and then north on US-89 across the high plain of Long Valley, is spectacular enough, but the longer route through the maple and aspen groves of the **Dixie National Forest** is even more dramatic. Halfway between Cedar City and US-89, Hwy-148 cuts sharply north through the eerie fringes of **CEDAR BREAKS NATIONAL MONUMENT**, where the soft sandstone has been eroded away into a fairyland of bizarre formations.

Cedar Breaks is in a sense just a small-scale version of Bryce Canyon to the east, but if you don't expect to pass that way it's well worth making the detour to come here. **Point Supreme**, where there's a small visitor centre (8am–6pm, June–mid-Oct only) and snack bar, is a mile into the park from the south, and gives the best view. Since most of Cedar Breaks is over 10,000 feet high it's usually quite cold; in fact the roads through are often blocked by snow until June. North of the monument, **Brian Head**, the highest town in Utah, is the site of southern Utah's only downhill ski resort ($20 per day; ☎677-2035); it's also a good starting point for cross-country tours of Cedar Breaks.

Heading east from Cedar Breaks towards Bryce Canyon, Hwy-143 passes through pine forests and across lava flows – there's a half-mile lava tube at **Mammoth Cave**, poorly signed south of Panguitch Lake in the middle of the forest. Beyond the lake the road drops down into the broad Sevier River valley at the squeaky-clean Mormon farming town of **PANGUITCH**, where you'll find eight petrol stations (one, *Todd's Truck Stop*, is open 24hr), a dozen $30-a-night motels, and not much else.

Bryce Canyon National Park

Named for an early settler who thought it was a wasteland, **BRYCE CANYON** is not really a genuine canyon. Nonetheless it deserves its national park status for the uncanny conglomeration of multihued, **strangely shaped stone figures** that fill a twenty-mile shelf along the eastern edge of the thickly forested Paunsaugunt Plateau, eight thousand feet above sea level. Like Cedar Breaks to the west, the weird formations here have been eroded out of the muddy sandstone by a combination of freezing winters (the temperature drops below zero two hundred nights out of the year) and summer rainstorms, which have left behind a veritable menagerie of rocks. Some resemble elephants, giraffes, or alligators; a good dozen or so look like **Elvis**. The racks of top-heavy pinnacles known as **"hoodoos"** were formed when the harder upper layers of rock stayed firm as the lower levels were worn away beneath them. These hoodoos – **Thor's Hammer**, visible from Sunset Point, is the most alarmingly precarious – look down into technicolour-toned ravines, all of which are far more vivid than the Grand Canyon and much more human in scale. The whole place is at its most inspiring in winter when the figures stand out from a blanket of snow.

The single road which runs south from Hwy-12 about 75 miles east of Cedar City passes by the entrance station before arriving at the **visitor centre** (daily 8am–5pm; ☎834-5322). On sale here is the illustrated *Bryce Canyon Auto and Hiking Guide* ($2.95), which explains the geology of Bryce and suggests a variety of hiking and driving tours. A couple of miles south, you come to a succession of scenic overlooks, and a network of trails drops down from the rim into **Bryce Amphitheatre** – remember that you'll have to walk back up the same distance that you go down. The two most popular overlooks are on either side of *Bryce Canyon Lodge* (see below): the more northerly, **Sunrise Point**, is fifty yards from the car park and so is slightly less crowded than **Sunset Point**, where most of the coach tours stop. A good hiking route (three miles total) descends steeply from Sunset Point through the cool 200-foot canyons of Wall Street, where a pair of 800-year-old fir trees stretch to reach daylight. It then cuts across into the basin known as the **Queen's Garden**, where the stout and remarkable likeness of Queen Victoria sits in majestic condescension – pointed out by a brass plaque – before climbing back up to the rim. Dozens of trails criss-cross the amphitheatre, but it's surprisingly easy to get lost, so don't stray from the marked routes.

Sunrise and Sunset points notwithstanding, the best view at both sunset and dawn (which is the best time for taking pictures) is from **Bryce Point**, at the southern end of the amphitheatre. From here, you can look down not only at the Bryce Canyon formations but also take in the grand sweep of the whole region, east to the **Henry Mountains** and north to the Escalante range. Most people only get as far as Bryce Amphitheatre, but the park stretches another 25 miles south, passing the intensely coloured **Natural Bridge**, an 85ft rock arch spanning a steep gully, at about the halfway point. For backpackers, the **Under-the-Rim Trail** winds from Bryce Point 22.6 miles to Rainbow Point, and numerous trails connect to the road above. It's also possible to avoid the crowds in summer by entering the park from below, via a two-mile trail and three-mile dirt road from the Hwy-12 village of **Tropic** (see opposite).

Practicalities

There's no regular scheduled transport to Bryce, though *Scenic Airlines* (☎1-800/634-6801) fly here from the Grand Canyon and will arrange ground transport; otherwise you'll have to drive or join a tour from St George (see p.705).

The best place to **stay**, if you manage to get a room, is the *Bryce Canyon Lodge* (May–mid-Oct only; ☎834-5361) one hundred yards from the rim between Sunrise and Sunset points, with double rooms from $65 and rustic cabins for a few dollars more. It also has a dining room, a grocery store, a laundromat and public showers. Much bigger, and open year-round, is *Ruby's Inn* (☎834-5341 or ☎1-800/528-1234) just north of the park entrance, where double rooms cost around $70 in summer, $35 in winter, and there's a large grocery store and restaurant. Both the *Bryce Village Motel* (☎834-5303) and the slightly more distant *Bryce Canyon Pines* (☎834-5336) along Hwy-12 west of Bryce are unpretentious motels, charging around $50 a night in peak season, half that in winter. The *Pines* also has a good restaurant.

The two **campgrounds** within the park are near the visitor centre; both *Sunset Campground*, near Sunset Point, and *North Campground* are first-come, first-served and cost $6 a night. There's a slightly more deluxe campground at *Ruby's Inn*. Backpackers can choose from dozens of sites below the rim, all south of Bryce Point; pick up the required free permit at the visitor centre, and take lots of water.

Bryce Canyon to Capitol Reef: Scenic Highway 12

Turning its back on the grand amphitheatre of Bryce Canyon, the tiny hamlet of **TROPIC** seems almost embarrassed about the flamboyant geological phenomena ranged along the ridge above it. The practical-minded people of this Mormon farming community (pop. 380), which strings along Hwy-12 eight miles from the park entrance, have managed to restore the cabin where **Ebenezer Bryce** lived – he's the man after whom the park is named, and the one who described it as "a helluva place to lose a cow" – but otherwise they don't go very far out of their way to please tourists. Bryce's log cabin now stands next to the *Pioneer Village* motel-cum-restaurant (☎679-8546), one of two in town. An unmarked road heads west from the cabin two miles to the park boundary, from where it's a two-mile hike up to the main formations.

At the even smaller speck of a town called **Cannonville**, nine miles south, a part-paved road turns sharply south toward **Kodachrome Basin State Park**, another collection of intensely coloured, strangely contorted stone hunks. What makes the formations here unusual is that they weren't so much eroded as extruded by mineral-laden geysers forcing their way up through softer stone, which has resulted in rounded, svelte shapes such as the phallic oddity that towers 150 feet over the attractive **campground** ($8, including hot showers).

Beyond Cannonville Hwy-12 curves along the edge of the Table Cliff Plateau before dropping down into the remote canyons of the **Escalante River**, said to be the last river system to be discovered within the continental US and site of some of the finest backpacking routes in the Southwest. As soon as you walk even a hundred yards off the main highway, you're in a wilderness which few travellers ever see.

ESCALANTE, 33 miles beyond Cannonville, is just another roadside town, with its two $30-a-night motels, the *Moqui* (☎826-4210) and the *Circle D* (☎826-4297); the latter also has a good cafe. The Escalante BLM **ranger station** (Mon–Fri 8am–4.30pm; ☎826-4291), a mile west of town, has up-to-date information and maps, and can suggest hiking or mountain biking trips into beautiful and relatively unvisited backcountry. From **Calf Creek**, sixteen miles east of Escalante, a well-marked trail leads just under three miles upstream to a lovely shaded dell replete with a 125ft waterfall; there's a nice campground ($4 per night) at the trailhead. More ambitious trips start from trailheads along the dusty but usually passable Hole-in-the-Rock Road, which turns south from Hwy-12 five miles east of town; from **Hurricane Wash**, 35 miles along, you can head to the sandstone bridges and arches of Coyote Gulch. The best times for hiking are late spring, when there's lots of water, and autumn, when the leaves turn colour.

Until the mid-1980s, when it was paved through to Capitol Reef, Hwy-12 ended at **BOULDER**, thirty miles beyond Escalante. **Anasazi State Park** (daily 9am–5pm; $1) here, which holds the excavated and partially reconstructed remains of a small Anasazi village, is set on a shallow knoll overlooking Boulder Creek. Beyond Boulder, Hwy-12 makes a gorgeous drive up onto the Aquarius Plateau, with marvellous vistas to the east across waves of gold and red sandstone outcrops; there's a lovely **campground** ($6) at Oak Creek fifteen miles along. Due east from Boulder the old dirt **Burr Trail** is (controversially) in the process of being paved, to provide easy access to the Waterpocket Fold and the southern reaches of Capitol Reef National Park.

Capitol Reef National Park

CAPITOL REEF sounds like something you'd be more likely to find off the coast of Australia than in the heart of the Utah desert, but in most respects its towering ochre, white, and red **rock walls** and deep **river canyons** are of a piece with the rest of the region. The outstanding feature is a multi-layered, thousand-foot-high reeflike wall of uplifted sedimentary rock, a section of which reminded an early traveller of the grand dome of the US Capitol. Stretching for over a hundred miles north to south, but only a few miles across, the seemingly impenetrable barrier of the **Waterpocket Fold** was warped upwards by the same process that lifted the Colorado Plateau, and the sharply defined sedimentary layers on display here trace over two hundred million years of geological activity. The Waterpocket Fold is sliced through in a number of places by deeply incised river canyons – some only twenty feet wide, but hundreds of feet deep – often accessible only on foot.

The one paved road through the park, Hwy-24, cuts across the northern half of the Fold, following the deep canyon of the Fremont River. Beneath the enormous and very prominent **castle**, the **visitor centre** (daily 8am–5pm; ☎425-3791) has explanatory exhibits and a campground ($6). To the east, the **Goosenecks Overlook** gazes down five hundred feet into the entrenched canyons cut by Sulphur Creek. In **Fruita** to the west, a schoolhouse and a thriving orchard are all that's left of a former Mormon community. Beyond the schoolhouse along the highway are the extraordinary **Fremont petroglyphs**, figures of Bighorn sheep and stylised spacepeople chipped into the varnished red rock a thousand years ago; a five-minute radio broadcast (AM 1540) describes their makers. Further along, four-and-a-half miles east of the visitor centre, one of Capitol Reef's best **day hikes** heads up along the gravelly river bed through **Grand Wash** – a beautiful (and usually quite cool) canyon where, it's said, Butch Cassidy and his gang used to hide out.

There are no other paved routes through the park, so to reach the spectacular back-country canyons you'll have to put up with many miles of dusty and spine-rattling roads – renting a mountain bike is a good idea. One popular dirt road heads twelve miles south from the visitor centre, past the top of Grand Wash to **Capitol Gorge** and back. A more adventurous sixty-mile loop trip explores the **Cathedral Valley** area in the north, while a 125-mile southern route starts off at the foot of the volcanic Henry Mountains, then follows the Burr Trail through Muley Twist Canyon (a good overnight stop), and continues west to the town of Boulder (see p.709). Detailed, well-illustrated maps and guides ($1) are available at the visitor centre.

The nearest food and lodging to Capitol Reef is eleven miles to the west, in the small town of **TORREY**, where for around $35 a night you can stay in the *Chuck Wagon* (☎425-3288), or the *Capitol Reef* (☎425-3271), which has a small cafe.

East of Capitol Reef

Fifty fairly desolate miles east of Capitol Reef along Hwy-24, you reach the tiny cross-roads of **Hanksville**. If you continue on Hwy-24 to the north, you come after about twenty miles to a 32-mile dirt road leading to a real anthropological and artistic wonder, **HORSESHOE CANYON**, a remote subsection of Canyonlands National Park. This pretty tree-lined canyon is remarkable for the hundreds of **pictographs** painted onto the red sandstone walls of the "Great Gallery", some time between 500 BC and 500 AD. The majority of the images show life-sized human figures, some weirdly elongated, others draped in robes. All are perfectly preserved, and together they form the greatest concentration of **ancient rock art** in the Southwest. To reach the paintings, follow the road signs to the Horseshoe Canyon trailhead, then hike a steep mile down into the canyon, and two miles upstream to the gallery. There are lots more ancient pictographs in The Maze section of Canyonlands, fifteen miles to the southeast (see p.712).

Back on Hwy-24, a mere half-mile further north, another side road to the east veers off to **GOBLIN VALLEY STATE PARK**, where thousands of gnome-like figures loom out of the soft Entrada sandstone. The Carmel Canyon trail loops for over a mile through a throng of misshapen rock pillars, many of which seem to have eyes and other human features. There's a well-equipped **campground** ($8) if you want to see the place by moonlight, when it looks especially spooky.

Green River

The uneventful riverside town of **GREEN RIVER**, just east of the Hwy-24 junction, is the largest community on a two-hundred-mile stretch of I-70. One very good reason to visit is the brand-new **John Wesley Powell River History Museum** (daily, summer 9am–9pm, otherwise 9am–5pm; $1). This recounts the epic journeys of the Canyonlands region's first true explorer, John Wesley Powell, featuring the anything-but-dry personal accounts of the men who first successfully navigated the Colorado River from near its source all the way through the Grand Canyon. An entertaining film and numerous models trace the development of river craft from Native American dugouts to turn-of-the-century steamships and today's motorised rafts, and the museum also has a wide range of information on Canyonlands and the rest of southern Utah. In summer **raft trips** from the museum dock float downriver to the **Crystal Geyser**, a hundred-foot cold-water gusher, and every Memorial Day hundreds of boats set out on weekend-long convoy trips that cruise down the Green River to its confluence with the Colorado, then head upriver to Moab.

Green River makes a very good base for exploring this part of Utah, with its dozen $30-a-night **motels**, including the *Robber's Roost*, 135 W Main Street (☎564-3452), and the *Oasis*, 118 W Main Street (☎564-8272), which also has a handy cafe.

Canyonlands National Park

Utah's largest and least-visited national park, **CANYONLANDS** displays red rock canyons and wild rivers in all their natural glory. Spread over 525 very remote square miles at the confluence of the Green and Colorado rivers, Canyonlands is divided into three very distinct sections (or four if you count the rivers themselves). As it's at least a one-hundred-mile drive from one to another, decide in advance which one best suits your interests. Most visitors choose the dramatic **Island-in-the-Sky** district, the highest and northernmost parcel, on a precipitous plateau some two thousand feet above the two rivers. South of here, the numerous sandstone spires and many narrow canyons of **The Needles** are a favourite destination for backpackers. Each of these districts has a state park along its approach road – **Dead Horse Point** and **Newspaper Rock** respectively. The wildest area of Canyonlands, requiring a long drive over very rough roads, is **The Maze**, a bizarre jumble of canyons, towers, buttes and mesas where you're unlikely to see another person. No public transport or guided bus tours go to any part of Canyonlands, though specialist companies will take you into the backcountry (see the box on p.714); the town of Moab (see below) has the nearest food and lodging as well as the park's headquarters.

Island-in-the-Sky and Dead Horse Point

Reached by a good road that climbs steadily up from US-191, 21 miles south of I-70, the **Island-in-the-Sky** district looks out over hundreds of miles of flat-topped mesas that drop in two-thousand-foot steps to the river. It's the highest, driest and most sparsely vegetated section (there's no water available anywhere on the plateau); from any of the half-dozen overlooks along the main roads you might catch a glimpse of the coyotes, foxes and Bighorn sheep which roam the rocky ledges below. The best panoramas of the lot come at the southern end of the main road, from **Grand View Point**. Another paved road cuts north from the heart of the park to the 1500ft crater of **Upheaval Dome**; just beyond the junction, a mile-long dirt road cuts west to the **Green River Overlook**, where you can peer down at the river as it flows through **Stillwater Canyon**. Near the overlook is the only **campground** (no water) in the district. There's a visitor centre (daily 8am–5pm) on the road in; just past here the **Shafer Trail** drops steeply down to the White Rim, a broad sandstone step one thousand feet above the rivers. An old mining road runs along this ledge above the Colorado, then back up along the rim of the Green River canyon, making a 110-mile loop trip that's ideal for mountain bike tourists; reservations (by post from the park HQ in Moab) are required for the backcountry campsites.

On the way in to the Island-in-the-Sky, a turnoff miles before the visitor centre cuts across south to **Dead Horse Point State Park**, a smaller but equally breathtaking version of Island-in-the-Sky, at the very tip of a narrow mesa, looking straight down two thousand feet to the twisting Colorado River. Cowboys used the mesa – under a hundred feet across at its thinnest point – as a natural corral, herding up wild horses then blocking them in behind a piñon pine fence which still marks the neck of the mesa. One band of horses was left here too long and died – hence the name. There's a **campground** ($8) and visitor centre two miles from the point.

The Needles and Newspaper Rock

Taking its name from the thousands of colourful sandstone pillars, knobs and hoodoos that punctuate its many lush canyons and basins, the **Needles** district allows a more intimate look at the Canyonlands environment than does Island-in-the-Sky. Here you're not always gazing thousands of feet downwards or scanning the distant horizon; instead you can wander through seemingly ceaseless acres of stone figures.

The road ends with a great collection of **mushroom-shaped hoodoos** at the **Big Spring Canyon Overlook**. You can hike 5.5 miles out to the Confluence Overlook, a thousand feet above the point where the Green River loses itself in the muddy waters of the Colorado. Various short walks head off the road at selected viewpoints; one of the best is **Pothole Point**, a mile before Big Spring Canyon. A longer day trip, or a good overnight hike, leaves from near the *Squaw Flat* **campground** ($5 April–Oct, when water is available; free rest of year) to the green meadow of Chesler Park, cutting through the narrow cleft of the Joint Trail. Check in at the visitor centre (daily 8am– 5pm) near the park boundary to get up-to-date information, as well as backcountry permits if you plan to camp out. The only way to **reach the river** from within the park is by taking the hot and dry trail down through Lower Red Canyon to Spanish Bottom; this is the start of the Cataract Canyon rapids, so don't try to swim across.

The 35-mile drive in to the Needles from US-191 is among the prettiest in the state, winding along Indian Creek through deep red rock canyons lined by pines and cotton-woods. **Newspaper Rock**, twelve miles in, is the best of many similarly named sites; here hundreds of tiny **petroglyphs**, many of which show deer, antelope, bear claws, and helmeted human figures, have been etched in the dark desert varnish of a red sandstone boulder by centuries of passing hunters and travellers. There's a lovely (free) streamside **campground** just across the road.

The Maze and the Rivers

Only about one in a hundred of the half a million visitors who come to Canyonlands every year makes it in to the harsh backcountry of the remote **Maze** district. Filling up the western third of the park, on the far side of the Colorado and Green rivers, the Maze is noted for its ancient rock-art panels (see Horseshoe Canyon, p.710) and for its many-fingered box canyons, accessible only by jeep or by long, dry hiking trails. If you're tempted, stop into the Hans Flat ranger station, 46 miles east of Hwy-24.

In many ways the best impressions of the Canyonlands region are to be had not from above but from the rivers below, looking up at the towering canyon walls and experiencing the restful solitude of the rushing waters. However, since there's no easy way in or out, you'll have to spend at least a week to get through, starting at Green River or Moab and being brought out at Lake Powell, a hundred or so miles down-stream. Much of the way the waters are smooth and unchallenging, but just beyond their confluence is the start of **Cataract Canyon**, which contains some of the most intense whitewater rapids in the US.

Arches National Park

Edward Abbey, who spent a year as a ranger at **ARCHES NATIONAL PARK** in the 1950s, wrote in *Desert Solitaire* that its arid landscape was as "naked, monolithic, austere and unadorned as the sculpture of the moon". It certainly is one of the least terrestrial places on this planet. Massive fins of red and golden sandstone stand to attention out of the bare desert plain, and over 1500 natural arches of various shapes and sizes have been cut into the rock by eons of erosive weathering. Apart from the single ribbon of black tarmac that snakes through the park there's nothing even vaguely human about it. The narrow, hunching ridges are more like dinosaurs' backbones than solid rock, and under a full moon, at twilight, or watching the lightning strikes of a distant thunderstorm, you can't help but imagine that the landscape has a life of its own.

While you could race through in a couple of hours, to do Arches justice you should plan to spend a whole day at the very least. A forty-mile road cuts uphill sharply from US-191 and the park **visitor centre** (daily 8am–4.30pm), where exhibits explain the fairly simple process by which the arches are formed and point out some of the more photogenic examples. The first main sight is **Courthouse Towers**, a huge chunk of red stone from where you hike a mile south through the vertically edged canyon called Park Avenue. Beyond here the road follows the foot of the **Great Wall**, a ten-mile stretch of salmon-coloured Entrada sandstone.

At roughly the centre of the park, **Balanced Rock** is a fifty-foot boulder atop a slender 75ft pedestal. A turning to the right (east) winds for about two miles through the Windows section, where a half-mile trail loops through a dense concentration of massive arches, some over 100 feet high and 150 feet across; a second trail, fifty yards beyond the main one, leads to **Double Arch**, a staunch pair of arches that together support another arch overhead. In the **Cove of Caves**, to the right on the way back, a dozen more arches form a semi-circular arcade at the top of a sandstone amphitheatre.

Beyond Balanced Rock the main road drops downhill for two miles past Panorama Point and the turnoff to **Wolfe Ranch**, where a century-old log cabin now serves as the trailhead for the three-mile round trip to the rather bulbous **Delicate Arch**, standing at the brink of a deep canyon, with the rugged La Sal mountains in the distance. Three miles beyond the Wolfe Ranch turnoff, the deep, sharp-sided mini-canyons of the **Fiery Furnace** section form a (usually quite cool) labyrinth, through which rangers lead hikes throughout the day during summer.

The road continues on to the **Devil's Garden** trailhead. Around a dozen named major arches, and many more that remain unnamed, are viewable along the four-mile round trip, including the mile-long **Landscape Arch**, 306 feet across. Arches' only **campground** ($5, water available March–Nov only) is across from the trailhead; check in at the visitor centre or get a permit there for backcountry camping, allowed anywhere in the park that's a mile from the road and a hundred yards from any trail. Rock-climbing is permitted except on named features, but it's easy to get stuck and rescues are expensive, so think before you set off.

Moab

The biggest centre in the Canyonlands of southeastern Utah, **MOAB** makes a pleasant surprise after the smug dullness of many other Utah towns. It may not look like much, but it's surrounded by some of the Southwest's most beautiful and unspoiled terrain, and its population is increasingly arts-orientated without being pretentious. As the obvious base from which to explore the nearby parks, Moab serves as the headquarters for most of Utah's adventure travel outfits; if you'd like to try river-rafting, mountain-biking, rock-climbing or even hang-gliding, this is the place to head for. The **tourist**

ADVENTURE TRAVEL OUTFITS IN SOUTHEAST UTAH

Some of the best of the many companies which run **adventure trips** through the back-country and along the raging waters of southern Utah are based in the **Moab** area. Such trips, which vary from half-day jaunts to week-long expeditions, can not only get you to places you'd never otherwise reach, but also give a sense of the region's natural splendour that can't be had from a car or on foot.

River Rafting

Among the dozen licensed operators who offer motorised one-day trips down the Colorado River from Moab for around $35 are *Adrift Adventures* (☎259-8594 or ☎1-800/874-4483); *Sherri Griffith Expeditions* (☎259-8229 or ☎1-800/332-3200); and *Tag-a-Long Tours* (☎259-8946 or ☎1-800/453-3292). **Oar-powered** trips are slower but much quieter, less expensive and in every way more pleasant than motorboat trips. Longer (two- to seven-day) trips head through Cataract Canyon and other wild Canyonlands spots.

Mountain Biking

The Moab area is ideally suited to mountain-bike touring. The most popular half-day route, the **Slickrock Bike Trail**, starts about three miles east of Moab, following a clearly marked and very challenging ten-mile loop over the sandstone knobs with views of the La Sal mountains and the Colorado River; wear a **helmet**, take lots of water, and keep an eye and an ear out for motorcyclists, who are also allowed on the trail.

Bike shops offering daily rentals and guided tours include the *Rim Cyclery* (☎259-5333 or ☎1-800/626-7335), 94 W 100 North Street; *Kaibab Mountain Bikes* (☎259-7423), 37 S 100 West Street, and *Nichols Bike Stop* (☎259-7882 or ☎1-800/635-1792).

Jeep Tours

Most of the thousands of miles of **jeep trails** around Moab were built years ago by miners and haven't been maintained since. The tourist office puts out a free map and guide to some of the more popular ones, and you can rent a four-wheel-drive jeep or pick-up truck from *North Main Service* (☎259-5242), at 284 N Main Street.

Guided jeep tours ($50–75 per day) are offered by *Lin Ottinger's Tours* (☎259-7312), *Canyonlands Tours* (☎259-5865 or ☎1-800/342-5938) and *Tag-a-Long Tours* (see above).

office at 805 N Main Street on the north side of town (☎259-8825 or ☎1-800/635-6622) has stacks of information (look out for the handy *Moab Happenings* newsletter) or you can find out about local events from the excellent *Back of Beyond Bookstore*, 83 N Main Street (☎259-5154), which has all the best hiking, cycling and natural history guides, a good selection of Beat and off-Beat literature, alongside *Earth First!* tracts and the complete works of Moab-based writers Edward Abbey and Zane Grey.

Moab is a young town, founded in the late 1800s but hardly a speck until the 1950s, when a local prospector, Charlie Sheen, discovered uranium in the nearby hills. Though the boom didn't last, within months the area was swamped by fortune hunters and quickly tripled in population (to around 4500); the whole story is told in the **Moab Museum**, 118 E Center Street (daily 1–9pm; donations), which also has exhibits on the region's prehistoric people, Ute Indians and the early Spanish and Yankee explorers. Moab is also the unlikely home of the **Hollywood Stuntman's Hall of Fame** (daily 9am–9pm; $3), 111 E 100 North Street, an extensive archive of odds and ends from Sean Connery's hairpiece to the hat Steve McQueen wore in *The Magnificent Seven*.

Innumerable movies, car commercials and MTV videos still get filmed in the nearby area, but otherwise Moab survives almost entirely off the tourist trade, with a dozen $25-a-night **motels** like the *Canyonlands*, 16 S Main Street (☎259-5167), and the *Apache*, 166 S 400 East Street (☎259-5727), where John Wayne stayed while filming *Rio Bravo* in the nearby canyons. Moab also holds the amiable *Lazy Lizard* (not-just-for-youth) **hostel** ($6 a night; ☎259-6057), 1213 S Hwy-191 on the south side of town (near the bowling alley), with a hot tub and very laid-back atmosphere. The people who run it can pick you up at the *Amtrak* stop at Thompson, or from *Greyhound* in Crescent Junction, the nearest public transport to Moab.

Eating options for the most part avoid the identikit franchise outlets of much of the Southwest, though Moab's first *McDonald's* did open in 1990. For breakfasts or burgers try the 24-hour *Westerner Grill*, 331 N Main Street, or the *Canyonlands Cafe*, 16 S Main Street; the old-fashioned soda fountain inside the *General Store* at 38 N Main Street does good sandwiches, and there's tasty **vegetarian** food at *Honest Ozzie's Desert Oasis*, 60 N 100 West Street. Both the *Rio Colorado*, 2 S 100 West Street, and *Mi Vida*, on the hill at 900 N Hwy-191, serve steaks and Southwest specialities and have full bars. For a cold **beer** after a day on the trails, head to *Woody's Tavern*, 221 S Main Street, or the *Outlaw Saloon*, 51 W Center Street.

Natural Bridges National Monument

One of the prettiest and least-travelled highways in southern Utah, **Hwy-95**, runs for over a hundred miles southeast from Capitol Reef, through dozens of red rock canyons and across the Dirt Devil and Colorado rivers, before topping out on the sagebrush plains of San Juan County. It's a fine drive in itself, but it also gives access to the marvellous collection of sandstone spans at **NATURAL BRIDGES NATIONAL MONUMENT**, forty miles west of US-191. Three canyons come together here, and at each junction the streams which carved them have also formed sandstone bridges, the largest of which, **Sipapu Bridge**, is 268 feet across at its base and over two-hundred-feet high. You can see the bridge from the eight-mile paved road which loops through the monument, or walk a few hundred yards down into the canyon for a closer look. **Kachina Bridge**, the next along the road, is nearly as high but twice as thick, and has Anasazi pictographs at its base. The oldest, slimmest and most fragile of the bridges is **Owachomo**, 1.5 miles up Armstrong Canyon or along the mesa-top road; it spans 180 feet but is only nine feet thick at its thinnest point. Besides the bridges, numerous **Anasazi ruins** are pointed out by markers along the road and the trails.

The **visitor centre** (daily 8am–4.30pm), three miles off Hwy-95, has trail guides ($1) and a slide show explaining how the bridges are formed, as well as a brief introduction to the Anasazi sites. Ambitious **hikers** can visit all three bridges, and many of the ruins, along an eight-mile circuit, but **camping** is allowed only in the small camp-ground near the visitor centre, which has the only drinkable water in the monument.

Blanding, Monticello and Grand Gulch

Due east from Natural Bridges forty miles along Hwy-95, solidly Mormon **BLANDING** offers little to the traveller apart from **Edge of the Cedars State Park**, a mile west. A small group of ruins, including a ceremonial kiva, has been restored, but surrounded as they are by suburban tract houses they're not exactly atmospheric. Inside the modern museum (daily 9am–5pm; $1) are dozens of carefully executed replicas of the Glen Canyon **Anasazi pictographs** now buried under Lake Powell.

The smaller town of **MONTICELLO**, 21 miles north of Blanding on US-191 near the turnoff for The Needles section of Canyonlands National Park (see above), makes a better base. Its strip of $30 **motels** includes *Canyonlands 6* at 197 N Main Street (☎587-2266) and *Navajo Trail* at 240 N Main Street (☎587-2251), and *The Chuck Wagon* **cafe** at 296 N Main Street is open all day. There's also a **cinema**, *The Movies* at 696 E Hwy-666 (☎587-2535), and a 24-hour *Trailside* petrol-station-and-general-store, at 251 N Main Street. As the seat of San Juan County, Monticello's the best place to pick up information on the region: the county **tourist office** is around the side of City Hall, 117 S Main Street (☎587-2231); the **National Park Service** have a handy office at 32 S 100 East

Street (☎587-2737); and the **BLM**, 435 N Main Street (☎587-2141), have stacks of information on the many "undiscovered" Anasazi sites scattered over southeastern Utah.

If you are interested in Anasazi culture, and want to experience it as closely as possible in its unreconstructed state, head to the **Grand Gulch Primitive Area**, which stretches for some fifty miles to the south of Natural Bridges Monument. The sharply twisting and, despite the ugly name, in places astoundingly beautiful canyon drops down to the San Juan River, and its sheer walls shelter dozens of undisturbed Anasazi cliff dwellings and hundreds of intriguing pictographs. Coyotes, mule deer, ringtailed cats and even a few mountain lions still roam the area. The Kane Gulch ranger station, five miles south of Hwy-95 along Hwy-261, marks the main trailhead; sign in here before heading off to explore, and don't disturb anything you come across. **Dark Canyon**, to the north of Natural Bridges, has yet more sites and is even less visited than Grand Gulch. (See the box on p.657 for more about the Anasazi.)

Mexican Hat, Bluff and the San Juan River

From Natural Bridges and the Grand Gulch area, Hwy-261 runs south for some 25 miles before coming to what looks like a dead end at the edge of Cedar Mesa. From here, high above the eerie sandstone towers of the **Valley of the Gods** (where much of *Thelma and Louise* was filmed) the road turns to gravel before dropping over a thousand feet in little over two twisting hairpin-turning miles down what's called the "**Moqui Dugway**". Six miles from the foot of the switchbacks, the barely marked Hwy-316 shoots across what seems like a flat valley floor to yet another overlook, this time high above the San Juan River at the aptly named **Goosenecks State Park**. A textbook example of what geologists call an entrenched meander, the river, a thousand feet below, snakes around in such convoluted twists and turns that it flows six miles in total for every one mile west.

Back on Hwy-261 and just south, **MEXICAN HAT**, now a sleepy river-rafting centre, was once a frenzied gold-mining camp – it takes its name from a hilarious **sandstone hoodoo**, right along the road, that looks more than a little like a south-of-the-border sombrero. It's just a cluster of buildings on the banks of the river, but it's good fun and makes a good base for visiting Monument Valley, twenty miles to the south (see p.695). The best place to **stay** is the *San Juan Inn* (☎683-2220), right on the river, which has doubles for $40 a night, its own grocery store and trading post, plus the amiable *Olde Bridge Bar and Grill*, with cold beers and Navajo tacos. The neighbouring *Canyonlands Motel* (☎683-2230) has more basic doubles from $25, summer only; *Peregrine River Outfitters* (☎683-2206) run a range of river tours.

Many of the rafts that come out of the water at Mexican Hat went in at **BLUFF**, twenty miles upstream. US-163, the road between, doesn't follow the river very closely but is still a pleasant drive, and the town itself has a number of **Mormon pioneer houses** along its back streets. Good **cafes** in Bluff include the *Sunbonnet* and the *Turquoise*, both open all day, and the *Cow Canyon Cafe* has delicious down-home dinners – and an enticing (and reasonably priced) resort, the *Recapture Lodge* (☎672-2281), which has double rooms from $30 a night and offers nightly slide shows and informal (and informative) guided tours of the surrounding landscape.

Hovenweep National Monument

In a gorgeous desert setting, miles from anywhere at the head of a narrow stream-cut canyon in the middle of nowhere, **HOVENWEEP NATIONAL MONUMENT** consists of the evocative remains of a small but self-sustaining ancient **Anasazi community**. Hovenweep is related to the bigger and better-known cities at Mesa Verde and Chaco Canyon, and if you've been to them you may be disappointed by the scale of things here; on the other hand, the breadth and completeness of the remains here afford a glimpse of Anasazi culture unavailable elsewhere. The one unique feature of Hovenweep is the series of **towers**, built of stone along the canyon rims and under the cliffs; there are also numerous kivas and pit houses and some rock art panels.

Getting out here to the Utah–Colorado border takes some doing. No matter which way you come you have to drive at least ten miles on unpaved roads; if it's raining, don't try. The best of half a dozen well-signed routes takes Hwy-262 east from US-191, midway between Bluff and Blanding; others come in from the north and south, and from Cortez, Colorado. All the routes converge at the small **visitor centre**, where rangers grow corn and other foodstuffs favoured by the ancients in the adjacent garden.

A half-mile loop, detailed in the **trail guide** (35¢), starts at the grandly named **Hovenweep Castle**, a short walk down from the visitor centre. This twin-towered structure was erected some eight hundred years ago at the edge of the canyon. Continuing around to the right, the trail drops down into the tree-shaded canyon to **Square Tower Ruin**, near the base of which is a small spring, the only water source for the entire three-hundred-strong community. Further along the canyon walls, the remains can be seen of the multistorey **Talus Pueblo** that used to reach up to Hovenweep Castle on the rim above; the rocky ruin has not been excavated, and it would be both unsafe and stupid to climb on it. The trail climbs back up to the top a hundred feet to the right, from where another trail leads through the sagebrush, cliff rose and junipers along the rim to **Tower Point**. Here another tower overlooks a fine view of two canyons, the desert plain, and the distant Ute Mountains.

Another, slightly longer (one mile total) but well worthwhile walk from the visitor centre heads west down into **Little Ruin Canyon**, passing by some (sadly much vandalised) Anasazi storerooms and half a dozen fine **petroglyphs** of snakes and birds, directly beneath Tower Point. On the south side of the canyon, you can climb up to the rim past some more ruins, one built underneath a large boulder, or work your way back to the north rim to examine the fortress-like **Stronghold House**, which was once the top of a series of structures stepping down to the canyon floor. The last of the ruins on this trail is the exceptionally well-built Unit-type House, inside which niches mark the angle of the sun at summer and winter solstice.

Suggestions that Hovenweep had some special astronomical significance seem more plausible once you've spent the night in the small **campground** here; the beautifully clear **night sky** displays more stars than you ever saw in your life.

Lake Powell and Glen Canyon National Recreation Area

Sadly but surely, the mighty rivers and canyons of southern Utah come to an abrupt and ignoble end at the Arizona border, where the **Glen Canyon Dam** stops them dead in the stagnant waters of **LAKE POWELL**. Ironically, the lake is named for John Wesley Powell, the first white man to explore the canyonlands in depth, and the first of any colour to run the Colorado River through the Grand Canyon. The roaring torrents with which he battled are now forever lost beneath these placid blue waters, and the blocked-up Colorado, Green, Dirty Devil, San Juan and Escalante rivers are now a playground for houseboaters and water-skiers. The construction of the dam in the early 1960s outraged **environmentalists** – Edward Abbey's *Monkey Wrench Gang* made their first big splash here, sabotaging bulldozers and simulating huge cracks in the dam at the opening ceremonies – and **anthropologists** – innumerable Anasazi pictographs are submerged hundreds of feet below the surface. It has created one of the most peculiar – and utterly unnatural – landscapes imaginable, the deep and tranquil lake a surreal contrast with the surrounding dry slickrock and sandstone buttes.

Lake Powell has 1960 miles of shoreline, which is more than the entire Pacific coast of the US, and 96 water-filled side canyons. The water level fluctuates considerably, so for much of the time the rocks to all sides are bleached for many feet above the current waterline, with a dirty-bath tidemark sullying the golden sandstone. Most of the many summer visitors bring their own boats, or rent a vessel from one of the three marinas that fringe the lake.

If you're passing through, by far the most accessible stop is **Wahweap Marina**, just off US-89 on the way between Zion and the Grand Canyon. From here you can take guided boat trips (daily, 7.30am & 1pm; $42) across the lake to the spectacular **Rainbow Bridge**. This fifty-mile round trip is the easiest way to see the lake's many landmarks – Gunsight Butte, Castle Rock, the Navajo Generating Station – and tour guides will point out which TV commercials were filmed where. Rainbow Bridge itself lies a mile or two down a side canyon, which narrows and winds until petering out at a jetty floating in a morass of pond scum. From there a ten-minute walk leads to the astonishing giant sandstone gateway, which springs up nearly 300 feet from just above the waterline, with Navajo Mountain visible through its magnificent smooth curve.

Another way to see the lake is to take the **ferry** ($9 per car) which links Hwy-276 between Halls Crossing and Bullfrog marinas two-thirds of the way up-lake; from here the Burr Trail heads across the Waterpocket Fold to the town of Boulder (see p.709). If you want to see more, and particularly if you want to explore the extensive backcountry lands to which the lake provides easy access, rent a **houseboat** from Wahweap or one of the other Lake Powell marinas; boats sleep four persons (or more) and cost from $400 for three nights in winter, $650 in summer. You can **camp** along the shore of the lake at each of the marinas, or pamper yourself by taking a $60 room at *Wahweap Lodge*, which also has some of the best food within a day's drive. All these facilities are owned and operated by *ARA Leisure Services* (☎602/269-9408 or ☎1-800/528-6154).

Self-guided tours of the **Glen Canyon Dam** start from the **visitor centre** (daily 9am–4pm) and climb down to the huge 1.1 kilowatt hydro-electric turbines. For the first eleven miles south, the Colorado River is relatively smooth-flowing, lined with sandy beaches and wildflowers and home to blue heron and golden eagles. Half-day rafting trips as far as Lee's Ferry provide an easy taster; if you keep going, the rapids begin and there's no way out before the Grand Canyon (see p.698).

The nearest budget accommodation to Lake Powell is across the Arizona border in **PAGE**, where you'll find petrol stations, motels, and cafes as well as banks with ATMs. You can continue on from here into the Navajo and Hopi lands of northeast Arizona.

Northern Utah: Salt Lake City

Compared to the scenic splendour of the southern half of the state, northern Utah holds little to interest the tourist. The **northeast corner** has coal mines, old railroad towns and, along the Wyoming border, the **Uinta Mountains**, uncrossed by road and showing hardly a sign of civilisation. From the **northwest**, the harshly alkaline Great Basin plain stretches uneventfully west across Nevada to the California border.

The dividing line between the comparatively lush eastern and the bone-dry western halves of northern Utah, the **Wasatch Front**, towers over **SALT LAKE CITY**, by far the largest and most cosmopolitan urban centre in Utah. This disarmingly pleasant and easy-going city is well worth a stopover of a couple of days, but not perhaps a thrilling destination in itself. Its setting is, however, superb, offering hiking or cycling in summer and fall and, in winter, some of the world's best skiing. People elsewhere in the US tend to imagine Salt Lake City as one step away from *The Stepford Wives* in terms of spontaneous public fun, and they're not far wrong. There is a fundamental lack of things to do, in the way of museums or other cultural diversions, but if you're willing to switch gears and slow down, its unhurried pace, and the lack of pretence and the positive energy of its people, can make for a surprisingly enjoyable experience.

Arrival, Getting Around and Information

Salt Lake City, slap in the centre of northern Utah, has the state's main **airport** and is well served by both *Amtrak* and *Greyhound*, so it's easy to reach and to leave. Both **buses** at 160 W South Temple Boulevard (left luggage lockers; ☎355-4684) and **trains**, 400 W South Temple Boulevard (☎364-8562), arrive downtown, and the airport is served by hourly local bus (#50).

This sprawling, mostly low-rise city incorporates a number of outlying communities like Provo, Bountiful, and Ogden, but most of what there is to see is concentrated in the walkable compact downtown area. *Utah Transit Authority* (*UTA*) provides a skeletal **public transport** system, and *Gray Line* (☎521-7060) and *Scenic West Tours* (☎572-2717) both offer a wide range of guided **coach tours**, from half-day and full-day jaunts around the city to multiday trips to the various national parks. To reach the best parts of the surrounding mountains, however, you'll need a car, or a cycle and strong legs; **bikes** can be rented from *Wasatch Touring*, 702 E 100 South Street (☎359-9631).

The Salt Lake City **visitors bureau** put out an immense and very helpful range of free information, available from their office in Terminal 2 of the airport (daily 9am–10pm), or downtown at 180 S West Temple Boulevard (daily 9am–5.30pm; ☎521-2868). For details on the rest of Utah, stop by the *Utah Travel Council* office (Mon–Fri 8am–5pm; ☎538-1030), across from the capitol. The main **post office** is at 250 W 200 South Street (Mon–Fri 8am–5.30pm, Sat 8am–1.30pm; ☎532-5902; zip code 84101).

Temple Square and Downtown Salt Lake City

The geographical – and spiritual – heart of Salt Lake City is **Temple Square**, the world headquarters of the **Mormon Church** (or Church of Christ of Latter Day Saints – LDS) and the only real public space in the whole city. Of its two **visitor centres**, north and south, the north has video introductions to Mormon belief – *Christ in America*, for example, explains how Jesus preached to the Native Americans after His resurrection – while the smaller south one displays replicas of the golden plates from which Joseph Smith transcribed the Book of Mormon. LDS literature is in theory available at both places, though they insist on having missionaries hand-deliver it to your home, and dozens of smiling young Mormon girls are on hand to answer none of your questions.

The architectural and religious focus here is the monumental **Temple** itself, completed in 1893 after forty years of intensive labour. The multispired granite edifice rises to 210 feet above the city – it's not the tallest building on the mainly flat skyline, but, thanks to its crisply angular silhouette, it's just about the only interesting one. Only confirmed Mormons may enter the Temple, and even they do so only for the most sacred LDS rituals – marriage, baptisms and "sealing", the joining of a family unit for eternity. Across the plaza from the Temple stands the odd oblong shell of the **Tabernacle**, concert hall and home to the world-renowned **Mormon Tabernacle Choir**. Free concerts take place at 9am on Sundays, and you can also attend rehearsals on Thursday evenings at 8pm; the marvellous organ is played at noon daily.

A block east of Temple Square along South Temple Street, the **Beehive House** is a plain white Puritan-style house with wraparound verandahs and green shutters. Erected in 1854 by church leader **Brigham Young**, it's now a small museum of pioneer life, restored to the style of the period. Free twenty-minute tours, which you have to join to see much of the house, are given at least every half-hour.

Just over West Temple Street from Temple Square is the one place you might actually plan to spend some time. The **Family History Library** (daily 9am–9pm; free) was set up by the LDS church so that its members could trace their ancestors and then baptise them into the Mormon faith by proxy, but it's open to all faiths. Without rival the most exhaustive genealogical library in the world, the library is housed in an attractive modern building and is surprisingly user-friendly, giving immediate access, through CD discs and banks of computers, to the birth and death records of over fifty countries dating back in many cases more than five hundred years. All you need is a person's name and place of birth, a few approximate dates and you're away; out of respect for the personal privacy of those still living, most of the information pertains to centuries prior to our own. Volunteers will help you if you need it, but leave you alone until you ask. Next door to the library, there's a free **Museum of Church History and Art** (daily 9am–9pm).

The area southwest of Temple Square is undergoing a rapid transformation, with a massive new "Salt Palace" convention centre and sports arena (home of the Utah Jazz basketball team) completed in 1991. The surrounding district of brick warehouses around the Union Pacific railway tracks is quickly filling up with designer shops and art galleries, signs that even Mormons can be yuppies. Further west, the "other side of the tracks" around the I-15 freeway, however, remains one of the city's most rundown and forgotten areas, the last resort of transient winos and Utah's growing homeless population.

Capitol Hill

Looking at the layout of Salt Lake City, you'd think that the Mormons would have located their Temple on the gentle hill above today's Temple Square. They chose not to, however, and when Utah became a state in 1896 the prominent site was adopted by the new state government. Considering the longstanding mutual distrust between the Mormon Church and the US government – in the 1870s and earlier the US Army was often on the verge of attacking the Mormons – the fact that the state government overlooks the Mormon headquarters shows how willing Mormon leaders were to accommodate US demands; they also dropped polygamy from the official church practices.

The grandly domed and imposing **Utah state capitol**, modelled as ever upon the US Capitol, is as much worth a visit as any of Salt Lake City's other buildings. Along with all the plaques and monuments you might expect to find, the corridors of power are packed full of earnest and rather diverting exhibits of great Utah moments: the basement area in particular is packed with anomalous historical what-nots, ranging from mining dioramas to the *Mormon Meteor*, the 18-cylinder, 750-horsepower car in which Ab Jenkins raced across the Bonneville Salt Flats in the 1950s (see opposite).

Now called **Capitol Hill**, the neighbourhood around the capitol holds some of Salt Lake City's finest turn-of-the-century homes, with dozens of ornate Victorian houses lining Main Street and Quince Street to the northwest; walking tour maps of the district are available from the *Utah Heritage Foundation*, 355 Quince Street. Directly opposite the front of the capitol stands another architectural landmark, **Council Hall**, the old Territorial Legislature building that was dismantled and rebuilt here in the 1960s. The main chamber off the entrance has been restored to its period appearance, and the rest of the building now houses the *Utah Travel Council* (see p.719).

Into the Mountains: Timpanogos Cave and the Alpine Loop

For **hiking information** on the countryside around Salt Lake City, call in at the Salt Lake Ranger District office of the US Forest Service, 6944 S 3000 East Street (☎524-5042) at the mouth of Big Cottonwood Canyon. Numerous canyon roads – **Emigration Canyon** (Hwy-65), **Big Cottonwood Canyon** (Hwy-190) and **Little Cottonwood Canyon** (Hwy-210), to name a few – head up from Salt Lake City into the foothills of the **Wasatch Front**. All are beautifully scenic, but perhaps the best way to get a feel for the bountiful wilderness that borders the city is to take the so-called **Alpine Loop** (Hwy-92), which starts twenty miles south of downtown Salt Lake off I-15.

From I-15, Hwy-92 follows the American Fork River east into the Uinta **National Forest**, reaching **Timpanogos Cave National Monument** ten miles on. From the visitor centre next to the car park (daily, summer only, 9am–3.30pm; $3), it's a moderately steep mile-and-a-half hike up to the mouth of the caves; be sure to bring a sweater or jacket because the temperature inside is rarely above 50°. Inside there's a magnificent array of stalactites and stalagmites; you can wander the mile or so underground on your own, or join one of the ranger-guided tours. On summer weekends the caves can often get extremely crowded, while in winter they close altogether.

From here Hwy-92 climbs steeply up behind 11,750ft **Mount Timpanogos**, allowing access to miles of unspoilt **hiking country**. It then drops down from the ridge into **Provo Canyon**, home of the *Sundance* ski resort and film institute, both owned and run by actor Robert *Sundance Kid* Redford, who lives here as well.

The Alpine Loop ends up back on the flatlands 45 miles south of downtown Salt Lake at the tidy little town of **Provo**, whose main feature is **Brigham Young University**, the Mormon-dominated college that has great sports teams – basketball and football especially – and such a squeaky-clean student body you'll feel like you stepped straight back into the Eisenhower years. Grab a bite to eat on campus, or in the town at *Clair's Cafe*, 154 University Avenue (☎373-4077), which has soups, sandwiches and good burgers for fair prices. Provo also has a few cheap **motels**.

The Great Salt Lake

The sole point of interest in the barren desert west of Salt Lake City, the **GREAT SALT LAKE** is the last remnant of a 20,000-square-mile inland sea that once stretched into Idaho and Nevada. Its contents have evaporated to such an extent that it's now the second-saltiest body of water in the world, so thick with various minerals as to be all but lifeless – though you can float in it if you don't mind getting coated. Years ago the lake's shores were lined with extravagant resorts, and its waters crossed by steamboats and pleasure cruisers; **Saltair**, the largest of the resorts, burned down in 1970 after years of disuse, but a small replica stands just off I-80 in Great Salt Lake State Park.

Those areas of the ancient sea that now lie west of the lake towards Nevada are used by the US military as a **bombing range** – this is where the flight crews of the *Enola Gay* trained before dropping the A-bomb on Hiroshima – and by thrill-seekers who come together here at the **Bonneville Salt Flats** every August to attempt to set world speed records: rocket-powered cars have raced across the desert at well over 600mph.

On the north side of the lake, the **Golden Spike National Historic Site** commemorates the place where the first transcontinental railroad linked the east and west coasts in 1869. Two competing companies, the *Central Pacific* from Sacramento, California, and the *Union Pacific* out of Omaha, Nebraska, raced across the country laying track in order to win massive US government subsidies; so great was their greed that they completed (and got paid for) over 200 miles of redundant parallel track across the Utah desert before Congress got wise and demanded they join the two lines at Promontory Point. The original junction was bypassed in 1904, and the tracks removed in 1942, so there's not much to see; a well-signposted **visitor centre** (daily 8am–6pm; $3), 29 miles west of I-15 via Hwy-83, has some good exhibits and the two original locomotives.

Salt Lake City Accommodation

Salt Lake City has a good **hostel** and a number of cheap **motels**, most of which are walkably close to the downtown centre, as well as some rather more luxurious hotels and B&B inns offering the usual homespun charm.

Avenues Youth Hostel, 107 F St (☎363-8137). Clean, standard rooms, five blocks east of Temple Square. Dorm beds $13, singles $20, doubles $28.

Colonial Village Motel, 1530 S Main St (☎486-8171). Basic motel, well out from the centre. $22.

Doubletree Inn, 215 W South Temple Blvd (☎531-7500). Plush modern hotel, with indoor pool, in Salt Palace complex. Doubles from $65.

Motel 6, 176 W 600 South St (☎531-1252). Standard rooms, near *Amtrak*. Doubles from $30.

Peery Hotel, 300 S 100 West St (☎521-4300 or ☎1-800/331-0073). Newly refurbished 1910 downtown landmark, with doubles $45–65 a night.

Pinecrest Bed and Breakfast Inn, 6211 Emigration Canyon Road (☎583-6663). Top-quality accommodation in six-acre pine forest, high above the city. Massive breakfasts, and doubles from $65.

Saltair Bed and Breakfast Inn, 164 S 900 East St (☎533-8184). Utah's oldest B&B, housed in landmark historic home. Doubles from $45.

Shilo Inn, 206 S West Temple Blvd (☎521-9500). Clean modern rooms in downtown tower, with pool, sauna and gym. Doubles from $60.

Travelodge-Temple Square, 144 West North Temple Blvd (☎533-8200 or ☎1-800/255-3050). Most central and least expensive of three local *Travelodges*. Doubles from $32.

Quality Inn-City Center, 154 W 600 South St (☎521-2930 or ☎1-800/228-5151). Spacious, recently remodelled downtown motel. Swimming pool, large doubles from $50.

Eating

Eating out in all-American Salt Lake City is not the most exciting event, but food is generally good value. A few comparatively stylish spots cater to upmarket professional types, but by and large places are unpretentious and family-oriented.

Bill and Nada's Cafe, 479 S 600 East (☎359-6984). All-American 1940s diner, open 24hr. Great for breakfast, but worth a visit anytime for its ace jukebox, the best west of Memphis – packed with Hank Williams, Patsy Cline, blues and be-bop tracks.

Market Street Grill, 48 Post Office Place (☎322-4668). The nearest Salt Lake City comes to a New York City bar and grill, serving up steaks and fresh fish dishes in the main room and all sorts of drinks in the adjoining *Oyster Bar*. Full meals from $12–25.

Lamb's Restaurant, 169 S Main St (☎364-7166). Great breakfasts, best eaten at the long shiny counter, and excellent-value set meals throughout the day in Utah's oldest restaurant.

Rio Grande, west end of 300 South St (☎364-3302). Spirited and stylish Mexican cantina housed in the old Denver and Rio Grande railway station, three blocks west of downtown.

Ristorante della Fontana, 336 S 400 East St (☎328-4243). Elegant Italian meals in converted church, complete with waterfall.

Ruth's Diner, 2100 Emigration Canyon Rd (☎582-5807). Bustling, anarchic burger bar housed in old railroad carriages in the mountains east of town. Great salads and the best breakfasts in Utah.

Santa Fe Restaurant, 2100 Emigration Canyon Rd (☎582-5888). Cosy but sophisticated restaurant whose eclectic menu features the best of Southwest cuisine as well as brilliantly presented grilled meats and fish. Main courses cost $9–20, or come for the excellent-value $12.95 Sunday brunch.

Star of India, 171 E 200 South St (☎363-7555). Good basic curries in no-frills downtown locale.

Drinking and Nightlife

Despite the bizarre (and slowly liberalising) prohibitions on alcohol, Salt Lake City doesn't roll up the pavements after the sun goes down. Several lively bars and clubs are worth checking out, of which many feature regular live music.

To find out about Salt Lake City's surprisingly broad range of fringe art, music and clubland happenings, pick up the two main papers, the Mormon-controlled *Desert News* and the comparatively liberal, non-LDS *Salt Lake Tribune*. If you're going to spend more than a day here, you'll have a better time if you head first to the *Cosmic Aeroplane* bookstore at 258 E 100 South Street and pick up free papers like the fortnightly *The Event* or the monthly *Catalyst*; or tune to community radio station KRCL 91FM .

The Bay, 404 S West Temple Blvd (☎363-2623). No booze, no smoking, but lots of young bodies grooving on the three-level dance floors.

Detour Club, 32 Exchange Place (☎355-8146). Underground gay bar, good sound system, stiff drinks; $5 membership.

Bar X, 155 E 200 South St. Lively downtown bar packed with urban cowgirls and pool sharks.

Salt Lake Coffee Roasters, 249 E 400 South St. Coffee bar open 7am until midnight, Mon– Sat.

Squatters Pub, 147 W 300 South St (☎363-2739). Casual, friendly brew-pub with a range of beers available until midnight every day.

Club Zephyr, 301 S West Temple Blvd (☎355-5646). Salt Lake's premier live venue, with semi-famous names most nights. Upmarket clientele, elegant decor, cover $5–15.

NEVADA

NEVADA is without doubt the most desolate state in the US, consisting largely of endless tracts of bleak empty desert. Its flat sagebrush plains are cut intermittently by angular mountain ranges, and the utter lack of rainfall or fertile soil has ensured its maintenance as untouched wilderness. Apart from the huge acreages given over to mining and to grazing cattle and sheep, much of Nevada is under the control of the US **military**, who use it to test aircraft and weapons systems, including Stealth fighters and atomic bombs. Notwithstanding the above caveats, there are dozens of intriguing small towns scattered around the state, some showing signs of the strong Basque influence (shepherding is big business). Many more are fairly decrepit roadside ghost towns, often little more than a petrol-station-cum-general-store, flanked by a saloon and perhaps a brothel – Nevada is the only US state not to have outlawed **prostitution**.

Though millions of people pass through on their way to and from California, there's only one real reason why anyone ever *visits* Nevada, and that is to **gamble**: as soon as you cross the state border, or stop in any town, you'll be attacked by a 24-hour-a-day onslaught of neon signs and gimmicky architecture, each advertising the best odds and biggest jackpots, nowhere more than in the surreal oasis of **Las Vegas**, in the southern corner of the state. Even the smaller and more down-to-earth settlements of **Reno** and **Carson City**, Nevada's capital, both revolve around the casino trade. One spinoff from the casinos' energetic pursuit of passing trade is that rooms and especially food are incredibly cheap, so if nothing else the towns make good places to break a long journey.

Getting Around Nevada

As there's almost nothing in Nevada outside of Las Vegas and Reno, it's hardly surprising that getting around the state's vast empty spaces is nearly impossible without a car. Buses, trains and planes stop in both the main cities, and if you're travelling across the country they're reasonable overnight stops. About the only other scheduled transport links Las Vegas with Death Valley and Reno with Lake Tahoe.

Las Vegas

When the bronzed visage of Engelbert Humperdinck – or whichever showbiz grizzly is gracing *Caesar's Palace* at the time – leers out from a Nevada billboard, you know you're approaching **LAS VEGAS**: a flat, sprawling, hot city that's almost entirely devoted to the worship of greed. The first hours in Las Vegas are like entering another world: one where the religion is luck, the language is money, and time is measured by revolutions of a roulette wheel. Once acclimatised, the whole spectacle is voyeuristically enjoyable (assuming you haven't pinned your hopes, and your savings, on the pursuit of a fortune). But it's not wise to stay too long – the ceaseless pursuit of dollars can quickly sap your faith in humanity.

Ironically, Nevada was the first state to outlaw **gambling**. Though it was made legal again in 1931, ostensibly to raise taxes for building schools, gaming remained fairly small scale until 1946, when mobster Bugsy Siegel opened the first major combined casino and hotel on what's now the Strip, the *Flamingo*. Its instant success cemented Las Vegas' links with organised crime and instigated the system of attracting people to the gaming tables with the bribe of bargain-priced beds, food, drink and entertainment, a policy that still holds today – Las Vegas is one of the **cheapest** places to sleep and eat in the US. Yet, despite the full-frontal glamour that assaults you from all corners, the

The telephone **area code** for the entire state of Nevada is ☎702.

enduring image isn't of high-spending playboys (who are seldom seen away from their complimentary hotel suites and secluded tables on the Strip), but of ordinary working people standing for hours at a stretch feeding quarters from buckets into slot machines.

It's the **Strip** that provides the most familiar image of Las Vegas, all flashing neon and spectacle. Here you'll find the largest and most glamorous **casino-hotels** – complete self-contained fantasylands of high-camp and genuine excitement. Huge moving walkways sweep you into the casinos, but once you're inside it can be almost impossible to find your way out; the action keeps going right around the clock and in this sealed and windowless environment you rapidly lose track of whether it's day or night. Even if you do manage to get back onto the streets during the day, the scorching heat is liable to drive you straight back in again; night is the best time to venture out, when the Strip's at its brightest and gaudiest. For perhaps 24 hours, it can all be absolutely exhilarating; once the novelty begins to pall, however, you may find yourself drawn to the lower-key pleasures of **downtown**, a more compact few blocks of casinos grouped around so-called "Glitter Gulch", the neon-illuminated junction of Main and Fremont streets. Downtown is three miles from the Strip, linked by the wide, ruler-straight, **Las Vegas Boulevard**, which is lined by petrol stations, fast-food drive-ins, and wedding chapels – getting married being simpler in Nevada than in any other state (no waiting and no blood tests; see Reno, p.728).

If, like most arrivals, you're in Las Vegas solely to gamble, there's not much to say beyond the fact that all the casinos are free, open 24 hours a day, with acres of floor-space packed full of ways to lose money: **one-armed bandits**, video **poker, blackjack** (21) with lightning-fast dealers, and loads of **craps, roulette** wheels and much much more. The casinos will just love it if you've come to play a **system**; with the odds stacked against you, your best hope of a large win is to bet your entire stake on one single play, and then stop, win or lose.

Frankly, the **rest of Las Vegas** needn't concern you at all. It's either given over to ordinary residential districts or to the business community – mining is the biggest industry after the gigantic tourist trade. Once the casinos are exhausted (or rather once *you're* exhausted) there's very little else. Once you're ready to escape, head to **Lake Mead** for a day water-skiing or just splashing about, or take advantage of the surprisingly cheap flights from Vegas to the **Grand Canyon**, and really get away from it all.

Arriving, Getting Around, and Information

By **train** you'll arrive in downtown Las Vegas: the station's platform leads directly into the *Union Plaza Hotel*, 1 Main Street. The *Greyhound* terminal (☎382-2640) is at 200 Main Street downtown, and arriving buses also stop on the Strip, outside the *Stardust Hotel*, 3000 N Las Vegas Boulevard. **Flights** land at **McCarran Airport**, a mile from the Strip and four from downtown. Many hotels have free buses to collect their guests, otherwise there are frequent minibuses to the Strip ($3) and downtown ($4.50).

Local buses are run by the *Las Vegas Transit System* (☎384-3540); the most useful route is #6 between the Strip and downtown, which runs 24 hours a day. The standard single fare on all buses is $1. Given the comparatively small area and lack of places to go beyond the two main districts, you're unlikely to need a **taxi**, though if you're feeling flush a cab between downtown and the Strip costs around $8. On Friday and Saturday nights especially, the Strip is so clogged with traffic that it's quicker to use the I-15 interstate to get around.

For **information**, pick up the free *What's On in Las Vegas, Today in Las Vegas* and *LVT*, which lie around hotel receptions and other public areas. They each carry details of accommodation, buffets, the latest shows, and assorted discount vouchers. There's also a **Convention and Visitors Bureau** at 3150 Paradise Road (Mon–Fri 8am–5pm; ☎733-2323), next to the vast Convention Center, near the Strip.

The Strip

The Strip (the 3000 blocks of Las Vegas Boulevard) gives full reign to the mythical Las Vegas gloss: the big shows, the big casinos, the big spenders. You'll find all three at **Caesar's Palace**; the moving walkway delivers you past a full-sized replica of Caravaggio's *David* into a vast labyrinth of slots and green baize, where half-naked male employees strut around dressed as Roman centurions and the waitresses are made up and attired to suggest a direct descent from Cleopatra. The nearby **Circus Circus**, a more family-orientated spot, attempts to pull in the punters by having live circus acts: a trapeze artist here, a fire-eater there, usually performing above dense crowds. At the far end of the Strip, **Excalibur**, with its vast drawbridge, crenellated towers, and relentless pseudo-medieval "pageantry", is also worth experiencing, while the ersatz Polynesia of the **Tropicana** across the road, while not exactly convincing, makes a great setting for some good-quality food and drink. The **Old-Tyme Gambling Museum** (daily 9am–1pm; $1) in the **Stardust Hotel**, 3000 N Las Vegas Boulevard, is a well-arranged collection detailing the intimate relationship between gambling and the American West (it was how the early pioneers passed the time, and what got quite a few of them killed), with great displays on the legendary figures of card-playing such as Wild Bill Hickok and Poker Annie – one of the few women to excel in what was a strongly male-dominated pursuit – and a mesmerising stock of one-armed bandits.

One haven of comparative serenity away from the relentless vulgarity of the casinos lies two miles east of the Strip: the **Liberace Museum** at 1775 E Tropicana Avenue (Mon–Sat 10am–5pm, Sun 1pm–5pm; $3.50). Popularly remembered as a beaming buffoon who knocked out torpid toe-tappers, the earlier days of Liberace (he died in 1987) make for interesting study. He began his career playing piano in the rough bars of his native Milwaukee; a decade later, in the 1950s, he was being mobbed by screaming adolescents and ruthlessly hounded by the scandal-hungry American press. All this is remembered by a yellowing collection of cuttings and family photos. The trappings of later wealth – electric candelabra, bejewelled quail eggs with inlaid-pianos, glittering cars and more – are here too, but overall the museum isn't the gathering of over-the-top kitsch you might expect. The music, on the other hand, piped into the scented toilets, hasn't improved with age.

Downtown Las Vegas

In **downtown Las Vegas**, the action centres around **Fremont Street**. Regular punters may have their own favourites, but the casinos here are all much the same; they have a friendlier feel than their flashy counterparts on the Strip and the odds are considered more favourable by those in the know. Several also hold free gambling lessons, though these should be treated with scepticism – it's unlikely they'll want you to win. All the casinos are close together and it's a simple business to walk from one to the next. The *Union Plaza*, facing the junction of Main and Fremont streets, has the most businesslike mood but is still good for a stroll around, while the least pretentious downtown joint is *El Cortez*, at the other end of Fremont Street. Of the others, squashed in between, *Binion's Horseshoe* is worth a look, mainly because it's the venue of the *World Series of Poker* each May, and sees some spirited wagering of all kinds year-round.

Lake Mead and the Hoover Dam

Almost as many people as go to Las Vegas visit **LAKE MEAD**, an artificial expanse of water about thirty miles southeast of the city. As with the similarly incongruous Lake Powell (see p.717) it makes a bizarre spectacle, the blue waters a vivid counterpoint to the surrounding desert, but it gets excruciatingly crowded all year round. You can sail, scuba-dive, water-ski or fish at various points along the five-hundred-mile shoreline; get the details and make bookings through any travel agent before arriving, and bear in mind that accommodation is limited to RV-dominated campgrounds.

Fifteen miles beyond Boulder City on US-93, through the rocky ridges of the Black Mountains, is the 1935 **Hoover Dam**, responsible for creating the lake in 1935. Designed to block the Colorado River and provide low-cost electricity for the cities of the Southwest, it's one of the tallest dams ever built (760ft high), composed of sufficient concrete to build a two-lane highway from the West Coast to New York. Informative half-hour **guided tours** (daily, summer 8am–6.45pm, otherwise 9am–4.15pm; $1) descend by lift to view the dam's insides. Without your own transport, the only way to get to Lake Mead and the dam from Las Vegas is on one of the many daily bus tours; the *Gray Line* (☎384-1234) price of $19.50 for a five-hour tour is fairly typical.

Moving on from Las Vegas

If you're relying on **public transport**, Las Vegas is a major connection point for **Death Valley** and the **Grand Canyon**. While there are no scheduled services, *LTR Stage Lines* (☎384-1230) run a charter bus to Death Valley; call to check on price and the current frequency of the service, which operates from September to May only.

Buses to the **Grand Canyon** run year-round courtesy of the *Nava-Hopi* line (☎774-5003), whose one daily service costs $25 one-way. That journey takes virtually the entire day, in searing desert heat, so you might consider **flying**, which offers the added bonus of aerial views of Lake Mead and the Canyon itself. *America West* (☎1-800/247-5692), *Scenic Airlines* (☎1-800/634-6801) and *Air Nevada* (☎1-800/634-6377) all operate several flights daily, with a bottom-rate single fare of around $50.

Las Vegas Accommodation

Although Las Vegas has some 85,000 motel and hotel rooms (most of them hitched to casinos so you never have to go outside), it's best to book **accommodation** ahead if you're on a tight budget, or arriving on Friday or Saturday – upwards of 200,000 people descend upon the city every weekend. If you're coming from anywhere else in the US, check local newspapers for advertisements outlining the latest Vegas accommodation bargains – virtually all hotels and motels offer discounts and food vouchers. Rooms are so cheap that there's no point in **camping**; but be sure to get the rate confirmed for the duration of your stay – that $25 room you found on Thursday may cost $100 on Friday.

AYH Youth Hostel, 1236 S Las Vegas Blvd (☎382-8119). Halfway between downtown and the Strip, charging members $9, non-members $12, with a $5 key deposit.

Caesar's Palace, 3570 S Las Vegas Blvd (☎731-7110 or ☎1-800/634-6001). Still the showcase of the Strip hotels. Doubles start at $100 a night, and keep going to well over $1000.

California Hotel, First St and Ogden Ave (☎385-1222). One of the most popular mid-range hotels in downtown Vegas, with doubles from $40.

Circus Circus, 2880 S Las Vegas Blvd (☎734-0410 or ☎1-800/634-3450). Hugely popular, family-orientated Strip hotel, with circus acts performing live above the casino floor. Doubles from $28.

El Cortez Hotel, Fremont St at Sixth St (☎385-5200 or ☎1-800/634-6703). Older and smaller than most, this recently modernised downtown hotel is one of the better bargains. Doubles from $20.

Excalibur, 3850 S Las Vegas Blvd (☎597-7777 or ☎1-800/937-7777). Arthurian legend built much larger than life, with drawbridges, turrets and nightly jousting matches; staff have to call guests *M'Lord* and *M'Lady*. It opened in 1990 as the largest hotel in the world. Doubles from $50.

Las Vegas Independent Hostel, 1208 S Las Vegas Blvd (☎385-9955). Cheap and cheerful hostel with bare-bones accommodation; $10 a night.

Motel 6, 195 E Tropicana Ave (☎798-0728). The largest branch of this nationwide chain; just off the south end of the Strip. Doubles from $25.

Nevada Hotel, 235 S Main St (☎385-7311). Basic but pleasant downtown doubles from $25.

Riviera, 2901 S Las Vegas Blvd (☎734-5110 or ☎1-800/634-6753). Among the older and larger Strip hotels, with one of the less intimidating casinos. Doubles from $60 a night.

Tropicana, 3801 S Las Vegas Blvd (☎739-2222 or ☎1-800/634-4000). The best and least posed of the Strip hotels, at least as far as non-gambling activities go, with swim-up gaming tables around the world's largest indoor–outdoor swimming pool. Doubles from $50 a night.

Eating, Drinking and Entertainment

Besides gambling, or just watching, the main forms of Las Vegas **entertainment** include credibility-straining "spectaculars" featuring golden-throated warblers and bad comedians, topped off with leggy dancing girls and thumping music. Show seats are $10 on average, but expect to pay (a lot) more if the likes of Frank Sinatra or Dean Martin are topping the bill. Tickets are available from the venues, or can be booked by phone. Full details of what's coming up are in the tourist magazines.

Eating is never difficult or expensive. Nearly all the casinos offer round-the-clock **buffets** available to everyone. **Breakfast**, normally served from 7am until 11am, is the least expensive meal of the day, with the basic versions costing from 99¢ – or even free with a voucher. A **buffet lunch** costs around $4 or $5, and is served until about 5pm, when it mutates into **dinner** and the price rises by a couple of dollars – although the food will often be exactly the same. The top spot for a full splurge is *Caesar's Palace*, particularly their $6.95 lunch, and the best value is either the *Golden Nugget* or *Circus Circus*.

Drinks – beer, wine, spirits and cocktails – are freely available in all the casinos to anyone gambling, and very cheap for anyone else. There are also hundreds of regular **restaurants** if you don't mind spending a bit more.

Battista's Hole in the Wall, 4041 Audrie St (☎732-1424). Pricey but stylish Italian food in a lively setting, enhanced by strolling accordion players and all-you-can-drink complimentary house wine.

Café Santa Fe, 1213 Las Vegas Blvd (☎384-4444). Great omelettes and fresh salads, and other meat-based all-American food.

Casa Tequila, 1815 E Charleston Blvd (☎384-0651). Mexican place offering an 11am–3pm lunch for $3, including a margarita.

Chapalas, 3335 E Tropicana Ave (☎451-8141). Daily happy hours, 3–6pm, with enormous helpings of Mexican food and cheap drinks.

Marie Callender's, 600 E Sahara Ave (☎734-6572). Known throughout the West Coast for its home-baked pies and great homemade soups.

Oh No Tokyo, 4455 W Flamingo Road (☎876-4455). Assorted sushi for $6, lunch or dinner, and a wide variety of other Japanese food.

Crossing Nevada

The bulk of Nevada – the largest but least populated state in the Southwest – is made up of dry, flat plains sliced by knife-edge volcanic mountain ranges. Called the **Great Basin** because its rivers and streams have no outlet to the ocean, the land here does have a certain eerie, even hypnotic, beauty. Its attractions are hard to pinpoint – a few ghost towns, many more odd places with nothing more than a petrol-station-cum-general-store and post office – but there is this indefinable, very American sense of the endless frontier, of wide open space, of room to move.

The main route across Nevada, **I-80**, shoots from Salt Lake City to Reno skirting dozens of bizarrely named small towns – Winnemucca, Elko, and Battle Mountain, for example – packed with casinos, bars, brothels, motels, and little else. The other main route, **US-50**, has the reputation of being the loneliest highway in America, with the least traffic and roadside life. Older and slower than I-80, it follows much the same route as did the riders of the Pony Express in the 1860s, though many of the towns along it have faded away, and some have been entirely abandoned, leaving behind whole blocks of uninhabited buildings. US-50 passes by Nevada's sole national park, the recently established **Great Basin National Park** in the eastern mountains, before it links up with I-80 at Reno, and then cuts off to the southwest to circuit magnificent **Lake Tahoe**, covered in the California chapter on p.817. One last main route, **US-95**, links Reno and Las Vegas, passing near Death Valley (see p.769) as well as Nevada's most famous and most evocative ghost town, **Goldfield**.

Great Basin National Park

Just over the Utah border, the **GREAT BASIN NATIONAL PARK** was formed in 1986 when the Lehman Caves National Monument and the Wheeler Peak Scenic Area were amalgamated. It's a distillation of the range of scenery the Nevada desert offers, from angular peaks to high mountain meadows cut by fast-flowing streams. The **Lehman Caves** are some of the most extensive and fascinating limestone caves in the country, not as big as Carlsbad Caverns (see p.664), but if anything more densely packed with intriguing formations. Daily ninety-minute tours ($3) of the caves leave every two hours from the **visitor centre** (daily 8am–5pm), five miles west of the hamlet of **Baker** near the mouth of the caves.

From the Lehman Caves, a twelve-mile road climbs the east flank of bald and usually snow-capped **Wheeler Peak**, and trails lead past alpine lakes and through a grove of gnarled, ancient bristlecone pines to the 13,063ft summit. Few people ever come here, but in winter the mountains and meadows make for excellent off-track cross-country skiing. The nearest real town, **ELY**, an hour's drive away, has two worthwhile museums – the entertaining **Northern Nevada Railway Museum** (daily 9am–4pm; $2) and the **County Museum** (daily 9am-3pm; free) as well as a dozen **motels** (try *Motel 6*, 770 Avenue O; ☎289-6671), and a handful of casinos and restaurants.

Elko

One of the few Nevada towns worth aiming for, if you're here at the right time of year, is **ELKO**, a straggling highway town a hundred miles from the Utah border. The self-proclaimed last real cowtown in the West is the centre of one of the largest open-range cattle-ranching regions in the US, and the fitting home of the annual **Cowboy Poetry Gathering**, held here every January. People get together in a sort of celebration of folk culture, telling stories around campfires, singing about the lonesome life on the range, and keeping alive the dying traditions and tales of the Wild West.

During the 72-hour party of the **National Basque Festival**, each Fourth of July weekend, hulking men throw huge logs at each other, amid a whole lot of carousing and downing platefuls of Basque food. The food is available year-round in restaurants like the *Nevada Dinner House*, two blocks south of the main drag at 351 Silver Street (☎738-8485). *Greyhound* and *Amtrak* both stop in Elko, and there are dozens of cheap motels, include the *El Neva*, 736 Idaho Street (☎738-7152). The Elko **visitors bureau** is at 700 Moren Way (738-4091 or ☎1-800/248-3556).

Reno and Around

If you don't make it to Las Vegas, you can get a feel for the non-stop, neon-lit gambler's lifestyle by stopping in **RENO**, on I-80, very near the California border. "The biggest little city in the world", as it likes to call itself, is a somewhat downmarket version of the glitz and glamour of Vegas, with miles of gleaming slot machines and poker tables, surrounded by tacky wedding chapels and quickie divorce courts. While the town itself may not be much to look at, its setting – at the foot of the snow-capped Sierra Nevada, with the Truckee River winding through the centre – is superb.

There are three things to do in Reno: gamble, get married, and get divorced. To get **married** you and your intended must be at least eighteen years of age and be able to prove it, swear that you're not already married and appear before a judge at the **Washoe County Court**, on the corner of Virginia and Court streets (daily 8am–midnight; ☎785-4172), to obtain a **marriage licence**, which costs $27. No waiting period or blood test is required. Civil services are performed for an additional $25, $30 during peak periods, at the **Commissioner for Civil Marriages** at 195 S Sierra Street. If you want something a bit more special, wedding chapels all around the city will help you tie the knot; across the street from the courthouse, the *Starlight Chapel* – "No Waiting, Just Drive In" – does the job for a bargain $30, providing a pink chintz parlour full of plastic flowers and heart-shaped seats. If it doesn't work out, you'll have to stay in Nevada for another six weeks before you can get a **divorce**.

Practicalities

An hourly, $2 bus connects Reno's Cannon International **airport** with the downtown casinos. *Greyhound* (☎322-2974) and *Amtrak*'s *California Zephyr* from Chicago both stop in the centre of town, on Second Street. The **visitor centre**, at 135 N Sierra Street (☎827-RENO or ☎1-800/FOR-RENO), can find you a cheap **place to stay**, and offer discount vouchers worth up to $15 in cash and $30 in credits for use in the nearby casinos. For sleeping you could also try *Circus Circus*, at 500 N Sierra Street (☎1-800/648-5010), or the *Grand Hotel*, at 239 E Plaza Street (☎322-2944), both of which have off-peak rooms from $20, though prices usually double on holiday weekends. Reno also has some pretty good **restaurants**, such as the tasty Italian *La Trattoria* at 719 S Virginia Street, and *Louis' Basque Corner*, 301 E Fourth Street (☎323-7203), which serves down-to-earth Basque cooking in comfortable surroundings. The casino food is as cheap as, and usually better than, what you'd get in Las Vegas.

Two-hour *Learn-to-Win Gaming Tours* (daily, noon & 2pm; $5) leave from next to the visitor centre, providing lessons in the basics of craps, roulette, and blackjack, before taking you on a guided tour of the backrooms of a casino – where you can watch the gamblers being watched from behind mirrors and on closed-circuit TV.

Carson City

US-395 heads south from Reno along the jagged spires of the High Sierra past Mono Lake, Mount Whitney and Death Valley (see p.769). Just thirty miles south of Reno, **CARSON CITY**, state capital of Nevada, is small by comparison but has a number of elegant buildings, some excellent historical museums and three world-weary casinos, populated mainly by old ladies armed with buckets of nickels which they pour ceaselessly into the one-armed bandits.

Carson City was named after frontier explorer Kit Carson in 1858, and is still redolent with Wild West history. A good introduction is the **Nevada State Museum** at 600 N Carson Street (daily 8.30am–4.30pm; $1.50), opposite the well-restored **state capitol**. Housed in a sandstone structure built during the Civil War as the Carson Mint, the museum covers the geology and natural history of the Great Basin desert, from prehistoric times up through the heyday of the 1860s, when the silver mines of the nearby Comstock Lode were at their peak. Amid the many guns and artefacts is the reconstructed **Ghost Town**, from which a tunnel allows entry down into a full-scale model of an **underground mine**, giving some sense of the cramped and constricted conditions in which miners worked.

Greyhound buses stop once a day in each direction between Reno and Los Angeles. There are a couple of $25 **motels** in town: the *Westerner* at 555 N Stewart Street (☎883-6565), behind the *Nugget* casino, and the *Trailside Inn* at 1300 N Carson Street (☎883-7300). The **Chamber of Commerce**, on the south side of town at 1191 S Carson Street (Mon–Sat 9am–5pm; ☎882-1565 or ☎1-800/634-8700), can help with practical details and runs architectural walking and driving **tours** of the town, particularly of the many fine 1870s Victorian wooden houses and churches on the west side.

Virginia City

Much of the wealth on which Carson City – and indeed San Francisco – was built came from the silver mines of the **Comstock Lode**, a solid seam of pure silver discovered underneath Mount Hamilton, fourteen miles east of Carson City off US-50, in 1859. Raucous **VIRGINIA CITY** grew up on the steep slopes above the mines, and a young writer named Samuel Clemens made his way west with his older brother, who'd been appointed acting Secretary to the Governor of the Nevada Territory, to see what all the fuss was about. His descriptions of the wild life of the mining camp, and of the desperately hard work men put in to get at the valuable ore, were published years later under his adopted pseudonym, **Mark Twain**. Though Twain also spent some time in the Gold Rush towns of California's Mother Lode on the other side of the Sierra – which by then were all but abandoned – his accounts of Virginia City life, collected in *Roughing It*, are a hilarious eyewitness account of the hard-drinking life of the frontier miners. There's not much to Virginia City nowadays, since all the old storefronts have been taken over by hot-dog vendors and tacky souvenir stands, but the surrounding landscape of arid mountains still feels remote and undisturbed.

travel details

TRAINS

Routes

• One train daily runs west from **Albuquerque** (at 5.10pm) via **Gallup** and **Flagstaff** to **Los Angeles**, and one east (at 1.45pm) to Lamy (connected by *Amtrak* bus with **Santa Fe**, fifteen miles away), **Dodge City** and **Chicago**.

• From **Salt Lake City**, one daily train (at 12.55am) heads west to **Las Vegas** and **Los Angeles**, and another (at 12.35am) to **Reno**, **Sacramento** and Oakland (for **San Francisco**). The daily eastbound train leaves Salt Lake City for **Denver** and **Chicago** at 5.15am.

• Three trains weekly in each direction connect **Los Angeles** with **El Paso** and **New Orleans**, via **Phoenix** and **Tucson**. Trains head east from **Los Angeles** (at 10.50pm) on Sun, Tues and Fri, and west from **El Paso** (at 2.25pm) on Tues, Thurs and Sun.

Journey Times

From **Albuquerque**: Gallup 2hr 20min; Flagstaff 5hr 15min; Los Angeles 15hr; Lamy 1hr; Dodge City 11hr; Chicago 25hr.

From **Salt Lake City**: Las Vegas 8hr; Los Angeles 15hr; Reno 9hr; Sacramento 14hr; Oakland 16hr 30min; Denver 14hr 30min; Chicago 35hr.

From **Los Angeles**: Phoenix 10hr 30min; Tucson 13hr; El Paso 17hr; New Orleans 43hr.

BUSES

All *Greyhound*.

From **El Paso**: to Las Cruces, Tucson, Phoenix and Los Angeles (6 daily; 50min, 6hr, 8hr, 16hr); to Whites City and Carslbad (3 daily; 3hr, 3hr 20min).

From **Santa Fe**: to Taos (4 daily; 1hr 30min); to Denver (4 daily, 6hr); to Albuquerque (7 daily, 1hr 30min).

From **Albuquerque**: to Gallup, Grants, Flagstaff (5 daily; 1hr 30min, 2hr 20min, 7hr); to Los Angeles (2 daily; 18hr).

From **Salt Lake City**: to Elko, Reno and San Francisco (3 daily; 3hr, 9hr 20min, 15hr); to Cedar City, St George, Las Vegas, Los Angeles (1 daily; 5hr, 6hr, 8hr, 14hr).

From **Las Vegas**: to Los Angeles (12 daily; 5hr 30min); to Phoenix (2 daily; 9hr).

For transport to the **Grand Canyon**, see p.698.

CHAPTER THIRTEEN

CALIFORNIA

P ublicised and idealised all over the world, **CALIFORNIA** really does live up to the myth. It's more than just a terrestrial paradise of sun, sand, surf and sea; it also has high mountain ranges, fast-paced glitzy cities, deep primeval forests and hot dry deserts. The landscape is also imbued with more **history** than you might expect, ranging from primitive rock carvings left by the aboriginal Native Americans, to the eerie ghost towns of the **Gold Rush** pioneers.

Having zoomed from the Stone Age to Silicon Valley in a couple of centuries, the West Coast is in some ways the ultimate "now" society. Anywhere so vulnerable to constant threat of the Big One – the **earthquake** that will one day drop half the state into the Pacific – is bound to have a sense of living for the moment. However, its supposed "superficiality", promoted as much by East Coast Americans as by foreigners, is largely fictitious. Though home to reactionary figures such as Ronald Reagan and Richard Nixon, it has also been the source of some of the country's most progressive **political movements**. The fierce protests of the Sixties may have died down, but California remains the heart of **liberal** America, at the forefront in issues such as environmental awareness, gay pride and social permissiveness. Economically, too, the region is crucial, whether it's in the long-established **film** industry, the recently ascendant **music** business, or even in the financial markets.

Distances in California can be huge, and visitors simply won't be able to see everything in a single trip; but in an area so varied it's hard to pick out specific highlights. **Los Angeles** is far and away the biggest and most stimulating city: a maddening collection of freeways, beaches, seedy suburbs, high-gloss neighbourhoods and extreme lifestyles that you should see at least once. From Los Angeles you can head south to the smaller, up-and-coming city of **San Diego**, with its broad, welcoming beaches and easy access to Mexico; or push inland to the **desert** areas. **Death Valley** is a barren and inhospitable landscape of volcanic craters and windswept sand dunes that in summer (when you can fry an egg on your car bonnet) becomes the hottest place on earth.

Most people, though, follow the shoreline north up the **central coast**: a gorgeous run which takes in lively small towns like Santa Barbara and Santa Cruz. California's second city, **San Francisco**, at the top end, is about as different from LA as it's possible to get: the oldest, most European-looking city, set on a series of steep hills, its wooden houses tumbling down to water on both sides. It is also well placed for the national parks to the east, such as **Yosemite**, where powerful waterfalls cascade into a sheer glacial valley, and **Sequoia** with its gigantic trees, as well as the ghost towns of the **Gold Country**. **North** of San Francisco the countryside becomes wilder, wetter and greener, approaching Oregon through spectacular and almost deserted volcanic tablelands.

The **climate** in **southern California** consists of endless days of summer sunshine, and warm dry nights – though **LA**'s notorious **smog** is at its worst when the temperatures are highest, in August and September. All along the **coast** mornings can be hazily overcast, especially in May and June; in exposed **San Francisco** it can be chilly all year, and fog rolls in to ruin many a pleasant sunny day. In winter, it can rain for weeks on end, causing massive mudslides that wipe out roads and hillside homes. Hiking trails in the **mountains** are blocked from November to June almost every year by the **snow** which keeps California's ski slopes among the busiest in the nation.

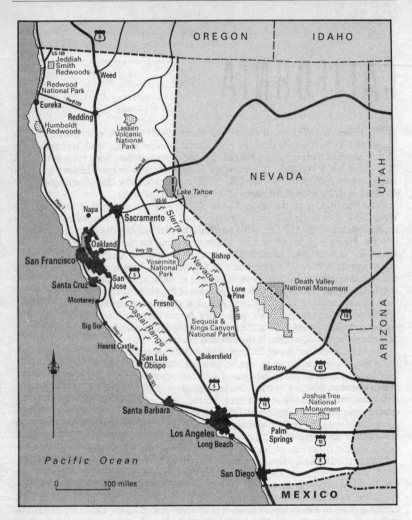

History

Around half a million people – almost half the population of what is now the US – were living in tribal villages along the West Coast when the Spaniard **Juan Cabrillo** first sighted San Diego harbour in 1542, and named **California** for an imaginary island (inhabited entirely by Amazons) from a Spanish novel. The British **Sir Francis Drake** landed near Point Reyes north of San Francisco in 1579, where the "white bancks and cliffes" reminded him of Dover. In 1602 **Sebastián Vizcaíno** bestowed most of the place-names that still survive; his exaggerated description of **Monterey** as a perfect harbour led later colonisers to make it the region's military and administrative centre. The Spanish occupation began in earnest in 1769, combining military expediency with missionary zeal. Father **Junipero Serra**, plus three hundred soldiers and clergy, first established a small mission and *presidio* (fort) at San Diego, before arriving in June 1770 at Monterey. By 1804, a chain of 21 missions, each a long day's walk from the next along the dirt path of *El Camino Real* (The Royal Road), ran from San Diego to San Francisco. The labour of the Indian converts was co-opted; though not all the Indians gave up without a fight, disease ensured that they were soon wiped out.

When Mexico gained its independence in 1821, in theory it also acquired control over California. However, by now the first **Americans**, males without exception, were beginning to turn up. The immense difficulty of getting to California – it took three months by sea via Cape Horn, or four months overland in a covered wagon – kept the population down to a mere ten thousand non-Indians in 1846. However, the growing belief that it was the **Manifest Destiny** of the United States to cover the continent from coast to coast soon led to diplomatic approaches from the US government, and to the **Mexican–American War**. Virtually all the fighting took place in Texas; Monterey was captured by the US Navy without a shot being fired, and by January 1847, the Americans controlled the entire West Coast. In 1850, California became the 31st US state.

By chance, a mere nine days before the treaty was signed that ended the war, flakes of **gold** were discovered by workmen in the Sierra Nevada. Prospectors flooded in, in the most madcap migration in history; it took just fifteen years to pick the gold fields clean. The completion of the **transcontinental railroad**, built using Chinese labourers, in 1869, was a major turning point. The crossing from New York now took just five days, and a railroad rate war brought fares down to as little as $1 for a one-way ticket.

California was perceived as immune to the worst effects of the **Great Depression** of the 1930s – thanks in part to the images of prosperity promulgated by its now-established **film industry**. From the Dust Bowl Midwest, entire families of "Okies" packed up everything they owned and set off for the farms of the Central Valley. Heavy industry came during **World War II**, in the form of shipyards and airplane factories, and many workers and military personnel stayed on afterwards. The aviation industry remains one of the West Coast's biggest employers.

As home to the **Beats** in the Fifties and the **Hippies** in the Sixties, and a host of radical political and ecological movements besides, California was at the cutting edge of cultural change. The illusions of the Flower Power days were shattered by Charles Manson, however, and once the anti-war struggle was over, popular culture seemed to withdraw into self-satisfaction. The easy-money boom of the Eighties in turn has now crash-landed in a tangled mess of scandal, and for California the Nineties have kicked off with a stagnant property market, rising unemployment, escalating gang violence and racial tensions in LA, and an appalling death toll from AIDS in San Francisco.

Getting Around California

If you want to explore and enjoy California to the full, you'll be glad of a **car**. A city such as Los Angeles couldn't exist without the automobile, and to drive down the coastal freeways invites irresistible mental images of Beach-Boy-style cruising.

Public transport is, however, adequate, with **bus** companies such as *Greyhound* and *Green Tortoise* (Los Angeles ☎310/392-1990; San Francisco ☎415/821-0803; toll-free ☎1-800/227-4766) linking all the main cities. *Amtrak* **trains** run up the coast from LA and San Diego; they don't go to San Francisco itself, but pass through nearby Oakland. Another line runs along the Central Valley and up to Oregon, but only connects with LA by bus. Cross-country routes head off through Nevada and Arizona. Foreign visitors can cut fares greatly by using the **Far Western Rail Pass** (see p.21).

For quick hops between the major cities – above all between LA and San Francisco – you can't beat **flying**. Services are extremely frequent, and prices competitive: *Southwest Airlines*, for example, have a $49 fare between any two Californian cities.

If you plan to do any **long-distance cycling**, cycling from north to south can make all the difference – the wind blows this way in the summer. Be careful if you cycle along Hwy-1 on the coast: it has heavy traffic, tight curves, and is prone to fog.

SAN DIEGO

Free from smog and jungle-like freeways, **SAN DIEGO**, set around a gracefully curving bay, represents the acceptable face of southern California. The second biggest city in California may be healthy, affluent and conservative, but it's also amiable, easy-going and far from smug. Though it was the site of the first mission in California, the city only really took off with the arrival of the Santa Fe Railroad in the 1880s, and in terms of trade and significance it has long played second fiddle to Los Angeles. However, during World War II the US Navy made it their Pacific Command Center, and the military continues to dominate the local economy, along now with tourism.

Arrival and Information

Both **trains** and **buses** leave you in the heart of downtown San Diego: *Greyhound* (☎239-9171) at Broadway and First Avenue is even more central then *Amtrak*'s Santa Fe Depot. Lindbergh Field **airport** is only two miles out, on bus #2 ($1.25).

Getting around without a car, by day at least, is easy. Seven companies operate an integrated **bus** system; the *Transit Store*, 449 Broadway (Mon–Sat 8.30am–5.30pm, Sun noon–5pm; ☎234-1060), has detailed timetables and sells passes. The tram-like **San Diego Trolley** covers the sixteen miles from the Santa Fe Depot to the Mexican border crossing at San Ysidro ($2; every 15min). The last trolley back from San Ysidro leaves at 1am, so you can if you want have an evening out south of the border. **Bicycle** rental shops include *Hillcrest Bike Shop*, 3934 Fifth Avenue, Hillcrest (☎296-0618).

The **visitor centre** is downtown at F Street and First Avenue (daily 8.30am–5pm; ☎236-1212), and the main **post office** is at 2535 Midway Drive, between downtown and Mission Beach (Mon–Fri 8.30am–5pm, Sat 8.30am–4.40pm; ☎293-5410; zip code 92138).

The City

You never feel under pressure in San Diego to do anything other than enjoy yourself. Though the work-hard play-hard ethic is as prevalent here as anywhere else in southern California, the accent is strongly on the second, more pleasurable, part of the equation. Indeed, the city, with its easily managed central area, scenic bay, 42 miles of beaches, and plentiful parks and museums, is hard not to like from the moment you arrive.

Downtown San Diego

Always vibrant and active, **downtown** San Diego is much the best place to start exploring. Since the late 1970s, several blocks of Twenties architecture have been stylishly renovated, while the sleek modern bank buildings symbolise the city's growing economic significance on the Pacific Rim. Downtown is safe by day, but it can be unwelcoming at night, and you should confine your after-dark visits to the restaurants and clubs of the comparatively well-lit and well-policed Gaslamp District.

The tall Moorish archways of the **Santa Fe Railroad Depot**, at the western end of **Broadway**, were built to welcome visitors to the 1915 Panama-California Exposition in Balboa Park, and still evoke a sense of grandeur. Broadway slices through the middle of downtown, its most hectic portion coming between Fourth and Fifth avenues. Shoppers, sailors, yuppies, and street bums linger around the fountains outside **Horton Plaza** (Mon–Fri 10am–9pm, Sat 10am–8pm, Sun 11am–6pm), San Diego's major upmarket shopping place, completed in 1985 for a cool $140 million. Its top level, with its open-air eating places, is the one to make for; although the food may be more

---

The telephone **area code** for San Diego and the surrounding area is ☎619.

expensive than in the streets, it's fun to sit over a coffee and watch the parade go by. Few of the stores are worth much more than a browse, but don't miss the 21ft-tall **Jessop Clock,** on level one, made for the California State Fair of 1907.

South of Broadway, the sixteen-block **Gaslamp District,** the heart of frontier San Diego, is now filled with smart streets lined with classy cafes, antique stores, art galleries – and gaslamps (albeit powered by electricity). A tad artificial it may be, but its late-nineteenth-century buildings can be intriguing to explore. One of the finest interiors in the city is in *Johnny's 801,* a seafood restaurant at 801 Fourth Avenue. Diners stuff themselves with crabs' legs beneath an epic stained glass dome and above a stunning tiled floor. Also worth a peek is the **Horton Grand** hotel, painstakingly rebuilt in Victorian style with original artefacts from one of the raunchiest hotels in the country.

The **Embarcadero,** beyond the new Convention Center, makes an enjoyable route to the **America's Cup Museum,** on the B Street Pier (daily 10am–6pm; $3). The controversy, intrigue and xenophobia which have dogged the cup ever since it was first competed for in 1851 are barely acknowledged; instead you see models and drawings of boats (and occasionally the cup itself). A few yards north, the **Maritime Museum** (daily 9am–6pm; $5) comprises three vintage sailing craft: the most interesting is the *Star of India,* built in 1863 and now the world's oldest still-afloat merchant ship.

Balboa Park and San Diego Zoo

Sumptuous **BALBOA PARK** contains one of the largest groupings of **museums** in the US. Yet its real charm is simply itself: its trees, gardens, traffic-free promenades – and a thumping concentration of Spanish colonial-style buildings. Within easy reach of downtown by **buses** #7, #16 or #25, the park is large but fairly easy to **get around** on foot – if you tire, there's a free Balboa Park tram. The cheapest way to see the museums is the $9 **Balboa Park Passport,** which allows admission to any four; it's available from the clearly signposted **information centre** (9.30am–4pm; ☎239-0512) inside the House of Hospitality. Most of the museums are closed on Mondays; and almost all are free on the first Tuesday of each month.

The high quality of the **Timkin Art Gallery** (Tues–Sat 10am–4.30pm, Sun 1.30–4.30pm; free), which has impressive works by Rembrandt and El Greco and a stirring collection of Russian icons, makes its stifling formality worth enduring. By contrast, the **San Diego Museum of Art** (Tues–Sun 10am–4.30pm; $5, students $2) has few individually striking items, but amongst its solid stock of European paintings are some exquisitely crafted pieces from China and Japan. Outside, don't miss the free **Sculpture Court and Garden,** with formidable works by Henry Moore and Alexander Calder. The **Museum of Man** (Tues–Sun 10am–4.30pm; $3, students $1), which straddles El Prado, veers from banal crafts demonstrations to excellent Native American displays.

In the much-hyped **Reuben H Fleet Space Theater and Science Center** (daily 9.45am–9.30pm; theater $4–6; science center $1), close to the Park Boulevard end of El Prado, the "gee whiz" kid-oriented exhibits are pretty lame, but the Space Theater's dome-shaped tilting screen and 152 loudspeakers can take you on stomach-churning trips into volcanoes, over waterfalls, even through outer space.

Across the plaza, the **Natural History Museum** (daily 10am–4.30pm; $4, students $1) has a great collection of fossils and an affecting section on threatened species of wildlife, which pulls no punches in explaining the issues. Just behind, in the **Spanish Village Arts and Crafts Center** (daily 11am–4pm; free), some 42 craftspeople practise skills such as painting, sculpture, photography, pottery and glass-working.

The enormous **San Diego Zoo** (daily March–Oct 9am–5pm, otherwise 9am–4pm), immediately north of the main museums, is one of the world's best. Its wide selection of animals – among them rare Chinese pheasants, Mhorr gazelles, and a freak-of-nature two-headed corn snake – are restrained in "psychological cages", without bars. Basic **admission** is $10.75; a *Deluxe Tour* ticket ($15) covers tours as well.

Old Town San Diego

In 1769, Spanish settlers chose Presidio Hill as the site of the first of California's missions. They soon began to build homes at the foot of the hill, which was dominated in turn by Mexican officials and then early arrivals from the eastern US. **OLD TOWN SAN DIEGO** is now a state historical park holding a number of original adobe dwellings, plus the inevitable souvenir shops. The shops and restaurants stay open until around 10pm, but the **best time** to be around is during the afternoon, to enter the more interesting of the adobes on the daily **free walking tour** (2pm). Details can be had from the **visitor centre** on San Diego Avenue (daily 10am–6pm).

The Spanish-style building now atop Presidio Hill is only a rough approximation of the original mission – moved in 1774 – but its **Junípero Serra Museum** (Tues–Sat 10am–4.30pm, Sun noon–4.30pm; $2) is an intriguing examination of the man who led the Spanish colonisation of California. The **Mission Basilica San Diego de Alcalá** itself was relocated six miles north to 10818 San Diego Mission Road (daily 9am–5pm; $1), to be near a water source and fertile soils – and to be safer from attack by Indians. The present building (on bus #43 from downtown) is still a working parish church, a peaceful complex that gives welcome respite from the nearby freeways. The mood is perhaps enhanced by its general decay. Walk through the dark and echoey church to the garden, where two small crosses mark the graves of Indian neophytes, making this California's oldest cemetery. A small **museum** holds craft objects and historical articles from the mission, including the crucifix held by Junípero Serra at his death in 1834. Despite accusations that the missionary campaign was one of kidnapping, forced baptisms, and virtual slavery, Serra was beatified in 1988, the Pope declaring him a "shining example of Christian virtue and the missionary spirit".

Hillcrest and Mission Bay

North of downtown and on the northwest edge of Balboa Park, **HILLCREST** is an increasingly lively and artsy area at the centre of the city's **gay community**. Go there either for something to eat – there's a selection of interesting cafes and restaurants – or simply to stroll around the fine gathering of Victorian homes.

Heading northwest towards the coast, you come to San Diego's most popular tourist attraction, in **MISSION BAY**. Exhibits and timetabled events at **Sea World** (daily 9am–dusk; $24.95) range from "performances" by killer whales and dolphins, to the eerie sight of the heads of hundreds of moray eels protruding from the hollow rocks of the "Forbidden Reef". All manner of sharks circle menacingly in the Shark House; the Penguin Exhibit is a mock Antarctica, in which hundreds of birds noisily jump around on ice and dive into the water, where they're visible through glass.

Anyone of a nervous disposition, or lacking a physique appropriate to bathing apparel, might find **MISSION BEACH**, just west, too hot to handle. On the other hand, the raver-packed sands, scantily clad torsos, and surfboard-clutching hunks may be precisely what you've come to the West Coast for. Despite first impressions, the city authorities are endeavouring to limit its anarchic hedonism – more families are using the area, but little impact has been made on the beach's freewheeling character.

Point Loma

The **Cabrillo National Monument** at the southern extremity of the hilly and very green peninsula of **POINT LOMA** was where Cabrillo and crew became the first whites to land in California. That's as far as the historical interest goes, for they quickly reboarded their vessel and sailed away. The startling views from this high spot, however, across San Diego Bay to the downtown skyline and right along the coast to Mexico, easily repay the journey here. A mile or two from the monument, a platform makes it easy to view the November to March **whale migration**, when scores of grey whales pass by on their way to their breeding grounds off Baja California, Mexico.

Accommodation

Accommodation is plentiful throughout San Diego, at prices to suit all pockets. The best-placed **campground** is *Campland on the Bay*, 2211 Pacific Beach Drive (☎1-800/BAY FUN), linked to downtown by bus #30.

Armed Services YMCA, 500 W Broadway (☎232-1133). Well-equipped budget option between the *Greyhound* and train stations. Dorm beds for *IYHA* members for $9, singles $20, doubles $35.

Balboa Park Inn, 4302 Park Blvd (☎298-0283). Sizeable gay-oriented bed and breakfast inn, in Hillcrest within walking distance of Balboa Park and its museums. Singles and doubles $65–100.

Beechwood Motel, 465 Fourth St (☎696-9694). Small and cosy, and within an easy walk of everything in downtown. Singles $19, doubles $30.

Churchill's Castle, 827 C St (☎1-800/621-5640). Bizarre downtown attempt to recreate a European castle, complete with turrets and moat. Singles $42, doubles $46.

Clarkes Flamingo Lodge, 1765 Union St (☎1-800/822-0133). Friendly hotel, whose high-camp tropical style is much appreciated by the predominantly gay clientele. Singles and doubles from $33.

The Maryland Hotel, 630 F St (☎239-9243). Amenable restored hotel, if somewhat lacking in frills, in a good downtown location. Singles from $17; doubles from $25.

Ocean Villa Motel, 5142 W Point Loma Blvd (☎224-3481). Usefully placed for the sands, with ocean-view rooms. Singles from $30, doubles from $35.

Point Loma AYH Hostel, 3790 Udal St (☎223-4778). Friendly hostel, six miles from downtown on bus #35 but ideal for the beach. Dorm beds; members $10, others $13.

YWCA, 1012 C St (☎239-0355). Atmospheric Twenties structure with women-only accommodation, in small dorms ($8.25 plus key deposit) or tidy private rooms: single $13, double $26.

Eating

Wherever you are in San Diego, you'll have few problems finding somewhere to **eat** that offers good food and good value. Everything from crusty coffeeshops to stylish ethnic restaurants are in copious supply.

The Brigatine, 2444 San Diego Ave. Sumptuous seafood in inventive styles in this award-winning, but not too expensive (especially during the 4–7pm happy hour) restaurant.

California Café, Top Floor, Horton Plaza. Good cheap California cuisine, with great daily specials.

Casa de Bandini, 2660 Calhoun St. Old Town Mexican lunch spot, in lovely landmark building.

Ichibin, 1449 University Ave. Few better places exist to enjoy quality Japanese cuisine.

Kung Food, 2949 Fifth Ave. Succulent vegetarian food, in a non-smoking environment.

The Red Onion, 3125 Ocean Front Walk. Beside the beachside boardwalk, with a riotous atmosphere as huge helpings of Mexican food are washed down with killer margaritas.

Stefano's, 3671 Fifth Ave. Finely prepared meals, a relaxing atmosphere and decent prices, makes this Hillcrest's top place for Italian food.

Thai Chada, 142 University Ave. Exquisite gourmet Thai dishes at modest cost, with heaps of care lavished on both food and service.

Nightlife

Though San Diego's money is lavished on classical music and opera, the crowds flock to beachside discos and boozy music venues. It may be narrow in scope, but there is at least plenty going on. For full listings, pick up the free *San Diego Reader*.

B St California Grill & Jazz Bar, 425 W B St (☎236-1707). Upmarket jazz haunt.

Blind Melons, 710 Garnet Ave, Pacific Beach (☎483-7844). Earthy, live blues every night.

Bodie's, 253 F St (☎236-08988). Rowdy bar with rock, blues and R&B combos nightly.

Club West Coast, 2028 Hancock St. Popular gay disco: expect loud sounds and blinding lights.

Shadows, 4046 30th St. Enjoyable, neighbourhood-style bar patronised by gay men and lesbians.

Spirit, 1130 Buenos Ave, Mission Bay (☎276-3993). Glam, metal, thrash and indie bands all get a look-in at this long-running alternative venue open every night.

TIJUANA: A TASTE OF MEXICO

You could hardly find a more intriguing day trip out from San Diego than **Tijuana**, just over the border in Mexico. Tijuana may not be the most interesting place in Mexico, but twenty million people every year cross here from the US. Most of them are Californians on day-long shopping expeditions, seeking a change from the local mall. And they find it: blankets, pottery, cigarettes, tequila, dentistry or car repair – everything is lower-priced in Tijuana than in the US, and all of it is hawked with enthusiasm.

Although you can't help but be made aware of the vast economic gulf separating the two countries – you're immediately confronted by beggars crouched in corners and dirty children scuffling for change – Tijuana is, in fact, one of the wealthiest Mexican cities. Things are much safer these days than a decade or so ago, when it really was a rough border town. The main streets and shopping areas are a mile or so from the border in downtown, where the major thoroughfare is Avenida Revolución. Stroll up and down for a while to get the mood and then retire to one of the many bars and watch the throng in the company of a sizeable margarita. At night, the action mostly consists of inebriated North American youths dancing themselves silly in flashy discos.

Heavy traffic, and insurance problems, make crossing into Mexico **by car** a bad idea; both the San Diego Trolley (p.734) and bus #932 run from San Diego. **Border formalities** are minimal: you only need a Mexican Tourist Card (free from consulates in the US or at the border) if you go further into the country. Returning to the US, however, even within a day, immigration procedures are stringent. If you want to stay the night, **hotels** are cheap, with many decent lodgings close to the centre. *Hotel del Mar*, Calle 1a 1948 (☎685-7302), and *Hotel San Jorge*, Avenida Constitución 506 (☎685-8540), both cost $7.50 for a double. The comparatively opulent *Hotel Nelson*, Avenida Revolución 502 (☎854303), charges $22. Dollars are accepted as readily as pesos, so there's no need to **change money**.

The Anza-Borrego Desert

Most of eastern San Diego County, which otherwise consists largely of sleepy suburban communities, is taken up by the 600,000-acre **ANZA-BORREGO DESERT**. Some of it can be covered by car, although four-wheel-drive vehicles are necessary for the more obscure – and most interesting – routes. The best **time to come** is in winter, when daytime temperatures stay around the mid-eighties. In the fiercely hot summer, the place is best left to the lizards, but when the desert **blooms**, between March and May, scarlet octillo, orange poppies, white lilies, purple verbena, and other wildflowers make a memorable – and fragrant – sight.

Historical reminders in the desert span Indian tribes, the first white trailfinders and Gold Rush times. In the west, Scissors Crossing, the junction of Hwy-78 and Hwy-2, was once on the **Butterfield Stage Route**, the first regular line of communication between the East and the newly settled West, which began service in 1857. **Box Canyon** is a passage carved through the rock by the Mormons in 1847. Some miles further on, the old adobe rest stop of **Vallecito Stage Station** gives a good indication of the privations of early desert travel. To the south, around Imperial Valley in the least-visited portion of Anza-Borrego, there's a vivid and spectacular clash as grey rock rises from the edges of the red desert floor. Hwy-22 leads east from Borrego Springs past a memorial to Peg Leg Smith, an infamous local spinner of yarns from the Gold Rush days who is celebrated by the **Peg Leg Liars Contest** on the first Saturday in April; anybody can get up before the judges and fib their hearts out.

For details on the many campgrounds in the park, call in at the **visitor centre** at 200 Palm Canyon Drive (June–Sept weekends and holidays 10am–3pm, rest of the year daily 9am–5pm; ☎767-5311), a mile or so west of Borrego Springs, the only sizeable town. **Hotels** here tend to be pretty expensive; only *Oases* at 366 W Palm Drive (☎767-5409) is at all affordable, with rooms from $42.

LOS ANGELES

The rambling metropolis of **LOS ANGELES** sprawls across a thousand square miles of a great desert basin, knitted together by an intricate network of high-speed freeways between the ocean and the snow-capped mountains. Its colourful melange of shopping malls, palm trees and swimming pools is at once bafflingly strange and startlingly familiar, thanks to the celluloid self-image that it has spread all over the world.

LA is a very young city; just a hundred years ago, it was a bicultural community of white American immigrants and wealthy Mexican ranchers, with a population of less than fifty thousand. Only on completion of the transcontinental railways in the 1880s did it really begin to grow. The old ranches were subdivided, and the enduring symbol of the city became the family-sized suburban house (with a swimming pool and two-car garage), set amidst the orange groves in a glorious land of sunshine. The real boom came after World War II in the mushrooming of the aeronautics industry – which still accounts for one in four jobs. While the population no longer doubles every ten years, it continues to soar.

The first-time visitor may well find Los Angeles thrilling and threatening in equal proportions; it's a place that picks you up and sweeps you along whether you want it to or not. Sure, it has its fine-art museums and so on, but what people really come here for is to experience the city that has come to epitomise the American Dream – most obviously in the fantasy worlds of **Disneyland** and **Hollywood**, but also in the half-flaunted and half-concealed opulence of Beverly Hills and Malibu.

Arriving and Information

All roads in southern California seem to lead to LA; plenty of travellers who try to avoid the city end up here anyway. Although LA is capable of bewildering people who've lived in it for years, however, it's really not that intimidating – just don't panic.

By Plane

All European and many domestic **flights** use Los Angeles International Airport – always known as **LAX** – sixteen miles southwest of downtown. Free 24-hour **shuttle buses** (line "C") connect with the LAX Transit Center at Vicksburg Avenue and 96th Street, where you can pick up **local buses**. Minibuses such as **Airport Shuttle** (☎971-8265), **SuperShuttle** (☎1-800/325-3948) and **Coast Shuttle** (☎310/417-3988) run all over town, delivering you to your door. Fares are generally around $15, with a journey time of between 30 and 45 minutes. **Taxis** from the airport are always expensive: around $25 to downtown, $30 to Hollywood and as much as $70 to Disneyland.

If you're arriving from elsewhere in the US, or Mexico, you might just land at one of the **other airports** in the LA area – at Burbank, Long Beach, Ontario or Newport Beach. RTD buses (☎626-4455) serve them all – see p.742.

By Bus or Train

The main **Greyhound** bus terminal (☎620-1200), at 208 E Sixth Street, is in a seedy section of downtown. Access is restricted to ticket holders and it's safe enough inside, but on leaving, make sure you turn left, across Los Angeles Street, and not right, into deepest Skid Row. The major local bus stops are three blocks on, along Broadway, in the heart of downtown. **Other Greyhound terminals**, elsewhere in LA, handle fewer services: in Hollywood at 1409 Vine Street; in Pasadena at 645 E Walnut Street; in Santa Monica at 1433 Fifth Street; and in Anaheim at 1711 S Manchester Boulevard.

Arriving in LA by **train** you'll be greeted with the expansive architecture of Union Station, 800 N Alameda Street (☎624-0171), on the north side of downtown.

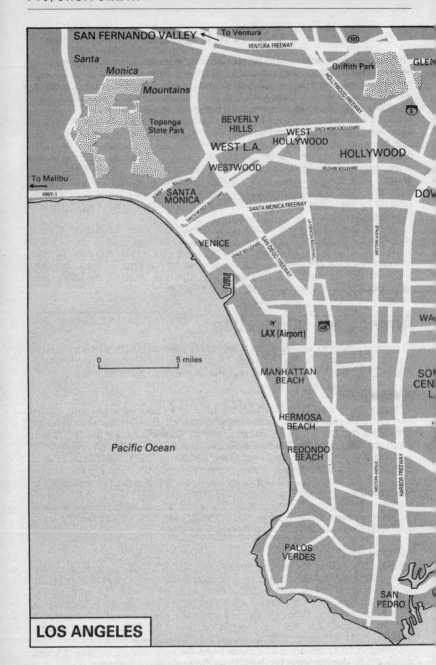

LOS ANGELES

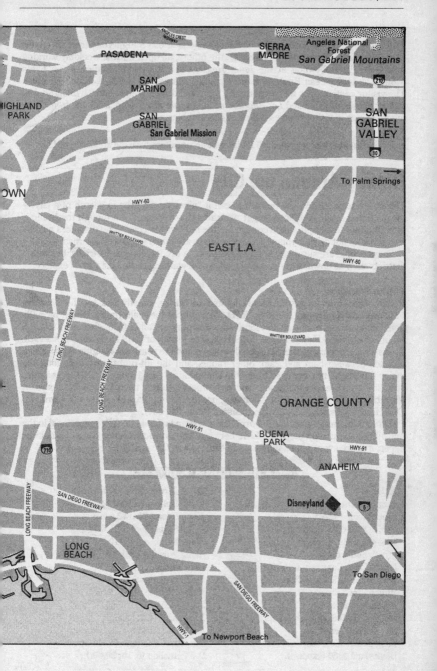

Information

LA has four **visitor centres**. The downtown one is at 695 S Figueroa Street (Mon–Fri 8am–5pm, Sat 8.30am–5pm; ☎689-8822); the others, all open normal weekday working hours, are in Hollywood at the *Janes House*, 6541 Hollywood Boulevard; in Santa Monica at 1400 Ocean Boulevard; and opposite Disneyland at 800 W Katella Avenue. The visitor centres offer free local **maps**, but you'd do better to spend $1.75 on *Gousha Publications*'s fully indexed *Los Angeles and Hollywood Street Map*, available from vending machines in visitor centres and most hotel lobbies.

> Unless otherwise specified, all LA **telephone numbers** have the area code ☎213.

Getting Around the City

The sheer scale of LA – its detractors call it "nineteen suburbs in search of a city" – means that it really *is* difficult to **get around** without a **car**. Even though the traffic is often bumper-to-bumper, the freeways are the only way to cover long distances quickly – so if you're not driving yourself, express buses are much the fastest alternative.

Some people are surprised to find pavements in LA, let alone pedestrians, but within districts such as downtown or central Hollywood, **walking** is the best way to explore.

Public Transport

Public transport in LA is mainly limited to **buses**, mostly run by the *Southern California Rapid Transit District* – **RTD**. We've listed the main routes below; for additional information, phone ☎626-4455 (6am–11.30pm), or call in (Mon–Fri only) at 419 S Main Street, 515 S Flower Street (level B of Arco Plaza), or 6249 Hollywood Boulevard. Buses on the major arteries between downtown and the coast run roughly every fifteen minutes between 5am and 2am; other routes, and the **all-night services** along the major thoroughfares, are less frequent. The standard **single fare** is $1.10; **transfers** cost 25¢ more; **express buses**, and any others using a freeway, are 35¢ extra. A **Monthly Pass** costs $42, or slightly more to include express buses. **Downtown DASH** buses also ply two downtown routes (Mon–Sat; 25¢).

Though the underground **Metrorail** train system is due to be fully operational in the mid-1990s, so far only the **Blue Line** between downtown and Long Beach is running; departures are every fifteen minutes and the one-way fare is $1.10.

MAJOR LA BUS ROUTES

RTD

From downtown to:

Santa Monica #22.

Venice #33, #333, #436 (express).

LAX #42, #439 (weekdays only), #607 (rush hours only).

Forest Lawn Cemetery #90, #91.

Exposition Park #40, #42, #81.

Huntingdon Library #79.

Burbank Studios #96.

San Pedro #446 (express), transfer to #146 for Catalina terminal.

Long Beach #60, #368, #456 (express).

Disneyland #460 (express).

To and from downtown:

Along Hollywood Blvd #1.

Along Sunset Blvd #2 .

Along Santa Monica Blvd #4 .

Along Melrose Ave #10 .

Along Wilshire Blvd #20, #21, #22.

Greyhound

From downtown to:

Hollywood (15 daily; 25min).

Santa Monica (9; 35min).

Long Beach (12; 35min).

Anaheim (14; 45min).

San Juan Capistrano (2; 1hr 30min).

San Fernando (6; 1hr 20min).

As well as downtown **walking tours**, there are innumerable **coach tours** of the city –
though only the "specialists" below show you anything you couldn't see more cheaply for
yourself. Costs are $25–40; most will collect you from your hotel.

WALKING TOURS

Los Angeles Conservancy. Downtown
treks on Saturday mornings (10am from the
Biltmore Hotel on Olive St; $5; ☎623-CITY).

MAINSTREAM COACH TOURS

Casablanca Tours, at the *Hollywood
Roosevelt*, 6362 Hollywood Blvd (☎461-0156).

Gray Line Tours and **Starline Tours,** at the
Janes House, 6541 Hollywood Blvd (☎856-
5900).

Hollywood Fantasy Tours, 1721 N Highland
Ave (☎1-800/782-7287).

Oskar J's Tours, 13455 Ventura Blvd (☎818/
785-4039).

SPECIALIST TOURS

The California Native, 6701 W 87th Place
(☎310/642-1140). One-day trip to the mountain and desert regions on the fringes of LA.

Grave Line Tours, PO Box 931694,
Hollywood (☎310/392-5501). Daily at noon, a
Cadillac hearse leaves from Hollywood Blvd
and Orchid Ave, pausing at the scene of nigh-
on every death, scandal, perverted sex act and
drugs orgy that ever tainted Hollywood.

Hollywood on Location, 8644 Wilshire Blvd
(☎310/659-9165). Inside info on movies and
TV shows being shot on location in LA, plus
directions on getting to them by car – but no
guarantee you'll see anything memorable.

Taxis don't cruise the streets: among the more reliable companies are *Independent
Cab Co* (☎1-800/521-8294) and *United Independent Taxi* (☎1-800/822-TAXI). The basic
fare is $1.90, plus $1.40 for each mile.

Cycling

Cycling in LA may sound perverse, but there are beach bike paths between Santa
Monica and Redondo Beach (see the Venice account on p.750), and from Long Beach
to Newport Beach, and many equally enjoyable inland pedals, notably around Griffith
Park (see p.748), the grand mansions of Pasadena and along the LA River.

The City

With only a finite amount of space between the desert, the mountains, and the ocean,
LA has long since filled in the gaps between what were once geographically isolated
and small communities. As a result, it's a massive conglomeration of interconnected
and not always well-defined districts, not all of which have that much in common.

If LA has a heart, however, it's **downtown**, in the centre of the basin. It offers a taste
of almost everything you'll find elsewhere around the city, from avant-garde art to the
abject dereliction of Skid Row, compressed into an area of small, easily walkable
blocks. The area **around downtown** contains some more elaborate Victorian suburbs,
Twenties Art Deco buildings, and the centre of LA's enormous Hispanic population.

A broad corridor runs 25 miles west from downtown to the coast. The first district
you come to, **Hollywood**, has streets caked with movie legend – even if the genuine
glamour is long gone. Adjoining **West LA** is home to the city's newest money, shown
off in Beverly Hills and along Sunset Strip. **Santa Monica and Venice** to the west are
the quintessential seafront LA of palm trees, white sands, and laid-back living, while
the coastline itself stretches another twenty miles down to **Malibu.**

Suburban **Orange County,** east of the Harbor Area, holds little of interest apart
from **Disneyland.** On the far side of the northern hills lie the **San Gabriel and San
Fernando Valleys,** distanced from mainstream LA life socially as well as geographically, and the butt of most Angeleno hick jokes.

Downtown LA

Downtown LA embraces LA's every social, economic and ethnic division. It's not the high-rise megalopolis you might expect; only the occasional towering office block punctuates its low and level skyline. During the post-war boom, as businesses spread out across the basin, it seemed to be heading for dilapidation and decay, but a recent revitalisation has given it a new life.

The whole area can easily be seen in a day on foot, aided by the odd ride on a 25¢ *DASH* bus. LA's original settlement on the **Northside** is the obvious first stop, before crossing into the brasher and more modern **Westside**, continuing through the chaotic streets of **central downtown**, and finally stepping into the strange blend of street bums and high-style art collections which makes up the **Eastside**.

The Northside

To see downtown LA, start at the beginning. **El Pueblo de Los Angeles**, off Alameda Street, was the site of the initial late eighteenth-century Mexican settlement of Los Angeles, and a few evocative early buildings remain in situ. The **plaza church**, the city's oldest, now serves as a sanctuary for Central American refugees. **Olvera Street**, which runs north from the plaza, contrived in part as a pseudo-Mexican village market, is saved only by its lighthearted grouping of food and craft stalls.

Union Station nearby provides different echoes of LA's roots. This magnificent example of mission-style municipal architecture, finished in 1939, is now barely used, although its projected use as a Metrorail terminal may bring back the crowds. Across the Santa Ana Freeway, the **Civic Center** is a collection of plodding bureaucratic office buildings around a lifeless plaza. The one exception is the Art Deco **City Hall**: familiar on TV through LA cop badges ever since *Dragnet*, this was as late as 1960 the city's tallest structure, and there's a 360° view from the observation deck of its 28-storey tower. On the south side of the plaza, free tours of the **Los Angeles Times** building (Mon–Fri 11am & 3pm) show how the West Coast's biggest newspaper is put together.

The Westside

Until a century ago the area south of the Civic Center, **Bunker Hill**, was LA's most elegant neighbourhood, its elaborate mansions and houses connected by funicular railway to the growing business district down below. Now it's been subsumed into the amorphous **Financial District**, forever sprouting colossal new fifty-storey towers. The largest and most ambitious of these, the billion-dollar **California Plaza** on Grand Avenue, is based around **MOCA** – the Museum of Contemporary Art (Tues, Wed, Sat & Sun 11am–6pm, Thurs & Fri 11am–8pm; $4, students $2, free Thurs 5–8pm). The museum opened at the end of 1986, funded by a one-percent tax on all new downtown construction. It justifies a visit for the playfully colourful building alone, designed by showman architect Arata Isozaki as a "small village in the valley of the skyscrapers". In addition to work by Franz Kline, Mark Rothko, Robert Rauschenberg and Claes Oldenburg – not necessarily their best pieces – and the impressive multimedia memorials of Antoni Tapiès, there's a compelling collection of paintings and sculpture by the rising stars you're likely to come across in trendy city galleries.

If MOCA's high-brow tone gets too demanding, there's relief in the shallow but amusing **Wells Fargo Museum** (Mon–Fri 9am–4pm; free) at the base of the shiny red towers of the *Wells Fargo Center*, telling the story of the bank of Gold Rush California.

A block away, the unmistakable shining glass tubes of the **Westin Bonaventure Hotel** defined the skyline of a futuristic Los Angeles in the movie *Bladerunner*. Its lobby doubles as a shopping mall and office complex – a disorientating Escher-style labyrinth of spiralling ramps and balconies that can only be negotiated with frequent recourse to the colour-coded map.

Central Downtown

Though it's hard to picture now, **Broadway** was once LA's most fashionable shopping and entertainment district. Today it's largely taken over by the cash-rich hustle and bustle of Hispanic clothing and jewellery stores, all to a soundtrack of blaring salsa music. Its most vivid taste is to be had amid the pickled pigs' feet and sheeps' brains inside the **Grand Central Market**, on Broadway between Third and Fourth. Right alongside, the whimsical terracotta facade of the 1918 **Million Dollar Theater** mixes buffalo heads with bald eagles. This is one of several Broadway movie palaces still in use; the **Los Angeles Theater** at 615 S Broadway is even more extravagant, built in ninety days for the world premiere of Charlie Chaplin's *City Lights* in 1931.

Around Downtown

The LA sprawl begins as soon as you leave downtown, the diverse environs of which tend to be forgotten quarters, scythed by freeways, and with large distances separating their few points of interest. They are too widely separated for it to make sense to try to see them consecutively; each is ten to thirty minutes by car or bus from the next.

MacArthur Park and Around

The dilapidated patches of green and large lake of **MacArthur Park** are the nearest open spaces to the sidewalks of downtown. Half a mile west, the seminal **Bullocks Wilshire** department store is the most complete example of late 1920s Art Deco in LA. *Bullocks* is still a retail business, but the merchandise on sale now is fairly dowdy.

The **Ambassador Hotel**, 3400 Wilshire Boulevard, is also rough around the edges these days and perhaps scheduled for demolition. Its *Cocoanut Grove* club flourished from the Twenties to the Forties, and the large ballroom (now closed) featured in the first two versions of *A Star is Born*. The kitchen, however, was the scene of the hotel's most notorious event. **Bobby Kennedy** was fatally shot here on June 5 1968, the day of his greatest political triumph – his victory in the California Democratic Primary.

The so-called "Miracle Mile" (see p.748) continues west from the *Ambassador*. Two blocks south of Wilshire, between Vermont and Western, **KOREATOWN** holds the largest concentration of Korean people outside Korea. It's five times larger – and infinitely more genuine and lively – than Chinatówn and Little Tokyo combined.

Exposition Park

Across Exposition Boulevard from the USC campus, south of downtown, is the sizeable **Exposition Park**, one of the most appreciated parks in LA. It retains a real sense of community, bolstered by its function as favourite lunchtime picnic place. The free **California Museum of Science and Industry** here, off Figueroa Street (daily 10am–5pm), contains enjoyable working models and thousands of pressable buttons – though its displays are uncritical and marred by a bizarrely sited *McDonalds* right in the middle. Just outside, the replica "classic" American diner in the **Hall of Health** (daily 10am–5pm; free) carries displays on what not to eat if you want to stay healthy.

In the neighbouring **Hall of Economics and Finance** (daily 10am–5pm; free), you can wreck the American economy with the aid of a few machines. If that seems too lightweight, head for the exhibitions on the history, art and culture of America's black communities in the **California Afro-American Museum** (daily 10am–5pm; free).

The **Los Angeles County Museum of Natural History** (April to Sept Tues–Fri 10am–5pm, Sat & Sun 9am–6pm, rest of the year Tues–Sun 10am–5pm; $3, students $1.50) is the nicest building in the park, with its echoey domes and travertine columns. Its tremendous stock of dinosaur skeletons includes the skull of a Tyrannosaurus Rex, and a Diatryma – a huge flightless bird. Other displays include Mayan pyramid murals and the complete contents of a Mexican tomb (albeit a reconstruction).

South Central LA

South Central LA hardly ranks on the tourist circuit, but it's a large and integral part of the city, whatever wealthy white LA might prefer to think. The population is mostly black with a few pockets of Hispanic and Asian, joined here and there by bottom-of-the-heap, working-class whites. It doesn't look so terribly rundown at first sight, mostly made up of detached bungalows enjoying their own patch of palm-shaded lawn, but just about all its people get an abysmal deal in schooling and work, and have little chance of climbing the social ladder and escaping. If you pass through, what's most striking is the sheer monotony: every block for twenty-odd miles looks much like the last, enlivened periodically by fast-food outlets, dingy supermarkets and uninviting factory sites.

The district of **Watts** achieved notoriety as the scene of the six-day **Watts Riot** of August 1965 which left 36 dead and innumerable buildings in charred ruins, and of the 1975 gun battle which put an end to the Symbionese Liberation Army (SLA), kidnappers of publishing heiress Patti Hearst. **Compton** too is renowned worldwide as the home of many of LA's **rappers** – NWA made their reputation with *Straight Outta Compton*. However, outsiders should not attempt to sniff out the local music scene.

THE GANGS OF LOS ANGELES

South Central LA is the heartland of LA's infamous **gangs**, said to number over seventy thousand members. The gangs have existed for forty years, but only recently, with the massive influx of drug money, has violence escalated and automatic weaponry (not least Uzi machine guns) become commonplace. Most fatalities (there are about five hundred a year) are a direct result of drug-trade rivalry, though there has lately been an increase in "drive-by shootings" – in which pedestrians are sprayed with bullets by a gunman emerging from a passing car. Not until the death of a single white professional woman in West LA in 1987 did a gang-related death attract much notice from the world outside. The resulting clampdowns have made little real headway in tackling the problem.

You're unlikely to see much evidence of the gangs beyond the occasional blue or red scarf (the colours of the Crips and Bloods, the two largest gangs) tied around a street sign to denote "territory"; and fortunately there's even less chance of witnessing inter-gang warfare. As for personal danger, passing through South Central LA by car is quite safe, but be wary, especially after dark, of delays at traffic lights.

Hollywood

If a single place-name encapsulates the LA dream of glamour, money and overnight success, it's **HOLLYWOOD**. Millions of tourists arrive on pilgrimages; millions more flock here in pursuit of riches and glory. Hollywood is a weird combination of insatiable optimism and total despair. It really *does* blur the edges of fact and fiction, simply because so much *seems* possible – and yet so little, for most people, actually is. Those who do strike it rich here get out as soon as they can, just as they always have; the big film companies, too, long ago relocated well away, leaving Hollywood in isolation, with prostitution, drug dealing and seedy bookstores as the reality behind the fantasy.

Central Hollywood

The myths, magic, fable and fantasy splattered throughout the few short blocks of **Central Hollywood** would put a medieval fairytale to shame. A rich sense of nostalgia pervades the area, giving it an appeal no measure of tourists or souvenir postcard stands can diminish. Although you're much more likely to find a porno theatre than spot a real star, the decline which blighted Hollywood from the early Sixties is fast receding. Nevertheless the place still gets hairy after dark, with on-leave marines strutting the sidewalks and adolescents cruising Hollywood Boulevard in customised autos.

A BRIEF HISTORY OF HOLLYWOOD

Hollywood started life as a temperance colony in 1887, intended to provide a sober God-fearing alternative to raunchy downtown LA, eight miles away by rough country road. The film industry was drawn here from the East Coast, for the guaranteed sunshine, diverse assortment of natural locations, and to dodge restrictive patent laws. The first studio opened in 1911, and within three years the place was packed with film-makers – such as Cecil B deMille who shared his barn-converted office space with a horse.

The ramshackle industry expanded fast, and eager new arrivals soon swamped the original inhabitants, outraging them with their hedonistic lifestyles. Once movie-making had proved itself to be a financially secure business – with the success of DW Griffith's *The Birth of a Nation* in 1915 – film production became highly specialised. Small companies either went bust or were incorporated into big studios. Hollywood has of course always had its creative side – such as the hard-bitten *film noir* style of the Forties – but big names, big bucks and conservatism are what have kept it alive. These days, with profits gnawed away by television and rock music, the industry rarely even thinks about taking risks.

The natural place to begin exploring Hollywood Boulevard is the junction of **Hollywood and Vine** – the classic location for budding stars to be "spotted" by big-shot directors and whisked off to fame and fortune. At no. 6608 Hollywood Boulevard, **Frederick's of Hollywood**, with its purple and pink facade, is Hollywood's idea of a landmark. Opened in 1947, it has been (under-) clothing Hollywood's sex-goddesses ever since, as well as mortal bodies all over the world via mail-order. Inside, the **lingerie museum** (free) displays some of the company's best corsets, bras and panties, donated by happy big-name wearers ranging from Lana Turner to Belinda Carlisle.

A little further on, the **Egyptian Theater** (no. 6708) was financed by impresario Sid Grauman, in a modest attempt to recreate the Temple of Thebes. The very first Hollywood premiere (*Robin Hood*) took place here in 1922, but sadly it's now divided into several smaller cinemas. Lovers of high camp should instead turn left for the **Max Factor Museum** at 1666 Highland Avenue (Mon–Sat noon–4pm; free). This commemorates the man who left his wig shop in Russia in 1904, and headed for Hollywood with a specially thinned grease-paint that turned out to be the perfect on-camera make-up.

No Hollywood visitor will want to miss the mundane yet magical foot and hand prints in the concrete concourse of the 1927 **Chinese Theater** at 6925 Hollywood Boulevard. Actress Norma Talmadge (supposedly by accident) trod in wet cement while visiting the construction site, and the practice has continued ever since, starting with Mary Pickford and Douglas Fairbanks Sr, at the opening of *King of Kings*. Through the halcyon decades, this was *the* spot for movie first-nights. As for the building, it's an odd western version of a classical Chinese Temple, replete with dodgy Chinese motifs and up-turned dragon tail flanks.

The **Roosevelt Hotel** opposite was movieland's first luxury hotel, its *Cinegrill* restaurant hosting the likes of WC Fields and F Scott Fitzgerald, not to mention hangers-on like Ronald Reagan. In 1929 the first Oscars were presented here, beginning the long tradition of Hollywood rewarding itself in the absence of honours from elsewhere.

Despite the beliefs of some of their loopiest fans, even the biggest Hollywood stars have been mortal; the many LA cemeteries which hold their tombs get at least as many visitors as the city's museums. In the southeast corner of the **Hollywood Memorial Cemetery**, near Santa Monica Boulevard and Gower Street, a mausoleum contains the resting place of **Rudolph Valentino**, the celebrated screen lover who died aged just 31 in 1926. To this day on each anniversary of his passing (23 August), at least one "Lady in Black" will likely be found mourning. The achingly ostentatious memorial to **Douglas Fairbanks Sr**, who with his wife Mary Pickford did much to introduce social snobbery among the movie-making people, is just outside.

Griffith Park

The gentle greenery and rugged mountain slopes making up vast **Griffith Park**, between Hollywood and the San Fernando Valley (daily 5am–10.30pm, mountain roads close at dusk; free), is a welcome escape from the mind-numbing hubbub of the city. The largest municipal park in the country, it's one of the few places where LA's multitude of racial and social groups at least go through the motions of mixing fairly happily together. Above the landscaped flat sections, the hillsides are rough and wild, marked only by foot and bridle paths, leading into desolate but appealingly unspoilt terrain that gives great views over the LA basin and out to the ocean. One way to explore is on a **rented bike** from *Woody's Bicycle World*, 3157 Los Feliz Boulevard (☎661-6665). The park is safe enough by day, but its reputation for after-dark violence is well founded.

The Hollywood Hills

The views from the **Hollywood Hills** take in a bizarre assortment of opulent properties. Around these canyons and slopes, which run from Hollywood itself into Benedict Canyon above Beverly Hills, mansions are so commonplace that only the half-dozen fully blown castles (at least, Hollywood-style castles) really stand out. On Mulholland Drive are Rudolph Valentino's extravagant **Falcon Lair**, Errol Flynn's **Mulholland House**, the former home of actress Sharon Tate, the last victim of the Manson family. Guided tours (p.743) can point out which is which, but for the most part you can't get close to the most elaborate dwellings anyway, and none is open to the public.

From more or less anywhere in Hollywood, you can see the **Hollywood sign**, erected as a property advertisement in 1923 (when it spelt "Hollywoodland"; the "land" was removed in 1949). The sign is also famous as a suicide spot, though few have followed the 1932 example of would-be movie star Peg Entwhistle. Hers was no mean feat, the sign being as hard to reach then as it is now: from the end of Beachwood Drive she picked a path slowly upward through the thick bush, to leap to her death from the fifty-foot "H". Attempting to reach it simply isn't worth the bother.

West LA

LA's so-called "Westside" begins immediately beyond Hollywood in **WEST LA**, bordered by the foothills of the Santa Monica Mountains to the north and the Santa Monica freeway to the south. West LA is at the sharp end of all that's new and happening in the city, though tucked away behind the showcase streets, the usual long residential blocks are only marginally less drab than normal.

The LA County Museum of Art

The **Miracle Mile** which stretches from downtown along Wilshire Boulevard was the premier property development of the Thirties. Though the enormous **LA County Museum of Art** or LACMA (Tues–Fri 10am–5pm, weekends until 6pm; $4, students $1.50) is one of the least impressive of its buildings, some of the collections of applied art here are among the best in the world. Despite the loss of Armand Hammer's fine stock of paintings to his own museum in Beverly Hills, it justifies a lengthy visit. The **Fearing Collection** of funereal masks and sculpted guardian figures from Pre-Columbian Mexico is highly impressive, but where the museum really excels is in its specialisations, notably the **German Expressionist** prints and drawings and the scrolls and ceramics in the **Pavilion for Japanese Art**.

An astonishing assortment of bones has been recovered from the adjacent **La Brea Tar Pits** (Tues–Sun 10am–5pm; $5, students $1.50). For thousands of years animals who tried to drink from the deceptive layer of water which covers this pool of smelly and still-seeping tar have found themselves stuck fast; it is now surrounded by life-sized models of victims such as mastodons and sabre-tooth tigers.

West Hollywood

Between Fairfax Avenue and Beverly Hills, **West Hollywood** was for many years notorious for after-hours vice clubs and general debauchery. These days it's much more upmarket, home to Los Angeles' prominent – and affluent – gay community. **Melrose Avenue**, LA's trendiest shopping street, runs parallel to the main drag, Santa Monica Boulevard, looking at times like something out of a low-budget 1950s sci-fi feature. Neon and art deco abound among a fluorescent rash of designer and secondhand boutiques, exotic antique shops, and avant-garde galleries.

Above West Hollywood, on either side of La Cienega Boulevard, is the roughly two-mile conglomeration of restaurants, plush hotels and nightclubs on Sunset Boulevard known as **Sunset Strip**, which remains one of LA's best areas for nightlife. These establishments first appeared in the early Twenties, along what was then a dusty dirt road linking the Hollywood movie studios with the West LA "homes of the stars". With the rise of TV the Strip declined, only reviving in the Sixties when a scene developed around the landmark *Whiskey-a-Go-Go* club, which featured seminal psychedelic rock bands such as Love and Buffalo Springfield.

Greta Garbo was only one of many stars to appreciate the quirky Norman castle that is the **Chateau Marmont Hotel**, towering over the east end of the Sunset Strip at no. 8221. Howard Hughes used to rent the entire penthouse so he could keep an eye on the bathing beauties around the pool below, and comedian John Belushi died of a heroin overdose here, in the hotel bungalow he used as his LA home.

Beverly Hills

Though **Beverly Hills** must be one of the world's wealthiest residential areas, the money is discreet rather than vulgar, revealed more by the immaculate shops (for example the high-fashion showcase of **Rodeo Drive**) and squeaky clean streets than ostentatious displays. It's not a particularly welcoming place, especially if your clothes don't match the quietly elegant attire of the residents.

Palatial estates lie hidden behind landscaped security gates in the verdant canyons and foothills above Sunset Boulevard. **Benedict Canyon Drive** climbs past a good number, beginning with the first and most famous: the lavish **PickFair** mansion at 1143 Summit Drive, built for Mary Pickford and Douglas Fairbanks in 1919. Further up, the secret passageways and large private screening room of Harold Lloyd's **Green Acres** survive intact, although the grounds, which contained a waterfall and a nine-hole golf course, have been broken up into smaller lots.

Westwood

West LA's most energetic district, **Westwood**, owes much of its youthful vitality to its proximity to the UCLA campus. Spanish Revival **Westwood Village** has a number of interesting shops and bookstores, and is LA's prime movie-going district. Wilshire Boulevard here exploded in the 1970s with oil-rich high-rise developments; now modest detached houses sit next to twenty-storey condominium towers in which penthouse apartments with private heliports sell for upwards of $12 million. Inside one such tower, on the corner with Westwood Boulevard, is the **Armand Hammer Museum of Art and Culture Center** (Wed–Mon noon–7pm; $4.50), amassed over seven decades by the flamboyant boss of Occidental Petroleum. Its Rembrandts and Rubens are less than stunning, but Van Gogh's intense and radiant *Hospital at Saint Remy* is a real jewel. The museum's costliest acquisition is also the most disappointing: the *Codex Hammer*, dreary pages of ramblings about hydraulics from the notebooks of Leonardo da Vinci.

Outside the museum, behind the tiny *Avco* cinema, Hammer's marble tomb in **Westwood Memorial Park** stands near the lipstick-covered plaque that marks the resting place of **Marilyn Monroe** – still decorated twice-weekly with a bouquet of red roses sent by Monroe's ex-husband, Joe DiMaggio.

Santa Monica, Venice and Malibu

Set along an unbroken twenty-mile strand of clean, white-sand beaches, the small, self-contained communities that line the **Santa Monica Bay** feature some of the best Los Angeles has to offer, with none of the smog or searing heat that can make the rest of the metropolis unbearable. The entire area is well served by public transport, near (but not too near) the airport, and a wide selection of cheap accommodation makes it a good base for seeing the rest of LA.

Santa Monica

Santa Monica is the oldest and biggest of LA's resort areas, perched on palm-tree-shaded bluffs above the blue Pacific. Once a wild beachfront playground, it's now a self-consciously healthy and liberal community, home to a large expatriate British community of writers and rock-stars, ranging from Rod Stewart to Johnny Rotten.

The Santa Monica beachfront grew into a giant funfair city when it was linked to downtown LA by the suburban streetcar system. It was the location for many of the underworld stories of Raymond Chandler, most memorably as "Bay City" in *Farewell My Lovely*, but today Chandler wouldn't recognise the place. The gambling ships and bathing clubs have gone, and Santa Monica is just another elegant seaside town.

Santa Monica reaches nearly three miles inland, but most things of interest are within a few blocks of the beach. The **visitor centre** (daily 10am–4pm; ☎310/393-7593) in a kiosk just south of Santa Monica Boulevard, along Ocean Boulevard in Palisades Park (the cypress-tree-lined strip along the top of the bluffs), makes a good first stop. Two blocks east of Ocean Boulevard, the **Santa Monica Promenade** is the closest the town comes to having a high street, a pedestrianised stretch popular with buskers and itinerant evangelists. Browse through the secondhand and fine art book shops, check out the latest Spanish-language movies, or, of a Wednesday, sample the weekly **farmers' market**, which sets up along Arizona Street on either side of the mall.

The real focal point of Santa Monica life is down below, on the **beach** and around **Santa Monica pier**, which boasts a giant helter-skelter and a well-restored 1922 wooden **carousel** – featured, along with Paul Newman, in the 1973 movie *The Sting*. The grand beach-houses just to the north of the pier were known as Hollywood's "Gold Coast"; the largest, now the **Sand and Sea** beach club, was built as the servants' quarters of a massive 120-room house, now demolished, that belonged to William Randolph Hearst. In the adjacent villa of MGM boss Louis B. Mayer, the Kennedy brothers were later rumoured to have had liaisons with Marilyn Monroe.

Venice

Immediately south of Santa Monica, **Venice** was laid out in the marshlands of Ballona Creek in 1905 by developer Abbot Kinney as a romantic twenty-mile network of canals, lined by sham palazzos and waterfront homes. It never really caught on, and the coming of the automobile finished it off altogether. Many of the canals were filled in, and the area fell into disrepair, being taken over by oil wells. Orson Welles' film *A Touch of Evil* starred the then-derelict Venice as a seedy border town.

Kinney was, however, ahead of his time. A fair bit of the original plan survives, and the pseudo-European atmosphere has made Venice one of the coast's trendier spots. Chic cafes and restaurants abound near the beach, and a strong alternative arts scene centres on the *Beyond Baroque* bookshop in the old City Hall at 681 Venice Boulevard.

The town's main artery, **Windward Avenue**, runs from the beach into what was the Grand Circle of the canal system. Its original Romanesque **arcade**, around the intersection with Pacific Avenue, is alive with health food shops, used-record stores, and roller-skate rental stands. The few remaining **canals** are just a few blocks south; some with their original quaint little bridges survive.

Venice Beach itself is the reason most people come here. Nowhere else does LA parade itself quite so openly and as sensuously as along the wide pathway of **Venice Boardwalk**, ever packed with people, people-watchers, jugglers, fire-eaters and roller-skating guitar players. South of Windward is **Muscle Beach**, a legendary outdoor weightlifting centre where serious-looking hunks of muscle pump some serious iron, and high-flying gymnasts swing on the adjacent rings and bars. Spend ten minutes watching and you'll find Narcissus is alive and well, and working on his biceps.

Outlets along Washington Street near the pier – such as *Spokes'n'Stuff* (☎310/650-1067) – rent out **bikes**. Incidentally, be warned that **at night** Venice Beach is taken over by street gangs, drug dealers and assorted psychos. Even walking on the beach after dark is illegal, and anywhere in the immediate vicinity you should take great care.

The J. Paul Getty Museum

Five miles along the curving Pacific Coast Highway ("PCH") from Santa Monica, a huge French chateau inadvertently marks the easily missed entrance to the **J. Paul Getty Museum** at 17985 PCH (Tues–Sun 10am–5pm; free; ☎310/458-2003), a fake Roman villa poised high above the ocean. Drivers must reserve parking space in advance; otherwise take RTD bus #434 from Santa Monica, and ask the driver for a free pass.

Two years after the museum opened in 1974, oil magnate John Paul Getty died, leaving it $1.3 billion. Obliged to spend five percent of its endowment – $100 million – every year, it can outbid anyone to get what it wants. Hence the inflation in international art prices – and allegations of shady behaviour among the museum's suppliers.

The quality of the **exhibits** is extraordinary. A formidable array of Getty's major interest, Greek and Roman statuary, includes the only remaining work (an athlete) of Lysippos, sculptor to Alexander the Great; a feast of ornate French furniture and decorative arts from the reign of Louis XIV, with clocks, chandeliers, tapestries and gilt-edged commodes, fills several overwhelmingly opulent rooms. Although Getty himself was much less interested in painting, a large collection has been amassed since his death, featuring all the major names from the thirteenth century to the present. Photography is represented by the works of Man Ray, Moholy-Nagy, and others.

Malibu

Malibu, at the top of the bay twenty miles north of Santa Monica, is a whole other world, its beach colony houses owned by those famous enough to need privacy and rich enough to afford it. It's not all that impressive on arrival, however, with ramshackle surf shops, fast-food stands and real estate agents scattered along PCH around the graceful **Malibu Pier**. **Surfrider Beach** here was the surfing capital of the world in the Fifties and early Sixties, seen in the many *Beach Blanket Bingo* movies of Annette Funicello and Frankie Avalon (the surf is at its best in late summer). Just beyond is **Malibu Lagoon State Park**, a nature reserve and bird refuge.

Most Malibu residences are tucked away in an insular community in the narrow canyons on the fringes of town. There's very little to see; if you must, you can come on foot or cycle a mile or so along PCH, on the other side of the hill. You'd do better, though, to visit **Trancas Market**, near the gated entrance to the colony – good both for star-spotting and stocking up on food and drink before a day on the sands.

Much of **Malibu Creek State Park**, at the crest of Malibu Canyon Road along Mulholland Drive, used to belong to *20th Century Fox*, who filmed many Tarzan pictures here, as well as the TV show *M.A.S.H.* The four-thousand-acre park includes a large lake, some waterfalls, and nearly fifteen miles of hiking trails.

Five miles along the coast from Malibu Pier, **Zuma Beach** is the largest and most crowded of the Los Angeles County beaches. Adjacent **Point Dume State Beach**, below the bluffs, is a lot more relaxed, and the rocks at its southern tip, **Pirate's Cove**, are a good place to look out for seals and migrating grey whales in winter.

The South Bay

South of Venice and Marina del Ray, the coast is dominated by the runways of LAX and the oil refineries of El Segundo. Beyond here begins the eight-mile coastal strip of the South Bay beach towns: **Manhattan Beach**, **Hermosa Beach** and **Redondo Beach**. These are poorer (though not poor), quieter, more suburban and smaller than the Westside beach communities. All three can make a refreshing break if you like your beaches without pretentious packaging. Each has a beckoning strip of white sand, and Manhattan and Hermosa especially are well equipped for surfing and beach sports. They're also well connected to the rest of the city, within easy reach of LAX and connected by regular buses (#439 and #443) to downtown LA.

Long Beach

Thanks to a billion-dollar clean-up, downtown **Long Beach** is not the seedy stamping-ground of off-duty sailors that it was just ten years ago. Pine Avenue is an enjoyable stretch of restored architecture and bargain-hunting antique stores, but the only reason you're likely to consider crossing to the far side of LA's massive Harbor (express bus #456 runs from downtown LA) is to see two specially imported attractions – the Spruce Goose and the Queen Mary (daily 10am–6pm; $17.50 for both).

It was over LA Harbor that the enormous **Spruce Goose** – the largest wooden plane ever constructed – skimmed in 1947, on its first and only flight. Built by Howard Hughes, it was intended to transport men and machinery to the beachheads of Europe; but the war ended well before it was finished, and Hughes was commonly suggested to be satisfying his own eccentricities at the taxpayers' expense (the nickname "Spruce Goose" was first applied in scorn by a congressman, and Hughes hated it). At least as interesting as the brief peeks into the cockpit and cargo hold are the short film-shows about the enigmatic Hughes himself. The **Queen Mary** – the *Cunard* flagship from the Thirties until the Sixties – is berthed next to the plane. It's now a luxury hotel, presenting a grossly sentimentalised version of its days of elegance and refinement.

Catalina Island

The enticing island of **Catalina**, twenty miles offshore, has been in private ownership since 1811, when the Gabrileño Indians were forced to resettle on the mainland. It remains a wilderness, devoted to the conservation of unique species such as the Catalina shrew (so rare that it's only been sighted twice), and tourism has been held largely at bay. Hotels are unobtrusive among the whimsical architecture, and cars are a rarity; the two thousand islanders walk, ride bikes or drive electric mokes. Return **ferry** trips to Catalina run several times daily from San Pedro and Long Beach ($20–28; *Catalina Cruises*, ☎1-800/888-5939, and *Catalina Express*, ☎519-1212). From Newport Beach, the *Catalina Passenger Service* (☎714/673-5245) runs a $20 daily round-trip.

The island's one offbeat town, **Avalon**, can be fully explored on foot in an hour. Begin at the sumptuous Art Deco **Avalon Casino**, built in the Twenties by William Wrigley Jr (of the Chicago-based chewing-gum dynasty). The collections at the adjoining **museum** (summer Mon–Sat 1pm–4pm & 8pm–10pm, Sun & hols 1–4pm; $2) include Native American artefacts from Catalina's past. On the slopes behind, the **Zane Grey Pueblo Hotel** is the former home of the Western author, who visited Catalina to film *The Vanishing American* and liked the place so much he never left.

The **Information Center** (☎1-800/428-2566) opposite the pier organises **tours** of the interior, and issues free permits to hikers and campers. Mokes and bikes can be rented from the stand opposite the *Busy Bee* restaurant on Bay Shore Drive.

Hotel **accommodation** in Avalon is much in demand, and pricey – often upwards of $80: the cheapest is usually the *Atwater* (☎1-800/4-AVALON), around $50; the only budget option is the **campground** (☎310/510-0303) on the town's western fringe.

Anaheim: Disneyland and Around

In the early 1950s, Walt Disney conceived a theme park where his already hugely popular cartoon characters – Mickey Mouse, Donald Duck, and the rest – could come to life, to enchant children and make their Uncle Walt even richer. **ANAHEIM** was chosen as the location for **Disneyland** on the basis that these acres of orange groves, thirty miles southeast of downtown, would become LA's next focus of population growth. Which indeed happened; the whole area is now overrun with hotels and restaurants (when Disney opened his next theme park, in Florida – see p.450 – he made sure he owned all of them too), and the boom doesn't look like slowing. If you're not coming to see Disneyland, you may as well give the place a miss: it hasn't an ounce of interest in itself.

Disneyland

1313 Harbor Boulevard, Anaheim. Summer daily 9am–midnight, rest of the year Mon–Fri 10am–6pm, Sat & Sun 10am–midnight. $27.50. 45 minutes by **car** from downtown using the Santa Ana Freeway. Six **trains** a day from downtown to Fullerton (30min) connect with *OCTD* buses #40 or #41. By **bus**, *Greyhound* takes 45min and RTD #460 takes 90min.

Few things come closer to reflecting the problem-free world dreamed of by average America than the simulated reality of **Disneyland** – the ultimate escapist fantasy, and the blueprint for imitations worldwide.

To make the most of Disneyland – and it's certainly a place to experience, at least once in your life – throw yourself right into it. Don't think twice about anything and go on every ride you can. The high admission price includes them all, although during peak periods each can entail queueing for hours. Remember, too, that the emphasis is on family fun; the authorities take a dim view of anything remotely anti-social, and eject those they consider guilty – stay sober, look normal, and smile a lot.

Among the best are two in **Adventureland**: the *Pirates of the Caribbean*, a boat trip through underground caverns, singing along with drunken pirates; and the *Haunted Mansion*, a riotous "doom buggy" tour in the company of the house spooks. **Tomorrowland** is Disney's vision of the future, where the *Space Mountain* rollercoaster zips through the pitch-blackness of outer space, and Michael Jackson dances in 3-D. The *Skyway* cable cars that connect it with the clever but cloyingly sentimental **Fantasyland** are the only spot in the park from which you can see the outside world.

As for **accommodation**, try to visit Disneyland just for the day and spend the night somewhere else. Most of the hotels and motels nearby cost well in excess of $70 per night (see p.756). You're not permitted to bring your own **food** to the park; you can only consume the fast-food produced on the premises.

Yorba Linda: the Richard Nixon Library and Birthplace

18001 Yorba Linda Boulevard. Mon–Sat 10am–5pm, Sun 11am–5pm. $4.95.

Mickey Mouse may be its most famous resident, but conservative Orange County's favourite son is former president **Richard Milhous Nixon**, born in 1913 in what's now the freeway-caged **Yorba Linda**, about eight miles northeast of Disneyland. His birthplace is a shrine to a man who forged a career from lies and secrecy, and finally resigned from the world's most powerful job in total disgrace. Oversized gifts from world leaders, amusing campaign memorabilia, and a laugh-a-line collection of obsequious letters written by and to Nixon form the core of the exhibition, but his distinctive persona is best enjoyed in the constantly running archive radio and TV recordings.

Nixon's face leers down in Big Brother fashion from almost every wall, but only inside the **Presidential Auditorium** do you get the chance to ask him a question. Many possibilities spring to mind, but the choice is limited to a small pre-programmed selection. Nixon's gaunt features fill the overlarge screen and provide the stock reply – as endearingly and believably as ever.

The San Gabriel and San Fernando Valleys

The northern limit of LA is defined by two long, wide valleys lying over the hills from the central basin, starting close to one another a few miles north of downtown and spanning outwards in opposite directions – east to the deserts around Palm Springs, west to Ventura on the central coast. You wouldn't miss an awful lot by not visiting the valleys at all, but they do give a picture of life in some of LA's more downbeat suburbs.

The San Gabriel Valley

Spreading east from **Pasadena**, ten miles north of Los Angeles, the **San Gabriel Valley** was settled by farmers and cattle ranchers on the lands of the eighteenth-century Mission San Gabriel. Pasadena itself is as much the home of the grand dames of Los Angeles society as it is to the "little old lady from Pasadena" of the Beach Boys song. A luxury resort in the 1880s, it then became a fashionable residential area. Downtown is undergoing a major renovation, modern shopping centres slipping in behind Edward Hopperish 1920s facades, but the historic parts have not been forgotten. Maps and booklets are to be had from the **Convention and Visitors Bureau** at 171 S Los Robles Avenue (Mon–Fri 9am–5pm, Sat 10am–4pm; ☎818/795-9311).

The **Norton Simon Museum** at 411 W Colorado Boulevard (Thurs–Sun noon–6pm; $5, students $2.50) is not one of LA's better-known museums, but its collection – ranging from Dutch paintings by Rembrandt and Frans Hals to Monet's *Mouth of the Seine at Honfleur* and Picasso's extraordinary *Woman with Book* – is consistently excellent. Your ticket stub entitles you to a free print from the superb museum **bookshop**.

South of Pasadena, in the dull, uppercrust little suburb of San Marino, the **Huntington Library**, off Huntington Drive at 1151 Oxford Road (Tues–Sun 1pm–4.30pm; advance reservations are required on Sun; free, parking $2), contains numerous manuscripts and rare books, such as a Gutenberg Bible and the **Ellesmere Chaucer**, a c.1410 illuminated manuscript of *The Canterbury Tales*. Paintings include Gainsborough's *Blue Boy* and Reynolds' *Mrs Siddons as the Tragic Muse*, and the whole ensemble is set off by acres of beautiful themed **gardens**.

The San Fernando Valley

The **San Fernando Valley**, spreading west, is *the* valley to most Angelenos: a sprawl of tract homes, mini-malls, fast-food drive-ins and auto parts stores. It has more of a middle-American feel than anywhere else in LA, inhabited – at least, in the popular LA imagination – by macho men and bimbo-esque "Valley Girls", speaking their own dialect of "Valley Talk". In the gateway town of **Glendale**, eight miles north of downtown, **Forest Lawn Cemetery** at 1712 S Glendale Avenue (daily 9am–5pm; free) was immortalised with biting satire by Evelyn Waugh in *The Loved One*. Among those buried here are Errol Flynn, Walt Disney, Clara Bow, Nat King Cole, Chico Marx, Clark Gable, and Jean Harlow, in a marble-lined room paid for by fiance William Powell.

Burbank and the Studios

The name of Hollywood may be synonymous with the movies, but the studios themselves, if they were there at all, moved out of Tinseltown long ago; the nitty-gritty business of actually making films goes on over the hills in otherwise boring **Burbank**.

Studios offering tours include **NBC**, at 3000 W Alameda Street (daily 9am–4pm, $7) and the technically oriented **Burbank Studios** (Mon–Fri at 10am, 10.30am, 2pm and 2.30pm; $20; ☎818/954-1744). The largest of the old backlots belongs to **Universal Studios**, whose four-hour tours (summer daily 8am–10.30pm, rest of the year Mon–Fri 10am–8pm, Sat & Sun 9.30am–8pm; $24.95) are more like a trip around an amusement park. You get to witness the fading miracle of the parting of the Red Sea, convincing Wild West shootouts, and the so-called Miami Vice Action Spectacular stunt show.

Los Angeles Accommodation

Finding a **place to stay** in LA is easy; finding somewhere cheap and well located is difficult, though not impossible. If you're not driving, either choose your base carefully, to avoid lengthy cross-town journeys, or divide your stay between several **districts**. Downtown has the best assortment of cheap hotels; Hollywood is more mid-range; and West LA, Santa Monica, Venice and Malibu are predominantly mid-to-upper range.

The nearest **campgrounds** to LA are along the Orange County coast.

Hostels

Hostels are dotted all over the city, though some limit stays to a few nights. Colleges and fraternity houses also let out space during summer; details from the *Pan-Hellenic Sorority Council* (☎310/206-1285) or the *Inter Fraternity Council* (☎310/825-8409).

Bill Baker International Youth Hostel (AYH), 8015 S Sepulveda Blvd (☎776-0922). Summer only. Near LAX on RTD bus #42. 7.30am–9pm, with an 11.30pm curfew. Members $7, others $10.

Centerpoint Backpackers, 11 South Venice Blvd (☎827-8811). Venice Beach lodging for $12.89.

Fullerton Hacienda Hostel (AYH), 1700 N Harbor Blvd (☎714/738-3721). New and comfortable, not far from Disneyland. 4pm–9.30am. *OCTD* bus #43A stops outside. Members $8.50, others $11.50.

Hollywood AYH Hostel, 1553 N Hudson Ave (☎467-4161). Close to Hollywood Blvd. Singles $29, doubles $39, dorms $9 for members, $11 for others (2-day maximum stay). No advance booking.

Huntington Beach Colonial Hostel (AYH), 421 Eighth St, Huntington Beach (☎714/536-3315). Four blocks from the beach, mostly double rooms. 4.30pm–9.30am, with an 11pm curfew. You can hire a key for $1 (plus $10 deposit). Members $7.50, others $9; ten-day stays for $65 if there's space.

Interclub Network Hostel, 2221 Lincoln Blvd, Venice (☎310/305-0250). Six-bed dorms, free shuttle bus to LAX. Closed 11am–4pm, with a 1am curfew. Five-day maximum stay. $12 per person.

Jim's at the Beach, 17 Brooks Ave, Venice (☎310/399-4018). Beachside dormitory rooms on production of a passport. $15 per night; $90 per week.

Los Angeles International Hostel (AYH), 3601 S Gaffey St, building #613 (☎310/831-8109). In the South bay area, overlooking the ocean. *RTD* bus #232 passes close by, *SuperShuttle* from LAX costs $13. Open 7–9.30am and 4pm–midnight. Members $9.25, others $12.25; private rooms $22.

Marina Hostel, 2915 Yale Ave, Marina del Rey (☎310/301-3983). On the edge of yachty Marina del Rey but only a mile from Venice Beach. No curfew, open 24 hours. $12 per person.

Mira Hershey Hall, 801 Hilgard Ave (☎310/825-3691). Two-bedded rooms on the UCLA campus, mid-June to mid-Sept, for $32. Book at least a month in advance.

Santa Monica International Hostel, 1436 Second St, Santa Monica (☎310/392-0325). Newly built *AYH* hostel just a few strides from the Santa Monica sands. Members $9, others $13.

Hotels, Motels & B&Bs

There are no booking agencies, and visitor centres do not reserve accommodation, so to be sure of a **hotel** or **motel** room you should make a reservation yourself as early as possible (six months ahead is not uncommon, but apart from in summer a month is often enough). Hotels are usually cheaper if booked by the week rather than the night.

Downtown and Around

Biltmore Hotel, 506 S Grand Ave (☎1-800/421-8000). Classical architecture combined with modern luxury to make your head swim. $190.

Brandon Hotel, 735 S Hartford Ave (☎483-0361). Between Seventh and Eighth streets – a dodgy neighbourhood but the hotel is safe and clean. $25–36.

The Eastlake Inn, 1442 Kellam Ave (☎250-1620). Meticulously restored Victorian house. $65–99.

Figueroa Hotel, 939 S Figueroa St (☎1-800/421-9092). Well-placed mid-range hotel. $72–84.

Jerry's Motel, 285 S Lucas Ave (☎481-0921). Small and good value. $37–40.

Mitchell Hotel, 1072 W Sixth St (☎481-2477). Slightly seedy but basically safe. $28.

Orchid Hotel, 819 S Flower St (☎624-5855). A simple walk to anywhere in downtown. $35.
Park Plaza, 607 S Park View St (☎384-5281). Sumptuous lobby, ordinary rooms. $40–45.
Terrace Manor, 1353 Alvarado Terrace (☎381-1478). Victorian house. $60–90.

Hollywood

Academy Hotel, 1621 N McCadden Place (☎465-1918). Small and pleasant. $40.

Holiday Inn Hollywood, 1755 N Highland Ave (☎1-800/465-4329). Expensive and massive, but perfectly placed. $89–132.

Hollywood Roosevelt, 7000 Hollywood Blvd (☎1-800/423-8262). The first hotel built for the movie greats, lately revamped and reeking with atmosphere – though the rooms are plain. $125.

Hotel Hollywood, 5825 Sunset Blvd (☎1-800/445-0021). The best at this price. $75.

St. Moritz Hotel, 5849 Sunset Blvd (☎467-2174). Poky, but the cheapest in central Hollywood. $25.

West LA

Bevonshire Lodge Motel, 7575 Beverly Blvd (☎936-6154). Well-situated motel. $44.

Chateau Marmont, 8221 Sunset Blvd (☎626-1010). Former haunt of Greta Garbo *et al*. $125 and up.

Deseret Motel, 10572 Santa Monica Blvd (☎310/474-2035). Faded and ordinary. $36–50.

Le Reve Hotel, 8822 Cynthia St (☎1-800/424-4443). A few blocks north of Santa Monica Blvd. Elegant suites in the style of a French provincial inn; $75 and up.

Santa Monica, Venice and Malibu

El Tovar by the Sea, 603 Ocean Ave, Venice (☎310/451-1820). Every room has a sea view. $75.

Hotel Carmel, 201 Broadway (☎310/451-2469). Near Santa Monica beach. $35 a night, $210 a week.

Hotel Santa Monica, 3102 Pico Blvd (☎1-800/231-7679). A mile from the beach. $50–65.

Malibu Riviera Motel, 28920 Pacific Coast Hwy (☎213/457-9503). $55 rooms just outside Malibu.

Venice Beach Hotel, 25 Windward Ave, Venice (☎310/399-7649). Relaxed atmosphere. $45.

Near LAX

Capri Motel, 8620 Airport Blvd (☎645-7700). A mile northeast of LAX. Swimming pool. $40–60.

The Cockatoo Inn, 4334 Imperial Highway (☎1-800/262-5286). Country-style inn in a faceless suburb just a stone's throw from LAX. Complimentary breakfast. $45–50.

Geneva Budget Motel, 321 W Manchester Blvd (☎677-9171). The cheapest in the area. $40.

The South Bay and Harbor Area

At Ocean Motel, 50 Atlantic Ave (☎310/435-8369). A serviceable base for Long Beach. $45.

Hotel Queen Mary, Pier J, Long Beach (☎1-800/421-3732). Cramped cabins. $80 and up.

Around Disneyland

Apollo Inn, 1741 S West St (☎714/772-9750). Good-value hotel owned by the Stovall family. $60.

The Disneyland Hotel, 1150 W Cerritos Ave (☎714/778-6600). The price does not include admission to the park, although the Disneyland monorail does stop right outside. $150 and up.

Motel 6, 921 S Beach Blvd (☎714/827-9450). The cheapest around. $35–45.

Park Place Inn, 1544 S Harbor Blvd (☎714/776-4800). Same management as *Apollo*. $60.

The San Gabriel and San Fernando Valleys

Belair-Bed & Breakfast, 941 N Frederic Ave (☎818/848-9227). The best value in Burbank. $35.

Econo Lodge, 1203 E Colorado Blvd, Pasadena (☎818/449-3170). Friendly budget chain. $40–45.

Gay Hotels

Coral Sands Hotel, 1730 N Western Ave (☎1-800/367-7263). Exclusively gay men. $80 and up.

The Selby Hotel, 1740 N Hudson Ave (☎469-5320). Solely for gay men. Shared bathrooms. $36.

Studio Hotel, 1611 Vista del Mar (☎460-6000). Art Deco hotel for men and women. $160 per week.

Los Angeles Eating

LA **eating** covers every extreme: whatever you want to eat and however much you want to spend, you're spoiled for choice. Try to take at least a few meals in the more exotic restaurants, if only to watch the city's many self-appointed food snobs going through their paces. If you simply want to load up quickly and cheaply, the options are almost endless, and include free food available for the price of a drink at happy hours.

Downtown

Bella Cucina, 949 S Figueroa St (☎623-0014). Fabulous pizzas and homemade pastas, with the accent on northern and rural Italian cuisine.

Clifton's Cafeteria, 648 S Broadway (☎485-1726). A cafeteria complete with redwood trees and a waterfall; the food is cheap and good too.

El Cholo, 1121 S Western Ave (☎734-2773). One of LA's first Mexican restaurants and still one of the best, despite the drunken frat-rats from USC.

Gorky's Café, 536 E Eighth St (☎627-4060). Round-the-clock diner that's a hangout for many painters, sculptors and general arty types. Excellent omelettes, soups and sandwiches at cheap prices.

Kingsley Gardens, 4070 W Third St (☎389-5527). A range of international meat-free dishes, plus a macrobiotic menu and a mouthwatering range of sugar-free desserts.

Miriwa, 750 N Broadway (☎687-3088). Cavernous and often crowded dim sum restaurant serving cheap and excellent food that's well worth the wait.

Mon Kee, 679 N Spring St (☎629-6717). For years this has been the best Chinese restaurant in LA, specialising in fresh seafood dishes: shrimp, deep-fried cod and a mouthwatering ginger crab.

Shibucho, 333 S Alameda St (☎626-1184). Excellent sushi bar in the heart of Little Tokyo; if possible, go with someone who knows what to order, as no one seems to speak English.

VIP Palace, 3014 Olympic Blvd (☎388-9292). Korean restaurant, strong on spicy barbecued beef.

Hollywood

Addis Ababa, 6263 Leland Way, a block south of Sunset Blvd (☎463-9788). Unpretentious Ethiopian food, served with fresh *injera* bread.

El Conchinito, 3508 W Sunset Blvd (☎668-7037). Halfway between a Mexican and Jamaican restaurant. Exotic-looking combinations of grilled meats and delicate sauces, and fresh fruit *licuados*.

Hampton's, 1342 N Highland Ave (☎469-1090). Over fifty styles of gourmet hamburgers.

Musso and Frank's Grill, 6667 Hollywood Blvd (☎467-7788). Since it opened in 1919, all the Hollywood bigwigs have come here – but at $15 for bacon and eggs, you pay for the atmosphere.

Paru's, 5140 Sunset Blvd (☎661-7680). Southern Indian food, all vegetarian and lightly spiced.

Shamshiry, 5229 Hollywood Blvd (☎469-8434). The best of the Iranian restaurants that have been established in West LA since the fall of the Shah, offering kebabs, pilafs and exotic sauces.

Village Coffee Shop, 2695 Beachwood Drive (☎467-5398). A classic laid-back coffeeshop in the hills below the Hollywood sign.

Yukon Mining Co, 7328 Santa Monica Blvd (☎851-8833). Excellent coffeeshop catering to the local gay community and the neighbouring senior citizens' home. Open 24 hours.

West LA

The Authentic Café, 7605 Beverly Blvd (☎939-4626). Santa Fe-style desert food; Mexican influenced, mixed in with spicy Chinese and the obligatory designer pizzas. Bring your own beer.

Border Grill, 7407½ Melrose Ave (☎658-7495). Quality Cajun cooking, with a host of daily specials.

Casa Carnitas, 4067 Beverly Blvd (☎667-9953). Tasty Mexican food from the Yucatan Peninsula: the dishes are unmistakably inspired by Cuban and Caribbean cooking; lots of seafood, too.

Chung King, 11538 W Pico Blvd (☎310/477-4917). The best neighbourhood Chinese restaurant in LA, serving spicy – and lately fashionable – Szechuan food: don't miss out on the *bum-bum* chicken.

Citrus, 6703 Melrose Ave (☎857-0034). Trendy and good upmarket restaurant, serving California cuisine in an outdoor setting indoors. Reservations are essential; lunch for two will be around $50.

Green's Soul Food, 5766 Rodeo Rd (☎295-9111). Ribs, cornbread, chitlins and black-eyed peas – Southern cooking at its best, and with a great jukebox.

The Gumbo Pot, 6333 W Third St in the farmers' market (☎933-0358). Delicious and dead-cheap Cajun cooking; try the *gumbo yaya* of chicken, shrimp and sausage, and the fruit-and-potato salad.

Mario's, 1001 Broxton Ave, Westwood (☎310/208-7077). Far and away the best pizza in West LA.

Patout's, 2260 Westwood Blvd (☎310/475-7100). Exquisite and authentic Cajun cooking in West LA, from gumbos to trout and crab in lemon. Expensive; even a light lunch is at least $25.

Ships, corner of La Cienaga and Olympic Blvd (☎310/652-0401). The best food of any coffeeshop in LA; try the *Ship Shape* hamburger, on sourdough bread, with a chocolate shake. Open 24 hours.

The Good Earth, 1002 Westwood Blvd (☎310/208-8215). The best of a chain of health-food restaurants: good food and friendly service at reasonable prices; also excellent breads and cakes.

Santa Monica, Venice and Malibu

Café Montana, 1610 Montana Ave (☎310/829-3990). Good breakfasts and excellent salads and grilled fish in this art gallery-cum-cafe on the newest strip of upmarket Santa Monica.

Café 50s, 838 Lincoln Blvd, Venice (☎310/399-1955). No doubts about this place: Ritchie Valens on the jukebox, burgers on the tables . . .

Chinois on Main, 2709 Main St (☎310/392-9025). LA's most popular restaurant, serving Chinese-style dishes like fresh fish in garlic and ginger. Very expensive, with lunches from $25.

Comeback Inn, 1633 W Washington Blvd (☎310/396-7255 or ☎310/396-6469). Carefully prepared vegan food, set off by live music in the evenings and on weekend afternoons.

Freddy's Cantina, 11520 W Pico Blvd (☎310/479-6149). Excellent and authentic enchiladas at William Burroughs' favourite (and relatively unknown) LA eatery.

Govinda's, 9624 Venice Blvd (☎310/836-1269). A range of meat-free dishes, from vegetarian Indian dishes to cauliflower quiche, complemented by a well-stocked juice bar.

Red Sea, 1551 Ocean Blvd (☎310/394-5198). Delectable Ethiopian food, cosy and well priced.

Todai, 201 Arizona Ave (☎310/451-2076). All-you-can-eat sushi is a long-accepted concept in LA; indulge to your heart's content for under $8 at lunchtime or $15 in the evening.

Inn of the Seventh Ray, 128 Old Topanga Rd, just off Topanga Canyon (☎310/455-1311). The ultimate New Age restaurant, serving vegetarian and other wholefoods. Excellent desserts, too.

Disneyland and Around

Angelo's, 511 S State College Blvd, Anaheim (☎714/533-1401). Straight out of *Happy Days*, drive-in complete with roller-skating car-hops and, incidentally, good burgers. Open until 2am on weekends.

Knott's Berry Farm, 8039 Beach Blvd, Buena Park (☎714/827-1776). Famous for delicious fried chicken long before Disneyland was around – and a fully fledged theme park in its own right.

The San Gabriel and San Fernando Valleys

Dr Hogly-Wogly's Tyler Texas Bar-B-Q, 8136 Sepulveda Blvd, Van Nuys (☎818/780-6701). Queue up for the chicken, sausages, ribs and beans, some of the best in LA.

Merida, 20 E Colorado Blvd, Pasadena (☎818/792-7371). Unusual Mexican restaurant, featuring dishes from the Yucatan Peninsula; try the spicy pork wrapped up and steamed in banana leaves.

Casa de Oriente, 2000 W Main St, Alhambra (☎818/282-8833). Dim sum at its best: pork baos, potstickers and dumplings, and delicious sweets.

Gen Mai-Sushi, 4454 Van Nuys Blvd (☎818/986-7060). Japanese-style vegetarian restaurant with brown rice, sushi and seasonal macrobiotic dishes.

Gay and Lesbian Restaurants

Casita de Campo, 1920 Hyperion Ave (☎662-4255). Great Mexican food, comfortable atmosphere.

Gloria's Cafe, 3603 W Sunset Blvd (☎664-5732). Popular local hangout that's a great spot for dinner, especially Cajun.

French Market Place, 7985 Santa Monica Blvd (☎654-0898). A themed eaterie that's at least as much fun as Disneyland.

Nightlife and Entertainment

Exploring the jungle of LA's **nightlife** can be great fun. Everyone you meet claims to be either a rock star or in the movies; half of them aren't lying. Even the quietest venue offers a chance to eavesdrop on a bit of vapid *Less Than Zero* dialogue; the wildest ones will take your breath away. In all the pubs, clubs and discos, you'll need to be 21 and will almost certainly be asked for ID.

The best sources of **listings** are *LA Weekly* and the more highbrow "Calendar" section in the *LA Times* at the weekend.

Bars and Pubs

That LA's **bars and pubs** are rarely the scruffy boozing places found elsewhere in the US is due at least in part to the easy availability of alcohol for home consumption, through any number of liquor stores and supermarket outlets.

Al's Bar, 305 S Hewitt St. At the heart of the Loft District art scene downtown; drink cans of cheap beer in small, smoke-filled rooms, with a pool table and occasional live acts.

Yee Me Loo, 690 N Spring St. A Chinatown bar that looks like a set from *Farewell My Lovely*.

Boardners, 1652 N Cherokee Ave, Hollywood. A likeably unkempt neighbourhood bar – a rarity in the heart of Hollywood but very welcome.

Gorky's, 1716 Cahuenga Blvd, Hollywood. A new branch of the famous downtown eaterie, worth a call for its big bar and great beers.

Musso and Frank's, 6667 Hollywood Blvd. If you haven't had a drink in this 1940s landmark bar, you haven't been to Hollywood. It also serves food.

The Power House, 1714 N Highland Ave. Enjoyable heavy-rockers' watering hole just off Hollywood Boulevard; few people get here much before midnight.

Barney's Beanery, 8447 Santa Monica Blvd. Well-worn pool-hall bar, stocking over two hundred beers. It also serves food.

The Ginger Man, 369 N Bedford Drive. Looks like a New York media-persons' bar but has the atmosphere of a neighbourhood pub; it also has a small cafe.

The Polo Lounge, 9641 Sunset Blvd, in the *Beverly Hills Hotel*. It's worth the price of a drink (at least $5) to watch Hollywood in action – mainly fat-cat producers making deals on the phone or showing off an endless stream of expensive young escorts.

McGinty's Irish Bar, 2615 Wilshire Blvd. Friendly, often raucous small pub with dartboards and, frequently, live music.

Rebecca's, 2005 Pacific Ave, Venice. The hottest bar in ever-so-trendy Venice, with an interior composed of crocodiles and octopi dangling from the rough wooden ceiling.

Clubs and Discos

LA's **clubs** are the wildest in the country, ranging from absurdly faddish hangouts to industrial noise cellars. The trendier side of the club scene is hard to pin down; check the *LA Weekly* or the *LA Reader* before setting out. There are further suggestions under "Gay and Lesbian LA".

Cocoanut Teaszer, 8117 Sunset Blvd (☎654-4773). Poseurs, rockers and voyeurs mix uneventfully on the two dance floors. No cover before 9pm, otherwise $5.

Mayan, 1038 S Hill St (☎746-4287). Get past the doorman and you're in with LA's coolest, eager to shake a leg in gorgeous surrounds. Friday and Saturday, downtown; $15.

Probe, 836 N Highland Ave, Hollywood (☎461-8301). Ultra-trendy but friendly club that hosts top DJs playing whatever's hot; $8.

Stock Exchange, 605 S Spring St (☎627-4467). A million-dollar sound and light system in the Art Deco interior of the old Pacific Stock Exchange downtown; LA's flashiest club. Wed–Sat; $15.

Twenty/20, 2020 Avenue of the Stars (☎937-2020). Hi-tech setting for hi-tech dance sounds, enjoyed by street-credible would-be socialites; $10–15.

1970, 5060 Sunset Blvd, Hollywood (☎669-1000). Seventies music (and dress) from the Sex Pistols to Sister Sledge. Sunday only; $5.

Bars and Clubs: Mainly for Men

Arena, 6655 Santa Monica Blvd (☎962-4485). Large dance floor throbbing to funk and hi-energy grooves – and sometimes live bands – on Wed, Sat and Sun; $8–10.

Le Bar, 2375 Glendale Blvd, Silverlake (☎660-7595). Quiet and welcoming, with a pool table.

Circus, 6655 Santa Monica Blvd (☎462-1291). A long-running disco with the latest dance music and three bars. Men only on Tues; gay men and women on Fri.

Catch One, 4067 W Pico Blvd (☎734-8849). Sweaty dance barn packed, mostly with gay men, every weekend; $5.

Corral Club, 3747 Cahuenga Blvd (☎818/796-6900). Male dancers and videos; no alcohol, the slogan is "hard men soft drinks".

Rage, 8911 Santa Monica Blvd (☎758-7243). Very flash gay men's club playing the latest hi-energy hits. Drinks are cheap, the cover varies.

Revolver, 8851 Santa Monica Blvd (☎550-8851). Watch yourself dance with yourself on giant video screens hanging above the dance floor. The definitive West Hollywood gay bar.

Bars and Clubs: Mainly for Women

Code Blue, 11150 Olympic Blvd (☎310/281-9903). Home to "the beautiful people" – the glamorous side of the women's movement.

Les Beans, 10836 Venice Blvd (☎310/836-6710). Feminist art gallery, coffeehouse, and vegetarian restaurant.

The Oxwood Inn, 13713 Oxnard St, Van Nuys (☎818/997-9666). After sixteen years in the same San Fernando Valley location, this country and western women's bar has become a mainstay. It's open Friday and Saturday nights, has no cover charge and features a pool table.

Peanut's, 7969 Santa Monica Blvd (☎654-0280). Eclectic, mixed crowd and a variety of bizarre side-shows, plus a massive dance floor. Men welcome most nights, call to check. Cover $6, $9 weekends.

Seven Hail Marys, call for location (☎310/672-0512). "A Club for Women with Alternative Rituals" the spiel goes; actually a Friday night haunt that plays Fifties, Sixties amd Eighties music. It also has a TV lounge equipped with biker magazines.

Live Music

LA has a near-overwhelming choice if you're looking for **live music**. Ever since the nihilistic punk bands – Circle Jerks, X, Black Flag – drew the city away from its cocaine-sozzled laid-back West Coast image, LA's **rock music** scene has been second to none. **Country music** is fairly prevalent, at least away from trendy Hollywood, and the valleys are hotbeds of country-folk and swing. **Jazz**, too, is played in a few genuinely authentic downbeat dives, though more commonly found being used to improve the atmosphere of a restaurant. **Salsa** remains immensely popular among LA's Hispanic population, and is found mostly in the bars of East LA; it's worth saying that (aside from the places we've listed) these are very male-orientated, and female visitors may well feel out of place.

The Baked Potato, 3738 Cahuenga Blvd, N Hollywood (☎818/980-1615). A small but near-legendary contemporary jazz spot, where many reputations have been forged; $8.

Birdland West, 105 W Broadway, Long Beach (☎310/436-9341). Very stylish jazz venue with good names. Cover varies.

Café Largo, 432 N Fairfax Ave (☎852-1073). Intimate cabaret venue which often features LA's more unusual live rock bands. Free–$10.

Casa Rivera, 9001 E Telegraph Rd, Pico Rivera, East LA (☎949-8381). Salsa most nights and *jaro-cho* music from Veracruz, a sort of festive mariachi, once a week. Cover $3 on Wed, Fri & Sat.

Club Lingerie, 6507 Sunset Blvd (☎466-8557). Long-enduring, stylish venue that's always at the forefront of what's new; $3–8. Intimate bar, music from rockabilly to jazz to post-industrial thrash.

Coffee Emporium, 4325 Glencoe Blvd, Marina del Rey (☎823-4446). A 1950s coffeehouse that leaps into the present with "New Age" jazz on Fri and Sat; $5.

Comeback Inn, 1633 Washington Blvd (☎310/396-7255). Cosy bar, jazz nightly at 9.15pm; $7.

Doug Weston's Troubadour, 9081 Santa Monica Blvd (☎310/276-6168). The best-known club for the heaviest riffs and shaggiest manes; $4–6.50.

The Foothill Club, 1922 Cherry Ave, Signal Hill (☎494-5196). A glorious country dance hall from the days when hillbilly was cool. Seven nights a week, doors open at 5pm; no cover.

Gazzari's, 9039 Sunset Blvd (☎310/273-6606). A temple of hard rock, with name-bands on Fri and Sat, hopefuls on Sun; $6–10.

Golden Sails Hotel, 6285 E Pacific Coast Highway (☎310/498-0091). Has some of the best reggae bands from LA and beyond on Fri and Sat; $5.

Kingston 12, 814 Broadway, Santa Monica (☎310/451-4423). Nightly reggae, nice and small. $10.

Longhorn Saloon, 21211 Sherman Way, Canoga Park (☎818/340-4788). Live country and blues-ish bands every night except Mon. Frequent star-studded jam sessions; $3.

Luminarias, 3500 Ramona Blvd, Monterey Park, East LA (☎268-4177). A hilltop restaurant where the live salsa is reckoned to be as good as the Mexican food; no cover.

McCabe's, 3103 W Pico Blvd, Santa Monica (☎310/828-4403). The back room of LA's premier acoustic guitar shop; long the scene of some excellent and unusual folk and country shows; $5–10.

Miami Spice, 13515 Washington Blvd, Venice (☎310/306-7978). Cuban restaurant with scintillating salsa sounds on Thurs and Sun; no cover.

Music Machine, 12220 W Pico Blvd (☎310/820-5150). The wildest club west of Hollywood for aspiring rock acts and more established blues and reggae; $4–8.

Nucleus Nuance, 7267 Melrose Ave (☎939-8666). A very small and very busy room whose bluesy-flavoured jazz is as much for dancing as listening to; $5.

The Palomino, 6907 Lankershim Blvd, North Hollywood (☎818/764-4010). Long the best place to catch visiting country and western singers, also good for R&B and the odd goth gig; $5–10.

Raji's, 6160 Hollywood Blvd (☎469-4552). Back room of an Indian restaurant that makes a good airing place for up-and-coming local rock bands; free–$5.

The Roxy, 9009 Sunset Blvd (☎310/276-2222). The showcase of the rock industry's new signings, intimate and with a great sound system. Also has "pay-to-play" nights for unknown bands; $8–15.

Whiskey-a-Go-Go, 8901 Sunset Blvd (☎310/652-4202). Recently done-up after many years as LA's most famous rock and roll club, nowadays mainly hard rock; $5–10.

Classical Music and Opera

LA has very few outlets for **classical music**. The *Los Angeles Philharmonic* perform regularly during the year, and the *Los Angeles Chamber Orchestra*, based at 315 W Ninth St (☎622-7001), appear sporadically at different venues.

The Ambassador Auditorium, 300 W Green St, Pasadena (☎622-7001). Superb acoustics and many international stars between September and May.

The Dorothy Chandler Pavilion, in the *Music Center*, 1365 N Grand Ave, downtown (☎972-7211 or ☎480-3232). Home to the LA Philharmonic (concerts Oct–May Mon–Sat 8pm, Sun 2.30pm).

The Hollywood Bowl, 2301 N Highland Ave, Hollywood (☎850-2000). The LA Philharmonic give open-air concerts here each Tues–Sat evening from July to September.

Orange County Performing Arts Center, 600 Town Center Drive, Costa Mesa (☎714/556-ARTS or ☎480-3232). Home of the Pacific Symphony Orchestra and Opera Pacific.

The Shrine Auditorium, 3228 Royal St (☎748-5116), box office at 655 S Hill St (☎749-5123). A bizarre building that hosts regular performances by choral and gospel groups.

Dance

The last fifteen years or so have seen an increase in **dance** activity in LA, with the *Los Angeles Ballet* and the *Joffrey Ballet* both relocating here from New York.

Japan America Theatre, 244 S San Pedro St (☎680-3700). Dance and performance works drawn from Japan and the Far East.

John Anson Ford Theater, 2850 Cahuenga Blvd (☎972-7200). Open-air venue, home in summer of the two-week Dance Kaleidoscope, organised by the *Los Angeles Area Dance Alliance (LAADA)* co-operative (☎465-1100), which produces the bi-monthly newsletter *Dance Flash*.

The Dorothy Chandler Pavilion, part of the *Music Center*, 1365 N Grand Ave (☎972-7211 or ☎480-3232). A venue of the *Joffrey Ballet* and other major names.

Santa Monica College Studio Stage, 1900 Pico Blvd, Santa Monica (☎310/4452-9214). Often stages daring new pieces by modern LA choreographers.

A CALENDAR OF LA'S FESTIVALS

January

1 Tournament of Roses in Pasadena. A parade of floral floats and marching bands along Colorado Boulevard.

February

Early Japanese New Year. Celebrated around Little Tokyo with traditional arts.

First full moon after 21 Chinese New Year. Three days of dragon-float street parades, based in Chinatown.

March

17 St Patrick's Day. A parade through downtown and related events all over the city, with some bars serving green beer.

End The Academy Awards are presented at the Shrine Auditorium.

April

Early The Blessing of the Animals. A long-established Mexican-originated ceremony thanking animals for their services to humans. Pets are blessed in Olvera Street, followed by a parade.

May

5 Cinco de Mayo. Day-long commemoration of the Mexican victory at the battle of Puebla (*not* Mexican Independence Day). A spirited parade in Olvera Street, celebrations with Mexican food, drink and music in most LA parks.

July

Middle Watts Jazz Festival. Two days of free music with the Watts towers as a backdrop.

August

First two weeks Culmination of the South Bay's International Surf Festival, where globally famed surfers compete.

September

4 LA's birthday. A civic ceremony and assorted street entertainment around El Pueblo de Los Angeles to mark the founding of the original pueblo in 1781.

Last two weeks LA County Fair in Pomona, in the San Gabriel Valley. The country's biggest; livestock shows, eating contests and fairground rides.

October

Second weekend LA Street Scene. Free rock music, fringe theatre and comedy on the streets of downtown. Usually running at the same time is the West Hollywood Street Festival, a display of handmade arts and crafts and a general slap-on-the-back for LA's newest constituent city.

November

End Hollywood Christmas Parade. The first and best of the many Yuletide events, with a cavalcade of mind-boggling floats.

Comedy Clubs

The Comedy Club, 49 S Pine Ave, Long Beach (☎310/437-5326). Mixed bag of stand-up comics.

Comedy & Magic Club, 1018 Hermosa Beach (☎310/372-1193). Strange couplings of naff magic acts and good-quality comedians.

The Comedy Store, 8433 W Sunset Blvd (☎656-6225). Popular comedy showcase spread over three rooms; you can usually turn up on spec at weekends. Always a good line-up too.

The Ice House, 24 N Mentor Ave, Pasadena (☎818/577-1894). The comedy mainstay of the valley, very established and fairly safe.

Igby's Cabaret, 11637 Tennessee Place (☎310/477-3553). Fairly new, boasting some surprise big-name turns alongside entertaining hopefuls.

LA Connection, 13442 Ventura Blvd, Sherman Oaks (☎818/784-1868). An improvisation showcase for highly rated obnoxiousness specialists. Seldom less than memorable.

Theatre

We've listed the pick of LA's very active **theatre** scene; *Theatrix* (☎466-1767) handles reservations and provides details on what's playing at several of the smaller venues.

Coronet Theater, 368 N La Cienega Boulevard (☎310/276-7461). Home of the LA Public Theater; productions include the odd famous name. Lively bar, patronised by excessively theatrical types.

Gene Dynarski Theater, 5600 Sunset Blvd (☎466-1767). Small-time character actor Dynarski built this likeable little theatre himself to rent out to small companies.

Groundling Theater, 7303 Melrose Ave (☎934-9700). Consistently interesting fringe venue.

Mark Taper Forum, 135 N Grand Avenue, downtown (☎972-7690). Theatre in the three-quarter round, frequently putting on innovative new plays.

Odyssey Theater, 12111 Ohio Ave (☎310/826-1626). Engaging productions of all kinds.

Powerhouse Theater, 3116 Second St, Santa Monica (☎310/392-6529). Experimental shows.

Schubert Theater, ABC Entertainment Center, Century City (☎310/553-9000). The only good thing about Century City is that you can come here to ogle the razzmatazz musicals.

Film

Many major feature films are released in LA months (sometimes years) before they play anywhere else in the world. Short seasons of **foreign-language films** often play at the eight *Laemmle Theaters*. If you're looking for a golden-years-of-film **atmosphere**, head for one of the historic downtown movie palaces (described on p.747), where the delirious furnishings may captivate your attention longer than the all-action triple-bills.

Bing Theater, at the County Art Museum, 5905 Wilshire Blvd (☎857-6010). Afternoon screenings of many neglected Hollywood classics, and it charges just $1.

Chinese Theater, 6925 Hollywood Blvd (☎468-8111). Landmark Art Deco cinema. Giant screen and six-track stereo sound, but limp MOR films.

Egyptian Theater, 6708 Hollywood Blvd (☎467-6167). Another legendary Hollywood venue, now split up and showing uninteresting programmes.

New Beverly Cinema, 7165 Beverly Blvd (☎938-4038). Imaginative cult double bills.

Nuart Theater, 11272 Santa Monica Blvd (☎310/478-6379). Rare classics and documentaries.

Gay and Lesbian LA

Although nowhere near as big as that of San Francisco, the **gay scene** in LA is far from invisible, and gay people are out and prominent right across the city. West Hollywood has a gay-led council and has become synonymous with the (affluent, white) gay life-style, not just in LA but all over California. The section of West Hollywood on Santa Monica Boulevard between Doheny Boulevard and Crescent Heights has many restaurants, shops and bars primarily aimed at gay men. The other overtly gay community is Silverlake, at its most evident along Hyperion Boulevard. We've listed gay accommodation, restaurants, bars and clubs in the relevant sections above.

The city's best known gay and lesbian bookshop is *A Different Light*, 4014 Santa Monica Blvd (☎668-0629). Magazines with good listings sections include *Compass*, *Dispatch*, *Edge*, and *Lesbian News*; and the *Gay Community Yellow Pages* (☎469-4454) is a comprehensive annual directory of gay businesses, publications, services and gathering places listed yearly. **The Gay and Lesbian Community Services Center**, 1213 H Highland Avenue (☎464-7400), is the community's prime resource for counselling, health testing and information.

Women's LA

It's hardly surprising that a city as big as LA should have such an organised **women's** network. **LA Woman** is the city's largest women's magazine, and the free **Women's Yellow Pages**, PO Box 66093, Los Angeles 90066 (☎310/398-5761), lists over 1400 women-owned businesses and services. All the following are good sources of general and detailed information. There's an inevitable crossover with the city's sizeable lesbian community – for bars catering only to women, see p.760.

Resource Centres

Connexxus Women's Center, 9054 Santa Monica Blvd (☎310/859-3960). Primarily lesbian in orientation, a drop-in centre offering group counselling and discussions.

International Gay/Lesbian Archives, Natalie Barney/Edward Carpenter Library, 1654 Hudson Ave (☎463-5450). Archives containing feminist books and periodicals. Mon–Fri noon–5pm.

The Women's Building, 1643 Eighteenth St, Santa Monica (no phone). Features everything from exhibits, performances and films to writing groups and various theme-related workshops.

The Shops

You can buy virtually anything, anywhere, anytime in LA; the big **department stores**, expansive **malls** and the thoroughly exclusive **Rodeo Drive** (see p.749) will have it if the ubiquitous run-of-the-mill retailers don't. A couple of the department stores – **Bullocks Wilshire**, at 3050 Wilshire Boulevard, and the **May Company**, 6067 Wilshire Boulevard – merit a call for their Twenties architecture rather than their uninspiring merchandise. **Neiman Marcus** at 9700 Wilshire Boulevard is more upmarket, selling everything from $5 Swiss truffles to his'n'her leopard skins. LA's massive **malls** often resemble self-contained city suburbs as much as shopping precincts. Swishest of all is the seven-acre **Beverly Center**, bordered by Beverly Boulevard and La Cienega Boulevard, and San Vicente Boulevard and Third Street, where you'll find designer stores, fourteen cinemas – and ample opportunities for star-gazing.

Clothes

American Rag, 150 S La Brea Ave. Classic American styles from the Thirties to the present day.

Atomic Age, 8308 W Third St. Men and women's clothes etc, from the Twenties to the Sixties.

The Back Room, 8525 W Pico Blvd. Cut-price stockist of women's designer clothes.

Ragtime Cowboy, 5332 Lankershim Blvd, N Hollywood. Secondhand American classics.

Third Faze, 1157 N La Brea Ave. A discount store that's constantly updating its stock: look for "$10 sales" when anything, trousers, shirts, skirts, sweaters, and silk ties, costs just that.

Books

Acres of Books, 240 Long Beach Blvd, Long Beach. LA's largest secondhand collection.

Bodhi Tree, 8585 Melrose Ave. New Age and occult books.

Book City, 6627 Hollywood Blvd. Tightly packed from floor to ceiling with eclectic titles.

Bookworks, 3517 Centinela Ave (☎310/398-1932). New and used women's books. Closed Mon.

Bread and Roses, 13812 Ventura Blvd, Sherman Oaks (☎818/986-5376). Store in the heart of the San Fernando Valley, catering to women of all social, racial, ethnic and sociological backgrounds.

A Change of Hobbit, 1853 Lincoln Blvd, Santa Monica. Packed with fantastic fiction.

Dangerous Visions, 13606 Ventura Blvd, in Sherman Oaks. SF and fantasy, especially for children.

Fowler Brothers, at 717 W Seventh St. LA's oldest, open since 1888, and one of the few small general bookshops to survive.

Hennessey and Ingalls, 10814 W Pico Blvd. An impressive range of art and architecture books which may otherwise be hard to find; also rare posters and catalogues.

Larry Edmunds Book Shop, 6658 Hollywood Blvd. Stacks of books on every aspect of film and theatre, and movie stills and posters.

Marlow's Bookshop, 6609 Hollywood Blvd. New and secondhand books, plus rare magazines.

Midnight Special, 1350 Santa Monica Blvd. Excellent for politics and social sciences.

Page One, 966 N Lake Ave, Pasadena (☎818/798-8694). Books by and for women.

Scene of the Crime, 13636 Ventura Blvd, in Sherman Oaks. New and used crime; everything from hard-boiled private dicks to whodunnits. Done up as an Agatha-Christie-style country mansion.

Sisterhood Bookstore, 1351 Westwood Blvd (☎310/477-7300). Westside landmark. Music, cards, jewellery and of course books, pertaining to the national and international women's movement.

Records

Aron's Records, 1150 N Highland Ave. Secondhand discs – all styles, all prices, huge stock.

House of Records, 2314 Pico Blvd. Singles from 1949 to the present.

Moby Disc, 14410 Ventura Blvd, Sherman Oaks. Secondhand and deletion stockist.

Mr Records, 2924 Wilshire Blvd. Rare items, especially obscure Beatles' waxings.

Music and Memories, 10850 Ventura Blvd, Studio City. Almost entirely devoted to Frank Sinatra, though they also stock singers who sound like Frank.

Poo-Bah Records, 1101 E Walnut Ave, Pasadena. American and imported New Wave.

The Record Connection, 8505 Santa Monica Blvd. Deleted Sixties stuff and classical rarities.

Rhino Records, 1720 Westwood Blvd. The biggest selection of international independent releases.

Vinyl Fetish, 7305 Melrose Ave. Besides the punk and post-punk merchandise, a good place to discover what's new on the LA music scene.

Listings

Airlines Most major airlines have offices at several locations around LA; these are just the main addresses: *American*, 6310 W Vincente Blvd; *British Airways*, 380 World Way West; *Continental*, 7700 World Way West; *Delta*, 529 W Sixth St; *Eastern*, 518 W Sixth St; *Northwest Airlines*, 504 W Sixth St; *TWA*, 508 W Eighth St. See "Basics" for toll-free numbers.

Airports *LAX* ☎310/646-5252; *John Wayne, Orange County* ☎714/834-2400; *Long Beach* ☎421-8293; *Hollywood/Burbank* ☎840-8847; *Ontario* ☎714/785-8838.

American Express Downtown at 901 W Seventh St (☎627-4800); in Beverly Hills at 327 N Beverly Drive (☎234-8277).

Babysitting Some hotels can arrange this, or try the *Baby Sitters Guild*, 6362 Hollywood Blvd (☎469-8246).

Beach Info Weather conditions ☎310/457-9701; surfing info ☎379-8471.

Chemists 24-hour pharmacies at *Thrifty's Drugs*, 333 S Vermont, downtown (☎735-7305), and *Kaiser Permanente* in the LA Medical Center, 4867 Sunset Blvd, Hollywood (☎667-8301).

Consulates *UK* 3701 Wilshire Blvd (☎385-0252); *Eire* 4021 Royal Oaks Place, Encino (☎818/981-6464); *Australia* 611 N Larchmont Blvd (☎469-4300); *New Zealand* 10960 Wilshire Blvd (☎310/477-8241).

Doctors *SOS Doctor* on call 24 hours a day: ☎222-1111.

Dental Treatment The cheapest place is the *USC School of Dentistry* (☎743-2800), on the USC campus, costing $20–200. Turn up and be prepared to wait all day.

Flea Markets/Swap Meets In Pasadena at the Rose Bowl, second Sunday of each month. In Orange County at the Costa Mesa Fairgrounds, each Saturday.

Hospitals with Casualty Departments Cedars-Sinai Medical Center, 8700 Beverly Blvd (☎310/855-6517); Good Samaritan Hospital, 616 Witmer St (☎397-2121); UCLA Medical Center, corner of Tiverton and Le Conte St in Westwood Village (☎310/825-2111).

Left Luggage At *Greyhound* stations and LAX for $1 a day ($2 for larger lockers). There's no left luggage at Union Station.

Post Offices The city's main post office is downtown at 901 S Broadway (☎617-4413), open Mon–Fri 8.30–6pm, Sat 7am–1.30pm. For Poste Restante, use zip code 90014.

Rape Hotline ☎262-0944.

Sport Baseball: the *LA Dodgers* (☎224-1400) play at Dodger Stadium near downtown, seats $4–10; *California Angels* (☎714/937-6761) at Anaheim Stadium in Orange County, seats $4–10. Basketball: the *LA Lakers* (☎637-1300) are at the Forum, in Inglewood, seats (often impossible to get) $10–20. Football: the *LA Rams* (☎714/937-6761) also play at Anaheim Stadium, seats $15–30; *LA Raiders* (☎747-7111) in the LA Coliseum, near downtown, seats $15–30. Hockey: *LA Kings* are also based at the Forum (☎310/419-3182), seats $10–25.

Ticketron The major LA office is 6060 W Manchester Ave (☎310/216-6666); they, or the phone book, will have details of the others.

Victims of Crime Resource Center ☎1-800/842-8467.

THE DESERTS

The **deserts** of Southern California occupy fully a quarter of the state. Untouched but for the three million acres used for military bases, this hot and inhospitable wilderness exerts a powerful fascination. There are two distinct regions: the **Colorado** or **Low Desert** in the south is the most easily reached from LA, containing the opulent artificial oasis of **Palm Springs** and the primeval expanse of **Joshua Tree**, and the **Mojave** or **High Desert**, dominated by **Death Valley**.

Low Desert

Most visitors to the Low Desert have no intention of getting away from it all. They head straight for where it's at – the irrefutable capital of the desert, **Palm Springs**. In these few square miles, overrun with the famous and the star-struck, the average age and average temperature are said to be about the same – a steady 88. Despite its shortcomings, you'll find it hard to avoid: it's the first stopping point east from LA on I-10, at the centre of the **Coachella Valley**, part of the most intensively productive agricultural area in the world, growing dates, oranges, lemons and grapefruits in vast quantities.

The sublime landscape of **Joshua Tree National Monument**, well worth a weekend spent taking in the sunsets and the howl of coyotes at twilight, lies one hour's drive east of Palm Springs, three and a half from LA, and is connected by bus from both.

Palm Springs

Sitting in lush farming land, replete with manicured golf courses, condominiums and millionaires, **PALM SPRINGS** does not conform to any typical image of the desert. The massive bulk of Mount San Jacinto glowers over its low-slung buildings, casting an instantaneous and welcome shadow over the town in the late afternoon. Ever since Hollywood stars first came here in the 1930s, the clean dry air and sunshine, just 120 miles east of LA, have made Palm Springs irresistible as a place to bring down stress levels. High-school kids arrive in their thousands for the drunken revelry of **Spring Break**, while others come specifically *not* to get drunk: the **Betty Ford Center** draws a star-studded patient list to its booze- and drug-free environment, attempting to undo a lifetime's behavioural disorders in a $20,000 two-week stay.

Palm Springs wasn't always like this. Once it was the domain of the **Cahuilla Indians**; they were allocated this land in the 1890s, but exact zoning was never settled until the 1940s, by which time the development of hotels and leisure complexes was well under way. Under an odd chequer-board system, every other square mile of Palm Springs forms part of the **Agua Caliente Indian Reservation**, and high rents have made this the richest tribe in America – over one hundred members of the Cahuilla have individual land-holdings worth $2 million or more.

Arrival and Information

Arriving by **car**, you drive into town on E Palm Canyon Drive. *Greyhound* **buses** (ten daily from LA) come in at 3111 N Indian Avenue (☎325-2053). *Desert Stage Lines* (☎367-3581) from the same terminal connect Palm Springs to Twentynine Palms and Joshua Tree. **Trains** link LA with **Indio**, 25 miles away from downtown Palm Springs and connected by *Sun Buses* (6am–6pm; ☎343-3451), which circulate all the local resorts.

The **visitor centre** is at 113 S Indian Avenue (Mon–Fri 9am–5pm; ☎327-7534).

The telephone **area code** for the California deserts is ☎619.

Downtown Palm Springs

Downtown Palm Springs stretches for about half a mile along Palm Canyon Drive, a wide, bright and modern strip full of expensive boutiques and restaurants. By day, people wear visors and swoon in air-conditioned shopping malls; by night, the youth take over and cruise the main drag in their four-wheel-drives with their stereos blaring.

The luxuriously housed **Desert Museum**, 101 Museum Drive (Tues–Fri 10am–4pm, Fri & Sat 10am–5pm; $3.50), is strong on Native American and Southwestern art, though its only permanent display is the late actor William Holden's collection of Asian and African works. Some surprisingly interesting natural science exhibits focus on the animal and plant life of the desert, demonstrating that it's not all sandstorms and rattlesnakes. There's an anarchic piece of landscape gardening at **Moorten's Botanical Gardens**, 1701 S Palm Canyon Drive (daily 9am–4pm; $2), a bizarre cornucopia of every desert plant and cactus, lumped together in no particular order but interesting for those who won't be venturing beyond town to see them in their natural habitat.

Several companies offer **celebrity tours** of the homes and country clubs of the international elite, the best of them being *Palm Springs Celebrity Tours*, 174 Palm Canyon Drive (☎325-2682). If you've got a car, you can do it yourself, with a map of the stars' homes from the visitor centre – but you'll miss the sharp anecdotal commentary.

Around Palm Springs

Most visitors to Palm Springs never leave the poolside, but a hardcore of desert enthusiasts still visit for the **hiking** and **riding** opportunities in the **Indian Canyons**, about three miles southeast of downtown along S Palm Canyon Drive. Centuries ago, ancestors of the Cahuilla developed extensive communities here, growing melons, squash, beans and corn. The canyons are about fifteen miles long, and can be toured by car, although it's worth walking at least a few miles; the easiest hiking trails lead past the waterfalls, rocky gorges and palm trees of **Palm Canyon** and **Andreas Canyon**. Some areas are set aside for the specific lunacy of **trailblazing** in jeeps and four-wheel-drives; rent your own vehicle from *Dune Off-Road Rentals*, 59755 Hwy-111 (☎325-0376), about four miles north of town, for around $50 for half a day, or take a **guided jeep adventure** with *Desert Adventures,* 68-733 Perez Road (☎324-3378), who offer excellent half-day tours of the Santa Rosa mountains for around $25 per hour, or $70 for half a day.

If the desert heat becomes too much to bear, large cable cars grind and sway over eight thousand feet up the **Palm Springs Aerial Tramway**, Tramway Drive, just off Hwy-111 north of Palm Springs (daily 8am–9pm; $13; ☎325-1391), passing through five climatic zones on the way to the top of Mount San Jacinto. There's a **bar** and **restaurant** at the Mountain Station up here. Concrete-paved trails (hardly the hiker's dream) stretch for a couple of miles around, and should sub-alpine ecology not interest you, there's always the option of a snowball fight.

Accommodation

Luxury **hotels** far outnumber the affordable variety in Palm Springs, but prices drop by as much as seventy percent as temperatures rise in summer. The north end of town, along Hwy-111, holds the cheaper places, virtually all of which have pools. The prices below are **summer rates**; add approximately $10 to $20 to get the winter rate.

Casa Cody, 175 South Cahuilla Rd (☎320-9346). The one affordable B&B inn. Attractive Southwestern-style buildings in a shady garden. Rooms from $45, apartments from $120 per night.

Desert Ho, 120 West Vereda Sur (☎325-5159). Small hotel, a mile or two north of downtown. Nine large rooms around a beautiful pool and gardens, facing Mt San Jacinto. Rooms from $48.

Desert Hotel, 285 N Indian Ave (☎325-3013). Probably the only place in town without a pool, but cheapest of the lot with doubles from $25.

Motel 6, 595 E Palm Canyon Drive (☎327-2004). Most central of the cheapies, this one is a ten-minute walk from downtown with a good pool and doubles from $32.

Eating and Drinking

The stifling desert heat suppresses even the healthiest of appetites; most people go all day on nothing, to find themselves suddenly ravenous at dusk. However, Palm Springs has a disappointing selection of **restaurants**; you can find better value, and a whole lot more life, in gay-oriented **Cathedral City** ("Cat City"), ten miles east along Hwy-111.

C.C. Construction Co, 68–449 Perez Road, Cathedral City. Seventies-style disco fun at the home of the "jig with a pig" evening; shimmy with a gay cop and mix with a good-natured drag-queen crowd.

Daddy Warbucks, 68–981 E Palm Canyon Drive, Cathedral City. A wild club scene with "whipped cream fighting" on Sunday and talent contests on Wednesday.

El Gallito Café, 68820 Grove Street, Cathedral City. Busy Mexican cantina that has the best food for miles and often queues to match – get there around 6pm to avoid the crowds.

Frying Fish, 123 N Palm Canyon Drive. Sushi for around $10 per enormous platter.

Louise's Pantry, 124 S Palm Canyon Drive. Fifties-looking diner, where none of the waitresses is under sixty and the servings are huge. Especially good for breakfast.

The Saloon, 225 S Indian Avenue. The best of Palm Springs' sorry bunch of bars, with a down-to-earth, beer & pretzels approach to drinking.

Le Vallauris, 385 West Tahquitz Way (☎325-5059 – reservations only). Excellent Californian/ French cuisine, though the price is around $50 per head. It bills itself as "*the* restaurant where the Stars entertain their friends"; and you may indeed run into one or two once-renowned artistes.

Wheel-Inn Eat, ten miles west on I-10 at the Cabazon exit (marked by two concrete dinosaurs). Humble, 24-hour desert truck-stop – so unpretentious they might never have heard of Palm Springs.

Joshua Tree National Monument

In a unique transitional area where the lower Colorado desert meets the high Mojave, the **JOSHUA TREE NATIONAL MONUMENT** protects 850 square miles of grotesquely gnarled and ragged trees. Each can reach up to forty feet in height, but they have to contend with extreme aridity and rocky soil, and the strain of their struggle to survive is evident. All around lie great heaps of boulders, pushed up by the San Andreas fault, their edges rounded and smooth from millenia of flash floods and winds.

This unearthly landscape is best appreciated at sunrise or sunset, when the desert floor is bathed in red light; at noon it can be a threatening furnace. The name "Joshua Tree", now familiar thanks to U2, was given by Mormons in the 1850s, who saw the craggy branches of the trees as the arms of Joshua leading them to the promised land.

It's wise to be selective in your explorations. As with any desert area, you'll find the heat punishing and an ambitious schedule impossible. Brief yourself at the visitor centres, and never venture anywhere without a map. Many roads are unmarked and restricted to four-wheel-drive use, in which case you shouldn't think about taking a normal car – you'll soon come to a grinding halt, and it could be quite a few panic-stricken hours before anybody finds you. If you're hiking, **stick to the trails**. Joshua Tree is full of abandoned gold mines: watch for loose gravel around openings, undercut edges, never trust ladders or timber, and bear in mind that the rangers rarely check mines for casualties. Even on the simpler trails, allow around an hour per mile.

One of the easiest hiking routes leads 1½ miles from Canyon Road, six miles from the visitor centre at Twentynine Palms, to **Fortynine Palms Oasis**. To the west of the oasis, quartz boulders tower around the *Indian Cove* campground; a trail from the eastern branch of the campground road heads to **Rattlesnake Canyon**, where, after rainfall, the streams and waterfalls break an otherwise eerie silence among the monoliths.

Moving south, follow the trails through **Hidden Valley**, where cattle rustlers used to hide out, to the rain-fed **Barker Dam**, to the east: Joshua Tree's crucial water supply, built by cattlemen around the turn of the century. One negotiable trail climbs past abandoned mining sites, where some buildings and equipment are still intact, to **Lost Horse Mine**, 450 feet up – once worth an average of $20,000 a week.

A brilliant desert panorama of badlands and mountains is to be had from the 5185ft **Key's View** nearby, from where Geology Tour Road leads down to the east through the best of Joshua Tree's **rock formations**.

Joshua Tree Practicalities

The monument is an hour's drive northeast from Palm Springs along Hwy-62, which leads to the **park headquarters** ($5 admission) at **Twentynine Palms**. In the absence of hotel accommodation in the monument itself, you may be glad of the good **motels** and scattering of restaurants here. The best of the lot is the New-Age-style *Twenty-Nine Palms Inn,* 73950 Inn Avenue (☎367-3505), where adobe cabins cost from $40 to $70 per person, per night. *Desert Stage Lines* **buses** (☎367-3581) arrive here from Palm Springs. There is another entrance and visitor centre at **Cottonwood**, seven miles north of I-10.

Joshua Tree has nine **campgrounds**, all concentrated in the northwest except for one at Cottonwood, but only two (*Black Rock* and *Cottonwood*) have water supplies. Camping is free, on a first-come-first-served basis, and no reservations are allowed.

High Desert

The **Mojave Desert**, known as the High Desert because on average it is two thousand feet above sea level, has no equals when it comes to hardship. Visitors are very thin on the ground; most simply race through on I-15 between LA and Las Vegas. If you do linger, you'll get the chance to see – and smell – what a desert is really like: a vast, impersonal, extreme environment, sharp with its own peculiar fragrance, and in spring alive with acres of fiery orange poppies and other brightly coloured wildflowers.

Most people prefer to do their sightseeing from the comfort of an air-conditioned car, though both *Greyhound* and *Amtrak* pass through Barstow en route to Las Vegas.

Barstow

BARSTOW, the one potential stop-off along the dusty, seemingly endless I-15, is a lacklustre small town. During the hottest part of the year it seems perpetually empty; everyone hides in their air-conditioned homes from the relentless sun. The one main road is lined with motels – rooms are $30 at *Torches Motel*, 201 W Main Street (☎256-3308), near the bus station – and restaurants (good Mexican food can be had at *Rosita's*, 540 W Main Street). At the junction of Barstow Road and I-15, the **California Desert Information Center** (daily 9am–6pm; ☎256-8617) has a good selection of maps, lodging and restaurant guides. You can **camp** in shaded canyons at the contrived **Calico Ghost Town** (daily 9am–5pm; $5), seven miles north along I-15.

Death Valley National Monument

DEATH VALLEY is an utterly inhuman environment: the hottest place on earth and almost entirely devoid of shade, much less water. Its sculpted rock layers form deeply shadowed, eroded crevices at the foot of sharply silhouetted hills, their exotic mineral content turning million-year-old mudflats into rainbows of sunlit phosphorescence, and comprise a nearly complete geological record of the past. It was named by a party of white settlers who stumbled through in 1849, looking for a shortcut to the Gold Rush towns; they managed to survive despite running out of food and water. For the next 75 years the only people willing to brave its hardships were miners, whose most successful endeavours were centred on borates, a harsh alkali used in detergent soaps.

Throughout the summer, the air temperature in Death Valley averages 120°F, and the ground can reach near boiling point. Better to come during the spring, when the wildflowers are in bloom, or from October to May when it's generally mild and dry.

The central north–south valley for which the monument is named contains its two main outposts: **Stovepipe Wells** and **Furnace Creek**, where the **visitor center** (daily 8am–9pm in winter, 8am–5pm in summer; ☎786-2331) is located. A $5 entrance fee is payable at the park entrance; the **ranger stations** close to the park boundaries provide free maps and up-to-date information on tours and activities.

Many of the most unusual sights are located south of Furnace Creek. A good first stop, seven miles along Hwy-178/Badwater Road, is the **Artist's Palette**, an eroded hillside covered in an intensely coloured mosaic of reds, golds, blacks and greens. Sixteen miles further south, **Badwater** is an unpalatable but non-poisonous thirty-foot-wide pool of water, loaded with chloride and sulphates, that's the only home of the soft-bodied Death Valley snail. A four-mile hike across the hot valley floor drops down to the **lowest point in the western hemisphere**, 282 feet below sea level.

Zabriskie Point, overlooking Badwater and the Artist's Palette off Hwy-190, four miles south of Furnace Creek, was the inspiration for Antonioni's eponymous 1960s film. The view is best during the early morning, when the pink and gold Panamint Mountains across the valley are highlighted by the rising sun.

Near Stovepipe Wells in the west spread fifteen rippled and contoured square miles of ever-changing **sand dunes**. A ten-mile dirt road west of the campground leads to sheer black-walled **Marble Canyon**, scratched with mysterious ancient petroglyphs.

Practicalities

Death Valley is a long way from anywhere; the only scheduled public transport is from **Las Vegas**, 140 miles to the southeast, from where the *LTR Stage Lines* (☎702/384-1230) leave roughly every other day from September to May, not at all in summer.

If you plan to **stay**, you must reserve ahead. The **Fred Harvey Consortium** (PO Box 1, Death Valley, CA 92328; ☎786-2345 or ☎1-800/622-0838) operates two pricey hotels on natural oases at Furnace Creek; the plush *Furnace Creek Inn* costs $175 to $250 a night, while the more reasonable *Furnace Creek Ranch* across the road about half a mile north charges $65 to $90 – and has the valley's best-value **restaurants** and a nice bar. Fred Harvey also offer regular three-hour **coach tours** ($21) in winter from the *Furnace Creek Inn*. The *Stovepipe Wells Village* (☎786-2387), on Hwy-190 about twenty miles northeast of Furnace Creek, has double rooms from $45; prices drop to $38 a night from June to August. **Camping** in one of the many National Park Service campgrounds costs $5 a night, and cannot be reserved. You could also stay **outside Death Valley** altogether, 35 miles past Furnace Creek in **Beatty**, Nevada: the *El Portal Motel* (☎702/553-2912) on the west side of town or the *Stagecoach Motel* (☎702/553-2419) on the east side both have double rooms for $35 a night, less in summer.

Outside the Valley

Hordes of overheated tourists queue to wander through the surreal luxury of **Scotty's Castle**, 45 miles north of the visitor centre and well beyond Death Valley itself. It was built during the 1920s as the desert retreat of Chicago insurance broker Albert Johnson, but named after "Death Valley" Scotty, who managed the construction and claimed the house was his own, financed by a hidden gold mine. **Tours** (daily 9am–5pm; $5) take in the ornate wooden ceilings, indoor waterfalls and a remote-controlled player piano; Johnson lost a fortune in the Wall Street Crash and had to abandon plans for swimming pools and elaborate gardens. The house remains as it was when he died in 1948. Scotty himself lived here until 1954, and is buried just behind the house.

Five miles west of Scotty's Castle gapes the half-mile **Ubehebe Crater**, the rust-tinged result of a massive volcanic explosion; half a mile south sits its thousand-year-old younger brother, **Little Hebe**. Beyond the craters the road continues west for another twenty dusty miles to **Racetrack Valley**, a 2½-mile long mudflat across which giant boulders seem slowly to be racing, leaving faint trails in their wake.

THE CENTRAL COAST

After the hustle of LA and San Francisco, the four hundred miles of coastline in between – the **central coast** – can seem like the land that time forgot: sparsely populated outside the few medium-sized towns, and lined by clean sandy beaches. This untouched environment is at its most dramatic at **Big Sur**, where the brooding Santa Lucia mountains rise steeply out of the thundering Pacific surf. The two largest towns in the region, **Santa Barbara** and **Santa Cruz**, are poles apart: Santa Barbara in the south is a wealthy resort; Santa Cruz in the north is a throwback to the Sixties. In between, languorous **San Luis Obispo** makes a good base for **Hearst Castle**, the hilltop palace of publishing magnate William Randolph "Citizen Kane" Hearst.

Almost all of the towns along the central coast grew up around Spanish **missions**, each sited a long day's walk from the next, and enclosed within thick walls to prevent Indian attack. **Monterey**, a hundred miles south of San Francisco, was the capital of California under Spain and Mexico, and retains more of its early nineteenth-century architecture than any other city in the state.

Amtrak's Coast Starlight **train** runs along the coast up to San Luis Obispo before cutting inland north to San Francisco; *Greyhound* **buses** stop at most of the towns, especially along the main highway, US-101. A better route, if you've got a car, is the smaller Hwy-1, which follows the coast all the way but takes twice as long.

Santa Barbara

The eight-lane coastal freeway that races past the oil wells and offshore drilling platforms slows to a leisurely pace a hundred miles north of Los Angeles at **SANTA BARBARA**. It's a conservative town – home to Ronald Reagan – but undeniably beautifully sited, on gently sloping hills above the Pacific. The insistent red-tiled roofs and white stucco walls of the low-rise buildings form a backdrop to some fine Spanish Revival architecture, while the golden beaches are wide and clean, lined by palm trees along a curving bay. However, the completion of the US-101 freeway in 1991, and the replacement of much of downtown by a vast shopping mall, are sure signs that it is slowly but surely turning into yet another identikit Southern California town.

The homogenised feel of Santa Barbara is no accident. Following a devastating earthquake in 1925, the entire town was rebuilt in the image of an apocryphal mission-era past, with numerous arcades linking shops, cafes and restaurants. **State Street** is the main drag, home to a friendly assortment of diners, bookshops, coffee bars and nightclubs catering for locals rather than visitors. The few remaining, genuine mission-era structures are preserved as the **Presidio de Santa Barbara** (Mon–Fri 10.30am– 4.30pm, Sat & Sun noon–4pm; donations), the centre of which, the two-hundred-year-old barracks, **El Cuartel**, stand two blocks off State Street on Perdido Street. The second-oldest building in California, this now houses historical exhibits and a scale model of the small Spanish colony. The more recent past is recounted in the nearby **museum** at 136 E de la Guerra Street (Tues–Sun noon–5pm; free).

State Street leads half a mile down from the town centre to wooden **Stearns Wharf**, built in 1872 and recently restored, with its seafood restaurants, ice cream stands and fish market, and magnificent **beaches** stretch away in either direction.

In the hills above the town is **Mission Santa Barbara** (daily 9am–5pm; $1), the so-called "Queen of the Missions", whose colourful twin-towered front is the most beautiful and impressive of all the California missions. A small **museum** displays historical artefacts from the mission archives.

The telephone **area code** for the central coast, from Santa Barbara to Big Sur, is ☎805.

Practicalities

Hourly *Greyhound* **buses** (☎965-3971) from LA and San Francisco stop downtown at 34 W Cabrillo Street; **trains** (☎687-6848) call once a day in each direction at the old Southern Pacific station at 209 State Street, a block west of US-101. The **visitor centre** is on East Beach at 1 Santa Barbara Street (☎966-9222). A free **shuttle bus** loops around Santa Barbara on weekdays, while the *Santa Barbara Metropolitan Transit District* (☎683-3702) covers the outlying areas for a flat fare of 50¢.

Rooms are generally expensive and hard to find; few places cost less than $75. The best options are the characterful old mission-style *Hotel State Street*, 121 State Street (☎966-6586), near the beach, where doubles cost $35 to $60, and the no-frills *Motel 6*, 443 Corona del Mar (☎564-1392), also costing from $35.

The two best-value **restaurants** in Santa Barbara are the Mexican seafood specialists *Pescado's*, 422 N Milpas Street (☎965-3805), and the upscale but not expensive New Mexican *Zia's*, at 421 N Milpas St (☎962-5391), but if you like fish there are plenty of other places to choose from along the north end of State Street.

There are **cafes**, **bars** and **clubs** all along State Street; *Joseppi's* at no. 434 (☎962-5516) is good for jazz, while *Carnaval* at no. 634 (☎962-9991) hosts biggish name indie bands. The *Sojourner Coffee House*, 134 E Canon Perdido (☎965-7922), serves coffee, beer, wine, and a range of vegetarian food, in a friendly, hippyish setting, with live music some nights.

San Luis Obispo

SAN LUIS OBISPO, ten miles northeast of the resort of Avila Beach and almost exactly halfway between LA and San Francisco, is a few miles inland, but makes the best base for exploring the nearby coast. Still primarily an agricultural market centre, it holds some of the central coast's best architecture, any number of good places to eat, a couple of pubs, and – outside summer holiday weekends – plenty of places to stay.

The compact core of San Luis is eminently walkable, centred around the late eighteenth-century **Mission San Luis Obispo de Tolosa** (daily 9am–5pm; free), a dark and unremarkable church that was the prototype for the now-ubiquitous red tiled roof, developed to replace the original, flammable thatch in response to Indian arson attacks. Between the mission and the tourist office, **Mission Plaza**'s terraces step down along San Luis creek, along which footpaths meander, criss-crossed by bridges every hundred feet and overlooked by shops and outdoor eateries on the south bank. **Higuera Street**, a block south of Mission Plaza, is the main drag, and springs to life on Thursdays for the **Farmers' Market**, when the street is closed to cars and filled with vegetable stalls, mobile barbeques and street-corner musicians.

Practicalities

The *Greyhound* terminal is at 150 South Street (☎543-2121), while *Amtrak* trains stop at the end of Santa Rosa Street, half a mile south of the business district. The **Chamber of Commerce** office is at 1039 Chorro Street (☎543-1323).

Monterey Street was the site of the world's first (long-gone) **motel** – the *Mo-tel Inn*. Rates in its modern counterparts are generally low. The English-owned *Adobe Inn*, 1473 Monterey Street (☎549-0321), has nice rooms from $55 a night. For a kitsch treat, look in on the shocking pink behemoth that is the *Madonna Inn*, 100 Madonna Way (☎543-3000). A waterfall flushes the gents' urinals (which look like whale mouths) and the rooms (from $80 a night) are decorated according to themes, ranging from fairy-tale princesses to cavemen. Higuera Street is the place to **eat**, especially during Thursday's market. *Brubeck's* at no. 726 (☎541-8688) serves salads and grilled fresh fish, with live jazz most nights; *Spike's* at no. 570 (☎544-7157) has a great selection of beers.

W R HEARST – CITIZEN KANE

Often portrayed as a power-mad monster – most memorably by Orson Welles in his thinly veiled *Citizen Kane* – **William Randolph Hearst** seems in retrospect more like a very rich, over-indulged little boy. Born in 1863 as the only son of a multi-millionaire mining engineer, he learned his trade in New York working for Joseph Pulitzer, the inventor of "Yellow Journalism". When he published his own *Morning Journal*, Hearst took Pulitzer's advice to heart, fanning the flames of American imperialism to ignite the Spanish-American War of 1898. As he told his correspondents in Cuba: "You provide the pictures, and I'll provide the war". Hearst eventually controlled an empire that during the 1930s sold twenty-five percent of the nation's newspapers – and sixty percent in California.

Despite his war-mongering and nationalism, Hearst was middle-of-the-road politically, a lifelong Democrat who served two terms in the House of Representatives but failed to be elected as Mayor of New York or President of the US. Besides his many newspapers, Hearst owned eleven radio stations and two movie studios, which he used to make his mistress Marion Davies a star. The Depression forced him to sell off most of his holdings, but he continued to exert power and influence until his death in 1951, aged 88.

Hearst Castle

Forty-five miles northwest of San Luis Obispo, hilltop **HEARST CASTLE** is one of the most extravagant houses in the world. Second only to Disneyland in the state, the home where publisher **William Randolph Hearst** held court over such guests as Winston Churchill, Charlie Chaplin, George Bernard Shaw and Charles Lindbergh now brings in over a million visitors a year. Its interior combines walls, floors and ceilings stolen from European churches and castles with Gothic fireplaces and Moorish tiles, and is bursting with Greek vases and medieval tapestries. Work on the 250,000-acre ranch began in 1919, managed by architect Julia Morgan, but was never actually completed: rooms would be torn out as soon as they were finished in order to accommodate yet more bits and pieces of old buildings. The main facade, a twin-towered copy of a Mudejar cathedral, stands at the top of steps which curve up from an expansive swimming pool filled with pure spring water and lined by a Greek colonnade.

Two-hour guided **tours** (summer daily 8am–5pm, winter 8am–3pm; $10; ☎927-2020) leave from the visitor centre on Hwy-1. Reservations are essential in summer.

Big Sur

The ninety wild and undeveloped miles of rocky cliffs of **BIG SUR** form a sublime landscape at the edge of a continent, where redwood groves line river canyons and the Santa Lucia mountains rise straight out of the blue Pacific. Only the occasional outpost interrupts the tortuous exhilarating route of **Hwy-1**, carved out of bedrock cliffs five hundred feet above the ocean, and **public transport** is limited to the twice-daily *MST* bus from Monterey. Hardly anyone braves the turbulent winters, when violent storms can sweep sections of the highway into the sea. Summer weekends see the roads and campgrounds packed to overflowing, but a mile or two's walk still gets you away from it all.

The southern coastline of Big Sur is relatively gentle, with sandy beaches hiding below crumbling yellow-ochre cliffs. **Esalen** is named for the Indians who once enjoyed its natural **hot spring**, on a cliff-top high above the raging Pacific surf. Since the 1960s, when people came to Big Sur to smoke pot and get back to nature, Esalen has been at the forefront of the "New Age" movement, and the spring is now owned and operated by the *Esalen Institute* (Mon–Fri midnight–5am; $5; ☎667-2335).

Three miles north of Esalen, **Julia Pfeiffer Burns State Park** has some of the best day hikes in the Big Sur area, including a twenty-minute walk along the cliffs from the parking area to see a waterfall crashing down into the sea. As well as a free and basic campground, the lovely old *Deetjen's Big Sur Inn* on Hwy-1 (☎667-2377) has rooms handcrafted from thick redwood planks for $55 to $110 a night and excellent food. There are good-sized cabins for $70 to $110 a night in the *Big Sur Lodge* (☎667-2171).

Further north, at **Nepenthe**, the rooftop *Cafe Amphora* offers affordable whole food and impressive views. Downstairs there's an outdoor sculpture gallery and a decent bookstore, including works by Henry Miller, who lived in the area until the 1960s. Big Sur's best beach is two miles north, where a barely marked road leads west from Hwy-1 a mile down Sycamore Canyon to **Pfeiffer Beach**, a white-sand beach dominated by a hump of rock whose colour varies from brown to red to orange in the changing light.

Two miles north of Pfeiffer Beach, and 65 miles north of Hearst Castle, Hwy-1 drops into the valley of the Big Sur River. In sheltered **Pfeiffer Big Sur State Park**, deep clear swimming holes form in the steep-walled river gorge during late spring and summer, and nude sunbathing is tolerated. A hiking trail leads half a mile up a canyon shaded by redwoods to the sixty-foot **Pfeiffer Falls**. The park is the centre for information on the region's many year-round **campgrounds**. All are available for up to $10 a night ($2 if you're on foot or bicycle) on a first-come, first-camped basis; only in Pfeiffer Big Sur State Park itself can you reserve a space, through MISTIX (☎1-800/444-7275).

Big Sur Village

The village of **BIG SUR**, just north of Pfeiffer Big Sur State Park, is probably the most feasible base for seeing Big Sur, with a long strip along Hwy-1 of places to sleep and eat. Accommodation gets very full in summer, but a night in one of the rustic (but rarely inexpensive) **mountain lodges** is well worth experiencing. Among those right on the river are *Fernwood* (☎667-2422), which has camping spots ($9–15) and simple cabins ($55–75), and the *River Inn Resort* (☎667-2700 or ☎1-800/548-3610), where rates vary from $45 to $130 a night, and there's a very good **restaurant**.

The Monterey Peninsula

The rocky headlands of the **Monterey Peninsula**, where gnarled cypress trees amplify the collision between the cliffs and the thundering sea, mark the northern edge of the Big Sur coast, a hundred miles south of San Francisco. The lively harbour town of **Monterey** was the capital of California under the Spanish and Mexicans, and retains many old adobe houses and places of genuine historic appeal alongside some overstated tourist traps. **Carmel**, on the other hand, three miles to the south, is a contrivedly quaint village of million-dollar holiday homes.

Arrival and Getting Around

If you're coming from the south, both *Greyhound* and *Amtrak* require you to change in the sprawling agricultural town of **Salinas** inland, and take a further 45-minute bus trip to 351 Del Monte Avenue in Monterey. **Getting around** the peninsula itself is surprisingly easy, on *Monterey-Salinas Transit* buses (7am–6pm; ☎899-2555). The most useful routes are bus #4 and #5 (Monterey–Carmel); #21 (Monterey–Salinas); and #1, (Monterey–Pacific Grove); there's also a free shuttle bus from downtown to the Aquarium on Cannery Row. Bus #22 runs to Big Sur twice a day, in summer only.

Another option is to **rent a bike**: the *Doubletree Inn* (☎649-4511) in Monterey, near Pacific House and the Wharf, rents out cruisers for $15 a day, and *Bay Bikes*, 640 Wave Street in Cannery Row (☎646-9090), have good-quality mountain bikes for $25 a day; they're also in Carmel (☎625-BIKE) on Lincoln between Fifth and Sixth streets.

The telephone **area code** for the Monterey Peninsula is ☎408.

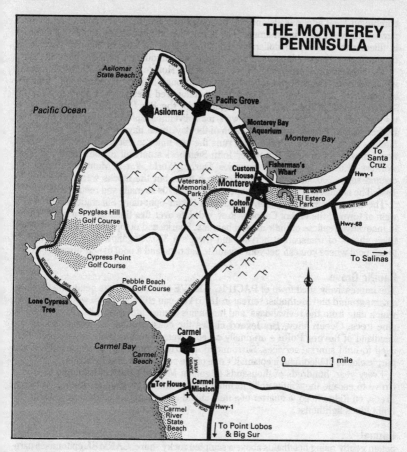

THE MONTEREY PENINSULA

Monterey

Though named by Vizcaino in 1602, **MONTEREY** was not colonised until 1770. Its claim to be the most historic city in California rests on its role thereafter as the military, administrative and commercial centre of a territory that extended east to the Rockies and north to Canada (with a non-native population of less than seven thousand). With the conjunction of the US takeover and the Gold Rush, Monterey suddenly became a backwater, hardly affected by the waves of immigration which followed.

Impressive vernacular colonial **buildings** now stand unassumingly in the compact town centre, within a few blocks of the tourist-thronged waterfront. A loosely organised **Path of History** connects the 35 sites of the **Monterey State Historic Park**, and park rangers lead guided walking tours on weekends (11am & 2pm; $3.50; ☎649-7118) from the Customs House, near the waterfront at the foot of Alvarado Street.

The best place to get a feel for life in old Monterey is at the **Larkin House**, on Jefferson Street a block south of Alvarado, home of the first and only American Consul to California. The New England-born Thomas Larkin, who was influential in persuading the Californians to turn towards the US and away from the erratic government of Mexico, is credited with developing the now-common Monterey style of architecture, combining local adobe walls and the balconies of a Southern plantation home with a puritan Yankee's taste in ornament. The house, the first two-storey adobe in California, is filled with millions of dollars' worth of antiques, and **tours** (hourly 10am–4pm, except Tues; $1) are obligatory. The gorgeous surrounding gardens are open all day.

The **Stevenson House**, a short way east at 530 Houston Street, is filled with memorabilia of Robert Louis Stevenson, who passed through in 1879. He witnessed Monterey in transition, and foresaw that its Mexican-influenced lifestyle was no match for the "Yankee craft" of the "millionaire vulgarians of the Big Bonanza". That catering to visitors has indeed become the town's main livelihood is evident around the tacky **Fisherman's Wharf**, where the catch-of-the-day these days tends to be overweight families from San Jose. A **bike path** runs the two miles to Pacific Grove, along what's now known as **Cannery Row** after John Steinbeck's portrait of the rough-and-ready workers of its thirty-odd fish canneries. During World War II Monterey caught and canned some 200,000 tons of sardines each year, but the stocks were exhausted by 1945. The abandoned canneries reopened in the 1970s as malls and restaurants.

The engaging **Monterey Bay Aquarium** (10am–6pm daily; $9, students $6), a mile west of town at the end of Cannery Row, exhibits over five thousand marine creatures in innovative replicas of their natural habitats. Sharks and octopi roam behind two-foot-thick sheets of transparent acrylic, and there's a 300,000-gallon Kelp Forest tank, a touch pool where you can pet your favourite bat rays, and a pool of **sea otters**.

Pacific Grove

The impressively sited town of **PACIFIC GROVE** at the end of the peninsula began as a campground and Methodist retreat in 1875. You can still see ornate wooden **cottages** which date from the revival days, and it remains a quiet little place, its streets lined by pine trees. **Ocean View Boulevard** circles the coast around the town, passing the headland of **Lovers Point** – originally called Lovers of Jesus Point – where preachers used to hold sunrise services. Surrounded in early summer by the colourful red and purple cloaks of blooming iceplant, it's one of the peninsula's best **beaches**.

Every year, hundreds of thousands of golden Monarch **butterflies** come to Pacific Grove to escape the winter chill, forming orange and black blankets on the **Butterfly Trees**, on Ridge Road, a quarter of a mile inland along Lighthouse Avenue towards the Point Pinos lighthouse.

Carmel

Set on gently rising headlands above a sculpted rocky shore, **CARMEL** epitomises parochial snobbery. The chance to catch a rare glimpse of ex-mayor Clint Eastwood may make the sterile shopping mall atmosphere worth bearing for an hour or so, but the real reason to come is the largely untouched nearby coastline. **Carmel Beach** is a tranquil cove of emerald blue water bordered by soft white sand and cypress-covered cliffs; the tides are deceptively strong and dangerous, so be careful if you chance a swim.

At the **Point Lobos State Reserve**, two miles south of Carmel on Hwy-1 ($5), a number of hiking trails give good views down into deep coves where sea otters may be seen surfing in the waves. The sea here is one of the richest underwater habitats in California, and grey whales are often seen offshore, migrating south in January and returning with young calves in April and early May. Because the point juts so far out into the ocean, chances are good of seeing them from as little as a hundred yards away.

Monterey Peninsula Accommodation

Hotel and B&B rates average $120 a night, but there are several **motels** along Fremont Street, two miles north of central Monterey. The **tourist office** at 380 Alvarado Street in Monterey (Mon–Fri 9am–5pm; ☎649-3200) has comprehensive listings and can tell you where to find the **youth hostel** (summer only) this year. The nearest **camping** is in Veteran's Memorial Park, site of Steinbeck's fictional *Tortilla Flat*, at the top of Jefferson Street in the hills above town.

Asilomar Conference Center, 800 Asilomar Blvd, Pacific Grove (☎372-8016). Rustic, hand-crafted cabins and modern lodges in splendid beachfront location. Doubles from $50 a night.

Carmel River Inn, Rio Road at Hwy-1, Carmel (☎624-1575). Clean and pleasant, no-frills motel, on the banks of the Carmel River, near the beach and Carmel Mission. Doubles from $45.

Motel 6, 2124 Fremont St, Monterey (☎646-8585). Basic, no-frills motel, but you'll have to reserve a room months in advance to avail yourself of their $40-a-night doubles.

Pacific Grove Motel, Lighthouse Ave at Grove Acre (☎372-3218). Basic, small motel in marvellous setting, 100 yards from the sea. Doubles $35 in winter, from $50 in summer.

Monterey Peninsula Eating

There are many excellent places to eat all over the peninsula. If you're on a tight budget, the best cheap eats are on the north side of Monterey along Fremont Street.

Cafe Fina, Fisherman's Wharf, Monterey (☎372-5200). Pasta dishes, wood-oven pizzas and, of course, grilled fresh fish in the Wharf's most style-conscious setting.

Fishwife Restaurant, 1996 Sunset Drive at Asilomar, Pacific Grove (☎375-7107). Long-standing local favourite, serving great food at reasonable prices in homey, unpretentious surroundings.

La Boheme, Dolores St between Ocean and 7th, Carmel (☎624-7500). Fine dining in a scaled-down replica of a French country hotel. Multi-course, *prix-fixe* meals for $17.50 plus wine and service.

Pepper's Mexicali Cafe, 170 Forest Ave, Pacific Grove (☎373-6892). Gourmet Mexican seafood Californified into healthy, high-style dishes that won't put too big a hole in your wallet.

Drinking and Nightlife

The clubs on the peninsula feature sedate live and canned music, though things pick up a bit with the world-class Monterey Jazz Festival in September (☎373-3366).

The Club of Monterey, Alvarado and Del Monte St (☎646-9244). Fairly young and upscale crowd at this DJ-dance club; darts and pool tables downstairs. Cover $1–8, with occasional live acts.

The Firehouse, 414 Calle Principal, Monterey (☎649-3016). Characterful cocktail lounge in historic brick fire station. Free live music at the weekend.

Monterey Brewing Company, 700 Cannery Row, Monterey (☎375-3634). Good, micro-brewed lagers and ales, bar food, and nightly live rock or blues bands.

Portofino Cafe, 620 Lighthouse Ave, Pacific Grove (☎373-7379). Casual cafe with acoustic folk and jazz musicians on weekend nights, cover under $5.

Santa Cruz

After the overcharged tourism of Monterey, the quiet easy-going community of **SANTA CRUZ**, seventy-five miles south of San Francisco, comes as a welcome surprise. Although in many ways it's the quintessential Californian coastal town, spread out at the foot of thickly wooded mountains beside a clean sandy beach, it has grown a bit too fast for comfort in the last few years, and the destruction wrought by the 1989 earthquake seems to have brought it up short – progress in repairing the damage has been very slow. In the Sixties, the Merry Pranksters turned the local youth on to LSD long before it defined a generation, and the area is still among the most politically and socially progressive in California. It's also surprisingly untouristed. No hotels spoil the miles of wave-beaten coastline; most of the land is agricultural, and roadside stands are more likely to sell apples or sprouts than postcards and souvenirs.

With much of the town centre now uninhabitable, the **Santa Cruz Boardwalk**, the last surviving beachfront amusement park on the West Coast, is the main focus for visitors (summer Mon–Fri 11am–7pm, Sat & Sun 11am–10pm, winter weekends only). Though packed at the weekend with teenagers on the prowl, most of the time it's a friendly funfair, where barefoot hippies mix with mushroom farmers and their families. The star attraction is the wild wooden roller coaster known as the **Big Dipper**.

The **beach** next to the Boardwalk is good enough but can get very rowdy. For a bit more peace and quiet, follow the coastline out of town to one of the smaller beaches hidden away at the foot of the cliffs. From **West Cliff Drive**, you'll see some of the biggest waves in California, not least at **Steamer Lane**, beyond the Municipal Pier. The ghosts of surfers past are animated at the **Surfing Museum** (daily noon–4pm; free) in the old lighthouse on the point, which holds surfboards ranging from early twelve-foot redwood planks to modern hi-tech multifinned cutters. A clifftop bicycle path runs two miles from here to **Natural Bridges State Park**, where waves have cut holes through the coastal cliffs, forming delicate stone arches (though three of the four bridges for which the park was named have since collapsed).

Practicalities

Greyhound buses from San Francisco stop four times a day at 425 Front Street (☎423-1800), in the centre of town, as do *Peerless Stages* from Oakland and San Jose, and *Green Tortoise*. The **Santa Cruz Visitors Bureau** is at 710 Front Street (Mon–Fri 9am–5pm; ☎425-1234). An excellent **public transport** system centres on the Metro Center at 920 Pacific Avenue. The basic fare is $1, and an all-day pass is $2. *Clark's Cyclery*, 927 Pacific Avenue (☎458-9551), rents **bikes** from $15 a day.

Though the characterful old *St George Hotel* was seriously damaged by the earthquake, Santa Cruz still has plenty of inexpensive places to **stay**. The cheapest of the lot, basically a bunk in a high school gym, is the *Santa Cruz Hostel*, 511 Broadway (☎423-8181; phone to check current location). *The Best Inn*, at 320 Ocean Street across the river (☎458-9220), has spartan doubles from $25, and the 1887 *Cliff Crest Inn*, 407 Cliff Street (☎427-2609), at the top of Beach Hill, charges from $80. Among several good seafront **restaurants** is the *Miramar*, 45 Municipal Wharf (☎423-4441); *El Paisano*, 605 Beach Street at Riverside (☎426-2382), serves great cheap Mexican food. The best **campground** around is at *New Brighton State Beach* (☎688-3241), three miles south on the edge of the beachfront village of Capitola.

Santa Cruz has the central coast's most enjoyable nightlife; the music in its unpretentious and unthreatening bars and nightclubs varies from heavy-duty surf-thrash to lilting reggae to the rowdy rock of local resident Neil Young. *The Catalyst*, 1011 Pacific Avenue (☎423-1336), is the best bet for catching big-name touring artists and up-and-coming locals, while the *Front Street Pub*, 516 Front Street (☎429-8838), offers home-brewed lagers and ales, and live music or comedians most nights.

The Coast North to San Francisco

Twenty-five miles up the coast from Santa Cruz, the beginning of the San Francisco Peninsula is marked by **Pigeon Point Lighthouse** (☎415/879-0633), where you can spend the night in the old lighthouse-keeper's quarters and soak your bones in a hot tub, cantilevered out over the rocks. Dorm beds cost $9 (plus $2 for non-AYH members) and private rooms for two people are $23. Pigeon Point took its name from the clipper ship, *Carrier Pigeon*, that broke up on the rocks off the point, one of many shipwrecks that led to the construction of the lighthouse in the late nineteenth century.

The cargo of one of these wrecked ships inspired residents of the nearby fishing village of **PESCADERO**, a mile inland, literally to "paint the town", using hundreds of pots of white paint that were washed up on the shore. The two streets of the small village are still lined by white, wooden buildings, and the descendants of the Portuguese whalers who founded the town keep up another, more enticing tradition, celebrating the annual **Festival of the Holy Ghost**, six weeks after Easter, with a lively and highly ritualised parade. Pescadero is well known as one of the best places to **eat** on the entire coast; an excellent restaurant, *Duarte's*, serving fish dinners and fresh fruit pies, and *Dinelli's Café* with Greek food and tasty fried artichoke hearts.

THE CENTRAL VALLEY

The vast **interior** of California is split down the middle by the Sierra Nevada mountains. The wide **Central Valley** in the west was made super-fertile by irrigation projects during the 1940s, and is now almost totally agricultural. Even if the nightlife begins and ends with the local ice cream parlour, after the big cities of the coast it can all be quite refreshing. However, the real reason to come here is to reach the **national parks** of **Sequoia** and **Kings Canyon** – whose huge trees form the centrepiece of a rich natural landscape – and **Yosemite**, where towering walls of silvery granite are invigorated by a number of cascading waterfalls. No roads penetrate the hundred miles of wilderness to the east, but the entire region is criss-crossed by hiking trails leading up into the pristine alpine backcountry of the **High Sierra**. When you see them from the eastern side, their Spanish name, *Sierra Nevada* ("snow capped sawblade"), perfectly describes the sharply serrated ridges that stand high above the deserted **Owens Valley**.

The arrow-straight I-5 barrels straight up from LA to San Francisco. Twice-daily **trains** and frequent *Greyhound* **buses** run through the valley, with bus connections from Fresno and Merced to Yosemite. Despite its sparse population, the Owens Valley is easy both to reach and to get around, with a daily *Greyhound* service along US-395 between LA and Reno, Nevada, and the *Trailhead Shuttle Service* ferrying hikers, bikers and skiers to the main High Sierra trailheads.

Bakersfield

The first town you come to across the rocky peaks north of Los Angeles, looming unappealingly out of a forest of oil derricks, is the flat and featureless **BAKERSFIELD**. While in itself it's almost entirely devoid of interest, it is the unlikely home of one of the liveliest **country music** scenes in the nation, stemming from the arrival during the Depression of midwestern farmers, who brought their hillbilly instruments and campfire songs with them. In the mid-Sixties, the gutsy honky-tonk style of Bakersfield artists such as Merle Haggard and Buck Owens challenged the slick commercial output of Nashville, but hopes of luring the major country music record labels to "Nashville West" foundered with the emergence of rivals like Austin, Texas.

Nevertheless, the numerous honky-tonks of Bakersfield are still jumping every Friday and Saturday night. There's never a cover charge, and live sets usually entail one band playing for four or five hours from around 8pm, with a fifteen-minute break every hour. Stetson hats and flowery blouses are the sartorial order of the day, and audiences span generations, ranging in age from 21 to 91. Most **venues** are hotel lounges or restaurant backrooms; one not to be missed is *Trouts*, 805 N Chester Avenue (☎805/399-6700), a country music bar that's been in business nearly forty years. Close by, you might also investigate *Cassidy's*, 4500 Pierce Road (☎805/631-9303) or *Junction Lounge*, 2620 Pierce Road (☎805/327-9651). Other worthwhile places lie half an hour's drive across town: *Brandy's Tavern*, 2700 S Union Avenue (☎805/831-9853), *Little Bit Country*, 3317 State Road (☎805/393-8044), and *Porter's House*, 10701 Hwy-78 (☎805/366-6000).

Practicalities

You have to come to Bakersfield from LA by *Amtrak* bus to catch the train through the valley to San Francisco and northern California, and several *Greyhound* routes require changes here too (1820 18th Street; ☎805/327-7371). The **visitor centre** is at 2101 Oak Street (Mon–Fri 8am–5pm; ☎805/861-2367). Cheapest **overnight stays** are at *EZ-8*, 2604 Pierce Road (☎805/322-1907), and the *Roadrunner Motel*, 2619 Pierce Road (☎805/323-3727), both $30 to $35; *Zingo's* at 2625 Pierce Road is a 24-hour truckstop where frilly-aproned waitresses deliver plates of diner staples.

Sequoia and Kings Canyon

The southernmost of the Sierra Nevada national parks, preserving ancient forests of giant sequoia trees, are **SEQUOIA** and **KINGS CANYON**. As you might expect, **Sequoia National Park** contains the thickest concentration – and the biggest specimens – of sequoias to be found anywhere, tending (literally) to overshadow its assortment of meadows, peaks, canyons and caves. **Kings Canyon National Park** has few big trees but compensates with a gaping canyon gored out of the rock by the Kings River as it cascades down from the High Sierra. The few established sights (like the drive-through Auto Log) of both parks are near the main roads, leaving the vast majority of the landscape untrammelled and unspoilt, but well within reach for willing hikers.

Arrival and Information

No **public transport** of any kind serves the parks, but by **car** things are pretty simple: the closest large town is **Visalia**, just under fifty miles distant on Hwy-198, or there's a slightly longer drive using Hwy-180 from Fresno. On payment of a **fee** of $5 per car, or $2 per person for those on foot, you'll be given a copy of *Sequoia Bark*, detailing numerous **guided hikes** and other activities. The two parks are separate but jointly run; **park headquarters** is on ☎565-3341, and **weather** and **road information** on ☎565-3306.

Sequoia National Park

While trees are seldom scarce in Sequoia National Park – where the giant sequoias can't grow there are thick swathes of pine and fir – the scenery varies. Paths lead through forests and meadows; longer treks rise above the treeline to the barren peaks of the High Sierras. Soon after entering the park, Hwy-180 becomes the **Generals' Highway** and climbs swiftly into the dense woods of the aptly labelled **Giant Forest**. **Giant Forest Village**, near the junction with Crescent Meadow Road, makes a good base for explorations. Six miles along a marked trail from the village (or a fifteen-minute walk off Crescent Meadow Road), the granite monolith of **Moro Rock** streaks wildly upward from the green hillside. Views from its remarkably level top can stretch 150 miles. A masonry staircase makes it easy to climb the rock, although the altitude can be a strain.

Continuing along Crescent Meadow Road you pass the **Auto Log,** chiselled flat for motorists to drive on to it, and go under the **Tunnel Log**, which fell across the road in 1937 and had a vehicle-sized hole cut through it. Further on, **Crescent Meadow** is, like other grassy fields in the area, more accurately a marsh, and too wet for the sequoias which form an impressive boundary around. A perimeter trail leads to **Log Meadow**. Hale Tharp, searching for a summer grazing ground for his sheep, was led here by Indians in 1856. He was not only the first white man to see the giant sequoias but the first to live in one – the hollowed-out **Tharp's Log**. Just north of Giant Forest on the Generals' Highway is the biggest sequoia of them all, the three-thousand-year-old, 275ft **General Sherman Tree**. While it's certainly a thrill to be face-to-bark with what is held to be the largest living thing on the planet, its extraordinary dimensions are hard to grasp alongside the almost equally monstrous sequoias around.

Whatever your plans, you should stop at **Lodgepole Village**, at the end of Tokopah Valley four miles from Giant Forest Village, for the geological displays and film-shows at the **visitor centre** (daily 8am–5pm). You can explore the glacial canyon on the **Tokopah Valley Trail**, which leads to the base of Tokopah Falls, beneath the 1600ft **Watchtower** cliff. The top of the Watchtower, with its great view of the valley, are accessible by way of the fatiguing but straightforward seven-mile **Lakes Trail**.

The telephone **area code** for the national parks of the central valley is ☎209.

Kings Canyon National Park

Kings Canyon National Park is wilder and less visited than Sequoia, with a maze-like collection of canyons and a sprinkling of isolated lakes – the perfect environment for careful self-guided exploration. To reach the canyon proper, you have to pass through **Grant Grove**, where there's a useful **visitor centre** (daily 8am–5pm) and the General Grant and Robert E Lee giant sequoias, as well as the massive stump of another which was taken to the 1875 World's Fair in Philadelphia to convince cynical easterners that such enormous trees really existed. A mile from Grant Grove, the **Big Stump Area** is named after the big stumps which litter the place – remnants from the first logging of sequoias carried out during the 1880s. A mile-long nature trail leads through this scene of devastation. It's hardly an enjoyable experience, even if you can spot the ageing remains of flumes used to transport logs to the valley.

Kings Canyon Highway, Hwy-180, descends from Grant Grove into the steep-sided Kings Canyon, cut by the furious gushings of various forks of the Kings River. Whether or not this is the deepest canyon in the US, as some would have it, its wall sections of granite and gleaming blue marble and the yellow pock-marks of yucca plants are magnificent. It's extremely perilous to wade into the river: people have been swept away even when paddling close to the bank in a seemingly placid section.

Once into the National Park proper, the canyon sheds its V-shape and gains a floor. **Cedar Grove Village** here is named for its proliferation of incense cedars. There's a **ranger station** across the river (Mon–Thurs 7am–3pm, Fri & Sat 7am–5pm). Apart from the scenery, you should look out for the **flowers**: Leopard lilies, shooting stars, violets, lupines and others, and a variety of birdlife. The longer hikes through the creeks, many seven or eight miles long, are fairly strenuous. An easy alternative, however, is to pootle around the beckoning green carpet of **Zumwalt Meadow**, four miles from Cedar Grove Village and a short walk from the road, beneath the forbidding grey walls of Grand Sentinel and North Dome.

Just a mile further, Kings Canyon Road comes to an end at **Copper Creek**. Thirty years ago it was sensibly decided not to allow vehicles to penetrate further. Instead the multitude of canyons and peaks which constitute the Kings River Sierra are networked by **hiking paths**, almost all best enjoyed armed with a tent and some provisions.

Accommodation and Eating in the Parks

The cheapest **rooms** are in the motels near the park entrances; *Snowline Lodge*, on Hwy-180 (☎336-2300), and the *Badger Creek Ranch Resort*, beside Hwy-245 (☎337-2340), both cost around $50. Inside the parks, all facilities are managed by *Guest Services Inc* (☎561-3314), with cabins at Giant Forest Village, Grant Grove and Cedar Grove. Space is at a premium during the high season (May–Oct), but you can usually pick up cancellations on the day. Summer prices range from $28 for basic cabins, to $97 for a deluxe version. In winter the cheaper cabins are too cold; a mid-range one costs around $35.

Recorded **camping** information for both parks is on ☎565-3351. In **Sequoia**, the busiest campground is *Lodgepole* (☎565-3338; bookable through *MISTIX*); Mineral King offers the basic *Atwell Mill* and *Cold Springs*. In **Kings Canyon**, the *Sunset*, *Azalea* and *Crystal Springs* campgrounds are all close to Grant Grove, and *Canyon View*, *Moraine*, *Sheep Creek* and *Sentinel* are dotted around Cedar Grove. At artificial Hume Lake, five miles north of Grant Grove, there's the large *Princess* campground. For **backcountry** camping, get a free permit from a visitor centre or ranger station.

There are **food** markets and cafeterias in the various villages, but the only fully fledged **restaurant** is *Giant Forest Lodge Dining Room* at Giant Forest Village. which provides a fitting culinary reward for a hard day's hiking, though you'll easily get through $20.

The Sierra National Forest

The entire gaping tract of land between Kings Canyon and Yosemite is taken up by the less-visited **SIERRA NATIONAL FOREST**. If you want to hike and camp in complete solitude, this is the place to do it. But don't try lone exploration without thorough planning, and don't expect a convenient bus to pick you up when you're tired. Public transport is virtually non-existent. For practical information in advance call in at the **forest information office**, 1130 O Street, in **Fresno** (Mon–Fri 8.30am–4pm; ☎487-5155).

Of the forest's two main regions, the **Pineridge** district, forty miles east from Fresno using Hwy-168, is the best for adventurous hiking. The most isolated alpine landscapes are around Kaiser Pass, where the campgrounds are all free, and there are rooms at the *Vermillion Valley Resort* close to Edison Lake. The sheer challenge posed by the rugged, unspoilt terrain of the adjoining **John Muir Wilderness**, with some of the starkest peaks and lushest alpine meadows of the High Sierra, can make the national parks look like holiday camps. Buses run to the trailheads from the resort; if you want to do some serious hiking, or even just spend the night camped out under the stars, you need a free permit from the **ranger station** (daily 7.30am–5pm, ☎841-3311) along Hwy-168, a mile south of Shaver Lake. Bad weather can strike even in late spring or early autumn, and the road and trails are often closed.

Further north, pine-fringed **Bass Lake** in the **Mariposa** district, just off Hwy-41 between Fresno and Yosemite, is the biggest tourist attraction in the forest. A stamping ground for Hell's Angels in the Sixties, it's now simply a good base for hiking and camping; you can get details from the **Mariposa Ranger District Office** in **Oakhurst** seven miles south (daily 8am–4.30pm; ☎683-4665). As an alternative to the fully equipped **campgrounds** around the lake, for which reservations are essential in summer (made via *MISTIX*), four-berth rooms at *Ducey's Bass Lake Lodge* on road 342 on its northern side (☎642-3131), or *Miller's Landing* on road 222 to the south (☎642-3633), cost as little as $30. Again, booking ahead is vital.

Yosemite National Park

More gushing adjectives have been thrown at **YOSEMITE NATIONAL PARK** than at any other part of California. However excessive the hyperbole may seem, the instant you turn the corner which reveals **Yosemite Valley** you realise it's actually an understatement – this is one of the world's most dramatic geological spectacles. Just seven miles long and at most one mile across, it's walled by near-vertical mile-high cliffs, streaked by cascading waterfalls and topped by domes and pinnacles which form a jagged silhouette against the sky. At ground level, grassy meadows are framed by oak, cedar and fir trees; deer, coyotes, and even black bears are not uncommon. Tourists are even more common, but the park is big enough to endure the crowds: you can visit at any time of year, even in winter when the waterfalls turn to ice and the trails are blocked by snow, and out of high summer the valley itself is rarely crammed.

Yosemite Valley was created by glaciers gouging through the canyon of the Merced River; the ice scraped away the softer granite but only scarred the harder sections, which became the present cliffs. The lake which formed when the glaciers melted eventually silted up to create the present valley floor. Native Americans lived here in comparative peace until the mid-nineteenth century, when the threatening approach of Gold Rush settlers led them to launch raiding parties. In 1851 Major James Savage's Mariposa Battalion trailed the Indians into the foothills and beyond, becoming the first whites to set foot in Yosemite Valley, and the Indians were soon moved out to make way for farmers, foresters and tourists. In 1864 Yosemite became the first State Park in the country.

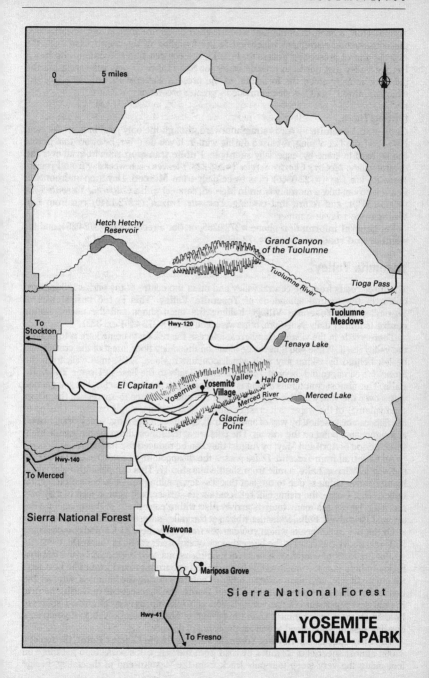

0   5 miles

Hetch Hetchy
Reservoir

Grand Canyon
of the Tuolumne

Tuolumne River

Tioga Pass

To
Stockton

Hwy-120

Tuolumne
Meadows

Tenaya Lake

El Capitan▲

Yosemite

Valley

Yosemite
Village

▲ Half Dome

Merced River

Merced Lake

▲Glacier
Point

Hwy-140

To Merced

Sierra National Forest

Wawona

●Mariposa Grove

Sierra National Forest

Hwy-41

↓To Fresno

YOSEMITE
NATIONAL PARK

John Muir, a Scottish immigrant who travelled the entire area on foot, spearheaded the conservation movement which led to the founding of the *Sierra Club*, with the express aim of preserving Yosemite. In 1913, the construction of a dam in the Hetch Hetchy Valley just north, to provide water for San Francisco, was a setback; but the publicity actually aided the formation of the present National Park Service in 1916, which promised – and has since provided – greater protection.

Getting There

Getting to Yosemite by car is straightforward, though the only road in from the east, Hwy-120 from Lee Vining, is closed during winter. If you do drive, be aware that **petrol** can be hard to come by, especially after 6pm. **Public transport** runs from all over the central valley. *McCoy's Charter Service* (☎268-2237) leaves each weekday from **Fresno**; *Yosemite Via Bus* (☎722-0366) runs twice daily from **Merced**. Day-trippers from **San Francisco** can take a morning **train** to Merced, connect with a *California Yosemite Tour* (☎383-15630), and return that evening. *Yosemite Transit* (☎372-1240) run from **Lee Vining** twice a day in summer.

For **general information** phone ☎372-0265, or (for a recording) ☎372-0264; and for **weather and road conditions** ☎372-4605.

Yosemite Valley

The three roads from the central valley end up in the centre of the park's 1200 square miles, in the natural splendour of **Yosemite Valley**. This is the busiest part of Yosemite, with **Yosemite Village** holding the main shops and the useful **visitor centre** (summer daily 9am–6pm, otherwise 9am–5pm; ☎372-4461 ext 333).

There's little in the village of any great interest; the reason to come here is to explore the valley itself. While you'll never be alone on the valley floor, most of the crowds can be left behind by taking any path which contains a slope. A 3½-mile walk from the *Sunnyside* campground, behind *Yosemite Lodge*, leads to the base of **Upper Yosemite Falls**. This almost continuous ascent is very sapping on the leg muscles, but you get fine views over the valley on the way up, and, at the end, a chance to appreciate the power (and volume) of the water as it crashes almost 1500 feet in a single cascade. The top of the falls can be reached by way of another trail, about six miles long, which branches off at a signposted point on the way up. The falls are at their most dramatic during the melt-water period of April and May; by August they can be reduced to a trickle.

An easy trail from *Yosemite Lodge* passes the disappointing Lower Yosemite Falls on the way to **Mirror Lake**, a mile from shuttle bus stop 17. This compellingly calm lake – its meditative stillness due to the fact that it's slowly silting up – lies beneath the great bulk of Half Dome, the rising cliff reflected on its surface, and is best seen in the early morning, before too many tourists arrive. Also within easy reach of the village are the sensual **Bridalveil Falls**, a slender ribbon at the valley's western end.

Of the two major peaks which you can see from the valley, **El Capitan**, rising some 3500 feet above the floor, is the biggest piece of exposed granite in the world, twice the size of the Rock of Gibraltar. A sense of its dimensions can be gleaned by the fact that rock-climbers fast become invisible to the naked eye from ground level. The best time for attempting an assault is early summer or autumn; during the height of summer the heat of the rock face can reach 100°F. **Half Dome**, the sheerest cliff in North America, is only seven percent off the vertical. You can hike up by way of a steel staircase hooked on to its curving back from the far end of Little Yosemite Valley; if you plan a one-day assault, you'll need to start at the crack of dawn.

The most spectacular views of Yosemite Valley are from **Glacier Point**, the top of a 3200ft almost sheer cliff, 32 miles by road from the valley. It's possible to get there on foot using the very steep four-mile track from the western end of the valley, beside

Hwy-41, though the lazy prefer to take the bus up (details below) and the trail down. The valley floor lies directly beneath the viewing point, and there are tremendous views across to Half Dome and the distant snow-capped summits of the High Sierra.

Practicalities

Everything commercial in Yosemite is run by the *Yosemite Park and Curry Company* (☎252-4848); prices are uniformly higher than outside the park, but not unaffordable. Of the **hotels** in the valley, *Yosemite Lodge* has some cabins for under $30 out of season, $40 in summer; rooms are much dearer, starting around $70, but you may get substantial reductions by waiting for cancellations. *Curry Village*, a mile from Yosemite Village, has similarly priced rooms but also offers fixed tents and cabins from $25.

Camping in the valley is only permitted in campgrounds, such as *Sunnyside Walk-In*, just west of *Yosemite Lodge*, which is popular with rock-climbers and has a bohemian reputation, and the calmer *Backpacker's Camp*. You must book ahead in summer, via *Ticketron* (☎1-800/452-1111); general information is on ☎372-4845.

As for **food**, there are stores, diners and snack bars in Yosemite Village, the best of which is *Degnan's Deli*, where massive sandwiches cost around $4. The *Mountain Room Broiler* at *Yosemite Lodge* is good but fairly pricey, while the baronial *Ahwahnee Dining Room* (☎372-1489) has the best (and most expensive) food in Yosemite. *Yosemite Lodge* also has the valley's liveliest **bar**.

Free **shuttle buses** loop around the valley in summer (7.30am–10pm). **Cars** spoil everybody's fun; if you drive in for the day, park at Curry Village. A number of **bicycle paths** cross the valley floor but **bike rental** is limited to outlets at *Yosemite Lodge* and *Curry Village*. There are also **guided tours** (☎372-1240), **hikes**, and **horseback trips**.

Outside the Valley

The **Mariposa Grove**, three miles east of Hwy-41 on a small road which cuts off just past the park's southern entrance, is the biggest and best of Yosemite's groves of **giant sequoia** trees. To get to the towering growths, walk the 2½-mile loop trail from the carpark at the end of the road, which is also served by a free tram from the entrance. The most renowned of the grouping, well marked along the route, is the **Grizzly Giant**, thought to be 2700 years old.

On the eastern edge of the park, the alpine **Tuolumne Meadows** have an atmosphere quite different from the valley; here, at 8500 feet, you almost seem to be level with the tops of the surrounding snow-covered mountains. The air always has a fresh, crisp bite, and early summer reveals a plethora of colourful wild blossoms. It's a better starting point than the valley for backcountry hiking into the High Sierras, where seven hundred-odd miles of trails, both long and short, criss-cross their way along the Sierra Nevada ridge. To use any of the primitive **backcountry campgrounds**, you must get a **wilderness permit**, available by post from the Wilderness Office, Box 577, Yosemite National Park, CA 95389, or from the nearest visitor centre no more than 24 hours in advance. Canvas **tent cabins** are available in Tuolomne in summer only for $35.

The High Sierra and Owens Valley

The towering **eastern** peaks of the **High Sierra** drop abruptly to the empty landscape of the **Owens Valley** far below. Almost the entire range is wilderness: well-maintained roads lead to trailheads at over ten thousand feet, providing access to the stark terrain of spires, glaciers and clear mountain lakes. US-395 is the lifeline of the area, travelled daily by *Greyhound* and with plenty of cheap motels. *Backpackers Shuttle Service* carry passengers from the Owens Valley to trailheads in the Eastern Sierra ($10 per person,

$20 minimum per trip; ☎873-4453), and many local outfits organise rock-climbing, ski-touring and cycling expeditions to get you to the great outdoors.

> The telephone **area code** for the High Sierra and Owens Valley is ☎619.

Mount Whitney

Rising out of the northern Mojave Desert, the Sierra Nevada Mountains announce themselves with a bang two hundred miles north of Los Angeles at 14,494ft **MOUNT WHITNEY**, the highest point in the continental US. A silver-grey knifelike ridge of pinnacles forms a nearly sheer wall of granite, dominating the small roadside town of **Lone Pine** eleven thousand feet below. **Motels** here include *Trails Motel* at 633 S Main Street (☎876-5555), and the *Frontier Best Western* (☎1-800/231-4731), 1008 S Main Street – both with doubles from $38. The *Sportsman Café* at 206 S Main Street and the *High Sierra Inn* across the road are decent places to eat. For more information, contact the **Chamber of Commerce** at 126 S Main Street (Mon–Sat 9am–5pm; ☎876-4444).

Many early Westerns, and the epic *Gunga Din*, were filmed in the **Alabama Hills** to the west, a rugged expanse of bizarrely eroded sedimentary rock. Some of the oddest formations are linked by the **Picture Rocks Circle**, a dirt road that loops around from Whitney Portal Road, passing rocks shaped like bullfrogs, walruses and baboons. There is a free **campground** at Tuttle Creek, on the south edge of the hills.

Two thousand or so eager mountaineers climb to the summit of Mount Whitney each summer, a strenuous 21-mile round-trip made especially difficult by the lack of oxygen. The ascent starts at dawn from the non-reservable **campground** (reachable on a shuttle bus) at the end of twisting Whitney Portal Road, which rises steeply from US-395. The trail cuts up past alpine lakes to boulder-strewn Trail Crest Pass, the southern end of the 220-mile John Muir Trail to Yosemite, then climbs along the top of vertical cliffs. At the rounded hump of the summit itself, a stone cabin serves as an emergency shelter.

Big Pine and the White Mountains

Nearly fifty miles north, hikes lead from the end of Glacier Lodge Road, ten miles west of nondescript **BIG PINE**, up to the **Palisades Glacier**, which is the southernmost glacier in the northern hemisphere. Along the opposite wall of the five-mile-wide Owens Valley, the bald, dry and inhospitable **White Mountains** are home to the gnarled **Bristlecone Pines**, the oldest living things on earth. Standing on the lower slopes, and often covered in snow until mid-June, some of these gnarled trees have been alive for over four thousand years. Battered and beaten by the harsh environment into contorted but beautiful shapes, even when dead they hang on without decaying for upwards of another thousand-odd years, slowly being eroded by wind-driven ice and sand.

Schulmann Grove, named for Dr Edmund Schulmann who discovered the trees in the mid-Fifties, is the most accessible collection, at the end of the paved road that twists up from Hwy-168. The mile-long Discovery Trail passes by some photogenic examples; another, longer, trail loops past the oldest tree, the 4700-year-old Methuselah. **Patriarch Grove**, eleven miles further, along a dusty dirt road that gives spectacular views of the Sierra Nevada to the west and the Great Basin ranges of the deserts to the east, contains the largest Bristlecone Pine, also over four thousand years old.

A couple of **motels** can be found along US-395 in Big Pine – the *Big Pine Motel* (☎938-2282) and the *Starlight Motel* (☎938-2011) both have doubles from $32.

The Bishop Area

BISHOP, to a Californian, means outdoor pursuits. The largest town (population 3500) in the Owens Valley, it's an excellent base from which to explore the mountains, and if you've ever wanted to try rock-climbing, hang-gliding, cross-country skiing or even fly-fishing, there's no better place to be. It's also easy to get to; besides *Greyhound* buses, two scheduled airlines serve the city daily from Los Angeles: *Alpha Air* (☎1-800/421-9353) and *Glazov Airlines* (☎1-800/456-4500), both for around $60. Innumerable motels and cheap restaurants can be found within a block of US-395 (Main Street in the town): the *Bishop Elms Motel*, 233 E Elm Street (☎873-8118); the *El Rancho Motel*, 274 W Lagoon Street (☎872-9251); and the *Thunderbird Motel*, 190 W Pine Street (☎873-4215), all have doubles from $35 a night. The **tourist office** at 690 N Main Street (☎873-8405) can provide details of the many **adventure travel specialists** based in town.

For information on **hiking** and **camping**, contact the ranger station at 798 N Main Street (☎873-4207). One of the most appealing destinations is the **Devil's Postpile National Monument**, some twenty-five miles northwest beyond the ski resort of **Mammoth Lakes**. A collection of slender, blue-grey basaltic columns, some as tall as sixty feet, the Postpile was formed as lava from a volcanic eruption cooled and fractured into multisided forms. The highlight of the monument is **Rainbow Falls**, reached by a two-mile hike along the San Joaquin River.

Mono Lake and Lee Vining

The blue expanse of **Mono Lake** sits in the midst of a volcanic, desert tableland at the north end of the valley. It looks like a science-fiction landscape, with two large islands, one bright white, the other shiny black, standing surrounded by salty, alkaline water. Strange sandcastle-like **tufa** formations have been exposed over the fifty years since the City of Los Angeles extended an aqueduct into the Mono Basin through an eleven-mile tunnel, dropping the **water level** by over forty feet and creating the biggest environmental controversy in California. Mono Lake is the primary nesting ground for the state's seagull population – twenty percent of the world total – and a prime stopover point for thousands of migratory geese, ducks and swans. As the levels drop, the islands in the middle of the lake, where the seagulls lay their eggs, become peninsulas, and the colonies fall prey to coyotes and other mainland predators. The landlocked water is becoming increasingly alkaline, threatening its unique eco-system.

For more details about Mono Lake and the fight for its survival, stop by the **visitor centre** (daily 9am–9pm), in the small town of **LEE VINING** on US-395. *Greyhound* buses from the south stop daily here at 2am, while the bus from Reno in the north comes in at the more reasonable 11am. There are a couple of **motels** along US-395: *El Mono Motel* (☎647-6310) and *Murphey's* (☎647-6316) both have doubles from $35. **Eat** at *Nicely's Coffee Shop*, a Fifties vinyl palace that opens at 6am; in summer, *Yosemite Transit* buses leave from the carpark at noon and 4pm for the trip into the park, costing $20. There are a number of **campgrounds** along Lee Vining Creek off the Tioga Pass Road, Hwy-120; stop by the **ranger station** (☎647-6525) one mile west of Lee Vining, for details, and to pick up wilderness permits for backcountry camping.

Northeast of Lee Vining, in a remote, high desert valley, stands a well-preserved and evocative relic of the gold-mining 1870s. **BODIE** is perhaps the best **ghost town** in the US, far enough out of the way to be relatively tourist-free. With thirty saloons and dancehalls and a population of ten thousand, it was once the raunchiest and most lawless mining camp in the west; over 150 wooden buildings survive in a state of arrested decay around the intact town centre, littered with old bottles and bits of machinery and old stagecoaches. The ruins of the mines themselves, in the hills east of town, are unfortunately off-limits to visitors due to their dangerously rundown state.

SAN FRANCISCO

SAN FRANCISCO proper occupies just 48 hilly square miles at the tip of a slender peninsula, almost perfectly centred along the California coast. Arguably the most beautiful, certainly the most liberal city in the US, it remains true to itself: a funky, individualistic, surprisingly small city whose people pride themselves on being the cultured counterparts to their cousins in LA – the last bastion of civilisation on the lunatic fringe of America. It's a compact and approachable place, where downtown streets rise on impossible gradients to reveal stunning views of the city, the bay and beyond, and blanket fogs roll in unexpectedly to envelop the city in mist. This is not the California of monotonous blue skies and slothful warmth – the temperatures rarely exceed the seventies, and even during summer can drop much lower.

The original inhabitants of this area, the **Ohlone Indians**, were all but wiped out within a few years of the establishment in 1776 of the **Mission Dolores**, the sixth in the chain of Spanish Catholic missions that ran the length of California. Two years after the Americans replaced the Mexicans in 1846, the discovery of gold in the Sierra foothills precipitated the riproaring **Gold Rush**. Within a year fifty thousand pioneers had travelled west, turning San Francisco from a muddy village into a thriving supply centre and transit town. By the time the **Transcontinental Railroad** was completed in 1869, San Francisco was a lawless, rowdy boomtown of bordellos and drinking dens.

Though a massive earthquake, followed by three days of fire, wiped out most of the city in 1906, recovery was rapid. In the decades which followed, writers like Dashiell Hammett and Jack London lived and worked here, as did Diego Rivera and other WPA-sponsored artists. Many of the city's landmarks, including Coit Tower and both the Golden Gate and Bay bridges, were built in the 1920s and 1930s. By World War II San Francisco had been eclipsed by Los Angeles as the main West Coast city, but it achieved a new cultural eminence with the emergence of the Beats in the Fifties and the hippy era of the Sixties, when the fusion of music, protest, rebellion and, of course, drugs pioneered in the Haight-Ashbury district. Traces of drop-out values linger some twenty-five years after 1967's "Summer of Love".

San Francisco was rocked once again by the earthquake of October 1989; as soon as the casualties had been taken care of and before electricity was restored, a party atmosphere took hold as people barbecued, stuck beers in ice boxes and rounded up neighbours in a show of community spirit and resolve in the face of disaster.

In an increasingly conservative America, San Francisco's reputation as a liberal oasis continues to grow – the city government's stance of offering support to soldiers unwilling to fight in the January 1991 conflict in Kuwait attracted widespread criticism elsewhere. As gay capital of the world it is handling a massive AIDS crisis with intelligence and dignity. Freedom is the key word, but with responsibility, and for all its failings – the level of homelessness, for example, is among the highest in the US – San Francisco remains one of the least prejudiced and most proudly distinct cities on earth.

Arrival and Information

All international and most domestic flights arrive at **San Francisco International Airport** (SFO), about fifteen miles south of the city. *San Mateo County Transit* (*SamTrans*) **buses** ($1.25) leave every half hour from the lower level of the airport; the #7F express takes around twenty-five minutes to reach the Transbay Terminal downtown, while the slower #7B stops everywhere and takes nearly an hour. On both, you're only allowed as much luggage as you can carry on your lap. The *San Francisco Airporter* bus ($4) picks up outside each baggage claim area every fifteen minutes and travels to the downtown hotels. The blue **Supershuttle** and the **Yellow Airport Shuttle** minibuses depart every five minutes from the upper level of the loop road and take passengers to any city-centre destination for around $12 a head. Be ruthless – competition for these is fierce and queues nonexistent. **Taxis** from the airport cost a hefty $30 to $35 (plus tip) for any downtown location, more for East Bay and Marin County. If you're planning to drive, the usual clutch of **car rental** agencies operate free shuttle buses to their depots.

Several domestic airlines (*America West, Southwest* and *Continental* are three) fly into **Oakland International Airport** (OAK; see p.809 for details), across the bay. This is actually closer to downtown San Francisco than SFO, and is efficiently connected with the city by the $2 *AirBART* shuttle bus from the Coliseum *BART* station.

Buses, Trains and Cycling
The San Francisco **Greyhound** terminal (☎433-1500) is on Seventh Street just south of Market Street, near the Civic Center. **Green Tortoise** buses (☎285-2441) disembark behind the Transbay Terminal on First and Natoma streets, also south of Market Street, near the Embarcadero *BART* station. **Amtrak** trains stop across the bay in **Richmond** (where you can transfer easily to *BART*) and continue to Oakland, from where a free shuttle bus will take you across the Bay Bridge to the Transbay Terminal.

Information
The **San Francisco Visitor Information Center**, in Hallidie Plaza at the end of the cable car line on Market Street (Mon–Sat 9am–5pm, Sun 9am–3pm; ☎974-6900), has free maps of the city and the Bay Area, and can help with lodging and travel plans.

> The telephone **area code** for San Francisco is ☎415;
> for the East Bay it's ☎510, and for San Jose it's ☎408.

Getting Around the City

Getting around San Francisco is simple. The city centre is small enough to walk around, and if the hills get a bit too breathtaking, there are always the famous cable cars (see p.793). Public transport is cheap, efficient and easy to use, both in the city and the surrounding Bay Area. Cycling and – outside the city centre – mountain biking are good options too, though you'll need stout legs to tackle the hills.

Muni
The city's public transport is run by the **San Francisco Municipal Railway**, or *Muni* (☎673-6864). A comprehensive network of **buses**, **trolley buses** and **cable cars** run up and over the city's hills, while the underground **trains** become **streetcars** when they emerge from the downtown metro system to split off and serve the suburbs. On buses and trains the flat **fare** (correct change only) is 85¢, $2 on cable cars; with each ticket you buy, ask for a **free transfer** – good for another two rides on a train or bus, and a fifty percent reduction on cable cars if used within ninety minutes.

A **24-hour pass** ($6), or a **three-day pass** ($10), good on all *Muni* services, can be bought from most Market Street stations. If you're staying more than a week or so, a **Fast Pass** costs $28 and is valid for unlimited travel on the *Muni* system and *BART* stations (see below) within the city limits for a full calendar month.

Muni trains run **throughout the night** on a limited service, except those on the M-Ocean View line, which stop around midnight. Buses run all night, but services are greatly reduced after midnight. For **more information** pick up the handy *Muni* map ($1.50) from the Visitor Information Center or bookshops.

SAN FRANCISCO PUBLIC TRANSPORT

Useful Bus Routes

#5 From the Transbay Terminal, west alongside Golden Gate Park to the ocean.

#7 From the Ferry Terminal (Market St) along Haight St to the ocean.

#15 From Third St (SoMa) to Pier 39, Fisherman's Wharf, via the Financial District and North Beach.

#20 (Golden Gate Transit) From Civic Center to the Golden Gate Bridge.

#38 from Geary St via Civic Center, west to the ocean along Geary Blvd.

#30 From the CalTrain depot in SoMa, north to Fisherman's Wharf via North Beach and the Financial District.

Muni Train Lines

Muni J-CHURCH LINE From downtown to Mission and East Castro.

Muni K-INGLESIDE LINE From downtown to Balboa Park.

Muni L-TARAVAL LINE From downtown west to the zoo and Ocean Beach.

Muni M-OCEAN VIEW From downtown west to Ocean Beach.

Muni N-JUDAH LINE From downtown west to Ocean Beach, via the Haight.

Other Transport Services

Various other public transport networks serve San Francisco and the Bay Area. Along Market Street downtown, *Muni* shares the station concourses with **BART**, the *Bay Area Rapid Transit* system, which runs to the East Bay and outer suburbs. The **CalTrain** commuter railway (depot at Fourth and Townsend streets, South of Market, or SoMA) links San Francisco along the Peninsula south to San Jose. **Golden Gate Ferry** boats leave from the Embarcadero, crossing the bay past Alcatraz to Marin County.

Taxis do not ply the streets. Phoning around, try *Veterans* (☎552-1300) or *Yellowcab* (☎626-2345). Fares are roughly $3 for the first mile, $1.50 per mile thereafter.

If you fancy **cycling**, *Park Cyclery* at 1865 Haight Street (☎221-3777) have touring bikes for $18 per day, and mountain bikes for $25 per day; weekly rates from $75.

Organised Tours

One way to orientate yourself is an **organised tour**. *Gray Line Tours* (☎558-9400), for example, whip you around the city in three fairly tedious hours for around $25 a head. Considerably more exciting are the two-hour **bay cruises** operated by the *Blue & Gold Fleet* (☎781-7877) from piers 39 and 40 – though at $17 a throw these don't come cheap either, and in any case everything may be shrouded in fog.

The best of the **walking tours** include *AM Walks* (1433 Clay St; $10; ☎928-5965), a witty, anecdotal early-morning trek; *Cruisin' the Castro* (375 Lexington St; $25; ☎550-8110), a fascinating tour of the gay community; and *Helen's Walk Tour* ($20; ☎524-4544), which leads you around the murals of the Mission.

The City

San Francisco is a city of hills. Becoming familiar with these is not just a good way to get your bearings; it will also give you a real insight into the city's class distinctions. As a general rule, geographical elevation means wealth – the higher you live, the better off you are. Commercial square-footage is surprisingly small and mostly confined to the downtown area, and the rest of the city is made up of distinct, primarily residential neighbourhoods, easily explored on foot. Armed with a good map you could plough through most of it in a day, but the best way to get to know San Francisco is to dawdle.

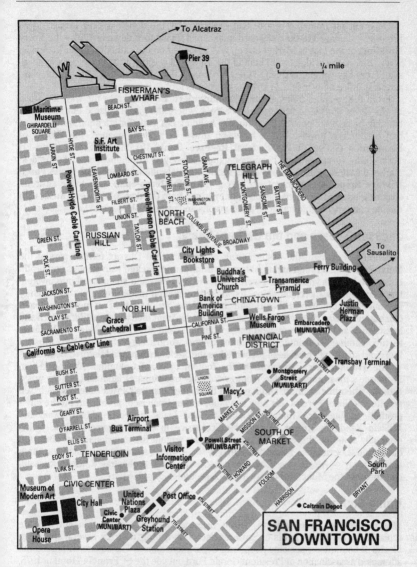

SAN FRANCISCO DOWNTOWN

Downtown: the Financial District

The top right-hand corner of the peninsula, bordered by I-80 to the south, US-101 to the west, and the water, makes up **downtown San Francisco**. North of the city's main artery, **Market Street**, the glass and steel skyscrapers of the **Financial District** have sprung up in the last twenty years to form its only real high-rise district. Sharp-suited workers clog the streets in well-mannered rush-hour droves, racing between their offices and the Montgomery *BART/Muni* station on Market Street.

Once cut off from the rest of San Francisco by the double-decker Embarcadero Freeway – damaged in the 1989 earthquake, and finally torn down in 1991 – the **Ferry Building**, at the foot of Market Street, was modelled on the cathedral tower in Seville, Spain. Before the bridges were built in the Thirties it was the arrival point for fifty thousand cross-bay commuters daily. A few ferries still dock here (see p.790), but the characterless office units inside do little to suggest its former importance.

From the vast and unimaginative **Embarcadero Center** across the way, it's a few blocks down Market to **Montgomery Street**, where the grand pillared entrances and banking halls of the post-1906 earthquake building era jostle for attention with a mixed bag of modern towers. For a hands-on grasp of modern finance, the **World of Economics Gallery** in the **Federal Reserve Bank**, 101 Market Street (Mon–Fri 10am–4pm), is unbeatable: computer games allow you to engineer your own stock-market disasters, while exhibits detail recent scandals and triumphs. The **Wells Fargo History Room**, 420 Montgomery Street (Mon–Fri 10am–5pm), traces the far-from-slick origins of San Francisco's big money, right from the days of the Gold Rush, with mining equipment, gold nuggets, photographs and even an old wagon.

Jackson Square and the Barbary Coast

A century or so ago, the eastern flank of the Financial District formed part of the **Barbary Coast**, a rough and tumble waterfront district packed with saloons and brothels where hapless young males were given *Mickey Finns* and shanghaied into involuntary servitude on merchant ships. Its wicked reputation made it off-limits for military personnel up until World War II, and many of the old dives died an inevitable death. During the 1930s, the Barbary Coast became a low-rent district, attracting writers and artists such as Diego Rivera, who had a studio on Gold Street at the height of his fame as the "communist painter sought after by the world's biggest capitalists". Most of these old structures have been preserved as the **Jackson Square Historic District**.

The **Transamerica Pyramid** at the foot of diagonal Columbus Avenue is San Francisco's most unmistakable (some would say unfortunate) landmark. There was a rumpus when this went up, and it earned the name "Pereira's Prick" after its LA-based architect William Pereira. It's now a symbol of San Francisco, prominent on the city's promotional literature. Rudyard Kipling, Robert Louis Stevenson, Mark Twain and William Randolph Hearst all rented office space in the *Montgomery Block*, which originally stood on this site, and regularly hung around the notorious *Bank Exchange* bar within. Legend also has it that Sun Yat-Sen – whose statue is in Chinatown, three blocks away – wrote the Chinese constitution and orchestrated the successful overthrow of the Manchu Dynasty from his second-floor office here.

Union Square

West of Kearny Street, around **Union Square**, the skyscrapers thin out and are replaced by the bright lights of San Francisco's **shopping district**: several spreading blocks of boutiques, speciality shops and department stores. The square witnessed the attempted assassination of President Gerald Ford outside the **St Francis Hotel** in 1975, and was also the location of Francis Ford Coppola's paranoid film, *The Conversation*, where Gene Hackman spied on strolling lovers. Many of **Dashiell Hammett's** detective stories, such as *The Maltese Falcon*, are set partly in the *St Francis*, in which he worked during the Twenties as a Pinkerton detective .

On Geary Street, on the south side of the square, the optimistically named **Theater District** is a pint-sized Broadway of restaurants, tourist hotels and serious and "adult" theatres – like New York's Broadway or London's Soho, the Theater District of San Francisco shares space with the less rarified institutions of porn and prostitution.

THE CABLE CARS

It was the invention of the **cable car** that made high-society life on San Francisco's hills possible and practical. Since 1873, these little trolleys have been an integral part of life in the city. At their peak, just before the 1906 earthquake, over six hundred cable cars travelled 110 miles of track throughout the city; by 1955, when usage had dwindled, nostalgic citizens voted to preserve the last seventeen miles as a moving historic landmark.

Today there are three lines. Two run from Powell Street to Fisherman's Wharf; the steepest and best climbs Nob Hill along California Street from the Embarcadero. The cars fasten on to a moving two-inch cable which runs beneath the streets, gripping on the ascent then releasing at the top and gliding down the other side. You can see the huge motors which power these cables in the **Cable Car Barn**, at Washington and Mason streets (daily 10am–5pm; free).

On the eastern side of the square, **Maiden Lane** is a chic little urban walkway that before the 1906 earthquake and fire was one of the city's roughest areas, where homicides averaged around ten a month. Nowadays, aside from some prohibitively expensive boutiques, its main feature is San Francisco's only **Frank Lloyd Wright** building, the pricey little **Circle Gallery** that was a try-out for the Guggenheim in New York.

Nob Hill

From Nob Hill, looking down upon the business wards of the city, we can decry a building with a little belfry, and that is the stock exchange, the heart of San Francisco; a great pump we might call it, continually pumping up the savings of the lower quarter to the pockets of the millionaires on the hill.

Robert Louis Stevenson

If the Financial District is representative of new money in the city, the posh hotels and masonic institutions of **Nob Hill**, just above, exemplify San Francisco's old wealth; it is, as Joan Didion wrote, "the symbolic nexus of all old California money and power". Once you've made the stiff climb up (or taken the cable car), there are very few real sights as such, but nosing around is pleasant enough, taking in the aura of luxury, and enjoying the views over the city and beyond.

This area became known as Nob Hill after the robber-baron industrialists who came to live here while running the Central Pacific Railroad. **Grace Cathedral** here is one of the biggest hunks of sham-Gothic architecture in the US. Construction began soon after the 1906 earthquake, but most of it was built, of faintly disguised reinforced concrete, in the early Sixties. The entrance is adorned with faithful replicas of the fifteenth-century Ghiberti doors of the Florence Baptistry.

Chinatown

Twenty-four square blocks of seeming chaos smack in the middle of San Francisco make up **Chinatown**. Dense, noisy, and colourful, the second-largest Chinese community outside Asia is almost entirely autonomous, with its own schools, banks and newspapers. It has its roots in the migration of Chinese labourers to the city after the completion of the Transcontinental Railroad. The city didn't extend much of a welcome: they were met by a tide of vicious racial attacks. Nowadays they have been joined by Vietnamese, Koreans, Thais and Laotians: by day the area seethes with activity, by night it's a blaze of neon. Overcrowding is compounded by a brisk tourist trade; sadly, Chinatown boasts some of the tackiest shops and facades in the city.

Gold ornamented portals and brightly painted balconies sit above the souvenir shops and restaurants of narrow **Grant Avenue**. Plastic Buddhas, floppy hats and chopsticks assault the eye from every doorway. This was once Dupont Street, a wicked ensemble of opium dens, bordellos and gambling huts policed, not to say terrorised, by Tong hatchet men. These days there's little trace of them on the streets, but the Mafia-style mob continues to operate, battling for a slice of the lucrative West Coast drug trade.

Parallel to Grant Avenue, **Stockton Street** is crammed with exotic fish and produce markets, bakeries and spice shops. The **Chinese Historical Society of America** at 17 Waverly Place (daily 9am–4pm; donations) has a small but worthy collection of photographs, paintings and artefacts. Also in Waverly Place, three opulent but skilfully hidden **temples** (numbers 109, 125 and 146), their interiors a riot of black, gold and vermillion, are still in use and open to visitors.

The best of Chinatown's very few **bars** is the dimly lit **Li Po's** at 916 Grant Avenue, a retreat from the confusion of the surrounding streets. Some of the more than one hundred restaurants (see p.801 for recommendations) are historical landmarks in themselves. **Sam Wo's**, at 813 Washington Street, is a cheap and churlish ex-haunt of the Beats where Gary Snyder taught Jack Kerouac to eat with chopsticks and had them both thrown out for his loud and passionate interpretation of Zen poetry.

One block further west, **Portsmouth Square** was the original centre of the city. Sam Brannan announced the discovery of gold here, transforming San Francisco from a sleepy Spanish pueblo into a rowdy frontier city.

North Beach

Resting in the hollow between Russian and Telegraph hills, and split by Columbus Avenue, **North Beach** likes to think of itself as the happening district of San Francisco. It has been a focal point for anyone vaguely alternative ever since the **City Lights Bookstore** opened in 1953. The first paperback bookshop in the US stands amid the flashing neon and sleazy clubs of Columbus Avenue at Broadway, open until midnight seven days a week, and is still owned by poet and novelist Lawrence Ferlinghetti. The **Beat Generation** made this the literary capital of California, achieving overnight notoriety when charges of obscenity were levelled at Allen Ginsberg's poem *Howl* in 1957. It was the hedonistic antics of the Beats, as much as their literary merits, which struck a chord, and North Beach came to symbolise a wild and subversive lifestyle. The roadtrips and riotous partying, the drug-taking and embrace of eastern religion were emulated nationwide; tourists poured into North Beach for "Beatnik Tours".

Next to the bookstore, **Vesuvio's**, an old North Beach bar where the likes of Dylan Thomas and Kerouac would get loaded, remains a haven for the lesser-knowns to pontificate on the state of the arts. At the crossroads of **Columbus and Broadway**, poetry meets porn in a raucous assembly of strip joints, rock venues and drag queens. Most famous, the now-derelict *Condor Club* is where Carol Doda's revealing of her silicone-implanted breasts started the topless waitress phenomenon. Her nipples are immortalised in neon above the door as a tribute to years of mammary fascination.

As you continue north on Columbus Avenue, you enter the heart of the old **Italian neighbourhood**, an enclave of narrow streets and leafy enclosures. Explorations lead to small landmarks like the **Café Trieste**, where the jukebox blasts out opera classics to a heavy-duty art crowd, toying with capuccinos and browsing slim volumes of poetry.

To the west of Columbus, **Russian Hill** was named for Russian sailors who died here in the early 1800s. There's always a tailback of cars waiting to drive down the tight curves of **Lombard Street**. Surrounded by palatial dwellings and herbaceous borders, Lombard is an especially thrilling drive at night, when the tourists leave and the city lights twinkle below. Even if you're without a car the journey up here is worth it for a visit to the **San Francisco Art Institute**, 800 Chestnut Street (Tues–Sat 10am–5pm; free), the oldest art school in the west, where the **Diego Rivera Gallery** has an outstanding mural done by the painter in 1931.

ALCATRAZ

Before the rocky islet of **Alcatraz** became America's most dreaded **high-security prison**, in 1934, it had been home to little more than the odd pelican (*alcatraz* in Spanish). Surrounded by the freezing, impassable water of San Francisco Bay, it made an ideal place to hold the nation's most wanted criminals – men such as Al Capone and Machine Gun Kelly. The conditions were inhumane: inmates were kept in solitary confinement, in cells no larger than five by nine feet, most without light. They were not allowed to eat together, read newspapers, play cards or even talk; relatives could visit for only two hours each month. Escape really was impossible. Nine men managed to get off the rock, but there is no evidence that any of them made it to the mainland.

Due to its massive running costs, the jail finally closed in 1963. The island remained abandoned until 1969, when a group of Native Americans staged an occupation as part of a peaceful attempt to claim the island for their people, citing treaties which designated all federal land not in use as automatically reverting to their ownership. Using all the bureaucratic trickery it could muster, the government finally ousted them in 1971, claiming the operative lighthouse qualified it as active.

At least 750,000 tourists each year take the excellent hour-long, self-guided audio **tours** of the abandoned prison, which include some sharp anecdotal commentary and possibly even the chance to spend a minute (it feels like forever) locked in a darkened cell.

Boats to Alcatraz leave from pier 41 (hourly from 9.15am, last boat back at 6pm; $8.15).

Fisherman's Wharf

San Francisco rarely goes out of its way to please the tourist, but with **Fisherman's Wharf**, and the nearby waterfront district, it makes a rare exception. An inventive use of statistics allows the area to proclaim itself the most-visited tourist attraction in the entire country; in fact this crowded and hideous ensemble of waterfront kitsch and fast-food stands makes a sad and rather misleading introduction to the city. It may be hard to believe, but this was once a genuine fishing port; the few fishing vessels that can still afford the exorbitant mooring charges are usually finished by early morning and get out before the tourists arrive. The shops and bars here are among the most overpriced in the city, and crowd-weary families do little to add to the ambience.

Two-hour **bay cruises** depart several times a day from piers 39 & 40 (see p.790).

The Tenderloin, Civic Center and South of Market

While parts of San Francisco may almost match the image of an urban utopia, the adjoining districts of **the Tenderloin**, **Civic Center** and **South of Market** (aka SoMa) reveal the harsh realities. With not a pretty tree-lined street nor a stunning view to be seen, these areas are a gritty reminder that not everybody has it so easy.

The majestic federal and municipal buildings of **Civic Center**, squashed between the Tenderloin and SoMa, can't help but look strangely out of sync, both with their immediate neighbours and with San Francisco as a whole. Their grand Beaux Arts style is at odds with the quirky wooden architecture of the rest of the city. At night, when the ritzy **War Memorial Opera House** and the giant aquarium-like **Louise M Davies Symphony Hall** swarm with well-heeled patrons of the ballet, opera and symphony hall, it all looks distinctly more impressive than by day.

It was at the huge, green-domed **City Hall**, on the northern edge of the dismal **United Nations Plaza**, that Mayor George Moscone and gay supervisor Harvey Milk were assassinated in 1978 (see below). Major works at the **Museum of Modern Art** (Tues–Sun 10am–4pm; $4.50), directly behind, include paintings by Jackson Pollock, Frida Kahlo and Diego Rivera. Dali, Matisse and Picasso are also represented, if not at their peak, and there's a good selection of twentieth-century photography.

Although traditionally one of San Francisco's least desirable neighbourhoods, **SoMa**, the district south of Market, enjoyed a renaissance in the 1980s. It's reminiscent in a way of New York's SoHo several years ago; many of its abandoned warehouses have been converted into studio spaces and art galleries, and the neighbourhood is now home to artists, musicians, hep-cat entertainers and trendy restaurants. This may well, however, be short-lived: SoMa is a prime piece of central real estate, and it's only a matter of time before the bulldozers move in and the artists move out. Ironically, the most talked-about of the projected buildings is a new home for the Museum of Modern Art.

Above all, SoMa is the nucleus of **clubland**, where the city's wildlife is at its best. Folsom Street was a major gay strip, the centre for much lewder goings-on than the Castro; in recent years the mix has become pretty diverse, though never tame.

The Mission

Low-rent, hip, colourful, and occasionally dangerous, **The Mission** is easily San Francisco's funkiest neighbourhood. A mile or so south of downtown, it is also the warmest, avoiding the summer fogs. As the traditional first stop for immigrants, the Mission serves as a microcosm of the city's history. It takes its name from the old **Mission Dolores**, 16th and Dolores (daily 10am–4pm; $1), the most ancient building to survive the 1906 earthquake and fire. Founded in 1776, it was the sixth in a series of missions built as Spain staked its claim to California; the graves of the Indians it tried to "civilise" can be seen in the cemetery next door, along with those of white pioneers.

The heart of the Mission lies in the restaurants, thrift stores, cafes and bookstores around 16th and Valencia. At the **Levi Stauss & Co** factory at 250 Valencia Street (Mon–Fri 10am–5pm; free), you can see how the world's most famous jeans are made. What really sets the Mission apart from other neighbourhoods, however, are its **murals** – there are over two hundred in all. A brilliant tribute to local hero **Carlos Santana** adorns three buildings where 22nd Street meets South Van Ness, while every possible surface on **Balmy Alley** between Folsom and Harrison off 24th Street (the axis of Latino shopping, with Nicaraguan, Salvadorean, Costa Rican, Mexican and other Latin American stores and restaurants) has been covered with murals depicting the political agonies of Central America.

The Castro

San Francisco's most progressive, if no longer most celebratory, neighbourhood has to be **the Castro**. As the city's avowed Gay Capital, it's the best barometer for the state of the AIDS-devastated gay scene. Some people insist that this is still the wildest place in town, others reckon it's a shadow of its former self; all agree that things are not the same as ten or even five years ago, when a walk down the Castro would have had you gaping at the revelry. Most of the same bars and hangouts still stand, but these days they're host to an altogether different, younger and more conservative breed. A visit to the district (inevitably somewhat voyeuristic) is a must if you're to get any idea of just what San Francisco is all about, though in terms of visible street life the few blocks from Market to 20th Street contain about all there is to see.

Harvey Milk Plaza, by the Castro MUNI station, is dedicated to the assassinated gay supervisor (or councillor), who owned a camera shop in the Castro. The man who shot Milk and Mayor George Moscone, Dan White, was a disgruntled ex-supervisor who resigned in protest at their liberal policies. At the trial, his plea of temporary insanity caused by harmful additives in his fast food – the "Twinkie defence" – won him a sentence of five years' imprisonment for manslaughter. The gay community reacted angrily; the riots that followed were among the most violent San Francisco has ever witnessed, with protesters marching into City Hall, burning police cars as they went.

Before heading down the hill into the heart of the Castro, take a short walk to the headquarters of the **Names Project** at 2362 Market Street (daily 10am–7pm). This sponsored the creation of "**The Quilt**" – a gargantuan blanket in which each panel measures six feet by three feet (the size of a gravesite) and bears the name of a man lost to AIDS. Made by their lovers, friends and families, the panels are stitched together and regularly tour the country and the world; it was spread on the Mall in Washington DC in 1987 and 1988 to dramatise the epidemic. Inside the showroom, you can see thousands of panels stored on shelves, and a few are hung up for display.

The junction of **Castro and 18th Street,** known as the "gayest four corners of the earth", marks the Castro's centre, cluttered with bookshops, clothing stores, cafes and bars. The side streets offer a slightly more exclusive fare of exotic delicatessens, fine wines and fancy florists, and enticingly leafy residential territory.

The zenith of the Castro's social calendar is **Halloween**, when six-foot beauties bedecked in jewels and ballgowns strut noisily through the streets. Those not in their finery strip down and take their carefully worked-on pectorals out for a stroll. The police block certain roads off, and turn a blind eye to minor indiscretions.

Haight Ashbury

The fame of **Haight Ashbury**, two miles west of downtown San Francisco, far outstrips its size. No more than eight blocks in length, centred around the junction of Haight and Ashbury streets, "The Haight" was a respectable Victorian neighbourhood-turned-slum until it transmogrified into the epitome of cool during the Sixties. Since then it's become gentrified, but it retains a collection of radical bookstores, laid-back cafes, record shops and secondhand clothing stores, and a smattering of residents still fly a slightly limp freak flag.

All there is to do in the Haight today is to stroll around what is still one of the best areas in town to **shop**. It shouldn't take more than a couple of hours to update your record collection, dress yourself up and blow money on books and beer. The eastern end of Haight Street, around the crossing with Fillmore Street, is the funkiest corner of the district. Known as the **Lower Haight**, and the centre of black San Francisco for decades, it is now emerging as the major stomping ground for the sort of fashion-victims usually spotted South of Market. Some of the city's best bars and meeting places are here, as well as a growing mix of ethnic restaurants.

THE HIPPIES

During the heady days of the massive "be-in" in Golden Gate Park in 1966 and the so-called "Summer of Love" the following year, no less than 75,000 pilgrims turned the busy little intersection of Haight Ashbury into the mecca of alternative culture.

Where Beat philosophy had emphasised self-indulgence, the **hippies**, on the face of it at least, stressed such concepts as "universal truth" and "cosmic awareness". Characters like Ken Kesey and his Merry Pranksters set a precedent of wild living and challenging authority. The use of drugs was seen as an integral – and positive – part of the movement. **LSD**, especially, which was not then illegal, was claimed as an avant-garde art form, pumped out in private laboratories and distributed by Timothy Leary and his supporters with a prescription – "Turn on, tune in, drop out" – that galvanised a generation into inactivity. Life in the Haight took on a theatrical quality: Pop Art found mass appeal, light shows became legion, and dress flamboyant. The psychedelic music scene, spearheaded by the Grateful Dead, Jefferson Airplane and Janis Joplin, became a genuine force nationwide, and it wasn't long before kids from all over America started turning up in Haight Ashbury for the free food, free drugs . . . and free love. Money became a dirty word, the hip became "heads", and the rest of the world were "straights".

Golden Gate Park

In a city which is hardly short of green space, **Golden Gate Park** stands out as not just the largest, but also the most beautiful, and the safest, of its parks. Spreading three miles or so west from the Haight as far as the Pacific, it was constructed on what was then an area of wild sand dunes, buffeted by the spray from the ocean. Despite the throngs of joggers, polo players, roller-skaters, cyclists and strollers, it never gets over-crowded and you can always find a spot to be alone.

Of the park's several museums, the **M H de Young Museum** (Wed–Sun 10am–5pm; $4, first Wed of each month and Sat mornings free) has a large and diverse range of painting and sculpture, while the **Asian Art Museum** (same times) is drearily exhaustive. The **California Academy of Sciences** (daily 10am–5pm; $4) opposite is a good place to amuse restless children, with its thirty-foot dinosaur skeleton and life-size replicas of humans throughout the ages. Over 14,500 specimens of aquatic life can be viewed in its **Steinhart Aquarium** (daily 10am–5pm; $3); the best are the alligators and other reptiles lurking in a simulated swamp. Slightly to the west is the **Japanese Tea Garden** (daily 8am–6pm; $2 admission charged 9am–5pm), dominated by a massive bronze Buddha. Bridges, footpaths, pools filled with carp, bonsai and cherry trees lend a peaceful feel. Busloads of tourists pour in; by far the best idea is to get here around 8am, for a breakfast of tea and fortune cookies in the tea house.

The Golden Gate Bridge and the Beaches

The orange towers of the **Golden Gate Bridge**, perhaps the best-loved symbol of San Francisco, are visible from almost every high point in the city. The bridge, which spans 4200 feet, had taken only 52 months to design and build when it was opened in 1937. Some quarter of a million people turned up for a sunrise party to celebrate its fiftieth anniversary in 1987; the winds were strong and the bridge buckled, but fortunately did not break. **Driving** across is a real thrill, racing under the towers, while the half-hour **walk** across allows you to take in its enormous size and absorb the views.

The **Fort Point National Historic Site** beneath the bridge gives a good sense of the place as the westernmost outpost of the nation. This brick fortress, built in the 1850s, has a dramatic site, the surf pounding away beneath the great span of the bridge high above – a view made famous by Kim Novak's suicide attempt in Alfred Hitchcock's *Vertigo*. A small **museum** (daily 9am–4pm; free) inside the fort shows some rusty old cannons and firearms.

San Francisco's best waters are to be found at the **beaches** at the tip of the peninsula, but beach culture doesn't exist here the way it does in southern California. Dangerous riptides and very cold water make it impossible to swim with any confidence, and nude sunbathing is about as adventurous as things get.

Inland, **Lincoln Park** is primarily a golf course, though it does have some striking trails. When open, the isolated, white-pillared **California Palace of the Legion of Honor** – it closed for a possible maximum of two years from March 1992 for renovation – is arguably San Francisco's best museum, as well as being its most beautifully located. Until a few years ago, the collection was mainly French and not particularly strong, but several new additions enabled it to emerge as the city's best assemblage of fine art. The **Renaissance** is represented with the works of Titian and El Greco, hung in high-ceilinged, well-lit, spacious marble halls. Some great canvases by Rembrandt and Hals, as well as Rubens' magnificent *Tribute Money*, are highlights of the seventeenth-century Dutch and Flemish collection. The **Impressionist** and **Post-Impressionist** galleries contain works by Courbet, Manet, Monet, Renoir, Degas and Cezanne. One enormous hall is filled with **Rodin** sculptures – bronze, porcelain and stone pieces including *The Athlete, Fugit Amor,* and a small cast of *The Kiss*.

Accommodation

Visitors count as San Francisco's number one business, and the city isn't short on places to stay. The **hotels and motels** have a good reputation for comfort and cleanliness. Hotels in the slightly seedy areas of South of Market and the Tenderloin start at around $25 per night or $100 a week, but don't expect a private bath or even toilet for that amount. In the glitzier areas around Union Square and Nob Hill it's hard to find a place for under $100 a night. As well as the **B&Bs** listed below, you could also contact a specialist agency such as *Bed and Breakfast International* (1181-B Solano Avenue, Albany, CA 94706; ☎525-4569) or *Bed and Breakfast San Francisco* (Box 349, San Francisco, CA 94101; ☎931-3083).

Both *Central Reservations of Hotel Group of America* (☎775-4600) on Market Street at Mason, or *Golden Gate Lodging Reservations* at 1030 Franklin Street (☎771-6915), will, for a small fee, find you a room from around $40 for a single, $50 a double. If all else fails and you've got a car, **motels** are legion along the highways and bigger roads throughout the Bay Area, at a standard rate of $35 to $45 a night. In all cases, bear in mind that all quoted room rates are subject to an **eleven percent room tax**.

Camping isn't really an option in San Francisco itself.

Hostels and YMCAs

European Guest House, 763 Minna St (☎861-6634). Dormitory-style accommodation with communal kitchen. No curfew; safe locker facilities. $11 per night per person.

Globe Hostel, 10 Hallam Place (☎431-0540). Funky, lively hostel with music room, sauna and no curfews. From $15 per person, per night.

International Network Cotel, 1906 Mission St (☎864-3629). Upmarket crash-pad with kitchen facilities. Dorm beds $10 per night. Private rooms $25–30.

San Francisco International Hostel, Building 240, Fort Mason (☎771-7277). On the waterfront between the Golden Gate Bridge and Fisherman's Wharf. Annoying 11pm curfew, but one of the most comfortable hostels around. $9 per person Nov–April; $9.50 May–Oct.

YMCA Central Branch, 220 Golden Gate Ave (☎885-0460). Singles $22, doubles $32.

Youth Hostel Central, 116 Turk St (☎346- 7835). Bit of a flophouse but dorms beds are just $8 per person. Private rooms for $15 (single) and $20 (double).

Hotels, Motels and B&Bs

Adelaide Inn, 5 Isadora Duncan Court, between Geary and Post (☎441-2261). Small downtown hotel with shared bathroom facilities. Doubles from $38.

Ansonia Hotel, 711 Post St (☎673–2670). Charming B&B inn, three blocks from Union Square downtown and cheap to boot, with breakfast and dinner included in the price. Rooms from $35.

Beresford Arms Hotel, 701 Post St (☎673-2600). Luxury B&B in the heart of town. Doubles $75.

Dolores Park Inn, 3641 17th St (☎621-0482). Tiny but elegant pension-style hotel in the Mission. Doubles from $35.

Edward II, 3155 Scott St (☎921-9776). Large and comfortable inn-style Northern Waterfront accommodation with free wine and breakfast. Doubles from $60.

Fairmont Hotel, 950 Mason St (☎772-5000). Most famous of the top-notch hotels, an over-ornate palace with seven restaurants, ten lounges and fantastic views from the rooms. $145–250 per night.

Gates Hotel, 140 Ellis St (☎781-0430). Super-cheap downtown location. Doubles from $35.

Golden City Inn, 1554 Howard St (☎431-9376). Best of the SoMa hotels, far from a doss-house and smack in the middle of the nightlife scene. Unbelievably good value with doubles for $23–28.

Grant Plaza Hotel, 465 Grant Ave (☎434-3883). Newly renovated Chinatown hotel. Doubles $40.

Hyde Plaza Hotel, 835 Hyde St (☎885-2987). Reasonable, no frills Tenderloin hotel with rooms from $25 per night.

The Mansion, 2220 Sacramento St (☎929-9444). Luxurious Victorian mansion up on the hill in Pacific Heights. $90 for a double.

Marina Motel, 2576 Lombard St (☎921-9406). Cheapest of the northern waterfront motels; under $30 per night.

Hotel Mark Twain, 345 Taylor St (☎673-2332). Elegantly decorated colonial-style hotel in the middle of the Theater District. Doubles from $79.

Metro Hotel, 319 Divisadero St (☎861-5364). Homely, clean and cheap. Doubles from $35.

Pensione International, 875 Post St (☎775-3344). Straightforward B&B accommodation downtown; $30 for a small double, with shared bathroom.

Pensione San Francisco, 1668 Market St (☎864-1271). A good base near the Civic Center, with doubles from $40.

La Quinta Inn, 20 Airport Blvd (☎583-2223). Overnight laundry service and a pool make this a comfortable stopover near the airport. Free shuttle service to the airport. Rooms from $65.

The Red Victorian Bed and Breakfast, 1665 Haight St (☎864-1978). Bang in the middle of the Haight Ashbury, a lively B&B that's a real relic of the Sixties. Rooms $45–70.

St Francis, 335 Powell St (☎397-7000). Truly grand hotel with a sumptuous lobby, five restaurants, an elegant bar and disappointingly plain rooms. $145–235.

Stanyan Park Hotel, 750 Stanyan St (☎751-1000). Gorgeous small Victorian hotel in a great setting across from Golden Gate Park, with friendly staff. Doubles for around $80.

Super 8 Lodge, 111 Mitchell Ave, South San Francisco (☎877-0770). Plain, motel-style accommodation near the airport. Free laundry service, breakfast and airport shuttle. Rooms from $53.

UN Plaza Hotel, Seventh and Market St (☎626-4600). Good location just opposite the Civic Center. Glitzy lobby and large, comfy rooms. Doubles from $55.

Washington Square Inn, 1660 Stockton St (☎981-4220). B&B bang on North Beach's lovely main square with rooms from $65.

Gay Men's Accommodation

Casa Loma Hotel, 600 Fillmore St (☎552-7100). Midsized, friendly hotel with sauna, jacuzzi, sundeck and a lively bar. Singles $30, doubles $38.

Gough Hayes Hotel, 417 Gough St (☎431-9131). Informal favourite in San Francisco, no private toilets but 24hr sauna and sundeck. Singles from $25, doubles from $29.

Inn on Castro, 321 Castro St (☎861-0321). Luxury B&B; not cheap, but worth it for the large rooms and good breakfasts. About two minutes' walk from the Castro. Singles $85, doubles $95.

Queen Anne Hotel, 1590 Sutter St (☎262-2663). Very much a gay hotel with overdone decor, full valet service and complimentary afternoon tea and sherry. Rooms $95 and up.

24 Henry, 24 Henry St (☎864-5686). Intimate guest house in a quiet street just off the heart of the Castro. Singles from $40, doubles $55 and up.

Women's Accommodation

Bock's Bed & Breakfast, 1448 Willard St. Secure and friendly hotel for women. Rooms from $35.

The Langtry, 637 Steiner St (☎863-0538). Nineteenth-century mansion. Each room is dedicated to a famous woman in history. Fabulous but not cheap with rooms at $75–200 per night.

Women's Hotel, 642 Jones St (☎775-1711). Comfortable, secure building, unfortunately situated in the unpleasant Tenderloin district. Weekly rates only: singles $100 per week, doubles $120.

Eating

With over four thousand restaurants crammed on to the small peninsula, and scores of bars and cafes which are open all day (and many all night), **eating** in San Francisco is never difficult. As well as ethnic cuisines of all kinds – watch out for **Mexican** food in the Mission, the **Italian** places in North Beach, and of course the **Chinese** restaurants in Chinatown – health-conscious San Francisco also has a wide range of **vegetarian** and **wholefood** restaurants. With the vineyards of Napa and Sonoma Valley on the city's doorstep, quality **wines** have a high profile in most San Francisco restaurants.

Budget Eating: Breakfasts and Burgers

Hamburger Mary's Organic Grill, 1582 Folsom St (☎626-5767). Rowdy restaurant, where punky waiting staff serve up burgers, sandwiches and several vegetarian options for less than $7.

Limbo, 299 Ninth Street (☎255-9945). Super cheap, ultra-trendy. Wholefood and burgers from $4.

Orphan Andy's, 3991 17th St (☎864-9795). Favourite hang-out in the Castro for filling burgers, omelettes and breakfasts.

Sparky's Diner, 240 Church St (☎621-6001). Inexpensive 24hr diner. Burgers, pastas and pizzas and delicious breakfasts, particularly a marvellous eggs florentine. Beer and wine as well.

Spaghetti Western, 576 Haight St (☎864-8461). Best breakfasts in town and a lively Lower-Haight crowd to look at while you chow down.

American, Californian, Italian and French

Bix, 56 Gold St (☎433-6300). Jackson Square restaurant kitted-out like an ocean liner, with torch singer, sax player and pianist. The food is great – straightforward, classic dishes. Book early. Dinner for two will be around $50, but if you're into elegant dining experiences you should definitely go.

Cafe Landais, 489 Third St (☎495-6944). SoMa bistro that's about the cheapest place for French food in town. Popular with connoisseurs on a budget.

Capp's Corner, 1600 Powell St (☎989-2589). Funky, family-style Italian restaurant in North Beach, with a fashionable clientele who line up for the big portions.

Ernie's, 847 Montgomery St (☎397-5969). Not cheap, but a lovely Victorian interior and an *haute cuisine* menu made famous by Hitchcock's *Vertigo* – it figured in some of the crucial scenes.

Il Pollaio, 555 Columbus Ave (☎362-7727). You'll be hard pushed to spend more than $6 for a good blow-out meal in this postage-stamp-sized restaurant.

Little Joe's, 523 Broadway (☎433-4343). Always a queue for tables, but worth it for the cheap, enormous portions of well-cooked food in this North Beach institution.

Tommaso's, 1042 Kearny St (☎398-9696). Always a wait for tables, but worth it to stuff yourself with these delicious pizzas and admire the scruffy decor and classical murals.

Trader Vic's, 20 Cosmo Place (☎776-2232). A San Francisco "society" institution. Ostensibly Polynesian/Indian, but ethnicity stops at the dinner plate. Dining moneyed-American style.

Washington Square Bar & Grill, 1707 Powell St (☎982-8123). Stylish grill – *the* place to see San Francisco society power-lunching. Food cooked to rich and heavy perfection; perhaps $15 per head.

Zuni Cafe, 1658 Market St (☎552-2522). The chic place to be and be seen, with Californian nouvelle cuisine portions as minimal as the elegant decor for around $30 a head with wine.

Asian and Middle Eastern

Bangkok 16, 3214 16th St (☎431-5838). Moderately priced Thai restaurant in the Mission, with a great selection for vegetarians or for meat-eaters they do a mean lamb saté.

Brandy Ho's Original Hunan, 217 Columbus Ave (☎788-7527). Excellent Hunan restaurant.

Celadon, 881 Clay St, Chinatown (☎982-1168). Fancy Cantonese restaurant. Far from bargain-basement food, but worth shelling out for the beautifully presented, fragrant dishes.

China Moon Cafe, 639 Post St (☎775-4789). Cantonese cuisine, excellent cheap dim sum lunches.

Empress of China, 838 Grant Ave (☎434-1345). The poshest Chinese place in town. An incredible selection of dishes, amazing views over North Beach. At least $18 for a main course.

Gaylord, Ghirardelli Square, 900 North Point, Fisherman's Wharf (☎771-8822). The best of San Francisco's very few Indian restaurants. Expect to pay around $15 for a main course.

Mamounia, 441 Balboa St (☎752-6566). Eat Moroccan food with your fingers and pay for it through the nose.

Manora's Thai Cuisine, 1600 Folsom St (☎861-6224). Massively popular, and you may have to wait, but it's worth it for light, spicy and fragrant Thai dishes at around $6 each.

Moshi Moshi, 2092 Third St (☎861-8285). Out-of-the-way gem of a Japanese restaurant in SoMa. Excellent sushi and seafood, moderately priced.

Mun's, 401 Balboa St (☎668-6007). Inexpensive and simple Korean food in the Western Addition.

New Asia, 772 Pacific Ave (☎391-6666). Amazing place for such a cramped neighbourhood. Some of the most authentic dim sum in town.

Silver Moon, 2301 Clement St (☎386-7852). Light Japanese seafood and vegetarian dishes.

Thep Phanom Restaurant, 400 Waller St (☎431-2526). Delicate decor and beautifully prepared Thai dishes in the Lower Haight. Only $7 for a main course, but expect to queue.

Yoshida-Ya, 2909 Webster St (☎346-3431). Genuine sushi bar; kick off your shoes and eat at low tables on futoned floors. Expect to pay around $20 a head, with a few drinks.

Mexican and Hispanic

El Cubane, 1432 Valencia St (☎824-6655). Big portions of Cuban food. Tues–Fri lunches for $4.

El Tapatio, 475 Francisco St (☎981-3018). Not as cheap as the Mission's Mexican restaurants, but the food in this North Beach eatery is notably better – and the margaritas larger.

El Tazumal, 3522 20th St (☎550-0935). Interesting Salvadorean place, small but lively. Tripe, tongue and spicy rice dishes for around $5 for a lunch and up to $9 for a dinner.

Mom's Cooking, 1192 Geneva St (☎586-7000). Small and crowded, on the fringes of the Mission. You may have to queue for the super-cheap fresh Mexican food.

Vegetarian and Wholefood

Amazing Grace, 216 Church St (☎626-6411). Highly rated vegetarian food for around $4 a dish.

Greens, Building A, Fort Mason Center, Fort Mason (☎771-6222). The city's only Zen Buddhist restaurant. Delicious macrobiotic and vegetarian food. Book in advance; $30 for a five-course dinner.

Marty's, 508 Natoma St (☎621-0751). Stuck down a little alley, this isn't the sort of place you'd stumble over, but if you're into macrobiotic food, you should definitely make the effort. Thurs–Sun only.

Nightlife and Entertainment

Compared to many US cities, where you need money and attitude in equal amounts, San Francisco's **nightlife** scene demands little of either. This is no 24-hour city, and the approach to socialising is often surprisingly low-key, with little of the pandering to fads and fashions that goes on in New York or LA. For $30 you can get a decent night out, including cover charge, a few drinks and maybe even a taxi home.

The Sunday *Chronicle*'s "Pink Pages" supplement, along with the free weekly *Bay Guardian* or the *San Francisco Weekly*, are the best sources of **listings**. BASS (☎893-2277) and *Ticketron* (☎392-7469) are the major **ticket** agencies.

Bars

Since its lawless, boomtown days, San Francisco has been a **drinking** town. Even as the rest of California cleans up its act, San Franciscans continue to indulge; the city's bars vary from seedy late-night dives to rooftop piano lounges touting glittering views.

Bouncers Bar, 64 Townsend St. Old waterfront hangout. Free live music and a very earthy crowd.

Brainwash, 1122 Folsom St. Great idea – cafe/bar and laundromat where you can have breakfast and a beer while you do your washing. Popular with the young and novelty-conscious.

Jimmy's West Point, 669 Haight St. The joint is jumping most nights at this black neighbourhood bar, where Philadelphia soul and Motown blare out relentlessly from the jukebox.

Perry's, 1944 Union St. Sophisticated meat-market, featured in Armistead Maupin's *Tales of the City* as the quintessential breeder bar.

The Rat and the Raven, 4054 24th St. Friendly, hard-drinking neighbourhood bar with pool, darts, and one of the best country music jukeboxes in town.

Rockin Robin's, 133 Beale St. Fifties rock and roll, and lots of boys in leather. Mon–Fri only.

Tropical Haight, 582 Haight St. Best decorated (tropical-themed) bar in the district.

The Uptown, 200 Capp St. Best of the Mission's neighbourhood bars, embracing an eclectic crowd who shoot pool, drink like fiends and fall around on the scruffy, leatherette upholstery.

Vesuvio's, 255 Columbus Ave. Legendary North Beach Beat haunt in the Fifties, next to *City Lights Bookstore*. Still caters to an arty but friendly crowd who prop up the bar into the small hours.

Gay and Lesbian Bars

San Francisco's **gay or lesbian bars** are many and varied, ranging from cosy cocktail bars to full no-holds-barred leather-and-chain hangouts. The scene may no longer be quite as wild as its reputation would have you believe, but at its best it can still be hard to beat.

Cafe Flore, 2298 Market St. Very much the in spot before dark. Attractive cafe with leafy outdoor area and no shortage of people sizing each other up.

The Corral, 2140 Market St. Country and western bar with large dance floor and cheerful crowd.

Castro Station, 456 Castro St. Noisy disco bar that packs 'em in even in the middle of the day. Very much the die-hard scene of the Seventies, with a fair number still in leather gear.

Eagle, 12th & Harrison St. Legendary SoMa biker bar. Not for wimps.

Francine's, 4149 18th St. Something of a female biker bar in the Castro – a friendly (if butch) joint with pool tables and the sort of women you'd want on your side if a fight started.

Midnight Sun, 4067 18th St. Young, white boys dressed to the nines and cruising like maniacs in this noisy Castro video bar.

Powerhouse, 1347 Folsom St. Full-on leather boys. Definitely not for the faint-hearted.

Rawhide, 280 Seventh St. If men in chaps are your scene, go no further than this dimly lit SoMa bar/dance club that plays country and western and bluegrass favourites.

Live Music: Rock, Jazz and Folk

San Francisco's **music scene** reflects the character of the city: laid-back, eclectic, and not a little nostalgic. The options for catching live music are wide and the scene is definitely on the up and up, with the city spawning some good young bands. The best of the music press, the free *BAM* (*Bay Area Music*), is available in most record stores, and carries exhaustive listings of events in the city and Bay Area.

Bahia Tropical, 1600 Market St (☎861-8657). Expensive, yuppie hangout and supper club with good Brazilian and samba bands. Cover $7.

Bajone's, 3140 Mission St (☎648-6641). Excellent nightly Latin jazz. Casual, unpretentious and genuine, with an unusual – and refreshing – age mix for San Francisco. $5 cover at weekends.

Full Moon Saloon, 1725 Haight St (☎775-6190). Pot luck – expect anything from reggae and funk to bluegrass. Consistently lively punters and good fun. No cover.

I-Beam, 1748 Haight St (☎668-6023). Haight-Ashbury's most famous venue. No place to see bands on the cheap, although midweek you can generally get in for around $5–10.

Jack's, 1601 Fillmore St (☎567-3227). Small, intimate bar. Jazz and blues nightly. No cover.

Nightbreak, 1821 Haight St (☎221-9008). Slightly shabby, small Haight venue. New wave and goth bands play to a matching crowd. Very dark, very loud, very crowded. A small cover at weekends.

Pasand Lounge, 1875 Union St (☎922-4498). Unusual club where you can come to eat Indian food and listen to very mellow jazz in the comfortable lounge. Open Wed–Sat. They sometimes make a small cover charge.

The Rite Spot Cafe, 2099 Folsom St (☎552-6066). Informal, cafe-style club with jazz and R&B bands. Snacks, drinks and coffee until 1am. Open Mon–Sat, small cover at weekends.

Roland's, 2513 Van Ness Ave (☎567-1063). Classic and Latin jazz in a dark, smoky atmosphere, for serious fans. Open Tues–Sun. Small cover at weekends.

The Saloon, 1232 Grant St (☎397-3751). Always packed, North Beach's best spot for R&B. Free.

The Stone, 412 Broadway (☎391-8282). Solid venue with consistently good billing of rock and new wave bands. Open until 6am Fri and Sat for a very danceable rock disco. Cover around $8.

Tar & Feathers, 2140 Union St (☎563-2612). Young, casual, country and western. The Marina's place to go for a few beers and a singalong when you can't face the singles bars.

The Tonga Room, basement of the *Fairmont Hotel*, 950 Mason St (☎772-5000). A must for fans of the ludicrous or just the very drunk. It's decked out like a Polynesian village, complete with a pond and simulated rain storms, and a grass-skirted band plays terrible jazz and pop covers on a raft in the middle of the water. Worth every penny of the cover charge and outrageously priced cocktails. Cover $4.

Clubbing

Trading on a reputation earned decades ago, the city's **nightclubs** continue to trail vapidly behind those of other large American cities. That said, the compensations are manifold – no queueing for hours, or high cover charges, ridiculously priced drinks and feverish posing. The greatest concentration of clubs is in **SoMa**, especially the area around 11th Street and Folsom.

Caesar's Latin Palace, 3140 Mission St (☎826-1179). A big laugh: relive Seventies disco-mania with Latin, jazz and disco rock. Naff enough to have achieved cult status. $6 cover.

Covered Wagon Saloon, 917 Folsom St (☎974-5906). One of the better SoMa places, especially on Thurs for the *Love Shack* hi-tech psychedelic night, and on Sat for hip-hop. Cover $4–6.

Crystal Pistol, 842 Valencia St (☎695-7887). One of the newer gay men's clubs, enjoying a very healthy patronage. Good dancing and a young, well-turned-out set.

DNA Lounge, 375 11th St (☎626-1409). The music changes nightly, but the young hipsters are the same. Large dance floor downstairs, comfy sofas in the mezzanine. Cover $7. Tues–Sun 9pm–4am.

DV8, 540 Howard St (☎777-1419). Huge, ornate and fashionable, about the only club in town worth dressing up for. High-energy funk and house music. Cover $10. Open Wed–Sat.

El Rio, 3158 Mission St (☎282-3325). Latin, jazz and samba are the speciality here, with live bands on Sunday, dancing to modern funk on Friday, and comedy cabaret on Wednesday in a friendly, anything-goes atmosphere. Open seven nights 3pm–2am, until 6am at weekends. No cover.

The Endup, Harrison and 6th St (☎495-9550). A mostly gay crowd. Good for the hard-core party animal – especially on "wet jockstrap night". Open from 6am Sat until 2am Mon. Small cover.

Esta Noche, 3079 16th Street (☎861-5757). Gay disco-mania Latin-style. Young men and their pursuers dance to a high-energy disco beat reminiscent of the 1970s.

Firehouse 7, 3160 16th St (☎621-1617). Not to be missed; bar/club with a broad cross-section of music styles and clientele. Reggae Wed, live music Fri, house music Sat. $3 cover at weekends.

The New Martini Empire, 1015 Folsom St (☎626-2899). Club with an international bent where you'll be able to hear Brazilian, salsa, Arabic, African and Soca. Open Fri–Sun. Cover $4.

Nightbreak, 1821 Haight St (☎221-9008). Small Haight club where the slogan is "All the funk that's fit to pump" – house, hip-hop and funk most nights, except for Wed when it becomes "Female Trouble", lesbian dance night. Small cover at weekends.

Rapture, 1484 Market St (no phone). Saturday night dance club for women. Tends to draw the younger, well-dressed lipstick-lesbian crowd.

Rock & Bowl, 1855 Haight St (☎752-2366). Try this one for a change – a bowling alley that turns up the music at weekends so that you can dance while you bowl.

The Stud, 399 Ninth St (☎863-6623). An oldie but a goodie. A gay scene mainstay for its energetic, uninhibited dancing and good times. No cover charge.

Townsend, 177 Townsend St (☎974-6020). A must for house fans, this place really cranks up the bass and keeps it blaring. Thurs–Sat. Cover $5.

Classical Music, Opera and Dance

Though the San Francisco arts scene has a reputation for provincialism, this is the only city on the West Coast to boast its own professional **symphony**, **ballet** and **opera** companies. These companies rely entirely on private contributions for their survival and cheap tickets are rare, if not non-existent. Look out also in summer for the **free concerts in Stern Grove** (at 19th Avenue and Sloat Blvd) where the symphony, opera and ballet give open-air performances for ten successive Sundays (starting in June).

Louise M Davies Symphony Hall, 201 Van Ness Ave (☎431-5400). Permanent home of the San Francisco Symphony. A year-round season of classical music and sometimes performances by other, often offbeat musical and touring groups. The least expensive seats go for around $20.

War Memorial Opera House, 401 Van Ness Ave (☎864-3330). The very opulent venue for both the San Francisco Opera Association, whose main thirteen-week season opens with great pomp at the end of September. In general, tickets for the June–July summer season are easier to come by. Expect to pay upwards of $40. The San Francisco Ballet (☎893-2277), which has gone from strength to strength since the appointment of Icelandic Helgi Tomasson as artistic director in 1985, appears here Jan–June.

Theatre

The majority of the **theatres** in downtown's Theater District are not especially innovative, but tickets are reasonably inexpensive – up to $20 a seat – and there's usually good availability. The *STBS* ticket booth in Union Square (Mon–Sat 11am–6pm; ☎433-7717) regularly has last-minute tickets for up to thirty percent off the price.

American Contemporary Theater, *Geary Theater*, 450 Geary St (☎775-5811). Despite the destruction of their theatre in the 1989 earthquake, the Bay Area's leading theatre group have bounced back, staging impressive plays from temporary bases around the city. Phone for current details.

Golden Gate Theater, 1 Taylor St (☎775-8800). San Francisco's most elegant theatre, with marble flooring, rococo ceilings and gilt trimmings. A pity the programme doesn't live up to the surroundings – generally a mainstream diet of Broadway musicals.

Lorraine Hansberry Theater, 25 Taylor St (☎474-8842). Radical young group of black performers. Traditional theatre as well as contemporary political pieces and jazz/blues musical reviews.

Theater on the Square, 450 Post St (☎771-6900). Converted Gothic theatre with drama, musicals, comedy and mainstream theatre pieces. San Francisco's main fringe venue.

The Magic Theater, Fort Mason Center, Building D (☎441-8822). Specialises in contemporary American playwrights and emerging new talent: Sam Shepard premieres his work here.

Theater Artaud, 450 Florida St (☎621-7797). Very modern theatre in a converted warehouse that tackles the obscure and abstract: always something interesting.

Theater Rhinoceros, 2926 16th St (☎861-5079). San Francisco's only uniquely gay theatre group. Lighter, humorous productions as well as those that confront gay issues.

Comedy Clubs

Holy City Zoo, 408 Clement St (☎386 4242). Supreme champion of the alternative circuit, *Holy City* plays host to the best of the genre in a small, funky club. Make an effort to go.

The Improv, 401 Mason St (☎441-7787). The chain store of the comedy world. Some good established talent and up-and-coming acts. Mon is the cheapest and best night to go.

Morty's, 1024 Kearny St (☎986-6678). Old North Beach club that evokes the Lenny Bruce era, even if none of the acts are quite as good as he was.

The Punch Line, 444 Battery St (☎397-7553). Frontrunner of the city's "polished" cabaret venues. Intimate, smoky feel; ideal for downing expensive cocktails and laughing your head off. The club usually hosts the bigger names in the world of stand-up, and is always packed.

Gay and Lesbian San Francisco

San Francisco is still the undoubted gay capital of the world, but the gay scene hasn't had much to celebrate in the last few years and there's been a definite move from the outrageous to the mainstream. The increasing number of gay activists in public office have become more conservative in approach, if not in policy. However, gay parties, parades and street fairs still swing better than most. If you're here in June, you'll coincide with the Gay and Lesbian Film Festival, Gay Pride Week, the Gay Freedom Day Parade and any number of conferences. Come October, the street fairs are in full swing and Halloween still sees some of the most outrageous carrying-on.

The 1980s also saw the flowering of a **lesbian** culture to rival the male 1970s upsurge, and while there still isn't anything like the number of women's bars and clubs that exist for men, they are catching up quickly. You'll find details of gay accommodation, bars and clubs under the relevant headings earlier in this chapter.

The Sentinel, Coming Up, The Bay Area Reporter and *Gay Times* are all free **publications** with listings of events, services, clubs and bars. *On Our Backs* and *Bad Attitude* are of particular use to lesbians. *The Gay Book* is a telephone-cum-resource book available from gay bookshops. The *AIDS Hotline* (☎863-2437) and the *Lesbian/Gay Switchboard* (☎841-6224) provide 24-hour counselling and advice. The *Gay Men's Group*, 450 Stanyan Street (☎750-5661), is good for contacts and advice on places to go.

Women's San Francisco

The flip side of San Francisco's gay revolution has in some women's circles led to a separatist culture, and women's resources and services are sometimes lumped together under the lesbian category. While this may be no bad thing, it can be hard to tell which organisations exist irrespective of sexuality. Don't let this stop you from checking out anything that sounds interesting; nobody is going to refuse you either entry or help if you're not a lesbian – support is given to anybody who needs it.

Contacts and Resources

Bay Area Resource Center, 318 Leavenworth St (☎474-2400). Services, info and clothing.

Rape Crisis Line (☎647-7273). 24hr switchboard.

Women's Building, 3543 18th St (☎431-1180). Central stop in the Mission for women's art and political events. A very good place to get information also – the women who staff the building are happy to deal with the most obscure of enquiries. Don't be afraid to ask.

Women's Health Center No.1, 3850 17th St (☎558-3908). Free contraception, AIDS testing, pregnancy testing and a well-women's clinic.

Women's Needs Center, 1825 Haight St (☎221-7371). Low-cost health care and referral service.

Women's Yellow Pages, 270 Napoleon St (☎821-1357). Call for a copy of this invaluable directory, with everything from where to stay to where to get your legs waxed.

Shops and Galleries

San Francisco does have the large-scale shopping facilities you'd expect in a major city, with the usual international names prominent in its downtown shop windows. However, most places are low-key and unpretentious. Not only does this mean slightly lower prices, but it also makes shopping a more pleasant, stress-free activity all round.

If you want to run the gauntlet of designer labels, or just watch the style brigades in all their consumer fury, **Union Square** is the place to aim for. Heart of the city's shopping territory, it has a good selection of big-name and chic stores – expense account stuff admittedly, but good for browsing, especially in the many art galleries.

Clothes

Aardvarks Odd Ark, 1501 Haight St (☎621-3141). Large secondhand clothing store in Haight Ashbury: stocks some junk, but also some priceless pieces and an infinite supply of perfectly faded Levis.

Mascara Club, 1408 Haight St (☎863-2837). Vintage clothing in the heart of Haight Ashbury, heavy on the psychedelic and more recently Wild Western garments.

Past Tense, 665 Valencia St (☎621-2987). Mission district store selling Thirties to Sixties collectable vintage clothing. One of the smarter secondhand stores.

Purple Heart, 1855 Mission St (☎621-2581). Top quality junk and kitsch.

San Francisco Symphony Thrift Store, 2223 Fillmore St (☎563-3123). Top-rate vintage clothing store in Pacific Heights, with flamboyant and original pieces going for top dollar.

Worn Out West, 1850 Castro St (☎431-6020). Gay secondhand cowboy gear store – a trip for browsing, but if you're serious about getting some Wild West kit, this is about the cheapest place in town to pick out a good pair of boots, stylish western shirts and chaps.

Books

Around the World, 1346 Polk St (☎474-5568). Musty, dusty and a bit of a mess, this is a great place for hours of poring over first editions, rare books and records.

Books Etc, 538 Castro St (☎621-8631). Stocks the gamut of gay publishing, from psychology to soft-core porn.

The Booksmith, 1644 Haight St (☎863-8688). Good general Haight Ashbury bookstore with an excellent stock of political and foreign periodicals.

City Lights Bookstore, 261 Columbus Ave (☎362-8193). America's first paperback bookshop, and still San Francisco's best. The range of titles includes their own publications.

A Different Light, 489 Castro St (☎431-0891). Well-stocked and diverse gay bookstore.

Modern Times, 968 Valencia St (☎282-9246). Largely radical feminist publications, but a hefty stock of Latin American literature and progressive political publications.

Small Press Traffic, 3599 24th St (☎285-8394). Don't be misled by the unprepossessing Mission storefront: this is San Francisco's prime outlet for independent, contemporary fiction and poetry, with an astounding range.

Tillman Place Bookstore, 8 Tillman Place, off Grant Ave, near Union Square (☎392-4668). Downtown's premier general bookshop, with a beautifully elegant feel.

Records

Aquarius Music, 3961 24th St (☎647-2272). Small neighbourhood store with friendly, knowledgeable staff. Admirably reluctant to stock CDs. Emphasis on indie rock, jazz and blues.

Discoteca Habana, 24th and Harrison St (no phone). Caribbean and samba recordings.

Embarcadero Discs and Tapes, 2 Embarcadero Center, the Embarcadero (☎956-2204). Not a piece of vinyl in sight – up-to-the-minute CDs and tapes.

Jack's Record Cellar, 254 Scott St (☎431-3047). The city's best source for American roots music – R&B, jazz, country and rock & roll.

Reckless Records, 1401 Haight St (☎431-3434). If you can't complete your Sixties collection here, you never will.

Record Finder, Noe and Market St (☎431-4443). One of the best independents, with a range as broad as it's absorbing. Take a wad and keep spending.

Record House, 1550 California St (☎474-0259). Nob Hill archive library of over 25,000 Broadway and Hollywood soundtracks. Great record-finding service.

Record Rack, 3987 18th St (☎552-4990). Castro 12" single emporium with a few albums, but the accent is definitely on stuff you can dance to.

Recycled Records, 1377 Haight St (☎626-4075). Good all-round new and used store for records, tapes and CDs, as well as a good selection of music publications.

Rooky Ricardo's, 448 Haight St (☎864-7526). Secondhand soul and funk, some albums but mostly 45s. Brilliant.

Rough Trade, 1529 Haight St (☎621-4395). Because of its London connections, this is the first place in town to get imports. Good reggae and indie rock.

Star Records, 551 Hayes St (☎552-3017). Secondhand rap, soul, jazz, gospel and reggae specialist, out in Western Addition. Any track ever cut by a black artist, you'll find here.

Art Galleries

American Indian Contemporary Arts, 685 Market St (☎495-7600). The only non-profit gallery in the country run by contemporary Native American artists.

Artspace, Ninth and Folsom St (no phone). Adventurous, avant-garde gallery that often exhibits video installations.

Atelier Dore, 771 Bush St (☎391-2423). Salon-style gallery. Historical genre paintings from California, as well as nineteenth- and twentieth-century black American painters.

Joseph Chowning Art Gallery, 1717 17th St (☎626-7496). Humorous and bizarre art.

Contemporary Realists Gallery, 506 Hayes St (☎863-6556). One of the more interesting galleries and the first California gallery dedicated to promoting current realist drawing.

Crown Point Press, 871 Folsom St (☎974-6273). With a showcase that changes monthly, you never know what to expect from one of SoMa's most eclectic galleries.

SF MOMA Rental Gallery, Building A, Fort Mason (☎441-4777). Large exhibition space of over 500 artists trying to break into the commercial art world.

Smile, A Gallery With Tongue In Chic, 1750 Union St (☎771-1909). From the whimsical to the very serious, this gallery is one of very few into it just for fun. They'll exhibit anything.

Listings

Airlines *American, Continental, Delta* and *United Airlines* are all at 433 California St; *British Airways*, Powell St; *TWA*, 605 Market St. Toll-free numbers are given in "Basics ".

American Express 237 Post St (☎981-5533). Mon–Fri 9am–5.30pm, Sat 9.30am–4.30pm.

Babysitting *Bay Area Babysitting Agency* (☎991-7474).

Consulates *United Kingdom*, 1 Sansome St (☎981-3030); *Ireland*, 655 Montgomery (☎392-4212); *Australia* (and also *New Zealand*), 360 Post St (☎362-6160); *Netherlands*, 601 California St (☎981-6454).

Disabled Visitors Most public buildings have been modified for disabled access, all *BART* stations are wheelchair accessible, and most buses have lowering platforms for wheelchairs – and, usually, understanding drivers. In San Francisco, the *Mayor's Council on Disabilities* puts out an annual guide for disabled visitors (Box 1595, San Francisco, CA; ☎554-6141).

Hospital The *San Francisco General Hospital*, 1001 Potrero Drive (☎821-8111), has a 24hr emergency walk-in service.

Passport and Visa Office I.N.S., 630 Sansome Street (☎705-4411).

Post Office Main post office with telephone and post restante facilities at Seventh & Mission. (Mon–Fri 9am–5.30pm, Sat 9am–1pm). Zip Code 94101.

Public Library Civic Center, between Market St and Van Ness Ave (☎558-3191). Mon–Sat 9am–6pm, until 9pm Tues and Thurs.

Sports Football's "side of the Eighties", the *San Francisco 49ers* (☎468-2249) play at Candlestick Park in South San Francisco, as do the baseball team, *San Francisco Giants* (☎467-8000). Ticket prices vary from $6 for standing room in the gods to $100 for a field-side box.

Telegrams *Western Union*, 697 Howard St (☎495-7301). Open daily 7am–midnight.

The Bay Area

Of the six million people who make their home in the vicinity of San Francisco, only a lucky one in every eight lives in the city itself. Everyone else is spread around the **Bay Area**, either down the peninsula or across one of the two impressive bridges that span the chilly waters of the exquisite natural harbour. In the **East Bay** are industrial Oakland and intellectual Berkeley. To the south lies the gloating new wealth of the **Peninsula**, known as "Silicon Valley" for the multibillion-dollar computer industries which have replaced agriculture in the last few decades. Across the Golden Gate Bridge to the north is the woody, leafy landscape and rugged coastline of **Marin County**, the Bay Area's richest suburb.

The East Bay

The largest and most-travelled bridge in the US, the **Bay Bridge** heads east from San Francisco, part graceful suspension bridge and part heavy-duty steel truss. Now recovered from its partial collapse during the 1989 earthquake, the Bay Bridge works a whole lot harder for a lot less respect than the more famous (and better-loved) Golden Gate: a hundred million vehicles cross it each year. The heart of the East Bay is **Oakland**, a hard-working, blue-collar city that was hideously scarred by the firestorm of October 1991. A few miles north is the image-conscious university town of **Berkeley** (pronounced as for Busby); the two communities all but merge into one city, with the hills above them topped by a twenty-mile string of forested **regional parks**.

The telephone **area code** for the Bay Area is ☎510.

Arrival, Getting Around and Information

Flights direct to the East Bay touch down at **Oakland Airport**, just outside town. The *AirBART Shuttle* van (every 15min; $2) connects to the Coliseum *BART* station, and there are also shuttle buses such as *Bayporter* ($15; ☎467-1800). The **Greyhound** station (☎834-3070) is in a dodgy part of northern Oakland on San Pablo Avenue at 21st Street. **Amtrak** terminates at 16th and Wood streets in West Oakland, but a better option is to get off at Richmond and change onto the ultra-modern **BART** trains. Three of these underground lines link San Francisco with the East Bay (Mon–Sat 6am–midnight, Sun 9am–midnight; fares 80¢–$3), heading their separate ways from downtown Oakland. *AC Transit* (☎839-2882) buses cover the entire East Bay area, running to Oakland and Berkeley from the Transbay Terminal in San Francisco.

There are **visitor centres** at 1000 Broadway near the 12th Street *BART* station in downtown Oakland (Mon–Fri 8.30am–5pm; ☎839-9000), and, less helpfully, at 1834 University Avenue in Berkeley (Mon–Fri 9am–4pm; ☎549-7000).

Oakland

OAKLAND, the workhorse of the Bay Area, is the largest port on the West Coast. It has also been the breeding ground of revolutionary **political movements**. In the Sixties, the city's fifty percent black population found a voice through the militant Black Panthers, and in the Seventies the Symbionese Liberation Army, kidnappers of heiress Patty Hearst, obtained a ransom of free food for the city's poor. It's not all hard graft: the climate is often sunny and mild when San Francisco is cold and dreary, and there's great hiking in the redwood- and eucalyptus-covered hills above the city.

Half a mile down Broadway from the recently spruced-up downtown – or direct by ferry from San Francisco – **Jack London Square** is Oakland's sole concession to the tourist trade. Stretching along the waterfront, this aseptic complex of boutiques and eateries is named for the writer, who grew up here as an orphaned delinquent, but is about as far from the spirit of the man as it's possible to get. **Gertrude Stein**, who was born in Oakland at around the same time as the macho and adventurous London, is barely commemorated – perhaps because she wrote "what was the use of me having come from Oakland, it was not natural for me to have come from there yes write about it if I like or anything if I like but not there, *there is no there there*" – a quote which has haunted Oakland ever since.

Joaquin Miller Park, the most easily accessible of Oakland's hilltop parks, stands above East Oakland. It was once home to the "Poet of the Sierras", Joaquin Miller, who made his name playing the eccentric frontier American in the salons of 1870s London. His poems weren't exactly acclaimed (his greatest poetic achievement was rhyming "teeth" with "Goethe"), but his prose account of the time he spent with the Modoc Indians near Mount Shasta (see p.822) remains powerful. His house, a small white cabin called **The Abbey**, still survives, as do the thousands of trees he planted.

Berkeley

BERKELEY is dominated by the **University of California**, whose grand buildings and thirty thousand students give off an energy that spills south down raucous **Telegraph Avenue**. The very name of Berkeley conjures up images of dissent. Among the sites of the almost-daily pitched battles of the Sixties and early Seventies, part of the broad campus revolt against the Vietnam War, was the now-seedy **People's Park**. Organised resistance to the university authorities' misguided plans to develop the site into student dormitories brought out the troops, who shot an onlooker dead by mistake. Even after the non-rebellious Eighties, the progressive legacy endures, noticeably in the agenda of the city council. When the university foolishly proposed to build volleyball courts in the middle of People's Park in late 1991, violent demonstrations returned to the streets once again.

Telegraph Avenue holds most of the studenty hangouts, and several fine bookshops. Older students congregate in **Northside**, popping down from their woodsy hillside homes to partake of goodies from "Gourmet Ghetto" – the restaurants, delis and bakeries on Shattuck Avenue. Along the bay itself is the **Berkeley Marina**, where you can rent windsurfing boards and sailboats or just watch the sun set behind the Golden Gate.

East Bay Accommodation

The only hostel in the East Bay is solely for men, but the **motels** and **hotels**, at around $35 a night, are slightly better value for money than their San Francisco equivalents.

Berkeley YMCA, 2001 Allston Way at Milvia St, a block from Berkeley *BART* (☎848-6800). Men-only bargain accommodation. First-come, first-served. Single rooms $22, with use of gym and pool.

Golden Bear Motel, 1620 San Pablo Ave, West Berkeley (☎525-6770). The most pleasant of the many motels in the "flatlands" of West Berkeley, though somewhat out of the way; $37 doubles.

Waterfront Plaza Hotel, 21 Jack London Square, Oakland (☎836-3800). Plush, modern hotel moored on the best stretch of the Oakland waterfront. Weekend doubles from $80.

London Lodge, 700 Broadway, downtown Oakland (☎451-6316). Spacious rooms, some of which have kitchens, make this a good option for families or groups. Doubles from $48.

Shattuck Hotel, 2086 Allston Way, Berkeley (☎845-7300). Central doubles from $85.

Eating

As befits the birthplace of California Cuisine, the Bay Area offers a choice of good **restaurants**. Berkeley is both an upmarket diner's paradise and a student town where you can eat cheaply and well, especially along and around Telegraph Avenue.

Alvita's Restaurant, 3522 Foothill Blvd, East Oakland (☎536-7880). Arguably the best Mexican restaurant in the Bay Area, with great *chiles rellenos, carnitas* and a range of seafood dishes.

Cha-Am, 1543 Shattuck Ave, North Berkeley (☎848-9664). Climb the stairs up to this unlikely, always crowded small restaurant for deliciously spicy Thai food at bargain prices.

Chez Panisse, 1517 Shattuck Ave, North Berkeley (☎548-5525). The first and still the best of the California Cuisineries – although at $50 a head *prix-fixe* you may prefer to try the comparatively cheap *Cafe* upstairs, especially if you don't have the obligatory three-months-in-advance reservation.

Gulf Coast Oyster Bar & Specialty Co, 736 Washington St, downtown Oakland (☎839-6950). Popular and reasonably priced Cajun-flavoured seafood restaurant.

Jade Villa, 800 Broadway, downtown Oakland (☎839-1688). For dim sum lunches or traditional Cantonese meals, this is one of the best places to go in Oakland's thriving Chinatown.

Juan's Place, 941 Carlton St, West Berkeley (☎845-6904). The original Berkeley Mexican restaurant, with great food (tons of it) and an interesting mix of people.

Tambo Cafe, 1981 Shattuck Ave near University Ave, Berkeley (☎841-6884). Brilliant, reasonably priced Peruvian food – including marvellous *ceviche* – served up fresh and fast.

Cafes and Bars

The many bohemian **cafes** of Berkeley are full from dawn to near midnight of earnest characters wearing their intellects on their sleeves; if you're not after a caffeine fix, you can generally get a glass of beer or wine. For serious drinking you're better off in one of the many **bars**, particularly in rough-hewn Oakland. Grittier versions of what you'd find in San Francisco, they're mostly blue-collar, convivial, and almost always cheaper.

Cafe Mediterranean, 2475 Telegraph Ave, Berkeley. Berkeley's oldest cafe, straight out of the Beat generation archives: beards and berets optional, books *de rigueur*.

Heinhold's First and Last Chance Saloon, Jack London Square, Oakland. Authentic waterfront bar that's hardly changed since the turn of the century, when Jack London himself drank here.

Larry Blake's, 2367 Telegraph Ave, Berkeley. Upstairs there's a small bar, downstairs there's a R&B club and large bar; in between the two there's a good-value restaurant.

Mama Bear's, 6536 Telegraph Ave, North Oakland. Women's bookshop, doubling as a cafe and meeting place. Open daily 10am–7pm, later for regular readings by lesbian and feminist writers.

The White Horse, 6560 Telegraph Ave at 66th St, North Oakland. Smallish, friendly mixed bar.

Live Music Venues

Nightlife is where the East Bay really comes into its own. **Discos** are virtually non-existent; however, dance music – from the likes of Oakland's own MC Hammer – is thriving, and **live music venues** range from smoky jazz cafes to sweaty R&B dives.

Berkeley's **Pacific Film Archives** at 2621 Durant Avenue (☎642-1412), perhaps the best **cinema** in California, puts on contemporary international films, plus old favourites. The free *East Bay Express* has the most comprehensive listings of **what's on**.

Ashkenaz, 1317 San Pablo Ave, Berkeley (☎525-5054). World music and dance cafe. Acts range from modern Afrobeat to the best of the Balkans. Kids and under-21s welcome. Admission $5–8.

Caribe Dance Center, 1408 Webster St, downtown Oakland (☎835-4006). For reggae, rockers, calypso, soca, dub, salsa or lambada, this new place is hard to beat. Admission $3–8.

Eli's Mile High Club, 3629 Martin Luther King Jr Way, North Oakland (☎655-6661). The best of the Bay Area blues clubs. Cover $5–8.

Gilman Street Project, 924 Gilman St, West Berkeley (☎648-3561). On the outer edge of the hardcore punk scene. No booze, all ages, admission $3–6.

Koncepts Cultural Gallery, 480 Third St, downtown Oakland (☎763-0682). Excellent, groundbreaking jazz club, hosting a wide variety of different acts. Admission $8–15.

The Peninsula

The city of San Francisco sits at the tip of a five-mile-wide **peninsula**. Home of old money and new technology, this stretches for fifty miles of relentless suburbia south from San Francisco along the bay to wind up in the futuristic roadside landscape of the so-called "Silicon Valley" near **San Jose**. There was a time when the region was covered with orange groves and fig trees, but the continuing computer boom – spurred by Stanford University in **Palo Alto** – has put paid to that. Surprisingly, most of the land along the **coast** – separated from the bayfront sprawl by a ridge of redwood-covered peaks – remains rural and undeveloped; it also contains some of the best **beaches** in the Bay Area, well served by public transport.

San Jose

But for the odd Burt Bacharach song, **SAN JOSE**, the fastest-growing city in America's fastest-growing state, is not strong on identity – though in area and population it's close on twice the size of San Francisco. Sitting at the southern end of the Peninsula, San Jose has in the past 25 years emerged as the civic heart of Silicon Valley, surrounded by miles of faceless hi-tech industrial parks where the next generations of computers are designed and crafted. Ironically, it's also one of the oldest settlements in California, though the only sign of that is the eighteenth-century **Mission Santa Clara de Asis**, on a pedestrianised stretch of San Jose's main drag, the Alameda.

The **Winchester Mystery House**, 525 S Winchester Boulevard, just off I-280 near Hwy-17 (daily 9.30am–4.30pm; $9), has to be seen to be believed. Sarah Winchester, heiress to the Winchester rifle fortune, was convinced upon her husband's death that he had been taken by the spirits of men killed with Winchester rifles, and believed that unless a room was built for each of the spirits and the sound of hammers never ceased, the same fate would befall her. Work on the mansion went on 24 hours a day for the next thirty years – stairs lead nowhere, windows open on to solid brick.

San Jose's **visitor centre** is at 333 W San Carlos Street (Mo ʁ–Sat 9am–5pm; ☎408/ 295-9600). Downtown **accommodation** options include the *Best Western Inn*, 455 S Second Street (☎408/298-3500), costing $55 a double, and the *Valley Inn*, 2155 The Alameda (☎408/241-8500) for $45. Budget **food** can be had at *Original Joe's*, 301 S First Street (☎408/292-7030). Grab a stool at the counter or settle into one of the comfy booths and enjoy a burger and fries or a plate of pasta at this San Jose institution, where $10 goes a long way. *Krung Thai Cuisine*, 1699 W San Carlos Street (☎408/295-5508), serves delicious, unusual seafood dishes and excellent satays.

The Coast

The **coastline** of the peninsula south from San Francisco is more appealing than inland – relatively undeveloped, with very few buildings, let alone towns, along the 75 miles of coves and beaches that extend down to the resort city of Santa Cruz. However, not until fifteen miles south of **Daly City** do you finally escape the suburban sprawl, at the clothing-optional sands of **Gray Whale Cove State Beach** (daily dawn–dusk; $2 to park). Despite the name it's not an especially great place to look for migrating gray whales, but there is a stairway from the bus stop down to a fine strand. Two miles south, the red-roofed buildings of the 1875 **Montara Lighthouse**, set among the wind-swept Monterey pine trees at the top of a steep cliff, have been converted into a **youth hostel** (☎728-7177), where dorm beds are $11 and you can rent bikes for $10 a day.

Marin County

Across the Golden Gate from San Francisco, **Marin County** (pronounced Ma-RINN) is an unabashed introduction to Californian self-indulgence: an elitist pleasure-zone of conspicuous luxury and abundant natural beauty, with sunshine, sandy beaches, high mountains and thick redwood forests. Often ranked as the wealthiest county in the US, Marin has drawn a sizeable contingent of wealthy young professionals to live in its swanky waterside towns – though many of the cocaine-and-hot-tub devotees who populated the place in the 1970s have traded in their drug habits for mountain bikes.

The modern **ferries** across the bay from San Francisco can make a great start to a day out. Boats to the chic bayside settlement of **Sausalito** leave from the Embarcadero (*Golden Gate Transit*; 5.30am–8pm, half-hourly at busy periods, every two hours at weekends; $3.50 single; ☎322-6600) or Pier 431/2 at Fisherman's Wharf (*Red and White Ferries*; $9 return; ☎546-2805).

Across the Golden Gate: The Marin Headlands

The largely undeveloped **Marin Headlands**, across the Golden Gate from San Francisco, afford some of the most impressive views of the bridge and the city behind. The coastline is much more rugged than it is on the San Francisco side, and it makes a great place for an aimless cliff-top scramble, in among the concrete remains of old forts and gun emplacements. Adjacent to the **visitor centre** (daily 8.30am–4.30pm; ☎331-1450), half a mile north of the bridge near the rocky cliffs and islets of the point, there's a wide sandy **beach** in between the chilly ocean and swimmably warm-water **Rodeo Lagoon**. The largest of the old army officers' quarters in the adjacent Fort Barry, half a mile to the east, has been converted into the spacious and homely **Golden Gate Youth Hostel** (closed 9.30am–4.30pm; ☎331-2777), an excellent base for more extended explorations of the inland ridges and valleys.

Sausalito

Pretty, smug little **SAUSALITO**, along the bay below US-101, was once a gritty community of fishermen and sea-traders, full of bars and bordellos. Now exclusive restaurants and pricey boutiques line its picturesque waterfront promenade, and expensive, quirky houses climb the overgrown cliffs above Bridgeway Avenue, the main road and bus route through town. Boats from San Francisco arrive next to the Sausalito Yacht Club in the town centre.

Casa Madrona at 801 Bridgeway Avenue (☎332-0502), a deluxe hideaway in the hills above the bay where rooms cost $100, is also a delectable seafood restaurant, with a great view of the harbour. Cheaper food can be found near the waterfront; **Greater Gatsby's**, 39 Caledonia Street (☎332-4500), is an inexpensive pizza parlour. The *no name bar*, 757 Bridgeway Avenue (☎332-1392), is a thriving ex-haunt of the Beats which still hosts poetry readings and evening jam sessions.

Mount Tamalpais and Muir Woods

Mount Tamalpais dominates the skyline of the Marin peninsula, hulking over the cool canyons of the rest of the county in a crisp yet voluptuous silhouette, and dividing the county into two distinct parts: the wild western slopes above the Pacific coast and the increasingly suburban communities along the calmer bay frontage. Panoramic Highway branches off from Hwy-1 along the crest through the centre of **Mount Tamalpais State Park**, which has some thirty miles of hiking trails and many campgrounds. Most of the redwood trees which once covered its slopes have long since been chopped down to build San Francisco's Victorian houses; one towering grove does remain, however, protected as the **Muir Woods National Monument** (daily 8am–sunset; free). It's a tranquil and majestic spot, with sunlight filtering three hundred feet down from the treetops to the laurel- and fern-covered canyon below. Being so close to San Francisco, Muir Woods is a popular target, and the trails nearest the car park have been paved and are often packed with coach-tour hordes.

Mill Valley

From the East Peak of Mount Tamalpais, a quick two-mile downhill hike follows the Temelpa Trail through velvety shrubs of chaparral, to the town of **MILL VALLEY**, the oldest and most enticing of the inland towns of Marin County. This was originally a logging centre, from which the destruction of the surrounding redwoods was organised, but for many years the town has made a healthy living out of tourism.

The town centres today around the *Book Depot and Cafe* (daily 7am–10pm), a popular bookshop, cafe and meeting place at 87 Throckmorton Avenue, with the town's **visitor centre** next door (Mon–Sat 9am–5pm; ☎388-9700). *Sweetwater* at no. 153 (☎388-3820) is a comfortable saloon which doubles as Marin's prime live music venue, with gigs ranging from jazz and blues all-stars to Jefferson Airplane survivors; the *Dipsea Cafe*, 1 El Paseo (☎381-0298), serves hearty diner food, especially good for breakfast. The *Motel Alto* at 817 Redwood Highway (☎388-6676) – take the Seminary Drive exit of US-101, and it's just west of the freeway – is the cheapest place to **stay**, with singles from $30 and doubles from $40.

Point Reyes National Seashore

The westernmost tip of Marin County comes at the end of the **Point Reyes National Seashore**, a near-island of wilderness surrounded on three sides by over fifty miles of isolated coastline – pine forests and sunny meadows bordered by rocky cliffs and sandy, windswept beaches. This wing-shaped landmass is a rogue piece of the earth's crust that has been drifting steadily northwards along the San Andreas Fault, having started some six million years ago as a suburb of Los Angeles. When the great earthquake of 1906 shattered San Francisco, the land here, at the epicentre, shifted over sixteen feet in an instant, though damage was confined to a few skewed cattle fences.

The **visitor centre** (daily 9am–5pm; ☎663-1092), two miles southwest of Point Reyes Station, has engaging displays on local geology and natural history, plus details of hiking trails. Just north, Limantour Road heads six miles west to the **Point Reyes Youth Hostel** (closed 9.30am–4.30pm; ☎663-8811) in an old ranchhouse, where dorm beds cost $11. Nearby **Limantour Beach** is good for swimming.

Eight miles west of the hamlet of Inverness, a turning leads down to **Drake's Beach**, the presumed landing spot of Sir Francis Drake in 1579. Appropriately, the coastline resembles the southern coast of England – cold, wet and windy, with chalkwhite cliffs rising above the wide sandy beach. The road continues west another four miles to the very tip of Point Reyes. A precariously sited **lighthouse** stands firm against the crashing surf, and the bluffs are excellent for watching sea lions and, in winter, migrating **grey whales**.

THE GOLD COUNTRY

The single most enduring image of California, after surfers and movie stars, is that of the rough and ready 49ers, who came from all over the world to get rich in the **Gold Country** of the Sierra Nevada, 150 miles east of San Francisco. The area ranges from the foothills near Yosemite two hundred miles north to the deep gorge of the Yuba River, with **Sacramento** as its largest city. Many of the mining camps that sprung up around the Gold Country vanished as quickly as they appeared, but about half still survive. Some are bustling resorts, standing on the banks of white-water rivers in the midst of thick pine forests; others just eerie ghost towns, all but abandoned on the grassy rolling hills. Most of the mountainous forest along the Sierra crest is preserved as near-pristine wilderness, with excellent hiking, camping and backpacking. There's great skiing in winter, around the mountainous rim of **Lake Tahoe** on the border between California and Nevada, aglow under the bright lights of the nightclubs and casinos that line its southeastern shore.

Sacramento

California's state capital, **SACRAMENTO**, in the flatlands of the Central Valley, was founded in 1839 by the Swiss **John Sutter**. He worked hard for ten years to build a busy trading centre and cattle ranch, only to be thwarted by the discovery of gold at a nearby sawmill in 1848. His workers quit their jobs to go prospecting, and thousands more flocked to the gold fields of the **Central Mother Lode** without any respect for Sutter's claims to the land. Sacramento became the main supply-point for the miners, and remained important as the western headquarters of the transcontinental railway. Flashy office towers and hotel complexes have now sprung from its rather suburban streetscape, enlivening the flat grid of leafy, tree-lined blocks, and going some way toward resurrecting the rowdy, free-for-all spirit of the city's Gold Rush past.

It's not especially prominent on most travellers' itineraries. There's not a great deal to see, though the wharves, warehouses, saloons and stores of the historic core along the **riverfront** have been restored and converted into the shops and restaurants of **Old Sacramento**. On the northern edge of the old town, the **California State Railroad Museum** (daily 10am–5pm; $3) brings together a range of lavishly restored 1860s locomotives, with "cow-catcher" front grilles and bulbous smokestacks. The old passenger station and freight depot a block south now serve as the summer depot for a refurbished **steam train** ($3) making a seven-mile, 45-minute round trip along the river.

Further east, and isolated from downtown, the dome of the **state capitol** stands proudly in a spacious green park two blocks south of the massive **K Street Mall**. Recently restored to its original elegance, and still the seat of state government, the luxurious building brims over with finely crafted details. Although you're free to walk around, you'll see a lot more if you take one of the free hourly **tours** (daily 9am–5pm).

Sutter's Fort (daily 9am–5pm; $1), on the east side of town at 27th and L streets, is a recreation of Sacramento's original settlement. An adobe house displays relics from the Gold Rush, and on summer weekends volunteers dress up and act out scenes from the 1850s. The adjacent **Indian Museum** (daily 10am–5pm; $1) on K Street displays tools, handicrafts and ceremonial objects of local Native Americans.

Practicalities

Trains come in at Fourth and I streets, near Old Sacramento, and an almost continuous stream of *Greyhound* buses (☎444-6800) arrives at 1107 L Street. The **airport** is twelve miles northwest: *Sacramento Airport Transit* vans (☎424-9640; $6) run downtown.

Sacramento's **visitor centre** is at 1421 K Street (Mon–Fri 8am–5pm; ☎442-5542). As well as the new *Gold Rush Home* AYH **Hostel**, at 1421 Tiverton Avenue (☎421-5954), there are plenty of cheap places to stay within walking distance of the city centre. The *Central Motel*, 818 16th Street (☎446-6006), has rooms from $35, while the *Briggs House*, 2209 Capitol Avenue (☎441-3214), is an attractive B&B half a mile from the state capitol, charging from $60 a night. *Annabelle's* at 200 J Street (☎448-6239) is a bustling Old Sacramento Italian restaurant, and *Rubicon Brewing Company*, 2004 Capitol Avenue, offers good Mexican bar food washed down by the flavourful house-brewed *Amber Ale*, and live jazz at weekends.

> The telephone **area code** for Sacramento, Lake Tahoe,
> and the northern Gold Country is ☎916; for the southern Gold Country, it's ☎209.

The Mines

In the romantic landscape of the **Gold Country**, overshadowed by the ten-thousand-foot granite peaks of the Sierra Nevada, fast-flowing rivers cascade through steeply walled canyons. In autumn, the flaming reds and golds of poplars and sugar maples on the slopes stand out against an evergreen background of pine and fir. The camps of the **southern mines** of the Gold Country were the liveliest and most uproarious of all the Gold Rush settlements, and inspired most of the popular images of the era: Wild West towns full of gambling halls, saloons and gunfights in the streets. Freebooting prospectors in these "placer" mines sometimes picked nuggets of gold out of the streams and rivers; further **north**, the diggings were far richer and more successful, but the gold was (and is) buried deep underground, and had to be pounded out of hardrock ore.

Sonora, Columbia and Jamestown

The centre of the southern mining district, and the easiest place to get to without a car, is **SONORA**, set on steep ravines roughly a hundred miles east of San Francisco. This friendly and animated logging town is more than just another tourist trap, with its appealing false-fronted buildings and Victorian houses on the main **Washington Street**. The *Tuolumne County Visitors Bureau*, 16 W Stockton Road (☎1-800/446-1333), a block from Washington Street, is the best source of **information**.

Sonora's one-time arch-rival, **COLUMBIA**, three miles north on Parrots Ferry Road, is now a ghost town, with a carefully restored Main Street that gives an excellent – if slightly contrived – idea of what Gold Rush life might have been like. In 1854 it was California's second largest city, and it missed becoming the state capital by two votes – just as well, since by 1870 the gold had run out and the town was abandoned.

Most of the saccharine-sweet village of **JAMESTOWN**, three miles south of Sonora, was burned down in 1966. Prior to that it was the location for *High Noon*, the train from which is now the biggest attraction of **Railton 1897 State Park**, a block east of Main Street – a collection of old steam trains that's open summer weekends, and offers half-day trips on restored local railways.

Practicalities

Calaveras Transit (☎209/728-1193) **buses** run to Sonora, once daily at 11am from the Pleasant Hill *BART* station, in the Bay Area, and three times daily from Stockton in the central valley. The nicest **place to stay** in Sonora is the *Ryan House*, 153 S Shepherd Street (☎533-3445), a very comfortable and welcoming B&B costing $70 for two; motels on Hwy-49 include the *Miner's Motel* (☎532-7850). For breakfast or lunch try *The Whitewater Cafe*, 79 N Washington Street (☎532-3543). Main Street Jamestown is lined by balconied old Gold Rush hotels like the *National* (☎984-3446) and the *Royal* (☎984-5271), both around $50 a night, and also holds a few good places to eat.

Grass Valley and Nevada City

The compact but still-thriving communities of **GRASS VALLEY** and **NEVADA CITY**, four miles apart in the Sierra Nevada mountains, were the most prosperous and substantial of the gold mining towns. Since the Sixties, artists and craftspeople – including songwriter Jonathan Richman – have settled in the elaborate Victorian homes of the surrounding hills and gorges. In Grass Valley, the **North Star Mining Museum** (daily, April–Oct 11am–5pm, irregular hours rest of year; donations) at the south end of Mill Street is housed in what used to be the powerstation for the North Star Mine. Its giant water-driven **Pelton wheel**, fitted with a hundred or so iron buckets, once powered the drills and hoists of the mine. Dioramas show the day-to-day working life of the miners, three-quarters of whom had emigrated here from the depressed tin mines of Cornwall (bringing the Cornish pasty with them).

The last mine in California to shut down was its richest, the **Empire Mine**, now preserved as a state park in the pine forests a mile east of Grass Valley (daily 9am–5pm; $1). It closed in 1956, after more than six million ounces of gold had been recovered, when the cost of getting the gold out of the ground exceeded $35 an ounce, the government-controlled price at the time. Most of the machinery has been dismantled, but there's a small but very informative **museum** at the entrance.

As well as the usual information, the Grass Valley **tourist office** at 248 Mill Street (Mon–Sat 10am–5pm; ☎273-4667) contains mementoes of Lola Montez, an Irish entertainer and former mistress of Ludwig of Bavaria who retired here after touring America with her provocative "Spider Dance" (and kept a grizzly bear in her front yard).

It's hard to pick out specific highlights of **Nevada City**; it's really the town as a whole that's worth seeing. The newly restored **Old Firehouse**, a lacy balconied and bell-towered piece of gingerbread, houses a small **museum** (daily 11am–4pm; donations) of local social history.

Greyhound stops four times a day at 123 Bank Street in Grass Valley from Sacramento via Auburn (☎272-9091), and the *Gold Country Stage* connects the two towns every half hour (daily 8am–5pm; $1 a trip, $2 for a day pass; ☎265-1411).

Grass Valley and Nevada City Accommodation

Accommodation in the revamped old Gold Rush hotels doesn't come cheap, but if you can afford to splash out on a B&B, Nevada City has some excellent options.

Airway Motel, 575 E Broad St, Nevada City (☎265-2233). Quiet, 1940s motel with swimming pool, ten minute's walk from centre of town. Doubles from $35 a night.

Annie Horan's, 415 W Main St, Grass Valley (☎272-2418). Sumptuous small home with antiques galore; rooms for two from $60 a night.

Downey House, 517 W Broad St, Nevada City (☎265-2815). Pretty 1870s Victorian home at the top of Broad Street looking out over the town and surrounding forest. Rooms from $60 a night.

Holbrooke Hotel, 212 W Main St, Grass Valley (☎273-1353 or ☎1-800/933-7077). Historic hotel, once visited by Mark Twain, and right in the centre of town. Doubles $65–120.

Eating and Drinking

Both Grass Valley and Nevada City have good places to eat and drink, as well as many bars and saloons, where you'll often be treated to free live music.

Gold Exchange Saloon, 158 Mill Street, Grass Valley (☎272-5509). Lively, unpretentious beer bar and saloon, great for quenching a thirst after a day's hiking, biking or prospecting.

The Live Wire, 11990 Plaza Drive, Grass Valley (☎477-0855). The Gold Country's main live venue. Headbanging metal music most nights, occasional bigger-name rockers and cabaret performers.

Main Street Cafe, 213 W Main Street, Grass Valley (☎477-6000). Casual but refined restaurant. An eclectic menu, from pastas to Cajun specialities. Recommended for grilled meats and fresh fish.

Marshall's Pasties, 203A Mill Street, Grass Valley (☎272-2844). Mind-boggling fresh pasties.

Lake Tahoe

One of the highest, largest, deepest, cleanest and coldest lakes in the world, **Lake Tahoe** is perched high above the Gold Country in an alpine bowl of forested granite peaks. Longer than the English Channel is wide, and more than a thousand feet deep, it's so cold that perfectly preserved cowboys who drowned over a century ago have been recovered from its depths. The sandy beaches around the shores attract thousands of families in summer, and in winter the snow-covered slopes of the nearby peaks are packed with skiers. The eastern third of the lake lies in Nevada, and gleams with the neon signs of flashy casinos; they offer cheap food, tawdry entertainment, and of course gambling, but not, unusually for Nevada, cheap rooms.

The prettiest part of the lake by far is along the southwest shore, at **Emerald Bay State Park**, ten miles from South Lake Tahoe, which has many good shoreline **camp-grounds**. A mile from the carpark, **Vikingsholm** is an unlikely reproduction Viking castle (summer daily 10am–4pm; $1). In **D L Bliss State Park**, two miles north, the fifteen-thousand-square-foot **Ehrman Mansion** (daily 11am–4pm; free) is decorated in Thirties-era furnishings; the extensive lakefront grounds were seen in *Godfather II*.

The rest of the 75-mile **drive** around the lake can be a bit of a disappointment; a better way to see it is to take a **paddlewheel boat** cruise on either the *Tahoe Queen* from South Lake Tahoe (daily 11am, 1.30pm and 4pm; $12.50; ☎541-3364) or the *MS Dixie*, from Zephyr Cove (daily at noon; $11; ☎702/588-3508).

Practicalities

Ten daily *Greyhound* buses from San Francisco and Sacramento stop at the Nevada casinos before returning to the **depot** (☎544-2241) at 1099 Park Avenue in South Lake Tahoe. Local **buses** serve the communities of Tahoe City and South Lake Tahoe; in the latter, you can rent **bicycles** from the *Clean Machine Bike Shop* (☎544-7160).

Both South Lake Tahoe and Tahoe City have dozens of bargain motels, though weekday rates from $30 can easily double at weekends, or in summer. The huge *Motel 6* at 2375 Lake Tahoe Boulevard, South Lake Tahoe (☎542-1400), costs from $38; the *Falcon Motor Lodge* in Tahoe City at 8258 North Lake Tahoe Boulevard (☎546-2583) has doubles from $35 a night. *Bobby's Cafe*, Hwy-267 at Hwy-28, King's Beach (☎546-2329), is an excellent and inexpensive North Shore diner. If you get stuck for a room, the visitor centre (☎1-800/288-2463) runs a free **reservation service**.

Truckee and Donner Lake

Twenty-five miles north of Lake Tahoe, **Donner Lake**, surrounded by alpine cliffs of silver-grey granite, was the site of a gruesome tragedy in 1846, when the **Donner Party**, heading for the Gold Rush, found their route blocked by early snowfall. They stopped and built crude shelters, hoping that the snow would melt; it didn't. Fifteen of their number braved the mountains in search of help from Sutter's Fort in Sacramento; only two men and five women made it, surviving by eating the bodies of the men who died. A rescue party set off immediately, only to find more of the same: thirty or so half-crazed survivors, living off the meat of their fellow-travellers. The horrific tale is recounted in the small **Emigrant Trail Museum** (daily 10am–4pm; $1), just off Donner Pass Road.

The small town of **Truckee**, three miles east, is a refreshing change from the tourist-dependent towns around Lake Tahoe, and lies on the main *Greyhound* (☎587-3882) and *Amtrak* routes. Its *Star Hotel/AYH Youth Hostel* at 10015 W River Street (☎587-3007), south of the river and the railway tracks, has dormitory beds for $12 and double rooms for $30 to $50. The *River Street Café*, on River Street at Hwy-267, is a good **place to eat**, while the *Bar of America* and *The Passage* at the east end of Commercial Row both have free **live music** most nights.

NORTHERN CALIFORNIA

The massive and eerily silent volcanic lands of **northern California** have more in common with Oregon and Washington than with the rest of the state. Its small settlements live by logging, fishing and farming, though locals have been joined in recent years by New Ageists and ex-hippies. Once you're past the atypically lush valleys of the **wine country**, the **coast** stretches for four hundred miles of rugged bluffs and forests. Trees are the big attraction, thousands of years old and hundreds of feet high, dominating a landscape swathed in swirling mists. The **Redwood National Park** teems with campers and hikers in summer, but out of season it can be idyllic. The remote wildernesses of the **interior** can be enchanting, especially around the **Shasta Cascade** and **Lassen Volcanic National Park**.

Public transport is, not surprisingly, scarce, though *Greyhound* buses run from San Francisco and Sacramento up and down I-5 and US-101.

The Wine Country

The warm and sunny hills of **Napa** and **Sonoma valleys**, an hour north of San Francisco, are by reputation if not statistically at the centre of the American wine industry; their 29,000 grape-acres turn out vintages to satisfy a snobbery every bit as rampant as in Europe. In summer, cars jam Hwy-29 through its heart, as visitors embark on a day's free drinking, thinly disguised as an avid interest in wine.

The Napa Valley

A 35-mile strip of gently landscaped hillsides, the **Napa Valley** looks like something you'd expect in rural England rather than beside the Pacific. Several of the large wineries at its southern end, such as the **Domaine Chandon**, off Hwy-29 at Yountville (Tues–Sun 11am–9pm; ☎944-8848), offer free tours, lasting a wearisome half-hour or so, followed by the chance to sample as many bottles as you like for around $4.

A little way up the valley at the pretty village of **St Helena**, the **Christian Brothers Vineyard**, Spring Mountain Road, off Hwy-29 (by appointment only; ☎967-3112, 10am–4pm), was the world's largest winery when erected in 1889, and turns out some of the best sparkling wines and champagnes in the valley. The **Berringer Brothers Winery** (daily 9.30am–4pm; closed Aug; ☎963-7115), modelled on a German Gothic mansion, has graced the cover of many a wine magazine. Spacious lawns and a grand tasting room, heavy on the dark wood, make for quite a regal experience.

Homely **Calistoga**, at the very tip of the valley, is well known for its mudbaths, whirlpools and mineral water. The **Chateau Montelena**, 1429 Tubbs Lane (☎942-5105), just north of town, is one of the valley's oldest and smallest wineries, with an impressive medieval facade. A mile further up the road, the **Old Faithful Geyser** (daily 9am–5pm; $3) spurts boiling water sixty feet into the air at fifty-minute intervals. The water source was discovered while drilling for oil here in the 1920s, when search equipment struck a force estimated to be up to a thousand pounds per square foot.

Practicalities

Greyhound buses connect Napa (1620 Main St; ☎226-1856) and Calistoga to San Francisco. The *Napa City Bus* (1130 First St; ☎255-7631) tours the valley. **Napa** itself is bland and expensive, but *Motel 6* at 3380 Solano Avenue (☎226-1811) has doubles from $45, and the *Red Hen Cantina*, 5091 St Helena Highway (☎255-8125), serves cheap pseudo-Mexican cuisine. In **Calistoga**, *Dr Wilkinson's Hot Springs*, 1507 Lincoln Avenue (☎942-4102), is a health spa and hotel, offering rooms and treatment from $70.

The Sonoma Valley

On looks alone the crescent-shaped **Sonoma Valley** beats Napa hands down. This altogether more rustic valley curves between oak-covered mountain ranges from the Spanish colonial town of Sonoma a few miles north along Hwy-12 to Glen Ellen. It's far smaller than Napa, and most of its wineries are informal, family-run businesses, where a charge for tasting is still frowned upon and visitors are few.

The restored **Mission San Francisco Solano de Sonoma** (daily 10am–5pm; free), just north of the spacious plaza in Sonoma, was the last and northernmost of the California missions, and the only one established in northern California by the nervous Mexican rulers, who were fearful of expansionist Russian fur-traders. Sonoma's wineries are concentrated a mile east, within walking distance, and include the grand old **Buena Vista Winery**, 18000 Old Winery Road (daily 10am–5pm; ☎938-1266), which has champagne cellars, tunnels of oak caskets and a high-ceilinged tasting room.

Practicalities

On weekdays, *Sonoma County Transit* (☎527-7665) buses link the town to Napa, and Santa Rosa in the north. **Accommodation** is pricey, though the *Sonoma Hotel*, 110 West Spain Street (☎996-2996), has antique crammed doubles from $65 per night – as well as a good bar and restaurant. For something more unusual, try *Little Switzerland* just west of town on Grove Street and Riverside Drive (☎938-9990). This former bordello has evolved into a cabaret with accordion and drums, serving bratwurst and goulash dinners – a full bar helps it all go down easier, but all the same, it's quite mad.

The Northern Coast

Rugged in the extreme, often foggy, always dangerous and thunderously dramatic, the **northern coast** is leagues away from the gentle, sun-drenched beaches of southern California. Sunbathing is right out, as is swimming; instead, don your hiking boots, wrap up warm and get out into the enormous forests.

The Sonoma Coast and Russian River

Despite the weekend influx from San Francisco, the villages of the **Sonoma Coast** and **Russian River Valley** seem all but asleep for most of the year. From tiny **Bodega Bay**, where Hitchcock filmed *The Birds*, a great thirteen-mile hike leads along the rugged cliffs to busy **Goat Rock Beach**, where the Russian River joins the ocean.

About ten miles up the warm and pastoral **Russian River Valley**, **Guerneville** is an (unofficial) gay resort. It offers plenty of places to stay – *The Willows*, 15905 River Road (☎869-3279), is a homely guest house with doubles from $60, while the **campground** at *Johnson's Resort* on First Street (☎869-2022) also has cabins from around $40 – as well as a lively nightlife. The *Rainbow Cattle Company* on Main Street and *Molly Brown's Saloon* on Old Cazadero Road are good for eating, drinking, and dancing in cowboy company. The **Armstrong Redwoods State Reserve**, two miles north, contains 750 very dense acres of enormous redwoods, interspersed by hiking and riding trails.

Monte Rio, five miles back down the river, is a lovely old resort town, at the entrance to the 2500-acre **Bohemian Grove**, where the richest and most powerful men in the country gather in privacy each July for a week of (supposedly male-only) high jinks.

The Mendocino Coast

Another hundred miles up the coast, **Mendocino** is weathered and almost cute, with a low-key, raffish charm and a plethora of art galleries, gift shops and boutique-delicatessens. Just south of town, hiking and cycling trails weave through the unusual

Van Damme State Park, on Hwy-1 (☎937-5804; $3), where the ancient trees of the **Pygmy Forest** are stunted to waist height because of poor draining and soil chemicals. Away from the waterfront, **rooms** can be as cheap as $40; the *Seagull Inn*, 44594 Albion Street (☎937-5204), puts on nightly jazz, and the friendly *Joshua Grindle Inn*, 4480 Little Lake Road (☎937-4143), has rooms from $48. Mendocino's oldest bar is *Dick's Place* on Main Street, with all the robust conviviality you'd expect from a spit-and-sawdust saloon. Of the town's **restaurants**, the *Wellspring* at 955 Ukiah Street is good for seafood.

Five miles north in the tiny village of **CASPAR**, an excellent **health spa** offers open-air hot tubs for $7 per hour. Caspar also has the best **bar** in the area, the *Caspar Inn*, which has a nightly billing of rock, jazz and rhythm and blues.

The Humboldt Coast

Humboldt is by far the most beautiful of the coastal counties – almost entirely forest-land, overwhelmingly peaceful in places, in others plain eerie. The impassable cliffs of **Kings Range** prevent even the sinuous Hwy-1 from reaching the "Lost Coast" of its southern reaches. To get there you have to travel US-101 through deepest redwood territory as far as **Garberville**, a one-street town with a few good bars, at the centre of the "Emerald Triangle" which produces the majority of California's largest cash crop, marijuana. Every August, the town hosts a **Reggae on the River** festival, costing $20.

Most of the town's **accommodation** is overpriced, though the scruffy *Johnston Motel*, 839 Redwood Drive (☎923-3327), costs $30. Garberville's **restaurants** and **bars**, such as *The Cellar*, at 728 Redwood Drive, turn out some great live bluegrass. The Italian food at *Sicilio's*, 445 Conger Lane, is cheap and reliable.

Redwood country begins in earnest a few miles north, at the **Humboldt Redwoods State Park**. The serpentine **Avenue of the Giants** weaves for 33 miles through trees which block all but a few strands of sunlight. This is the habitat of *sequoia sempervirens*, a coastal redwood with ancestors dating back to the dinosaurs. Some are over 350ft tall. The three **campgrounds** fill quickly in summer; you must book (☎946-2436).

The tiny company town of **Samoa**, a few minutes by car from industrial **Eureka**, holds the last remaining cookhouse in the west. Lumbermen came to the **Samoa Cookhouse** to eat gargantuan meals after a day of felling redwoods; the oilskin table-cloths and burly workers have gone, but the lumbercamp style remains, with long tables and colossal portions of red meat.

Arcata, twelve miles across the bay from Eureka, is a small college town with an earthy, mellow pace, a few raunchy bars, and some excellent white-sanded and wind-swept beaches to the north. Three blocks from the *Greyhound* station on Tenth Street, the *Arcata Crew House Hostel*, 1390 I Street (May–Sept only; ☎822-9995), has rooms for $8.75 per night; the *Fairwinds Motel*, 1674 G Street (☎822-4824), costs from $38. The working *Humboldt Brewery*, 856 Tenth Street, has its own bar and cheap restaurant.

BIGFOOT COUNTRY

Willow Creek, forty miles east of Arcata, is the gateway to "Bigfoot Country". Reports of giant 350- to 800-pound humanoids wandering the forests of northwestern California have circulated since the late nineteenth century, fuelled by long-established Indian legends, but weren't taken seriously until 1958, when a road maintenance crew found giant foot-prints. Thanks to their photos, the Bigfoot story went worldwide. Since then, there have been over forty separate sightings of Bigfoot prints. At the crossroads in Willow Creek is a huge wooden replica of the man-ape, with slanted forehead, flared nostrils and short ears, an identikit of the creature who in recent years has added kidnapping to his list of alleged activities. A small visitor centre here has details of Bigfoot's escapades, as well as information on the adjacent Hoopa Valley Indian Reservation, which has often been the site of violent confrontation between Native Americans and whites over fishing territory.

The Redwood National Park

Thirty miles north of Arcata, the small town of **Orick** marks the southern limit, and busiest section, of the enormous **REDWOOD NATIONAL PARK**. **Tall Trees Grove** here is home of the world's tallest tree – a mighty 367-footer. Many visitors hike to it on the 8.5 mile trail from the **ranger station** (daily 8am–5pm; ☎488-3461), but if you're unsure of your footing in the dense undergrowth, there's also a **shuttle bus** ($3).

The varied **Prairie Creek** area further north is the only place in the park where you can take **ranger tours** of the wild and damp profusion. These leave from the ranger station on US-101 (daily, summer 8am–6pm, winter 8am–5pm, ☎488-2171), beside the meadows of **Elk Prairie**, which is roamed by Roosevelt elk and even bears. A line of **restaurants** along US-101 as you approach Prairie Creek have the bad taste to serve wild boar roasts, elk steaks and the like, as well as more traditional dishes. One mile north, a magnificent redwood, more than a hundred metres tall, overlooks the road.

Spectacular coastal views can be had from trails in the **Klamath** area, especially the **Klamath Overlook**, on Requa Road about three quarters of a mile down to the sea. You can drive through, jump over, or lumber under all the sculpted **Trees of Mystery** (daily 8am–6pm; free), except the impressive **Cathedral Tree**, where nine trees have grown from one root structure to form a spooky circle. The **Redwood Hostel** (☎482-8265) on US-101 has rooms at around $17 per night.

The park headquarters are in **Crescent City** at 1111 Second Street (☎464-6101), but you can pick up information all over the park. There are **campgrounds** everywhere; three that have showers and water are *Prairie Creek* on US-101; *Mill Creek*, eight miles south of Crescent City; and *Jedediah Smith*, five miles north of Crescent City on Smith River. If you must come in summer, make reservations on ☎452-1950; and if things get really desperate, head up US-101 and look for **motels** around Crescent City.

The Northern Interior

The remote **northern interior** of California, cut off from the coast by the **Shasta Cascade** range and dominated by forests, lakes, and mountains, is largely uninhabited too, and infrequently visited. I-5 leads through the heart of this near wilderness, forging straight through the unspectacular farmland of **Sacramento Valley** to **Redding** – the regions' only buses follow this route. Redding isn't much of a place in itself, but it's a good base for the **Whiskeytown-Shasta-Trinity area** and the more demanding **Lassen National Volcanic Park**. The volcanic **Lava Beds** at the very northeastern tip of the state are for most of the year inaccessible.

Redding and Shasta

REDDING itself is basically a railway centre, a characterless assembly of cheap lodgings and little else whose streets only really brighten during midsummer when the tourists hit town. Its **motels** are concentrated along Market Street (Hwy-273) and Pine Street, four blocks from the *Greyhound* station (☎241-2643). *Budget Lodge*, 1055 Market Street (☎243-4231), has rooms from around $35. Down the road a little, the *Redding Lodge*, 1135 Market Street (☎243-5141), offers slightly more luxurious rooms from $40.

SHASTA, ten miles west of Redding, is altogether more appealing. These half-ruined brick buildings were once a booming gold-mining town, literally at the end of the road from San Francisco and on the very edge of the wilderness. The **courthouse** has been turned into a museum (daily 10am–3pm; $2), full of mining paraphernalia; the gallows and prison cells are a grim reminder of the once daily executions.

The precipitous Hwy-299 leads from Shasta into the **Whiskeytown-Shasta-Trinity National Recreation Area**, where three lakes – Clair Eagle, Whiskeytown and Shasta – have artificial beaches, forests and camping facilities designed to meet the needs of water-skiers, sailors and wilderness hikers. Sadly, during summer it's completely congested, and severe drought in the last few years has led to receding water levels, evidenced by the red band of hitherto unexposed rock just above the surface of the water. An extensive system of tunnels, dams and aqueducts directs the plentiful waters of the Sacramento River to California's central valley to irrigate cash crops. The lakes are pretty enough, but residents complain they're not a patch on the wild waters that used to flow from the mountains before the Central Valley Project came along in the 1960s.

The lone peak of 14,162ft **Mount Shasta**, still considered active though it hasn't erupted for two hundred years, dominates the landscape for a hundred miles all around. A scenic road branches off I-5 and pushes eight thousand feet up the slopes to the tiny town that describes itself as "the best kept secret in California": **MOUNT SHASTA**, hard under the enormous bulk of the mountain. It's a rewarding journey, and easily done by *Greyhound* (305 N Mt Shasta Blvd; ☎926-3797), which connects the town with Redding in the south and Oregon in the north.

If you want to **stay** in Mount Shasta, the *Mountain View Lodge,* 305 McCloud Road (☎926-4704), and the *Das Alpenhaus Motel,* 504 Mount Shasta Boulevard (☎926-4617), both have rooms for around $30 or $40. Really nice places like the *McCloud Guest House,* 606 W Colombero Drive (☎964-3160), set in the former headquarters of the old logging company, will set you back about $65. The picturesque *Lake Siskiyou Campground* (☎926-2618) is in a wood four miles west of town. For **eating**, *Bellissimo's,* at 204 E Lake Street, serves delicious well-priced meals, while the excellent Italian *Mike and Tony's,* 501 Mount Shasta Boulevard, is a bit more expensive.

Lassen National Volcanic Park

Around forty miles directly east from Redding are the pine forests, crystal-green lakes and boiling thermal pools of the **Lassen National Volcanic Park**. A forbidding climate, which brings up to fifty feet of snowfall each year, keeps the area pretty much uninhabited outside the brief June-to-October season. **Mount Lassen** itself last erupted in 1915, when the peak blew an enormous mushroom cloud some seven miles skyward, tearing the summit into chunks that landed as far away as Reno; scientists predict that it is the likeliest of all the West Coast volcanoes to blow again.

The thirty-mile tour of the park along Hwy-89 from **Manzanita Lake** in the north should take no more than a few hours. The explosion of seventy years ago denuded the **devastated area**, ripping out every tree and patch of grass. Slowly the earth is recovering a green blanket, but the most vivid impression is one of complete destruction. Marking the halfway point, **Summit Lake** is a busy camping area set around a beautiful icy lake, close to which are the park's most manageable hiking trails. From a parking area to the south (eight thousand feet up), the steep five-mile ascent to Lassen Peak begins. Experienced hikers can do it in four hours, but wilderness seekers will have a better time pushing east to the steep trails of the **Juniper Lake** area.

Continuing south along Hwy-89, Lassen's indisputable show-stealers are **Bumpass Hell** and **Emerald Lake**, the former (named after a man who lost a leg trying to cross it) a steaming valley of active pools and vents which bubble away at a low rumble all around. The trails are sturdy and easy to manage, but *never* venture off them. The crusts over the thermal features are often brittle, and breaking through could plunge you into very hot water. Before leaving the park at **Mineral**, make an effort to stop at **Sulphur Works**, an acrid cauldron of steam vents. A magnificent but gruelling trail leads for a mile around the site to the avalanche-prone summit at **Diamond Peak**, and great views over the entire park and forestland beyond.

Visitor centres at Manzanita and Mineral (daily 8.30am–4.30pm; ☎335-4266) have free maps and information on the park.

Lava Beds National Monument

Lava Beds National Monument (May–Sept only), in the far northeastern corner of the state, is the most remote and forgotten of California's parks. The history of these volcanic caves and huge black lava flows is as violent as the natural forces that created them. Before the Gold Rush the area was home to the **Modoc** Indians, but repeated and bloody confrontations with miners led the government to order them into a reservation shared with another, traditionally enemy, tribe. After only a few months the Modocs drifted back to the isolation of the lava beds, and in 1872 the Army was sent in. Fifty-two Modoc warriors, under the leadership of "Captain Jack", held back an army twenty times the size of theirs for five months from a natural fortress of caves now known as **Captain Jack's Stronghold** at the northern tip of the park. On the outside the stronghold looks like nothing special, but a trail into the darkness reveals a subterranean labyrinth of passageways. You're allowed to explore the caves alone, but that takes considerable nerve, and most opt for the ranger-led tours which leave daily at 2pm from the **visitor centre** near the entrance (daily 8.30am–5.30pm; ☎667-2283).

This entrance is in the southeastern corner of the park along Hwy-139, 160 miles from Redding. The town of **TULELAKE** 25 miles north is your last chance to buy supplies – there's nothing in the park itself – and has several roadside budget **motels** and a few cheap restaurants. Both the *Park Motel* (☎667-2913) and the *Ellis Motel* (☎667-5242) have rooms starting from $28 per night.

travel details

TRAINS

Routes

• One train each way every day runs along the coast between **Los Angeles** and Oakland (for **San Francisco**), continuing via Sacramento and Redding to Seattle.

• Eight trains per day connect **Los Angeles** and **San Diego**, with stops including Fullerton where a bus connects for **Disneyland**.

• Three trains daily in each direction connect Oakland (for **San Francisco**) with **Bakersfield** (from where a connecting bus makes the 2hr 30min journey to **Los Angeles**). From both Merced and Fresno train stations, you can pick up buses to **Yosemite**.

• One train daily leaves **Los Angeles** for **New Orleans**, via Phoenix and Houston.

• Three trains daily connect **Los Angeles** with **Chicago**; two run via Flagstaff and Albuquerque, the other via Las Vegas, Salt Lake City and Denver.

• One train daily connects Oakland (for **San Francisco**) with **Chicago**, via Sacramento, Truckee, Reno, Salt Lake City, and Denver.

Journey Times

From Los Angeles: Oakland 10hr 30min; Sacramento 13hr; Redding 16hr; Seattle 34hr; Fullerton 34min; San Diego 2hr 50min; Las Vegas 7hr; New Orleans 40hr; Chicago 51hr.

From Oakland (San Francisco): Merced 3hr; Fresno 4hr; Bakersfield 6hr; Sacramento 2hr 30min; Truckee 5hr 30min; Reno 6hr 30min; Chicago 52hr.

BUSES

All *Greyhound* unless otherwise stated.

From San Diego to Tijuana, Mexico (14 daily; 50min); Borrego Springs (2; 2hr 50min); Scissors Crossing (3; 2hr 35min); Anaheim (12; 2hr 15min); Long Beach (7; 2hr 15min); Los Angeles (22; 2hr).

From Los Angeles one a day, leaving at 5pm for Lone Pine (6hr); Bishop (7hr); Lee Vining (9hr) and Reno (13hr). Note that this bus arrives at most places in the middle of the night.

From Los Angeles to Las Vegas (13 daily; 6hr 15min); San Francisco (9; 11hr); San Diego (7; 3hr); Palm Springs (10; 3hr); Barstow (13; 4hr); Santa Barbara (15; 2hr); San Luis Obispo (10; 5hr 30min); Salinas (9; 8hr); Bakersfield (18; 1hr 25min); Visalia (6; 6hr 15min); Merced (9; 9hr); Stockton (11; 6hr 45min).

From Palm Springs *Desert Stage Lines* to Joshua Tree (4 daily; 1hr 30min).

From Lee Vining to Yosemite (2 daily; 2hr).

From Merced to Yosemite (3 daily; 2hr 25min).

From San Francisco to Los Angeles (9 daily; 11hr); San Diego (11; 10hr 30min); Sacramento (4; 2hr); Redding (4; 7hr 30min); Portland (4; 16hr); Seattle (4; 20hr); San Jose (6; 1hr); Salinas (9; 2 hr 30min); San Luis Obispo (8; 6hr); Santa Barbara (8; 9hr); Santa Cruz (4; 2hr 30min); Monterey (4; 3hr 30min); Modesto (8; 2hr 10min); Merced (8; 3hr 20min); Visalia (2; 5hr); Bakersfield (7; 7hr 20min); Sacramento (25; 2hr); Truckee (3; 4hr 30min); Reno (14; 5hr 30min); South Lake Tahoe (11; 6hr).

From Oakland and San Jose *Peerless Stages* to Santa Cruz (7 daily; 2 hr).

From Fresno to Merced (15 daily; 1hr 10min); Modesto (*7; 2hr 10min); Stockton (9; 3hr); Yosemite (5 a week; 3hr).

From Eureka to Redding (2 daily; 4hr).

From Sacramento to Redding (4 daily; 3hr 30min); Auburn (8; 1hr); Grass Valley (4; 2hr); Truckee (5; 2hr); Reno (18; 3hr); Placerville (6; 1hr 30min); South Lake Tahoe (12; 4hr).

Green Tortoise (see "Basics") runs three times weekly along the coast between San Francisco and Los Angeles, and also run tours of northern California and Yosemite.

CHAPTER FOURTEEN

THE PACIFIC NORTHWEST

The two northern Pacific states of **WASHINGTON** and **OREGON** are similar in both topography and climate. Significantly cooler than California to the south – and hence spared most of the damaging effects of over-tourism – both are split in half by the great north–south spine of the **Cascade Mountains**, with their western portions far more inviting, both as places to live and places to visit.

To the **west** the rains that come in from the ocean, if not quite as unceasing as local folklore might suggest, have created a verdant and rugged landscape, thick with woodlands that on the **Olympic Peninsula** become mini-rainforests. This fertile land is where the population is most heavily concentrated, although the principal cities are not along the exposed coast itself, which remains in a remarkably pristine state, scattered with remote driftwood-strewn beaches. Both **Seattle** and **Portland** lie roughly fifty miles inland, on the route of the I-5 highway which runs from Canada to California. Seattle, the commercial and cultural capital of the Northwest, is nonetheless a major port, perched on the edge of the beautiful island-strewn **Puget Sound**, with a busy network of local and long-distance ferries among the container traffic. Portland lies in the rich farmlands of the Willamette valley, long the historic heartland of Oregon.

Across the Cascades, the **east** is far drier and less hospitable, often indeed verging on desert. Only **Spokane** of the towns is of any appreciable size, though the enduring pioneer spirit means that there tend to be surprises lurking in unexpected places along the way.

History

The first inhabitants of the Americas are believed to have reached the continent across a land bridge over what is now the Bering Strait between Siberia and Alaska. Thus the Pacific Northwest could well have been the earliest populated area of the United States. Little evidence remains of the Native American presence, though the perfectly preserved five-hundred-year-old settlement at **Makah Bay** – engulfed by one freak mudslide and recently exposed by another – provides a great opportunity to appreciate how the local Indians once lived.

Not until late in the eighteenth century was there a significant white presence in the region, and that was very much confined to trading and exploration along the coast rather than permanent settlement. Russian trappers began to make their way down from the north, while European sea captains such as Cook and Vancouver came in search of the mythical **Northwest Passage**. A brief period of hectic competition, in which entrepreneurs of many nationalities vied for hefty fur-trading profits, only came to an end when the whole coast was all but "trapped out". Lewis and Clark, who came hurtling along the Columbia River Gorge in 1804, were the first whites to cross the interior of the continent, and within forty years settlers were streaming in along the Oregon Trail. By the time another forty years had passed, the railways had reached Portland and Seattle, Chief Joseph of the Nez Percé had made his last despairing bid on behalf of the displaced Native Americans (see p.640) and both Oregon and Washington had achieved statehood.

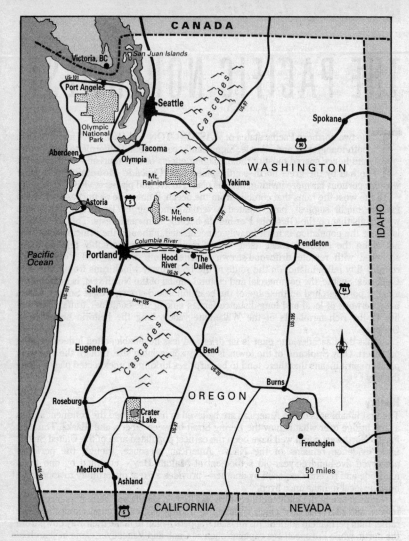

WASHINGTON

Although revitalised **Seattle** is one of America's most popular cities in which to live, its main virtue for the tourist is as a base for exploring the **Puget Sound** and its glorious rural scenery. Cross an island or two, and you come to the **Olympic Peninsula**, its rugged mountains home to rare elk and lush vegetation that merges into rain forest to the west, and with wilderness beaches on its Pacific edge unchanged since Native Americans launched their whaling canoes. Further south, the **lower coast** is more accessible but not as appealing, splodged with industrial towns and holiday resorts.

It has to be said, though, that whatever the tourist board may claim, western Washington is for most of the year very wet: only the summers (late June to September) are usually warm and blue-skied. But even through a haze of fine grey drizzle, the region is incredibly beautiful, and it's very much worth planning to tackle at least a few of its well laid-out and manageable hiking trails.

The parched prairies and canyon-lands of eastern Washington are in stark contrast. If a cross-country trek takes you through Yakima or Spokane, the Grand Coulee Dam is worth a detour; otherwise it would require a major expedition to bring you out here.

Getting Around Washington

All the main cities of the Pacific Northwest are served by both **trains** and **buses**. **Seattle** is regularly connected with **Portland** along the route of the I-5 interstate. *Amtrak* and *Greyhound* run west from **Seattle** across the Cascades to **Spokane** and beyond. *Greyhound* also run south from Ellensburg in **central Washington** via Yakima into Oregon; *Green Tortoise* serve several of the same routes, and *Greyhound* and *Empire Lines* connect **Spokane** with the Grand Coulee Dam and Yakima.

Getting to and along the coast is more of a problem. Buses from Seattle cross the **Kitsap Peninsula**, and provide access to Olympic National Park from Port Angeles on the **Olympic Peninsula**. Most areas not covered by *Greyhound* have local buses, but no buses follow the western side of the Olympic Peninsula. The roads here can be pretty tortuous, and you never know when some vast logging lorry is going to hurtle around the next corner, so it's no place to cycle. In general, your own transport is necessary for detailed exploration.

In the Seattle and Puget Sound area, **ferries** are a faster and more enjoyable option (but often a much more expensive one) for getting around to such places as **Whidbey Island**, the **San Juan Islands**, and the **Olympic Peninsula**. There are also long-distance routes, to **Canada** and on to **Alaska**.

Seattle

Curved around the shore of Elliott Bay, with Lake Washington behind and the snowy peak of Mount Rainier hovering faintly in the distance, **SEATTLE** is beautifully set. Its insistently modern skyline of glass skyscrapers gleams across the bay, emblem of two decades of vigorous urban renewal. In many ways it feels like a new city, groping for a balance between the smart high-rises and a downbeat streetlife that reflects its tough past, its old centre now restored as a colourful historic district.

Seattle's **beginnings** were inauspiciously muddy. Flooded out of its first location on the flat little peninsula of **Alki Point,** the town shifted over in the 1850s to what's now Pioneer Square, renaming itself after a local Native American chief. This was soggy ground, and the small logging community built its houses on stilts. As the surrounding forest was gradually felled and the wood shipped out, Seattle grew slowly until the impetus provided by the Klondike Gold Rush of 1897 put it firmly on the national map. World War I boosted the shipbuilding trade, and the city was soon a large industrial centre – with a significant place in US labour history. Trade unions grew strong, based on the shipworkers, and the *Industrial Workers of the World*, or "Wobblies", co-ordinated the USA's first general strike here on February 6 1919.

Since the turn of the century, the **Boeing** airline corporation has been crucial to the city's well-being, booming during World War II and employing one in five of Seattle's workforce by the 1960s. The obvious prosperity *Boeing* and more recent success stories such as computer software giant *Microsoft* have brought the city jars with a surprisingly large and visible community of teenage runaways and homeless people on the streets.

Arrival, Information and Getting Around

Flights land at Seattle/Tacoma's **Sea-Tac Airport**, fourteen miles south of downtown. There's a **visitor information kiosk** (daily 9.30am–7.30pm) in front of the baggage carousel. Outside, the *Gray Line Airport Express* **bus** ($5) leaves every half hour for the thirty-minute journey downtown, dropping off at major hotels, though further along, the local *Metro* bus makes regular runs along much the same route for 85¢ and takes only ten minutes more. Hwy-99, the Pacific Highway, leads into town.

Arriving **by car**, you'll probably come in on **I-5**, the main highway between California and Canada; for downtown, take the Stewart Street or Union Street exit. The **Amtrak** station at Third Avenue and Jackson Street, just south of downtown, and **Greyhound**, at Eighth Avenue and Stewart Street to the east (☎624-3456), are both an easy bus ride from downtown accommodation. *Green Tortoise* drops off and picks up at Ninth Avenue and Stewart Street (☎324-RIDE). For **information**, walk a couple of blocks towards downtown (the less rundown-looking direction) from *Greyhound*, to the **Seattle-King County Visitor's Bureau**, 666 Stewart Street under the Vance Hotel (Mon–Fri 8.30am–5pm, summer also Sat 10am–4pm; ☎447-4240).

City Transport

It's best to **get around** either on foot or on the free downtown **buses**. Cross out of the free zone, and you pay as you get off; come back in and you pay as you enter. Single fares vary between 55¢ and $1, and tickets are valid for an hour. **Day passes** ($1; bought from the driver) are available on weekends and holidays: **three-day passes** ($5) can be purchased at the **Metro Customer Assistance Offices** (☎447-4800) at Fourth and Seneca or Second and Marion, and can be used on the overhead **monorail** (otherwise 60¢) between downtown and the Seattle Center, and on the waterfront **streetcar** (60¢).

The City

Of Seattle's various districts **downtown**'s main attractions are the busy stalls and cafes of **Pike Place Market** and the restored nineteenth-century **Pioneer Square**, lined with taverns. A stroll along **the waterfront** lets you enjoy fabulous views of Elliott Bay. At the **Seattle Center** in the north, the **Space Needle** presides over a collection of theatres and museums. A couple of the city centre's outlying districts are often livelier than downtown: **Capitol Hill**'s cafes and bars form the heart of the city's gay scene, and the **University District** is a studenty area of cheap cafes and uptempo nightlife.

Pike Place Market and the Waterfront

Farmers first brought their produce to **Pike Place Market** (close to the youth hostel, at the bottom of Pike Street) in 1907, lowering food prices by selling straight from the barrow. The market prospered during the Depression, but by the 1960s it was shabby and neglected, and the authorities decided to flatten the area altogether. Horrified protesters campaigned to preserve this as the affordable domain of the elderly and poor, and after a sharp fight, Seattlites voted overwhelmingly to do so. The restoration has been highly successful; the whole place bustles with energy, and a real attempt has been made to stay true to its roots, even if upscale restaurants are inevitably creeping in. Street entertainers play to busy crowds, smells of coffee drift from the cafes, and stalls are piled high with lobsters, crabs, salmon, vegetables and fruit. Further into the long market building, handmade jewellery, woodcarvings and silk-screen prints are on sale, while over the street small shops stock a massive range of ethnic foods.

The telephone **area code** for Seattle and western Washington is ☎206.

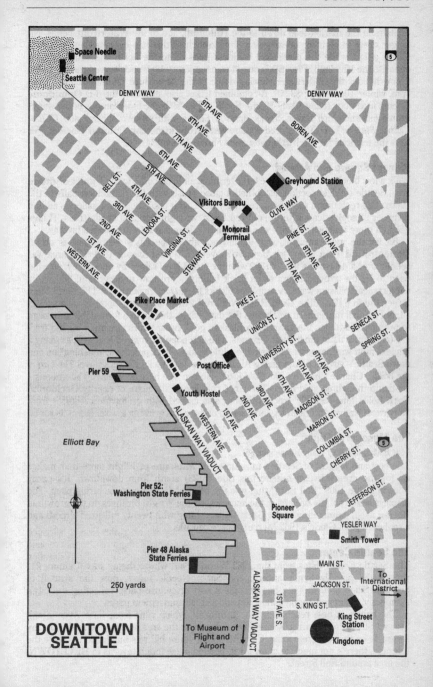

Space Needle

Seattle Center

DENNY WAY

DENNY WAY

9TH AVE.

8TH AVE.

7TH AVE.

BOREN AVE.

6TH AVE.

5TH AVE.

BELL ST.

4TH AVE.

Greyhound Station

3RD AVE

Visitors Bureau

OLIVE WAY

LENORA ST.

2ND AVE.

PINE ST.

9TH AVE.

1ST AVE.

Monorail Terminal

VIRGINIA ST.

8TH AVE.

7TH AVE

WESTERN AVE.

STEWART ST.

Pike Place Market

PIKE ST.

UNION ST.

SENECA ST.

SPRING ST.

UNIVERSITY ST.

6TH AVE.

Post Office

5TH AVE.

Pier 59

4TH AVE

Youth Hostel

3RD AVE.

MADISON ST.

2ND AVE.

ALASKAN WAY VIADUCT

1ST AVE.

MARION ST.

WESTERN AVE.

COLUMBIA ST.

Elliott Bay

CHERRY ST.

JEFFERSON ST.

Pier 52:
Washington State Ferries

Pioneer
Square

YESLER WAY

Smith Tower

Pier 48 Alaska
State Ferries

MAIN ST.

To
International
District

0   250 yards

JACKSON ST.

1ST AVE. S.

S. KING ST.

ALASKAN WAY VIADUCT

King Street
Station

DOWNTOWN
SEATTLE

To Museum of
Flight and
Airport

Kingdome

Stairs in the market lead down to the **Hillclimb**, and to the **Waterfront** below. No longer deep enough for ocean-going ships, much of this has become cluttered with tourist shops while the port's real business goes on to the north and south. Almost opposite the Hillclimb, **Pier 59** is an old wooden jetty which once served the tall ships; it now houses the underwater viewing dome of the **Aquarium** (summer daily 10am–7pm, winter 10am–5pm; $3.50). A combined ticket also admits to the 3-D **Omnidome** cinema next door (daily 10am–10pm). South of Pier 59 is the most famous of the waterfront's fish-and-chips stands, *Ivar's Acres of Clams*, with its own special stop (*"Clam Central Station"*) on the restored vintage **waterfront streetcar**. **Colman Dock** at Pier 52 is the terminal for the *Washington State Ferries* (see p.834).

Pioneer Square and Around

Walk a few blocks inland from the ferry terminal and you come to the **Pioneer Square** area. Seattle's oldest section, it too had a close brush with the demolition balls of the 1960s. The restoration work is more glossy here, with bookshops and galleries adding a veneer of sophistication to the old red brick, wrought iron and shady trees. Things get a bit more raucous at night, when rock music booms out from assorted taverns.

By far the most amusing way to find out about the city's seamy past is on an **Underground Tour** from *Doc Maynard's* tavern, 610 First Avenue ($4). This area was rebuilt after a disastrous fire in 1889 with the street level raised by one storey, so what used to be the ground floors of its brick buildings are now underground, linked by subterranean passageways. A couple of blocks from *Doc Maynard's*, at 117 South Main Street, the free **Klondike Gold Rush National Park** (daily 9am–5pm) is not a park at all, but a small museum. It celebrates the days when, thanks to a formidable campaign to promote Seattle as the gateway to Alaskan gold, prospectors streamed in, and traders (and con-artists) made their fortunes. The dog population fared less well, as many a hapless mutt was harnessed to a sledge while gold-seekers practised "mushing" up and down Seattle's streets before facing Alaskan snow (see Jack London's novel *The Call of the Wild*). Charlie Chaplin's *The Gold Rush* – shown free here on weekend afternoons – sends up the whole gold fever. The large cobblestoned square of nearby **Occidental Park** holds four recently erected totem poles carved with grotesque creatures from Northwest Native American legends, a sign of the city's growing awareness of its roots.

The Museum of Flight

9404 E Marginal Way (daily 10am–5pm; $5).

The best and biggest of Seattle's museums, the **Museum of Flight** more than makes up for the dreary twenty-minute bus ride (#123) south from downtown. It's partly housed in the 1909 "Red Barn" that was the original *Boeing* manufacturing plant. The displays lead from the dreams of the ancients, via the Wright brothers, to the growth of Boeing itself, culminating in the Great Gallery, hung with twenty full-sized aircraft and a replica of John Glenn's 1962 Mercury space capsule.

The Seattle Center

The Seattle Center dates from the 1962 World's Fair, whose theme was "Century 21" (hence the spindly flying-saucer-tipped Space Needle tower, now the symbol of Seattle). Since then the site has become a sort of culture park, collecting the city's symphony, ballet and opera, a museum and a small amusement park.

The centre is best reached by the **monorail**, which runs from Fifth Avenue and Stewart Street downtown (60¢ one-way) and crosses the area now known as the **Denny Regrade** on thin concrete stilts. Considering an entire hill was bulldozed to create the Regrade, there's not much to show for it, beyond a few tough taverns in **BELLTOWN**, the area around Bell Street.

The monorail drops you close to the **Space Needle**, which now feels oddly dated, but still exudes a fair amount of glamour, especially at night, when it's lit up and the revolving restaurant is in full swing. The view from the observation deck, where there's a bar, is unmatched (summer daily 7.30am–1am, Sept Sun & Thurs 9am–midnight, Fri & Sat 9am–1am, winter Sun & Thurs 10am–midnight, Fri & Sat 10am–1am; $4).

The **Seattle Art Museum** (Tues, Weds, Fri & Sat 10am–5pm, Thurs 10am–9pm, Sun noon–5pm; $4) has recently moved to a new Robert Venturi-designed building on First Avenue, which shows off its eclectic collections of African and Pacific art to great effect.

Nearby, the excellent **Pacific Science Center** (summer daily 10am–6pm, otherwise Mon–Fri 10am–5pm, weekends 10am–6pm; $4) is easily recognised by its white arches. This is full of bright and innovative exhibits on science-based topics, sometimes linked to cultural issues; the permanent *Sea Monster House* exhibit, for example, recreates a turn-of-the-century Native American home.

Capitol Hill

CAPITOL HILL, a fifteen-minute bus ride east of downtown, has been the closest the city has to an alternative centre since young gays, hippies and assorted radicals moved in during the Sixties and Seventies. The shops and cafes around **Broadway**, the main street, are now pretty mainstream, but the concentration of easy-going restaurants, coffeehouses and bars provide good day-time cafe-sitting and night-time drinking.

The northern end of the district is quietly wealthy. Mansions built on Gold Rush fortunes sit sedately around **Volunteer Park**, where the **Conservatory**'s hothouses (summer daily 10am–7pm, winter 10am–4pm; free) contain flowers, shrubs and orchids from jungle, desert, and rain forest. Ten blocks east, **Washington Park** stretches away to the north, encompassing the **Arboretum**, where the trees are especially beautiful in autumn. At the south end of the park, the immaculate **Japanese Gardens** (March–Nov daily 10am to around 5pm depending on the season; $1.50) flash banks of pink flowers beside neat little pools.

The University District

Across Union Bay from the park, the **University** (or "U") **District** is livelier than Capitol Hill: a busy hotchpotch of coffeehouses, cinemas, clothes, book- and record shops, catering to the University of Washington's 34,600 students. The area centres on University Way, known as **"the Ave"** and lined with cheap ethnic restaurants and the cavernous *University Bookstore* – an excellent place to seek out a cheap meal (see *Eating*) or the lowdown on the student scene.

There are a couple of museums on the sedate nineteenth-century **campus**. The pale brick **Henry Art Gallery**, at Fifteenth Avenue NE and NE 41st Street (Tues, Wed & Fri 10am–5pm, Thurs 10am–7pm, weekends 11am–5pm; $2), houses American and European paintings from the last two centuries, and mounts small, innovative shows. The **Thomas Burke Memorial Museum**, on the campus' northwest corner at Seventeenth Avenue and NE 45th Street (Mon–Fri 10am–5.30pm, Sat & Sun 9am–4.30pm; free), has carved totem poles, painted wooden masks from the Northwest coast, plaited fibre fans from Polynesia and sorcery charms from New Guinea.

Ballard and the Ship Canal

The "U" district and Seattle's other northern neighbourhoods are sliced off from the rest of town by water. Lake Union, in the middle, is connected to the larger Lake Washington to the east, and the sea to the west by the **Lake Washington Ship Canal**. The procession of boats passing through the locks near the mouth of the canal makes pleasant viewing (bus #17 from downtown). Migrating salmon bypass the locks via a **fish ladder**, laid out with viewing windows. In peak season (late summer for salmon, autumn and early winter for trout) the water is full of enormous leaping fish.

Behind the locks is Salmon Bay, with **Fisherman's Terminal** on its south side crowded with Seattle's fishing fleet and selling freshly caught fish. On the northern side of Salmon Bay, **BALLARD** (reachable by several buses from downtown) was settled by Scandinavian fishermen, whose history is outlined at the **Nordic Heritage Museum**, 3014 NW 67th Street (Tues–Sat 10am–4pm, Sun noon–4pm; $3). Bar a couple of nightspots, there's little else to see.

Accommodation

While there's no shortage of hotel space in Seattle, it can be difficult to find the middle ground between smart, expense-account-type places and seedy dives. Two specialist **B&B agencies** are *Pacific B&B* (701 NW 60th Street; ☎784-0539), who can find rooms for between $40 and $100, and the statewide *Washington Bed and Breakfast Guild* (2442 NW Market Street, #355, Seattle, WA 98107).

Seattle International Youth Hostel, 84 Union St, behind Pike Place Market (☎622-5443). Comfortable, modern and well-equipped. Dorms for $10 (AYH members) or $13 (non-members) a night, although there's a midnight curfew and you'll need a sheet sleeping bag. Closed 10am–5pm.

College Inn, at 4000 NE University Way in the U District (☎633-4441). Very popular, friendly B&B that's well worth the extra cost. Doubles from $40 including a full breakfast.

Commodore Hotel, 2013 Second Ave (☎448-8868). Cheap but cheerless downtown hotel – doubles with bath from $35, and a few dorm beds for $11 a night.

Gaslight Inn, 1727 15th Ave (☎325-3654). Capitol Hill landmark home converted into attractive B&B, with its own swimming pool. Doubles cost $55–75.

Motel 6, 18900 S 47th Ave (☎241-1648). Cheapest of the nationally known motels, but it's miles out of town near the airport; exit 152 from I-5. Doubles from $35.

Pacific Plaza, 400 Spring St (☎623-3900 or ☎1-800/426-1165). Newly renovated 1920s hotel, half-way between Pike Place Market and Pioneer Square, with doubles from $63 a night.

St Regis Hotel, 116 Stewart St (☎448-6366). Scruffy but well located, cheap and safe downtown hotel, with doubles from $32, $5 more with bath.

YMCA, 909 Fourth Ave (☎382-5000). Clean, safe and open to men and women. Dorms $17, private rooms from $38 single, $44 double – more for private TV and bath. Weekly rates from $160.

YWCA, 1118 Fifth Ave (☎461-4888). Women only, with large clean rooms from $24 single, $35 double; add $5 for a private bath. Weekly rates from $150.

Eating

You won't have to spend a fortune in Seattle's elegant new French restaurants to **eat** well: between the coffeeshops of Capitol Hill, the ethnic restaurants of the University District, and above all Pike Place Market there are some excellent pickings. **Seafood** is the speciality, and even if your budget won't stretch to salmon or crab, you'll be able to afford fish and chips, or a steaming bowl of clam chowder.

Byzantion, 806 E Roy St. Reasonably priced Greek in elegant Capitol Hill setting.

Cause Celebre, Mercer St and E Fifteenth Ave. First-class wholefood and cheerful service.

Chile Pepper, 5000 University Way. Good cheap Mexican food.

Deluxe Bar and Grill, 625 Broadway E St. Casual Capitol Hill restaurant serving nachos, salads and pasta, at outdoor tables.

Kokeb, 926 Twelfth Ave. Low-priced and spicy Ethiopian food on Capitol Hill.

Last Exit on Brooklyn, 3930 Brooklyn Ave at NE 40th St, University District. Warm, late-opening coffeehouse; classic student hangout.

Mikado, 514 S Jackson St, International District. Classy Japanese restaurant with a good sushi bar – but not cheap.

The Unicorn, 4550 University Way. British-style pub, with Cornish pasties, steak-and-kidney pies and British beer.

Viet My, 129 Prefontaine Place, International District. Authentic Vietnamese cooking.

Nightlife

Jimi Hendrix was born in Seattle (his *Spanish Castle Magic* celebrated a now-defunct Seattle nightclub), and Ray Charles came here to make his name. Sadly, the current music scene doesn't quite live up to the past, but taken on its own laid-back terms Seattle's **nightlife** isn't bad, particularly if all you're after is a convivial atmosphere and a beer or two. As far as drinking goes, **taverns** in Washington sell beer and wine but not spirits, while **bars** sell everything but must be attached to a restaurant.

Downtown, there's no better introduction to the tavern scene than **Pioneer Square**, where bars such as *Doc Maynard's*, *Old Timer's Cafe* and the *Central Tavern* often host bands. Look out for "joint cover nights", when you can get into five or six venues for as many dollars. Seattle's lively and well-organised **gay scene** is focused around the Capitol Hill district.

For what's on **listings**, *The Weekly*, 75¢ from boxes on the streets, is good for reviews and theatre, cinema and arts listings, and the Friday editions of *The Seattle Times* and *Seattle Post Intelligencer* supply live-music details.

Backstage Club, 2208 NW Market St, Ballard. Quality jazz, rock, reggae or folk acts.

Comet Tavern, 922 E Pike St. Counter-cultural Capitol Hill drinking place. Smoky pool tables.

DJ's Nightlife, 1501 E Olive Way. A tavern/dance club mostly for gay men.

The Double Header, 407 Second Ave. The oldest gay bar around, with pool tables and live bands nightly.

Murphy's Pub, 2110 N 45th St. Massive beer list and live folk music, often Irish, for no cover.

New Melody Tavern, 5213 NW Ballard Ave. Barn-like place, lacking atmosphere, but puts on classy jazz, bluegrass and folk.

Scarlet Tree, 6521 Roosevelt Way. Sweaty rhythm & blues venue.

Spinnaker's, 6413 NW Seaview, Shilshole Bay. High-tech and sophisticated dance club, with great sea view. A small cover ($5) at weekends.

Wildrose Tavern, 1021 E Pike St. A popular venue for gay women, with decent food and often live music or entertainment.

Dance, Classical Music, Opera, Theatre and Film

The **Seattle Center** is the base for the city's cultural institutions: the *Pacific Northwest Ballet* (☎628-0888), the *Seattle Symphony Orchestra* (☎443-4747) and the *Opera Association* (☎443-4711) take it in turns to use its Opera House. Tickets ($10–55) tend to sell out in advance, particularly for the *Opera Association*; but there are sometimes reduced-price last-minute returns.

Theatre is Seattle's strongest suit. The longest-established small company is the *Seattle Repertory Company* (☎447-2222) at the Seattle Center. For more offbeat and adventurous productions, and sparse classics, try the *Empty Space* in Pioneer Square at First and Jackson (☎467-6000). Seattle's most politically right-on company is *The Group*, based in the U District's Ethnic Cultural Theater, 3940 Brooklyn NE (☎543-4327), next to the *Last Exit* cafe.

May's **Seattle International Film Festival** centres on independent venues such as the Art Deco *Egyptian*, in an old Masonic Temple at 801 E Pine Street (☎323-4978), and the *Market Theater*, on Lower Post Alley near Pike Place Market (☎382-1171).

Listings

Airlines *British Airways* 1315 Fourth Ave; *Delta* 410 University St; *Northwest Airlines* 402 University Ave; *TWA* 1001 Fourth Ave.

Airport *Sea-Tac International Airport*, 18612 Pacific Hwy S (information ☎433-5217).

British Consulate On the 8th floor of the First Interstate Center at Third and Madison (☎622-9253). Surprisingly friendly, though they may well refer you to the dragons in LA.

ONWARDS TO CANADA AND ALASKA

VICTORIA on Vancouver Island in Canada is just four or five hours by ferry from Seattle. From May to October, *BC Steamship Company* (☎441-5560) runs the *Princess Marguerite* and the slower *Vancouver Island Princess* daily from Seattle's Pier 69 to Victoria ($30 single, $40 return for passengers, $50 each-way for a car plus driver). You can get there quicker with the *Victoria Clipper* catamaran, also from Pier 69 (☎448-5000), which only takes two hours and thirty minutes but costs twice as much ($70 return, no cars).

The much more expensive **Alaska Marine Highway** is a weekend-long ferry ride that winds between islands and a fjord-lined coast from Seattle to **SKAGWAY**, Alaska. Ferries leave Seattle's Pier 48 (☎623-1149) every Friday at 8pm, May–October, earlier in winter. For more details see p.867.

Chemist *LD Bracken Prescription Pharmacy* 1303 Fourth Ave (☎622-2110).

City Tours *Gray Line* (☎626-5208) runs guided half-day tours by coach and by boat (more fun but less comprehensive), both pricey at $16 each but not a bad way to see the city if you've got more cash than time. Pick-up and drop-off is at major downtown hotels.

Local Ferries *Washington State Ferries*, tickets from Pier 52, Colman Dock (☎464-6400), run to Winslow and Bremerton.

Post Office/post restante The main post office is at Union St and Third Ave downtown (Mon–Fri 8am–5.30pm; ☎442-6255); zip code 98101.

Rape Crisis Line 24 hours; ☎632-7273.

Resource Center for the Handicapped 20150 NE 45th Ave (☎362-2273).

Sport Seattle's main sports (and concert) arena is the huge concrete **Kingdome**, a few blocks south of Pioneer Square. It's home to football's *Seahawks* and baseball's *Mariners*.

Around Seattle: Bainbridge Island

For a brief escape from Seattle, **BAINBRIDGE ISLAND**, a serene half-hour ferry ride across Elliott Bay, is well worth the trip. *Washington State Ferries* leave every hour from Pier 52 ($4 return for foot passengers, $7 car; avoid rush hours), landing in **WINSLOW** – a town so small that once you've admired the harbour and had lunch, you'll probably be ready to head back. This green and rural island is mostly private land; if you want to pitch a tent, there's **camping** at the far end in Fay Bainbridge State Park. *Kitsap Transit* (☎373-2877) runs a limited bus service across the island.

The Puget Sound

The broad and deep **Puget Sound** hooks far into Washington state, a clutter of tiny islands and ragged peninsulas teeming with yachts, ocean-going ships, fishing trawlers, and even nuclear submarines (on the Kitsap Peninsula). At first, the dense forest deterred homesteaders, but soon small logging communities sprang up, and the sound became a vital waterway. As more and more settlers arrived, the demand for Native American land grew, and in the 1850s treaties confining Indians to reservations were put before tribal leaders. Some signed, including Chief Seattle of the Suquamish; but others refused, and accusations of forgery flew. A legacy of injustice was created, with which modern courts still struggle.

The southern end of the sound is increasingly urban. There's little to attract visitors to polluted **Tacoma** or the small state capital of **Olympia**, but mountains, forests and lakes are all around. Popular weekend escapes include the rural parts of **Whidbey Island**, and the beautiful **San Juan Islands** further north.

Tacoma

The first explorers to come to **TACOMA** thought its deep Commencement Bay far superior to Seattle. It's hard to avoid passing through the city, set squarely on the main Seattle–Portland route, but there's no great reason to prolong your stay. These days it's better known for the smell and dirt of its industry – the Environmental Protection Agency has listed it as one of the USA's most dangerously polluted areas – and the strong military presence, with large bases nearby.

The main approach to town is along sleazy Pacific Avenue, with its pawn shops and boarded-up buildings, dividing the town centre from the industrial port area below. To the left of Pacific Avenue, the new **Broadway Plaza** pedestrian area attempts to inject new life into the ailing city centre, at its heart the elegant white **Pantages Center**, a 1918 Vaudeville theatre which now serves as Tacoma's Performing Arts Center (☎591-5894 for details). A short walk away at 12th and Pacific, the **Tacoma Art Museum** (Mon–Sat 10am–4pm, Sun noon–5pm, closed holidays; free) has a few Renoirs, a Pissarro and a Degas among American paintings, together with Chinese jade and robes.

Heading north, Ruston Way curves around Commencement Bay, past the abandoned chimney of the *Asarco* copper refinery, just closed after years of spewing out arsenic. At its tip, **Point Defiance Park** (beaten only by New York's Central Park as the USA's largest urban open space) has beaches, gardens, and trails through acres of shady virgin forest. Here also are a **zoo and aquarium** (summer daily 10am–7pm, winter 10am–4pm; $3.50); **Camp Six** (Memorial Day to Labor Day only Mon–Fri 11am–5pm, weekends 11am–6pm; free), a reconstructed logging camp; and **Fort Nisqually** (summer daily noon–6pm, winter daily 1–4pm; free), a reconstruction of the 1833 Hudson's Bay Company trading post, in the days of the fur traders.

Practicalities

Tacoma's *Greyhound* station is at 1319 Pacific Avenue (☎383-4621), a short if not pleasant walk from downtown; *Amtrak* at 1001 Puyallup Avenue is less central. *Pierce Transit* (☎581-8000 or ☎1-800/562-8109) run **local buses** downtown from here and also connect with Seattle's local *Metro* buses, offering a bargain-rate route between the two cities. Maps are available at the helpful **Chamber of Commerce**, 950 Pacific Avenue (Mon–Fri 8.30am–5pm; ☎383-2459).

For **food and entertainment** in Tacoma, apart from the Pantages Center the best places are out of downtown. The *Antique Sandwich Shop*, 5102 N Pearl Street, near Point Defiance Park, is an offbeat cafe which often has live folk or classical music in the evenings. Also a short way out, *Engine House No. 9* at 611 N Pine Street is a lively and late-opening tavern/cafe bedecked with firefighters' helmets. **Hotels** downtown are either too smart or too grim: if you have a car, keep going the few miles north to *Motel 6* at 5201 20th Street in Fife (☎922-1270), where clean rooms cost $32 a double, or **camp** at **Dash Point State Park**, 5700 SW Dash Point Road, Federal Way, five miles northeast of Tacoma with wide beaches and hiking trails. Another alternative is to take one of the hourly ferries which take fifteen minutes to reach the pleasant, cycleable **Vashon Island**. The **AYH Hostel** here, 168th – Cove Road – and 121st Avenue (members $9 a night, non-members $12; ☎463-2592) may be far from the harbour but, housed partly in a hand-built log cabin and partly in tepees, it makes a pleasant change.

Olympia and Around

Just a muddy little logging community when picked as Washington's territorial capital in 1853, **OLYMPIA** has never really grown into the metropolis its founders hoped for. A top-heavy load of weighty architecture eclipses its rather small centre; you can but wonder at the sheer energy of the pioneers, who plotted something along the lines of

St Paul's Cathedral in what was then a backwoods beset by Native American uprisings. Only completed in 1928, the **Legislative Building** (Mon–Fri 8am–5pm; free) is an imposing Romanesque structure, hung with a massive brass Tiffany chandelier.

Eight blocks south, the small **Washington State Capital Museum**, 211 W 21st Avenue (Tues–Fri 10am–4pm, Sat & Sun noon–4pm; donation), set in a 1920s mansion, juxtaposes a restored well-to-do dining room with displays of Native American basketwork and local natural history, inadvertently underlining a vast cultural gap. In the other direction, the **town centre** offers a few streets of shops and restaurants, presided over by the chateau-like **Old Capitol** at Seventh Avenue between Washington and Franklin streets, its turreted roofs and arched windows facing a green town square. If you've come here to **eat**, try the *Urban Onion*, 117 E Legion Way (closed Sun), across the square from the Old Capitol, which serves its own herb and onion bread. Failing that there's *The Spar*, a few blocks away at 114 E Fourth Avenue – a Thirties diner with a long, curved counter.

A short drive or bus ride (#12 or #13 from Capitol Way and 15th Street) north of Olympia, tiny **TUMWATER** was Washington's first pioneer community, settled in 1845 by a group which included Bing Crosby's grandparents. Its name comes from the tumbling water of the Deschutes River, which now goes into the making of Olympia beer at the **Pabst (Olympia) Brewing Company**, by the Tumwater turning (exit 103) off I-5 (tours and tastings daily 8am–4.30pm; free). Smelling strongly of hops, the brewery overlooks **Tumwater Falls**, now enclosed in a park but once a rich salmon-fishing site for the Nisqually tribe.

Olympia Practicalities

Greyhound is at Capitol Way and Seventh Avenue (☎357-5541), about five blocks north of the Capitol Campus; the *Amtrak* station is about eight miles southeast and not on the bus route. *Intercity Transit* (☎786-1881) runs **local buses**.

Olympia's **Visitor Information Center** (Mon–Fri 9am–5pm; ☎357-3370) is just across from the *Pabst* brewery. In-town **accommodation** is geared towards business visitors; in Tumwater, *Motel 6*, 400 W Lee Street (☎754-7320), has doubles for $32. East of town, *Holly Motel*, 2816 Martin Way (☎943-3000), has doubles from $30; exit 109 off I-5. There's **camping** at forested **Millersylvania State Park**, 12245 Tilley Road south of Olympia, two miles east of I-5 (exit 99), and in **Capitol Forest** fifteen miles west.

Whidbey Island

With sheer cliffs and craggy outcrops, rocky beaches and prairie countryside, **WHIDBEY ISLAND** is a favourite retreat for the Puget Sound's city-dwellers. In its north is a large naval base, but in the southern and central parts, narrow country roads wind through farmland and small villages.

Coming **from Seattle**, the quickest route here is to head north to Mukilteo (near Everett) and catch the ferry to Whidbey's southern tip; boats run every half-hour, and single fares are around $3 per person, $5 with a car. There's also a stopping *Greyhound* from Seattle to Anacortes across the island on Mondays, Wednesdays and Fridays, and Whidbey has its own (somewhat sketchy) bus system, *Island Transit* (☎321-6688). Another ferry leaves Keystone, in the middle of the island, for the Olympic Peninsula every ninety minutes or so, dropping at Port Townsend; single fares are around $3.50 per person, $7 with a car.

The Mukilteo ferry lands at the small town of CLINTON, but **LANGLEY** further around the east coast makes a better first stop, its short high street of old-west wooden storefronts set on a bluff overlooking the water. The **Chamber of Commerce** (☎321-6765) in the small arcade carries information. If you're here in the evening, the *Dog House Tavern* is a convivial gathering place and restaurant.

The middle part of the island is a National Historic Reserve called **Ebey's Landing**. Showcase **COUPEVILLE** here, with its nineteenth-century sea captains' houses, is far more appealing than OAK HARBOR, Whidbey's largest town and the site of most of its motels. On the edge of Coupeville, the *Tyee Motel*, 403 S Main Street by Hwy-20 (☎678-6616), has doubles from around $33; the *Captain Whidbey Inn*, two miles west of Coupeville on Penn Cove, is a lovely B&B costing upwards of $80 per night, serving superb food (☎678-4097). **Bed and breakfast** prices elsewhere start at around $65, and you need to book in advance; contact *Whidbey Island Bed and Breakfasts*, PO Box 259, Langley, WA 98260 (☎321-6272). Whidbey's four state parks all offer **camping**.

The San Juan Islands

North of Whidbey Island, midway between the Washington coast and Canada, the beautiful **San Juan Islands** scatter across the northern reaches of the Puget Sound, and entirely upstage the rest of the inlet. Every summer brings more visitors than the islands can really accommodate, especially on the largest, San Juan and Orcas. You'll need to book somewhere to stay in advance, though even in July and August peaceful corners can be found.

Getting There
Washington State Ferries run about eight boats a day, more in summer, to the islands from **ANACORTES** – an as-yet unreconstructed fishing town at the end of Hwy-20, reachable on *Evergreen Trailways'* daily buses from Seattle. The ferry only stops at four of the 172 islands, but the slow cruise through the archipelago is a delight. Motorists should get to the port early; pedestrians and cyclists have less hassle. Summer fares are around $25 return for a car and driver, $8 for foot-passengers to San Juan island. One ferry a day (more in summer) goes on to Sidney in British Columbia.

If you want to catch an early ferry (the first one leaves before 6am) from Anacortes you may well decide to spend the night. The *Islands Motel*, 3401 Commercial Avenue (☎293-4644), is one of several $35-a-night roadside motels, while the *Majestic*, 419 Commercial Avenue (☎293-3355 or ☎1-800/950-3323), is a recently renovated grand old hotel with plush doubles from $75, which also has the best restaurant (and bar) in Anacortes. Incidentally, **petrol** on the islands is considerably more expensive than on the mainland, so drivers will save by filling up in Anacortes first.

San Juan Island
SAN JUAN, the ferry's last stop, is the only island where the ferry drops you in a town. Though small, **FRIDAY HARBOR** is the largest town in the archipelago and the best place to rent the necessary transport. The *Friday Harbor Motor Inn*, 410 Spring Street, rents out **cars and mopeds** (and runs tours), while **bikes** can be had from *Island Bicycle* at 380 Argyle Street. Ask for advice on cycling routes – and maps, essential on such twisting and badly marked roads – at the **information center** (daily 8am–4.30pm, longer in summer), nearby at First and Spring streets.

Friday Harbor's cafes, shops and waterfront make for pleasant wandering. There's a **Whale Museum** on First Street, but to see the real thing, head past past the coves and bays on the island's west side to **Limekiln Point State Park**. Orcas come here in summer to feed on migrating salmon, and there's usually at least one sighting a day.

Camping is the obvious way to stay on San Juan island, but neither of its (not particularly exciting) national parks has sites. There's a very pleasant cyclists-only camp, the *Pedal Inn* at 1300 False Bay Drive, and *Lakedale Campground* is four miles from the ferry on Roche Harbor Road and reachable by bus. In Friday Harbor, the *Elite Hotel* on First Street (☎378-5555) is the island's best budget deal (where it's essential to book ahead, especially in July and August), with dorm beds from $13, and shared rooms from $25; no kitchen but no curfew. A mile out of town on Guard Street, doubles at the friendly and easy-going *Island Lodge* (☎378-2000) start at $55, less out of season.

There are plenty of places to **eat** in Friday Harbor: *Cannery House* (lunch only) at the top of First Street offers a wonderful view and Mexican-style food; the *Electric Company*, 175 First Street, has live music at weekends. If you're setting off early, the *San Juan Donut Shop*, 209 Spring Street, serves hefty breakfasts from 5am.

Orcas Island

Horseshoe-shaped **ORCAS ISLAND** is quieter than San Juan, its several holiday resorts tucked away in distant coves. The tiny community of **ORCAS**, where the ferry lands, is no exception, with little beyond the grand Victorian **Orcas Hotel** (☎376-4300), which is good for a leisurely breakfast and has rooms from $55. You can rent **mopeds** from *Key Moped Rentals* (☎376-2474) at *The Shoals*, a cafe above the ferry dock; there are no bikes for rent on the island, and the terrain is in any case rather hilly.

Most visitors head ten miles north through the farmlands to the main town, **EASTSOUND**, where the **visitor information** kiosk on North Beach Road, just past Eastsound Square, can provide maps. Its handful of shops and restaurants include *Doty's Cafe*, a homey diner a block inland from the waterfront, and the more upscale *Outlook Inn*, west of the centre. There's also a small Orcas Island Historical Museum (summer only, daily 9am–5pm; donations). Two miles west, at the end of W Beach Road, the *Beach Haven Resort* (☎376-2288) is a great place to stay, its fifty-year-old beachfront log cabins lined up along a densely wooded, sunset-facing cove; in summer the cabins are only available by the week, out of season they go from $60 a night.

The island's real highlight is a little further on at **Moran State Park**, where miles of hiking trails wind through dense forest and open fields to freshwater lakes, as well as up to the summit of **Mount Constitution**. Its four **campgrounds** fill up early in summer.

Doe Bay Village Resort (AYH), Star Route 86 (☎376-2291 or 376-4755), tucked round to the east on a secluded bay, is a lovely place, where cabins go from around $28, cottages $45–70, dorm beds $9.50 to $12.50. The excellent facilities, including an open-air **spa**, can also be used by day visitors ($5).

North to Bellingham and Mount Baker

The I-5 speeds north past the Puget Sound along the mainland towards the Canadian border, cutting past forests, lakes and, eventually, distant Mount Baker. Sprawling **BELLINGHAM** is the first sizeable town you come to, with several **motels** around exit 252 off I-5. *Mac's Motel*, at Samish and Maple Street (☎734-7570), and *Motel 6* (☎671-4494) at 3701 Byron Avenue, which crosses Samish Way, both have rooms for around $35 double. Women can stay at the *YWCA*, 1026 N Forest Street (☎734-4820), not far from the *Greyhound* station at 1329 N State Street (☎733-5251) and the **local bus** terminal. Bellingham's most appealing section is the restored railway community of **Fairhaven Village**, a pleasant drive or bus ride around the bay, and the best place to find **food and drink**. *Tony's* at 1101 Harris Ave is a lovely coffeeshop, sometimes hosting live music, while across the road, *Bullie's* has an extraordinary list of beers.

Natural sights bring most people to the area. **Parks** surrounding the city are laid out with hiking trails, and beyond them to the east are the foothills of **MOUNT BAKER**, 56 miles along Hwy-542. Lummi tribal mythology has this as a sort of Ararat, surviving the legendary Great Flood to provide sanctuary for a Native American Noah in his giant canoe, but it's better known today for its **skiing**, with a seven-month season from early November until May, and the best early snow in the Northwest (ski information on ☎734-6771). There's plenty of good **camping** in the area. Near Bellingham, try **Larrabee State Park**, seven miles south of the city on Hwy-11, or on the way to Mount Baker, **Silver Lake Park**, up Silver Lake Road north of Maple Falls.

The Olympic Peninsula

The broad mass of the **Olympic Peninsula** projects across the Puget Sound, sheltering Seattle from the open sea. Small logging communities are sprinkled around its edges, but at the core the Olympic mountains thrust upwards, shredding rain clouds as they drift in from the Pacific and drenching the surrounding area. In the western river valleys, the dense vegetation thickens into rain forest, and the forests and lonely Pacific beaches provide cover for a huge variety of wildlife and seabirds.

Port Townsend

With its brightly painted Victorian mansions, convivial cafes and vigorous cultural (and counter-cultural) scene, **PORT TOWNSEND** has always had aspirations beyond its small-time logging roots. A would-be San Francisco since the nineteenth century, it was poised for Puget Sound supremacy in the 1890s, when confident predictions of a railway terminus lured in the rich, and Gothic mansions sprang up above the flourishing port. Unfortunately for the investors, the railway never arrived, and the town was left with a glut of stylish residences and a very small business district.

As with many other US port towns, Port Townsend's physical split – half on a bluff, half at sea-level – reflects nineteenth-century social divisions, when wealthy merchants built their houses uptown, well above the noise and brawl of the port. The downtown area is at the base of the hill, its shops and pleasant cafes centring on **Water Street** – lined with proud 1890s brick and stonework. In recent times the old mansions have been restored, and the town has mellowed into an artsy community with hippy undertones and a fair amount of charm.

A good reason for coming here is to enjoy the annual **music festivals** at **Fort Worden**, two miles north – *Jazz Port Townsend* towards the end of July, the *Hot Jazz* festival in February and *American Fiddler Tunes* in early July – for all of which you need to book accommodation well ahead. The well-preserved nineteenth-century fort itself, the set for the film *An Officer and a Gentleman*, makes rather bleak viewing.

Practicalities

Pick up a map and information in Port Townsend at the very helpful **Chamber of Commerce**, 2437 Sims Way (☎385-2722), west on Hwy-20. The **AYH youth hostel** at **Fort Worden** (☎385-0655) offers the cheapest beds; there's also a **campground**. Another **youth hostel** (May–Sept only; ☎385-1288) and **campground** are twenty miles west at **Fort Flagler**, on the tip of rural Marrowstone Island – usually pretty empty, probably because of the lack of public transport, though cyclists might bear it in mind. Otherwise, there are plenty of plush bed and breakfasts around, and the *Port Townsend Motel*, 2020 Washington Street (☎385-2211), costs around $50 for a double.

Port Townsend is the peninsula's best place for **eating and drinking**; try the *Salal Cafe*, 634 Water Street, or *Bread and Roses* at 230 Quincey Street. For more substantial meals, the *Fountain Cafe*, 920 Washington Street, serves classy seafood and pasta. *Russell's Back Alley Tavern*, down an alley off Water and Tyler streets, has live music Wednesday to Sunday evenings.

Port Angeles

Originally named "Puerto de Nuestra Senora de los Angeles" by the Spanish in 1791 (the post office later insisted one Los Angeles was enough), **PORT ANGELES** is the peninsula's main town and the most popular point of entry into the Olympic National Park. Though its setting is lovely, it's very much a working town, the main strip of motels and restaurants making few concessions to quaintness. Timber is Port Angeles' real business, but the harbour has its own harsh beauty: industrial chimneys are back-dropped by mountains, and out in the bay, cormorants fly over the fishing boats.

The two parallel one-way main drags, First Street and Front Street, are cluttered with **motels** (book ahead on summer weekends). The rooms at *Aggies*, 602 E Front Street (☎457-0471), for around $50 a double are palatially large, though *Dan Dee Motel*, 132 E Laurisden Boulevard (☎457-5404), is cheaper at around $30. To get to any of the many excellent **campgrounds** in the Olympic National Park, you need your own transport: six miles south of Port Angeles along Hurricane Ridge Road, the *Heart o' the Hills* is one of the best. For breakfast or lunch, try the tiny *First Street Haven* cafe, 107 E First Street; for dinner, the innovative vegetarian *Coffee House Restaurant and Gallery*, 118 E First Street, practically opposite, has low prices and a pleasant atmosphere.

Port Angeles has the peninsula's best **transport connections**: *Greyhound*, at 215 N Laurel Street (☎452-7611), run daily to Seattle, while local *Clallam Transit* buses go part-way to Port Townsend (change to a *Jefferson Transit* bus at Sequim), into the national park and west around the peninsula to Neah Bay and Forks. *Black Ball Transport* (☎457-4491) run **ferries** to Victoria in Canada for a bargain $5 walk-on fare one-way, $22 with car. The **visitor centre** is at 121 East Railroad Street, near the ferry terminal (summer daily 7am–10pm, winter 10am–4pm; ☎452-2363).

The Olympic National Park

Theodore Roosevelt created the **Olympic National Park** in 1909, partly to ensure the survival of the rare *Roosevelt elk*; it now has the largest remaining herd in the US. Much of the peninsula is protected land, and large areas of national forest surround the national park. Some logging is allowed; the timber trade brought settlers here in the first place, almost every town has a sawmill, and logging is still crucial for local jobs. However, the opportunities for spectacular camping, hiking and wildlife-watching are attracting more and more visitors, and ecologists now reluctantly favour tourism as the lesser of environmental evils.

The **Olympic National Park Visitor Center** is in Port Angeles, at the top of Race Street (summer 8am–8pm, winter 8am–4pm; ☎452-4501), an excellent source of maps and hiking information (be sure to get the free *Northern Olympic Peninsula's Visitor's Guide*). The weather can be dodgy so carry raingear; there's a fair amount of snow even as late as June.

No roads cross the park, but many run into it, so you'll probably end up making several forays into different sections around the peninsula's western rim. *Gray Line* (☎457-4140) run $12 excursions in summer, while in winter *Clallam Transit* buses climb seventeen miles of precipices to **Hurricane Ridge** for cross-country skiing. A **lodge** on the ridge has tourist facilities and information, and **trails** lead off – through masses of wild flowers in summer – to isolated spots.

Neah Bay and the Makah Indians

A perfectly preserved ancient settlement of the sea-going **Makah Indians** – buried for five hundred years, Pompeii-like, by a mudslide – was revealed at Lake Ozette by another mudslide in 1970. The first witnesses encountered bizarre scenes of instantaneous ageing – green alder leaves, lying where they fell centuries ago, shrivelled as soon as they were exposed. Eleven years of excavation have uncovered thousands of artefacts: harpoons, intricately carved seal clubs, watertight boxes made without the use of metal, bowls, toys – all belonging to a period before trade with Europeans. They are displayed at the **Makah Cultural and Research Center** (summer daily 10am–5pm, otherwise Wed–Sun 10am–5pm; $2) in the small and rundown village of **NEAH BAY**, the home of the few remaining Makah. It can be reached by *Clallam Transit* buses.

There are a couple of **motels**: the *Thunderbird* (☎645-2450) with doubles from around $45, and the slightly cheaper *Tyee Motel* (☎645-2223). If you've got your own transport, *Hilden's Motel* (☎645-2306), east of Neah Bay at Bullman Beach, is a better bet at around $40. The village's two cafes are friendly places, but the food isn't great: try the *Breakwater Inn* on Hwy-112 near Seiku – or bring a picnic.

The Peninsula's Ocean Beaches

The wild, lonely Pacific **beaches** that start near Neah Bay and stretch down the Olympic Peninsula's west side still look exactly as they did before the pioneers got here: black rocks point out of a grey sea, populated mostly by seabirds. With their strong currents (and dramatic tides – get hold of a tide-table), these beaches aren't really suitable for swimming, but the hiking can be magnificent. Even if you have **your own transport**, you can expect to do a lot of walking – the roads tend to be rough, and many peter out altogether.

Cape Flattery at the northern corner of the Makah Reservation is comparatively accessible, by an unpaved road, from Neah Bay. A short hike leads to the cape which once "flattered" Captain Cook with the hope of finding a harbour and is the USA's northwesternmost point (excluding Alaska). Below the cape, the waves have worn caves into the sheer rock of the cliff-face, while opposite on **Tatoosh Island**, coastguards run a remote lighthouse. **Beaches** at the south of the cape include **Hobuck** and the crescent-shaped **Shi-Shi**.

The Rain Forests

Incredible though it seems in cool Washington, the river valleys of the western peninsula produce an environment akin to a jungle, as the Olympic rain combines with riverwater from the mountains to exert the overwhelming growing-power associated with much warmer climates. Temperate rain forests are rare, but the peninsula's mild climate and more than twelve feet of annual watering have produced giant trees; mosses cling to the bark and hang in pendants from the branches, filtering the sunlight – while below, three hundred different species of plants fight for space, crowding the ground with ferns, mushrooms and more mosses. The only way to get through the forest is on the specially cleared **trails**, which tend to get slippery as moss grows back again – bring footwear that grips.

The Hoh River Rain Forest

The most popular of the rain forest areas, the **Hoh River Rain Forest** has the only large **visitor centre** (daily 9am–5pm), nineteen miles along Upper Hoh River Road, which leaves US-101 twelve miles south of Forks. You can explore the rain forest along two short trails, the three-quarter mile Hall of Mosses Trail or the slightly longer Spruce Trail, which reaches the Hoh River on a circuit through the forest. More energetic hikers can follow the 36-mile Hoh River Trail right up to the base of 8000-foot Mt Olympus. Climbing the ice-covered peak is a major undertaking; if you just want to camp out along the route, check in with the rangers and get a free **Backcountry Permit**. Cougars and other beasts are still very much present in the park.

Kalaloch and the Queets River Rain Forest

US-101 runs right along the coast beyond the Hoh River, passing a continous strand of windswept beaches. One of the prettiest spots, **KALALOCH**, has a couple of campgrounds and the very pleasant *Kalaloch Lodge* (☎962-2271), which has a good restaurant and large ocean-view rooms from $55 a night. A **ranger station** on the south edge of the short built-up strip has lots of information and suggestions for hiking trips.

South of Kalaloch, US-101 cuts inland around the Quinault Indian Reservation, while the Queets River, and a 25-mile-long dirt road, head inland to the **Queets River Rain Forest**, the least visited of the three main rain forest areas. The luxuriant flora and fauna along the well-marked path includes the **world's tallest Douglas Fir** tree – 220 feet tall and 45 feet in circumference.

Lake Quinault and the Quinault Rain Forest

The most easily accessible and perhaps most beautiful of all the rain forests is the **Quinault Rain Forest**, around the shores of Lake Quinault. The lake itself was already a popular resort area when Teddy Roosevelt visited in the 1900s and decided to proclaim it part of an expanded Olympic National Park. Many thick and impressive groves fan off from the road, but in places it feels a bit overdeveloped. Motels, cafes and lodges like the rustic *Quinault Lodge* (☎288-2571 or ☎1-800/562-6672), where rooms cost $85, line the southern shore.

One of the best short hikes starts from the ranger station just north of the lodge, climbing up and along a small stream through some textbook rain forest vegetation. A huge expanse of dense overgrowth covers the eastern shore of the lake, around which winds a narrow but definitely passable road, perfect for a mountain bike tour. The best **camping** is on the northeast shore, at the **July Creek Campground.**

Accommodation near the Park

Most of the best options for **accommodation** within reach of the park area are in and around **FORKS**. The *Miller Tree Inn* (☎374-6806), five hundred yards east of the town's only set of traffic lights, is a relaxed B&B charging $40–45 for a double in high season (less in winter). *Olympic Suites* (☎374-5400 or ☎1-800/262-3433), on the north side of town, also has doubles from $40. Twenty miles south of Forks, the small but very friendly *Rain Forest AYH Hostel* (☎374-2270), off US-101 four miles before **Ruby Beach**, puts mattresses in the barn when its twelve **hostel beds** are full.

Washington's Lower Coast

As you head south along the Washington coast, the roads improve but the scenery gradually grows tamer. Wilderness beaches give way to holiday resorts, dense virgin forest to privately owned timber land, thinned by logging and replanting and punctuated by completely bald patches of "clear-cutting".

At the southern end of the Olympic Peninsula, US-101 hugs the coast for a stretch before looping awkwardly inland around the **Quinault Indian Reservation**. There have been numerous plans to build a coast road, but the Quinault tribe has so far vetoed them to preserve its beaches. Routes therefore become somewhat contorted, the main highway travelling inland as far as industrial **Aberdeen** in the bay of Gray's Harbor, where Hwy-109 sneaks back up the coast, ending abruptly at **TAHOLAH** at the reservation's centre. (It is possible to hike through the beaches and forests in groups led by Native Americans; contact the Tribal Office in Taholah on ☎276-8211).

The next indentation is muddy **Willapa Bay**, ringed by oyster beds and wildlife sanctuaries. At the base of **Long Beach Peninsula**, **Cape Disappointment** hooks into the mouth of the wide Columbia River, the boundary with Oregon. Before the US-101 toll bridge, and just past tiny **Chinook**, turn-of-the-century **Fort Columbia** (grounds open: summer daily 8am-dusk, winter closed Mon & Tues), houses an Interpretive Center portraying early military life, as well as displays on the local Chinook Indians. The cheapest place to stay is in the fort's old hospital, now an **AYH Youth Hostel** (summer only; ☎777-8755).

This region is covered by two **local bus** services: *Grays Harbor Transit*, based in Hoquiam (☎1-800/562-9730), runs north to Lake Quinault, west along the ocean up to Taholah, and inland to Olympia in the east. It connects with *Pacific Transit* (☎642-4475) at Aberdeen, which then runs south as far as Astoria in Oregon.

The Cascade Mountains

The serene beauty of the snow-capped and pine-covered **Cascade Mountains** conceals awesome volcanic power – as proved by the 1980 explosion of **Mount St Helens**. But away from the grey scar left by the blast, the Cascades offer mile upon mile of forested wilderness, sheltering all kinds of wildlife and traversed by a skein of beautiful trails – which, for all but a few summer months, you'll need snowshoes to follow. Deservedly the most popular access-point is **Mount Rainier**, set in its own national park and accessible from Tacoma or Seattle. Further afield, the **North Cascades** demand more time; Hwy-20, the high mountain road that crosses them, is by far the most spectacular route to the east.

The North Cascades and the Cascade Loop

When Hwy-20 opened up the rugged **North Cascades** to an admiring public in 1972, the towns of the eastern foothills got together and came up with the **Cascade Loop**, to channel tourist traffic their way. It's only feasible during the summer, as snow otherwise closes the mountain passes and completely covers the hiking trails. The towns themselves are best taken simply as bases between trips into the gorgeous scenery, for all their efforts to attract visitors. **WINTHROP**, for example, has dressed itself up in Wild West regalia (befitting its status as the original setting for *The Virginian*).

LEAVENWORTH, on the other hand, has turned Bavarian. Bikes are for rent from *Icicle Bicycle* (☎548-7864), and you can pitch a tent at the **campgrounds** ten miles down Icicle Creek Road (last on the left at the far end of town). In town, the *Edelweiss* on Front Street (☎548-7015) is a **hotel** with one double room at $20, and more at around $33. The **ranger station** just off US-2 provides trail guides and hiking information. *Greyhound* continues to the apple-growing centre of **WENATCHEE**, where a strip of cheap **motels** lines N Wenatchee Avenue.

Wenatchee is connected by *Empire Lines* buses to the resort of **CHELAN**. From the Boat Dock, a mile south, a **ferry**, the *Lady of the Lake* (☎682-2224), sails slowly up long thin **Lake Chelan**, leaving daily in summer at 8.30am and returning early evening ($25). It's a pleasant cruise, stopping briefly at the lake's mountainous western tip in **STEHEKIN**, an isolated village otherwise accessible only by hiking trail or air-taxi ($40 each way from Chelan; ☎682-5555). If you want to explore the North Cascades, you can rent bikes and canoes from the *North Cascades Lodge* (☎682-4711), which also runs a shuttle-bus deeper into the mountains. Rooms at the lodge start at $65 for a double and can be hard to get, so it makes sense to bring a tent. For camping and hiking information (and, for some of the trails, a wilderness permit), visit the **ranger station** in Stehekin, the helpful **Chelan ranger station**, 428 W Woodin Avenue, at the south end of town by the lake (Mon–Sat 8am–4.30pm), or the **National Park Headquarters**, 800 State Street (Mon–Fri 8am–4.30pm) in **Sedro Woolley**.

From Leavenworth, US-2 runs west through the Cascades over Steven's Pass, emerging north of Seattle. Alternatively, US-97 branches off south through the Swauk Mining District, where prospectors once dug for gold. Just off the highway, tiny, ramshackle **LIBERTY** is a curious if gimmicky ghost town, with a year-round population of around seven, still promoting gold-panning from its grocery store – about the only solid-looking building there.

Mount Rainier National Park

Set in its own National Park, **MOUNT RAINIER** is the tallest and most accessible of the state's Cascade peaks. Recurrent jokes characterise its name as a description of its weather: often very wet, with heavy snowfalls during the long winter season. Not until late June or July does the snow-line creep up the slopes, unblocking roads and revealing a web of hiking trails. But in summer, when the deer, mountain goats and marmots reappear, and meadows sprout alpine flowers, the mountain makes for some perfect – and not always tough – hiking.

Admission to the national park is $5 per car, $2 per hiker or cyclist. Its four entrances all lead to distinct sections, though in summer you can drive between the **Nisqually entrance** in the southwest corner and the smaller entrance to the southeast.

Only the Nisqually section is kept open year-round (for cross-country skiing; the others open around June). It's the only part you can see by public transport – confined to pricey day-trips with *Gray Line* from Seattle (☎626-5208; $35; May–Oct only) – and is just short of **LONGMIRE**, around sixty miles southeast of Tacoma on Hwy-7, then Hwy-706. Here, a **hiker information centre** has plenty of trail information. In winter you can rent skis, and year-round the *National Park Inn* offers accommodation (doubles from $45 without bath). Ring ☎569-2275 for reservations here and at the cosy *Paradise Inn* (May–October; doubles from $48 without bath) in **PARADISE**, further up the mountain beyond waterfalls of melted glacier snow. This is a short walk from another, larger **visitor centre**, and several routes begin here.

Paradise is also the starting point for the highly serious undertaking of **climbing the peak**. Unless you're very experienced (and even then, you have to register with rangers) do it with the guide service, *Rainier Mountaineering Inc* in Paradise (☎569-2227), who offer three-day courses – one day's practice, then the two-day climb – and rent out equipment for around $275.

Other Entrances

During summer it's possible to drive from Paradise along rugged **Stephen's Canyon Road** to the park's southeastern corner. Here, the **Ohanapecosh visitor centre** is set in deep forest, near the trout-packed Ohanapecosh River. Two further entrances are accessible from Seattle and the west: the **White River entrance** on Hwy-410 in the northeastern corner leads to the **Sunrise visitor centre** and wonderful views of Emmons Glacier and the mountain's crest; the **Carbon River entrance** on Hwy-165 in the northwest is the least used, and has no visitor centre. There are **campgrounds** near each entrance; for overnight backpacking you'll need a wilderness permit (free from any ranger or visitor centre).

Mount St Helens

The Klickitat Indians who called **MOUNT ST HELENS** *Tahonelatclah* ("Fire Mountain") knew what they were talking about. A perfect snow-capped peak, long popular with scout camps and climbing expeditions, Mount St Helens suddenly exploded in May 1980, leaving a charred area of almost total destruction.

Visiting the devastation is fascinating but slow. You'll need your own transport, and the roads are narrow and twisting; most are closed by snow for much of the year, and some are shut for reconstruction (call ☎274-4038 for an update). There's no obvious base – it's possible to do it in a day from Portland, but this is a heavy drive, and you're probably better off finding a **motel** somewhere nearby. There's a *Motel 6* at 106 Minor Road, KELSO – exit 39 off I-5 (doubles $30; ☎425-3229), and plenty of **camping** in the national forest surrounding the blast area; *Iron Creek Campground* on national forest route 25 is closest.

THE ERUPTION OF MOUNT ST HELENS

From its first rumblings in March 1980, Mount St Helens became a big tourist attraction. Residents and loggers working the forests were evacuated and roads were closed, but by April the entrances to the restricted zone around the steaming peak were jammed with reporters and sightseers. Impatient residents were soon demanding to be let back to their homes. Even the official line became blurred when Harry Truman, a local pensioner who refused to move out, became a national celebrity and was, incredibly, congratulated on his "common sense" by Washington's governor.

A convoy of homeowners was waiting at the barriers, about to go and collect their possessions, when the explosion finally came on May 18 – not upwards but sideways, ripping a great chunk out of the mountainside. An avalanche of debris slid into Spirit Lake, raising it by two hundred feet and turning it into a steaming cauldron of mud. Heavy clouds of ash suffocated loggers on a nearby slope, and drifted east to smother the town of Yakima several feet deep.

Fifty-seven people died on the mountain: a few were there officially, but most, like Harry Truman, had ignored the warnings. The wildlife population was harder hit: about a million and a half animals – deer, elk, mountain goats, cougar and bear – were killed, and thousands of fish were boiled alive in sediment-filled rivers. There were dire economic effects, too, as falling ash devastated the land, and millions of feet of timber were lost.

The main **visitor centre** (summer daily 9am–6pm, winter daily 9am–5pm; ☎247-5473), just west of TOUTLE off I-5, is worth dropping into, for exhibits, interpretive programmes and a free film, as well as lots of useful information. You can't see anything of the actual blast area from here, but by the time Hwy-504 is re-opened beyond the visitor centre you'll be able to drive well up into the devastated area. At the end of the road, two more visitor centres, one at **Coldwater Ridge** and another at **Johnson Ridge**, above Spirit Lake, are due to open in 1992 and 1994 respectively. In the meantime, the **two other routes** up the mountain both involve backtracking to I-5 from the visitor centre and at least a further three-hour drive.

Clogged by cars in summer, route 26 winds round hairpin bends through dark green forest, until bald, spikey trees signal a sudden change: thousands of grey tree-skeletons lie in combed-looking rows, knocked flat in different directions as the blast waves bounced off the hillsides. The wastage is staggering: the trees were deliberately left to rot, as the decaying wood helps to regenerate the soil and provides cover for small animals and insects. Despite signs of renewal – the odd patch of grass or young tree – it's a stark scene. Beside the road, the wrecked car of a couple who ducked the entry restrictions has been left where it was blown by the blast, the rusty roof crushed in. This road ends by a viewpoint across a lake part-jammed with fallen trees; another, narrow route 99, leads on to **Windy Ridge**, an outcrop which overlooks the crater itself – apparently the best view of all, but only accessible once the road is reconstructed.

Eastern Washington

Big, dry and empty, eastern Washington has more in common with neighbouring Idaho than with the green western side of the state. Faded olive-coloured sagebrush covers mile upon mile, and huge reddish rocks loom over the prairies – the powerful landscape of a thousand westerns. The towns, though, are no-nonsense agricultural and commercial centres, and only **Spokane** has any degree of cultural life. The **Grand Coulee Dam** is an engineering marvel with emotive echoes of the Depression, while at **Walla Walla**, near the border with Oregon, are the remains of the home of Marcus Whitman, massacred by Cayuse Indians.

> The telephone **area code** for eastern Washington is ☎509.

Ellensburg

If you're travelling east beyond the mountains by *Greyhound* along I-90, your first major stop will be **ELLENSBURG**, a dusty little town with a red-brick core. On Labor Day weekend (early Sept), the **Ellensburg Rodeo** fills the town with Stetsoned cowboys (and cowgirls) who rope steers, ride bulls and sit on bucking broncos, accompanied by much pageantry. For tickets, call the Rodeo Ticket Office (☎1-800/637-2444).

Greyhound (☎925-1177) and *Empire Lines* stop at Oakanogan Street and Eighth Avenue. The **Chamber of Commerce**, a short walk away at 436 N Sprague Street (Mon–Fri 8am–5pm; ☎925-3137), can provide a downtown map and advice on **accommodation** (book ahead for rodeo time). The *Rega Lodge*, in Motel Square at Sixth and Water Street (doubles around $35; ☎925-3116), is close to downtown. As for **eating**, the Art Deco *Valley Cafe*, 105 W Third Street, is by far the nicest place in town.

Yakima

YAKIMA, to the south, is not about to win any beauty contests: the railway yard, busy with freight trains, is its real centre of gravity. The attractions are few, though it is a base for exploring the Cascades or the wineries of the Yakima Valley to the east. *Greyhound* stop at 602 E Yakima Avenue (☎457-5131), sharing the depot with *Empire Lines*. Pick up a map at the **Visitors and Convention Bureau** at 10 N Eighth Street at E Yakima Avenue (Mon–Fri 8.30am–5pm; ☎575-1300), a short walk away. There are plenty of motels along N First Street, and the central **YWCA**, at 15 N Naches Avenue (☎248-7796), has beds for women from $8.

A couple of new projects aim at cheering up the part of downtown that hasn't been scooped into the main mall. Where Yakima Avenue crosses Front Street, the brightly painted train carriages of **Track 29** house a small collection of shops and food stalls. Opposite, **Yesterday's Village and Farmer's Market** is trying to turn the old Fruit Exchange building into a nostalgic antiques-and-crafts mall. Also in this area, the *Brewery Pub*, 25 N Front Street, serves *Grants* ales from the brewery next door and pub-type **food** in a friendly atmosphere; there are plenty of diner-style restaurants north of here up N First Street.

South through the Wine Country

US-97 runs south from Yakima to Toppenish and the **Yakima Nation Museum** (rough timings only: daily 9am–5pm, closed Jan and Feb; free Mon, otherwise $2; ☎865-2800). In a sort of stone wigwam, the museum (subtitled *the Challenge of Spilyay* – Spilyay being the Yakima version of the recurrent Indian coyote figure) outlines Yakima traditions in a series of big tableaux. The presentation is self-consciously evocative of Indian rituals; information plaques are written in simple, fairy-tale language.

Back on I-82, **wineries** are thickly scattered throughout Yakima Valley. All have tasting-rooms; the Yakima visitors bureau has wine-tour leaflets, or just follow the signs.

Walla Walla: the Whitman Mission

WALLA WALLA, south and east on US-12, is an uneventful college and agricultural town, known best for its mild onions, eaten raw like apples. There's little to see now, but this was the place where the missionary **Dr Marcus Whitman** arrived from the East Coast in 1836. He made little headway in his bid to convert the Cayuse Indians from their nomadic ways into crop-growing Christian citizens, and soon turned his attention to white settlers. In 1843, Whitman guided the first wagon-train across the Oregon Trail: his mission became a refuge for sick and orphaned travellers. The Cayuse eyed the ever-increasing emigrants warily, and when measles spread among the tribe, suspicions grew that they were being poisoned, particularly as Dr Whitman could help (some) whites but few of the Indians – who had no natural immunity to the epidemic. Half the tribe died. Whitman must have known the tribal tradition that medicine-men were directly liable for the deaths of their patients, but continued to take on even hopeless cases. In November 1847 a band of Cayuse Indians murdered Whitman, his wife Narcissa and several others. Fifty more, mostly children, were taken captive, and although they were later released, angry settlers raised volunteer bands against the Cayuse. When the story hit the newspapers back east, it generated such a tide of fear about Indian uprisings that the government finally declared the Oregon land (then including Washington) an official US territory, which meant the army could be sent in to protect the settlers – with drastic implications for the Indians.

The site where the **Whitman Mission** was burnt down by the Cayuse (summer daily 8am–8pm, rest of the year 8am–4.30pm; free), seven miles west of Walla Walla, is bare but effective. Simple marks on the ground show its one-time layout, and a visitor's centre shows a film on Whitman's life.

Greyhound stops in Walla Walla at 315 Second Street (☎525-9313), a couple of blocks from the **Chamber of Commerce**, Sumach and Colville streets (Mon–Fri 9am–5pm). The *Whitman Motor Inn*, 107 N Second Avenue (☎525-2200), has doubles from $50 and an excellent restaurant, while the *Tapadera Budget Inn*, 211 N Second Avenue (☎1-800/722-8277), starts at $32. For women, the centrally located *YWCA* at First and Birch streets (☎525-2570) has single rooms from $15 a night.

Spokane

The wide open spaces and plain little towns of eastern Washington don't really prepare you for **SPOKANE**. Just a few miles from the Idaho border, it's the region's only real city, and its scattering of grandiose late nineteenth-century buildings – built on the spoils of the Coeur d'Alene silver mines, just over the state divide – sport some unexpectedly elegant, almost Colonial touches. But its heyday came and went, and shades of the down-at-heel freight town it became haunt the modern city. It's not a place to linger long, but its pleasant parks and unusual architecture can easily fill a day or so.

In summer at least, the town's focal point is **Riverfront Park**. Set beside the Spokane River, this was originally planned by Frederick Olmsted of Central Park fame, though it was not laid out as specified until just before the 1974 World's Fair. At the back of the park, the river tumbles down a series of rocky shelves known as **Spokane Falls**, once a fishing site for the Spokane Indians and later the home of the first pioneers. The **Gondola Skyride** cablecars (summer daily 11am–9pm; $3) run across the river from the west end of the park.

The main concentration of relics of Spokane's early grandeur is several blocks southwest on W Riverside Avenue, where neo-Classical facades cluster around Jefferson Street. At the **Museum of Native American Cultures**, in the northern part of town at 200 E Cataldo Street (Mon–Sat 9am–6pm, Sun noon–6pm; $2), a fine collection takes in prehistoric artwork from Central and South America – weavings, images, odd little dolls – as well as a number of small tableaux showing excruciating initiation ceremonies, where the candidates are suspended from hooks embedded in their chests.

Practicalities

Greyhound (☎624-5251) and *Empire Lines* (☎624-4116) **buses** share a depot at 1125 Sprague Avenue, a few blocks from the **Chamber of Commerce** at Riverside Avenue and Jefferson Street (Mon–Fri 8.30am–5pm). *Amtrak* trains pull in at W First and Bernard Street. The cheapest place to **stay** is the *Brown Squirrel AYH Hostel*, W 1807 Pacific Avenue (☎838-5968), ten minutes by bus west of downtown. *Motel 6* near the airport in the west at 1508 S Rustle Street (☎459-6120) starts at $32, while the more central *Shilo Inn* at E 923 Third Ave (☎535-9000) charges $52 and upwards. There's **camping** in *Riverside State Park* (☎456-3964), six miles northwest off Hwy-291.

For **eating and drinking**, *Morelands*, at 216 Howard Street, has good cafeteria lunches; nearby, *Cyrus O'Leary's*, W 516 Main Street, serves a reasonably priced menu to rowdy teenagers. Over at 313 Riverside Avenue, *Auntie's Bookstore and Cafe* offers soups, salads, and a quieter atmosphere. At W 230 Riverside, *Henry's Pub* is packed for live rock, Wednesday to Saturday nights. *Knights Diner*, near the Native American museum at N 2442 Division Street, is a beautiful old train carriage in which an astoundingly dexterous chef dishes out large platefuls. Big-name rock groups often appear at **Spokane Coliseum**, N 1101 Howard Street (☎456-3204), also the venue for sporting events (including the odd **rodeo**).

The Grand Coulee Dam and Around

The huge **Grand Coulee Dam** – the largest concrete structure in the world – is around eighty miles west of Spokane. When work began in 1933, it was as much a political icon as an engineering feat. Probably the most ambitious scheme of the New Deal, it was a symbol of hope which provided jobs for hundreds of workers from all over the country, notably the dustbowl regions further east. Folk singer Woody Guthrie worked on the Bonneville Dam lower down the river and was commissioned to write some twenty songs about the Columbia project. These were originally played at local rallies, held to raise investment money and combat propaganda from the private power companies whose interests lay in keeping power production in their own hands. Glowing with optimism, the songs underline the promise the dam held for impoverished working people.

Grand Coulee Dam is now the world's biggest producer of hydro-electricity, and has certainly controlled flooding lower down the Columbia. But the power-guzzling demands of industry switched attention and resources from irrigation, and Guthrie's vision of "green pastures of plenty from dry desert ground" has been much slower to get underway – even now, only half the area originally planned has been irrigated. The whole story is detailed in the **visitor centre**, Hwy-155 on the west side of the dam, which also runs tours of the dam and its generating plants (summer daily 8am–10pm, rest of the year daily 8.30am–5pm). As for the **dam itself**, it's initially something of an anti-climax. It just doesn't look that big, a trick of the huge-scale scenery that surrounds it.

If you need to stay here, the twin neighbouring towns of **COULEE DAM** and **GRAND COULEE** have a few motels and fairly dire restaurants. More appealingly, there are more than thirty **campgrounds** scattered around the long, spindly reservoir of Lake Roosevelt, becoming more woody and secluded as you get further north. *Empire Lines* run a daily service from Spokane to Grand Coulee.

Dry Falls

South of the Grand Coulee Dam, Hwy-155 follows the shore of Banks Lake through more of the Columbia Basin's big country. **Dry Falls**, a few miles beyond Dry Falls Dam, had their moment of glory during the Ice Age when the Columbi poured a tremendous torrent over a drop twice as high and almost four times as wide as Niagara. It must have been quite a sight, but a waterfall without water is not that impressive, and all you can see today is a canyon-walled hole, the remnants of a lake lurking apologetically in its flat-bottomed depths.

OREGON

For nineteenth-century pioneers, driving in covered wagons over the mountains and deserts of the Oregon Trail, **Willamette Valley** was the promised land. Rich and fertile, it became the home of Oregon's first settlements and towns, and the valley is still the heart of the state's social, political and cultural existence. Nonetheless, the pace remains firmly provincial and there's a somewhat dreamy Sixties-orientated culture. Even **Portland** can feel very much like an overgrown village. **Salem**, the state capital, and student-oriented **Eugene**, at the foot of the valley, have a similar atmosphere.

Just beyond Portland, waterfalls cascade down mossy cliffs along the **Columbia River Gorge**, and south of here the twisting path of an old pioneer road leads through more gorgeous scenery around **Mount Hood**. Several highways link the Willamette Valley to the rugged Oregon **coast**, where wide expanses of sand are broken by jagged, black monoliths; white lighthouses look out from stark headlands; and rough cliffs conceal small, sheltered coves. Dramatically varied, the coast takes in acres of sand-dunes and dense forests – not as warm as its Californian counterpart but every bit as appealing. As for towns, there are a couple of working ports and several small resorts, busy in summer, half-deserted and lashed by waves and wind out of season.

Eastern Oregon was only settled on any scale once the prime land in the west was already taken, and the process involved not only ferocious Indian campaigns but also the bitterly violent "range wars" between sheep-farmers and terrorist "sheepshooters" associations of cattle-ranchers. Sheep and cows now safely graze, and some small towns still celebrate their cowboy roots with annual rodeos.

Getting Around Oregon

Portland is well connected by train and bus along the line of highway I-5, to **Seattle** in the north and California to the south. *Amtrak* and *Greyhound* also follow the line of I-84 east from **Portland** as far as Pendleton and then south towards Boise in Idaho. Bus routes radiate from Portland out to **Spokane** in Washington, across **southern** and **central Oregon**, out to the coast, and south towards California.

Though not all the **coast** is served by buses – there's nothing, for example, between Tillamook and Lincoln City – it's excellent for cycling, very level if a bit windy. Once again, if you want to get any distance off the beaten track – and certainly if you're planning to **hike** – getting hold of your own transport can make all the diference. It's worth noting that **hitching** in Oregon is, strictly speaking, illegal.

The telephone **area code** for all Oregon is ☎503.

Portland

Small, friendly **PORTLAND** is not the most obvious tourist destination. It has museums, galleries and parks, a colourful weekend market and any number of cheerful coffeehouses, bars and plenty of jazz music; and as a base for exploring the surrounding countryside, it's hard to beat. But there are no really major sights, and only a patchy nightlife – though its fans say that's half the appeal.

The city was named after Portland, Maine, after a coin toss between its two East Coast founders in 1845 ("Boston" was the other option). Its location on a deep part of the Willamette River, near fertile valleys, made it a perfect trading port, and it grew fast, gentrifying quickly and replacing its clapboard houses with ornate Florentine facades and Gothic towers and gables. Through the nineteenth century – until the new ports in the Puget Sound gained ascendancy – it was a raunchy, bawdy place, notorious for gambling, prostitution and opium dens.

Now Portland is scrupulously salvaging what's left of its past, while risking the odd splash of Post-Modernist architectural colour (one splash, in fact, but it is an odd one). City planners in the Seventies faced a downtown in tatters, part-gentrified, part low-life waterfront, its historic buildings decayed or sacrificed to carparks and expressways. There's been much assiduous gap-filling since, and today, overlooked by extensive parkland on the green west hills, Portland is almost a very attractive city.

Arriving, Information and Getting Around

Greyhound, at 550 NW Sixth Avenue (☎243-2357), and *Amtrak*, 800 NW Sixth Avenue, are either in or very close to the local bus system's downtown free-ride zone. *Green Tortoise* (☎225-0310) drop off and pick up at the *University Deli* cafe at 616 SW College Street. **Portland International Airport** is in the far northeast of the city. Two buses into town leave from right outside the doors; the express *RAZ* ($6) drops off regularly at major hotels, and the cheaper local *Tri-Met* bus (#12; 90¢) runs to SW Sixth Avenue and Main Street downtown. **Max**, Portland's new light-railway, shunts tourists between downtown and the old town, then carries commuters over the river to the suburbs.

Portland's a compact city, divided in half by the Willamette River. The downtown area, where you'll probably spend most time, is on the west bank; the east is mostly residential. You can see much of it on foot: the friendly **visitor centre**, in the Willamette Center, 26 SW Salmon Street (Mon–Fri 8.30am–5pm; ☎222-2223), can provide maps and information. The **bus system** is based at the downtown "transit malls" along Fifth Avenue (southbound) and Sixth Avenue (northbound). Each bus shelter has a small symbol – brown beaver, blue snowflake, purple rain – as a route code. The nearby **Tri-Met Customer Assistance Office** on Pioneer Square (Mon–Fri 8am–6pm; ☎233-3511) can sort you out if you find it confusing. Buses are free in the downtown zone, and otherwise 90¢ to $1.20 (all-day passes cost $3). Portland's **post office** is at 715 NW Hoyt Street (Mon–Fri 8.30am–8pm, Sat 8.30am–5pm; ☎294-2424; zip code 97208).

The City

When the sun shines, **Pioneer Courthouse Square** is Portland's focal point, filled with music and people. Red-bricked and lined with curving steps, the square is the centrepiece of downtown's new look – a compact mix of gleaming new offices and crumbly old plasterwork, punctuated by small grassy parks. This is where to find the malls, theatres and the main museums.

A block up from the transit malls along Fifth and Sixth avenues, **Broadway** pulls together Portland's mix of decayed grandeur and new wealth, prestigious hotels sharing space with great white crumbling movie palaces. One such, the grand *Portland*, has been restored as part of the **Portland Center for the Performing Arts**. Across the park, next to the columned front of the **Masonic Temple**, is the long, low facade of **Portland Art Museum** (Tues–Thurs 11am–7pm, Fri 11am–9.30pm, Sat & Sun noon–5pm; $2.75, free Tues 4–7pm). The collection is wide ranging and well laid-out, with haunting Northwest Indian masks, squat Mexican statues, ancient Chinese figures – and one of Monet's *Waterlilies*. Opposite the museum, beside an old, ivy-covered church, the free **Oregon Historical Center** (Mon–Sat 10am–4.45pm) has fascinating displays on Oregon's covered-wagon past, and an excellent little bookshop.

At the junction of Madison Street and Fifth Avenue is Portland's one sight of national, if not world, renown – Michael Graves' **Portland Building**, a concoction of concrete, tile and glass, adorned with rosettes and pink and blue tiling. It's quite possible to walk straight past without realising this is anything special; in fact it was the USA's first post-modern building. On closer examination it's certainly eclectic: an uninhibited (some say flippant) re-working of classical and other motifs that outraged conservatives and

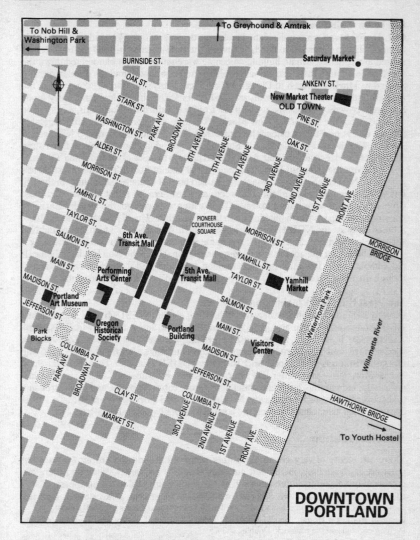

DOWNTOWN PORTLAND

delighted the avant-garde. Portland relished the controversy, going so far as to hoist an enormous kneeling copper figure of *Portlandia* above the main entrance.

A few blocks further east, the **riverfront** has recently been rescued from over a century of burial beneath wharves, warehouses, and, more recently, an express highway, and is now lined by the mile-long **Waterfront Park**. Just behind the park around Salmon Street, the modern, grey and glassy **World Trade Center** houses a carousel (daily 11am–5pm) and the **Carousel Museum** – really a workshop for restoring the wooden animals. A couple of blocks over, around First and Yamhill, the small **Yamhill Historic District** is lined with 1890s buildings. **Yamhill Marketplace** (actually built in 1982) has a couple of produce stalls, though most of its stands now serve hot food.

Old Town, Chinatown and Nob Hill

Old Town, seven rather desolate blocks north, was where Portland was originally founded. The area tended to flood, and when the railway came in 1883 the town centre shifted away; its big, ornate buildings became warehouses and it plummetted down the social scale, though there are now a few bistros and boutiques amid the dereliction. The **Saturday Market** (March to Christmas Sat 10am–5pm, Sun 11am–4.30pm) packs the area around Burnside Bridge with arts and crafts stalls, street musicians, spicy foods and lively crowds. Across an angular plaza from the **Skidmore Fountain**, a colonnade stretches from the side of the **New Market Theater**, a restored theatre-cum-vegetable market that is now full of cafes. The **American Advertising Museum**, 9 NW Second Avenue (Wed–Fri 11am–5pm, Sat–Sun noon–5pm; donation), gives a fascinating account of the rise of advertising, from printed posters to tapes of old radio and TV ads.

Away from the river, up Burnside, the oriental gate at Fourth Avenue marks what's left of **CHINATOWN**. This was once the second largest Chinese community in the US, but white unemployment in the 1880s led, as elsewhere, to racist attacks, and most Chinese workers were forced to leave. The further west you go, the sleazier Burnside becomes, though it's worth pushing on to the labyrinthine *Powell's Bookstore* at no. 1005. A bus ride away, the **NOB HILL** district (or "North West Section") focuses around NW 23rd Avenue and NW 21st Avenue: the name was borrowed from San Francisco by a grocer who hoped the area would become as fashionable as the Nob Hill back home. It did, almost, and a few multicoloured wooden mansions add a San Franciscan tinge – though the main interest up here is the neighbourhood's cafes and restaurants.

The West Hills and Washington Park

Directly behind Nob Hill are the wooded bluffs of elegant **WEST HILLS**. A special bus (#63) winds to the green and leafy **Washington Park**, home to a **zoo** (daily 9.30am–7.30pm; $3). In summer, there are free evening concerts for visitors; **Zoo Jazz** on Wednesdays and **Zoo Grass** (bluegrass) on Thursdays. Across the car park, the **Oregon Museum of Science and Industry (OMSI)** (summer Tues–Sat 9am–9pm, Sun & Mon 9am–6pm, winter Sat–Thurs 9am–5pm, Fri 9am–8pm; $4.50), is a "hands-on" set-up: kids thump, jump and shout at the more robust exhibits, and play astronauts to discover the mysteries of gravity. Nearby, the **World Forestry Center** (daily 10am–5pm; $2) goes in for similar tactics, not least in its seventy-foot "talking" tree.

Accommodation

There are plenty of very cheap old **hotels** scattered around the downtown area, but most are fairly shabby, inside and out. Hostel rooms are better value, and there are dozens of motels off the interstates and along Sandy Boulevard in the northeast .

Clinkerbrick House, 2311 NE Schuyler (☎281-2533). This peaceful Dutch Colonial B&B inn, some way out from the centre, has a lovely garden and comfortable rooms from $60 a night.

General Hooker's House, 125 SW Hooker St (☎222-4435). Small and relaxed B&B inn, offering evening cocktails on the roofdeck. Doubles $50–75.

Heathman Hotel, 1009 SW Broadway (☎241-4100 or ☎1-800/551-0011). Restored downtown landmark, with elegant teak-panelled interior. It would be a standout anywhere. Rooms start at over $110.

Mallory Hotel, 729 SW 15th Ave at Yamhill (☎223-6311 or ☎1-800/228-8657). Old and well-worn, with comfortable if slightly spartan doubles from $45, just a few blocks from Pioneer Square.

Portland International AYH Hostel, 3031 SE Hawthorne Blvd (☎236-3380). Cheery old Victorian house, across the river in a lively neighbourhood. Dorm beds $9 AYH members, $12 non-members.

Travelodge, 949 E Burnside St (☎234-8411). Standard motel, half a mile east of Pioneer Square. $35.

Youth Hostel Portland International, 1024 SW Third St (☎241-2513). Privately run, with a funky feel, and open 24 hours. Dorm beds $10, private rooms $15–20.

YWCA, 1111 SW Tenth St (☎223-6281). Clean and central – right next to the downtown arts centre – but its very few rooms are often booked solid months in advance. Doubles $20, for women only.

Eating

Friendly and unpretentious are the two words that come to mind most often to describe Portland's **eating** options, the bulk of which are concentrated in the downtown area, with quite a few in the Nob Hill area to the northwest and a handful on the less-touristed east side of the river, on and around Hawthorne Boulevard.

Brasserie Montmartre, 626 SW Park Ave (☎224-5552). Pseudo-Left Bank bistro. Free live jazz and good food. Not exactly cheap, but the only place to get fresh pasta with pesto and scallops at 2am.

Dan and Louis Oyster Bar, 208 SW Ankeny St (☎227-5906). Good cheap Old Town seafood.

Cisco and Pancho's, 107 NW Fifth Ave (☎223-5048). Lively, inexpensive Tex-Mex restaurant with free live jazz or blues most evenings.

Jake's Famous Crawfish, 401 SW 12th Ave (☎226-1419). Portland's prime spot for fresh seafood, though at weekends it's packed. The daily fish specials are excellent and not exorbitantly priced.

L'Auberge, 2601 NW Vaughn St (☎223-3302). Exquisite French dishes with a nouvelle emphasis on fresh local ingredients; prix fixe meals start at $35, plus wine. Cheaper menu in the upstairs bar.

McCormick and Schmick's, 235 SW First Ave (☎224-7522). Excellent fish restaurant, with a variety of ultra-fresh nightly specials, and a lively oyster bar.

Metro on Broadway, 911 SW Broadway St (☎295-1200). A dozen distinct low-priced stands offer food from around the world, under one roof; live jazz piano most evenings.

Old Wives' Tales, 1300 E Broadway St (☎238-0470). Feminist cafe with great breakfasts, sandwiches and innovative vegetarian dishes.

Vat and Tonsure, 822 SW Park Ave (☎227-1845). Unreconstructed Beat Generation hangout, energised by good-sized portions of bistro-style food, copious amounts of wine, and reasonable prices.

Drinking and Nightlife

Portland's streets can seem pretty quiet at night, but there's a lot more going on here than you might at first think. **Coffeehouses** and dozens of **bars** form the fulcrum of a lively scene, and the city is a beer-drinker's heaven, with dozens of local microbreweries. For **music**, the place to head is downtown, on- and off-Broadway. *The Downtowner* and *Willamette Week*, and the younger and livelier *PDXS*, available free on most street corners, have up-to-the-minute listings of what's on and where.

Bars, Pubs and Coffeehouses

B Moloch's, 901 SW Salmon St (☎221-5700). Crowded downtown brew-pub, with beer ranging from *Widmer's* weisen lagers to *Deschutes'* Black Butte Porters, and good-value designer pizzas.

Cafe Omega, 711 SW Ankeny St (☎226-2508). Hyper-trendy, post-industrial, 24-hour Old Town espresso bar just off Burnside St, next to the *Elvis is King* sound and light automated freak show.

Dublin Pub, 6821 SW Beaverton Hillsdale Hwy (☎297-2889). Traditional Irish pub, with regular live folk music, including bagpipes, and well-kept pints of Guinness. A short walk from the youth hostel.

Produce Row Cafe, 204 SE Oak St (☎232-8355). Just across the river amongst the still-working fruit-and-vegetable warehouses, with about a million different beers and gigantic sandwiches to help soak it up. Pool tables and a varied crowd keep things interesting.

Rimsky Korsakoffee House, 707 SE 12th Ave (☎232-2640). Looks like someone's house from the outside, but inside live chamber music enlivens a very pleasant if slightly cliquish cafe.

Music Venues

Cafe Vivo, 555 SW Oak Ave (☎228-8486). Lively jazz and blues venue.

East Avenue Tavern, 727 E Burnside St (☎236-6900). Located about half a mile east of the river, with nightly Irish, folk or bluegrass music.

Key Largo, 31 NW First Ave (☎223-9919). Tropical decor, steamy dance floor, and the hottest blues bands. Cover at weekends only.

Melody Ballroom, 615 SW Alder (☎232-2759). Cavernous old dancehall, a prime venue for up-and-coming pop bands and touring indie stars.

Satyricon, 125 NW Sixth Ave (☎243-2380). Somewhat forbidding post-punk club in a seedy neighbourhood, mixing live bands and various oddball acts. Cover free–$5, and good bar food.

The Hobbit, 4420 SE 39th Ave (☎771-0742). Well out from downtown, but worth the ride for the city's best late-night live jazz, from trad through bebop and beyond. Cover free–$12.

Parchman Farm, 1204 SE Clay St (☎235-7831). Intimate club; good pizzas, great jazz, no cover.

The City, 13 NW 13th Ave (☎224-2489). Portland's largest and liveliest gay nightclub, with huge dance floors and occasional live acts. Thurs–Sun only, till 4am Fri and Sat; cover $2–6.

Portland Underground, 333 SW Park Ave (☎775-7232). All sorts of bands, plus rappers and live DJs mixing up a range of house and reggae and generally artsy, alternative sounds; cover under $5.

Red Sea, 318 SW Third Ave (☎241-5450). Small dance floor in the back of an Ethiopian restaurant, grooving most nights to DJ'ed reggae and rockers tunes. No cover, strong drinks.

Classical Music, Theatre and Cinema

The opening of the *Performing Arts Center* on Broadway, coupled with the opulent restoration of the *Arlene Schnitzer Concert Hall* next door, has given Portland's **arts scene** a new lease on life; for what's on and ticket information, call the **events hotline** on ☎233-3333. The **Oregon Symphony Orchestra** perform at the concert hall (☎243-7350) from September to April; tickets range from $15 to $40 for evening performances, but you can catch a Sunday afternoon concert for as little as $7. **Free concerts** are held in Pioneer Square, Waterfront Park, and at the zoo in the summer, as well as year-round at the *Old Church*, Eleventh Avenue and Clay Street downtown, every Wednesday at noon.

The *Performing Arts Center* (☎248-4496) is the focus of Portland's **theatre** scene. One of its two small auditoria, the cherrywood-panelled *Intermediate Theatre*, is also the main venue for the local chamber orchestra and ballet companies; the other, the high-tech *Winningstad Theatre*, is used by the *Storefront Theater*, performing tough, original plays; and *New Rose Theater*, who tend to keep more to the classics. A few blocks away at SW Third Avenue and Clay Street, the *Civic Auditorium* (☎248-4496) is a venue for big musical extravaganzas, operas and the *Oregon Shakespeare Festival* (Oct–Feb).

You'll find listings and reviews of all sorts in the free *Willamette Week*.

Around Portland: Columbia River Gorge and Mount Hood

The **Columbia River Gorge**, twenty miles northeast of Portland, was scoured deep and narrow by huge glaciers and rocks during the Ice Age. Now it's covered with green fir and maple trees, which turn fabulous shades of gold and red in the autumn, and narrow white waterfalls cascade down its sides. The best way to see the gorge is by **car**, allowing plenty of time – whatever the tourist leaflets say, it's much better not to attempt the gorge and Mount Hood in one day. A nice **Mount Hood Loop** takes in both areas, but leaves no time for walking. *Greyhound* stop at **Cascade Locks**, and more scenic – but brief – day **tours** are run from Portland during the summer by *Gray Line* ($25; ☎226-6755).

Early British explorers such as Drake and Cook accidently missed the Columbia River. It was left to the American trader Robert Gray to cross the sandbar at its mouth in 1792 and sail into Oregon's interior. More interested in buying furs than making maps, he didn't follow the river very far, and its first non-native explorers in fact came down the Columbia the other way – a tired Lewis and Clark, on the last stage of their 1804 trek. Forty years later, the gorge became the final leg of the Oregon Trail, negotiated by pioneer families on precarious rafts.

Mount Hood is the tallest of the Oregon Cascades. The highest point on the loop road, **Barlow Pass**, is named after Samuel Barlow, a wagon-train leader who blazed the first trail around the gorge. Much of the **Barlow Road** is still followed by Hwy-26, including the steep ridges where wagons frequently skidded out of control and plummeted downhill. You can still see deep gashes on some of the trees where ropes were fastened to check the wagons' descent.

Shortly after Hwy-35 meets Hwy-26, a turning up the mountain leads to the solid stone **Timberline Lodge** (☎272-3311), another New Deal scheme which is now a year-round ski resort, good for hiking in summer; rooms cost from around $55 double. Out of season, the deserted roads around here can feel downright eerie, especially once the realisation begins to dawn that *Timberline* was the set for the horror film *The Shining*.

South through the Willamette Valley

South of Portland, highway I-5 threads towards the Californian border along a series of inland valleys. It bypasses historic **OREGON CITY**, thirteen miles south of Portland. Set by the falls of the Willamette River (and connected by the city's *Tri-Met* bus service), this was the first state capital, at the end of the Oregon Trail. Today, the split-level town consists of a short, turn-of-the-century high street, connected by steps, steep streets and a cliff-face elevator to an uptown area of old wooden houses set on a bluff.

Salem: the State Capital

The build-up of motels and fast-food chains that ushers you into **SALEM** is deceptive for what is in fact a small and rather staid little town, content dutifully to point visitors around its quota of attractions, but not expecting them to linger. Its showpiece is the 1869 **Reed Opera House**, now a mall full of antique shops. A short walk from the downtown shopping area the tall, white, Vermont-marble **capitol building** is topped with a large gold-leaf pioneer, axe in hand, eyes towards the West. Next to the capitol, tree-lined **Willamette University** is the oldest university in the West.

Salem is a possible day trip from Portland (just an hour away). *Greyhound* is at 450 Church Street NE (☎362-2428), *Green Tortoise* drops off at the Bingo truckstop, exit 263 from I-5, and *Amtrak* is at 13th and Oak streets. The best **place to stay** for women is the *YWCA*, 768 State Street (☎581-9922), next to the university, at around $15 a day. Space is tight, as also at the *YMCA*, 685 Court Street (☎581-9622), two blocks away. There are plenty of motels: *Motel 6*, quite a way out at 2250 Mission Street SE (☎588-7191), has doubles for $33. **Camping** options are limited to the *KOA* site, 1596 Lancaster Drive SE (☎581-6736), on the outskirts of town; 26 miles east of Salem, **Silver Falls State Park**, 20024 Silver Falls Highway (☎873-8681), has a much more attractive location. The area around the university is not the busy **food** scene you might expect, though *Murphy's*, 515 12th Street SE, is a pleasant bar and restaurant. *Euphoria Cafe* on Court Street sells good homemade food during the day.

Eugene

EUGENE dominates the lower end of the Willamette Valley – a lively social mix of students and professionals, loggers and hippies. It's Oregon's second largest centre, and has been a cultural focus since the days of the travelling theatre groups last century. Now, beyond the standard downtown shopping malls, Eugene's markets make colourful wandering, and ethnic eateries are out in force. The **University of Oregon** campus in the city's southeast corner lends a youthful feel. Its **Museum of Art** (Wed–Sun noon–5pm; free) has a strong Asian collection.

Eugene is also a **sports** capital – the runner Mary Decker Slaney (of the famed dispute with Zola Budd) hails from here, and locals even claim to have started the Seventies jogging revolution. Trails and paths abound for runners and cyclists, both in the city centre and along leafy river banks. The ideal way to get around is a bike, which can be rented from *Pedal Power*, 245 6th Street, or the *Bicycle Barn*, 460 Coburg Road.

Though short on sights as such, Eugene offers two big markets, especially the weekly **Saturday Market** (Eighth and Oak between April and Christmas), which is something of a carnival, with live music and street performers. Tie-dye and wholefoods set the tone, but rastas, skateboarders, punks and students join in. **Fifth Street Market** to the north is more touristy, though still lively, set in a converted chicken processing plant and selling arts, crafts, and clothes, as well as a huge variety of ethnic food, from Chinese to Mexican to fish and chips.

Greyhound are at Tenth Avenue and Pearl Street (☎344-6265), *Amtrak* pull in at Fourth Avenue and Willamette, and *Green Tortoise* stop at Fifteenth Avenue and Kincaid Street (☎937-3603). There's a **visitor centre** downtown at 307 W Seventh Avenue (Mon–Fri 8.30am–5pm; ☎484-5307). *Motel 6* offer $29 doubles at 3690 Glenwood Drive (☎687-2395), a mile from the university, two from downtown, and *Eugene Motor Lodge Motel* is more central at 476 E Broadway (☎344-5233); doubles from $32. **Campgrounds** are much further out: *Fern Ridge Lake* is the closest, twelve miles west on US 126.

With over fifteen thousand students to feed, Eugene has plenty of places to **eat**. *Cafe Zenon*, 898 Pearl Street, is an eclectic but pricey bistro; the cheaper *Keystone Cafe*, 395 W Fifth Street, serves high-quality American and Mexican food. To the east, *Old Town Pizza* at 174 E Broadway is the best of many pizza places, while opposite the university, *Taylor's Bayou Kitchen*, 394 E 13th Street, has good, well-priced Cajun cooking and nightly live music. The **WOW Hall**, 291 W 8th Street (☎687-2746), once a meeting hall for the "Wobblies", is an informal venue for up-and-coming bands.

The **Oregon Country Fair**, a big hippy-flavoured festival of music, arts, food and dancing, is held twenty minutes west on US-26 in **VENETA** on the second weekend in June ($5 on the first day, $6 a day thereafter). Traffic then is heavy, and even with a car it's easier to take the local *LTD* buses, which run every half-hour during the fair for 25¢.

South to California

South of Eugene along I-5, almost to the California border, **GRANTS PASS** lies on the Rogue River, which tumbles vigorously from the Cascades. It earns its living mainly from taking visitors **whitewater rafting**. Half a day will cost around $40, a full day $50 – the **visitor centre**, just off I-5 at 1501 NE Sixth Street (☎1-800/547-5927 or ☎476-7717) can provide brochures from more than two dozen *licensed* (and so safer) river guides.

The Oregon Caves
At the small town of **CAVE JUNCTION** there's a turning off Hwy-199 for the **Oregon Caves**, Oregon's only national monument, tucked in a wooded canyon at the end of a narrow, twisting road (*Greyhound* run to Cave Junction, but you have to cover the last twenty miles to the caves yourself). It's actually one enormous cave, with smaller passages leading off. The dripping marble walls are covered with elaborate stalactites and stalagmites. Organised (and very cold) tours of the caves run all year round (75min; $6; ☎592-3400). Eight miles from Cave Junction, the **Fordson Home Hostel**, 250 Robinson Road (☎592-3203), offers a cheap bed ($3–6), camping and $2 discount off entry to the caves for non-Americans. There's plenty of other camping around, either at the two US Forest Service campgrounds near the caves or at *Woodland Echoes Motel and Campground*, 7901 Caves Highway (☎592-3406; motel rooms around $20 a night).

Ashland and the Shakespeare Festival
Throughout Oregon, small **ASHLAND** is identified with William Shakespeare; a real anomaly among the timber and dairy-farming towns of the south. For fifty years, the **Oregon Shakespeare Festival** has been held here each summer, packing audiences into the half-timbered **Elizabethan Theater**. It may all be phony, but Ashland is no more tacky than Shakespeare's real birthplace, and in some ways has the distinct edge. Its setting, between the Cascade and the Siskiyou mountains, is magnificent, there's good skiing in the winter and river-rafting in summer, performance standards are high,

and there's some excellent contemporary fringe theatre – not to mention pleasant cafes and a young, friendly atmosphere when the nearby college is in session.

The **festival** runs from February to October. Shakespeare is performed at the *Elizabethan* and the modern *Angus Bowmer* theatres, both in **Lithia Park**, while the smaller *Black Swan*, off Pioneer Street, stages contemporary plays (☎482-2111; $10–18 though sometimes half-price on the day; standing at the *Elizabethan* for $5). Contemporary drama comes cheaper ($5–10): try the *Actors' Workshop Theater*, 295 E Main Street (☎482-9659; tickets from *Blue Dragon* bookshop), the *Oregon Cabaret Theater*, in a renovated pink church at First and Hagerdine Street (☎488-1926), or the *New Playwright's Theater*, 31 Water Street (☎482-9286).

The **Chamber of Commerce** is at 110 E Main Street; *Greyhound* stop at 91 Oak Street (☎482-2516). For **accommodation**, the Ashland *AYH Youth Hostel*, 150 Main Street (☎482-9217 – book ahead), or one of the **motels** along Main Street should suffice. There are a few $30-a-night motels along here, such as the *Manor Motel*, 476 N Main Street (☎482-2246). Otherwise rooms in town are relatively expensive, especially the numerous B&Bs which charge up to $150.

There are also quite a few good places to eat and drink, ranging from soup-and-sandwich spots like the *Ashland Bakery Cafe,* 28 E Main Street, to more upscale haunts like *Alex's Plaza Restaurant,* 35 N Main Street; the best place to drink is the *Rogue River Brewery,* 31-B Water Street just off N Main Street, which has a dozen of Oregon's best micro-brewed beers as well as pizzas and nightly live music.

The Oregon Coast

Although the **Oregon coast** is as beautiful as any in the West, the Californian sun (summer temperatures here stay in the sixties and seventies) draws off the tan-seeking masses, leaving Oregonians to hike and clam-dig along their own four hundred miles, all of it public land. State park after state park lines the shore, scattering campgrounds thickly; hostels appear at strategic intervals, while extensive and often isolated beaches offer a multitude of free activities, from beach-combing for Polynesian glass floats and sea-carved driftwood, to shell-fishing, whale-watching, or, in winter, storm-watching. This isn't to say that Oregon has escaped commercialism: small fishing towns, hard-hit by decline, are jumping onto the tourism bandwagon as fast as they can, and it's a lucky traveller who finds a cheap room without booking ahead in July and August.

The coast is almost perfect for cycling (pick up the *Coast Bike Route Map* from the tourist board). US-101 follows the coast right down to the Californian border, and you can escape onto the many smaller "scenic loop" roads.

Astoria

ASTORIA, at the mouth of the Columbia River, was founded by John Jacob Astor in 1811, in the hope of establishing his own fur-trading empire. In fact "Fort Astoria" survived eighteen months, before selling out to the British: Washington Irving tells the saga in his novel *Astoria*. A small replica of the old fort stands at Fifteenth and Exchange streets, but nowadays Astoria is really a working port, with enough history to attract a few tourists, but little of the razzmatazz of the communities further south.

The road into Astoria runs parallel with the waterfront – crammed with saloons and brothels in the nineteenth century, many equipped with built-in trap doors for shanghai-ing drunken customers, who might wake up halfway across the Pacific. It all got so out of hand at one point that workers on quayside canneries carried guns to get themselves safely to the nightshift. Things are much tamer now, but exhibits from Astoria's seafaring past are on display at the huge **Columbia River Maritime Museum**, at 17th and Marine Drive (summer daily 9.30am–5pm, winter Tues–Sun 9.30am–5pm; $2.50).

From Marine Drive, numbered streets climb towards the elegant uptown area. On top of Coxcomb Hill, the **Astoria Column** is coated with a faded mural depicting the town's early history, and offers a good view. The nearby **Indian Burial Canoe** is a memorial to Chief Comcomly of the Chinook. He was on amiable terms with the first settlers, one of whom married his daughter, until he caught his son-in-law hoeing potatoes (woman's work in the chief's opinion). Comcomly's son, on the other hand, is said to have proposed to **Jane Barnes**, a barmaid from Portsmouth who arrived on an English ship in 1814 to become, Astorians claim, the first white woman in the Northwest. Jane turned him down, which wrought havoc with local race relations but is commemorated each year by **Jane Barnes Day**, held in the second week of May.

South and west of town, you can visit Lewis and Clark's reconstructed 1808 winter base at **Fort Clatsop** (summer daily 8am–6pm, winter 8am–5pm; free) before continuing to **Fort Stevens State Park** off US-101, with its trails, camping and miles of beaches. Fortifications were first put up at Fort Stevens to guard against Confederate raiders during the Civil War, though **Battery Russell** was part of World War II defences. It did get shelled one night by a passing Japanese submarine, which makes it, incredibly, the only military installation on the mainland US to have been fired on by a foreign power since 1812.

The *Greyhound* station is at 364 Ninth Street (☎325-5641), connected daily with Portland. **Local buses** run around Astoria, south to Seaside, and up the Washington coast. The **visitor centre** is in the south at 111 W Marine Drive (summer daily 8am–8pm, winter Mon–Fri 8am–6pm, weekends 10am–6pm). You can **camp** at *Fort Stevens State Park* (see above), or stay in one of the **motels** along West Marine Drive, such as the *Lamplighter*, at no. 131 (☎325-4051) or the *Rivershore* at no. 59 (☎325-2921). **Bed and breakfast** at *Franklin St Station*, 1140 Franklin Street (☎325-4314), is $50 a double. There's a **youth hostel** across the Columbia River in *Fort Columbia State Park* (see p.842). For **food**, the *Pacific Rim Restaurant*, 229 W Marine Drive, is a long way out and a bit shabby but has excellent pasta and pizza. More centrally, the tiny *Columbian Cafe*, 1114 Marine Drive, has tasty vegetarian food.

Seaside

Seventeen miles down the coast from Astoria, **SEASIDE** is an endearingly tacky holiday resort, with a long sandy **beach** and a few places to stay. The *Riverside Inn*, 430 S Holladay Drive (☎738-8254), officially a bed and breakfast, is a good cut above the average motel: the *Holladay Motel*, 426 S Holladay Drive (☎738-6529) next door, is cheaper. Seaside is on the *Greyhound* route between Portland and Astoria.

Cannon Beach

In the summer buses continue nine miles south from Seaside to the more upmarket **CANNON BEACH**, home of a **sandcastle competition** held each May. Past subjects have included dinosaurs, sphinxes, even a Crucifixion. **Accommodation** is tight, especially during the competition. Both *Mcbee Motel*, close to the beach at 888 S Hemlock Street (☎436-2569), and *Hidden Villa* at 188 E Van Buren Street (☎436-2237), have doubles from around $35. For **food**, N Hemlock Street is the best bet. *Lazy Susan Cafe* at no. 126, next to the *Coaster Theater*, does excellent health food, and the *Bistro* at no. 263 has tasty seafood and the town's best bar.

Lincoln City

There's no avoiding **LINCOLN CITY** if you're driving. Probably the ugliest town on the coast, it sprawls along the highway for seven congested, motel-lined miles. **Greyhound** buses, 316 SE US-101 (☎994-8418), reappear here, running to Portland and south, so you might end up staying – in which case the **visitor centre** is on US-101 at 40th (Mon–Fri 9am–5pm, Sat 10am–5pm, Sun 10am–4pm; ☎1-800/452-2151). Of the many **motels**, the

City Center, 1014 NE US-101 (☎994-2612), is clean and has doubles from $31; the *Nidden Hof*, 136 NE US-101 (☎1-800/98COAST), is slightly more expensive.

Newport

NEWPORT, 26 miles further on, is another fishing town labouring to turn itself into a resort – this time a surprisingly chic one, with the smart new *Mariner Square* development right opposite the dented metal walls of the old canneries. The place has an artsy undertone, manifest in a new Performing Arts Center and two small art museums on long, uncrowded **Nye Beach**.

The highlight of its good budget **accommodation** is the *Sylvia Beach Hotel*, 267 NW Cliff (☎265-5428), which aims to encourage would-be writers, with a cosy attic library and dorm beds at $20 a night, including breakfasts. Other rooms, decorated in the styles of various writers, are small and pricey: $50 to $110 for a double. The *Penny Saver*, 710 N Coast Highway (☎265-6631), is a good **motel** costing around $35. Complete motel and **campground** listings are available from the **Chamber of Commerce**, 555 SW Coast Highway (summer Mon–Fri 8.30am–5pm, Sat & Sun 10am–4pm, winter Mon–Fri 8.30am–5pm). For **food**, the *Whale's Tale* on Bay Boulevard has a good, varied menu and live music at weekends. Nearby is the pleasant *Canyon Way Restaurant and Bookstore*, 1216 SW Canyon Way; at Nye Beach, the *Chowder Bowl* is good value, as is the Italian *Don Petrie's*, across the road. *Greyhound* is at 956 SW 10th Street (☎265-2253).

Bandon

Twenty-four miles south of industrial COOS BAY, at the mouth of the Coquille River, easy-going **BANDON** combines old town restoration with a strong New Age presence, and has become an arts and crafts centre. It was originally a Native American settlement, which developed with the onset of the Gold Rush. This century began rather ominously, when townsfolk dynamited Tupper Rock, a sacred tribal site, to build the sea wall, and the town was cursed to burn down three times: it's happened twice so far, in 1914 and 1936, and the superstitious are still waiting.

Bandon's main attraction today is the unusual rock formations along its rugged **beach**. Magnificent in stormy weather, the prolific quantities of shellfish make this a prime venue for **crabbing** and **clamming**. Bandon's history is on display at the **Coquille Museum**, overlooking the river mouth (summer Tues–Sun 1pm–4pm, rest of the year Thurs–Sun 1pm–4pm), and the **Bold Duck** paddle steamer runs daily cruises along the river ($8 for two hours).

The best place to **stay**, overlooking the harbour at 370 First Street, is the *Sea Star Guest House* (☎347-9632), with doubles from $33–50 in the summer. Right in front of that is the associated *Sea Star Hostel*, just off US-101 on Second Street (☎347-9533), which has a friendly cafe downstairs, and the **visitor centre** (daily 9am–5pm; ☎347-9616) is just across the road. The **food** at *Andrea's Old Town Cafe*, a block away on Baltimore Street, is good value for money. There's **camping** just north of town at **Bullards Beach State Park**, where a lighthouse stand, guard over miles of wind-swept wilderness.

South to California

Towns are fewer and further between as you travel south along US-101, which passes dozens of secluded **beaches**. *Greyhound* stops at the *Port Orford Motel* in tiny **PORT ORFORD**, on its way south to the terminal at 310 Colvin Street in **GOLD BEACH**. This small town is where the wild **Rogue River** reaches the sea, and is largely devoted to whitewater rafting expeditions, up canyons and through roaring rapids into the depths of the **Siskiyou National Forest**. The **Chamber of Commerce**, 510 S Ellensburg Street (Mon–Fri 9am–5pm, weekends 10am–4pm; ☎452-2334), has all the details.

Central and Eastern Oregon

Once you cross the Cascades, Oregon, like Washington, grows warmer, drier, and wilder; green valleys give way to scrubby sageland, bare hills and stark rock formations, fringed with juniper. The landscape is volcanic and often alien, with cracked lava flows, abrupt cone-like hills, and high craters such as lovely **Crater Lake** in the south. The **east**, though seldom visited, can be surprisingly beautiful, with the prehistoric **John Day Fossil Beds** along US-26, and the remote, snow-capped Wallowa Mountains overlooking the long, deep slash of **Hells Canyon**.

Bend and Around

BEND is the best base in Central Oregon, giving access both to Cascade grandeur and the eerie landscape of Oregon's Lava Lands. It's a pleasant enough little town, eagerly benefitting from the recent explosion of interest in outdoor pursuits.

The *Greyhound* from Portland arrives a mile east of the town centre (☎382-2151). **Local buses** run to nearby towns and cross the Cascades on Hwy-20 west to Sweet Home, where there are connections on to the coast. You can pick up **information** at the Central Oregon Welcome Center on US-97 just north of town (☎1-800/547-6858 or ☎382-8334).

Lots of cheapish (though often full) **motels** line Third Street (US-97). Try the *Royal Gateway*, 475 SE Third Street (☎382-5631), or the *Edelweiss Motor Inn*, 2346 Division Street (☎382-6222), both with doubles for around $25. There's summer **camping** in *Tumalo State Park* (☎388-6055), five miles along US-20 northwest. For **eating**, Bend has several pricey little bistros like the *Old Bend Blacksmith Shop and Broiler*, 211 Greenwood Avenue; cheaper meals can be found at *D&D Bar and Grill*, 927 NW Bond Street and, opposite, *Arvard's Lounge and Cafe*, 928 NW Bond Street. *Deschutes Brewery and Public House*, nearby at 1044 Bond Street, is a **brew-pub** with a very good selection of micro-brewed ales and stouts, and also serves exceptionally fresh food.

Mount Bachelor and the Cascades Lake Highway

The largest ski resort in the Northwest is at **Mount Bachelor**, 22 miles southwest of Bend, its Olympic-standard facilities open from mid-November to as late as July, snowfall permitting. Mount Bachelor is also the first stop on the **Cascade Lakes Highway**, known as "Century Drive" – a hundred-mile mountain loop road which gives access to trailheads into the **Three Sisters**, or further south, the **Diamond Peak** wilderness areas, and a sprinkling of campgrounds. Get details at the **Deschutes National Forest Office**, 1645 East Hwy-20 (☎388-2715), or the Lava Lands Visitors Center (see below).

The Lava Lands

The **Lava Lands** cover a huge area of central Oregon, though the greatest concentration of weird lava formations – neat conical buttes, caves and the frozen forms of trees – is in the Bend area. They date back seven thousand years to the explosions of mounts Newberry and Mazama, which dumped enormous quantities of ash and pumice across the region. The **Lava Lands Visitors Center** (daily in summer; ☎593-2421) is an excellent source of maps and information on the many hiking trails; it's eleven miles south of Bend on Hwy-97, near the spectacular dark cinder cone of **Lava Butte**.

A mile south, off US-97, the **Lava River Cave** (summer daily 8.30am–6pm; $1, plus 50¢ for a lamp), is a subterranean passage into the volcanic underworld. Most of the lava which created the cave eventually cooled and hardened around the still-molten centre of the flow. When this drained away, it left an empty lava-tube, over a mile long, discovered only when part of the roof fell in. There are all kinds of formations along the chilly cave, but even if you have a lantern it's hard to see much beyond the next few steps.

ANTELOPE AND THE BHAGWAN

In 1981, followers of the Indian guru Bhagwan Shree Rajneesh bought a ranch near **ANTELOPE** (fifty miles east of Warm Springs Reservation on Hwy-218), and converted it into an agricultural commune. Bhagwan's red-dressed followers were a middle-class and apparently idealistic lot. Their mish-mash of eastern philosophy and western therapies initially raised sympathetic interest across Oregon – and eyebrows in conservative Antelope. Despite the commune's agricultural success in this relatively depressed region, relations disintegrated fast, especially when Rajneeshis took over the town council – and "peace patrols" appeared, clutching semi-automatic weapons.

The Rajneeshis' hold on the community was fairly short-lived. Just before the local elections, they began to bus in street-people from across the US and register them to vote. Many vagrants turned up in neighbouring towns (without the promised ticket home), saying they'd been conned, drugged or both. Worse, an outbreak of salmonella poisoning turned out to have been a Rajneeshi strategy for laying low the voting opposition. When the law eventually moved in on the commune – by now an armed fortress – they discovered medical terrorism (more poisoning, the misdiagnosis of AIDS) had been used on Rajneeshis themselves in an internal power struggle. The culprits were jailed and commune members dispersed. The Bagwhan meanwhile, after a bungled attempt to flee the country, was deported to India (where he soon died), and his fleet of Rolls Royces sold off, along with the ranch. By 1986, the embattled Antelope was quiet again, and a plaque on a new memorial flagpole in the town centre is dedicated to the triumph of the Antelope community over the "Rajneesh invasion".

Crater Lake and Klamath Falls

The Northwest's best-looking volcanic crater, now preserved as Oregon's only National Park, is just over a hundred miles south of Bend. The shell of Mount Mazama holds the blue, deep and resoundingly beautiful **Crater Lake**. The explosion which created the lake was 42 times greater than the Mount St Helens blast; the two islands you see in it are the tips of two mini-volcanoes which began to grow again within the hollowed mountain-top. In its snow-covered isolation, the lake is awe-inspiring; in summer too it's spectacular, when wildflowers bloom and wildlife emerges from hibernation.

You need a car to get here, though only the southern of the two approach roads (off Hwy-62, which leads off US-97) is kept open year-round. The northern acess road (off Hwy-138) is closed from mid-October to July, as is the "Rim Drive" around the crater's edge. At tiny **Rim Village**, the National Park maintains a summer-only **visitor centre**, and there's also a cafe, and a **lodge** offering rooms for around $40 (☎594-2511).

There are two **campgrounds** near the lake, and cheap motels in and around **KLAMATH FALLS**, sixty-odd miles away on the enormous Upper Klamath Lake. This logging and agricultural town is a nexus for public transport; *Greyhound* arrive from Portland and Eugene at 1200 Klamath Avenue, and *Amtrak*, 1600 Oak Street, also crosses the mountains. While the town has few actual sights, you can at least be sure of a cheap **room** and some sort of a **meal**. The **visitor centre**, 125 N Eighth Street (Mon–Fri 8.30am–5pm; ☎884-5193), has maps and listings, or try the *Pony Pass Motel*, 75 Main Street (doubles at around $29; ☎884-7735).

East on US-26: the John Day Fossil Beds

Further north, US-26 is the more rewarding road east, emerging from a brief green passage through the **Ochoco National Forest** into a bare, sun-scorched landscape of ochres and beige. Many features of the area are named after John Day, a fur-trapper from the Astoria colony, who early in the nineteenth century fell victim to local Indians and was later discovered wandering robbed, lost and naked. Of especial importance are the **John Day Fossil Beds**, a little way north of US-26, which hold some of the most revealing fossil formations in the US. These were preserved in a layer of volcanic ash as the Cascades sputtered into being, just after the extinction of the dinosaurs.

The **Painted Hills** unit, down a side road six miles west of one-horse MITCHELL, is the most accessible of the three widely separated fossil-bed sites. Striped in shades of rust and brown, the hills look like sandcastle mounds, the smooth surface quilted with rivulets worn by draining water. Back on US-26, just before **Sheep Rock**, is a turning for an area known as **Blue Basin**, a natural amphitheatre where a trail leads past perspex-covered fossil exhibits, including a tortoise that hurtled to its death millions of years ago and a sabre-toothed cat.

John Day Town, and on to Baker

Small, dry **JOHN DAY** is, despite its size, the largest town along US-26, with a handful of motels and restaurants and the fascinating **Kam Wah Chung & Co Museum**, next to the City Park (summer only Mon–Thurs 9am–noon & 1pm–5pm, Sat & Sun 1–5pm; $1.50), once the home of a famed Chinese herbalist.

The road leads after eighty miles to more substantial **BAKER**, well equipped with motels. The *New Image Motor Inn*, 134 Bridge Street (doubles $30; ☎523-6571), is the best value, and the area is sprinkled with campgrounds; details from the **Chamber of Commerce**, 490 Campbell Street (☎523-5855). Public transport reappears at this point – *Greyhound*, 1932 Main Street, and *Amtrak*, 2803 Broadway, both run to Portland, though there's no local transport once you're here. You'll find **restaurants** around Main Street.

La Grande and Around

From Baker, I-84 runs north through cattle-grazing rangeland and into the **Grande Ronde Valley** – large, round, flat and rimmed by mountains. Now mostly drained to become farmland, this was once a marsh, fatally boggy to pioneer wagons, forcing the Oregon Trail to keep to the higher but tougher ground around the hills as it headed northwest towards the Blue Mountains.

The centre of the valley is **LA GRANDE**, a simple lumber-and-railway town linked with Portland by *Greyhound* (2108 Cove Avenue) and *Amtrak*. The **visitor centre** at 1502 N Pine Street, near the railway station (Mon–Fri 8.30am–5pm; ☎963-8588), has maps and information. **Motels** gather along Adams Avenue (US-30) and prices aren't bad: try *Broken Arrow Lodge*, 2215 East Adams (☎963-7116), with doubles at around $35, or, more pleasantly, splash out on B&B at the luxurious *Stange Manor* at 1612 Walnut Street (☎963-2400) – doubles from around $60. There's **camping** at Morgan Lake, two miles west down B Avenue. **Restaurants** also line up on Adams Avenue; *Mamacita's* at 110 Depot Street is best for Mexican food.

Pendleton

From La Grande I-84 follows the Oregon Trail northwest to **PENDLETON**, on the same *Greyhound* and *Amtrak* routes. The town cultivates a cowboy image, holding the immensely popular annual four-day **Pendleton Round-Up** in mid-September; tickets from the Round-Up Association, PO Box 609, Pendleton, OR 97801 (☎276-2553 or ☎1-800/824-1603 inside Oregon; $7–12 per rodeo session).

The **Chamber of Commerce** in Pendleton is at 25 SE Dorion Avenue (Mon–Fri 9am–5pm; ☎276-7411), a short walk from *Greyhound*, as is *Longhorn Motel*, 411 SW Dorion Avenue (☎276-7531), with doubles from around $28. Further out, *Motel 6*, 325 SE Nye Avenue (☎276-3160), southeast of town near exit 210 off I-84, has doubles for $32. Book early at round-up time.

Joseph and the Wallowa Mountains

The **Wallowa Mountains**, reached by leaving I-84 at La Grande and heading east on Hwy-82, are one of eastern Oregon's loveliest and least-discovered areas. Set at the northern tip of glacially carved Wallowa Lake, the mountains rearing behind, the tiny town of **JOSEPH** is a perfect spot to spend the night. *Wallowa Valley Stage* (☎569-2284) run a daily van service from La Grande. There are a handful of **motels** here, but with just a little more money (doubles from $50), the friendly *Bed, Bread and Trail* **bed and breakfast inn**, 700 S Main Street (☎432-9765), includes a big morning feed. The sad story of the Nez Percé Indians (see p.640) is detailed alongside an attic-like collection of pioneer bits and pieces at the small **Wallowa County Museum** on Joseph's Main Street (officially daily 10am–5pm, but in practice less often; donation requested).

A mile or so south of Joseph, mountain-rimmed **Wallowa Lake** is supposedly inhabited by an Indian version of the Loch Ness monster. At its far end, the **state park** has **camping**, and the **Wallowa Lake Tramway** cable-car sets off up into the mountains, where short trails lead to magnificent overlooks (summer daily 10am–4pm; May 16–June 7 weekends only, $8). Much of the mountain scenery behind Joseph belongs to the **Eagle Cap Wilderness** area, whose lakes, streams and peaks are accessible only along trails (no roads). Backcountry hiking and camping here really is remote – contact the **Forest Service station** by Hwy-82 in Enterprise (☎426-3151) for details.

Hells Canyon

West of Joseph, along the Idaho border, the Snake River has carved the deepest canyon on the continent, a thousand feet deeper than the Grand Canyon. **Hells Canyon** is what's known as a low-relief canyon, edged by a series of gradually ascending false peaks – so it doesn't have the overwhelming impact of the steep-walled Grand Canyon. But it's impressive, with the Seven Devils mountains rising behind and the river glimmering in its depths. It has since time immemorial been a winter sanctuary for wildlife and Indians, and stone tools and rock-carvings have been found at old Nez Percé village sites. For more on the area, which extends into Idaho, see p.639.

The Nez Percé are long gone, but the canyon is now preserved as the **Hells Canyon National Recreation Area**: deer, otters, mink, black bears, mountain lions and elk live here, along with rattlesnakes and black widow spiders. Mechanical vehicles are banned above water-level in much of the canyon (boats along the Snake are allowed), so you can only explore on foot or horseback. There are roads through the rest of the recreation area, but they tend to be rough and slippery, and many are closed by snow for much of the year: check with the **rangers** in Enterprise (☎426-3151) or Baker (☎523-6391) before you set out.

Of the two ways to reach the canyon from Oregon – via Enterprise and Joseph, west of La Grande, or, to the south, via Halfway, west of Baker – the former gives the ultimate view from **Hat Point** on Hwy-350. Tiny tin-roofed **HALFWAY** makes a good base for exploring the southern end of the canyon: rooms at *Granites Motel* (☎742-5868) go for around $30 a double, and *Clear Creek Farm* (☎742-2233/2238; call for directions from the town) is a lovely, rural **bed and breakfast** with doubles from around $45.

Hwy-86 winds towards the canyon from Halfway, meeting the Snake River at Oxbow Dam, where a rough Forest Service road leads on to Hells Canyon Dam, the launching-point for **jet boat** and **raft trips** through the canyon. *Hells Canyon Adventures Inc* (☎785-3352) run sightseeing tours from $25 per person during the summer. Skimming over whitewater rapids, the boats take you between the deceptively low, bare hills, past rocks faintly coloured with ancient Indian rock carvings, to an old pioneer homestead. This company also operates a "drop-off" service, taking you to hiking trails along the canyon and picking you up either later in the day or the week (fee from $25 per person).

travel details

TRAINS

Routes

• Three daily *Amtrak* trains each way between **Seattle** and **Portland** stop at Tacoma, East Olympia, Centralia, Kelso-Longview and Vancouver (WA). One connects the two cities with Los Angeles, stopping south of Portland at Salem, Albany, Eugene, Chemult and Klamath Falls. Another connects them with Chicago (via Salt Lake City and Denver), stopping east of Portland at Hood River, The Dalles, Hinkle-Hermiston, Pendleton, La Grande, Baker and Ontario (OR).

• A daily train each way between **Seattle** and Chicago along the northern route stops at Edmonds, Everett, Wenatchee, Ephrata and Spokane. An *Amtrak* bus meets the westbound train at Spokane (at 3am!) and runs to **Portland** via Pasco, Wishram, Bingen-White Salmon and Vancouver (WA).

• One *Amtrak* bus per day runs from **Seattle** to Vancouver BC; another runs from Vancouver BC to Everett to connect with the Seattle train.

Journey Times

From **Seattle**: Tacoma 1hr; **Portland** 4hr; Everett 1hr; Wenatchee 4hr; Spokane 7hr; Vancouver BC (by bus) 3hr 30min; Los Angeles 35hr; Chicago 58hr.

From **Portland**: Salem 1hr; Albany 1hr 40min; Eugene 2hr 20min; Klamath Falls 7hr; Hood River 1hr 20min; Pendleton 4hr; La Grande 6hr; Baker 7hr; Spokane (by bus) 7hr.

BUSES

Greyhound

From **Seattle** to Sea-Tac Airport (4 daily; 25min); Tacoma (9; 45min); Olympia (8; 2hr); Castle Rock (1; 3hr 25min); Longview (5; 3–4hr 30min); **Portland** (10; 2 express buses 3hr 15min, others up to 5hr); Everett (6; 40min); Mt Vernon (6; 1hr 30min); Bellingham (6; 2hr 10min); Vancouver BC (7; 3hr 20min–5hr); Winslow (2; 1hr); Poulsbo (2; 1hr 15min); Port Ludlow (2; 2hr); Sequim (2; 2hr 30min); Port Angeles (2; 3hr); Anacortes (2; 2hr, except Mon, Wed and Fri, when a third bus runs via Whidbey Island); Leavenworth (3; 3hr); Cashmere (3; 3hr 15min); Wenatchee (3; 3hr 30min); (5; 2hr); Ellensburg (7; 2hr); Yakima (4; 3hr); Toppenish (2; 4hr 30min); Richland (3; 5hr 30min); Pasco (3; 6hr 20min); Walla Walla (2; 7hr); Spokane (7; 5hr 15min–8hr).

From **Portland** to Oregon City (1 daily; 1hr 30min); Salem (9; 1–1hr 30min); Eugene (10; 3hr); Grants Pass (5; 7hr); Medford (7; 6–8hr); Ashland (5; 7–9hr); Klamath Falls (3; 7–8hr); San Francisco (4; 16–30hr); Bend (2; 45min); Boise (1; 13hr); Spokane (1; 9hr, change in Biggs); Yakima (1; 8hr).

From **Yakima** to Goldendale (1 daily; 1hr 30min); Biggs OR (1; 2hr).

Green Tortoise

From **Seattle** twice weekly to **Portland** (4hr 15min).

From **Portland** twice weekly to Salem (1hr 45min), Eugene (3hr 15min), Ashland (10hr), and San Francisco (20hr). Also Bend (2 daily; 4hr); Pendleton (2; 4hr); La Grande (2; 5hr 30min); Baker (2; 6hr).

From **Bend** to Burns (1 daily; 3hr 30min); Ontario (1; 7hr 15min).

Empire Lines

From **Spokane** to Grand Coulee (1 daily; 2hr 30min), with connections to Chelan, Brewster, Okanogan, Wenatchee, Ellensburg and Yakima.

FERRIES

Washington State Ferries unless otherwise stated.

To Alaska from Seattle (1 weekly; leaves Friday evening, arrives Skagway Monday afternoon).

To Bremerton from Seattle (15 daily; 1hr).

To the San Juan Islands from Anacortes (8 daily; to Orcas 1hr 30min, to Friday Harbour 2hr).

To Whidbey Island: from Mukilteo to Clinton (from 6am to 1am every half-hour; 20min); from Port Townsend to Keystone (Mon–Thurs 7 daily, twice as many Fri–Sun; 30min).

To Vashon Island: from Point Defiance to Tahlequah (18 daily; 15min); from Fauntleroy, W Seattle, to Vashon (around every half-hour from 5.25am–1.40am; 15min).

To Victoria from Seattle (*BC Steamship Company* May–Oct 2 daily; 4–5hr, also a catamaran 2 1/2hr); from Anacortes via the San Juans (1; 3hr); from Port Angeles (*Black Ball Transport* summer 5, spring and autumn 2; 1hr 15min).

To Winslow from Seattle (at least hourly from 6.20am–2.40am; 35min).

CHAPTER FIFTEEN

ALASKA

The sheer size of **ALASKA**, more than double the area of Texas, is hard to comprehend. America's **northernmost, westernmost** and, because the Aleutians stretch across the 180th meridian, its **easternmost** state would, if superimposed onto the Lower 48 – the rest of the continental United States – stretch from the Atlantic to the Pacific. This vast expanse holds America's highest mountains, huge icefields and glaciers, active volcanoes, fjords, sweeping plains and dense forests. Wildlife may be under threat elsewhere, but here it is abundant, with grizzly bears standing twelve feet tall, moose stopping traffic in downtown Anchorage, and king salmon weighing more than eighty pounds.

Alaska is often called the **"last frontier"**, and in many ways it represents what early America did for the first settlers: an endless, undeveloped space in which to stake one's claim and set up a life without interference. Today this "great land" is inhabited by a mere 500,000 people, more than half of whom live in Anchorage. Only twenty percent of residents were actually born here. Over the years, thousands have been lured by the promise of wealth – **oil** and the **fishing** industry being the most recent equivalents to the **gold rush** of the nineteenth century. As a rule of thumb, the more winters you have endured, the more Alaskan you are. However, Alaska's **native peoples**, who don't have the option of returning to the lower 48 if things don't work out, have been left behind in the state's economic boom, and make up the poorest section of the population.

Travelling around Alaska is not for everyone. The state has few "sights" as such; the land itself is the attraction. To make the most of it, you need to have an enthusiasm for striking out on your own, and to be prepared to rough it. If you plan to **camp**, you'll need the best possible gear – a strong, waterproof tent, a fibre-filled sleeping bag, and cooking equipment. Binoculars are an absolute must, as, rather more mundanely, is bug spray. The **mosquito** is referred to as the "Alaska state bird", and only a repellent with 100 percent DEET will keep the insects away. On top of that, of course, there's the **climate**. Winter temperatures drop low as -40°F; and the summers, especially in the southeast, can be very wet, with temperatures ranging from 40°F at night to an average daytime high of 65°F. Remarkably, in the interior in summer it often gets as hot as 80°F.

Except for the youth hostels in the major towns, there is little budget **accommodation; transport**, thanks to the long distances, is far from cheap; and eating and drinking is at least twenty percent more expensive than in the lower 48.

History

Alaska has been inhabited for longer than anywhere else in the Americas; it was here, across the land bridge that spanned what is now the Bering Sea, that human beings first reached the "New World". These first settlers can be classified into four groups. The **Aleuts**, in the fog-bound, inhospitable Aleutian islands, built underground homes and hunted sea mammals for food and clothing, while the **Athabascans** herded caribou in the interior. The warrior **Tlingit**, who were more affluent and had more complex social structures, lived in the warmer coastal regions of the southeast, while the **Inuits** (also known as the Eskimos) inhabited the northwestern coast, living off sea mammals such as bow whales. Their famous **igloo** ice-houses were seldom used as permanent dwellings, but rather as temporary lodging during whale-hunts. Descendants of all these groups remain in Alaska today, living in much the same way as their ancestors.

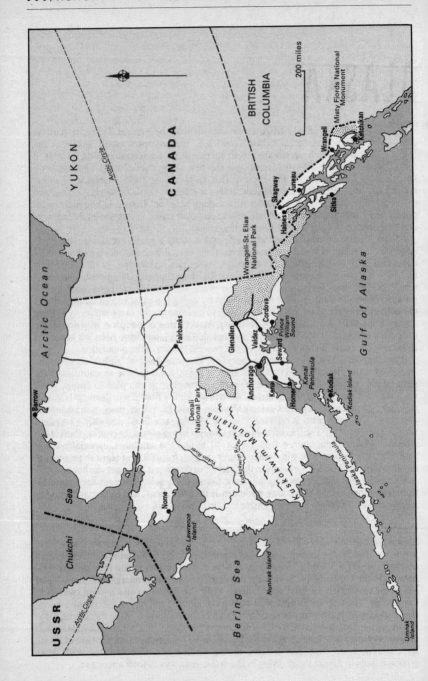

In 1741, a Dutch explorer, **Vitus Bering**, working for the Czar of Russia, sailed into the Prince William Sound, and became the first white man to set foot on Alaskan soil. He died before he could return to Russia, but his crew reported huge numbers of **sea otters** and **seals** – whose **furs** were ideal for making hats – in Alaska's coastal waters. Russians, and later, Britons and Spaniards, joined in the ensuing slaughter, both of the otters and the Aleuts, who were enslaved and forced to hunt for the fur traders. By 1799 the Russians had decimated all the sea otter colonies in the Aleutians and around Kodiak, and had pressed on as far west as present-day Sitka, where they set up a fort.

During the 1860s, when Russia hit economic difficulty due to the collapse of the fur trade and the disastrous Crimean War, it proposed the sale of its lands to America. On October 18 1867, Secretary of State William Seward **purchased Alaska** for $7,200,000 – less than 2¢ per acre. Although the unpopular deal was referred to as "Seward's Folly" or "Seward's Icebox", Alaska soon turned out to be a literal gold mine. **Gold** was discovered in the late 1800s in southeast Alaska and near Nome on the Bering Strait, and subsequently near Fairbanks in 1902. As the second wave of fortune-seekers hit Alaska, the government began to take a more active interest in its affairs. In 1912 the Territory of Alaska was set up, and it was finally granted statehood in 1959, along with Hawaii.

In 1942, after the Japanese occupied two of the Aleutian islands, the huge **US military** build-up that was to last all through the Cold War began with the construction of the **Alcan Highway** to link Alaska to the rest of America. Alaska's next boom followed with the discovery of **oil** in 1968 at Prudhoe Bay on the Arctic ocean, when fortune-seekers headed to Alaska to construct and work on the trans-Alaska pipeline which runs to Valdez on the Prince William Sound. Today, despite price fluctuations, Alaska still derives much of its wealth from "black gold"; indeed, instead of paying income tax, each resident receives an annual dividend cheque of around $1000. But the state is still in economic transition. The once lucrative fishing and lumber industries are giving way to tourism as the state's major source of income, and the ethical question of how best to use Alaskan lands in the future has led to bitter controversy.

Getting To and Around Alaska

For many people, the drive up to Alaska through Canada is one of the major highlights of a visit to the state. Originally built by the military in just eight months, the **Alaska Highway**, or **Alcan**, which can be accessed from Washington, Idaho and Montana, used to have a well-merited reputation as consisting of 1500 fearsome miles of dirt, gravel, steep descents and thick mud. These days the road is completely paved, with plenty of service stations, campgrounds and hotels, but it remains as beautiful as ever, and it still demands a spirit of adventure from drivers who attempt it.

A number of **bus** companies, including *Greyhound*, run from Seattle to Alaska on the Alcan, usually in summer only, for around $250, though the *Greyhound* Ameripass is only valid as far as Whitehorse in the Yukon, not in Alaska itself. *Alaskon Express*, controlled by *Gray Line of Alaska* (☎277-5581), run summer buses from Whitehorse to Haines, Skagway and Fairbanks. *Green Tortoise* (see p.21) run trips from San Francisco.

Though Anchorage is no longer quite the major air crossroads it once was, it's still easy to fly to Alaska. It is, however, very expensive. Most flights from the lower 48 are routed through Seattle, although some non-stop services are available from major cities. The round-trip fare from Seattle is around $300.

Alaska Marine Highway

The **ferries** of the 2200-mile **Alaska Marine Highway** cover many areas otherwise only reachable by air, operating two separate and unconnected systems. The most popular route is along the **Inside Passage** in the southeast, which runs for more than a thousand miles from **Bellingham**, Washington, just north of Seattle, through a wonderland of pristine waters, towering glaciers and untouched forests to **Skagway** at the top of the panhandle. Stops include Ketchikan, Juneau and Haines. The whole trip takes two and a half days and costs $235 for walk-on passengers, plus $241 extra for a small car. It is possible to sleep – and even to pitch a tent – on the covered, heated, upper deck.

The **Southwest Ferry** system connects the Kenai Peninsula and the Prince William Sound to the Aleutians. Fares are expensive and vary widely, with charges levied on kayaks, cars and bicycles. It's a good idea to book ahead in the summer. Although standby space is available, standby passengers risk being off-loaded at each port of call as the ferry takes on passengers with reservations.

For information on either route, contact the **Alaska Marine Highway**, PO Box R, Juneau, AK 99811-2505 (☎1-800/642-0066 or ☎465-3941).

Getting Around

Getting around Alaska on the cheap can be tough; **public transport** is limited, and many areas other than the most popular tourist spots are only accessible by **plane**, which is quick and convenient, but invariably pricey. **Hitching** is hard work, simply due to the lack of traffic, but, with enough time, it can be done, and is more acceptable here than elsewhere in the nation.

The **Alaska Railroad** was constructed between 1915 and 1923 to transport supplies from the southern ports to the mines in the interior; it runs nearly five hundred miles north from Seward on the Kenai peninsula to Fairbanks. Trains are clean, comfortable and generally reliable, and have dining cars in the summer. The Railroad also offers special tours. For details, contact the Alaska Railroad Corporation, PO Box 107500, Anchorage, AK 99510-7500 (☎1-800/544-0522 or ☎265-2494).

Visitors intending to **drive** around Alaska should pick up a copy of *The Milepost*, which provides mile-by-mile information on the entire Alaska Highway System, including the Alcan, and is available throughout the state for $16.95. An **emergency kit** is essential, especially in winter, as distances between cities are long and traffic can be sparse even on major routes. Conditions on the roads can change rapidly – for the latest information, call ☎243-7675. Avalanches are a serious threat, as are collisions with wild animals, especially moose. Drivers on gravel roads are advised to keep speeds low, especially when passing other vehicles, as rocks often fly up and shatter windscreen. Petrol stations are often few and far between, and charge wildly varying prices.

Travelling by **plane** is not always more expensive than the bus. The most frequently used airlines include *Alaska Air* (☎1-800/426-0333); *Markair* (☎1-800/426-6784), which goes to the bush towns, Kodiak and the Aleutians; *ERA Aviation* (☎243-3300) in the southcentral region, and, for access to even the remotest parts of the bush, *Ryan Air* (☎248-0695). Flights to the least accessible reaches are taken on the notorious **bush planes**; although nerve-wracking, these offer the most breathtaking views, and can be the experience of a lifetime for those who have enough cash.

Southeast Alaska

With its heavy rainfall and lush vegetation, **Southeast Alaska** – also known as the **Panhandle** – may lack the vast openness of the interior, but its narrow fjords, steep mountains, glaciers and thick conifer forests are awesome in their own right. **Ketchikan**, the state's southernmost city, makes a suitably pretty introduction, while **Juneau**, the capital, and **Haines** and **Skagway** at the northern end of the Panhandle, all set amid magnificent scenery, are redolent of the old gold-mining days.

The region's first settlers, the **Tlingit** (pronounced *Klingit*), were joined in the 1800s by white frontiersmen, and today its small communities resound with tales of extraordinary endurance, folly and cruelty. On July 17 1897, a steamer arrived in Seattle from

> The telephone **area code** for the entire state of Alaska is ☎907.

the Yukon territory of Canada, carrying 68 miners and around $800,000 worth of gold. Rumours of large gold deposits in the Klondike region were thereby confirmed, and the news spread like wildfire across the US – in the midst of a depression caused in part by a shortage of gold. The rush of hopefuls was truly colossal. Many families cashed in their last possessions to buy a ferry ticket north, and even the Mayor of Seattle resigned to hop aboard one of the countless overloaded ferries up the west coast.

By far the best way to travel the region is on the Marine Highway. For a true outdoor adventure, you can rent a cabin in the Tongass National Forest – into which most of southeast Alaska falls – for around $20 per night; get details from the US Forest Service in Juneau (see p.871) or Ketchikan (see below). The cabins are usually booked up well in advance, but they keep a list of recently cancelled reservations.

Ketchikan

As the first stop on the Alaska Marine Highway, **KETCHIKAN**, which sits on an island about six hundred miles north of Seattle, is described as Alaska's "first city". The state's fourth largest city is also a strong contender to be the nation's wettest, with an annual precipitation of up to 165 inches. Ketchikan stretches five miles along the **Tongass Narrows**, its compact and historic downtown wedged between the water and the forested slopes of **Deer Mountain**. Much of the town is built on steep hills, propped up on wooden pilings, with wooden boardwalks and staircases.

White settlement reached Ketchikan in the early 1880s, attracted by the abundant local salmon in the area. By 1883 the first of dozens of canneries had opened in what was soon to be the "salmon capital of the world". Tall forests of cedar, hemlock and spruce, which had provided timber for Tlingit homes and totems, also fed the town's first sawmill, built in 1903. The timber and fishing industries have declined since then, though both are still major employers. On the Fourth of July, a **Logger's Festival** includes axe flinging and various hair-raising contests involving chainsaws.

Arrival and Information

Ketchikan's **ferry terminal** (☎225-6181) is about a mile northwest of town on the N Tongass Highway; a city **bus** stops here every hour until 6.45pm. The **airport**, served by *Alaska Airlines* (☎225-2141), is a five-minute ferry ride ($4) across the Narrows from town. Opposite the cruiseship dock, the **visitor centre**, 131 Front Street, provides maps and a walking tour of town (daily 8am–5pm; ☎225-6166). Close by, in the pink building on Federal Street, is the US Forest Service Information Center (☎225-2148).

Southern Exposure (☎225-6044), 507 Stedman Street, rents kayaks and organises paddling in the Narrows – six hours costs $60 – plus longer expeditions further afield. *North Wind Expeditions* (☎225-4751), who have a booth on the dock near the visitor centre, give guided tours of the rainforest, which usually cost about $30 for half a day.

The Town

The best way to get acquainted with Ketchikan's historic buildings is to take the visitor centre's hour-long walking tour. **Creek Street**, a newly restored boardwalk along Ketchikan Creek, used to be the town's red light district, but today all the former houses of ill-repute are given over to boutiques and cafes. *Dolly's House*, 24 Creek Street, formerly the home and workplace of Dolly Arthur, the town's most famous madam, is now a small museum stuffed with saucy memorabilia (hours vary; $2; ☎225-6329).

Totem poles, usually carved from cedar, were used by the Tlingit to honour the dead, to record history, and to tell stories. You'll see many colourful replicas of old poles around town, but fifteen of the best are to be found in the **Totem Bight State Park**, attractively set on a forested strip of coast overlooking the Narrows, about ten miles north of town on the Tongass Highway. On the way there, you pass old floating homes built on logs in the bay. **Saxman Totem Park**, three miles south of town, displays the world's largest standing collection of poles – including one featuring a likeness of Abe Lincoln – transported in the Thirties from old southeastern communities and beautifully restored. Check with the visitor centre for any available guided tours; without help, it takes a lot of imagination to decipher the strange images. In town, the **Totem Heritage Center** on Deermount Street (☎225-5900) exhibits over thirty nineteenth-century poles, and puts on an informative film show, as well as holding workshops on traditional native crafts (Mon–Sat 8am–5pm, Sun 9am–4pm; $1.50, free on Sun).

Across Ketchikan Creek from the Totem Heritage Center, the **Deer Mountain Salmon Hatchery** is next to the City Park at the top of Park Avenue. Each year, 300,000 silver and king salmon are raised and released into the creek; by the end of summer, it's teeming with returning fish who have swum upstream to spawn and die. You can watch the fish jump the falls from the Park Street Bridge. The fish ladder, which supposedly helps the salmon up the boiling waterfall, is not all that useful – in autumn, the banks of the creek are littered with dead fish.

Misty Fjords National Monument

Twenty-two miles from Ketchikan, but only accessible by boat or floatplane, the awe-inspiring **Misty Fjords National Monument** consists of 2.2 million acres of deep fjords flanked by sheer granite walls approaching 3000 feet. As befits its name, the Monument is at its most atmospheric when swathed in low-lying mists. Day-long guided tours with *Outdoor Alaska* (☎225-6044), 215 Main Street, Ketchikan, cost $135.

Accommodation

Hotels in Ketchikan range from very pricey to cheap and run-down, but there shouldn't be a problem finding somewhere to stay. *Ketchikan B&B* (☎225-8550) arranges accommodation in private homes from around $50. There are no official **campgrounds** in town; the closest is in the attractive *Ward Lake Recreation Area*, about five miles northwest of the ferry terminal.

Alaska Rainforest Inn, 2311 Hemlock St (☎225-9500). A mile from the ferry terminal, with bunks for $21, or rooms which sleep four for $45.

Ketchikan Youth Hostel (AYH), in the United Methodist Church, 400 Main St (☎225-3319). Very basic hostel with beds for $7, open May–Sept only.

The New York Hotel, 207 Stedman St (☎225-0246). Nicely restored joint overlooking the small boat harbour. Doubles $79.

The Union Rooms, 319 Mill St (☎225-3580). Doubles with shared bath from $49.

Eating

Cheap food in Ketchikan tends to be rather good. Several greasy joints along Front Street serve tasty breakfasts and dinners. It's also renowned as a wild "party town", its bars teeming with cannery workers eager to forget the sight and smell of raw fish.

Chico's, 435 Dock St (☎225-2833). Great Mexican food and pizza, dinners starting at $8.50.

Diaz Chinese Restaurant, 335 Stedman St (☎225-2257). Good-value Chinese and Filipino dishes.

Five Star Cafe, Creek St (☎247-7827). Well-prepared, healthy food, including the piggish peanut butter, tahini, honey and banana sandwich.

The Ketchikan Cafe, 314 Front St (☎247-CAFE). "English-style fish'n'chips" for $4.95.

The Potlatch Bar, Stedman and Thames streets. No-frills pub overlooking the small boat harbour.

Roller Bay Cafe, 1287 Tongass Ave (☎225-0696). Cocktails and seafood on the waterfront.

The Sourdough Bar, 301 Front St (☎225-2217). Much-loved local bar decorated with photos of shipwrecks.

Juneau

The sophisticated and vibrant city of **JUNEAU** is unlike any other state capital in the nation. Only accessible by sea or air, it is an exceptionally picturesque place, butted up against the **Gastineau Channel**, with steep, narrow roads clawing up into the rainforested hills behind. Gold features heavily in its history. In 1880, two prospectors – one of them Joe Juneau – made **Alaska's first gold strike** in the rainforest along the banks of the Gastineau Channel. Named Gold Creek, the camp grew rapidly in size and importance, and, until the last mine was shut down in 1944, this was the world's largest producer of low-grade ore.

Juneau was made territorial capital in 1906. In the early Eighties, there was much talk of moving the state government from Juneau to Willow, a small town north of Anchorage. Many Alaskans see the benefit of having a more easily accessible capital, but few favour the costs the transition would incur, and for the moment the issue appears to have been laid to rest. Aside from government, fishing and tourism have replaced mining. In summer, downtown is a seething mass of cruiseship passengers, but there is a lot more to do in Juneau than shop for souvenirs – particularly in April, when the city hosts the annual state folk festival.

Arrival, Information and Getting Around

The **Marine Highway ferry terminal** (☎465-3941) is about fourteen miles northwest of downtown at Auke Bay. Because the daily ferries from Bellingham arrive at unearthly hours, getting into town can be a problem. An *MGT bus* (☎789-5460) usually leaves the terminal about fifteen minutes after the ferry arrives, dropping off at the airport and many of the downtown hotels ($9). Alternatively, you could walk one mile along the road towards town and catch the *Capital Transit* (☎789-6901) bus #3 at Maidenhall Loop Road, which costs $1 and runs every hour from 7am. The ferry dock is not to be confused with the cruiseship terminal in town. Juneau's **airport** (☎789-7281) is about ten miles out, towards the ferry terminal. You can get into town for $6 on the *Eagle Express* bus (☎586-2660) from the Airport Mall.

The **Davis Log Cabin**, 134 Third Street, carries information about Juneau and the surrounding area (June–Sept daily Oct–May Mon–Fri; ☎586-2284), and there's an **information booth** at the Marine Park on the waterfront, at the cruiseship dock (May–Sept daily 9am–6pm). A 24-hour events hotline on ☎586-JUNO will keep you up to date. The **Forest Service Information Center**, in Centennial Hall at the corner of Willoughby Avenue and Egan Drive, has films and exhibits on the region's attractions (June–Aug daily 9am–6pm; Sept–May Mon–Sat 8am–5pm; ☎586-8751).

Juneau's Parks and Recreation Department (☎586-5226) organises communal **hikes** which attract up to sixty people; if you'd prefer to go it alone, invest in one of two books widely available locally: the *Juneau Trail Guide*, published by the forest service ($3), or *90 Short Walks around Juneau*. D M Bicycles (☎586-2277), at 217 S Franklin Street, rents out **mountain bikes** for $5 per hour, $25 per day, and offers customised area tours. Next door, *Alaska Discovery* (☎463-5560) organises sea-kayaking and rents out double kayaks for $50 per day. *Alaska Rainforest Tours* (☎463-3466), 369 S Franklin Street, organises all manner of tours in Juneau and the surrounding region.

In and Around Juneau

Setting off from the kiosk in Marine Park, it takes an hour and a half to follow the self-guided Juneau walking tour. The onion-domed **St Nicholas Russian Orthodox Church**, on Fifth and Gold streets, contains icons and religious treasures, while the **Alaska State Museum**, 395 Whittier Street, covers native culture, the Russian heritage and the first gold strikes. Its pride and joy is the log book in which Bering reported his first sighting of Alaska (Mon–Fri 9am–6pm, Sat & Sun 10am–6pm; $2).

Juneau's gold-studded past remains important to its tourist industry. Just ten minutes from downtown, the **Last Chance Mining Museum**, containing relics from the mining era, is due to reopen soon. Even if it is not yet open, the walk there, half a mile northeast along Basin Road, is very beautiful, meandering along a cascading river through lush rainforest. Dozens of hiking trails branch off from the Basin Road, including the extensive **Perseverance Trail** system.

The old **Treadwell Mine**, across the Gastineau Channel – reached by taking the bus to Sandy Beach on Douglas Island – was one of Alaska's most impressive mines, producing $67 million dollars of gold at a time when gold was worth less than $20 per ounce. On April 21 1917, it collapsed after being flooded by a freak tide. Miraculously, no one was hurt, but it was closed shortly afterwards. The Treadwell Mine Historic Trail leads to those ruins that remain, including old foundations and a waterlogged entrance.

The **Mendenhall Glacier**, thirteen miles from downtown, is, like so many things in Alaska, of superlative proportions: twelve miles long and one and a half miles wide at the face. Should your knowledge of cirques and striations be a little rusty, the **visitor centre** on its east side has films and other information (daily 8.30am–6pm; ☎789-0097). Hiking trails include the **West Glacier Trail**, on which you can explore the ice caves.

Capital Transit buses leaves hourly every day except Sunday from downtown to the glacier; get off at Glacier Spur Road for the visitor centre, or at Montana Creek Road for the West Glacier trail. *Alaska Travel Adventures* (☎789-0052) organises four-hour float trips on the Mendenhall River, with wonderful views of the great lumbering flow of ice. The cost, including lunch, is $75.

Accommodation

There are plenty of motels near downtown, and the *Alaska B&B Association*, 3444 Nowell Street (☎586-2959), reserves rooms for between $40 and $65. *Mendenhall Lake Campground*, accessible by buses #3 or #4 and a short hike, is spectacularly situated near the glacier. *Auke Village Campground*, with views of the ocean, is a smaller place two miles north of the ferry terminal.

Alaskan Hotel and Bar, 167 S Franklin St (☎586-1000). Pleasant old hotel in the heart of downtown, with one of the finest bars in Juneau. Doubles are $45 with shared bath.

Driftwood Lodge Motel, 435 Willoughby Ave (☎586-2280). One block from the waterfront, with rooms including kitchenettes from $49. Transportation to and from the airport and ferry terminal.

Inn at the Waterfront, 455 S Franklin St (☎586-2050). Recently remodelled hotel opposite the cruiseship terminal, with doubles from $40. Its restaurant is good for breakfast.

Juneau International Hostel, 614 Harris St (☎586-9559). Clean and comfortable, in an old home near downtown, with dorm space for $11 for non-members.

Eating

The good downtown bars and restaurants quickly fill with cruiseship passengers, so where you eat may depend entirely on where you can find a space. For a summertime feast in beautiful surroundings, head out to the *Gold Creek Salmon Bake* on Basin Road at the *Last Chance Basin* (☎586-1424). The eat-till-you-drop deal, costing $20, includes salad and delicious salmon served at sheltered outdoor tables, with live music.

Alaskan Hotel and Bar, 167 S Franklin St. Great bar, with occasional live music.

Armadillo Tex-Mex Cafe, 431 S Franklin St (☎586-1880). Huge plates of nachos start at $5.50, or try the Enchiladas Azteca, served with beans, rice and guacamole for $10.

The Cookhouse, 278 Franklin St (☎463-3658). BBQ ribs and big burgers. Prime rib sandwich and fries for $7.50.

The Heritage Coffee Company and Cafe, 174 S Franklin St (☎586-1088). Popular hangout for excellent coffee and huge sandwiches from $5.

Red Dog Saloon, S Franklin St. Touristy bar opposite the cruiseship terminal with a carefully fabricated olde worlde ambience.

Haines

Although it lacks the fascinating history of other southeastern communities, **HAINES**, at the northern end of the Lynn Canal fjord on a peninsula between the Chilkat and the Chilkoot rivers, is a real "Alaskan experience", recently the location for the filming of Jack London's *White Fang*. When the weather is clear, it is nothing short of spectacular, with snow-covered **Mount Ripinsky** rising up behind, the **Chilkoot and Chilkat mountains** hemming it in on either side, and glaciers spilling out into the deep fjord. The Tlingit fished and traded here for years before the first missionaries arrived in 1881 and named the settlement for a prominent Presbyterian, Mrs F Haines.

Today Haines survives on timber and fishing, and is fast becoming a popular tourist spot, even if few cruiseships stop here. Most visitors use Haines as a base to explore the surrounding wilderness; the hiking is tremendous, with fabulous views of the town, the fjord, and the surrounding mountains and glaciers. In August the town hosts the **Southeast Alaska Fair**, with great food, crafts, pig-racing and log-rolling.

The Town

Apart from its art galleries and craft shops, mainly concentrated around the visitor centre, Haines itself holds little interest. However, the small **Sheldon Museum**, at the bottom of Main Street, has a rather abstract collection of native crafts and historical artefaçts, a good bookshop, a movie about eagles and a mediocre slide show on "life in Haines" (daily; $2).

In response to the general lawlessness of the gold rush era, and territorial disputes with Canada, **Fort William H Seward** was established here in the early 1900s, and served as Alaska's only barracks for twenty years. On the west side of town, it's now buzzing with fairgrounds, a reconstructed Totem Village, and displays of native crafts, as well as replicas of a traditional Tlingit house and a trapper's cabin. During the summer, the Chilkat Dancers perform in native costumes at the **Chilkat Center for the Arts**, in Fort Seward's recreational centre, south of town between Totem Street and Mud Bay Road ($7; ☎766-2160).

Each autumn, the world's largest gathering of **bald eagles** flocks to the banks of the Chilkat River to feed on an unusually late chum salmon run (delayed by a hot spring that keeps the river from freezing). By November over three thousand of the endangered eagles, America's national bird, are gathered at the **Chilkat Bald Eagle Reserve**, nine miles out of town on the Haines Highway. *Chilkat Guides* (☎766-2491), on Beach Road below Fort Seward, organises four-hour float trips ($60) down the river through the Reserve. You may even see bears, wolves and moose.

Practicalities

Haines' **ferry terminal** (☎766-2111) is about four miles west of town. The *Haines Streetcar* shuttle service (☎766-2819) meets all ferry arrivals, and there are also taxis. *Alaskon Express* (☎1-800/544-2206) leaves Haines three times a week in the summer for Haines Junction in Canada, Anchorage and Fairbanks. *Sockeye Cycles* (☎766-2869), in the alley south of Main Street, rents out bikes and organises group tours.

The town's **visitor centre**, at Second Avenue at Willard Street (☎766-2234), has all kinds of maps and information about the nearby state parks and Glacier Bay. Of central **accommodation** options, the *Mountain View Motel*, Mud Tract Road, Fort Seward (☎766-2900), has doubles for $60, while at the *Officer's Inn B&B*, Fort Seward (☎766-2000), doubles with shared bathrooms are $50. *Bear Creek Camp and Hostel*, two miles out of town on Small Tract Road (☎766-2259), provides dorm beds at $12 for non-members, and cabins, which sleep up to four people, for $30. The owners will collect you from the ferry terminal. The wooded *Port Chilkoot Camper Park* (☎766-2755) is centrally located near Fort Seward on Mud Bay Road and Third Avenue.

As well as standard **eating** places such as the *Bamboo Room*, on Second Avenue near Main Street (☎766-9101), where breakfasts such as jalapeno-filled Spanish omelettes cost about $4, Haines has a few more upmarket possibilities. *The Fort Seward Lodge* (☎766-2009) specialises in prime rib and crab, and on summer evenings between 5pm and 8pm you can eat as much salmon as you can manage for $20 at the *Port Chilkoot Potlatch* on the Fort Seward Parade Grounds (☎766-2003).

Skagway

SKAGWAY, the northernmost stop on the Marine Highway, sprang up overnight in 1897, as a trading post serving Klondike gold rush pioneers about to set off on the five-hundred-mile **trail**. It was also the last stop before the harrowing White Pass Trail, known as the "Dead Horse Trail", on which over three thousand horses perished in just one year. Having grown from one cabin to a town of twenty thousand in three months, Skagway was reported to be "hell on earth". It boasted over seventy bars and hundreds of prostitutes, and was controlled by organised criminals, including the notorious Jefferson Soapy Smith, renowned for cheating hapless prospectors out of their gold (see also p.593). One of his scams was to operate a bogus telegraph office through which he concocted countless false messages from loved ones in the lower 48 urgently demanding money, which "Soapy" , of course, took responsibility for sending. He finally met a nasty end in 1899 after a shoot-out with Frank Reid, head of a vigilante group.

By 1899, the gold rush was over, and Skagway's population was dwindling fast. However, the completion in 1900 of the **White Pass and Yukon Railway** from Skagway to Whitehorse, the Yukon capital, ensured the town's survival. Though the railway officially closed down in 1982, it reopened in 1988 for summer excursions, a characteristic move for one of Alaska's most tourism-conscious towns. The eight hundred residents have gone to great lengths to maintain the original appearance of their town, much of which lies in the **Klondike Gold Rush National Historic Park**, and to cynical visitors the wooden sidewalks have something of the feel of a Hollywood film set. Skagway's charm is also its curse, and in the summer it gets packed out, with as many as three cruiseships calling in each day. However, from mid-September to early May most places in town are closed, and it becomes far more sedate, indeed almost eerie.

Many people head north from Skagway on the **Klondike Highway**, which connects with the Alaska Highway close to Whitehorse. Still more visitors come to follow the footsteps of the original stampeders, and hike the 33-mile **Chilkoot Trail**, sometimes called the world's longest museum.

Arrival, Information and Getting Around

Marine Highway **ferries** (☎983-2941) arrive every day a few minutes southwest of Broadway Street, the main thoroughfare. The **train station** (☎983-2217) is a block off Broadway Street on Second Avenue, offering daily rail service to Whitehorse and the White Pass Summit. *Alaskon Express* **buses** to Anchorage ($194) and Fairbanks ($177) leave three times weekly (overnight) from the *Westmark Inn* on Third Avenue (☎983-2241), which is the place to buy tickets. Several tours leave from the small hut on the corner of Broadway Street and Sixth Avenue (☎983-2523), including a trip up the Klondike Highway to White Pass, and a $25 city tour. They also rent bikes and operate a shuttle to Whitehorse for $50.

Skagway is very compact, and most of the sights can be seen easily on foot. The National Park Service **visitor centre**, between Second Avenue and Broadway Street, holds talks, leads walking tours, and has historical displays and an impressive movie about the gold rush, as well as maps and information on the Chilkoot Trail (June–Aug daily 8am–8pm; May & Sept 8am–6pm; ☎983-2921). Skagway's **CVB** is a block off Broadway Street in the City Building (Mon–Fri 9am–6pm; ☎983-2854).

The Town

The facade of the remarkable **Arctic Brotherhood Hall** on Broadway Street between Second and Third avenues, built in 1899 by a fraternity of gold miners who paid their dues solely in nuggets, is decorated with over twenty thousand pieces of driftwood. You can see antiques from the gold rush days at the small **Trail of 98 Museum**, on Seventh Avenue, just off Broadway Street (daily 8am–8pm; $2). A block away, at the corner of Sixth Avenue and Broadway Street, the **Days of 98 Show** is a reasonably entertaining historical musical about Soapy Smith ($12).

About one and a half miles north of town, the **Gold Rush Cemetery** is the final resting place of many of the stampeders. Among them are Soapy Smith and Frank Reid, who according to his gravestone "gave his life for the honor of Skagway"; a local prostitute, on the other hand, is remembered for "giving her honor for the life of Skagway".

If you've had enough of Soapy and his cronies, you may feel like **hiking**; one option is to follow State Street out of town, and, just before you reach the river, take the sign-posted trail off to the right to the 300-foot-high Reid Falls. Two other favourite trails are the **Dewey Lakes** system, which pass pretty subalpine lakes and tumbling waterfalls, and the trek along the waterfront west of town to **Smuggler's Cove**.

The Chilkoot Trail

Alaska's most famous and popular trail, the 33-mile **Chilkoot Trail** is a "wilderness museum" which starts in **Dyea**, seven miles from Skagway, and ends in **Lake Bennett** in Canada, climbing through rainforest to Arctic tundra. Following the exact footsteps of the original Klondike prospectors at the turn of the century, it is strewn with haunting reminders of the past, including old mining dredges and gold-rush ghost towns.

The three- to five-day hike can be strenuous, especially the final ascent from Sheep Camp (1000ft) to Chilkoot Pass (3550ft). You must be self-sufficient for food and fuel, and be prepared for foul weather, especially howling winds. **Campgrounds** line the trail, as well as **cabins** with stoves and firewood, but these are often fully booked in the summer. There are also **ranger stations** at Dyea, Sheep Creek and Lindeman City. Dyea is accessible by trail, and the **White Pass and Yukon Railway** has a service for hikers returning to Skagway. Miniature carriages, or "casey cars", run from Lake Bennett to Frazer on the Klondike Highway for $14, and to Skagway for $69.

Accommodation

Skagway has a **youth hostel**, and a pleasantly secluded **campground** at 14th Avenue and Broadway Street, near the railway, but most other **accommodation** is expensive.

The Golden North Hotel, Broadway St (☎983-2294). Skagway's most famous hotel, built in 1898. All rooms are decorated with gold-rush antiques and have large cast-iron bathtubs. $70.

The Skagway Home Hostel, Third Ave and Main St (☎983-2181). Homely and welcoming, one of the finest hostels in the state, despite its strict 10.30pm curfew. $10 per night, $15 for non-members.

The Skagway Inn B&B, Seventh Ave and Broadway St (☎983-2289). Doubles from $55.

Eating and Drinking

Most of Skagway's **bars** and **restaurants** lie in the touristy area on Broadway Street between Second and Seventh streets.

Northern Lights, Broadway St, between Fourth and Fifth avenues (☎983-2225). Italian food, with pizza from $10 and pasta from $8.

The Prospectors Sourdough, Broadway St, between Third and Fourth avenues (☎983-2865). All-you-can-eat salad bar for $6.50.

The Red Onion Saloon, Second Ave and Broadway St. Best bar in town with live music, excellent pizza, and Alaska amber beer on tap.

Sourdough Cafe, Broadway St, between Third and Fourth avenues (☎983-2291). Across the street from the *Prospectors Sourdough*, with all-you-can-eat spaghetti dinners with salad and bread, for $12.

Anchorage

Wedged between the two arms of the Upper Cook Inlet and the imposing Chugach Mountains to the east, **ANCHORAGE** is the major metropolis in South Central Alaska. Home to over seventy percent of Alaska's population, it serves as the transportation centre for the whole state.

By the time **Captain James Cook** came up what is now the Cook Inlet in 1778, in search of a Northwest Passage to the Atlantic, Russian fur-trappers had already started to settle the area, trading copper and iron for fish and furs with the Indians. Though Cook was sure that this inlet was not the passage, he sent boats out in a southeasterly direction to investigate. When they were forced to turn back by the severe tides, Cook named this the **Turnagain Arm**; on May 30 a group landed at Possession Point to claim the land in the name of King George III.

Anchorage itself began life in 1915 as a small tent city for construction workers on the Alaska Railroad. During the Thirties, hopefuls fleeing the Depression came pouring in from the lower 48, and World War II – and the construction of the **Alcan Highway** – further boosted the city's size and strategic importance. The opening of the international **airport** established Anchorage as the "Crossroads of the World", and statehood in 1959 brought yet more optimistic adventurers to the city

On Good Friday 1964, North America's strongest ever **earthquake**, measuring 8.6 on the Richter scale, devastated much of downtown, but ironically Anchorage emerged stronger than ever from the consequent building boom. In the early Seventies, the discovery of **oil** in Prudhoe Bay led to an influx of construction workers, earning six-figure incomes working on the Alaska pipeline. However, Anchorage has suffered since the oil crisis in the mid-Eighties.

Today, this sprawling city is a combination of old and new, ugly urban blight and rural parks. Very cosmopolitan, with many ethnic groups (the most significant of whom are the native Alaskans), it also has its fair share of poverty, homelessness and crime. Downtown Anchorage can seem faceless, heaving with bars, malls and snack joints, but the city's setting, minutes away from snowy mountains and glaciers, makes it very definitely something more than Anytown, USA.

Arrival, Getting Around and Information

Anchorage's **airport** is seven miles west of town, served five times daily by the *People Mover* bus (see below). Check the timetable outside the terminal. If you arrive at an inconvenient time you can take a **taxi** ($9–12 to downtown) or a hotel courtesy van (provided by most larger hotels, although you may need a reservation). The *Dynair Charter* shuttle service (☎243-3310) costs $5 to downtown. The **train station** (☎265-2494) is at the edge of town on Second Avenue.

Most of the major sights downtown are easily reached on foot, but the best way to get around is by **bike**. *Downtown Bicycle Rental*, 145 W Sixth Avenue (☎276-5293), rents mountain bikes for $14 per day. *People Mover* **buses** cover the city and the surrounding area – known together as the "bowl" – between 5am and midnight, for a 75¢ flat fare. However, they're few and far between; sometimes there's only one every ninety minutes. Schedules cost 50¢ from the *Transit Center* office on Sixth Avenue and G Street (Mon–Fri 9am–5pm), or call *Rideline* on ☎343-6543.

The main information and assistance office downtown is the **Log Cabin Visitor Information Center**, on the corner of Fourth Avenue and F Street (daily May–Sept 7.30am–7pm; Oct–April 8.30am–6pm; ☎274-3531). Their three-hour self-guided **downtown walking tour** makes a pleasant and easy way to explore Anchorage; you can also join the guided tours of the town's historic buildings organised by Anchorage Historic

Properties, in the Old City Hall next door (summer only; $2). For a recorded message detailing events in town, call the *All About Anchorage* hotline (☎276-3200).

Diagonally across the street from the Log Cabin, the **Alaska Public Lands Information Center** has natural history information, maps, and brochures about Alaska's parks. They can help plan trips into the interior, and also make reservations both for accommodation and the shuttle bus to Denali National Park – important during the busy summer months (daily 9am–7pm; ☎271-2737).

Onward from Anchorage

You can get to practically anywhere in Alaska from Anchorage. Regular **bus** services include *Caribou Express* (☎278-5776), 501 L Street, who run to Fairbanks and Homer for very reasonable rates; *Alaska Denali Transit* (☎273-3331/☎733-2601), whose daily buses from the youth hostel go to Denali, Kenai, Homer and Fairbanks; *Alaska Direct* (☎277-6652 or ☎1-800/478-7228), which heads twice a week for Skagway and White Horse in Canada, and also puts on a fortnightly service to Minneapolis; and *Alaskon Express* (☎452-2843), which departs three times a week for Skagway. If you have a bit more cash to spare, *Gray Line of Alaska* (☎277-5581), 547 W Fourth Avenue, offers **narrated trips** to most major cities, including Fairbanks and Valdez, and sightseeing tours out to the glaciers.

Alaska Airlines (☎243-3300) and *Markair* (☎243-1541) provide the state's most comprehensive network of **flights**. An express **train** service to Fairbanks, which passes Denali National Park, leaves Anchorage at 8.30am, arriving in Denali at 3.45pm, and in Fairbanks at 8pm. From Anchorage to Denali costs $78; the trip to Fairbanks, with a stopover in Denali, is $108. Reserve at the Second Avenue station or any travel agency; the Alaska Railroad also offers assorted train, bus and boat packages, including a three-day *Interior Alaska Excursion*, which includes a trip to Denali Park, a riverboat tour in Fairbanks and a flight back to Anchorage for $526.

The Town

Travellers eager to rush off into the so-called "real" Alaska tend to overlook Anchorage as a destination, dismissing it simply as a place to make their next connection. There is, however, plenty to see in town, and it's worth spending some time here experiencing big-city Alaska, as uncompromisingly "real" as any of the state's natural wildernesses.

Anchorage is laid out in a grid pattern; numbered avenues run east–west, and lettered streets run north–south. The **Anchorage Museum of History and Art**, A Street and Seventh Avenue, includes a massive (six by ten foot) oil painting of Mount McKinley by Sydney Laurence, and life-size dioramas of Alaskan history (daily 9am–6pm; $3). With its modest displays on the state's flora and fauna, the **Alaska Wildlife Museum**, 844 Fifth Avenue, is less inspiring, but offers useful snippets on the natural wonders you can expect to see when you head out of the city (daily 9am–9pm; $5). The **Imaginarium**, 725 Fifth Avenue, is more exciting, especially for the young at heart, with hands-on displays to tell you whatever you need to know about glaciers, the Northern Lights, polar bears and the private life of the dopey-looking moose (Mon–Sat 11am–6pm; $4).

Around the corner, the **Visual Arts Center**, at the corner of Fifth Avenue and G Street, has a collection of contemporary local and national works (Mon–Sat 10am–6pm; $1), but by far the most impressive range of Alaskan artefacts in town is in the private collection of the **Heritage Library Museum**, in the *National Bank of Alaska* on the corner of Northern Lights Avenue and C Street. Exhibits include paintings, photographs, old newspapers, rare books and maps, tools and weapons and old costumes including bizarre-looking parkas made from walrus intestines (Mon–Fri noon–5pm; free; ☎265-2834 for details of tours).

Anchorage also offers some great **shopping**. The gift shop in the **Alaska Native Medical Center**, on Third Avenue and Gambell Street, has a fine selection of authentic native crafts for sale, including jackets and moccasins. All profits go to the improvement of health care for native Alaskans (Mon–Fri 10am–2pm). There are also original handicrafts for sale at the *Alaska Native Arts and Crafts Showroom*, 333 W Fourth Avenue, which specialises in jewellery and beadwork (Mon–Fri 10am–6pm, Sat 10am–5pm).

Delaney Park, known as the Park Strip, running parallel to Ninth Avenue from A to P streets, once marked the boundary between the original city and the wilderness. It's a popular spot to play baseball, tennis, soccer and basketball, or to simply hang out.

If you're tiring of noise and crowds, head northwest of the city to **Earthquake Park**, at the end of Northern Lights Boulevard, which offers restorative views of the mountains. The park's rather paltry trails are not really worth bothering with, however.

The **Alaska Zoo**, at Mile 2 on O'Malley Road, is quite small but offers a nice sample of Alaska's famous wildlife, including a pair of grizzlies, a polar bear, wolves and moose – although gawping at creatures trapped in cages, while only a few miles out of the city limits many more of them are actually roaming free, is more than a little incongruous (daily 10am–6pm; $5).

Over 120 miles of **cycling trails** criss-cross the town through parks and woodland. The **Coastal Trail**, which starts at the bottom of Second Avenue and runs along the Cook Inlet to Kinkaid Park, is a great afternoon walk or bike ride – you might see beluga whales feeding in the waters of the inlet.

Chugach State Park

The 495,000-acre **Chugach State Park**, just fifteen minutes' drive from Anchorage, is one of America's largest, a huge wilderness of mountains, lakes and wildlife traversed by hiking trails (some open to mountain bikes). In the winter, you can go dog sledding, snowmobiling and cross-country skiing. The two-hour hike up to the top of **Flattop Mountain** (4500ft) is highly popular, although steep and rocky in parts, and you should be prepared for sudden weather changes and dangerous situations. There have been serious accidents here, and recently a nine-year-old boy fell to his death. However, there are spectacular views of Anchorage, the Cook Inlet and the mountains behind, and, on clear days, you may be able to see Mount McKinley. In winter, adventurous souls "glissade" down the steeper sections of the trail. Details on the park's extensive trail system are available from the Alaska Public Lands Information Center (see above). Check the large, detailed maps posted at the trailheads, or pick up the very informative *55 Ways to South Alaskan Wilderness*, available in most Anchorage bookshops and sport stores.

Unfortunately, the *People Mover* does not go all the way to the park, but bus #92 from downtown runs to the corner of Hillside Drive, from where you can walk or hitch. The last bus leaves for downtown at 5.30pm.

Accommodation

Inexpensive **accommodation** in Anchorage can be hard to find, especially in the summer, and many places are reserved months in advance. Downtown, the hotels are nearly all prohibitively expensive, but there is a **hostel**, and several campgrounds in the "bowl", as well as many **B&Bs** that charge from $45. Free B&B reservation services include *Stay with a Friend*, 3605 Arctic Boulevard, Suite 173 (☎258-4036), and *Alaska Sourdough B&B Association*, 889 Cardigan Circle (☎563-6244).

Anchorage Hotel, 330 E St (☎1-800/544-0988). Historic hotel that survived the earthquake. In the summer, rooms begin at $139, but rates are much lower in winter.

Anchorage International Hostel, 700 H St (☎276-3635). Welcoming, cosy, and very central, a block south of the Transit Center. Dorm beds for $10 for members, $13 for non-members – reserve well ahead in the summer.

The Ingra House, 641 Ingra St (☎278-9656). Rooms with shared bathroom, kitchen and sitting area, starting from $48 for doubles ($155 weekly). No alcohol allowed.

Sixth and B B&B, 145 W Sixth Ave (☎279-5292). Doubles for $55, with free bikes for guests.

Eating

Anchorage is home to countless fast-food joints and snack bars, with plenty of small, reasonably priced cafes downtown. The best of its restaurants, however, are along L Street overlooking the Inlet. Cheaper ethnic food is also excellent; don't leave without trying one of the many Oriental restaurants.

Cyrano's Bookstore and Cafe, 413 D St (☎274-2599). Great surroundings in a lively bookshop (open until 2am on Saturday). Sandwiches, soups, occasional live entertainment, free papers and taped classical music.

Downtown Deli, 525 W Fourth Ave (☎274-0027). Old Anchorage institution; not particularly cheap for a deli (entrees start at $7), but serving bagels, pastrami and lox to rival New York's best.

Maharaja's, 328 G St (☎272-2233). Excellent Indian cuisine, with an all-you-can-eat lunch buffet.

La Mex, Sixth Ave and I St (☎274-7678). Mexican food; try the sizzling beef fajitas with rice, beans and guacamole ($11.50). Famed for their B-B-Q baby-back ribs. Inexpensive lunch specials.

The Old Anchorage Salmon Bake Restaurant, 251 K St (☎279-8790). Alaskan seafood restaurant, popular with package tours. Massive mixed platters for $15.95. Only open May–Sept.

Peggy's Restaurant, 675 Fifth Ave (☎258-7599). Good family dining and homemade pies, a little way out of town.

Simon and Seaforts, 420 L St (☎274-3502). One of the best of the big-name restaurants, with gorgeous views over the Inlet and wondrous seafood from around $15. Reservations recommended.

Thai Cuisine, 444 H St (☎277-8424). One of the best of Anchorage's many Thai restaurants.

Wings'n'Things, 529 I St (☎277-6257). "Nuclear hot" chicken wings (ten for $5) and fine sub sandwiches.

Entertainment and Nightlife

There are lots of good **bars** in downtown Anchorage, and the atmosphere varies as much as the clientele. However, Anchorage is a macho city, and women travellers may not find its "Bohemian" side quite as endearing as many locals seem to think it is. Many innocent-looking bars turn out to be strip joints, filled with leering, jeering, Alaskan "real men". **Spenard Road**, between Northern Lights Boulevard and International Airport Road, is the city's self-consciously sleazy vice district.

On the more highbrow side of things, not much can lure Alaskans indoors during the summer, so there are few summer performances, but during the rest of the year, the **Center for Performing Arts** (☎263-2787) has a huge variety of shows, plays, opera and concerts. The **Anchorage Opera** (☎279-2557) performs tragedies from late September to early October, operettas from late January to early February, and musicals at the beginning of April. In the summer, the *ACRO Theater*, 700 G Avenue, has free film shows about Alaska's history and native culture (Tues & Thurs 2pm & 3pm; ☎263-4545). *Cyrano's Cinema*, part of the restaurant and bookshop at 413 D Street (see above), shows foreign and classic movies ($4; ☎274-0064). For further details of happenings in town, call the events line on ☎263-2901.

Chilkoot Charlie's, 2435 Spenard Rd (☎272-1010). Anchorage's busiest bar; a huge, sawdust-on-the-floor, wild-time kind of place. Six bars, live music, and a diverse lot of customers. They serve standard bar food, with frequent lunchtime specials for $3. Their motto is "We screw the other guy and pass the savings on to you!".

Darwin's Theory, 426 G St (☎277-5322). Quiet neighbourhood bar.

Downbeat, 3230 Seward Hwy (☎274-2328). Students' hangout underneath a restaurant, with unusually good music for this part of the world.

Jens's, 36th Ave and Arctic St. Trendy, arty cafe-bar, south of downtown.

South of Anchorage

Seward Highway, which heads south out of Anchorage, offers fantastic views as it follows Turnagain Arm to Portage. Along the way, signs in several lay-bys explain the surrounding environment – watch out for beluga and killer whales in mid- to late summer, as well as mountain goats on the cliffs above the road.

Visits to **Portage Glacier**, about ninety minutes from Anchorage, are made especially memorable by its fascinating **visitor centre**, which includes a mock-up walkthrough ice cave, an observation deck, a large film theatre and compendious information about the local wriggly ice worm. The centre is about seven miles up, situated on the shore of Portage Lake – which, incidentally, is sterile, so don't expect to see any marine life. Narrated **boat rides**, which leave six times daily during the summer (and costs $20), are a great way to see the glacier up close. *Gray Line of Alaska* combine round-trip transportation from Anchorage with the boat ride for $50.

Trains to Portage ($15) continue to Whittier (an additional $8) on the Prince William Sound, from where an Alaska Marine Highway ferry heads to Valdez (see p.883).

The Kenai Peninsula

Beyond Portage, Seward Highway skirts the end of the Turnagain Arm and enters the **Kenai Peninsula**, "Anchorage's playground". At over nine thousand square miles, the peninsula is larger than many states in the lower 48, and offers an endless diversity of activities and scenery. For those relying on public transport, **Homer**, at the end of the highway, is the final destination, roughly four hours' drive from Anchorage.

Trails branch off all along the highway to provide excellent hiking in the **Kenai mountains**. Five-day hikes on the **Resurrection Trail** run from the small gold-mining community of **Hope**, on the Turnagain Arm, and come out on the **Sterling Highway** about fifty miles east of Soldotna. Cabins along the trail must be rented in advance. For more information on hiking and camping in the Kenai Peninsula, contact the Public Lands Information Center in Anchorage (see p.877).

The most popular pastime in the Kenai Peninsula is **fishing**. Cast aside any assumptions that this is a tranquil activity – "combat fishing", which often entails hauling in a brute that might weigh over sixty pounds, is pretty aggressive stuff. The king salmon run starts in late May, when thousands of anglers stand elbow to elbow along the Kasilof, Russian and Kenai rivers in pursuit of the millions of fish that return to spawn.

Campgrounds along the rivers fill up fast, but in July and August hungry bears join in the fun and games, and most of the crowds go home. Frequently changing regulations limit fishing, so call the Department of Fish and Game in Juneau (☎344-0541) before you set out. **Permits**, widely available in shops, cost $10 for one day, $15 for three, and $30 for two weeks.

Homer

At the end of the Sterling Highway, **HOMER**, located on the edge of Kachemak Bay, is the Kenai Peninsula's southernmost town, roughly 230 miles by road from Anchorage. It is also its most appealing, to the extent that it's sometimes called the "Shangri-La of Alaska". From the shores of the bay, a thin five-mile finger of land – the "**Spit**" extends out into the dark waters, where glaciers spill off forested mountains.

The Russians were the original settlers of the bay, drawn by the abundance of **coal**, and by the mid-1800s, several American companies had followed suit. In 1896, Homer Pennock, a gold-seeker from Michigan, set up the community that still bears his name. Today, the village depends heavily on **fishing**. For some years, every summer, young people from the lower 48 have arrived here in droves to work on the boats or in the cannery. Unfortunately, due to the recent decline in the price and quantity of salmon in Alaska, it remains to be seen whether this tradition will continue to flourish.

Homer's other main industry, **tourism**, is under no such threat. Due to its dramatic surroundings and "mild" winters (temperatures only drop to 20°F below zero), people have been attracted to this pretty fishing village for years. The resident population is younger and more mixed than elsewhere in the state, and there is a thriving arts community, with many galleries. Outdoor lovers will also appreciate the opportunity to explore some of Alaska's finest scenery and see its marine wildlife.

Arrival, Information and Getting Around

Homer's **airport** is two miles east of town on Kachemak Way. *ERA Aviation* (☎235-5205) and *Southcentral Air* (☎235-6172) both operate regular flights to Anchorage for around $60. The **Alaska Marine Highway** office (Mon–Fri 9am–1pm; ☎235-8849) is at the end of the Spit; there are twice-weekly services to Seldovia and Kodiak.

Although small, Homer is quite spread out. Most hotels, restaurants and shops are in town, and there are two kitschy **boardwalks** on the Spit where many of the tour operators are concentrated. The main **visitor centre** is at 3776 Lake Street (☎235-7740), and there's another information office on the Spit, open daily. There is no public transport in town, but hitching is seldom a problem, and you can rent **mountain bikes** for $20 per day from *Quiet Sports* (☎235-8620), on Pioneer Avenue across from the library, who also have a good stock of camping gear.

The Town

The **Pratt Museum** on Bartlett Street in downtown Homer features high-quality works by local craftspeople, as well as Inuit and Indian artefacts, aquariums and historic Homer oddities (daily 10am–5pm; $3). The oldest of the town's many **galleries** is the *8 x 10 Studio*, 581 Pioneer Avenue, which shows local art works in a log cabin.

Many of Homer's most popular activities, however, revolve around the Spit. Apart from all the beachcombing, clamming, sunbathing and general touristy hubbub of the Spit itself, the prime attraction is to get out onto the waters of **Kachemak Bay**. If you plan to do so, call in first at the **Alaska National Marine Wildlife Refuge** office at 202 Pioneer Avenue (☎235-6546), for its displays and videos about marine wildlife.

A large proportion of the Alaskans who visit Homer each summer come for the excellent **halibut fishing**. These large flat fish, considered by some to be better eating than salmon, average around fifty to one hundred pounds, but have been known to come in at over three hundred pounds; a full day's excursion with any of dozens of charter companies costs around $125. If you don't mind joining in with the crowds, it's cheaper and simpler to visit the small pond on the Spit known as the **fishing hole**, which fills up with salmon at certain times in the summer. Each year the hole is stocked with thousands of king, red and silver salmon smelt, which are then released. After several years at sea, the fish return to the hole; unable to spawn – salmon spawn in freshwater – the lost fish swim around aimlessly until snagged.

Homer itself has few hiking trails, but there are scores in **Kachemak Bay State Park**, across the bay from town. These 250,000 acres of forested mountains, glaciers, pristine fjords and inlets are home to a huge variety of wildlife, including seals, sea otters and whales, as well as eagles, puffins and countless other bird species.

To get to the park, try *Central Charters* (☎235-7847) on the Spit, which has various wildlife sightseeing tours and water taxis, and will drop you off at the park and pick you up the following day for about $45. The *Danny J*, bookable through *Central Charters*, makes two daily trips to the lovely and very tiny arts community of **Halibut Cove**, on the south shore of the bay, including a brief stop at **Gull Island**, a rookery of over 15,000 seabirds. The early trip costs $35, but it's cheaper if you travel in the evening.

Trailheads are concentrated in and around Halibut Cove. It is possible to hike any one of the trails in a day, though if you wish to spend more time here, the park has several **campgrounds**. As with all hiking in Alaska, you must be well provisioned, treat water before drinking, and dress appropriately for the inevitable wet, boggy conditions. The most popular hike, up to the **Grewingk Glacier**, is an easy three-and-a-half-mile trek above the spruce and cottonwood forest to the foot of the glacier, from where you get splendid views of the bay.

The **Alaska Department of Natural Resources**, which maintains the park, has stations in Homer (☎235-7024) and Herring Cove (no phone). Their maps, which mark the hiking trails, are available from tour operators and the visitor centre.

Accommodation

All of Homer's several **hotels** and **B&Bs** can be fully booked in midsummer. The visitor centre can help you find a room, and there is **camping** in town, across the bay in the state park, or, most popularly, on the Spit. The $3 fee for camping on the Spit doesn't seem to apply to the beach across from the *Sawlty Dog Saloon* known as "tent city", where a large summer community of "Spit-rats" resides while working in the canneries or on the boats. There are toilets next to the *General Store*, but, for a shower, you'll have to head back to the *Washboard Laundry*, about half a mile off the Spit.

The Driftwood Inn, 135 W Bunnel Ave (☎235-0019). Located on the edge of the bay, this is the most pleasant hotel in Homer, with a variety of facilities such as barbecue and shellfish cookers, and free fish-cleaning. Rooms cost $60–85.

Heritage Hotel, 147 E Pioneer Ave (☎235-7787). Log-built hotel in centre of town. Doubles with bath from $68.

Oomiak B&B Hostel, 1680 East End Rd (☎235-2949). One of the least expensive places to stay, with hostel rates at $10, and double rooms $35. Call before heading out there; it's one and a half miles east of the town centre.

Pioneer B&B, 243 Pioneer Ave (☎235-5670). In the centre of Homer, with self-contained rooms that sleep four for $65, and a small basement unit for $35.

Eating and Drinking

Many unremarkable cafes on the Spit cater to the crowds of day-trippers, but the best **restaurants** are in town. For **nightlife**, head for the colourful bars, or to the relaxed *Pier One Theatre* (☎235-7333), next to the fishing hole on the Spit (May–Sept only).

Alice's Champagne Palace, Pioneer Ave (☎235-7560). Live music venue with large dance floor.

Cafe Cups, 162 W Pioneer Ave (☎235-8330). A bit expensive, but worth it for the innovative cuisine.

Don Jose's, 127 W Pioneer Ave (☎235-7963). Large Mexican platters or pizza, $7–15.

Fresh Sourdough Express Bakery and Cafe, 1316 Ocean Drive (☎235-7571). Good all-you-can-eat breakfast for $8.

The Sawlty Dog Saloon, the Spit (☎235-9990). It's hard to miss this Homer landmark; a log-built bar with a lighthouse tower, at the end of the Spit.

Smoky Bay Co-op Natural Food Store, Pioneer Ave and Bartlett St (☎235-7242). Wholefood shop with great lunches from $5.

The Prince William Sound

The **Prince William Sound** is a wilderness of steep fjords and mountains, glaciers and marine wildlife, covering over 15,000 miles of Southcentral Alaska. Sheltered by the Chugach Mountains in the north and east, and the Kenai Mountains in the west, and taking up most of the Chugach National Forest, the sound has, as yet, a relatively low-key tourist industry, and its economy is heavily reliant on timber, fish and mining. **Valdez**, at the end of Alaska's oil pipeline, and **Cordova**, a modest and untouristy fishing community, both make good bases for visits to the awesome **Columbia Glacier**, a dazzling blue-white bank of ice which covers over four hundred miles and rises nearly three hundred feet, and frequently calves icebergs off its face into the sea with a great thundering roar.

On Good Friday 1989, the infamous **Exxon Valdez oil spill** destroyed a lot of the region's natural beauty. Although the long-term effects have obviously yet to be determined, the spill fortunately affected just twenty percent or so of the Prince William Sound, and did not damage the salmon in the Copper River Basin.

Valdez

VALDEZ, the northernmost ice-free port in the Western hemisphere, rose to fame in the late 1800s during the gold rush, when thousands of prospectors arrived to head up the Valdez Trail to the mines around Fairbanks. The gold boom passed, and with the 1923 completion of the Alaska railroad between Fairbanks and Seward, Valdez shrank in size and importance, depending on fish canneries and occasional military use for its economic survival. Nature conspired to finish the town off on Good Friday 1964. The epicentre of North America's largest **earthquake** (see also p.877) was just forty-five miles away. Shock waves turned the ground beneath the town to quivering jelly, breaking roads, toppling buildings, and killing 33 people. A tidal wave completed the devastation. However, the residents refused to be intimidated, and, with the help of the Army Corps of Engineers, moved more than sixty buildings to a more stable site four miles away, where the "new" Valdez struggled on. All that remains on the old site is a simple plaque dedicated to those who died.

The town's fortunes rose again during the 1970s, when **oil** was found beneath Prudhoe Bay, and Valdez became the southern terminus of the 800-mile **trans-Alaska pipeline**, which carries one and a half million barrels of oil per day.

Although 1989's *Exxon Valdez* oil spill was an ecological disaster for the area, it triggered an economic boom for the city in the form of the massive **cleanup**, which cost *Exxon* and the government over one hundred billion dollars. Eleven thousand workers in over one thousand boats and three hundred planes scoured the beaches; the rate for an eighteen-hour day of scrubbing rocks by hand was $24 per hour. The cleanup was declared officially over in 1991.

Today, the economy depends on oil, fishing and tourism. Known as "little Switzerland" for its backdrop of steep mountains, glaciers, waterfalls and an annual snowfall of over five hundred inches, Valdez offers great hiking, fishing and wildlife viewing. However, it is also very wet, with rain seven days out of ten. In summer, low clouds and constant drizzle may obscure the mountains and the harbour, and in winter, the town is often blocked by enormous snowdrifts (in 1952 they reached record levels of 974 inches). Locals take a perverse pride in their inclement weather, and insist that the world is cut off from Valdez, rather than the other way round.

The **Valdez Town Museum**, in the Centennial building on Egan Drive, carries detailed displays on the role of the oil business (daily 9am–8pm; $1). It also has exhibits on nineteenth-century mining, the 1964 earthquake and the Columbia Glacier. A few blocks south of the museum, near the small boat harbour, **Point of View Park** offers good views of the old (pre-earthquake) town and the monstrous *Alyeska* **pipeline terminal**, which lies fourteen miles away, across the bay. Various tour operators, such as *Gray Line* (☎835-2357), can take you there.

The **Salmon Spawning Viewpoint** on Crooked Creek, about half a mile out of town on the Richardson Highway, is a great spot to observe returning salmon in midsummer. Several charter companies on the harbour offer salmon- and halibut-**fishing trips** (about $90–120 per person), as well as sightseeing tours of the Prince William Sound and the Columbia Glacier (expect to pay $70 per person).

Practicalities

Valdez is the only town on the Sound to have **road** access, but many visitors arrive on the **Alaska Marine Highway**. The ride, if the weather is clear, offers superb views both of the fabulous Columbia Glacier and of an abundance of wildlife. The **ferry terminal** is in the city dock at the end of Hazelet Avenue (☎835-4436). *Gray Line* operates a **bus** service to and from Anchorage, leaving from the *Westmark Hotel* (Mon–Sat 8am; ☎835-2357). Also from the *Westmark*, *Alaska-Yukon* **coaches** (☎835-4391) run three times a week to Fairbanks. The **airport** is five miles out, on Airport Road, with two or three daily flights to Anchorage provided by *ERA Aviation* (☎835-2595).

As well as details of pipeline tours, the **visitor centre**, 245 East North Harbour Road, offers bike rental and a left-luggage service (daily 8am–8pm; ☎835-2330). Valdez has very little by way of inexpensive **accommodation**. The *Totem Inn*, at Richardson Highway and Meals Avenue (☎835-4443), is a comfortable hotel, with a big log fire and hunting trophies in the lounge, where rooms start at $80; they also do salmon bakes. Just outside town on Richardson Highway, the *Village Inn* (☎835-2437) is a bargain for large groups, with cabins that sleep six for $80 per night. If you want to **camp**, the *Valdez Glacier Campground*, behind the airport five miles from town, is somewhat impractical for those without transport. An alternative is to join the cannery workers who spend the entire summer in tents on the appropriately named **Hotel Hill**, behind the small boat harbour. The park service requires a $3 fee, but often fails to collect.

The *Pipeline Club* at the *Valdez Motel*, 136 Egan Drive (☎835-4332), does good steak and seafood **dinners**; its bar is where Captain Hazelwood of the *Exxon Valdez* was drinking on the fateful night. Greek and Italian meals at the *Pizza Palace*, 210 Harbor Road (☎635-2368), are a bit cheaper, and there's a great view from the bar. *Tim's Quarter Pounder*, in Acres Mall (☎835-2853), serves great burgers and Mexican food.

Cordova

Far quieter than Valdez, and only accessible by sea or air, **CORDOVA** is an unpretentious community set in forests and mountains on the eastern edge of the Sound. Once a boomtown on the railroad transporting copper from the mines near McCarthy, about one hundred miles northeast, Cordova became dependent on **fishing** after the mines closed in the late Thirties. At first it reeled from the effects of the oil spill but, fortunately, it now seems that most of the salmon and halibut have survived. The Copper River Delta, about twenty miles away, remains one of the world's richest salmon-spawning grounds, as well as a major homing ground for America's migratory birds.

Arrival and Information

There is no road access to Cordova; flights land at the **airport** twelve miles from town on the Copper River Highway. *Alaska Airlines* (☎424-7151), *North Pacific Airlines* (☎424-3777) and *Wilbur's Flight Service* (☎424-5695) all offer service from Anchorage – *Wilbur* also goes to Valdez. A bus between the airport and the main hotels in town costs around $8. The **ferry** stops three times a week a mile north of town on Ocean Dock Road (☎424-7333), before heading on to Valdez and the Kenai Peninsula. The **Chamber of Commerce** on First Street has the usual brochures and maps (Tues, Thurs & Sat 1–4pm; ☎424-7260).

The Town

There are few sights in untouristy Cordova; the **small boat harbour** is the core of the town's activity, particularly when the fleet is in, from May until September. The **Cordova Museum** on First and Adams streets has quirky exhibits on local history, including the evolution of the little ice worm who lives in the glaciers and the funky annual festival that celebrates its existence (Tues–Fri 1–5pm, Sat 1–7pm; free).

A walking tour details those original buildings that survived the earthquake, but most visitors are eager to get out on to the **Copper River Highway** – originally intended to connect Cordova with the rest of Alaska, but abandoned after the 1964 earthquake. This superb fifty-mile drive takes you through the **Copper River Delta**, one of the nation's best sites for bird-watching. Over two hundred species nest here on their migrations, including rare trumpeter swans, great blue herons and bald eagles. Furthermore, much of the area has been given over to a wildlife refuge where you might see moose, bears and beavers. It's a wonderful – and tranquil – site for fishing, rafting or bird-watching.

At the end of the Highway stands the collapsed **Million Dollar Bridge**, an architectural triumph constructed between two active glaciers at great risk in 1906. Destroyed during the earthquake, it remains out of use, but the views it offers of the Miles and Childs glaciers are truly breathtaking. The latter, to the west of the bridge, is particularly noisy, especially in summer; the crash of calved icebergs resounds for miles and can cause huge waves, which are liable to fling hapless salmon ashore.

It's difficult to travel the Highway without your own car, and car rental in town isn't cheap (the *Reluctant Fisherman* charges about $50 per day plus 50¢ per mile; the trip out to Childs Glacier will thus cost well over $100). The cheapest tour out to the Bridge is offered by *Alaska Seacoast Charters* (☎424-7742) – around $25 per person.

Accommodation

Most of Cordova's **hotels** are booked up in the summer, but **B&Bs** are a good option; check with the Chamber of Commerce for availability. There are also forest cabins ($20 per night) near the Copper River Delta, administered by the Forest Service in the old post office on Second Avenue (Mon–Fri 8am–5pm; ☎424-7661). Official **campgrounds** line the beautiful Copper River Highway, but real back-to-nature types prefer "Hippy Cove", two miles north of town on Orca Road, where flower children and cannery workers mingle freely.

Alaskan Hotel and Bar, First St (☎424-3288). The cheapest hotel in town, with doubles from $60. Reserve ahead in summer.

Oystercatcher B&B, Third St and Council Ave (☎424-5154). Old B&B with rooms and hearty cooked breakfasts from $50.

Prince William Sound Motel, 501 First St (☎424-7772). Friendly hotel with rooms from $70.

Eating and Nightlife

There are plenty of cheap places to eat in town, especially along First Street. Cordova is pretty quiet at night, with bars catering mostly to local fishermen and regulars. The bar in the *Alaskan Hotel* is a favourite, as is the pricier *Reluctant Fisherman* (see below). On the Copper River Highway, overlooking Eyak Lake, the *Powderhouse Bar* is a lively venue putting on folk, blues and country music. Cordova's annual **iceworm festival** in the first week of February is an excuse for much drinking and revelry.

Killer Whale Cafe, First St (☎424-7733). Popular backpackers haunt over a bookshop, serving soup, sandwiches and muffins at low prices, and with great views over the harbour.

Reluctant Fisherman, 407 Railroad Ave (☎424-3272). Superb seafood from $20.

Sourdough Cafe, First St (☎424-5494). Hearty home-cooking and the obligatory sourdough pancakes. Large meals start at around $7.

Interior Alaska

Interior Alaska cannot fail to live up to expectations of the vastness of the Great Land. Its scenery is writ large, with enormous mountain ranges and major rivers, and, due to the cold climate and short summers, it's far less forested than elsewhere in the state. More than just a wilderness, the Interior is home to a fantastic proliferation of **wildlife**

– moose, dall sheep, grizzly bears and eagles, and huge herds of caribou sweeping over seemingly endless stretches of Arctic tundra. The jewel of the region is **Denali National Park**, about one hundred miles south of Fairbanks; but don't venture there without a strong insect repellent – summer temperatures often reach the 80s, and the mosquitoes are the worst in the state.

Denali National Park

A visit to **DENALI NATIONAL PARK**, 237 miles north of Anchorage, is one of the real highlights of any Alaska itinerary. This six-million-acre wildlife reserve is named after its most famous denizen, **Mount McKinley**, which Native Americans referred to as *Denali*, "the Great One". Although an early adventurer named the mountain McKinley, after the governor of Ohio who later became the 25th US president, Alaskans have never really taken to the name, and still refer to both the mountain and the park by their original title. Whatever you choose to call it, North America's tallest mountain towers 20,320 feet above sea level, isolated above the surrounding hills. The rise from base to peak is 15,000 feet, one of the highest uplifts in the world, and the view from a low vantage point rivals that of even Mount Everest. On a clear day, standing by a lake or on the tundra, one's view is dominated by the snow-covered massif, its white glow a sharp contrast to the warm colours around it. However, as the mountain creates its own weather, it is frequently shrouded in clouds.

Only park buses, a few tour operators and permit-holders are allowed to travel the one road into the park, a policy which ensures that the native flora and fauna remain, for the most part, undisturbed. Tourists on *Denali Shuttle* **buses**, on the lookout for the "Big Four" – dall sheep, moose, caribou, and of course, grizzly bears – are rarely disappointed; the sharp-eyed bus drivers pull over to point out animals, and a good pair of binoculars is a definite boon. Travel on the buses is free of charge once you've paid the $3 park admission fee; pick up tickets two days in advance from the new **visitor centre** (May–Sept daily 5.45am–8pm; ☎683-1266), just inside the park entrance. This is where you register for the park, and you can stock up on books, pamphlets and information about organised hikes, or attend seminars and talks by rangers. You can also pick up bus tickets three to twenty-one days in advance from the **Alaska Public Lands Center** in Anchorage (see p.877).

Hikers interested in seeing more of Denali than is visible from the bus should obtain permits from the Backcountry Desk (daily 8am–8pm). With the permit, rangers also distribute bear-resistant food containers. The idea is to disassociate human smells and food, thus sparing bears from becoming dependent on hikers, and hikers from becoming food for bears. Special "camper buses" carry hikers with backcountry permits into the park; riders are free to get off in their assigned section and start hiking. There are no trails across the tundra; just choose a good landmark and head towards it. It's not a bad idea to reconnoitre the park on a full-day bus trip in order to choose where you might like to hike on subsequent days. Walking can be very boggy, so keep to the dry river beds for an easier time. If there's room, buses also carry **mountain bikes**; cyclists can be dropped off wherever they like, but are obliged to keep to the roads.

More adventurous **activities** are available in the Denali area. Several **rafting** companies take two-hour trips down the Nenana River: all offer a gentle "scenic float", and an eleven-mile "Canyon Run" through churning whitewater. Water levels on the Nenana change frequently with both rain and glacial melt, so enquire first if you're only interested in "big" water. *Owl Rafting* (☎683-2215) is the largest outfitter and has the best safety record. Trips cost $36 per person.

For close-up views of Mount McKinley without the effort, **flight-seeing tours** cost about $120 per hour. *Denali Air* (☎683-2261) have an office at the *Denali National Park*

> Call ☎452-PARK for recorded information about Denali National Park.

Hotel. Denali Wings fly from the *Historic Healy Hotel*, a few miles north of the park; they are a little cheaper, and offer a free shuttle from nearby hotels. *ERA Helicopters* (☎683-2574), at Mile 238 on the Parks Highway, do fifty-minute tours for $155 per person.

Getting There

Driving up to Denali from Anchorage, along the George Parks Highway, takes about five hours. At mile 98.7 comes the turnoff to the small town of **TALKEETNA**, which is the centre for climbers attempting Mount McKinley. Talkeetna is worth the extra half-hour drive for its small-town-Alaska feel, combined with an international flavour as climbers from all over the world gather to prepare for their assaults on the mountain. In midsummer, the town also hosts a bluegrass festival.

The **Alaska Railroad** is an easy and comfortable way to get to the park. Trains leave Anchorage daily in summer at 8.30am; the trip to the station at Denali, one and a half miles inside the park entrance, takes around eight hours and costs $85 one-way. You can also buy a through ticket to Fairbanks, and make a stopover in the park along the way.

The *Alaska Sightseeing Company* (☎452-8518) and *Denali Express* (☎274-8539) both have daily **bus trips** from Anchorage to Fairbanks via Denali during the summer. *Denali Express* is the cheapest, charging $75 to Denali, and an additional $25 to continue from Denali to Fairbanks. *Princess Tours*, 612 W Fourth Avenue, Anchorage (☎276-7711), and *Gray Line of Alaska*, 547 W Fourth Avenue, Anchorage (☎277-5581), have their own glass-topped dome cars, complete with restaurant and bar, which make expensive daily trips from Anchorage to Denali Park and Fairbanks, giving good views of wildlife and Mount McKinley.

Hitching along the Parks Highway is quite easy, especially during the summer when there are more than twenty hours of daylight.

Accommodation

The only **hotel** within the park boundaries, the *Denali National Park Hotel*, operated by *ARA Services* (☎276-7234), is open between mid-May and mid-September. The hotel is just across from the train station. In addition to the usual facilities, it boasts a 300-seat auditorium which hosts National Park Service programmes, and a bar and restaurant in a renovated railroad car. This is much the most convenient place to stay at Denali, but it's usually fully booked, and double rooms cost a hefty $113.

ARA Services also run the comfortable *McKinley Chalet* (☎276-7234) just outside the park, a couple of miles beyond the entrance, which has a swimming pool, sauna and hot-tub, in addition to a good restaurant (expensive) and beautiful views of the Nenana River. Double rooms cost $133. Among several other mid- to high-priced hotels on the developed strip outside Denali, the *Denali Grizzly Bear Cabins* (☎683-2696) has cabins at around $49 per night, as well as campsites.

Denali also has six **campgrounds**, in which spaces – costing $12 per night – have to be reserved at the visitor centre. Campers may stay as long as a fortnight, but must book the entire stay in advance. Those with camping permits may take their cars into the first 29 miles of the park. The space restrictions will all seem worthwhile when you're inside the park, and find that you don't have to contend with crowds on anything like the same scale as Yosemite or Yellowstone.

Several spots immediately outside the park handle the overflow. *Lynx Creek Campground* (☎683-2547) is right in the centre of the developed strip and convenient for restaurants and shops.

Fairbanks

FAIRBANKS, about 360 miles north of Anchorage, is at the end of the Alaska Highway and definitely at the end of the road for most tourists. Its central location makes it the focal point for the tiny villages scattered around the surrounding wilderness, and a staging post for North Slope villages such as **Barrow** and the oil community of **Prudhoe Bay**. These northern areas are accessible by air and the **Dalton Highway**, also known as the Haul Road.

The town was founded accidentally when, in 1901, Captain E T Barnette's steamship ran aground in the shallows of the Chena River. Unable to transport the supplies he was carrying, Barnette set up shop in the wilderness and catered to the few miners trying their luck in the area. The following year, with the beginnings of the gold rush, a tent city sprang up on the site.

In 1908, at the height of the gold stampede, Fairbanks had a population of 18,500. Due to the difficulty in retrieving gold from the frozen bedrock, however, mining activity declined, and by 1920 the population had dwindled to only 1100, although as the seat of Alaska's Federal Court System, and the terminus of the Alaska Railroad, Fairbanks survived even after the gold rush petered out.

Due to its strategic position, Fairbanks has benefited greatly from **military** spending in the last fifty years, and still has three military bases. In the mid-Seventies, it became the transport centre for the **Alaska Pipeline** project; pipeline construction and other oil-related activities brought a rush of workers seeking wages of up to $1500 per week and the population reached an all-time high. Fairbanks was stretched to the seams, with just about everything but bars and prostitutes in short supply. The city's economy dropped dramatically with the oil crash, and unemployment had hit twenty percent before government spending put the city back on track.

Fairbanks is a flat and somewhat ugly city, but it's surrounded by beautifully wooded rolling hills, accented by the distant Alaska Range, and tourism is increasingly important. The spectacular **Northern Lights** are a major attraction, as is the **Ice Festival** in mid-March, when the North American Open Sled Dog Championships take place on the frozen downtown streets. The Festival is perhaps most famous for its ice-sculpting competition; the impressive design and detail which goes into these large works makes it well worth braving the evil subzero temperatures.

Summer visitors should try to catch the **World Eskimo/Indian Olympics** in July. Competitors from around the state compete in the traditional skills of subsistence living, as well as ear pull, knuckle hop, and high kick, where age and wisdom often defeat youth and strength. It all takes place in the *Alaskaland Civic Center Theater* (☎452-6646).

Fairbanks is remarkable for inflicting exceptional extremes of climate, found in few other places on earth. Temperatures of -40°F are not uncommon, but the thermometer can rise to over 90°F in summer. Because the city sits just 150 miles south of the Arctic Circle, above which the sun neither sets during the summer nor rises during the winter, Fairbanks also has very long days. The shortest day of the year has less than four hours of sunlight, the longest has over 21. Both can be disconcerting, and residents suffer from a high rate of depression. In summer, midnight baseball games under natural light are great fun, but stumbling out of a bar at 2am into bright sunshine can be really perturbing.

Arrival, Information and Getting Around

Driving or hitching the 653 miles from Haines is the preferred method of getting to Fairbanks, but *Markair, Alaska Airlines, United* and *Delta* all have daily **flights** to Fairbanks from Anchorage. Also from Anchorage, the *Alaska Sightseeing Company* (☎452-8518) and *Denali Express* (☎274-8539) make daily **bus trips**. *Alaskon Express*

THE NORTHERN LIGHTS

The **Aurora Borealis**, or Northern Lights, give their brightest and most colourful displays in the sky above Fairbanks. The lights are caused by highly charged particles, released by solar storms and carried to earth on the solar wind. Once they reach the earth's magnetic field, the particles are deflected to the polar regions and release light. From the ground they are viewed as dancing walls of light ranging across the spectrum.

(☎452-2843) costs $177 from Skagway, $156 from Haines. The two-day bus trip stops overnight at Beaver Creek, where you make your own sleeping arrangements.

The 358-mile drive down the **Parks Highway** via Denali National Park is along an excellent, seldom-crowded road. Views en route include Mount McKinley, the entire Alaska Range, and, of course, plentiful wildlife. The **Alaska Railroad** offers the most relaxing and scenic trip to Fairbanks from Anchorage, for $108 round trip (daily in summer) or $70 off-season, (Sat only). Those planning to stay in Fairbanks less than a week can take advantage of the Fly/Rail package, under which you do one leg of the journey by train and the other on *Markair* for $189 ($162 off-season).

Although Fairbanks is not a large city, it is quite spread out. Numbered avenues run parallel to the Chena River, getting higher as you head south. The **visitor centre**, 550 First Avenue (daily 8am–5pm; ☎456-5774), organises free **walking tours** daily in summer at 10am and 3pm. For information on area parks, including Denali, the useful **Public Land Information Center** is at 250 N Cushman Street (☎451-7352). The town has two **bus** lines, but routes and schedules change frequently, so call ☎459-1011 for information or collect a schedule from *Transit Park* between Fifth and Sixth avenues.

The Town

One of the state's best **museums** can be found on the attractive campus of the University of Alaska, on the northern edge of town. Displays include native and pioneer relics, plus northern wildlife and histories of Alaska and Fairbanks (daily 9am–7pm; $3). The university is also the best place in town to view Mount McKinley and the Northern Lights. For those interested in earthquakes, the **Geophysical Institute** (☎474-7243) has an excellent tour. The city bus will get you there.

The forty-acre **Alaskaland** complex on the banks of the Chena River celebrates Alaskan history in a very touristy, but friendly way, and admission is free. Log cabins from Fairbanks' original downtown have been relocated here, and the "Mining Valley" pays homage to the early prospectors. You can even try your hand at gold panning. The **Crooked Creek and Whiskey Island Line Railroad** encircles the entire complex. Numerous free shuttle buses head out from the major hotels in town, and there is sometimes a bus from the visitor centre.

In the summer, the **Riverboat Discovery** (☎479–6673), a restored paddle steamer, operates a four-hour narrated tour down the Chena to the Tanana River, stopping at an Indian trappers' camp and an Athabascan village with assorted tourist kitsch and demonstrations of native crafts.

Accommodation

There are dozens of **motels** and **hotels** in downtown Fairbanks, but they can be very pricey, while many of the cheap motels on the edges of town are pretty dodgy. **B&Bs** are plentiful, with rooms from $50; the *Fairbanks B&B Registry* (☎452-4957) has details. The **youth hostel** is currently seeking a new location, having moved from the Tanana Fairgrounds. Temporarily, the owner is putting people up in his home at 1641 Willow Street, but space is limited so do call first (☎456-4159). For camping, the **Alaska Division of Parks** operates the *Chena River State Campground* (☎451-2695), a few miles south on University Avenue and accessible by bus from Transit Park.

Alaskan Motor Lodge, 419 Fourth Ave (☎452-4800). Quiet rooms with TV, from $60.

Fairbanks Hotel, 517 Third Ave (☎456-6440). Adequate rooms downtown, from $40.

Yukon Yonda's, 2521 Old Steese Hwy (☎457-1884). An unusual place to stay, 13 miles northeast of town. Accommodation, for $50 per night including breakfast, is in the old cook shack, which has its own kitchen and is lit by oil lamps. The friendly staff will collect you from Fairbanks if necessary, and will teach you everything you need to know about life in the bush, including how to tap birch trees to make beer. You can also pan for gold in their private mine.

Eating

Apart from fast-food joints, cheap food is difficult to find in Fairbanks, although there are a number of good spots to eat, and drink, out near the university. For the truly famished, there's a massive **salmon bake** in **Alaskaland Park**, with all-you-can-eat salmon, halibut and ribs for $16.

Food Factory, 36 College Rd (☎452-3313). Hefty home-cooked cheesesteaks and ice-cold beers, all around $5–6.

Golden Exchange Bar and Grill, 500 First Ave (☎452-1978). Pricey, but well worth it.

Jay Bird's Wingworld, 201 Old Steese Hwy (☎452-4017). Inexpensive chicken wings and wonderful halibut in beer batter.

Whole Earth Grocery and Deli, College Rd and Deborah St (☎479-2062). Healthy eating near the university.

Outside Fairbanks: Two Hot Springs

Of the various **hot springs** in the vicinity of Fairbanks, which gush from the frozen ground at temperatures ranging from 120 to 150°F, the most popular, with the best facilities, are the **Chena Hot Springs**, sixty miles to the east. **Rooms** at the fully equipped resort (☎452-7867) are priced from $55 to over $100 per night, and **camping** is available. Walking in the area is especially enjoyable after a soak in the steaming natural spring waters; if you're not staying at the resort, it costs $7 per day to use the indoor hot tubs.

The **Circle Hot Springs**, 130 miles northeast of Fairbanks along scenic Steese Highway, were discovered in 1893 by a prospector trailing a wounded moose. Long popular with locals, they now cater to tourists, with a lodge which charges $60 to $90 per night (☎520-5113), a large swimming pool and various outdoor activities. For budget travellers, the lodge has **hostel** rooms which cost $20 for the first adult and $10 for each one thereafter.

travel details

TRAINS

Routes

• The **Alaska Railroad** has one daily service in each direction in summer, and one weekly service in winter, between Seward on the Kenai Peninsula and Fairbanks, via Anchorage and Denali National Park.

• There are also several trains each day between Anchorage and Whittier on the Prince William Sound.

• **White Pass and Yukon Route** has a daily service from Skagway to Bennett, BC, and Whitehorse, YT.

Journey Times

From Anchorage: to Denali National Park 7hr; Fairbanks 11hr.

BUSES

Bus services by companies such as **Alaskon Express**, **Alaska Intercity Line**, **Alaska-Denali Transit**, **Alaska-Yukon Express**, **Alaska Direct**, are detailed throughout this chapter. All routes are served less frequently in winter; the main routes in summer are:

From Anchorage: to Whitehorse (2 weekly); Haines (2 weekly); Skagway (4 weekly); Valdez (1 daily); Denali (1 daily); Fairbanks (1 daily).

FERRIES

For details on the two separate services of the **Alaska Marine Highway** – one along the Inside Passage in the southeast, the other in the southwest between Cordova, Valdez and Homer – see p.868.

CHAPTER SIXTEEN

HAWAII

D espite their isolation, two thousand miles out in the Pacific, the islands of
HAWAII belong very definitely to the United States. If you're expecting an
unspoiled South Seas idyll, forget it. This is where Americans come on honeymoon, or when they win the lottery, and the fantasy of a dream holiday in
Paradise remains firmly rooted in the creature comforts of home. With six million tourists per year – including over a million Japanese, each said to spend a daily average of
$586 – the islands can seem like a gigantic theme park.

On the other hand, with its **volcanoes**, palm-fringed **beaches**, verdant **valleys**, glorious **rainbows**, and awesome **sea cliffs**, Hawaii is one of the most spectacularly beautiful places on earth. The resort developments can be hard to take, and you can't help
but be aware of how much of what was unique has gone; but on every island it's still
easy to hike into pristine **wilderness**. It doesn't all have to cost a fortune, either; there
are plenty of **budget** facilities if you know where to look. The only major expense you
really can't avoid, other than on Oahu, is **car** rental, and rates are probably the cheapest in the nation. If you do have money, of course, the possibilities are endless.

Honolulu, by far the largest city of the fiftieth state, and with its resort annex of
Waikiki the main tourist centre, is on **Oahu**. The biggest island, **Hawaii** itself, is
known as the **Big Island**, in a vain attempt to avoid confusion. **Maui** and **Kauai** also
attract mass tourism, while smaller **Molokai** is starting to gear itself up.

The islands share a similar topography and **climate**. The ocean winds from the northeast shed their rain on that, **windward**, coast, keeping it wet and green; the southwest
or **leeward** coasts can be almost barren, and so make ideal locations for big resort
hotels. Rainfall is at its heaviest from December to March, but temperatures remain
consistent at between 70°F and 85°F. Thanks to the usual American vacation patterns,

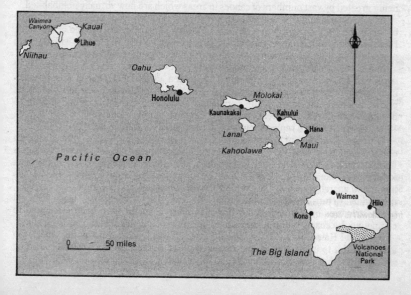

Christmas and mid-summer are far more expensive times to visit than the "off-seasons" of September to December and April to May. Prices for the cheaper accommodation options (below $50) do not fluctuate very much, but in high season the more expensive places may cost as much as fifty percent more than the prices given in this chapter.

History

Each of the Hawaiian islands in turn was forced up like a vast mass of candle drippings by submarine volcanic action, all fuelled by the same "hot spot" below the seabed, which has remained stationary as the Pacific plate drifted above. The oldest islands are now mere atolls way off to the northwest; the process is continuing at Kilauea on the Big Island, with lava exploding into the sea to add new land day by day.

Until less than two thousand years ago, these unknown specks in the ocean were populated only by the mutated descendants of what few organisms had been carried here by wind or wave. Though carbon dating suggests that *someone* was here in the second century AD – possibly the legendary dwarf-like *menehune* – the first known human inhabitants were the **Polynesians**, who arrived in two separate migrations; one from the Marquesas in the eighth century, and another from Tahiti four or five hundred years later. (Though justly famous for their navigational skills, they only undertook such long-distance canoe voyages in exceptional circumstances.)

The first European to cross the Pacific, Magellan, saw not a single island; no western ship chanced upon Hawaii until **Captain Cook** arrived at Kauai in January 1778. He was amazed to find a civilisation sharing a culture – and language – with the peoples of the south Pacific. The Hawaiians too were amazed, having long since lost contact with the outside world. Cook himself was killed in Hawaii in 1779 (see p.909), but he had started an irreversible process of change. The first Polynesians had brought the plants and animals necessary to create a self-sufficient way of life. Westerners took things further, and in reshaping the islands to suit their economic and agricultural needs decimated most of the indigenous flora and fauna – as well as the Hawaiians themselves. Cook's men estimated that there were a million islanders; the figure today is roughly the same, but a mere eight thousand **pure-blood Hawaiians** are left. The geographical distribution has changed too; it's striking how often the accounts of the early explorers describe being greeted by vast numbers of canoes in areas which are now virtually uninhabited.

As well as bringing venereal and other diseases, Cook's voyage opened the fur trade between the Pacific northwest and China. Passing ships regularly traded arms to the Hawaiians, and within a few years, chief **Kamehameha** of the Big Island, with the help of westerners and their cannons, became the first king to unite all the islands.

In a sense, ancient Hawaii had no economy, not even barter; the abundant fruits of earth and sea were simply shared out. The sudden advent of capitalism was devastating. When the fur traders realised that Hawaiian **sandalwood** fetched enormous prices in China, the mass of the population abandoned taro-farming and fishing to become wage-slaves. The great forests were almost entirely denuded by the end of the 1820s, at which point a replacement industry appeared – **whaling** (see p.913).

With the dislocation of traditional ways, Hawaiian **religion** fell apart. After the death of Kamehameha in May 1819, the female regent Kaahumanu set out to break the **kapu** (*tabu*) system which held society together. Her public defiance of the injunctions forbidding women to eat alongside men, or to eat bananas or pork, threw the islands into moral anarchy – just as the first Puritan **missionaries** arrived from New England, determined to turn Hawaii into the Promised Land. Their wholehearted capitalism and harsh strictures on the easy-going Hawaiian lifestyle might have been calculated to compound the chaos. White advisers and ministers soon dominated the government.

In the old Hawaii there was no private land; all was held in trust by the chief, who apportioned it to individuals at his continued pleasure only. After a misunderstanding with the British consul almost resulted in the islands' permanent cession to Britain, the king was requested to "clarify" the situation. In 1848 all the land was parcelled out, to native Hawaiians only, but within two years the *haole* (non-Hawaiians) too were allowed to buy and sell land. The jibe that the missionaries "came to Hawaii to do good – and they done good" stems from the speed with which they amassed vast acreages; their children became Hawaii's wealthiest and most powerful class.

While the Civil War severely disrupted whaling, it triggered a Hawaiian **sugar** boom, to replace southern sugar in the markets of the north. From then on, the machinations of the sugar industry to get favourable prices on the mainland moved Hawaii inexorably towards **annexation** by the US. In 1887 an all-white (and armed) group of "concerned businessmen" forced King David Kalakua to surrender power to an assembly elected by property owners (of any nationality) rather than citizens. When after his death his sister Liliuokalani announced her desire to proclaim a new constitution, the businessmen called in the US warship *Boston*, then in Honolulu, and declared a provisional government. US President Grover Cleveland (a Democrat) responded that "Hawaii was taken possession of by the United States forces without the consent or wish of the government of the islands. . . . (It) was **wholly without justification** . . . not merely a wrong but a **disgrace**." With phenomenal cheek, the provisional government rejected his demand for the restoration of the monarchy by saying the US should not "interfere in the internal affairs of their sovereign nation". They found defenders in the Republican US Congress, and declared themselves a Republic on July 4 1894.

A Republican President, McKinley, came to office in Washington in 1897, arguing that "annexation is not a change. It is a consummation." The strategic value of Pearl Harbor was emphasised by the Spanish-American war in the Philippines; and on August 12 1898 Hawaii was formally annexed as a territory of the United States. At this point there was no question of Hawaii becoming a state; the whites were outnumbered ten to one, and had no desire to afford the natives the protection of US labour laws, let alone to give them the vote (one leader, Sanford Dole, said that natives couldn't expect to vote "simply because they were grown up"). Furthermore, as the proportion of Hawaiians of Japanese descent (*nisei*) increased (to 25 percent by 1936), Congress feared the prospect of a state whose people might consider their primary allegiance to be to Japan.

Consequently, Hawaii was for the first half of this century the virtual fiefdom of the so-called **Big Five**, conglomerations started by the missionary families and rooted in their massive land holdings. By controlling agriculture (owning 96 percent of the sugar crop), they also dominated transport, banks, utilities, insurance – and government.

The inevitable integration of Hawaii into the American mainstream was hastened by its crucial role in the war against Japan – with the clear support of the *nisei* – and the expansion of tourism thereafter. The islands finally became the fiftieth of the United States in 1959, after a plebiscite showed a 17- to-1 majority in favour. The only group to oppose statehood was the few remaining native Hawaiians. Since then support has grown for **Hawaiian sovereignty**, on the basis that those of Hawaiian descent should gain at least the rights already held by Native American nations on the mainland.

Modern Hawaii

Roughly sixty percent of the million-plus modern Hawaiians were born here. Around one third are Caucasian (many of them US military personnel), one third Japanese, and one sixth Filipino. The economy has shifted firmly away from agriculture; those green fields that survive do so mainly because they look prettier than building sites, and in Maui for example they have to import agricultural labourers from Mexico, as the locals prefer more lucrative employment in hotels and tourism.

The dreams of American business leaders that Hawaii could replace Hong Kong as the financial centre of the Pacific are turning sour now that Japanese money looks set to reap the benefits. The need to import virtually all the basics of life has resulted in an extraordinarily high **cost of living** (the *Paradise Tax*, as they call it). In particular, the cost of buying or renting a home is so high that many islanders find themselves either obliged to work at two jobs, or simply to sleep on the beaches.

Visitors in search of the **ancient Hawaii** will find that few vestiges remain. What is presented as "historic" usually post-dates the missionary impact. The "old towns" are pure nineteenth-century Americana, with false-front stores and raised wooden boardwalks. The ruins of temples (*heiaus*) to the old gods still stand in some places – notably on the Big Island – and committed campaigners work to revive traditional philosophies, but the closest Hawaii comes to a state religion now appears to be Elvis-worship. Authentic **hula** dancing is a powerful art form, but you're far more likely to encounter it bastardised in some kind of "Polynesian spectacular" – perhaps a **luau** or "traditional feast". Usually dire tourist money-spinners, *luaus* do at least provide an opportunity to sample Hawaiian **foods** such as *kalua* pig, baked underground, and *lomi-lomi* (raw salmon). *Poi* – a paste made from mashed taro root – remains a staple of the diet, much as it was when one of Captain Cook's men described it as "a disagreeable mess".

The Hawaiian **language** most obviously endures in place names and music. At first glance it looks unpronounceable – especially as it is written using a mere twelve letters (the five vowels, plus *h*, *k*, *l*, *m*, *n*, *p* and *w*). Each letter is enunciated individually – apostrophes indicate a pause for breath. Hawaii itself is more correctly written (and pronounced) *Hawai'i*, but for visual clarity we've omitted the apostrophes in this book.

Getting To and Around Hawaii

Honolulu, just under six hours by plane from the US West Coast, is one of the world's busiest centres for air traffic. *Hawaiian Air* has the best return fares from **LA**, **San Francisco** and **Seattle** ($319–359); *Continental* and *America West* cost $400 to $500. Many flights to the US from **Australia** – such as all on *Continental* – include free stopovers in Hawaii. **European** travellers should buy all-inclusive tickets from Europe.

Hawaiian Air (Oahu ☎537-5100; US ☎1-800/367-5320; Britain ☎0293/774412) and *Aloha Air* (Oahu ☎833-3219; US ☎1-800/323-3345) connect the major islands, usually several times daily, for a standard single fare of around $65 (early morning and late night, $50; reduced rates for several tickets bought at once).

With the exception of Oahu, **bus** services on the islands barely exist. Several companies run **bicycle tours**, including *Island Bicycle Adventures* (PO Box 458, Volcano HI96785; ☎967-8603, or ☎1-800/233-2226 in the US).

> The telephone **area code** for all Hawaii is ☎808.

OAHU

Three quarters of Hawaii's population live on **OAHU**, which has monopolised the islands' trade and tourism since the first white sailors realised **Pearl Harbor** to be the finest deep-water harbour in all the Pacific. Virtually all visitors to Hawaii still arrive in **Honolulu** – albeit by air now rather than by sea – and the majority remain there for their entire vacation. Oahu has learned to live with the tourists by effectively confining them to the tower block enclave of **Waikiki**, just east of downtown Honolulu; there are very few rooms anywhere else. In much the same way, the **military** – the other mainstay of the economy – are closeted away in relatively inconspicuous camps. On any one day, the numbers of military personnel and tourists on Oahu are roughly the same.

Overcrowding and rampant development mean that Oahu could never be recommended over the **Neighbor Islands** (as the other Hawaiian islands are collectively known), but it is still possible to get a real flavour of Hawaii by staying here. There are some excellent **beaches**, with those on the north shore a haven for **surfers** and campers, and the cliffs of the **windward** side are awesome.

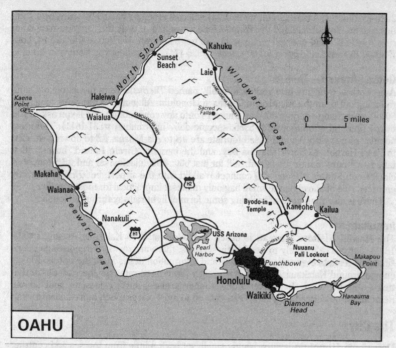

OAHU

Honolulu

Until the Europeans came, **HONOLULU** was insignificant; soon so many foreign ships were using adjacent Pearl Harbor that it had become King Kamehameha's capital, and it remains the economic centre of the island. However, although Honolulu does cover a long (but always pretty narrow) strip of southern Oahu, **downtown** is a manageable size, and a lot quieter than the glamour of its name might lead you to expect. The tourist hotels, and consequently a lot of Honolulu's hustle, are concentrated among the skyscrapers of the very distinct area of **Waikiki**, a couple of miles east.

The setting is beautiful, right on the Pacific and backed by dramatic *pali* (cliffs) and the extinct volcanoes of **Punchbowl** (a military cemetery) and **Diamond Head**; but then beauty is not so rare a commodity on Hawaii, and there are plenty of other places to see this sort of scenery without a city slapped down in the middle of it. What attracts most visitors to stay in Honolulu is the sheer **hedonism** of shopping, eating and generally hanging out in the sun. Hawaii's broad ethnic mix, and Honolulu's status as a major crossroads for world travellers, make it a cosmopolitan place where there's always something happening (and everything is for sale). It's also the centre of an exemplary **public transport** system, making it easy and cheap to explore the whole island.

Arrival and Information

The runways of Honolulu's **International Airport**, just west of downtown, extend out to sea on a coral reef. There are plenty of **car rental** outlets at the airport, but a car is not especially desirable in Honolulu, what with city traffic and very hefty parking fees in Waikiki. The nine-mile drive to Waikiki – not at all a scenic route – takes anything from

25 to 75 minutes. A **taxi** (*SIDA*, ☎836-0011) will cost around $20, and two **minibus** shuttles cost $6. You should find the *Waikiki Express* waiting outside the baggage area; if not ring ☎942-2177 and one will pick you up. To get back from Waikiki to the airport, both *Waikiki Express* and *Airport Motor Coach* (☎926-4747) will collect you from your hotel.

Getting Around – *TheBus*

A network of over fifty **bus** routes, officially named *TheBus*, covers the whole of Oahu, radiating out from the Ala Moana Center in Honolulu. All journeys, however long, cost 60¢ – exact change only – with free transfers onto any connecting route if you ask as you board (general enquiries ☎848-5555; specific daily information ☎531-1611). The most popular routes with Waikiki-based tourists are #8 to Ala Moana, #2 to downtown, #20 to Pearl Harbor, #22 to Hanauma Bay, and the bargain "Circle Island" buses which take four hours to tour the island, still for just 60¢: #52 (clockwise) and #55 (counterclockwise). Routes #19 and #20 connect Waikiki with the airport, but *TheBus*'s strictly enforced rule of allowing one small bag only makes it impractical for most travellers.

There is also much talk of building some form of light railway through Honolulu.

Information

The **Hawaii Visitors Bureau** is based in Waikiki at 2270 Kalakaua Avenue (☎923-1811), but you're unlikely to need their services; there are racks of free listings magazines and leaflets everywhere you turn, and information desks in all the hotels. Kiosks on and around Kalakaua Avenue offer greatly discounted rates for the various "**activities**" – island tours, helicopter rides, dinner cruises, surfing lessons, and so on. Remember, however, that *TheBus* can get you to most places much more cheaply.

The City

Downtown Honolulu is surprisingly small, set back a little from the sea and centring around a spacious plaza on King Street which includes **Iolani Palace** and the **State Capitol**. The palace was built for King David Kalakaua in 1882, and apart from its *koa*-wood floors contains little that is distinctively Hawaiian (Wed–Sat 9am–2.15pm; $5; ☎522-0832). Across the road is a colourful statue of Kamehameha I.

To reach the nearby ocean, pedestrians have to negotiate fearsome traffic. Although the sea may be turquoise, the shorefront is concrete, not beach, and you can't wander along it for any distance. Free elevators go to the top (tenth) floor of the **Aloha Tower** on pier 9, which as the city's tallest building once served to greet all new arrivals to Honolulu. The view is little short of ugly, but is good for orientation. East towards Diamond Head is the new black glass of Restaurant Row (see below), loomed over by the two stereo-speakers of the Waterfront Towers condominiums. Even the oldest surviving building, the 1920 Hawaiian Electric Water Plant, is a bit of a monstrosity, and that is due to be torn down. To the west (where planes swoop down to land at the airport) is Pearl Harbor; a giant pineapple in the distance marks the *Dole* factory.

The **Hawaii Maritime Center** (daily 9am–5pm; $7; ☎536-6373), almost at the foot of Aloha Tower, documents Hawaii's seafaring past in superb detail, from ancient migrations through white contact, nineteenth-century trade and twentieth-century cruises. A stunning film from 1922 (with Clara Bow in a bit part) shows the true-life drama of whaling, and there's a wall of gigantic historic surfboards. In the adjacent dock are the fully rigged four-master *Falls of Clyde* and the replica Polynesian canoe *Hokulea*, which has three times crossed the Pacific using traditional methods of navigation.

On the way towards the massive Ala Moana shopping mall, the **Artist Guild** (☎531-2933) in the **Ward Warehouse** at 1050 Ala Moana Boulevard sells individual pieces by over two hundred artists. It's well worth a look – assuming you don't go for the Wyland school of art so evident elsewhere, romanticising whales as interplanetary voyagers.

Chinatown

If you get off *TheBus* #2 from Waikiki at the junction of Hotel and Bishop streets, you'll find yourself at the gleaming hi-tech Executive Center in the heart of downtown Honolulu. Just five minutes' walk away down Hotel Street, the fading green wooden clapboard storefronts of **Chinatown** seem like another world. These narrow streets leading down to the Nuuanu Stream were traditionally the city's red-light district, and are still characterised by pool halls, massage parlours and heavy-duty bars.

The **Chinatown Visitor Center** (daily 10am–4pm; $2; ☎524-3409) in the Maunakea Marketplace, at Hotel and Maunakea streets, traces the area's history since the first Chinese arrived in 1788, covering its near-destruction in January 1900, when an attempt to burn out a plague epidemic went hideously wrong. The centre also gives contemporary information on shops and restaurants. The oriental food specialities at **Oahu Market**, on N King and Kekaulike streets, make for fascinating browsing.

Bishop Museum

The anthropological collection at the **Bishop Museum**, back from the ocean at 1525 Bernice Street (daily 9am–5pm; $6; ☎847-3511), demonstrates the reality of Polynesian culture, as opposed to the fakery of Waikiki. Three floors of one of Hawaii's oldest houses display magnificent feather cloaks and Japanese samurai armour, and a full-size sperm whale hangs in the central well. There are also excellent special exhibitions for kids, and a planetarium. *TheBus* #2 from Waikiki stops two blocks away on Kapalama Street; there's also a direct shuttle from the *Hilton Hawaiian Village* (☎922-1770).

Pearl Harbor

Almost the whole of **Pearl Harbor**, the principal base for the US Pacific fleet, is off limits to visitors. However, the surprise Japanese attack of December 7 1941, which an official US inquiry called "the greatest military and naval disaster in our nation's history", is commemorated by a simple white memorial set above the wreck of the battleship **USS Arizona**, still discernible in the clear blue waters. More than 1100 of its crew – who had earned the right to sleep in late that Sunday morning by coming second in a military band competition – are entombed there.

Free tours to the ship operate between 8am and 3pm each day, but it can be two or three hours after you pick up your numbered ticket at the Visitor Center (daily 7.30am–5pm; hours on ☎422-0561, queries on ☎422-2771) before you are called to board the ferry across the bay. A significant proportion of the 1.5 million annual visitors are Japanese; a remarkably even-handed 20-minute film pays tribute to "one of the most brilliantly planned and executed attacks in naval history", and books and charts are on sale telling the Japanese side of the story. The USS Arizona memorial was partly financed by Elvis Presley's 1961 Honolulu concert, his first show after leaving the Army.

Pearl Harbor is just over one hour from Waikiki, beyond the airport, on *TheBus* #20.

Punchbowl

High above Honolulu, lush lawns growing in the caldera of an extinct volcano are the emotive setting for the **National Memorial Cemetery of the Pacific** (summer daily 8am–6.30pm; winter 8am–5.30pm), in which are buried the dead of all US Pacific wars, including Vietnam. Hawaiian shuttle astronaut Ellison Onizuka is also here. The site is said to have been an ancient sacrificial temple, and is on *TheBus* route #15 from town.

Waikiki

Waikiki is very nearly an island, all but separate from Honolulu between the sea and the Ala Wai canal (which provides the drainage to make its incredible high-rise profusion possible). The site, once home to King Kamehameha I, may be venerable, but these days its only *raison d'être* is rampant commercialism. It would just about be possible to survive here with very little money, buying snacks from the omnipresent *ABC* convenience stores, but there would be no point – there's nothing to see, and the only thing to do apart from surf and sunbathe is to buy, anything and everything.

Most of your time in Waikiki will be spent strolling up and down seafront **Kalakua Avenue**, resisting or succumbing to temptation as you see fit. The most striking thing about the parallel **Waikiki Beach** is quite how narrow it is, a thin strip of shipped-in sand that in a French Riviera sort of way is nonetheless attractive. Compared to other Hawaiian beaches, it's overcrowded and small, but then it serves a different function; no-one is trying to "get away from it all", they're there to be seen.

Diamond Head

Waikiki's most famous landmark is the pinnacle of **Diamond Head**, just to the east. Named for the erroneous belief of a party of English sailors that they'd found diamonds on its slopes, it's another extinct volcano. The lawns of the crater interior are oddly bland, almost suburban in fact, but a straightforward hiking trail leads up to a panorama of the whole coast, and passes through a few of an enormous network of tunnels built by the military during World War II. *TheBus* #57 stops on the road nearby.

Hanauma Bay

A few miles further on, the magnificent crescent-shaped **Hanauma Bay**, formed when the wall of a crater collapsed to let in the sea, is renowned as Oahu's best place to **snorkel**. It makes a nice excursion, and the sea is full of brightly coloured fish queueing for food; but it has to be said that overuse has all but killed off the coral near the shore. Coach parties have now been banned, but the damage is done. Some patches of living coral, and bigger fish, can be seen if you swim out to the deeper waters beyond the inner reef (inviting coral cuts that can take weeks to heal). Snorkelling equipment is available for $5 rental (bring a deposit). The beach is closed on Wednesday mornings.

TheBus #22 ("The Beach Bus") runs right to the bay every forty minutes; #58 drops you on the main road ten minutes' walk up.

Accommodation

You'll find all ranges of accommodation in Waikiki; the highest rates will bring absolute luxury, but it's possible to pay much less. Pick up a copy of the Hawaii Visitors Bureau's *Hawaii On A Budget* for lists of cheaper alternatives on all the islands.

Big Surf Hotel, 1690 Ala Moana Blvd (☎946-6525). Compact hotel offering clean basic rooms with minimal extra frills and facilities. $35–39.

Driftwood Hotel, 1696 Ala Moana Blvd (☎1-800-669-7719). Seventy-room hotel near Ala Moana mall, with generally good facilities. The cheaper rooms are spartan but adequate. $35–55.

Hale Aloha AYH Hostel, 2417 Prince Edward St (☎926-8313). $12, members only. A few doubles at $26. Three-day maximum stay.

Honolulu International AYH Hostel, 2323-A Seaview Ave (☎946-0591). Well back from the sea, near the University in Manoa Valley. $9 members, $12 non-members.

InterClub Hostel Waikiki, 2413 Kuhio Ave (☎924-2636). Friendly small hotel (no chores). Dorm rooms, no reservations, $18.

Outrigger, innumerable locations around Waikiki, mostly skyscrapers (reservations ☎1-800-733-7777). At the *Ala Wai Terrace*, 1547 Ala Wai Blvd, rooms are $45–50; the *Waikiki Surf* at 2200 Kuhio Ave charges $60–65; most of the others will have rooms for under $75. If you request it when you arrive at an *Outrigger*, you can have a free *Dollar* rental car for every day of your stay.

Waikiki Joy, 320 Lewers St (☎923-2300). One of the new generation of small-scale "boutique hotels". Friendly and personalised top-of-the-range accommodation. $89 and upwards.

Waikiki Prince, 2431 Prince Edward St (☎922-1544). Small, basic but perfectly adequate budget hotel near the beach. $31–43.

Eating

Honolulu offers so many **food** possibilities that recommendations are inevitably highly personal. Check out also **Restaurant Row** near the Harbor, while for **snacks** and fast food the assorted ethnic kitchens in **Makai Market** in the Ala Moana Center, and the **International Food Court** in Waikiki's International Market Place (where lunches are accompanied by live Polynesian music and dance), are hard to beat.

Columbia Inn, 645 Kapiolani Blvd, Waikiki (☎531-3747). Long-standing traditional diner, 6am–1am. Late-night snacks and good full meals for $7–15. The shrimp tempura is recommended.

New Orleans Bistro, 2139 Kuhio Ave, Waikiki (☎926-4444). Pricey Cajun and Creole dishes – crawfish and even alligator. Virtually all entrees are $17–20, but there's live jazz every night until 2am.

Perry's Smorgy, 2380 Kuhio Ave, Waikiki (☎926-0184). Very popular open-air place for all-you-can-eat buffets (with hordes of scavenging birds). $4.45 breakfast (7–10.30am), $5.95 lunch (11am–2.30pm), $7.95 dinner (5–9pm). Also at *Outrigger Waikiki* and *Coral Seas Hotel*, 250 Lewers St.

Quintero's, 2334 S King St, Honolulu (☎944-3882). Genuine Mexican food, fresh and tasty. $7–10.

Ruffage Natural Foods, 2443 Kuhio Ave, Waikiki (☎922-2042). Tiny place tucked away on Kuhio, with cheap vegetable and tofu dishes, plus sushi from $9.50. Until 10pm.

Wong and Wong, 1023 Maunakea St, Honolulu (☎521-4492). Popular and very cheap, right in Chinatown. Vegetarian dinner $4, fish $8, and there's even frog on the menu.

Yakiniku Camellia, 2494 S Beretania St, Honolulu (☎944-0449). Excellent Korean barbecue. Marinated meats and vegetables to cook at your table. Lunch $7.95 , dinner $11.95, open to 11pm.

Yanagi Sushi, 762 Kapiolani Blvd, Waikiki (☎537-1525). Authentic and extremely popular sushi bar and Japanese restaurant; a full meal will cost upwards of $17.

Entertainment and Nightlife

Various free magazines will make sure you get details of musical and other attractions during your visit. The **bars** of Chinatown are the most raucous in town, but way too hair-raising for most tastes. Otherwise the clubs and discos are pretty mainstream.

Anna Banannas, 2440 S Beretania St (☎946-5190). Reasonable bar, live music Wed–Sun 9.30pm.

Hula's Bar and Lei Stand, 2103 Kuhio Ave (☎923-0669). Waikiki's most popular gay venue.

Partner's, 802 Kapiolani Blvd (☎545-7810). Women's bar and disco, open until 2am.

Studebakers, Restaurant Row (☎526-9888). Fifties-style nightspot, age 24 or over, with free buffet.

Wave Waikiki, 1877 Kalakua Ave (☎941-0424). Loud heavy rock, live and on record, 10pm–4am.

Listings

Babysitting *Aloha Babysitting Service* (☎732-2029).

Bicycle Rental Waikiki options include *Aloha Funway* (☎942-9696) and *The Bike Way* (☎538-7433).

City and Island Tours *Polynesian Adventure Tours* (☎922-0888); full day $45–60, half-day $22–25.

Dinner Cruises *Ali'i Kai Catamaran* (☎522-7822) leaves Pier 5 at 5.30pm daily; hotel pick-up.

Disabled Information *Commission on Persons with Disabilities*, 5 Waterfront Plaza, Suite 210, 500 Ala Moana Blvd, Honolulu HI 96813. *Handicabs of the Pacific* (☎524-3866) run taxis for the disabled.

Diving *Aloha Dive Shop* (☎395-5922) and *Dan's Dive Shop* (☎536-6181) run introductory courses.

Doctor 24-hr *Doctors on Call service* ☎926-4777; but the fee is $85.

Hospital Queen's Medical Center ☎538-9011; emergency ☎547-4311.

Luaus The biggest "Polynesian feast" is *Paradise Cove* (☎973-5828; $40). Hundreds daily are bused 30 miles (sing-alongs compulsory) to eat indifferent food, get drunk, and make fools of themselves.

Post Offices At 330 Saratoga Road, Waikiki (☎941-1062); 3600 Aolele St, Honolulu (☎423-3990; zip code 96813); and Ala Moana Center (☎946-2020).

Submarine *Atlantis Submarines* (☎522-1710); one-hour dives to an artificial reef for around $85.

Surf *KPOI Surf Report* (☎521-7873) gives latest surfing/snorkelling information.

Tattoos *China Sea Tattoo*, 10033 Smith St, Chinatown (☎533-1063). Traditional Polynesian tattooing.

Telephone Cheap calls from *Phone Line Hawaii* in Waikiki's International Market Place.

SEA, SURF AND SAFETY

Drownings in Hawaii are all too common. In many places the waves come sweeping in from 2000 miles of open ocean, onto beaches – magnificent to look at – unprotected by any reef. Not all beaches have lifeguards and warning flags; unattended beaches are not necessarily safe. Look for other bathers, but whatever your experience elsewhere don't assume you'll be able to cope with the same conditions as the local kids. Don't rush into the water, watch the sea carefully before going in, and never take your eyes off it thereafter. Fierce **rogue waves** can appear from the blue to drag waders – or even those walking along the shore – far out to sea in seconds, and powerful **undertows** may not be detectable until too late. If you do get swept out, wait until the big waves die down, even if it takes hours. Never attempt to swim where waves are breaking right on the reef.

Sea creatures to avoid include *wana* – black spiky **sea urchins**, Portuguese Men of War **jellyfish**, and **coral** in general, which can give painful infected cuts. **Shark attacks** are much rarer than popular imagination suggests; those which do occur are usually due to "misunderstandings", such as spear-fishers inadvertently keeping sharks from their catch, or surfers idling on their boards looking a bit too much like turtles from below.

Assuming that you're self-destructive enough to want a **tan**, take exposure to the harsh tropical **sun** in moderation; a mere twenty minutes is the safe recommendation for the first day. Even on overcast days your skin still absorbs most of the harmful UV rays.

Ocean Fun

The nation that invented **surfing** – long before the whites came – remains its greatest arena. The sport was popularised earlier this century by Olympic swimmer Duke Kahanamoku, using a twenty-foot board; these days most are around six-foot. Smaller **boogie boards**, which you don't stand on, make an exhilarating initiation. **Windsurfing** too is rapidly growing, using the same favourite beaches, usually on the north shore of each island. **Snorkelling** and **diving** are top-quality, although Hawaii's **coral** has fewer brilliant hues than in warmer equatorial waters – and in places it's just plain dead. Two-day diving courses cost around $300. **Snuba**, basically snorkelling with a longer tube, is less demanding. For the sedentary, **submarines** are in action on Oahu and Hawaii.

Snorkel sets are widely available for around $5 per day (or buy your own). A week's rental at the excellent **Snorkel Bob's** outlets costs $15. "Snorkel Bob" also writes entertaining handbooks to having a good time on each island, and can be found at:

Oahu: 819 Kapahiulu Ave, Honolulu (☎735-7944), on the road out to Hanauma Bay.

Big Island: 75-3831 Kahakai St, Kailua-Kona (☎329-0770).

Maui: 34 Keala Place, Kihei (☎879-7449) and at *Napili Village Hotel*, Lahaina (☎669-9603).

Kauai: 4480 Auhukini Road, Lihue (☎245-9433) very near the airport.

Windward Oahu

Much the most spectacular moment of a tour of Oahu comes as you cross the Koolau Mountains on the **Pali Highway** (Hwy-61) to see the sheer green cliffs of the windward side of the island, swirling with mists. The highest spot, just four miles out of Honolulu heading northeast, is the **Nuuanu Pali Lookout**. King Kamehameha finalised his conquest of Oahu here in 1795, forcing hundreds of enemy warriors over the edge of the cliffs; Mark Twain saw the battlefield seventy years later, littered with skulls.

The wide highway is barely adequate for its role as a major commuter thoroughfare connecting Honolulu with **Kailua** and **Kaneohe**, and a new tunnel is being dug which will inevitably bring further "development" to the windward side. Apart from the inaccessible cliffs a few miles inland, there's little worth seeing. **Sea Life Park** at Makapuu Point (Thurs, Fri & Sun 10am–10pm, otherwise 10am–5pm; $12.50), for example, is a dismal and heavily commercial theme park. The replica Japanese Buddhist **Byodo-In Temple** off Hwy-83, however, should not be missed (8.30am–4.30pm; $2).

Oahu's leading paying attraction, with one million annual visitors, is the **Polynesian Cultural Center** at Laie (Mon–Sat 12.30–9pm; $25; ☎293-3333). This haphazard mixture of real and bogus Polynesia – in which the history is firmly on the bogus side – is owned by the Mormons, and staffed by students at Brigham Young University right behind it. The imposing white Mormon Temple nearby was the first to be built outside the continental United States. *TheBus* #52 takes roughly two hours to get this far.

At **Amorient Aqua Park** a little further on in Kahuku (☎293-8661), delicious fresh (cooked) shrimps are on sale for immediate consumption at the picnic tables.

All the windward beaches are public, but use proper paths to reach them.

North Shore Oahu

The **surfing beaches** of northern Oahu are famous the world over, but they're barely equipped for tourists. **Waimea**, **Sunset** and **Ekuhai** beach parks (the latter is home of the Banzai Pipeline) are all laid-back roadside stretches of sand, where you can usually find a quiet spot to yourself. Sunset is best for savouring the atmosphere, though surfers can be an exclusive bunch. The tame summer waves may make you wonder what all the fuss is about; if you see them at full tilt in the winter you'll have no doubts.

HALEIWA is the main surfers' hangout, combining alternative shops and cafes with upfront tourist traps. *Jim's at the Beach*, at 61-545 B Pohaku Loa Way (☎637-5100), has dorm beds for $15, and assorted informally let (double) rooms in the area go for around $25 per day or $150 per week. The friendly *Coffee Gallery* at 66-250 Kamehameha Hwy, (☎637-5571), one of several places displaying advertisements, is open each day from dawn until 9.30pm, serving health food and featuring occasional live music.

Leeward Oahu

The leeward (Waianae) coast of Oahu, customarily dismissed as "arid", is only so by Hawaiian standards. It certainly has its share of fine beaches, the best being **Makaha Beach Park** (served by *TheBus* #51). However, the traditionally minded inhabitants of towns such as **Nanakuli** are not disposed to welcome the encroachment of hotels and golf courses, and visitors tend to be treated with a degree of suspicion. The further north you go the stronger the military presence becomes, with soldiers in camouflage blending into the green valleys. You are not encouraged to attempt an island circuit; the last stretch of road, through a military reservation, is deliberately left unpaved.

THE BIG ISLAND

The **Big Island** of **HAWAII** is indeed big – it could accommodate all the other islands with room to spare. With a population of only 100,000, less than half what it was in Captain Cook's day, and a comparatively low level of tourism, there's far more space than on Oahu or Maui. The development that will surely come may put an end to that, but for the moment there are sleepy old towns all over the island, unchanged for a century. The few resorts are in the least beautiful areas, built on the barren lava flows of the **Kona** coast to catch maximum sunshine.

What's more, the Big Island is still growing. The continuing eruption of the **Kilauea** volcano means that the southern shore is inching ever further out to sea. Roads and even towns are wiped off the map; pristine beaches of jet-black sand appear overnight. **Hawaii Volcanoes National Park**, which includes **Mauna Loa** as well as Kilauea (though not **Mauna Kea**, higher than either at 13,796 feet), is absolutely compelling;

you can explore steaming craters and cinder cones, venture into the rainforest, and – for the moment at any rate – approach within a few feet of the eruption itself. The summits of Mauna Loa and Mauna Kea have the clearest air on earth – and numerous astronomical observatories to take advantage of it – but down below, when the trade-winds drop, the island is prone to a choking sulphurous volcanic haze known as "**vog**".

As befits the birthplace of **King Kamehameha**, the base from which he became the first man to rule all the Hawaiian islands, more of the ancient Hawaii survives on the Big Island than anywhere else. **Puuhonua O Honaunau** National Historical Park preserves a temple complex which served as a "place of refuge" for *kapu*-breakers and defeated warriors, just a few miles from the site of Captain Cook's death, and there are further temples and *heiaus* north along the Kohala coast. **Waipio Valley**, where Kamehameha spent his youth, remains as lush and green as ever, all the more magical for the knowledge that six further impenetrable valleys lie beyond it.

Flights to Hawaii arrive at either **Hilo** on the rainy east coast, or the resort of **Kona** (also known as Kailua), which is a much less genuine place but not quite big enough to be offensive. If you don't rent a **car**, you probably won't be able to get to most of the interesting sites; occasional buses link Hilo and Kona, and there are expensive organised coach tours to specific attractions, but public transport is all but non-existent.

Windward Hawaii

Almost all the rain that falls on the slopes of Mauna Kea flows back down to the sea on the eastern side of the Big Island. Numerous streams and waterfalls nourish dense junglelike vegetation; the main road north along the coast from Hilo is alive with colourful orchids, and most of the state's commercial tropical gardens are in this area. Hilo is the only sizeable base for travellers, though there are small hotels in several places.

Hilo

Although it's the Big Island's capital, and largest town, just 35,000 people live in **HILO**, which remains endearing and unpressured. Despite the construction of the only airport on the island which can accept jumbo jets direct from the mainland, mass tourism has never taken off. Quite simply, it rains too much. However, the rain falls mostly at night, and America's wettest city blazes with wild orchids and tropical plants.

Historically, Hilo's role as the island's main port gave it an unusually radical labour force. From the Thirties onwards, Hilo's workers spearheaded successive campaigns against the "Big Five" who dominated the Hawaiian economy. Fifty were injured, though none died, in the "Hilo Massacre" of August 1 1938, when strikers were attacked by armed police, and further strikes in 1946 and 1949 were instrumental in ending the long-term Republican domination of state politics.

Hilo has always been at the mercy of the twin natural forces of fire and water. Cataclysmic tidal waves killed 96 people in April 1946, and a further 61 in May 1960. Countless lava flows have also threatened to engulf it; in 1881 Princess Ruth (see p.908) summoned up all her *mana*, watched by missionaries and journalists, to halt one on the edge of town, while in 1984 another flow stopped eight miles short.

Arrival and Orientation

Downtown Hilo is compact and very walkable, around the junction of the seafront Kamehameha Avenue, and Waianuenue Avenue which heads towards the Saddle Road across the island. However, the urban area extends for several miles, and the **airport** at **General Lyman Field** (☎935-0809), on the eastern outskirts, is well beyond walking distance. If you're not renting a car at the airport, a taxi into town will cost around $5.

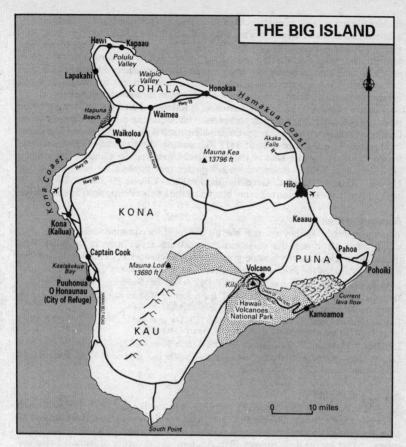

THE BIG ISLAND

(Map of the Big Island of Hawaii showing locations including Hawi, Kapaau, Polulu Valley, Waipio Valley, Lapakahi, KOHALA, Honokaa, Hamakua Coast, Hapuna Beach, Waimea, Hwy-19, Waikoloa, Akaka Falls, Mauna Kea ▲13796 ft, Kona Coast, Hwy 19, Hwy 190, Saddle Road, Hilo, KONA, Keaau, Kona (Kailua), Captain Cook, Kealakekua Bay, Puuhonua O Honaunau (City of Refuge), Mauna Loa ▲13680 ft, Hawaii Belt Road, Volcano, Kilauea, Hawaii Volcanoes National Park, PUNA, Pahoa, Pohoiki, Current lava flow, Chain of Craters, Kamoamoa, KAU, South Point; scale 0–10 miles)

The **Hawaii Visitors Bureau** is at 180 Kinoole Street (Mon–Fri 8am–noon & 1–4.30pm; ☎961-5797). Hilo's *Mass Transportation Agency* (25 Aupuni St; ☎935-8241) operate a very small-scale **city bus** service (only two per day), as well as scheduled buses across to Kona from the Mooheau Bus Terminal on Kamehameha Avenue.

Exploring Hilo

There is a simple and tragic reason why **downtown Hilo** looks so appealingly low-key, with its modest streets and wooden stores: all the buildings which stood on the seaward side of Kamehameha Avenue were destroyed by the two *tsunami*. After 1960 there was felt to be no point attempting to rebuild the "little Tokyo" that had housed Hilo's predominantly Japanese population, and the seafront is now occupied by a succession of pleasant gardens. Besides plenty of conventional shopping, Hilo has a seafront **market** on Wednesday and Saturday mornings. If you want to **swim**, follow Kamehameha Avenue for four miles beyond Banyan Drive to tiny **Richardson's Beach**.

The focus of the two-part **Lyman Museum** at 276 Haili Street (Mon–Sat 9am–5pm; ☎935-5021; $3.50) is the original 1830s **Mission House**, furnished in dark *koa* wood, which belonged to Calvinist missionaries David and Sarah Lyman. Their congregation numbered merely twenty until the charismatic Titus Coan arrived in 1835, and aided by a fortuitous tidal wave in 1837, started a Revival – complete with speaking in tongues – which baptised thousands of ordinary Hawaiians but antagonised his superiors. The museum next door starts with a fascinating set of **ancient weapons** and then documents Hawaii's various **ethnic groups**, including the Portuguese shipped in 1878 from the overpopulated but similarly volcanic Azores, who brought the *braginha* which became the ukelele, and the first Japanese arriving from Hiroshima, Hilo's sister city.

A couple of miles up Waianuenue Avenue, at **Rainbow Falls**, just to the right of the road, a spectacular wide waterfall plummets 100ft across the mouth of a huge cavern. Continue another two miles to reach the bubbling natural jacuzzis of the **Boiling Pots**.

The **Hilo Tropical Gardens** at 1477 Kalanianaole Avenue (daily 8.30am–5.30pm; free; ☎935-4957) are the best of the commercial gardens. To admire extraordinary plants in a less formal setting, take a self-guided tour through the rainforest of the **Hawaii Tropical Botanical Gardens** (daily 8.30am–4.30pm; $10; ☎946-5233), which sweep down to the sea seven miles out of town on the lovely **Peepeekeo Scenic Drive**.

Accommodation

When people say, as they do, that there's not much **accommodation** in Hilo, they simply mean that it (and the whole eastern coast) has fewer major resort hotels than usual. There are, however, several possibilities; the cheaper ones tend to be in town rather than around the loop of **Banyan Drive** on the seafront near the airport.

Country Club Hotel, 121 Banyan Drive (☎935-7171). At $35, the cheapest on Banyan Drive.
Dolphin Bay Hotel, 333 Iliahi St (☎935-1466). Just across the Wailuku River from the town centre. A very friendly place, popular with budget travellers, with doubles at $42.
Hawaii Naniloa Hotel, 93 Banyan Drive (☎969-3333). The grandest of Hilo's options, with luxury rooms from $89 and superb views across the bay towards Mauna Kea.
Hilo Bay AYH Hostel, 311 Kalanianaole Ave (☎935-1383). Rooms at $26–30; non-members $3 extra.
Lanikai Hotel, 100 Puueo St (☎935-5556). Near the *Dolphin Bay*, and considerably more rundown and basic, but significantly cheaper at $28.

Eating and Nightlife

Most of Hilo's (eminently missable) **nightlife** is in the Banyan Drive hotels, though there are a few shows at downtown's newly restored *Palace Theatre*. **Restaurants** all over town include several cheap Japanese and Oriental options. You might also like to get up at 7am for the daily **Suisan Fish Auction**, at the corner of Banyan Drive and Lihiwai Street, where you can buy from the night's catch of marlin and other big fish.

Fiascos, 200 Kanoelehua Ave (☎935-7666). All-American but adventurous menu, salad bar. $6–10.
Karrots, 197 Keawe St (☎935-6191). Wholefood restaurant and juice bar. Breakfast for around $3.
Lisa's Kitchen, 333 Keawe St (☎961-5656). Cheap lunches and takeouts; some Japanese dishes.
Nihon Cultural Center, 123 Lihiwai St (☎969-1133). Next to the Fish Auction and Liliuokalani Gardens. Full Japanese meals and sushi too, with exquisite fresh fish and magnificent views. $5–15.
Roussels, 60 Keawe St (☎935-5111). French Creole; formal but good, $13–22. Occasional live jazz.

North from Hilo

The **Hamakua coast** extending north from Hilo is prime sugar-growing country. At first the fields are crammed into narrow rain-carved "gulches"; further north the land spreads out and there's room for larger plantations. It's well worth driving the **Belt Road** (Hwy-19), clinging to the hillsides and crossing ravines on slender bridges. For an easy glimpse into the interior, head into the mountains after fifteen miles to the 450ft **Akaka Falls**. A fifteen-minute loop trail through the forest, festooned with wild orchids, offers a variety of views of Akaka and other junglelike tropical waterfalls.

Waipio Valley

Hwy-240, which turns northwards off the Belt Road at **HONOKAA**, comes to an abrupt end after nine miles at the edge of **WAIPIO VALLEY**. As the southernmost of six successive sheer-walled valleys, this is the only one accessible by land – and it's as close as Hawaii comes to the classic South Seas image of an isolated and self-sufficient valley, dense with fruit trees and laced by footpaths leading down to the sea. Just off the black-sand beach (greyish in fact) of his boyhood home, Kamehameha the Great fought Kahekili of Oahu in the inconclusive but bloody "Battle of the Red-Mouthed Gun" of 1791, in which for the first time Hawaiian fleets were equipped with cannons, operated by foreign gunners. Spectacular waterfalls cascade down the valley's flanks, but recurrent tidal waves have meant that only a few taro farmers now live here. A more recent threat has come from Japanese developers, who plan to build two golf courses.

It's perfectly possible to walk down the steep track into Waipio, but most visitors take tours in the four-wheel-drive vehicles of the *Waipio Valley Shuttle* (daily 8am–4pm; $25; ☎775-7121), based at the *Last Chance Store* in Kukuihaele a mile from the end of the road. You can also tour by horse-drawn wagons ($35; ☎775-9518) or on horseback ($65; ☎775-7291). The only **accommodation** in the valley is Tom Araki's rudimentary "No-Name Hotel" (contact ☎775-2368 in Hilo), where very basic rooms in an idyllic banana-grove setting cost $15, and are often booked months ahead. You can also **camp** discreetly on the beach, for which officially you need a permit from the Hamakua Sugar Company (☎776-1211). Back in Honokaa, rooms at the *Hotel Honokaa Club* (PO Box 185; ☎775-0678) cost $32, or around $50 at the *Waipio Wayside B&B* (☎775-0275). Rough-and-tumble Honokaa holds a **Western Week** each May, featuring rodeo.

Pahoa and the Southeast

The southeastern corner of the Big Island is off the usual tourist trail. **PAHOA** in particular has gone its own sweet way, its distinctive blend of lawless cowboy town and hippy hangout probably due to its alleged role as the island's main marijuana-growing area. Businesses along the rudimentary boardwalks include a New Age bookstore and cafe, the *Naung Mai Thai Kitchen* (☎965-8186) serving plenty of vegetarian options, and *Luquin's* Mexican restaurant (☎965-9990). The *Bamboo House* is a small and friendly B&B with $45 double rooms (enquire at *Pahoa Natural Groceries* or ring ☎965-8322).

At **Pohoiki**, seven miles southeast, a jagged expanse of black rocks and sand is pummelled by ferocious surf. Following the coast south from here you rejoin Hwy-130 from Pahoa shortly before it is blocked by lava flows from Kilauea.

Hawaii Volcanoes National Park

The southern and smaller two of the Big Island's volcanoes, **Mauna Loa** and **Kilauea**, jointly constitute **HAWAII VOLCANOES NATIONAL PARK**, thirty miles from Hilo and eighty from Kona. It's possibly the most dramatic of all the US national parks; as well as two active volcanoes, of which at least one is likely to be erupting before your eyes, it includes desert, arctic tundra, and the Wao Kele O Puna **rainforest**, where plans to drill for geothermal energy are currently the subject of fierce debate.

Evidence is everywhere of the awesome power of the volcanoes to create and destroy; no map can keep up with the latest whims of the lava flow. Whole towns have been engulfed, and what were once prized beachfront properties lie buried hundreds of yards back from the sea. No one knows quite where they are – there's nowhere for surveyors to get their bearings. There are no towns left on the southern coast. The Hawaiians abandoned their villages 150 years ago, after a succession of terrible tidal waves; now the Americans too have been driven out.

Kilauea Caldera

The headquarters of the park ($5 admission) is on the rim of Kilauea Caldera. Both the **visitor centre** (daily 7.45am–5pm; ☎967-7311) and the fascinating **Jaggar Museum** of geology (daily 8.30am–5pm; ☎967-7643) on **Crater Rim Drive** offer basic orientation.

Kilauea is said to be the home of the volcano goddess **Pele**, who has followed the "hot spot" from island to island. In 1824 Queen Kapiolani, a recent convert to Christianity, defied her by descending into the crater, reading aloud from her Bible, eating the *tabu* red ohelo berries, and throwing stones into the pit. When Mark Twain came here, he saw a dazzling lake of liquid fire; since a huge explosion in 1924 it's been shallower and quieter, a black dusty expanse dotted with hissing steam vents. The three-mile **Halemaumau Trail** leads across the crater floor, now (mostly) solid.

The **Devastation Trail** is a boardwalk laid across the scene of a 1959 eruption; scientists are monitoring how long it takes for vegetation to re-establish itself. Most of what you see is new growth – fresh lava is full of nutrients, and rainwater and seeds soon collect in the recesses – but a few older trees survived partial submersion in ash by growing "aerial roots" some way up their trunks. Around the cinder cone of **Puu Puai**, the land is utterly barren, scattered with bleached dead branches.

Thurston Lava Tube was created when the surface of a lava stream, exposed to the air, hardened; just below, the now-protected lava was able to keep flowing 28 miles to the sea with only a slight loss of temperature. It's now a damp empty tunnel, an illuminated segment of which is open. Gigantic ferns grow over the top, and a few roots have worked their way through cracks in the rock to dangle from the ceiling. Outside, the native red-billed *iiwi* bird can always be heard, if not seen.

Stretching away southwest of Kilauea, the **Kau Desert** receives plenty of rainfall – but it's a natural sulphurous acid rain, composed of volcanic fumes carried by the trade-winds, and far too noxious to support life.

Chain of Craters Road

The Chain of Craters road winds down from Crater Rim Drive, steering to the sea in sweeping curves around a succession of cones and vents. An occasional dead white tree trunk or flowering shrub pokes up. If Hawaii is the place where they paved paradise and put up a parking lot, then here paradise is fighting back. Fresh sheets of lava are constantly oozing down the slopes and covering the road. When they build the road again on top of the new flow, more lava covers it. From high on the hillside it looks like a stream of black tarmac, an ever-widening highway down to the endless blue ocean.

The **black sand beach** at **KAMOAMOA** was created literally overnight in January 1988 by the explosive impact of lava striking the sea; there it was the next morning, two miles long and absolutely jet black, made up of rounded glass-like fragments.

Approaching the Eruption

For the past eight years, though the exact site has varied, it has been possible to walk across the congealed lava blocking Chain of Craters Road and see molten rock gush from the earth – sometimes directly into the sea. The account here may already be out of date; a **Volcano Update** information line (☎967-7977) has the latest details (for information on tours run by park rangers, ring ☎967-7311).

A wooden shack on wheels – of necessity, periodically shifted – at the end of the road hands out warnings that new lava is unstable and may collapse at any time, and that it's best to avoid clouds of hydrochloric acid. There's no set path to follow, you just pick your way through a disarray of broken slabs. Every surface is like sandpaper, a fall can shred your skin, and the ground can be searingly hot. It's essential to carry water.

Pele was the most capricious of Hawaiian deities; chiefs and priests tested their spiritual strength (*mana*) by controlling her outbursts. Sacred sites too could possess *mana*; and sure enough one of Hawaii's oldest temples is the only manmade structure to survive in this wasteland. A few miles away, the **Star of the Sea** church stands forlorn beside Hwy-30, moved bodily from doomed Kalapana before its *mana* could be put to the test. **Wahaula Heiau** ("the Temple of the Red-mouthed God") stayed put, relying on an impeccable five-century record of human sacrifice to Pele. Perhaps it's not so surprising that the lava flowed to either side of its stone walls, built on high ground; the chill wind that swirls around the sacrificial platform suggests deeper forces at play.

Every day, extremely self-confident – or stupid – hikers continue past the rough noticeboards reading "EXTREME DANGER: Do not go beyond this point", and approach the conflagration, even prodding with sticks at the eggshell crust. Many stay out all night to marvel at the glowing orange rivers of molten rock, somehow considering themselves impregnable. Nature seems to concur; there has yet to be a serious injury, after eight years of such nocturnal hikes. If you try it, be sure to carry a flashlight for the long walk back across the treacherous lava.

Accommodation and Eating

The small and inconspicuous town of **VOLCANO** just before the park entrance on the Hilo side provides the best places to **stay** in the vicinity. Both *My Island B&B*, run by local expert Gordon Morse (PO Box 100; ☎967-7216) and *Volcano B&B* at 19-3950 Keonelehua Street (☎967-7779) have rooms for $50. The famous *Volcano House* on the very edge of the crater within the park (PO Box 53; ☎967-7321) is not literally the same building as Mark Twain stayed in, and although the views are spectacular, it's expensive ($125 for a room overlooking the crater) and generally unsatisfactory. Neither is it a good place to **eat**; the restaurant at *Volcano Golf & Country Club* (☎967-7331) is much better value, and various stores in Kiluaea sell provisions. Note that there are no facilities of any kind – no food, no gas – along Chain of Craters Road or down by the ocean.

The Kona Coast

Hawaii's leeward **Kona coast** divides into two distinct areas. To the north of its only sizeable community, **Kona**, a long bleak slope of barren lava trails from dormant Mauna Kea down to the sea. Thanks to the relentless sun on its magnificent beaches, luxury hotels dot the shoreline, incongruous green patches in the wasteland. Southwards, the hillsides are more fertile, and although the condos are spreading, you can still get a real feel of the old Hawaii, in the land where Captain Cook met his end.

Kona (Kailua)

Although the Big Island's main resort is officially called Kailua, and its postal address is "Kailua-Kona", confusingly enough everyone refers to it simply as **KONA**. It's reasonably attractive, and has played its part in Hawaiian history, but its summer-holiday seafront of fast-food restaurants and souvenir shops could be anywhere; and the windborne "vog" means that the atmosphere can be as bad as in Los Angeles or London.

Arrival and Information

Open-plan **Keahole Airport** is on a field of black lava nine miles north of Kona. It has the usual car rental places; otherwise a shared *Gray Line Limousine* into town costs around $12, and a cab $30. Once in Kona, a regular **shuttle bus** runs the six-mile length of Alii Drive every ninety minutes (7.45am–9.15pm; $1). One daily bus follows Highway 11 round to Hilo, leaving Kona just before 6am and returning in the evening.

The **Hawaiian Visitors Bureau** is in Kona Plaza on Alii Drive (Mon–Fri 8am–noon & 1–4.30pm; ☎329-7787), as is the well-stocked *Middle Earth* bookstore. **Bicycles** can be rented from *Hawaiian Pedals* in the Kona Inn Shopping Village (☎329-2294).

The Town

Hulihee Palace (daily 9am–4pm; $4; ☎329-1877) stands square-on to the ocean in the middle of Kona. Built as the governor's residence in 1838, it's not all that imposing from the outside. Within, it's notable for massive *koa*-wood furnishings, made to fit the considerable girth of the various members of the Hawaiian royal family who later lived here, such as the redoubtable four-hundred-pound Princess Ruth. The 1836 **Mokuaikaua Church** opposite was the first in Hawaii, and acts in part as a museum of the early days of Hawaiian Christianity, setting out to debunk the popular notion of the missionaries as having been primarily concerned with feathering their own nests. A peculiar "sausage-tree" from Mozambique stands in the grounds.

Nearby, the *King Kamehameha Hotel* (see below) dominates the northern end of the bay. King Kamehameha's funeral rites were performed in the **Ahuena Heiau** which juts into the sea in front of its beach. Tours on *Atlantis Submarines* leave from here, descending one hundred feet to the coral reef, accompanied by the *Star Wars* theme, to see a frenzy of feeding fish and the occasional lurking shark (☎329-6626; $74).

South Kona Accommodation

Alii Drive is lined for about five miles south from Kona with hotels and condos, but none of them offers much by way of cheap accommodation. The listings below therefore include a couple of places a bit further along the coast.

Hotel King Kamehameha, 75-5660 Palani Road (☎329-2911 or ☎1-800-733-7777). Rooms at Kona's grandest hotel start at $99. Hunter S Thompson abandoned a monstrous demented dog in one of the plushest suites. The *heiau* is the backdrop to a *luau* (Tues, Thurs & Sun; $42), at which the baked pig is supplemented with raw fish, Hawaiian and Japanese dishes, and Polynesian entertainment.

Kona Lodge & Hostel at Honalo, eight miles south of Kona (PO Box 645, Kealakekua; ☎322-8136). Dorm beds in very basic rooms are $14 (AYH members $12), private doubles are $29. Set in nice gardens, on the main road well above the sea.

Kona Tiki Hotel, at the one-mile marker on Alii Drive (PO Box 1567; ☎329-1425). Sandwiched between the main road and the sea, with standard rooms at $45.

Manago Hotel, on Hwy-11 in Captain Cook (PO Box 145, Captain Cook; ☎323-2642). Hawaii's best value. Very comfortable ocean-view rooms, in flower-filled Japanese gardens, $35–38; with shared bathrooms, $23. Cheaper weekly rates. Run by the same friendly family since 1917. Good Japanese/American restaurant (closed Mon). Reserve three months ahead; one month is pushing it.

Eating and Drinking

Competition ensures that the bars and restaurants of central Kona – especially those along the seafront – are well priced, though the relentless holiday atmosphere means the place can seem a bit unreal.

Banana Bay, at the *Kona Bay Hotel*, 75-5739 Alii Drive (☎329-1393). $4.95 breakfast buffet in central Kona hotel (where rooms start at $62).

Jennifer's Korean BBQ, Luhia St, Kailua-Kona (☎326-1155). Lunch and dinner from $6. Not a buffet but you do cook it yourself.

Kona Amigos, Alii Drive (☎326-2840). Restaurant (until 10pm) and bar (until midnight) in Kona Square opposite the *King Kamehameha*. Mexican/Hawaiian cuisine; *mahi-mahi fajitas* for $7.

Ocean View Restaurant, Alii Drive (☎329-9998).Very cheap Hawaiian and Oriental food overlooking the sea; traditional fish dishes. Closed Mon.

Kealakekua Bay

Kealakekua Bay, a dozen miles south of Kona, was where Captain Cook was killed on his second voyage to Hawaii (see box). One of ancient Hawaii's major population centres, it's now barely inhabited, and the white **obelisk** on the death site – which is legally a small piece of England – is all but inaccessible. You can only get to within a mile of it by car, to the beach at **Napoopoo** across the bay, though you'll glimpse it

THE DEATH OF CAPTAIN COOK

Captain James Cook sailed into Kealakekua Bay on January 17 1779 at a singularly auspicious moment. The *makahiki* festival, at the temple of the god **Lono**, was at its height; Lono's return, circling Hawaii on a floating island of tall trees, had long been prophesied. As the billowing sails of the *Resolution* (originally a "Whitby cat", built to transport coal from Newcastle down the English coast) hove into view, they looked just like the cloth-draped sticks which were Lono's emblems. Cook and his men were welcomed as honoured guests, and fed and feted for three long weeks before they set off once more across the ocean, having dismantled the temple for firewood.

A week later they returned, forced back by a storm which left their ship in tatters – and this time the islanders were not so hospitable, far from keen to part with further scarce resources. On February 14, Cook led a landing party of nine men in an attempt to kidnap the local chief and effect the return of a stolen small boat. In an undignified scuffle, surrounded by thousands of hostile warriors including the future Kamehameha the Great, he was stabbed and died at the water's edge, unable as a non-swimmer to reach safety. His body was treated as appropriate for a dead chief; the skull and leg bones were kept, and the rest cremated (though his heart was eaten by children who mistook it for a dog's). His crew, however, were far from mollified by the eventual return of just a few charred bones.

Whether the Hawaiians believed Cook to be Lono is debatable, despite the various coincidences; they were certainly puzzled and cautious, testing Cook to see just what sort of creature he might be. That he failed such tests, for example by groaning when struck a severe blow instead of maintaining a godlike tranquillity, is hardly surprising.

from the road on the way down. The bay itself is the best place on the Big Island for **snorkelling**, even if there are sharks further out. It's also possible to hike down to the monument from the town of **CAPTAIN COOK**; in fact this is the track to follow to reach the sea if you're staying at the *Manago Hotel* (see opposite).

Puuhonua O Honaunau – "The City of Refuge"

Puuhonua O Honaunau National Historical Park (7.30am–5.30pm; $1; ☎328-2288), four miles on from Kealakekua, is the single most evocative historical site in all the Hawaiian islands, jutting into the Pacific on a small peninsula of jagged black lava. The grounds include a palace, with fishpond and private canoe landing, and three *heiaus* (altars), guarded by large carved effigies of gods – reproductions, but still eerie in their original setting. An ancient **"place of refuge"** lies firmly protected behind the mortar-less masonry of the sixteenth-century **Great Wall**. Those who broke ancient Hawaii's intricate system of *kapu* (*tabu*) – perhaps by treading on the shadow of a chief, or fishing in the wrong season – could expect summary execution . . . unless they fled to the sanctuary of such a place as this. As chiefs lived on the surrounding land, transgressors had to swim through the shark-infested seas. If successful, they might be absolved and released overnight. In times of war, non-combatants came here to sit out the conflict.

North Kona

There's nothing to call a town on the coast north of Kona, but there are several spectacular sandy beaches, safe for swimming in summer though with tempestuous winter surf – the long crescent of **Hapuna Beach** is the best. Each of the extraordinary **hotels** along the shore has been designed as a self-contained oasis in this inhospitable lava desert. The *Hyatt Regency* (rooms $235 and up; ☎885-1234), for example, is ludicrously ostentatious, its rooms reached by electric boats or monorail – and consumes four percent of all the island's energy. The *Royal Waikoloan* (☎885-6709) offers a couple of good restaurants, and is half the price – which is still $110. It also has its own field of petroglyphs.

Kohala

The green slopes of **Kohala Mountain** at the northern tip of the Big Island come as a refreshing change after barren Kona. The sugar industry here is dying away, yet to be replaced by tourism, so old-style plantation towns such as **HAWI** survive virtually unchanged. It's rundown in an appealing sort of way, the all-purpose general stores still floored with creaking planks. In **KAPAAU**, the birthplace of Kamehameha (who was brought up in Waipio Valley, hidden from his enemies) is marked by his statue. Identical to that in Honolulu, this is in fact the original, lost at sea near the Falklands, and then miraculously recovered after the insurance money had paid for a new one. The *Deli Cafe* opposite (☎889-5822) does basic snacks, with vegetarian options.

Polulu Valley at road's end is the last of the chain of inaccessible valleys which begins with Waipio, and for the moment is every bit as pristine. Plans exist for a restaurant at the lookout, to be followed no doubt by paving the path down to the black sand beach. The fear of *tsunami* which led the Hawaiians to abandon these once densely populated valleys is probably their best defence against the rapacity of the developers.

An illuminating insight into the ancient way of life can be had at **Lapakahi State Historical Park**, a partly reconstructed 600-year-old village (daily 8am–4pm; free). The waters off its small beach are a marine conservation area, great for snorkellers.

Waimea and Inland Hawaii

Inland Hawaii comes as a surprise; pastoral meadows roll over gentle hills where once stood forests of sandalwood. This is cattle-ranching country, most of it – ten percent of the island – owned by the United States' largest private ranch, the **Parker Ranch**.

WAIMEA (also known as **Kamuela**) is not the company town it once was – the Parker Ranch now employs just one hundred of its eight thousand inhabitants – but more of a sophisticated country-town resort, which retains traces of its cowboy past. You can no longer tour the ranch itself, just an interesting **Visitor Center** (Mon–Sat 9am–4pm; $5; ☎885-7311) in town, with a good section on surfer Duke Kahanamoku, and the nearby **Parker Ranch Homes** (Tues–Sat 10am–5pm; $7.50, or $10 for both). The reconstructed 1840s *koa*-wood house of the ranch's founder now adjoins the very un-Hawaiian home of Richard Smart, the current (sixth-generation) owner. Inspections of his rather dubious pastel-yellowing furnishings are accompanied by recordings of this former actor singing Broadway favourites; when he's at home he sings along too.

Other than assorted shopping malls, Waimea's main alternative attraction is the eclectic and eccentric **Kamuela Museum** (daily 8am–4pm; $2.50; ☎885-4724).

Practicalities

B&B is booming in Waimea; in fact there's little else. Barbara Campbell's own *Waimea Gardens Cottage* (☎885-4550) costs around $70, and she also coordinates *Hawaii's Best B&Bs* (PO Box 563, Kamuela 96743), a selection of carefully vetted Big Island properties costing from $60 to $100. *Merriman's* in Opelo Plaza (☎885-6822) is deservedly the most fashionable **restaurant**, for its innovative cuisine, but entrees cost up to $20. *Auntie Alice's* in the Parker Ranch Shopping Center (☎889-0206) is good for cheap snacks.

The Saddle Road

The car rental companies prefer you not to cross the Big Island on the **Saddle Road** between Mauna Kea and Mauna Loa. It's not an especially bad road, but there are no facilities, and it would be a nuisance to rescue you after a breakdown. If you do choose to chance it, you get some great views of the volcanoes – and a good deal of mist too.

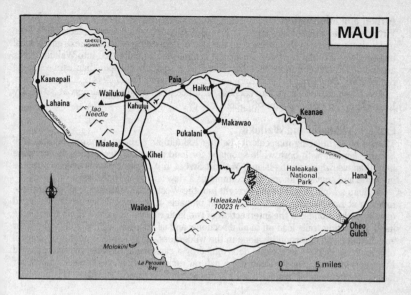

MAUI

The island of **MAUI**, the second largest in the Hawaiian chain, is the fastest-growing rival to Oahu in terms of attracting tourists – with all that entails. Whereas in 1956 only one percent of all visitors to Hawaii came to Maui, the figure these days is more like one third. Opponents of plans to extend Kahului Airport to accommodate jumbo jets fear things are going too far. What were remote unspoiled beaches twenty years ago, around **Kaanapali** and **Kihei** for example, have been swamped by ugly sprawling resorts, and **Lahaina**, once "whaling capital of the world", is now just another tourist trap. Traffic clogs the roads, and most towns consist of little more than a succession of malls.

On the other hand, the crowds come to Maui for the good reason that it's still beautiful. It may lack man-made "sights", but there's still plenty of dramatic scenery left to explore, and this is probably the best equipped of all the islands for **activity** holidays – whale-watching, windsurfing, diving, sailing, snorkelling, cycling. Temperatures along the coast can be searing, especially at Lahaina, but it's always possible to get somewhere cooler. **Upcountry Maui**, on the slopes of the mighty **Haleakala** volcano, is a delight, well away from the bustle; **Makawao** and **Paia** here make good alternative hangouts, if short on accommodation. The tortuous road out west to **Hana** does not quite merit its legendary status, but with its waterfalls and ravines it outclasses anything on Oahu.

Kahului and Wailuku

Half of Maui's 86,000 inhabitants – the workers who keep this fantasy island going – live in the twin towns of **KAHULUI** and **WAILUKU**, to the north of the "neck" connecting its two mountainous sections. The land here can be so flat you fear the waves will wash right over it. Kahului is the main commercial centre; Wailuku, if not aesthetically pleasing, is unusual for Maui in feeling like a genuine community, and with its cheap hotels and restaurants – and the stunning **Iao Needle** nearby – it makes a good central base.

Arrival and Information

Virtually all visitors to Maui arrive at **Kahului Airport**, which is well placed for all the major destinations. In the absence on the island of anything other than extremely local bus services, a rental car from the airport is almost essential; a taxi into Wailuku costs around $8, to Lahaina more like $30. **Bicycles** – scarcely cheaper than cars – can be rented from *The Island Biker* in Kahului Shopping Center (☎877-7744).

The **Hawaiian Visitors Bureau** has an office just outside the airport at 380 Dairy Road (Mon–Fri 8am–4.30pm; ☎871-8691).

Exploring Kahului and Wailuku

There's no sightseeing to speak of in either Kahului or Wailuku, though you may well become familiar with both while shopping for food and other necessities, better value here than elsewhere on the island. **Market Street** in Wailuku contains several interesting curio and souvenir shops, and commands a view across to Haleakala.

Wailuku's Main Street heads straight into the West Maui Mountains, stopping three miles in at **Iao Needle**, a stunning 1200ft pinnacle of green-clad lava. It stands, head usually in the clouds, at the intersection of two lush valleys; you can't climb the needle itself, but hiking trails lead off in all directions, and as very few visitors follow them for any distance you can soon be alone in the wilderness. King Kamehameha won control of Maui here in 1790, in a battle determined by a cannonade directed by two captured European gunners. On the road up, a natural rock formation has become known for fairly – but not very – obvious reasons as the **John F Kennedy Profile**.

Accommodation

As most of the Maui resorts are long oceanfront strips of expensive hotels, where you have to drive just to get to a shop or restaurant, there's a lot to be said for a cheap and simple room in Wailuku.

Banana Bungalow, 310 N Market St, Wailuku (☎244-5090, ☎1-800-846-7835 from the US). Newly renovated and extremely convivial budget hotel with Maui's cheapest accommodation. $13 for a dorm bed; $35 for a bare, basic double room. Informal meals, organised trips, cut-price car rental.

Mark Edison's Lodge, Iao Valley Rd (☎242-5555). Motel rooms in Iao Valley for $55.

Northshore Inn, 2080 Vineyard St, Wailuku (☎242-8999). $15 dorms, $32 single, $45 double. Much the same communal feel as *Banana Bungalow*.

Eating

Wailuku has several of Maui's best-value restaurants, some near *Banana Bungalow* on Market Street, others in Lower Main Street as it loops down towards Kahului Harbor.

Siam Thai, 123 N Market St (☎244-3817). Fiery Thai curries and lots of vegetarian choices. $6–8.

Tasty Crust, 1770 Mill St (☎244-0845). Basic home-cooking, especially good value for breakfast.

Tipanan, 1276 Lower Main St (☎244-9466). Cheap and tasty Filipino specialities. $6–8.

Tokyo Tei, 1063 Lower Main St (☎242-9630). Very popular for the cheapest Japanese food around.

West Maui

It's easy to state the disadvantages of staying on Maui's **west coast**: the prices are higher, it's well away from the best beaches and sights of the island, and the long drive around is often made much worse by the volume of traffic. Holiday-makers come for the guarantee of sun, then spend their days in expensive air-conditioned hotels and shopping centres of the two main resorts, **Lahaina** and **Kaanapali**. One real plus is that development has sensibly been restricted to the *makai* (oceanward) side of the Honoapiilani Highway, leaving the inland hills and valleys largely untouched except by drifting rainbows.

Lahaina

The square at the heart of modern **LAHAINA** is all but filled by a magnificent **banyan tree**, its branches pushing pack into the earth to become sturdy additional trunks. Just in front, in the small boat harbour, the replica square-rigged *Carthaginian* houses a **maritime museum** (Mon–Sat 9am–4.30pm, Sun 11am–4pm; $3). **Pioneer Inn** nearby is Lahaina's main social centre, well worth wandering into for a beer, if not exactly quiet.

Otherwise, a walk up Front Street and back down Wainee Street just about covers what Lahaina has to offer; but it may well take you some time, as the concentration of tourist shops, fast-food places and so on is phenomenal. The one respite is the views out to sea, towards the island of Lanai. These cramped streets make **parking** a terrible business, incidentally; the only free public parking is at Front and Prison streets.

Accommodation

If you do have the money to spend on resort-style accommodation, Lahaina and the coast northwards have some good options; otherwise the availability of rooms at the historic *Pioneer Inn* may well determine whether you come here at all.

Maui Islander, 600 Wainee St (☎667-9766). Very central low-key top-range accommodation, $83 up.

Pioneer Inn, 658 Wharf St (☎661-3636). Characterful and very lively old hotel, right in the thick of things. Rooms in the old building (above the bar) start at $30; in the newer, $70.

Tony's Place, 13 Kauala Rd (☎661-8040). B&B near the beach, basic doubles $55.

WHALE-HUNTING AND WHALE-WATCHING

The first **whaling ships** arrived in Hawaii in 1820, the same year as the missionaries – and had an equally dramatic impact. With the ports of Japan closed to outsiders, Hawaii swiftly became the centre of the industry. Any Pacific port of call would have seemed a godsend to the whalers, who were away from New England for three years at a time, and paid so badly that most were either fugitives from justice or just plain mad (see p.167). Hawaii was such a paradise to as fifty percent of each crew would desert, to be replaced by native Hawaiians, born seafarers eager to see the world. Soon King Kamehameha IV had established his own whaling fleet, and the economy adapted to meet the sailors' needs. The Big Island turned to raising cattle, and Maui began to grow vegetables.

Until the 1840s, Honolulu, which permitted drinking, was the whalemen's favourite port. Then the twin attractions of potatoes and prostitution lured them to **Lahaina** as well, which by 1857 had grown to a length of several miles. The sea was calm enough for ships to dock along the open roadstead, and a grass-covered marketplace stood beside a central canal. Both Lahaina and Honolulu were notorious as entrance points for disease; not just syphilis, but also influenza, measles, typhoid and smallpox.

At the peak of the trade, almost six hundred whaling vessels docked in Honolulu in a single year. Decline came with the Civil War, when many ships were bought up in order to be sunk as a blockade of Confederate ports, and, with the 1871 disaster, when 31 vessels lingered in the Arctic too long, became frozen in, and had to be abandoned.

Whale-watching

Ironically, the waters just off western Maui are now one of the world's best areas for whale-watching and research. Between January and March each year, and for up to a month either side of that, **humpback whales** use the ocean channels here as both sanctuary and playground. They did not do so in the nineteenth century, although they would have been safe enough, as humpbacks were not then hunted. When caught with the old technology, they sank uselessly to the bottom of the sea.

The whales are often clearly visible from the shore, but specific whale-watching trips can take you much nearer (with money-back guarantees if you don't see one). Operators include *Pacific Whale Foundation* ($25; ☎879-8811) and *Maui Princess* ($25; ☎661-8397). You might also see whales during a Molokini snorkel trip (p.915) or similar excursion.

Food

Lahaina's many malls contain a tremendous selection of restaurants and takeaways, not all of them good by any means but covering a wider spectrum than the hotels.

Golden Palace, Lahaina Shopping Center (☎661-3126). Good-value Chinese with varied menu. $8.

Lahaina Tasca, 608 Front St (☎661-8001). Highly imaginative *tapas* bar, serving inventive seafood dishes. In theory tasters are $6, but a full meal can easily work out at $25. Open until midnight.

Musashi, Lahaina Square, Wainee St (☎667-6207). Sushi until 9pm, and full Japanese menu. $12–20.

Sunrise Cafe, 693 Front St (☎661-4710). Seafront French food, until midnight. Light lunches $5–8.

Kaanapali

KAANAPALI, just a few miles north but reliably cooler, was never a town; fields of sugarcane were replaced in the Sixties by high-rise hotels and condos, each no doubt comfortable enough but soulless en masse. There are several reasonable **beaches** around – swimming and snorkelling are best at **Black Rock**, in front of the *Sheraton* – but otherwise the main attraction is the **whaling museum** in the Whalers Village mall (daily 9.30am–10pm). Grisly but fascinating exhibits include a cast-iron "try pot", used for reducing whale blubber at sea; such pots gave rise to the stereotyped but not entirely untrue image of cannibals cooking missionaries in big black cauldrons.

A free shuttle bus connects Kaanapali with Lahaina, and a trolley operates within the resort. The warnings of the rental car companies concerning the **Kahekili Highway**, which looks on the map like a good route to continue around northwest Maui and back to Wailuku, should be taken seriously; it's an exceptionally dangerous drive.

Kihei and Wailea

Maui's other main resort area is south of Kahului, across the isthmus. The long strip of hotels, malls and condos begins at **KIHEI**, with the road heavily built up to both sides, but thins out beyond the manicured lawns of **WAILEA** near some superb beaches. **Paluea Beach** is ideal for families; **Little Beach**, reached by a trail from cactus-lined Makena (or Big) Beach, is famous for (illegal) nudism. A very rough one-lane track, with minimal visibility, peters out altogether just before **La Perouse Bay**. Once a significant population centre, the beach here is good for snorkelling, and **dolphins** regularly come to play with swimmers, though you're forbidden to encourage them.

None of the **accommodation** here is cheap, though rooms at *Wailana Sands*, 35 Walaka Street (☎879-2026), start at $45, and off-season condos at *Nani Kai Hale*, 73 N Kihei Road (☎879-9120), can drop to around $50. For **snacks**, the 24-hour *Paradise Fruit* stand at 1913 S Kihei Road (☎879-1723) serves fresh juices, shakes and sandwiches. *Royal Thai Cuisine* in Azeka Shopping Center, 1280 S Kihei Road (☎874-0813), is a good-value Thai restaurant, and there's a *Perry's Smorgy* here too (see p.899).

Upcountry Maui

Not always is Hawaii a man tarnished by civilisation. Central Maui, in the last century "a dreary expanse of sand and shifting sandhills, with a dismal growth ... of thornless thistles", is now a pastoral idyll, thanks to an ingenious system of irrigation channels.

The highway to the top of **Haleakala** rises higher, faster, than any road on earth, starting in the rich meadows where Jimi Hendrix's *Rainbow Bridge* concert was filmed. Beyond the exclusive homes and white clapboard churches, it climbs past purple-blossoming jacaranda, firs and eucalyptus to reach open ranching land and then ascends in huge curves to the volcanic desert and the crater itself.

Haleakala

Though **HALEAKALA** is the world's largest dormant volcano, you may not appreciate its full ten thousand feet until you're at the top. Shield volcanoes are not as dramatic as the classic cones, and the summit is often obscured by cloud. That it hasn't erupted for two hundred years doesn't necessarily mean it won't ever again – in 1979, for example Haleakala was thought more likely to explode than Mount St Helens (see p.844).

The higher reaches of the mountain are a **national park**, which is kept open non-stop (admission $3). Manhattan would fit comfortably into the awe-inspiring **crater**, almost eight miles across, which was for the ancient Hawaiians a site of deep spiritual power. The most popular time to come is for the **sunrise**; the **visitor centre** at the top operates from just before dawn until 3pm (weather ☎572-7749; information ☎572-9306). Hiking trails of varying difficulty cross the crater floor, where a berth in a **cabin** costs around $10 (allocated by lottery; apply three months in advance to Box 369, Makawao HI 96768). Some **camping** is also permitted.

Makawao and Paia

Both **MAKAWAO**, five miles up from the ocean, and **PAIA**, beside it near the great surfing beach of **Hookipa**, are a world away from Maui's luxury resorts. These laid-back little country towns seem to be populated mainly by Californian veterans of the Sixties; not exactly Hawaiian, but pleasant places to hang out.

Neither has much formal accommodation, but advertisements at the wholefood store *Mana Foods*, 49 Baldwin Avenue, Paia (☎579-8078), offer rooms in the area for around $25. The friendly *Casanova's* at 1188 Makawao Avenue in the centre of Makawao (☎572-0220) has Italian lunch specials for around $6, and live music at night, in part thanks to the local community of rock exiles. Paia has several good eating options, with fresh fish at *Paia Fishmarket*, 101 Hana Highway (☎579-8030), and the more expensive but greatly recommended *Mama's Fish House*, 799 Poho Place (☎579-9672), set next to the sea a mile along the Hana Highway. Vegetarians will be glad of *The Vegan*, at 115 Baldwin Avenue, Paia (closed Mon; ☎579-9144).

MAUI ACTIVITIES

Promotional hand-outs, and free newspapers such as *Maui Beach Press*, will familiarise you with a wide range of possible tours and activities. Agencies throughout the island, especially along Front Street in Lahaina, offer cut-price deals well below advertised rates.

Molokini

Maui's best-known **snorkelling** and **diving** spot is the tiny crescent of Molokini, all that's left poking above the sea of a once-great volcano. There's no beach, or landfall of any kind, but you do see a lot of fish, including deep-water species. Countless cruises leave early each morning (to avoid the worst of the heat) from Maalea Harbor.

Official rates vary from $40 to $70; vessels range from the 16-passenger racing yacht *Suntan Special* ($59; ☎874-0332) up to the 150-seater *Prince Kuhio* ($65; ☎242-8777).

Downhill Cycle Rides

One of Maui's more unusual opportunities is to be taken by van to see the dawn on top of Haleakala, and then to roll on a bicycle thirty-nine miles down to Paia by the sea – without pedalling once. Even Vice-President Dan Quayle managed it, in March 1990, accompanied by six uzi-toting Secret Service men on mountain bikes. Serious cyclists may find the trip frustrating, particularly as you're obliged to keep pace with the slowest in your group; complete novices or the unfit shouldn't try; the in-betweens think it's great.

Companies running trips (with pick-ups anywhere on Maui) include *Cruiser Bob's Downhill*, based in Paia (☎667-7717), and *Maui Downhill* in Kahului (☎871-2155).

The Road to Hana

The rains which fall on Haleakala cascade down Maui's long windward flank, covering it in thick junglelike vegetation. Convicts in the Twenties hacked out a road along the coast which has become a major tourist attraction in its own right, twisting tortuously in and out of gorges, past innumerable waterfalls, and over more than fifty tiny one-lane bridges. All year round, and especially in June, the route is ablaze with colour, from orchids up to rainbow eucalyptus and African tulip trees with their orange blossom.

The usual day's excursion is roughly sixty miles (or two to three hours) each way from Paia, to Oheo Gulch just past Hana. Don't attempt it if it's raining, but in good weather the road is nothing like as difficult as its reputation suggests. However, drivers miss much of the scenery, and may prefer to take an **organised tour** with *No Ka Oi Scenic Tours* (☎871-9008) or *Polynesian Adventure Tours* (☎877-4242).

Keanae

The views from the Hana Highway are the main thing, but halfway along, a side road down to the peninsula of **KEANAE** brings you to a small Hawaiian village with taro fields and a fine old church. Banana trees and birds of paradise grow in abundance, and the ocean surf comes crashing in on sharp headlands of black *aa* lava.

YMCA **Camp Keanae**, on the main highway just before the turning, is a **youth hostel** (once a prison) with dorm beds at $8 per night, for a maximum of three days. You must book ahead via Maui YMCA (95 Mahalini St, Wailuku HI 96793; ☎244-3253).

Hana

The former sugar town of **HANA** itself might seem a disappointment at the end of the road; really it's a pleasant enough little community that isn't especially interested in attracting tourists. *Hasegawa's General Store* is a friendly place to pick up supplies, and there's a delightful **red sand beach** reached by a trail from the end of Uakea Road.

Rooms at the deluxe *Hotel Hana-Maui* (☎248-8211) *start* at $295; the Japanese-style *Heavenly Hana Inn* (☎248-8442) out towards the tiny airport is better value, from $75.

Beyond Hana

A mile or two past Hana, a dirt track leads to the banyan-shaded oceanside cemetery of **Palapala Hoomau** church, where **Charles Lindbergh** was buried in 1974. The first man to fly the Atlantic, who retired to Maui for privacy, was a notorious Nazi sympathiser who once told the *Reader's Digest* that aviation is "one of those priceless possessions which permit the White Race to live at all in a sea of Yellow, Black, and Brown".

The gorgeous scenery of **Oheo Gulch**, part of Haleakala National Park, is ten miles out of Hana. Waterfalls tumble down the hillside to oceanfront meadows. If you hike up, you soon escape the crowds and reach cool rock pools which are ideal for swimming; most visitors stroll down to the **Seven Sacred Pools**. The newly coined name is just a gimmick used to promote Hana tours, and in its time has been attached to other features along the way, but even if they're not sacred the pools are certainly special.

If you're congenitally averse to going back the same way you came, in normal conditions (but *not* rain) it is possible to follow the road right around southern Maui, although it has several rocky and unpaved stretches. At first the countryside is lovely, dotted with exclusive homes whose owners would prefer this not to become a standard tourist loop, and passing a small black sand beach, the 1859 church at Huailoha, and the last-chance store at Kaupo. It then climbs thirty miles up bleak lava fields and rounds the corner to give spectacular views out to the island of **Kahoolawe** (a naval bombing range until 1990, when President Bush finally succumbed to pressure from Hawaiian activists). You're now back in upcountry Maui, and soon come to the **Tedeschi Winery** (daily 9am–5pm; ☎878-6058), Hawaii's only vineyard.

MOLOKAI

Halfway between Oahu and Maui, little MOLOKAI is the least touristed of the major Hawaiian islands. It doesn't have a single traffic light or elevator; a brief visit is a chance to feel how Hawaii must have been fifty years ago. The capital, **Kaunakakai**, is one dusty street of wooden falsefront stores, the scenery of **Kalaupapa Peninsula** and **Halawa Valley** is unspoiled, and gigantic **Papahoku Beach** is usually deserted. The downside is that agriculture is on the decline, and Molokai has the highest unemployment in the United States; some islanders have to commute to factory jobs in Maui.

Eastern Molokai

Halawa Valley is perhaps the finest of all Hawaii's "lost valleys", an absolute gem an hour's drive east of Kaunakakai. The first view from the **overlook** is staggeringly beautiful, with Moaula Falls high in the distance half-hidden by clouds, and the rich green valley with its black sand beach below. You can continue down to the beach, where the shore is taken up with lush meadows filled with bright wild flowers, or hike for an hour up to the foot of the falls. The pool there is supposedly home to a giant lizard.

The highest **sea cliffs** in the world, four thousand feet high, are further around the northern coast; the only way to see them (other than by air – scheduled flights south from Molokai pass over them, as do helicopter trips) – is on a boat trip with Glenn Davis from Halawa (no phone; write to Box 350, Kaunakakai, HI 96748).

Kalaupapa Peninsula

The flat peninsula of **Kalaupapa** on Molokai's northern shore was created by a lava flow at the base of a colossal cliff, and was so naturally isolated that King Kamehameha IV made it a **leper colony**. Sufferers from all the islands were sent here to live out their days, forced to say goodbye forever to their homes and families. The Belgian priest **Father Damien**, who arrived here in 1873, was the first to concern himself with the welfare of the lepers, greatly improving their conditions before he succumbed to the disease himself. Robert Louis Stevenson sprang to his defence with an impassioned tribute when his reputation was maligned, and he is a likely candidate for sainthood.

In the 1940s, new drugs made leprosy (Hansen's Disease) no longer contagious, and the need for isolation disappeared. Many of the patients, guaranteed homes in Kalaupapa for life, are still there, conducting tours of the settlement. Daily **mule treks** descend from the overlook above ($90; ☎567-6088), and you can also hike ($30) or fly ($80). A deeply grooved path climbs from the overlook to a not-especially **Phallic Rock**.

Western Molokai

The few resort hotels at the west end of Molokai are a surreal testament to the wonders a bit of water can work in a volcanic wasteland. They can't be claimed to have any character; on the other hand, **Papahoku Beach** is phenomenal. Stretching for miles of empty white sands and magnificent pounding surf, it's so massive that unscrupulous developers were able to cart much of it off to Waikiki before anyone realised.

Mauna Loa on the road down used to be a **Dole** pineapple town, and in antiquity was the birthplace of *hula*. This enclave amidst the fields is now a sleepy sort of alternative arts community. There's a nice *General Store*, and the *Big Wind Kite Factory* makes kites and sells artefacts from Bali and Nepal alongside Molokai "Red Dirt" T-shirts. At the top end of town you can walk out to the old cemetery along a path of that red dirt.

Molokai Practicalities

Molokai's **airport** is in the centre of the island, with rental cars and taxis but no public transport. The *Maui Princess* **ferry** (☎553-5736 on Molokai; ☎661-8397 on Maui) sails twice daily between Kaunakakai and Lahaina on Maui.

Rooms in **Kaunakakai** at the *Pau Hana Inn* (☎1-800-423-MOLO or ☎553-5347), which with its spreading banyan tree and low-slung buildings has a lot of style, start at $45; at the bizarre-looking but comfortable *Hotel Molokai* (same phone) they're $59. **East** of Kaunakakai, *Honomuni House* is a B&B in a really nice setting eighteen miles along the road to Halawa (☎558-8383; $65 double). Diana and Larry Swenson (☎558-8394) rent an apartment nearby for $50 for two, $66 for four, two-night minimum stay. In the **west**, *Kaluakoi Hotel* (☎1-800-777-1700) costs $90, and *Paniolo Hale* (☎1-800-367-2984 or ☎552-2731), more human in scale and less antiseptic, is $85, or $105 for four.

Good **food** can be had in Kaunakakai at the *Pau Hana Inn* and the rough and ready *Mid-Nite Inn* (☎553-5302) on the main street. *Outpost Natural Foods* (☎553-3377) behind the *Chevron* garage do wholefood snacks and smoothies. The wooden-verandahed *JoJo's Cafe* is a nice place to eat in **Mauna Loa** (☎552-2803; closed Wed & Sun).

KAUAI

Although no point on the tiny island of **KAUAI** is as much as eleven miles from the sea, the variety of its landscapes is quite incredible. This is the oldest of the major islands, and erosion has had that many more million years to sculpt it into fantastic shapes. The mist-shrouded extinct volcano **Mount Waialeale** at its heart is the world's wettest spot, draining into a high land-locked swamp, full of unique plants and animals. Nearby **Waimea Canyon** is on a scale to rival the Grand Canyon, while along the north shore are the vertiginous green cliffs of the awe-inspiring **Na Pali** coast.

Kauai does have its share of upscale resorts, busy belt roads, and overcrowded beaches; but it also has marvellous "secret" hideaways, and for **hikers** it offers unparal-lelled opportunities to escape into untouched wilderness, only accessible on foot. In terms of nightlife, fine dining and so on – or for that matter museums and high culture – there's little to do. Kauai is a place to be active, on sea and land; and if you only go on one **helicopter** flight in your life, do it here. You may never see scenery like this again.

Lihue

Most flights to Kauai arrive at the capital, **LIHUE**. It's roughly at the midpoint of the circle-island highway (prevented from completing a loop by the Na Pali cliffs), and has the few cheap hotels around, but as a base it's pretty undistinguished. The population is just five thousand, and downtown consists of a few tired-looking plantation-town streets, well back from the sea and surrounded by a conglomeration of anonymous malls.

The central **Kauai Museum** at 4428 Rice Street (Mon–Fri 9am–4.30pm, Sat 9am–1pm; $3; ☎245-6931) traces the history of the island from the mythical *menehune* through Captain Cook's landfall in January 1778 and on to its sugar-growing heyday. Kauai was the one island not conquered by Kamehameha the Great; he spent six years amassing a fleet which never sailed, and settled in the end for accepting economic trib-ute. A couple of miles south, **Grove Farm Homestead** on Nawiliwili Road is a restored plantation home (tours Mon, Wed & Thurs, 10am & 1pm; $3; reserve on ☎245-3202).

Arrival and Information

Lihue's **airport** is only two miles from downtown; a **taxi** into town costs roughly $5, to Wailua or Kapaa more like $15. All the usual **car** rental outlets are here, as are the island's **helicopters**. *South Sea Helicopters* (☎245-7781) are typical of many companies in offering basic tours from $130; shopping around in the malls, and checking out free-sheets like *Kauai Beach Press*, you should find discounts. The **Hawaii Visitors Bureau** is in town at 3016 Umi Street (Mon–Fri 8am–4.30pm; ☎245-3971).

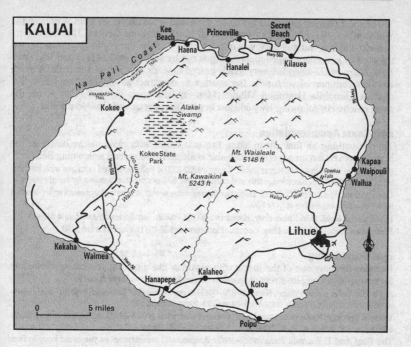

KAUAI

Na Pali Coast
Kee Beach
Haena
Princeville
Secret Beach
Kilauea
Hwy-560
Hanalei
AWAAWAPUHI TRAIL
KALALAU TRAIL
PIHEA TRAIL
Kokee
Alakai Swamp
Mt. Waialeale 5148 ft
Kapaa
Waipouli
Kokee State Park
Opaekaa Falls
Mt. Kawaikini 5243 ft
Wailua
Wailua River
Kekaha
Waimea
Waimea Canyon
Lihue
Hwy-50
Hanapepe
Kalaheo
Koloa
Poipu

0   5 miles

Accommodation

Lihue is the one town on Kauai with cheap hotel rooms for visitors from other islands.

Garden Island Inn, 3445 Wilcox Rd, Kalapaki Beach (☎1-800-648-0154). Surprisingly cheap tourist accommodation down by the beach. $45–50.

Hale Lihue Motel, 2931 Kalena St (☎245-3151). Basic accommodation from $20.

Motel Lani, 4240 Rice St (☎245-2965). Very central, well-kept motel. Doubles from $27, triples $37.

Tip Top Motel, 3173 Akahi St (☎245-2333). A reasonable standard for $30.

Eating

The ethnic mix in Lihue, and its working population, mean that its restaurants offer a wide range of cuisines and prices. The malls are, of course, full of fast-food options.

Casa Italiana, 2989 Haleko Rd (☎245-9586). Dinner only, closed Sun. Pasta and seafood from $10.

Hamura Saimin, 2956 Kress Street (☎245-3271). Family-run communal Japanese food counter, open very late. Standard bowls of *saimin* (noodles) under $3, shrimp $3.75.

Rosita's, Kukui Grove Shopping Center (☎245-8561). Good Mexican food, though the Center itself isn't all that exciting. Lunch specials from $6, live music Fri & Sat until 10pm.

East Kauai

Just north of Lihue up the eastern shore of Kauai, the three communities of **WAILUA**, **WAIPOULI** and **KAPAA** blend into each other in a long strip of malls, condos and hotels. All the way along there's an exposed thin strip of beach, fine for sunbathing but not as good for swimmers and surfers as those further up.

The most popular tourist attraction on the island is the excursion from Wailua up the Wailua River, the only navigable river in all Hawaii, to **Fern Grotto**. This large, fern-bedecked, damp and dull cave was immortalised by Elvis Presley in *Blue Hawaii*, and the crowds in the large open-topped barges run by *Smith's* (☎822-4111) and *Waialeale Boat Tours* (☎822-4909) are very much geared towards that sort of schmaltz. A much worthier commercial venture is the attempt to construct an idealised ancient settlement at **Kamokila Hawaiian Village** (Mon–Sat 9am–4pm; $5; ☎822-1192) beside the river, reached by following Hwy-580 just beyond the spectacular **Opaekaa Falls**.

East Coast Accommodation

There's nothing all that cheap along the east coast, with most of the hotels in the luxury bracket, but on a more manageable scale there are several welcoming B&Bs.

Royal Drive Cottages, 147 Royal Drive, Kapaa (☎822-2321). Fully equipped cottages with kitchenettes beyond the falls. Knowledgeable and friendly host. $75 per night, discounts for longer stays.

Coco Palms, Wailua (☎822-4921). Definitive honeymoon resort in ersatz Polynesian style; worth a look but wildly expensive at over $200.

Hotel Coral Reef, 1516 Kuhio Hwy, Kapaa (☎1-800-843-4659). Small friendly hotel, just $40–45.

Plantation Hale, 484 Kuhio Hwy, Coconut Plantation (☎822-4941). Condos from $100.

East Coast Eating

Kapaa is the only one of the towns with anything like a centre; you can window-shop for restaurants along its street of wooden stores fronted by a beach park.

A Pacific Cafe, Kauai Village, Kapaa (☎822–0013). Very popular for its exotic, eclectic (and expensive) Pacific cuisine. Dinner only, Wed–Mon 5.30–10pm, around $30.

Perry's Smorgy, Kauai Beachboy Hotel, Coconut Plantation (☎822–3111). As on the other islands, all-you-can-eat buffets at $4.45 breakfast, $5.95 lunch, $7.95 dinner.

The King And I, Waipouli Plaza (☎822–1642). As good a Thai restaurant as you could hope to find. Vegetarian specialities, lots of fresh herbs, $6–8 for entrees.

North Kauai

That part of northern Kauai which is unique and unspoiled seems to be diminishing all the time. The astonishing valleys of the **Na Pali coast** itself must surely remain inviolate – though accessible enough by canoe to sustain large Hawaiian populations, their awesome walls shield them from any attempt to build roads in. But the bulldozers are inching ever closer. The spanking new resort of **Princeville**, which began life as a sugar plantation in 1860, is quite clearly on the point of ruining a considerable area of oceanfront, with its airport, golf courses and homes for millionaires such as Sylvester Stallone.

Secret Beach

Long golden **Secret Beach** is Kauai's best-looking beach, though swimming is usually unsafe. Hidden away from the road, it's an unofficial centre for campers and nudists. Driving up Hwy-56 from the south, pass **Kilauea** and then turn right at Kalihiwai. Take the second right, which is a dirt track leading to a parking area. The beach is a ten-minute walk down through the woods. At the far end there's a waterfall of beautiful fresh mountain water, and there are often spinner dolphins just offshore, especially around the picturesque 1913 Kilauea **lighthouse**. The cliffs above are a bird sanctuary.

Hanalei

For the moment, major development stops beyond Princeville, which is mainly due to the fact that the road crosses seven successive one-lane bridges. The first is over the Hanalei River, where the valley stretching away inland is a National Wildlife Refuge.

Here rare species of Hawaiian ducks, coots and stilts are protected by the preservation of their major habitats – natural wetlands and taro ponds. As a result, this is a rare chance to see a Hawaiian landscape relatively unchanged since ancient times.

The small town of **HANALEI** is set around a magnificent bay – the name in fact means "crescent bay". There are quite a few low-key apartments for rent, but the area has very little formal accommodation. All the roadside beaches from here on are good, especially for snorkelling; at **HAENA**, the *Camp Naue* YMCA is right on the beach, with $10 dorm beds and $8 camping spaces (contact ☎246-9090 in Lihue on weekdays, or the camp caretaker on ☎826-6419 at weekends). Hanalei has several **restaurants**; the wooden *Tahiti Nui* (☎826–6277) is particularly nice, with its authentic Tahitian decor, rattan screens and old prints. Dinner costs between $12 and $18, there's a *luau* on Wednesdays, and Fridays, for $35, and live country music on Sundays, and Mondays.

The Na Pali Coast

The lush valleys of the **Na Pali coast**, separated by knife-edge ridges of rock often thousands of feet high but just a few feet thick, make Kauai one of the great hiking destinations of the world. Although many of the best views (other than from a helicopter) are from the trails in Kokee State Park (see overleaf) or boat trips out at sea, the **Kalalau Trail** along the shore is unforgettable. The full eleven miles to Kalalau Valley is arduous, and gets progressively more dangerous; in places you have to scramble along a precipitous (and shadeless) wall of crumbly red rock.

However, the first two miles of the trail, to **Hanakapiai Beach**, are probably the most beautiful. They're steep but straightforward, passing through patches of dense vegetation where you clamber over the gnarled root systems of the baffling *hala* (or pandanus) tree. Creepers and vines hang down, and it's all pretty exposed to the sun. From the beach, a further hour's hike (off the main trail), which requires a lot of climbing up little rock faces and over fallen trees, leads inland to the natural amphitheatre of the towering **Hanakapiai Falls**. An absolute minimum to get to the falls and back from the trailhead at Kee Beach would be four and a half hours.

Hikers and campers doing anything more than a day-hike must obtain (free) permits from the State Parks Office (3060 Eiwa St, Lihue; Mon–Fri 8am–4.15pm; ☎245–4444). It's in your own interest to do so; there are a lot of accidents and drownings along the way, and they need a record of who may be missing.

Several stores in the small **Ching Young Village** mall in Hanalei specialise in equipping hiking and other expeditions. *Captain Zodiac* (☎826–9371 or ☎926-9192) offer motorised rubber **raft trips** up the coast (varying lengths cost $50–105). Quite how far they get depends on the weather, but they're absolutely exhilarating, racing at top speed into caves, through tunnels, and under waterfalls – and you get a snorkelling stop too. If you have a camping permit, they'll drop you off at the far end of the trail for $60 one-way or $110 return; for this you have to go on (and return by) the 6.15am boat. *Jungle Bob's* (☎826–6664) offer books, maps and plenty of first-hand trail information, renting tents and backpacks. Next door, *Pedal'n'Paddle* (☎826-9069) rents out bikes ($20) as well as canoes and kayaks ($35–55) for use on the rivers and inland waterways.

South Kauai

POIPU, the southernmost point on Kauai, is the island's principal beach resort, but apart from good surf and snorkelling it has very little of interest, and there's no real point basing yourself here. *Gloria's Spouting Horn B&B* at 4464 Lawai Beach Road (☎742–6995) has **rooms** for around $60; for good value food, get a giant pizza at the welcoming *Brick Oven* (closed Mon; ☎332-8561) on the main road through **Kalaheo**.

West Kauai

Two of the major scenic attractions in all Hawaii, the gorge of **Waimea Canyon** and **Kokee State Park** with its views of the Na Pali cliffs to one side and the sodden Alakai Swamp to the other, can only be reached from the west coast of Kauai. The coast itself, however, is nondescript. **WAIMEA**, the largest town, is just one short street at the foot of the road up to the canyon. The statue of **Captain Cook**, which commemorates his "discovery" of Hawaii here on January 20 1778, is an exact replica of one in Cook's home town of Whitby, England. A little way upstream along the Waimea River, near an alarming wooden suspension bridge, the uninspiring **Menehune Ditch** is said to be the remains of an aqueduct built by the mythical *menehune*. *Waimea Plantation Cottages* (☎338-1625) are exactly what they sound like: self-contained cottages for $65 per night.

Waimea Canyon and Kokee State Park

It's not unreasonable to call **Waimea Canyon** the "Grand Canyon of the Pacific". It may not be quite as deep, at three thousand feet, but the colours – all shades of green against the bare red earth – and the way it all manages to fit into such a tiny island, are absolutely breathtaking. The road from Waimea climbs beside the widening gorge, until after eight miles the mile-wide canyon can be seen in all its splendour. Each of the roadside lookouts is worth stopping for. Erosion by torrential rains created this landscape, but the process began when a massive geological fault almost split Kauai in two.

Explore Kokee Park as early in the day as possible; by late morning the valleys may fill with mist and cloud. Numerous trails head off to both sides of the highway. Although the ranger station at **KOKEE**, the park headquarters, is often unstaffed, you can pick up detailed information from the small but informative **Kokee Museum** nearby, where displays centre on the indigenous wildlife. Kauai is the only island where mongooses have not killed off most native **birds**, and at this height mosquitoes are no threat either, so some of the world's rarest species (such as the *o'o a'a*) survive here and nowhere else.

Around $45 per night rents one of the *Kokee Lodge Housekeeping Cabins* (PO Box 819, Waimea, Kauai, HI 96796; ☎335-6061). There's also free **camping**, with permits from the parks office in Lihue (see previous page). *Kokee Lodge* has lunch specials for $7.

Awaawapuhi Trail
The **Awaawapuhi Trail** drops steeply from the road beyond Kokee, passing through three miles of dense forest before abruptly emerging at a staggering view of a valley open only to the ocean, tucked between the Na Pali cliffs. The sheer razorback ridges are almost vertical, even if they are somehow covered with clinging vegetation.

Kalalau Lookout and Pihea Trail
A few miles further up, **Kalalau Lookout** stands over the valley where the Kalalau Trail ends (see previous page) – though to attempt a descent would be certain suicide. The **Pihea Trail** follows the course of a lunatic attempt to extend the road beyond its current end. At times it narrows to a few feet, with precipitous drops to either side. Visibility can drop to nothing, as the clouds siphon across the ridges. Inland lies the **Alakai Swamp**, where the heaviest rainfall on earth collects in the volcanic rock. You can hike in, but that involves wading thigh-deep through patches of cloying sticky black swamp mud, and potentially damaging a unique environment. Better to remain here above, listening to the shrills and whistles and buzzes of a jungle without mammals or snakes, and watching the darting flashes of colour. Giant ferns dangle above the trail, and orchids gleam from the undergrowth, while the trees – especially in June – erupt into brilliant flowering displays.

PART THREE

THE
CONTEXTS

A CHRONOLOGICAL INDEX

Throughout this book, we've covered the history of the various colonies, states and communities of North America in as much detail as space will allow. The chronology below is designed as a readily accessible means of drawing together the many disparate historical and cultural trends that have contributed towards the development of the modern United States. Most of the topics and incidents mentioned are covered in more detail at the relevant point in the book; we've provided page references as appropriate.

BC	30,000 BC Aleuts, Inuits and Athabascans cross frozen straits from Asia to America → p.865. 6000 BC With the giant bison and other oversized mammals hunted to extinction, nomadic peoples start to settle in agricultural communities. 1000 BC First terraced villages in New Mexico.	
AD	0 The Moundbuilders in Ohio Valley establish trading links throughout the continent. 1–550 Anasazi Basketmakers on the Colorado → p.657. 700 Pueblo culture begins to develop in the Southwest → p.657. 750 Polynesian voyagers from the Marquesas arrive in Hawaii → p.892.	500 Caddo build city of Cahokia around what is now St Louis.
1000	1000 Norse sailors touch on northeast coast; repelled by Algonquin → p.143. 1100–1500 Navajo and Apache migrate from western Canada to the Southwest. Second wave of Polynesian settlers reach Hawaii from Tahiti → p.892. 1200 Southeastern Creek build city of Etowah in Georgia. 1492 First voyage of Christopher Columbus. 1497 John Cabot touches on Labrador → p.143.	1066 Eruption of Sunset Crater in Arizona leads to rapid agricultural development → p.682. 1100–1276 "Golden Age" of Anasazi in Southwest → p.657 and others; construction of Cliff Palace in Mesa Verde → p.611, and White House in Canyon de Chelly → p.690. 1170 Hopi establish Old Oraibi, → p.692. Acoma Pueblo founded → p.662. 1276–99 Great Drought disperses Anasazi → p.657.

1500	1521 Ponce de León lands in Florida → p.425.		
	1524 Verrazano sails up the Hudson River → p.200.		
	1540 Francisco Vásquez de Coronado treks north from Mexico in search of cities of gold, and comes across the Grand Canyon → p.643.		
	1541 De Soto reaches the mouth of the Mississippi.	1550s The League of the Iroquois extends from Massachusetts to Ohio, Canada to Kentucky.	1542 De la Vega, member of De Soto's Florida expedition, publishes first comprehensive description of the new land.
	1565 First permanent white settlement founded by Spain in St Augustine, FL → p.445.		
	1579 Sir Francis Drake claims California for England → p.732.		
	1585 Sir Walter Raleigh lands on Roanoke Island and founds first British settlement, which vanishes mysteriously a few years later → p.350 .	1586 Sir Francis Drake destroys St Augustine → pp.425, 445.	1589 Richard Hakluyt prints anthology of travellers' impressions of America.
1600	1604 French establish colony at Mount Desert Island, Maine → p.200.		
	1607 Colony of Virginia founded at Jamestown; Captain John Smith encounters the Powhatan → p.307.		
	1609 Spanish establish Santa Fe as northern capital of their colonial empire → p.652.		
	1620 Pilgrims land at Plymouth → pp.143, 160.	1619 First black slaves introduced in Virginia → p.300.	
	1626 Dutch found New Amsterdam → p.99.	1600s The introduction of horses by the Spanish enables the development of the culture of the Plains Indians → p.496.	
	1630 Boston founded as Puritan "City Upon A Hill" → p.144.		
	1636 New England colonists massacre the Pequot of southern Connecticut.		
	1638 Swedes settle in Delaware.	1639 Harvard College founded → p.153.	1643 Roger Williams publishes guide to the languages and customs of Native Americans in New England → p.170.
	1664 British take control of New Amsterdam and rename it New York → p.101.		
	1673 Marquette and Joliet get to the northern reaches of the Mississippi River.	1675 "King Phillip" leads Wampanoag in final doomed resistance to white presence in New England → p.143.	

1680 Pueblo Indians temporarily drive Spanish out of much of the Southwest → p.651.		
1682 William Penn founds Pennsylvania as Quaker Colony → p.113.	1692 Salem witchtrials → p.159.	

1700	1718 New Orleans founded by the French → p.470.		
	1733 Georgia settled at Savannah → p.373.		
	1741 Vitus Bering lands in Alaska, presaging large-scale presence of Russian fur-traders in the region → p.867.		
	1755 French Acadians ("Cajuns"), expelled from Nova Scotia in Canada, settle in Lousiana → p.484.	1760 Pontiac of the Ottowa joins forces with French in resisting English expansion into Great Lakes area.	
	1763 British victory in French and Indian War confirms their control of eastern continent → p.127.		
	Spain cedes Florida to Britain → p.445.		
	1764 French hand Louisiana over to Spanish → p.469.		
	1770 Spanish establish first of trail of Catholic missions along the California coast → p.732.		
	1773 Growing protest at burden of English taxation finds expression in the Boston Tea Party → p.152.		
	1775 First shots of Revolutionary War fired at Concord and Lexington → p.154.		
	1776 Declaration of Independence signed → p.116.		
	1778 Captain Cook encounters Hawaiian islands → p.892.		
	1781 Cornwallis surrenders on behalf of Britain at Yorktown → p.310.	1779 Captain Cook dies in Hawaii → p.909.	
	Florida returns to Spanish control → p.425.	1787–88 Draft constitution enshrines distinction between federal government and states' rights, allowing each state to adopt its own stand on slavery. → pp.99, 113, 170, 177.	1782 Publication of de Crèvecoeur's *Letters from an American Farmer* → pp.167, 940.

		1789 First meeting of US Congress; George Washington becomes President → p.283. 1791 First ten amendments to constitution ratified as the Bill of Rights. 1793 Eli Whitney's invention of the cotton gin → p.181, and Samuel Slater's water-powered textile mill → p.172, mark beginning of industrialisation.	1789 Olaudah Equíano (Gustavus Vassa) publishes first-hand account of his kidnapping into slavery and life as a slave → p.937.
1800	1800 Washington DC built as national capital → p.285. 1801 Louisiana ceded by Spanish to French → p.470. 1803 The Louisiana Purchase: President Jefferson buys the Louisiana territory from France for $15 million → pp.470, 551, 591, 589. 1804–1806 Lewis and Clark expedition from St Louis to Oregon to map out new territory → pp.551, 576, 589, 636, 640, 825, 854. 1815 Andrew Jackson's victory at the Battle of New Orleans ends the "1812 War" with Britain for control of the seas → pp.471, 478. 1819 Spain cedes Florida to the US → p.425. 1825 Erie Canal opens crucial trade route between New York and Great Lakes → pp.101, 107. 1835 Texan Revolution → p.496; Battle of the Alamo → p.505. 1836–1845 Texas an independent Republic → pp.495–96. 1846–48 War between the US and Mexico results in the cession of California and much of the Southwest to the United States → pp.643, 647, 733. 1848 Mormons arrive in Utah → p.703.	1802 West Point Military Academy formed → p.102. 1808 Importation of slaves prohibited by Congress. 1820 The Missouri Compromise permits slavery to continue in the southern states → p.200. 1820s Sequoyah develops written Cherokee language and publishes the *Cherokee Phoenix* newspaper → p.390. 1838 Cherokee Indians forced onto Trail of Tears → p.390.	1832 Frances Trollope publishes *Domestic Manners of the Americans*. 1835 De Tocqueville's *Democracy in America* appears. 1839 Abner Doubleday pioneers baseball at Cooperstown, New York → p.106. Edgar Allen Poe publishes *The Fall of the House of Usher*. 1842 Charles Dickens makes extensive lecture tour and publishes *American Notes*.

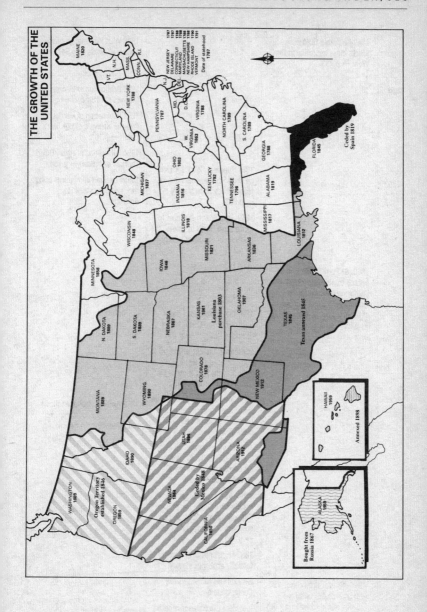

THE GROWTH OF THE UNITED STATES

Date of statehood 1787

NEW JERSEY 1787
DELAWARE 1787
CONNECTICUT 1788
MARYLAND 1788
MASSACHUSETTS 1788
NEW HAMPSHIRE 1788
RHODE ISLAND 1790
VERMONT 1791

MAINE 1820
VT.
N.H.
MASS.
CONN.
R.I.
N.J.
MD.
DEL.
D.C.

NEW YORK 1788
PENNSYLVANIA 1787
W. VIRGINIA 1863
VIRGINIA 1788
NORTH CAROLINA 1789
S. CAROLINA 1789
GEORGIA 1788
FLORIDA 1845
Ceded by Spain 1819

OHIO 1803
MICHIGAN 1837
INDIANA 1816
KENTUCKY 1792
TENNESSEE 1796
ALABAMA 1819
MISSISSIPPI 1817
LOUISIANA 1812

ILLINOIS 1818
WISCONSIN 1848
MINNESOTA 1858
IOWA 1846
MISSOURI 1821
ARKANSAS 1836

N. DAKOTA 1889
S. DAKOTA 1889
NEBRASKA 1867
KANSAS 1861
OKLAHOMA 1907
Louisiana purchase 1803

TEXAS 1845
Texas annexed 1845

MONTANA 1889
WYOMING 1890
COLORADO 1876
NEW MEXICO 1912

WASHINGTON 1889
OREGON 1859
Oregon Territory established 1846
IDAHO 1890
UTAH 1896
ARIZONA 1912

NEVADA 1864
CALIFORNIA 1850
Ceded by Mexico 1848

HAWAII 1959
Annexed 1898

ALASKA 1959
Bought from Russia 1867

	1849 California Gold Rush sparks mass migration to the West → p.733.		1848 Walt Whitman publishes *Leaves of Grass* → p.947.
1850			1851 Publication of Herman Melville's *Moby Dick* → p.167.
			1852 Publication of Harriet Beecher Stowe's *Uncle Tom's Cabin* → p.181.
			1854 Publication of Henry David Thoreau's *Walden* → p.154.
		1857 Supreme Court decision on Dred Scott appears to give federal backing to slavery → p.552.	1850s German immigrants bring the "hamburg steak" to America.
		1859 John Brown attempts to incite slave revolt by raiding the US Arsenal at Harper's Ferry → p.318	
	1860–61 Pony Express mail service from Missouri to California survives for 18 months before being driven out of business by the telegraph → p.559.	1860 Following election of President Lincoln, South Carolina secedes from US → p.359	
		1861 Eleven southern states join to form the Confederate States of America → p.409.	
		Confederate forces attack US garrison at Fort Sumter → p.361; the first shots of the Civil War → pp.301, 345.	
		1863 After a run of Confederate successes, Union victory at Gettysburg marks a turning point in war → p.126.	1862 Anthony Trollope follows in his mother's footsteps and publishes *North America*.
		1864 Navajo rounded up in Canyon de Chelly, Arizona by Kit Carson and deported to New Mexico → p.690.	
		1864–65 General Sherman marches his Union troops through Georgia, destroying southern economy and morale → p.370.	
		1865 Thirteenth amendment formally abolishes slavery.	
		General Lee surrenders the Confederate army → p.346.	
		President Lincoln assassinated five days after war ends.	
		Ku Klux Klan formed by ex-Confederate soldiers → p.346.	

	1867 US purchases Alaska from Russia → p.847.	1867 Reconstruction imposed on southern states by often corrupt Northern Republican "carpetbaggers" → p.346.	1869 First inter-collegiate football game.
	1869 Transcontinental Railroad opens → p.733.	1869 Wyoming grants all women the vote → p.613.	1870 Atlantic City's Boardwalk opens → p.135.
		1873 Jesse James Gang stages first ever train robbery → p.559.	
1875		1876 Custer's Seventh Cavalry wiped out at Little Bighorn by Sioux and Cheyenne under the leadership of Sitting Bull; US Army responds by stepping up campaign to drive the Plains Indians onto reservations → p.628.	1875 First Kentucky Derby → p.382.
			1876 Publication of Mark Twain's *Tom Sawyer* → p.549.
		1877 Crazy Horse murdered, Oglala Sioux deported to Missouri → p.573.	
		1878 Billy the Kid comes to prominence in Lincoln County Wars → p.666.	
		1881 Gunfight at the OK Corral → p.674.	1882 Oscar Wilde lectures Colorado miners on etiquette.
			1883 Buffalo Bill's Wild West Show starts touring → p.618.
		1890 Ghost Dance cult sweeps Native Americans; massacre at Wounded Knee → p.583.	1886 Statue of Liberty unveiled → p.58.
			1891 Tchaikovsky conducts on opening night of New York's Carnegie Hall → p.71.
			1892 *Coca-Cola* company established in Atlanta → p.367.
	1897 Alaskan Gold Rush → p.867.		1896 Basketball invented in Massachusetts → p.168.
	1898 Hawaii annexed as a territory of the USA → p.893.		
	1899 Spain cedes Puerto Rico, Guam and the Philippines to the USA.		
1900			1902 "Jazz" music heard for the first time in the red-light district of New Orleans → p.481.
			1903 Henry Ford founds F*ord Motor Company* → p.234.

		1905 Industrial Workers of the World (the "Wobblies") hold first convention in Chicago → p.631.	1903 Wilbur and Orville Wright make first ever powered flight → p.350.
		1906 San Francisco earthquake kills 100 people → p.788.	1906 William S Kellogg invents corn flakes in Battle Creek MI as a therapy for mental patients.
			Upton Sinclair's *The Jungle* exposes conditions in Chicago's Stockyards → p.258.
			1911 First Indianapolis 500 motor race → p.244.
	1914 Opening of Panama Canal.	1915 Ku Klux Klan claims a million members. Joe Hill executed in Utah → p.703.	1915 D W Griffith's melodrama *Birth Of A Nation* has sympathetic portrayal of the Ku Klux Klan → p.354.
		1917 President Wilson abandons isolationism; US enters World War I.	1920 Boston Red Sox sign Babe Ruth for a record $125,000.
		1920 The 18th Amendment to the Constitution, forbidding the "manufacture, sale, or transportation of intoxicating liquers" introduces total Prohibition to the US. The 19th Amendment grants all US women the vote.	1922 The Will Hays Code imposes rigorous censorship on on-screen lewdness.
1925			1925 First presentation of *Grand Ole Opry* show on Nashville radio → p.394.
		1927 Sacco and Vanzetti executed in Boston → p.144. Charles Lindbergh makes first flight across the Atlantic → p.292	1927 Hollywood's transition to sound; Al Jolson stars in *The Jazz Singer*.
		1929 Al Capone's St Valentine's Day Massacre in Chicago. Wall Street Crash.	1928 Walt Disney produces first Mickey Mouse film, *Steamboat Willie*.
		1934 FBI shoot John Dillinger, Public Enemy No. 1, in Chicago → p.257.	1931 Empire State Building constructed → p.68.
		1930s Depression hits US; President Franklin Roosevelt instigates New Deal programme → p.347.	1934 Laurel and Hardy star in *Sons of the Desert* → p.1.
		1933 Prohibition ends.	
		1935 Amelia Earhart makes first flight from Hawaii to California.	1936 Robert Johnson records *Crossroads Blues* → p.415.
			1939 John Steinbeck's *The Grapes of Wrath* published → pp.541, 942.

		1939 *Gone With the Wind* stars Vivien Leigh and Clark Gable → pp.368, 490.
		John Ford's *Stagecoach* stars John Wayne → p.695.
		1940 First *Kentucky Fried Chicken* diner opens → p.380.
	1941 Japanese attack Pearl Harbor; US enters World War II → p.897.	1941 Orson Welles' *Citizen Kane* → p.773.
		Dedication of Mount Rushmore → p.587.
		1941 Glenn Miller records *Chattanooga Choo-Choo* → p.389.
		Jackie Robinson becomes first black player in Major League baseball.
1946 Philippines granted independence; Guam and Puerto Rico maintained as protectorates.	1945 First atomic bomb detonated in New Mexico → p.666	1943 Frank Sinatra drives bobby-soxers wild at New York's *Paramount Theater*.
		1946 Bugsy Siegel opens the *Flamingo*, Las Vegas' first resort casino → p.723.
1950	1950 Senator Joseph McCarthy spurs the House Un-American Activities' Committee into investigating supposed Communist infiltration in all walks of American life, including Hollywood.	1951 Ronald Reagan co-stars in *Bedtime for Bonzo*.
		1954 Elvis records *That's All Right Mama* in Sun Studios, Memphis → p.401.
	1954 Supreme Court outlaws segregation in schools (Brown vs. Topeka).	1954 Marlon Brando stars in *On The Waterfront*.
	1955 Black protesters boycott segregated buses in Montgomery, Alabama → p.410.	1955 James Dean stars in *Rebel Without A Cause*.
		Disneyland opens in Anaheim, California → p.753.
1958 NASA set up. First US space satellite put into orbit.	1957 Riots engulf Little Rock High School, Arkansas, after enrolment of nine black students → p.537.	1957 The publication of Allen Ginsberg's *Howl* and Jack Kerouac's *On The Road* kicks off the so-called Beat Generation.
1959 Alaska and Hawaii granted statehood → pp.867, 893.		1959 Buddy Holly, Ritchie Valens and the Big Bopper die in plane crash → p. 526.
		Berry Gordy Jr sets up *Motown Records* → p.233
		Marilyn Monroe stars in *Some Like It Hot*.

		1961 President John Kennedy instigates abortive invasion of Cuba at Bay of Pigs → p.430.	1961 Andy Warhol screen-prints cans of *Campbell's Soup*.
		1962 Riots on University of Mississippi campus protesting against enrolment of the first black student → p.417.	1962 James Brown records *Live At The Apollo* → p.79.
		1963 March on Washington culminates in Dr Martin Luther King Jr's "I have a dream" speech → p.290.	
		1963 Assassination of President Kennedy → p.519.	
		1964 President Johnson deepens American commitment in Vietnam.	
		1965 Malcolm X assassinated in Harlem → p.945.	1965 Timothy Leary, Ken Kesey and the Merry Pranksters, the Grateful Dead and the Hell's Angels all active in San Francisco → p.797.
		President Johnson steers through passage of Voting Rights Act; 250,000 new black voters register before the end of the year.	Bob Dylan records *Highway 61 Revisited* → p.280.
		25000 march from Selma to Montgomery, Alabama → p.411.	
		Six-day riot in Watts, Los Angeles, leaves 36 dead → p.746.	
		1967 Over 200,000 Americans involved in anti-Vietnam demos in San Francisco and New York. Norman Mailer and Joan Baez among those arrested at anti-war demo outside the Pentagon. Muhammad Ali stripped of World Heavyweight Boxing Championship following his refusal to be drafted.	1967 "Summer of Love" in San Francisco's Haight-Ashbury district → p.797.
			Green Bay Packers win first Superbowl.
		1968 Assassination of Dr Martin Luther King Jr in Memphis → p.401.	
		Random police brutality scars Democratic Convention in Chicago → p.247.	
		Tommy Smith and John Carlos give Black Power salute at Mexico Olympics.	
	1969 Neil Armstrong and Buzz Aldrin make one giant leap for mankind on the moon.	1969 Sharon Tate brutally murdered in Hollywood; Charles Manson's "Family" held responsible.	1969 Woodstock Festival held in upstate New York → p.102.

		1969 Gay men battle police on streets of New York City → p.65.	
		Native Americans occupy Alcatraz → p.795.	
		1970 Six students shot dead during anti-war demonstrations at Kent State University, Ohio, and Jackson State, Mississippi.	
		1970–72 As US involvement in Vietnam draws to an end, President Nixon illegally authorises bombing of Cambodia and Laos.	
		1972 Break-in at Democrat headquarters in Watergate building linked to Richard Nixon's re-election organisation, *CREEP*.	1972 Francis Ford Coppola's *The Godfather* opens.
		1974 President Nixon is obliged to become the first president ever to resign.	1974 Symbionese Liberation Army kidnap Patty Hearst; demand that food be distributed among the poor of San Francisco → p.809.
1975			1977 George Lucas produces *Star Wars*.
			John Travolta stars in *Saturday Night Fever*.
			Elvis dies in Graceland → p.401.
			Roots attracts nightly TV audience of 80 million.
		1978 Gay Supervisor Harvey Milk and Mayor George Moscone shot in San Francisco → p.795–96.	
		1979 Nuclear leak at Three Mile Island in Pennsylvania.	1979 Sugarhill Gang release *Rappers' Delight*.
		1980 Continuing detention of US hostages in Iran scuppers President Carter's chances of re-election and paves way for Ronald Reagan.	
		1983 US Marines land in Grenada.	1982 Alice Walker publishes *The Color Purple*.
	1983 Development of Star Wars space-defence programme announced → p.601.	1984 Democrats adopt Geraldine Ferraro as first female candidate for US vice-president.	Release of Michael Jackson's *Thriller* video spurs growth of MTV.
			1984 Bruce Springsteen records *Born In The USA*.
	1986 Space shuttle *Challenger* explodes on take-off.		Arnold Schwarzenegger is the *Terminator*.
			Madonna's *Like A Virgin* hits number 1.

		1986 US Air Force bombs Libya. Irangate scandal reveals that Ollie North set up arms-for-hostages deals with the Iranians.	
		1987 "The Quilt" spread on the Mall in Washington DC as memorial to AIDS fatalities → p.797.	1987 God threatens to call Oral Roberts home → p.542.
		1988 Early campaign successes make Jesse Jackson the first-ever black front-runner for the presidency.	
		1989 US troops blast Noriega out of Panama with rock'n'roll.	
		1990 Abortion declared a capital crime in Utah → p.703.	1990 Donald Trump's Taj Mahal casino opens in Atlantic City → p.136.
			Success of Fox TV's *Simpsons* dents domination of network TV by the Big Three – ABC, CBS and NBC.
		1991 US Army leads allied forces in Operation Desert Storm.	1991 Concerted campaign to censor Two Live Crew's rap lyrics and Robert Mapplethorpe's photography → pp.228 and 296.

BOOKS

It would be futile to attempt to provide a comprehensive overview of American literature in the limited space available. The following bibliography is, therefore, a personal selection of those books which proved most useful or enjoyable during the preparation of this guide.

HISTORY AND SOCIETY

James Baldwin, *No Name On The Street*, *The Fire Next Time*, *Evidence Of Things Not Seen*, and many others (Laurel). The most brilliant prose stylist of twentieth-century America. Stunningly incisive accounts of the black experience in the cities of the USA, although Baldwin was such a powerful polemicist that he was occasionally swept away by his own rhetoric.

John W Blassingame, *Black New Orleans 1860–1880* (Phoenix). Comprehensive and impressively detailed history of urban blacks during Reconstruction.

Hugh Brogan, *Penguin History of the USA* (Penguin). Good, up-to-date and very complete history of the United States.

Dee Brown, *Bury My Heart At Wounded Knee*. Twenty years on from its first publication, this remains the best narrative of the impact of white settlement and expansion on Native Americans across the continent.

Peter Carroll and David Noble, *The Free and the Unfree: A New History of the USA* (Penguin). A good interpretive history of American political development, focusing on the wide gap between those who hold power and those who are disadvantaged on grounds of race, sex or class.

Gavan Daws, *Shoal of Time* (University of Hawaii Press). A somewhat long, dry read, but still the most comprehensive history of Hawaii.

Frederick Douglass et al, *The Classic Slave Narratives* (Mentor, US). Compilation of ex-slaves' autobiographies, ranging from Olaudah Equiano's kidnapping in Africa and global wanderings to Frederick Douglass' eloquent denunciation of slavery. Includes Harriet Jacobs' story of her escape from Edenton, North Carolina – see p.349.

Michael Kioni Dudley, *A Hawaiian Nation* (Na Kane O Ka Malo). Immensely readable, if short, two-volume account of Hawaiian history and theology, which culminates in the well-argued *Call For Hawaiian Sovereignty*.

Frances Fitzgerald *Cities on a Hill* (Picador). Intelligent, sympathetic exploration of four of the odder corners of American culture, including San Francisco's gay Castro district and the Rajneeshi community in eastern Oregon – see p.861.

U S Grant, *Personal Memoirs* (Da Capo, US). Encouraged by Mark Twain, the Union general and subsequent president wrote his autobiography just before his death, in a (successful) bid to recoup his horrendous debts. At first the book feels oddly downbeat, but the man's down-to-earth modesty grows on you.

James R Grossman, *Land of Hope* (University of Chicago). Scholarly yet moving account of the exodus of Southern blacks to northern cities, specifically Chicago, during the early twentieth century. Though it focuses on the broader social and economic issues, it also manages to bring to life the individual stories involved.

Frederick Hoxie (ed), *Indians in American History* (Harlan Davidson). Eye-opening collection of essays focusing on the role of Native Americans in US history, and presenting them as active and aware (if hopelessly out-gunned) players rather than passive victims. Filled with illustrations and extensive quotes from journals and contemporary accounts of Native Americans from across the US.

J B Jackson, *American Space* (W W Norton). Engagingly written work which traces the transition of America from a rural to an urban and industrialised nation in the crucial decade immediately after the Civil War.

Charles Jencks, *The New Moderns* (Academy Editions). Occasionally impenetrable, always opinionated academic study of neo-modernist architecture as designed by Philip Johnson, Peter Eisenman and Richard Meier. Interviews and lots of glossy photographs lighten the tone.

Roger G Kennedy, *Rediscovering America* (Houghton Mifflin). Collected essays by one of America's most readable historians, looking behind the gloss of conventional tellings to reveal something of the real story of how America came to be.

Meriwether Lewis and William Clark, *The Original Journals of the Lewis and Clark Expedition, 1804–1806* (Dodd, Mead and Co., New York, o/p). Eight volumes of meticulous jottings by the Northwest's first inland explorers, scrupulously following President Jefferson's orders to record every detail of flora, fauna and native inhabitant.

James M McPherson, *Battle Cry Of Freedom* (Penguin). Extremely readable history of the Civil War which integrates and explains the complex social, economic, political and military factors into one concise volume. Highly recommended.

Stephen Singular, *Talked To Death* (Berkley, US). Gripping investigation into the death of Denver DJ Alan Berg and his neo-Nazi killers; the basis of Oliver Stone's movie *Talk Radio* – see p.641.

Hunter S Thompson, *The Great Shark Hunt* (Picador). The most accessible and varied collection of the maverick Dr Gonzo's journalistic rantings on contemporary American life and politics. Spiced up by tales of his own anarchic love of good times, guns and gambling.

Mark Twain, *Roughing It, Life on the Mississippi*, and many others (Penguin Classics, etc). Mark Twain was by far the funniest and most vivid chronicler of nineteenth-century America. *Roughing It*, which covers his early wanderings across the continent, all the way to Hawaii, is absolutely compelling.

Geoffrey C Ward, with Ric and Ken Burns, *The Civil War* (Bodley Head). Marvellous illustrated history of the Civil War, designed to accompany the recent TV series and using hundreds of the same photographs.

Juan Williams, *Eyes On The Prize* (Harrap). Informative and detailed accompaniment to the excellent TV series, covering the Civil Rights years from the early Fifties up to 1966, with lots of rare and some very familiar photos.

BIOGRAPHY AND ORAL HISTORY

Maya Angelou, *I Know Why The Caged Bird Sings* (Virago). First volume of an autobiographical sequence which provides an ultimately uplifting account of how a black girl transcended her traumatic childhood in 1930s Arkansas.

William F Cody, *The Life Of Hon William F Cody, Known As Buffalo Bill* (University of Nebraska Press). Larger than life autobiography of one of the great characters of the Wild West. Particularly treasurable for the moment when he refers to himself more formally as "Bison William".

Henry Hampton and Steve Fayer, *Voices of Freedom* (Bantam). Hugely impressive oral history of the Civil Rights movement, heavily drawn from the TV series.

Langston Hughes, *The Big Sea* (Pluto). Autobiography of one of the major lights of the Harlem Renaissance. Occasionally descends into namedropping, but at its best sensitively evokes the tensions of an era when black artists came into their own, at the expense of becoming the latest fashion for wealthy whites. Hughes' homosexuality isn't covered, which says a lot about the political ambivalence of the times.

Joyce Johnson, *Minor Characters* (Picador). Johnson, Jack Kerouac's girlfriend and "muse", tells her own story and those of the other women in the 1950s East Village scene, revealing the stiflingly reactionary male elitism of the Beats.

Malcolm X, with Alex Haley, *The Autobiography of Malcolm X* (Penguin). Searingly honest and moving account of a progress from street hoodlum to political leadership. Written on the hoof over a period of years, it traces the development of Malcolm X's thought before, during and after his split from the Nation of Islam. The conclusion, when he talks about his impending assassination, is painful in the extreme.

Marion Meade, *What Fresh Hell is This?* (Mandarin). Lively biography of darkly witty writer Dorothy Parker. Successfully evokes the tensions and excitement of the literary New York of the 1920s and 30s, in particular the notorious "Round Table".

Muhammad Ali, *The Greatest* (o/p but widely available). Powerful and entertaining autobiography of the Louisville boy who grew up to become world heavyweight boxing champion. The most memorable parts deal with his fight against the Vietnam draft and the subsequent stripping away of his world championship status.

Tony Parker, *A Place Called Bird* (Pan). Fascinating oral history based on interviews with the inhabitants of a tiny town in the very centre of Kansas, the heartland of the Midwest.

Ishbel Ross, *Rebel Rose* (Mockingbird). Evocative Rebel-yelling biography of Rose Greenhow, glamorous Washington socialite and remarkably brave Confederate spy. Works equally well as an exciting tale of political espionage and an impeccably detailed historical document.

Quinta Scott and Susan Croce Kelly, *Route 66* (University of Oklahoma Press). Moving oral histories and monochrome photographs trace the life span of the now abandoned 2000-mile highway immortalised in film, novels and song.

Joanna L Stratton, *Pioneer Women* (Simon and Schuster). Original memoirs by women – mothers, teachers, homesteaders and circuit riders – who ventured across the Plains from 1854 to 1890. Lively, superbly detailed accounts, with chapters on journeys, homebuilding, daily domestic life, the church, the cowtown, temperance and suffrage.

Studs Terkel, *American Dreams Lost and Found* (Grafton). Interviews with ordinary American citizens. As illuminating a guide to US life as you could hope for.

Frank Waters, *Book Of The Hopi* (Penguin, US). Extraordinary insight into the traditions and beliefs of the Hopi, prepared through years of interviews and approved by tribal elders.

ENTERTAINMENT AND CULTURE

Kenneth Anger, *Hollywood Babylon* (Arrow). A vicious yet high-spirited romp through Tinseltown's greatest scandals, amply illustrated with gory and repulsive photographs, and always inclined to bend the facts for the sake of a good story. A seldom-seen second volume covers more recent times, but was hurriedly put together and shoddily researched.

Thomas A Bass, *The Newtonian Casino* (Penguin). Daydreaming gamblers will love this account of an attempt to beat the casinos in Las Vegas by a bunch of Californian college dropouts with computers hidden in their shoes.

Thomas Boswell, *How Life Imitates The World Series and Time Begins On Opening Day* (Sportspages). Boswell elevates baseball into something higher than a mere sport. Full of perceptive insights and amusing anecdotes.

Peter Guralnick, *Sweet Soul Music* (Penguin). A history of southern rhythm'n'blues, packed with obsessive detail on all the great names – Solomon Burke, Otis Redding, James Brown.

Charlotte Greig, *Will You Still Love Me Tomorrow?* (Virago). Enthusiastic feminist appraisal of (predominantly American) girl groups from the Fifties (the Chantels and the Crystals) through to contemporary rap stars like Salt'n'Pepa. Lots of photos and personal recollections make it a great read.

Gerri Hershey, *Nowhere To Run: The History of Soul Music* (Pan). Definitive rundown on the evolution of soul music from the gospel heyday of the Forties through the Memphis, Motown and Philly scenes to the sounds of the early Eighties. Strong on social commentary and political background and studded with anecdotes and interviews.

Nicky Horne, *The Complete American Football Book* (Robson). Very basic, flick-through high-colour read for newcomers to the sport.

Bill Malone, *Country Music, USA: A Fifty Year History* (University of Texas). An academic but thoroughly engrossing study of the roots and development of country music up to 1968.

Greil Marcus, *Mystery Train* (Penguin). Intelligent and absorbing overview of American popular music, from Robert Johnson to Elvis Presley and Randy Newman.

Robert Palmer, *Deep Blues* (Papermac). Readable history of the development and personalities of the Delta Blues.

Randall Reise, *Nashville Babylon*. Thrashes the squeaky clean image of the country music scene. Cocaine, whiskey, infidelity, murder, rape, and other skeletons are dug up from the cupboards of some of the most unlikely characters.

John Williams, *Into The Badlands* (Paladin). Williams' interviews with a batch of America's very best crime writers build a picture of the underbelly of US society from the Montana mountainsides of James Crumley to the mean streets of Elmore Leonard's Detroit. He lapses into sexism, however, when dealing with Chicago's Sara Paretsky, who "is learning as she goes along".

Edmund Wilson, *Patriotic Gore* (Hogarth Press). Fascinating eight-hundred-page survey of the literature of the American Civil War, which in its own right serves as an immensely readable narrative of the conflict.

TRAVEL WRITING

Edward Abbey, *The Journey Home* (Plume). Hilarious accounts of whitewater rafting and desert hiking trips alternate with essays, by the man who inspired and helped the radical environmentalist movement Earth First!. All of Abbey's many books, especially *Desert Solitaire*, a journal of time spent as a ranger in Arches National Park, make great travelling companions.

James Agee and Walker Evans, *Let Us Now Praise Famous Men* (Picador). A deeply personal but also richly evocative journal of travels through the rural lands of the Depression-era Deep South, complemented by Evans' powerful photographs.

Stephen Brook, *New York Days, New York Nights* (Picador). An Englishman's drily witty impressions of the Big Apple, with chapters on every aspect of the place from flotation chambers to Jewish restaurants. Brook's *Honky Tonk Gelato* (also in Picador) treats Texas in a similar, if sometimes patronising, vein.

Bill Bryson, *The Lost Continent* (Sphere). Using his boyhood home of Des Moines in Iowa as a benchmark, the author travels the length and breadth of America to find the perfect small town. At times hilarious but marred by some very smug, self-indulgent comments.

Robert L Casey, *Journey to the High Southwest* (Globe Pequot, US only). Practical and personal description of exploring the canyon country and Anasazi sites of the Southwest.

J Hector St-John de Crèvecoeur, *Letters from an American Farmer and Sketches of Eighteenth-Century America* (Penguin). First published in 1782, a remarkable account of the complexities of Revolutionary America.

Ian Frazier, *Great Plains* (Faber). An immaculately researched and well-written travelogue containing a wealth of information on the people of the American prairielands from Native Americans to the soldiers who staff the region's many nuclear installations.

Bill Kaysing, *Great Hot Springs of the West* (Capra Press). If you like the idea of soaking your bones in pools of naturally hot water in some of America's most beautiful locales, this fact-packed guidebook will point you in the right direction.

Roger G Kennedy, *Smithsonian Guides to Historic America* (Stewart Tabori & Chang). Profusely illustrated series of twelve guidebooks, treating specific US regions from a conventional but deeply informed historical standpoint, with a strong emphasis on architecture.

Jack Kerouac, *On The Road* (Penguin). Definitive account of transcontinental Beatnik wanderings which now reads as a curiously dated period piece. Not as incoherent as you might expect.

James A MacMahon (ed), *Audobon Society Nature Guides* (Alfred A Knopf). Attractively produced, fully illustrated and easy to use guides to the flora and fauna of seven different US regional ecosystems, covering the entire country from coast to coast and from grasslands to glaciers.

Virginia and Lee McAlester, *A Field Guide to American Houses* (Knopf). Well illustrated and engagingly readable guide to America's rich variety of domestic architecture, from pre-colonial to post-modern.

John McPhee, *Encounters with the Arch Druid* (Farrar, Straus and Giroux). In three interlinked narratives, environmental activist and Friends of the Earth founder David Brower confronts developers, miners and dam builders, while trying to protect three different American wilderness areas – the Atlantic shoreline, the Grand Canyon, and the Cascades of the Pacific Northwest.

William Least Heat Moon, *Blue Highways* (Picador). Account of a mammoth loop tour of the US by backroads, in which the author interviews ordinary people in ordinary places. A good overview of rural America, with lots of interesting details on Native Americans.

Jonathan Raban, *Old Glory* (Picador). A somewhat pompous though always interesting account of Raban's journey on a small craft down the Mississippi River from the headwaters in Minnesota to the bayous of Louisiana.

Bernard A Weisberger (ed), *The WPA Guide to America*. Prepared during the New Deal as part of a make-work programme for writers, these guides paint a fairly comprehensive portrait of 1930s and earlier America. Also available are state by state guides, most of them out of print but easily found in US libraries and secondhand bookshops.

Edmund White, *States of Desire: Travels in Gay America* (Picador). A revealing account of life in gay communities across the country, focusing heavily on San Francisco and New York.

FICTION

Nelson Algren, *A Walk on the Wild Side* (Penguin). Bleak novel charting the decline of a youth who flees his Tex-Mex border town after raping a girl and embarks upon a hobo life, ending up in the sleazy red light district of New Orleans.

Paul Auster, *New York Trilogy* (Faber). Three Borgesian investigations into the mystery and madness of contemporary New York. Using the conventions of the detective novel, Auster unfolds a disturbed and disturbing picture of the city.

James Lee Burke, *Black Cherry Blues* (Mysterious Press). Cajun cop Dave Robicheaux sets out to expose alliances between government and organised crime in the beautiful environs of Louisiana and Montana. A detective book that has it all.

George Washington Cable, *The Grandissimes* (Penguin Classics). Romantic saga of Creole family feuds, written at the turn of the century but set during the Louisiana Purchase. Superb evocation of steamy Louisiana, elite Creole lifestyle and the resistance of New Orleans to its Americanisation. Apparently shocking at the time for its sympathetic portrayal of blacks.

Willa Cather, *Death Comes for the Archbishop* (Virago). Melodramatic title for a sober but very emotive fictionalised biography of the first archbishop of Santa Fe. *The Professor's House* (Vintage) has a similar feel for the history of the Southwest, reaching back to the Anasazi.

Michael Chabon, *The Mysteries of Pittsburgh* (Serpent). A just-graduated gangster's son learns about life during a sweltering Pittsburgh summer.

Kate Chopin, *The Awakening* (The Womens Press). Subversive story of a bourgeois married woman whose fight for independence ends in tragedy. Swampy turn-of-the-century Louisiana is portrayed as both a sensual hotbed for her sexual awakening and as her eventual nemesis.

James Crumley, *The Wrong Case* (Vintage US). The lack of an intricate plot is more than compensated for by accounts of Montana scenery and the hapless detective Milo Milodragonovic, a man with a drink problem and a knack for doing things the hard way. An enjoyable, easy read.

Ivan Doig, *English Creek* (Penguin US). The tribulations of the McCaskill family in the hard times of Thirties Montana, illuminated in lovely prose which at times moves a little slowly. The heir to Guthrie's crown (see below).

John Dos Passos, *USA* (Penguin). Hugely ambitious novel (originally a trilogy) which grapples with the US in the early decades of this century from every possible angle. Gripping human stories with a strong political and historical perspective.

Louise Erdrich, *The Beet Queen* (Pan). Slightly offbeat tale of passion and obsession amongst poor white North Dakota folk – particularly women – set against the backdrop of an economy and culture changing with the introduction of sugar beet as a crop in the 1940s. Erdrich's *Love Medicine* (Futura) describes two Native American families on a North Dakota reservation, the strong women who hold them together, and the tensions between tradition and "progress".

William Faulkner, *The Reivers* (Penguin). The last and most humorous work of this celebrated highbrow southern author. *The Sound and the Fury*, a fascinating study of prejudice, set like most of his books in the fictional Yoknatapawpha County in Mississippi, is a much more difficult read.

A B Guthrie Jr, *Big Sky* (Time Life US). When first published in the Thirties it shattered the credibility of the mythical west peddled by Hollywood. Realistic historical fiction at its very best, following desperate mountain man and fugitive Boone Caudill whose idyllic life in Montana was ended by the arrival of white settlers.

Thomas Harris, *The Silence of the Lambs* (St Martins). Bleak chronicle of fin-de-siècle America featuring Hannibal the Cannibal, one of fiction's most terrifying serial killers, and Clarice Starling, trainee FBI agent who establishes a relationship with him in order to track down a killer who skins his female victims.

George V Higgins, *Penance for Jerry Kennedy* (Abacus). Crime thriller written almost entirely in the dialogue of Boston lowlifes and crooked lawmen.

Tony Hillerman, *The Dark Wind* and many others (Sphere). The adventures of Jim Chee of the Navajo Tribal Police on the reservations of northern Arizona, forever dabbling in dark and mysterious forces churned up from the Anasazi past.

Chester Himes, *Cotton Comes to Harlem, Blind Man with a Pistol*, and many others (Allison & Busby). Action-packed and uproariously violent novels set in New York's Harlem, starring the much-feared detectives Coffin Ed Johnson and Grave Digger Jones.

Zora Neale Hurston, *Spunk* (Camden). Short stories celebrating black culture and experience from around the country, by a writer from Florida who became one of the bright stars of the Harlem cultural renaissance in the 1920s.

Garrison Keillor, *Lake Wobegon Days* (Faber). Wry, witty tales about a mythical Minnesota small town. Pokes fun at the rural Midwest with an affectionate finger.

Harper Lee, *To Kill A Mockingbird* (Pan). Classic tale of racial conflict and society's view of an outsider, Boo Radley, as seen through the eyes of children.

Elmore Leonard, *Freaky Deaky* (Penguin). One of the funniest of Leonard's tough, brutal thrillers. Set in Detroit, it follows two former Sixties radicals who turn to crime.

Jack London, *The Call of the Wild and Other Stories* (Penguin). London's short story about a tame dog discovering the ways of the wilderness while forced to pull sleds across the snow and ice of Alaska's Klondike made him into the world's best-selling author almost overnight.

Norman MacLean, *A River Runs Through It* (University of Chicago). Unputdownable – the best ever novel about fly-fishing, set in beautiful Montana lake country.

Armistead Maupin, *Tales Of The City* (Black Swan). Long-running saga comprised of sympathetic and entertaining human tales of life in San Francisco, that also work surprisingly well as suspenseful stand-alone novels. The fact that most of the characters are gay has meant that over the years the series has become a chronicle of the impact of AIDS on the city.

Carson McCullers, *Member of the Wedding* (Penguin). McCullers is unrivalled in her sensitive treatment of misfits, in this case the attitude of a small southern community to a deaf mute.

Jay McInerney, *Bright Lights, Big City* (Flamingo). Mid-Eighties cult book, with noticeable undertones of Salinger's *Catcher in the Rye*, which follows a struggling New York yuppie from one cocaine-sozzled nightclub to another.

Herman Melville, *Moby Dick* (Penguin and others). Compendious and compelling account of nineteenth-century whaling, packed with details on American life from New England to the Pacific.

Margaret Mitchell, *Gone With The Wind* (Pan). Worth a read even if you know the lines of Scarlett and Rhett off by heart.

Toni Morrison, *Beloved* (Picador). Exquisitely written ghost story by one of America's most brilliant contemporary novelists, tracing the painful lives of a group of freed slaves after Reconstruction, and the obsession a mother develops after murdering her baby daughter to spare her a life of slavery.

Flannery O'Connor, *A Good Man is Hard to Find* (Women's Press). Short stories, featuring strong, obsessive characters, that explore religious tensions and racial conflicts in the Deep South.

Grace Paley, *The Little Disturbances of Man* (Virago) Shrewd love-hate stories set in the immigrant Jewish communities of New York.

Marge Piercey, *Braided Lives* (Penguin). Story of two friends who met at college and never let go, with much good detail on Fifties Detroit and New York.

Anne Rice, *Interview with the Vampire* (Futura). One of a series of sensual, chilling vampire novels set in Louisiana.

Paul Rudnick, *Social Disease* (Penguin). Extremely funny, irreverent, wicked and, at times, slapstick send-up of Manhattan night-owls.

J D Salinger, *The Catcher in the Rye* (Penguin). Brilliant novel of adolescence, tracing Holden Caulfield's sardonic journey through the streets of New York.

John Steinbeck *The Grapes of Wrath* (Pan). The classic account of a migrant family forsaking the Midwest for the Promised Land. Steinbeck's light-hearted but crisply observed novella *Cannery Row* (Pan) captures daily life on the pre-war Monterey waterfront, and the epic *East of Eden* (Pan) updates and re-sets the Bible in the Salinas Valley and details three generations of familial feuding.

Peter Taylor, *Summons To Memphis* (Penguin). Warm tale of a wealthy Tennessee family who make a downmarket move from Nashville to Memphis during the Thirties.

John Kennedy Toole, *A Confederacy of Dunces* (Penguin). Anarchic black tragicomedy in which the pompous and repulsive antihero Ignatius O Reilly wreaks havoc through an insalubrious and surreal New Orleans.

Andrew Vachss, *Flood* (Pan). Vachss' vigilante-like detective operates among New York's child-molesters, porno merchants and sex offenders in some of the most violent, hard-hitting and disturbing crime fiction on the market.

Alice Walker, *In Love and Trouble* (The Women's Press). Moving and powerful stories of black women in the South. *The Color Purple* is far more sensitive and less glamorous than you might expect from Spielberg's movie.

Eudora Welty, *The Ponder Heart* (Virago) Quirky, humorous evocation of life in a backwater Mississippi town. Her most critically acclaimed work, *The Optimist's Daughter*, explores the tensions between a judge's daughter and her stepmother.

Tom Wolfe, *The Bonfire of the Vanities* (Picador). Sherman McCoy is a Wall Street dealer who finds he can't live on $1 milion a year; his downfall begins when he inadvertently drives into the Bronx. It's no literary masterpiece and the black characters are very unconvincing, but it remains a reasonable revelation of New York in the late Eighties.

Richard Wright, *Native Son* (Penguin). A harrowing story about Bigger Thomas, a black chauffeur who accidently kills his employer's daughter. The story develops his relationship with his lawyer, the closest he has ever come to being on an equal footing with a white.

BIOGRAPHIES

The following are some of the many personalities from American history whose names recur throughout this book. You can find detailed page references for all of them in the main index, which begins on p.948.

Susan B Anthony (1820–1906). Pioneer suffragette and president of the US suffragist society from 1892 to 1900, Anthony began her campaigning career in the temperance movement. She was also a committed abolitionist, published the New York liberal paper *The Revolution* (1868–70), and advocated equal pay for women, as well as donning bloomers to protest against the constrictive nature of women's clothing.

Louis Armstrong (1900–1971). New Orleans-based jazz trumpeter, known as Satchmo (from "satchel mouth"). Credited with devising the scat style of improvisational singing, and for his individualistic style which foregrounded the solo performance above that of the band. Well known for his humour and affability, Armstrong also appeared in a number of Hollywood films.

Benedict Arnold (1741–1801). Revolutionary commander who shifted his allegiance to the British in 1779, but soon lost popularity with loyalists for leaving his British contact, Major John Andre, to be captured and hanged as a spy.

Chuck Berry (born 1926). Rock'n'roll pioneer born in (*Johnny B*) Goode Street, St Louis. Consummate lyricist, red-hot guitarist, and sharp businessman.

Billy the Kid (1859–81). The subject of innumerable Wild-West legends, former busboy William Bonney made his name in the Lincoln County Wars in New Mexico. His brief and bloody career ended at the hands of Pat Garrett.

Daniel Boone (1735–1820). Legendary hunter, trapper and explorer. One of the first whites to cross the Appalachians and stake out Kentucky for settlement.

John Brown (1800–59). Fervent white abolitionist who, as part of a grand plan to set up a free state for escaped slaves, seized the US Armory at Harpers Ferry. After a short battle, Brown was captured, tried and hanged for treason.

Calamity Jane (1852–1903). Bawdy frontierswoman, cook, dancer, prostitute and camp follower, who in 1876 took up as bullwhacker for the gold rush camps in South Dakota. "Calam" travelled with Wild West shows but was fired for boozing and brawling.

Al Capone (1899–1947). Bootlegger and gangster who controlled the Chicago underworld during the 1920s, and later died in Florida of syphilis.

Andrew Carnegie (1835–1919). Scots-born industrialist and philanthropist, responsible for major innovations in the steel industry. By the close of the nineteenth century, when US steel production outdid that in Britain, most of it came from Carnegie's "vertically integrated" company – which owned the coal fields and the ships and railroads for transportation of the supplies to the mills.

Kit Carson (1809–68). Carson, who moved to Taos in 1826 and became a guide on the Santa Fe Trail and "mountain man", was later instrumental in rounding up the Navajo from Canyon de Chelly.

William "Buffalo Bill" Cody (1846–1917). Pony Express rider and Indian scout immortalised by the dime novels of Ned Buntline. His Wild West show toured all over the world.

Francisco Vázquez de Coronado (1510–1554). Spanish explorer who travelled through the Southwest as far as Kansas in search of cities of gold. When he eventually threw in the towel in 1542 and returned to Mexico, he faced a series of indictments for his lack of success.

Crazy Horse Ta-Sunko-Witko (1842?–1877). Oglala Sioux leader, and one of the most able and determined Native American warriors. Prominent in the Fetterman Massacre, Battle of the Rosebud and Custer's Last Stand. Murdered at Fort Robinson, Nebraska.

Davy Crockett (1786–1836). Frontiersman, Indian fighter and Tennessee politician, who perished at the Alamo with all the other American volunteers. Popularly represented as a backwoods boy in a raccoon hat, with no education but the gift of the gab, Crockett was, in fact, less unconventional than his legend suggests.

George Armstrong Custer (1839–76). Legendary US Cavalry general whose first big mistake – leading over two hundred troops into an ambush at Little Bighorn – was his last.

John Dillinger (1902–34). Bankrobber whose criminal activities earned him the title of Public Enemy Number One. After being set up by the legendary "Lady in Red", Dillinger was killed by FBI agents outside a Chicago movie theatre.

Walt Disney (1901–66). Inventor of Mickey Mouse, Donald Duck and Disneyland, Disney was also Hollywood's Last Tycoon, singlehandedly controlling a vast media and entertainment empire.

Frederick Douglass (1817?–95). Escaped slave who rose to prominence as a writer and orator in the abolitionist movement.

W E B Du Bois, (1868–1963). Black intellectual and civil rights activist best known for his debates with Booker T Washington (see below) in the early part of this century, and his role in forming the National Association for the Advancement of Coloured People. A long-time campaigner for the independence of African colonies, he joined the Communist Party in 1961 and emigrated to Ghana where he renounced his US citizenship.

Bob Dylan (born 1941). North-country Minnesota boy who redefined himself first as Woody-Guthrie-style folkie and later as enigmatic rock star. The endearing elliptical games of his youth have long since grown wearisome in a man of 50, but he can still write songs to equal his best.

Amelia Earheart (1897–1937). Pioneer aviatrix, the first woman to fly solo across the Atlantic (in 1932), and the first person ever to fly the perilous route from Hawaii to California (1935). Both she and her navigator vanished without trace on an attempted round-the-world flight, and were last contacted just near the international date line.

Thomas Edison (1847–1931). Mercurial inventor and entrepreneur who developed the light bulb, motion pictures and phonograph records. He also founded General Electric, still one of the largest US corporations.

Thomas Stearns Eliot (1888–1965). Born beside the Mississippi in St Louis, Eliot reversed the usual American pattern and moved east, first to Harvard and then England, where he was awarded the Nobel Prize for Literature for a body of poetry including *The Wasteland* and *The Four Quartets*.

Henry Ford (1863–1947). Michigan farmer's son and industrial genius who pioneered assembly-line production in his car factories. A vehement right-winger, particularly on trade union and racial issues.

Benjamin Franklin (1706–90). Printer, inventor, diplomat and politician, responsible amongst other things for publishing *Poor Richard's Almanac* (a litany of mottos advocating prudence and honesty), setting up America's first public library, the invention of bifocal glasses and early experiments with electricity. Franklin also helped draft the Declaration of Independence, and went to France to seek aid for the revolutionary cause.

Geronimo (1829–1909). Brilliant Chiricahua Apache leader who battled the US Army in Arizona and New Mexico throughout the 1880s. Despite US promises, after surrendering he and his people were deported to Florida.

Ulysses Simpson Grant (1822–85). At the start of the 1860s, the 38-year-old Ulysses Grant was finding it difficult to hold down a part-time job in his brother's saddle shop; within ten years he had led the Union armies to victory in the Civil War, and become president of the US.

William Randolph Hearst (1863–1951). Publishing magnate and role model for *Citizen Kane*, whose inflammatory "yellow journalism" kindled public support for the Spanish-America War.

Billie Holiday (1915–59). Definitive song stylist – not quite blues, not quite jazz – who made her greatest recordings with Lester Young and Duke Ellington.

Buddy Holly (1936–59). Bespectacled kid from Lubbock, Texas, who died at 22 but was the first and the greatest of rock's singer-songwriters.

Henry Hudson (1565–1611). English explorer whose expedition for the Dutch East India Company to find a route from Europe to Asia through the Arctic led to the discovery of the Hudson River in 1609 – which he mistakenly believed would lead to the Pacific – and formed the basis for Dutch colonisation in the New World.

Howard Hughes (1905–76). Business magnate and Hollywood film producer (*Hell's Angels*, 1930; *Scarface*, 1932), who became increasingly eccentric after an aircraft crash in 1946. Twenty years later, he sold his majority holding in *TWA* for $500,000,000 and lived from then on in complete seclusion in sealed-off hotel suites.

Andrew Jackson (1767–1845). Military general who was a major light in the Revolutionary War. His defeat of the British in New Orleans in 1815 led to huge popular support, and he was elected seventh US president (Democrat) in 1829. The first president from west of the Appalachians, Jackson had much grass-roots support in Tennessee, and his election is seen as the first truly democratic choice in the nation's history.

Rev Jesse Jackson (born 1941). Black religious and political leader whose Rainbow Coalition has come to represent the most viable progressive alternative to the centrist Democratic Party.

Thomas Jefferson (1743–1838). Author of the Declaration of Independence, third US president, and slave-owner, Jefferson was a strong advocate of freedom of the press and of religion, as well as being an accomplished architect.

Lyndon Baines Johnson (1908–73). Brash Texan Democrat sworn in as president two hours after John Kennedy's assassination in 1963. Johnson pushed through liberal civil rights and social welfare bills, but his failure to deal with the increasingly horrific mess of Vietnam left him obliged not to seek re-election in 1968.

Robert Johnson (1911?–38). Seminal Delta bluesman, whose songs were imbued with such a brooding aura that he was rumoured to have sold his soul to the Devil. The clearest, earliest forerunner of rock'n'roll.

Kamehameha the Great (1760?–1819). The first man to unite the Hawaiian islands – by terror, force of personality, and shrewd exploitation of European expertise.

Helen Keller (1880–1968). Despite being struck blind and deaf by scarlet fever as an infant, Keller's writings and activism made her an inspirational early leader in the movement for equal rights for disabled people.

John Fitzgerald Kennedy (1917–63). When elected in 1960, Kennedy was the youngest ever, and the first Catholic, president. His liberal domestic policies (known as "new frontier" programmes) and success in securing the nuclear test ban treaty with the USSR and Britain won him huge popularity, as did his superficially glamorous life with wife Jackie. His assassination in Dallas, on November 22 1963, might be said to mark the beginning of a long period of disillusionment and hopelessness in the American psyche.

Dr Martin Luther King Jr (1929–68). Baptist minister who was the main black spokesperson during the Civil Rights years, and was awarded the Nobel Peace Prize after his "I have a dream" speech. Remembered by a public holiday in most states, and a street name in most major cities.

General Marie Joseph Paul Yves Roch Gilbert du Motier Lafayette (1757–1834). French aristocrat, known as "the hero of two worlds" for supporting the Americans in the Revolutionary War, who went on to fight with the revolutionary bourgeoisie in France. A great friend of George Washington, Lafayette advocated religious tolerance and the abolition of slavery.

Robert Edward Lee (1807–70). Confederate Civil War general, considered one of the outstanding military strategists of all time. Enjoyed early success by whipping the vastly superior Union forces under the incompetent McClellan, but crashed to defeat at Gettysburg.

Meriwether Lewis (1774–1809) and **William Clark** (1770–1838). Jointly famed as leaders of the first exploratory expedition west from the Mississippi to the Pacific in 1804–1805. Lewis' journals and Clark's drawings are invaluable documents of pre-conquest western US.

Abraham Lincoln (1809–65). To northerners at least, the most revered of all US presidents. The son of a Kentucky backwoodsman, he taught himself law and later entered Illinois politics, beating better-known opponents for the 1860 Democratic presidential nomination. He led the Union through the Civil War, but was shot five days after the Confederate surrender.

Charles Lindbergh (1902–74). In 1927, Lindbergh became the first person to complete a solo flight across the Atlantic, in the *Spirit of St Louis*, named for his home town. Tickertape parades feted him across the continent, and the "Lindy Hop" was named for him. The kidnapping and murder of his infant son was one of the most notorious crimes of the Thirties, but his pronounced Nazi sympathies progressively lost him public support.

Huey Long (1893–1935). Flamboyant, populist governor of Louisiana known as the "Kingfish". His radical social welfare policies and tax reforms boosted the morale of poor rural whites during the Depression, and as senator, in the last three years of his life, he claimed his "Share the Wealth" programme would make "every man a king". However, his corrupt and intimidating style of government made him plenty of enemies, and he was eventually assassinated in still-mysterious circumstances in Baton Rouge.

Joe Louis (1914–81). Black Detroit heavyweight boxer who took the world championship from Mussolini-sidekick Primo Carnera in 1937 and retained it for twelve years.

Malcolm X (1925–65). Successful burglar who came into contact in prison with the teachings of Elijah Muhammad's Nation of Islam, rose to become its leading minister and spokesperson, and then broke with the organisation after a trip to Mecca and tour of Africa. Malcolm occasionally worked with Dr Martin Luther King Jr during his civil rights campaigns, and for many people his militant approach remains more persuasive than Dr King's.

Joseph McCarthy (1909–57). Republican Senator for Wisconsin, notorious for his hysterical and unproven charges of Communist subversion in high government circles. President Truman called him a "pathological character assassin" and his career was ended when the Senate censured him for unconstitutional behaviour.

J Pierpoint Morgan (1837–1913). The quintessential New York financier, Morgan achieved sufficient wealth to buy out Andrew Carnegie and served as a broker between world governments.

Muhammad Ali (born 1941). Heavyweight boxer who upon winning the world title from Sonny Liston in 1964 announced that he was a member of the Nation of Islam. Within three years his anti-war stance – "no Vietcong ever called me nigger" – had cast him into the wilderness, but eventually America took him to its bosom once more.

Carry Nation (1846–1911). Temperance activist and suffragette whose tendency to take an axe to saloons after storming in, singing hymns and bellowing Biblical insults, won her no popularity with the official temperance movement (although she made lots of money on lecture tours). Frequently imprisoned, she paid her fines from souvenir axe sales.

Richard Nixon (born 1913). From his earliest days as Eisenhower's vice-president – a position obtained with the help of his maudlin "Checkers" speech, about his little puppy dog – Nixon was the man American liberals most loved to hate. That he emerged from the turmoil of 1968 as America's president made a mockery of the idea that the Sixties would turn out to be a progressive decade. The seemingly relentless progress of his latest rehabilitation, following the disgrace of Watergate, has much to do with an enduring and perverse media fondness for him.

Annie Oakley (1860–1926). Performer with Buffalo Bill's Wild West show. Nicknamed "Little Miss Sure Shot", she once shot the cigar from the mouth of Kaiser Wilhelm.

Georgia O'Keeffe (1887–1986). Prolific painter whose stark, brightly coloured abstractions of flowers and the Southwest desert have won her acclaim as one of the greatest modern US artists.

Dolly Parton (born 1946). Country singer, movie star, perennial talk-show guest and part-owner of a theme park.

William Penn (1644–1718). British Quaker, often imprisoned in England for his beliefs. He gradually softened towards other doctrines, and campaigned strongly against any form of persecution, eventually establishing the colony of Pennsylvania as a refuge for religious minorities.

John Wesley Powell (1834–1902). After losing an arm in the Civil War, Powell headed west to lead the first group of white men through the rivers and canyons of the Colorado Plateau.

Elvis Presley (1935–77). Poor white boy from Tupelo, Mississippi, who moved to Memphis and became the first and the greatest white rock'n'roll star. Whether you blame Colonel Tom Parker or Elvis' own enfeebled intellect, within a couple of years he was throwing away his magnificent voice on empty show-tunes, and embarking on the long road to Hamburger Heaven.

Paul Revere (1735–1818). Silversmith and unofficial political leader of the mechanic class in Boston in the period leading up to the Revolutionary War. As principal rider for Boston's Committee of Safety, in April 1775 he made the famed horseback journey from Boston to Concord to warn the rebels that the British were coming; thus started the War of Independence.

John D Rockefeller (1839–1937). Petroleum magnate whose *Standard Oil* company dominated the US and international markets from the 1880s to 1911, when the government dissolved his monopoly. Also a great philanthropist, in his later years he gave away his money – over half a billion dollars.

Franklin Delano Roosevelt (1882–1945). Four-term Democratic president, crippled by polio in 1920, who steered the country through the Depression with the closest the US has ever come to having socialist policies: his "New Deal" provided work for the unemployed and enforced collective bargaining with unions. His wartime leadership was often criticised, especially, with hindsight, his appeasement of Stalin.

Theodore (Teddy) Roosevelt (1858–1919). Explorer, writer, soldier and Republican president from 1901 to 1909. His "square deal" policies, which included "trust busting" and government arbitration in wage disputes, were seen to serve the public interest over Big Business, and he won the Nobel Peace Prize in 1906 for mediating an end to the Russo-Japanese War. In 1912 he founded the Progressive Party and ran (unsuccessfully) for president as an independent, advocating a strong social service state.

Dred Scott (1795?–1858). Black slave who made constitutional history as the plaintiff in a widely publicised but unsuccessful test case, in which he sought his freedom on the grounds that his master had taken him to live in a free state. The ruling effectively allowed slavery in US territories and was a leading factor in the build-up to the Civil War.

William Tecumseh Sherman (1820–91). The Union general who burned Atlanta and boasted about it in his memoirs, and invented the blitzkrieg by laying waste to Georgia. The bane of his later life was to be greeted at all official functions with *Marching through Georgia*, a song he detested. His son, a Jesuit priest, had to be forcibly persuaded from attempting his own march thirty years later.

Frank Sinatra (born 1915). Italian boy from Hoboken, NJ, who made his name thrilling bobby-soxers with New York's Tommy Dorsey Band in the early Forties and has barely let up since. One of the few singers to turn into a decent movie actor.

Sitting Bull Tatanka Iyotake (1834–90). Chief of the Dakota Sioux and leader of the Native American forces at the Battle of Little Bighorn. Pursued by the army, he escaped to Canada but surrendered in 1881. Killed by police in the attempt to suppress the 1890 Ghost Dance movement.

Bruce Springsteen (born 1949). New Jersey singer-songwriter known as "the Boss". His energetic and poignant articulations of white, male, working-class America are often dismissed as machismo; President Reagan missed the point completely in the 1980s and announced his approval of Springsteen's *Born in the USA*, mistaking its ironic blue-collar disillusionment for reactionary blue-eyed patriotism.

Harriet Beecher Stowe (1811–96). Though she had little firsthand experience of the South, Stowe's *Uncle Tom's Cabin* aroused the world in fierce opposition to slavery. Abraham Lincoln greeted her witrh the words "so this is the little lady that made this great big war".

Peter (Petrus) Stuyvesant (1592–1672). Early governor of all Dutch colonies in North America, known as "Peg-leg Pete" for his wooden leg. He arrived in New Amsterdam (now New York) in 1647, doubling the colony's size and population, but was so unpopular, ignoring all appeals for self-government, that in 1664 he was forced to surrender the colony to the British. His farm, the Bowerie, gave the district in New York City its name.

Harriet Tubman (1820–1913). Escaped from slavery in Maryland in 1849 to become the leading abolitionist voice in the pre-Civil War years. Led hundreds of slaves to freedom on the Underground Railway and served as a nurse and spy for Union forces during the war.

Nat Turner (1800–31). Black preacher who led five other Virginia slaves on a murderous rampage, killing over fifty whites, mostly with knives and axes, in a single day. In reaction, whites murdered hundreds of blacks and enacted an even more repressive regime.

Mark Twain (1835–1910). The great American humorist and novelist, whose works provide the most vivid imaginable account of pioneer days across the continent, was also a powerful polemicist for liberal causes, and pioneered white-suit chic long before Tom Wolfe. He pursued his desire to typeset his own books, and break free from the evil machinations of self-important publishers, almost to the point of bankruptcy.

George Wallace (born 1919). Segregationist three-times Alabama governor; received 13 percent of the popular vote in the 1968 presidential election and looked set to increase his tally in the 1972 race before he was shot and paralysed. Towards the end of his political career he eschewed his previous racist policies and was re-elected governor in 1982.

Booker Taliaferro Washington (1856–1915). Controversial self-taught black educationalist who founded Tuskegee University. His 1901 book *Up From Slavery* proposed that blacks should abandon campaigns for voting rights and instead gain skills to work for economic gains.

John Wayne (1907–79). Alias "the Duke": movie macho man, legendary boozer, Reagan role model and right-wing crank.

Walt Whitman (1819–92). Writer and poet whose *Leaves of Grass*, first published in 1848, is among the most original and passionate works of American literature.

Hank Williams (1923–53). Country music legend whose compositions (*I Saw The Light*, *Jambalaya*, etc) are still Nashville standards. A drink- and drug-sodden lifestyle accounted for his premature death.

Frank Lloyd Wright (1867–1959). Prolific architect who came to prominence around 1900 with a series of prototypical suburban houses and went on to design such landmarks as New York's Guggenheim Museum.

Wilbur (1867–1912) and **Orville** (1871–1948) **Wright**. Bicycle shop proprietors from Dayton, Ohio, who went on to greater things at Kitty Hawk, North Carolina, when they made the world's first ever powered flight on December 17 1903 – it lasted twelve seconds.

Brigham Young (1801–77). The son of near-illiterate Vermont farmers, Young led the Mormons to Utah following the assassination of Joseph Smith in 1844. More of a pragmatist than a theologian, he confronted the full force of the US to establish a permanent home for his people.

INDEX

ROUGH GUIDES – THE FULL LIST

EUROPE
- Amsterdam
- Barcelona and Catalunya
- Berlin
- Brittany and Normandy
- Crete
- Czechoslovakia
- Eastern Europe
- Europe
- France
- Germany
- Greece
- Holland, Belgium and Luxembourg
- Hungary
- Ireland
- Italy
- Paris
- Poland
- Portugal
- Prague
- Provence and the Côte d'Azur
- The Pyrenees
- Scandinavia
- Sicily
- Spain
- Tuscany and Umbria
- Venice
- Yugoslavia

Forthcoming:
- Bulgaria
- Romania
- St Petersburg
- Cyprus
- Albania

NORTH AMERICA
- California and West Coast USA
- Florida
- New York
- San Francisco and the Bay Area
- USA
- Canada

CENTRAL AND SOUTH AMERICA
- Brazil
- Guatemala and Belize
- Mexico
- Peru

AFRICA
- Egypt
- Kenya
- Morocco
- Tunisia
- West Africa
- Zimbabwe and Botswana

ASIA & AUSTRALASIA
- Hong Kong and Macau
- Israel and the Occupied Territories
- Nepal
- Turkey

Forthcoming:
- Thailand
- Australia

ROUGH GUIDE SPECIALS

- Mediterranean Wildlife
- Women Travel: Adventures, Advice and Experience
- Nothing Ventured: Disabled People Travel the World

Forthcoming:

- World Music: the Complete Handbook (large format, fully illustrated)

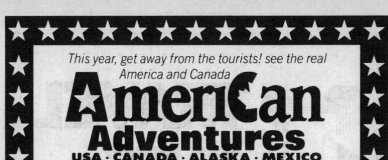

BEFORE YOU TRAVEL THE WORLD, TALK TO AN EXPERIENCED STAMP COLLECTOR.

At STA Travel we're all seasoned travellers so we should know a thing or two about where you're headed. We can offer you the best deals on fares with the flexibility to change your mind as you go – without having to pay over the top for the privilege. We operate from 120 offices worldwide. So call in soon.

74 and 86 Old Brompton Road, SW7, 117 Euston Road, NW1. London.
Manchester. Leeds. Oxford. Cambridge. Bristol.
North America **071-937 9971.** Europe **071-937 9921.** Rest of World **071-937 9962**
(incl. Sundays 10am-2pm). **OR 061-834 0668 (Manchester)**
Africa Desk 071-465 0486.

WHEREVER YOU'RE BOUND, WE'RE BOUND TO HAVE BEEN.

STA TRAVEL

 Retail Agents for ATOL Holders